CW00621364

THE DIRECTORY OF
MODERN
MILITARY WEAPONS

General Editor
CHRIS BISHOP

GREENWICH EDITIONS

This edition published by Greenwich Editions in 1999
10 Blenheim Court
Brewery Road
London N7 9NT

Copyright © 1999 Orbis Publishing Ltd.
Copyright © 1999 Aerospace Publishing

This revised and updated edition is based on material previously published
as part of the reference set *War Machine*.

Conceived and produced by
Amber Books Ltd
Bradley's Close
74-77 White Lion Street
London
N1 9PF

Editorial Consultants: Chris Chant, Bob Jackson, Ian V. Hogg and
 Antony Preston.

ISBN 0-86288-237-0

Printed in Singapore.

Contents

Contents

Introduction

The 20th century has turned out to be perhaps the most turbulent and destructive century in history, with two World Wars and innumerable smaller ones, to ensure that not a year, not even perhaps a day, has passed without someone, somewhere, being involved in armed conflict. In the circumstances, therefore, it is timely to take this overview of the world's military equipment, for on past form it would seem highly probable that some of it will be put to use in the coming century.

Studying the pages which follow will reveal the level of technology which modern armaments have reached, and it would be pertinent to stop for a moment and contemplate just how far man's martial attainments have come in one hundred years.

The soldier of 1900 had a repeating rifle, a bayonet and a shovel; his accompanying artillery fired over

USS McFaul, a US Navy DDG 51 Class Aegis guided-missile destroyer, commissioned in April 1998. Shown here during sea trials, the ship was named after a US Navy SEAL who died during the US invasion of Panama in 1997.

open sights at enemies it could see, and every gun on the battlefield had been brought there by animal power. Apart from the remote possibility of an observer in a tethered balloon, he was under no threat from the sky. There were, in all the world, possibly two thousand machine-guns; there were no rockets, no submachine guns, no hand or rifle grenades, no high explosive shells, no smoke shells, no poison gases

Technically, the sailor of 1900 was ahead of his land companion; he sailed in a steel armoured ship driven by turbine engines, with hydraulic or electrical power moving his huge guns and hoisting his ammunition. He had self-propelled torpedoes, contact or command-operated mines, and experiments in wireless communication were proceeding with some success. But he still ran around in bare feet and practised cutlass drill.

Introduction

The soldier of the 21st century carries an automatic rifle capable of firing 600 shots a minute; he probably has a device on his belt for determining his position from a satellite; he or a companion will be carrying a radio and data link which links his squad to the rest of the army. Instantly available to him are machine-guns, mortars, artillery of all shapes and sizes, rockets, missiles and tanks. Like almost everyone else on the battlefield, today's soldier will have arrived there in an armoured vehicle of some sort. He watches the skies for ground attack aircraft or helicopters, and looks also to the sky for support.

The sailor, too, has advanced; his ship will be smaller, more agile, and packed with electronic devices for determining his position and that of his enemy, for plotting the tactical picture, for controlling his weapons. He has guns, torpedoes, depth charges, mines and missiles at his disposal. He has aviation as part of his force, and like the soldier regards it both as a threat and an aid.

The aviator had no equivalent in 1900 and has therefore made a much faster progress than his companions. He, more than all others, relies entirely upon technology to get his machine into the air, maintain it there, direct it, seek out enemies, communicate with comrades-in-arms and direct his multitude of highly complicated weapons.

All these weapons, and many others, will be described in the pages which follow; some are so new that their operators are still learning how to use them; others have been in service for some time, others are on the way out but reveal the direction in which development has been taking place in recent years. But one thing should be borne in mind when contemplating the future of warfare: the cost. Today one single warship costs more than the entire annual budget for the Royal Navy in 1900. One combat aircraft costs more then an entire squadron did in 1914. Today's private soldier gets considerably more remuneration than his comrade in arms at the beginning of the century. And the cost of maintaining an armoured division in combat for a single day runs into millions of dollars, when a single anti-tank missile costs $15,000 (£9,000) and a round of ammunition for a tank gun $800 (£500) per shot.

So the formation of armed forces today has become a circular effect; highly technical weapons are expensive; but since they are 'force multipliers' – in other words, they can have the same effect as several cheaper weapons – they are cost-effective. They also require less human intervention, so the armed force becomes smaller. Since the force becomes smaller it can afford more expensive weapons...one wonders where the circuit will end.

But the inescapable practical conclusion is that all-out, full-scale warfare is no longer an economic possibility for any nation, no matter how rich. On the other hand, 'low intensity' or 'brush-fire' warfare becomes more and more probably as nationalist and ethnic tendencies overflow into armed aggression, as was seen across the globe during the late 20th century. A study of these pages will show that this is well to the fore in most military minds today. Armies, navies and air forces are being fine-tuned to cater for this form of warfare and also, more and more, for the peace-keeping and policing operations which can sometimes forestall outright warfare and bring about an amicable settlement of the dispute.

Whatever the coming century brings, the armed forces of the world are prepared for it; provided, of course, that it doesn't go on too long or become too expensive.

Ian V. Hogg
1999

The World's Main Battle Tanks

Tracing its ancestry back to the Soviet T-34 of World War II, the main battle tank (MBT) emerged in the post-war era. It has now reached such a level of technological excellence that it is hard to see how it can be improved, and harder still to see how improvement can be afforded.

The collapse of the Soviet Union, from the late 1980s in to the early 1990s, and the consequent removal of the major threat to the West of the past 50 years - that of the Soviet tank forces sweeping across Germany - has led to a reduction in both the development and the production of main battle tanks. Until one can be sure what form the battle will take, tank design can only be a matter of speculation, and it would seem that 'peace-keeping' and similar operations are likely to be all that Western armies are expected to do in the future. So for the present, the tank forces of the Western and NATO nations are being whittled away and the development of replacement vehicles appears to have stalled.

Such is not the case elsewhere. Russia still produces tanks, ostensibly for export as well as for her own forces, and there can be little doubt that design bureaux are still industriously at work on further generations. Virtually every country outside the immediate political orbit of NATO and the NATO-aligned bloc have tank-building and tank-design facilities and appear to be using them to a greater or lesser degree. No longer do these countries automatically turn to

The M1A2 Abrams, the latest production model of the standard US MBT, entered service in 1993. It has the same 120-mm gun as the M1A1; the differences are mainly in its systems.

Russia, the United States or Britain when shopping for a new tank; modern technology is there for the taking, and within the next 20 years we may well see the world's best tanks coming from some entirely new source.

Any future advances in tank technology will be expensive and extremely complicated. Potential customers might well ask if these are justified by the improvement in performance. Tank development has reached a plateau of perfection from which it is going to take some unimaginable technological leap to progress. If we study the major MBTs of today we find that, irrespective of nationality, they all have very similar shapes, thickness of armour, engines,

performance. They also have similar guns, ammunition and ballistics. Any tanks that deviate from this formula are usually distinguished by unreliability and erratic behaviour. The determining factor in any future tank conflict is going to be the state of training of the individual tank crews and their commanders.

TAM Medium Tank

For many years the World War II Sherman tank was the backbone of Argentinian armoured units. By the early 1970s these were becoming increasingly difficult to maintain and a decision was taken to obtain a new tank. Most of the tanks available at that time weighed 40 tonnes or more and were therefore too heavy to pass safely over many of the bridges in the country. A decision was then taken to have a new tank designed specifically to meet the requirements of the Argentinian army, and the development contract for this was subsequently awarded to the West German company of Thyssen Henschel, which was at that time building the Marder MICV (mechanized infantry combat vehicle) for the West German army. The first prototype of the new tank, called **TAM** (Tanque Argentino Mediano) was completed in 1976, a further two vehicles being completed the following year. This tank was accepted for service with the Argentinian army and a factory for production of the vehicle was established near Buenos Aires. About 200 TAMs were built before production ceased in 1986. None were used during the Falklands campaign of 1982. To work with the TAM the VCTP infantry fighting vehicle was developed by Thyssen Henschel and

150 were built before financial restrictions stopped production in 1986.

The hull of the TAM is based on that of the Marder MICV, of which over 2,000 are now in service with the West German army. The driver is seated at the front of the vehicle on the left with the powerpack (engine and transmission) to his right. The glacis plate is well sloped to give the best possible protection within the weight limits of the vehicle. The armour does not compare very well with that fitted to MBTs such as the Leopard 1 and AMX-30, however. The three-man all-welded turret is at the rear of the vehicle, with the commander and gunner on the right and the loader on the left. The main armament comprises a 105-mm gun fitted with an extractor to remove fumes when the gun is fired; this has an elevation of +18° and a depression of −7°. A 7.62-mm (0.3-in) machine-gun is mounted co-axially with the main armament, and a similar weapon can be mounted on the turret roof for anti-aircraft defence. Four Wegmann dischargers can be fitted on each side of the turret, and these fire smoke or fragmentaton grenades. Totals of 50 rounds of 105-mm and 6000 rounds of 7.62-mm (0.3-in) ammunition are carried in the TAM.

Using the chassis of the TAM/

VCTP, an armoured recovery vehicle (VCRT) and an SP155-mm howitzer (VCA155) were developed 1988–93 to prototype stage. The TAM tank was tested by Peru and Panama

The TAM tank has been designed by the West German company of Thyssen Henschel for the Argentinian army and is based on the chassis of the Marder MICV. Well over 100 of these have now been built in Argentina.

Specification
Crew: 4
Weight: 30.5 tonnes (loaded)
Engine: MTU 6-cylinder diesel developing 720 hp (537 kW)
Dimensions: length (with gun forward) 8.23 m (27 ft 0 in); length (hull) 6.77 m (22 ft 2½ in); width 3.25 m (10 ft 8 in); height (turret top) 2.42 m (7 ft 11¼ in)

Performance: maximum road speed 75 km/h (46.6 mph); maximum range 550 km (342 miles); fording 1.4 m (4 ft 7 in); gradient 65%; vertical obstacle 1 m (3 ft 3⅓ in); trench 2.5 m (8 ft 2½ in)

Type 59 Main Battle Tank

Following the ending of the Chinese civil war in 1949, the Communist Chinese army was based on a more permanent basis, but much of its equipment was obsolete or in urgent need of repair including a number of American and Japanese tanks of World War II vintage. The USSR soon supplied large numbers of armoured vehicles including T-34/85 tanks, SU-100 100-mm tank destroyers, and BTR-40 and BTR-152 armoured personnel carriers. In the early 1950s these were followed by a quantity of T-54 MBTs, and production of the type was subsequently undertaken in China under the designation **Type 59** MBT. The first production models were very austere and were not fitted with a stabilization system for the 100-mm Type 59 gun or with any night-vision equipment. Later vehicles were fitted with a full range of infra-red night-vision equipment for the commander, gunner and driver, as well as a stabilization sytem. The 7.62-mm (0.3-in) bow-mounted and 7.62-mm (0.3-in) co-axial machine-guns are designated Type 59T, while the Russian-designed 12.7-mm (0.5-in) DShKM machine-gun mounted on the loader's cupola is designated Type 54 by China. The British company MEL has provided small quantities of pas-

sive night-vision equipment for the Type 59 MBT, including the driver's periscope and the commander's and gunner's sights. More recently a number of Type 59s have been observed with a laser rangefinder mounted externally above the gun mantlet. This is in a very exposed position, however, and is therefore vulnerable to small arms fire and shell splinters.

The Type 59 was replaced by the Type 69, which was first seen in 1982. The principal change being the use of a 100-mm smooth-bore gun instead of the 100-mm rifled gun of the T59. Next came the Type 79, made in relatively small numbers in the mid-1980s, that was simply a Type 69 fitted with a new 105-mm rifled gun and with some modifications to the engine and transmission. This series of tanks had now reached its limit and a fresh design was begun in the mid-1980s, resulting in the Type 80, first seen in 1988.

The Type 80 employed a new torsion bar suspended chassis, new diesel powerpack, and a 105-mm rifled gun. It had laser rangefinding, a stabilised fire control systems and the gun could use either Chinese or Western ammunition. An improved model, the Type 85-II, appeared in

1989; this had a welded steel turret and an advanced computerised fire control system. Finally, in 1992, the Type 90 was revealed, a further improvement on the basic Type 80 design which mounts a 125-mm smooth-bore gun fed by an automatic loading mechanism which allowed the crew to be reduced to three men. Numbers of Type 90 have been licence built in Pakistan.

Specification
Crew: 4
Weight: 36 tonnes
Engine: V-12 diesel developing 520 hp (388 kW)

The Chinese-built Type 59 is essentially a Soviet T-54. Later production Type 59s have infra-red night vision equipment and an externally mounted laser rangefinder.

Dimensions: length (with gun forward) 9.0 m (29 ft 6 in); length (hull) 6.17 m (20 ft 3 in); width 3.27 m (10 ft 9 in); height 2.59 m (8 ft 6 in)
Performance: maximum road speed 50 km/h (31 mph); maximum range 400 km (249 miles); fording 1.4 m (4 ft 7 in); gradient 60%; vertical obstacle 0.79 m (2 ft 7 in); trench 2.68 m (8 ft 9½ in)

Type 74 Main Battle Tank

The **Type 74** MBT has been designed to meet the requirements of the Japanese Ground Self-Defense Force (JGSDF) by Mitsubishi Heavy Industries. The first prototype, called the **STB**, was completed in 1969, and the first production vehicles followed in 1975. By early 1983 about 300 Type 74 MBTs had been completed, and production was expected to continue until at least the mid-1980s.

The main armament consists of the proven British Royal Ordnance Factories 105-mm L7A1 gun, for which a total of 55 rounds of ammunition are carried; there are also a 7.62-mm (0.3-in) co-axial machine-gun and a 12.7-mm (0.5-in) machine-gun on the roof for anti-aircraft defence. Three smoke dischargers are mounted on each side of the turret, firing forwards. The fire-control system includes a ballistic

computer and a laser rangefinder to enable the exact range to the target to be determined, so increasing the possibility of a first-round hit. Some models have an infra-red/white-light searchlight mounted to the left of the main armament, and the driver is also provided with infra-red night-vision equipment.

The most unusual feature of the Type 74 is its hydro-pneumatic suspension, which enables the driver quickly to adjust the height of the vehicle to suit the type of ground being crossed or to

meet different tactical situations. The ground clearance can be varied from 0.2 to 0.65 m (7.9 to 25.6 in), and the driver can even tilt the nose or back of the tank, or have one side of the tank higher than the other. The 105-mm gun has an elevation of +9.5° and a depression of −6.5°, but with the suspension raised at the front and lowered at the rear this can be increased to +15°, the reverse producing a depression of −12.5°; this is a very useful feature when the tank is firing from behind a crest or from a reverse slope.

The Type 90 MBT was developed to replace the Type 74; prototypes appeared in 1988 but production was delayed due to the usual financial restrictions and it is unlikely that the Type 74 will be entirely replaced by the Type 90 within the century.

The Type 90 is armed with a 120-mm smoothbore gun built under licence from Rheinmetall of Germany. The turret design also shows affinities with the German Leopard II MBT, and the gun is fed by an automatic loading system which holds 16 ready-use rounds. The fire control system is based upon thermal imaging and laser rangefinding and has a highly advanced automatic tracking facility. Power is provided by a super-charged diesel engine delivering 1500 bhp and giving the 50-tonne tank a speed of 70 km/hr (43.8 mph). An armoured recovery vehicle on the same chassis has been developed and produced in small numbers.

Specification
Crew: 4
Weight: 38 tonnes (loaded)

Engine: Mitsubishi 10-cylinder diesel developing 750 hp (560 kW)
Dimensions: length (with gun forward) 9.41 m (30 ft 10½ in); length (hull) 6.7 m (21 ft 11¾ in); width 3.18 m (10 ft 5¼ in); height (overall) 2.67 m (8 ft 9 in)

Performance: maximum road speed 53 km/h (33 mph); maximum range 300 km (186 miles); fording 1 m (3 ft 3⅓ in); gradient 60%; vertical obstacle 1 m (3 ft 3⅓ in); trench 2.7 m (8 ft 10¼ in)

The Type 74 MBT entered service in 1976. An unusual feature of the vehicle is its hydro-pneumatic suspension, allowing the driver to adjust the height of the suspension to suit the type of terrain being crossed.

SWEDEN

Stridsvagn 103 (S-tank) Main Battle Tank

In the period immediately after World War II, light tanks formed the bulk of the Swedish army's tank strength. To meet the country's immediate requirements for tanks some 300 Centurions were purchased from the UK. Development of a heavy tank (the KRV) armed with a 150-mm smooth-bore gun was started with Landsverk responsible for the chassis, Volvo for the powerpack and Bofors for the armament. At the same time Sven Berge of the Swedish army was designing a new concept in AFVs in that the gun was fixed to the chassis and not mounted in a turret. Traverse was to be obtained by turning the tank on its vertical axis and elevation/depression by lowering or raising the suspension at front or back. Test rigs proved the basic concept and in 1958 Bofors was awarded a contract for two prototypes of the turretless tank. At the same time development of the KRV was stopped. The first two prototypes were completed in 1961 but so certain was the Swedish army that the concept was sound that it had, in 1960, placed a pre-production order for a further 10 vehicles. Total development costs of the **Stridsvagn 103** tank, which is commonly known as the **S-tank**, was under £9 million. The first production vehicles, which differed only in minor details from the prototypes, were completed in 1966 and production continued until 1971, by which time 300 had been built.

The main armament of the S-tank is a modified version of the British 105-mm L7, and this is fed from a 50-round magazine located in the hull rear. The ammunition mix depends on the tactical situation but could comprise 25 APDS, 20 HE and five Smoke. A maximum of 15 rounds a minute can be fired. A 7.62-mm (0.3-in) machine-gun is mounted on the commander's cupola and a further two 7.62-mm (0.3-in) machine-guns are fixed on the left side of the hull, firing forwards. A total of 2,750 rounds of 7.62-mm (0.3-in) ammunition is carried. Mounted on the roof of the vehicle are two Lyran laun-

Bofors S-tank showing external stowage boxes at hull rear and dozer blade in retracted position under nose. Flotation screen is in lowered position.

chers for illuminating targets at night.

The engine and transmission are at the front of the vehicle, and the powerpack consists of a British Rolls-Royce K60 multi-fuel engine developing 240 bhp/179 kW (to be replaced by a Detroit Diesel) and a Boeing 553 gas turbine developing 490 shp (366 kW). In normal use the tank is powered by the diesel, the turbine being engaged when the vehicle is in combat or moving across country demanding a higher power-to-weight ratio.

The driver is seated on the left of the hull and has a combined periscope and binocular sight with a magnification of ×1, ×6, ×10 or ×18, the right eyepiece having a graticule sight. The radio operator is to the rear of the driver and faces the rear. The commander is on the right and his observation equipment includes a combined periscope and optical sight that is almost identical to that of the driver and enables him also to aim and fire the gun. The commander's OPS-1 sight is fully stabilized and can be traversed through 208°. In a typical engagement the commander first observes the target then uses the handle bars on the tiller columns to lay the armament onto the target, the type of ammunition is then selected and loaded and the gun is fired. The empty cartridge case is ejected through the hull rear.

The suspension is of the hydro-pneumatic type and allows the armament/hull to have an elevation of +12° and a depression of −10°. The main drawback of the S-tank is that it cannot fire on the move. This is of no great

drawback to Sweden, however, as her armed forces will probably be engaged in defensive rather than offensive operations.

Mounted under the nose of the tank is a dozer blade which is used to prepare defensive positions. Carried around the top of the hull is a flotation screen which can be erected in 20 minutes, and the tank is then propelled in the water by its tracks at a speed of 6 km/h (3.7 mph).

Specification
Crew: 3
Weight: 39 tonnes
Engines: diesel developing 240 hp (119 kW) and a Boeing 553 gas turbine developing 490 shp (366 kW)

Dimensions: length (with gun) 8.99 m (29 ft 6 in); length (hull) 7.04 m (23 ft 1 in); width 3.26 m (10 ft 8⅓ in); height (overall) 2.5 m (8 ft 2½ in)
Performance: maximum road speed 50 km/h (31 mph); maximum range 390 km (242 miles); fording 1.5 m (4 ft 11 in); gradient 60%; vertical obstacle 0.9 m (2 ft 11½ in); trench 2.3 m (7 ft 6½ in)

Bofors Strv 103B (or S-tank), which has a 105-mm gun fixed to the hull with the weapon being aimed in elevation and depression by adjusting the hydro-pneumatic suspension. The gun is fed by an automatic loader, enabling 15 rounds per minute to be fired.

AMX-30 Main Battle Tank

When the French army was re-formed after the end of World War II its initial tank fleet comprised Sherman tanks and a few French-designed ARL 44s. All of these were replaced from the mid-1950s by the American M47, which was supplied to France in large numbers by the United States under the Mutual Defense Aid Program (MDAP). In 1956 France, West Germany and Italy drew up a requirement for a new MBT lighter and more powerfully armed than the M47 which was then being used by all three countries. France and West Germany each went ahead and built prototypes of a new MBT to meet this specification, the French contender being the **AMX-30**, and the West German vehicle the Leopard 1. It was expected that one of these two tanks would be adopted by both countries, but in the end each adopted its own tank. The AMX-30 was designed by the Atelier de Construction d'Issy-les-Moulineaux (AMX), which has designed most French AFVs since World War II. The first prototypes were completed in 1960, and the first production tanks were completed by the Atelier de Construction Roanne in 1966. By 1982 some 2,000 had been built, half for the French army and half for export. The AMX-30 is also manufactured under licence in Spain for the Spanish army.

The AMX-30 is the lightest of the first generation of NATO tanks, and has a hull of rolled steel plates welded together; the three-man turret is of cast construction. The main armament consists of a 105-mm gun with a 20-mm cannon co-axial with the main armament and a 7.62-mm (0.3-in) machine-gun on the commander's cupola. The co-axial weapon is unusual in that it can be elevated independently of the main armament to +40°, enabling it to be used against low-flying aircraft and helicopters. A total of 47 rounds of ammunition is carried for the 105-mm gun, of which 19 are in the turret and

French Army AMX-30 showing 105-mm type CH-105-F1 gun whose main anti-tank round is the OCC (HEAT), which has a muzzle velocity of 1000 m (3,280 ft) per second and will penetrate 400 mm (15¾ in) of armour at an incidence of 0 degrees. More recently an APFSDS (OBUS Flèche) has been introduced into French army service, but not exported.

Main armament of the AMX-30 is a 105-mm rifled gun, which can fire standard NATO ammunition as well as French-designed rounds.

the remaining 28 in the hull. Totals of 1,050 rounds of 20-mm and 2,050 rounds of 7.62-mm ammunition are also carried. Types of ammunition fired by the 105-mm gun include HEAT, HE, Smoke and Illuminating, while a new APFSDS round has been introduced recently. The latter is called the Obus Flèche, and with a muzzle velocity of 1525 m (5,005 ft) per second will penetrate 150 mm (5.9 in) of armour at an angle of 60° at a range of 5,000 m (5,470 yards). The current production model of the AMX-30 for the French army is the **AMX-30 B2**, which has a number of improvements including an integrated fire-control system that includes a laser rangefinder and a LLLTV system; its automotive improvements include a new transmission.

The basic AMX-30 chassis has given birth to a very large family of related vehicles. The **AMX-30D** armoured recovery vehicle is designed to recover and repair damaged vehicles in the field, and has a dozer/stabilizer blade mounted at the front of the hull, two winches, and an hydraulic crane on the right side of the hull for changing engines and other components in the field. The **AMX-30 bridgelayer** has a scissors bridge which can be used to span gaps of up to 20 m (65 ft 7½ in). The chassis is also used to carry and launch the Pluton surface-to-surface tactical nuclear missile, which is used only by the French army. The combat engineer tractor, the **AMX-30 EBG**, is still under development and will be used by the French corps of en-

gineers. The chassis is also used for the French version of the Euromissile Roland SAM system and the SA-10 Shahine SAM system which has been developed by Thomson-CSF to meet the requirements of the Saudi Arabian army. A twin 30-mm self-propelled anti-aircraft gun system, the AMX-30-S 401 A, has also been developed for Saudi Arabia, this providing close-in protection for the SA-10 batteries. The **GCT** is essentially a modified AMX-30 chassis with a new turret fitted with a 155-mm howitzer that is provided with an automatic loader and enables the weapon to fire eight rounds a minute until its ammunition supply is exhausted. The GCT is now in service with the French army and Saudi Arabia and has more recently been ordered by Iraq.

AMX-30 of the French army showing its cross-country mobility. This is one of the few Western MBTs that is not now fitted with a stabilization system for the main armament, and cannot therefore fire on the move.

Specification
Crew: 4
Weight: 36 tonnes
Engine: Hispano-Suiza 12-cylinder diesel developing 720 hp (537 kW)
Dimensions: length (with gun forward) 9.48 m (31 ft 1 in); length (hull) 6.59 m (21 ft 7 in); width 3.1 m (10 ft 2 in); height (overall) 2.86 m (9 ft 4 in)
Performance: maximum road speed 65 km/h (40 mph); maximum range 500 to 600 km (311 to 373 miles); gradient 60%; vertical obstacle 0.93 m (3 ft 0⅔ in); trench 2.9 m (9 ft 6 in)

AMX-32 Main Battle Tank cutaway drawing key

1 DI VT 13 TV camera
2 Elevation sensor
3 M581 gunner's telescope
4 Gunner's panel

5 Gunner's TV monitor
6 Gun gyro-accelerometer box
7 Tank commander's TV monitor
8 Tank commander's panel
9 Turret gyro-accelerometer box
10 Cupola

11 M527 tank commander's telescope
12 Radio sets
13 NBC compartment
14 Flux valve
15 Case
16 Radiator (engine cooling)

Leclerc MBT

This tank first appeared as the AMX-32 and was originally designed by the Atelier de Construction d'Issy-les-Moulineaux specifically as an export MBT for those countries who required more firepower and better armour protection than was available on the current AMX-30 MBT. The first prototype, armed with the same 105-mm gun as the contemporary AMX-30 was shown in 1979, but the second prototype, shown in 1981, had a new 120-mm gun as well as improved armour protection. By this time the French Army had begun to pay attention, and using the AMX-32 as their starting point, now produced a specification for an 'EPC' or 'Engin Principal du Combat'. The new design was officially named the 'Leclerc' in January 1986.

The layout of the Leclerc is conventional, with the driver at the front, two-man crew in the turret, and the engine and transmission at the rear. Main armament comprises a 120-mm smooth-bore gun developed by the Etablissement d'Etudes et de Fabrications d'Armement de Bourges (EFAB) with a vertical sliding breech block. The 52-calibre length barrel is fitted with a thermal sleeve and an air-blast system which ejects any fumes remaining in the barrel after the gun is fired. Two types of ammunition have been developed, APFSDS with a muzzle velocity of 1790 m (5,350 ft) per second, and a HEAT/multi-purpose round with a muzzle velocity of 1100 m (3,445 ft) per second. The 120-mm gun is chambered so as to accept the same STANAG-4385 range of ammunition as used with the

Leopard 2 MBT in service with the West German and Dutch armies. The German gun is, though, of 44 calibre length, and thus the French gun develops a higher velocity.

The gun is fed by an automatic loader mounted in the turret bustle. Loaded from the outside of the tank, this carries 22 rounds of ready-use ammunition. The device is programmed to recognise up to six different types of ammunition and select them on command. A further 18 rounds are carried in a reserve drum alongside the driver, and these can be loaded into the auto-loader inside the tank as required.

The auto-loaded consists of a series of circular troughs linked together to form an endless chain. When the loader is activated, the gun is automatically depressed and aligned with the loader, and the selected round is brought to the loading station and then rammed into the gun breech. The entire auto-loader is separated from the crew space by blast walls, and a blow-out panel in the top of the turret bustle will yield first in the event on an ammunition explosion and thus direct any blast away from the crew space. Should the auto-loader cease to function, the gunner can manually load, using the ammunition from the reserve drum. The auto-loader will permit a sustained rate of fire of about 12 rounds per minute to be achieved.

Mounted co-axially to the left of the main armament is a 12.7-mm Browning machine gun. A 7.62-mm AAT-F2 machine gun is mounted on the commanders cupola, and can be aimed and fired by remote control

from within the turret. Mounted on each side of the rear part of the turret is a bank of nine launcher tubes which can be used to discharge smoke grenades, infra-red missile decoys and anti-personnel munitions.

The fire control system is based upon a thermal-imaging unit, with laser rangefinder and fire control computer, allied to a gyroscope position finder and navigation platform. Gun sights and controls are duplicated so that the gun can be aimed and fired by either the commander or the

AMX-32 has a redesigned turret and hull front with improved armour protection. The fire control system includes a laser rangefinder and a roof-mounted stabilized sight.

gunner.

The Leclerc is powered by a 1500 bhp 'Hyperbar' V-8 diesel engine; this is coupled to a five-forward, two-reverse speed SESM 500 automatic transmission. This combination allows acceleration from 0–32 km/h (0–20 mph) in five seconds. A total of 1100 litres of fuel give the vehicle a range of 550 km (335 miles).

Specification:
Crew: 3
Weight: 52 tonnes
Engine: SACM-1500 V-8, 1500 bhp at 2500 rpm
Dimensions: length (gun forward) 9.87 m (32ft 4in); hull length 6.88 m (22ft 6in); width 3.71 m (4ft 1in); height to turret roof 2.46 m (8 ft)
Performance: max road speed 72 km/hr (44 mph); max range 550 km (335 miles); vertical obstacle 1.25 m (4 ft); trench 3 m (9ft 9 in); fording 1 m (3ft 3in); 4 m (13ft 2in) with preparation)

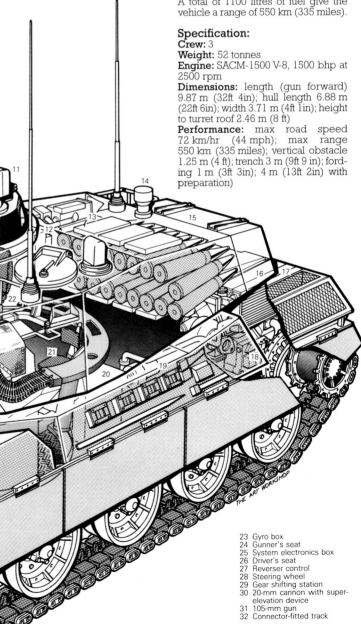

17 Oil cooler (gearbox cooling)
18 Hydraulic mechanism box
19 Air supply dust remover
20 Air filter
21 Loader's seat
22 Tank commander's seat

23 Gyro box
24 Gunner's seat
25 System electronics box
26 Driver's seat
27 Reverser control
28 Steering wheel
29 Gear shifting station
30 20-mm cannon with super-elevation device
31 105-mm gun
32 Connector-fitted track

Chieftain Mk 5 Main Battle Tank

The **Chieftain** MBT was designed by the Fighting Vehicles Research and Development Establishment (now the Military Vehicles and Engineering Establishment) in the late 1950s as a successor to the Centurion tank. The first prototype was completed in late 1959 with a further six prototypes following in 1961-62. The Chieftain was accepted for service with the British army in May 1963 and two production lines were laid down, one at the Royal Ordnance Factory Leeds and the other at Vickers at Elswick (Newcastle-upon-Tyne). Until the introduction of the Leopard 2 into the West German army in 1980, the Chieftain was the best armed and armoured MBT in the world. About 900 Chieftains were built for the British army, Kuwait also ordering 165, and Oman taking delivery of a small quantity in 1981. But the largest export order was placed by Iran, which ordered over 700 MBTs, plus ARVs and bridgelayers as well as 187 Improved Chieftains. In 1974 Iran ordered 125 **Shir 1** and 1,225 Shir 2 MBTs (the latter a new design) but this order was cancelled by the new regime. The Shir 1 became the Khalid and further development of the Shir 2 resulted in the Challenger which entered service with the British Army in 1983.

The layout of Chieftain is conventional, with the driver at the front, turret in the centre (with the commander and gunner on the right and the loader on the left), and the engine and transmission at the rear. To reduce overall height, the driver sits in a reclined position, lying almost horizontal when driving with the hatch closed. The turret is of all-cast steel construction with the front well sloped to provide the maximum possible protection. The commander has a cupola that can be traversed through 360°, and mounted externally on this is a 7.62-mm (0.3-in) machine-gun which can be aimed and fired from within the turret.

The main armament of the Chieftain is a 120-mm L11A5 series rifled gun designed by the Royal Armament Research and Development Establishment at Fort Halstead. This fires separate-loading ammunition (divided projectile and charge). The main advantages of this type of ammunition over the conventional fixed round is that the ammunition is easier to handle in the cramped confines of the tank turret, and that as the bagged charges are stowed in special water-filled containers below the turret ring, there is less risk of an explosion. Types of projectile that can be fired include APDS-T (training round is DS-T), HESH (training round is SH/Practice) and Smoke. Soon to be introduced into service is the APFSDS-T projectile which will have a long rod-penetrator and will be capable of penetrating the armour of all known MBTs in service today.

British army Chieftains are now being fitted with the Marconi Space

Until the introduction of the West German Leopard 2 with its 120-mm gun, the British Chieftain with its 120-mm rifled gun was the most well-armoured and powerful tank in NATO. More recently a 120-mm APFSDS-T round has been introduced to enhance its combat effectiveness.

and Defence systems Improved Fire Control System (IFCS) which, when used in conjunction with the laser rangefinder manufactured by Barr and Stroud, enables targets to be hit at ranges of well over 2010 m (2,200 yards).

Mounted co-axially with the 120-mm gun is a 7.62-mm (0.3-in) machine-gun and located on each side of the turret is a bank of six electrically-operated smoke dischargers. A total of 64 rounds of 120-mm ammunition (projectiles and charges) and 6,000 rounds of 7.62 mm (0.3-in) machine-gun ammunition are carried. The NBC pack is mounted on the turret bustle, and a fire detection and extinguishing system is mounted in the engine compartment. Night-vision equipment is of the infra-red type with an infra-red/white-light searchlight mounted on the

left of the turret. This has a range of 1000 m (1,100 yards) in the infra-red role and 1500 m (1,640 yards) in the white-light role. Thermal imaging night-vision equipment will be introduced in the mid-1980s.

Variants of the Chieftain include an armoured recovery vehicle and a bridgelayer. The latter can lay a Number 8 tank bridge which is of the scissor type and can span a gap of up to 22.86 m (75 ft 0 in) or a Number 9 tank bridge which can span a gap of up to 12.192 m (40 ft 0 in). The Chieftain can also be fitted with a hydraulically-operated dozer blade at the front of the hull for the clearance of battlefield obstacles and the preparation of fire positions.

Specification
Crew: 4

Weight: 55 tonnes
Engine: Leyland 6-cylinder multi-fuel developing 750 bhp (560 kW)
Dimensions: length (with gun forward) 10.795 m (35 ft 5 in); length (hull) 7.518 m (24 ft 8 in) width 3.657 m (11 ft 8½ in); height (overall) 2.895 m (9 ft 6 in)
Performance: maximum road speed 48 km/h (30 mph); maximum road range 400 to 500 km (250 to 310 miles); fording 1.066 m (3 ft 6 in); gradient 60%; vertical obstacle 0.914 m (3 ft 0 in); trench 3.149 m (10 ft 4 in)

British Chieftain MBT with 120-mm L11A5 rifled tank gun, which has a thermal sleeve to reduce distortion, and is also used by Iran, Kuwait, Oman and probably Iraq.

Challenger Main Battle Tank

In 1974 Iran ordered 125 Shir 1 and 1,225 **Shir 2** MBTs from Royal Ordnance Factory Leeds. The Shir 1 was essentially a late-production Chieftain, already entering service with Iran in large numbers, with a new powerpack consisting of a 1,200-bhp (895-kW) Rolls-Royce diesel, coupled to a David Brown TN37 automatic transmission and fitted with an Airscrew Holden cooling system. Armament was the 120-mm L11A5 rifled gun connected to a Marconi Space and Defence Systems Improved Fire Control System (IFCS) and a Barr and Stroud laser rangefinder. The Shir 2 was a brand new design and had the same powerpack, armament and fire-control system as the Shir 1, but had a hull and turret of Chobham armour which would provide a high degree of protection against all battlefield weapons, especially missiles with their HEAT warheads. It also had hydrogas suspension which gave an excellent ride across rough country as well as being easy to maintain and repair in the event of battlefield damage.

The British army was to have replaced its Chieftains with a British/West German design, but this fell by the wayside in March 1977 and the UK went ahead on its own with a new project designated MBT-80. With the fall of the Shah of Iran the massive Iranian order was cancelled before deliveries could start, although by that time the Shir 1 was already in production at the Royal Ordnance Factory Leeds. Jordan eventually placed an order for 278 Khalid MBTs essentially similar to the Shir 1; deliveries of these began in 1981, and are still under way.

In 1980 the British Ministry of Defence announced that the MBT-80 project had been cancelled as not only was it getting too expensive but its in-service date was slipping. Instead an initial order was placed with Leeds for 237 examples of the **Challenger** MBT, this being basically the Shir 2 with modifications to suit it for a European rather than Middle Eastern climate. The first production Challengers were handed over to the British army in March 1983, and four regiments are expected to be equipped with the tank within the British Army of the Rhine. It is anticipated that a further order will be placed to enable at least half of the Chieftains of the Royal Armoured Corps to be replaced.

The first production vehicles will be fitted with the standard Royal Ordn-ance Factory Nottingham 120-mm L11A5 rifled gun but at a later date this will be replaced by the new high-technology gun now under advanced development by the Royal Armament Research and Development Establishment (RARDE) at Fort Halstead. This weapon will be of electro-slag refined steel (ESR) with a new split breech design, and will be able to fire projectiles with a much higher muzzle velocity, providing increased penetration compared with current projectiles. It will also be able to fire, as will the current L11A5, the new Royal Ordn-ance Factory Birtley APFSDS-T projectile which will defeat all known armours.

One of the first Challenger MBTs for the British army, which accepted the tank in March 1983. This retains the 120-mm gun of the earlier Chieftain but has a new powerpack and Chobham armour.

Specification
Crew: 4
Weight: 60 tonnes
Engine: Rolls-Royce 12-cylinder diesel developing 895 kW (1,200 hp)
Dimensions: length (with gun forward) 11.55 m (37 ft 10¾ in); length (with gun to rear) 0.87 m (32 ft 4⅔ in); width 3.51 m (11 ft 6¼ in); height 2.89 m (9 ft 5¾ in)

Performance: maximum road speed 56 km/g (35 mph); maximum range (estimated) 500 km (310 miles); fording 1.07 m (3 ft 6 in); gradient 60%; vertical obstacle 0.91 m (3 ft 0 in); trench 3 m (9 ft 10 in)

Tank Battles of the Iran-Iraq War

An Iraqi T-62 at speed, pictured early during that country's advance into Iran.

In 1979 the Shah of Iran was overthrown, bringing to an end a regime that had been in power for some 37 years and had in recent years built up one of the most powerful and well-trained armed forces in the Middle East. The strength of the Iranian army included three armoured and three infantry divisions, plus four independent brigades which were equipped with some 900 Chieftain tanks, 400 M47 and M48 tanks, 460 M60A1 tanks, over 250 Scorpion reconnaissance vehicles, many APCs (armoured personnel carriers) plus self-propelled guns and self-propelled howitzers, and (most importantly) mobile air-defence systems.

At this time the Iraqi army had a strength of some four armoured, four infantry and two mechanized brigades plus two special-forces brigades, one independent brigade and the Republican Guard Brigade. All major equipment was Russian, including over 2,000 T-54, T-55 and T-62 MBTs.

Border flare-ups

When the Shah was in power there was little trouble between the two countries as in 1975 a treaty was negotiated to redefine the mutual borders. But from May 1979 there were a number of clashes along the Iranian/Iraqi border, and between April and July some 30,000 Iraqis of Iranian origin were expelled from Iraq; in September 1980 President Hussein cancelled the 1975 treaty between the two countries. On 20 September Iraqi aircraft bombed a number of airfields in Iran, and two days later the Iraqi army advanced into Iran. According to Iraq, all she wished was to return to Iraqi sovereignty parts of the Shatt-al-Arab waterway and territory ceded to Iran in 1975.

Iraqi forces advanced on three main axes, towards Qasr-e-Shirin in the north, Mehran in the centre, and (the most important of the three) Susangerd and Khorramshahr in the south. Iraq hoped that such a move would quickly lead to the downfall of the regime of Ayatollah Khomeini. Iraq succeeded in crossing the border, but the depth of penetration varied considerably. Most of the successes were in the southern thrust, with Khorramshahr falling after a bitter struggle. Iran did mount minor counterattacks in the northern and central sections, usually with little armour or artillery support, and did regain some of its lost territory.

In January 1981 the Iranians mounted a much larger counterattack south of Susangerd in the southern sector. This was a complete failure as the tanks were apparently unsupported by infantry, and the terrain, which at that time of year is soft, was unsuitable for tanks. It is believed that Iraq lost about 50 T-62s with Iran losing well over 100 Chieftains and M60A1s.

Armour turn-round

In the first year Iraq lost about 250 or 300 tanks, and Iran probably about the same number. Then early in 1982 it was reported that Iraq had captured some 50 operational Chieftains abandoned by their Iranian crews; M60A1s and Scorpions were also captured. When well-crewed, the Iranian Chieftains with their 120-mm rifled guns have been more than a match for the 100-mm gunned T-54s and T-55s, and the 115-mm gunned T-62s of the Iraqi army.

By 1981 both countries were in dire need of additional supplies of equipment, especially new vehicles. Iran succeeded in getting spare tank parts (probably for her M48s and M60s) from Israel, as well as from Syria, Libya and some Soviet bloc countries. Iraq was still receiving supplies (including anti-tank missiles) from France and the USSR as well as from North Korea, North Vietnam and Egypt, the last supplying mainly ammunition, and T-54 and T-55 tanks which were becoming surplus as a result of deliveries of more modern American equipment. Early in 1983 Iraq started to receive considerable amounts of equipment from China, including the Type 69 MBT which was supplied via Saudi Arabia.

C-1 Ariete Main Battle Tank

In the late 1970s the OTO-Melara company developed their OF-40 MBT, hoping for its adoption by the Italian Army. Although some were sold to various Arab states, the Italians did not adopt it. Instead, in 1982 the Italian Army issued a completely new specification for a new MBT, and OTO-Melara joined with IVECO, the vehicle builders, to develop a suitable design. The first prototype of the C-1 Ariete was built in 1986; five more followed, trials were conducted, and in 1988 the Italian Army placed an order for 200 tanks. This was to be followed by a further 500 of an improved 'Mark 2' model by the end of the century, but financial considerations slowed down the programme.

The hull of the Ariete is of welded steel, with additional armour across the frontal arc, giving full protection against attack from anything less than 120-mm calibre. The layout has the driver front and right, the turret central and the engine and drives at the rear. Beside the driver is a reserve magazine containing 27 rounds of ammunition for the main armament. The interior is protected by a fire and explosion detection and suppression system.

The main armament is a 44-calibre-length smoothbore 120-mm gun manufactured by OTO-Melara, which is generally based upon the German 120-mm gun design and which is capable of firing the same STANAG-4385 NATO-standard ammunition. Indeed, although APFSDS and HEAT rounds were developed by SNIA of Italy in the early 1990s, it seems that current ammunition is being bought-in from Germany and no manufacture takes place in Italy. A total of 40 ready-use rounds are carried in the tank. There is a 7.62-mm machine gun mounted co-axially with the main armament, and another 7.62-mm machine gun on the turret for anti-aircraft protection.

The turret is sloped sharply at the front, in a similar manner to the US M1 Abrams, and houses the commander, gunner and loader. Ammunition is stowed in the bustle and can be replenished from outside the tank. The fire control and surveillance system uses a 360° roof-mounted sight for the commander, a roof-mounted sight for the gunner, laser rangefinder, ballistic sensors for bore wear, meteorological conditions and tank attitude, and a ballistic computer programmed for the ammunition options. The gunner is has a thermal imaging camera sight, the picture from which is available on a video screen in front of the commander. The gunner's controls permit him to utilise the various sighting options according to the visibility and weather conditions.

Power is provided by an IVECO power pack comprising a IVECO V-12 turbo-charged diesel engine coupled to a German ZF LSG3000 automatic transmission giving four forward and two reverse speeds which is built under licence by IVECO. There are seven roadwheels on each side of the tank, carried on a torsion-bar suspension system.

The interior of the tank is ventilated by a selectable NBC system; in the 'unprotected' mode it acts simply as a ventilation system, drawing in air and roughly filtering it. In the 'protected' mode the filtration is to a far higher standard. Stale air is ejected at the left rear of the turret.

Specification:
Crew: 4
Weight: 54 tonnes
Engine: IVECO V-12 turbo-charged diesel, 1250 bhp at 2300 rpm.

OF-40 MBT of the Dubai army (part of the United Arab Emirates), which has ordered 18 vehicles with an option on a further 28. This MBT uses automotive components of the West German Leopard 1 and is armed with a 105-mm gun and two 7.62-mm (0.3-in) MGs. The fire-control system includes a laser rangefinder and a ballistic computer.

Dimensions: length (gun forward): 9.67 m. hull length 7.59 m; width: 3.60 m; height to turret roof 2.50 m.
Performance: max road speed 65 km/hr. max range 550 km; vertical obstacle 2.1 m; trench 3.0 m; fording 1.20 m (4 m with preparation)

Leopard 1 Main Battle Tank

When the West German army was reformed it was initially equipped with American M47 and M48 tanks, both of which were armed with a 90-mm gun. A decision was soon taken that the former would be replaced by a more modern tank armed with a 105-mm gun, and two design teams (called A and B) were selected to build prototypes of vehicles for comparative trials. At the same time France built prototypes of the AMX-30 to replace its American-supplied M47s. It had been expected that either the West German MBTs or the French AMX-30 would become the common MBT of both armies, but in the end each country went its own way. In the case of West Germany, further development of the team A design resulted in the standardization of the vehicle as the **Leopard 1**. The first production tanks were completed by Krauss-Maffei of Munich in September 1965 and production continued until 1979. A total of 2,437 MBTs

was built for the West German army in four basic models designated **Leopard 1A1** (with additional armour this became the **Leopard 1A1A1**), the **Leopard 1A2**, the **Leopard 1A3** (with a new welded turret) and the **Leopard 1A4** (with a new welded turret and new fire-control system). The Leopard 1 was also adopted by Australia (90 vehicles), Belgium (334), Canada (114), Denmark (120), Italy (920, of which 720 were built in Italy by OTO Melara), the Netherlands (468) and Norway (78). Production was resumed by Krauss Maffei and Krupp MaK in 1982 to meet further orders from Greece (106) and Turkey (77).

The Leopard 1 is armed with the proven British Royal Ordnance Factories Nottingham L7 series rifled tank gun, and can fire a variety of ammunition including APDS, APFSDS, HEAT, HESH and Smoke, a total of 60 rounds being carried. A 7.62-mm (0.3-in) machine-gun is mounted co-axially

with the main armament, a similar weapon is mounted on the turret roof for use in the anti-aircraft role, and four three-barrelled smoke dischargers are mounted on each side of the turret, firing forwards. A gun stabilization system is fitted, enabling the main armament to be laid and fired whilst the tank is moving across country. Leopard 1s have an NBC system and a full set of night-vision equipment for the commander, gunner and loader. When originally introduced, the latter was of the first-generation infra-red type but this is now being replaced by the second-generation passive type.

A wide range of optional equipment has also been developed for the Leopard 1 including a schnorkel which enables the tank to ford deep rivers and streams to a maximum depth of 4 m (13 ft 1½ in). An hydraulic blade can be mounted at the front of the hull and this is operated by the driver to clear or prepare battlefield obstacles. Most West German and Dutch Leopards are having appliqué armour fitted to their turrets to give increased

armour protection against missiles and HEAT projectiles.

The basic Leopard 1 chassis has been the basis for a complete family of vehicles which have been designed to support the MBT on the battlefield. All of the specialized versions, with the exception of the Gepard, have been designed and built by MaK of Kiel who have also built a few of the Leopard 1 MBTs.

Specification
Crew: 4
Weight: 40 tonnes
Engine: MTU 10-cylinder diesel developing 830 hp (619 kW)
Dimensions: length (with gun forward) 9.543 m (31 ft 4 in); length (hull) 7.09 m (23 ft 3 in); width 3.25 m (10 ft 8 in); height (overall) 2.613 m (8 ft 7 in)
Performance: maximum road speed 65 km/h (40.4 mph); maximum range 600 km (373 miles); fording 60%; vertical obstacle 1.15 m (3 ft 9¼ in); trench 3 m (9 ft 10 in)

WEST GERMANY

Leopard 2 Main Battle Tank

Leopard 2 MBT of the West German army, which will take delivery of 1,800 vehicles by 1986. The 7.62-mm (0.3-in) MG3 machine-gun can be mounted at the commander's or loader's station and provides short range anti-aircraft protection. On either side of the turret is a bank of eight electrically-operated smoke dischargers.

In the late 1960s West Germany and the USA were jointly developing a new MBT designated MBT-70. In 1970 this was cancelled as a result of rising costs, and West Germany went ahead to develop a new MBT eventually known as the **Leopard 2**. This is fact incorporated the engine, transmission and certain other components of the MBT-70. A total of 16 hulls and 17 turrets was built to test various suspension, armaments (105-mm or 120-mm smooth-bore guns) and fire-control combinations. A special version was also built at a later date to meet the requirements of the US Army; this was called the **Leopard 2(AV)** and was armed with the standard 105-mm L7 rifled gun.

After trials had been carried out, the Leopard 2 was accepted for service by the German army, and in 1977 an order was placed for 1,800 Leopard 2 MBTS, of which Krupp MaK built 810 and Krauss-Maffei of Munich the remaining 990 The first production tanks were handed over to the West German army in 1979, but it was not until 1992 that the final deliveries were made. In 1979 the Netherlands army selected the Leopard 2 to replace its ageing Centurion MBTs and AMX-13 light tanks armed with a 105-mm gun; a total of 445 Leopard 2 to be delivered by 1986. The first was handed over in 1982 and the final deliveries were on time in July 1986.

In 1983 the Swiss Army, after evaluation of the US M1 Abrams and the Leopard 2, decided upon the latter and ordered 380 tanks. Of these, the first 35 were made by Krauss-Maffei in Germany and the remainder under licence in Switzerland by Contraves, the final deliveries taking place in 1993.

The Leopard 2 is armed with a Rheinmetall-developed 120-mm smooth-bore gun which fires two main types of ammunition, namely HEAT-MP-T (High Explosive Anti-Tank Multi-Purpose Tracer) and APFSDS-T (Armour-Piercing Fin-Stabilized Discarding-Sabot Tracer); in each case there is also a practice round. The former is used against all battlefield targets, including field fortifications and lighter vehicles, while the latter is the main tank-killing round and is said to be able to penetrate the frontal armour of all current tanks including the Soviet T-64 and T-72. The ammunition, also developed by Rheinmetall, is unusual in that it has a combustible cartridge case, so that after the gun is fired all that remains of the cartridge is the base stub which is ejected into a bag under the breech of the gun. A total of 42 rounds of 120-mm ammunition is carried, compared with 60 rounds for the first-generation Leopard 1 with its 105-mm gun. This is not a great drawback as the 120-mm round has greater penetration and the fire-control system gives a much greater hit probability. A 7.62-mm (0.3-in) machine-gun is mounted co-axially with the main armament, and a similar weapon is mounted on the turret roof for anti-aircraft defence. On each side of the turret are eight smoke dischargers, firing forwards.

The commander of the Leopard 2, who sits on the right of the turret, is provided with a stabilized roof-mounted sight which has a variable magnification of ×2 and ×8; this can be traversed through 360° for observation and can also be used to lay and fire the main armament. The gunner, who is seated forward and below the commander, also has a stabilized sight, but his incorporates a laser rangefinder and a thermal image unit, both of which are linked to the fire-control system. The main armament is fully stabilized and standard equipment includes passive night-vision equipment, an NBC system, a fire extinguishing system and a schnorkel for deep wading.

The hull and turret of the Leopard 2 incorporate advanced armour which gives it a high degree of battlefield survivability, especially against anti-tank weapons with HEAT warheads. The Leopard 2 is powered by a multi-fuel engine developing 1,500 hp (1119 kW), which gives the Leopard 2 a power-to-weight ratio of 27 hp (20 kW) per tonne compared with just under 20 hp (15 kW) per tonne for the final production models of the Leopard 1. This gives the tank greater acceleration and improved cross-country mobility, which promote survivability on the battlefield.

Specification

Crew: 4
Weight: 55.15 tonnes
Engine: MTU 12-cylinder multi-fuel developing 1,500 hp (1119 kW)
Dimensions: length (with gun forward) 9.668 m (31 ft 8⅔ in); length (hull) 7.772 m (25 ft 6 in); width 3.7 m (12 ft 1⅔ in); height (overall) 2.79 m (9 ft 1¾ in)
Performance: maximum road speed 72 km/h (45 mph); maximum range 550 km (342 miles); gradient 60%; vertical obstacle 1.1 m (3 ft 7¼ in); trench 3 m (9 ft 10 in)

USA

M60A1-3 Main Battle Tank

The M60A3 is the most widely used American MBT and is the latest development of the M60, which entered service in 1960. It is armed with a 105-mm M68 gun and has an advanced fire control system that includes a stabilization system, passive night vision equipment, laser rangefinder and a ballistic computer.

In 1956 further development of the M48 tank to incorporate a new engine and a larger-calibre main armament: the British 105-mm L7AI barrel fitted with an American-designed breech. The L7A1 was subsequently made under licence in the USA under the designation M68 and fitted to all production examples of the M60 series (with the exception of the M60A2) and to the M1 Abrams, which was also produced by General Dynamics.

The M60 entered service with the US Army in 1960 but was soon succeeded in production by the **M60A1** which had a number of modifications including a redesigned turret which offered greater ballistic protection.

The **M60A2** was fitted with a new turret armed with a 152-mm weapon system which could fire the Shillelagh missile or a range of conventional ammunition with a combustible cartridge case. A total of 526 M60A2s was built, but the armament proved to be a failure and the vehicles withdrawn. The chassis was used for modification into specialist vehicles.

The final production model was the **M60A3**, which was produced at the Detroit Tank Plant now operated by the Land Systems Division of General Dynamics who took over Chrysler Defense Inc. during 1982. The M60A3 has many improvements over the earlier M60A1 including a Hughes Aircraft Laser Tank Fire Control System, the Tank Thermal Sight, the main armament stabilised in both elevation and traverse, a new AVDS-790-ZA RISE (Reliability Improved Selected Equipment) engine, new tracks with replaceable pads, new searchlight over the main armament, thermal sleeve for main armament, new co-axial 7.62-mm (0.3-in) machine-gun, and British six-barrelled smoke dischargers mounted on each side of the turret. These improvements were then retrofitted into M60AI vehicles, which became M60A3s.

The M60A3 carried a total of 63 rounds of ammunition for the 105-mm gun, of which 26 were carried in the forward part of the hull, 13 in the turret for ready use, 21 in turret bustle and three under the gun. A 7.62-mm (0.3-in) machine gun is mounted co-axially with the main armament, and a 12 7-mm (0.5-in) machine-gun is mounted in the commander's cupola, primarily for air defence.

Production of the M60A3 was completed in 1984, by which time over 13,000 vehicles had been built for home and export. In addition to being used by the US Amy and US Marines. the M60 series was also used by Austria, Egypt. Iran, Israel, Italy, Jordan, Morocco, Saudi Arabia, Sudan, Tunisia and the Yemen Arab Republic (North Yemen). In the early 1990s, the replacement of the M60 by the M1 Abrams and the reduction in US Army strength, 2000 or more M60A3 tanks were made available for NATO armies including those of Portugal. Greece, Spain and Turkey. Numbers are still held by US National Guard regiments.

There were two main versions of the M60: the **M60 Armoured Vehicle Launched Bridge** and the **M728 Combat Engineer Vehicle**. The M60 AVLB has a scissors bridge on top of the bull, and this is launched over the front of the vehicle to span gaps of up to 18.3 m (60 ft). Numbers were purchased by Singapore and Spain. The M728 CEV has a hull and turret similar to those of the M60AI, but is armed with a 165-mm demolition gun which fires a HESH (High Explosive Squash Head) rounds to demolish battlefield fortifications and pillboxes, and carries a collapsible A-frame for engineer lifting tasks. It is used by Saudi Arabia and Singapore.

Specification (M60A3)

Crew: 4
Weight: 52.60 tonnes
Engine: continental 12-cylinder diesel 750 bhp at 2400 rpm
Dimensions: length (gun forward) 9.44 m (30 ft); hull length 6.95m (22ft 8 in); width 3.63 m (11ft 9in); height to turret roof 3.27 m (10ft 7 in)
Performance: max road speed 48 km/hr (30 mph); max range 480 km (300 miles); vertical obstacle 0.91 m (36 in); trench 2.59 m (8ft 5in); fording 1.21 m (4 ft); 2.4 m, (7ft 9in) with preparation

M1 Abrams Main Battle Tank

In the 1960s West Germany and the USA started the joint development of a new MBT known as the MBT-70 but this was cancelled in July 1970. The USA went on to develop a version called the XM803, but this too was soon cancelled as it would be too expensive and complicated Two years later the Detroit Diesel Allison Division of the General Motors Corporation and the Defense Division of the Chrysler Corporation were each awarded contracts to design a new MBT which would have much improved armour protection and greater mobility than the M60 then in production. After extensive trials the Chrysler design was accepted and in 1976 the company was awarded a development contract including the construction of 11 pilot vehicles which were completed in 1978. This XM1 was eventually standardised as the M1 Abrams MBT, the first production tank being in 1980, and by early 1983 over 700 M1s had been built and two plants were each turning out 30 tanks a month. The US Army required a total of 8,113 M1s by 1988.

The hull and turret of the M1 were of advanced compound armour and provided the greatest degree of protection ever incorporated into an American MBT. Main armament was the 105-mm M68 gun as mounted in the current M60 series but a much improved fire-control system was installed, which included a laser rangefinder and thermal imaging system that allowed the tank to engage targets by both day and night. The gun was stabilised in both elevation and traverse and so could

The M1 Abrams, with its 105-mm M68 rifled gun, advanced armour and gas turbine, is now operational with the US 7th Army in West Germany. Its fire control system, incorporating thermal sights, laser rangefinder and stabilization system, enables it to engage and destroy enemy tanks in a variety of environmental conditions.

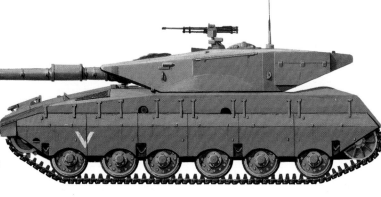

be aimed and fired while the vehicle is moving across country. A total of 55 rounds of 105-mm ammunition was carried of which 44 were in the turret bustle (22 on each side) and separated from the crew by sliding doors. A 7.62-mm (0.30-in) machine gun was mounted co-axially with the main gun, and a similar weapon was mounted at the loaders hatch. The commander had a 0.5-in (12 7-mm) machine-gun on the turret for air defence. Mounted on each side of the turret was a bank of six smoke dischargers.

It was always intended that the 105-mm gun was to be an interim measure, and in 1985 the **M1A1** Abrams appeared, mounting the Rheinmetall 120-mm smoothbore gun. In addition it had improved armour, an improved NBC/air conditioning system and changes in the torsion bar suspension system. The turret now carried 40 rounds of ammunition. By April 1993, when production ceased, a total of 4798 M1A1 Abrams tanks had been built.

In 1988 General Dynamics were contracted to improve the design. The result was the **M1A2**, which entered service in 1993. This uses the same

120-mm smoothbore gun and the changes are almost entirely concerned with the navigation, surveillance and fire control systems.

The M1 Abrams is the first production tank to be powered by a gas turbine engine, installed following trials in an M48 tank. The gas turbine takes up much less room than a diesel, and is easier to service or replace in the field if it breaks down. On the other hand it uses more fuel than a diesel engine, a factor which tends to negate the space saved in the first place.

Specification (M1A1)
Crew: 4
Weight: 57.15 tonnes
Engine: Lycoming gas turbine developing 1500 bhp at 30,000 rpm
Dimensions: length (gun forward) 9.83 m (32 ft); hull length 7.92 m (25 ft 9 in); width: 3.66 m (11 ft10in); height to turret roof 2.44 m (7 ft 9 in)
Performance: max road speed 72 km/hr.(45 mph) max range 465 km; (20 miles); vertical obstacle 1.06 m (3 ft 6in); trench 2.74 m (9 ft); fording 1.22 m (4 ft); (max 1.98 m, 6 ft 6in)

Merkava Main Battle Tank

In the 1960s the backbone of the Israeli Armoured Corps was the British-supplied Centurion MBT (which was subsequently rebuilt and fitted with a 105-mm gun to become known as the Upgraded Centurion), Sherman (most of which have now been rebuilt for specialized roles such as command vehicles, ambulances, recovery vehicles, mortar carriers and self-propelled howitzers) and the American M48. After the 1967 Middle East war Israel became concerned that in the future she would not be able to obtain AFVs from her traditional suppliers (the UK, France and the USA). Moreover, many of the tanks from these sources did not meet Israel's unique requirements.

Under the direction of General Tal, Israel started to develop its own MBT, named **Merkava** (or Chariot). This was announced in 1977, and the first production vehicles were completed in 1979. It was estimated that by 1982 at least 250 vehicles had been built. The Merkava was used in action for the first time against Syrian armoured units operating in southern Lebanon in the summer of 1982.

The layout of Merkava is unique in that the whole front of the vehicle is occupied by the engine, transmission, cooling system and fuel tanks. The driver is seated just in front of the turret on the left. The turret, which is of cast and welded construction, is situated well to the rear of the hull with the commander and gunner on the right

Israeli army Merkava MBT armed with a 105-mm M68 gun, as fitted to the M48A5 and M60 series of MBT. The Merkava was first used in combat in the 1982 invasion of the Lebanon, when it engaged and defeated Syrian T-72s. It can carry infantrymen, additional ammunition or a number of stretcher patients in the hull rear.

and the loader on the left. The turret is well sloped to give the greatest possible degree of armour protection and its small cross section makes it a very difficult target. At the rear of the hull is a compartment which can be used to carry additional ammunition or (supposedly) four stretcher patients or 10 fully equipped infantrymen. A hatch is provided in the hull rear to allow for the rapid exit of the tank crew or infantrymen. Standard equipment includes a full range of night-vision equipment, an NBC system and a special fire detection and extinguishing system which is automatically activated when a projectile penetrates the vehicle.

The main armament is the proven 105-mm rifled tank gun, which can fire a wide range of ammunition including the new APFSDS-T round (the M111) developed by Israel Military Industries. During the recent fighting in the

Lebanon this round proved capable of penetrating the Soviet T-62 and T-72 MBTs over their frontal arc. The 105-mm gun has an elevation of +20° and a depression of −8.5°. Turret traverse and gun elevation/depression are electro-hydraulic, with manual controls for emergency use. A stabilization system is fitted, enabling the gun to be aimed accurately and fired while the vehicle is moving across country. The Elbit fire control system includes a computer and laser rangefinder.

Compared with other MBTs developed in recent years, the Merkava has a very low speed and poor power-to-weight ratio, but it has been designed for a different tactical situation to that found in Central Europe. It should also be remembered that Israel has had more experience of successful armoured warfare since World War II than any other country. In designing

the Merkava the Israelis have placed great emphasis on crew survivability. With a national population of only four million, every trained crew man is a very valuable person who must be given the maximum possible protection.

Specification
Crew: 4
Weight: 56 tonnes
Engine: V-12 diesel developing 900 hp (671 kW)
Dimensions: length (with gun forward) 8.36 m (27 ft 5¼ in); length (hull) 7.45 m (24 ft 5¼ in); width 3.72 m (12 ft 2½ in); height (roof) 2.64 m (8 ft 8 in)
Performance: maximum road speed 46 km/h (28.6 mph); maximum range 500 km (311 miles); gradient 60%; vertical obstacle 1 m (3 ft 3⅓ in); trench 3 m (9 ft 10 in)

T-62 Main Battle Tank

The **T-62** is a further development of the T-54/T-55 tank with a slightly longer hull to accommodate the turret with its 115-mm smooth-bore gun. The T-62 was first seen in public during a parade held in Red Square (Moscow) during 1965, although it is now known to have entered production in about 1961. The T-62 remained in production until the early 1970s and a number were also produced under licence in Czechoslovakia, mainly for the export market. The T-62 was more expensive to produce than the earlier T-54/T-55 and for this reason the T-55 remained in production for many years after the more modern T-62 had been phased out of production.

The 115-mm U-5TS smooth-bore gun is fitted with a bore evacuator and is fully stabilized in both elevation and traverse. An unusual feature of the T-62 is that it has an integral shell case ejection system which is activated by the recoil of the gun. This ejects the empty case out through a trapdoor in the turret rear, but this has reduced the rate of fire to about four rounds a minute as the gun has to elevate to +3° 30′ for this to be carried out.

Three main types of ammunition are fired by the 115-mm gun, namely HE-FRAG-FS, or High Explosive Fragmentation Fin-Stabilized, with a muzzle velocity of 750 m (2,460 ft) per second; HEAT-FS, or High Explosive Anti-Tank Fin-Stabilized, with a muzzle velocity of 900 m (2,955 ft) per second and capable of penetrating over 430 mm (16.9 in) of armour at any range; and the deadly APFSDS, or Armour-Piercing Fin-Stabilized Discarding-Sabot, with a muzzle velocity of 1680 m (5,510 ft) per second and a very flat trajectory, and capable of penetrating 330 mm (13 in) of armour at a range of 1000 m (1,095 yards). A total of 40 rounds of 115-mm ammunition is carried, of which four are ready rounds in the turret, and of the rest 16 are to the right of the driver and 20 in the rear of the fighting compartment. A 7.62-mm (0.3-in) PKT machine-gun is mounted co-axially with the main armament; for this weapon 2,500 rounds of ammunition are carried.

Standard equipment on all T-62s includes infra-red night-vision equipment for the commander, gunner and driver, an unditching beam which is carried at the rear of the hull, a turret ventilation system to remove fumes when the gun is fired, a nuclear collective protection system, and the capability of injecting diesel fuel into the exhaust to provide smoke screen. The vehicle carries 675 litres (148.5 Imp gal) of fuel internally with a further 285 litres (63 Imp gal) externally on the running boards, and this total gives the T-62 a road range of 450 km (280 miles). A further two drum-type fuel tanks can be fitted on the hull rear; these each hold some 200 litres (44 Imp gal) of fuel, increasing road range to some 650 km (404 miles). All T-62s can ford rivers to a depth of 5.5 m (18 ft 0½ in) with the aid of a schnorkel erected over the loader's hatch. A centralized fire-extinguisher system is provided for the engine and fighting compartments, and this can be operated automatically or manually by the commander or driver.

Soviet T-62 tanks advance through an artillery barrage during training exercises. This tank was first used operationally in the Middle East.

Specification
Crew: 4
Weight: 40 tonnes
Engine: V-12 water-cooled diesel developing 580 hp (433 kW)
Dimensions: length (with gun forward) 9.335 m (30 ft 7½ in); length (hull) 6.63 m (21 ft 9 in); width 3.3 m (10 ft 10 in); height 2.395 m (7 ft 10¼ in)
Performance: maximum road speed 50 km (31 mph); maximum road range 650 km (404 miles); gradient 60%; vertical obstacle 0.8 m (2 ft 7½ in); trench 2.85 m (9 ft 4¼ in)

T-64 Main Battle Tank

In the 1960s the Russians built prototypes of a new MBT which became known as the **M-1970** in the West in the absence of any known Soviet designation. This vehicle had a new suspension consisting of six small dual road wheels with the drive sprocket at the rear, idler at the front and four track return rollers supporting the inside of the track only. All previous MBTs designed in the USSR since World War II (the T-54, T-55 and T-62) had been characterized by larger road wheels with no return rollers. The turret of the M-1970 was similar to that of the T-62 and was armed with the same 115-mm smooth-bore gun. Further development of the M-1970 resulted in the **T-64** MBT which was placed in production at one tank plant in the USSR. Production vehicles were armed with a 125-mm gun which was later fitted to the T-62 MBT. So far the T-64 has not been identified as being in service with any other country whereas the later T-72 has been exported on a wide scale, both within the Warsaw Pact and overseas with production now being undertaken both in Czechoslovakia and Poland. Some reports have stated that the T-64 was such a poor design and so plagued with mechanical troubles that it was only in production for a few years, although several thousands were built. The other theory is that the T-64 has advanced armour (especially on the glacis plate) and for this reason was never exported, even to trusted members of the Warsaw Pact.

The layout of the T-64 is similar to that of the T-72, with the driver's compartment at the front, turret in the centre and engine and transmission at the rear. The driver is seated in the centre with a well-shaped glacis plate (probably of laminate armour) to his front. A vee-type splashboard on the glacis

plate stops water rushing up when the vehicle is fording a deep stream. When driving in the head-out position, the driver can quickly erect a cover over his position to protect himself against rain and snow.

The turret design is similar to that of the T-72 but is not thought to have advanced armour. The gunner is seated on the left and the tank commander on the right; no loader is required as an automatic loading mechanism is provided for the 125-mm gun, which is assumed to be the same as that of the T-72.

Armament is identical to that of the T-72 and consists of a fully stabilized 125-mm smooth-bore gun, a 7.62-mm (0.3-in) machine-gun co-axial with the main armament, and a 12.7-mm (0.5-in) machine-gun on the commander's cupola. The T-64 has an NBC system and a full range of night-vision equipment and, like most other Russian MBTs, it can be fitted with a front-mounted dozer blade and various types of mine-clearing systems such as roller or plough.

The only known variant is the **T-64K** command vehicle which carries a 10.0 m (32 ft 9⅔ in) high telescopic mast. When erected over the turret, this is held in position by stays that are pegged to the ground, preventing the tank from moving off quickly.

Specification
Crew: 3

The T-64 has only been seen in service with the USSR, and by all accounts has been unsuccessful and was replaced by the much improved T-72.

Weight: 38 tonnes
Engine: 5-cylinder diesel developing 700 to 750 hp (522 to 560 kW)
Dimensions: length (overall) 9.10 m (29 ft 10¼ in); length (hull) 6.40 m (21 ft 0 in); width (without skirts) 3.38 m (11 ft 1 in); height 2.30 m (7 ft 6½ in)
Performance: maximum road speed 70 km/h (43 mph); maximum range 450 km (280 miles); fording 1.4 m (4 ft 5½ in); gradient 60%; vertical obstacle 0.915 m (3 ft 0 in); trench 2.72 m (8 ft 11 in)

T-72 Main Battle Tank

The T-64 soon showed itself to be highly complicated and expensive to manufacture and maintain in the field. In the late 1960s an alternative design was begun. This appeared in 1971 as the T-72 and some 20,000 were later built. It remained available on the export market well into the 1990s.

The T-72 used a similar layout to the T-64, and some of the T-64's components. The hull used compound armour and the glacis plate was 200-mm thick, while the cast steel turret was 280-mm thick. The driver sits in the front of the hull, and other crew members, the commander and the gunner, occupy the turret. There is a combined day/night sight in the front of the turret, together with an infra-red searchlight. An unusual fitment was an optical stereoscopic rangefinder mounted across the turret front, later replaced by a laser rangefinder. Examples of the earlier model are still to be found in the armies of some Middle Eastern countries. This rangefinder was stabilised in the vertical plane and was capable of measuring to a range of 4 km (6.4 miles); its output was coupled to an electronic fire control computer linked to the gunner's optical sight. Night firing was performed by using the infra-red searchlight to illuminate the target and then switching in the infra-red component of the day/night sight. This system was replaced in later models by advanced fire control equipment.

The T-72 was driven by a transverse-mounted V-12 multi-fuel engine connected to a manual transmission giving seven forward and one reverse speed. There are six road-wheels on each side, with torsion-bar suspension instead of the T-64s variable hydro-pneumatic suspension.

Main armament is a 125-mm smooth-bore gun which fired APFSDS and HEAT-FS projectiles; it was then modified and provided with a gun-launched missile carrying a shaped charge warhead and capable of reaching to 4 km (6.4 miles) by riding on a projected laser beam. The conventional ammunition is carried in a rotary 'carousel' storage device which lies on the turret floor, while an autoloader occupies much of the turret rear. Ammunition – projectile and separate cartridge – is withdrawn from the carousel to the auto-loader and then rammed into the breech. Unfortunately the auto-loader went through several years of development before it was reliable; stories have been told of it attempting to ram the gunner into the breech instead of the projectile. On a good day it can reach a rate of eight rounds per minute. A 7.62-mm PKM machine gun is co-axially mounted alongside the main gun,

Provisional drawing of T-72 MBT with the commander's cupola fitted with 12.7-mm AA MG traversed rear. At hull rear are the long range fuel tanks that can be quickly jettisoned. Side skirts provide defence against ATGWs with their HEAT warheads.

and a 12.7-mm NSV heavy machine gun is mounted on top of the turret.

Eventually the T-72 was known to be in service with: Algeria. Bulgaria. Cuba Czechoslovakia. East Germany, Finland, Hungary. India. Iraq, Libya, Poland, Romania, Syria, Yugoslavia and, of course, the USSR. The T-72 was first used in combat by Syria against Israeli armoured units in southern Lebanon during the summer of 1982, where it was discovered that the 105-mm M68 APFSDS projectile and the TOW missile could both defeat the T-72's frontal armour.

A number of variant models of the **T72** have been developed, though the difference between them is often difficult to detect. The **T72K** is provided with additional communication equipment for formation commanders. The **T72A** has the optical rangefinder removed and replaced by a laser rangefinder. The **T72B** appeared in 1984 with increased frontal turret armour and an additional layer of armour in the glacis plate, doubtless as a result of the Syrian experiences. The **T72BV** is a T72B with explosive

reactive armour added; while the **T72B1** is the T72B with even thicker armour and a new fire control system. The basic T72 can also be found fitted with various types of mine roller or mine plough, according to whatever is fashionable at the time, and there are numbers of **BREM** armoured recovery and repair vehicles and **IMR-2** combat engineer vehicles built on the basic T72 chassis.

The T-72 was licence-built as the M84 in Yugoslavia for several years, , and in Romania where it was known as the TR-125. About 1100 were also built under licence in India.

Specification:
Crew: 3
Weight: 44.5 tonnes
Engine: V-12 multi-fuel developing 840 bhp at 2000 rpm
Dimensions: length (gun forward): 9.53 m. hull length 6.95 m; Width: 3.59 m; height to turret roof 2.22 m.
Performance: max road speed 60 km/hr. max range 480 km; vertical obstacle 0.85 m; trench 2.80 m; fording 1.8 m (5 m with preparation)

T-80 Main Battle Tank

Development of the T80 began in the early 1970s; pre-production models were tested from 1976 onwards, and full production began in about 1983. It has been estimated that perhaps 20,000 have been built; almost all have been issued to Russian first-line formations, though a small number are believed to have been supplied to India and Syria for trials.

The design follows generally upon the T-64 and T-72 patterns, with the driver in front, two-man turret in the centre of the hull, and engine and transmission at the rear. Much use has been made of compound laminated armour, and there is a permanently mounted bulldozer blade under the nose of the tank. The turret is also of compound armour and most service vehicles appear to be fitted with ERA (Explosive Reactive Armour) modules around the turret and on various parts of the hull. The commander is seated on the right side of the turret and the gunner on the left.

The main armament is the same 2A46M1 125-mm smoothbore gun as used in the late-production T-72 tanks. It is provided with an APFSDS projectile with a velocity of 1825 m/sec (1996 yd/sec) which is claimed to be capable of defeating 300-mm of armour at 60° angle of impact, though the range at which this is achieved is not stated. Considering that British 105–mm spun APDS could achieve this at 910 m (1000 yd) range forty years ago, it appears that the Russian 125-mm gun is not so efficient as might be expected.

The 125-mm gun can also launch the 9M119 'Kobra' gun-launched missile. This is a laser beam-riding missile which is fired like a gun projectile but which then picks up the transmitted beam from a laser projector on the tank. The gunner keeps his sight aligned on the target and the missile follows the sight alignment to a maximum range of about 4 km (6.4 miles) . It is provided with a shaped-charge warhead which should be able to defeat about 650–700 mm (25.6-77.6 in) of armour. The gun is provided with an automatic loading system mounted in the rear of the turret, and is also fitted with a thermal sleeve and fume extractor. A 7.62-mm machine gun is mounted co-axially, and a 12.7-mm NSV machine gun is mounted on the turret for use by the commander.

The T-80 is driven by a gas turbine engine coupled to a manual transmission system giving five forward and two reverse speeds. There are six roadwheels on each side, with torsion-bar suspension replacing the somewhat temperamental hydro-pneumatic suspension used on the T-64.

Other equipment includes a snorkel system for deep fording, an NBC system for filtering ventilation air, and night vision surveillance equipment for all three crew members. The fire control system is not known in detail, but is assumed to be an improvement on previous systems and to incorporate the usual thermal imaging night vision sight, laser

rangefinder and ballistic computer.

Known variants of the T-80 include the T-80K with ceramic armour on the turret; and the T-80BK with additional communications equipment for the use of formation commanders.

Specification:
Crew: 3
Weight: 42.5 tonnes
Engine: 1000 bhp gas turbine
Dimensions: length (gun forward): 9.90 m. hull length 7.40 m; width: 3.40 m; height to turret roof 2.20 m.

In March 1983 the US Department of Defense allocated the T-80 designation to the late production model of the T-72 MBT, although Soviet sources have given the latter the designation T-74.

Performance: max road speed 70 km/hr. max range 450 km; vertical obstacle 1.0 m; trench 2.85 m; fording 1.8 m (5 m with preparation).

Armoured Vehicles of the 1950s & 1960s

This chapter looks back at an interesting 'shake-down' period, in which armies and designers tried to guess which way warfare would evolve and how to design suitable vehicles for it. It was the era in which the true main battle tank was born and in which tank design moved beyond the scope of private enterprise.

The period 1950–70 was an interesting one for the watcher of armoured fighting vehicles (AFVs). The chaotic tank design race of the war years had barely subsided, and the appearance of the Soviet JS3 tank in the Berlin Victory Parade was causing shudders in the West.

The first major post-war change was the adoption of heavy tanks, a response to the Soviet JS3 and T-10. Two of these were the US M103 and the British Conqueror, which shared the same gun, based on the US 4.7-in AA weapon and firing a cumbersome brass-cased round. The British then put an experimental 183-mm gun into the Conqueror. But the facts were inescapable: these tanks were too heavy, too complex to maintain, and required separate logistic support. Within a decade they had gone.

Anti-tank missile systems were in their earliest days, and an Australian design, the Malkara tank destroyer, was a fair example. The massive HESH warhead could take out a tank with one blow, but the launcher was vulnerable and the missile inaccurate. In those days the M56 Scorpion and M50 Ontos self-propelled anti-tank guns probably seemed better value.

Old tanks never die; an elderly T-54 given a new lease of life by fitting a new 120-mm gun and a modern fire control system.

Gradually the concept of the all-purpose tank, explored by the British Centurion and US M48, took hold and the main battle tank was born. The Soviet T-54 edged out the T-10 and became the grandfather of a dynasty of tank designs. The Vickers MBT represented one of the last attempts at private enterprise. From now on the military design bureaux would produce their specifications, and though private contractors might bid, making minor design changes, they could no longer develop a stock model for general sale.

Airborne and light forces were also in the post-war picture: the Soviet N-ASU-57 gun was an example of an airborne self-propelled weapon which probably had greater propaganda value than it did tactical value.

Finally, the Panhard EBR was a pointer to the armoured cars of the future, while the Swiss Pz68 MBT represented a last 'home-grown' design. The financial realities of AFV technology meant that tank manufacture was henceforth undertaken by government-backed consortia.

M48A3 Main Battle Tank

USA

When the Korean War broke out in 1950, the USA had no medium tanks in production. As an interim measure the turret of the T43 medium tank then under development was put onto the chassis of the M46A1 tank and this entered production as the M47, well over 8,000 being built. The M47 has long been phased out of US Army service but remains in service with many countries including Greece, Italy, Spain, Pakistan and Portugal, to name but a few. Design work on a new medium tank, also armed with a 90-mm gun, started in the early 1950s under the designation T48, and this was ordered into production even before the first prototypes had been completed. The first production vehicles were completed at the Delaware Tank Plant, operated by the Chrysler Corporation, in July 1952, when the widow of General George Patton christened

M48A2 of the US Army with commander's and loader's hatch in the open position. By late 1983 the US Army still had over 2,000 of these vehicles on strength.

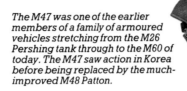

The M47 was one of the earlier members of a family of armoured vehicles stretching from the M26 Pershing tank through to the M60 of today. The M47 saw action in Korea before being replaced by the much-improved M48 Patton.

the type **Patton**. With such a short development period, which was justified by the international situation at that time, there were many problems with the early M48s, including poor reliability and a very short operating range of only 70 miles (113 km). The M48 was followed by the **M48A1**, **M48A2** and finally **M48A3**. The last had many modifications as a result of problems with the earlier vehicles, and was powered

by a Teledyne Continental AVDS-1790-2A diesel which increased the operational range of the tank to some 288 miles (463 km).

Production of the M48 series continued until 1959, by which time over 11,700 had been built. The M48 was succeeded in production by the M60 series, which itself is a further development of the M48. The M48 is still used by many countries around the world including Greece, Iran, Israel, Jordan, South Korea, Lebanon, Morocco, Norway, Pakistan, Portugal, Somalia, Spain, Taiwan, Thailand, Tunisia, Turkey, the USA and West Germany.

The M48, M48A1, M48A2 and M48A3 are all armed with a 90-mm gun, with a 7.62-mm (0.3-in) machine-gun mounted co-axially with the main armament and a 0.5-in (12.7-mm) machine-gun mounted in the commander's cupola. To extend the type's operational life, the **M48A5** was developed in the mid-1970s. This is essentially any one of the earlier models rebuilt and fitted with a 105-mm M68 gun (as fitted to the M60 series), a 7.62-mm (0.3-in) M60D machine-gun on the turret roof, a new powerpack and many other detailed modifications. From 1975 Anniston Army Depot converted well over 2,000 of the older M48 series MBTs to the M48A5 configuration, and apart from two battalions in Korea these are all deployed in the USA. The United States has also supplied many countries with kits to enable them to convert their existing

stocks of M48s to M48A5 standard. The West German company Wegmann has converted some 650 M48A2 tanks into the **M48A2GA2** version for the West German army. These have the British 105-mm L7A3 gun, new ammunition racks, new commander's cupola, passive night-vision equipment, Wegmann smoke dischargers and modifications to the fire-control system.

The automotive components of the M48 were also used in the **M88** ARV and the **M53** and **M55** self-propelled artillery weapons. Variants of the M48 include the **M67**, **M67A1** and **M67A2** flamethrower tanks (none of which are at present in front-line service) and the **M48** AVLB which is widely used in the US Army and has a scissors bridge launched over the front of the vehicle. Several countries, including Iran, Israel, Spain, Taiwan and Turkey have used the upgraded M48 with replacement engines, guns and fire control equipment, while the German firms of Wegmann and Krauss-Maffei collaborated to build the 'Super M48' as a private venture. This used a new German engine, new turret and British 105-mm gun. Numbers of German M48s were also converted into mine-clearing and armoured recovery vehicles.

The M48 series has seen combat with the United States and Vietnamese armies in South Vietnam, with the Pakistani army against India, and with the Israeli army against Jordan, Egypt and Syria. It has now proved to be a reliable tank, and when fitted with the 105-mm L7A3 or M68 gun can counter most tanks likely to be encountered on the battlefield today, especially when firing the new types of APFSDS-T ammunition developed by the United States, Israel and the United Kingdom.

Specification
Crew: 4
Weight: 47.17 tonnes
Engine: Continental AVDS-1790-2A 12-cylinder diesel developing 750 bhp (560 kW)
Dimensions: length (with gun forward) 8.686 m (28 ft 6 in); length (hull) 6.882 m (22 ft 7 in); width 3.631 m (11 ft 11 in); height 3.124 m (10 ft 3 in)
Performance: maximum road speed 48.2 km/h (30 mph); maximum range 463 m (288 miles)); fording 1.219 m (4 ft 0 in); gradient 60%; vertical obstacle 0.915 m (3 ft 0 in); trench 2.59 m (8 ft 6 in)

An early production M60 tank crosses a pontoon bridge. The M60 was virtually an upgunned M48 with an improved engine; it was quickly replaced by the M60A1, which had a completely redesigned turret.

USA
M50 Ontos tank destroyer

In the early 1950s the US Marine Corps issued a requirement for a highly mobile tank destroyer, and in October 1951 authorization was given for the building of no less than five prototype vehicles, all of which had various numbers of recoilless rifles as their main armament. These were built and tested, and in February 1953 approval was given for the procurement of 24 models of the **T165** which was armed with six 106-mm recoilless rifles. Trials with the first of these vehicles showed that some work was required with the mounting, fire-control system and suspension. The remaining vehicles were built to a slightly modified design and designated the **T165E2**. Following trials with the latter vehicles, and more modifications, the vehicle was finally accepted for service with the US Marine Corps and in 1955 was standardized as the Rifle, **Multiple, 106-mm Self-Propelled, M50** or, as it was normally called, the **Ontos** (Greek for The Thing). In August 1955 Allis Chalmers was awarded a production contract for 297 vehicles, which were all completed by November 1957. At a later date it was decided to replace the original General Motors petrol engine with a Chrysler petrol engine developing 180 hp (134 kW) and subsequently, in June 1963, the original manufacturer was awarded a contract to rebuild 294 M50 vehicles to the new configuration known as **M50A1**, at the same time a number of other minor improvements were made to the vehicle. The M50 was used in South Vietnam and in the Dominican Republic, but it has now

been retired from service with the US Marine Corps without a direct replacement, although ground- and vehicle-mounted TOW ATGWs carry out a similar function.

The vehicle was armed with six M40A1C recoilless rifles mounted on a common mount at the rear of the hull. These had a traverse of 40° left and right with an elevation of +20° and a depression of −10°, elevation and traverse all being manual. The top four recoilless rifles were fitted with a 12.7-mm (0.5-in) M8C spotting rifle: the weapons were first lined up with the optical sight and the spotting rifle was then fired, a hit on the target being indicated by a puff of smoke, whereupon the gunner knew that the recoilless rifle was correctly aligned with the target. One or more of the recoilless rifles could be fired, maximum effective range being about 1100 m (1,200 yards) although maximum range was over 7000 m (7,655 yards). The ammunition was of the fixed type and included HEAT (High Explosive Anti-Tank) and HEP-T (High Explosive Plastic-Tracer), the latter type being known as HESH in British service. Totals of 18 rounds of 106-mm and 80 rounds of spotting ammunition were carried. In addition an M1919A4 7.62-mm (0.3-in) machine-gun was fitted to the top of the mount for local protection.

The driver was seated at the front of the hull on the left, with the engine to his right and the very cramped crew compartment at the rear; entry to the latter was effected via two doors in the

hull rear. The engine was coupled to a General Motors Corporation (Allison Division) XT-90-2 cross drive transmission that transmitted power to the drive sprockets at the front of the hull.

The chassis was also used for a number of experimental vehicles but none of these, including several armoured/infantry carriers, entered production or service.

Specification
Crew: 3
Weight: 8.64 tonnes
Dimensions: length 3.82 m (12 ft 6⅜ in); width 2.60 m (8 ft 6¼ in); height 2.13 m

M50 Ontos tank destroyer as used by the US Marine Corps. Note the 12.7-mm spotting MGs above the top four 106-mm recoilless rifles. Once these had been fired the crew had to leave the vehicle to reload them.

(6 ft 11⅞ in)
Powerplant: one General Motors Corporation Model 302 petrol engine developing 145 hp (108 kW)
Performance: maximum road speed 48 km/h (30 mph); maximum road range 240 km (150 miles); gradient 60 per cent; vertical obstacle 0.76 m (30 in); trench 1.42 m (4 ft 8 in)

USA
M56 90-mm airborne self-propelled anti-tank gun

Apart from hand-held weapons, the most important anti-tank weapon used by US airborne forces in World War II was the jeep-towed 57-mm anti-tank gun M1, which was essentially the British 6-pdr made in the United States. After the war a requirement was issued for a highly mobile self-propelled anti-tank gun that could be air-dropped by parachute during the initial phases of airborne operations and have a firepower similar to that of a tank. Two prototypes of a vehicle called the **T101** were built by the Cadillac Motor Car Division of the General Motors Corporation. Further development resulted in the improved **T101E1** which was eventually standardized as the **Gun, Anti-tank, Self-propelled 90-mm M56**, or more commonly the **Scorpion**. Production was undertaken by the Cadillac Motor Car Division between 1953 and 1959. In the US Army the M56 was issued only to the 82nd and 101st Airborne Divisions, but was replaced in the 1960s by the M551 Sheridan Armored Reconnaissance/Airborne Assault Vehicle. A few M56s were supplied to Spain and Morocco, and some were also deployed by the US Army to Vietnam, where they were used mainly in the fire-support role.

The hull of the M56 was of all welded and riveted aluminium construction, with the engine and transmission at the front, gun in the centre and the crew area at the rear. The engine was coupled to a General Motors Corporation (Allison Division) transmission with one reverse and two forward ranges which in turn supplied power to the final drives on each side. The suspen-

M56 90-mm self-propelled anti-tank gun, which was often called the

Scorpion. This was developed specifically for the US 82nd and 101st Airborne Divisions. Its main drawback, apart from the recoil when the 90-mm gun was fired, was the complete lack of armour protection for the gun crew apart from the small shield. A total of 39 rounds of fixed 90-mm ammunition was carried for the gun, which had a maximum effective range of about 1500m (4920ft).

sion was of the torsion-bar type with four rubber-tyred road wheels, idler at the rear and drive sprocket at the front; there were no track-return rollers. The track consisted of a steel-reinforced endless rubber-band.

The main armament was a 90-mm gun M54 fitted with a muzzle brake and a vertical sliding breech block. The gun had an elevation of +15° and depression of −10°, and a traverse of 30° left and right, all manual. A total of 29 rounds of fixed ammunition was car-

One of the prototypes of the M56, then designated the T101, shortly after the 90-mm gun had fired, showing the gun recoilling to the rear and the forward part of the chassis lifting clear of the ground. The dust often obscured the gunner's line of sight for the next shot.

ried under and to the rear of the gun; AP-T, APC-T, HE-T, HEAT, HEAT-T, HEP-T, WP, TP-T, HVAP-T and HVTP-T rounds could be fired. The main drawback of the M56, which had much better firepower than the M41 light tank with its 76-mm gun, was that the chassis was too light and when the 90-mm gun was fired the vehicle often moved several feet and the target was obscured by dust from the muzzle brake.

Another drawback was the complete lack of armour protection for the crew, apart from the very small shield. The driver was seated to the left of the gun with the gunner to the rear; the latter was provided with a sight with a magnification of ×4.1 or ×8.

The chassis of the M56 was also used as the basis for a number of other vehicles including an armoured personnel carrier with a much higher superstructure with the troop compartment at the rear, 81-mm and 107-mm self-propelled mortar carriers, a 106-mm M40 recoilless anti-tank gun carrier, a missile launcher and an anti-aircraft vehicle fitted with four 12.7-mm (0.5-in) M2HB machine guns; none of these entered production or service.

Specification
Crew: 4
Weight: 7.03 tonnes
Dimensions: length (including gun) 5.841 m (19 ft 2 in); length (hull) 4.555 m (14 ft 11⅓ in); width 2.577 m (8 ft 5½ in); height 2.067 m (6 ft 9⅓ in)
Powerplant: one Continental 6-cylinder petrol engine developing 200 bhp (149 kW)
Performance: maximum road speed 45 km/h (28 mph); maximum road range 225 km (140 miles); gradient 60 per cent; vertical obstacle 0.762 m (30 in); trench 1.524 m (5 ft 0 in)

USA

M103 heavy tank

The standard American heavy tank at the end of World War II was the M26 Pershing, which saw action in the closing months of the European campaign; in the post-war period this was reclassified as a medium tank and again saw combat in Korea. Development of heavy tanks continued in the USA, a number of prototypes being built including the T29, T30, T34 and T32. With the advent of the Cold War design work commenced on three new tanks, the T41 light tank which was standardized as the M41, the T42 medium which resulted in the M47, and the **T43**. Trials with prototypes of the last revealed numerous deficiencies especially in the areas of turret and gun control equipment, and in the sighting system, none of which met the specifications of the user. Trials with modified vehicles designated **T43E1** showed that over 100 additional modifications were required, but the vehicle was eventually standardized as the **Tank, Combat, Full Tracked, 120-mm, M103**. A total of 200 vehicles was built by Chrysler at the Detroit Tank Plant between 1952 and 1954 for deployment with the 7th Army in Europe, where it was found that the weight and small range of action made the type difficult to employ. There were also

M103 heavy tank showing external 12.7-mm M2 anti-aircraft machine-gun on the commander's cupola. The M103 was designed to provide long-range support to the 90-mm armed M48 tanks and to counter the Soviet IS-3 tanks with their 122-mm guns. They were deployed to Europe but were soon phased out of service. In many respects the M103 was essentially a scaled-up M48 tank.

constant reliability problems, and the M103s were phased out of service with the US Army in the 1960s. A number were supplied to the US Marine Corps, and in the 1960s 153 vehicles were fitted with a type of new engine, which increased operational range from 130 to 480 km (80 to 300 miles); these were designated **M103A2**. They have since been phased out of service with the US Marine Corps, and none was supplied to any foreign countries under the MAP. The role of the M103 was to provide direct assault and long-range anti-tank support to the M47 and later the M48 (a similar role to that of the

British Conqueror heavy tank developed at the same time).

In many respects the M103 was virtually a scaled-up M48, with the driver at the front, turret and fighting compartment in the centre, and the engine and transmission at the rear. The commander's cupola, which was provided with an externally mounted 12.7-mm (0.5-in) M2HB machine-gun for anti-aircraft defence, was in the centre of the turret at the rear, while the gunner and one of the loaders were seated forward on the right with the second loader on the left. The torsion-bar suspension consisted of seven dual rub-

ber-tyred road wheels (with the drive sprocket at the rear and idler at the front) and six track-return rollers.

Main armament comprised a 120-mm rifled gun with an elevation of +15° and a depression of −8°, turret traverse being 360°. Ammunition was of the separate-loading type, and a total of 38 rounds (38 projectiles and the same number of charges) was carried. The following types of ammunition could be fired: AP-T, HE, HE-T, WP, WP-T and TP-T. A 7.62-mm (0.3-in) machine-gun was mounted co-axial with the main armament, and 5,250 rounds of ammunition were carried for this; stowage was provided for 1,000 rounds of 12.7-mm (0.5-in) ammunition. Standard equipment included crew compartment heaters, deep-fording equipment, infantry telephone and a fire extinguishing system.

To support the M103 the **M51** armoured recovery vehicle was built on the same chassis. This was fitted with a rear spade, winches and a heavy-duty crane for changing major components in the field.

Specification
Crew: 5
Weight: 56.7 tonnes
Dimensions: length (gun forwards) 11.32 m (37 ft 1½ in); length (hull) 6.98 m (22 ft 11 in); width 3.76 m (12 ft 4 in); height 2.88 m (9 ft 5⅜ in)
Powerplant: one Continental AV-1790-5B or 7C V-12 petrol engine developing 810 hp (604 kW)
Performance: maximum road speed 34 km/h (21 mph); maximum road range 130 km (80 miles); gradient 60 per cent; vertical obstacle 0.91 m (36 in); trench 2.29 m (7 ft 6 in)

One of the prototypes of the M103A1E1, with its turret traversed to the rear and the gun travel lock in the open position. The M103, like the similar British Conqueror heavy tank of the same period, was difficult to use operationally in West Germany because of its size and weight, which also made it difficult to conceal.

Conqueror heavy tank

In 1944 authorization was given to commence the **A45** tank project as the replacement for the **A43 Black Prince**, which itself was based on the Churchill infantry support tank. The A45 was intended to work with the A41 Centurion tank and share a number of common automotive components. In 1946 it was decided to develop a whole new range of armoured vehicles including the **FV200 Universal Tank** family, and in addition to the **FV201** basic gun tank a number of specialized vehicles were proposed including an AVRE, mine-clearing vehicle of the flail type, bridgelayer, ARV, assault personnel carrier, and a number of specialized vehicles for the Royal Artillery. The FV200 series was based on the A45 but had a longer hull, and the first prototype was completed in 1948. It was soon realized that many of the proposed variants were not feasible: the bridgelayer, for example, would be too large for the standard LCT. A decision was therefore taken to continue development of the Centurion as a gun tank and as the basis for a complete family of specialized vehicles. This proved to be a wise decision, and the Centurion family became the most successful tank of the post-war period, remaining in service to this day.

There was, however, a requirement for a heavy gun tank, the **FV214**, and the FV201 was used as the basis for this vehicle. To provide some experience with a tank of this size a chassis was fitted with the complete turret of the Centurion Mk 3 tank and called the **FV221 Medium Gun Tank Caernarvon**.

Just under 200 **FV214 Conqueror** tanks were built between 1955 and 1958, the majority of these being deployed to the British Army of the Rhine where they were issued to some of the armoured regiments on the basis of a troop of three vehicles or one Conqueror per Centurion squadron. The

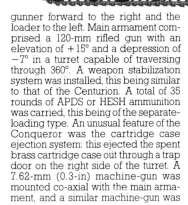

Conqueror heavy tank clearly showing its 120-mm gun that fired separate loading ammunition, and the commander's cupola, which was also fitted with a rangefinder and a 7.62-mm (0.3-in) anti-aircraft MG.

only advantage of the Conqueror over the Centurion with the 20-pdr gun was the former's improved armour protection and longer range of its main armament. Its major disadvantages were that it was too large, too heavy and difficult to maintain. The Conquerors were all withdrawn in the mid-1960s with the arrival of the Centurion with the 105-mm gun, and most ended up on ranges as hard targets, although one or two have been preserved.

In all there were over 30 projected models on the FV200 chassis, but the only model to see service apart from the Conqueror tank was the **FV219 ARV Mk 1**. One of the more interesting projects was the **FV215b** heavy-self-propelled anti-tank gun which had the engine moved forward to enable a limited-traverse turret (armed with a 180-mm gun) to be mounted at the rear.

The layout of the Conqueror was conventional, with the driver at the front on the right and ammunition to his left; turret and fighting compartment in the centre; and engine and transmission at the rear. The commander was provided with his own cupola in the centre of the turret at the rear, with the

The Conqueror was produced to provide long-range fire support to the Centurion, but was phased out of service in the 1960s.

gunner forward to the right and the loader to the left. Main armament comprised a 120-mm rifled gun with an elevation of +15° and a depression of −7° in a turret capable of traversing through 360°. A weapon stabilization system was installed, this being similar to that of the Centurion. A total of 35 rounds of APDS or HESH ammunition was carried, this being of the separate-loading type. An unusual feature of the Conqueror was the cartridge case ejection system: this ejected the spent brass cartridge case out through a trap door on the right side of the turret. A 7.62-mm (0.3-in) machine-gun was mounted co-axial with the main armament, and a similar machine-gun was

mounted on the commander's cupola for anti-aircraft defence.

Specification
Crew: 4
Weight: 65 tonnes
Dimensions: length (gun forwards) 11.58 m (38 ft 0 in); length (hull) 7.72 m (25 ft 4 in); width 3.99 m (13 ft 1 in); height 3.35 m (11 ft 0 in)
Powerplant: one 12-cylinder petrol engine developing 810 bhp (604 kW)
Performance: maximum road speed 34 km/h (21.3 mph); maximum road range 155 km (95 miles); gradient 60 per cent; vertical obstacle 0.91 m (36 in); trench 3.35 m (11 ft 0 in)

Centurion Main Battle Tank

The **Centurion** was developed during World War II as a cruiser tank under the designation **A41**, the first prototypes being completed early in 1945 and armed with the 17-pounder gun. The A41 was subsequently renamed the Centurion and entered production shortly after the end of the war. By the time production was completed in 1962, some 4,423 examples had been completed at four plants, namely the Royal Ordnance Factories at Leeds and Woolwich (early vehicles only), Leyland Motors at Leyland and Vickers at Elswick. The **Centurion Mk 1** and **Mk 2** were armed with the 17-pounder (76.2-mm gun), and the **Centurion Mk 3** with the 20-pounder (83.4-mm) gun. A total of 13 basic marks of Centurion were fielded, many of these having no less than three submarks. For example, the **Centurion Mk 10** was a **Mk 8** with more armour and a new 105-mm L7 gun, the **Centurion Mk 10/2** was Mk 10 with ranging machine-gun. All though its British army life the Centurion had the standard Rolls-Royce Meteor petrol engine which was a development of the Merlin aero engine. The Centurion was replaced as a gun tank in the British army by the Chieftain, but the last Centurions, used as observation post vehicles by the Royal Artillery, were not phased out of service until

very recently.

Many countries placed orders for the Centurion, and early in 1983 gun Centurions were still in service with Denmark, Israel, Jordan, the Netherlands, Somalia, South Africa, Sweden and Switzerland. Many of these countries have rebuilt the vehicle to extend its life well into the 1990s. For example Israel has replaced the petrol engine by a Teledyne Continental AVDS-1790-2A diesel coupled to an Allison CD-850-6 automatic transmission, this giving the tank a maximum speed of 27 mph (43 km/h) and a cruising range twice that of the Mk 5 hull on which the conversion is based. The Israeli Centurions, which when rebuilt are redesignated **Upgraded Centurion**, all have the 105-mm gun and carry additional ammunition.

There have been many specialized versions of the Centurion, including a variety of self-propelled weapons including the 25-pounder, 5.5-in and 180-mm guns, and a 120-mm tank destroyer. Versions that remain in service include the **Centurion Mk 2 ARV** fitted with large spades at the hull rear and a winch with a capacity of 31 tonnes, which with snatch blocks can be increased to 90 tonnes. The **Centurion/ AVRE (Assault Vehicle Royal Engineers)** is used only by the British

army and is fitted with a turret-mounted 165-mm demolition gun for the destruction of battlefield fortifications and a dozer blade at the front of the hull. It can also carry a fascine (large bundle of wood) which can be dropped into anti-tank ditches to enable following vehicles to cross, as well as tow a trailer carrying the ROF Giant Viper mine-clearance equipment. The **Centurion BARV** (Beach Armoured Recovery Vehicle) is another specialized version unique to the British army, and this is used to recover disabled vehicles on an invasion beach, as well as to push landing craft off the beach. The BARV was successfully used during the British landings at San Carlos Water in the Falklands. Other versions include the **Centurion AVLB** (armoured vehicle-launched bridge) and target tanks, while the Israelis have fitted a number of vehicles with special dozer blades and roller-type mine-clearing equipment.

The reason why the Centurion has been such a successful design is that it has been able to accept more armour and a larger gun (from the 17-pounder to the 20-pounder and finally to the famous 105-mm L7 gun) as the threat and technology have changed. All models have been fitted with a gun

stabilization system which keeps the gun on the target when the tank is moving across country, and many countries today are now installing advanced fire-control systems which include a laser rangefinder. The Centurion has seen combat with the British army in Korea, with the Australian army in Vietnam, with the Indian army against Pakistan, and with the armies of Israel, Egypt and Jordan in the Middle East. To many people, the Centurion has been the most successful tank design in the history of armoured warfare.

Specification
Crew: 4
Weight: 51.82 tonnes
Engine: Rolls-Royce Meteor Mk IVB V-12 petrol developing 650 bhp (485 kW)
Dimensions: length (with gun forward) 9.854 m (32 ft 4 in); length (hull) 7.823 m (25 ft 8 in); width 3.39 m (11 ft 1½ in); height (without AA MG) 3.009 m (9 ft 10½ in)
Performance: maximum road speed 34.6 km/h (21.5 mph); range 190 km (118 miles); gradient 60%; vertical obstacle 0.914 m (3 ft 0 in); trench 3.352 m (11 ft 0 in)

Vickers Main Battle Tank

Vickers' Elswick facility built many of the 4,423 Centurion MBTs built by 1961, but the company realized that for many countries Centurion's successor, the Chieftain, would be too heavy and too expensive. At about the same time the Indian army issued a requirement for a new MBT, and in 1961 the Vickers proposal was accepted. This was based on the company's private-venture design which had become known as the Vickers Main Battle Tank (VMBT). This used the proven 105-mm L7 series gun as well as some of the components of the Chieftain MBT, which was then about to enter production at both Royal Ordnance Factory Leeds and Vickers Elswick facility, including the 12.7-mm (0.5-in) ranging machine-gun, Leyland L60 engine, TN12 transmission, auxiliary engine, brakes and steering. The first two prototypes were completed in 1963 and by the following year a production line had been established in India, the first tank being completed in 1965 from components supplied by Vickers. But as time went on India produced more and more of the tank and by 1982 some 1,200 had been built, with production continuing. In 1968 Kuwait ordered 70 Vickers Mk I MBTs which were delivered between 1970 and 1972.

Vickers continued development of the tank with its own funds, the first stage being the replacement of the L60 engine by a Detroit Diesel, followed by a new all-cast turret with a welded bustle which could be fitted with different types of fire-control system. In 1977 Kenya ordered 38 Vickers Mk III MBTs plus three ARVs; these were delivered by 1980, and a second order was placed in 1978 for a further 38 MBTs plus four ARVs, all these being delivered by late 1982.

In 1981 Nigeria ordered 36 MBTs plus six ARVs and five AVLBs. These are being built at Vickers Defence Systems' new Armstrong Works, which were opened late in 1982. The famous old Elswick works, which produced armoured fighting vehicles and artillery pieces for some 100 years, has now been closed down and demolished.

The Mk III is also armed with the 105-mm L7 mounted in a turret which can be traversed through 360° and provides the gun with elevation of +20° and depression −10°. A 7.62-mm (0.3-in) machine-gun is mounted co-axially with the main armament, and a similar weapon is mounted on the commander's cupola. The latter can be aimed and fired from within the turret and be elevated to +90°. A bank of six electri-

cally-operated smoke dischargers is mounted on each side of the turret. The Nigerian vehicles are fitted with the Marconi Radar SFCS-600 (Simplified Fire Control System) which gives a high probability of a first-round hit. This system is now being fitted to some of the Indian Mk I MBTs. The commander has a Pilkington PE Condor day/night sight which enables him to lay and fire the main armament. As usual a whole range of optional equipment can be fitted to the Vickers Mark III MBT, including various radio installations, passive night-vision equipment, fire extinguishing system, a 0.5-in (12.7-mm) M2 HB machine-gun to replace the standard 7.62-mm (0.3-in) co-axial machine-gun, deep fording kit, full air filtration and pressurization, heater and so on.

The Vickers Armoured Bridge-laying Vehicle (VABV) is fitted with a bridge 44 ft (13.41 m) long, which is launched hydraulically over the front of the vehicle. The Vickers Armoured

Recovery Vehicle (VARV) is provided with a front mounted dozer/stabilizing blade and a winch with a maximum capacity of 25 tonnes which can be increased to 65 tonnes if required. Some vehicles have a hydraulic crane to enable them to change powerpacks (engine and transmission) in the field.

Vickers Mk I MBT with turret traversed to the right firing its 105 mm L7 rifled tank gun during a demonstration at the Royal Armoured Corps gunnery range at Lulworth. The Mk I is in service with Kuwait and India and is also manufactured in the latter country under the name of the Vijayanta; over 1200 have been built there.

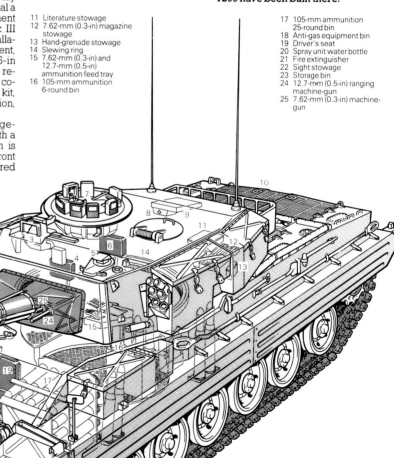

Vickers Mk I Main Battle Tank cutaway drawing key

1 QF 105-mm high-velocity gun
2 Smoke dischargers
3 Gunner's periscope sight
4 Gunner's seat
5 Loader's periscope
6 Commander's seat
7 Commander's cupola
8 First-aid box
9 Map board
10 Access to engine and transmission
11 Literature stowage
12 7.62-mm (0.3-in) magazine stowage
13 Hand-grenade stowage
14 Slewing ring
15 7.62-mm (0.3-in) and 12.7-mm (0.5-in) ammunition feed tray
16 105-mm ammunition 6-round bin
17 105-mm ammunition 25-round bin
18 Anti-gas equipment bin
19 Driver's seat
20 Spray unit water bottle
21 Fire extinguisher
22 Sight stowage
23 Storage bin
24 12.7-mm (0.5-in) ranging machine-gun
25 7.62-mm (0.3-in) machine-gun

The hull of the Vickers Mk III MBT can also be fitted with the Vickers Ship-building and Engineering Limited turret armed with a 155-mm howitzer which can fire an HE round to a maximum range of 26,250 yards (24000 m), or to 32,800 yards (30000 m) with a rocket-assisted projectile (RAP).

Specification
Crew: 4
Weight: 38.7 tonnes
Engine: 12-cylinder diesel developing 720 hp (537 kW)
Dimensions: length (with gun forward) 32 ft 1¾ in (9.788 m); length (hull) 24 ft 9¾ in (7.561 m); width 10 ft 4¾ in

(3.168 m); height (overall) 10 ft 2 in (3.099 m)
Performance: maximum road speed 31 mph (50 km/h); range 375 miles (600 km); gradient 60%; vertical obstacle 3 ft 0 in (0.914 m); trench 8 ft 0 in (2.438 m)

Vickers Mk III MBT of the Kenyan army, who took delivery of 76 vehicles plus seven armoured recovery vehicles between 1979 and 1982. It is now in production for Nigeria, who have also ordered the ARV plus the bridgelayer tank. The Mk I is powered by the Detroit Diesel engine.

 UK
Hornet Malkara tank destroyer

The **Hornet Malkara** weapon system was developed in the 1950s to give the Royal Armoured Corps a long-range anti-tank capability. At one time it was to have replaced the Conqueror heavy tank, but in the end it was only issued to the Parachute Squadron, Royal Armoured Corps, which used it until it was replaced in the 1970s by the Ferret Mk 5, which has four British Aerospace Dynamics Swingfire wire-guided ATGWs. The Parachute Squadron, RAC, consisted of a Squadron HQ; three guided-weapon troops each with a Ferret scout car, four Hornet Malkara launcher vehicles, a resupply vehicle and a REME resupply vehicle; a reconnaissance troop with six Ferrets; a missile resupply troop; an administration troop; and an REME attachment.

The Hornet Malkara essentially consisted of a modified Humber 1-tonne (4×4) armoured truck chassis with a launcher arm mounted at the rear of the hull for two Malkara wire-guided anti-tank missiles. For travelling the latter were lowered to the rear of the hull, but when the vehicle was deployed for action these were raised above the roof of the vehicle to fire over the cab.

The missile itself was developed in Australia by the Government Aircraft Factories, the Aeronautical Research Laboratories and the Weapons Research Establishment of the Australian Ministry of Supply, with the Royal Aircraft Establishment in England assisting. The co-ordinating design authority in England was the British Aircraft Corporation, later British Aerospace.

The operator was seated in the cab of the vehicle on the left, and he controlled the missile by a joystick which transmitted electrical signals along a wire unreeled from the missile sight. The operator observed the missile via a roof-mounted periscope sight with a magnification of ×10, and to assist him in keeping track of the missile the latter was fitted with flares. In addition the missile, which took 28 seconds to reach its maximum range of 4000 m (4,375 yards), could be launched up to 80 m (90 yards) away from the vehicle with the aid of a separation sight and controller. In addition to the two missiles in the ready-to-launch position, a further two missiles were carried; it took about two minutes to reload.

At launch the missile weighed just over 91 kg (200 lb), of which 27 kg (60 lb) comprised the HEAT warhead, which even today remains the largest warhead ever fitted to an ATGW sys-

Hornet Malkara tank destroyer in the travelling configuration, with the launcher and its two missiles in retracted position at hull rear. This was used by the Parachute Squadron, Royal Armoured Corps to give airborne troops a long range anti-tank capability; it was replaced by the Ferret Mk 5 with the Swingfire missile system. For economic reasons the Parachute Squadron, Royal Armoured Corps has now been disbanded.

tem and would deliver a knock-out blow to any tank in service at that time, including the Soviet IS and T-10 series of heavy tank. The missile was about 1.98 m (6 ft 6 in) long, 20.32 cm (8 in) in diameter and 0.79 m (2 ft 7¼ in) in span. There were four forward wings (two for yaw and two for pitch, the former each being fitted with a flare for tracking) and four stabilizing fins. The two-stage solid-fuel booster/sustainer rocket motor was mounted at the rear with the bobbin and associated wire in the centre of the missile.

The Hornet Malkara was designed specifically for paradropping, and could be ready for action about 10 mi-

nutes after landing. Although it was never used in anger, many of the features of the missile system, such as the joystick control and very useful separated sight capability, were later used in the British Aerospace Swingfire ATGW system, which is today the standard long-range ATGW of the British army; at present this is manned by the Royal Artillery, although it could soon be transferred to the Royal Armoured Corps.

Specification
Crew: 3
Weight: 5.8 tonnes
Dimensions: length 5.05 m (16 ft 7 in);

width 2.22 m (7 ft 3½ in); height 2.34 m (7 ft 8 in)
Powerplant: one Rolls-Royce B60 Mk 5A 6-cylinder petrol engine developing 120 bhp (89 kW)
Performance: maximum road speed 64 km/h (40 mph); maximum road range 402 km (250 miles); gradient 60 per cent; trench not applicable

Hornet Malkara tank destroyer with missiles in ready-to-launch position, and showing the optical sight in the roof of the vehicle. The missile could also be launched away from the vehicle.

ASU-57 airborne
self-propelled anti-tank gun

The **ASU-57** (ASU being the Soviet designation for airborne assault gun and 57 for the calibre of the gun) was developed in the 1950s specifically for use by the Soviet airborne divisions and was seen in public for the first time during a parade held in Red Square, Moscow, during 1957. The gun is a development of the World War II ZIS-2 M1943 anti-tank gun while its engine is from the Pobeda civilian car, and the vehicle may well be related to the OSU-76 self-propelled gun which was only developed to the prototype stage.

The hull of the ASU-57 is of welded aluminium construction with a uniform thickness of only 6 mm (0.24 in), which makes it very vulnerable. The engine is at the front on the right with the cooling system on the left and transmission at the very front. The open-topped crew compartment is at the rear with the driver and loader on the right, and the commander, who also acts as the gunner, on the left. Forward of the driver and commander is an armoured flap which contains two vision blocks; when the vehicle is not in the combat area this flap can be folded forwards to give improved vision. The top of the ASU-57 can be covered by a tarpaulin cover, and an unditching beam is often carried at the rear, this latter being a common feature on Soviet armoured vehicles. The torsion-bar suspension consists of four single rubber-tyred road wheels with the drive sprocket at the front and fourth road wheel acting as the idler, and two track-return rollers. The ASU-57 can ford to a depth of 0.7 m (28 in) but has no NBC system.

The vehicle is armed with a Ch-51 or Ch-51M rifled gun offset slightly from the vehicle's centreline. The Ch-51 was the first model to enter service

ASU-57 airborne self-propelled anti-tank gun, armed with a 57-mm CH-51M gun with a double baffle muzzle brake. For many years this was the main self-propelled anti-tank gun of the Soviet airborne divisions but has now been replaced by the ASU-85, which has a bigger gun and much improved armour protection.

and has a long barrel with a multi-slotted muzzle brake. This was followed by the Ch-51M, which has a shorter barrel with a double-baffle muzzle brake. Both weapons have a vertical sliding breech-block and hydro-spring recoil system, and fire the following types of fixed ammunition: HE fragmentation (muzzle velocity 695 m/2,280 ft per second), AP-T (muzzle velocity 980 m/3,215 ft per second and capable of penetrating 85 mm/3.35 in of armour at 0° at a range of 1000 m/1,095 yards), and HVAP (capable of penetrating 100 mm/ 3.94 in of armour at 0° at a similar range). A total of 30 rounds of ammunition is carried, and it is estimated that a well trained crew can fire a maximum of 10 rounds a minute. The gun has manual elevation and traverse, the former being from −5° to +12°, and the latter 8° left and 8° right. The vehicle is often used to carry four paratroops, and a 7.62-mm (0.3-in) machine-gun is carried. This can be dismounted for use in the ground role.

ASU-57 advances across the snow while in the background an 85-mm auxiliary propelled anti-tank gun is positioned. Note the unditching beam carried on the left side of the hull of the ASU-57, and the driver's head in an exposed position.

Each Soviet airborne division has three rifle regiments, and each of these had one battalion each with three six-gun batteries with ASU-57s, giving the division a total of 54 such weapons. In the USSR the ASU-57 is now used only for training as it has been replaced in front line use by the ASU-85, which not only has a more powerful gun but also much improved armour protection. It is interesting to note that the ASU-57 was developed at roughly the same time as the American M56 self-propelled anti-tank gun with its 90-mm gun.

When originally introduced, the ASU-57 was packed in a special container and two of these were carried under a Tupolev Tu-4 heavy bomber, one under each wing. On the Antonov An-12 introduced in the late 1950s, two

ASU-57s could be carried internally on individual pallets. Such pallets were provided with parachutes and a retro-rocket system to soften the impact on landing.

Specification
ASU-57 (with CH-51M gun)
Crew: 3
Weight: 3.35 tonnes
Dimensions: length (including gun) 4.995 m (16 ft 4⅔ in); length (hull) 3.48 m (11 ft 5 in); width 2.086 m (6 ft 10 in); height 1.18 m (3 ft 10½ in)
Powerplant: one M-20E 4-cylinder petrol engine developing 55 hp (41 kW)
Performance: maximum road speed 45 km/h (28 mph); maximum road range 250 km (155 miles); gradient 60 per cent; vertical obstacle 0.5 m (20 in); trench 1.4 m (4 ft 7 in)

T-10 heavy tank

During World War II the USSR developed a series of heavy tanks including the IS-3 and IS-4 (alternatively JS-3 and JS-4) which were armed with a potent 122-mm gun firing separate-loading ammunition and were provided with excellent armoured protection. Post-war this basic type saw service in the Middle East with Egypt, and some captured by Israel in the 1967 war were then used for static defence on the Suez Canal against their former owners.

In the immediate post-war period the USSR continued the development of heavy tanks as did the United States (the M103) and the United Kingdom (the Conqueror), and among further prototypes built were the IS-5, IS-6, IS-7, IS-8 and IS-9. The last was accepted for service as the **T-10**, an improved later model being called the **T-10M**. It is believed that at least 2,500 production tanks were built before production was completed in the late 1950s. The T-10 was never exported, and was withdrawn from service in the 1970s when it became obvious that, even upgraded, it was unlikely to survive for long on a modern battlefield. The main role of the T-10 was to provide long range fire support for the T-54/T-55 tanks armed with 100-mm guns, and also to lead an armoured thrust through

T10 heavy tank, showing 12.7mm DShKM anti-aircraft machine gun on the commander's cupola. In spite of periodic updating, it remained basically a World War II tank and was retired to the reserve in the 1970s and eventually scrapped in the 1980s.

areas with a high degree of anti-tank defences, where the T-10's heavy armour protection would have proved most useful.

The hull of the T-10 is of rolled steel armour: the front is 230 mm (9.06 in) thick, the sides and upper front are 120 mm (4.72 in) thick, and the remainder of the hull varies from 20 mm to 80 mm (0.79 to 3.15 in) thick. The turret is all cast: the turret mantlet is 250 mm (9.84 in) thick, the sides are 100 mm (3.94 in) thick and the rear is 25 mm (1 in) thick. The driver is seated at the front of the hull and the other three crew members in the turret, with the commander and gunner on the left and the loader on the right. The engine and transmission are at the rear of the hull.

Main armament consists of a 122-mm

gun that is provided with a double-baffle muzzle brake and a bore evacuator to remove fumes from the barrel. It fires separate-loading ammunition (projectile and charge) of the following types: APC-T which will penetrate 185 mm (7.28 in) of armour at 1000 m (1,095 yards), HEAT which will penetrate 460 mm (18.1 in) of armour at a similar range, and HE fragmentation which is used against troops in the open and other soft battlefield targets. Separate-loading ammunition had to be used as otherwise the complete round would have been too heavy and difficult for handling in the cramped confines of the turret. A total of 30 rounds (30 projectiles and the same number of charges) is carried. A 12.7-mm (0.5-in) DShKM machine-gun is

mounted co-axial with the main armament, and a similar weapon is mounted on the loader's cupola for anti-aircraft defence.

The T-10 was succeeded by the T-10M, which has the following recognizable alterations: the 12.7-mm (0.5-in) DShKM machine-guns have been replaced by the more powerful 14.5-mm (0.57-in) KPV series, which is used in a number of other Soviet AFVs including the BRDM-2 (4×4) reconnaissance vehicle and the BTR-60PB (8×8) APC; the 122-mm gun has a multi-baffle muzzle brake in place of the double-baffle muzzle brake; the main armament is stabilized in both horizontal and vertical planes; infra-red night-vision equipment has been installed, as has an overpressure NBC system; and finally a large sheet-metal stowage box is often mounted externally at the turret rear. There are no known variants of the T-10 heavy tank, although several variants of the earlier IS-3 remain in service to this day.

Specification
Crew: 4
Weight: 50 tonnes
Dimensions: length (including gun) 9.875 m (32 ft 4¾ in); length (hull) 7.04 m (23 ft 1 in); width 3.566 m (11 ft 8½ in); height 2.25 m (7 ft 4½ in)
Powerplant: one V-12 diesel develop-

ing 700 hp (522 kW)
Performance: maximum road speed 42 km/h (26 mph); maximum road range 250 km (155 miles); gradient 62 per cent; vertical obstacle 0.9 m (35½ in); trench 3.0 m (9 ft 10 in)

T-10M heavy tank, which had its 12.7-mm machine-guns replaced by 14.5-mm KPVs, and has a multi-baffle muzzle brake for the 122-mm gun, infra-red night vision equipment for the commander, gunner and driver, and an overpressure system.

T-54 Main Battle Tank

In 1946 the USSR designed a new medium tank called the T-44, and this was produced in small numbers between 1945 and 1949 although it was not considered to be a satisfactory design. In 1946 prototypes of a new design, the **T-54**, were completed and this type entered production several years later. The T-54 and its variants were built in larger numbers than any other Russian tank to appear after World War II, and by the time production of the improved **T-55** was completed in 1980-1 it is estimated that well over 50,000 vehicles had been built. The series was also built in Czechoslovakia and Poland for both the home and export markets, while the Chinese produced an almost identical version designated Type 59. Further development of the T-54 and T-55 resulted in the **T-62**.

The T-54 has an all-welded hull divided into three compartments (driver's at the front, fighting in the centre, and engine and transmission at rear). The driver is seated at the front of the hull on the left and steers the tank with conventional sticks. An unusual feature of the T-54 is that it has a 7.62-mm (0.3-in) machine-gun fixed in the centre of the glacis plate to fire forwards, this being fired when the driver presses a button on his right steering lever. The commander and gunner are seated on the left of the turret, with the loader on the right. The turret is a casting with the top welded into position. One of the major weaknesses of the T-54 series has been its engine and transmission, which have proved very unreliable in service.

The main armament consists of a 100-mm gun, which was developed from a naval weapon of the same calibre and also used in a modified form in the SU-100 tank destroyer developed in World War II. A well-

The T-54 tank was developed in the late 1940s and has probably been produced in greater numbers than any other Soviet tank in the post-war period. It has also been produced in China, Poland and Czechoslovakia and has seen combat in countless campaigns since World War II, especially in the Middle East, where it has been used by the Arab states against Israel.

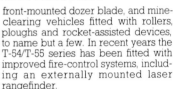

trained crew can fire about four rounds per minute, and the types of ammunition that can be fired includes AP-T, APC-T, HE, HE-FRAG, HEAT-FS and HVAPDS-T. The last was introduced some time after the T-54 entered production and will penetrate well over 200 mm (7.9 in) of armour at a range of 1000 m (1,095 yards). A total of 34 rounds of 100-mm ammunition is carried, a poor quantity when compared with contemporary Western tanks. One of the major drawbacks of the T-54 family is that the main armament can only be depressed to −4°, which makes firing from a hill or reverse slope almost impossible. A 7.62-mm (0.3 in) SGMT is mounted co-axially with the 100-mm gun, and a similar weapon is mounted in the bow. A 12.7-mm (0.5-in) DShKM anti-aircraft machine-gun is mounted on the loader's hatch. The tank does not have smoke dischargers as it can lay its own smoke screen by injecting diesel fuel into the exhaust pipe on the left side of

the hull just above the track.

The basic T-54 was improved as the years went by. The **T-54A** included stabilization of the 100-mm gun in the vertical plane. The **T-54B** was the first production model to incorporate infra-red night-vision equipment, subsequently retrofitted to earlier vehicles, and its armament was stabilized in both the horizontal and vertical planes. The **T-54C** was not fitted with an AA MG, although such a weapon was refitted at a later date. The T-55 succeeded the T-54 in production in the late 1950s and has numerous improvements including more ammunition stowage, new 7.62-mm (0.3-in) machine-guns, and improved NBC protection. There have been countless versions of the T-54 family, including a flamethrower tank, armoured recovery vehicles (including Russian, Polish and Czech versions), bridgelayers (built by East Germany, Czechoslovakia and the USSR), dozer tanks, a combat engineer vehicle fitted with an hydraulic crane and

front-mounted dozer blade, and mine-clearing vehicles fitted with rollers, ploughs and rocket-assisted devices, to name but a few. In recent years the T-54/T-55 series has been fitted with improved fire-control systems, including an externally mounted laser rangefinder.

The T-54/T-55 series has seen extensive combat in the Middle East, North Africa, Angola and the Far East. On a one-for-one basis Western tanks of the same period, such as the British Centurion and American M48, have proved more than a match for the T-54/T-55, especially during the fighting between Israel and Egypt and Syria.

Specification
Crew: 4
Weight: 36 tonnes
Engine: V-12 diesel developing 520 hp (388 kW)
Dimensions: length (with gun forward) 9 m (29 ft 6⅓ in); length (hull) 6.45 m (21 ft 2 in); width 3.27 m (10 ft 8¾ in); height (turret roof) 2.4 m (7 ft 10½ in)
Performance: maximum road speed 48 km/h (30 mph); maximum range 400 km (249 miles); fording 1.4 m (4 ft 7 in); gradient 60%; vertical obstacle 0.8 m (2 ft 7½ in); trench 2.7 m (8 ft 10¼ in)

Soviet T-54 series tanks lined up in a street in Prague during the unrest in Czechoslovakia in 1968. The white stripes have been a common marking on Soviet vehicles when invading other countries.

Soviet T-54 with turret traversed to the rear, and the loader manning the 12.7-mm DShKM anti-aircraft machine-gun. The tank can also lay its own smokescreen by injecting diesel fuel into the exhaust outlet.

EBR heavy armoured car

The Panhard EBR (Engin Blindé de Reconnaissance, or armoured reconnaissance vehicle) has the distinction of being probably the oldest design of armoured car still in service in the world today. Its origins can be traced to 1937, when Panhard and Levassor of Paris started design work on a new armoured car that would have superior cross-country mobility to the 4×4 armoured cars then in use with the French army. The first prototype was completed in 1939 and was armed with a 25-mm cannon and a co-axial 7.5-mm (0.295-in) machine-gun. Its most unusual feature was that of its eight road wheels, the four centre ones (two on each side) were fitted with steel rims for improved traction. For road use these were raised clear of the ground by a hydro-pneumatic unit operated by the driver, and lowered again when crossing country. The prototype was taken to North Africa when World War II broke out, and its eventual fate is unknown.

After the end of the war the French army issued a requirement for a new heavy armoured car and, after a number of proposals from French companies had been studied, Panhard and Levassor was awarded a contract for an 8×8 vehicle while Hotchkiss was awarded a contract for a 6×6 vehicle. Each company built two prototypes for evaluation by the French army, and the Panhard and Levassor vehicle was subsequently selected for service as the EBR. The first production vehicles were completed in 1950. Production was completed in 1960 after some

From 1950 to 1972 the Panhard EBR was the standard heavy armoured car of the French army, although its design dates back to before World War II. An unusual feature of the vehicle is that its centre road wheels, which have steel rims, are normally raised when travelling on roads and lowered only when going across country, so improving ground traction in mud and soft soils.

1,200 vehicles had been built. In addition to the French army, the type was also exported to Mauritania, Morocco and Tunisia. An armoured personnel carrier version, the **EBR VTT**, was also developed by Panhard on the same chassis, and a few of these were exported to Portugal where they have been used mainly for internal security use. Today the EBR remains in service with the French army, although it is slowly being replaced by the much more sophisticated and expensive AMX-10RC (6×6) armoured vehicle which is also amphibious. It is expected that the EBR will not finally be phased out of service until 1987, some 50 years after it was first designed.

The driver is seated at the front, with commander and gunner in the centre of the vehicle, the engine in the floor and the second driver at the rear. The EBR is fitted with an FL-11 oscillating turret armed with a 90-mm gun, 7.5-mm (0.295-in) co-axial machine-gun and two banks of two electrically oper-

ated smoke-dischargers. In an oscillating turret the gun is fixed in the upper part of the turret which pivots on the lower part of the turret. The 90-mm gun fires the following types of fixed ammunition: HEAT (muzzle velocity 640 m/2,100 ft per second), high explosive (muzzle velocity 635 m/2,085 ft per second), smoke (muzzle velocity 750 m/2,460 ft per second) and canister for close defence. A total of 43 rounds of 90-mm and 2,000 rounds of 7.5-mm (0.295-in) ammunition is carried. Another unusual feature of the EBR is that the drivers at the front and rear are each provided with a fixed 7.5-mm (0.295-in) machine-gun firing forwards, although in peace time this is rarely fitted. As with many armoured vehicles developed in the 1950s, the EBR is not fitted with an NBC system and has no infra-red night-vision equipment.

Some vehicles were fitted with the FL-10 turret of the AMX-13 light tank armed with a 75-mm gun fed by two revolver type magazines, each holding

six rounds of ammunition. These allowed 12 rounds to be fired very quickly, after which the magazines had to be reloaded manually from outside the vehicle. The main drawback of this combination was that the weight of the vehicle went up to over 15 tonnes, while overall height also increased and so facilitated detection in the field.

Specification
Crew: 4
Weight: 13.5 tonnes
Dimensions: length (gun forwards) 6.15 m (20 ft 2 in); width 2.42 m (7 ft 11¼ in); height 2.32 m (7 ft 7⅓ in)
Powerplant: one Panhard 12-cylinder petrol engine developing 200 hp (149 kW)
Performance: maximum road speed 105 km/h (65 mph); maximum range 650 km (404 miles); gradient 60 per cent; vertical obstacle 0.4 m (15¾ in); trench 2.0 m (6 ft 7 in)

Pz 68 Main Battle Tank

Like many other countries after the end of World War II, Switzerland turned to the UK to meet its immediate needs for a MBT and ordered some 200 Centurions, a further 100 being obtained from South Africa. The Federal Construction Works at Thun, which had already designed and built prototypes of the NK I 75-mm self-propelled anti-tank gun and the NK II 75-mm assault gun, completed the prototype of a Swiss designed MBT in 1958. This was armed with a 90-mm gun and called the **KW 30**; a second prototype was completed in 1959. Between 1960 and 1961 10 pre-production tanks were built under the designation **Pz 58**; these were armed with the British 20-pounder gun as then installed in the Centurion. In 1961 an order was placed for 150 production vehicles armed with the 105-mm L7 gun. Under the designation **Pz 61** these were delivered to the Swiss army between 1965 and 1966.

The Pz 61 was followed in production by the **Pz 68**, which had a number of modifications including the replacement of the co-axial 20-mm cannon by a 7.5-mm (0.295-in) machine-gun; other alterations include a gun stabilization system, wider tracks and increased length of track in contact with the ground. A total of 170 Pz 68s was built between 1971 and 1974; these were followed by 50 **Pz 68 Mk 2** (delivered in

Pz68 MBT of the Swiss army, showing the thermal sleeve fitted to the 105-mm gun. This tank has now been replaced by the German Leopard 2, built in Switzerland.

1977), 110 **Pz 68 Mk 3** (delivered in 1978/79) and finally 60 **Pz 68 Mk 4** which were delivered between 1981 and 1982.

The layout of the Pz 68 is conventional, with the driver at the front, turret in the centre, and engine and transmission at the rear. The turret is of cast steel construction with the commander and gunner on the right and the loader on the left. Unlike many tanks, in the Pz 68 the loader operates the anti-aircraft machine-gun, so allowing the tank commander to carry out his proper role of commanding the tank. The main armament consists of a 105-mm gun with an elevation of +21° and a depression of −10°; there is a 7.5-mm (0.295-in) co-axial machine-gun and a similar anti-aircraft machine-gun. Three smoke dischargers are mounted on each side of the turret and

more recently most vehicles have been fitted with two Bofors Lyran launchers on the turret roof to provide target illumination at night.

Using the chassis of the Pz 68 several variants have been developed including the **Entpannungspanzer 68** ARV, the **Brückenpanzer 68** armoured bridgelayer and a target tank. Prototypes of an anti-aircraft tank (armed with twin 35-mm cannon) and a 155-mm self-propelled gun were built, but these were not placed in production. The ARV is fitted with a stabilizer/dozer blade at the front of the hull, an A-frame which can lift 15 tonnes and an hydraulic winch with a capacity of 25 tonnes increasable to 75 tonnes with the aid of snatch blocks.

The Pz 61 and Pz 68 have not been among the more successful of post-war designs, and in 1979 a report stated

that there were some 50 faults in the Pz 68; some of these were quite serious, including short track life, gun not staying on the target and cracking fuel tanks.

Specification
Crew: 4
Weight: 39.7 tonnes
Engine: MTU 8-cylinder diesel developing 660 hp (492 kW)
Dimensions: length (with gun forward) 9.49 m (31 ft 1⅔ in); length (hull) 6.98 m (22 ft 11 in); width 3.14 m (10 ft 3⅔ in); height (including AA MG) 2.88 m (9 ft 5½ in)
Performance: maximum road speed 55 km/h (34 mph); maximum range, road 350 km (217 miles); fording 1.1 m (3 ft 7⅓ in); gradient 60%; vertical obstacle 1 m (3 ft 3⅓ in); trench 2.6 m (8 ft 6⅓ in)

Light Tanks and Reconnaissance Vehicles

Once too weak and poorly armed to take care of themselves, light armoured vehicles today could outgun a World War II battle tank. New armament and improved protection has given the light and agile armoured vehicle a new lease of life.

World War II showed that the light tank as a combat vehicle was obsolete, but that there was a requirement for a nimble armoured vehicle for reconnaissance and scouting purposes. This led to a number of armoured car designs. There was a brief period in the 1960s when air-mobility became fashionable and one or two light tank designs were suggested. Air-portable they might have been, fighting vehicles they were not. An air-landed force is restricted in the armour it can deploy, but the ground force is under no such restriction, and light armour is unlikely to survive for long.

The current crop of armoured cars and light armoured vehicles owe their existence to the advances in gun and ammunition technology of the past 30 years. An armoured car of today can mount a gun of much greater power than could a main battle tank (MBT) of World War II and the projectile it fires can do more damage that its wartime equivalent. Consequently it can perform its scouting tasks in the knowledge that if it meets trouble, it can take care of itself. This is an improvement on the old armoured cars which, if they were lucky, had a 20-mm cannon for defence.

A prototype of the US CCV-L light tank being loaded into a C-130 Hercules aircraft in a demonstration of air-portability. The CCV-L developed into the M8 armoured gun system (AGS).

The selection that follows in this chapter covers a wide span, from the British Ferret, which would not have looked out of place in 1944, to the AMX-10RC, which resembles a tank with wheels. The M551 Sheridan exemplifies the dangers of exceeding one's technological reach: the gun-launched missile was ahead of its time, but costly.

The Cascavel represented the early arms industry in Brazil, an industry which has since achieved several notable designs which have sold well within South America and beyond. The two Alvis designs, the Saladin and the Scorpion, show the British Army's flirtation with a wheeled armoured personnel carrier (APC) and its longer-lasting affair with a

lightweight highly mobile tank. The three French designs of armoured car – the AMX-10RC, the Sagaie and the AML-90 – show the gradual progression from a scouting role to a fighting one, and the two light tanks, the Austrian SK105 and the French AMX-13, show some remarkable similarities for designs which were 20 years apart.

SK-105 Light Tank/Tank Destroyer

The **Jagdpanzer SK-105** was designed by Steyr in the mid-1960s to meet an Austrian army requirement for a highly mobile and hard-hitting tank destroyer suitable for operation in Austria's unique terrain. The first prototype was completed in 1967, and production began in the early 1970s. By early 1983 about 400 vehicles had been built, 150 for the Austrian army and the remainder for the export market, in which sales have been made to Argentina, Bolivia, Morocco, Nigeria and Tunisia. The engine, transmission, tracks, suspension and many other automotive components are identical to those of the Steyr-Daimler-Puch family of tracked vehicles, which have also been exported in large numbers.

The hull of the SK-105 is of all-welded steel armour, with the driver's compartment at the front, the turret in the centre, and the engine and transmission at the rear. Over its frontal arc the vehicle has complete protection from attack by all weapons up to 20-mm calibre, protection against small arms fire being provided over the remainder of the vehicle.

The turret is a modified version of the French Fives-Cail-Babcock FL-12 as installed on the AMX-13 light tank, and is of the oscillating type, with the gun fixed to the upper part, which pivots on the lower part. The commander is seated on the left and the gunner on the right, both with a hatch cover and observation devices. The main armament comprises a 105-mm (4.13-in) gun fitted with a thermal sleeve and a muzzle-brake; elevation is +13° and depression −8°, and turret traverse is 360°. Ammunition stowage is provided for totals of 44 105-mm (4.13-in) main armament rounds and 2,000 rounds of 7.62-mm ammunition for the co-axial machine-gun. The 105-mm (4.13-in) gun is fed by two revolver-type magazines in the turret bustle, this enabling the gun to fire until the ammunition is exhausted. One of the crew then has to leave the vehicle in order to reload the magazines. The empty brass cartridge cases are ejected from the turret through a small trap in the bustle. The

fire-control system includes telescopes for both the commander and gunner, with an infra-red/white-light searchlight above this. The latter enables targets to be engaged at night. Mounted on each side of the turret is a bank of three electrically-operated smoke-dischargers.

The engine and transmission are at the rear, the latter being a ZF manual box with six forward and one reverse gears. Suspension is of the torsion-bar type, and consists of five dual rubber-tyred road wheels with the drive sprocket at the rear, idler at the front and three track-return rollers. Standard equipment includes an NBC system and a heater.

Variants of the SK-105 include the **Greif** armoured recovery vehicle, a pioneer vehicle and a driver training vehicle. The Greif is fitted with a 6-tonne hydraulic crane, a dozer/stabilizer blade at the front of the hull, a winch with a capacity of 20 tonnes, and full provision for carrying spare parts and tools.

Specification
Crew: 3
Weight: 17.5 tonnes
Dimensions: length (including gun) 7.763 m (25 ft 5⅔ in); length (hull) 5.58 m (18 ft 3⅔ in); width 2.50 m (8 ft 2½ in); height 2.529 m (8 ft 3½ in)
Powerplant: one Steyr 6-cylinder

The SK-105 light tank/tank destroyer climbs an incline, showing the turret roof at the rear with an infra-red/white light searchlight mounted above. The 105-mm (4.13-in) gun is fed by two revolver-type magazines, each of which hold six rounds of fixed ammunition for ready use.

diesel developing 320 hp (239 kW)
Performance: maximum road speed 65 km/h (40 mph); maximum range 520 km (325 miles); fording 1.00 m (3 ft 3 in); vertical obstacle 0.80 m (2 ft 7½ in); trench 2.41 m (7 ft 11 in)

ENGESA EE-9 Cascavel Armoured Car

For many years the standard armoured car of the Brazilian army was the US 6×6 M8 Greyhound that was developed in the early 1940s and armed with a 37-mm gun. By the late 1960s spares for the vehicle were becoming difficult to obtain, and its armament was obviously inadequate. The São Paulo company ENGESA had already converted many trucks, for example from 6×4 to 6×6 configuration, so giving them an excellent cross-country mobility. ENGESA then went on to develop two armoured vehicles to meet the requirements of the Brazilian army: these were the 6×6 **EE-9 Cascavel** armoured car and the 6×6

The latest production ENGESA EE-9 Cascavel armoured car, showing the laser rangefinder mounted externally over the 90-mm (3.54-in) gun and 7.62-mm machine-gun mounted externally at the commander's station. This vehicle has been widely used by the Iraqi army during the recent conflict with Iran.

EE-11 Urutu armoured personnel carrier, which shared many common automotive components although their layouts are quite different. The first prototype of the EE-9 Cascavel, named after a Brazilian snake, was completed in 1970 and was followed by a batch of pre-production vehicles before the first production vehicles were completed at the company's new facility at São José dos Campos in 1974. Since then large numbers have been built not only for the Brazilian army but also for many other countries around the world including Bolivia, Chile, Colombia, Cyprus, Gabon, Iraq, Libya, Tunisia and Uruguay, to name a few. The Cascavel has been used operationally by the Iraqi army in the the recent war with Iran.

Although some five different marks of the Cascavel have now been produced, the layout of all EE-9s is essentially the same. The armour is of an unusual design developed by the company in conjunction with the University of São Paulo, and consists of an outer layer of hard steel with an inner layer of softer steel roll-bonded and heat-treated to give the maximum possible protection within the weight limit of the vehicle; increased protection is provided over the frontal arc.

The driver is seated at the front of the vehicle on the left, with the two-man turret in the centre, and the engine and transmission at the rear. The engine is either a Detroit Diesel or a Mercedes-Benz diesel, coupled to an automatic or manual transmission. Spare parts for both the engine and transmission are available from commercial sources all over the world. All six wheels are powered, power-assisted steering is provided on the front two wheels. The rear suspension is of the ENGESA-designed Boomerang type that gives excellent cross-country mobility.

The initial **Cascavel Mk I** had the same gun as the M8, but all of these vehicles have now been rebuilt with the ENGESA turret armed with a 90-mm (3.54-in) gun. The **Cascavel Mk II** was for export only, and has a French Hispano-Suiza H-90 turret armed with a 90-mm (3.54-in) DEFA gun. The other models, the **Cascavel Mks III, IV** and **V**, have a two-man ENGESA-designed turret armed with a 90-mm (3.54-in) Cockerill Mk III gun (produced in Brazil by ENGESA), a 7.62-mm machine-gun mounted co-axially with the main armament, and a 12.7-mm or 7.62-mm machine-gun mounted on the roof for anti-aircraft defence.

As with most armoured cars today, a wide range of optional equipment can be fitted to the Cascavel, including a fire-control system, a laser rangefinder mounted externally over the main armament, a laser rangefinder operating through the gunner's sight, day/night sights for commander and gunner, an NBC system, and a ventilation system. All current models have a central tyre-pressure regulation system to enable the driver to adjust the ground pressure to suit the terrain.

Specification
Crew: 3
Weight: 12 tonnes
Dimensions: length (gun forward) 6.22 mm (20 ft 5 in); length (hull) 5.19 m (17 ft 0⅓ in); width 2.59 m (8 ft 6 in); height 2.29 m (7 ft 6 in)
Powerplant: one Detroit Diesel 6V-53 6-cylinder diesel developing 212 hp (158 kW)
Performance: maximum road speed 100 km/h (62 mph); maximum range 1000 km (620 miles); fording 1.00 m (3 ft 3 in); gradient 60%; vertical obstacle 0.60 m (1 ft 11⅔ in); trench not applicable

M551 Sheridan light tank

In the mid-1950s the only mobile weapons with a direct-fire capability in the American airborne divisions were the 76-mm (3-in) M41 light tank and the 90-mm (3.54-in) M56 self-propelled anti-tank gun. In 1959 a requirement was issued for a new air-portable vehicle to replace both the M41 and M56, and development of such a vehicle started under the name **Armored Reconnaissance/Airborne Assault Vehicle (AR/AAV)** and the designation of the **XM551**. The Allison Division of General Motors was subsequently awarded the development contract, and a total of 12 prototypes was built. In 1965 a four-year production contract was awarded to the company, although at that time the vehicle had not been fully accepted for service. Production continued until 1970, by when a total of 1,700 vehicles had been built. The XM551 was officially classified fit for service in 1966 and called the **M551 General Sheridan**. Although it was evaluated by a number of countries the type was never sold overseas, though it was deployed with the US Army to Europe, South Korea and Vietnam. In the last theatre the M551 earned itself a bad reputation, many faults soon becoming apparent, especially with the 152-mm (6-in) main armament, the powerpack and the very thin belly armour, which provided little protection from mines, one of the more common Vietcong weapons.

In the late 1970s the M551 was generally withdrawn from first-line service, though numbers were retained by Airborne formations and the tank was employed during in the invasion of Panama in 1989 and in the Gulf War of 1991. Large numbers are also used by the National Training Center at Fort Irwin, California, where they have been modified to resemble Soviet vehicles such as the ZSU-23-4 23-mm self-propelled anti-aircraft gun, BMP-1 MICV and the 122-mm (4.8-in) M-1973 self-propelled howitzer.

The hull of the M551 is of welded aluminium construction, while the turret is of steel contruction. The driver is seated at the front in the centre, the turret is in the centre of the hull, and the engine and transmission are at the rear. Suspension is of the torsion-bar

Above: M551 Sheridan, as deployed to Vietnam, showing extensive external turret stowage and additional protection for the commander.

type, and consists of five dual rubber-tyred road wheels with the drive sprocket at the rear and idler at the front; there are no track-return rollers. A flotation screen is carried collapsed around the top of the hull and when this has been erected the M551 is fully amphibious, being propelled in the water by its tracks at a speed of 5.8 km/h (3.6 mph).

The main armament consists of a M81 152-mm (6-in) gun/missile launcher that can fire a Shillelagh missile or one of four types of combustible-case conventional ammunition, namely HEAT-T-MP, WP, TP-T and canister. The last was of some use in Vietnam for beating off massed guerrilla attack at close quarters. The mix of conventional ammunition and missile depended on the mission being undertaken, but was typically 20 conventional rounds and eight missiles. A 7.62-mm machine-gun was mounted co-axial with the main armament and a 12.7-mm machine gun, with a shield, was mounted on top of the commander's cupola for local and anti-aircraft defence. Space was so cramped inside

the M551 that much of the machine-gun ammunition was carried externally on the sides of the turret.

Specification
Crew: 4
Weight: 15.83 tonnes
Dimensions: length 6.299 m (20 ft 8 in); width 2.819 m (9 ft 3 in); height (overall) 2.946 m (9 ft 8 in)
Powerplant: one Detroit Diesel 6V-53T 6-cylinder diesel developing 300 hp (224 kW)
Performance: maximum road speed 70 km/h (43 mph); maximum range

A standard Sheridan during tests at Fort Knox. About 1700 Sheridans were built between 1966 and 1970 but they were a technological step too far and gave persistent trouble in service. Withdrawn in the late 1970s, those which were not scrapped were converted to resemble Soviet vehicles for use at the National Training Center, Fort Irwin.

600 km (310 miles); fording amphibious; gradient 60%; vertical obstacle 0.838 m (2 ft 9 in); trench 2.54 m (8 ft 4 in)

Lynx Command and Reconnaissance Vehicle

When the M113 armoured personnel carrier entered production at FMC's facility at San Jose in 1960, it was realized that in addition to being used for a wide range of roles its automotive component could also be used in other armoured vehicles. At that time the US Army had already selected the M114 vehicle to carry out the role of command and reconnaissance, but the M114 did not prove a successful design and it has long been phased out of service, and it was never sold overseas. FMC then designed and built a command and reconnaissance vehicle using automotive components of the diesel-powered M113A1, and this was subsequently selected by Canada, which ordered 174 vehicles under the name **Lynx**, and by the Netherlands, which ordered 250 vehicles. all of these were delivered by 1968. The vehicle is often called the M113 and a half!

In comparison with the M113 the Lynx has a lower-profile hull, the powerpack repositioned to the rear, and one road wheel less on each side. The hull is of all-welded aluminium construction that provides the crew with complete protection from small arms fire and shell splinters. The driver is seated at the front of the vehicle, with the commander to his rear and right. The radio operator/observer is seated to the left rear of the commander. The engine compartment is at the rear of the hull on the right side, with access hatches in the roof and hull rear.

Suspension is of the torsion-bar type, and consists of four dual rubber-tyred road wheels on each side with the drive sprocket at the front and the idler at the rear; there are no track-return rollers. The Lynx is fully amphibious, being propelled in the water by its tracks at a speed of 5.6 km/h (3.5 mph). Before the vehicle enters the water a trim vane is erected at the front of the hull, electric bilge pumps are switched on, and rectangular covers erected around the air inlet and exhaust louvres on the hull top to stop water entering the engine compartment, the vehicle having very limited freeboard. Vehicles such as the M113 and the Lynx can cross only calm rivers and lakes, open-sea landings almost inevitably resulting in swamping.

The commander of the Lynx has an M26 hand-operated turret, with vision blocks for all-round observation and an externally-mounted standard 12.7-mm M2HB machine-gun for which

Lynx Command and Reconnaissance vehicle of the Canadian Armed Forces, armed with a 12.7-mm M2HB machine-gun forward and a 7.62-mm machine-gun at the rear. A bank of three electrically-operated smoke dischargers is mounted either side of the hull front.

1,155 rounds of ammunition are carried. The radio operator/observer has a pintle-mounted 7.62-mm machine-gun with 2,000 rounds. In addition a bank of three electrically-operated smoke-dischargers is mounted at the front of each side of the hull firing forwards.

The Dutch vehicles have a slightly different internal layout, and as originally supplied were slightly lighter. More recently all of these vehicles have been fitted with a Swiss Oerlikon-Buhrle GBD-AOA one-man turret armed with a 25-mm KBA-B cannon. This has three rates of fire: single-shot, 175 rounds per minute and 570 rounds per minute. Two hundred rounds of ready-use ammunition are carried for the cannon, of which 120 are high explosive and the other 80 armour-piercing. An added advantage for the Dutch is that this Oerlikon cannon (in a different one-man power-operated turret) is also installed in the FMC-designed armoured infantry fighting vehicles of the Dutch army, so assisting in ammunition commonality.

Specification
Crew: 3
Weight: 8.775 tonnes

Dimensions: length 4.597 m (15 ft 1 in); width 2.413 m (7 ft 11 in); height (including armament) 2.171 m (7 ft 1½ in)
Powerplant: one Detroit Diesel Type 6V53 6-cylinder diesel developing 215 hp (160 kW)
Performance: maximum road speed 70.8 km/h (44 mph); maximum range 523 km (325 miles); fording amphibious; gradient 60%; vertical

All Dutch vehicles have now been fitted with a Swiss Oerlikon-Buhrle one-man turret armed with a 25-mm KBA-B cannon. This is also fitted to the Dutch army's Armoured Infantry Fighting Vehicles, thus ensuring ammunition supply on the battlefield.

obstacle 0.609 m (2 ft 0 in); trench 1.524 m (5 ft 0 in)

Daimler Ferret Scout Car

Following the success of the Daimler Dingo scout car in World War II, the British War Office issued a requirement for a new scout car in 1946 and in the following year Daimler Ltd of Coventry was awarded the development contract. The first prototype was completed in 1949, and after user trials the vehicle was accepted for service as the **Ferret** scout car, although it was at one time to be called the **Field Mouse**. Production continued at Daimler for the home and export markets until 1971, by which time just over 4,400 vehicles had been built. In 1985 the Ferret was still being used in some numbers by the British army and by some 30 other countries in almost ev-

ery part of the world with the exception of the Americas.

All versions of the Ferret have the same basic layout, with the driver at the front, the commander/gunner in the centre, and the engine and transmission at the rear. The all-welded steel hull has a maximum thickness of 12 mm (0.47 in) and provides the crew

A Daimler Ferret Mk 1 scout car (left) armed with a Bren light machine-gun, and a Ferret Mk 2/3 on the right armed with a 7.62-mm machine-gun. A total of 4409 vehicles were built for home and export markets by the time production was completed in 1971.

with complete protection from small arms fire and shell splinters. Steering is on the front four wheels but is not power assisted.

The **Ferret Mk 1** has an open top and is armed simply with a pintle-mounted 7.62-mm Bren or a Browning machine-gun. The **Ferret Mk 1/2** has a three-man crew and a low-profile turret with an externally-mounted machine-gun. The **Ferret Mk 2/3** has a one-man turret armed with a 7.62-mm machine-gun with an elevation between −15° and +45°, turret traverse being 360°. This turret is almost the same as that fitted to the Alvis Saracen armoured personnel carrier. The **Ferret Mk 2/2** was an interesting model developed locally in the Far East, and was a Ferret Mk 2 with an extension collar between the hull top and turret base to give the commander much improved all-round observation. As far as it is known none of this particular model remain in service. The **Ferret Mk 2/6** is the Ferret Mk 2/3 with a British Aircraft Corporation (now British Aerospace Dynamics) Vigilant ATGW mounted on each side of the turret, a further two missiles being carried in reserve on the left side of the hull. The Vigilant was a first-generation wire-guided missile and had a maximum range of 1375 m (1,500 yards), and could be launched from within the vehicle or away from the vehicle with the aid of a separation sight and cable. The **Ferret Mk 3** and **Ferret Mk 4** were essentially earlier versions rebuilt to incorporate stronger suspension units, larger tyres and a flotation screen carried collapsed around the top of the hull; this could be quickly erected by the crew to make the vehicle fully amphibious, being propelled in the water by its wheels.

The **Ferret Mk 5** was the final version, and all of these were rebuilds of earlier vehicles. It has the stronger suspension, larger tyres, flotation screen and a turret in each side of which were two launcher bins for the British Aerospce Dynamics Swingfire ATGW with a range of 4000 m (4,375 yards). These could knock out the heaviest tank, and could be launched from within the vehicle or away from

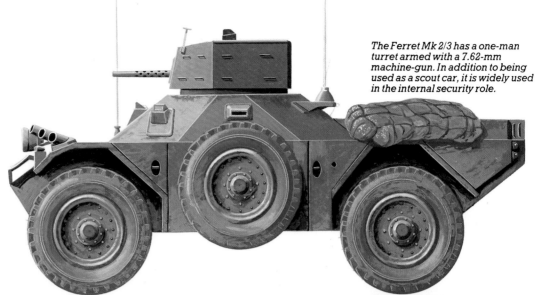

The Ferret Mk 2/3 has a one-man turret armed with a 7.62-mm machine-gun. In addition to being used as a scout car, it is widely used in the internal security role.

the vehicle with the aid of a separation cable and sight. The Ferret Mk 5 was also armed with a 7.62-mm machine-gun and, like all Ferrets, smoke-dischargers. This model is no longer in service with the British army and was not exported.

Specification
Daimler Ferret Mk 2/3
Crew: 2
Weight: 4.395 tonnes
Dimensions: length 3.835 m (12 ft 10 in); width 1.905 m (6 ft 3 in); height 1.879 m (6 ft 2 in)
Powerplant: one Rolls-Royce 6-cylinder petrol engine developing 129 hp (96 kW)
Performance: maximum road speed 93 km/h (58 mph); maximum range 306 km (190 miles); fording 0.914 m (3 ft 0 in); gradient 46%; vertical obstacle 0.406 m (1 ft 4 in); trench 1.22 m (4 ft 0 in) with one channel

The Fox is a Jaguar-powered development of the late production Ferret family. Capable of 104 km/h (64.6 mph) on roads, the Fox is armed with the 30-mm Rarden cannon.

UK
Alvis Scorpion Reconnaissance Vehicle

In the late 1960s the British army decided to build two new reconnaissance vehicles, one tracked and the other wheeled, and these became known as the **Combat Vehicle Reconnaissance (Tracked)** or **Scorpion** and the Combat Vehicle Reconnaissance (Wheeled), or Fox. In 1967 Alvis was awarded a contract to build 17 prototypes of the Scorpion, the first of which was completed in 1969. Trials were so successful that it was accepted for service the following year. Late in 1970 the Scorpion was also ordered by Belgium and an assembly line for the vehicle was set up at Malines in Belgium. First production Scorpions were delivered to the British army in 1972, and by 1985 total orders had passed the 3,000 mark and production was continuing. In addition to being used by the United Kingdom (army and Royal Air Force Regiment) and Belgium, the Scorpion is also used by Brunei, Eire, Honduras, Iran, Kuwait, Malaysia, New Zealand,

Nigeria, Oman, Tanzania, Philippines and the United Arab Emirates.

The Scorpion has a hull and turret of all-welded aluminium construction. The driver is seated at the front on the left, the engine is to his right, and the two-man turret is at the rear. Suspension is of the torsion-bar type, and consists of five road wheels with drive sprocket at the front, idler at the rear; there are no track-return rollers. A flotation screen is carried collapsed around the top of the hull, and once this has been erected the vehicle is propelled in water by its tracks at a speed of about 6 km/h (3.7 mph).

The basic Scorpion has a 76-mm (3-in) gun (a lightened version of that carried in the Saladin armoured car) with an elevation of −10° to +35°; turret traverse is 360°. A total of 40 rounds of ammunition is carried, and this can be a mixture of canister, HESH, HE, smoke (base ejection) and illuminating. A 7.62-mm machine-gun is mounted co-axial with the main arma-

ment, and the machine-gun can be used as a ranging as well as a secondary weapon; a total of 3,000 rounds of ammunition are carried for this weapon. The vehicle is also available with a diesel engine in place of the standard petrol engine, and this model has a much increased operating range.

On the same basic chassis a complete family of light tracked vehicles has been developed. **Striker** is the anti-tank model and has five British Aerospace Swingfire ATGWs in the ready-to-launch position. **Spartan** is the troop carrier and can carry four fully equipped troops in addition to its three-man crew. The ambulance model, which is unarmed, is called the **Samaritan**, while the command model, which like Samaritan has a much higher roof, is called the **Sultan**. The recovery model, which uses the same hull as the Spartan, is called the **Samson** and has winches, spades and other specialized equipment. The **Scimitar** has

the same hull as the Scorpion but has a two-man turret armed with the same 30-mm Rarden cannon as fitted to the Fox CVR(W). More recently the **Stormer** armoured personnel carrier and the **Streaker** high-mobility load-carrier have been developed, both based on the chassis of the Spartan and developed with company rather than government money.

Specification
Crew: 3
Weight: 8.073 tonnes
Dimensions: length 4.794 m (15 ft 8¾ in); width 2.235 m (7 ft 4 in); height 2.102 m (6 ft 10¾ in)
Powerplant: one Jaguar 4.2-litre petrol engine developing 190 hp (142 kW)
Performance: maximum road speed 80 km/h (50 mph); maximum range 644 km (400 miles); fording 1.067 m (3 ft 6 in); gradient 60%; vertical obstacle 0.50 m (1 ft 8 in); trench 2.057 m (6 ft 9 in)

Alvis Saladin Armoured Car

Following the success of the AEC Mk III and Daimler Mk II armoured cars during World War II the British army issued a requirement for a new armoured car with a 2-pdr gun. But it was soon decided that this weapon would be ineffective against the newer vehicles expected in the 1950s, and the Armament Research and Development Establishment then designed a new 76-mm (3-in) gun called the L5.

The chassis of the **Saladin**, or **FV601**, is very similar to that of the FV603 Saracen armoured personnel carrier, which was also under development by Alvis at that time. Because of needs of the guerrilla war in Malaya, development of the Saracen was given precedence over that of the Saladin, and because of the high work load at Alvis the first six preproduction Saladins were built by Crossley Motors at Stockport in Cheshire.

The Saladin was accepted for service with the British army in 1956, and production started two years later at Alvis in Coventry. Production continued for the home and export markets until 1972, by which time 1,177 vehicles had been completed. In British army service the Saladin has now been replaced by the Alvis Scorpion tracked vehicle, which is armed with a new version of the 76-mm (3-in) gun called the L23. A small number of Saladins remain in service in Cyrpus with the British army, and the type is also used by Bahrain, Ghana, Indonesia, Jordan, Kenya, Kuwait, Lebanon, Libya, Oman, Nigeria, Portugal, Sierra Leone, Sri Lanka, Sudan, Tunisia, United Arab Emirates and both North and South Yemen, although in some cases spares must be a major problem as the UK is no longer handling spares for some countries as a result of political considerations.

The hull of the Saladin is of all-welded steel armoured construction that varies in thickness from 8 mm (0.31 in) up to 16 mm (0.63 in); the turret has a maximum thickness of 32 mm (1.25 in) at the front and 16 mm (0.63 in) at the sides and rear. The driver sits at the front of the vehicle with excellent vision to his front and sides. The other two crew members are seated in the turret with the commander, who acts as the loader, on the right and the gunner on the left. The engine and trans-

mission are at the rear of the hull. All six wheels of the Saladin are powered, with steering on the front four wheels. The vehicle can still be driven with one wheel blown off.

The 76-mm (3-in) gun is mounted in a turret that can be traversed manually through 360°; the gun itself can be elevated from −10° to +20°. A total of 42 rounds of fixed ammunition can be carried, the type being identical to those used in the L23 gun of the Scorpion and including canister, HESH, SH/P, HE, HE/PRAC, smoke (both base ejection and phosphorus) and illuminating. A 7.62-mm machine-gun is mounted co-axial with the main armament, and a similar weapon is mounted on the turret roof for anti-aircraft defence. A total of 2,750 rounds of 7.62-mm ammunition is carried. Mounted on each side of the turret is a bank of six electrically-operated smoke-dischargers.

There were very few variants of the Saladin, one of the more interesting ones being the amphibious model. This was fitted with a flotation screen around the top of the hull, and when this had been erected the vehicle could propel itself on water with its wheels.

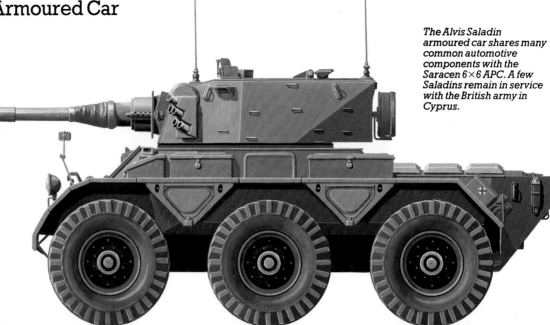

The Alvis Saladin armoured car shares many common automotive components with the Saracen 6×6 APC. A few Saladins remain in service with the British army in Cyprus.

Specification
Crew: 3
Weight: 11.59 tonnes
Dimensions: length (including gun) 5.284 m (17 ft 4 in); length (hull) 4.93 m (16 ft 2 in); width 2.54 m (8 ft 4 in); height 2.93 m (9 ft 7⅓ in)
Powerplant: one Rolls-Royce B80 8-cylinder petrol engine developing 170 bhp (127 kW)
Performance: maximum road speed 72 km/h (45 mph); maximum range

400 km (250 miles); fording 1.07 m (3 ft 6 in); gradient 46%; vertical obstacle 0.46 m (1 ft 6 in); trench 1.52 m (5 ft 0 in)

The Saladin is armed with a 76-mm (3-in) gun; a lightened version is fitted in the more recent Scorpion, and fires the same range of fixed ammunition. Between 1958 and 1972 Alvis of Coventry built 1177 Saladins for the home and the lucrative overseas markets.

AMX-13 Light Tank

The **AMX-13** light tank was one of the three armoured vehicles designed in France immediately after the end of World War II, the other being the Panhard EBR heavy armoured car and the AMX-50 MBT which did not enter service as large numbers of M47s soon became available from the United States. The AMX-13 was designed by the Atelier de Construction d'Issy-les-Moulineaux, the numeral 13 in the designation being the originally specified design weight in tonnes. The first prototype was completed in 1948 and production was under way at the Atelier de Construction Roanne (ARE) by 1952. The AMX-13 continued in production at the ARE until the 1960s, when space was needed for the AMX-30 MBT and AMX-10P IFV family. Production of the whole AMX-13 family, including the light tank, was transferred to Creusot-Loire at Chalon-sur-

Saône, where production continues to this day. By early 1983 over 3,000 vehicles had been built and the type remains in service with Algeria, Argentina, Chile, Djibouti, Ecuador, France, El Salvador, India, Indonesia, Ivory Coast, Lebanon, Morocco, Nepal, Peru, Singapore, Tunisia and Venezuela. The AMX-13 was also used by a number of other countries such as India, Israel, the Netherlands and Switzerland, but most of these have now been sold. The chassis of the

The AMX-13 light tank is fitted with an oscillating turret in which the gun is fixed in the upper part, which in turn pivots on the lower part. The gun can fire until its 12 rounds of ready-use ammunition are exhausted, and then two six-round magazines have to be reloaded manually from outside the vehicle by a crewman.

AMX-13 (extensively modified in many cases) has been used as the basis for one of the most complete family of vehicles ever developed; this includes the 105-mm (4.13-in) **Mk 61** self-

AMX-13 light tank fitted with an FL-10 two-man turret armed with a 75-mm (2.95-in) gun. Other versions were armed with 90-mm (3.54-in) or 105-mm (4.13-in) guns.

propelled howitzer, 155-mm (6.1-in) **Mk F3** self-propelled gun, **AMX-13 DCA** twin 30-mm self-propelled anti-aircraft gun system, **AMX VCI** infantry fighting vehicle and its countless variants, **AMX VCG** engineer vehicle, AMX-13 armoured recovery vehicle and the AMX-13 armoured bridge-layer.

The original model of the AMX-13 was fitted with the FL-10 turret armed with a 75-mm (2.95-in) gun and a 7.62-mm co-axial machine-gun. This turret is of the oscillating type and the 75-mm (2.95-in) gun is fed by two revolver-type magazines, each of which holds six rounds of ammunition. The basic types of ammunition were fixed HE and HEAT, the latter capable of penetrating 170 mm (6.7 in) of armour. This model was used in some numbers by Israel during the 1967 Middle East war, but its gun was found to be ineffective against the frontal armour of the Soviet T-54/T-55 MBTs supplied to Syria and Egypt, so it was soon phased out of service, most ending up in Singapore or Nepal.

At a later date all 75-mm (2.95-in) models of the French army were fitted

with a 90-mm (3.54-in) gun which would fire canister, HE, HEAT and smoke projectiles, although more recently a APFSDS projectile has been developed that can penetrate a triple NATO tank target at an incidence of 60° at a range of 2000 m (2,190 yards). The 105-mm (4.13-in) gun model was designed specifically for the export market and has the heavier FL-12 turret, which is also fitted to the Austrian SK-105 light tank/tank destroyer.

The basic AMX-13 is powered by a petrol engine with an operative range of between 350 and 400 km (220 and 250 miles), but recently Creusot-Loire have replaced this with an American GM Detroit Diesel developing 280 hp (209 kW) and this gives an operational range of 500 km (310 miles) as well as reducing the risk of fire.

Specification
AMX-13 (90-mm gun)
Crew: 3
Weight: 15 tonnes

Dimensions: length (including gun) 6.36 m (20 ft 10⅓ in); length (hull) 4.88 m (16 ft 0 in); width 2.50 m (8 ft 2½ in); height 2.30 m (7 ft 6½ in)
Powerplant: one SOFAM 8Gxb 8-cylinder petrol engine developing 250 hp (186 kW)
Performance: maximum road speed 60 km/h (37 mph); maximum range 350-400 km (220-250 miles); fording 0.60 m (1 ft 11⅔ in); gradient 60%; vertical obstacle 0.65 m (2 ft 1⅔ in); trench 1.60 m (5 ft 3 in)

AMX-10RC Reconnaissance Vehicle

The AMX-10RC (6×6) reconnaissance vehicle is the replacement for the old Panhard EBR-75 (8×8) armoured car.

Since 1950 the standard heavy armoured car of the French army has been the 8×8 Panhard EBR, which can trace its development back to the period before World War II. In the 1960s the French army issued a requirement for a new armoured car that would have a more powerful gun and a sophisticated fire-control system, have good cross-country mobility and be fully amphibious. The result is the **AMX-10RC**, the first of whose three prototypes was completed in 1971. Following trials with the French army, the type was accepted for service and production got under way at the Atelier de Construction Roanne, where the AMX-10P MICV and the AMX-30 MBT family are produced. The first French army units were issued with the vehicle in 1979.

In spite of being an expensive and complicated machine, the AMX-10RC has proved to be a most effective vehicle and has been supplied to Morocco and Qatar. A version with a 90-mm gun is also produced for export.

The hull and turret of the AMX-10RC are of all-welded aluminium construction, with the driver seated at the front left, the turret in centre and engine and transmission at the rear. The 6×6 suspension is unusual in that the driver can adjust its ground clearance to suit the type of ground being crossed and even tilt it from side to side. For example, when travelling on roads the ground clearance is 330 mm (13 in), while for cross-country travel it is

470 mm (18½ in). Many of the automotive components, including the engine and transmission, are identical with those of the AMX-10P tracked MICV; and like the MICV the wheeled AMX-10RC is also skid-steered.

The vehicle is fully amphibious, being propelled in the water by two waterjets at the rear of the hull. Designed in the UK but manufactured in France under licence, this propulsion produces a maximum water speed of 7.2 km/h (4.5 mph). Before the vehicle enters the water a trim vane is erected at the front of the hull and the bilge pumps are switched on.

The commander and gunner are seated on the right on the turret, with the loader on the left. The main armament comprises a 105-mm (4.13-in) gun with an elevation of +20° and a depression of −8°; turret traverse is

360°. A 7.62-mm machine-gun is mounted co-axial with the main armament. Totals of 40 105-mm (4.13-in) and 4,000 7.62-mm rounds are carried. Two electrically-operated smoke dischargers are mounted on each side of the turret rear and fire forwards.

The fire-control system is the most sophisticated of its type installed in any vehicle of this class, and includes a laser rangefinder, a computer and a low-light TV system with a screen for both the commander and driver. This fire-control system enables stationary and moving targets to be engaged by day and night.

Four types of ammunition are provided for the 105-mm gun: APFSDS, HEAT, HE and WP smoke. The APFDS has a muzzle velocity of 1400 m/sec (1531 ft) and can easily defeat the standard NATO heavy tank target at a

range of 1000 metres. The HEAT shell is fully capable of defeating 100-mm of armour at an angle of impact of 70° at any range, though it is not normally used at ranges much over 2000 metres.

Specification
Crew: 4
Weight: 15.8 tonnes
Dimensions: length (gun forward) 9.15 m (30 ft 0¼ in); length 6.35 m (20 ft 10 in); width 2.95 m (9 ft 8 in); height 2.68 m (8 ft 9½ in)
Powerplant: one 8-cylinder diesel developing 260 hp (194 kW)
Performance: maximum road speed 85 km/h (53 mph); maximum range 800 km (500 miles); fording amphibious; gradient 60%; vertical obstacle 0.70 m (2 ft 3¼ in); trench 1.15 m (3 ft 9 in)

Panhard ERC Sagaie Armoured Car

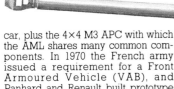

For many years the backbone of the Panhard armoured vehicle production has been the 4×4 AML light armoured car, plus the 4×4 M3 APC with which the AML shares many common components. In 1970 the French army issued a requirement for a Front Armoured Vehicle (VAB), and Panhard and Renault built prototype vehicles in both 4×4 and 6×6 configurations, all of them fully amphibious. This competition was won by Renault, and since then large numbers of 4×4 and 6×6 vehicles have been built. Using the technology gained in this competition Panhard then started design work on a new range of 6×6 vehicles that would include both an armoured car and an armoured personnel carrier. The former made its first appearance in 1977 as the **ERC** (**Engin de Reconnaissance Canon**, or cannon-armed reconnaissance machine), while the APC is known as the **VCR** (**Véhicule de Combat à Roues**, or wheeled combat vehicle). Production commenced in 1979 and the ERC is now in service with, or has been ordered by Argentina (Marines), France, Iraq, Ivory Coast, Niger and Mexico.

The vehicle can be fitted with a wide range of turrets on the same basic chassis. The driver is seated at the front, the turret is in the centre, and the engine and transmission are at the rear. All six road wheels are powered; power-assisted steering is provided on the front two wheels. An unusual feature of the ERC is that the centre pair of wheels can be raised off the ground for road travel and lowered again for cross-country travel. The basic vehicle is fully amphibious,

being propelled in the water at a speed of 4.5 km/h (2.8 mph) by its wheels, or by two optional waterjets at a speed of 9.5 km/h (5.9 mph). Before the vehicle enters the water a trim vane is erected at the front of the hull and two schnorkels are erected at the rear.

The basic vehicle can be fitted with a wide range of turrets including the GIAT TS-90, Hispano-Suiza Lynx 90, Hispano Suiza 60-20 Serval and EMC 81-mm mortar turrets, and a two-man turret with twin 20-mm or 25-mm cannon for use in the anti-aircraft role is also available.

The model selected by the French army (for use by its rapid intervention force) is fitted with the GIAT TS-90 turret and called the **ERC-90 F4 Sagaie**. This is armed with the long-barrelled 90-mm (3.54-in) gun with an elevation of +15° and a depression of −8°. The gun can fire the following types of fixed

ammunition: canister, HE, HEAT, smoke and APFSDS. The last has a muzzle velocity of 1350 m (4,430 ft) per second and will penetrate 120 mm (4.72 in) of armour at an incidence of 60°. A 7.62-mm machine-gun is mounted co-axial with the main armament, and two electrically-operated smoke-dischargers are mounted on each side of the turret. Twenty rounds of 90-mm (3.54-in) and 2,000 rounds of 7.62-mm machine-gun ammunition are carried.

Optional equipment includes an air-conditioning system, additional ammunition stowage, laser rangefinder, passive night-vision equipment, NBC system, anti-aircraft machine-gun, additional elevation of the 90-mm (3.54-in) gun to +35°, various types of fire-control system and a land navigation system, the last being essential when the vehicle is operating in the desert.

The Panhard ERC Sagaie armoured car is fitted with a GIAT TS-90 turret, armed with a 90-mm (3.54-in) gun.

Specification
Crew: 3
Weight: 7.65 tonnes
Dimensions: length (including gun) 7.693 m (25 ft 2¾ in); length (hull) 5.083 m (16 ft 8 in); width 2.495 m (8 ft 2¼ in); height 2.254 m (7 ft 4¾ in)
Powerplant: one Peugeot V-6 petrol engine developing 155 hp (116 kW)
Performance: maximum road speed 100 km/h (62 mph); maximum range 800 km (500 miles); fording amphibious; gradient 60%; vertical obstacle 0.80 m (2 ft 7½ in); trench 1.10 m (3 ft 7½ in)

Panhard AML-90 Armoured Car

The French army used large numbers of British-built 4×4 Daimler Ferret scout cars in North Africa in the 1950s, and decided to procure a similar vehicle but with a wider range of armament installations. After evaluation of prototype vehicles, the design from Panhard was selected. Production commenced in 1960 under the designation **AML** (**Automitrailleuse Légère**, or light armoured car), and since then well over 4,000 vehicles have been built in several variants, with production continuing to this day for export. The type is also built in South Africa by Sandock Austral for the South African army, which calls the type the **Eland**. The AML, which is in service with well over 30 countries, shares 95 per cent of its automotive components with the Panhard M3 armoured personnel carrier, and many countries operate fleets of M3s and AMLs with the obvious financial, logistical and training advantages.

The layout of all variants is similar, with the driver at the front, the two-man turret in the centre (with an entry door in each side of the hull) and the engine and transmission at the rear.

One of the most common models is the **AML-90**, the latest version of this being called the **Lynx 90**. This has a two-man turret designed and built by

Hispano-Suiza and armed with a GIAT 90-mm (3.54-in) DEFA gun, a 7.62-mm co-axial machine-gun and a 7.62-mm anti-aircraft machine-gun. The 90-mm (3.54-mm) gun can fire a wide range of fixed ammunition, including HEAT, HE, smoke and canister. The HEAT round will penetrate 320 mm (12.6 in) of armour at an incidence of 0° or 120 mm (4.72in) of armour at an incidence of 65°. Totals of 21 rounds of 90-mm (3.54-in) and 2,000 rounds of 7.62-mm ammunition are carried. Optional equipment for this turret includes passive night-vision equipment, powered controls and a laser rangefinder.

The **HE 60-7** turret has a 60-mm breech-loaded mortar and two 7.62-mm machine-guns, the **HE 60-12** turret a similar mortar and a 12.7-mm machine-gun, and the **HE 60-20** turret has the 60-mm mortar and a 20-mm cannon. The breech-loaded mortar is used both in the indirect and direct fire modes, and is very useful in guerrilla-type operations as it can be fired over hills and buildings.

One of the more recent models is the **HE 60-20 Serval** turret with a 60-mm long-barrel mortar mounted in the turret front with a 20-mm cannon and 7.62-mm machine-gun mounted externally at the turret rear. For the export market an anti-aircraft model of the AML

was developed fitted with a two-man **SAMM S530** turret armed with twin 20-mm cannon, each with 300 rounds of ready-use ammunition. Turret traverse and weapon elevation is powered so enabling aircraft and helicopters to be engaged successfully.

More recently, scout car versions of the AML have been developed that are fitted with various combinations of 7.62-mm and 12.7-mm machine-guns on pintle mounts or in turrets. These have a lower profile than the 90-mm (3.54-in) gun models, are lighter, much cheaper and well suited for the light reconnaissance role.

As usual a wide range of optional equipment can be fitted, including passive night-vision equipment, an air-conditioning system and a complete NBC system. An amphibious kit was developed, but as far as is known this was not produced in quantity.

The AML-90 has been one of the most successful wheeled AFVs in the post-war era, with over 4000 being built in France and South Africa. This model has a 90-mm (3.54-in) gun.

Specification
Crew: 3
Weight: 5.5 tonnes
Dimensions: length (including gun) 5.11 m (16 ft 9¼ in); length (hull) 3.79 m (12 ft 5¼ in); width 1.97 m (6 ft 5½ in); height 2.07 m (6 ft 9½ in)
Powerplant: one Panhard 4-cylinder petrol engine developing 90 hp (67 kW)
Performance: maximum road speed 90 km/h (56 mph); maximum range 600 km (375 miles); fording amphibious; gradient 60%; vertical obstacle 0.30 m (1 ft 0 in); trench 0.80 m (2 ft 7½ in) with one channel

BRDM-1 Amphibious Scout Car

In the period immediately after World War II the BA-64 light armoured car (developed in 1942) remained the standard reconnaissance vehicle of its type in the Soviet army. From the late 1950s this was rapidly replaced by the 4×4 **BRDM-1** amphibious scout car, which was also used by the Warsaw Pact countries and exported to a number of countries in Africa and the Middle East. It was not used by Hungary, however, as that country decided to build a similar vehicle called the **FUG** (or **OT-65**), which is very similar in appearance but has the engine at the front instead of the rear. The FUG is also used by Czechoslovakia and Poland. In most Soviet units the BRDM-1 has now been replaced by the much improved BRDM-2 vehicle.

The layout of the BRDM-1 is similar to that of a car with the engine and transmission at the front, driver and commander in the centre and a small crew compartment at the rear. The only means of entry are by hatches in the roof and rear of the crew compartment. Between the front and rear wheels on each side of the hull are two belly wheels, which are powered and lowered to the ground by the driver when the vehicle is crossing ditches or rough terrain. This feature was also adopted by the later BRDM-2. A central tyre pressure regulation system is standard, and this allows the driver to inflate or deflate the tyres according to the conditions: for example, the tyres are deflated for sand crossings, while on roads they are fully inflated. The BRDM-1 is fully amphibious, being propelled in the water at a speed of 9 km/h (5.6 mph) by a single waterjet at the rear of the hull. Before the vehicle enters the water, a trim vane is erected at the front of the hull and the bilge pumps are switched on.

The BRDM-1 is normally armed with a single 7.62-mm SGMB machine-gun mounted on the forward part of the roof with a total traverse of 90° (45° left and right) elevation being from −6° to +23.5°. A total of 1,070 rounds of

ammunition is carried. Some vehicles have been observed with a similar weapon at the rear and a 12.7-mm DShKM machine-gun at the front.

The **BRDM-U** command vehicle has additional communications equipment, while the **BRDM-rkh** radiological/chemical reconnaissance vehicle is used to mark lines through contaminated areas. Mounted at the rear of the hull are two racks that contain the marking poles and pennants; when required, these racks swing through 90° over the rear of the vehicle so allowing the poles with their attached pennants to be put into the ground.

There are also three versions of the BRDM-1 fitted with ATGWs. The first model has three AT-1 'Snapper' ATGWs with a range of 2500 (2,735 yards). The missiles on their launcher arms are carried under armour protection and raised above the roof of the vehicle for launching. The second model is similar but has four 'Swatter' missiles with a range of 3000 m (3,280 yards); for some reason this mounting was not adopted outside the Warsaw Pact. The last model to enter service has six 'Sagger' ATGWs with a maximum range of 3000 m (3,280 yards); additional missiles are carried in the hull. This wire-guided missile, which proved to be highly effective in the 1973 Middle East war, can be launched from within the vehicle or up to 80 m (87.5 yards) away from it with the aid of a separation sight.

Specification
Crew: 5
Weight: 5.6 tonnes
Dimensions: length 5.70 m (18 ft 8½ in); width 2.25 m (7 ft 4⅔ in); height 1.90 m (6 ft 2¾ in)
Powerplant: one 6-cylinder petrol engine developing 90 hp (67 kW)
Performance: maximum road speed 80 km/h (50 mph); maximum range 500 km (310 miles); fording amphibious; gradient 60%; vertical obstacle 0.40 m (1 ft 3¾ in); trench 1.22 m (4 ft 0 in)

Above: Soviet BRDM-1 (4×4) amphibious scout cars, with roof hatches open, ford a stream. The vehicle is propelled in the water by a single waterjet at the rear of the hull, which gives it a maximum speed of 9 km/h (5.6 mph). When travelling across rough country belly wheels are lowered between the front and rear axles.

Below: A Soviet BRDM-1 with four AT-2 'Swatter' ATGWs in the foreground, and a BRDM-1 with three AT-1 'Snappers' in the background. The 'Snapper' has a maximum range of 2500 (8202 ft), while the 'Swatter' has a range of 3000 (9842 ft). Both missiles have a HEAT (High Explosive Anti-Tank) warhead.

BRDM-2 Amphibious Scout Car

The 4×4 **BRDM-2** amphibious scout car was developed as the successor to the earlier **BRDM-1**, and was first seen in public in 1966, although it entered service some years before that date. The most significant improvements of the BRDM-2 over the earlier vehicle can be summarized as better vision for the commander and driver, more powerful armament mounted in a fully enclosed turret, a more powerful engine that gives higher road and water speeds, an NBC system, and longer operational range.

The BRDM-2 has now replaced the BRDM-1 in most Soviet units, and is also in service with almost 40 countries all over the world, seeing action in such places as Angola, Egypt, Iraq, Syria and Vietnam.

The all-welded steel hull of the BRDM-2 is only 7 mm (0.275 in) thick, apart from the nose plate which is 14 mm (0.55 in) thick, and the underside of the belly which is only 2 or 3 mm (0.08 or 0.12 in) thick and makes the vehicle very vulnerable to mine explosions. The driver and commander are seated at the front of the vehicle. Each has to his front a windscreen

that is covered in combat by an armoured hatch. Over each of their positions is a single-piece hatch cover that opens vertically; these are the only means of entry into the vehicle for the four-man crew. The turret, which has no roof hatch, is the same as that fitted to the Soviet 8×8 BTR-60PB and Czech 8×8 OT-64 Model 2A armoured personnel carriers, and is armed with a 14.5-mm KPV heavy machine-gun and a co-axial 7.62-mm PKT machine-gun. The weapons have an elevation of +30° and a depression of −5°, and turret traverse is 360°. Totals of 500 rounds of 14.5-mm and 2,000 rounds of 7.62-mm ammunition are carried. The KPV is a highly effective weapon and can fire an API projectile that will penetrate 32 mm (1.26 in) of armour at a range of 500 m (545 yards).

A BRDM-2 ATGW carrier, with a launcher for six AT-3 'Sagger' ATGWs in the raised position, ready for firing. This model was used successfully by the Egyptian army in the 1973 Middle East campaign. The missiles can be launched from or away from the vehicle.

The engine and transmission are at the rear of the vehicle. Like the earlier BRDM-1 the BRDM-2 has two belly wheels that can be lowered to the ground on each side of the hull to enable ditches and rough country to be crossed with ease. The vehicle also has a central tyre pressure regulation system, infra-red night-vision equipment, an NBC system, radios, a navigation system and a winch mounted internally at the front of the hull.

The basic BRDM-2 chassis has formed the basis for a whole family of more specialized vehicles including the **BDRM-2-rkh** radiological/chemical reconnaissance vehicle and the BRDM-2U command vehicle, which does not have a turret.

The first ATGW model was armed with six 'Sagger' ATGWs with a range of 3000 m (3,280 yards), and this **BTR-40PB 'Sagger'** model was widely used by Egypt during the 1973 Middle East war. A version with 'Swatter' ATGWs is also in service, but the latest model is armed with five 'Spandrel' ATGWs in the ready-to-launch position on the hull top. These missiles, which operate in a similar manner to the Euromissile HOT, have a range of at least 4000 m (4,375 yards). The SA-9 'Gaskin' sur-

Most BRDM-2 ATGW versions were armed with 'Sagger', but some carried the earlier 'Swatter' missile.

face-to-air missile also uses the BRDM-2 chassis and has four missiles in the ready-to-launch position; each Soviet armoured and motorized rifle division has 16 of these systems. The SA-9 has also been used in combat in the Middle East, most recently with the Syrian forces during the Israeli invasion of the

Lebanon in the summer of 1982.

Specification
Crew: 4
Weight: 7 tonnes
Dimensions: length 5.75 m (18 ft 10⅓ in); width 2.35 m (7 ft 8½ in); height 2.31 m (7 ft 7 in)

Powerplant: one V-8 petrol engine developing 140 hp (104 kW)
Performance: maximum road speed 100 km/h (62 mph); maximum range 750 km (465 miles); fording amphibious; gradient 60%; vertical obstacle 0.40 m (1 ft 3¾ in); trench 1.25 m (4 ft 1 in)

Former USSR

PT-76 Amphibious Tank

The PT-76 light tank is now being replaced in many Soviet units by special models of the BMP-1 (reconnaissance) vehicle.

The Soviet Union developed light tanks with an amphibious capability in the 1920s and these were used with varying degrees of success during World War II. The **PT-76** light amphibious tank was designed in the immediate post-war period by the design team responsible for the IS series of heavy tanks. For many years the PT-76 was the standard reconnaissance vehicle of the Soviet army, and was used alongside the 4×4 BRDM-1 and BRDM-2 amphibious scout cars. In many Soviet units the type has now been replaced by MBTs such as the T-62, T-64 and T-72. Although production of the PT-76 was completed many years ago, the tank is still used by at least 25 countries. It has seen action with the Indian army during the conflict with Pakistan, with the Egyptian army during the 1967 Middle East war, with the North Vietnamese army during the Vietnamese war, and more recently with the Angolan army during operations in South West Africa.

The chassis of the PT-76 was subsequently used for a large number of other vehicles including the **BTR-50** amphibious APC and the launcher for the FROG (Free Rocket Over Ground) missile system.

The hull of the PT-76 is of all-welded steel construction and provides the crew with protection from small arms fire only: any additional armour would have increased the type's weight to the point that it would not have been amphibious. The driver is seated at the front in the centre, the two-man turret is in the centre of the vehicle, and the engine and transmission are at the rear. The torsion-bar suspension consists of six single road wheels, with the drive sprocket at the rear and the idler at the front; there are no track-return rollers.

The main armament consists of a 76-

mm (3-in) D-56T gun with an elevation of +30° and a depression of −4°, turret traverse being 360°. A 7.62-mm SGMT machine-gun is mounted co-axial with the main armament, and more recently some vehicles have been observed fitted with a 12.7-mm DShKM anti-aircraft machine-gun on the turret roof. Totals of 40 rounds of 76-mm (3-in) and 1,000 rounds of 7.62-mm ammunition are carried. Several types of fixed ammunition can be fired, namely AP-T, API-T, HE-FRAG, HEAT and HVAP-T. The HEAT projectile can penetrate 120 mm (4.72 in) of armour at 0°, while the HVAP-T projectile can punch through 58 mm (2.28 in) of armour at 1000 m (1,095 yards) or 92 mm (3.62 in) at 500 m (545 yards). The lack of armour penetration against more recent tanks must have been one of the reasons why the PT-76 has been phased out of service with many Soviet units.

The most useful feature of the PT-76 is its amphibious capability, which is the reason why the type has also been used by the Polish and Soviet Marines. In the water the tank is powered by two waterjets at a maximum speed of 10 km/h (6.2 mph). The only preparation required before entering the water is the raising of the trim vane at the front of the hull, the activation of the bilge pumps and the engagement of

the waterjets. Maximum waterborne range is about 65 km (40 miles). To enable the driver to see forwards when afloat his centre periscope can be raised above the hatch cover. Standard equipment includes infra-red lights, but no NBC system is installed.

Specification
Crew: 3
Weight: 14 tonnes
Dimensions: length (with armament) 7.625 m (25 ft 0¼ in); length (hull) 6.91 m (22 ft 8 in); width 3.14 m (10 ft 3⅔ in); height 2.255 m (7 ft 4¾ in)
Powerplant: one V-6 6-cylinder diesel

developing 240 hp (179 kW)
Performance: maximum road speed 44 km/h (27 mph); maximum range 260 km (160 miles); fording amphibious; gradient 60%; vertical obstacle 1.10 m (3 ft 7⅓ in); trench 2.80 m (9 ft 2 in)

PT-76 Model 2 light amphibious tanks come ashore from landing craft of the Red Banner Northern Fleet. Note the turret hatch cover open and the trim vane at the front in the raised position. Main armament comprises a 76-mm (3-in) gun and 7.62-mm co-axial machine gun.

Spähpanzer 2 Luchs Reconnaissance Vehicle

When the West German army was reformed in the 1950s it had insufficient time to have equipment designed to meet its own requirements, and it therefore had to take what was on offer from the American or European manufacturers. To meet this requirement for a reconnaissance vehicle it selected the French Hotchkiss carrier fitted with a turret armed with a Hispano-Suiza 20-mm cannon, this variant being designated the **SPz 11-2**. This suffered from a number of drawbacks as it was not amphibious and its petrol engine gave an operating range of only about 400 km (250 miles).

In the mid-1960s a complete family of 4×4, 6×6 and 8×8 trucks, 4×4 and 6×6 (later to become the Transportpanzer, or Fuchs) armoured amphibious load-carriers, and an 8×8 amphibious armoured reconnaissance vehicle were developed, all sharing many common automotive components that were in most cases already in production for a civilian application. Prototypes of the 8×8 amphibious armoured reconnaissance vehicle were designed and built by Daimler-Benz and a consortium of companies known as the Joint Project Office (JPO) in 1968, and in 1971 the Daimler-Benz model was selected for production. For a variety of reasons production was undertaken by Thyssen Henschel, which built a total of 408 vehicles called the **Spähpanzer 2 Luchs** for the West German army between 1975 and 1978. The Spz 2 was offered on the export market, but for most countries it proved too expensive.

The hull of the Luchs is of all-welded steel construction, with the front part of the turret and the hull providing protection against attacks from 20-mm projectiles and the remainder proof

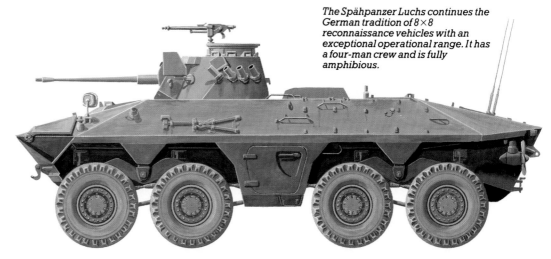

The Spähpanzer Luchs continues the German tradition of 8×8 reconnaissance vehicles with an exceptional operational range. It has a four-man crew and is fully amphibious.

against small arms fire and shell splinters. The driver is at the front left, the two-man turret in the centre, the engine at the rear on the right side, and the co-driver, who also operates the radio, on the rear on the left side, seated facing the rear. In an emergency the rear driver can quickly take control and drive the vehicle out of trouble. The Luchs has a maximum speed of 90 km/h (56 mph) in both directions. It also has an exceptionally large operating range of 800 km (500 miles).

The Rheinmetall TS-7 turret is armed with a dual-feed Rheinmetall MK 20 Rh 202 cannon, for which 375 rounds of ammunition are carried in the turret. Turret traverse and weapon elevation (from −15° to +69°) is powered, turret traverse being 360°. A 7.62-mm MG3 machine-gun is mounted on the turret roof for anti-

aircraft defence and 1,000 rounds of ready-use ammunition are provided for this weapon. On each side of the turret is a bank of four electrically-operated smoke-dischargers, all firing forward.

The driver has powered steering to reduce fatigue when driving over long distances or across rough country, and he can select either steering on the front four wheels or on all eight wheels; the latter turning radius is only 11.5 m (37 ft 8¾ in).

The Luchs is fully amphibious, being propelled in the water at a speed of 9 km/h (5.6 mph) by two steerable propellers mounted under the hull at the rear, one on each side. Before the vehicle enters the water the trim vane is erected at the front of the hull and the three bilge pumps are switched on.

The Luchs also has an NBC system,

and the original range of infra-red night-vision equipment is now being replaced by the passive type. Standard equipment includes a pre-heater for the batteries, engine and transmission oil and cooling liquid, all essential for winter operations in Germany.

Specification
Crew: 4
Weight: 19.5 tonnes
Dimensions: length 7.743 m (25 ft 4¾ in); width 2.98 m (9 ft 9⅓ in); height (including AA MG) 2.905 m (9 ft 6⅓ in)
Powerplant: one 10-cylinder diesel developing 390 hp (291 kW)
Performance: maximum road speed 90 km/h (56 mph); maximum range 800 km (500 miles); fording amphibious; gradient 60%; vertical obstacle 0.60 m (1 ft 11⅔ in); trench 1.90 m (6 ft 3 in)

FIAT Type 6616 Armoured Car

During World War II the Italian army used scout cars and armoured cars on quite a large scale, but in the post-war period no vehicles of this type were developed as the Italian army did not have an operational requirement for a vehicle of this type. Then in the early 1970s FIAT and OTO-Melara developed the **Type 6616** armoured car and the **Type 6614** armoured personnel carrier. In both cases FIAT was responsible for the powerpack and automotive components, plus final assembly, while OTO-Melara supplied the armoured hull and turret. The first prototype of the Type 6616 was completed in 1972, and 50 vehicles were subsequently ordered by the Italian government for the Carabinieri. Since then sales have also been made to Peru, Somalia and several other undisclosed countries.

The hull of the Type 6616 is of all-welded steel construction with a uniform thickness of 8 mm (0.315 in), somewhat thin when compared with other vehicles in this class. The driver is seated at the front of the vehicle on the left, with vision blocks giving good vision to the front and sides. The two-man turret is in the centre of the vehicle, with the engine and transmission at the rear.

The Type 6616 is fully amphibious, being propelled in the water by its wheels at a speed of 5 km/h (3.1 mph); all the preparation that is required be-

fore entering the water is to switch on the bilge pumps and pressurize the submerged mechanical components. Unlike most other comparable vehicles, the Type 6616 requires no trim vane at the front of the hull.

The commander is seated on the left and gunner on the right of the turret, each man being provided with an adjustable seat, observation equipment and a single-piece hatch cover. The communications equipment is mounted in the turret bustle. The main armament comprises a West German Rheinmetall 20-mm Mk 20 Rh 202 cannon with an elevation of +35° and a depression of −5°; turret traverse is 360°. Turret control is electric, with traverse at a maximum of 40° per second and weapon elevation at a maximum of 25° per second. A total of 400 rounds of 20-mm ammunition is carried, of which 250 are for ready use and 150 in reserve. A useful feature of the weapon, which is also installed in the West German 8×8 Luchs amphibious reconnaissance vehicle and the Marder MICV is that the empty cartridge cases are ejected outside the turret automatically, and therefore do not clutter up the crew compartment. A 7.62-mm machine-gun is mounted co-axial with the main armament, and 1,000 rounds are carried for this. Mounted on each side of the turret is a bank of three forward-firing electrically-operated smoke-dischargers.

Standard equipment includes a front-mounted winch with a capacity of 4500 kg (9,921 lb), while optional equipment includes an NBC system, a full range of passive night-vision equipment for commander, gunner and driver, and a fire-extinguishing system.

One of the main drawbacks of this vehicle on the export market is its small-calibre gun. More recently FIAT has fitted the basic Type 6616 chassis with a new two-man OTO-Melara turret armed with a 90-mm (3.54-in) Cockerill Mk III gun and a co-axial 7.62-mm machine-gun, so giving the vehicle the capability to engage much heavier vehicles than in the past.

Specification
Crew: 3
Weight: 8 tonnes

The FIAT Type 6616 armoured car is a joint development between FIAT and OTO Melara, and shares many common components with the Type 6616 APC. It is, however, under-armed, and for this reason a model with a 90-mm (3.54-in) two-man turret has recently been built. This has the Belgian Cockerill gun used in many AFVs.

Dimensions: length 5.37 m (17 ft 7½ in); width 2.50 m (8 ft 2½ in); height 2.035 m (6 ft 8 in)
Powerplant: one FIAT diesel developing 160 hp (119 kW)
Performance: maximum road speed 100 km/h (62 mph); maximum range 700 km (435 miles); fording amphibious; gradient 60%; vertical obstacle 0.45 m (1 ft 5¾ in); trench not applicable

Tracked APCs and MICVs

What began as simply a 'battle taxi' to get vulnerable infantry close to their objective in safety has now become a fighting vehicle in its own right. In many ways, APCs and MICVs have taken over the tank's original role – that of helping the infantry onto their objective.

The Saxon went into service with the British Army in 1976. It is capable of travelling over very rough terrain and is fitted with a 7.62-mm machine-gun for low-level air defence (LLAD).

The armoured personnel carrier (APC) was born in World War II. Redundant tanks and lightly armoured half-tracks were put to use to carry the infantry through the fire-swept area of No Man's Land and deliver him to a covered position close to his objective, where he then dismounted to fight on foot in the usual manner. In the post-war years there was some desultory development of APCs, some of which were given machine-guns and some of which allowed the 'passengers' to fire their personal weapons through ports in the sides. But it was left to the Germans to take the APC to its logical conclusion and give the infantry section its own armed and armoured vehicle.

For most countries the object had been to keep the result as simple and cheap as possible, but the Germans developed a vehicle to a very high specification. The rest of the Western world thought they had made a mistake, until they came to develop their own designs; then, after various failures and second attempts, they slowly realized that the Germans had been right to aim high to start with. The Germans also got their mechanized infantry combat vehicle (MICV) at a bargain price, because by the time the rest of the world had caught up, the cost of MICVs had escalated. What they had overlooked was that the Germans, with their experience on the Eastern Front in 1941–44, understood more about the tactical requirements of MICVs than anyone else in the world.

The basic proposition is that the vehicle delivers the squad to its jumping-off position and then acts as a fire support vehicle. In fact, it was to do exactly what the original tanks of 1916 were designed to do: accompany the foot soldier, deal with obstacles, and assist in taking the objective. Unfortunately, people look at the MICV (or IFV – infantry fighting vehicle) and think of things to put in it, so one will find an air defence missile launcher, some mines, a surveillance radar – whatever is the flavour of the month. There is a danger of the infantryman becoming a sort of military plumber, who examines the problem, then goes back to his van for the right tool. Packing more equipment into the vehicle has, in some cases, led to a reduction in the number of men carried, which is self-defeating.

AMX-10P mechanized infantry combat vehicle

The **AMX-10P** is the replacement for the AMX-VCI, and was designed by the Atelier de Construction d'Issy-les-Moulineaux in the mid-1960s, production being undertaken from 1972 at the Atelier de Construction Roanne (ARE), where production of the AMX-30 MBT is undertaken together with that of the AMX-10RC (6×6) reconnaissance vehicle which is automotively related to the AMX-10P even though it is a wheeled vehicle. First production vehicles were completed in 1973, and since then more than 2,000 vehicles have been completed for the French army and for export to countries such as Greece, Indonesia, Mexico, Qatar, Saudi Arabia and the United Arab Emirates.

The AMX-10P has a hull of all-welded aluminium, with the driver at the front left, engine to his right, two-man turret in the centre and troop compartment at the rear. The eight troops enter and leave the vehicle via a power-operated ramp in the hull rear; there is a two-part roof hatch above the troop compartment. Apart from the roof hatches and two firing ports in the ramp, there is no provision for the troops to use their rifles from within the vehicle. The power-operated turret is armed with a 20-mm dual-feed (HE and AP ammunition) cannon with a co-axial 7.62-mm (0.3-in) machine-gun; mounted on each side of the turret are two smoke-dischargers. The weapons have an elevation of +50° and a depression of −8°, turret traverse being 360°. Totals of 800 rounds of 20-mm and 2,000 rounds of 7.62-mm (0.3-in) ammunition are carried.

The AMX-10P is fully amphibious, being propelled in the water by water-jets at the rear of the hull, and is also fitted with an NBC system and a full range of night-vision equipment for the commander, gunner and driver.

Variants of the AMX-10P include an ambulance, a driver training vehicle, a repair vehicle with crane for lifting engines, an anti-tank vehicle with four HOT ATGW in the ready-to-launch position, an **AMX-10PC** command vehicle, a RATAC radar vehicle, artillery observation and fire control vehicles, an **AMX-10TM** mortar tractor towing 120-mm (4.72-in) Brandt mortar and carrying 60 mortar bombs, 81-mm

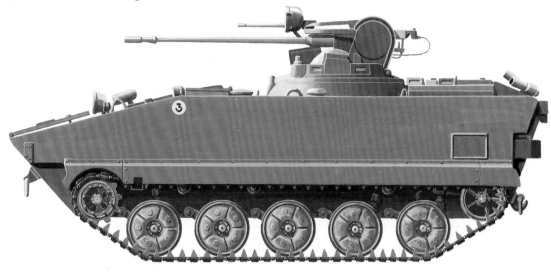

Above: The AMX-10P has a two-man power-operated turret armed with a 7.62-mm (0.3-in) machine-gun and a dual-feed 20-mm cannon. In the future it is probable that the latter will be replaced by a 25-mm weapon, which will have improved penetration characteristics against more recent vehicles.

Right: French infantry dismount from the rear of their AMX-10P MICV, which forms the basis for a complete family of vehicles including command post, HOT anti-tank, mortar tractor, fire control, artillery observation, repair vehicle, ambulance, radar and fire support.

(3.19-in) fire-support vehicle and the **AMX-10 PAC 90** fire-support vehicle. The last has already been adopted by the Indonesian marines and has a GIAT TS-90 two-man turret armed with a 90-mm (3.54-in) gun, for which 20 rounds of ammunition are carried, and a 7.62-mm (0.3-in) co-axial machine-gun. As with most main vehicles today, a wide range of options is offered including an anti-aircraft machine-gun and various types of fire-control equipment. In addition to its three-man crew of commander, gunner and driver, the AMX-10 PAC 90 carries four infantrymen in the rear. The vehicles delivered to In-

donesia have improved amphibious characteristics and they are meant to leave landing craft offshore rather than just cross rivers and streams, as is the basic vehicle. Indonesia also took delivery of a number of AMX-10Ps with the original two-man turret replaced by a new one-man turret at the rear armed with a 12.7-mm (0.5-in) M2 HB machine-gun.

Specification
AMX-10P
Crew: 3+8

Weight: 14200 kg (31,305 lb)
Powerplant: one HS-115 V-8 water-cooled diesel developing 280 hp (209 kW)
Dimensions: length 5.778 m (18 ft 11 in); width 2.78 m (9 ft 1 in); height (hull top) 1.92 m (6 ft 4 in) and (overall) 2.57 m (8 ft 5 in)
Performance: maximum road speed 65 km/h (40 mph); maximum range 600 km (373 miles); fording amphibious; gradient 60 per cent; vertical obstacle 0.70 m (2 ft 4 in); trench 1.60 m (5 ft 3 in)

AMX VCI infantry combat vehicle

To meet a French army requirement for an infantry combat vehicle Hotchkiss, which is no longer involved in the design, development or production of vehicles, built a number of prototypes in the early 1950s, but these were all rejected. It was then decided to build an IFV based on the chassis of the AMX-13 light tank, which was then already in large scale production for both the French and other armies. Following trials with prototype vehicles, the **AMX VCI** was adopted by the French army, first production vehicles being completed at the Atelier de Construction Roanne in 1967. Since then some 3,000 vehicles have been built for the home and export markets. Once the Atelier de Construction Roanne (ARE) started to turn out the AMX-30 MBT, production of the AMX-13 light tank family, including the VCI, was transferred to Creusot-Loire at

Chalon-sur-Saone, where the VCI remains in production today at a low level. The French army currently calls the vehicle the Vehicule de Combat d'Infanterie (infantry fighting vehicle), although it had a number of earlier names. In many respects the VCI was an advance on other Western vehicles of its period as not only was it fitted with a machine-gun turret for suppressive fire, but the infantry could also use their rifles from within the vehicle. The major drawback of the VCI was its lack of amphibious capability, and when originally deployed it was not fitted with an NBC system or night-vision equipment. The VCI remains in service with the French army, although it is being replaced by the AMX-10P, and is also used by Belgium, Ecuador, Indonesia, Italy, Morocco, Venezuela and the United Arab Emirates.

The AMX VCI is of all-welded steel

AMX VCI infantry fighting vehicle of the French army fitted with a cupola mounted machine-gun. The troop compartment at the rear of the hull is

provided with firing ports. In the French army this is now slowly being replaced by the amphibious AMX-10P MICV.

construction, with the driver at the front left, engine to his right, commander and gunner in the centre and the troop compartment at the rear. The last are provided with doors in the rear, and hatches in the side are provided with four firing ports each. Torsion-bar suspension consists of five single rubber-tyred road wheels, with the drive sprocket at the front and idler at the rear; there are four track-return rollers.

In addition to the basic VCI, which carries 10 fully equipped troops as well as its three-man crew, there were also ambulance, command, cargo, combat engineer, anti-tank (with ENTAC wire-guided missiles), RATAC radar, artillery fire-control, mortar-carrier (both 81-mm/3.19-in and 120-mm/4.72-in weapons) and support vehicles, the last carrying the remainder of the gun crew and additional ammunition for the 155-mm (6.1-in) Mk F3 self-propelled gun.

More recently the manufacturer has offered a diesel conversion package for the VCI and all other members of the AMX-13 light tank family. In this the original petrol engine is replaced by the well-known Detroit Diesel 6V-53T engine developing 280 hp (208 kW) for improved operational range, slightly higher speed and reduced fire risk.

Specification
AMX VCI
Crew: 3+10
Weight: 15000 kg (33,069 lb)

Powerplant: one SOFAM 8-cylinder petrol engine developing 250 hp (186 kW)
Dimensions: length 5.70 m (18 ft 8 in); width 2.67 m (8 ft 9 in); height (hull top) 2.1 m (6 ft 11 in) and (overall) 2.41 m (7 ft 11 in)
Performance: maximum road speed 60 km/h (37 mph); maximum range 350 km (218 miles); fording 1.00 m (3 ft 3 in); gradient 60 per cent; vertical obstacle 0.65 m (2 ft 2 in); trench 1.60 m (5 ft 3 in)

UK

FV432 armoured personnel carrier

After the end of World War II various prototypes of full-tracked armoured personnel carriers were built in the UK, but it was not until 1962 that one of these, the **FV432**, was accepted by the British army. The FV432 is member of the **FV430** series of vehicles which also includes the **FV433** Abbot 105-mm (4.13-in) self-propelled gun built by Vickers at its Elswick facility in Newcastle between 1964 and 1967. Production of the FV432 and its many variants was undertaken by GKN Sankey between 1963 and 1971, about 3,000 being built in all. Although offered overseas it was never purchased by any country as by that time the very similar American M113 APC was already in volume production for the US Army, and this was much cheaper than the FV432. For a short period the FV432 was commonly known as the **Trojan**.

The basic role of the FV432 is to transport British infantry across the battlefield; when close to its objective the infantry dismount and continue the assault on foot. The main difference between the M113 and the FV432 is that the latter has a hull of welded steel construction while the former has a hull of welded aluminium. The driver is seated at the front on the right, with the commander to his rear and the power-pack to his left. The troop compartment is at the rear of the hull, with entry to this compartment via a large single door in the hull rear. Hatches are provided over the top of the troop compartment, but there is no provision for the infantry to use their weapons from within the vehicle. The 10 infantrymen carried are seated five on each side of the hull facing each other on seats that can be quickly folded up to enable cargo to be carried. The vehicle is fitted with night-vision equipment and was also one of the first vehicles of its type to be fitted with an NBC system, which supplies clean air to the troops and crew. When introduced into service the FV432 was fitted with a flotation screen attached to the top of the hull; when this was erected the vehicle could propel itself across lakes and rivers with its tracks. These screens have now been removed as they were easily damaged and prone to damage in time of war from small arms fire and shell splinters. The basic vehicle is fitted with a 7.62-mm (0.3-in) machine-gun in an unprotected mount, but many vehicles have now been fitted with a turret-mounted 7.62-mm (0.3-in) machine-gun over the troop compartment.

In addition to being used as a troop carrier, the FV432 is also used for a wide range of other roles including ambulance, command with extensive

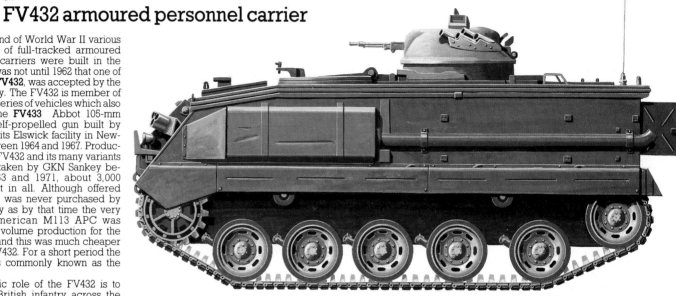

An FV432 fitted with a Peak Engineering one-man turret armed with a 7.62-mm (0.3-in) machine-gun and four electrically-operated smoke dischargers on either side. When fitted with this turret the roof hatches over the troop compartment cannot be used. The FV432 is in service only with the British army.

communications equipment installed, 81-mm (3.19-in) mortar carrier, mine-layer towing the Bar minelaying system and fitted with the Ranger anti-personnel mine scatter on the roof, radar carrier (such as the ZB 298 surveillance radar or the Cymbeline mortar/artillery-locating system), artillery fire-control vehicle with the Field Artillery Computer Equipment (FACE), and specialized vehicles for the Royal Signals. The maintenance carrier is called the **FV434** and can change Chieftain engines in the field, while the anti-tank member of the family is the FV438 which has Swingfire ATGWs. From the late 1980s the FV432 has been supplemented in service by the 'Warrior' MCV-80.

Specification
FV432
Crew: 2+10
Weight: 15280 kg (33,686 lb)
Powerplant: one Rolls-Royce K60 6-cylinder multi-fuel engine developing

240 bhp (170 kW)
Dimensions: length 5.251 m (17 ft 7 in); width 2.80 m (9 ft 2 in); height (with machine-gun) 2.286 m (7 ft 6 in)
Performance: maximum road speed 52.2 km/h (32 mph); maximum range 483 km (300 miles); fording 1.066 m (3 ft 6 in); gradient 60 per cent; vertical obstacle 0.609 m (2 ft 0 in); trench 2.05 m (6 ft 9 in)

An FV432 APC at speed. In many respects this vehicle is similar to the American M113, but it has steel rather than aluminium armour and, as built, was fitted with a multi-fuel engine and a complete NBC system.

GKN Warrior Mechanised Combat Vehicle

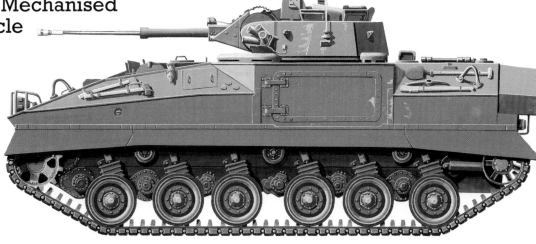

Originally called the MCV-80, the Warrior infantry combat vehicle was developed by GKN Sankey to meet the requirements of the British army. After trials of the prototypes in 1984, the design was approved and, the first production vehicles appeared in December 1986. The first Warrior-equipped infantry battalion was fully operational in the summer of 1988. The initial production of 1048 vehicles for 13 battalions was later reduced to 789 vehicles and eight battalions.

The hull of the vehicle is all-welded aluminium, giving greater protection than the FV432. The driver is at the front on the left side, and the power-pack is to his right. The engine is a Perkins Condor CV-8 diesel, coupled to an American Allison automatic transmission manufactured under licence in Britain by Perkins Engines.

The two-man power-operated steel turret, built by Vickers Defence Systems, is in the left centre of the hull with the commander on the left, and the gunner on the right. Both men have a Pilkington day/night sight, and there are additional vision devices for all-round surveillance. Main armament comprises a 30-mm Rarden cannon which was already in service with the British arm in the CVR(W)) Fox light armoured car and the Scimitar. Mounted co-axially with the main armament is a Hughes 7.62-mm (0.3-in) EX-34 Chain Gun which is manufactured under licence in the United Kingdom by the Royal Ordnance Factory at Nottingham. On the outside of the turret are two groups of four electrically-fired smoke grenade dischargers.

The troop compartment is at the rear of the and the eight infantrymen leave via a power-operated door in the rear of the hull. Over the top of the troop compartment are double roof hatches and two periscopes for use by the infantry section. There is no provision for the infantry to aim and fire their weapons from within the vehicle as is the case with the

Above: The GKN Warrior MCV entered service in 1986 and is now firmly established as a vehicle capable of fighting its way to the objective or acting as a fire support unit for the dismounted troops normally carried inside it. It has a two-man power-operated turret with a 30-mm cannon.

American M2 Bradley, West German Marder and Soviet BMP. There is ample room in the vehicle for personal equipment and space to carry sufficient supplies of food and ammunition for a 48-hour period.

Suspension is of the torsion-bar type with six road wheels, and the drive sprocket is at the front with the idler at the rear; there are three track-return rollers. The British army did not require it to be amphibious. It is fitted with an NBC system and a full range of night vision equipment.

Variant models include an artillery observation vehicle with a dummy gun and additional communications and surveillance equipment; an anti-tank vehicle equipped with the MILAN wire-guided missile; a repair and recovery type; an infantry command vehicle; and specially equipped models for operations in Arctic and desert conditions. Prototypes have been constructed with a 90-mm turret-mounted gun, with the HOT anti-tank missile system, and with the TRIGAT anti-tank

missile system. It is likely that this will enter service with the British army once the TRIGAT system is in production. Numbers of the basic Warrior vehicle have been sold to Kuwait.

Specification:
Crew: 2 + 8
Weight: 24.5 tonnes
Engine: Perkins CV-8 diesel, 550 bhp at 2300 rpm
Dimensions: length 6.34 m (20ft 9in); width 3.03 m(9ft10in); height to turret

Unlike the M2 Bradley and the Marder, the Warrior does not have any firing ports in the rear compartment. It is fitted with an NBC system and a full range of night vision equipment.

roof 2.79 m (9ft 2in)
Performance: max road speed 75 km/hr (45 mph); max range 660 km (402 miles); vertical obstacle 0.75 m (2ft 5in); trench 2.5 m (2 ft 8 in); fording 1.3 m (4 ft 3in)

VCC infantry armoured fighting vehicle

OTO Melara of La Spezia, well known as a manufacturer of naval weapons, have been engaged in the design and production of armoured vehicles since the 1960s and have built several thousand M113 armoured personnel carriers for the Italian army under licence from FMC of the United States. While the M113 is an excellent vehicle, it suffers from the major drawback of having an unprotected 12.7-mm (0.5-in) machine-gun mounting and no provision for the infantry to fire their weapons from within the vehicle with any degree of safety. The Automotive Technical Service of the Italian army subsequently modified the M113 and after trials this was adopted by the Italian army under the designation of the **VCC-1**, or more commonly the **Camillino** and well over one thousand of these have now been delivered to the Italian army, with final deliveries taking place in 1983. From 1983 there were delivered to Saudi Arabia 200 vehicles fitted with the Emerson Improved

TOW launcher as fitted to the M901 Improved TOW Vehicle (ITV).

The forward part of the VCC-1, which was deployed to the Lebanon in 1983, is identical to the M113, with the driver at the front left and the engine to his right. The rest of the vehicle is new, the commander being seated to the rear of the driver and provided with a cupola and periscopes. The 12.7-mm (0.5-in) machine-gun is to the right of the driver in a cupola that can be traversed through 360°, lateral and rear armour protection being provided. The troop compartment is at the rear and in each side of the hull top, which is chamfered inwards on its upper part, are two firing ports each surmounted by a vision block. There is a

An Italian OTO Melara Infantry Armoured Fighting Vehicle with a roof-mounted 20-mm cannon. This is a further development of the M113, which has been built under licence by the company.

further firing port in the power-operated ramp in the hull rear. In the centre of the hull at the rear is a machine-gunner, who has an externally mounted 7.62-mm (0.3-in) machine-gun. To make more room in the troop compartment the fuel tank has been removed and the diesel fuel is now carried in two panniers externally at the hull rear, one on each side of the ramp. When the infantry fire their weapons from within the troop compartment there is a considerable build-up of fumes, which can be dangerous, so two roof-mounted fans are fitted to remove these fumes.

The VCC-1 is fully amphibious, being propelled in the water by its tracks at a speed of 5 km/h (3.1 mph). Before the water is entered a trim vane is erected at the front of the hull and the two electric bilge pumps are switched on. These pump out any water that seeps into the vehicle through door seals or through the hatches.

Under contract to the Italian army OTO Melara is now designing the **VCC-80** IFV, which will weigh about 20 tonnes and be fitted with a two-man power-operated turret armed with a 20-mm cannon and a 7.62-mm (0.3-in) co-axial machine-gun. For the export market OTO Melara has recently developed the **C 13** APC, which has a very low profile and can be fitted with a variety of weapons including a 25-mm cannon and a 90-mm (3.54-in) Cockerill Mk 3 gun.

Specification
VCC
Crew: 2+7

Weight: 11600 kg (25,573 lb)
Powerplant: one GMC Model 6V-53 6-cylinder water-cooled diesel developing 215 bhp (160 kW)
Dimensions: length 5.041 m (16 ft 9 in); width 2.686 m (8 ft 10 in); height (12.7 mm MG) 2.552 m (8 ft 4 in) and (hull top) 1.828 m (6 ft 0 in)
Performance: maximum road speed 64.4 km/h (40 mph); maximum range 550 km (342 miles); fording amphibious; gradient 60 per cent; vertical obstacle 0.61 m (2 ft 0 in); trench 1.68 m (5 ft 6 in)

Marder mechanized infantry combat vehicle

When the West German army was reformed in the 1950s its first mechanized infantry combat vehicle was the SPz 12-3 based on a Swiss chassis and subsequently manufactured both in England and West Germany. A decision was taken at an early stage that a complete family of vehicles would be developed that would use the same basic chassis. The first members of this family to enter service were the **Jagdpanzer Kanone** with a 90-mm (3.54-in) gun and the **Jagdpanzer Rakete** armed with SS.12 ARGWs (recently replaced by HOT). After many different prototypes had been built and subjected to extensive tests one of these was finally adopted by the West German army as the **Marder Schützenpanzer Neu M-1966**, and Rheinstahl (now Thyssen Henschel) was selected as prime contractor with MaK of Kiel as the second source. First production vehicles were delivered late in 1970 and production continued until 1975, by which time 3,000 vehicles had been built. The Marder was not exported overseas although recently Saudi Arabia has shown some interest in the vehicle.

At the time of its introduction the Marder was the most advanced MICV in the West, and even today it is matched only by the more recent Bradley infantry fighting vehicle. The Marder has excellent armour protection and a high cross-country speed to enable it to operate with the Leopard 1 and Leopard 2 MBTs as part of the combined-arms team.

The driver is seated at the front left with one infantryman to his rear and the engine to his right. The two-man power-operated turret (commander and gunner) is in the centre of the vehicle with the troop compartment at the rear. The infantry enter and leave via a power-operated ramp in the hull rear, and on each side of the troop compartment are two spherical firing ports, each with a roof-mounted periscope above it to enable infantrymen to aim and fire their rifles from within the vehicle.

The turret is armed with a dual-feed 20-mm Rh 202 cannon and a co-axial 7.62-mm (0.3-in) machine-gun. These can be elevated from −17° to +65°,

Above: Recently many Marders have been fitted with new passive night vision equipment and a Euromissile MILAN ATGW system. In the future the 20-mm cannon will be replaced by a 25-mm weapon to enable the vehicle to defeat the latest Soviet light combat vehicles, such as the BMP-2.

turret traverse being 360°. In the future the 20-mm cannon will be replaced by a Mauser 25-mm weapon firing ammunition with better armour-piercing characteristics to enable it to combat recent Soviet vehicles such as the BMP. Some Marders have recently been fitted with a Euromissile MILAN ATGW launcher on the turret to enable them to engage MBTs out to a maximum range of 2000 m (2,190 yards). Mounted above the rear troop compartment is a remote-controlled 7.62-mm (0.3-in) machine-gun.

Variants of the Marder in service with the West German army include the Roland SAM system with two missiles in the ready-to-launch position and a further eight in reserve, and another model with a surveillance radar on a hydraulically-operated arm that can be raised above the top of the vehicle for increased radar coverage.

The chassis of the Marder is also used as the basis for the Argentine

TAM medium tank and its variants, including the **VCTP** infantry combat vehicle and the **VCTM** 120-mm (4.72-in) mortar carrier; none of these vehicles were used during the Falklands campaign of 1982.

Specification
Marder
Crew: 4+6
Weight: 28200 kg (62,169 lb)
Powerplant: one MTU MB 833 6-cylinder diesel developing 600 hp (447 kW)
Dimensions: length 6.79 m (22 ft 3 in);

The Marder was the first MICV to enter service in the West, and is fitted with a two-man power-operated turret armed with a 20-mm cannon and a 7.62-mm (0.3-in) machine-gun. It has not so far been exported.

width 3.24 m (10 ft 8 in); height (overall) 2.95 m (9 ft 8 in)
Performance: maximum road speed 75 km/h (46.6 mph); maximum range 520 km (323 miles); fording 1.50 m (4 ft 11 in); gradient 60 per cent; vertical obstacle 1.00 m (3 ft 3 in); trench 2.50 m (8 ft 2 in)

Pbv armoured personnel carrier

Although the Swedish army deployed tanks well before World War II, it was not until the post-war period that the first full-tracked armoured personnel carriers were fielded. These were called the **Pbv 301** and were essentially the older Strv m/41 light tank stripped down to the basic chassis and rebuilt as an armoured personnel carrier. This was armed with a 20-mm cannon and could carry eight fully-equipped infantrymen as well as the two-man crew. The conversion work for the Pbv 301 was carried out by Hägglund & Söner between 1962 and 1963. Even before this work had started the Swedish army realized that this would only be a interim solution as the basic chassis was so old. Design work on the new **Pbv 302** armoured personnel carrier started in 1961 and progress was so quick that the first prototypes were completed in the following year. After the usual trials the company was

awarded a full-scale production contract and production was undertaken from 1966 to 1971. The Pbv 302 was not sold abroad, although it was offered to several countries. The main reason for this lies with the fact that the export of defence equipment is subject to such strict controls that Sweden can deal with only a very few countries.

In some respects the Pbv 302 is very similar in layout to the American M113, although the Swedish vehicle has some noticeable features that, when the vehicle was introduced, put it some way ahead of its competitors. The hull is of all-welded steel armour with the driver in the centre at the front, the gunner to the left rear and the commander to the right rear. Main armament comprises 20-mm Hispano cannon mounted in a turret with a traverse of 360°, weapon elevation being from −10° to +60°. The cannon can fire either high explosive (in belts of 135 rounds) or armour-piercing (in 10-round magazines) ammunition. The same turret has also been fitted to a number of other vehicles including M113s of the Swiss army and EE-11 (6×6) vehicles of Gabon. The troop compartment is at the rear of the hull, with the 10 infantrymen seated five along each side facing inwards. No firing ports are provided, although hatches over the troop compartment allow the troops to fire their weapons from within the vehicle. The infantry enter and leave the vehicle via two doors in the hull rear. The Pbv 302 is fully amphibious, being propelled in the water by its tracks.

The basic vehicle can also be used as an ambulance or a cargo carrier, while more specialized versions include an artillery command vehicle, an armoured observation post vehicle and a fire direction-post vehicle. The prototype of the **Pbv 302 Mk 2**

armoured personnel carrier has been built by Hägglund & Söner as a private venture. This has a separate cupola at the rear for the squad commander, a Lyran flare system and other minor modifications. The company has also proposed that the vehicle be converted into a mechanized infantry fighting vehicle with 25-mm cannon and sloping hull sides (like those of the Italian IFV) provided with firing ports and vision blocks.

Specification
Pbv 302
Crew: 2+10
Weight: 13500 kg (29,762 lb)
Powerplant: one Volvo-Penta Model THD 100B 6-cylinder inline diesel developing 280 hp (209 kW)

Dimensions: length 5.35 m (17 ft 7 in); width 2.86 m (9 ft 5 in); height (turret top) 2.50 m (8 ft 2 in) and (hull top) 1.90 m (6 ft 3 in)
Performance: maximum road speed maximum road speed 66 km/h (41 mph); maximum road range 300 km (186 miles); fording amphibious; gradient 60 per cent;

Above: The Pbv 302 APC is only used by the Swedish army, and is fitted with a turret-mounted 20-mm cannon. Before entering water the bilge pumps are switched on and the trim vane erected at the front.

Swedish infantrymen dismount from the rear of their Pbv 302 armoured personnel carrier. The Pbv 302 was one of the first vehicles of its type to enter production with a fully enclosed weapon station.

vertical obstacle 0.61 m (2 ft 0 in); trench 1.80 m (5 ft 11 in)

SWITZERLAND
MOWAG Tornado mechanized infantry combat vehicle

The MOWAG company has been engaged in the design and development of tracked and wheeled vehicles since just after World War II, and in the early 1960s it was awarded a contract from the West German government for the construction of prototype of a mechanized infantry combat vehicle that eventually became known as the Marder. In the 1970s the company developed as a private venture the very similar **Tornado** MICV, whose latest version, called the **Improved Tornado**, was announced in 1980. At this time the Swiss army's standard APC is the American M113, though many of these have been fitted with a Swedish turret armed with a 20-mm cannon. As the Swiss Army was about to equip with Leopard 2 MBTs, it was reasonable to assume they would be in the market for an armoured personnel carrier.

The hull of the Improved Tornado is of all-welded steel construction and probably has better protection against armour-piercing projectiles than most vehicles on the market today as its sides and front are so well sloped for the maximum possible protection. The driver is at the front of the vehicle on the left, with the commander to his rear and the engine and transmission to his right. In the centre of the hull can be mounted a wide range of armament installations depending on the mission

requirement. One of the most powerful installations is the Swiss Oerlikon-Bührle two-man power-operated Type GDD-AOE turret, which has an externally mounted 35-mm KDE cannon fed from two ready-use magazines each holding 50 rounds. One could hold armour-piercing rounds to engage other vehicles while the other could hold high explosive rounds for use against softer target such as trucks. Mounted co-axially with the 35-mm cannon is a 7.62-mm (0.3-in) machine-gun with 500 rounds of ready-use ammunition for the engagement of soft targets. The infantrymen are seated in the troop compartment at the hull rear, and enter and leave via a power-operated ramp. On each side of the troop compartment are spherical firing ports that allow some of the troops to fire their weapons from within the vehicle. If required, two remote-controlled 7.62-mm (0.3-in) machine-guns can be fitted (one on each side) at the rear on the troop compartment roof. These are almost identical to those fitted to the Marder, also built by MOWAG. Each mount can be traversed through 230° and the machine-guns can be elevated from −15° to +60°.

In spite of its many virtues, the Improved Tornado failed to attract many buyers; it was expensive, and

there were cheaper alternatives available. Mowag continued to promote the design until 1990, after which they concentrated on their more successful wheeled vehicles (such as their eight-wheeled 'Piranha') and the Improved Tornado was abandoned.

Specification
MOWAG Tornado
Crew: 3+7
Weight: 22300 kg (49,162 lb)
Powerplant: one Detroit Diesel Model 8V-71T diesel developing 390 hp (290 kW)
Dimensions: length 6.70 m (22 ft 0 in);

The Tornado MICV has been developed by MOWAG of Switzerland as a private venture. This particular Tornado has a turret-mounted 25-mm cannon and two machine-guns at the rear.

width 3.15 m (10 ft 4 in); height (hull top) 1.75 m (5 ft 9 in) and (turret top) 2.86 m (9 ft 5 in)
Performance: maximum road speed 66 km/h (41 mph); maximum road range 400 km (249 miles); fording 1.30 m (4 ft 3 in); gradient 60 per cent; vertical obstacle 0.85 m (2 ft 9 in); trench 2.20 m (7 ft 3 in)

M2 Bradley Infantry Fighting Vehicle

For many years the United States had a requirement for a mechanized infantry combat vehicle, but it is only in the last two years that this ambition has been realized with the introduction into service of the **M2 Bradley Infantry fighting Vehicle**. Back in the early 1960s prototypes of the **MICV-65** were designed, built and subsequently tested (as was the XM765 based on the well known APC), but in 1972 FMC was awarded the development contract for a new vehicle called the **XM723**, which was to be armed with a 20-mm cannon. No sooner had prototypes of this been built and started tests than there was another change of plan. At that time the US Army also had a requirement for the **XM800 Armored Reconnaissance Scout Vehicle** (ARSV) and prototypes of both tracked and wheeled vehicles were built and tested. It was then decided to develop a vehicle to meet both the MICV and scout requirements and at the same time a decision was taken that both vehicles would have the same basic hull and be fitted with a two-man turret armed with a 25-mm cannon and a twin TOW ATGW launcher. The chassis of the XM723 was used for both vehicles, the Infantry Fighting Vehicle becoming the **XM2** and the **Cavalry Fighting Vehicle** the **XM3**, with the whole family called the Fighting Vehicle System (FVS). These vehicles were soon standardized as the M2 and **M3**, the first production vehicles coming off the production line at San Jose, California, in 1981. The US Army has a requirement for just under 7,000 of these vehicles and in 1984 production was running at the rate of about 600 per year. The M2 Bradley is almost identical to the M3 except that the latter has no firing port, carries a total of five men (compared with 10 in the M2) and is provided with much more ammunition.

The hull of the M2 is of welded aluminium armour with an additional layer of spaced laminate armour fitted to the hull front, sides and rear to give much increased protection against most battlefield weapons. The driver is at the front of the hull on the left, with the powerpack to his right. The two-man power-operated turret is in the centre of the hull with the commander on the right and gunner on the left. The main armament is a Hughes Helicopter 25-mm dual-feed Chain Gun which can defeat Soviet light armoured vehicles when firing APDS ammunition; there is

Above: An M2 Bradley Infantry Fighting Vehicle with the twin TOW launcher retracted. This vehicle is entering service in increasing numbers with the US Army, with 600 vehicles being produced.

also a 7.62-mm (0.3-in) co-axial machine-gun and a twin launcher on the left side of turret for the Hughes TOW ATGWs. A stabilization system is fitted which allows the gunner to aim and fire the 25-mm cannon while moving at speed across country. The troop compartment is at the rear and provided with six firing ports and periscopes to allow the embarked men to fire their 5.56-mm (0.22-in) weapons from within the vehicle. A full range of night-vision equipment is fitted for the commander, gunner and driver, and there is an NBC system. The Bradley is a highly effective vehicle and plays a key role in the US Army's combined-arms team concept. It has many critics, though, who say that it is too large, expensive and difficult to maintain, and will be unable to operate with the M60 and M1 tanks as it has much inferior armour protection to these MBTs.

Specification
M2 Bradley
Crew: 3+7
Weight: 22666 kg (49,970 lb)
Powerplant: one Cummins VTA-903T 8-cylinder diesel developing 500 hp 9373 kW)
Dimensions: length 6.453 m (21 ft 2 in);

width 3.20 m (10 ft 6 in); height (overall) 2.972 m (9 ft 9 in)
Performance: maximum road speed 66 km/h (41 mph); maximum range 483 km (300 miles); fording amphibious; gradient 60 per cent; vertical obstacle 0.914 m (3 ft 0 in); trench 2.54 m (8 ft 4 in)

The M2 Bradley IFV has been designed to operate alongside the M1 Abrams Main Battle Tank on the modern battlefield. The twin TOW missile launcher gives the Bradley a significant anti-tank capability.

Armoured Infantry Fighting Vehicle

The shortcomings of the M113 armoured personnel carrier were realized by the US Army in the late 1960s, and in 1967 FMC was awarded a contract to build two prototypes of a new vehicle called the **XM765**. This was essentially a M113 with a fully-enclosed weapon station and with the troop compartment at the rear modified for firing ports and observation devices in the upper part of an inward-sloping hull top. The US Army did not adopt this vehicle, however, going on to develop a much heavier and more complex vehicle eventually standardized as the M2 Bradley Infantry Fighting Vehicle, which is also built by FMC Corporation.

FMC realized, though, that the new US Army infantry fighting vehicle

would be too complex, heavy and expensive for many countries around the world, so with company funds started a development of the XM765 which finally resulted in the **Product Improved M113A1**. This was not placed in production but did result in another vehicle with rearranged interior layout called the **Armoured Infantry Fighting Vehicle**. Following a number of demonstrations in Europe and elsewhere, the Netherlands became (in 1975) the first country to adopt the

The Dutch army uses a version of the AIFV fitted with the Emerson twin TOW launcher, as fitted to the M901 Improved TOW Vehicles of the US army, which has two missiles in the ready-to-launch position.

vehicle with an initial order for 850 vehicles. This was followed by the Philippines with an order for about 30 vehicles and in 1981 Belgium ordered 514 AIFVs and 525 M113A2s which are now being built under licence in Belgium.

Like the M113 series, the hull of the AIFV is of welded aluminium armour construction, but in addition has a layer of appliqué steel armour added to the front, sides and rear for increased protection. The driver is at the front left, with the engine to his right and the commander to his rear. The commander has a cupola with observation devices. The power-operated turret is to the right of the commander and is armed with a 25-mm Oerlikon dual-feed cannon; a 7.62-mm (0.3-in) machine-gun is mounted co-axially to the left of the 25-mm cannon. The turret is provided with both day and night observation devices. The seven infantrymen are seated in the rear of the vehicle and enter via a power-operated ramp as in the standard M113. A hatch is provided above the troop compartment, and there are five firing ports with observation devices. A wide range of optional equipment can be fitted including an NBC system, heater and different armament options.

The basic vehicle is fully amphibious, being propelled in the water by its tracks. Compared with the earlier

M113 the AIFV has improved armour protection, improved fire power (25-mm cannon in turret instead of a 12.7-mm/0.5-in machine-gun in an unprotected mount) and improved mobility (improved suspension and more powerful engine).

The Dutch army is using the AIFV as the basic member of a whole family of vehicles including an anti-tank vehicle with the Emerson Improved TOW system, a command vehicle, a tractor for the 120-mm (4.72-in) Brandt mortar, a radar vehicle, a cargo carrier and an ambulance.

Specification
AIFV
Crew: 3+7
Weight: 13687 kg (30,175 lb)
Powerplant: one Detroit Diesel 6V-53T V-6 diesel developing 264 hp (207 kW)
Dimensions: length 5.258 m (17 ft 3 in); width 2.819 m (9 ft 3 in); height (overall) 2.794 m (9 ft 2 in)
Performance: maximum road speed

The Armoured Infantry Fighting Vehicle has been developed by the FMC Corporation specifically for the export market, and fills the gap between the basic M113 APC and the more expensive M2 Bradley IFV.

61.2 km/h (38 mph); maximum range 490 km (305 miles); fording amphibious; gradient 60 per cent; vertical obstacle 0.635 m (2 ft 1 in); trench 1.625 m (5 ft 4 in)

 JAPAN
Type 73 armoured personnel carrier

When the Japanese Ground Self-Defense Force was formed in the 1950s its first armoured personnel carriers were half-tracks supplied by the United States. The first Japanese-designed vehicle to enter service was the **Type SU 60** APC which was produced by Mitsubishi Heavy Industries and the Komatsu Manufacturing Corporation, final deliveries being made in the early 1970s. The Type SU 60 is not amphibious, has a four-man crew and can carry six fully equipped troops. Over 400 of these are in service and variants include an NBC detection vehicle, 81-mm and 107-mm (3.19-in and 4.2-in) mortar-carriers and a dozer. The **Type 73** is now supplementing the Type SU 60 but production is at a very low rate, some times as low as six per year, and by 1984 about 150 had been built with production still under way.

The Type 73 has a hull of all-welded aluminium armour with the commander, driver and bow machine-gunner at the front. The 7.62-mm (0.3-in) machine-gun in the bow is unique and can be traversed 30° left, right, up and down, and a similar weapon is installed in the earlier Type SU 60 APC. The engine is towards the front on the left, with troop compartment at the rear. Entry to the latter is via two doors rather than a power-operated ramp as in the M113 APC and M2 Bradley IFV. One of the nine infantrymen normally mans the roof-mounted 12.7-mm (0.5-in) machine-gun, which is on the right side of the vehicle and can be aimed and fired from within the vehicle. The cupola can be traversed through 360° and the weapon elevated from −10° to +60°. The infantry are seated on benches down each side of the troop compartment facing each other; the ben-

ches can be folded up to allow stores and other equipment to be carried. On each side of the troop compartment are two T-type firing ports, although these have a limited value compared with the firing ports/vision blocks fitted to vehicles such as the West German Marder. Another unusual feature of the Type 73 is that mounted on the very rear of the hull roof on each side is a bank of three electrically-operated smoke-dischargers, which fire forwards. In action these would be fired when the vehicle was under attack so that it could withdraw to the rear.

The Type 73 has night-vision equipment and an NBC system, but is only amphibious after lengthy preparation. This preparation includes flotation aids along side of the hull and attached to the road wheels, a trim vane mounted at the front of the hull, and boxes fitted

around the air inlet, air outlet and exhaust pipes on the roof of the vehicle. If the last were not fitted any surge of water over the roof would soon get into the engine.

Unlike many current APCs there is only one known variant of the Type 73, namely the **Type 75** self-propelled ground-wind measuring unit that is used with the 130-mm (5.12-in) multiple rocket-launcher and uses some automotive components of the Type 73.

The Type 73 is still used as a troop transporter, but the major combat role has now been taken by the Mitsubishi Type 89 MICV, armed with an Oerlikon 35-mm cannon and two anti-tank guided missiles on its turret. It has a two-man crew and has the capacity to carry seven fully-equipped soldiers in the troop compartment.

The Japanese Type 73 APC and the earlier Type SU 60 APC are the only vehicles of their type with a bow-mounted 7.62-mm (0.3-in) machine-gun.

Specification
Type 73
Crew: 3+9
Weight: 13300 kg (29,321 lb)
Powerplant: one Mitsubishi air-cooled diesel developing 300 hp (224 kW)
Dimensions: length 5.80 m (19 ft 1 in); width 2.80 m (9 ft 2 in); height (with MG) 2.20 m (7 ft 3 in) and (hull) 1.70 m (5 ft 7 in)
Performance: maximum road speed 70 km/h (45 mph); maximum range 300 km (186 miles); fording amphibious; gradient 60 per cent; vertical obstacle 0.70 m (2 ft 4 in); trench 2.00 m (6 ft 7 in)

Steyr 4K 7FA armoured personnel carrier

Between 1961 and 1969 Oesterreichische, which was taken over by Steyr-Daimler-Puch in 1970, built 450 full-tracked armoured personnel carriers for the Austrian army, the final production model being **Schützenpanzer 4K 4FA** with a more powerful engine. In addition to the usual specialized versions, the Austrian army uses two basic models of the 4K 4FA, the **SPz G2** fitted with an Oerlikon-Bührle one-man turret armed with a 20-mm cannon and the **SPz G1** fitted with a 12.7-mm (0.5-in) M2 HB machine-gun.

In 1976 Steyr-Daimler-Puch completed the prototype of the **SPz 4K 7FA** APC which had much improved armour protection as well as the more powerful engine and upgraded transmision of the SK-105 tank destroyer with 105-mm (4.13-in) gun that by then was already in production for the Austrian army and was subsequently adopted by many other countries. The first production 4K 7FA APCs were completed in 1977, and since then sales have been made to Austria, Greece (where the vehicle is manufactured under licence as the **Leonidas**), Nigeria and Tunisia.

The all-welded steel hull of the SPz 4K 7FA provides the crew with protection from 20-mm projectiles over the frontal arc, and accommodates the driver at the front left with the engine to his right and the troop compartment at the rear. The gunner is seated to the rear of the driver, and his cupola is provided with a two-part hatch cover that when in the vertical position provides protection to his sides, the 12.7-mm (0.5-in) machine-gun being provided with a shield to provide frontal protection. On the rear of the gunner's cupola are four smoke-dischargers firing to the rear. The eight troops enter and leave the vehicle through twin doors in the hull rear, and sit in two

rows of four down the middle of the vehicle facing outwards. Over the top of the troop compartment is a two-piece hatch cover that opens to each side, and around the roof can be mounted up to four 7.62-mm (0.3-in) machine-guns; to fire these weapons the troops have to expose their heads and shoulders above the roof. Standard equipment includes heating and ventilating systems, and passive night-vision equipment can be installed if required.

As usual the chassis has been used as the basis for a complete family of vehicles. The infantry fighting vehicle has ball mounts for two rifles in each side of the hull with periscopes above for aiming the weapons. The fire-support model, which has yet to enter production, has a GIAT TS 90 turret armed with a long-barrelled 90-mm (3.54-in) gun that fires APFSDS-T ammunition. There are also command, ambulance (unarmed), mortar-carrier (81-mm/3.19-in and 120-mm/4.72-in) and two anti-aircraft vehicles. Neither of the latter has yet entered production. One is fitted with the French ESD turret and armed with twin 20-mm cannon, while the other has a complete surveillance and tracking system and is armed with twin 30-mm cannon in a turret designed by Thomson-CSF.

Specification
SPz 4K 7FA
Crew: 2+8
Weight: 14800 kg (32,628 lb)
Powerplant: one Steyr 6-cylinder

The Steyr-Daimler-Puch 4K 7FA-K SPz infantry fighting vehicle is a further development of the basic 4K 7FA which is used by Austria, Greece (manufactured under licence), Morocco, Nigeria and Tunisia. It shares many common components with the SK 105 tank destroyer.

liquid-cooled diesel developing 320 hp (238 kW)
Dimensions: length 5.87 m (19 ft 3 in); width 2.50 m (8 ft 2 in); height (without MG) 1.69 m (5 ft 7 in)
Performance: maximum road speed 63.6 km/h (41 mph); maximum range 520 km (323 miles); fording 1.00 m (3 ft 3 in); gradient 75 per cent; vertical obstacle 0.80 m (2 ft 7 in); trench 2.10 m (6 ft 11 in)

M-980 mechanized infantry combat vehicle

The first Yugoslav-designed and -built armoured personnel carrier to enter service was the **M-60P**. In appearance and role this was similar to other vehicles developed in this period, such as the American M113, and was designed to transport men across the battlefield where they would dismount and fight on foot. Realizing the obvious shortcomings of this vehicle, Yugoslavia then started design work on a mechanized infantry combat vehicle which finally appeared in 1975 under the designation **M-980**. The short development period was made possible by the decision to incorporate a number of proven components from other sources, often from outside the country. For example, the engine came from Renault (formerly Saviem) of France and is also installed in the GIAT AMX-10P vehicle, while the road wheels are similar to those of the Soviet PT-76 light amphibious tank family and the 'Sagger' ATGW is fitted to a wide number of Soviet vehicles including MICVs, APCs and tank destroyers.

In many respects the design of the M-980 is very similar to that of the Soviet BMP-1, which is also used by Yugoslavia in small numbers. The driver is seated at the front of the vehicle on the left, with the vehicle commander to his rear and the engine to his right. The one-man turret is in the centre of the vehicle and armed with a 20-mm cannon with an elevation of +75° and a depression of −5°; mounted co-axially to the right of this is a 7.62-mm (0.3-in) machine-gun. The high elevation of these weapons enables them to be used against low-flying aircraft and helicopters. Mounted externally on the right rear of the turret are two Soviet AT-3 'Sagger' wire guided anti-tank missiles. The troop compartment is at the rear, and entry to this is via two doors in the hull rear. Over the top of the troop compartment are roof hatches and firing ports (with periscopes above) to enable the troops to fire their weapons from within the vehicle.

The M-980 is fully amphibious, being propelled in the water by its tracks; before the vehicle enters the water a trim vane is erected at the front of the hull and the bilge pumps are switched on. It is also fitted with a fire-extinguishing system, an NBC pack and a smokelaying system.

As far as it is known there are no variants of the M-980, although command vehicles and other specialized versions probably exist. In some respects this vehicle is an improvement over the Soviet BMP-1 as it has two rather than one 'Sagger' missile in the ready-to-launch position, and its 20-mm cannon is probably more suited to

the role of the vehicle than the 73-mm (2.87-in) gun of the BMP-1. It is of note that the latest Soviet BMP has had the 73-mm (2.87-in) weapon replaced by a smaller 30-mm calibre gun, and most Western vehicles of this type are armed with weapons in the 20- to 30-mm range rather than heavy weapons such as the 73-mm (2.87-in) gun of the BMP-1.

Specification
M-980
Crew: 2+8
Weight: 13000 kg (28,660 lb)
Powerplant: one HS 115-2 V-8 diesel

A Yugoslav M-980 mechanized infantry combat vehicle, showing the twin launcher for AT-3 'Sagger' ATGWs above the turret roof. The engine is as used in the French AMX-10P.

developing 260 hp (194 kW)
Dimensions: length 6.40 m (21 ft 0 in); width 2.59 m (8 ft 6 in); height (overall) 2.50 m (8 ft 2 in)
Performance: maximum road speed 60 km/h (37 mph); maximum range 500 km (310 miles); fording amphibious; vertical obstacle 0.80 m (2 ft 8 in); trench 2.20 m 7 ft 3 in)

BMD airborne combat vehicle

The Soviet Union has for some time placed great emphasis on its airborne forces, and for many years has had at least seven airborne divisions maintained at full strength. In the past the only armoured vehicles these divisions have used have been the 57-mm ASU-57 or the 85-mm (3.35-in) ASU-85 or the 85-mm (3.35-in) ASU-85 self-propelled anti-tank guns. To give these units increased firepower and mobility once they have been landed behind enemy lines the **BMD** airborne combat vehicle was designed, and this entered service in 1970. Today each Soviet airborne rifle division has 330 of these vehicles in various configurations, although it is uncertain whether or not all seven of these divisions have their full complement of vehicles. While the Soviet Union has considerable airborne forces, it does not have the capability to lift more than one airborne rifle division at any one time. The BMD was used to spearhead the invasion of Afghanistan in 1979, and there is also evidence that it has been used operationally elsewhere.

The layout of the vehicle is unusual, the driver being seated at the front of the hull in the centre with the commander to his left and the bow machine-gunner to his right. The latter operates the two single 7.62-mm (0.3-in) machine-guns mounted internally at the front of the hull, one on each side. The turret, which is identical to that fitted to the BMP-1, is in the centre of the hull and is armed with a 73-mm (2.87-in) gun, a 7.62-mm (0.3-in) co-axial machine-gun and a launcher rail for the AT-3 'Sagger' ATGW mounted above the main gun. To the rear of the turret is a small compartment with seats for the senior gunner, the grenade-launcher and his assistant; the

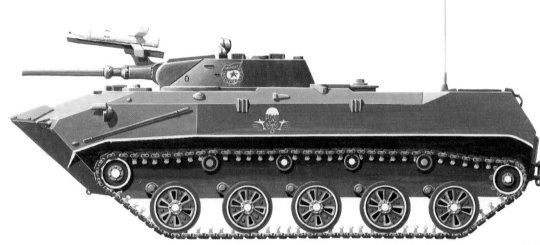

only means of entry to this compartment is via the concertina type roof hatch. The independent suspension of the BMD consists of five road wheels, with drive sprocket at the rear and idler at the front; there are four track-return rollers. An unusual feature of this suspension is that a hydraulic system is incorporated that allows the ground clearance of the vehicle to be altered from 100 mm to 450 mm (4 in to 18 in), a factor of some importance for airborne operations.

The BMD is fitted with an NBC system and a full range of night-vision equipment. It is also fully amphibious, the only preparation required being the erection of the trim vane at the front of the hull and the engagement of the bilge pump.

The command version of the BMD is called the **BMD-U** (command), and this

has a longer chassis with six road wheels on each side and no turret. There is also an 82-mm (3.23-in) mortar version that has seen action in Afghanistan. More recently some BMDs have been observed with the launcher rail for the 'Sagger' ATGW replaced by that for a shorter-range AT-4 'Spigot' on the turret roof; if required the launcher can be dismounted for use in the ground role.

The BMD can be carried slung under a heavy-lift helicopter or dropped from transport aircraft by parachutes; the Antonov An-22 'Cock' is believed to be able to carry at least three BMDs.

Specification
BMD
Crew: 7
Weight: 6700 kg (14,771 lb)

The BMD airborne combat vehicle is used only by the Soviet Air Assault Divisions and has been operated extensively in Afghanistan. Its turret is similar to that fitted to the BMP-1 MICV, although some BMDs have a roof-mounted Spigot ATGW in place of the AT-3 'Sagger' ATGW.

Powerplant: one V-6 liquid-cooled diesel developing 240-hp (179 kW)
Dimensions: length 5.40 m (17 ft 9 in); width 2.63 m (8 ft 8 in); height 1.62 m to 1.97 m (5 ft 4 in to 6 ft 6 in)
Performance: maximum road speed 70 km/h (43 mph); maximum range 320 km (200 miles); fording amphibious; gradient 60 per cent; vertical obstacle 0.80 m (2 ft 8 in); trench 1.60 m (5 ft 3 in)

BMP-1 mechanized infantry fighting vehicle

The **BMP-1** was developed as the replacement for the BTR-50 armoured personnel carrier and caused a major stir throughout Western armies when it rolled through Red Square for the first time in 1967. Previous armoured personnel carriers simply transported the infantry to a point near the scene of action, where it dismounted to attack the objective on foot. The BMP-1 not only has firing ports that allow all of the embarked troops to fire their weapons from within the vehicle in relative safety, but also a 73-mm (2.87-in) cannon and a wire-guided anti-tank missile. Since the introduction of the BMP-1 several countries have also developed mechanized infantry combat vehicles: the West German Marder (20 mm cannon), the French AMX-10P (20-mm cannon) and most recently the US M2 Bradley (25-mm cannon) are all good examples. The Marder has recently been fitted with an externally mounted MILAN ATGW, but although this is more accurate than the 'Sagger' fitted to the BMP-1 it has a shorter range. The M2 has a twin launcher for the TOW ATGW which has a longer range than the 'Sagger' and is much more accurate.

The layout of the BMP-1 is unusual, with the driver at front left, the commander to his rear and the engine on the right. The turret is in the centre of the hull and the infantry compartment at the rear. The eight infantrymen are

seated four down each side, back to back, and enter the vehicle via twin doors in the hull rear. Over the top of the troop compartment are roof hatches. The main drawback of this arrangement is that the troop commander is out of immediate contact with the men he must command in battle. The 73-mm (2.87-in) gun is fed from a magazine that holds 40 rounds of HEAT (high explosive anti-tank) or HE-FRAG (high explosive fragmentation) ammunition, and there is a 7.62-mm (0.3-in) co-axial machine-gun. Turret traverse is electric, with manual controls for emergency use. The main drawbacks of the 73-mm (2.87-in) low-pressure gun are its low muzzle velocity and its lack of accuracy in high winds. To fire with any chance of a first-round hit the BMP-1 must first halt. The 'Sagger' ATGW is mounted on a launcher rail over the 73-mm (2.87-in) gun and controlled (via a joystick) by the gunner. The missile has a maximum range of 3000 m (3,280 yards), but takes 27 seconds to reach this range.

The BMP-1 is fitted with a full range of first-generation infra-red night-vision equipment for the commander, gunner and driver, as well as an NBC system. It is fully amphibious with hardly any preparation, being propelled in the water by its tracks.

In addition to the basic BMP-1 there are also command versions of the vehicle, a radar carrier fitted with two-man

turret armed with a 7.62-mm (0.3-in) machine-gun and fitted with a 'Small Fred' mortar/artillery-location radar on turret rear, and a reconnaissance vehicle that has a turret fitted with the same 73-mm (2.87-mm) gun. Shown for the first time in the 1982 Red Square parade was yet another version that is sometimes called the **BMP-2**. This has a new two-man turret armed with a new long-barrelled rapid-fire cannon with a 'Spandrel' ATGW launcher mounted on the turret roof, and fitted with three smoke-dischargers on each side of the turret.

Specification
BMP-1
Crew: 3+8
Weight: 13500 kg (29,762 lb)

Soviet BMP-1 mechanized infantry combat vehicles in support of their dismounted infantry. In this photograph none of the vehicles have the AT-3 'Sagger' wire-guided anti-tank missile mounted above the 73-mm gun.

Powerplant: one 6-cylinder diesel developing 300 hp (224 kW)
Dimensions: length 6.74 m (22 ft 1 in); width 2.94 m (9 ft 8 in); height (overall) 2.15 m (7 ft 1 in)
Performance: maximum road speed 80 km/h (50 mph); maximum range 500 km (248 miles); fording amphibious; gradient 60 per cent; vertical obstacle 0.80 m (2 ft 8 in); trench 2.20 m (7 ft 3 in)

BTR-50PK armoured personnel carrier

The **BTR-50P** was the first full-tracked armoured personnel carrier to enter service with the Soviet army in the mid-1950s, and is essentially the chassis of the PT-76 amphibious light tank with its turret removed and a superstructure added to the forward part. The commander and driver are seated under armour protection at the front of the vehicle, while the 10 infantrymen are seated in the troop compartment on bench seats that run across the width of the vehicle. The main drawback of this model is the complete lack of any overhead armour protection for the infantry carried and additionally there is no NBC system. The main armament consists of a 7.62-mm (0.3-in) machine-gun on a pintle mount at the front of the crew compartment. On the rear engine decking ramps are provided so that a 57-mm (2.24-in) or 85-mm (3.35-in) anti-tank gun could be carried and, if required, even fired from the vehicle. The next major model to enter service was the **BTR-50PK**, which has a fully enclosed troop compartment and is fitted with an NBC system. Armament consists of a roof-mounted 7.62-mm (0.3-in) machine-gun that provides no protection for the gunner. The Czechs have also built an improved version of the BTR-50PK called the **OT-62**, this being distinguishable from the Soviet vehicle by its lack

of chamfer between the side and top of the hull. There are two command versions of the vehicle called the **BTR-50PU** (command) **Model 1** and **BTR-50PU Model 2**. Both of these have a fully enclosed crew compartment, the former having one projecting bay and the latter two. These command vehicles have additional communications equipment and can be recognized by their radio aerials, external stowage and a generator; the last removes the need for the main engine to be run when the vehicle is being used in the static mode.

The basic vehicle has been out of production for some time, and in many Soviet units the type has been replaced by the BMP-1 MICV. Two new versions have recently been noticed by Western intelligence, however, these being the **MTK** mine-clearing vehicle and the **MTP** technical support vehicle. The former is fitted with a launcher on the rear deck that fires explosive tubes across the minefield: these fall to the ground and are then detonated, hopefully detonating the mines in the process. In concept this is similar to the British Giant Viper system. The MTP has much higher roof with chamfered sides and supports the BMP in the forward battlefield area, it having better cross-country capability than the trucks normally used in this

role.

Even in 1984, the BTR-50P and its variants are still used by some 30 countries in Europe, the Middle East and elsewhere. The type was used in Vietnam by the North Vietnamese army and in the Middle East campaigns by Syria and Egypt. The last used the BTR-50P with some success in crossing the Suez Canal during 1973. Whereas most western APCs (such as the American M113 and British FV432) are propelled in the water by their tracks, the BTR-50P is propelled in the water by waterjets at a speed of 11 km/h (6.8 mph).

Specification
BTR-50PK
Crew: 2+10
Weight: 14200 kg (31,305 lb)
Powerplant: one Model V-6 6-cylinder inline water-cooled diesel developing 240 hp (179 kW)
Dimensions: length 7.08 m (23 ft 0 in); width 3.14 m (10 ft 4 in); height (without armament) 1.97 m (6 ft 6 in)
Performance: maximum road speed 44 km/h (27 mph); maximum range 400 km (273 miles); fording amphibious; gradient 70 per cent; vertical obstacle 1.10 m (3 ft 7 in); trench 2.80 m (9 ft 2 in)

Soviet BTR-50PK armoured personnel carriers. This model has overhead armour protection for the troop compartment. The original BTR-50P has an open-topped troop compartment, which makes the 10 seated infantry men very vulnerable to shells and mortar bombs bursting overhead.

MT-LB multi-purpose tracked vehicle

In the period immediately after World War II the Soviets introduced the AT-P armoured tracked artillery tractor, which could tow anti-tank guns and howitzers up to 122 mm (4.8 in) in calibre. This has now been replaced by the **MT-LB** multi-purpose armoured vehicle, which is used for a wide range of roles in addition to its role of towing anti-tank guns such as the 100-mm (3.9-in) T-12.

The crew compartment is at the front, with the engine to the rear of this on the left and the troop compartment at the rear. The 11 infantrymen are seated on canvas seats down each side of the troop compartment that can be folded up to allow cargo to be carried. The infantry can quickly leave the vehicle through two large doors in the hull rear, and two hatches are provided over the top of their compartment. Mounted at the front of the hull on the right side is a manually-operated turret armed with a 7.62-mm (0.3-in) machine-gun. The road wheels are similar to those on the PT-76 amphibious light tank and the BTR-50 series armoured personnel carrier. The torsion-bar suspension consists of six road wheels, with the drive sprocket at the front and idler at the rear. The MT-LB is normally fitted with 350-mm (13.8-in) wide tracks, but when operating on snow-covered ground these can be replaced by the much wider 565-mm (22.25-in) wide tracks, which give a lower ground pressure and therefore better mobility.

The MT-LB is fully amphibious, being propelled in the water by its tracks at a speed of between 5 and 6 km/h (3 to 4 mph), and has infra-red night vision equipment and an NBC system.

In some areas of the Soviet Union where terrain is swampy or normally covered by snow, the MT-LB is used in

Above: The MT-LB multi-purpose armoured vehicle is a member of a family of vehicles that all share the same automotive components.

place of the BMP mechanized infantry combat vehicle.

As usual the MT-LB chassis has been used for a number of specialized applications including the **MT-LBU** (command), **MT-SON** with 'Pork Trough' radar mounted on roof, MT-LB with 'Big Fred' artillery/mortar locating radar on roof at rear, MT-LB armoured engineer vehicle with dozer blade and **MTL-LB** repair vehicle. The last is used for repair and recovery operations in the forward area and fitted (at the front) with an A frame, plus a winch and a full range of tools and other specialized equipment. The chassis is also used as the basis for the SA-13 surface-to-air missile system that has four missiles in the ready-to-launch position. Automotive components of the MT-LB, including the engine and transmission, are also used in the 122-mm (4.8-in) 2S1 self-propelled howitzer which entered service in the 1970s and is now widely used by the Soviet Union as well as

being exported to many countries.

Specification
MT-LB
Crew: 2+11
Weight: 11900 kg (26,235 lb)
Powerplant: one V-8 diesel developing 240 hp (179 kW)
Dimensions: length 6.454 m (21 ft 2 in); width 2.85 m (9 ft 4 in); height (turret) 1.865 m (6 ft 5 in)

The MT-LB amphibious vehicle is used for a wide range of roles such as artillery prime mover, command post, cargo carriers and an armoured personnel carrier.

Performance: maximum road speed 61.5 km/h (38 mph); maximum range 500 km (310 miles); fording amphibious; gradient 60 per cent; vertical obstacle 0.70 m (2 ft 3 in); trench 2.70 m (8 ft 10 in)

A New Generation of Fighting Vehicles

When armoured vehicle designers finally shook off the shackles of World War II the results were a little mixed; but some turned out to be winners. Early 1980s designs reflected the West's continued preoccupation with Soviet armour, the needs of 'brush-fire wars' and the escalating costs of armoured vehicle development.

The 1980s introduced a number of new designs to the world's armies. This section is representative of the sort of equipment that was on offer in the early part of the decade. The ever-present threat from the massive Soviet tank armies on the far side of the Inner German Border is reflected in the potent design of the French AMX-40 MBT and in the little Panhard VBL scout car. There were a number of people who felt that a light, nimble inconspicuous vehicle with a missile on it might be a better investment that a 40-tonne tank.

Another of the current bogeymen was the overpowering strength of the Soviet air forces in terms of ground-attack aircraft, and the Marconi Marksman anti-aircraft tank shows the sort of response which this generated. However, the response that the vehicle itself generated was less enthusiastic: after a small sale to Finland, the Marksman never hit the bull's-eye again

The Wiesel air-portable vehicle, which is still in service with the German Army, demonstrates an early concern with what is now called 'rapid response' forces. By the 1980s it was apparent that airborne operations were no longer viable; no vast caravans of

The Vickers Mark Eleven, revealed in 1993, is still under development. It is fully amphibious and is armed with a 105-mm gun plus 12.7-mm machine-gun.

troop-carrying aircraft packed with parachute troops could hope to survive in the face of modern missile defences. Thus a light armoured vehicle to accompany such a force was no longer required. But a light armoured vehicle which could be quickly air-lifted to some small 'brush-fire war' and used to separate dissidents or rebels and

defuse a tense situation – this made sense, and the Wiesel, two of which can be lifted by a CH-53 helicopter, and similar vehicles were the result.

By the early 1980s the price of main battle tanks had exceeded the million-dollar mark and showed no sign of slowing down its rate of increase. Cheaper armoured vehicles which could

pack as much punch as a tank began to look attractive: hence the Panhard Sagaie 2 armoured car which, armed with a 90-mm gun, could actually out-perform quite a number of elderly tanks. The Sagaie 2 itself did not make much of an impression, but it was the precursor of improved models and similar vehicles from other makers.

Marksman air-defence system

Mechanized forces have always been vulnerable to attack from the air, but in recent years this threat has grown with the advent of new and dedicated attack aircraft which can fly very low and attack targets on the first pass. The introduction of the attack helicopter carrying guided missiles, rapid-firing cannon and unguided rockets has added a new dimension to land combat.

A number of countries in the West have fielded complete self-propelled anti-aircraft systems (for example the West German Gepard and French AMX-30 DCA) to protect mechanized forces against attack by such aircraft and helicopters.

Marconi Command and Control Systems has designed and built air-defence radars for land and sea applications over a period of many years, and some years ago undertook a market survey which showed that there was a gap in the market for a complete all-weather air-defence turret which could be fitted onto existing Chieftain, Challenger, Centurion, T-54/T-55, Type 59, M48, M60 and Vickers tank chassis with the minimum of modification. By using a chassis already in service the user would have significant cost advantages as not only would the crews already be familiar with the automotive aspects of the chassis but spare parts would already be available.

The first prototype of this air-defence turret, called **Marksman**, was completed in mid-1984 and shown for the first time at the British Army Equipment Exhibition on the Vickers Mk 3 MBT chassis.

Major sub-contractors to Marconi Command and Control Systems are Vickers Defence Systems of Newcastle upon Tyne, which built the all-steel turret, and Oerlikon-Bührle, which supplied the twin 35-mm KDA cannon and ammunition.

The turret is of all-welded construction providing the crew with complete protection from small arms fire and shell splinters. The commander sits on the left and the gunner on the right, and in addition to having periscopes for all-round observation with the hatches closed, each has a roof-mounted gyro-stabilized sight with magnifications of ×3 and ×10. The gunner's sight also has a laser rangefinder.

The turret armour provides complete protection against 14.5-mm (0.57-in) rounds over the frontal arc and against 7.62-mm (0.3-in) armour-piercing bullets over the remainder.

Mounted on the roof of the turret is a Series 400 radar, which is unusual in that it uses a single antenna for surveillance and tracking, and this has a maximum range in the surveillance mode

of about 12 km (7.5 miles).

A considerable amount of effort has gone into the design of the fire-control system to make its operation as simple as possible. The complete system includes the roof-mounted radar, computer, transmitter, synthesizer, signal processing unit, control console (visible to both crew members), data extraction unit and radar power amplifier. The system has a number of operating methods, including fully automatic. In this mode the radar picks up the target, checks that it is hostile and then starts to track the target; the turret is then traversed, the guns elevated, and the gunner informed when the target is within effective range; all the gunner then has to do is press the firing button.

The cannon can also be laid with the aid of the roof-mounted sights, this being of particular use when electronic countermeasures are being used to degrade the performance of the radar.

The 35-mm cannon are the same as those installed in Gepard and the gunner can select single shots, burst or full automatic fire. Each cannon has 230 rounds of ready-use air defence ammunition and 20 rounds of APD-T (Armour-Piercing Discarding-Sabot Tracer) for engaging ground targets.

By the early 1990s the Marksman turret has been tested on several MBT chassis with success, and a quantity have been supplied to Finland where they were fitted into T-55 MBT chassis and are still in service.

With the ominous exception of Britain, most armies use a mixture of guns and missiles to defend themselves against air attack. Marksman is an AA gun system developed by Marconi and is able to fit on to most tank chassis with minimal modification.

Specification
Marksman
Crew: 2
Armament: two 35-mm cannon
Ammunition: 230 anti-aircraft and 20 anti-armour rounds per barrel
Turret traverse: 360°
Cannon elevation: −10° to +85°
Weight: 11000 kg (24,250 lb)

Vickers Mk 7 main battle tank

In the late 1970s Vickers Defence Systems designed and built as a private venture the Valiant MBT which made its first public apperance during the 1980 British Army Equipment Exhibition. This was armed with a 120-mm (4.72-in) Royal Ordnance tank gun and a Marconi fire-control system, and was designed to have the new Chobham armour. The Valiant was demonstrated in the Middle East but no orders were placed.

Vickers Defence Systems then discovered that a number of customers believed that the turret of the Valiant could be married to a chassis incorporating automotive components of the Leopard 2 MBT currently in service with the West German and Dutch armies, and also ordered by the Swiss army. The first prototype of this tank, called the **Vickers Mk 7**, was completed in mid-1985 and later in that year went to Egypt for trials. This tank has been designed specifically for the export market as the British army is

already taking delivery of the heavier Challenger MBT armed with the same gun.

The Vickers Mk 7 is fitted with the standard Royal Ordnance 120-mm L11A5 tank gun, a McDonnell Douglas Helicopters 7.62-mm (0.3-in) Chain Gun being mounted co-axial with the main armament. A total of 38 rounds of 120-mm and 3,000 rounds of machine-gun ammunition are carried.

As an alternative to the L11A5 a West German Rheinmetalal 120-mm

smoothbore gun can be installed.

The Vickers Mk 7 has a Marconi Command and Control Systems Centaur 1 fire-control system: both the commander and gunner can aim and fire the gun, and the main armament is stabilized in both elevation and traverse. The commander is provided with a roof-mounted French SFIM panoramic sight that allows him to scan through 360° without moving his head. The sight also incorporates a laser rangefinder. The gunner has a Vickers telescopic laser sight and a roof-mounted periscope sight.

Also mounted on the turret roof is a Philips UA9090 gyro-stabilized panoramic sight which provides a thermal picture on a TV screen at both tank commander's and gunner's positions. A very useful auto-scanning device is fitted: this scans a pre-set arc, and if there is a change in the thermal picture an alarm sounds, so alerting the crew.

The MTU diesel engine is coupled to Renk HSWL 354/3 automatic transmission with four forward and two reverse gears.

Standard equipment includes an NBC pack and a fire-extinguishing system for engine compartment. Optional equipment includes a roof-mounted anti-aircraft machine gun, a fully automatic fire detection and suppression system for the crew compartment, and an air-conditioning system which is essential in the Middle East.

The idea found no buyers, and Vickers abandoned it in order to concentrate on Challenger II.

The Vickers Mk 7 is a private venture by the company aimed purely at the export market. It combines the turret of the Valiant MBT, which failed to gain any orders, with automotive components of the German Leopard 2. It carries the powerful Royal Ordnance 120-mm (4.72-in) gun.

Specification
Vickers Mk 7
Crew: 4
Weights: empty 52640 kg (116,050 lb); loaded 54641 kg (120,460 lb)
Powerplant: one MTU MB 873 Ka 501 12-cylinder turbocharged diesel developing 1,500 bhp (1119 kW)
Dimensions: length, gun forward 10.95 m (35 ft 11 in) and hull 7.72 m (25 ft 4 in); width 3.43 m (11 ft 3 in); height overall 3.00 m (9ft 10 in)
Performance: maximum road speed 72 km/h (45 mph); range 500 km (310 miles); fording 1.7 m (5 ft 7 in); vertical obstacle 1.1 m (3 ft 7 in); trench 3.0 m (9 ft 10 in); gradient 60 per cent, side slope 30 per cent

---

ENGESA EE-T1 Osorio main battle tank

Since the early 1970s the ENGESA company has built over 4,000 of its Jararac 4×4 scout cars, EE-9 Cascavel 6×6 armoured cars and EE-11 Urutu 6×6 armoured personnel carriers, sales having been made to virtually every continent. Several years ago the company decided to design and build a new MBT which would meet the needs of both the home and export markets. The first prototype, armed with the combat-proven British Royal Ordnance 105-mm (4.13-in) rifled tank gun, was completed in 1985. This was demonstrated in Saudi Arabia late in 1985 and the second prototype, armed with a French GIAT 120-mm (4.72-in) smoothbore gun, was completed early in 1986. Vickers Defence Systems of the UK designed both the 105-mm and 120-mm turrets specifically to meet the requirements of ENGESA.

The **EE-T1 Osorio** has an all-welded hull and turret. The conventional layout locates the driver at front left, the turret in the centre, and the engine and transmission at the rear. The 12-cylinder turbocharged diesel is coupled to a fully automatic transmission with four forward and two reverse gears.

The suspension is of the hydropneumatic type and has been designed by Dunlop of the UK. It has six road wheels with the drive sprocket at the rear and idler at the front; there are three track-return rollers.

Turret traverse is electric, and controls are provided for both tank commander and gunner. At present two fire-control systems are available for the EE-T1 Osorio. The first option is a an integrated fire-control system in which the gunner has a day/night sight with a laser rangefinder and the commander a day/night sight. The second fire-control option includes a stabilization system for the main armament allowing the gun to be fired against moving targets while the tank itself is moving across country. The tank commander has a roof-mounted SFIM stabilized periscopic sight with a laser rangefinder, while the gunner also has an SFIM stabilized sight with laser rangefinder. To enable targets to be detected and engaged at night, mounted on the turret roof is a Philips stabilized thermal camera which provides a TV picture on screens at the commander's and gunner's positions.

The Osorio is not a particularly innovative tank design, but it is an attractive MBT for smaller countries which lack their own manufacturing capability and for whom the latest European or American vehicles are too big, too complicated and too expensive.

Mounted on each side of the turret is a bank of electrically-operated smoke-dischargers, and optional equipment (apart from the choice of main armament and fire-control systems) includes an NBC system, a fire detection and suppression system, a land navigation system, a laser detector and indirect fire control equipment.

Development of the Osorio has been completed, and all that is now required is the financial go-ahead from the Brazilian government.

Specification
EE-T1 Osorio
Crew: 4
Weights: empty 37000 kg (81,570 lb); loaded 39000 kg (85,979 lb)
Powerplant: one 12-cylinder diesel developing 1,000 hp (745 kW)
Dimensions: length, gun forward 9.995 m (32 ft 9.5 in) and hull 7.08 m (23 ft 2.75 in); width 3.26 m (10 ft 8.3 in); height 2.371 m (7 ft 9.3 in)
Performance: maximum road speed 70 km/h (43.5 mph); maximum range 550 km (342 miles); fording 1.20 m (3 ft 11 in); vertical obstacle 1.15 m (3 ft 4 in); trench 3.0 m (9 ft 10 in); gradient 60 per cent; side slope 30 per cent

Osorio is offered with a choice of armament, either the proven British 105-mm gun used all over the world or the French GIAT 120-mm smoothbore. The turrets for both weapons were designed by Vickers Defence Systems to ENGESA's requirements.

Type 63 light tank

After the end of World War II the USSR supplied China with a significant amount of military equipment including T-54 MBTs and PT-76 light amphibious tanks. Further development of the latter by China resulted in the **Type 63 light tank**, which has been in service with the Chinese army for many years and has seen combat in the hands not only of the Chinese army but also of the Pakistani army (against India) and of the North Vietnamese army (against South Vietnam).

In many respects the Type 63 has a number of significant improvements over the original Soviet PT-76, including a four-man crew, increased firepower and (as it has a more powerful engine) a greater power-to-weight ratio which gives much improved road and water speeds.

The hull of the Type 63 is, like that of the PT-76, very large to allow the vehicle to float without any preparation apart from erecting the trim vane at the front of the hull and switching on the bilge pumps. The Type 63 is propelled in the water at a maximum speed of 12 km/h (7.5 mph) by two water jets mounted at the rear of the vehicle.

Main armament comprises an 85-mm (3.34-in) gun which fires a variety of ammunition including armour-piercing HE, HE, HEAT and smoke; 47 rounds of ammunition are carried. A 7.62-mm (0.3-in) machine-gun (for which 1,000 rounds are carried) is mounted co-axial with the main armament, and a 12.7-mm (0.5-in) machine-gun (for which 500 rounds are carried) is mounted on the turret roof for anti-aircraft defence.

The turret and hull are of welded steel construction with a maximum thickness of 14 mm (0.55 in), which is sufficient to provide protection against small arms fire and shell splinters only. If the armour was any thicker then the vehicle would require a flotation screen to be amphibious.

Suspension is of the torsion bar type, and consists of six large rubber-tyred road wheels with the idler at the front and drive sprocket at rear; there are no track-return rollers.

In the Chinese army four Type 63 light tanks can be found in the reconnaissance platoon of each armoured regiment, while there are 10 in the reconnaissance company of each armoured division. The vehicle is also still in service with North Korea, Sudan and Vietnam, and is still offered on the export market.

Specification
Type 63
Crew: 4
Weights: empty 16700 kg (36,816 lb); loaded 18700 kg (41,226 lb)
Powerplant: one Type 12150-L 12-cylinder diesel developing 400 hp (299 kW)
Dimensions: length, gun forward 8.437 m (27 ft 8.2 in) and hull 7.125 m (23 ft 4.5 in); width 3.20 m (10 ft 6 in); height without machine-gun 2.522 m (8 ft 3.3 in)
Performance: maximum road speed 64 km/h (40 mph); range 370 km (230 miles); fording amphibious; vertical obstacle 0.87 m (2 ft 10 in); trench 2.9 m (9 ft 6 in); gradient 60 per cent; side slope 30 per cent

Above: The Type 63 amphibious light tank was one of the first AFVs to be produced by China. Sharing many components with the Type 77 armoured personnel carrier, it is a development of the Soviet PT-76 and has seen action in Vietnam and Pakistan.

Below: The Type 63 needs only to erect its trim vane and switch on the bilge pumps before entering the water. It has a more powerful engine than the PT-76, which gives it correspondingly faster speeds both on land and in the water.

BMP-2 mechanized infantry combat vehicle

The **BMP-2** mechanized infantry fighting vehicle is a further development of the BMP-1 and was first observed in public during a parade held in Red Square, Moscow, late in 1982, although it entered service with the Soviet army several years before that. Since then it has also been observed in service with the Czech army.

The basic chassis of the BMP-2 is very similar to that of the original BMP-1 which entered service with the Soviet army in the early 1960s, but has a new turret and different crew positions. On the BMP-1 the commander was seated behind the driver and

therefore had poor observation to the right side of the vehicle. In the BMP-2 the commander now sits in the much enlarged turret alongside the gunner, and has excellent all-round battlefield observation.

The BMP-1 is armed with a 73-mm (2.87-in) weapon that fires a fin-stabilized HEAT (High Explosive Anti-Tank) or HE-FRAG (High Explosive Fragmentation) round, with a 7.62-mm (0.3-in) co-axial machine-gun, and with a 'Sagger' wire-guided anti-tank weapon mounted above the main armament. The 73-mm gun suffered from a number of drawbacks and is ineffective in high winds, while the

first-generation 'Sagger' missile needed a well-trained gunner to ensure a first-round hit.

These major disadvantages have been overcome in the BMP-2, as the armament now comprises a 30-mm rapid-fire automatic cannon which can be elevated to +74°, so enabling it to be used against low-flying aircraft and helicopters. The gunner can select either single shots or one of two rates of automatic fire (200/300 or 500 rounds per minute) and 500 rounds of HE-T (High Explosive – Tracer) and AP-T (Armour-Piercing – Tracer) are carried. A 7.62-mm PKT machine-gun is mounted co-axial with the main arma-

ment.

Mounted on the turret roof is an AT-4 'Spigot' anti-tank guided weapon, which has a maximum range of 2000 m (2,187 yards) and is fitted with a HEAT warhead. All the operator has to do to ensure a hit is to keep the crosswires of his sight on the target. (On the earlier AT-3 'Sagger' he had to operate a small joystick.)

In addition to being able to inject diesel fuel into the exhaust to lay its own smoke screen, the BMP-2 has a bank of three electrically-operated smoke-dischargers mounted on each side of the turret towards the rear. More recent BMP-2s have appliqué armour on their turret sides.

Seven fully-equipped infantrymen are carried, compared with eight in the earlier vehicle: one man is seated to the rear of the commander, and the other six in the troop compartment at the rear facing outwards, each being provided with a firing port with an observation periscope above.

Like the BMP-1, the BMP-2 is fully amphibious, being propelled in the water by its tracks. Before entering the water a trim vane is erected at the front of the vehicle and the bilge pumps are switched on.

Specification
BMP-2
Crew: 3+7
Weight: loaded 14600 kg (32,187 lb)
Powerplant: believed to be one Type 5D20 turbocharged 6-cylinder water-cooled diesel developing 350 hp (261 kW)
Dimensions: length 6.71 m (22 ft 0.2 in);

width 3.09 m (10 ft 1.7 in); height 2.06 m (6 ft 9 in)
Performance: maximum road speed 60 km/h (37.3 mph); range 500 km (311 miles); fording amphibious; vertical obstacle 0.7 m (2 ft 3 in); trench 2.0 m (6 ft 7 in); gradient 60 per cent; side slope 30 per cent

Above: The BMP-2 is a new version of the BMP Mechanized Infantry Combat Vehicle, and substitutes a 30-mm cannon for the 73-mm smooth bore gun of the first model. It also carries AT-4 'Spigot' ATGMs in place of outdated AT-3 'Sagger' missiles.

Below: Like most Soviet AFVs, the BMP-2 is able to lay a smokescreen by injecting diesel fuel directly into the exhaust, but it also carries a bank of electrically operated smoke dischargers on the turret sides. Some BMP-2s have been sporting appliqué armour on their sides.

Former USSR
T-72 main battle tank

For many years there has been much confusion in the West as to exactly which main battle tanks the USSR has produced in quantity in recent years. This problem has been compounded by the fact that different countries give different designations to the same vehicle.

From recent information it appears that the USSR has mass produced two MBTs in the last 15 years. The T-64 entered production in 1967 and remained in production until 1981. This was built in fairly large numbers, but so far has been identified in service only with the Soviet army. The basic tank has the same armament as the later T-72 and is fed by an automatic loader, so enabling the crew to be reduced to just three men (commander, gunner and driver). From most reports there were many problems with the T-64 once it reached the troops, especially with the engine, transmission, suspension and automatic loader. In addition

to the basic gun tank there is a version, the T-64B, that fires a 'Cobra' guided missile in the long-range anti-tank role.

The **T-72** MBT entered production in 1971, and in 1986 was being produced in at least three plants in the USSR as well as in Czechoslovakia and Poland. Production of modified versions is also being undertaken in India and Yugoslavia.

The T-72 and its later variants have now been identified in service with Algeria, Bulgaria, Cuba, Czechoslovakia, East Germany, Hungary, India, Iraq, Libya, Poland, Romania, Syria, the USSR and Yugoslavia. Finland is expected to take delivery of its vehicles in the near future.

The 125-mm (4.92-in) gun is fed by an automatic loader which first inserts the projectile and then the charge into the breech. Three types of ammunition are carried: APDSDS (Armour-Piercing Fin-Stabilized Discarding-Sabot), HEAT – FS (High Explosive Anti-Tank

– Fin-Stabilized), HE-FRAG (FS) (High Explosive-Fragmentaion Fin-Stabilized). A 7.62-mm (0.3-in) machine-gun is mounted co-axial with the main armament, and a 12.7-mm (0.5-in) machine-gun is mounted on the commander's cupola. Like other Soviet armoured vehicles, the T-72 can lay its own smoke screen by injecting diesel fuel into the exhaust.

Since the T-72 first appeared a number of improvements have been carried out, including the installation of a laser rangefinder, additional armour protection, smoke grenade launchers on each side of the turret and so on. The late production T-72 is known as the **T-74** in the USSR, although the USA calls it the **T-80**.

The area of greatest confusion on the T-72/T-74 is its armour. It is assumed that the hull front is of a laminate armour, but it is believed that the turret is of conventional armour.

Variants of the T-72 include a com-

mand vehicle, another firing the 'Cobra' anti-tank missile and the **BREM-1** armoured recovery vehicle.

Specification
T-72
Crew: 3
Weights: empty 39000 kg (85,979 lb); loaded 41000 kg (90,388 lb)
Powerplant: one V-12 diesel developing 780 hp (582 kW)
Dimensions: length, gun forward 9.24 m (30 ft 3.8 in) and hull 6.95 m (22 ft 9.6 in); width without skirts 3.60 m (11 ft 9.7 in); height with machine-gun 2.37 m (7 ft 9.3 in)
Performance: maximum road speed 60 km/h (37 mph); range 480 km (298 miles); fording 1.4 m (4 ft 7 in); vertical obstacle 0.85 m (2 ft 10 in); trench 2.8 m (9 ft 2 in); gradient 60 per cent; side slope 40 per cent

203-mm M1975 self-propelled gun

Apart from self-propelled anti-tank guns such as the ASU-57 and ASU-85 developed specifically for use by the airborne forces, the Soviet army in the post-war period has relied on artillery towed by full-tracked prime movers or by 6×6 trucks to provide fire support for its mechanized units.

The various Middle East conflicts clearly showed, however, that towed artillery cannot hope to keep up with mechanized forces moving at speed across country, tanks and troop carriers in these wars often outrunning their support artillery.

In the early 1970s the Soviets thus introduced two self-propelled artillery pieces into service, the 122-mm (4.8-in) **2S1** (called the **M1974** in NATO) self-propelled howitzer and the 152-mm (5.98-in) **2S3** (called the **M1973** in NATO) self-propelled gun/howitzer. Although these vehicles have different hulls they are very similar in layout to the US 155-mm (6.1-in) M109 series of weapons, which has been in service for over 25 years.

Since then the Soviets have introduced at least three other new self-propelled artillery pieces. The **2S5** 152-mm self-propelled gun was first seen in the late 1970s and is believed to consist of the chassis of the GMZ minelayer with a long-barrelled 152-mm weapons mounted at the rear. No protection is provided for the crew against shell fragments. The ordnance is believed to fire a standard HE projectile to a range of 27000 m (29,530 yards) or a rocket-assisted projectile to a range of perhaps 37000 m (40,465 yards). It also has a nuclear capability.

In the mid-1970s the Soviet army introduced a 203-mm (8-in) self-propelled howitzer which has been given the NATO designation **M1975** in the usual absence of any official Soviet designation. The M1975 is believed to be employed at front level, and has the distinction of being the largest armoured vehicle in service at the present time.

The fully enclosed armoured cab is at the front of the vehicle, with the engine to the rear. The weapon itself is mounted at the very rear of the hull, and when travelling is held in position by a lock above the cab roof. Before the weapon can be fired a large hydraulically-operated blade is lowered at the rear of the hull to provide a more stable firing platform, and mounted on the right side of the chassis is a hydraulic loading system to help lift the heavy projectiles and charges into the breech.

It is probable that a few rounds of ready-use ammunition are carried on the actual vehicle, though the main supply of ammunition and most of the gun crew are carried in another tracked and armoured supporting vehicle.

Like the 2S5, the M1975 suffers from one major disadvantage: there is no protection for the gun crew when the vehicle is in action.

No firm details of the types of ammunition fired by the M1975 are yet available, but it is likely that the weapon has both nuclear and conventional capabilities, and it is generally comparable to the American M110/M110A1/M110A2 self-propelled howitzers that have been in service for many years.

Also introduced in the mid-1970s was a 240-mm (9.45-in) self-propelled mortar which has also been called the M1975 (this being the year it was first seen by Western intelligence). Like the 203-mm M1975 self-propelled gun, it has yet to make a public appearance and no firm details are available.

Since the early 1970s the Soviets have been manufacturing an expanding range of self-propelled artillery which now includes the massive M1975 203-mm weapon, the world's largest AFV. It is assumed to fire nuclear as well as conventional ammunition.

Specification (provisional)
M1975
Weights: empty 37000 kg (81,570 lb); loaded 40000 kg (88,183 lb)
Powerplant: one diesel developing 450 hp (336 kW)
Dimensions: length, with gun 12.80 m (42 ft 0 in) and hull 10.50 m (34 ft 5.4 in); width 3.50 m (11 ft 5.8 in); height 3.50 m (11 ft 5.8 in)

AMX-40 main battle tank

Unlike West Germany, the UK and the USA, France has not developed a second-generation MBT such as the Leopard 2, Challenger or M1/M1A1. The standard French army MBT is still the AMX-30, whose design can be traced back to the late 1950s. This is now being modernized until the new French army MBT, the so called Engin Principal de Combat (recently renamed the Futur Char, or future tank) enters production.

GIAT realized that there would be a big gap between the end of AMX-30 production and the beginning of EPC production, so a decision was taken to build a new MBT specifically for the export market.

The first tank built was the so called AMX-32, which was based on the AMX-30 but fitted with a 120-mm (4.72-in) gun, new armour, improved fire-control system and some automotive improvements. Its crucial power-to-weight ratio was below that of the AMX-30, however, and the AMX-32 has not been sold. It is now offered only with the standard 105-mm (4.13-in) gun as installed in the AMX-30.

In 1983 GIAT unveiled the **AMX-40** MBT, which is a brand new design and has significant improvements over the earlier AMX-30 in the three key areas of tank design: armour, mobility and firepower. The AMX-40 has been designed specifically for the export market and by early 1986 four prototypes had been completed and one of these is believed to have been tested in the Middle East. The AMX-40 has also been offered to the Spanish army

Above: The AMX-40 carries laminate armour over the hull front to give improved protection against HEAT ammunition. It carries its ammunition in the turret bustle, which, if penetrated, will explode upwards and away from the crew compartment.

Right: The French army is still stuck with a first-generation tank, the AMX-30, and the promised 'future tank' is still a long way off. GIAT has developed a much-improved MBT for the export market, the AMX-40, which is armed with a 120-mm smooth-bore gun.

which has a requirement for new MBT with a 120-mm gun.

The armour over the frontal part is of the laminate type and provides protection against HEAT (High Explosive Anti-Tank) rounds with a calibre of up to 100 m (3.94 in).

The layout of the AMX-40 is similar to that of other French MBTs, with the driver at the front left, the turret in the centre (with the commander and gunner on the right and the loader on the left) and the engine and transmission at the rear.

The AMX-40 is powered by a Poyaud diesel engine which gives a power-to-weight ratio of around 25 hp (18.6 kW) per tonne, a very significant improvement over current French MBTs. The engine is coupled to a West German ZF automatic transmission for ease of handling and reduced driver fatigue.

The main armament comprises a 120-mm smoothbore gun which fires ammunition with combustible cartridge case. Ammunition stowed in the turret bustle is separated from the crew compartment by bulkheads and if a round penetrates the turret bustle the force of the exploding ammunition is vented upward rather than into the crew compartment.

The design was completed and prototypes tested by 1986, but then the French Army produced its specification for the new tank if required. And it bore no resemblance to the AMX-40; the army wanted a three-man crew, automated loading and several other features which would demand a total re-design. The AMX-40 was no longer considered for French adoption, and although it was offered on the export market until the early 1990s, there were no takers and the design was abandoned.

Specification
AMX-40
Crew: 4
Weights: empty 41000 kg (90,388 lb); loaded 43000 kg (94,798 lb)
Powerplant: one Poyaud 12-cylinder diesel developing 1,100 hp (820 kW)
Dimensions: length, gun forward 10.04 m (32 ft 11.3 in) and hull 6.80 m (22 ft 3.7 in); width 3.36 m (11 ft 0.3 in);

height overall 3.08 m (10 ft 1.3 in)
Performance: maximum road speed 70 km/h (44 mph); range 600 km (373 miles); fording 1.30 m (4 ft 3 in); vertical obstacle 1 m (6 ft 7 in); trench 3.20 m (10 ft 6 in); gradient 70 per cent; side slope 30 per cent

Although heavier than the AMX-30, the AMX-40 is still a very agile MBT thanks to its Poyaud diesel engine, which gives a power-to-weight ratio of 18.6 kW per tonne. Its automatic transmission reduces driver fatigue.

FRANCE
Panhard VBL scout car

Some years ago the French army issued a requirement for a small, light and fast armoured vehicle which would be able to carry out two basic roles on the battlefield: anti-tank armed with the Euromissile Milan anti-tank guided weapon, and reconnaissance/scout armed with machine-guns. Five manufacturers submitted designs for this competition, and Panhard and Renault were each awarded a contract to deliver three prototypes for trials with the French army.

Following these trials the Panhard VBL (Véhicule Blindé Leger) was accepted for service although no immediate production order was placed because of a shortage of funding. The total French army requirement is for a total of 3,000 vehicles (1,000 in the anti-tank role and the remaining 2,000 in the scout/reconnaissance role).

Panhard was convinced that its design would win the French army competition, so it built additional prototypes with its own funds and embarked on an intensive overseas marketing drive which involved the despatch of vehicles to many parts of the world. This marketing effort was successful to the extent that Mexico placed an order for 40 VBLs in 1984, an these had all been delivered by late 1985. Of these 40 vehicles, 32 were armed with machine-guns and the remaining eight with Milan anti-tank guided weapons.

The hull of the Panhard VBL is of all-welded steel armour and provides the crew with protection from small arms fire and shell splinters. The small size and rapid acceleration of the vehicle also increases its survivability on the battlefield.

To reduce both initial procurement costs and life cycle costs, proven commercial automotive parts have been used in the design of the VBL: for example, the diesel engine is from the Peugeot 505 and 605 civilian cars and the Peugeot P4 4×4 light vehicle already entering service with the French army in significant numbers as the replacement for the Hotchkiss M201 jeep, while the West German ZF fully automatic transmission is used in many civilian cars.

The layout of the vehicle is conventional, with the engine and transmission at the front, the driver and commander in the centre and space for a third man, weapons or other specialized equipment in the rear. Bulletproof windows (providing the same degree of protection as the hull) are provided for all crew members, and standard equipment on French army vehicles will include an NBC system, heater and communications equipment. The combat tyres allow the VBL to travel a distance of 50 km (31 mph) at a speed of 30 km/h (19 mph) after they have been damaged by enemy fire.

The vehicle is fully amphibious with very little preparation, and is moved in the water by a propeller at the rear of the hull.

The anti-tank model has a three-man crew and is armed with a Milan anti-tank guided missile launcher with six missiles and a 7.62-mm (0.3-in) machine-gun with 3,000 rounds of ammunition. The scout model normally has additional communications equipment, a two-man crew and armament comprising a 7.62 mm or 12.7-mm (0.5-in) machine-gun.

The Panhard light armoured vehicle is designed as a reconnaissance scout car and anti-tank guided weapons platform carrying Milan missiles. It is fully amphibious and is fitted with an NBC system and combat tyres.

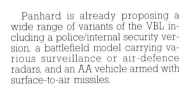

Panhard is already proposing a wide range of variants of the VBL including a police/internal security version, a battlefield model carrying various surveillance or air-defence radars, and an AA vehicle armed with surface-to-air missiles.

Specification
VBL
Crew: 2 or 3
Weights: empty 2850 kg (6,283 lb); loaded 3550 kg (7,826 lb)
Powerplant: one Peugeot XD 3T 4-cylinder turbocharged diesel developing 105 hp (78 kW)

The Panhard VBL has a propeller at the rear of the hull and needs little preparation to enter the water. Many proven commercial automative parts are used in the VBL, including the engine from the Peugeot 505 civilian car.

Dimensions: length 3.82 m (12 ft 6.4 in); width 2.02 m (6 ft 7.5 in); height without weapons 1.70 m (5 ft 6.9 in)
Performance: maximum road speed 100 km/h (62 mph); range 1000 km (621 miles); fording amphibious; gradient 50 per cent; side slope 30 per cent

Panhard Sagaie 2 armoured car

In 1977 Panhard unveiled its private-venture range of 6×6 armoured vehicles, which included a family of armoured cars and a complete family of armoured personnel carriers all using identical automotive components with obvious training, logistical and cost advantages to the user.

The armoured car family was commonly known as the Engin de Reconnaissance Cannon (ERC) and included the ERC 90 F4 Sagaie 1, ERC 90 F1 Lynx, ERC 60/20 Serval, ERC 20 Kriss, and ERC 60/12 Mangouste. These were originally developed specifically for the export market, but the Sagaie 1 was subsequently adopted by the French army.

The Sagaie 1 is fitted with a two-man GIAT turret armed with a 90-mm (3.54-in) gun firing a range of ammunition including APFSDS (Armour-Piercing Fin-Stabilized Discarding-Sabot).

In 1985 Panhard announced that it had developed the Sagaie 2 armoured car and that one overseas country had already placed an order for the vehicle. The Sagaie 2 has a slightly longer and wider hull, and instead of the 90-mm GIAT TS-90 turret it is fitted with the SMM TTB-1900 turret, which has the same gun as the TS-90 turret. The SAMM turret has much improved armour protection, however, and is available with a wide range of turret controls, fire-control systems and optical devices. Two types of ammunition stowage are available, one having 35 rounds of 90 mm ammunition of which 13 are ready for immediate use, and the other 32 rounds of which 10 are for ready use.

The original Panhard Sagaie 1 was powered by a single Peugeot V-6 petrol engine developing 155 hp (116 kW), but the Sagaie 2 is powered by two Peugeot XD 3T 4-cylinder turbocharged diesels which develop a total of 196 hp (146 kW); these engines are also used in the Panhard VBL 4×4 light armoured vehicle. As an alternative the Sagaie 2 can be powered by two V-6 petrol engines developing a total of 290 hp (216 kW) which gives an exceptionally high power-to-weight ratio.

The Sagaie 1 and 2 have full 6×6 drive with powered steering on the front road wheels only. An unusual feature is that when travelling on roads the centre wheels can be raised clear of the ground, so reducing resistance and saving wear on the tyres. The wheels are normally lowered for cross-country use.

As with most armoured vehicles today a wide range of optional equipment can be installed, including a NBC system, a heater or air conditioning system, night vision equipment for the commander, gunner and driver, and a land navigation system.

Specification
Crew: 3
Weights: loaded 10000 kg (22,046 lb)
Powerplant: two Peugeot XD 3T 4-cylinder diesels developing a total of 196 hp (146 kW), or two Peugeot 6-cylinder petrol engines developing a total of 290 hp (216 kW)
Dimensions: length, gun forward 7.97 m (26 ft 1.8 in) and hull 5.57 m (19 ft 3.3 in); width 2.70 m (8 ft 10.3 in); height

Panhard's private venture range of 6×6 armoured cars has attracted a number of export orders as well as interest from the French army. The ERC 90 has seen action in Chad's interminable civil war, and now equips part of the French rapid deployment force.

2.30 m (7 ft 6.6 in)
Performance: maximum road speed 100 km/h (62 mph); maximum road range 600 km (373 km); fording 1.2 m (3 ft 11 in); vertical obstacle 0.8 m (2 ft 7.5 in); trench 0.8 m (2 ft 7.5 in); gradient 50 per cent; side slope 30 per cent

The Sagaie 2 was unveiled in 1985 and several, fitted with the 90-mm gun turret, were purchased by Gabon. It has a new turret and better armour protection and is offered with a wide range of fire controls systems and optical devices.

Wiesel air-portable armoured vehicle

Today the West German army has one three-brigade airborne division, and this uses the Faun Kraka 4×2 light cross-country vehicle for a wide range of roles including the carriage of TOW and Milan anti-tank guided weapons.

Many years ago the West German army issued a requirement for a new light armoured tracked vehicle for use by the airborne brigades, and Porsche was subsequently awarded a development contract. After prototypes had been built and tested, the whole project was shelved as the West German ministry of defence found that it could not fund all of its projects.

More recently this **Wiesel** has been tested by the US Army, while in 1984

The Wiesel will provide West German paratroops with the sort of mobile fire support the ASU light tanks provide for the Soviet airborne forces. Two models are planned: one with a 20-mm canon, seen here, and another mounting TOW anti-tank guided missiles.

the West German army announced that it was to fund final development of the Wiesel air-portable armoured vehicle and to purchase 312 production variants with first deliveries due in 1989.

Two basic models of the Wiesel are to be produced, one armed with a Hughes TOW anti-tank guided missile and the other with a 20-mm cannon.

The first of these has a three-man crew and is armed with a Hughes TOW anti-tank guided missile launcher on an elevating pedestal which can be traversed 45° to each side of the centreline, and elevated and depressed 10°. Seven TOW missiles are carried, of which two are for ready use. In action, as soon as it has launched two missiles, the vehicle changes its firing position (to avoid being detected by the enemy) and loads another pair of TOWs.

The second model is armed with a Rheinmetall 20-mm dual-feed cannon in a turret which can be traversed 110° left and right while the cannon has an elevation of +45° and a depression of −10°. Some 400 rounds of 20-mm ammunition are carried, of which 160 rounds are for ready use and the remainder in reserve. This version has a two-man crew.

The hull of the Wiesel is of all-welded steel armour construction providing protection from small arms fire and shell splinters. The engine is at the front left and coupled to a fully-automatic transmission. The driver is seated at the front on the right, so leaving the complete rear of the vehicle clear for a weapons station.

As the Wiesel has been designed for air transport it is very compact and difficult to detect on the battlefield. A Sikorsky CH-53 helicopter, as used by West Germany, can carry two Wiesel vehicles, while a Lockheed C-130 Hercules transport aircraft can carry three internally and the Transall C.160 four.

The manufacturer has suggested that the Wiesel could be adopted for a wide range of other missions, all using the same basic chassis or a slightly longer chassis with an additional road wheel on each side. These variants include an anti-tank model with a turret for HOT missiles in the ready-to-launch position, an anti-aircraft model with Stinger surface-to-air missiles, a recovery vehicle, an ambulance, a reconnaissance vehicle, a command and control vehicle, a battlefield surveillance model and an armoured personnel carrier, to name but a few.

Specification
Wiesel (with TOW launcher)
Crew: 3
Weights: empty 2030 kg (4,475 lb); loaded 2750 kg (6,063 lb)
Powerplant: one 5-cylinder turbocharged diesel developing 86 hp (64 kW)
Dimensions: length 3.265 m (10 ft 8.5 in); width 1.82 m (5 ft 11.7 in); height 1.875 m (6 ft 1.8 in)
Performance: maximum road speed

Two Wiesels can be carried by a Sikorsky CH-53 helicopter and four by a Transall C-160 transport aircraft. The vehicle may be used for a variety of other roles including mobile SAM system, APC and command vehicle.

80 km/h (50 mph); range 200 km (124 miles); vertical obstacle 0.4 m (1 ft 4 in); trench 1.2 m (3 ft 11 in); gradient 60 per cent; side slope 30 per cent

---

M1A1 Abrams main battle tank

The first M1 Abrams MBT came off the production line at the Lima Army Tank Plant in February 1980, the initial vehicles from the Detroit Arsenal Tank Plant following two years later. The basic M1 is armed with a standard 105-mm (4.13-in) M68 rifled tank gun of the type also installed in the M48A5 and M60/M60A1/M60A3 MBTs. The M68 is essentially the British L7 gun, developed in the 1950s, but fitted with an US breech mechanism.

Some years ago the USA decided to adopt the West German Rheinmetall 120-mm (4.72-in) smoothbore gun already selected for the Leopard 2 MBT for an improved version of the M1, which was given the development designation **M1E1**. After the usual trials and modifications, this vehicle was accepted for service as the **M1A1 Abrams**, the first two production vehicles being completed August 1985. Other armament is a 12.7-mm (0.5-in) commander's machine-gun and a 7.62-mm (0.3-in) loader's machine-gun.

The 120-mm Rheinmetall gun is built under licence in the USA under the designation M256, with Honeywell responsible for the complete range of ammunition together with its combustible cartridge case. In addition to the making of the West German APFSDS-T (Armour-Piercing Fin-Stabilized Discarding-Sabot – Tracer) and HEAT-MP-T (High Explosive Anti-Tank – Multi-Purpose – Tracer), Honeywell has also developed new types with much improved armour-penetration characteristics.

In addition to the 120-mm gun, the M1A1 has a number of other improvements including increased armour protection and an integrated NBC system which not only provides the four-man crew with conditioned air for breathing but also supplied cooling or heating as long as the crew are wearing their protective suits and masks.

At one time both the Detroit Arsenal

In August 1985 the first M1A1 was completed, and has now replaced the M1 in production. Armour protection has been increased and an integrated NBC system fitted.

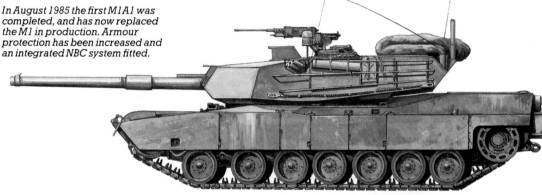

Tank Plant and the Lima Army Tank Plant were producing both the M1 and M1A1, but from early 1986 only the M1A1 was in production. At present there are no plans for the 105-mm armed M1 to be upgunned with the 120-mm gun.

As the M1/M1A1 will remain in service until the 21st century many other improvements are already under development, including a new and safer laser rangefinder, an improved commander's weapon station with panoramic sight, and a rapid refuelling capability.

The M1 Abrams has already been evaluated by Saudi Arabia and Switzerland, but so far no export orders have been placed.

At present there are no variants of the M1/M1A1, although under development by BMY is the **Heavy Assault Bridge** which uses a M1 chassis. It is probable that an armoured recovery vehicle will be developed on the M1 chassis as the current M88A1 is not powerful enough to handle the M1A1.

Undergoing trials is the **Tank Test Bed** which is a M1 chassis with an externally-mounted 120-mm gun, the three-man crew being safely seated within the hull.

The production M1A1s carry the same Rheinmetall 120-mm smooth-bore gun as the Leopard 2; it has a combustible case and fires APFSDS ammunition. The M1A1 will be the MBT of the US Army until well into the 21st century.

Specification
M1A1
Crew: 4
Weight: loaded 57154 kg (126,000 lb)
Powerplant: one Avco Lycoming AGT-1500 gas turbine developing 1,500 hp (1118 kW)
Dimensions: length, gun forward 9.83 m (32 ft 3 in) and hull 7.925 m (26 ft

0 in); with 3.658 m (12 ft 0 in); height overall 2.896 m (9 ft 6 in)
Performance: maximum road speed 67 km/h (41.6 mph); range, road 465 km (288 miles); fording 1.219 m (4 ft 0 in); vertical obstacle 1.066 m (3 ft 6 in); trench 2.743 m (9 ft 0 in); gradient 60 per cent; side slope 30 per cent

Close Combat Vehicle – Light

The Ordnance Division of the FMC Corporation of San Jose, California, is the largest manufacturer of tracked vehicles in the West, having produced over 70,000 units in the M113 series of armoured personnel carriers and over 2,000 Bradley Infantry Fighting Vehicles, plus large numbers of armoured amphibious tracked vehicles, reconnaissance vehicles, M59s and Armoured Infantry Fighting vehicles.

Several years ago the company realized that the US Army would require a highly mobile armoured vehicle armed with a 105-mm (4.13-in) standard main gun for use with its light divisions. A decision was then taken to design and build a prototype of the **Close Combat Vehicle – Light (CCV – L)** with company money.

The first prototype of the CCV – L was unveiled late in 1985 and attracted a great deal of interest as its crew had been reduced to just three men (commander, gunner and driver) by the installation of an automatic loader for the main armament.

The prototype cost $26 million to build, of which around $14 million came from FMC and the remainder from the many subcontractors involved in the project.

To reduce development time and cost, proven automotive components have been used in the design of the CCV – L: for example, the engine uses many parts of the 8V-92TA engine installed in the Heavy Expanded Mobility Tactical Truck which has been in service with the US Army for some

The three-man CCV-L has been built by FMC's ordnance division as a private venture intended for the US Army's light divisions. It carries a modified version of the 105-mm gun carried by M48s, M60s and M1s but has a West German low recoil system and an automatic loader.

years, the transmission is from the FMC-built Bradley IFV, and parts of the suspension are from the M113A2.

The main armament comprises a 105-mm M68A1 gun of the type installed in the M48A5, M60/M60A1/M60A3 and M1 MBTs already in service with the US Army, but in this application fitted with a West German Rheinmetall low recoil system. The automatic loader for the main armament has been designed by FMC Northern Ordnance Division, which has some 40 years of experience in designing and building automatic loaders mainly for naval applications. The automatic loader makes possible a rate of fire of 12 rounds per minute. Nineteen rounds are carried in the automatic loader, with a further 24 rounds carried elsewhere in the hull.

The turret traverse and weapon elevation systems are based on those installed in the M1. The gunner has a stabilized day/night sight with laser rangefinder, while the commander has periscopes for all-round observation and an independent thermal viewer which can be traversed through 360° and has a day/night capability.

The US Army has a requirement for a vehicle it calls the Armoured Gun System (AGS) and hoped to get some funding for this in the FY87 budget, but this has been disapproved. So far three US companies have built vehicles which could meet the AGS requirement: these are the FMC Close Combat Vehicle – Light, the Cadillac Gage Stingray and the Teledyne Continental Motors General Products Division TCM-20.

Specification
CCV – L
Crew: 3
Weights: empty 17509 kg (38,600 lb); loaded 19414 kg (42,800 lb)
Powerplant: one Detroit Diesel Model 6V-92 TA 6-cylinder diesel developing 552 hp (412 kW)
Dimensions: length, gun forward 9.37 m (30 ft 9 in) and hull 6.20 m (20 ft 4 in); width 2.69 m (8 ft 10 in); height 2.36 m (7 ft 9 in)
Performance: maximum road speed 70 km/h (43.5 mph); range 483 km (300 miles); fording 1.32 m (4 ft 4 in); vertical obstacle 0.76 m (2 ft 6 in); trench 2.13 m (7 ft 0 in); gradient 60 per cent; side slope 40 per cent

---

Stingray light tank

Since the early 1960s the Cadillac Gage Company has built over 3,500 of its Commando range of 4×4 multi-mission vehicles, most of which have been exported. More recently the company has developed and placed in production the V-300 6×6 and Commando Scout 4×4 vehicles, while the Commando Ranger 4×4 light armoured personnel carrier has been built in large numbers for the the US Air Force base-production role.

Some years ago Cadillac Gage realized that there was a need for a light tank with good cross-country mobility, the combat-proven 105-mm (4.13-in) tank gun, and simplicity of operation and maintenance. With this requirement in mind the company designed and built the **Stingray** light tank, whose prototype was unveiled for the first time late in 1984.

To reduce development and procurement costs, proved and in-production automotive components have been used wherever possible: for example, the suspension is the same as that on the M109 self-propelled howitzer used by more than 20 countries.

The turret and hull are of all-welded steel armour construction providing complete protection from small arms fire and shell splinters. If required, additional armour can be added, for example of the reactive type which provides protection against HEAT projectiles.

Main armament comprises a British Royal Ordnance Nottingham 105-mm rifled tank gun which fires an identical range of ammunition to that of the L7/M68 gun used in many MBTs (including the Leopard 1, M48A5, M60, M1,

The Stingray light tank weighs little over 17 tons, but has the firepower of a main battle tank. Costs have been minimized by the use of automotive parts already in production; for example, the suspension is the same as that of the M109 SP gun.

Merkava and some models of the Centurion) and including the recent APFSDS-T (Armour-Piercing Fin-Stabilized Discarding-Sabot – Tracer).

Mounted co-axial with the main armament is a 7.62-mm (0.3-in) machine-gun for the engagement of soft targets such as trucks or infantry, while a 7.62-mm or 12.7-mm (0.5-in) machine-gun is mounted on the roof for anti-aircraft defence. Mounted on each side of the turret is a bank of electrically-operated smoke-dischargers.

The turret has power controls, and the prototype Stingray has a Marconi Command and Control System computerized digital Fire-Control System, which gives a high first-round hit probability. As an option a stabilization system can be installed, allowing the main armament to be laid and fired while the Stingray is moving across country.

As with most armoured vehicles today, a wide range of optional equipment is available to suit different user's requirements: for example, a land

Right: Given the vulnerability of many MBTs to HEAT warheads, the light armour of Stingray is not necessarily a great disadvantage. A stabilization system can be fitted, enabling the main armament to be aimed and fired while the vehicle is moving.

navigation system, a laser rangefinder, an NBC system, and a fire detection and suppression system.

Between 1989 and 1991 Thailand purchased 106 Stingray tanks. In 1993 the FMC CCV-L was selected for the US AGS programme, after which development of Stingray went to a very low priority.

Specification
Stingray
Crew: 4
Weights: empty 17237 kg (38,000 lb);
loaded 19051 kg (42,000 lb)
Powerplant: one Detroit Diesel Model 8V-92 TA diesel developing 535 hp (399 kW)
Dimensions: length, gun forward 9.35 m (30 ft 8 in) and hull 6.30 m (20 ft 8 in); width 2.71 m (8 ft 11 in); height overall 2.54 (8 ft 4 in)
Performance: maximum road speed 69 km/h (43 mph); range 483 km (300 miles); fording 1.22 m (4 ft 0 in); vertical obstacle 0.76 m (2 ft 6 in); trench 1.69 m (5 ft 7 in); gradient 60 per cent; side slope 30 per cent

Fahd armoured personnel carrier

For many years one of the standard wheeled armoured personnel carriers of the Egyptian army has been the Walid. This 4×4 vehicle is essentially a West German Magirus Deutz truck chassis fitted with an armoured body designed and built in Egypt. In many respects the Fahd fulfils a similar role to that of the Soviet BTR-40 vehicle which has also been used by the Egyptian army. The BTR-40 does, however, suffer the major disadvantge in having an open-topped troop compartment, so making the troops vulnerable to shell splinters.

The **Fahd** 4×4 armoured personnel carrier has been designed and built by the Kadar Factory for Developed Industries in Heliopolis not only to meet the demanding requirements of the Egyptian army but also for the export market. The vehicle was first shown in public late in 1984 and is expected to enter production in the very near future.

The vehicle consists basically of the proven Daimler-Benz LAP 1117/32 4×4 truck chassis fitted with a fully armoured body that provides complete protection against penetration from 7.62-mm×54 armour-piercing projectiles and shell splinters.

The commander and driver are seated at the very front of the vehicle, with the troop compartment at the rear. The 10 fully equipped infantrymen are seated down the centre of the vehicle, and enter and leave via a rear hatch, of which the upper part opens upwards and the lower part folds down to provide a step.

In the sides and rear of the troop compartment are firing ports, each

with a bulletproof vision block above it, allowing the infantrymen to fire their weapons from within the vehicle.

The standard commercial Mercedes-Benz six-cylinder diesel engine is coupled to a fully automatic gearbox and a two-speed transfer case. Steering is power-assisted to reduce driver fatigue, and standard equipment includes a tyre pressure-regulation system that allows the driver to adjust the pressure to suit the type of ground being crossed, this being of great use when the Fahd is crossing desert terrain. The wide low-pressure tyres are of the run-flat type, and allow the vehicle to travel for a distance of 50 km (31 miles) at a speed of 30 km/h (18.6 mph) if they are punctured by small arms fire or shell fragments.

As usual, the Fahd can be fitted with a wide range of optional equipment

including a front-mounted winch (used to recover other vehicles or itself), night-vision equipment and an NBC pack.

The basic vehicle is at present unarmed, although a wide range of armament systems can be fitted including a 7.62-mm (0.3-in) or 12.7-mm (0.5-in) machine-gun, or a 20-mm cannon. The type can also operate in the anti-tank role with wire-guided anti-tank systems such as the Euromissile Milan. More specialized variants include a command post with extensive communications equipment, a recovery vehicle, a reconnaissance vehicle, a multiple rocket – launcher, a forward ambulance and a supply carrier.

Specification
Fahd
Crew: 2 + 10

Soon to enter producton, the Fahd APC is based on a Daimler-Benz truck chassis and can carry 10 fully-equipped troops. Firing ports in the side and rear allow them to fire their weapons from the vehicle.

Weights: empty 9100 kg (20,026 lb); loaded 10900 kg (24,030 lb)
Powerplant: one Mercedes-Benz OM-352 A 6-cylinder turbocharged diesel developing 168 hp (125 kW)
Dimensions: length 6.00 m (19 ft 8.2 in); width 2.45 m (8 ft 0.5 in); height 2.10 m (6 ft 10.7 in)
Performance: maximum road speed 90 km/h (56 mph); maximum range 800 km (497 miles); fording 0.7 m (2 ft 4 in); vertical obstacle 0.5 m (1 ft 4 in); trench 0.8 m (2 ft 8 in); gradient 70 per cent; side slope 30 per cent

---

122-mm SP122 self-propelled howitzer

Until the recent introduction of the US M109A2 155-mm (6.1-in) self-propelled howitzer, virtually all Egyptian artillery was towed, most of this having been supplied by the USSR and including large numbers of excellent 122-mm (4.8-in) D-30s, whose ammunition Egypt has been making for some years. More recently Egypt has started to produce the D-30 for both the home and export markets.

The Egyptian army decided that it wanted a self-propelled version of the D-30 more advanced than the Syrian version, which was essentially an old T-34/85 tank with its turret replaced by a D-30 firing over the rear engine decking; no protection is provided for the gun crew from small arms fire and shell splinters.

In 1984 it was announced that BMY of the USA and Royal Ordnance of the UK had each been awarded contracts to design and build a self-propelled version of the D-30 which would eventually be made in Egypt. The prototypes made their first official appearance at a defence exhibition in Cairo late in 1984.

The BMY entry in this competition consists essentially of a M109 chassis with a new fixed superstructure at the rear: in the forward part of this is the D-30 howitzer, which has an elevation of +70° a depression of −5° and a traverse of 30° left and right. Some 85 rounds of 122-mm ammunition are carried, of which five are normally HEAT (High Explosive Anti-Tank). Mounted on the roof is a 12.7-mm (0.5-in) M2 HB

machine-gun, for which 500 rounds of ammunition are carried.

Rather than use an existing chassis Royal Ordnance Leeds designed a new vehicle from scratch of all welded steel construction rather than aluminium as used in the BMY entry. The reason for this was that steel is easier to weld than aluminium, and Egypt already has extensive experience in using this material in other armoured vehicle programmes.

The layout of the Royal Ordnance D-30 self-propelled howitzer is similar to the BMY type, but is much more compact. The driver is at the front left with engine to his right and the gun compartment at rear. Weapon elevation, depression and traverse are identical to the BMY vehicle, and 80 projectiles and charges are carried. A 12.7-mm M2 HB machine-gun is carried on the roof for anti-aircraft defence.

The Perkins diesel engine is coupled to a fully automatic Self-Changing Gears six-speed transmission. Some parts of the suspension are also used in the Royal Ordnance Nottingham Combat Engineer Tractor already in service with the British and Indian armies.

Egypt has been manufacturing the Soviet D-30 122-mm gun for some years, and invited Royal Ordnance and BMY in the USA to produce a self-propelled version. Royal Ordnance have designed a completely new chassis, which may also be used for a whole family of AFVs.

However, in spite of prolonged testing of both designs in the late 1980s, the Egyptian government declined to order any equipments. Which is scarcely surprising; a 4.8 inch gun on an 18-ton vehicle is simply too much vehicle for too little gun.

Specification (provisional)
SP122
Crew: 5
Weights: empty 17500 kg (38,580 lb);

loaded 20000 kg (44,092 lb)
Powerplant: one Perkins TV8.540 eight-cylinder diesel developing 300 hp (224 kW)
Dimensions: length 7.70 m (25 ft 3 in); width 2.82 m (9 ft 3 in); height 2.69 m (8 ft 10 in)
Performance: maximum road speed 55 km/h (34 mph); range 300 km (186 miles); fording 1.0 m (3 ft 3 in); vertical obstacle 0.75 m (2 ft 6 in); trench 2.2 m (7 ft 3 in); gradient 60 per cent; side slope 30 per cent

Amphibians and Over-snow Vehicles

Highly specialized and often strange-looking, amphibious and over-snow vehicles are designed to go where others fear to tread. You may never need one of these specialists, but when you do need one, nothing else will do.

M113 APCs crossing a river during exercises in Korea. This photograph shows exactly what the 'trim vanes' on the front of these vehicles are there for.

It is doubtful whether anyone before World War II gave the slightest consideration to the problems inherent in driving tanks across deep snow. When the Soviets put their final T-34 prototype together in 1940, they made sure that its tracks were wider than was hitherto thought necessary, so that the T-34 had a quite remarkable performance

across snowfields. Even so, little notice was taken of the snow problem elsewhere until the 1960s when the Swedes developed the Bv 202. By this time NATO was functioning, and various armies used to temperate or even tropical climes found themselves in North Norway and similar places. The Bv 202 became very popular, and similar vehicles

appeared elsewhere. However, oversnow vehicles are a highly specialized breed and they are not found in very great numbers.

Amphibians had been closely examined in pre-war days. Christie had demonstrated an amphibian tank on the Hudson River in the 1920s. But as with many new ideas of the 1919–36 period, it was ruled too costly.

The first successful amphibian was designed, not as a land vehicle for water but as a boat that could operate on land. In 1935 German Army engineers needed a boat which could assist in building bridges but was able to move across country with the bridging train. The result, the Landwasser-schlepper, took seven years to perfect.

In the end it was the American automobile industry that produced the two amphibians which were to serve the Allied armies and also act as guides to future designers: the amphibious Jeep and the DUKW, or 'Duck'. The former was a useful light vehicle for overcoming flooded ground and crossing rivers. It made itself particularly useful in North-West Europe in 1944–45 when inundation was part of the German defensive strategy. The DUKW was a 2.5-tonne truck converted to float, and it crossed rivers and served as a ferryboat to bring supplies from ships off shore until suitable harbours could be found. And, as the following pages show, when post-war designers required a cargo amphibian, they simply produced a clone of the DUKW. The engineering may have improved a little, but the basic approach remains the same.

FIAT Type 6640A amphibious vehicle

FIAT is the largest manufacturer of wheeled military vehicles in Italy, and it was natural that when the Italian Home Office Civil Protection and Fire Fighting Department issued a requirement for an amphibious vehicle some years ago that FIAT should tender a vehicle. This entered production under the designation **FIAT Model 6640A**, and can carry a maximum payload on land or water of 2140 kg (4,718 lb).

The hull of the FIAT Model 6640A is of all-welded aluminium construction with a maximum thickness of 4 mm (0.16 in), and is divided into three compartments: engine at the front, crew in the centre and freight at the rear. The engine is coupled to a manual gearbox with five forward and one reverse gear and a torque converter. The suspension, front and rear, consists of an independent strut and link with helical spring and rubber bump stop, with a hydraulic shock absorber. Steering is power-assisted, and on land the vehicle has a turning radius of 7.5 m (24.6 ft).

The crew compartment in the centre is provided with windows and side-screens, and this and the load compartment to the rear can be covered by bows and a tarpaulin cover. When afloat the vehicle can be powered by its wheels or a four-blade screw type propeller with a Kort nozzle, steering being accomplished by a rudder coupled to the steering wheel. Mounted at the front of the vehicle is a winch with a maximum capacity of 3000 kg (6,614 lb). Three bilge pumps are provided as standard, one in the engine compartment (separated from the crew compartment by a fireproof bulkhead) and another two under the cargo area.

Production of the FIAT Model 6640A has now been completed, but further development has resulted in the **FIAT Type 6640G** which was announced in 1980 and, according to FIAT, is not in production. The main difference between this and the earlier vehicle is the

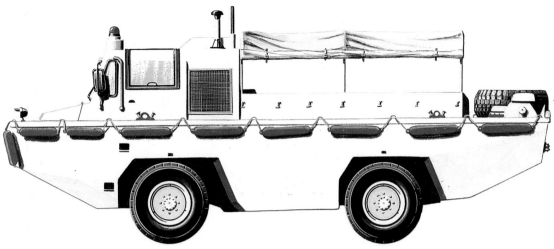

Type 6640G's longer wheelbase and more powerful engine, the latter developing 195 hp (145 kW) and coupled to a fully automatic gearbox with three forward and one reverse gear. The cab is now fully enclosed and provided with a heater, and the vehicle is propelled in the water by a single waterjet under the hull rear.

Specification
FIAT Type 6640A
Crew: 1 + 1
Combat weight: 6950 kg (15,322 lb)
Powerplant: one FIAT Model 8060.02 6-cylinder diesel developing 117 hp (87 kW)
Dimensions: length 7.30 m (23 ft 11.4 in); width 2.50 m (8 ft 2.4 in); height overall 2.715 m (8 ft 10.9 in)
Performance: maximum road speed 90 km/h (56 mph); maximum water speed with propeller 11 km/h (6.8 mph) or with wheels 5 km/h (3.1 mph); range on land 750 km (466 miles); range on water with propeller 60 km (37 miles) or with wheels 30 km (18 miles); fording amphibious; gradient 50 per cent; trench not applicable; vertical obstacle 0.43 m (1 ft 5 in)

The aluminium-hulled Type 6640A is in paramilitary service with the Italian home office, used for civil protection and also in the fire service.

The Type 6640A has a cargo capacity of some 3000 kg (6,614 lb) capable of 90 km/h (56 mph) on land; on water it can be manoeuvred by wheels or by a propeller. As with many modern amphibians, the vehicle bears a resemblance to the pioneering American DUKW of World War II.

GAZ-46 MAV amphibious vehicle

During World War II Canada, the UK and the USA shipped vast quantities of military equipment to the Soviet Union, including Ford GPA 4×4 amphibious jeeps and DUKW 6×6 amphibious load-carriers. These were used to ferry men, equipment and supplies across the many rivers in eastern Europe during the push back into Germany. After the end of the war the Soviet Union decided to design two similar vehicles, the **GAZ-46 MAV** being the equivalent of the Ford GPA and the BAV 485 the equivalent of the DUKW. Initial production GAZ-46 vehicles were built on the GAZ-67B 4×4 chassis which was produced during World War II, while later production vehicles were based on the post-war GAZ-69 4×4 500-kg (1,102-lb) light vehicle, which entered production at the Gorki plant in 1952. The main role of the GAZ-46 MAV, apart from its basic role of transporting men and light supplies across rivers and lakes, was in river reconnaissance, but from the late 1950s this role was taken over by the much more capable BRDM-1 4×4 amphibious scout car. In the 1950s the East Germans produced a not dissimilar 4×4 light vehicle for their army under the designation P2M and subsequently developed an amphibious version of this under the designation **P2S**. This was not produced in large numbers and is no longer in service. The P2M was replaced in production by the P3 but the amphibious version of this vehicle did not enter production.

The hull of the GAZ-46 MAV is of all-steel construction with the engine compartment at the very front, the passenger area in the centre, and a spare wheel and tyre carried horizontally on the rear deck. The driver and vehicle commander have individual seats and to their rear is a three-man bench seat. The windscreen can be folded down onto the bonnet, and if required a tarpaulin cover can be erected over the crew area. The engine is coupled to a manual gearbox with three forward and one reverse gear and a two-speed transfer case. The vehicle is powered in the water by a single three-blade propeller mounted under the very rear of the hull and driven from the main engine; before the vehicle enters the water a trim vane is erected at the front to stop water swamping the en-

American aid to the Soviet Union during World War II included large numbers of amphibious trucks, which were of such value that the Red Army copied the concept post-war; the 4×4 GAZ-46 MAV amphibious truck appeared in the late 1940s.

gine and crew compartments. The vehicle has a maximum payload of 500 kg (1,102 lb) and can tow a trailer or light weapon (a mortar or anti-aircraft gun) of similar weight.

Specification
GAZ-46 MAV
Crew: 1+4
Combat weight: 2480 kg (5,467 lb)
Powerplant: one M-20 4-cylinder petrol engine developing 55 hp (41 kW)
Dimensions: length 5.06 m (16 ft 7.2 in); width 1.735 m (5 ft 8.3 in); height with hood up 2.04 m (6 ft 8.3 in)
Performance: maximum road speed 90 km/h (56 mph); maximum water speed 9 km/h (5.6 mph); range 500 km (311 miles); fording amphibious; gradient 60 per cent; trench not applicable

Still in use after more than 30 years, the GAZ-46 amphibian is being replaced in front-line service by BRDM scout cars. With a carrying capacity of 500 kg (1102 lb), it should be regarded as an amphibious field car.

 Former USSR

PTS amphibious vehicle

The **PTS** amphibian entered service with the Soviet army in the mid-1960s, and in comparison with the earlier K-61 amphibian has a greatly increased load-carrying capability, slightly higher speed on both land and water, and can also tow a trailer when afloat. The PTS has a steel hull with the crew compartment at the very front of the hull and the cargo area stretching back right to the rear. The crew compartment, unlike those on the earlier K-61 and BAV-485, is fully enclosed, the two-man crew entering via two circular roof hatches. An NBC system is provided to enable the vehicle to operate in an NBC-contaminated area. The engine is beneath the vehicle, with the exhaust pipes on top of the cargo compartment on each side, a configuration which in certain conditions could permit exhaust fumes to be blown back into the cargo area, an unfortunate situation when troops are being carried. The PTS can carry a maximum of 5000 kg (11,023 lb) of cargo on land and 10000 kg (22,046 lb) on water, or up to 70 or so fully equipped troops. Cargo and vehicles such as a Ural-375D 6×6 4000-kg (8,818-lb) truck can be loaded into the PTS via the rear tailgate, which has two integral loading ramps. The suspension of the vehicle is of the torsion-bar type with six dual rubber-tyred road wheels, plus a drive sprocket at the front and an idler at the rear; there are no track-return rollers. The vehicle is driven in the water by two propellers mounted in tunnels under the rear of the hull, and steered by two rudders. Before the vehicle enters the water a trim vane is erected at the front to stop water swamping the forward part of the vehicle, and the bilge pumps are switched on. All vehicles have a front-mounted winch (to recover other vehicles and equipment, or to assist in self-recovery), night driving equipment, a searchlight mounted on top of the crew compartment, radios and an intercom.

The PTS can also tow the specially

The PTS has been in Egyptian service for some years, its amphibious carrying capacity having been used to good effect during the Yom Kippur war of 1973.

developed **PKP** boat-shaped two-wheel trailer, which is provided with ramps to enable cargo to be loaded. This has two sponsons, one on each side: for land travel these are folded on top of the trailer, but before entering the water they are swung through 180° and locked in position to provide additional buoyancy. The trailer is used to carry a 122-mm (4.8-in) D-30 howitzer while the PTS vehicle carries the truck, ammunition and crew.

The latest production version is the **PTS-M**, which has minor differences including increased fuel capacity. The only known variant is one used by Poland, which has a rocket-propelled

mine-clearing system mounted in the rear. In addition to being used by most members of the Warsaw Pact, the PTS is also operated by Egypt, Iraq and Syria.

Specification
PTS
Crew: 1+1
Combat weight: on land 22700 kg (50,045 lb) and on water 27700 kg (61,068 lb)
Powerplant: one V-54P diesel developing 350 hp (261 kW)
Dimensions: length 11.50 m (37 ft 8.8 in); width 3.30 m (10 ft 10 in); height 2.65 m (8 ft 8.3 in)

Water-driven by twin tunnel-mounted propellers at the rear, the large PTS is capable of carrying up to 10000 kg (22,046 lb) on water, or up to 70 men. The crew compartment at the front of the vehicle is fully sealed against NBC (Nuclear, Biological, Chemical) contaminants.

Performance: maximum road speed 42 km/h (26 mph); maximum water speed 10.6 km/h (6.5 mph); range 300 km (186 miles); fording amphibious; gradient 60 per cent; vertical obstacle 0.65 m (2 ft 1.6 in); trench 2.5 m (8 ft 2.4 in)

BAV-485 amphibious carrier

Following the successful use of American-supplied DUKW 6×6 amphibious vehicles by the Soviet army during World War II, it was decided to build a similar vehicle but based on a Soviet truck chassis. This finally appeared in the early 1950s as the BAV-485, sometimes called the ZIL-485. The layout of the BAV-485 is similar to that of the American DUKW with the engine and transmission at the front, crew seats to the rear of the engine compartment, and the cargo area at the rear. A maximum of 2500 kg (5,511 lb) of cargo or 25 fully equipped troops can be carried. The crew at the front are provided with a windscreen which can be folded forwards, and if required bows and a tarpaulin cover can be erected over the crew and troop compartments. A major improvement over the original American DUKW is the installation of a drop-down tailgate at the very rear of the cargo compartment, which enables light vehicles, mortars and light artillery weapons to be loaded very quickly. The engine is coupled to a manual gearbox with five forward and one reverse gear, and a two-speed transfer case. The main brakes are pneumatic, with a mechanical parking brake that operates on the rear wheels only. The BAV-485 is powered in the water by a single three-blade propeller mounted under the rear of the hull, and before the vehicle enters the water bilge pumps must be switched on.

The basic BAV-485 was based on the ZIL-151 6×6 2500-kg (5,511-lb) truck chassis built by the Likhachev Motor Vehicle Plant in Moscow between 1947 and 1958. Later production vehicles were based on the ZIL-157 6×6 2500-kg (5,511-lb) truck chassis built at the same plant between 1958 and 1961, this model being designated the BAV-485A. The major difference between the BAV-485 and the later BAV-485A is that the former has external air lines for the central tyre pressure-regulation system while the latter has internal air lines which are less easily damaged. The central tyre

pressure-regulation system is a common feature on Soviet wheeled armoured vehicles and military trucks, and enables the driver to adjust the ground pressure to suit the ground being crossed. It is by no means a new idea, however, as the Americans had a similar system on their DUKWs during World War II. Some BAV-485s have been observed with a 12.7-mm (0.5-in) DShKM heavy machine-gun for anti-aircraft defence, this being mounted on the forward right side of the troop compartment.

Specification
BAV-485
Crew: 1+1
Combat weight: on land and on water 9650 kg (21,275 lb)
Powerplant: one ZIL-123 6-cylinder petrol engine developing 110 hp (82 kW)
Dimensions: length 9.54 m (31 ft 3.6 in); width 2.845 m (9 ft 4 in); height 2.66 m (8 ft 8.7 in)
Performance: maximum road speed 60 km/h (37.3 mph); maximum water speed 10 km/h (6.2 mph); maximum

Derived directly from the wartime 6×6 DUKW provided under Lend-Lease, the BAV-485 is a watertight boat-like body on a Soviet truck chassis.

road range 480 km (298 miles); fording amphibious; gradient 60 per cent; vertical obstacle 0.4 m (1 ft 4 in); trench not applicable

Based upon ZIL trucks, the BAV-485 largely serves in second-line units of the Warsaw Pact.

K-61 amphibious carrier

The K-61 tracked amphibious load carrier was developed in the period immediately after World War II and can carry a maximum payload of 3000 kg (6,614 lb) on land and 5000 kg (11,023 lb) on water. In the troop transport role it can carry a maximum of 60 fully equipped troops. The K-61 was first seen in Soviet army use in the early 1950s, and was subsequently exported to most members of the Warsaw Pact as well as to Egypt and Vietnam. Egypt used the K-61 in the 1973 Middle East conflict to carry supplies across the Suez Canal. In Soviet frontline units the K-61, which is sometimes known as the GPT, has been replaced by the more recent PTS tracked amphibious vehicle, which has not only a greater payload capacity but also a higher road speed and increased operating range.

The K-61 tracked amphibious carrier has an all-steel hull with the engine and crew compartment at the very front. The cargo/troop area runs almost the whole length of the K-61, and to facilitate the loading of vehicles a large tailgate is provided. To protect the

crew and cargo against bad weather, bows and a tarpaulin cover can be fitted over the whole of the cargo area. The suspension on each side consists of seven very small road wheels with the drive sprocket at the front and idler at the rear, and there are seven slides to support the tracks as they return.

The K-61 is driven in the water by two propellers mounted under the hull rear, these being driven by a power take-off from the main engine.

In addition to carrying troops and cargo, K-61 vehicles have been used to carry a wide range of engineer equipment and weapons such as the

The view from above displays the large capacity and the loading ramps incorporated into the tailgate. Normal load can include trucks, artillery pieces or mortars.

122-mm (4.8-in) M1938 (M30) towed howitzer, 76-mm (3-in) or 85-mm (3.35-in) anti-tank guns, mortars, 14.5-mm (0.57-in) ZPU-2 twin and ZPU-4 quadruple towed anti-aircraft guns, and light vehicles such as the GAZ-63. For heavier equipments one K-61 would carry the weapon while another ferried the towing vehicle.

Specification
K-61
Crew: 1+1
Combat weight: on land 12550 kg (27,668 lb) and on water 14550 kg (32,077 lb)
Powerplant: one YaAZ-M204VKr 4-cylinder water-cooled diesel developing 135 hp (100 kW)

East Germany has the K-61 on its inventory, as have most of the Warsaw Pact nations. It has seen combat service with Egypt, in 1973, and also equips the Vietnamese army.

Dimensions: length 9.15 m (30 ft 0.2 in); width 3.15 m (10 ft 4 in); height 2.15 m (7 ft 0.6 in)
Performance: maximum land speed 36 km/h (22 mph); maximum water speed 10 km/h (6.2 mph); maximum range 260 km (162 miles); fording amphibious; gradient 40 per cent; vertical obstacle 0.65 m (2 ft 1.6 in); trench 3 m (9 ft 10 in)

GT-S tracked oversnow vehicle

The **GT-S**, sometimes called the **GAZ-47**, is believed to have been the first tracked amphibious oversnow vehicle to enter service with the Soviet army after World War II. During this conflict the Soviet army used a number of oversnow vehicles including several sled-type vehicles with a propeller at the rear. The GT-S was designed to carry a maximum payload of 1000 kg (2,205 lb) and to tow a trailer (or weapon such as a 120-mm/4.72-in mortar) weighing up to 2000 kg (4,409 lb).

The engine, more commonly the GAZ-61, is at the very front of the vehicle and coupled to a manual gearbox with four forward and one reverse gear. Some vehicles were fitted with the less powerful GAZ-47. The commander and driver are seated to the immediate rear of the engine, and behind them is the cargo area extending to the very rear of the vehicle. This cargo area is normally covered by a tarpaulin cover with small windows in the sides and rear. The tracks are 300 mm (11.81 in) wide and give a ground pressure of 0.24 kg/cm² (3.4 lb/sq in) loaded. The suspension is of the torsion-bar type and consists of five large rubber-tyred road wheels, the last road wheel on each side acting as the idler, and a drive sprocket at the front; there are no track-return rollers. As with the later oversnow vehicles, the GT-S is fully amphibious without preparation, being propelled in the water by its tracks.

One of the more interesting versions of the GT-S was the **LFM-RVD-GPI-66**, on which the tracks are replaced by cylindrical steel pontoons powered by the main engine. This model has a much higher water speed of 20 km/h (12.4 mph), but is wholly impractical on hard surfaces such as roads.

The GT-S has been replaced in production by the **GT-SM**, which has a

The GT-SM is an enlarged and more powerful version of the GT-S, with six road wheels per side instead of the five of the earlier model. It is in extensive Soviet service.

Wartime experience with fighting in the snow led to the development of the GAZ-47, or GT-S oversnow

longer chassis with six instead of five road wheels, and is powered by a more powerful GAZ-71 V8 water-cooled petrol engine developing 115 hp (86 kW). This gives it higher road and water speeds, and the vehicle's wider tracks give a lower ground pressure and therefore better mobility across snow and swampy ground.

Specification
GT-S
Crew: 1+1
Combat weight: 4600 kg (10,141 lb)

vehicle. The 1000-kg (2,205-lb) payload makes the GT-S equivalent to a light truck.

Powerplant: one GAZ-61 6-cylinder water-cooled petrol engine developing 85 hp (63 kW)
Dimensions: length 4.90 m (16 ft 1 in); width 2.435 m (8 ft 0 in); height 1.96 m (6 ft 5.2 in)
Performance: maximum road speed 35 km/h (21.7 mph); maximum water speed 4 km/h (2.5 mph); maximum range 725 km (450 miles); fording amphibious; gradient 60 per cent; trench 1.3 m (4 ft 3.2 in); vertical obstacle 0.6 m (1 ft 11.6 in)

Above: Fully amphibious without prior preparation, the GT-S has been in service since 1955, and was manufactured until 1970. It is being replaced by the enlarged GT-SM.

CAMANF amphibious truck

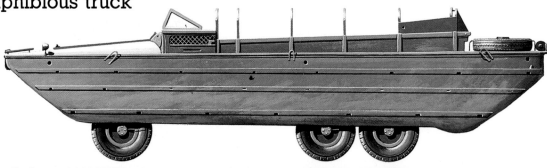

The Brazilian marines come under operational control of the Brazilian navy and have about 15,000 men organized into one amphibious division, one reinforcement command and an internal security force. Its vehicles include ENGESA EE-11 Urutu amphibious armoured personnel carriers, EE-9 Cascavel armoured cars, LARC-5 4×4 amphibious cargo-carriers and **CAMANF** amphibious trucks. On order are a small number of FMC LVTP7A1 amphibious armoured assault vehicles from the USA.

After the end of World War II Brazil was supplied with a number of American DUKW 6×6 amphibious vehicles, but by the 1970s these were becoming difficult to maintain and operate, and as with all petrol-engined vehicles there was the ever-present risk of fire. Biselli Viaturas e Equipamentos Industriais of Sao Paulo had for some time been supplying the Brazilian armed forces with equipment, including tank transporters, and in the mid-1975s started design work on the CAMANF (Caminhao Anfibio, or amphibious truck) and in the late 1970s the first batch of 15 vehicles was delivered to the Brazilian marines. The vehicle is essentially a 6×6 version of a Ford F-7000 chassis fitted with a watertight body. Some sources have indicated that it is almost identical to the original American body with modifications to suit the requirements of the Brazilian marines, including a much stronger bow to enable the vehicle to operate in rougher water and to push beached landing craft back into the water.

In appearance the CAMANF is almost identical to the American DUKW designed in the early days of World War II, with the engine compartment at the front and the crew and

Having used the DUKW for many years, the Brazilian replacement is virtually identical, but with minor modifications to suit Brazilian maritime requirements. Maximum water speed is 14 km/h (8.7 mph).

troop compartment towards the rear. The cargo area is provided with removable bows and a tarpaulin cover, and a ring-mounted 12.7-mm (0.5-in) M2 HB anti-aircraft machine-gun can be fitted over the right side of the crew compartment. The vehicle can carry a load of 5000 kg (11,023 lb) on land and very calm water, but in rougher water it is limited to 2500 kg (5,511 lb). Before entering the water a trim vane is erected at the front of the vehicle and the bilge pumps are switched on. The CAMANF is propelled in the water by a single propeller mounted under the rear of the hull. All six wheels are fitted with a tyre pressure-regulation system that allows the commander to adjust the tyre pressure to suit the type of ground being crossed. Tyres are all 9.00×20, and a spare wheel and tyre are carried on the rear of the vehicle.

Specification
CAMANF
Crew: 1+2
Combat weight: 13500 kg (29,762 lb)
Powerplant: one Detroit-Diesel Model 40-54N diesel engine
Dimensions: length 9.50 m (31 ft 2 in); width 2.50 m (8 ft 2.4 in); height 2.65 m (8 ft 8.3 in)
Performance: maximum road speed 72 km/h (45 mph); maximum water speed 14 km/h (8.7 mph); maximum

The 5000-kg (11,023-lb) payload of the CAMANF is considerably reduced in rough water, but the bow has been strengthened so that handling in such conditions is improved.

road range 430 km (267 miles); fording amphibious; gradient 60 per cent; trench not applicable; vertical obstacle 0.4 m (1 ft 3.7 in)

Pegaso VAP 3550/1 amphibious vehicle

In Spain, as in most countries the marines come under the operational control of the navy. Today the Spanish marines consist of a force of about 12,000 men organized into five garrison regiments and one regiment that comprises two infantry, one support and one logistics battalion. Equipment includes M48 tanks, LVTP7 amphibious assault vehicles, 106-mm (4.17-in) recoilless rifles, 105-mm (4.13-in) OTO Melara pack howitzers, 105-mm (4.13-in) M52 self-propelled howitzers and **Pegaso VAP 3550/1** amphibious vehicles. The last was designed by ENASA to meet the requirements of the Spanish navy for an amphibious wheeled vehicle that could be launched from a Landing Ship Tank (LST) while carrying a payload of 3000 kg (6,614 lb), reach the coast under its own power and then travel inland to a point where the cargo would be unloaded with the assistance of an onboard crane.

The VAP 3550/1 uses many of the automotive components from the Pegaso 3045 4×4 and Pegaso 3050 6×6 series of trucks which have been produced in large numbers for the Spanish army, navy, air force and marines over the last 15 years. This makes for easier training and reduced maintenance.

The hull of the VAP 3550/1 is of all-welded steel construction with a maximum thickness of 6 mm (0.24 in), and is divided into a number of watertight

compartments; if any one of these is punctured the vehicle will not sink. The crew compartment is towards the front of the vehicle, with the driver seated on the left and the other two crew members to his right; the top, front and sides of the crew compartment are covered, but the back is open. The cargo compartment is in the centre and is normally fitted with removable bows and a tarpaulin cover; there is no provision for loading wheeled vehicles, the normal role of the vehicle being the carriage of bulk cargo. To the rear of the cab is a hydraulic crane with an extending jib which can lift a maximum load of 350 kg (772 lb).

The engine compartment is at the rear with the air inlet/air outlet louvres and exhaust pipe mounted above it. The engine is coupled to a manual gearbox with six forward and one reverse gear and a two-speed transfer case. Steering is power-assisted on the front wheels.

Unlike many amphibians, which are impelled on the water by propellers, the VAP 3550/1 is powered by two waterjets, one mounted on each side of the hull rear, and these give excellent waterborne manoeuvrability. The vehicle is also fitted with two automatic bilge pumps with a maximum capacity of 3600 litres (792 Imp gal) per hour and two pumps with a maximum capacity of 6000 litres (1,320 Imp gal) per hour, while at the very front is a winch with a

capacity of 4500 kg (9,921 lb) for self-recovery operations.

In addition to serving with the Spanish navy and marines, the type has been exported: seven were delivered to Mexico in 1982, and a quantity is reported to have been supplied to Egypt. The Italian company Astra has a licence to build this vehicle.

Specification
Pegaso VAP 3550/1
Crew: 1+2
Combat weight: 12500 kg (27,558 lb)
Powerplant: one Pegaso 9125/5 diesel developing 190 hp (142 kW)
Dimensions: length 9.058 m (29 ft

Designed to operate from Spanish navy LSTs (Landing Ships Tank), the Pegaso VAP 3550/1 is powered in water by two waterjets driving the vehicle at some 55 kts when afloat. Standard payload is 3000 kg (6,614 lb).

8.6 in); width 2.50 m (8 ft 2.4 in); height to top of cab 2.50 m (8 ft 2.4 in)
Performance: maximum road speed 87 km/h (54 mph); maximum water speed 10 km/h (6.2 mph); range on land 800 km (497 miles); range on water 80 km (49.7 miles); fording amphibious; gradient 60 per cent; trench not applicable

LVTP7 armoured amphibious assault vehicle

After the evaluation of a number of proposals for a new armoured amphibious assault vehicle to replace the LVTP5 family, the FMC Corporation was awarded a development contract by the Naval Ship Systems Command and the first of 15 **LVTPX12** prototypes were completed in 1967. Following trials, the vehicle was standardized as the **LVTP7 (Landing Vehicle Tracked Personnel Model 7)**, and in 1970 FMC was awarded a contract for 942 vehicles at total value of $78.5 million. The first vehicles were completed in 1971 and production continued until 1974. In addition to the US Marine Corps, sales of the LVTP7 and its variants were also made to Argentina (21), Italy (25), South Korea (61), Spain (19), Thailand (23) and Venezuela (11). The type's only combat use, apart from peacekeeping duties in Lebanon, has been with the Argentine marines during the 1982 invasion of the Falklands, when one vehicle was knocked out by the Royal Marines with a Carl Gustav light anti-tank weapon.

More recently the LVTP7A1 has entered production for the US Marines, and most of the original LVTP7 vehicles are to be brought up to this improved standard, which includes replacement of the original Detroit-Diesel engine by a Cummins diesel, and incorporation of passive night-vision devices, a smoke-generating capability, a fire-suppression system, improved ventilation for the troop compartment, a Position Location and Reporting System and improvements to the 12.7-mm (0.5-in) weapon station. For trials purposes three LVTP7 vehicles have recently been fitted with a one-man turret armed with a 40-mm grenade-launcher and a 12.7-mm (0.5-in) machine-gun, but no production orders have yet been placed.

The LVTP7 has a hull of all-welded aluminium construction with the driver at the front on the right and the vehicle commander to his rear. The engine and transmission are at the front, with the one-man turret (armed with a 12.7-mm/0.5-in machine-gun) on the right; 1,000 rounds of ammunition are carried for this weapon. The troop compartment is at the rear of the vehicle, and the normal means of entry and exit to this is a large power-operated ramp in the hull rear. Over the top of the troop compartment is a three-part roof hatch that opens sideways to enable cargo and troops to be loaded when the vehicle is alongside ships. The 25 marines are seated on three bench seats, one down each side of the hull and one in the centre; the last can be folded to

Storming ashore from their LVTP7 amphibians, these US Marines form part of the largest amphibious force in the world. Their armoured vehicle is an important component in US power projection capabilities.

enable up to 4536 kg (10,000 lb) of cargo to be carried.

Suspension of the LVTP7 is of the torsion-bar type, and consists of six dual rubber-tyred road wheels, with a drive sprocket at the front and idler at the rear; there are no track-return rollers. When afloat the vehicle is normally propelled by two waterjets at the hull rear, one on each side, but if these fail the LVTP7 can also be propelled by its tracks at the slower speed of 7.2 km/h (4.5 mph).

On the basic hull of the LVTP7 several specialized versions of the vehicle have been developed. The command model, the **LVTC7**, has extensive communications equipment and a 12-man crew. The recovery member of the family is the **LVTR7**, which is fitted with a winch for recovery of vehicles, a crane for changing components in the field, and a complete set of tools and other specialized equipment. There was to have been an engineer vehicle with hydraulically-operated dozer blade (at the front of the hull) and a mine-clearing system, but this was not placed in production although a prototype was built. There was also to have been a 105-mm (4.13-in) howitzer model to replace the LVTH6, but this did not reach even the prototype stage. Undergoing trials in 1984 was an LVTP7 with the turret of the Sheridan light tank armed with a 105-mm (4.13-in) gun. The chassis of the LVTP7 was also used as the basics-for the **Mobile Test Rig** which was armed with a laser to shoot down aircraft. This was successfully tested in the mid-1970s but did not enter service.

Specification
LVTP7
Crew: 3+25
Combat weight: 22837 kg (50,348 lb)
Powerplant: one Detroit-Diesel Model 8V-53T developing 400 hp (298 kW)
Dimensions: length 7.943 m (26 ft 0.7 in); width 3.27 m (10 ft 8.7 in); height overall 3.263 m (10 ft 8.5 in)
Performance: maximum road speed 64 km/h (40 mph); maximum water speed 13.5 km/h (8.5 mph); maximum road range 482 km (300 miles); fording amphibious; gradient 60 per cent; trench 2.438 m (8 ft 0 in); vertical obstacle 0.914 m (3 ft 0 in)

Left: The LVT7 series are not small vehicles, being 7.94 m (26 ft 1 in) in length, and weighing in at 22838 kg (50,348 lb). Only the superpowers can afford to develop such armoured vehicles specifically for their amphibious forces.

Above: With a seven-hour waterborne endurance, the LVTP7 can be launched up to 50 km (31 miles) from the beach, and carry up to 25 fully-armed troops or over 4500 kg (9,900 lb) of cargo in the basic version.

LARC-5 amphibious cargo carrier

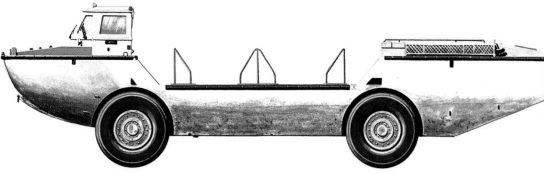

In the 1950s the US Transportation Engineering Command issued a requirement for a vehicle capable of transporting 4356 kg (10,000 lb) of cargo from ships lying offshore, across the beach and then to inland dumps. Development of this vehicle, subsequently called the **Lighter Amphibious Resupply Cargo 5-ton (LARC-5)** was carried out by the Borg Warner Corporation. Production was initially undertaken by the Adams Division of Le Tourneau Westinghouse, but final production came from Condiesel Mobile Equipment Division, and between 1962 and 1968 about 950 vehicles were built. In addition to being used by the US Army, the LARC-5 is also known to be in service with Australia, West Germany and Argentina. The last used the vehicle during its invasion of the Falklands in 1982, but by the time of the islands' recapture by the British all of the vehicles had been returned to the mainland.

The hull of the LARC-5 is of all-welded aluminium construction with the cab at the front of the vehicle, cargo areas in the centre and the engine compartment at the very rear. The cab, which is open at the rear, has seats for the driver and two passengers and is provided with a magnetic compass, a heater and windscreen defroster, a portable fire extinguisher, a radio, and a portable lamp and cable. If required, the rear of the cab can be shielded by a fabric cover.

The cargo area is open on the top, but fabric curtains reinforced with stranded wire rope can be installed on each side to protect the cargo from spray. In place of cargo up to 20 fully equipped troops can be carried by the LARC-5, and some vehicles have been fitted to the rear of the cab with a hydraulically-operated boom that can lift a maximum load of 2495 kg (5,500 lb).

The engine compartment is fully enclosed and provided with a fire extinguisher operated from the cargo-deck rear bulkhead. The first production vehicles were powered by a petrol engine but final examples have a diesel engine which reduces the danger of fire.

Above: LARC-5 has been in service since 1962, providing transportation for up to 20 fully equipped troops or 4356 kg (10,000 lb) of cargo.

On roads 4×2 drive is normally used, the 4×4 drive being engaged only when the vehicle is being driven across country; a two-speed transfer case is fitted (high and low ranges). The LARC-5 is powered in the water by a three-blade propeller mounted under the hull at the rear. Both power-operated and manual bilge pumps are fitted for the disposal of any water that seeps into the vehicle. The LARC-5 has no suspension as such, the 18.00×25 tyres absorbing all of the shock. Steering is power-assisted on the front wheels only.

Specification
LARC-5
Crew: 1+2
Combat weight: 14038 kg (30,948 lb)
Powerplant: one Cummins V8 diesel developing 300 hp (224 kW)
Dimensions: length 10.668 m (35 ft 0 in); width 3.149 m (10 ft 4 in); height overall 3.034 m (9 ft 11.4 in)
Performance: maximum road speed 48.2 km/h (30 mph); maximum water speed 16 km/h (10 mph); maximum road range, empty 402 km (250 miles); fording amphibious; gradient 60 per cent; trench not applicable; vertical obstacle about 0.5 m (1 ft 7.7 in)

An LARC-5 of the Australian Army negotiates rough surf, giving a good impression of the conditions that any modern amphibious supply vehicle has to cope with in order to be effective.

LARC-15 amphibious cargo carrier

The **Lighter Amphibious Resupply Cargo 15-ton (LARC-15)** is a member of a family of 4×4 vehicles designed to meet the requirement of the US Army to transport cargo from ships, over the beach and on to points inland. The other vehicles are the smaller LARC-5 and the much larger LARC-60. The LARC-15 was designed by the Ingersoll-Kalamazoo Division of the Borg Warner Corporation, production being undertaken by the Military Products Division of the Fruehauf Corporation. The first production vehicles were completed in the mid-1960s. The only known operators of the LARC-15 are the USA and West Germany.

The LARC-15 has been designed to carry a maximum load of 15 US tons (13608 kg/30,000 lb) and operate in surf up to 3.048 m (10 ft) high. A major difference between the LARC-5 and the LARC-15 is that the latter has the engine compartment and cab at the rear to make possible the incorporation of a hydraulically-operated bow ramp for the onloading of tracked and

wheeled vehicles. Typical loads can include a 155-mm (6.1-in) M114 towed howitzer, whose crew, ammunition and 2½-ton 6×6 towing vehicle are carried in another LARC-15. The sides of the freight area can be fitted with fabric curtains reinforced with stranded wire rope to stop spray reaching the cargo, and with these curtains removed cargo can be loaded and unloaded from the side with the aid of a fork-lift truck.

The engines are mounted under the fully enclosed cab, which can be removed as a complete unit. The engines are coupled to a transmission and a two-speed transfer case (high and low), and in the water the vehicle is propelled by a four-blade propeller mounted under the rear of the hull; waterborne steering is via the wheels and a rudder. The vehicle has no suspension system, the large 24.00×29 tyres absorbing the shock. Steering is power-assisted and the driver can select one of three different modes; two-wheel, four-wheel and oblique

The LARC-15 is the larger brother of the LARC-5, with a capacity of 15 US tons (13608 kg/30,000 lb). Large trucks can thus be carried, but on-land performance is limited when carrying large loads.

(also known as crab), the last being used in very difficult conditions such as those likely to be found on many beaches.

The **LARC-60** was the first of the LARCs to be developed (in the early 1950s) by the Pacific Car and Foundry Company of Renton, Washington. Its normal maximum load of 60000 kg (132,276 lb) can be increased to 100000 kg (220,460 lb) in an emergency, and like other LARCs it was widely used in South Vietnam to transport cargo from ships onto the beach, where it was unloaded into trucks for transportation to supply dumps inland. An unusual feature of the LARC-60 is that it is powered by four engines, one powering each of the four road wheels. When afloat, the vehicle is powered by two propellers at the rear, each of these being driven by two engines.

The large 36.00×41 tyres are fitted with a central tyre pressure-regulation system, a feature very useful for crossing deep sand as the pressure can be decreased for improved traction.

Specification
LARC-15
Crew: 1+1
Combat weight: 34100 kg (75,177 lb)
Powerplant: two Cummins V8 diesels each developing 300 hp (224 kW)
Dimensions: length 13.716 m (45 ft 0 in); width 4.419 m (14 ft 6 in); height with cab 4.724 m (15 ft 6 in)
Performance: maximum road speed 50 km/h (31 mph); maximum water speed 15 km/h (9.3 mph); maximum road range, empty 482 km (300 miles); fording amphibious; gradient 40 per cent; trench not applicable; vertical obstacle not known

An early LARC-15 is seen with ramp lowered and an M-56 self-propelled anti-tank gun prepared to unload.

The bulk of the vehicle enables it to operate through up to 3.05 m (10 ft) of surf

WEST GERMANY
EKW Bison amphibious truck

The **EKW Bison** 4×4 amphibious truck has been developed as a private venture by the Eisenwerke Kaiserlautern Goppner company of West Germany for both civil and military applications, and was seen in public for the first time in 1982. EWK has considerable experience in the development of amphibious vehicles, having already designed the **ALF-2** amphibious fire tender, the **M2** amphibious bridge/ferry systems used by the British, West German and Singapore armies, and more recently the **APE** 4×4 amphibious armoured reconnaissance vehicle. The last was developed to meet the requirements of the West German army but has yet to enter production because of a shortage of funds.

The Bison has a fully enclosed forward control cab with the engine to its rear. The engine is coupled to a fully automatic transmission with six forward and one reverse gear. The load area is at the rear and provided with drop sides, bows and a tarpaulin cover. The normal load is 5000 kg (11,023 lb), but in an emergency a total of 7000 kg (15,432 lb) of cargo can be carried. Before the vehicle enters the water a trim vane is erected at the front, and the flotation bags are extended to each side and inflated with the aid of an APU-driven pump; the flotation bags give additional buoyancy when the Bison is afloat. The APU also provides the power for the two propellers which are mounted at the rear of the hull. These propellers have been designed by Schottel and can be traversed through 360° for increased waterborne manoeuvrability. (Schottel propellers are fitted to many of the armoured fighting vehicles used by the West German army, including the 6×6 Transportpanzer and the 8×8 Luchs reconnaissance vehicle.) Steering is power-assisted to reduce driver fatigue, and dual brakes are fitted as standard (hydraulic on the front wheels and pneumatic on the rear). The Bison is also fitted with a central tyre pressure-regulation system that allows the driver to adjust the tyre pressure to suit the type of terrain being crossed. The Soviets have fitted such a system to most of their wheeled armoured vehicles and many of their cross-country trucks since shortly after the end of World War II.

Another West German designer of

amphibious vehicles is Hans Trippel, who has been working on such vehicles for some 50 years and has recently designed the Trippel 4×4 550-kg (1,212-lb) light vehicle which is propelled in the water by two propellers (mounted at the hull rear), each of which can be traversed through 360°. A bilge pump is fitted as standard and this is automatically activated when the vehicle enters the water, so there is no possibility of the driver forgetting to switch it on. This vehicle has yet to enter production for military use.

Specification
Bison
Crew: 1+1
Combat weight: 16000 kg (35,274 lb)
Powerplant: one KHD V8 air-cooled diesel developing 320 hp (239 kW)
Dimensions: length 9.34 m (30 ft 7.7 in); width 2.5 m (8 ft 2.4 in); height to cab roof 2.96 m (9 ft 8.5 in)
Performance: maximum road speed 80 km/h (49.7 mph); maximum water speed 12 km/h (7.4 mph); maximum road range 900 km (559 miles); fording amphibious; gradient 60 per cent; trench not applicable; vertical obstacle not available

The EKW Bison was originally designed for civil use in underdeveloped regions, but the obvious military applications of such a vehicle were soon to lead to forces interest.

The 5000-kg (11,023 lb) capacity Bison is driven by two steerable Schottel propellers at speeds of up to 12 km/h (7.4 mph). As a private

venture, the EKW Bison has yet to be ordered for military purposes, but development is complete.

Type 60 oversnow vehicle

The Japanese northern island of Hokkaido is often covered in snow, and this factor led the Japanese Ground Self-Defence Force to the procurement of two full-tracked oversnow vehicles, the **Type 60** and **Type 61**, both designed and built by the Komatsu Manufacturing Company and the Ohara Ironworks. The Type 60, which is also called the **Medium Snow Mobile**, has been designed to carry a total of 10 men (including the driver) or 900 kg (1,984 lb) of cargo, and to tow a trailer or weapon weighing 1500 kg (3,307 lb). The engine is at the front of the Type 60 and coupled to a manual gearbox with four forward and one reverse gear, while the suspension is of the bogie/torsion-bar type with eight dual road wheels, return rollers, drive sprocket and idler. The cargo area is at the rear and provided with a drop tailgate; it is normally covered with removable bows and a tarpaulin cover.

The Type 61 oversnow vehicle, also called the **Large Snow Mobile**, is similar in appearance to the Type 60 but can carry 1280 kg (2,822 lb) of cargo or tow a maximum load of 3200 kg (7,055 lb), and as such is often used to tow ski-fitted artillery such as the 105-mm (4.13-in) M101 which is the standard weapon of its type in the Japanese Ground Self-Defence Force. The Type 61 is powered by an Isuza DA-120T 6-cylinder water-cooled diesel developing 155 hp (116 kW), coupled to a manual gearbox with five forward and one reverse gear.

Specification
Type 60
Crew: 1+9
Combat weight: 3770 kg (8,311 lb)
Powerplant: one Toyota 6-cylinder water-cooled petrol engine developing 105 hp (78 kW)
Dimensions: length 4.07 m (13 ft 4.2 in); width 1.98 m (6 ft 6 in); height 2.05 m (6 ft 8.7 in)
Performance: maximum road speed 36 km/h (22 mph); maximum water speed not applicable; maximum range 135 km (84 miles); fording not known; gradient 60 per cent; trench 1.066 m (3 ft 6 in); vertical obstacle 0.5 m (1 ft 7.7 in)

Evolved from the civilian Komatsu KC-20 designed for use in the northern Japanese island of Hokkaido, the Type 60 was adopted in 1960 by the Japanese Ground Self-Defence Force, largely for use in the same location.

Bombardier Snowmobile oversnow vehicle

The Industrial Division of Bombardier Limited of Quebec has for many years been involved in the design and production of a variety of tracked and semi-tracked oversnow vehicles for the civilian market. More recently it has undertaken production of some 2,000 M35 CDN 6×6 2½-ton trucks for the Canadian Armed Forces, and is building the West German Iltis 4×4 light vehicle for both the Belgian and Canadian forces. The very small **Bombardier Bombi** oversnow vehicle has been used by the Canadian Armed Forces as part of the United Nations forces operating in the Sinai desert, where the type's very low ground pressure makes it equally at home on sand as on snow. The **Bombardier Ski Doo Elite Snowmobile**, which can carry two passengers, has been tested by the US Marine Corps as a reconnaissance vehicle for possible use in Norway and elsewhere. The full-tracked **Bombardier Skidozer**, which is available with either a petrol or a diesel engine, is used by a number of countries in a military role, although it was not originally designed for this purpose.

The **Bombardier Snowmobile** oversnow vehicle is used by the Canadian Armed Forces in northern Canada as a general utility vehicle, and in appearance is very similar to a coach but the engine is at the rear and coupled to an automatic gearbox with three forward and one reverse gear. The front suspension consists of coil springs and hydraulic shock absorbers and is normally fitted with tyres, though these can be replaced by skis. The rear suspension on each side consists of four rubber-tyred road wheels on trailing arms, fitted with 420 mm (16.5 in) wide tracks which consist of rubber belts with steel crosslinks.

The personnel enter via a large door in the forward part of the vehicle, and there is also a door in the rear and an emergency roof hatch. Steering is of the power-assisted rack and pinion type, and standard equipment includes a heater and defroster, two fuel tanks, wing mirrors, front and rear lights, dry type paper air cleaner, block heater and full instrumentation.

Purchased by the Canadian Armed Forces for use in the wastes of northern Canada, the Bombardier Snowmobile, like many other such vehicles, was originally designed for civil rather than military use.

The Bombardier Bombi has found an unusual use for its abilities with the Canadian contingents of the UN forces in the Middle East, its low ground pressure being as suited to sand as to snow.

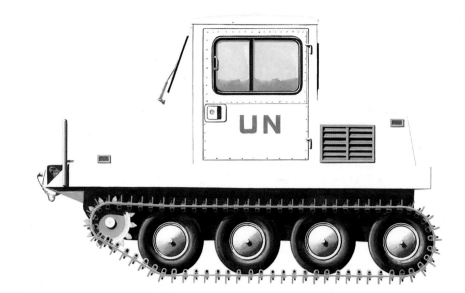

Specification
Bombardier Snowmobile
Crew: 1+11
Combat weight: 2337 kg (5,152 lb)
Powerplant: one Chrysler Model 318 V8 petrol engine developing 187 hp (139 kW)
Dimensions: length 5.38 m (17 ft 7.8 in); width 1.95 m (6 ft 4.8 in); height 2.06 m (6 ft 9 in)
Performance: maximum road speed 64 km/h (40 mph); maximum water speed not applicable; maximum range 320 km (199 miles); fording not known; gradient not known; trench not applicable; vertical obstacle not known

Bv 202 tracked oversnow vehicle

The first oversnow vehicle used in any numbers by the Swedish army was the US Weasel, which was developed by Studebaker during World War II and used both in Europe and the Far East. By the mid-1950s these were becoming difficult to maintain and operate, so the Swedish army approached a number of national companies with a proposal to build a new vehicle. As none of them showed any real interest, the Swedish army itself built prototypes which were completed in 1958. These were followed by additional vehicles incorporating improvements as a result of trials with the original test rigs and prototypes. Once the design had been finalized, the complete production programme was put out to tender, and in 1961 Bolinder-Munktell was awarded the first production contract for the vehicle, which was called the **Bv 202**.

The Bv 202 remained in production for almost 20 years, final deliveries being made in 1981. In addition to those for the Swedish army, sales were also made to Finland, the Netherlands, Norway, Turkey and the UK. The last uses its vehicles for a wide range of roles such as command, cargo-carrying and towing the 105-mm (4.13-in) Light Gun on skis. The Royal Marines and Royal Artillery used the vehicle during the 1982 Falklands campaign, where it proved to be one of the few vehicles able to traverse the boggy terrain. In the Swedish army the Bv 202 is now being supplemented by the much improved Bv 206 built by Hägglund & Söner, although it will be many years before the older vehicle is phased out of Swedish service. The Bv 202 is also used for a number of civil roles in Sweden and countries where its low ground pressure enables it to cross with ease terrain such as swamp, mud and snow.

The Bv 202 consists of two units, front and rear, connected by an articulated joint. The front unit contains the engine, transmission, driver and commander, while the rear unit carries the load which can be 800 kg (1,764 lb) across country or 1000 kg (2,205 lb) on roads. The commander and driver are seated in a fully enclosed cab pro-

Naturally, Scandinavia has proved a fertile ground for the design of oversnow vehicles, with the Swedish Bv 202 being in service with several countries, including Turkey and the UK.

vided with a heater, but the rear unit has only a tarpaulin cover for the troops sitting on a bench seat down each side; if required, however, the rear unit can also be fitted with a heater. The vehicle is fully amphibious, being propelled in the water by its tracks.

When in production the vehicle was offered with a number of options such as a fully enclosed rear unit with stowage rack on top, a torque converter, a cold starting device and a tropical kit. Late-production vehicles had a slightly more powerful engine and a different transmission which gave a slight increase in carrying capacity on roads, and across country.

Specification
Bv 202
Crew: front unit 2 and rear unit 8
Combat weight: 4200 kg (9,259 lb)
Powerplant: one Volvo B18 4-cylinder petrol engine developing 91 bhp (68 kW)
Dimensions: length 6.172 m (20 ft 3 in); width 1.759 m (5 ft 9.3 in); height 2.21 m (7 ft 3 in)
Performance: maximum road speed 39 km/h (24 mph); maximum water speed 3.3 km/h (2 mph); maximum range 400 km (249 miles); fording amphibious; gradient 60 per cent; trench not available; vertical obstacle 0.5 m (1 ft 7.7 in)

A British Army Bv 202 comes ashore from an SRN-6 hovercraft on the coast of Norway. It was used effectively on the peat bogs of the

Falkland Islands, where the low ground pressure was a great advantage.

Bv 206 tracked oversnow vehicle

The **Bv 206** was developed from 1974 by Hägglund & Söner to meet the requirements of the Swedish army for a vehicle to replace the Bv 202 tracked oversnow vehicle. After trials with three batches of prototypes, the Swedish army placed an initial order for production vehicles in 1979, the first of them delivered in 1981. The Swedish army has a requirement for some 4,000 Bv 206s, and export orders have already been placed by Finland, Norway, the UK and the USA, while trials vehicles have been ordered by Canada and Italy. In the US Army the Bv 206 is known as the **Small Unit Support Vehicle M973**, and 268 vehicles have been ordered to replace the old M116 tracked oversnow vehicles which have been in service in Alaska since the 1960s.

Like the Bv 202, the Bv 206 consists of two units, front and rear, connected by a steering unit. The front unit contains the engine and transmission and has seats for five or six men, while the rear unit has seating for 11 men. When used in the cargo-carrying role, the Bv 206 can move a maximum of 600 kg (1,323 lb) in the front unit and 1400 kg (3,086 lb) in the rear unit.

The basic Bv 206 has fully enclosed front and rear bodies of fire-resistant glassfibre reinforced plastic. Each body unit is provided with a heater, which is essential in Sweden during the winter months. The basic vehicle is fully amphibious, being propelled in the water by its tracks. As an option the standard Ford V6 water-cooled petrol engine can be replaced by a Mercedes-Benz 5-cylinder inline turbocharged diesel developing 125 bhp (93 kW).

The anti-tank member of the family is the **Pvbv 2062**, which has an open-topped front body in which is mounted a Bofors 90-mm (3.54-in) recoilless rifle, the rear unit being used for ammunition. The front unit is provided with special roll-over protection bars which can be quickly lowered in action to allow the recoilless rifle to be used. In the future the 90-mm (3.54-in) recoilless rifle will be replaced by the Bofors BILL anti-tank guided missile, while for trials purposes the vehicle has already been fitted with the Hughes TOW anti-tank guided weapon, already used by the Swedish army. The command post version of the Bv 206 is the **Rabv 2061**, and this is fitted with extensive communications equipment. It has also been suggested that the Bv 206 could be fitted with the Swedish Giraffe surveillance radar (on a hydraulically-operated mast) for use in conjunction with the Bofors RBS 70 surface-to-air missile already fielded by the Swedish army.

Specification
Bv 206
Crew: front unit 5 or 6 and rear unit 11
Combat weight: 6340 kg (13,977 lb)
Powerplant: one Ford Model 2658E V6 petrol engine developing 136 bhp (101 kW)
Dimensions: length 6.86 m (22 ft 6 in); width 1.85 m (6 ft 0.8 in); height 2.40 m (7 ft 10.5 in)
Performance: maximum road speed 55 km/h (34 mph); maximum water speed 3 km/h (1.86 mph); maximum range 330 km (205 miles); fording amphibious; gradient 60 per cent; trench not available; vertical obstacle 0.5 m (1 ft 7.7 in)

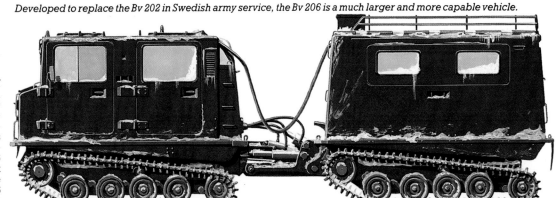

Developed to replace the Bv 202 in Swedish army service, the Bv 206 is a much larger and more capable vehicle.

Above: The Bv 206 has been fitted with a variety of weapons, including a TOW anti-tank missile mount. It has been ordered by several nations, including the USA, UK, Canada and Italy.

Right: The Bv 206 can transport five or six men in the front section and up to 11 in the rear section. Total cargo capacity is 2000 kg (4,409 lb) in the two sections. Both sections are driven, but the engine and transmission is in the front.

In winter, the Bv 206 enters its element, its fully heated enclosed cabins ensuring crew comfort in the often bitterly cold northern Swedish climate. The Bv 206 is fully amphibious, being propelled in water by its tracks.

Wheeled Armoured Personnel Carriers 1

The wheeled armoured personnel carrier (APC) has become one of the mainstays of modern forces and services and the boundary between an APC and a fighting vehicle is becoming somewhat indistinct.

A South African Ratel shows off its suspension on a concrete test track. Developed by Sandock-Austral (now Reumech Sandock), the Ratel went into production in the 1970s.

As this chapter and the next illustrate, the wheeled armoured personnel carrier is one of the most popular and prolific of military vehicles, and one which has also managed to move beyond the confines of solely military use to find a good deal of employment with other forces. The police and security forces in some of the more lively parts of the world are frequently seen to use them for effective anti-terrorist and other civil defence roles.

The wheeled APC's popularity stems, principally, from its relatively low first cost, especially when compared with the tracked armoured personnel carrier. It benefits from much lower running costs too.

The vehicles on display in this chapter range from the relatively simple - such as the German TM-170 - to the really quite complex - such as the South African Ratel. They also bring out the point that once you decide on a wheeled armoured personnel carrier there are not very many shapes to choose from. Compare, for example, the Renault VAB, the German Transportpanzer and the Spanish BMR-600. On a day with poor visibility and at a distance you would have a hard time telling one from another.

Another common feature of wheeled armoured personnel carriers is their longevity, which no doubt stems from their comparative mechanical simplicity and ease of maintenance. Once introduced into service, they tend to stay there until they fall to pieces.

Although some of the vehicles in this section date from the early 1960s they can all still be found in service with at least one military force somewhere in the world, even if it is not the one which originally purchased them. It is also worth remarking that in recent years several of the larger and better-armed armoured personnel carriers have been given gun turrets and firing ports - the Ratel, for example, can mount a 20-mm cannon or a 90-mm gun, whilst the BMR-600 can be fitted with a variety of weapons, including a 90-mm gun for the fire support role. These additions turn APCs into infantry fighting vehicles, although in most cases the aim has been to provide a powerful disincentive to riots and civil disorder rather than a military vehicle.

Renault VAB armoured personnel carrier

Some years ago the French army decided to issue its infantry battalions with both tracked and wheeled armoured personnel carriers, the former being the AMX-10P built by the ARE. To meet the requirement for the wheeled vehicle, designated **VAB** (*Véhicle de l'Avant Blindé*, or front armoured vehicle), prototypes were built by Panhard and Saviem/Renault in both 4×4 and 6×6 configurations. In May 1974 the Renault design was selected, and first production vehicles were delivered to the French army in 1976. The total French army requirement is for at least 4,000 vehicles, and production is already running at between 30 and 50 vehicles per month. The VAB has been offered on the export market, and by mid-1984 over 800 had been exported, sales having been made to the Ivory Coast, Cyprus, Lebanon, Mauritius, Morocco, Oman, Qatar and the United Arab Emirates. Of these Morocco is the largest operator, having purchased over 400 vehicles; some of these have already been lost in the fighting in the Sahara against the Polisario guerrillas.

The VAB is currently produced in 4×4 and 6×6 configurations, the latter costing about 10 per cent more but having greater cross-country capability. At present the French army uses only the 4×4 model.

The VAB has a hull of all-welded steel armour construction with the driver and commander at the front (the latter also operating the roof-mounted 7.62-mm/0.3-in machine-gun), the engine compartment to their immediate rear, and the troop compartment at the rear of the hull; an aisle connects the front of the vehicle with the troop compartment. The infantry enter and leave via two doors in the hull rear, and the troops are seated five down each side facing the centre. The VAB is fully amphibious, being propelled in the water by its wheels or, as an option, by two waterjets at the rear of the hull. Standard equipment on French army vehicles includes an NBC system and passive night-vision equipment.

French army VABs are fitted with a cupola-mounted 7.62-mm (0.3-in) machine-gun, but a wide range of other armament options is available, including turret-mounted 12.7-mm (0.5-in) machine-guns and 20-mm cannon. The basic vehicle has also been adopted for a wide range of other roles including a forward ambulance, internal security vehicle, command vehicle, repair vehicle, 81-mm mortar carrier, 120-mm (4.72-in) mortar tower, anti-aircraft vehicle (with twin 20-mm rapid-fire cannon or short range

Above: At present the French army uses only the 4×4 VAB, which is slightly cheaper than the 6×6. This particular VAB is not fitted with water jets under the hull at the rear, or with a roof-mounted weapon station, which normally carries a 7.62-mm (0.3-in) MG.

SAMs) and anti-tank vehicle. There are two versions of the latter, the **UTM 800** and the **Mephisto**. The former has a turret with four HOT ATGWs in the ready-to-launch position, while the latter has a similar number of HOT ATGWs on a launcher retracted flush along the top of the hull until it is required for action.

To reduce operation and procurement costs, well tried commercial components have been used in the design of the VAB range of armoured vehicles. Using the same automotive components, Renault has designed the **VBC 90** 6×6 armoured car which is now in service with Oman and the French Gendarmerie.

Specification
VAB (4×4 model)
Crew: 2+10
Combat weight: 13000 kg (28,660 lb)
Powerplant: one MAN 6-cylinder inline diesel developing 235 hp (175 kW)
Dimensions: length 5.98 m (19 ft 7.4 in); width 2.49 m (8 ft 2 in); height without armament 2.06 m (6 ft 9 in)
Performance: maximum road speed 92 km/h (57 mph); maximum road range 1000 km (621 miles); fording amphibious; gradient 60 per cent; vertical obstacle 0.6 m (2 ft 0 in); trench not applicable

Above: A Renault VAB (6×6) for the export market, fitted with the new Creusot-Loire one-man turret armed with a 20-mm cannon. The VAB can be fitted with a wide range of armament systems to enable it to undertake different roles on the battlefield.

Below: A Renault VAB (4×4) vehicle used by the French army and fitted with the RATAC (Radar de Tir pour Artillerie de Campagne) radar on the roof. This can detect, identify, locate and automatically track a variety of ground targets, including armoured vehicles.

Berliet VXB-170 armoured personnel carrier

After World War II Berliet was a major supplier of trucks to the French army, and in the late 1960s designed and built the prototype of a wheeled APC called the **BL-12** which used a number of standard heavy duty commercial components. Further development of this resulted in the **VXB-170** which was subsequently adopted by the French Gendarmerie as well as Gabon and Senegal. In 1975 Berliet was taken over by the Renault group, who had by then already built prototypes of 4×4 and 6×6 vehicles to meet the French army VAB requirement. With the accept-

ance of the Renault/Saviem vehicle to meet this requirement, production and marketing of the VXB-170 ceased as there was no point in two parts of the same group producing vehicles of a

A Berliet VXB (4×4) armoured personnel carrier at speed with armoured shutters over the driver's windscreens in the open position. When in a combat zone these cover the windscreens, and the driver then sees the terrain ahead through three roof-mounted periscopes, replaceable from inside the vehicle.

similar nature.

The hull of the VXB-170 is of all-welded steel construction with a maximum thickness of 7 mm (0.27 in). The driver is seated at the front of the hull in the centre with a large windscreen to his front and a smaller one on each side. In an internal security situation these windscreens are covered by armoured flaps and the driver then observes the terrain ahead through three roof-mounted periscopes. The troops enter the vehicle through three doors, one in each side and the third in the hull rear on the right side. Hatches are provided in the roof, and as usual a wide range of armament installations could be fitted. The vehicles used by the French Gendarmerie have a small SAMM one-man turret armed with a 7.62-mm (0.3-in) machine-gun and a 40-mm grenade-launcher which can be elevated from −15° to +60°; the grenade-launcher is normally used to launch tear gas grenades to disperse crowds.

The engine compartment is at the rear of the vehicle on the right side, and the diesel engine is coupled to a pre-selective gearbox with six forward and one reverse gear and a two-speed transfer case. Steering is power-assisted to reduce driver fatigue, and the suspension consists of helical springs and hydraulic shock absorbers. The VXB-170 is fully amphibious, being propelled in the water by its wheels at a speed of 4 km/h (2.5 mph); waterjets were offered as an option,

but as far as it is known these were never fitted to any production APCs. Vehicles used by the French Gendarmerie have a hydraulically-operated obstacle-clearing blade at the front of the hull, and optional equipment includes bullet-proof tyres, night-vision equipment, a winch and a heater.

Berliet offered three families of the VXB-170: one was for internal security use and the two others were the light reconnaissance vehicle and the light combat vehicle. These were offered with a wide range of weapon options including the Hispano-Suiza turret armed with twin 7.62-mm (0.3-in) machine-guns and a 60-mm breech/muzzle-loaded mortar, and the H-90 turret armed with a 90-mm (3.54-in) gun and a 7.62-mm (0.3-in) co-axial machine gun; both turrets were at that time standard for the Panhard AML-90 light armoured car.

Specification
VXB-170
Crew: 1+11
Combat weight: 12700 kg (27,997 lb)
Powerplant: one Berliet V 800 M V-8 diesel developing 170 hp (127 kW)
Dimensions: length 5.99 m (19 ft 8 in); width 2.50 m (8 ft 2.4 in); height without armament 2.05 m (6 ft 8.7 in)
Performance: maximum road speed 85 km/h (53 mph); maximum road range 750 km (466 miles); fording amphibious; gradient 60 per cent; vertical obstacle 0.3 m (1 ft 0 in); trench not applicable

Infantry armed with 9-mm MAT 49 sub-machine guns remount their Berliet VXB 170 (4×4) armoured personnel carrier while the 7.62-mm (0.3-in) machine-gunner prepares to give covering fire if required. The largest user of the VXB is the French Gendarmerie.

A Berliet VXB 170 (4×4) armoured personnel carrier with all roof hatches open. When the Berliet company was taken over by Renault the VXB family was phased out of production as the Renault VAB (4×4 and 6×6) series had more scope for further development.

FRANCE
Panhard VCR armoured personnel carrier

Following the success of its AML and M3 range of 4×4 armoured vehicles, Panhard went on to develop the ERC 6×6 armoured car and **VCR** 6×6 armoured personnel carrier, which share over 90 per cent common automotive components such as engine, transmission, suspension, steering and wheels. The first prototype of the VCR (*Véhicule de Combat à Roues*, or wheeled combat vehicle) was shown in 1977, the first production vehicles being completed just two years later. The VCR has been designed specifically for the export market, and known sales have been made to Argentina, Iraq and the United Arab Emirates.

The VCR has an all-welded hull which varies in thickness from 8 to 12 mm (0.315 to 0.47 in), the very front of the vehicle being almost identical with that of the Panhard M3 4×4 armoured personnel carrier. The driver is seated at the front with the engine to his right rear and the commander to his left rear. Both have a single-piece

hatch cover and periscopes for observation. The troop compartment is at the rear and has twin doors in the hull rear, with roof hatches and firing observation ports in the upper part. The main armament is normally mounted over the forward part of the troop compartment and can consist of a pintle-mounted 7.62-mm (0.3-in) or 12.7-mm (0.5-in) machine-gun, or a turret with similar weapons or a 20-mm cannon. An unusual feature of the VCR is its wheel arrangement as all six wheels are powered, with power-assisted steering on the front wheels only. When the VCR is travelling on roads, the centre road wheel on each side is normally raised off the ground. The VCR is fully amphibious, being propelled in the water by its wheels at a speed of 4 km/h (2.48 mph). Optional equipment includes an air-conditioning system, passive night-vision equipment, an NBC system and a front-mounted winch for self-recovery or assisting other vehicles.

The first model to enter production

was the **VCR/TH** anti-tank vehicle, of which 106 have been supplied to Iraq. This is fitted with the Euromissile UTM 800 turret with four HOT ATGWs in the ready-to-fire position and a further 10 missiles in the hull. Mounted over the rear part of the troop compartment is a remote-controlled 7.62-mm (0.3-in) machine-gun. This model has a crew of four and has been used in the fighting between Iraq and Iran. The ambulance version is the **VCR/IS**, and has a higher roof so the medical staff can stand up. This can carry six seated and two stretcher patients or four stretcher patients plus the three-man crew consisting of commander, driver and medical orderly. The ambulance version is known to have been supplied to the United Arab Emirates. The command post version is the **VCR/PC**, which has communications equipment and mapboards. The repair vehicle is the **VCR/AT**, fitted with a block and tackle for lifting out engines and other components; it carries a full range of spares and tools, but no winch.

There is also a 4×4 model of the VCR which has recently entered production for an undisclosed country, and this can be propelled in the water by two waterjets at a speed of 7.2 km/h (4.5 mph). For trials purposes one prototype of the VCR 4×4 has been fitted with the Euromissile Mephisto anti-tank system.

Specification
VCR
Crew: 3+9
Combat weight: 7000 kg (15,432 lb)
Powerplant: one Peugeot PRV V-6 petrol engine developing 155 hp (115.6 kW)
Dimensions: length 4.565 m (14 ft 11.7 in); width 2.495 m (8 ft 2.2 in); height without armament 2.03 m (6 ft 8 in)
Performance: maximum road speed 100 km/h (62 mph); maximum range 800 km (497 miles); fording amphibious; gradient 60 per cent; vertical obstacle 0.8 m (2 ft 7.5 in); trench 1.1 m (3 ft 7.3 in)

A standard Panhard VCR/TT armoured personnel carrier with a 20-mm cannon over the forward part of the troop compartment and a 7.62-mm (0.3-in) machine-gun at rear.

The Panhard VCR/TH anti-tank vehicle is fitted with a Euromissile UTM-800 one-man turret armed with four Euromissile HOT long-range anti-tank weapons.

The Panhard ENC 81-mm mortar gun carrier is a member of the ERC range of armoured cars which shares common components with the VCR range of APCs.

This Panhard VCR/TT armoured personnel carrier is fitted with a one-man turret armed with a 20-mm cannon. All VCRs are fully amphibious without preparation.

Panhard M3 armoured personnel carrier

The **M3** armoured personnel carrier was designed as a private venture by Panhard, and the first production vehicles were completed in 1971. The vehicle uses 95 per cent common automotive components with the Panhard AML armoured car, of which some 4,000 have now been built by Panhard or manufactured under licence in South Africa by Sandock-Austral. This enables a country to purchase a fleet of armoured cars and personnel carriers which share the same components, permitting significant savings in training and spare parts holdings. Over 25 countries have now purchased the vehicle, some for army use and some for police use. For example, Algeria has recently taken delivery of 44 vehicles for its *gendarmerie* fitted with a one-man turret armed with a machine-gun. It also has the VPC, VAT, VLA and VTS variants (see below) in service.

The hull of the M3 is of all-welded steel armour construction which varies in thickness from 8 to 11 mm (0.315 to 0.43 in). The driver is seated at the front of the hull, with the engine to his immediate rear. The engine is coupled to a manual gearbox with six forward and one reverse gear, and power is transmitted to the four road wheels by drive shafts that run inside the hull. The troop compartment is at the rear of the hull, a single door being provided in each side of the hull and twin doors in the hull rear. In the upper part of the hull side, which slopes inwards, are three hatches hinged at the top, these enabling troops to use their small arms from within the vehicle. The main armament is normally mounted in the roof to the rear of the engine compartment, this armament ranging from a turret with single or twin 7.62-mm (0.3-in) machine-guns to a power-operated turret with a 20-mm cannon. Over the rear of the troop compartment is a small hatch on which is normally installed a rail mount with a 7.62-mm (0.3-in) machine-gun.

The M3 is fully amphibious, being propelled in the water by its wheels at a speed of 4 km/h (2.48 mph), but it can only operate in lakes and rivers with a slow current. Many vehicles are fitted with channels which can be quickly removed and placed in front of the vehicle to allow it to cross ditches and other battlefield obstacles. If required, the M3 can be fitted with passive night-vision equipment for the driver, an air-conditioning system (essential in the Middle East) and smoke dischargers. The basic M3 has also been adopted for a number of more specialized roles.

This Panhard M3 armoured personnel carrier has the driver's hatch open and is fitted with a Creusot-Loire STB shield with a 7.62-mm (0.3-in) machine-gun. Designed as a private venture, the M3 has been purchased by more than 25 countries, with more than 4000 vehicles in service.

A standard Panhard M3 armoured personnel carrier showing rear troop doors and a roof-mounted 7.62-mm (0.3-in) machine-gun. All M3s are fully amphibious.

The anti-aircraft model is called the **M3 VDA** and is fitted with a power-operated turret armed with twin 20-mm cannon. The **M3 VAT** repair vehicle has a full range of tools and is fitted with a jib for lifting engines in the field. The **M3 VPC** command vehicle has extensive communications equipment. The ambulance model of the family is called the **M3 VTS** and is unarmed. The engineer vehicle version is the **M3**

The anti-aircraft member of the family is called the M3 VDA and is fitted with a one-man turret armed with twin 20-mm cannon.

VLA, and is fitted with a hydraulically-operated dozer blade at the front of the hull for clearing obstacles.

Specification
M3
Crew: 2+10
Combat weight: 6100 kg (13,448 lb)
Powerplant: one Panhard Model 4 HD 4-cylinder petrol engine developing

This Panhard M3 is used in the fire support role and is fitted with a Brandt Type HB 60-mm breech/muzzle loaded mortar in a special mount.

90 hp (67 kW)
Dimensions: length 4.45 m (14 ft 7.2 in); width 2.40 m (7 ft 10.5 in); height without armament 2.00 m (6 ft 6.7 in)
Performance: maximum road speed 90 km/h (56 mph); maximum ange 600 km (373 miles); fording amphibious; gradient 60 per cent; vertical obstacle 0.3 m (11¾ in); trench with one channel 0.8 m (2 ft 7.5 in) or with three channels 3.1 m (10 ft 2 in)

ACMAT armoured personnel carrier

For well over 25 years the Ateliers de Construction Mécanique de l'Atlantique (ACMAT) have been building a wide range of 4×4 and 6×6 cross-country trucks which have exceptional range and durability. These have been sold to more than 30 countries in Africa, the Middle East and the Far East. The company also realized that there was a market for an armoured personnel carrier on the same chassis and has therefore recently introduced the **TPK 4.20 VSC**, which is now in service with a number of countries including Gabon and the Ivory Coast.

The layout of the TPK 4.20 VSC is similar to that of a truck, with the engine at the front, commander and driver in the centre and the troop compartment at the rear. The commander and driver each have a windscreen to their front which can be quickly covered by an armoured shutter, a side door with a bullet-proof window in its upper part, and a single-piece hatch cover above their position.

An ACMAT VSC armoured personnel carrier with an open-topped troop compartment, in which can be mounted an 81-mm mortar or other types of weapons. The ACMAT armoured vehicles have exceptional range and durability.

The troops are seated on bench seats down each side of the vehicle, and can exit quickly through the two doors in the hull rear. If required, firing ports and/or vision blocks can be provided in the sides and rear of the troop compartment, and a 7.62-mm (0.3-in) or 12.7-mm (0.5-in) machine-gun turret can be mounted on the roof of the vehicle to give covering fire while the infantry dismount from the vehicle. Another model of the vehicle has an open-topped rear troop compartment with sides that can quickly folded down on the outside.

The well proven Perkins six-cylinder diesel engine is coupled to a manual gearbox with four forward and one reverse gear and a two-speed transfer case. Steering is of the worm and nut type, and the exceptional operating range of 1600 km (994 miles) results from the large-capacity fuel tank, which holds 370 litres (81.4 Imp gal). A spare wheel and tyre is normally carried on the wall to the immediate rear of the commander's and driver's position. Optional equipment includes an air-conditioning system, essential in many parts of the world if the infantry

are to arrive at their objective in any condition to fight, and different radio systems. Other armament options include a Euromissile MILAN ATGW system with additional missiles carried internally in the troop compartment, and an 81-mm Brandt mortar firing to the rear. In most infantry battalions six or eight mortars are normally issued to provide immediate and close-range support for the infantry. Artillery support is normally not organic to an infantry battalion, although for some missions (for example a long-range patrol in North Africa by a battalion of infantry in ACMAT trucks), it would often have a battery of four 105-mm (4.13-in) howitzers towed by similar vehicles.

Specification
TPK 4.20 VSC
Crew: 2+8
Combat weight: 7300 kg (16,094 lb)
Powerplant: one Perkins Model 6.354.4 6-cylinder diesel developing 125 hp (93 kW)
Dimensions: length 5.98 m (19 ft 7.4 in); width 2.07 m (6 ft 9.5 in); height 2.21 m (7 ft 3 in)
Performance: maximum road speed

95 km/h (59 mph); maximum range 1600 km (994 miles); fording 0.8 m (2 ft 7.5 in); gradient 60 per cent; trench not applicable

An ACMAT VBL light armoured car with all hatches closed and fitted with a one-man Creusot-Loire turret armed with one machine-gun.

SPAIN

BMR-600 infantry fighting vehicle

In the early 1970s the Spanish army issued a requirement for a 6×6 infantry fighting vehicle which was subsequently developed by ENASA and the Spanish army under the designation **Pegaso 3.500**, later **BMR-600** (*Blindado Medio de Ruedas*, or wheeled medium armoured vehicle). This was tested alongside the Swiss MOWAG Piranha 6×6 and French Renault VAB 6×6 vehicles, and accepted for service against a total requirement for at least 500. The company have now developed a complete family of vehicles using the same basic chassis, namely the **Pegaso 3560/1** armoured personnel carrier, the **Pegaso 3560/3** 81-mm mortar carrier, the **Pegaso 3560/4** 120-mm mortar towing vehicle, the **Pegaso 3560/5** battalion command vehicle and the **Pegaso 3564** fire-support vehicle which can be fitted with a variety of turrets such as the French TS-90 two-man turret armed with a 90-mm (3.54-in) gun. The **Pegaso 3562 VEC** cavalry scout vehicle has a brand new hull but uses the same automotive components as the basic infantry fighting vehicle, and is fitted with a two-man power-operated turret armed with a 20-mm or 25-mm cannon; this model is already in service with the Spanish army.

The hull of the BMR-600 armoured personnel carrier is of all-welded aluminium construction which provides complete protection against 7.62-mm (0.3-in) armour-piercing rounds over the frontal arc and 7.62-mm (0.3-in) ball over the remainder of the vehicle. The driver is seated at the front of the vehicle on the left with the machine-gunner/radio operator to his rear and the engine compartment to their right. The troop compartment is at the rear of the hull, and has accommodation for 11 fully equipped troops who enter and leave the vehicle through a power-operated ramp in the hull rear. Depending on the model, firing ports and/or vision blocks are provided in the troop compartment to allow the troops to fire their weapons from within the vehicle. The main armament normally

comprises a 7.62-mm (0.3-in) externally-mounted machine-gun, although other weapon stations can be fitted.

The vehicle is fully amphibious, and if required can be delivered with waterjets which give it a maximum water speed of 10 km/h (6.2 mph). Steering is powered to reduce driver fatigue, and is unusual in that it is on both the front and rear axles. The engine is coupled to an automatic transmission with six forward and one reverse gear, torque converter and hydraulic retarder.

Vehicles used by the Spanish army have a machine-gun with an elevation of +60° and a depression of −15° in a turret capable of 360° traverse. Some 2,500 rounds of ammunition are carried for this weapon. For trials purposes a BMR-600 has been fitted with the Euromissile HCT turret with four HOT wire-guided anti-tank missiles in the ready-to-launch position, additional missiles being carried in reserve. An anti-aircraft version with a 20-mm Meroka cannon or missiles is also being proposed.

Specification
BMR-600
Crew: 2+11
Combat weight: 13750 kg (30,313 lb)
Powerplant: one Pegaso 9157/8 6-cylinder diesel developing 306 hp (228 kW)
Dimensions: length 6.15 m (20 ft 2.1 in); width 2.50 m (8 ft 2.4 in); height to hull top 2.00 m (6 ft 6.7 in)
Performance: maximum road speed 100 km/h (62 mph); maximum range 700 km (435 miles); fording amphibious; gradient 68 per cent; vertical obstacle 0.8 m (2 ft 7.5 in); trench 1.2 m (3 ft 11.2 in)

A BMR-600 infantry fighting vehicle as used by the Spanish army and fitted with a one-man turret armed with a remote-controlled 12.7-mm (0.5-in) M2 HB machine-gun. An

unusual feature of this vehicle is that both the front and rear axles can be steered and the suspension adjusted to suit the type of terrain being crossed.

A BMR-600 used in the fire support and anti-tank role, and fitted with the French GIAT TS-90 turret armed with the long-barrelled 90-mm gun which can fire a wide range of fixed ammunition, including APFSDS.

BLR-600 armoured personnel carrier

The **BLR-600** (*Blindado Ligero de Ruedas*, or wheeled light armoured vehicle) is one of two armoured vehicles of the wheeled type currently being produced by Empresa Nacional de Autocamiones, the other being the BMR-600 6×6 infantry fighting vehicle. The BLR 4×4 vehicle is designed mainly for internal security operations, however, and is used in this role by the Spanish army and Spanish civil guard. Many of the automotive components are taken from standard commercial vehicles already in production.

The layout of the BLR is unusual, the commander and driver being seated at the front of the vehicle with excellent observation to the front and sides, a essential requirement for an internal security vehicle. The 12 fully equipped men are seated to the rear of the commander and driver and along the sides of the hull at the rear. The engine, coupled to an automatic transmission with torque converter and transfer case, is in the centre of the hull at the rear. No less than four doors are provided, one in each side and two in the rear, so that in the event of an ambush the troops quickly leave the vehicle through at least one of the doors. There are four hatches in the roof in addition to a cupola located on the forward part of the roof and armed with a 7.62-mm (0.3-in) machine-gun, with a shield to protect the gunner from enemy small arms fire. Depending on the actual model, firing ports and/or vision blocks are provided in the sides and rear of the troop compartment to allow the men to fire their weapons from within the vehicle.

The basic BLR is fitted with a six-cylinder water-cooled diesel developing 220 hp (164 kW), but the type is also available powered by a diesel engine developing only 170 hp (127 kW).

In many riot situations, petrol bombs are thrown at the internal security vehicles, and in addition to being fitted with the normal fire-suppression system in its engine compartment, the BLR has in each of the four road wheels hub outlets for fire suppressant in case the tyres catch fire. The tyres are fitted with puncture-proof Hutchinson O-rings. The commander's and driver's windows can be quickly covered by shutters, and each is provided with a standard water washer and another one filled with solvent to deal with paint or other liquids on the windscreens.

In addition to the less powerful engine already mentioned, the BLR can also be fitted with a wide range of optional equipment including a manual transmission in place of the automatic transmission, CS gas dischargers, loudspeakers (also essential in IS operations to warn crowds to disperse), power-take-off and so on.

More recently Empresa Nacional Santa Barbara, Macosa and Land Rover Santana have developed the BMU-2 armoured personnel carrier based on a long wheel base Land Rover chassis which is made in Spain by Land Rover Santana. This can carry six men including the driver and can be fitted with light weapons, although the manufacturer has suggested that it could also be fitted with a 106-mm (4.17-in) M40 series recoilless rifle for use in the anti-tank role.

Specification
BLR-600
Crew: 3 + 12
Combat weight: 11600 kg (25,574 lb)
Powerplant: one Pegaso 9220 6-cylinder diesel developing 220 hp (164 kW)
Dimensions: length 5.65 m (18 ft 6.4 in); width 2.5 m (8 ft 2.4 in); height without armament 1.99 m (6 ft 6.3 in)
Performance: maximum road speed 86 km/h (53.4 mph); maximum range 800 km (497 miles); fording 1.1 m (3 ft 7.3 in); gradient 75 per cent; vertical obstacle 0.6 m (1 ft 11.6 in); trench not applicable

The BLR (Blindado Ligero de Ruedas) was designed by Empresa Nacional de Autocamiones (who also build the BMR-600 IFV) mainly for use in the internal security role. It is now used by the Spanish army and Civil Guard. Armament normally comprises a 7.62-mm (0.3-in) or 12.7-mm (0.5-in) machine-gun.

A BLR (4×4) armoured personnel carrier from the rear with all of its doors in the open position. The large number of doors and hatches allows the 12 troops carried to quickly leave the vehicle in the event of an ambush. Firing ports and vision blocks are fitted.

Ratel 20 infantry fighting vehicles

For many years the British-supplied Alvis Saracen 6×6 armoured personnel carrier was the standard vehicle of its type in the South African army. When it became apparent that future supplies of armoured vehicles and their all-essential spare parts were in some doubt, the South Africans decided to build a new vehicle to meet their own requirements. Then as now, Sandock-Austral was building a modified version of the Panhard AML 4×4 light armoured car for the South African army under the name Eland, and the task of designing and building the new vehicle was given to this company. The first prototype was completed in 1976, the first production vehicles being completed just two years later, a remarkable achievement by any standards. Since then some 1,000 examples of the **Ratel** have been built for the home market and for export to Morocco. The South African army used the type operationally for the first time in Operation 'Reindeer' in May 1978, and since then Ratels have been used on many of the deep strikes into Angola, where the type's large operating range has proved to be very useful. The Moroccans have used them against the Polisario guerrillas in the Sahara desert.

The basic vehicle is called the **Ratel 20** and carries a total of 11 men in the form of the commander and gunner in the turret, the driver at the front, the anti-aircraft machine-gunner at the rear and seven fully equipped infantry. The two-man turret is armed with a French-designed 20-mm dual-feed cannon and co-axial 7.62-mm (0.3-in) machine-gun, a similar weapon being located on the turret roof for anti-aircraft defence. Mounted on each side of the turret are two smoke-dischargers, and there is a 7.62-mm (0.3-in) anti-aircraft machine-gun at the right rear of the hull roof. The **Ratel 60** has a similar crew, but has a two-man turret armed with a 60-mm breech-loaded mortar, a 7.62-mm (0.3-in) co-axial and a 7.62-mm (0.3-in) anti-aircraft machine-gun. The **Ratel 90** is the fire-support vehicle and has a two-man turret armed with the same 90-mm (3.54-in) gun as fitted to the Eland light armoured car, together with a 7.62-mm (0.3-in) co-axial and 7.62-mm (0.3-in) anti-aircraft machine-gun. Some 69 rounds of 90-mm (3.54-in) ammunition are carried, 29 in the turret and 40 in the hull, these being of the HEAT (high explosive anti-tank) or HE (high explosive) types. The command member of the family has a nine-man crew consisting of the commander, driver, main gunner and six command staff, and is armed with a turret-mounted 12.7-mm (0.5-in) M2 HB machine-gun and two 7.62-mm (0.3-in) anti-aircraft machine-guns. This variant has map boards, a pneumatically-operated mast, intercom, internal loudspeakers, public address system and three radios for communication with other vehicles and higher command staff.

A Ratel logistic support vehicle was developed, which would carry sufficient containerised fuel, ammunition and rations for a Ratel section to operate autonomously for eight days, but this was not adopted. In the late 1980s two further variants, an 81-mm mortar carrier and a special version with a turret-mounted 'Swift' anti-tank guided missile launcher, were placed in service.

Specification
Ratel 20
Crew: 11
Combat weight: 19000 kg (41,888 lb)
Powerplant: one Model D 3256 BTXF 6-cylinder diesel developing 282 hp (210 kW)
Dimensions: length 7.212 m (23 ft 8 in); width 2.516 m (8 ft 3 in); height overall 2.915 m (9 ft 6.8 in)
Performance: maximum road speed 105 km/h (65 mph); maximum range 1000 km (621 miles); fording 1.2 m (3 ft 11.2 in); gradient 60 per cent; vertical obstacle 0.35 m (1 ft 1.7 in); trench 1.15 m (3 ft 9.3 in)

Transportpanzer 1 armoured personnel carrier

In the mid-1960s the West German army decided to develop a complete new range of vehicles sharing many common components; the range included 4×4, 6×6 and 8×8 trucks, an 8×8 armoured reconnaissance vehicle and 4×4 and 6×6 armoured personnel carriers. The 8×8 armoured reconnaissance vehicle finally emerged as the Luchs, of which 408 were built between 1975 and 1978. In the end only the 6×6 armoured personnel carrier entered production as the **Transportpanzer 1**. In 1977 Thyssen Henschel was awarded a production contract for 996 vehicles, the first of which was completed in 1979. The 4×4 was then developed into the APE amphibious engineer reconnaissance vehicle by EWK, but this was never placed in production. In 1983 Venezuela ordered about 10 Transportpanzer vehicles fitted with a 12.7-mm (0.5-in) and a 7.62-mm (0.3-in) machine-gun, and these were delivered by late 1983.

When used as an armoured personnel carrier the Transportpanzer can carry 10 fully equipped troops in addition to the commander and driver. In the West German army, however, the Transportpanzer is normally used for more specialized roles. The NBC reconnaissance vehicle, of which 140 are being built, is fitted with NBC detection equipment, and devices for taking soil samples and for marking the ground. The engineers have 220 vehicles which they use for carrying mines and demolition equipment about the battlefield. The electronic warfare version is the **TPz-1 Eloka** and has a large number of antennae on the roof and a generator to provide sufficient power to run the equipment. The supply units have 220 vehicles to supply forward units with ammunition and other essential supplies, and this model can also be used as a forward ambulance carrying up to four stretcher patients. The radar carrier has a RASIT battlefield surveillance radar mounted on a hydraulic arm which is raised above the roof of the vehicle, and this can be operated up to 30 m (98 ft) from the vehicle by remote control. There is also a command and control model with extensive communications equipment and a generator at the rear. The West German army vehicles are normally armed with a 7.62-mm (0.3-in) machine-gun above the commander's position but other weapons can be fitted on the roof of the troop compartment, including a 20-mm cannon. Mounted on the left side of the hull is a bank of six smoke dischargers firing forwards.

The commander and driver are seated at the front of the Transportpanzer

Above: Thyssen-Henschel of Kassel are now building 996 Transportpanzer 1 (6×6) Fuchs amphibious vehicles for the West German army, which will be used in a wide range of roles including that of NBC reconnaissance vehicle, load carrier and engineer vehicle.

Right: The Transportpanzer 1 is fully amphibious, being driven through water at up to 10.5 km/h (6.5 mph) by twin propellers.

with the engine immediately behind them on the left and the troop compartment at the rear; a small aisle connects the front and rear compartments. The latter has seats down each side, and these seats can be quickly folded to allow cargo to be carried. The compartment has two doors in the rear, roof hatches and three vision blocks. The Transportpanzer is fully amphibious, being propelled in the water by two propellers at the rear of the hull for a maximum water speed of 10.5 km/h (6.5 mph). All West German vehicles have an NBC system and passive

night-vision equipment. Steering is power assisted on the front two axles.

For the export market a wider range of variants is offered, such as anti-tank vehicles with HOT, TOW or MILAN ATGWs, mortar carriers, a recovery vehicle and even an infantry fighting vehicle with firing ports and a turret-mounted 25-mm cannon.

Specification
Transportpanzer 1
Crew: 2+10

Combat weight: 17000 kg (37,479 lb)
Powerplant: one Mercedes-Benz OM 402A V-8 diesel developing 320 hp (239 kW)
Dimensions: length 6.76 m (22 ft 2.1 in); width 2.98 m (9 ft 9.3 in); height without armament 2.30 m (7 ft 6.5 in)
Performance: maximum road speed 105 km/h (65 mph); maximum range 800 km (497 miles); fording amphibious; gradient 70 per cent; trench 1.6 m (5 ft 3 in)

Condor armoured personnel carrier

Following the success of the UR-416 armoured personnel carrier, Thyssen Henschel decided to develop a new vehicle with improved armour protection, greater speed and range, increased load-carrying capability, fully amphibious performance and able to mount heavier armament installations. The first prototype of this vehicle, called the **Condor**, was completed in 1978 and an initial sale was soon made to Uruguay. In 1981 Malaysia placed its largest ever order for armoured vehicles when 459 Condors were ordered

from Thyssen Henschel and 186 SIB-MAS 6×6 vehicles from Belgium.

The Condor has an all-welded steel hull which provides the crew with protection from small arms fire and shell splinters. Wherever possible standard automotive components (such as the engine and transmission) are taken from commercial sources to keep costs to a minimum. The Condor has a three-man crew consisting of the commander, who would normally dismount with the troops, the gunner and the driver, and carries nine fully equipped

infantrymen. The driver is seated at the front left with the commander to his rear, each having a single-piece hatch cover that opens to the rear. The driver has excellent vision to his front and sides through large bullet-proof windows. In the combat area these would normally be covered by quickly erectable armoured shutters, forward observation then being maintained via a roof-mounted periscope. The engine compartment is to the right of the driver, and the troop compartment at the rear. Entry to the latter is effected via

three doors, one in each side and one in the rear. The infantry sit on individual seats and can use their weapons from within the vehicle via firing ports and/or vision blocks. The main armament installation is normally in the centre of the hull, and can range from a turret with one or twin 7.62-mm (0.3 in) machine-guns right up to a power-operated turret with a 20-mm cannon. For the anti-tank role the vehicle has already been fitted, for trials purposes, with the Euromissile HOT turret with four ATGWs in the ready-to-launch

Left: A Thyssen Henschel Condor (4×4) armoured personnel carrier with a Rheinmetall TUR-1 one-man turret armed with twin 7.62-mm (0.3-in) machine-guns. In 1981 Malaysia ordered a total of 450 Condors, and all of these have now been delivered. The vehicle is fully amphibious.

Right: A Thyssen Henschel Condor (4×4) armoured personnel carrier fitted with a one-man turret armed with a 20-mm cannon and co-axial 7.62-mm (0.3-in) machine-gun. In addition to its three-man crew of commander, gunner and driver it can also carry 12 fully-equipped troops and their supplies.

position, additional missiles being carried in the hull. When fitted with a one-man turret accommodating a 20-mm cannon and a 7.62-mm (0.3-in) machine-gun, totals of 220 rounds of 20-mm and 50 rounds of 7.62-mm (0.3-in) ready-use ammunition are carried. The turret can also be fitted with smoke-dischargers or grenade-launchers on each side.

The Condor is fully amphibious, being propelled in the water by a single rear-hull propeller at a speed of 8 km/h (5 mph); before the vehicle enters the water a trim vane is erected at the front of the hull and the bilge pumps are switched on. The Condor can be equipped with a wide range of optional equipment such as passive night-vision devices, an NBC and/or air-conditioning system, various intercoms and radios, and a winch. The last is suggested as standard equipment for many parts of the world, for although the Condor has excellent amphibious capability, like most other vehicles it sometimes needs assistance in order to leave a river when the banks are very steep.

Specification
Condor
Crew: 3+9
Combat weight: 12000 kg (26,455 lb)
Powerplant: one Daimler-Benz OM 352A 6-cylinder diesel developing 168 hp (125 kW)
Dimensions: length 6.05 m (19 ft 10.2 in); width 2.47 m (8 ft 1.2 in); height without armament 2.10 m (6 ft 10.7 in)
Performance: maximum road speed 100 km/h (62 mph); maximum range 900 km (559 miles); fording amphibious; gradient 60 per cent; vertical obstacle 0.55 m (1 ft 9.7 in); trench not applicable

---

UR-416 armoured personnel carrier

The Daimler-Benz Unimog 4×4 was developed originally as a civilian vehicle in the period after World War II and soon established an excellent reputation for its cross-country capabilities. Development has continued, and the Unimog range of trucks, with typical payloads of one to four tonnes, is today used by many armed forces around the world, including those of Argentina, West Germany, New Zealand and Australia to name but a few.

In the early 1960s Rheinstahl Maschinenbau (now part of the Thyssen group) saw that there was a considerable overseas market for an armoured personnel carrier based on the chassis of the Unimog 4×4 truck, and the first **UR-416** prototype was completed in 1965. Production got under way four years later. By 1984 almost 1,000 vehicles had been completed, with sales made to countries in Black Africa, North Africa, South and Central America and the Far East, as well as to some European countries. European operators deploy the type mainly for airport patrol and riot control, while other countries use them for reconnaissance as well as their designed roles of carrying troops. The UR-416 is a relatively inexpensive vehicle and is simple to maintain and operate. Spare parts are not a problem as the chassis is identical to that of the Mercedes-Benz Unimog light truck.

The all-welded hull is 9 mm (0.35 in) thick and provides the crew with protection from small arms fire and shell splinters. The commander and driver are seated at the front with the eight fully equipped troops to their rear, three down each side facing outwards and two at the rear facing the rear. Firing ports are provided in the hull sides and rear to allow the troops to fire their rifles from inside the vehicle, and if required these standard ports can be replaced by spherical firing ports and an observation block which allows each man to fire his rifle or submachine gun from within the vehicle in complete safety. The UR-416 has two roof hatches, the forward one normally being fitted with a 7.62-mm (0.3-in) machine-gun that can also be provided with a shield.

As with most vehicles of this type, the UR-416 can be fitted with a wide range of optional equipment such as a rear-mounted winch with a capacity of 5000 kg (11,023 lb), passive or active night-vision equipment, an obstacle-clearing blade at the front of the hull, a public address system, flashing lights, a heater, a fire extinguisher, an air-conditioning system and run-flat tyres. In addition to the normal pintle-mounted 7.62-mm (0.3-in) machine-gun, other armament installations that can be fitted include a turret with one or two 7.62-mm (0.3-in) machine-guns, a turret with a 20-mm cannon, or a special cupola for use in internal security roles with vision devices and the ability to mount a rifle to engage snipers. More specialized versions include a repair vehicle complete with jib crane and a complete set of tools, an ambulance, and a command vehicle with extensive communications equipment. It was also proposed that the UR-416 could be fitted with a recoilless rifle or anti-tank guided missiles for use in the anti-tank roles, but as far as is known neither of these were placed in production.

Specification
UR-416
Crew: 2+8
Combat weight: 7600 kg (16,755 lb)
Powerplant: one Daimler-Benz OM 352 6-cylinder diesel developing 120 hp (89 kW)
Dimensions: length 5.21 m (17 ft 1 in); width 2.30 m (7 ft 6.5 in); height without armament 2.225 m (7 ft 3.6 in)
Performance: maximum road speed 85 km/h (53 mph); maximum range 600 to 700 km (373 to 435 miles); fording 1.4 m (4 ft 7 in); gradient 75 per cent; vertical obstacle 0.55 m (1 ft 9.7 in); trench not applicable

Above: Thyssen Maschinenbau UR-416 armoured personnel carrier.

The Thyssen Maschinenbau UR-416 armoured personnel carrier is based on the chassis of the Mercedes-Benz Unimog (4×4) vehicle, which has exceptional cross-country mobility and is easy to maintain and operate.

TM 170 armoured personnel carrier

Using company money, Thyssen Maschinenbau of Witten-Annen has developed three light armoured personnel carriers of the wheeled variety, all of them using proven and common commercial components to keep procurement and operating costs to an absolute minimum. The vehicles are the **TM 170, TM 125** and the **TM 90**. The largest member of the family is the TM 170, which has a two-man crew and can carry 10 fully equipped infantrymen, although more often than not it is used in the internal security role for the rapid and safe transport of riot squads to spots at which they are needed.

In the early 1960s Bussing and Henschel in West Germany built some 600 of the Swiss-designed MOWAG MR 8 series of 4×4 armoured personnel carriers for the Federal German border police, although at a later date some of these were transferred to the state police. By the early 1980s it had been decided to start replacing this old vehicle with a more modern type, and after looking at the various vehicles on offer, the border police and state police selected the TM 170 under the designation **SW4**, the SW1 being the basic MR 8, the SW2 being the same vehicle with a turret-mounted 20-mm cannon and the SW3 an armoured version of the Mercedes-Benz light jeep type vehicle. At least 250 examples of the SW4 are required, although funding problems have meant that the initial order was for only 87 vehicles, the first of these being delivered in 1983.

The TM 170 has a hull of all-welded steel construction with the engine at the very front of the hull and coupled to a manual gearbox with four forward and one reverse gear. For road use the driver would normally select 4×2 (rear wheels only) drive, while for cross country the front axles would also be engaged for 4×4 (all wheel) drive. The commander and driver have bullet-proof windows to their front, and in combat these are covered by armoured shutters, observation then being obtained through roof-mounted periscopes. An entry door is provided in each side of the hull and rear, and firing ports and/or vision blocks enable the troops or police to aim their weapons safely from inside the vehicle. The basic vehicle is fully amphibious, being propelled in the water by its wheels; before the vehicle enters the water a trim vane is erected at the front of the hull. For increased water speed the TM 170 can be fitted with waterjets, which give a maximum speed of 9 km/h (5.6 mph). A variety of armament stations can be fitted on the roof including turret- or pintle-mounted 7.62-mm (0.3-in) machine-guns or even 20-mm cannon. Specialized equipment for the riot-control role includes a hydraulically-operated dozer blade at the front of the hull (for clearing street barricades and pushing cars and other obstacles out of the way) and a special observation cupola.

The TM 125 is slightly smaller than

the TM 170, has a crew of two and can carry 10 fully equipped men. The TM 90 is an armoured patrol vehicle rather than an armoured personnel carrier and has a crew of four, including the driver.

Specification
TM 170
Crew: 2 + 12
Combat weight: 9500 kg (20,944 lb)
Powerplant: one Daimler-Benz OM 352 supercharged diesel developing 168 hp (125 kW)
Dimensions: length 6.10 m (20 ft 0 in); width 2.45 m (8 ft 0.5 in); height 2.22 m

A Thyssen Maschinenbau TM 170 (4×4) armoured personnel carrier with the hatches over the windscreen in the lowered position. The TM 170 has been selected by the West German Border Guard and State Police to replace the old SW1 and SW2 vehicles.

(7 ft 3.4 in)
Performance: maximum road speed 100 km/h (62 mph); maximum range 670 km (416 miles); fording amphibious; gradient 80 per cent; vertical obstacle 0.5 m (1 ft 7.7 in); trench not applicable

---

PSZH-IV armoured personnel carrier

In the 1960s Hungary developed the FUG 4×4 amphibious scout car, which it uses in place of the Soviet BRDM vehicle. Further development resulted in a vehicle which was seen in the mid-1960s and called the **FUG-66** or **FUG-70**. It was originally thought that this was the replacement for the original FUG and that it would be used in place of the Soviet BRDM-2 4×4 amphibious scout car. After some time it was discovered that the new vehicle was in reality called the **PSZH-IV** and that its role was that of a personnel carrier, not an amphibious scout vehicle.

The hull of the PSZH-IV is of all-welded steel construction with a maximum thickness of 14 mm (0.55 in). The commander and driver are seated at the front of the vehicle, each being provided to his front with a windscreen that can be quickly covered by an armoured shutter with an integral periscope. Above their position is a single-piece roof hatch and to each side is a vision block. Mounted in the centre of the roof is a one-man turret armed with a 14.5-mm (0.57-in) KPVT machine-gun with a 7.62-mm (0.3-in) PKT machine-gun mounted co-axially to the left. Both weapons have an elevation of +30° and a depression of −5°, turret traverse being 360°. Totals of 500 rounds of 14.5-mm (0.57-in) and 2,000 rounds of 7.62-mm (0.3-in) ammunition are carried. The turret is of Hungarian design and is not the same as that fitted to the Soviet BRDM-2 amphibious scout car and a number of BTR-60 and OT-64 series of armoured personnel carriers.

The troops enter and leave the PSZH-IV through a door in each side of

the hull; each door is in two parts, upper and lower, and opens towards the front of the vehicle. The engine, which is the same as that installed in the earlier FUG amphibious scout car, is mounted at the rear of the hull. The PSZH-IV is fully amphibious, being propelled in the water at a speed of 9 km/h (5.6 mph) by two waterjets at the rear of the hull. Before the vehicle enters the water the bilge pumps are switched on and a trim vane is erected at the front of the hull (when not required the latter is stowed on the glacis plate). Like most Warsaw Pact vehicles developed in recent years, the PSZH-IV is fitted with a central tyre-pressure regulation system (allowing the driver to adjust the tyre pressure to suit the type of ground being crossed),

an NBC system and infra-red night-vision equipment for the gunner and commander.

There are a number of variants of the PSZH-IV including two command vehicles (one with and the other without the turret), an ambulance model (although loading of stretchers cannot be considered to be an easy occupation) and an NBC reconnaissance vehicle. The last is probably provided with equipment to detect NBC agents and then drop pennants into the ground to mark a path through the contaminated area.

Specification
PSZH-IV
Crew: 3 + 6
Combat weight: 7500 kg (16,535 lb)
Powerplant: Caspel 4-cyinder diesel

When the PSZH-IV was first seen in the early 1960s its role was believed to be that of a reconnaissance vehicle, but it was later discovered that it was in fact an armoured personnel carrier and carried six troops in addition to its three-man crew consisting of a commander, gunner and driver.

developing 100 hp (74.57 kW)
Dimensions: length 5.70 m (18 ft 8.4 in); width 2.50 m (8 ft 2.4 in); height 2.30 m (7 ft 7 in)
Performance: maximum road speed 80 km/h (50 mph); maximum range 500 km (311 miles); fording amphibious; gradient 60 per cent; vertical obstacle 0.4 m (1 ft 3.7 in); trench 0.6 m (1 ft 11.6 in)

BTR-152 armoured personnel carrier

The Soviet Union did not employ a tracked or wheeled armoured personnel carrier during World War II, and her infantry normally went in on foot or were carried on tanks. The **BTR-152** was first seen in public during 1951, but probably entered service several years before then. The vehicle consists basically of a ZIL-151 truck chassis fitted with a fully armoured body, later production vehicles from the BTR-152V1 onwards being based on the improved ZIL-157 truck chassis. From the early 1960s it was replaced in front-line Soviet motorized rifle divisions by the BTR-60 series of 8×8 armoured personnel carriers, which have better cross country capabilities. The BTR-152 and its variants have been widely exported by the Soviet Union, and even in 1984 the type remains in service with some 30 countries all over the world, and the BTR-152 has seen action in the Middle East (with Syria, Iraq and Egypt), Africa and the Far East.

The first model to enter service was the BTR-152, and has an open-topped troop compartment, in which the 17 troops sit on bench type seats running across the hull. The second model to enter service was the **BTR-152V1**, which retained the open-topped troop compartment but was fitted with a front-mounted winch and a central tyre-pressure regulation system with external air lines. The latter system enables the driver to adjust the tyre pressure to suit the type of ground being crossed. The **BTR-152V2** was not fitted with a winch, but did have a tyre-pressure regulation system. The **BTR-152V3** had winch, infra-red night-vision equipment and a central tyre-pressure regulation system with internal air lines more robust than those of the external system. The main drawback of these versions was the open-topped troop compartment, which left the infantry vulnerable to overhead shell bursts. This was rectified with the introduction of the **BTR-152K** which had full overhead protection. In all ver-

Above: A BTR-152 (6×6) armoured personnel carrier fitted with a central tyre pressure regulation system that allows the driver to adjust the pressure to suit the type of ground being crossed.

Right: Soviet BTR-152 (6×6) armoured personnel carriers being supported by T-54 tanks. Until the introduction of the BTR-60 (8×8) armoured personnel carrier in the 1960s the BTR-152 was the standard vehicle of the Soviet motorized rifle divisions.

sions of the BTR-152 firing ports are provided in the sides and rear of the troop compartment. The infantry enter and leave the vehicle via two doors in the rear of the hull.

The command version is called the **BTR-152U** and has a much higher roof so the command staff can work while standing; it also has an armoured roof. The anti-aircraft model is the **BTR-152A**, which has at its rear a mount with twin 14.5-mm (0.57-in) KPV heavy machine-guns that can be elevated from −5° to +80° with turret traverse through 360°. During the fighting in the Lebanon in 1982, the Israeli army captured a number of BTR-152s from the

PLO: these vehicles had the towed ZU-23 twin 23-mm mounted in the rear, these being much more effective than the 14.5-mm (0.57-in) KPVs.

The first armoured personnel carrier to be deployed by the Soviet Union after World War II was in fact the **BTR-40** 4×4 vehicle, which was based on a modified GAZ-63 truck chassis. This could carry eight troops in addition to its two-man crew and was also used as a reconnaissance vehicle until the introduction of the BRDM-1 in the 1950s. Both the BTR-40 and BTR-152 were normally armed with a pintle-mounted 7.62-mm (0.3-in) machine-gun.

Specification
BTR-152V1
Crew: 2+17
Combat weight: 8950 kg (19,731 lb)
Powerplant: one ZIL-123 6-cylinder petrol engine developing 110 hp (82 kW)
Dimensions: length 6.83 m (22 ft 4.9 in); width 2.32 m (7 ft 7.3 in); height 2.05 m (6 ft 8.7 in)
Performance: maximum road speed 75 km/h (47 mph); maximum road range 780 km (485 miles); fording 0.8 m (2 ft 7.5 in); vertical obstacle 0.6 m (1 ft 11.6 in); trench 0.69 m (2 ft 3.2 in)

BTR-60P series armoured personnel carrier

The BTR-152 6×6 armoured personnel carrier introduced into the Soviet army during the 1950s had a number of major shortcomings, including poor cross-country mobility (as it was based on a truck chassis) and lack of an amphibious capability. In the late 1960s the **BTR-60P** was introduced, and this and later variants have now replaced almost all BTR-152s used by the Soviet army, in which the BTR-60 series is normally used by the motorized rifle divisions while the tank divisions have the BMP-1 tracked MICVs. The BTR-60 series has been exported to some 30 countries, and Romania has produced a modified version under the designation **TAB-72**. The BTR-60 has seen action in many parts of the world, most recently in Grenada when a few BTR-60PBs were encountered and quickly destroyed by United States forces.

The members of the BTR-60 series are all fully amphibious, being propelled in the water by a single waterjet under the rear of the hull at a speed of 10 km/h (6.21 mph), and have a similar layout with the commander and driver at the front, troop compartment in the centre and the two petrol engines at

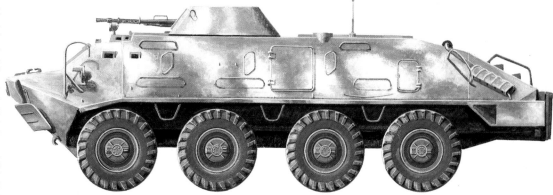

A BTR-60PB (8×8), which has the same turret as fitted to the BRDM-2 (4×4) scout car and the Czech OT-64C (8×8) vehicle.

the rear. Each engine drives one side of the vehicle. Power-assisted steering is provided on the front two axles.

The first model to enter service was designated BTR-60P, and has an open-topped troop compartment. This carried a total of 16 infantrymen who were seated on bench seats across the hull. Armament normally consisted of one 12.7-mm (0.5-in) and two 7.62-mm (0.3-in) machine-guns. This was soon replaced in production by the **BTR-60PA**,

which has a fully enclosed troop compartment and carries a maximum of 16 troops, although its normal complement is 12. This model is generally armed with a pintle-mounted 7.62-mm (0.3-in) machine-gun. The **BTR-60PB** is similar to the BTR-60PA but is fitted with the same one-man manual turret as installed on the BRDM-2 4×4 scout car and the Czech OT-64C(1) armoured personnel carrier, used by Czechoslovakia and Poland (as the

SKOT-2A) in place of the Soviet vehicle. The infantry carried by the BTR-60PA and the BTR-60PB can aim and fire their weapons from within the vehicle, although they normally have to dismount by climbing through the roof hatches. The command version of the vehicle is called the **BTR-60PU** and has additional communications equipment; there is also a forward air control vehicle, basically the BTR-60PB with the armament removed and an observation window in the forward part of the turret.

The BTR-60PB is now being replaced in the Soviet Union by the **BTR-70**, which is very similar in appearance and has the same turret, but introduces a slightly more powerful engine and has improved seating and exit arrangements for the infantry, the roof hatches being supplemented by a small door in the lower part of the hull between the second and third road wheels. The BTR-70 has seen action in Afghanistan, where a number have been fitted with a 30-mm grenade-launcher on the roof.

Specification
BTR-60PB
Crew: 2 + 14
Combat weight: 10300 kg (22,708 lb)

A BTR-60PB (8×8) armoured personnel carrier, powered by two petrol engines, each of which drives four wheels on one side of the vehicle. When afloat the vehicle is propelled in the water by a single water jet mounted in the hull rear.

Powerplant: two GAZ-49B 6-cylinder petrol engines each developing 90 hp (67 kW)
Dimensions: length 7.56 m (24 ft 9.6 in); width 2.825 m (9 ft 3.2 in); height to top of turret 2.31 m (7 ft 6.9 in)
Performance: maximum road speed 80 km/h (50 mph); maximum road range 500 km (311 miles); fording amphibious; gradient 60 per cent; vertical obstacle 0.4 m (1 ft 3.7 in); trench 2.0 m (6 ft 7 in)

A BTR-60PB (8×8) armoured personnel carrier swims ashore from a landing ship of the Soviet navy during exercises in the Red Banner Caucasian Military District.

OT-64 armoured personnel carrier

Rather than employ the Soviet BTR-60P series of 8×8 armoured personnel carriers, Czechoslovakia and Poland decided to develop their own vehicle. This entered service in 1964 and in addition to being used by Czechoslovakia and Poland has also been exported to Hungary, India, Libya, Morocco, Sudan, Syria and Uganda. The main advantages of the **OT-64** over the Soviet vehicle are that the former is powered by a diesel instead of two petrol engines (giving a longer operational range and reduced risk of fire) and that the troop compartment is fully enclosed. The OT-64 is heavier than the Soviet vehicle, however, and has a lower power-to-weight ratio. Many of the automotive components of the OT-64 are also used in the TATRA 813 range of 8×8 cross-country vehicles, which are widely used for civil and military applications.

The hull of the OT-64 is of all-welded steel construction that provides protection from small arms fire and shell splinters, maximum hull armour thickness being 10 mm (0.39 in). The commander and driver are seated at the front of the vehicle with the engine to their immediate rear. The troop compartment is at the rear of the hull, and access to this is gained via two doors in the hull rear. Roof hatches are provided over the top of the troop compartment, and firing ports are located in the side and rear. The OT-64 is fully amphibious, being driven in the water by two propellers mounted under the hull rear at a speed of 9 km/h (5.6 mph); before the vehicle enters the water a trim vane is erected at the front of the hull and the bilge pumps are switched on. All vehicles have night-vision equipment, front-mounted winch and an NBC system.

The original member of the family, the **OT-64A** (or **SKOT** in Poland) was sometimes fitted with a roof-mounted 7.62-mm (0.3-in) machine-gun. The **OT-64B (SKOT-2)** has on the roof to the rear of the engine compartment a plinth on which is mounted a 7.62-mm (0.3-in) or 12.7-mm (0.5-in) machine-gun fitted with a shield. The **OT-64C(1)**

or **SKOT-2A** has a one-man turret identical with that fitted to the BTR-60PB 8×8 APC and the BRDM-2 4×4 scout car; this turret is armed with a 14.5-mm (0.57-in) and a 7.62-mm (0.3-in) machine-gun. Some vehicles have been fitted with a wire-guided 'Sagger' ATGW on each side of the turret to give the vehicle an anti-tank capability. The **OT-64C(2)** or **SKOT-2AP** is used by Poland and has a new turret with a distinctive curved top which has the same armament as the turret of the OT-64C(1) but with an elevation of +89.5° to enable them to engage aircraft and helicopters. Other more specialized versions include a recovery vehicle and at least two command vehicles designated **R-2** and **R-3**.

Czechoslovakia also still uses a number of **OT-810** half-track vehicles. During World War II the Germans made the SdKfz 251 half-track at the Skoda plant in Pilsen, where production continued after the end of the war. In the 1950s many of these vehicles, by then designated the OT-810, were rebuilt and fitted with a diesel engine and overhead armour protection for the troop compartment. Most of the OT-810s have now been fitted with the 82-mm (3.23-in) M59A recoilless gun for use in the anti-tank role.

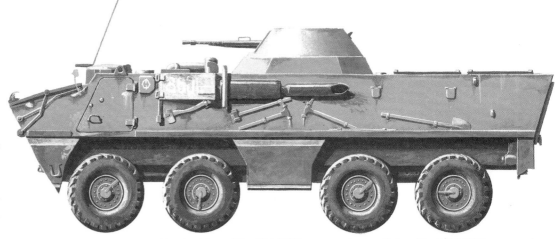

Above: The OT-64C(1) armoured personnel carrier and its earlier models are used by Czechoslovakia and Poland in place of the Soviet BTR-60 series.

Below: The OT-64C(1) armoured personnel carrier has the same one-man turret as fitted to the Soviet BRDM-2 (4×4) and BTR-60PB (8×80) vehicles.

Specification
OT-64C(1)
Crew: 2 + 15
Combat weight: 14500 kg (31,967 lb)
Powerplant: one Tatra V-8 diesel engine developing 180 hp (134 kW)
Dimensions: length 7.44 m (24 ft 5 in); width 2.55 m (8 ft 4.4 in); height overall

2.06 m (6 ft 9 in)
Performance: maximum road speed 94.4 km/h (59 mph); maximum road range 710 km (441 miles); fording amphibious; gradient 60 per cent; vertical obstacle 0.5 m (1 ft 7.7 in); trench 2.0 m (6 ft 7 in)

Wheeled Armoured Personnel Carriers 2

The flexibility and simplicity of the modern wheeled armoured personnel carrier (APC) has led to its continued popularity with military forces and to its becoming a common feature in the arsenals of civil defence forces.

Following on from the previous chapter, this section shows a wide range of wheeled APCs and again illustrates their tendency to remain in service for long periods. The DAF YP408 was first built in 1964 and is still to be found patrolling airports and military garrisons in the Netherlands. The British Saracen and Humber FV1600 are even older, dating from the middle of the 1950s, but both are now retired from British service, although they will doubtless appear in other countries for a few more years.

The Swiss MOWAG series has met with mixed fortunes; of the models shown here, only the Piranha has survived. It has been modified frequently to meet the demands of an ever-changing market and has appeared in a bewildering variety of models over the years. A GKN Defence Piranha family of APCs is in production under licence in the UK; the Piranha has also been built in Canada and Chile.

A strange feature of the wheeled APC is the apparent inability of the great US automobile industry to produce a satisfactory design. Only Cadillac Gage have persisted with their various models since the 1950s, although it seems unlikely that

The Piranha 6 x 6 Grizzly APC was developed by the Swiss MOWAG company. The turret is part of the TOW anti-tank guided weapon (ATGW) system.

their sales could have paid for the vast amount of development work which has taken place.

The US Army has always had a reluctance to employ wheeled armoured vehicles; they could scarcely get rid of their wartime armoured cars fast enough once World War II had ended and have bought a bare minimum of wheeled vehicles since, largely for

policing purposes. Had it not been for sales to other countries, the US armoured car business would have collapsed years ago.

The British Saxon APC has now entirely replaced the Saracen and Humber vehicles in infantry divisions. Other forces have received the Saxon, and some have been modified so that they approximate to a fighting vehicle.

The tendency now, in the late 1990s, appears to be towards the more expensive type of APC, and there are more 8 x 8 and even 10 x 10 designs on offer today than ever before. Experience has shown that a wheeled APC or IFV (infantry fighting vehicle) can carry the same armour and armament as a tracked one and has a better survivability rate.

DAF YP-408 armoured personnel carrier

Since well before World War II DAF has been a major supplier of wheeled vehicles to the Royal Netherlands army, and in 1958 it built prototypes of an eight-wheeled armoured personnel carrier. With a number of modifications and the replacement of the Hercules JXLD petrol engine by a more powerful DAF diesel engine, this was accepted for service as the **DAF YP-408**, the first production vehicles being delivered in 1968 and final deliveries taking place in 1968. A total of 750 vehicles were built for the Dutch army and five are used by Surinam, these latter being passed on when the Dutch withdrew in the 1970s. In the Dutch army the YP-408 is now rapidly being replaced by the YPR-765, which is the Dutch version of the FMC Armoured Infantry Fighting Vehicle, and it is expected that all YP-408s will have been phased out of service by 1988 at the latest.

The hull of the YP-408 is of all-welded steel construction which varies in thickness from 8 mm (0.315 in) to 15 mm (0.59 in). The engine is at the front, the commander and driver are to the rear of the engine compartment, and the troop compartment is at the rear. The diesel engine is coupled to a manual gearbox with five forward and one reverse gear and a two-speed transfer box. The YP-408 has a total of eight road wheels (four on each side), but only six of these are powered, making the YP-408 an 8×6 vehicle; it is the second pair of road wheels which is unpowered. Steering is power-assisted on the front four wheels, and the tyres have reinforced side walls that enable the vehicle to be driven for a distance of 50 km (31 miles) at a reduced speed after they have been punctured. The driver is seated on the left with the commander/machine-gunner to his right. The 12.7-mm (0.5-in) M2 machine-gun can be traversed through 360° and elevated from −8° to +70°.

The 10 fully equipped troops enter and leave the YP-408 through two doors in the hull rear, and are seated five down each side facing each other.

Hatches are provided over the top of the troop compartment. Standard equipment includes a heater, but the YP-408 lacks an NBC system and amphibious capability. If required, infra-red equipment can be fitted for the driver and the machine-gunner.

The basic armoured personnel carrier is called the **PWI-S(GR)**, this standing for the **Pantser Wagen Infanterie-Standaard(Groep)**; the platoon commander's vehicle is the **PWI-S(PC)**, and has a crew of nine and additional communications equipment; and the battalion or company commander's vehicle is the **PWCO**, this having a crew of six, additional communications equipment and mapboards. The ambulance model, which is unarmed, is the **PW-GWT** which can carry two stretcher patients and four seated patients plus its three-man crew (driver and two medical orderlies). The DAF YP-408 APCs were withdrawn from general service with the Dutch Army in early the 1990s, but a number were retained and are still use by airport security patrols, border guards and military police. The Army's requirement for the APC role was filled by the American FMC Armoured Infantry Fighting Vehicle, described elsewhere, built in Holland under licence.

Specification
YP-408
Crew: 2+10
Combat weight: 12000 kg (26,455 lb)
Powerplant: one DAF Model DS 575 6-cylinder diesel developing 165 hp (123 kW)
Dimensions: length 6.23 m (20 ft 5.3 in); width 2.40 m (7 ft 10.5 in); height (including MG) 2.37 m (7 ft 9.3 in)
Performance: maximum road speed 80 km/h (50 mph); maximum road range 500 km (311 miles); fording 1.2 m (3 ft 11 in); gradient 60 per cent; vertical obstacle 0.7 m (2 ft 4 in); trench 1.2 m (3 ft 11 in)

The YP-408MT tows a French-built Brandt 120-mm mortar, and transports the seven-man mortar team as well as up to 50 mortar bombs. The machine-gun is a Browning M2 HB 12.7-mm and is operated by the vehicle commander.

First produced in 1968, the 8×6 DAF YP-408 is soon to be replaced by the tracked FMC infantry fighting vehicle. With a crew of two, the YP-408 can transport up to 10 fully-equipped infantrymen, but has no NBC protection or amphibious capability.

MOWAG Roland armoured personnel carrier

The **MOWAG Roland** 4×4 is the smallest vehicle currently produced by the MOWAG company of Kreuzlingen, Switzerland, and is used mainly in the internal security role. The first prototype was completed in 1963, the first production vehicles being completed the following year. Known operators of the Roland include Argentina, Bolivia, Chile, Greece, Iraq, Mexico and Peru. The hull of Roland is of all-welded steel armour construction that provides the crew with complete protection from 7.62-mm (0.3-in) small arms fire. The driver is at the front, the crew compartment in the centre and the engine at the rear on the left side; there is also an aisle in the right side of the hull that leads to a door in the hull rear. The driver has a roof hatch, and there is a single door in each side of the hull. In each of the three doors is a firing port (with a vision block above) which allows three of the embarked infantrymen to fire their rifles or sub-machine guns from within the vehicle in safety.

The basic Roland was designed from the outset for relatively easy conversion to a number of roles, including those of personnel, cargo or ammunition carrier, reconnaissance, command and communications post or, as illustrated, for the ambulance role.

In the centre of the roof is installed the main armament; this is normally a simple cupola with an externally mounted 12.7-mm (0.5-in) or 7.62-mm (0.3-in) machine-gun. One of the alternative weapon stations is a turret on top of which is a remotely-controlled 7.62-mm (0.3-in) machine-gun fired from within the turret.

The petrol engine is coupled to a manual gearbox with four forward and one reverse gear and a two-speed transfer case. More recent production Rolands are offered with an automatic gearbox to reduce driver fatigue.

When used in the internal security role, the Roland is normally fitted with an obstacle-clearing blade at the front of the hull, a public address system, wire mesh protection for the head-lamps and sometimes the vision blocks as well, a siren and flashing lights. Another option is MOWAG bulletproof cross-country wheels. These consist of metal discs on each side of the tyre, the outside ones having ribs which assist the vehicle when crossing through mud.

In the late 1960s the company designed and built another 4×4 armoured personnel carrier called the **MOWAG Grenadier**, which can carry a total of nine men including the commander and driver. This model was sold to a number of countries but is no longer offered, having been replaced by the Piranha range of 4×4, 6×6 and 8×8 armoured vehicles. Typical armament installations for the Grenadier included a one-man turret armed with a 20-mm Hispano-Suiza cannon and a turret with twin 80-mm (3.15-in) rocket-launchers. The vehicle is fully amphibious, being propelled in the water by a propeller under the rear of the hull. Waterborne steering is accomplished by turning the steering wheel in the normal manner to move two parallel rudders mounted to the immediate rear of the propeller.

Specification
Roland
Crew: 3+3
Combat weight: 4700 kg (10,362 lb)
Powerplant: one V-8 petrol engine

developing 202 hp (151 kW)
Dimensions: length 4.44 m (14 ft 6.8 in); width 2.01 m (6 ft 7 in); height (with turret) 2.03 m (6 ft 8 in)
Performance: maximum road speed 110 km/h (68 mph); maximum range 550 km (341 miles); fording 1.0 m (3 ft 3.4 in); gradient 60 per cent; vertical obstacle 0.4 m (1 ft 4 in); trench not applicable

The anti-tank Roland is armed with three Messerschmitt-Bölkow-Blohm Mamba wire-guided anti-tank missiles. The equipment is mounted directly onto the remote-controlled 7.62-mm machine-gun turret.

SWITZERLAND
MOWAG MR 8 series armoured personnel carriers

Since the end of World War II the MOWAG company has manufactured a wide range of tracked and wheeled armoured fighting vehicles aimed mainly at the export market, and has also built prototypes of armoured vehicles for foreign governments. For example, MOWAG built some of the prototypes of the West German Marder mechanized infantry combat vehicle. In the 1950s a 4×4 series of armoured vehicles were designed and built under the company designation **MOWAG MR 8**, and this was subsequently adopted by the West German border police in two configurations, the **SW1** and the **SW2**. The first batch of 20 or so vehicles was supplied direct by MOWAG, but main production was undertaken in West Germany by Henschel and Büssing. Total production in West Germany amounted to about 600 vehicles.

The SW1 (**geschützter Sonderwagen Kfz 91**) is the armoured personnel carrier model and accommodates five men plus the commander and driver, while the SW2 has a slightly different hull top and is fitted with a one-man turret armed with a 20-mm Hispano-Suiza cannon plus four smoke-dischargers mounted on each side of the turret to fire forwards.

The same basic hull is used for both the SW1 and SW2, with slight differences to the roof. In the SW1 the commander and driver are seated at the front of the hull with a windscreen in front of each man; these windscreens can be quickly covered by armoured shutters with integral vision blocks. The driver also has a roof hatch above his position for driving in the head-out position. The troop compartment is at the rear of the vehicle with the engine compartment to its left. In each side of the hull is a two-part door that opens left and right; each door has a vision block and a firing port. Over the top of the troop compartment are two roof hatches and an unusual cupola. The latter is fixed but split down the middle so that it can be opened vertically if required; in each half are three fixed vision blocks. When the cupola is in

the normal position complete visibility is possible through 360°.

Unlike more recent MOWAG wheeled armoured vehicles, the MR 8 series vehicles have no amphibious capability and are not fitted with an NBC system or any type of night vision equipment, although both of the latter could have been fitted if so required by the user.

MOWAG continued to develop the MR 8 series for other export markets, and these variants included the **MR 8-09** sporting a one-man turret armed with a 20-mm cannon, the **MR 8-23** that had a two-man turret armed with a 90-mm (3.54-in) gun and a 7.62-mm (0.3-in) co-axial machine-gun, and the **MR 9-32** fitted with a 120-mm (4.72-in) mortar at the rear of the hull. The last version had an open-top hull, and before the mortar could be fired it had to be lowered to the ground. In spite of these variations the MR 8 series found few buyers; the only considerable sale was to the West German Border Police, and when East and West Germany were re-united the orientation and equipment of this force changed considerably. The MR vehicles have been allowed to 'waste out' and few now remain in use.

Specification
MR 8
Crew: 2+5
Combat weight: 8200 kg (18,078 lb)
Powerplant: one Chrysler Type R 361 6-cylinder petrol engine developing 161 hp (120 kW)
Dimensions: length 5.31 m (17 ft 5 in); width 2.2 m (7 ft 3 in); height (hull) 1.88 m (6 ft 2 in)
Performance: maximum road speed 80 km/h (50 mph); maximum range 400 km (248 miles); fording 1.1 m (3 ft 7 in); gradient 60 per cent; vertical obstacle 0.4 m (1 ft 4 in); trench not applicable

West German Bundesgrenzschutz (BGS, or Federal Border Police) parade with their armoured but unarmed MR 8 (model SW1) *personnel carriers. The first Swiss-built models were delivered in 1959/60, subsequently built in the Federal Republic.*

The SW2 model of the MR 8, also used by the BSG, differs in being armed with an Hispano 20-mm cannon and having a crew of four instead of *seven. Smoke dischargers are mounted on each side of the 20-mm turret.*

✚ MOWAG Piranha armoured personnel carrier

The **MOWAG Piranha** range of 4×4, 6×6 and 8×8 armoured personnel carriers was designed by MOWAG in the late 1960s, and the first prototype was completed in Switzerland in 1972, with first production vehicles following four years later. As with all recent MOWAG vehicles, the Piranha family was a private venture and developed without government support. In 1977 Canada decided to adopt the 6×6 version and production was undertaken in Canada by the Diesel Division of General Motors Canada, 491 being built for the Canadian Armed Forces between 1979 and 1982. Canada uses three versions of the 6×6 Piranha: the 76-mm (2.99-in) **Cougar Gun Wheeled Fire Support Vehicle**, which has the same two-man turret as the British Combat Vehicle Reconnaissance (Tracked) Scorpion; the **Grizzly Wheeled Armoured Personnel Carrier**, which has a one-man turret armed with a 12.7-mm (0.5-in) and a 7.62-mm (0.3-in) machine-gun and has a three-man crew consisting of commander, gunner and driver plus six fully equipped troops; and the **Husky Wheeled Maintenance and Recovery Vehicle**, which supports the other vehicles in the field. In addition to being used by Canada, the Piranha range of vehicles is used also by Chile (licence production), Ghana, Liberia, Nigeria and Sierra Leone, and in 1983 the 6×6 model was evaluated by the Swiss army as an anti-tank vehicle fitted with the Hughes TOW anti-tank system. After evaluating a number of different vehicles both tracked and wheeled, the USA selected the 8×8 version of the Piranha to meet its requirement for a Light Armored Vehicle (LAV) and the first of these was completed for the US Marine Corps in late 1983. These have a two-man power-operated turret armed with a Hughes Helicopters 25-mm cannon (as fitted to the Bradley) and a co-axial 7.62-mm (0.3-in) machine-gun. Variants required by the US Marines include a logistics support vehicle, a command vehicle, a repair vehicle, a mortar carrier and an anti-tank model. The US Army withdrew from the programme early in 1984.

The hull of the Piranha is of all-welded steel construction, which provides protection from small arms fire. On the six-wheeled version the driver is at the front on the left with the commander to his rear and the engine to the right. The troop compartment is at the rear of the hull, and entry to this is gained via two doors in the hull rear. Armament depends on the role, but can range from a single-man turret up to a two-man power-operated turret armed with a 90-mm (3.54-in) Cockerill gun. If a heavy weapon such as this is fitted, however, the commander is normally in the turret and a reduced number of troops is carried.

All members of the Piranha family are fully amphibious, being propelled in the water by two propellers at the rear of the hull. Optional equipment includes such things as night vision equipment, an NBC system, an air-conditioning system (essential in the Middle East) and so on.

Specification
Piranha (6×6 version without armament)
Crew: 2+12
Combat weight: 10500 kg (23,148 lb)
Powerplant: one Detroit Diesel 6V-53T developing 300 hp (224 kW)
Dimensions: length 5.97 m (19 ft 7 in), width 2.50 m (8 ft 2.4 in); height 1.85 m (6 ft 1 in)
Performance: maximum road speed 100 km/h (62 mph); maximum range 600 km (373 miles); fording amphibious; gradient 70 per cent; vertical obstacle 0.5 m (1 ft 8 in); trench not applicable

The 4×4 version of the Piranha has a maximum load of 10 infantrymen and, as here, can be armed with a remote-controlled 7.62-mm machine-gun mount. All of the Piranha family are fully amphibious, being driven by twin propellers in water.

Armed with the Belgian Cockerill 90-mm gun, the 6×6 Piranha is capable of fulfilling the infantry support role so often required of the modern infantry fighting vehicle. Such a large weapon is mounted at the expense of the number of troops carried.

AV Corporation Dragoon APC

In the late 1970s the US Army Military Police issued a requirement for a vehicle which would be airportable in a Lockheed C-130 Hercules transport aircraft and be suitable for both air base protection and convoy escort. The requirement lapsed, but the Verne Corporation went ahead and with its own money built two prototypes of a vehicle which was eventually called the **Verne Dragoon**. In appearance the Dragoon is very similar to the Cadillac Gage V-100 and V-150 range of 4×4 multi-mission vehicles, but shares many common components with the M113A2 full-tracked armoured personnel carrier and the M809 6×6 5-ton truck, which are used all over the world. From the M113A2 the Dragoon uses the engine, starter, periscopes, bilge pumps, switches, electrical and hydraulic components (to name but a few), with the obvious logistical advantages.

The hull of the Dragoon is of all-welded steel construction which provides the crew with complete protection from 5.56-mm (0.22-in) and 7.62-mm (0.3-in) small arms fire and shell splinters. The driver is seated at the front on the left with another crew

Although apparently very similar to the well established Cadillac Gage Commando range, the Dragoon is designed for maximum commonality with the existing US Army inventory. As is usual today, a variety of weapons can be fitted, including the Arrowpointe 90-mm turret with the Mk III Cockerill 90-mm gun.

member to his right, the main crew compartment is in the centre, and the engine is at the rear of the hull on the right side (on the Cadillac Gage vehicles it is on the left side), and an aisle connects the main crew compartment with the door in the hull rear. The troops normally enter and leave the vehicle via a door in each side of the hull, the lower part of each door folding down to form a step while the upper part hinges to one side. Firing ports with a vision block above are provided in the sides and rear of the crew compartment. The diesel engine is coupled to an automatic transmission with five forward and one reverse gear and a single-speed transfer case, and steering is hydraulic on the front axle. The Dragoon is fully amphibious, being propelled in the water by its wheels at a speed of 4.8 km/h (3 mph), with three bilge pumps extracting any water that seeps in through the door and hatch openings.

When being used as a basic armoured personnel carrier the Dragoon is normally fitted with an M113 type cupola with a pintle-mounted 12.7-mm (0.5-in) or 7.62-mm (0.3-in) machine-gun to allow the maximum number of troops to be carried. Other armament installations are available, however, including two-man power-operated turrets armed with a 25-mm cannon or a 90-mm (3.54-in) gun, 7.62-mm (0.3-in) co-axial and 7.62-mm (0.3-in) anti-aircraft machine-guns. More specialized versions include com-

mand, engineer, anti-tank (with TOW ATGWs), recovery and internal security vehicles.

In 1982 a number of Dragoons were supplied to the US Army and US Navy. At that time they were manufactured by the Arrowpoint Corporation, and they and Verne now joined together to form the A.V. Corporation. A considerable range of variant models, including mortar carriers, electronic warfare vehicles, missile carriers, 90-mm gun vehicle and an armoured maintenance vehicle have been developed, and sales have been made to Thailand and Venezuela, in addition to further numbers supplied to United States forces.

Specification
Dragoon
Crew: typically 3+6
Combat weight: typically 12700 kg (27,998 lb)
Powerplant: one Detroit Diesel Model 6V-53T diesel developing 300 hp (224 kW)
Dimensions: length 5.588 m (18 ft 4 in); width 2.438 m (8 ft 0 in); height (hull top) 2.133 m (7 ft 0 in) but varies with weapon fit
Performance: maximum road speed 116 km/h (72 mph); maximum road range 1045 km (650 miles); fording amphibious; gradient 60 per cent; vertical obstacle 0.99 m (3 ft 3 in); trench not applicable

The electronic warfare Dragoon is undergoing trials with the US Ninth Infantry division. Roles include the jamming of high speed communications, and advanced battlefield direction finding.

Seen on deployment to Egypt, the long-range video optical surveillance vehicle offers commanders a highly mobile, armoured observation capacity, giving real-time communication.

Cadillac Gage V-150 Commando armoured personnel carrier

In the early 1960s the Cadillac Gage Company of Detroit, Michigan, started to design a multi-purpose armoured vehicle which was finally unveiled in 1963 as the **Cadillac Gage V-100 Commando.** Trials were so successful that the type entered production the following year for the export market. The conflict in South Vietnam soon showed that there was an urgent need for a wheeled vehicle for patrolling air bases, fuel dumps and other high risk areas as well as escorting convoys from one base to another, and soon significant numbers of vehicles were shipped to South Vietnam for use by the South Vietnamese army and the United States forces (including the military police and US Air Force).

The first model was powered by a Chrysler petrol engine, and was followed by the much larger **V-200 Commando** with a more powerful engine, greater weight and increased load-carrying capability. The V-200 was sold only to Singapore and is no longer offered by the company. In the early 1970s the V-100 and V-200 were replaced in production by the **V-150 Commando,** which is still the current production model. The V-150 introduced a number of improvements, the most significant of which is the installation of a diesel engine which gives the vehicle a much increased range of action as well as reducing the risk of fire. So far over 4,000 V-100, V-150 and V-200 armoured vehicles have been built, and known purchasers have included Bolivia, Botswana, Cameroun, Dominican Republic, Ethiopia, Haiti, Gabon, Guatemala, Indonesia, Jamaica, Kuwait, Malaysia, Oman, Panama, Philippines, Saudi Arabia,

Singapore, Somalia, Sudan, Taiwan, Thailand, Tunisia, Turkey, United States and South Vietnam. The stretched model of the V-150, the **V-150 S**, was entered in the Light Armored Vehicle (LAV) competition together with the new 6×6 Cadillac Gage V-300 Commando, but this competition was won by the Canadian 8×8 vehicle based on the Swiss Piranha.

The V-150 Commando is called a multi-mission vehicle as it can be used for a wide range of roles. In the basic armoured personnel carrier model it has a three-man crew (commander, gunner and driver) and can carry nine fully equipped troops, who enter and leave the vehicle via doors in the hull

sides and rear. A very wide range of armament installations can be fitted, including a one-man turret with various combinations of 7.62-mm (0.3-in) and 12.7-mm (0.5-in) machine-guns; a two-man power-operated turret with 90-mm (3.54-in) or 76-mm (2.99-in) gun and 7.62-mm co-axial and 7.62-mm (0.3-in) anti-aircraft machine-guns; and a turret with 20-mm cannon and 7.62-mm co-axial and 7.62-mm anti-aircraft machine-guns. There is also an anti-aircraft vehicle with a 20-mm Vulcan six-barrelled anti-aircraft weapon, a mortar carrier with an 81-mm mortar, an anti-tank vehicle with the Hughes TOW anti-tank guided weapon, a command vehicle with raised roof to allow

the command staff to work in the upright position, a riot control vehicle, and a recovery vehicle.

Specification
V-150 Commando
Crew: 3+9
Combat weight: 9888 kg (21,800 lb)
Powerplant: one V-8 diesel developing 202 bhp (151 kW)
Dimensions: length 5.689 m (18 ft 8 in); width 2.26 m (7 ft 5 in); height (hull top) 1.981 m (6 ft 6 in)
Performance: maximum road speed 88.5 km/h (55 mph); maximum range 643 km (400 miles); fording amphibious; gradient 60 per cent; vertical obstacle 0.609 m (2 ft 0 in)

Developed from the V-100 of 1962, the V-150 entered production in 1971. A wide range of armament can be fitted, including the two-man 25-mm gun turret.

Cadillac Gage V-300 Commando armoured personnel carrier

In the last 20 years the Cadillac Gage Company of Detroit, Michigan has built some 4,000 of its Commando range of 4×4 multi-mission vehicles in three models: the V-100, V-150 (current production model) and V-200. In recent years, however, there has been a trend to 6×6 vehicles with their increased load-carrying capabilities, and for this reason in 1979 the company as a private venture built two prototypes of the **Cadillac Gage Commando V-300** 6×6 vehicle which can be used for a wide range of roles, including use as an armoured personnel carrier. In 1982 Panama placed an order for 12 V-300 vehicles, which were all delivered the following year. Four different models were selected by Panama: a fire-support vehicle with 90-mm (3.54-in) Cockerill gun, a recovery vehicle, and two types fitted with different machine-gun installations. Cadillac Gage also supplied three V-300s for the US Army and US Marine Corps Light Armoured Vehicle (LAV) competition; of these one was fitted with a two-man turret armed with a 90-mm (3.54-in) Cockerill Mk III gun, while the other two were fitted with a two-man turret armed with the Hughes Helicopters 25-mm Chain Gun as installed in the FMC M2 and M3 tracked vehicles. In the end, however, the LAV programme was won by General Motors of Canada with an 8×8 version of the MOWAG Piranha.

The layout of the V-300 is quite different from that of the V-150. The driver is seated at the front left with the engine to his right. The engine is coupled to a fully automatic Allison MT-643 transmission with four forward and one reverse gear and a two-speed transfer case. In addition to his roof hatch the driver also has a small hatch in the left side of the hull. The troop compartment is at the rear, and the troops enter and leave via the two doors in the hull rear; in addition there are hatches in the roof and firing ports with a vision block in the sides and rear.

The V-300 can be fitted with a wide range of armament installations, all in a

The V-300 has been developed as a private venture by Cadillac Gage. Heaviest of the wide range of weapons operable is the Cockerill Mk III 90-mm gun, mounted in a Cadillac Gage two-man turret. For air defence a 7.62-mm machine-gun is pintle mounted.

turret designed and built by Cadillac Gage. Among the two-man installations is a turret armed with a 90-mm (3.54-in) Cockerill Mk III gun, or British ROF 76-mm (2.99-in) gun or 25-mm Hughes Helicopters Chain Gun, or 20-mm cannon; there is also a one-man turret with a 20-mm cannon, and in all of these a 7.62-mm (0.3-in) machine-gun is mounted co-axial with the main armament and a similar weapon can usually be mounted on the roof for anti-aircraft defence. The one-man turret can have single or twin 7.62-mm (0.3-in) machine-guns or a combination of 7.62-mm (0.3-in) and 12.7-mm (0.5-in) machine-guns. A simple alternative to the turrets is a ring mounting with a 7.62-mm (0.3-in) or 12.7-mm (0.5-in) machine-gun.

Variants of the V-300 include an ambulance with a higher roof, an anti-tank vehicle fitted with the same TOW launcher as fitted to the M901 Improved TOW Vehicle (ITV), and an 81-mm mortar carrier.

The vehicle is fitted with a front-mounted winch and is fully amphibious, being propelled in the water by its wheels at a speed of 5 km/h (3 mph).

Specification
V-300 Commando
Crew: 3+9 (commander, gunner, driver and 9 infantry)
Combat weight: typically 13137 kg (28,962 lb)
Powerplant: one VT-504 V-8 turbocharged diesel developing 235 hp (175 kW)

The Hughes Helicopter 25-mm Chain Gun has been fitted to the V-300 Commando. The two-man turret has a co-axial 7.62-mm machine-gun,

Dimensions: length 6.40 m (21 ft 0 in); width 2.54 m (8 ft 4 in); height (hull top) 1.981 m (6 ft 6 in) but varies with weapon fit
Performance: maximum road speed

and smoke dischargers have been mounted on the side. An extra machine-gun can be fitted on top of the turret.

93 km/h (58 mph); maximum road range 700 km (435 miles); fording amphibious; gradient 60 per cent; vertical obstacle 0.609 m (2 ft 0 in); trench not applicable

---

Cadillac Gage Commando Ranger armoured personnel carrier

Developed to meet USAF base security requirements, the Ranger is also tasked with escorting ordnance convoys.

The US Air Force has hundreds of vast bases spread all over the world, and in recent years these have become possible targets for terrorists and other fringe groups as these bases not only contain highly expensive aircraft and/or missiles but also radars and other surveillance devices, fuels and all types of ordnance ranging from ammunition and conventional aircraft bombs up to nuclear warheads. To protect these assets the US Air Force issued a requirement for a vehicle which it called a Security Police Armored Response/Convoy Truck which, in addition to carrying out patrols on air bases, would also escort convoys carrying ordnance to and

from bases, or even from the storage dump on the airfield to the aircraft itself.

After studying a number of proposals, in early 1979 the US Air Force selected the **Cadillac Gage Commando Ranger** armoured personnel carrier to meet its requirements. The first of these was handed over in the following year, and by 1984 some 700 had been delivered. The US Air Force calls the vehicle the **Peacekeeper**, and sales have also been made by the company to Luxembourg (these are the only armoured vehicles operated by this country) and more recently some have been sold to Indonesia together with a number of Cadillac Gage Commando Scout 4×4 reconnaissance vehicles.

The Commander Ranger is based on a standard Chrysler truck chassis suitably modified and with a shorter wheelbase. (The wheelbase of a vehicle is the distance between the first and last axles.) The full armoured body provides the crew with protection from small arms fire and shell splinters. The engine is at the front of the vehicle and coupled to an automatic transmission with three forward and one reverse gear and a two-speed transfer case. Steering is integral with pump

assistance, and suspension front and rear consists of leaf springs and double-acting hydraulic shock absorbers.

The commander and driver are seated to the rear of the engine, each being provided with a bulletproof window to his front and a rearward-opening side door that has a bulletproof vision block and a firing port underneath; in addition there is a firing port between the driver's and commander's windscreens.

The six men sit three down each side in the rear, and enter via two doors in the hull rear. Each of these doors has a firing port, and the left one also has a vision block. In each side of the troop compartment is a vision block and a firing port. In the roof is a hatch on which a variety of light armament installations can be fitted, including a simple shield with a 7.62-mm (0.3-in) machine-gun or a turret with twin 7.62-mm (0.3-in) machine-guns.

Standard equipment includes internal lighting, an air-conditioning system, a heater, two-speed wipers and a windscreen defogger. Optional equipment includes 24-volt electrics in place of the normal 12-volt system, and a winch. Specialized versions include a command vehicle and an ambulance.

Specification
Commando Ranger
Crew: 2+6
Combat weight: 4536 kg (10,000 lb)
Powerplant: one Dodge 360 CID V-8 petrol engine developing 180 hp (134 kW)
Dimensions: length 4.699 m (15 ft 5 in); width 2.019 m (6 ft 7.5 in); height 1.981 m (6 ft 6 in)
Performance: maximum road speed 112.5 km/h (70 mph); maximum range

The Ranger interior is insulated and air-conditioned, lessening crew fatigue considerably. The interior can be fitted for command and communication equipment or for two crew and six passengers.

556 km (345 miles); fording 0.457 m (1 ft 6 in); gradient 60 per cent; vertical obstacle 0.254 m (10 in); trench not applicable

 UK
Humber FV1600 APC

When World War II was over, the British army drew up its requirements for a complete new generation of wheeled military vehicles including a 1-ton truck which was eventually produced by Humber/Rootes. In the early 1950s the Alvis Saracen 6×6 armoured personnel carrier started to enter service, but as there would clearly be insufficient of these to go around it was decided to build an armoured personnel carrier on the **Humber FV1600** series truck chassis. This armoured personnel carrier was not designed to operate with tanks, but rather to transport the infantry from one part of the battlefield to another, where they would dismount and fight on foot. About 1,700 vehicles were eventually built, the bodies being provided by GKN Sankey and the Royal Ordnance Factory at Woolwich. By the 1960s the FV432, also designed and built by GKN Sankey, was entering service in increasing numbers so the **Humber APCs** were phased out of service and placed in reserve or scrapped. The flare-up in Northern Ireland in the late 1960s meant that many of these vehicles were returned to service, and in 1984 these were still in use with the British army in Northern Ireland.

Many of the APCs in Northern Ireland have now been modified for use in the internal security role, being fitted with additional armour protection to stop 7.62-mm (0.3-in) armour-piercing rounds and barricade-removal equipment at the front of the hull.

The basic armoured personnel carrier model is the **FV1611**, and normally carries six or eight men in the rear with the commander and driver sitting at the front to the rear of the engine. Both the commander and driver are provided with a door in the side, and there are twin doors in the rear. A total of six firing ports/observation blocks are provided in the rear troop compart-

Above: The FV1609 model of the Humber one-ton armoured personnel carrier entered service in the early 1950s. With an open top, capacity was two crew and up to eight troops.

ment, (two in each side and one in each of the rear doors). The ambulance member of the family is the **FV1613**, which has a two-man crew and can carry three stretcher or eight seated patients, and the radio vehicle is the **FV1612**. The anti-tank version was called the **Hornet/Malkara**, or **FV1620**, and had two Malkara long range anti-tank guided missiles in the ready-to-launch position. This model is no longer in service with the British Army.

Specification
FV1611 'Pig'
Crew: 2+6 (or 2+8)
Combat weight: 5790 kg (12,765 lb)
Powerplant: one Rolls-Royce B60 Mk 5A 6-cylinder petrol engine developing 120 bhp (89 kW)

Dimensions: length 4.926 m (16 ft 2 in); width 2.044 m (6 ft 8.5 in); height 2.12 m (6 ft 11.5 in)
Performance: maximum road speed 64 km/h (40 mph); maximum range 402 km (250 miles); trench not applicable

The FV1600 vehicles have now been withdrawn from service completely and replaced by Saxon APCs, described elsewhere.

Alvis Saracen armoured personnel carriers

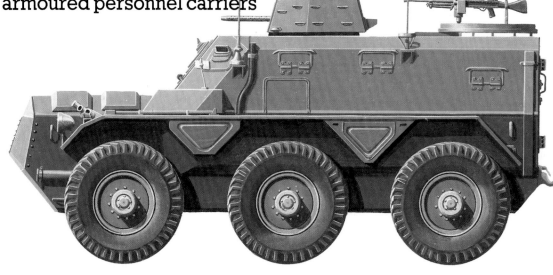

After the end of World War II the Fighting Vehicles Research and Development Establishment (FVRDE) designed in the UK a complete family of wheeled armoured vehicles known as the FV600 series which included the FV601 Saladin armoured car and the FV603 Saracen armoured personnel carrier. The requirement for the latter was much more urgent because of the guerrillas being encountered in Malaya, so development of this version took precedence, and the first prototypes were completed in early 1952, production vehicles following by December of the same year. Production of the whole FV600 series was undertaken by Alvis Limited at Coventry, and 1,838 vehicles had been completed by the time production came to an end in 1972. Throughout the 1950s the Saracen was the only real armoured personnel carrier in service with the British army, used in the Far East and Middle East (for example Aden and Libya) as well as in the United Kingdom and with the British Army of the Rhine. From the early 1960s replacement of the Saracen in the BAOR started by the FV432 full-tracked armoured personnel carrier, which has better cross-country performance, improved armour protection and longer operational range. In 1984 the Saracen remained in service with the British army in Northern Ireland, where it is used in internal security operations, with the Territorial Army and in Hong Kong. Sales of the Saracen were also made to Indonesia, Jordan, Kuwait, Lebanon, Libya, Nigeria, Qatar, South Africa, Sudan, Thailand, the United Arab Emirates and Uganda.

Although the FV603 Saracen had the same automotive components as the FV601 Saladin 6×6 armoured car, its layout was quite different with the engine at the front and troop compartment at the rear. The driver is seated in the centre, with the section commander to his left rear and radio operator to his right rear. To their rear are the eight infantrymen, who are seated on individual seats (four down each side of the hull facing inwards). The troops enter and leave via twin doors in the hull rear, and firing ports are provided in the sides and rear. On the forward part of the roof is a manually-operated turret with a 7.62-mm (0.3-in) machine-gun (this turret is identical with that fitted to some Ferret scout cars), and over the rear part of the troop compartment is a 7.62-mm (0.3-in) Bren light-machine gun for air defence.

Steering is hydraulically assisted on the front four wheels, and the vehicle can be driven with one wheel missing from each side. Some vehicles supplied to the Middle East were not fitted with a roof.

There were not many variants of the Saracen as the FV602 ambulance was cancelled fairly early on in the development programme. The FV604 is a command vehicle, while the FV610 is also a command vehicle with a much higher roof to allow the command staff to work standing up. The FV611 is an ambulance model and also has a higher roof. The FV610 was also fitted with the Robert surveillance radar but this never entered service; the same fate befell the 25-pdr self-propelled gun version and a roller-type mine-clearing vehicle.

Specification
Saracen
Crew: 2+10
Combat weight: 8640 kg (19,048 lb)
Powerplant: one Rolls-Royce B80 Mk 6A 8-cylinder petrol engine developing 160 hp (119 kW)
Dimensions: length 5.233 m (17 ft 2 in); width 2.539 m (8 ft 4 in); height (overall) 2.463 m (8 ft 1 in)
Performance: maximum road speed 72 km/h (44.7 mph); maximum road range 400 km (248 miles); fording 1.07 m (3 ft 6 in); gradient 42 per cent; vertical obstacle 0.46 m (1 ft 6 in); trench 1.52 m (5 ft 0 in)

First produced in 1952, the FV 603 Saracen APC was a member of a family of 6×6 vehicles. The turret mounts a 0.30-calibre machine-gun.

Versions of the Saracen include the FV 604 command vehicle, seen landing from a Mexefloat while on exercise with the 13/18 Hussars in Cyprus. Notice the extensive external stowage, the auxiliary generator on the front wing and the lack of the machine-gun turret.

GKN Sankey Saxon armoured personnel carrier

The GKN-Sankey AT105 has been designed to meet an army requirement for a wheeled APC in the 1980s and 1990s. The turreted AT105E can carry up to 10 troops.

In the early 1970s GKN Sankey built the AT100 4×2 and AT104 4×4 vehicles as a private venture, these being aimed mainly at the internal security role. The former never entered production, but about 30 AT104s were built for the Dutch state police and Royal Brunei Malay Regiment. These were followed by the GKN Sankey AT105 which was subsequently called the Saxon. This is a completely new design and uses many common automotive components from the Bedford MK 4×4 4-tonne truck, which is the standard vehicle in its class in the British army and many other armed forces around the world. Production of the AT105 started by 1976, and by 1984 about 200 had been sold to Bahrain, Kuwait, Malaysia and Oman. The British army purchased three for evaluation purposes in the 1970s, and in 1983

placed an order for 50 further vehicles. The first of these were delivered early in 1984, and by the early 1990s a total of some 624 were in service; less than the original requirement of 1000 vehicles. The Saxon is primarily used in infantry divisions, leaving the more expensive Warrior for use by troops in armoured divisions. Saxon has also been issued to Territorial battalions and has replaced the Humber one-ton armoured truck for internal security duties.

The AT105 Saxon has a hull of all-welded steel construction that provides complete protection against small arms fire and shell splinters, including 7.62-mm (0.3-in) armour-piercing rounds; indeed the vehicle is one of the best armoured vehicles of its type available in the world today. Both left-hand and right-hand drive models are available, the driver being seated right at the front of the vehicle with the engine to his left or right. The troop compartment is at the rear of the hull, and twin doors are provided in the hull rear and a single door in each side to allow for the rapid exit of troops. British army vehicles do not have the left door installed as external bins are fitted for the stowage of personnel kit and supplies. The commander's cupola in the roof of the Saxon is fixed and fitted with an observation block in each of the four sides for all-round

observation; a 7.62-mm (0.3-in) machine-gun is mounted on a DISA mount for ground and anti-aircraft fire. A wide range of other armament installations can be fitted, including turret-mounted 7.62-mm (0.3-in) and 12.7-mm (0.5-in) machine-guns or anti-riot weapons. If required firing ports and/or vision blocks can be installed in the troop compartment. An unusual feature of the Saxon is that its mudguards are of light sheet steel construction which will blow off in the event of the vehicle hitting a mine so that the blast is not contained under the hull.

Variants of the Saxon proposed by the manufacturer include a command vehicle, a mortar carrier, an armoured ambulance and various anti-riot versions, including one with an obstacle-clearing blade at the front of the hull.

GKN Sankey has also designed the **Simba** range of armoured vehicles which can be used as armoured personnel carriers or as weapon carriers with a wide range of armament installations up to 90 mm (3.54 in) in calibre.

Specification
Saxon
Crew: 2×8
Combat weight: 10670 kg (23,523 lb)
Powerplant: one Bedford 500 6-cylinder diesel developing 164 bhp (122 kW)

The AT105P, seen outside the UK Ministry of Defence, has a commander's cupola with pintle-mounted 7.62-mm GPMG. The cupola can be removed and replaced by one of a number of alternative armament installations.

Dimensions: length 5.169 m (16 ft 11.5 in); width 2.489 m (8 ft 2 in); height 2.86 m (9 ft 4.6 in)
Performance: maximum road speed 96 km/h (60 mph); maximum range 510 km (317 miles); fording 1.12 m (3 ft 8 in); gradient 60 per cent; vertical obstacle 0.41 m (1 ft 4 in); trench not applicable

---

ENGESA EE-11 Urutu armoured personnel carrier

In 1970 the Brazilian company EN-GESA, which had for some years been successfully converting 6×4 and 4×2 trucks into 6×6 and 4×4 models for increased cross-country mobility, turned its attention to the development of a range of 6×6 wheeled vehicles to meet the requirements of the Brazilian armed forces. In 1970 prototypes of the ENGESA EE-9 Cascavel armoured car and **ENGESA EE-11 Urutu** armoured personnel carrier made their first appearance. Production of these started in 1974 at a new plant at Sao Jose dos Campos, and by early 1984 some 3,000 EE-9s and EE-11s had been built, most of them for export, especially to the Middle East.

The layout of both vehicles is quite different although they both share many common automotive components such as engine, transmission and suspension. In the EE-11 the driver is seated at the front on the left side with the engine to his right and the troop compartment to his rear. The troops can enter the vehicle via a door in the side of the hull or through two doors in the hull rear. Over the top of the troop compartment are four roof hatches, two on each side, which open outwards, while forward of this is the main armament installation. This can range from a pintle- or ring-mounted 12.7-mm (0.5-in) M2 HB machine-gun, via a turret armed with a 20-mm cannon and a co-axial 7.62-mm (0.3-in) machine-gun, right up to a two-man turret armed with a 90-mm (3.54-in) gun, 7.62-mm (0.3-in) co-axial and 7.62-mm (0.3-in) anti-aircraft machine-gun. This turret is similar to that fitted to the EE-9 armoured car, but has no bustle and the 90-mm (3.54-in) gun has a reduced recoil length. Firing ports and/or vision blocks can be installed in the troop compartment to enable the troops to

fire their weapons from within the vehicle if required. The infantry sit on seats down each side of the hull facing each other, and these seats can be folded up to allow cargo to be carried. The EE-11 is fully amphibious, being propelled in the water at a speed of 8 km/h (5 mph) by two propellers at the hull rear. Before the vehicle enters the water a trim vane is erected at the front of the hull by the driver, who does so without leaving his seat, and the electric bilge pumps are switched on. The **EE-11 Mk 2** is available with a Detroit Diesel or a Mercedez-Benz diesel engine coupled to an automatic transmission, although the original **EE-11 Mk 1** had a manual transmission. All models now have a central tyre pressure regulation system that enables the driver to adjust the tyre pressure to suit the type of ground being crossed, and optional equipment includes a winch, night vision equipment, an NBC system and various radio installations.

A whole range of versions of the basic vehicle has now been designed by the company, including ambulance, cargo, command, recovery, anti-tank and anti-aircraft vehicles. The anti-tank model has MILAN or HOT ATGWs, while the anti-aircraft has a French ESD turret with twin 20-mm cannon and a surveillance radar. When fitted with the two-man 90-mm (3.54-in) turret the EE-11 is known as the **Urutu Armoured Fire Support Vehicle** (AFSV), and this is known to be used by Tunisia. The recovery vehicle has a hydraulically-operated crane for changing components in the field, and a winch for recovering other vehicles.

Specification
EE-11
Crew: 2+12 (commander, driver and 12 infantry)

Combat weight: 13000 kg (28,660 lb)
Powerplant: one Detroit Diesel 6V-53N 6-cylinder diesel developing 212 hp (158 kW)
Dimensions: length 6.15 m (20 ft 2 in); width 2.59 m (8 ft 6 in); height (without armament) 2.09 m (6 ft 10.3 in)
Performance: maximum road speed 90 km/h (56 mph); maximum road range 850 km (528 miles); fording amphibious; gradient 60 per cent; vertical obstacle 0.6 m (1 ft 11.6 in): trench not applicable

The ENGESA EE-11 Urutu armoured personnel carrier has a crew of two and can carry up to 12 fully armed infantrymen. Basic armament is a 12.7-mm (0.50-in) M2 HB heavy machine-gun.

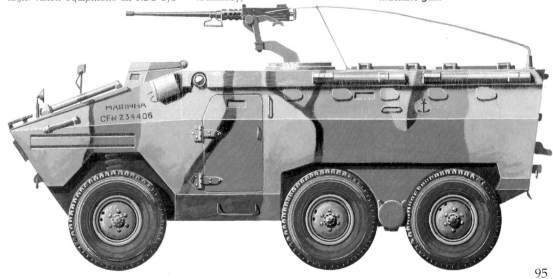

Left: The EE-11, in production since 1974 has been successful in the export market. This version is equipped with a Swedish-designed Hagglunds turret armed with a 20-mm cannon from Hispano. A 7.62-mm machine-gun can also be fitted.

Above: The 3,000 or more Urutus manufactured have carried a wide variety of weapon systems. This model is equipped with a Euromissile MILAN ATGW system and a 7.62-mm M1919 machine-gun.

SIBMAS armoured personnel carrier

In the mid-1970s the Belgian company B N Constructions Ferroviaires et Métalliques started development, as a private venture, of a 6×6 armoured personnel carrier which would have a number of common and proven commercial components. The first **SIBMAS** prototype was completed in 1976, the second following in 1979. One of these was tested by the Royal Malaysian army in competition with a number of vehicles submitted from other European, North American and South American companies. In the end Malaysia selected two vehicles to meet its requirements, namely the Condor 4×4 from Thyssen Henschel of West Germany and the Belgian SIBMAS 6×6. The order for the latter, valued at about £50 million, was placed in 1981, and the first vehicles were delivered in 1983. Two versions have been ordered by Malaysia: 24 examples of the **SIBMAS Armoured Recovery Vehicle (ARV)** and 162 examples of the **SIBMAS Armoured Fire Support Vehicle 90 (AFSV-90)**. The latter has a two-man turret designed and built by Cockerill and armed with a 90-mm (3.54-mm) Cockerill Mk III gun, 7.62-mm (0.3-in) co-axial and 7.62-mm (0.3-in) anti-aircraft machine-gun, and fitted with an OIP fire-control system.

The hull of the SIBMAS is of all-welded steel construction which provides the crew with complete protection from small arms fire and shell splinters. The driver is seated at the front of the vehicle, with the crew compartment in the centre and the engine at the rear of the vehicle on the left side, an aisle connecting the troop compartment with a door in the hull rear being fitted on the right side. Doors are provided in each side of the hull, and there are hatches over the troop compartment. Depending on the model, firing ports and/or vision blocks can be fitted in the sides and rear of the troop compartment. The engine is coupled to a fully automatic ZF transmission with six forward and one reverse gear and a hydrodynamic torque converter. Steering is power-assisted on the front wheels, and if required the vehicle can be fitted with a hydraulically-operated winch to assist in self-recovery or in the recovery of other

vehicles.

The basic model is fully amphibious without preparation, being propelled in the water by its wheels at a speed of 4 km/h (2.4 mph). The SIBMAS can also be fitted with two propellers at the hull rear to provide a maximum water speed of 11 km/h (6.8 mph). Other optional equipment includes night vision equipment, an air-conditioning system, a heater and an NBC system.

Other armament installations can also be fitted including the French ESD turret with twin 20-mm anti-aircraft cannon and a surveillance radar, the Lynx 90 turret with a 90-mm (3.54-in) gun, the Serval 60/20 turret, and a wide range of light armament installations such as twin 7.62-mm (0.3-in) machine-guns. The main armament installation is normally mounted to the rear of the driver's position, and a 7.62-mm (0.3-in) machine-gun can be mounted over the aisle at the right rear of the vehicle. More specialized versions of the SIBMAS include ambulance, command and cargo vehicles.

Specification
SIBMAS
Crew: 3+11
Combat weight: 14500 kg to 16500 kg (31,967 to 36,376 lb) depending on role and armament

Powerplant: one MAN 6-cylinder turbocharged diesel developing 320 hp (239 kW)
Dimensions: length 7.32 m (24 ft 0 in); width 2.50 m (8 ft 2.4 in); height (hull) 2.24 m (7 ft 4.2 in)
Performance: maximum road speed 100 km/h (62 mph); maximum road range 1000 km (621 miles); fording amphibious; gradient 70 per cent; vertical obstacle 0.6 m (1 ft 11.6 in); trench 1.5 m (4 ft 11 in)

The SIBMAS 6×6 APC was designed as a private venture. It can be armed with the French SAMM TTB 120 20-mm two-man turret.

The major export success to date for the SIBMAS has been the 186 vehicle sold to Malaysia. Most of the vehicles have been the Cockerill Mk III armed AFSV-90 version, for use as Armoured Fire Support Vehicles.

BDX/Valkyr armoured personnel carrier

In the early 1970s Technology Investments of Ireland designed and built the prototype of a 4×4 armoured personnel carried called the **Timoney**, and after trials with several prototype vehicles the Irish army finally ordered 10 vehicles in two batches of five. In 1976 Beherman Demoen of Belgium obtained a licence from Technology Investments to manufacture the Timoney armoured personnel carrier in Belgium. The Belgian government placed an order for a total of 123 vehicles under the designation **BDX**, and these were all built between 1978 and 1981. Of the 123, 43 were delivered to the Belgian air force for the defence of air bases, while the remainder were supplied to the Gendarmerie. All of the air force vehicles have a 7.62-mm (0.3-in) machine-gun, while the Gendarmerie vehicles comprise 13 fitted with an 81-mm mortar, 41 in the armoured personnel carrier role and the remaining 26 fitted with a front-mounted dozer blade.

The BDX was also tested in a number of other countries including Malaysia, but the only order obtained was placed by Argentina, which ordered five vehicles for use in the internal security role.

More recently Vickers Defence Systems of the United Kingdom have undertaken further development of the BDX which has resulted in the **Valkyr**, whose first two prototypes were completed in 1982 and the third in 1984. The Valkyr has many significant improvements over the original vehicle and is considered by many to be a new vehicle. It is powered by a proven General Motors Model 4-53T diesel coupled to a fully automatic AT-545 transmission with four forward and one reverse gear. Two basic models of the Valkyr are being offered, an armoured personnel carrier and a weapons platform which has a slightly lower profile and has already been experimentally fitted with a variety of weapons stations including a French turret armed with a 90-mm (3.54-in) gun and the Belgian CM-90 Cockerill turret armed with the 90-mm (3.54-in) Cockerill Mk III gun, 7.62-mm (0.3-in) co-axial and 7.62-mm (0.3-in) anti-aircraft machine-guns.

When used as an armoured personnel carrier the vehicle normally has a two-man crew consisting of the commander/machine-gunner and driver, and can carry 10 fully equipped troops, who can rapidly leave the vehicle via twin doors in the hull rear. If required the Valkyr can be fitted with firing ports and/or vision blocks and a wide range of options including air-conditioning, riot-control equipment and night vision devices. It is fully amphibious, being propelled in the water by its wheels, although as an option waterjets can be fitted to provide a much higher water speed.

In addition to armoured personnel carrier and fire-support vehicle models, a wide range of other variants are possible such as forward ambulance, command post vehicle, mortar carrier, and anti-tank vehicle fitted with turret mounted ATGWs.

Combat weight: 10700 kg (23,590 lb)
Powerplant: one Chrysler V-8 water-cooled petrol engine developing 180 hp (134 kW)
Dimensions: length 5.05 m (16 ft 7 in); width 2.50 m (8 ft 2.4 in); height (hull top) 2.06 m (6 ft 9 in)
Performance: maximum road speed 100 km/h (62 mph); maximum range (road) 500 to 900 km (310 to 560 miles);

Specification
BDX
Crew: 2 + 10

The Vickers Valkyr, while based upon the Timoney/BDX design, is of significantly improved capability. As has become the norm with modern APCs, the Valkyr can be fitted with a wide range of weapon systems.

fording amphibious; gradient 60 per cent; vertical obstacle 0.4 m (1 ft 4 in); trench not applicable

---

Tipo 6614 armoured personnel carrier

Some years ago Fiat and OTO-Melara designed and built prototypes of a 4×4 armoured car (the Tipo 6616) and a 4×4 armoured personnel carrier (**Tipo 6614**), both of which had identical automotive components although their layouts were quite different. Many of the automotive components of these vehicles are taken from standard commercial vehicles to keep costs to a minimum as well as making spare parts easier to obtain on a worldwide basis. The Tipo 6616 is used in small numbers by the Italian police, and known export customers include Libya, Peru, Somalia and Tunisia. It is estimated that about 400 vehicles at least had been built by 1984, and licence production is also undertaken in the Republic of Korea by Asia Motors Incorporated, who call the vehicle the **KM900**.

The hull of the Tipo 6614 armoured personnel carrier is of all-welded steel construction that varies in thickness from 6 mm (0.24 in) to 8 mm (0.315 in), and this provides protection against 7.62-mm (0.3-in) small arms fire and light artillery splinters. The driver is seated at the very front of the vehicle on the left side with the engine to his right. The troop compartment is toward the rear, and the 10 fully equipped troops, including the commander, sit on individual bucket type seats that can be quickly folded up. The troops enter and leave via a door in each side of the hull, or over a power-operated ramp in the hull rear. A total of 10 firing ports is provided, with a vision block above each; four of these ports are in each side of the hull (including one in the door) and one on each side of the rear ramp. Over the top of the troop compartment is a two-part roof hatch that opens to each side, while to the front of this is the main armament installation. This is normally an M113-type cupola with a single-piece hatch cover that opens to the rear, periscopes for all-round observations and a 12.7-mm (0.5-in) M2 HB machine-gun. A turret armed with twin 7.62-mm (0.3-in) machine-guns can also be installed. One of the more unusual versions offered has a multiple rocket launcher, this consisting of an Italian 48-round 51-mm system which can be fired by remote control at a rate of 10 rounds per second. Other variants include a mortar carrier which is known to be used by Peru, an ambulance and a command vehicle.

The Fiat engine is coupled to a manual gearbox with five forward and one reverse gear and a two-speed transfer case. The Tipo 6614 is fully amphibious, being propelled in the water by its wheels at a speed of 4.5 km/h (2.8 mph), and before the vehicle enters the water the four electrically-operated bilge pumps are switched on to pump out any water that enters the vehicle through the door or ramp seals. As usual a range of optional equipment is available apart from the different weapon stations, these including various types of passive night vision equipment, a spare wheel and holder (often mounted on the roof of the troop compartment), smoke dischargers, an air-conditioning system, a fire extinguishing system, and a front-mounted winch with a capacity of 4500 kg (9,221 lb) and 40 m (131 ft) of cable. This last would be used to recover other vehicles or to assist in self-recovery.

Specification
Tipo 6614
Crew: 1 + 10
Combat weight: 8500 kg (18,739 lb)
Powerplant: one Model 8062.24 supercharged liquid-cooled diesel developing 160 hp (119 kW)
Dimensions: length 5.86 m (19 ft 2.7 in); width 2.50 m (8 ft 2.4 in); height (hull top) 1.78 m (5 ft 10 in)
Performance: maximum road speed 100 km/h (62 mph); maximum range 700 km (435 miles); fording amphibious; gradient 60 per cent; vertical obstacle 0.4 m (1 ft 4 in); trench not applicable

Seen fording a stream, the Type 6614 APC (left) shares many components with the Type 6616 armoured car. The APC can transport 10 men in addition to the driver, with usual armament being a 12.7-mm MG.

Light Vehicles

Tanks and combat vehicles are the glamourous tip of the iceberg. Beneath are layers of very ordinary vehicles which carry out the day-to-day jobs necessary to an army's survival – delivering rations, mail, fuel, carrying troops here and there. But even a humble delivery truck can show some differences in military use.

The M998 HMMWV – the 'Hummer' or 'Humm-Vee' – appeared in prototype in 1980. It can carry a variety of weapons, including the TOW anti-tank system and Stinger surface-to-air missiles.

According to a German military historian more than a century ago, 'names, gaudy uniforms, orders, and an empty stomach, all things which a philosopher treats with contempt, play a decisive part in war'. Armies know this and arrange for mail, uniforms, orders and food, among many other things, to be supplied on a regular basis. And the supply of these items involves transport, which means the plain sort of trucks which we see here. Some of them – the Jeep, the Land Rover, the GAZ – have extended their influence beyond the military sphere and have become commercial successes. But they all have certain things in common – robustness, reliability and a capacity to take overloading and hard treatment in their stride. They are also remarkably long-lived. Armies are not particularly concerned with trends in body shape: once a design is accepted it goes on being produced as long as the military require it. Only when the tooling begins to wear will the makers suggest that a slight change might be in order.

By now, though, some of the vehicles shown here have finally been pensioned off: the original Jeep and the Hotchkiss copy, for example, are now avidly sought after by military vehicle collectors. The latest American equivalent of the Jeep, the High Mobility Multi-purpose Wheeled Vehicle (HMMWV) is a good deal more complex and expensive than the Jeep ever was, but it is snapped up whenever a specimen appears on the commercial market.

Recent developments in light vehicles include small 'all-terrain vehicles' for a variety of purposes. They form an agile platform for Special Forces to conduct raids and similar operations, whilst with a utilitarian body they are invaluable for carrying ammunition and other vital supplies in difficult terrain such as swamps or sandhills. There have also been moves to fit these vehicles with radio control and weapons – mainly anti-tank rockets – and, by using a video camera, drive them by remote control out on to the battlefield to discharge their weapons at a target and then return to reload. As a method of conducting war without personal risk, it has its points, but it promises to be an expensive pastime.

M37 light vehicle

The Beep (4×4) light vehicle, or to give its official designation, the T214, was widely used as a command/radio vehicle and forward ambulance during World War II, and was placed back in production to meet Korean War requirements. This was replaced by the **M37**, also produced by Dodge, who built over 125,000 vehicles between 1950 and 1970 for the US Army and many other countries around the world. The M37 was replaced in many units in the 1970s by the M715 series, but insufficient of these were built to replace the M37 on a one-for-one basis.

The basic M37 truck was designed to carry 907 kg (2,000 lb) of cargo on roads or 680 kg (1,500 lb) of cargo across country, and can also tow a trailer weighing 2722 kg (6,000 lb) on roads or 1815 kg (4,000 lb) across country.

In layout the M37 is similar to a standard commercial pick-up, with the engine at the front, the driver and two passengers in the centre, and the cargo area at the rear. The last has a drop tailgate, folding troop seats down each side, removable front rack bows and a tarpaulin cover. The cab has a windscreen that can be folded forward onto the bonnet, on each side a door whose top can be removed, and a removable tarpaulin cover. Some vehicles were fitted with a front-mounted winch for recovery operations, and a deep-fording kit can be fitted which enables the M37 to ford to a depth of 2.133 m (7 ft).

There are a number of variants of the M37, including the **M43** ambulance which has a fully enclosed steel body and can carry eight seated or four stretcher patients and a medical attendant. The rear compartment is provided with a heater and a light. The command post model is similar to the basic cargo model but has side curtains with windows, and internally has a folding table and map light, and can be fitted with communications equipment. The telephone maintenance truck is the **M201** which has an all-steel body with compartments for tools and spare equipment.

The M37 was also made under licence in Canada in the 1950s by Chrysler at Windsor, Ontario, these being called the **M37CDN** cargo vehicle, **M43CDN** ambulance and

An M37 (4×4) cargo truck, complete with bows and a tarpaulin cover over the rear compartment. The latter is provided with a drop tailgate and fold-up troop seats down each side.

M152CDN fully enclosed panel truck. One of the more unusual Canadian models was an M37CDN with a pedestal mount to the cab rear for launching anti-tank guided weapons.

In the 1950s Japan produced two vehicles very similar to the M37. These were the **Nissan Q4W73** (4×4) 750-kg (1,653-lb) truck and the **Toyota 2FQ15L** (4×4) with a similar carrying capability. Both of these are used by the Japanese Ground Self-Defence Force, and the Nissan vehicle has also been built under licence in India for the Indian army. The Toyota model was also used by United States forces in the Far East, South Vietnam and South Korea. The South Vietnamese fitted many of their vehicles with additional armour protection for convoy escort work and for the patrol of air bases and other targets.

Above: Between 1950 and 1970 Dodge built more than 130,000 of these M37 (4×4) cargo trucks for the US armed forces. This particular vehicle has a front-mounted winch.

Below: The ambulance member of the family is designated the M43, and can carry four stretcher patients plus an attendant, or eight seated patients and an attendant.

Specification
M37
Crew: 1+2 (plus 6/8 in rear)
Weight: empty 2585 kg (5,699 lb) and loaded 3493 kg (7,700 lb)
Powerplant: one Dodge T245 6-cylinder petrol engine developing 78 bhp (58 kW)
Dimensions: length 4.81 m (15 ft 9 in); width 1.784 m (5 ft 10 in); height 2.279 m (7 ft 6 in)
Performance: maximum road speed 88.5 km/h (55 mph); maximum range 362 km (225 miles); gradient 68 per cent; fording 1.066 m (3 ft 6 in)

M38 light vehicle

At the outbreak of the Korean War in 1950, the standard American light vehicle was still the Jeep. But the rapid expansion of the US Army meant that there were insufficient Jeeps, even when units in Europe and elsewhere were robbed of their vehicles. To meet this urgent need the civilian **Willys CJ3A** was fitted with a 24-volt electrical system (to enable it to be fitted with radios), semi-floating rear axle and a deep-fording kit (to enable it to ford to a depth of 1.879 m/6 ft 2 in), and this was standardized as the **M38**. In appearance it was similar to the Jeeps of World War II, and could carry a payload of 544 kg (1,200 lb) on roads or 363 kg (800 lb) across country, and could tow a trailer weighing 907 kg (2,000 lb) on roads or 680 kg (1,500 lb) across country. It could also be fitted with a front-mounted winch.

The M38 was in production from 1950 to 1952, when it was replaced by the **M38A1**, which is powered by a four-cylinder petrol engine developing 72 bhp (53.69 kW), has a longer wheelbase, possesses greater operational range thanks to the provision of a larger-capacity fuel tank, and has the same payload capability as the basic M38. The M38A1 is distinguishable from the M38 as the former has distinct curved sides to the bonnet, while the latter has a flat bonnet that is almost identical to that of the World War II Jeep.

An M38A1 (4×4) light vehicle of the Spanish marines, fitted with radios for use in the command role.

The layout of the M38 is conventional, with the engine at the front, the driver and one passenger in the centre, and a bench seat for a further two passengers at the rear. The windscreen folds forward onto the bonnet and a canvas top, stowed at the rear when not required, can be quickly erected when the windscreen is raised. Variants of the later M38A1 included the **M38A1C**, which carried a 106-mm (4.17-in) recoilless rifle in the rear that could be fired from the vehicle or dismounted for ground use and also had a split windscreen so that the barrel could be locked along the centre of the vehicle for travelling. The ambulance model of the M38A1 was the **M170**, which could carry three stretcher or six seated patients.

The M38 and M38A1 were replaced in the US Army by the M151 light vehicle, but they remain in service with many other countries around the world, and the type was also made under licence in Canada as the **M38CDN** and **M38A1CDN**, both of

which will soon be replaced by the West German Volkswagen Iltis light vehicle built under licence.

In the early 1960s Willys-Overland became Kaiser Jeep, which later became the Jeep Corporation, a subsidiary of the American Motors Corporation, which manufactures a wide range of 4×4 vehicles for the civilian market. Military versions of some of these vehicles are also produced for the export market including the **AM7**, **AM8** and **AM10**, which all have different wheelbases and payloads, although they are all powered by the same Model 258 engine.

Specification
M38
Crew: 1 + 1 (plus 2 in rear)
Weight: empty 1247 kg (2,749 lb) and loaded 1791 kg (3,948 lb)
Powerplant: one Willys MC 4-cylinder petrol engine developing 60 bhp (44.7 kW)
Dimensions: length 3.377 m (11 ft 1 in); width 1.574 m (5 ft 2 in); height 1.879 m

(6 ft 2 in)
Performance: maximum road speed 88.5 km/h (55 mph); maximum range 362 km (225 miles); gradient 65 per cent; fording 0.939 m (3 ft 1 in)

The forward ambulance version of the M38 is the M170, which has a longer wheelbase and can carry three stretcher or six seated patients.

USA
M151 light vehicle

The **M151** is at present one of the most widely used light vehicles in the world, but its development can be traced back to a requirement issued in 1950 for a new ¼-ton vehicle to replace the M38 which was then entering production at Willys. Development of the new vehicle was undertaken by the Ford Motor Company, the first prototypes being completed in 1952 and further prototypes in 1954 under the designation **XM151**. Further development of the latter resulted in the **XM151E1** of steel construction, and in the **XM151E2** of aluminium construction. The former was eventually selected for production, and the first vehicles came off the production line at Ford's Highland Park Plant in 1960 under the designation **M151**. In 1984 the vehicle was in service with some 100 armies in almost every corner of the world, but production is now undertaken by AM General Corporation at its Sound Bend Facilities. This company has produced over 100,000 vehicles, though none of the type have been ordered by the US Army in recent years as the engine does not meet stringent emission standards. Thus all production is now for export. The M51 has seen action with American forces in Vietnam, where the vehicle was used for a wide range of roles, some even being fitted with armour protection.

The original M151 was followed in production by the **M151A1**, which had improved suspension, while the **M151A2** that followed in 1970 had modified lighting, two-speed wipers, modified rear suspension, collapsible steering wheel and a dual brake system. The **M151A2LC** has different gearbox, transfer box and suspension. There are many variants of the M151 including the **M107/M108** communications vehicles, **M718** ambulance which can carry one stretcher and three seated patients (or various combinations of stretcher patients and sitting patients), and the **M825** fitted with the M40 106-mm (4.17-in) recoilless rifle.

The basic M151 series can carry 554 kg (1,221 lb) on roads or 362 kg (798 lb) across country, and can tow a trailer weighing 970 kg (2,138 lb) on

An M151 (4×4) light vehicle with the canopy erected. AM General is still producing this vehicle to meet foreign military sales as the United States armed forces have not purchased any M151 series for some five years.

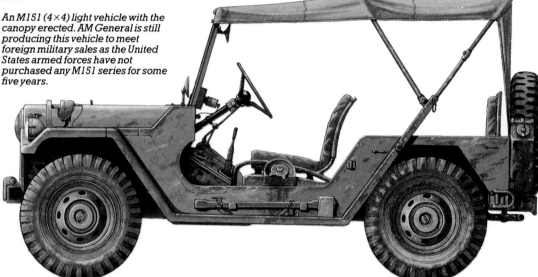

roads or 680 kg (1,499 lb) across country. A variety of kits can be fitted including a heater, fully enclosed hard top, searchlight, front-mounted winch, 100-amp alternator and a kit to enable the vehicle to ford to a depth of 1.524 m (5 ft), the last kit being widely used by the US Marine Corps when driving the vehicle out of landing craft during amphibious operations.

The layout of the vehicle is similar to other vehicles of this type, with the engine at the front, the driver and one passenger in the centre, and a bench seat at the rear. The engine is coupled to a manual gearbox with four forward and one reverse gear and a single-speed transfer box that enables the driver to select either 4×4 or 4×2 drive. The suspension, front and rear,

Below: Since 1960 the M151 has been the standard light vehicle of the US Army and many other armies in every corner of the world. From 1984 it will start to be replaced by the High Mobility Multi-purpose Wheeled Vehicle, or Hummer.

consists of coil springs and hydraulic shock absorbers.

The M151 is widely used by the US Army to mount such weapons as 7.62-mm (0.3-in) or 12.7-mm (0.5-in) machine-guns or the Hughes TOW ATGW system. The M151 will soon start to be replaced by the High Mobility Multi-purpose Wheeled Vehicle (also built by AM General), which will have greatly increased carrying capability and better off-road performance.

Specification
M151
Crew: 1+1 (plus 2 in rear)
Weight: empty 1012 kg (2,231 lb) and loaded 1575 kg (3,472 lb)

Powerplant: one 4-cylinder petrol engine developing 72 hp (53.69 kW)
Dimensions: length 3.352 m (11 ft 0 in); width 1.58 m (5 ft 2 in); height 1.803 m (5 ft 11 in)
Performance: maximum road speed 106 km/h (66 mph); maximum range 483 km (300 miles); gradient 60 per cent; fording 0.533 m (1 ft 9 in)

An M151 (4×4) light vehicle of 17th Cavalry with a pintle-mounted 7.62-mm (0.3-in) M60 machine-gun during Operation 'Junction City', Phase II, in South Vietnam, 1967.

 UK
Land Rover 1-Tonne light vehicle

When the long-wheelbase **Land Rover** was introduced into service in the 1950s, it was more than adequate to tow weapons such as the OTO Melara 105-mm (4.13-in) Model 56 Pack Howitzer used by the Royal Artillery from 1960. It was realized that in the future heavier weapon systems would be introduced into service, so a requirement was drawn up for a 4×4 vehicle with a cross-country payload of 1000 kg (2,205 lb) and also the ability to tow a powered trailer carrying 1500 kg (3307 lb). This vehicle was subsequently designed by Land Rover in co-operation with the Military Vehicles and Engineering Establishment at Chertsey, Surrey. The first prototypes were completed in the mid-1960s, but as a result of trials a number of modifications were carried out and it was not until 1975 that the first production **Land Rover 1-Tonne** vehicles were issued to British army units. For a variety of reasons less than 3,000 vehicles were built, most of them being supplied to the British army and Royal Air Force, although overseas sales were made to Australia (for the Rapier SAM), Egypt (for the Swingfire ATGW system) and Luxembourg. The main reason for this relative short production run, almost insignificant by Land Rover standards, was that it was designed specifically for military use, whereas the basic Land Rover was developed as a commercial vehicle but later adopted by the military.

In the British army the Land Rover 1-Tonne is used to tow the Royal Ordnance Factory Nottingham 105-mm (4.13-in) Light Gun, to carry 81-mm (3.19-in) mortar teams in UK-based infantry battalions, to carry MILAN anti-tank teams (two launchers and 14 missiles), and to tow the Rapier SAM launcher, its missile resupply trailer and the Blindfire radar system. There is also a model with a fully enclosed body for use in the ambulance role, and this can carry four stretcher or six sitting patients in addition to its crew. Another fully enclosed body version is used in the communications/electronic warfare role.

The Land Rover 1-Tonne is of the forward control type, with the driver at the front right and passenger on the left with the engine between and below their seats. The engine is basically a standard commercial model (but with a reduced compression ratio to enable it to run on low-octane fuels) and is coupled to a manual gearbox with four forward and one reverse

gear. The transfer box is of the two-speed type with permanent four-wheel drive. The cargo is at the rear and has bows and a tarpaulin cover.

For air transport the complete hood, body sides, windscreen, bumpers, doors, bows and tarpaulin cover can be quickly removed, so reducing the overall weight of the vehicle to only 1580 kg (3,483 lb).

Now that the Land Rover 1-Tonne is out of production, the **Gomba Stonefield** (4×4), **Dosco HS 100-4** (4×4) and **Reynolds Boughton** (4×4) ranges of trucks are being offered by British industry to fill the gap in the market. The Gomba Stonefield has already been recommended for use as the towing vehicle for the 105-mm (4.13-in) Light Gun, and this vehicle is now in service with the Malaysian army.

Specification
Land Rover 1-Tonne
Crew: 1+1 (plus 8 in rear)
Weight: empty 1924 kg (4,242 lb) and loaded 3120 kg (6,878 lb)
Powerplant: one Rover V-8 petrol engine developing 128 bhp (95.5 kW)
Dimensions: length 4.127 m (13 ft 6 in); width 1.842 m (6 ft 1 in); height 2.138 m (7 ft 0 in)
Performance: maximum road speed 120 km/h (74 mph); maximum range 560 km (348 miles); gradient 60 per cent

Above: The 1-Tonne Land Rover was developed specifically to meet the requirements of the British armed forces by Land Rover and the Military Vehicles and Engineering Establishment. Typical roles in the British army include towing the 105-mm (4.13-in) Light Gun and the Rapier surface-to-air missile.

Below: A 1-Tonne Land Rover towing a trailer. In addition to the British army and Royal Air Force Regiment, sales were also made to Luxembourg, Egypt (for the Swingfire ATGW system), and to Australia for the Rapier. It is no longer in production and was not produced in very large numbers.

Citroën Méhari Armée light vehicle

The **Citroën Méhari Armée** is typical of the many standard commercial vehicles that have been adopted to meet military requirements with a minimum of changes. In times of peace light vehicles, apart from the periods when they are on exercises, spend much of their time on normal roads and have little occasion to use their all-wheel drive. The 4×4 vehicles are not only expensive to procure, but also tend to be uneconomic on fuel.

After looking at a number of vehicles on the market the French army chose the Méhari to meet its requirements for a vehicle suitable for use in rear areas where little cross-country capability is required, and some 10,000 have now been delivered, not only to the French army, but also the *gendarmerie*, air force and navy, with additional export sales being made. Typical roles include cargo carrying with a maximum load of 405 kg (894 lb), and command when fitted with radios. The type is not used to mount any type of weapon system.

The civilian model is produced in such exotic colours as TP orange and beige, but the military vehicles are in various shades of sand or green. The Méhari Armée has an all-steel chassis with a plastic body. This requires hardly any maintenance as it will not rust. The basic model has the engine at the front, seats for the driver and one passenger in the centre (each with a safety door chain), and an additional two-man seat that folds down at the rear to provide a large cargo area. The windscreen folds forwards onto the bonnet and a black cotton canopy can be fitted over the body; if required, a complete hood with transparent side panels and doors can be installed. The utility model is similar, but to the rear of the driver and passenger seat is a flat load area. Like the basic model it has a windscreen and canopy, and can be fitted with a complete hood.

The engine is coupled to a manual gearbox with four forward and one reverse gear, there being no transfer box as it is only a 4×2 vehicle. Both the front and rear axles are suspended by arms with lateral interplay on spiral springs, with hydraulic shock absorbers at each wheel station. Even though this is only a 4×2 vehicle the Méhari Armée does have some cross-country capability, and it is so light that it can be easily manhandled in the field.

The Citroën company has more recently developed another light vehicle that is available in both 4×4 and 4×2 configurations. This is the **A FAF** and has a maximum payload of 400 kg (882 lb). It is powered by a petrol engine developing 28.5 hp (21 kW) in the 4×2 configuration, or 34 hp (25.3 kW) in the 4×4 configuration. Both versions use automotive components from the civilian A type 4×2 vehicle, of which many millions have been built. The 4×4 model was selected by Burundi and in 1981 by the French army which placed an order for 5,000 vehicles, while the 4×2 model is produced under licence in Greece by the National Motor Company (NAMCO) as the **Pony**, which is used by the Greek army in a number of roles.

Specification
Citroën Méhari Armée
Crew: 1+1
Weight: empty 585 kg (1,290 lb) and loaded 990 kg (2,183 lb)
Powerplant: one AK 2 2-cylinder air-cooled petrol engine developing 26 hp (19.4 kW)
Dimensions: length 3.52 m (11 ft 7 in); width 1.53 m (5 ft 0 in); height 1.635 m (5 ft 4 in)
Performance: maximum road speed 100 km/h (62 mph); maximum range 300 km (186 miles); gradient 40 per cent; fording 0.30 m (1 ft 0 in)

Above: A Citroën Méhari Armée (4×2) light vehicle, used in the command role with a radio fitted in the rear of the vehicle. This vehicle was originally developed for the civilian market, but was then found to be suitable for a wide range of rear area duties where all-wheel drive is not essential.

Below: A basic Citroën Méhari Armée (4×2) light vehicle, with the hood folded down at the rear. An unusual feature of this vehicle is that its body is of all-plastic construction, which is rust free and therefore requires little or no maintenance. The vehicle is used by all three arms of the French forces.

Peugeot P4 light vehicle

Since the 1950s the standard light vehicle of the French army has been the Hotchkiss M 201, and to find a replacement for this type the French army held a competition for which three manufacturers each provided four vehicles. Each of the three French manufacturers selected foreign vehicles, Peugeot selecting a Mercedes-Benz vehicle, Renault the Italian FIAT 1107 AD which it renamed the TRM 500, and Citroën the West German Volkswagen Iltis (already in service with the West German army) which it renamed the C 44. In 1981 the **Peugeot P4** was selected, and the first of 15,000 vehicles were delivered in the following year.

In the basic model the engine is at the front, the driver and one passenger in the centre, and the cargo area at the rear. The last has a two-man bench seat down each side, and this can be folded down to provide more space;

Five variants of the Peugeot P4 range of vehicles are (left to right) short wheelbase; short wheelbase with 7.62-mm (0.3-in) machine-gun; long wheelbase command vehicle; short wheelbase with MILAN ATGW; and long wheelbase troop carrier. The French army has ordered only the short wheelbase version.

the opening tailgate also carries the spare tyre. The engine is coupled to a manual gearbox with four forward and one reverse gear and a two-speed transfer box is fitted. The suspension front and rear consists of coil springs and double-action shock absorbers. The basic model is powered by the XN8 four-cylinder inline petrol engine, but the P4 is also offered with the XD3 four-cylinder diesel which develops 75 hp (56 kW) and gives a much better fuel consumption when being driven at a speed of 60 km/h (37 mph), though at 90 km/h (56 mph) fuel consumption is identical with that of the petrol engine. Standard equipment includes inertia seat belts, towing eyes at the front, a trailer hook at the rear and a 24-volt electrical system. Optional equipment includes a 15-litre (3.3 Imp gal) fuel can, power take-off front and rear, power-assisted steering, front locking differential and a front-mounted winch. Winches are available on most light vehicles as an optional extra and can be used for self recovery or for recovering other vehicles. In the former case the end of the cable is attached to a tree or other solid object and the vehicle winches itself out of trouble.

In French army service some vehicles will be fitted with twin light machine-guns for use in the reconnaissance role, while others will be used to carry MILAN anti-tank teams around the battlefield, each team having one launcher and four missiles.

There is also a long-wheelbase version, which has not been adopted by the French army so far; this can carry 10 men (two in the front as normal and a further eight in the rear seated four down each side). Fully enclosed versions of both the standard- and long-wheelbase versions are available for use in the command and ambulance roles.

Peugeot has also built a 4×4 version of the standard civilian **Peugeot 504** pick-up truck, and some of these have recently been ordered by the French marines as it has a useful payload of 1110 kg (2,448 lb), good ground-clearance and a high road speed. In addition to the basic pick-up model, station wagon and ambulance versions are also offered.

Specification
Peugeot P4
Crew: 1 + 1 (plus 4 in rear)
Weight: empty 1680 kg (3,704 lb) and loaded 2280 kg (5,026 lb)
Powerplant: one XN8 4-cylinder petrol engine developing 83.5 hp (62 kW)
Dimensions: length 4.12 m (13 ft 6 in); width 1.70 m (5 ft 7 in); height 1.95 m (6 ft 5 in)
Performance: maximum road speed 122 km/h (76 mph); maximum range 500 km (311 miles); gradient 70 per cent; fording 0.60 m (2 ft 0 in)

 FRANCE
Hotchkiss M 201 light vehicle

The Free French Forces used the American-supplied Jeep in large numbers during World War II, and these proved so successful that in the early 1950s Hotchkiss-Brandt of Paris obtained a licence to start production in France, for both the civilian and military markets. The first production models of this **Hotchkiss M 201** were completed in 1953 and production continued until 1969, by which time over 40,000 had been built. In addition to being used by the French armed forces the M 201 was supplied to many countries in North Africa and also to Belgium. In the French armed forces its replacement by the Peugeot P4 (4×4) vehicle, which has greater load-carrying capability, has recently started. The M 201 will be around for many years yet, however, and surplus vehicles are already finding their way onto the civilian market.

The M 201 is almost identical to the wartime Jeep with the engine at the front, driver and one passenger in the centre, and a seat for a further two passengers at the rear. With the windscreen erected a canopy can be fitted to the M 201 to provide protection for the crew. The engine is coupled to a manual gearbox with three forward and one reverse gear and a two-speed transfer box. Suspension consists of semi-elliptical springs and hydraulic shock absorbers. The vehicle can carry a maximum load of 400 kg (882 lb) and tow a trailer weighing up to 500 kg (1,102 lb).

The M 201 has been used as a weapons carrier and fitted with 7.62-mm (0.3-in) or 12.7-mm (0.5-in) machine-guns, 106-mm (4.17-in) M40 type recoilless rifles (which can also be dismounted for use in the ground role) and ENTAC ATGWs. In the last model a total of four missiles were carried in the ready-to-launch position, a further three missiles being carried in reserve; this model was used by France and Belgium, but the missiles have now been replaced by the longer-range Euromissile MILAN system. The vehicle is also fitted with extensive communications equipment for use in the command role, and some have even been fitted with battlefield surveillance radars to detect enemy movements some distance away.

The basic military model has a wheelbase of 2.03 m (6 ft 8 in), but a longer model was built with a wheelbase of 2.53 m (8 ft 4 in) and greater carrying capability.

Once the M 201 had gone out of production, a number of manufacturers proposed vehicles to fill this gap: at the time there was no French army requirement for a new vehicle, but new countries that were previously French colonies or who had a strong French bias still looked to France for their requirements. This gap was eventually filled by the **SAMO** light vehicle, which is available in both standard- and long-wheelbase configurations, with a petrol or diesel engine, and with a wide range of optional equipment such as heavy-duty axles, 24-volt electrical system, long-range fuel tanks and a winch. This has been exported to a number of countries including the Central African Republic, Chad, Upper Volta and Burundi.

Specification
Hotchkiss M 201
Crew: 1 + 1 (plus 2 in rear)

Weight: empty 1120 kg (2,469 lb) and loaded 1520 kg (3,351 lb)
Powerplant: one 4-cylinder petrol engine developing 61 hp (46 kW)
Dimensions: length 3.36 m (11 ft 0 in); width 1.58 m (5 ft 2 in); height 1.77 m (5 ft 10 in)
Performance: maximum road speed 100 km/h (62 mph); maximum range 348 km (216 miles); gradient 65 per cent; fording 0.533 m (1 ft 9 in)

Above: The M 201 (4×4) light vehicle was in production by Hotchkiss-Brandt in Paris from 1953 to 1969 for both the civilian and military markets. It is almost identical to the Jeep used by the Allied armies during World War II, and it is only now being replaced in the French army by the Peugeot P4 (4×4) light vehicle, which is based on a West German design.

Right: A Hotchkiss M 201 (4×4) light vehicle of the French army fitted with four Aérospatiale ENTAC wire guided anti-tank missiles. For travelling, these missiles are retracted to the rear of the driver and missile operator. In the French army ENTAC has now been replaced by the MILAN ATGW.

Steyr-Puch 700 AP Haflinger light vehicle

The **Steyr-Puch 700 AP Haflinger** light vehicle was designed in the early 1950s specifically for use in mountainous terrain, and was in production between 1959 and 1974, by which time the Pinzgauer was firmly established as its successor with its much improved cross-country performance and increased load-carrying capability. The Haflinger has an unusual layout, with the driver at the very front on the left, with one passenger to his right and a further two passengers to the rear. At the rear is a very small cargo-carrying area, which can be increased by folding flat the back two seats. When the vehicle is being used in the troop-carrying role the windscreen is normally erected and a canvas top with removable side doors is fitted.

The engine is mounted under the very rear of the hull which has enabled the load-carrying area to be retained,

but it has also meant that the fording capability of the vehicle is limited. The engine is coupled to a manual gearbox (with four forward and one reverse gears) which transmits power to all four wheels, which have 165×12 tyres. Vehicles produced after 1967 have a manual gearbox with five forward and one reverse gear, a significant improvement over the earlier model as no transfer box is fitted. From 1967 the vehicle was produced with a slightly more powerful engine. Optional equipment included a winch with a

A Steyr-Puch Haflinger (4×4) light vehicle with a canvas top and the side removed to show the seating arrangements. The two-cylinder petrol engine is under the rear and is coupled to a manual gearbox with four forward and one reverse gear.

capacity of 1500 kg (3,307 lb), a power take-off for running accessories such as a power saw, and a snow plough. There was also a model of the Haflinger with a slightly longer wheelbase and slightly greater load-carrying capability.

In its military role, the Haflinger was often used as a weapons platform. The Austrian army has used the vehicle to mount the standard 12.7-mm (0.5-in) M2 HB machine-gun on a pintle in the centre of the vehicle, or the old American 57-mm (2.24-in) M18A1 recoilless

Two Haflinger (4×4) light vehicles of the Austrian army. The one on the left is armed with a 12.7-mm (0.5-in) M2 HB machine-gun, and that on the right with a 57-mm recoilless rifle for use in the anti-tank role. This vehicle was in production between 1959 and 1974.

anti-tank rifle. Both the Swiss and Swedish armies have used the vehicle as an anti-tank platform with six Bofors Bantam wire-guided anti-tank missiles facing the front and another eight missiles facing the rear.

Specification
Steyr-Puch Haflinger
Crew: 1+3
Weight: empty 645 kg (1,422 lb) and loaded 1200 kg (2,645 lb)
Powerplant: one Model 700 AP 2-cylinder petrol engine developing 24 hp (18 kW)
Dimensions: length 2.85 m (9 ft 4 in); width 1.40 m (4 ft 7 in); height 1.74 m (5 ft 8 in)
Performance: maximum road speed 75 km/h (46.6 mph); maximum range 400 km (248 miles); gradient 65 per cent; fording 0.40 m (1 ft 4 in)

Mercedes-Benz light vehicle

The Mercedes-Benz company of West Germany has for many years produced a wide range of trucks that are widely used by the military, including the famous Unimog range which is available in models with cross-country payloads of between 1 and 5 tonnes. To complement these vehicles it was decided to design a new **Mercedes-Benz light vehicle** which would have a cross-country payload of 750 kg (1,654 kg) and be able to tow a 2500-kg (5,511-lb) trailer on roads or a 750-kg (1,654-lb) trailer across country. This vehicle was not adopted by the West German army, which selected the West German Volkswagen Iltis. The vehicle was entered by Peugeot in the competition for a successor to the Hotchkiss M 201 light vehicle used by the French army, winning the competition in the form of the Peugeot P4 which is now in service with the French army in a number of variants.

Production of this vehicle is undertaken in Austria by GFG, which built 7,500 vehicles in 1980, mostly for the civilian market. GFG was established by Daimler-Benz and Steyr-Daimler-Puch, the former company supplying the axles, transmission and engine and the latter the body and chassis. This vehicle has been adopted by the Norwegian army, which ordered an initial batch of 450, and some were obtained by Argentina, only to be captured by the British in the Falklands. These captured vehicles are now used by the British forces alongside their

Land Rovers, spare parts being obtained from normal commercial sources in Europe!

The layout of the vehicle is different to that of the Land Rover with the engine at the front, driver and one passenger in the centre, a seat for two passengers to the rear and a small cargo area at the back. The rear seats can be folded down to provide space for cargo, which can be loaded through a door in the rear, although the short-wheelbase vehicle has a drop-down rear like the Land Rover. The basic model is available with four different engine options, a four- or five-cylinder diesel or a four- or six-cylinder petrol engine, the latter two offering the highest performance. The engine is coupled to a manual gearbox with four forward and one reverse gear and a transfer-box; for road operations the vehicle is normally driven in 4×2 configuration.

In addition to the normal four-seater version, there is also a station wagon type with a fully enclosed body and twin doors at the rear, and a long-wheelbase model with a van type body; although these are aimed mainly at the civilian market, the van type model has obvious potential for use as a command vehicle or ambulance.

As with most vehicles today a range of optional equipment can be fitted including an electrically-operated winch mounted at the front, different tyres, front and rear differential locks, a trailer coupling, a tow hook on the

A Mercedes-Benz (4×4) light vehicle with the windscreen folded forwards and the hood removed to allow installation of a pintle-mounted 12.7-mm (0.5-in) M2 HB machine-gun in

front, a trailer hook at the rear and additional protection for the radiator and engine.

Specification
Mercedes-Benz light vehicle
Crew: 1+1 (plus 2 in rear)
Weight: empty 1670 kg (3,682 lb) and

the rear. Light vehicles with similar armament installations are used by almost every country in the world for reconnaissance.

loaded 2400 kg (5,291 lb)
Powerplant: one OM616 4-cylinder diesel developing 65 hp (49 kW)
Dimensions: length 4.145 m (13 ft 6 in); width 1.70 m (5 ft 7 in); height 1.995 m (6 ft 7 in)
Performance: maximum road speed 117 km/h (72 mph); gradient 80 per cent; fording 0.60 m (2 ft 0 in)

Volkswagen Iltis light vehicle

The standard light vehicle of the West German armed forces for many years was the **Auto-Union Lkw** (4×4), which could carry 250 kg (552 lb) of cargo. Between 1958 and 1968 over 55,000 of these were built at Ingolstadt for both civil and military use. The Lkw was to have been replaced by the so called Europe Jeep designed to carry 500 kg (1,102 lb) of cargo and also have an amphibious capability, but after prototypes had been built by two competing teams (each having one manufacturer from West Germany, Italy and France), the whole project was dropped. The West German army then issued a new requirement for a vehicle that would carry 500 kg (1,102 lb) of cargo across country, but which was not required to be amphibious. To meet this requirement prototype vehicles were built by Daimler-Benz and Volkswagen, and in 1977 the latter type was selected and an order placed for 8,800 **Volkswagen Iltis** vehicles. The first of these were handed over in 1978, and production has now been completed for the West German armed forces. The Iltis was entered in the French army competition for a new light vehicle by Citroën under the designation **Citroën C 44**, but this competition was eventually won by Peugeot P4 based on a West German

Mercedes-Benz design. More recently the Iltis has been selected by the Canadian Armed Forces to replace its obsolete M38 vehicles which have been in service for some 30 years, and production will be undertaken in Canada by Bombardier Incorporated.

The Iltis has a pressed steel body with the engine at the front, driver and one passenger in the centre, and cargo area at the rear. The last has a seat which can be folded down to increase the load area. In inclement weather the windscreen is raised and the folding hood and removable sidescreens fitted. The engine is coupled to a manual gearbox with five forward and one reverse gear and a two-speed transfer box. When driving on roads the front axle is normally disengaged so the vehicle becomes a 4×2. Suspension front and rear consists of semi-elliptical leaf springs and double-acting hydraulic shock absorbers.

The basic vehicle is used for normal duties in the front-line area, but more specialized versions include a cable-layer for use by signal units, a command vehicle with communications equipment, an artillery survey vehicle, an ambulance and an anti-tank vehicle with Euromissile MILAN ATGWs. This last model is the replacement for the Lkw with Cobra ATGWs that were

launched over the rear of the vehicle.

The West German Army also uses a number of **Volkswagen 181** (4×2) light vehicles for general duties where a 4×4 capability is not essential, and numbers of these vehicles were supplied to Austria, Denmark and France for military use.

Specification
Volkswagen Iltis
Crew: 1 + 1 (plus 2 in rear)
Weight: empty 1550 kg (3,417 lb) and loaded 2050 kg (4,520 lb)
Powerplant: one 4-cylinder petrol engine developing 75 hp (56 kW)

A Volkswagen Iltis (4×4) vehicle with the hood folded down at the rear. This is now the standard vehicle in its class in the West German armed forces, and is now being manufactured under licence in Canada by Bombardier Incorporated.

Dimensions: length 3,887 m (12 ft 9 in); width 1.52 m (5 ft 0 in); height 1.857 m (6 ft 1 in)
Performance: maximum road speed 130 km/h (80 mph); maximum range 500 km (311 miles); gradient 70 per cent; fording 0.60 m (2 ft 0 in)

UAZ-469B light vehicle

In 1960 the Ul'yanovsk Motor Vehicle Plant, which was then building the UAZ-69 and UAZ-69A (4×4) light vehicles, built the prototype of a new vehicle called the **UAZ-469**, which used many components of the **UAZ-450** range of 4×4 forward control vehicles designed mainly for civilian use. This was not placed in production and further development resulted in the **UAZ-469B** which entered production in 1972 and has now replaced almost all of the UAZ-69 and UAZ-69A light vehicles in the armies of the USSR and of most other members of the Warsaw Pact. The UAZ-469B uses the engine, transmission, axles, brakes and other parts of the **UAZ-452** series of 4×4 light vehicles, which are used in both civilian and military roles. The vehicle has been widely exported outside the Soviet Union, especially to the Middle East, and is available on the civilian market as the **Tundra**.

The main improvements of the UAZ-469B over the earlier vehicle include slightly increased payload, greater road speed and much longer operational range.

The layout of the UAZ-469B is conventional, with the engine at the front and the driver and passenger in the centre (each with a side door); to their rear is a three-man bench seat with a door on each side, and a further two men can sit at the rear, one on each side, facing each other. The windscreen can be folded forward onto the bonnet, the tops of the doors removed and the canvas top folded down. When carrying seven men the freight payload of the vehicle is only 100 kg (220 lb), but when only the driver and one passenger are carried this payload is increased to 600 kg (1,323 lb). The vehicle can also tow an unbraked trailer weighing a total of 600 kg (1,323 lb), or 2000 kg (4,409 lb) if braked.

The four-cylinder petrol engine is coupled to a manual gearbox with four forward and one reverse gear and a two-speed transfer case. The suspension consists of semi-elliptical springs and hydraulic shock absorbers; 8.40×15 tyres are fitted all round, and a spare wheel and tyre are located on the rear.

In addition to the basic model, which is widely used by the Soviet army, there is also an ambulance model designated the **UAZ-469G** which can carry four stretcher patients in addition to the driver, a fully enclosed van-type vehicle used for a variety of roles, and another that has equipment fitted at the rear of the hull that dispenses pennants into the ground to designate clear lanes through NBC-contaminated areas.

Although the UAZ-469B is the most widely used light vehicle, it is not the only one of its type in the Soviet Union. The **VAZ-2121** (4×4) light vehicle has been used for a number of military applications and is sold in the West as the **Niva**. The Lutsk Motor Vehicle Plant has developed the **LuAZ-967M** amphibious battlefield medical reconnaissance vehicle as well as the **LuAZ-969** (4×4) light vehicle which is used mainly for civilian applications, although its automotive components are used in the LuAZ-967M.

In general terms, Soviet trucks and light vehicles have not proved so popular in the Middle East and elsewhere as their Western counterparts have, as the latter are found to be more reliable.

Specification
UAZ-469B
Crew: 1 + 1 (plus 7 in rear)
Weight: empty 2290 kg (5,048 lb) and loaded 1540 kg (3,395 lb)
Powerplant: one ZMZ-4151M 4-cylinder water-cooled petrol engine developing 75 hp (56 kW)
Dimensions: length 4.025 m (13 ft 2 in); width 1.785 m (5 ft 10 in); height 2.015 m (6 ft 7 in)
Performance: maximum road speed 100 km/h (62 mph); maximum range 750 km (466 miles); gradient 62 per cent; fording 0.80 m (2 ft 8 in)

A UAZ-469B (4×4) light vehicle, which entered production in 1972. It is used by every arm of the Soviet forces and has been exported on a large scale.

GAZ-69 series

The **GAZ-69** series is the Soviet equivalent of the Jeep, and entered production at the Gor'ky Motor Vehicle Plant in 1952, although in 1956 production was transferred to the Ul'yanovsk Motor Vehicle Plant and the vehicle was subsequently redesignated **UAZ-69**. Production continued well into the 1960s, the type's replacement, the UAZX-469B, entering production in 1972.

The basic GAZ-69 has a conventional layout with the engine at the front, the driver and one passenger in the centre, and the cargo at the rear. The last has a bench seat down each side. The windscreen can be folded forward onto the bonnet, and the crew and cargo/passenger area can be covered by a quickly-removable cover that is stowed at the rear when not in use. The GAZ-69 can carry a maximum load of 500 kg (1,102 lb) and tow a trailer weighing a maximum of 850 kg (1,874 lb).

The M-20 petrol engine is coupled to a manual gearbox with three forward and one reverse gear, a two-speed transfer box being standard. Suspension front and rear consists of semi-elliptical springs with hydraulic shock absorbers. Late production vehicles were of the UAZ-69M standard with a more powerful engine.

The **GAZ-69A** (later **UAZ-69A**) has four doors, two on each side, and can carry five men and 100 kg (220 lb) of cargo.

As with most vehicles of this type the chassis has been used for a number of applications. The GAZ-69 anti-tank vehicle has been rebuilt to the rear of the driver/passenger area and carries four AT-1 'Snapper' wire-guided anti-tank missiles, which are launched to the rear of the vehicle with the operator either a short distance away from the vehicle (controlling the missiles with a separation sight and controller)

or from within the cab (a window in the right side being provided for this purpose). This particular vehicle has seen combat in the Middle East.

The chassis was also used as the basis for the **GAZ-46** or **MAV** amphibious vehicle, which is similar in concept to the American Ford GPA (4×4) vehicle supplied to the Soviet Union during World War II and based on a Jeep chassis. The GAZ-46 was used to carry out reconnaissance of river crossing points, but this role has now been taken over by amphibious armoured vehicles such as the BRDM-1 and BRDM-2.

A GAZ-69 (4×4) light vehicle, used in the anti-tank role with a four-round launcher for Snapper ATGWs at the rear. In this photograph the wire-guided ATGWs are not fitted. The launcher is covered when travelling.

One of the more unusual models is that fitted with DIM mine-detection equipment. When travelling this equipment rests on the roof of the vehicle, but when required for use is swung through about 140° to project over the front of the vehicle, where it is supported by two small rubber tyres. The vehicle is driven along the road at low speed, and when the sensor detects a mine or other metallic object the vehicle automatically stops and an alarm sounds. Once the exact position of the mine has been determined its position is marked and the vehicle withdrawn to the rear while it is neutralized.

A GAZ-69 (4×4) light vehicle with the top in the raised position. This entered service with the Soviet armed forces in 1952, but has now been replaced in most units by the UAZ-469B, which has a slightly greater payload.

A GAZ-69 (4×4) light vehicle, which has seats for the driver and one passenger at the front and a bench seat down each side at the rear. The windscreen is in the raised position but the cover is not erected. On the left side of the vehicle is the spare wheel and tyre.

Specification
GAZ-69

Crew: 1+1 (plus 4 in rear)

Weight: empty 2175 kg (4,795 lb) and loaded 1525 kg (3,362 lb)

Powerplant: one M-20 4-cylinder petrol engine developing 52 hp (39 kW)

Dimensions: length 3.85 m (12 ft 8 in); width 1.85 m (5 ft 2 in); height 2.03 m (6 ft 8 in)

Performance: maximum road speed 90 km/h (56 mph); maximum range 530 km (330 miles); gradient 60 per cent; fording 0.55 m (1 ft 10 in)

Fiat 1107 AD light vehicle

When the Italian army was re-formed its requirement for a light vehicle was met by the **Fiat AR-51** which was powered by a four-cylinder petrol engine developing 53 hp (39.5 kW); this was succeeded in production by the **AR-55** and finally by the **AR-59**. All these vehicles have a similar layout with the engine at the front, driver and one passenger in the centre, and cargo area at the rear, the last having a

bench seat down each side for two men. An interesting feature of these vehicles was that the side doors could be swung back through 180° and clipped to the sides so allowing the crew to leave the vehicle rapidly in an emergency.

The AR-59 was replaced in production by the **Fiat 1107 AD** (4×4) light vehicle which has a maximum payload of 750 kg (1,653 lb) across country and

can tow a 1740-kg (3,836-lb) trailer on roads or a 900-kg (1,984-lb) trailer across country.

The Fiat 1107 AD entered production in 1974 for both the civilian and military markets. It is also produced under licence in Yugoslavia for the army (as was the earlier AR-59 under the name of the **Zastava**) and was entered in the French army's competition for a new light vehicle by Renault

under the designation **Renault TRM 500**, although this competition was won by Peugeot.

The body of the Fiat 1107 AD is of all-steel construction, with the engine at the front, driver and two passengers in the centre (with a door on each side opening to the front) and the cargo area at the rear. The last has a bench seat down each side for two men, and can be loaded via the tailgate, on

The Fiat 1107 AD (4×4) chassis is used for a number of applications, such as this forward ambulance with bodywork by Grazia. In addition to the military, civilian authorities such as ambulance and fire brigades use the military-type chassis where an off-road capability is required.

which the spare wheel is carried. The basic model has a windscreen that folds forward onto the bonnet and a removable canvas top and side curtains. The Fiat 1107 AD is also produced with a fully enclosed hard-top body and there is also a long-wheelbase version that can carry a total of nine men.

The petrol engine is coupled to a manual gearbox with five forward and one reverse gear and a two-speed transfer box. Suspension is of the independent McPherson type with longitudinal torsion bar. Each front wheel station has a single hydraulic shock absorber while each rear wheel station has two hydraulic shock absorbers, because the loaded vehicle has more weight on the back of the vehicle than the front.

More recently the company has offered the type with a diesel engine for longer operational range. Standard equipment for the military model includes a pintle towing hook at the rear to enable trailers and light weapons to be towed, towing eyes at the front, pick and shovel, a fire-extinguishing system, and a heating and defrosting system; options include a petrol engine that will run on low-octane fuel and special equipment such as engine protection and a fuel filter between pump and carburettor.

The vehicle can be adapted as a communications vehicle or ambu-

lance, and a number of companies in Italy have made use of the chassis for other applications, one such being ASA for the **Guardian** internal security vehicle, which was used in small numbers by the Italian peacekeeping force in Lebanon early in 1984.

Specification
Fiat 1107 AD
Crew: 1+2 (plus 4 in rear)
Weight: empty 2420 kg (5,335 lb) and loaded 1670 kg (3,682 lb)
Powerplant: one 4-cylinder petrol engine developing 80 hp (59.7 kW)

Dimensions: length 3.775 m (12 ft 5 in); width 1.58 m (5 ft 1 in); height 1.901 m (6 ft 3 in)
Performance: maximum road speed 120 km/h (74.5 mph); maximum range 400 km (249 miles); gradient 100 per cent; fording 0.70 m (2 ft 3 in)

DAF YA 126 weapons carrier

Since well before World War II Van Doorne's Automobielfabriek of Eindhoven has been a major supplier of wheeled transport vehicles to the Dutch army. In the immediate postwar period the company, which today is known as DAF Trucks, produced a complete range of new transport vehicles for the Dutch army, the smallest member of this family being the **DAF YA 126** (4×4) weapon carrier. The prototype of this was completed in 1950, and production was undertaken at Eindhoven between 1952 and 1960. The type is still in service, but has been replaced in many units by DAF trucks with an increased payload.

The layout of the DAF YA 126 weapons carrier is conventional, with the engine at the front, the driver and one passenger in the centre, and the cargo area at the rear. The windscreen can be folded down onto the bonnet and the rear cargo area can be covered by removable bows and a tarpaulin cover. Four troops can be seated down each side of the cargo area and the dropdown tailgate facilitates the loading and unloading of supplies. The engine of the YA 126, which is the same as that installed in the **DAF YA 314** (6×6) 3000-kg (6,614-lb) truck, is coupled to a manual gearbox with four forward and one reverse gear and a two-speed transfer case. The front and rear wheels, which have 9.00×16 tyres, are suspended on two longitu-

dinal trailing arms connected at the front with transversely mounted tubular beams containing torsion bars. Between the upper trailing arms and the chassis auxiliary rubber springs are fitted, and each wheel also has a hydraulic shock absorber.

On each side of the vehicle is a spare wheel and tyre; these are free to rotate and so assist the vehicle in overcoming obstacles, a similar arrangement being used on the **DAF YA 328** (6×6) 3000-kg (6,614-lb) cargo truck.

Some vehicles were fitted with a winch with a capacity of 2500 kg (5,512 lb), and variants included a workshop vehicle, fully enclosed van-type ambulance that can carry a maximum of four stretcher patients, and a command/radio vehicle.

To meet the requirements of the Dutch army for a light utility vehicle, the DAF company designed the **DAF 55 YA** (4×2) which is based on standard and proven commercial components. This was eventually standar-

A DAF YA 126 (4×4) weapons carrier, with bows and a tarpaulin cover erected over the troop compartment at the rear. To assist with self-recovery and to recover other vehicles that became stuck, a number of Dutch army YA 126 vehicles were fitted with a winch.

dized as the **DAF 66 YA**, and a total of 1,200 vehicles were delivered between 1973 and 1977. In addition to the driver, this vehicle can carry three passengers and 400 kg (881 lb) of cargo. To increase the load-carrying area the two rear seats can be folded down. Typical roles for the DAF 66 YA include rear-area military policing where good off-road performance is not required, casualty evacuation with two stretcher patients plus the medical attendant and driver, and radio carrying.

The Dutch army is also a large user of the Land Rover (4×4) vehicle, including a number supplied to meet its own specific requirements.

Specification
DAF YA 126
Crew: 1+1 (plus 8 in rear)
Weight: empty 4230 kg (9,325 lb) and loaded 3230 kg (7,121 lb)

Powerplant: one Hercules JXC 6-cylinder petrol engine developing 102 hp (76 kW)
Dimensions: length 4.55 m (14 ft 11 in); width 2.10 m (6 ft 11 in); height 2.20 m (7 ft 3 in)
Performance: maximum road speed 84 km/h (52 mph); maximum range 330 km (205 miles); gradient 65 per cent; fording 0.76 m (2 ft 6 in)

A DAF YA 126 (4×4) weapons carrier, which was in production for the Dutch army between 1952 and 1960. An unusual feature of this vehicle is that the spare wheel on each side is free-wheeling and assists the YA 126 in overcoming obstacles while crossing rough country.

Japanese light vehicles

In the early 1950s Mitsubishi Motors Corporation obtained a licence from the American Jeep manufacturer Willys to undertake production of the Jeep in Japan for both civilian and military roles. The **Mitsubishi J54A**, powered by a four-cylinder petrol engine developing 75 hp (56 kW), was the standard ¼-ton vehicle of the Japanese Self-Defence Forces for many years. This has now been replaced by the **J25A** which has the military designation **Type 73**; this is powered by a diesel for increased fuel efficiency. The Type 73 is very similar in appearance to the Jeeps used by the Allies during World War II, and has an identical layout with the engine at the front, driver and one passenger in the centre, and two seats at the rear. One of the distinguishing features of these vehicles is that each of the headlamps at the front has vertical bars to protect it from damage. As usual there are many variants of Jeep used by the Japanese Ground Self-Defence Force, including a reconnaissance vehicle fitted with a pintle-mounted 7.62-mm (0.3-in) machine-gun, and an anti-tank vehicle with the 106-mm (4.17-in) M40 recoilless rifle, KAM-3D (Type 64) or the more recent KAM-9 (Type 79) anti-tank missiles, the last having a much longer range.

In addition to Mitsubishi, the Nissan Motor Company and Toyota also manufacture light vehicles. These are designed for civilian applications but are used by many armies around the world. The **Nissan Patrol** vehicle is produced in standard open-type as well as hard-top, pick-up and long-wheelbase configuration. It has also been built under licence in India by Mahindra and Mahindra, which has supplied many vehicles to the Indian armed forces for a wide range of roles including anti-tank (with recoilless rifles), command (with radios) and reconnaissance. One of the more unusual versions used by the Indian army has three SS.11 wire-guided anti-tank missiles over the roof, firing forward. India has also exported vehicles to other countries, and recently supplied some 4,000 Jeep kits for assembly in Iran.

The **Toyota Land Cruiser** is used by many countries in Africa and the Far East, and is available in three different wheelbases (standard, long wheelbase and super long wheelbase), the first two of these being used by the military. They are available with four-

or six-cylinder petrol or diesel engines, the petrol engine being preferred in many parts of the third world as there are more petrol than diesel stations.

If one excludes the United States and the Soviet Union, the British Land Rover was for many years the most widely used vehicle of its type, but in recent years the Japanese have been making steady inroads to many traditional Land Rover markets, and in 1980 alone Nissan and Toyota between them built some 150,000 4×4 light vehicles for the home and export markets, although most of these were for civilian rather than military use.

Specification
Mitsubishi J25A
Crew: 1+1 (plus 2 in rear)
Weight: empty 1420 kg (3,130 lb) and loaded 1900 kg (4,189 lb)
Powerplant: one 4-cylinder diesel developing 80 hp (59.7 kW)
Dimensions: length 3.75 m (12 ft 4 in); width 1.655 m (5 ft 5 in); height 1.95 m (6 ft 5 in);
Performance: maximum road speed 90 km/h (56 mph); maximum range 500 km (311 miles); gradient 60 per cent; fording 0.5 m (1 ft 8 in)

Above: A long-wheelbase Mitsubishi (4×4) light vehicle, which can carry six men instead of the four men of the normal version. These are used for a wide range of roles including that of anti-tank, fitted with ATGWs; command, fitted with radios; and forward ambulance.

Below: Mitsubishi (4×4) light vehicles of the Japanese Ground Self Defence Force (JGSDF) fitted with 7.62-mm (0.3-in) machine-guns on pintle mounts at the rear for use in the reconnaissance role. Latest versions of the vehicle have a diesel engine for longer range.

Multiple Rocket Launchers

What began as a cheap and somewhat haphazard weapon has progressed, thanks to the application of technology, into an expensive and more predictable weapon. However, the jury is still out on just how effective the rocket launcher is.

Rockets have been part of the artillery armoury for just over 200 years, but they went out of fashion in the 1890s. They did not really regain their place in the battle line until World War II, when both Germany and Russia put multiple rocket launchers into the field. Britain developed the rocket as an anti-aircraft weapon, but then used these for ground bombardment in the final months of the war. The principal drawback with rocket launchers was that, compared with guns, they were inaccurate. Spin stabilization helped to improve matters, but large rockets had to be fin-stabilized, and as soon as the wind hit the fins, accuracy vanished. The rocket launcher was an 'area weapon', and treated as such it was devastating. As the Russians proved, if you lined up a few hundred launchers and fired them, the amount of explosive dumped onto the enemy was vast, far greater than the same number of guns could achieve.

But the inaccuracy label stuck, and besides the Russians few people took much interest in free-flight rockets. They were cheap and they made a big bang at the target, if could get to it. In the nuclear age, lining up several launchers was no longer feasible.

A Brazilian SS-30 rocket being fired from its AV-LMU armoured launch vehicle. This truck forms part of the ASTROS (Artillery SaTuration ROcket System) system, developed by Avibras.

Technology improved the rockets. With more precise design and manufacture, more accurate methods of measuring wind and other factors, by using computers to determine exactly how to adjust the initial aim to compensate, overall accuracy improved. Then technology took another step forward and began developing rockets with multiple warheads, or warheads filled with independent munitions, mines, or bomblets capable of defeating armour. With this sort of payload, pinpoint accuracy was not so vital, since the bursting warhead scattered the sub-munitions all around the target area.

This type of rocket – exemplified by the MLRS – saw action in the 1991 Gulf War, and appears to have operated satisfactorily. As the following pages show there is no shortage of rocket designs on offer all over the world. But there is still that question at the back of the artilleryman's mind: will it hit the target? There is simply not enough data or experience of the use of modern rockets in war for us to make assumptions.

Light Artillery Rocket System (LARS)

The 110-mm (4.33-in) Light Artillery Rocket System (LARS) was developed in the mid-1960s and accepted into West German army service in 1969. It is issued on the scale of one battery of eight launchers per army division, each battery also having two 4×4 truck-mounted Fieldguard fire-control systems and a resupply vehicle with 144 rockets. Following upgrading to the LARS II standard, each launcher is now mounted on the rear of a 7000-kg (15,432-lb) MAN 6×6 truck chassis and consists of two side-by-side banks of 18 launcher tubes. The fin-stabilized solid propellant rockets can all be fired within 17.5 seconds, manual reloading taking approximately 15 minutes. The minimum and maximum ranges are 6 km (3.73 miles) and 14 km (8.7 miles) respectively. There are seven types of warhead that can be fitted to the rocket, these including the DM-711 mine dispenser with five parachute-retarded AT-2 anti-tank mines, the DM-21 HE-fragmentation, and the DM-701 mine dispenser with eight AT-1 anti-tank mines. A total of 209 LARS II launchers is in service with the West German army at present, and these are likely to be relegated to reserve units as the MLRS is phased into service during the late 1980s and early 1990s.

Specification
LARS II
Combat weight: 17480 kg (38,537 lb)
Crew: 3
Chassis: 7000 kg (15,432 lb) MAN 6×6 truck
Calibre: 110 mm (4.33 in)
No. of launcher tubes: 36
Rocket length: not known
Rocket weight: not known
Warhead types: HE-fragmentation, submunition, smoke, practice, radar target
Warhead weights: not known

Called the Artillerie Raketenwerfer 110SF by the West German army, the system is issued on the scale of one battery per division, each battery having two Swiss Contraves Fieldguard radar fire control systems on a 4×4 truck chassis and a resupply vehicle with 144 rockets.

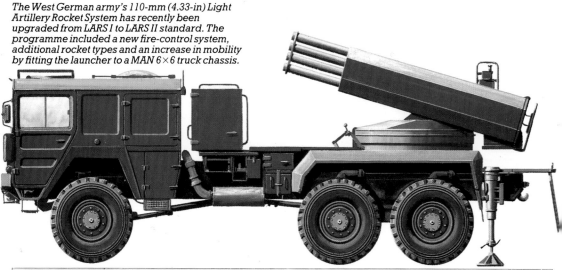

The West German army's 110-mm (4.33-in) Light Artillery Rocket System has recently been upgraded from LARS I to LARS II standard. The programme included a new fire-control system, additional rocket types and an increase in mobility by fitting the launcher to a MAN 6×6 truck chassis.

BM-21 multiple rocket-launcher

The 122-mm (4.8-in) BM-21 MRL entered service in the early 1960s and has since become the standard MRL of the Warsaw Pact and most Soviet-supplied client states. Variants of the system have also been manufactured in China (the 40-round Type 81 MRL), Egypt (a straight 40-round copy and modified 21- and 30-round systems, together with the Sakr-18 and Sakr-30 systems), India (the 40-round LRAR system) and Romania (a 21-round launcher on a Bucegi SR-114 lorry chassis). In the Warsaw Pact the BM-21 is found on both the Ural-375D 6×6 truck and, more recently, the ZIL-131 truck in a modified 36-round version identified as the M1976 by NATO. There is also a 12-round launcher mounted on a small 4×4 vehicle, the M1975, which is in service with Soviet airborne troops as a replacement for the older towed 140-mm (5.5-in) MRLs. During the 1982 Israeli invasion of Lebanon the Israeli army came across a 30-round BM-21

The standard Warsaw Pact Multiple Rocket Launcher is the 122-mm (4.8-in) BM-21, with a 40-round launcher mounted on the rear of a Ural-375 6×6 truck chassis. Several countries have copied the system, while others have built their own versions.

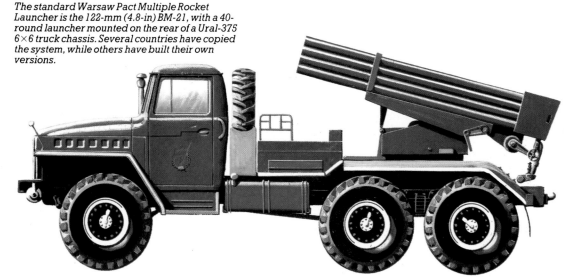

variant mounted on the rear platform of a Japanese Isuzu 6×6 truck which is identical in most respects to the Egyptian 30-round system mounted on the same chassis but is actually manufactured in North Korea under the designation BM-11.

The BM-21 is normally found in battalions of 18 integrated into the divisional artillery regiment, but a number of Category 1 motorized rifle divisions also have regimental batteries of six BM-21s or M1976s in service. The 122-mm rocket can be fitted with a smoke, HE-fragmentation, incendiary or chemical warhead, and the launcher can be filled with mixed loads if required. Most of the BM-21 variants have now been used in combat throughout the world, the latest Soviet systems having been blooded in Afghanistan against the guerrillas there. A number of local guerrilla forces such as the PLO have also taken

parts of the BM-21 launcher to produce home-built systems for use in their internal conflicts. The PLO MRLs saw considerable use in the battles in and around Beirut from 1982 onwards.

Specification
BM-21
Combat weight: 11500 kg (25,353 lb)
Crew: 6
Chassis: Ural-375D 6×6 truck
Calibre: 122 mm (4.8 in)
No. of launcher tubes: 40
Length of rocket: standard 3.23 m (10.6 ft), and short 1.91 m (6.3 ft)
Weight of rocket: standard 77 kg (169.75 lb), and short 45.8 kg (100.97 lb)
Warhead types: HE-fragmentation, incendiary, smoke, chemical
Warhead weight: 19.4 kg (42.77 lb)
Maximum range: standard 20.38 km (12.66 miles), and short 11 km (6.84 miles)

The BM-21 is seen in a Moscow parade with several 200-mm (7.87-in) four-round BMD-20 multiple rocket systems in front. In recent years the Soviets have also produced 36-round and 12-round MRLS, code-named M1976 and M1975 respectively by NATO, based on the BM-21 system.

BM-24 multiple rocket-launcher

Introduced into service during the early 1950s, the 240-mm (9.45-in) **BM-24** MRL has now been replaced in front-line service by either the 122-mm (4.8-in) BM-21 or the 220-mm (8.66-in) BM-27 systems, and is now usually found in Soviet second-line units and the strategic reserve stockpile for issue during wartime to mobilized divisions. The BM-24 has been widely exported and has seen widespread use with the Arab armies in the Middle East against Israel.

The system was originally mounted on the rear of the 2500-kg (5,512-lb) ZIL-151 6×6 truck, but is now to be found on the ZIL-157 truck chassis. The launcher consists of two rows of six tubular frame rails with two stabilizer jacks and armoured window shutters that need to be lowered for firing. Israel was so impressed by the system when it was used against its forces that it adopted captured BM-24s as one of the Israeli army's standard MRL systems. A new rocket was manufactured for the launcher, and the equipments were grouped into independent MRL artillery battalions which were used in combat during the 1973 'Yom Kippur' and 1982 'Peace for Galilee' wars. The new Israeli Military Industries rocket is 1.29 m (4.23 ft) long and weighs

The 12-round 240-mm (9.45-in) BM-24 Multiple Rocket Launcher entered service with the Soviet army in the early 1950s and is now found only in training units and the strategic war reserve for mobilization units.

110.5 kg (243.6 lb) with a 48.3 kg (106.5-lb) HE-fragmentation warhead of superior performance to that of the original Soviet type. The maximum range is slightly less than that of the Soviet rocket at 10.7 km (6.65 miles).

The Soviets also mounted a 12-round 240-mm launcher on the rear of an AT-S medium artillery tractor under the designation **BM-24T** for use by

armoured units, but as far as it is known this is no longer in service, the tractors having been converted back to their original use.

Specification
BM-24
Combat weight: 9200 kg (20,283 lb)
Crew: 6

Chassis: 2500-kg (5,512-lb) ZIL-157 6×6 truck
Calibre: 240 mm (9.45 in)
No. of launcher rails: 12
Length of rocket: 1.18 m (3.87 ft)
Weight of rocket: 112..5 kg (248 lb)
Warhead types: HE-fragmentation, smoke, chemical
Warhead weight: 46.9 kg (103.4 lb)
Maximum range: 11 km (6.84 miles)

Following the 1967 war between the Arabs and the Israelis, the latter came into possession of large numbers of BM-24s as war booty. These were promptly refurbished and issued to independent MRL battalions of the Israeli army, who used them against the Arabs in 1973 and in Lebanon in 1982.

The adoption of the BM-24 into Israeli army service resulted in Israel Military Industries manufacturing a new rocket for the system that has greater lethality than the original Soviet model, although maximum range of the rocket has been marginally reduced.

BM-22 multiple rocket launcher

The 16 round 220-mm (8.99-in) BM-22 MRL was active in the Soviet Army in the mid-1970s and is found in selected Category 1 motorised rifle and tank division artillery regiment rocket launcher battalions and at battalion strength in the combined arms army artillery brigades. In the tank army the artillery brigade has been replaced by an MRL regiment of three battalions with 72 BM-22s. At front level the system has been integrated into the rocket launcher brigade of the artillery division. The BM22 provides chemical HE and submunition (including anti-personnel, incendiary, and minelet) supporting fire to first-echelon manoeuvre units during offensive and defensive operations. The launcher comprises one layer of four tubes on two layers of six tubes, and is carried on the rear platform of a ZIL-135 8×8 truck chassis. A rapid-reload system allows a second ZIL-135 carrying 16 reload rounds to transfer its load within five minutes. For firing four stabilizer jacks have to be lowered, two at the rear and one on each side of the vehicle. It is believed that the system has also been exported in limited numbers to Syria for combat evaluation against Israel.

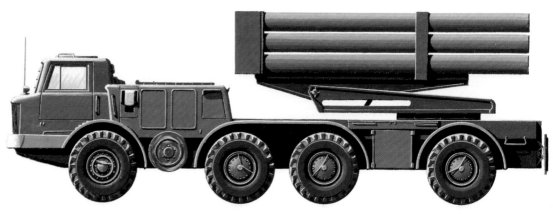

Specification
BM-22
Combat weight: 22750 kg (50.155 lb)
Crew: 6
Chassis: ZIL-135 8 x 8 truck
Calibre: 220 mm (8.66 in)
No. of launcher tubes: 6

Length of rocket: 4.8 m (15.75 ft)
Weight of rocket: 360 kg (793.7 lb)
Warhead types: HE-fragmentation, chemical, submunition
Warhead weights: not known
Maximum range: 40 km (24.85 miles)

The most recent Soviet rocket launcher system to enter service is the 220-mm (8.66-in) 16 round BM-22 mounted on the rear of the ZIL-135 8 x 8 truck chassis. In operational characteristics it is very similar to the American MLRS.

Brazilian multiple rocket-launcher systems

Since the early 1960s the Brazilians have been developing MRL systems both for the home and export markets. The first was the **FGT-108RA1** which is currently used by the Brazilian army, Brazilian marines and Iraq. It utilizes a single-stage solid-propellant 108-mm (4.25-in) calibre rocket fired from a 16-round launcher which is mounted either on the back of a light 4×4 vehicle or, more normally, on a two-wheeled trailer. The crew consists of four and a battery of these weapons has four launchers.

The X2A1 trailer used for the FGT-108 was also the basis for the next system, the 36-round **SBAT-70** launcher. This fires a modified version of the standard 70-mm (2.76-in) Avibras folding-fin aircraft rocket which can be fitted with one of seven different types of warhead. Although not operational with the Brazilian army the SBAT-70 has been produced for several unidentified export customers.

Avibras also adapted its 127-mm (5-in) calibre air-to-surface rocket in the same way to produce the **SBAT-127** system for export. This utilizes a 12-rail launcher for either trailer or vehicle mounting, but has the choice of only two different-weight HE-fragmentation warheads. The maximum range is achieved at a launcher elevation of 47°.

These systems were followed by two experimental research rockets, the **FGT X-20** and **FGT X-40** to improve long-range rocket technology. These were followed in the early 1980s by a request to Avibras from a foreign country, believed to be Iraq, to design a mobile MRL system. With the aid of Brazilian army inputs this resulted in the **Astros II** modular mobile MRL system mounted on identical 10000-kg (22,046-lb) Tectran 6×6 truck chassis. The three variants are the 32-round **SS-30**, the 16-round **SS-40** and the four-round **SS-60**, which differ only in the size and weight of the rockets they fire.

The X-40 is the largest of the Brazilian rockets, and is fired from the XLF-40 version of the X1A1/X1A2 series light tank. Although at one time thought to be an operational system, it is now known to be used in armament research trials.

This is the Tectran 6×6 truck chassis launcher for the SS-30 rocket. The modular design can be clearly seen, with the four eight-round launch tube containers located within the firing platform on the truck's rear deck.

A typical battery is believed to comprise from four to eight launchers with optional radar fire-control vehicles. The crew consists of three men, with reloading undertaken from other trucks using module rocket pods. Iraq ordered 60 batteries of the Astros II and is already using the system in combat against Iran. Libya is also believed to have ordered a few batteries, while the Brazilian army is known to be interested.

Specifications

FGT-108
Combat weight: 802 kg (1,768 lb)
Crew: 4
Chassis: X2A1 trailer
Calibre: 108 mm (4.25 in)
No. of rocket tubes: 16
Rocket length: 0.97 m (3.18 ft)
Rocket weight: 17 kg (37.5 lb)
Warhead type: HE-fragmentation
Warhead weight: 3 kg (6.6 lb)
Maximum range: 7 km (4.35 miles)

SBAT-70
Combat weight: 1000 kg (2,205 lb)
Crew: 4
Chassis: X2A1 trailer
Calibre: 70 mm (2.76 in)
No. of rocket tubes: 36
Rocket length: not known
Rocket weight: 9 kg (19.84 lb)
Warhead types: HEAT, HE-fragmentation, HE-anti-tank/anti-personnel, anti-personnel flechette, smoke, practice
Warhead weight: 4 kg (8.8 lb)
Maximum range: 7.5 km (4.66 miles)

SBAT-127
Combat weight: not known
Crew: 4
Chassis: trailer or vehicle
Calibre: 127 mm (5 in)
No. of launcher rails: 12
Rocket length: not known
Rocket weights: 48/61 kg (105.8 lb/134.5 lb)
Warhead type: HE-fragmentation
Warhead weights: 22/35 kg (48.5/77.2 lb)
Maximum ranges: 14 km/12.5 km (8.7/7.77 miles)

Astros II
Rocket: SS-30
Crew: 3
Chassis: 10000-kg (22,046-lb) Tectran 6×6 truck
Calibre: 127 mm (5 in)
No. of launch tubes: 32
Rocket length: 3.9 m (12.8 ft)
Rocket weight: 68 kg (149.9 lb)
Maximum range: 30 km (18.64 miles)
Warhead types: HE

Rocket: SS-40
Crew: 3
Chassis: 10000-kg (22,046-lb) Tectran 6×6 truck
Calibre: 180 mm (7.09 in)
No. of launch tubes: 16
Rocket length: 4.2 m (13.78 ft)
Rocket weight: 152 kg (335.1 lb)
Maximum range: 35 km (21.75 miles)
Warhead types: HE, submunition

Rocket: SS-60
Crew: 3
Chassis: 10000-kg (22,046-lb) Tectran 6×6 truck
Calibre: 300 mm (11.81 in)
No. of launch tubes: 4
Rocket length: 5.6 m (18.37 ft)
Rocket weight: 595 kg (1,311.7 lb)
Maximum range: 60 km (37.28 miles)
Warhead types: HE, submunition

The fire control system for the Astros II modular multiple rocket system can be the Swiss Contraves Fieldguard J-band radar, with a 300-m (984.25-ft) to 20000-m (65616.8-ft) range. It is used to plot rocket trajectories and hence calculate the impact point.

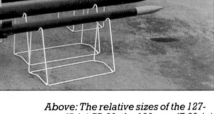

Below: The 70-mm (2.76-in) SBAT-70 36-tube trailer-mounted rocket-launcher system is based on the standard Avibras folding-fin aircraft rocket, and is currently being offered on the export market.

Above: The relative sizes of the 127-mm (5-in) SS-30, the 180-mm (7.09-in) SS-40 and 300-mm (11.81-in) SS-60 artillery rockets can be seen here. The two larger rockets have cluster munition warheads with dual effect anti-armour anti-personnel bomblets.

Above: Smallest of the Astros II artillery rockets fired from the Tectran 6×6 truck launcher is the 127-mm (5-in) calibre SS-30, which has a range of 30 km (18.75 miles). A total of 32 launch tubes are fitted to this configuration of the launcher.

Multiple Launch Rocket System (MLRS)

Initiated as a feasibility study in 1976, the concept definition phase of the **General Support Rocket System (GSRS)** was contracted to five different firms. After evaluation of these, Boeing Aerospace and Vought Corporation (now LTV Aerospace and Defence Company) were asked to compete in the follow-on validation stage. At the same time the system was directed towards a standard NATO weapon design. The trials were held in 1979 and early 1980, with the result that Vought was chosen as the winner. In the same year the GSRS title was changed to the definitive **Multiple Launch Rocket System (MLRS)**.

The first production battery of Self-Propelled Launcher Loaders (SPLL), based on the M2 IFV chassis, was delivered to the US Army in 1982, with a total of 805 by the late 1990s.

Launchers purchased by other armies include 55 for France, 150 for Germany, 24 for Italy, 59 for the UK, 22 for the Netherlands, 150 for Japan and 132 for Turkey. With the exception of Japan and the Netherlands, the majority of these SPLLs have been built in Europe by an international consortium, which is also manufacturing the rockets.

Each SPLL carries 12 rockets in two six-round pods, and can be self-loaded from a resupply vehicle within 10 minutes. Four warheads have or are in the process of being developed for the single-stage solid-propellant rocket. These are the basic Phase I submunition model with a range of about 30 km (18.6 miles) carrying 644 M77 dual-purpose shaped-charge blast-fragmentation bomblets each weighing 0.23 kg (0.51 lb) and capable of piercing some 100 mm (3.94 in) of armour plate; the Phase II mine-dispenser model, with 28 AT-2 parachute-retarded anti-tank mines de-

veloped by West Germany, allowing a rocket range of 40 km (24.9 miles); the Phase III submunition model with six individual active-radar terminally-guided shaped-charge free-fall weapons allowing a rocket range of 42 km (26.1 miles); and a US only chemical warhead containing approximately 41.7 kg (92 lb) of binary nerve gas chemical agents.

Further studies are being carried out to see if lightweight three- or six-round rocket pods based on the MLRS design can be mounted on more mobile chassis types for use by the new US Army lightweight divisions.

Specification
MLRS
Combat weight: 25191 kg (55,536 lb)
Crew: 3
Chassis: M2 IFV
Calibre: 227 mm (8.94 in)
No. of launcher tubes: 12
Rocket length: 3.94 m (12.93 ft)
Rocket weight: 308 kg (679 lb)
Warhead types: submunition, chemical
Warhead weights: not known
Maximum ranges: see text

Designed for all-terrain mobility, the Self-Propelled Launcher-Loader (SPLL) is fitted with two pods of six 227-mm (8.94-in) calibre rockets, which can be rapidly replaced.

A Multiple Launch Rocket System (MLRS) vehicle fires one of its 227-mm (8.94-in) rockets. Based on the M2 Infantry Fighting Vehicle chassis, the MLRS has already been ordered by the American, French, Italian, West German and British armies, and is expected to be chosen by the Dutch army to replace or supplement current tube artillery.

Type 67 multiple rocket-launcher

Developed in 1965 by a division of the Nissan Motor Company Ltd, the 307-mm (12.09-in) Type 67 MRL entered service with the Japanese Ground Self-Defence Force in 1968. The system consists of a 4000-kg (8,818-lb) Hino 6×6 truck chassis fitted with two launch rails for the Type 68 rocket. Another Hino 6×6 truck acts as the resupply vehicle and carries six reload rounds, which are transferred to the launcher by a hydraulic crane. Before firing three truck stabilizers have to be lowered to the ground, one on each side of the vehicle and one at the rear. The Type 67 is used by artillery units and some 50 in-service systems complement the similar number of 15-km (9.3-mile) 130-mm (5.12-in) 30-round Type 75 MRLs mounted on a derivative of the Type 73 tracked APC

which are used by the mechanized and armoured brigades. More modern systems to eventually replace the Type 67 and Type 75 are already under investigation, with the former likely to be mounted on a tracked chassis to improve mobility over rough terrain.

Specification
Type 67 MRL
Combat weight: not known
Crew: 4-6
Chassis: 4000 kg (8,818-lb) Hino 6×6 truck
Calibre: 307 mm (12.09 in)
No. of launch rails: 2
Rocket length: 4.5 m (14.76 ft)
Rocket weight: 573 kg (1,263.2 lb)
Warhead type: HE-fragmentation
Warhead weight: not known
Maximum range: 28 km (17.4 miles)

Right: The two Type 68 307-mm (12.09-in) solid fuel rockets are seen on the launch rails of a Hino 6×6 truck-mounted Type 67 launcher of the Japanese Ground Self-Defence Force. The rocket has a range of 28 km (17.5 miles) and is fitted with an HE warhead.

A Type 67 rocket launcher is seen in travelling order with two Type 68 rockets in position on the launch rails. Another Hino 6×6 truck fitted with a hydraulic crane and carrying six reload rounds is used to resupply the vehicle.

RM-70 multiple rocket-launcher

First seen during 1972, the 122-mm (4.8-in) calibre **RM-70** MRL is an armoured version of the Czech Tatra 813 8×8 truck with the Soviet 40-round BM-21 launcher and a reload pack of 40 rounds mounted to the rear of the cab for rapid reloading. The vehicle is fitted with a central tyre pressure-regulation system (to allow adjustment to suite the type of terrain being cros-

sed) and, if required, a BZT dozer blade for preparing its own fire positions and clearing obstacles. The scale of issue of the RM-70 is one battalion of 18 launchers in three batteries per Czech army tank and motorized rifle division. The RM-70 is also known to be in service with the East German and Libyan armies and, it is believed, with selected Category 1 divisions of

the Soviet army.

Two types of fin-stabilized rocket are fired, a short round with a range of 11 km (6.84 miles) and the standard long round with a range of 20.38 km (12.66 miles). It is also possible to fire the short round with an additional motor to increase the range to 17 km (10.56 miles). However, this version together with the short one are more

likely to be encountered in the single-tube launcher used by guerrilla forces throughout the world.

Specification
RM-70
Combat weight: 33700 kg (74,296 lb)
Crew: 6
Chassis: 7900-kg (17,417-lb) Tatra 813 8×8 truck

Calibre: 122 mm (4.8-in)
No. of launcher tubes: 40
Rocket lengths: standard 3.23 m
(10.6 ft), and short 1.91 m (6.27 ft)
Rocket weights: standard 77 kg
(169.75 lb), and short 45.8 kg
(100.97 lb)
Warhead types: HE-fragmentation,
incendiary, smoke, chemical
Warhead weight: 19.4 kg (42.77 lb)
Maximum ranges: standard 20.38 km
(12.66 miles), and short 11 km (6.84
miles)

*The Czechoslovakian army has
adopted its own version of the
standard Soviet 122-mm (4.8-in)
multiple rocket launcher system
known as the RM-70, the major
difference being that the new version
has a complete 40-round reload pack
of rockets to speed up reloading.*

Yugoslav multiple rocket-launchers

The Yugoslav army uses two types of
128-mm (5.04-in) MRL, the 32-round
towed **M-63 Plaman** and the truck-
mounted 32-round **YMRL-32 Oganj**.
The former was developed in the late
1950s and early 1960s, and is mounted
on a split-trail carriage. It fires the 8.6-
km (5.34-mile) range spin-stabilized
M-63 rocket, which is 0.81 m (2.66 ft)
long, weighs 23.1 kg (50.93 lb) and has
a 7.6-kg (16.75-lb) HE-fragmentation
warhead. An improved version with a
wider carriage has also been built,
while both 16-round and 8-round
variants are available for export on
carriages or vehicle mounts if required.

The YMRL-32 (a NATO designation
in the absence of the official Yugoslav
designation) was developed in the
early 1970s and is based on the
FAP2220BDS 6×6 truck fitted with a
32-round launcher and a reload pack
of 32 rounds on the rear platform. The
rocket fired by this system is of a newer type, 2.6 m (8.53 ft) long, 65 kg
(143.3 lb) in weight with a maximum
range of 20 km (12.43 miles) and an
HE-fragmentation warhead weighing
20 kg (44 lb). Reloading of the tubes

takes approximately two minutes
when using the reload pack.

The M-63 is normally found in battalions of three batteries, each with four
launchers, while the YMRL-32 is found
in batteries of six vehicles. It is believed that both systems have been
exported, but the only known user outside Yugoslavia is Cyprus, which has a
few YMRL-32 systems.

Specification
M-63
Combat weight: 2134 kg (4,705 lb)
Crew: 3-5
Chassis: two-wheeled trailer
Calibre: 128 mm (5.04 in)
No. of launcher tubes: 32
Length of rocket: 0.81 m (2.66 ft)
Weight of rocket: 23.1 kg (50.93 lb)
Warhead type: HE-fragmentation
Warhead weight: 7.6 kg (16.75 lb)
Maximum range: 8.6 km (5.34 miles)

YMRL-32
Combat weight: (estimated) 13000 kg
(28,660 lb)
Crew: 6
Chassis: 10000-kg (22,046-lb) FAP
2020BS 6×6 truck

Calibre: 128 mm (5.04 in)
No. of launcher tubes: 32
Length of rocket: 2.6 m (8.53 ft)
Weight of rocket: 65 kg (143.3 lb)
Warhead type: HE-fragmentation
Warhead weight: 20 kg (44 lb)
Maximum range: 20 km (12.43 miles)

*The 128-mm (5.04-in) M-63 Plaman
multiple rocket launcher is used in
battalions of three batteries, each
with four launchers, to support
Yugoslavian infantry units.*

*Although supplied with many weapons by the Soviet Union, Yugoslavia chose
to develop the YMRL 32 Oganji 128-mm (5.04-in) multiple rocket launcher on
the FAP 2220BDS 6×4 truck chassis as its standard self-propelled system. It is
used by the army's armoured and mechanized units.*

IMI multiple rocket launcher

Work on the Israeli 290-mm (11.42-in) medium artillery rocket began in 1965 and the system entered service in the 1970s as a four-round frame launcher mounted on a Sherman tank chassis. Used in combat during the 1982 'Peace for Galilee' Israeli invasion of Lebanon, this **Israel Military Industries MRL** is now being mounted on converted Centurion MBT chassis in a new four-round tube launcher arrangement. The Centurion has a crew of four, who take cover within the vehicle for firings. A full salvo takes less than 10 seconds to be fired, the launch vehicle then moving to a prearranged location for reloading from a supply truck. The reloads are first lowered to the ground

and placed on a special frame by the truck's crane. The Centurion then positions itself and hydraulically lifts the frame to the same height as the launch tubes and slides the rockets into the tubes. This entire operation takes only 10 minutes, the Centurion operations being controlled by only one man. The warhead used is of the HE-fragmentation type although submunition types are known to have been developed and used in combat against Syrian air-defence systems.

Specification
IMI MRL
Combat weight: 50800 kg (111,995 lb)
Crew: 4

Chassis: Centurion MBT
Calibre: 290 mm (11.42 in)
No. of launcher tubes: 4
Rocket length: 5.45 m (17.88 ft)
Rocket weight: 600 kg (1,322.8 lb)
Warhead types: HE-fragmentation, submunition
Warhead weight: 320 kg (705.5 lb)
Maximum range: 25 km (15.5 miles)

The original version of the Israel Military Industries 290-mm (11.42-in) Medium Artillery Rocket System is seen mounted on a Sherman tank chassis in a four-round frame rack. The current version employs cylindrical counter-launcher tubes on a Centurion MBT chassis.

Valkiri multiple rocket-launcher

Development of the 127-mm (5-in) **Valkiri** started in 1977 as a counter to the Soviet 122-mm (4.8-in) BM-21 MRLs and other long-range artillery pieces in service with neighbouring African countries. The first systems entered service in late 1981 with the South African army, and are deployed with artillery regiments in batteries of eight launchers that are tasked either to work on their own or with more conventional tube artillery to attack area targets such as guerrilla camps, troop or artillery concentrations, and soft-skinned vehicle convoys. The system consists of a 24-round launcher mounted on the rear hull of a 4×4

SAMIL truck chassis with overhead canopy rails so as to make it appear to be just a normal truck when travelling. A second 5-ton truck with 48 reload rounds is assigned to each Valkiri. The full load of 24 rounds can be fired in 24 seconds, reloading taking about 10 minutes. The solid-propellant rocket is fitted with an HE-fragmentation warhead filled with some 3,500 steel balls to give a lethal area of some 1500 m² (16,146 sq ft). The range can be varied from a minimum of 8 km (5 miles) to a maximum of 22 km (13.67 miles) depending upon which spoiler rings are fitted to the rocket body.

Above: The highly mobile Valkiri is ideally suited for the South African mechanized cross-border raids against SWAPO guerrilla bases and Angolan army units deep within Angola itself.

Below: Overhead canopy rails are fitted to the Valkiri launcher in order to camouflage the vehicle to appear as a normal South African Army SAMIL 20 4×4 light truck. With the canopy down it is almost impossible to tell the difference.

The launch signature of the Valkiri is minimal. This helps the system to avoid counter-battery fire from the long-range Soviet-supplied artillery pieces belonging to surrounding African states and guerrilla forces.

Specification
Valkiri
Combat weight: 6440 kg (14,198 lb)
Crew: 2
Chassis: 2200-kg (4,850-lb) SAMIL 20 4×4 truck
Calibre: 127 mm (5 in)
No. of launcher tubes: 24
Rocket length: 2.68 m (8.79 ft)
Rocket weight: not known
Warhead type: HE-fragmentation
Warhead weight: not known
Maximum range: 22 km (13.67 miles)

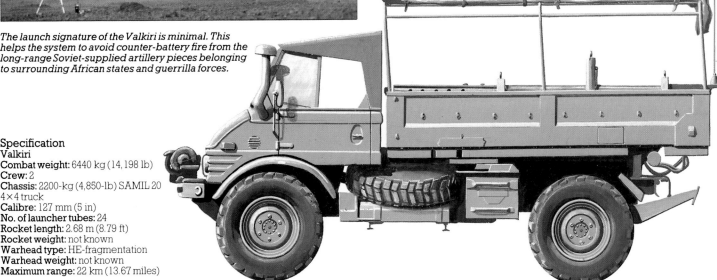

Egyptian multiple rocket-launchers

The Egyptian arms industry produces copies of the Soviet 132-mm (5.2-in) rocket for the army's elderly BM-13-16 Soviet systems and 122-mm (4.8-in) rockets for its BM-21 systems. It has also reverse-engineered the latter to produce a new 30-round launcher mounted on a Japanese 2500-kg (5,512-lb) Isuzu 6×6 truck chassis as well as the more usual 40-round version on a Soviet 3500-kg (7,716-lb) ZIL truck. The former is very similar in appearance to the North Korean BM-11 variant of the BM-21, which is mounted on the same chassis.

In addition to the reverse-engineered models two new systems have also been designed and built for the Egyptian army. These are the 122-mm calibre **Sakr-18** and the 122-mm calibre **Sakr-30** MRLs. The former has a range of 18 km (11.18 miles) and is built in 21-round, 30-round and 40-round versions mounted on lorry chassis types. It utilizes a 3.25-m (10.66-ft) long, 67-kg (147.7-lb) weight rocket fitted with a 21-kg (46.3-lb) submunition warhead containing either 28 anti-personnel or 21 anti-tank bomblets.

The Sakr-30 has a range of 30 km (18.64 miles) and fires three types of rocket which vary in length from 2.5 m (8.2 ft) to 3.16 m (10.37 ft). The longest weighs 63 kg (138.9 lb) and carries a 24.5 kg (54-lb) warhead which delivers five anti-tank mines. The medium-length round at 3.1 m (10.17 ft) weighs 61.5 kg (135.6 lb) and carries a sub-munition-dispensing 23-kg (50.7-lb) warhead with either 28 anti-tank or 35 anti-personnel bomblets as payload. The anti-tank bomblet is the same as that used in the SAKR-18, and can pierce over 80 mm (3.15 in) of armour, while the anti-personnel bomblets of both systems are lethal to a radius of 15 m (49.2 ft) from the point of detonation. The smallest round weighs 56.5 kg (124.6 lb) and has a basic 17.5-kg (38.6-lb) HE-fragmentation warhead. The increased range over the BM-21 and SAKR-18 systems has been achieved by using an improved light-weight rocket motor and case coupled with a new composite bonded star-grain propellant instead of the standard Soviet double-base grained

propellant used in the shorter-range systems.

For infantry and anti-guerrilla use the 12-round 80-mm (3.15-in) **VAP** light vehicle-mounted MRL has been produced. This is mounted on a pedestal which is fitted in the rear of a 4×4 jeep-type vehicle and is fired by remote control. The 1.5-m (4.92 ft) long 12-kg (26.5-lb) fin-stabilized rocket can be fitted with either a HE-fragmentation or an illuminating warhead. The maximum range is 8 km (5 miles)

There is also a specialized system for laying down smoke screens. This can be found either as a 12-round rectangular frame launcher in the rear of a Walid 4×4 wheeled APC or as quadruple box-like launchers mounted on each side of a T-62 MBT turret. The

The Egyptians use locally-made 12-round rocket launchers on the rear of Walid 4×4 APCs to fire 80-mm (3.15-in) D-3000 smokescreen rockets to hide major troop and armour attacks.

Right: An Egyptian army VAP-80 light vehicle mounted 80-mm (3.15-in) rocket launcher system with the 12-round launcher elevated to the firing position. The 12-kg (26.6-lb) rocket has a range of 8 km (5 miles).

rocket fired in both cases is the 80-mm (3.15-in) calibre 1.51 m (4.95 ft) long D-3000 which can form a smoke screen that lasts up to 15 minutes. A full 12-round salvo from a Walid can form a 1000-m (3,281-ft) long smoke screen of sufficient thickness and duration to cover most actitivies.

Below: Walid APCs of the Egyptian army parade through Cairo carrying 12-round rocket launchers. These can fire a salvo of smoke rockets to create a smokescreen up to 1000 m (1,094 yards) long, which can last 15 minutes in favourable wind conditions.

Type 63 and Type 81 107-mm multiple rocket-launchers

Developed in the late 1950s as the replacement for the 102-mm (4.02-in) six-round Type 50 MRL, the 107-mm (4.21-in) system is issued on the scale of 18 launchers per Chinese infantry division.

The basic **Type 63** 12-round launcher has three rows of four barrels and is mounted on a rubber-tyred split-pole trailer carriage. For firing the wheels are removed and the launcher is supported by two legs at the front and the two trails at the rear, the latter being fitted with spades. A lighter model is used by the Chinese airborne and mountain infantry units, and this can be dismantled into loads for carriage by men or horses.

To increase mobility the launcher can also be mounted on the rear of a 4×4 truck fitted with an enlarged cab to accommodate the crew of four and 12 reload rounds. The launcher can either be remote-fired from the vehicle or dismounted for use as on its normal towing carriage. This variant is known as the **Type 81**.

The 107-mm systems have seen extensive combat service throughout the world, the Chinese having used them against the Vietnamese, the Vietnamese against the Americans, Chinese and Kampucheans, the Ira-

Below: The 107-mm (4.21-in) 12-round Type 63 rocket launcher is in widespread use with the People's Liberation Army. The rocket can also be fired on its own and is currently being used by the Afghanistan Mujahideen guerrillas.

Above: Type 81 is the Chinese designation for a Type 63 12-round MRL mounted on a 4×4 truck with an enlarged cab which accommodates the crew and 12 reloads.

nians against the Iraqis, and the Palestinians against the Israelis and Shi'ites, to name but a few. Both HE and incendiary rounds have been used.

Specification
Type 63
Combat weight: 602 kg (1,327 lb)
Crew: 4
Chassis: two-wheeled trailer
Calibre: 107 mm (4.21 in)
No. of launcher tubes: 12
Rocket length: 0.84 m (2.76 ft)
Rocket weight: 18.8 kg (41.45 lb)

Warhead types: HE-fragmentation, incendiary
Warhead weights: 8.33 kg (18.36 lb) and 7.54 kg (16.62 lb)
Maximum ranges: 8.5 km (5.28 miles) and 7.9 km (4.9 miles)

Type 63 and Type 70 130-mm multiple rocket-launchers

The Chinese have indigenously designed and built two types of 19-tube 130-mm (5.12-in) calibre MRL systems, the **Type 63** mounted on the rear platform of the 2500-kg (5,511-lb) NJ-230 4×4 truck in two variants, and the **Type 70** mounted on the top of the Type YM531 tracked APC, to replace elderly Soviet systems. The major difference in the truck-mounted variants is that the second has a covered crew cabin. All three types are grouped into batteries of six launchers, the truck-mounted systems serving in the artillery's MRL regiments and the APC systems serving in the armoured divisions. The launch tubes are arranged in two rows, with a top one of 10 over a lower row of nine. Both systems are in production and have seen combat use with the Chinese and Vietnamese armies during their short border war in 1979. The North Korean army is also known to have the truck-mounted system in service, and may well be building it under licence in North Korean state arsenals as part of that country's arms-building programme.

Specification
Type 70
Combat weight: 13400 kg (29,542 lb)
Crew: 6
Chassis: Type YW531 tracked APC
Calibre: 130 mm (5.12 in)
No. of launch tubes: 19
Rocket length: 1.05 m (3.45 ft)
Rocket weight: 32.8 kg (72.3 lb)
Warhead type: HE-fragmentation
Warhead weight: 14.7 kg (32.4 lb)
Maximum range: 10.37 km (6.44 miles)

The Type 70 Multiple Rocket System is of 130-mm (5.12-in) calibre and is the tracked vehicle-mounted version of the Type 63 system. The vehicle used is the Type YW531 APC.

Below: The Type 70 carries 19 130-mm (5.12-in) rocket tubes on a YM531 APC chassis, and saw action in 1979 during the border clashes with Vietnam. North Korea has adopted the truck-mounted system, the Type 63.

Above: A six-launcher battery of Type 70 130-mm (5.12-in) MRLs opens fire during a People's Liberation Army exercise. The Type 70 MRLs serve with armoured divisions, and the truck-mounted models with the infantry.

Self-Propelled Guns and Howitzers

Self-propelled (SP) guns and howitzers are still the only weapon systems which can deliver fire deep into enemy territory 24 hours a day in all weathers. And modern technology has increased their area of influence and decreased their vulnerability on the battlefield.

Three 203-mm M110 SP howitzers of the British Army passing in review before the Captain-General, Royal Artillery. An American weapon, the M110 first entered service in 1963.

Self-propelled artillery was originally developed to provide armoured divisions with artillery support which could move at the same pace and across the same terrain as tanks. There seems to be little difference in the mobility of the armoured division and the infantry division, and hence SP guns have been accepted into every sort of formation. Towed guns still exist, but in the larger calibres they invariably have auxiliary propulsion fitted.

The 155-mm howitzer is the most common weapon in this class; this is due to a decision taken by NATO in the 1960s that 155-mm would be the standard close-support gun calibre. Once the calibre was standardized, a large family of ammunition was developed around a NATO-standard gun chamber, and it made sense for new guns to conform. Improvement in performance is achieved by lengthening the barrel and improving the propellant charges. In World War II the standard length of barrel for a 155-mm howitzer was 20 calibres

(20 x 155 mm = 3.10 m). This remained unchanged until the 1970s, since when it has crept up, until now the 52-calibre barrel is becoming the norm. Maximum range has also increased, from a wartime figure of 14.9 km (9.3 miles) to 30 km (18.8 miles) today. Added to this, specialist ammunition means 40–45 km (64–72 miles) is within the scope of modern self-propelled artillery, giving each gun vast coverage within its zone of fire.

Today it is important that SP artillery be able to conceal itself while still under control of a central authority that directs fire from widely dispersed guns onto a single target. It is no longer practical to deploy guns which simply become attractive targets. By dispersing the guns but concentrating their fire, survivability is improved. This tactic has become much easier to perform and more effective with the use of the Global Positioning System allied to inertial platforms on the guns so that they can constantly update their own position. Given this, and the co-ordinates of a target sent by the command post, each gun uses its fire control computer to calculate firing data and apply corrections for meteorological and other conditions.

Mk 61 105-mm Self-Propelled Howitzer

The development by the Atelier de Construction d'Issy-les-Moulineaux of the AMX-13 light tank in the late 1940s laid the basis for one of the largest families of tracked vehicles ever developed. At an early stage the French army issued a requirement for a 105-mm (4.13-mm) self-propelled howitzer, and it was decided to base this **Mk 61** equipment on a modified AMX-13 tank chassis. After trials with prototype vehicles, the equipment was placed in production at the Atelier de Construction Roanne in the late 1950s under the designation **Obusier de 105 Modèle 50 sur Affût Automoteur** for the French army. It was withdrawn from French first-line service and replaced by the 155-mm GCT in the late 1980s, with some still held in reserve. In addition to being used by the French army, it has been purchased by Morocco, Israel and the Netherlands, the last having a longer 30-calibre barrel. The type has already been phased out of service with the Israeli army, having been replaced by the 155-mm (6.1-in) M109A1; in the French army it is being replaced by the 155-mm (6.1-in) GCT self-propelled weapon.

The vehicle is of all-welded steel construction that provides the crew with protection from small arms fire and shell splinters. The engine and transmission are at the front, the driver is on the left side, and the fully enclosed gun compartment is at the rear. Access hatches are provided in the roof and rear, and the commander has a cupola with periscopes for all-round observation. The suspension is of the well-proven torsion-bar type, and consists on each side of five rubber-tyred road wheels, with the drive sprocket at the front, the idler at the rear and three track-return rollers. Hydraulic shock absorbers are provided at the first and last road wheel stations. The tracks are steel, but can be fitted with rubber pads to reduce damage to the road surface.

The 105-mm (4.13-in) howitzer has a double-baffle muzzle-brake, and can be elevated from −4° 30′ to +66°; traverse is 20° left and right. Traverse and elevation are both manual. Various types of standard 105-mm (4.13-in) separate-loading ammunition can be fired, including an HE projectile weighing 16 kg (35.3 lb) to a maximum range of 15000 m (16,405 yards) and a HEAT projectile which will penetrate 350 mm (13.8 in) of armour at an incidence of 0° or 105 mm (4.13 in) of armour at 65°. A total of 56 rounds of ammunition is carried, and of these six are normally HEAT rounds. A 7.62-mm (0.3-in) or 7.5-mm (0.295-in) machine-gun is mounted externally on the roof for anti-aircraft defence, and a similar weapon is carried inside the vehicle for use in the ground role, 2,000 rounds of ammunition being carried for these weapons. The Mk 61 does not have an NBC system, and has no amphibious capability.

One of the drawbacks of the Mk 61 is the limited traverse of the ordnance.

The prototype of a similar vehicle but fitted with a turret that could be traversed through 360° was built but not placed in production, although a few were purchased for trials purposes by Switzerland. By the time the turret version was ready most countries had already decided to replace their 105-mm (4.13-in) equipment with more effective 155-mm (6.1-in) weapons, and in most cases chose the American M109. The chassis of the Mk 61 was also used for trials with the Roland surface-to-air missile system and as a minelayer, but neither of these variants entered production. A similar chassis is also used for the AMX-13 DCA twin 30-mm self-propelled anti-aircraft gun produced for the French army in the 1960s.

The Mk 61 is one of the many vehicles based on the AMX-13 light tank chassis. Obsolete by modern standards, it is still available to special order.

Specification
Crew: 5
Weight: 16500 kg (36,375 lb)
Dimensions: length 5.70 m (18 ft 8½ in); width 2.65 m (8 ft 8¼ in); height 2.70 m (8 ft 10¼ in)
Powerplant: one SOFAM 8Gxb 8-cylinder petrol engine developing 250 hp (186 kW)
Performance: maximum road speed 60 km/h (37 mph); maximum range 350 km (217 miles); gradient 60%; vertical obstacle 0.65 (2 ft 2 in); trench 1.60 m (5 ft 3 in)

Mk F3 155-mm Self-Propelled Gun

In the period immediately after World War II the standard self-propelled howitzer of the French army was the American 155-mm (6.1-in) M41 Howitzer Motor Carriage, essentially the M24 Chaffee light tank chassis fitted with a slightly modified version of the standard M114 towed howitzer. This was replaced in the 1960s by the 155-mm (6.1-in) **Mk F3** self-propelled gun, which is basically a shortened AMX-13 light tank chassis with 155-mm (6.1-in) gun mounted at the rear of the hull. The ordnance is based on the Modèle 50 towed weapon of the same calibre. In addition to being used by the French army, the Mk F3 is used by Argentina, Chile, Ecuador, Kuwait, Morocco, Qatar, Sudan, United Arab Emirates and Venezuela. It will be replaced in the late 1980s in French service by the 155-mm (6.1-in) GCT. Production of the Mk F3, along with other members of AMX-13 light tank family, was originally undertaken at the Atelier de Construction Roanne, a French government facility, but as this plant tooled up for production of the AMX-30 MBT, AMX-30 variants and the AMX-10P family, production of the whole AMX-13 family, including the Mk F3, was transferred to Creusot-Loire at Châlon-sur-Saône, where production continues today, although at a much lower rate.

The 155-mm (6.1-in) ordnance is mounted at the very rear of the chassis and can be elevated from 0° to +67°, with a traverse of 20° left and right up to an elevation of +50° and of 16° left and 30° right from +50° up to the maximum elevation. Elevation and traverse are both manual. When travelling the ordnance is held in a travel lock and

The Mk F3 is widely used in a number of Middle East and South American countries, including Argentina.

traversed 8° to the right. The 33-calibre barrel has a double-baffle muzzle-brake and a screw breech mechanism. Ammunition is of the separate-loading type, and the following can be fired: high explosive with a maximum range of just over 20000 m (21,875 yards), illuminating and smoke to a range of 17750 m (19,410 yards), and a rocket-assisted projectile to a range of 253300 m (27,670 yards). Rate of fire for the first few minutes is three rounds per minute, but when the Mk F3 is used in the sustained fire role the rate is one round a minute. Before firing commences two spades are manually released at the rear of the hull and the vehicle then reversed backwards to provide a more stable firing platform.

A major disadvantage of the Mk F3 (in addition to the total lack of protection for the gun and its crew) is that only the driver and commander can be carried in the actual vehicle. The remainder of the gun crew are carried in an AMX VCA (Véhicule Chenillé d'Ac-compagnement, or tracked support vehicle) or 6×6 truck which also carries 25 projectiles, charges and associated fuzes. The VCA can also tow an

The Mk F3 in firing position with its recoil spade down. The total lack of gun and crew protection is self-evident.

ARE 2-tonne F2 ammunition trailer which carries an additional 30 projectiles and charges.

The Mk F3 can ford to a depth of 1 m (3 ft 3 in) but has no NBC system; active or passive night-vision equipment can be installed, and all vehicles have direct and indirect sights, and a loud-speaker and cable. The basic vehicle is powered by a petrol engine, but if required this can be replaced by a General Motors Detroit Diesel 6V-53T developing 280 hp (209 kW). This produces a slightly higher road speed and, most important of all, an increased operational range from 300 to 400 km (185 to 250 miles).

Specification
Crew: 2
Weight: 17400 kg (38,360 lb)
Dimensions: length (gun forward) 6.22 m (20 ft 5 in); width 2.72 m (8 ft 11 in); height 2.085 m (6 ft 10 in)
Powerplant: one SOFAM 8Gxb 8-cylinder petrol engine developing 250 hp (186 kW)
Performance: maximum road speed 60 km/h (37 mph); maximum range 300 km (185 miles); gradient 40%; vertical obstacle 0.60 m (2 ft 0 in); trench 1.50 m (4 ft 11 in)

FRANCE
GCT 155-mm Self-Propelled Gun

For many years the standard self-propelled weapons of the French army have been the 155-mm (6.1-in) Mk F3 and the 105-mm (4.13-in) Mk 61. The former suffered a major disadvantage in that its weapon was in an unprotected mount with limited traverse and most of the gun crew had to be carried in another full-tracked vehicle that also carried the ammunition. In the late 1960s a new self-propelled gun called the **GCT** (Grande Cadence de Tir) was developed on a slightly modified AMX-30 MBT chassis. The first prototype was completed in 1972, and following trials with a pre-production batch of 10 vehicles production got under way in 1977. For a number of reasons Saudi Arabia was the first country to deploy the GCT; they ordered 51 systems plus a complete fire-control system. The French army designates the GCT the **155 AU F1**, and deploys it in regiments of 18 weapons (three batteries each with six GCTs). More recently Iraq has placed an order for 85 GCTs, and these are now being delivered. The GCT is manufactured at the Atelier de Construction Roanne with the assistance of many other GIAT establishments all over France.

As mentioned above, the chassis is similar to that of the AMX-30 MBT but with a new all-welded turret in the centre fitted with a 155-mm (6.1-in) 40-calibre barrel that has a multi-baffle muzzle-brake and a vertical sliding wedge breech block. Elevation is from −4° to +66° at a rate of 5° per second, and turret traverse is 360° at the rate of 10° per second. Turret traverse and gun elevation are hydraulic, with manual controls for emergency use.

The major feature of the GCT is the automatic loading system for a total of 42 projectiles and a similar number of cartridges carried in racks in the turret rear. Ammunition mix depends on the tactical situation, but can consist of 36 (six racks of six) HE and six (one rack of six) smoke projectiles. Access to the ammunition racks for reloading purposes is via two large turret doors in the rear. The four-man crew can reload the GCT in 15 minutes, and if required loading can be undertaken while the weapon is being fired. The automatic loading system enables a rate of eight rounds per minute, and the gunner can select either single shots or six-round bursts, the latter taking just 45 seconds. When manual loading is used, two to three rounds per minute can be fired.

The GCT is provided with the usual range of conventional shells, high explosive, smoke and illuminating, propelled by a seven-zone bag charge system giving a maximum range of 23,300 m (25,480 yards). It also has an Extended-Range Full-Bore Base Bleed HE shell ranging to 39,000 m (42,650 yards) with a special charge; and two cargo projectiles, one loaded with 63 dual-purpose anti-tank/anti-personnel grenades and the other with six 2.2 kg (4.8 lbs) anti-tank mines.

A 7.62-mm (0.3-in) or 12.7-mm (0.5-in) machine-gun is mounted on the turret roof for anti-aircraft defence, and two electrically-operated smoke-dischargers are mounted on each side of the turret. Standard equipment of all vehicles includes night-vision equipment and a ventilating system, while optional equipment includes an NBC pack, muzzle velocity measuring equipment and various fire-control devices. For trials purposes the turret of the GCT has also been fitted to the

Although meant to replace the Mk F3 in French service, the GCT was first deployed by Saudi Arabia, since when it has been adopted by Iraq and used in the Gulf War. The automatic loading system enables the GCT to fire up to eight rounds per minute.

Leopard 1 MBT chassis but this combination has not so far been adopted by any country.

Specification
Crew: 4
Weight: 42000 kg (92,595 lb)
Dimensions: length (gun forward) 10.25 m (33 ft 7½ in); length (hull) 6.70 m (22 ft 0 in); width 3.15 m (10 ft 4 in); height 3.25 m (10 ft 8 in)
Powerplant: one Hispano-Suiza HS 110

The GCT is seen here with its ordnance at its maximum elevation of 66 degrees.

12-cylinder water-cooled multi-fuel engine developing 720 hp (537 kW)
Performance: maximum road speed 60 km/h (37 mph); maximum range 450 km (280 miles); gradient 60%; vertical obstacle 0.93 m (3 ft 0⅔ in); trench 1.90 m (6 ft 3 in)

USA
M52 105-mm Self-Propelled Howitzer

The **M52** 105-mm (4.13-in) self-propelled howitzer was developed to meet the requirements of the United States Field Artillery in the period immediately after World War II, and uses many automotive components common to the M41 light tank. Production started in 1951 at the Detroit Tank Arsenal under the designation **T98E1**, this being standardized subsequently as the M52. From the early 1960s the weapon was replaced by the 105-mm (4.13-in) M108, which itself was soon replaced by the 155-mm (6.1-in) M109 self-propelled howitzer based on the same chassis as the M108. The main reasons for the replacement of the M108 and M52 by the M109 was the latter's 155-mm (6.1-in) projectile, which is much heavier and has a greater HE content, and is therefore considerably more effective. It also has the longer range of 14000 m (15,310 yards) and can fire a wider selection of ammunition, eventually including tactical nuclear ammunition. Another advantage of the M109 over the M52 is

Although replaced in US Army service by the M109 series, the M52 can still be found in a number of NATO and Far Eastern countries.

its greater operating range of 390 km (240 miles) thanks to the use of a diesel engine.

The M52 has long been replaced in US army service by the M108 and M109, but is still used by Belgium, Greece, Italy, Japan, Spain and Turkey.

The hull and turret of the M52 are of 12.7-mm (0.5-in) welded steel armour, with the engine and transmission at the front of the hull and the turret at the rear. Suspension is of the torsion-bar type, and consists of six road wheels on each side with the rearmost of these acting as the idler; the drive sprocket is at the front and there are four return rollers. The fully enclosed turret is at the rear and is unusual in that it accommodates the driver. The turret can be traversed 60° left and right. Main armament consists of the 105-mm (4.13-in) M49 howitzer with an elevation of +65° and a depression of −10°; elevation/depression and turret traverse are manual. The M49 has a very short barrel, and a total of 102 rounds of ammunition is carried, of which 21 rounds are located in a vertically-mounted revolver-type rack (commonly called the Lazy Susan) at the left rear of the turret. Additional ammunition is stowed in the turret and under the hull at the rear. The 105-mm (4.13-in) howitzer has a maximum range of 11270 m (12,325 yards). The howitzer was cleared to fire the following types of ammunition (not all of these are used today): chemical, anti-personnel, high explosive, high explosive plastic, high explosive rocket-assisted (with a range of 15000 m/16,400 yards), leaflet, illuminating, smoke, and tactical CS. Both direct (anti-tank) and indirect sights are fitted, although the former would only be used as a last resort. A 12.7-mm (0.5-in) Browning anti-aircraft machine-gun is mounted on the commander's cupola for anti-aircraft use; 900 rounds of ammunition are carried for this weapon.

Standard equipment includes a heater, a turret-mounted ventilator (essential to remove fumes from the turret when the ordnance is fired), an auxiliary generator so that the batteries will not quickly run down, a bilge pump and a fixed fire-extinguishing system. The M52 has no NBC system and no amphibious capability, although it can ford to a depth of 1.219 m (4 ft), but some vehicles have been fitted with infra-red driving lights.

Specification
Crew: 5
Weight: 24040 kg (53,000 lb)
Dimensions: length 5.80 m (19 ft 0⅓ in); width 3.149 m (10 ft 4 in); height (with AA MG) 3.316 m (10 ft 10¼ in)
Powerplant: one Continental AOS-895-

3 6-cylinder petrol engine developing 500 hp (373 kW)
Performance: maximum road speed 56.3 km/h (35 mph); maximum range 160 km (100 miles); gradient 60%; vertical obstacle 0.914 m (3 ft 0 in); trench 1.828 m (6 ft 0 in)

The extensive stowage spaces for reserve ammunition and the turret revolver-type 'Lazy Susan' 21-round ready-use rack can clearly be seen in this rear view of a US Army M52. It was about to fire on an exercise in 1959.

M109 155-mm Self-Propelled Howitzer

The **M109** 155-mm (6.1-in) self-propelled howitzer is the most widely used self-propelled artillery weapon in the world today. Its development can be traced back to 1952, when the requirement was issued for a new self-propelled howitzer to replace the 155-mm (6.1-in) M44. At that time the 110-mm (4.33-in) T195 self-propelled howitzer was already being designed, and it was decided to use its hull and turret as the basis for the new weapon, which would be armed with a 156-mm (6.14-in) howitzer. But in 1956 it was decided to stick to a 155-mm (6.1-in) calibre for commonality in NATO, and in 1959 the first prototype was completed under the designation T196. There were numerous problems with this equipment, and much redesign work had to be carried out to improve its reliability. At the same time a decision was taken that all future American AFVs would be powered by diesel engines for greater operating range, so the vehicle was redesignated **T196E1** with such a powerplant. In 1961 this was accepted for service as the M109 self-propelled howitzer, and the first production vehicles were completed in late 1962 at the Cleveland Army Tank Plant, this facility being run by the Cadillac Motor Car Division. At a later date the plant was run by Chrysler, but in the 1970s all production of the M109 series was taken over by Bowen-McLaughlin-York (BMY), where production of the latest version continues today.

In the United States Army the M109 is issued on the scale of 54 per armoured and mechanized division (three battalions each of 18 vehicles, each battalion having three batteries of six M109s). In addition to the US Army and US Marine Corps, the M109 is used by Austria, Belgium, Canada,

The basic M109 self-propelled howitzer mounting the short barrel M126 howitzer barrel. The M109 series is the most widely used of all self-propelled weapons and has seen extensive combat service throughout the world, as well as seeing constant adaptation and updating.

Denmark, Ethiopia, West Germany, Greece, Iran, Israel, Italy, Jordan, Kampuchea, Kuwait, Libya, Morocco, the Netherlands, Norway, Oman, Pakistan, Peru, Portugal, Saudi Arabia, South Korea, Spain, Switzerland, Taiwan, Tunisia, Turkey and the United Kingdom. It has been used in action in a number of conflicts in the Middle East (by Iran and Israel) and the Far East (by the USA in Vietnam and by Kampuchea).

The hull and turret of the M109 are of all-welded aluminium construction. The driver is seated at the front on the left, with the engine compartment to his right, and the turret is at the rear. The suspension is of the well-tried torsion-bar type, and consists of seven road wheels with the drive sprocket at the front and the idler at the rear; there are no track-return rollers. Standard equipment includes infra-red driving lights and an amphibious kit enabling the vehicle to propel itself across slow-flowing rivers with its tracks.

The M109 has a 155-mm (6.1-in) howitzer M126 with an elevation of +75° and a depression of −5°. Turret traverse is 360°, and both gun elevation and turret traverse are powered, with manual controls available for emergency use. The ordnance has a large fume extractor, large muzzle-brake and a Welin-step thread type breech block. Normal rate of fire is one round per minute, but for short periods three rounds per minute can be attained. The weapon can fire a wide range of projectiles including high explosive (maximum range 14320 m/15,660 yards), illuminating, tactical nuclear, smoke, tactical CS and Agents VX or GB. A total of 28 projectiles and charges is carried. A 12.7-mm (0.5-in) M2HB machine gun is mounted on the commander's cupola for anti-aircraft defence, and 500 rounds are provided for this weapon.

One of the reasons that the M109 has

been in production for so long is that its basic chassis has proved capable of constant updating and of accepting longer-barrelled ordnance that fires projectiles to a greater distance.

Specification
Crew: 6
Weight: 23786 kg (52,440 lb)
Dimensions: length (gun forward) 6.612 m (21 ft 8¼ in); length (hull) 6.256 m (20 ft 6¼ in); width 3.295 m (10 ft 9¾ in); height 3.289 m (10 ft 9½ in)
Powerplant: one Detroit Diesel Model 8V-71T diesel developing 405 bhp (302 kW)
Performance: maximum road speed 56 km/h (35 mph); maximum range 390 km (240 miles); gradient 60%; vertical obstacle 0.533 m (1 ft 9 in); trench 1.828 m (6 ft 0 in)

M107 175-mm Self-Propelled Gun

In the 1950s the standard 203-mm (8-in) self-propelled howitzer of the US Army was the M55, which had the chassis and turret of the M53 155-mm (6.1-in) self-propelled gun. The main drawbacks of both these weapons were that at a weight of about 45 tons they were too heavy for air transport and their petrol engines gave them an operating range of only 260 km (160 miles). In the mid-1950s a decision was taken to design a new family of self-propelled artillery that would share a common chassis and mount, be air-portable, and come into and be taken out of action quickly. Prototypes were built by the Pacific Car and Foundry Company under the designations 175-mm (6.89-in) self-propelled gun **T235**, 203-mm (8-in) self-propelled howitzer T236, and 155-mm (6.1-in) self-propelled gun T245. Further development, including the replacement by diesels of the petrol engines for increased operational range, resulted in the T235 being standardized as the **M107** and the T236 as the M110. The chassis of the family was also used as the basis for a number of armoured recovery vehicles (ARVs) but in the end only the T120E1 was placed in production as the M578 light ARV; this serves with many countries including the United States.

Production of the M107 was undertaken initially by the Pacific Car and Foundry Company, the first vehicles being completed in 1962 and the first battalion forming at Fort Sill (home of the US Field Artillery) in early 1963. At a later date production was also undertaken by FMC, and from 1965 to 1980

by Bowen-McLaughlin-York.

The US Army deployed the 175-mm (6.89-in) M107 in 12-gun battalions at corps level but in recent years all of these weapons have been converted to the 203-mm (8-in) M1102 configuration as this has a range of just over 29000 m (31,715 yards) with a HERA (High Explosive Rocket Assist) projectile. The M107 was also exported to Greece, Iran, Israel, Italy, South Korea, the Netherlands, Spain, Turkey, the United Kingdom and West Germany; many of these countries are now also converting their M107s to the M110A2 configuration.

The chassis of the M107 is fully described in the entry for the M110. The 175-mm (6.89-in) gun has an elevation of +65° and a depression of −2° and traverse is 30° left and right. Traverse and elevation are powered, although manual controls are provided for emergency use. Only one round was ever standardized for US Army use, the HE M437A1 or M437A2 which with a charge three propellant had a maximum range of 32700 m (35,760 yards), although a special round is used by Israel with a range of some 40000 m (43,745 yards). To assist the crew in loading the 66.78-kg (147-lb) projectile, a rammer and loader assembly is mounted at the rear of the chassis. This lifts the projectile from the ground, positions in and then rams it into the chamber. The charge is then loaded and the ordnance fired. Only two projectiles and charges are carried on the M107, which has a total crew of 13, of whom five (driver, commander and

three gunners) travel on the M107. The remainder are carried in the M548 tracked cargo carrier that also carries the bulk of the ammunition. Some countries use 6×6 trucks to support the M107, but often these have poor cross-country mobility compared with the M107. The M107 is normally fitted with infra-red night-vision equipment, but does not have an NBC system. It has no amphibious capability although it can ford to a depth of 1.066 m (3 ft 6 in).

Specification
Crew: 5+8
Weight: 28168 kg (57,690 lb)
Dimensions: length (gun forward)

A US Army M107 in travelling order. All of these vehicles have now been converted to the M110A2 configuration by replacing the 175-mm (6.8-in) gun.

11.256 m (36 ft 7¾ in); length (hull) 5.72 m (18 ft 9 in); width 3.149 m (10 ft 4 in); height 3.679 m (12 ft 0 in)
Powerplant: one Detroit Diesel Model 8V-71T diesel developing 405 hp (302 kW)
Performance: maximum road speed 56 km/h (35 mph); maximum range 725 km (450 miles); gradient 60%; vertical obstacle 1.016 m (3 ft 4 in); trench 2.326 m (7 ft 9 in)

M110 203-mm Self-Propelled Howitzer

The **M110** 203-mm (8-in) self-propelled howitzer uses the same chassis and mount as the 175-mm (6.89-in) M107 self-propelled gun and details of its development are given in the entry for the M107. The M110 entered service with the US Army Field Artillery in 1963, and is issued today on the scale of one battery of four per infantry division and one battalion of 12 for each armoured and mechanized division. Production was originally completed in the late 1960s but was resumed in the 1970s by Bowen-McLaughlin-York (BMY) and the latest models remain in current production. In addition to being used by the US Army and US Marines, the M110 is operated by Belgium, Greece, Iran, Israel, Italy, Japan, Jordan, the Netherlands, Pakistan, Saudi Arabia, South Korea, Spain, Taiwan, the United Kingdom and West Germany. This list includes those on order and in many cases, especially in Europe, the M110s are being upgraded with the aid of kits supplied by the United States.

The chassis of the M110 is of all-welded steel construction with the driver seated under armour on the front at the left, with the engine compartment on his right and the howitzer on its mount on top of the chassis at the rear. Suspension is of the torsion-bar type and consists of five large road wheels with the rearmost acting as the idler; the drive sprocket is at the front and there are no track-return rollers. The suspension can be locked when the M110 is in the firing position to provide a more stable firing platform.

The 203-mm (8-in) M2A2 howitzer

was developed well before World War II and is located on the mount M158, this allowing an elevation of +65° and a depression of −2°, with traverse 30° left and right. Elevation and traverse are hydraulic, with manual controls for emergency use. The M2A2 has no muzzle brake or fume extractor and has an interrupted screw breech block. At the rear of the chassis is a rammer and loader assembly to lift the projectile from the ground, position it and ram it into the chamber. The following projectiles can be fired: high explosive (weight 92.53 kg/204 lb to a maximum range of 16800 m/18,375 yards), high explosive (carrying 104 or 195 grenades), Agents GB or VX, and tactical nuclear. Only two projectiles and charges are carried on the M110, others being provided from the M548 carrier that also transports the remainder of the crew. The complete crew of the M110 consists of 13 men, of whom

five (commander, driver and three gunners) are on the actual vehicle.

One of the main drawbacks of the M110 is the complete lack of any protection for the gun crew from shell splinters, small arms fire and NBC agents. A protection kit is being developed and is expected to be fielded soon.

All American M110s have now been upgraded to **M110A1** or **M110A2** standard. The former has a longer barrel and fires an HE projectile to a maximum range of 21300 m (23,300 yards) or a HE rocket-assisted projectile to 29100 m (31,825 yards); other rounds available are Improved Conventional Munitions, Agents GB or VX, Binary or tactical nuclear. The **M110A2** is almost identical to the M110A1 but has a muzzle-brake which enables it to fire charge nine of the M118A1 propelling charge whereas the M110A1 can go only up to charge eight.

A US Army M110A2. This differs from previous M110 versions in having a long, muzzle-braked barrel. All of the M110 series in the US Army will eventually be fitted with a crew shelter and NBC system, to rectify the original lack of cover for the gun crew.

Specification
Crew: 5+8
Weight: 26536 kg (58,500 lb)
Dimensions: length (gun forward) 7.467 m (24 ft 6 in); length (hull) 5.72 m (18 ft 9 in); width 3.149 m (10 ft 4 in); height 2.93 m (9 ft 7¼ in)
Powerplant: one Detroit Diesel Model 8V-71T diesel developing 405 bhp (302 kW)
Performance: maximum road speed 56 km/h (35 mph); maximum range 725 km (450 miles); gradient 60%; vertical obstacle 1.016 m (3 ft 4 in); trench 2.362 m (7 ft 9 in)

Israeli Self-Propelled Artillery

In the 1950s the Israelis used a wide range of towed artillery weapons to provide fire support for their mechanized units, but it was soon realized that such artillery could not keep up with these highly mobile forces when they deployed to the desert, where roads were nonexistent. Israel therefore purchased quantities of the American World War II **Priest** 105-mm (4.13-in) and French 105-mm (4.13-in) **Mk 61** self-propelled howitzers despite the fact that they felt, as did most members of NATO at that time, that the 155-mm (6.1-in) projectile was much more effective than the 105-mm (4.13-in) shell because of the former's greater content of high explosive.

The first self-propelled weapon of 155-mm (6.1-in) calibre to enter service with the Israeli army was the **M-50**, which was developed in France by the Etablissement d'Etudes et Fabrications d'Armement de Bourges and entered service in 1963. This system was essentially a rebuilt Sherman tank chassis with the engine moved forward to the right of the driver to enable a French 155-mm (6.1-in) Modèle 50 howitzer (which in its towed configuration was used by Israel at that time) to be mounted in an open-topped compartment at the rear of the hull. When the vehicle is deployed in action, the two doors open to each side of the hull rear revealing horizontal ammunition racks and a tailgate folded down to provide space for the crew to operate the howitzer. Additional ammunition storage space is provided under the mount, and external stowage compartments are provided in each side of the hull. The 155-mm (6.1-in) howitzer fires an HE projectile weighing 43 kg (95 lb) to a maximum range of 17600 m (19,250 yards). Maximum elevation of the howitzer is +69° but traverse is very limited. The M-50 has a crew of eight men and weighs 31000 kg (68,340 lb) fully loaded. The main drawback of the system, which was used for the first time in the 1967 Middle East War, is the lack of any overhead protection for the crew from shell splinters and small arms fire.

The M-50 was followed in Israeli service by the **L-33** (named after the length of the ordnance in calibres) which was developed in Israel by Soltam and this saw action for the first time in the 1973 Middle East War. This is based on the M4A3E8 Sherman chassis, which has Horizontal Volute Spring Suspension (HVSS) rather than the Vertical Volute Spring Suspension (VSS) of the M-50, and gives a much improved ride across country. The original petrol engine has been replaced by a Cummins diesel for a much increased operational range.

The 155-mm (6.1-in) M-68 gun/howitzer is almost identical to the standard towed weapon and is mounted in the forward part of the superstructure with an elevation of +52°, a depression of −3° and a traverse of 30° left and right. Weapon elevation and traverse are manual. The ordnance has a single-baffle muzzle brake, fume extractor, gun travel lock and a horizontal sliding semi-automatic breech block.

To assist in maintaining a high rate of fire and in loading the ordnance at any angle of elevation, a pneumatic rammer is installed. The weapon fires an HE projectile weighing 43 kg (95 lb) to a maximum range of 21000 (22,965 yards) at maximum charge; smoke and illuminating projectiles can also be fired. A total of 60 projectiles and charges is carried, 16 of which are for ready use. A 7.62-mm (0.3-in) machine-gun is mounted on the roof for local and anti-aircraft defence.

The hull is of all-welded steel construction and provides the crew with complete protection from small arms fire and shell splinters. Entry doors are provided on each side of the hull, and ammunition resupply doors are fitted in the hull rear; ammunition can be loaded via these doors when the weapon is still firing. The driver is seated at the front on the left with the commander to his rear; the anti-aircraft machine-gunner is in a similar position on the opposite side, and each of these crew members is provided with a roof hatch and bulletproof windows to their front and side for observation.

Unlike the earlier M-50 conversion, which entailed moving the engine forward, the L-33 has its engine at the rear, power being transmitted to the transmission at the front of the hull by a two-part propeller shaft.

As a private venture Soltam has also developed the 155-mm (6.1-in) self-propelled howitzer M72. This is a turret that weighs 14000 kg (30,865 lb) complete with ammunition and can be fitted onto a variety of tank chassis including the M60 and M48. The prototype has already been fitted onto a Centurion tank chassis for trials purposes. The prototype has a 33-calibre barrel but a 39-calibre barrel can be fitted, this allowing a 43-kg (95-lb) projectile to be fired to a range of 23500 m (25,700 yards). So far this turret system has not been adopted by the Israeli army as it already has some 200 American supplied M109A1 and M109A2 self-propelled artillery weapons in service.

Specification
Soltam L-33 155-mm Self-Propelled Gun/Howitzer
Crew: 8
Weight: 41500 kg (91,490 lb)
Dimensions: length (gun forward) 8.47 m (27 ft 9½ in); length (hull) 6.47 m (21 ft 2¾ in); width 3.50 m (11 ft 6 in); height 3.45 m (11 ft 3¾ in)
Powerplant: one Cummins diesel developing 460 hp (343 kW)
Performance: maximum road speed 36.8 km/h (23 mph); maximum range 260 km (162 miles); gradient 60%; vertical obstacle 0.91 m (3 ft); trench 2.30 m (7 ft 6½ in)

Above: The crew of a 155-mm (6.1-in) L-33 man their vehicle during an exercise. The L-33 was first extensively used in combat during the 1973 war.

Below: Oldest of the self-propelled guns in Israeli service is the 155-mm (6.1-in) M-50. This entered service in 1963 and is still in service today with reserve units.

Below: The Israeli Army is the only Western nation to use 160-mm (6.3-in) self-propelled mortars. The high angle of fire proved extremely useful in the mountain fighting against Syrian troops during the 1982 invasion of Lebanon.

JAPAN

Type 75 155-mm Self-Propelled Howitzer

When the Japanese Ground Self-Defense force was formed in the 1950s all its artillery was of towed types and supplied by the United States. With increased mechanization taking place in the 1960s, the United States also supplied 30 105-mm (4.13-in) M52 and 10 155-mm (6.1-in) M44 self-propelled howitzers. In the later 1960s development of indigenous 105-mm (4.13-in) and 155-mm (6.1-in) self-propelled howitzers started in Japan, the former eventually being standardized as the Type 74 and the latter as the **Type 75**. Only 20 of the Type 74 were built as a decision was taken to concentrate on the more effective 155-mm (6.1-in) system.

So far about 50 Type 75s have been built, with Mitsubishi Heavy Industries responsible for the hull and final assembly, and Japan Iron Works/Nihon Seiko for the gun and turret. The Japanese Ground Self-Defense Force expects to have 200 Type 75s in service by the late 1980s.

In many respects the Type 75 is similar to the American M109, with the engine and transmission at the front and the fully enclosed turret at the rear. The six-man crew consists of the commander, layer, two loaders and radio operator in the turret, and the driver at the front. The hull and turret are of all-welded aluminium construction, which provides the crew with complete protection from small arms fire and shell splinters. The suspension is of the torsion-bar type, and consists

of six road wheels on each side, the rearmost serving the idler; the drive sprocket is at the front, and there are no return rollers.

The 30-calibre barrel has an interrupted screw type breech block, a fume extractor and a double-baffle muzzle-brake. When the Type 75 is travelling the barrel is normally held in a travel lock mounted on the glacis plate. The ordnance has an elevation of +65° and a depression of −5°, and the turret can traverse 360°. Weapon elevation and turret traverse are hydraulic, with manual controls provided for emergency use. Before fire is opened, two spades are manually lowered to the ground at the rear of the hull to provide a more stable firing platform.

The Type 75 can fire 18 rounds in three minutes, such a rate being achieved by the use of two drum-type magazines (one on each side of the turret and containing nine projectiles each, a two-part extending loading tray and an hydraulic rammer. Once the gun has fired, it automatically returns to an angle of +6° for reloading. The breech is opened, the extending loading tray positioned, the projectile is then charge loaded with the aid of the hydraulic rammer, the breech closed, the loading tray returned to normal position and the weapon fired again. The drum magazines are rotated electrically or manually and can be reloaded from outside the vehicle via two doors/hatches in the turret

rear. In action the Type 75 would probably fire 12 or 18 rounds before moving off to a new fire position before the enemy could return fire. In addition to the 18 projectiles in the two magazines, a further 10 projectiles are carried internally as are 56 fuzes and 28 bagged charges. Mounted externally at the commander's station is a standard 12.7-mm (0.5-in) M2HB machine-gun with a shield.

Standard equipment includes infra-red night-vision lights, a fire extinguishing system, an NBC pack, a turret ventilator and a crew compartment heater. An amphibious kit was developed but not adopted, but the Type 75 can ford to a depth of 1.3 m (4 ft 3 in) without preparation.

The Type 75 self-propelled howitzer is essentially a Japanese-designed and built counterpart to the American M109.

Specification
Crew: 6
Weight: 25300 kg (55,775 lb)
Dimensions: length (gun forward) 7.79 m (25 ft 6⅔ in); length (hull) 6.64 m (21 ft 9½ in); width 3.09 m (10 ft 1¾ in); height (without MG) 2.545 m (8 ft 4 in)
Powerplant: one Mitsubishi 6-cylinder diesel developing 450 hp (336 kW)
Performance: maximum road speed 47 km/h (29 mph); range 300 km (185 miles); gradient 60%; vertical obstacle 0.70 m (2 ft 3 in); trench 2.50 m (8 ft 2½ in)

ITALY

Palmaria 155-mm Self-Propelled Howitzer

The **Palmaria** 155-mm (6.1-in) self-propelled howitzer has been developed by OTO-Melara specifically for the export market, and shares many common components with the OF-40 MBT which is already in service with Dubai. The first prototype was completed in 1981, and production vehicles were completed the following year. The type has so far been ordered by ordered by Libya (200), Nigeria (25) and Argentina (20 turrets for local assembly to TAM tanks).

The layout of the Palmaria (named after an Italian island) is similar to that of a tank with the driver at the front of the hull, turret in the centre and the engine and transmission at the rear. The major difference beteen the chassis of the Palmaria and that of the OF-40 MBT is that the former has thinner armour and is powered by a V-8 diesel developing 750 hp (559 kW) whereas the OF-40 has a V-10 diesel developing 830 hp (619 kW).

The 155-mm (6.1-in) 41-calibre barrel is fitted with a fume extractor and a multi-baffle muzzle-brake. The turret has 360° traverse and the ordnance can be elevated from −4° to +70° hydraulically, with manual controls for emergency use. An unusual feature of the Palmaria is the installation of an auxiliary power unit to provide power for the turret, thus conserving fuel for the main engine. The Palmaria is available with a normal manual loading system or a semi-automatic loading system. With the latter, a three-round burst can be fired in 30 seconds and then one round every 15 seconds can

Specifically developed to export, the Palmaria has now been bought by Libya, Nigeria and Oman. An additional 25 turrets are being supplied to Argentina for fitting on the TAM tank chassis.

be maintained until the 23 ready-use projectiles have been fired; a further seven projectiles are stowed elsewhere in the hull. Once the ordnance has fired, it automatically returns to an elevation of +2°, the breech opens, the projectile is loaded with power assistance, the charge is loaded manually, the breech is closed and the ordnance can be fired again.

A complete range of ammunition has been developed for the Palmaria by Simmel: the range consists of four different rounds, each of which weighs 45.5 kg (100 lb). The high explosive, smoke and illuminating projectiles have a range of 24000 m (26,245 yards), and the rocket-assisted projectile has a range of 30000 m (32,800 yards). The extra range of the RAP has a penalty, however, in as much as it is achieved only at the expense of HE content, which is 8 kg (17.6 lb) compared with 11.7 kg (25.8 lb) in the normal projectile.

A 7.62-mm (0.3-in) machine-gun is mounted at the commander's station on the right side of the turret roof, and four electrically-operated smoke dischargers can be fitted to each side of the

turret if required.

A wide range of optional equipment can be fitted, including passive night-vision equipment and an NBC system. Standard equipment on all vehicles includes a hull escape hatch, bilge pumps and an automatic fire-extinguishing system. Track skirts help to keep down dust when the vehicle is travelling across country.

One of the prototypes of the OTO Melara Palmaria, based on the chassis of the OF-40 MBT but fitted with a smaller diesel engine.

Specification
Crew: 5
Weight: 46000 kg (101,410 lb)
Dimensions: length (gun forward) 11.474 m (37 ft 7¾ in); length (hull) 7.40 m (24 ft 3⅓ in); width 2.35 m (7 ft 8½ in); height (without MG) 2.874 m (9 ft 5¼ in)
Powerplant: 8-cylinder diesel developing 750 hp (559 kW)
Performance: maximum road speed 60 km/h (37 mph); maximum range 400 km (250 miles); gradient 60%; vertical obstacle 1.00 m (3 ft 3 in); trench 3.00 m (9 ft 10 in)

Abbot 105-mm Self-Propelled Gun

After the end of World War II the standard self-propelled gun of the British Royal Artillery was the 25-pounder Sexton, which was designed and built in Canada. Prototypes of various self-propelled guns were built on a modified Centurion tank chassis, including one with a 25-pounder gun and the other with a 140-mm (5.5-in) gun. By the 1950s these calibres were not standard within NATO, which was standardizing on 105-mm (4.13-in) and 155-mm (6.1-in) rounds. To meet the Royal Artillery's immediate requirements for SP weapons of the latter calibre, quantities of American M44 self-propelled howitzers were supplied while development concentrated in England on the 105-mm (4.13-in) self-propelled gun which used the engine, transmission and suspension of the FV432 series of APC. Vickers of Elswick was awarded a contract to build 12 prototypes, of which six were powered by a petrol engine and six by a diesel engine. Following trials with these prototypes the company was awarded a production contract, series vehicles being built between 1964 and 1967. The British Army adopted the FV435 Abbot in the early 1960s, equipping field regiments supporting armoured divisions. It was also used by training establishments in Britain and Canada. It failed to sell to others because it was too expensive and complicated. The Value Engineered Abbot was developed in 1976; this was the standard Abbot but with some of the fitments removed. Night vision and NBC equipment, flotation screen and fire warning system were omitted, and the steel tracks had no rubber pads. India purchased 68 which are still in service.

The hull and turret of the Abbot are of all-welded steel which provides the four-man crew with complete protection from small arms fire and shell splinters. The driver is seated at the front on the left, with the engine to his right. The turret is mounted at the very rear of the hull, with the commander and gunner on the right and the loader

Used in the Field Regiments of the Royal Artillery, the Abbot is supported by the amphibious 6×6 Alvis Stalwart High Mobility Load Carrier with prepacked ammunition pallets, and is capable of operating in an NBC environment.

on the left. In addition to the commander's cupola and loader's roof hatches a large door is provided in the hull rear which is also used for ammunition supply. The Abbot is fitted with an NBC system, infra-red driving lights and, when originally introduced into the British army, with a flotation screen; the last has now been removed.

Main armament consists of a 105-mm (4.13-in) gun manufactured by the Royal Ordnance Factory Nottingham, a 7.62-mm (0.3-in) Bren light machine-gun at the commander's station for use in the anti-aircraft role, and one bank of three electrically-operated smoke dischargers on each side of the turret. The 105-mm (4.13-in) gun has a double-baffle muzzle-brake, a fume-extractor and a semi-automatic breech. Traverse is powered through 360°, while elevation is manual from −5° to +70°. The gun has a maximum range of 17000 m (18,600 yards) and fires the following types of separate-loading ammunition: HE, HESH, SH/PRACT, smoke (three types) and illuminating. A total of 40 projectiles is carried.

The ammunition of the Abbot is also used in the Royal Ordnance Factory Nottingham 105-mm (4.13-in) Light Gun, whose ordnance has been developed from the L13A1 gun of the Abbot.

Replacement of the Abbot became vital when the 155mm (6.1-in) calibre

was declared NATO standard for close support guns. Initial replacement was the M109A2, which has since itself been replaced by the AS-90.

Specification

Crew: 4
Weight: 16556 kg (36,500 lb)
Dimensions: length (gun forward) 5.84 m (19 ft 2 in); length (hull) 5.709 m (18 ft 8¾ in); width 2.641 m (8 ft 8 in); height (without armament) 2.489 m (8 ft 2 in)

Powerplant: one Rolls-Royce 6-cylinder diesel developing 240 hp (179 kW)
Performance: maximum road speed 47.5 km/h (30 mph); maximum range 390 km (240 miles); gradient 60%; vertical obstacle 0.609 m (2 ft 0 in); trench 2.057 m (6 ft 9 in)

Eventually to be replaced in the late 1980s by the SP-70 155-mm (6.1-in) gun, the Abbot is no longer fitted with a flotation screen.

Bandkanon 1A 155-mm Self-Propelled Gun

For many years Bofors has been well known for its expertise in the design, development and production of guns and their associated ammunition systems for both army and naval applications. This work was put to good use in the development of the **Bandkanon 1A** 155-mm (6.1-in) self-propelled gun for the Swedish army. The first prototype was completed in 1960, and after extensive trials and some modifications the equipment was placed in production from 1966 to 1968. The Bandkanon 1A has the distinction of being the first fully automatic self-propelled gun to enter service with any army. It is also the heaviest and slowest, factors which make the equipment very difficult to conceal and of limited mobility.

The hull and turret are of all-welded steel construction that varies from 10 mm (0.4 in) to 20 mm (0.8 in) in thickness. The vehicle uses many automotive components of the Bofors S-tank, including the powerpack and

suspension. The engine and transmission are at the front of the hull, with the driver seated to the immediate front of the turret. Suspension is of the hydropneumatic type and consists of six road wheels, with the drive sprocket at the front and the last road wheel acting as the idler. To provide a more stable firing platform the suspension can be locked.

The turret is mounted at the rear of

the hull, and is in two parts with the 155-mm (6.1-in) ordnance mounted between them. In the left part are the commander, gun layer and radio operator, while in the right part are the loader and 7.62-mm (0.3-in) anti-aircraft machine gunner. Turret traverse is manual, 15° left and right when the ordnance is above 0° in elevation, reducing to 15° left and 4° right when the ordnance is below 0° Elevation is

electric from +2° to +38°, and manual from −3° to +40°.

The 155-mm (6.1-in) ordnance has a pepperpot muzzle-brake, no fume-extractor and a semi-automatic wedge breech block that opens downwards. An unusual feature of the ordnance is that it has a replacable liner. When travelling, the ordnance is held in position by a lock pivoted at the front of the hull.

Although the first fully automatic self-propelled gun, the Bandkanon 1A was only procured in small quantities by the Swedish army because of size and lack of mobility.

The ammunition is fed from a 14-round clip carried externally in an armoured magazine at the rear of the hull. This clip consists of seven compartments, each of which contain two rounds of ammunition, these being fed to the breech by a loading tray before being rammed into the breech by a rammer. The loading tray and rammer are operated by springs that are cocked by the run-out of the gun. The first round has to be manually loaded but after this the sequence is fully automatic and the gunner can select single shots or fully automatic. The empty cartridge cases are ejected from the breech to the rear. Once the clip of ammunition has been expended a fresh clip is brought up by truck, the ordnance is elevated to +38°, covers on the magazine are opened vertically, a hoist on the upper part of the turret slides along the slide bar before picking up the clip and placing it in the magazine, the doors are then closed and the hoist is returned to travelling position. Fire can then be resumed. This whole sequence takes just two

The Bandkanon 1A prepares to fire. The unique 14-round armoured magazine is at the rear of the hull; once expended it can be reloaded in less than two minutes from a resupply truck.

minutes.

The 155-mm (6.1-in) projectile has a range of 25600 (28,000 yards). For some time it has been reported that a rocket-assisted projectile is under development that will have a range of about 30000 m (32,800 yards).

Specification
Crew: 5
Weight: 53000 kg (116,845 lb)
Dimensions: length (gun forward) 11.00 m (36 ft 1 in); length (hull) 6.55 m (21 ft 6 in); width 3.37 m (11 ft 0⅔ in); height (including AA MG) 3.85 m (12 ft 7½ in)
Powerplant: one Rolls-Royce diesel developing 240 hp (179 kW) and Boeing gas turbine developing 300 shp (224 kW)
Performance: maximum road speed

28 km/h (17.4 mph); maximum range 230 km (143 miles); gradient 60%;

vertical obstacle 0.95 m (3 ft 1½ in); trench 2.00 m (6 ft 6¾ in)

DANA 152-mm Self-Propelled Howitzer

The Czech 152-mm (6-in) VZ/77 DANA was the first wheeled self-propelled howitzer to enter service. Wheeled SP artillery equipments have a number of advantages over their more common tracked counterparts. They are cheaper and easier to manufacture and to maintain, are less heavily stressed than tracked vehicles, are more economical of fuel and they have a much greater strategic mobility as wheeled armoured vehicles are much faster than their tracked counterparts and have a greater operational range. South Africa introduced their G6 6 x 6 155-mm (6.1-in) wheeled SP howitzer in 1983 and since then several other designs have appeared.

The DANA, first seen at a military parade in 1980, is based on the 8 x 8 Tatra 815 truck, which probably has the best off-road performance of any truck in existence. The driver and gun commander are seated at the front, there is a fully-enclosed split turret in the centre and the armoured engine compartment is at the rear. The amour is of all-welded steel and provides complete protection from small arms fire and shell splinters.

The engine is coupled to a six-speed manual gearbox which transmits power to a two-speed transfer box. Steering is power-assisted on the front four wheels and a central tyre-pressure regulation system allows the driver to adjust the tyre pressure to suit the type of ground being crossed.

The turret consists of two compartments, between which sits the gun. In the right-hand compartment is the ammunition handler who sets fuzes on the shells before they go to the automatic loader; the shells are held vertically in the rear of this compartment. In the left-hand compartment are the propelling charges, the gunlayer and the loader.

Before firing commences three hydraulically operated stabilizers (one at the rear of the hull under the engine compartment and one on each side between the second and third axles) are lowered to the ground

Right: Only Czechoslovakia among the Warsaw Pact armies uses the DANA wheeled gun. The DANA is based on the 8×8 Tatra 815 high mobility truck chassis.

Below: The DANA is a cheaper but more roadworthy alternative to the tracked self-propelled guns now entering the Warsaw Pact inventories.

to provide a firm platform and relieve the vehicle suspension of the firing shock. The breech is opened manually for the first round; thereafter the breech opened automatically on run-out and closes after loading. The automatic loading mechanism lies behind and above the breech and is operated by the loader. A total of 60 rounds are carrier ready for use. The standard shell weighs 43.5 kg (95.8 lbs) and has a maximum range of 18,700 m (20,450 yds). The gun is also provided with a cargo shell containing 42 anti-tank/anti-personnel bomblets; this has a maximum range of 28,230 m

(30,875 yd).

The turret has a limited traverse of 112.5° either side of zero, and the gun elevates from −4° to +70°. Fire can be opened within two minutes of reaching a firing position, and the vehicle can be out of action in less than one minute. NBC protection by over-pressuring the cabins, is provided, and hydraulic power for traverse, elevation, loading and the stabilising jacks is by means of a pump driven by the vehicle engine, with manual back-up.

The 152-mm DANA has been exported to Libya, Poland and Russia. A version with a NATO-standard

155-mm howitzer has been produced for general export.

Specification:
Crew: 5
Weight: 25.1 tonnes
Engine: Tatra V-12 turbo-charged air-cooled diesel, 3,450 bhp at 2,500 rpm
Dimensions: length (gun forward) 11.16m (36ft 7in); width 3.0m (9ft 9in); height to turret roof 2.85m (9ft 4in)
Performance: max road speed 80 km/hr (50 mph); max range 740 km (450 miles); vertical obstacle 0.6 m (1ft 10in); trench 2.0 m (6ft 6in); fording 1.40 m (4 ft 7in)

M1973 152-mm Self-Propelled Gun/Howitzer

The **M1973** 152-mm (6-in) self-propelled gun/howitzer is known as the **2S3** in the Soviet Union, and is issued on the scale of 18 per tank division and a similar number per motorized rifle division. The equipment is also known to be used by East Germany, Iraq and Libya. Its chassis is a shortened version of that used for the SA-4 'Ganef' surface-to-air missile system and GMZ armoured minelayer, which have both been in service with the Soviet Union for many years.

The M1973 has three compartments, that for the driver at the front, that for the engine to its right and that for the turret at the rear, the last being slightly forward of the very rear as it has such a large overhang. The torsion-bar suspension consists of six road wheels, with a distinct gap between the first and second and the third and fourth road wheels; the drive sprocket is at the front with the idler at the rear, and there are four track-return rollers.

The commander's cupola is on the roof of the turret, on the left side, and this is fitted with a 7.62-mm (0.3-in) machine-gun for local and anti-aircraft defence. This is the only hatch in the roof, but there is also a hatch in the right side of the turret. In the hull rear is a large hatch that opens downwards, and on each side of this is one circular hatch. These, and the two square openings in the turret rear, are believed to be used for the rapid loading

Known as the SO-152 Akatsiya (Acacia) in Soviet army service, this vehicle forms the basis for a standard chassis design used for other purposes, including the SA-4 'Ganef' launcher and the GMZ minelayer.

of projectiles and fuses.

The ordnance is based on the 152-mm (6-in) D-20 gun/howitzer but with a bore evacuator, which helps stop fumes from entering the crew compartment when the breech is opened, to the rear of the double-baffle muzzle-brake. The ordnance fires an HE projectile weighing 43.5 kg (95.9 lb) to a maximum range of 18500 m (20,230 yards). Other projectiles that can be fired include HEAT (this will penetrate 300 mm/11.8 in of armour at 1000 m/1,095 yards), HE extended range (with a claimed range of 24000 m/26,245 yards), HE RAP (with a claimed range of 37000 m/40,465 yards), illuminating, smoke and 2-kiloton tactical nuclear. A total of 40 projectiles and charges is carried, and maximum rate of fire is four rounds per minute. The ordnance has an elevation of +60° and a depression of −4°; turret traverse is 360°.

Unlike the 122-mm (4.8-in) M1974 self-propelled howitzer, the M1973 does not have amphibious capability, although it can ford to a depth of 1.5 m (4 ft 11 in). The M1973 is fitted with an NBC system, and with night-vision equipment for the commander and driver.

In recent years the Soviet Union has developed and placed in production at least three new weapons, a 152-mm (6-in) self-propelled gun, a 203-mm (8-in) self-propelled howitzer and a 240-mm (9.45-in) self-propelled mortar. It is believed that the last is probably an updated version of the 240-mm (9.45-in) M240 towed weapon which fires a chemical, high explosive fragmentation or nuclear projectile to a maximum range of 9700 m (10,610 yards). Photographs of the 152-mm (6-in) gun were released by the United States in 1982 and showed a chassis similar to that of

the M1973 but with the ordnance in an unprotected mount on the top rear of the chassis. The ordnance is not fitted with a fume extractor, and when travelling is clamped in position. Located at the rear of the hull is a large spade.

Specification
Crew: 6
Weight: 25000 kg (55,115 lb)
Dimensions: length (gun forward) 8.40 m (27 ft 6⅔ in); length (hull) 7.80 m (25 ft 7 in); width 3.20 m (10 ft 6 in); height 2.80 m (9 ft 2¼ in)
Powerplant: one V-12 diesel developing 520 hp (388 kW)
Performance: maximum road speed 55 km/h (34 mph); maximum range 300 km (186 miles); gradient 60%; vertical obstacle 1.10 m (3 ft 7 in); trench 2.50 m (8 ft 2½ in)

M1974 122-mm Self-Propelled Howitzer

In the period after World War II the Soviet Union placed its main emphasis on the continuing development of towed artillery whereas NATO emphasized self-propelled weapons. Although the latter are much more expensive to build, maintain and operate they do have many advantages over their towed counterparts, including increased cross-country mobility, full armour protection for the crew and ammunition, the possibility of an NBC system, and a reduction in the time necessary for the equipment to be brought into and taken out of action. The Soviet Union did continue to develop specialized tank destroyers such as the ASU-57 and ASU-85, but it was not until 1974 that the first 122-mm (4.8-in) self-propelled howitzer made its appearance during a parade in Poland, although it had doubtless already entered service with the Soviet Union by this date. NATO calls this 122-mm (4.8-in) self-propelled howitzer the **M1974**, this being the year when it was first seen, while the Soviet designation is **2S1**. The system is also used by Algeria, Angola, Czechoslovakia, Ethiopia, East Germany, Hungary, Iraq, Libya, Syria and Yugoslavia, and licensed production may well take place in Czechoslovakia and/or Poland. In the Soviet army the M1974 is employed on the scale of 36 per motorized rifle division and 72 per tank division.

The layout of the M1974 is similar to that of the American M109 with the engine, transmission and driver at the front and the fully enclosed turret at the rear. The suspension is adjustable, and consists of seven road wheels with the drive sprocket at the front and the idler at the rear; there are no track-return rollers. For normal use 400-mm (15.75-

The M1974 has the Soviet designation SO-122 Gvozdika (Carnation) and is fully amphibious, unlike the SO-152. The chassis is also used for the TT-LB (or ACRV in NATO circles), a mine-clearing vehicle, and for a new chemical warfare reconnaissance vehicle.

in) wide tracks are fitted, but when operating in the snow or swampy areas 670-mm (26.4-in) wide tracks are fitted to reduce the vehicle's ground pressure as much as possible. Standard equipment includes an NBC system and a full suite of night-vision equipment for the driver and commander. The M1974 is fully amphibious, being propelled in the water by its tracks at a speed of 4.5 km/h (2.8 mph).

The turret is fitted with a modified version of the standard 122-mm (4.8-in) D-30 towed howitzer, which has an elevation of +70° and depression of −3°; turret traverse is 360°. Turret traverse and weapon elevation are electric, with manual control for emergency use. The ordnance has a double-baffle muzzle-brake, a fume-extractor and a semi-automatic vertical sliding breech block; an ordnance travel lock is mounted on top of the hull. The howitzer fires an HE projectile weighing 21.72 kg (47.9 lb) to a maximum range of 15300 m (16,730 yards), and can also fire chemical, illuminating, smoke and HEAT-FS projectiles. The last is used to engage tanks and will penetrate 460 mm (18.1 in) of armour at an incidence of 0° at a range of 1000 m (1,095 yards). It is also re-

ported that an HE RAP is available, and that this has a maximum range of 21900 m (23,950 yards). A normal ammunition load consists of 40 projectiles: 32 HE, six smoke and two HEAT-FS. It is believed that a power rammer is fitted to permit a higher rate of fire (five rounds per minute) and also to enable the ordnance to be loaded at any angle of elevation.

The chassis of the M1974 is also used for a number of armoured command and reconnaissance vehicles (ACRVs) fitted with the 'Big Fred' artillery/mortar-locating radar, and for a specialized mine-clearing vehicles. The latter is similar in concept to the British Giant Viper.

Specification
Crew: 4
Weight: 16000 kg (35,275 lb)
Dimensions: length 7.30 m (23 ft 11½ in); width 2.85 m (9 ft 4 in); height 2.40 m (7 ft 10½ in)
Powerplant: one YaMZ-238V V-8 water-cooled diesel developing 240 hp (179 kW)
Performance: maximum road speed 60 km/h (37 mph); maximum range 500 km (310 miles); gradient 60%; vertical obstacle 1.10 m (3 ft 7 in); trench 3.00 m (9 ft 10 in)

Two of the 25 SO-122 guns currently credited with being in service with the Hungarian army.

Self-Propelled Anti-Aircraft Guns

Given the apparent size of the threat from the air, you might expect self-propelled (SP) anti-aircraft guns to form a large part of a modern army. You would be wrong. Modern SP anti-aircraft guns are complex and expensive weapon systems, and most armies simply do not have the money to spare.

The Bofors Trinity is a 40-mm close-in anti-aircraft weapon system that can be carried by a range of armoured vehicles. In this case it is mounted on a modified Piranha APC chassis.

In June 1944 the German Panzer columns attempting to move forward against the Allied invasion troops were torn to pieces by ground-attack aircraft and were unable to move in daylight. You might expect the major armies of the world today to be well fitted out with mobile air defence weapons with which to protect their armoured columns while on the move. However, they are not.

The only major European armies to have acted are the German (not surprisingly) and the Russian. Both forces are equipped with suitable anti-aircraft tanks which can take their place in the armoured column and deliver self-contained protection. The British and the French appear to ignore the possibility of air attack, while the Americans utilize an elderly twin 40-mm type and a number of 20-mm Gatling guns, neither of which are capable of dealing with a modern armoured ground-attack aircraft.

The absence of hardware is not because suitable designs have not been forthcoming. There is no shortage of ideas in this field.

Indeed, if the US Army's M247 Sgt York is anything to go by, there have been too many ideas. But while they appear at exhibitions, very few of them ever make it into military service. The reason is, of course, money. There are an infinite number of items an army wants, a smaller number that they actually need, and a finite amount of money to spend. And mobile air defence is low on the list of requirements.

A modern self-propelled system needs to carry its own radar, both for surveillance and target acquisition and for tracking. Moreover, it needs to have an electro-optical sighting system so that electronic counter-measures can be ignored and the equipment can still have a day and night capability. It requires an advanced ballistic computer, a laser rangefinder... and none of it is cheap. And, ideally, it has to have two or more reliable and destructive guns fed with modern and expensive ammunition.

In spite of all these obstacles manufacturers keep trying. More recently they have tried adding a few missiles to the gun vehicle. Unfortunately, as the threat of major war recedes, so does the threat of enemy air superiority, and mobile air defence slips even further down the list.

Type 63 twin 37-mm self-propelled AA gun

The 'Chinese Type 63' SP anti-aircraft gun is a classic example of over-estimating the opposition and erecting a structure of supposition on relatively slender evidence, a pastime of intelligence staffs the world over.

Some time in the middle 1960s the South Vietnamese Army captured a self-propelled AA gun from the North Vietnamese. It was immediately seized and shipped off to the USA for evaluation by intelligence experts, and their subsequent report gave the following information:

To meet its needs for a self-propelled anti-aircraft gun system China has used the T-34 series tank chassis with its turret replaced by a new open-topped turret armed with twin 37-mm anti-aircraft guns; this gun was already in service with the Chinese army, mounted on a four-wheeled carriage. The chassis of the Type 63 is identical to that of the tank, with the driver at the front left and bow machine-gunner to his right, though it is probable that the bow machine-gun was removed. The turret is in the centre of the hull with the engine and transmission at the rear.

The twin 37-mm cannon are recoil-operated and have cyclic rate of fire of 160 to 189 rounds per minute, but practical rate of fire per barrel is 80 rounds a minute Weapon elevation and turret traverse are manual, which would be a major tactical drawback in the engagement of aircraft flying at low level and high speed. Only optical sights are hired. with no provision at all for radar fire-control. The ammunition is fed to each weapon in clips of five rounds, some ready-use ammunition being stowed inside the turret with the bulk of the ammunition stowed externally in panniers on each side of the hull. Two basic types of ammunition are fired, FRAG-T (fragmentation-tracer) being used against aerial targets, and AP-T (armour-piercing tracer) being used against armoured targets such as light tanks. Both projectiles have a muzzle velocity of 880 m (2,887 ft) per second. and the AP-T round will penetrate 37-mm (14 in) of armour at a range of 1000 m (1,095 yd) or 46 mm (18.4 in) of amour at a range of 500 m (347 yd) penetration being better at shorter ranges because of the projectile's higher velocity. Effective anti-aircraft range is 3000 m (3,280 yards), although maximum vertical range is

The Type 63 is a weapon of limited capability. Mounted onto an unmodified T-34 tank hull, the open turret has no provision for radar fire control, and the optically sighted weapons are elevated and traversed manually.

6700 m (21,980 ft).

The equipment was subsequently placed on display in the Ordnance Museum at Aberdeen Proving Ground.

And there the matter rested for several years, even though no other example of the Type 63 was ever captured or even seen. It was not until well over twenty years later, when information on weapon development at last began to emerge from China, that it became apparent that there never had been a Type 63 gun equipment. The specimen captured in Vietnam had been just that – a specimen, the only one of its kind, cobbled together by some unknown and unrecorded North Vietnamese workshop from a redundant tank chassis and a twin 37-mm gun mount, probably from a naval origin, encased in a home-made shielded turret. Whatever its effectiveness as an air defence weapon might have been, it was certainly effective in diverting the energies of several intelligence experts for quite a long time.

Specification (provisional)
Type 63
Crew: 6
Weight: 32000 kg (70,547 lb)

Dimensions: length (guns forward) 6.432 m (21 ft 1 in); length (hull) 7.53 m (24 ft 8 in); height (turret top) 2.995 m (9 ft 10 in)
Powerplant: one V-12 water-cooled diesel developing 500 hp (373 kW)
Performance: maximum road speed 55 km/h (34 mph); maximum range

This Type 63 was supplied to the Viet Cong, from whom it was captured by the US Forces during the Vietnam war.

(road) 300 km (186 miles); gradient 60 per cent; vertical obstacle 0.73 m (2 ft 5 in); trench 2.5 m (8 ft 2 in)

BTR-152A twin 14.5-mm self-propelled AA gun

While the ZSU-57-2 twin 57-mm SPAAG was the first purpose-built weapon of its type to be introduced into the Soviet army in large numbers during the post-war period, the **BTR-152A** (6×6) and BTR-40A (4×4) entered service some years before. In both cases these were essentially armoured personnel carrier chassis with the normally-towed twin 14.5-mm (0.57-in) KPV heavy machine-guns turret-mounted in the troop compartment at hull rear. The turret is designated the ZPTU-2 and can be traversed through 360°, the weapons being able to elevate −5° to +80°. The KPV machine-gun is also fitted in a number of Soviet armoured vehicles including the BRDM-2 (4×4) amphibious scout car and the BTR-60PB and BTR-70

(8×8) armoured personnel carriers. It was also installed as the co-axial and anti-aircraft weapon of the T-10M heavy tank, which is no longer in front-line service with the Soviet Union. There are also three versions of the towed KPV heavy anti-aircraft machine-gun: the ZPU-1 (single), ZPU-2 (twin) and ZPU-4 (quadruple). In the Warsaw Pact most of the towed ZPUs have been replaced by the 23-mm ZU-23 anti-aircraft gun, and the BTR-152A and BTR-40A each remain in front line service only outside the Soviet Union.

The KPV heavy machine-gun has a

The BTR-152A has been used operationally in Vietnam and the Middle East in both AA and fire support roles.

cyclic rate of fire of 600 round per minute per barrel, but its practical rate of fire is 150 rounds per minute per barrel. The method of operation is gas-assisted short recoil. The barrel is air-cooled, is fitted with a flash eliminator and a handle for carrying out quick changes, and is chromium-plated internally to reduce barrel wear. Two types of ammunition, API and HEI-T, are fired. The armour piercing incendiary round is used mainly against armoured vehicles and will penetrate 32 mm (1.29 in) of armour at a range of 500 m (547 yards). The high explosive

incendiary-tracer (HEI-T) round is used against aircraft. Only optical sights are fitted, there being no provision for radar fire-control. This limits the system's capability to clear-weather operations only. The lack of power traverse and elevation also limits the system's capability to engage fast-moving targets at low level.

In addition to being used in its originally-designed anti-aircraft role in the Middle East and Vietnam, the system has also been used in the ground fire-support role, in which its high rate of fire has proved most useful. During the

fighting in the Lebanon in the summer of 1982 the Israeli army captured a number of BTR-152 APCs with the more effective twin 23-mm ZU-23 cannon mounted in the rear, but as far as is known this was a local modification.

One of the more interesting local modifications carried out by Egypt on the BTR-152 was the installation of the Czech quadruple 12.7-mm (0.5-in) M53 machine-gun mounting in the rear of the vehicle. The weapons have a lower cyclic rate of fire than the KPV and also a shorter effective range.

Specification
BTR-152A
Crew: 4
Weight: 9600 kg (21,164 lb)
Dimensions: length 6.83 m (22 ft 5 in); width 2.32 m (7 ft 7 in); height (overall) 2.70 m (9 ft 2 in)
Powerplant: one ZIL-123 6-cylinder petrol engine developing 110 hp (82 kW)
Performance: maximum road speed 65 km/h (40 mph); maximum range 780 km (485 miles); gradient 55 per cent; vertical obstacle 0.60 m (2 ft); trench 0.69 m (2 ft 3 in)

ZSU-57-2 twin 57-mm self-propelled AA gun

The **ZSU-57-2** was the first post-war Soviet self-propelled anti-aircraft gun to be introduced on a large scale and was first seen in public during November 1957. The chassis of the ZSU-57-2 is essentially a lightened version of the

The first purpose-built self-propelled AA gun to be introduced into the Soviet inventory, the ZSU-57-2 is in wide use with Soviet-supplied forces, although no longer in front-line Soviet use.

T-54 MBT with thinner armour protection and one road wheel less on each side, though the length of track on the ground remains identical. The guns fire the same ammunition and have the same performance as the widely used towed 57-mm S-60 anti-aircraft gun. In the ZSU-57-2 designation ZSU means that the equipment is a self-propelled anti-aircraft gun system, 57 is for the calibre of the weapons (57-mm) and 2 is for the number of guns. The system was widely deployed by the Soviet Union but has now been replaced in all front line units by the ZSU-23-4 self-propelled anti-aircraft gun system. It is still used by Algeria, Angola, Bulgaria, Cuba, East Germany, Egypt, Ethiopia, Finland, Hungary, Iran, Iraq, North Korea, Poland, Romania, Syria and Yugoslavia. In 1982 the Syrian army made extensive use of the ZSU-57-2 in the ground-support role during fighting in the Lebanon.

The chassis is of all-welded steel construction, with the driver at the front left, the other five crew members in the open-topped turret in the centre of the hull, and the engine and transmission at the rear. Suspension is of the torsion-bar type with the drive sprocket at the rear and the idler at the front; there are four road wheels but no track-return rollers. As the ZSU-57-2 is lighter than the T-54 tank on which it is based it has a higher power-to-weight ratio of 18.56 hp/tonne and a lower ground pressure. To extend its operating range to 595 km (370 miles), long-range fuel tanks can be fitted at the rear of the hull.

The twin 57-mm cannon are power-operated from −5° to +85° at 20° per second, with turret traverse through 360° at a speed of 30° per second; manual controls are provided for emergency use.

Each gun has a cyclic rate of fire of 105 to 120 rounds per minute, though the practical rate of fire is 70 rounds per minute. Ammunition is fed to each weapon in clips of four rounds, the empty cartridge cases and clips being deposited onto a conveyor belt under the weapon. This runs to the turret rear and drops the empty cartridge cases and clips into the large wire basket mounted externally at the turret rear.

The following types of fixed ammunition can be fired: FRAG-T (fragmentation-tracer) and APC-T (armour piercing capped-tracer). The former is used mainly against aerial targets while the latter, which will penetrate 96 mm (3.7 in) of armour at a range of 1000 m (1,094 yards), is used against ground targets such as tanks and APCs. Effective anti-aircraft range is 4000 m (4,375 yards) with maximum vertical range 8800 m (28,870 ft). Max-

imum horizontal range is 12000 m (13,125 yards), although fire control would be a major problem at such long ranges.

Specification
ZSU-57-2
Crew: 6
Weight: 28100 kg (61,949 lb)
Dimensions: length 8.48 m (27 ft 10 in); length (hull) 6.22 m (20 ft 5 in); width 3.27 m (10 ft 9 in); height 2.75 m (9 ft)

Powerplant: one Model V-54 V-12 diesel developing 520 hp (388 kW)
Performance: maximum road speed 50 km/h (31 mph); maximum range 420 km (260 miles); gradient 60 per cent; vertical obstacle 0.80 m (2 ft 7 in); trench 2.70 m (2 ft 8 in)

In the ground support role the ZSU-57-2 (as used by Syria in Lebanon) has proved extremely potent.

ZSU-23-4 quadruple 23-mm self-propelled AA gun

The **ZSU-23-4** was developed in the 1960s as the replacement for the 57-mm ZSU-57-2 self-propelled anti-aircraft gun system. Although the ZSU-23-4's 23-mm cannon has a shorter range than the earlier weapon, the system is much more effective as it has a radar fire-control system and a much higher rate of fire. Since being introduced into the Soviet army on a large scale it has also been exported to almost every country that has received Soviet military equipment, including Afghanistan, Algeria, Angola, Bulgaria, Cuba, Czechoslovakia, East Germany, Egypt, Ethiopia, Hungary, India, Iran, Iraq, Jordan, Libya, Mozambique, Nigeria, North Korea, North Yemen, Peru, Poland, Romania, Somalia, South Yemen, Syria, Vietnam and Yugoslavia. In addition to seeing extensive action during the conflict in Vietnam, the ZSU-23-4 also proved to be one of the most effective systems during the 1973 Middle East war: Soviet-supplied missiles such as the SA-6 'Gainful' forced Israeli aircraft to fly at low altitude, where they encountered the ZSU-23-4 and the SA-7 man-portable missiles. In the Soviet army, who call the system the Shilka, the ZSU-23-4 is issued on the scale of 16 systems per division and normally operates in pairs.

The chassis of the ZSU-23-4 is very similar to that of the SA-6 'Gainful' SAM system, and uses automotive components of the PT-76 amphibious light tank family. It is of all-welded steel construction with a maximum thickness of 15 mm (0.6 in) at the front and 10 mm (0.4 in) over the remainder of the vehicle including the turret, and this provides protection only against small arms fire and shell splinters. The driver is seated at the front of the hull on the left, with the turret in the centre, and engine and transmission at the rear. Suspension is of the torsion-bar type and consists of six single rubber-tyred road wheels with the drive sprocket at the rear and idler at the front. A gas turbine is installed in the rear to provide power for the turret and other systems while the main engine is not running.

The commander, search radar operator/gunner and rangefinding number are all seated in the large flat turret. Main armament consists of four AZP-23 23-mm gas-operated cannon with a cyclic rate of fire of 800 to 1000 rounds per minute per barrel. These weapons have an elevation of +85° and a depression of −4° in a turret

Seeing extensive operational use in Vietnam and the Middle East, the ZSU-23-4 (called 'Shilka' in Soviet service) proved one of the most effective air defence weapons of the 1970s. The four-barrelled weapon can provide radar-directed fire in bursts of up to 50 rounds at a time.

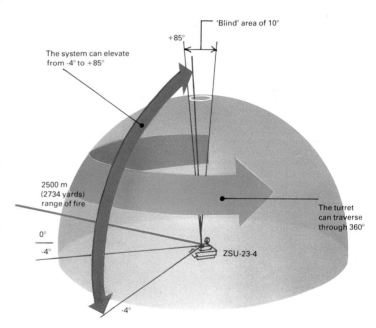

capable of traversing through 360°. Turret traverse and weapon elevation are powered, manual controls being provided for emergency use. The gunner can select 3/5-, 5/10- or 50-round bursts, and the cannon have an effective anti-aircraft range of 2500 m (2,735 yards) and a similar range in the ground-target role. Each cannon is provided with 500 rounds of ready-use ammunition; the two types normally fired are API-T (armoured-piercing incendiary-tracer) and HEI-T (high explosive incendiary-tracer). The ZSU-23-4 is fitted with a fire-control system that includes a radar scanner mounted on the turret rear, sights and a fire-control computer. Target can be engaged while the vehicle is travelling across country, but where possible the ZSU-23-4 would stop to provide a more stable firing platform.

Specification
ZSU-23-4
Crew: 4
Weight: 19000 kg (41,888 lb)
Dimensions: length 6.54 m (21 ft 5 in); width 2.95 m (9 ft 8 in); height (without radar) 2.25 m (7 ft 4 in)
Powerplant: one V-6R diesel developing 280 hp (210 kW)
Performance: maximum road speed 44 km/h (27 mph); maximum road range 260 km (162 miles); gradient 60 per cent; vertical obstacle 1.10 m (3 ft 7 in); trench 2.80 m (9 ft 2 in)

'Blind' area of 10°

+85°

The system can elevate from -4° to +85°

2500 m (2734 yards) range of fire

0°

−4°

ZSU-23-4

The turret can traverse through 360°

−4°

The ZSU-23-4 can throw up a wall of impenetrable fire covering a hemisphere of 2500 m (2,734 yards) around itself. Its radar can pick up targets 20 km (12 miles) out, and its computer automatically bears the guns onto the hapless intruder. Able to quickly traverse through 360° and elevate from −4° to +85°, the system can kill anything that enters its zone.

ZSU-23-4s are seen in Egyptian service prior to the 1973 war with Israel. In combination with the SA-6 'Gainful' missile system, the guns wrought havoc for a time amongst Israeli ground attack aircraft.

Soviet 'Shilkas' on the move, with armament and radar systems at the ready. The Soviet army normally operates the weapons in pairs, with some 16 systems being the normal complement per division.

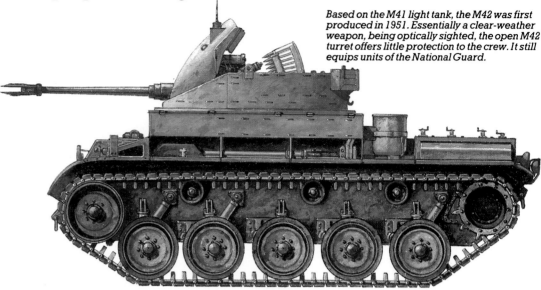

M42 twin 40-mm self-propelled AA gun

During the latter half of World War II the United States developed a series of tracked vehicles (the Light Combat Team) which included the M24 Chaffee light tank, M37 105-mm (4.13-in) howitzer motor carriage, M41 155-mm (6.1-in) howitzer motor carriage and M19 twin 40-mm self-propelled anti-aircraft gun system. After the end of the war a new family of light vehicles was developed, this including a light tank called the M41 (or Walker Bulldog) while the anti-aircraft gun system, which had the same automotive components but a different hull, was called the **M42**, or more commonly the **Duster**. The turret of the M42 is the same as that of the earlier M19, though in the former it is mounted in the centre of the hull and in the latter at the rear of the hull. The M42, whose development designation was T141, was in production from 1951 to 1956 and about 3,700 equipments were built, the majority by the Cadillac Motor Car Division of the General Motors Corporation at the Cleveland Tank Plant. Late production equipments were called the **M42A1**, the major difference being the fuel injection system for the engine. One of the main drawbacks of the M42, along with other members of this family, was its use of a petrol engine, which resulted in a very short operating range. Today the M42 is still used by the US Army National Guard (eight battalions), as well as by Austria, Greece, Japan, Jordan, Lebanon, Saudi Arabia, Taiwan, Thailand, Turkey and Venezuela. It was used successfully in Vietnam by both the US and South Vietnamese armies, although its primary role was in the ground-support fire role rather than the air-defence role for which it was originally designed.

The hull and turret of the M42 are of all-welded steel construction, with the commander and driver seated in the front of the vehicle, turret with other four crew members located in the centre, and the engine and transmission installed at the rear. Suspension is of the well-tried torsion-bar type, and consists of five dual rubber-tyred road wheels, with the drive sprocket at the rear and idler at the front; there are three track-return rollers.

Based on the M41 light tank, the M42 was first produced in 1951. Essentially a clear-weather weapon, being optically sighted, the open M42 turret offers little protection to the crew. It still equips units of the National Guard.

Right: M42A1 vehicles wait on the range firing line at Dina Beach in the Panama Canal Zone. By 1967, when the photograph was taken, the Dusters were nearing the end of their front-line service, although still being used operationally in Vietnam.

The turret and weapons are power-operated; the turret can be traversed through 360° at 40° per second, and the guns can be elevated from −3° to +85° at a speed of 25° per second. Manual controls are provided for emergency use. A total of 480 rounds of ammunition is carried, and the guns have a practical rate of fire of 120 rounds per minute per barrel with an effective anti-aircraft range of 5000 m (5,470 yards). The gunner can select single shots or full automatic fire, and four types of ammunition carried are AP-T, HE-T, HEI-T and TP-T. A 7.62-mm (0.3-in) M60 or M1919A4 machine-gun is mounted externally on left rear of turret for local defence, and 1,750 rounds of ammunition are carried for this weapon.

The M42 is essentially a clear-weather system as its fire-control system consist of an M38 computing sight, M24c reflex sight and a speed ring sight. Efforts were made to fit a radar fire-control system, but this idea was eventually dropped.

Specification
M42
Crew: 6
Weight: 22452 kg (49,497 lb)
Dimensions: length (guns forward)
6.356 m (20 ft 10 in); length (hull) 5.819 m (19 ft 1 in); width 3.225 m (10 ft 7 in); height 2.847 m (9 ft 4 in)
Powerplant: one Continental AOS-895-3 6-cylinder air-cooled petrol engine developing 500 bhp (373 kW)
Performance: maximum road speed 72.4 km/h (45 mph); maximum range 161 km (100 miles); gradient 60 per cent; vertical obstacle 0.711 m (2 ft 4 in); trench 1.829 m (6 ft)

M163 Vulcan 20-mm self-propelled AA gun

In the early 1960s Rock Island Arsenal developed two 20-mm Vulcan air-defence systems. The self-propelled model was based on a modified M113 APC chassis and was designated the **XM163** (the chassis being the XM741) while the towed model was the XM167. These were subsequently accepted for service as the **M163** and M167 respectively. The former was produced by the General Electric Company of Burlington, Vermont, and was soon deployed to South Vietnam where it was widely used in the ground fire-support role. In the US Army the M163 is deployed in composite battalions, each of which has two batteries each with 12 Chaparral SAM launchers and two batteries each with 12 M163s. The towed M167 is used mainly by the air-mobile and air-assault divisions. In addition to the United States, the M163 is also used by Ecuador, Israel, Morocco, North Yemen, South Korea and Tunisia. In the regular US Army the M163 will be replaced by the M247 DIVAD, then

being passed on to the National Guard, which at present operates the old twin 40-mm M42 self-propelled anti-aircraft gun system.

The M163 consists of a standard M113 chassis on top of which has been mounted an electrically-operated turret fitted with a 20-mm six-barrelled M61 series cannon, a US Navy Mk 20 lead-computing sight, and an EMTECH range-only radar located on the right side of the turret. The turret can be traversed through 360° at a speed of 60° per second and the gun elevated from −5° to +80° at 45° per second. Manual controls are provided in case of power failure. The 20-mm cannon, which is a development of the weapon originally designed for the Lockheed F-104 Starfighter in the

Standard anti-aircraft gun in US Army service, the Vulcan is available in tracked self-propelled (M163) and wheeled towed (M167) forms.

1950s and still fitted in aircraft such as the General Dynamics F-16, has two rates of fire in this application, 1,000 and 3,000 rounds per minute. The former is normally used for engagement of ground targets, while the higher rate of fire is used against aerial targets. The gunner can select 10-, 30-, 60- or 100-round bursts, and 1,100 rounds of ready-use ammunition are carried, with a further 1,000 rounds in reserve. Ammunition types that can be fired include APT (armour piercing tracer), TP (target practice), HEI (high explosive incendiary), TPT (target practice tracer) and HEI-T (high explosive incendiary-tracer). All have a muzzle velocity of 1030 m (3,380 ft) per second. Maximum effective range in the anti-aircraft role is 1600 m (1,750 yards) and in the ground role 3000 m (3,280 yards). A typical target engagement is described in the entry for the Vulcan Commando air-defence system, which has been developed specifically for the export market.

The US Air Force has a requirement for a Mobile Weapon System (MWS) to defend its airfields against ground attack from helicopters, and General Electric has recently been awarded a contract for a MWS which will consist of a M113A1 chassis fitted with a power-operated turret armed with a 30-mm GAU-8 cannon which would have ammunition interoperability with the Fairchild A-10A Thunderbolt II aircraft

of the USAF's Tactical Air Command.

Specification
M163
Crew: 4
Weight: 12310 kg (27,139 lb)
Dimensions: length 4.86 m (15 ft 11 in); width 2.85 m (9 ft 4 in); height (overall) 2.736 m (8 ft 11 in); height (hull top) 1.83 m (6 ft 0 in)

Powerplant: one Detroit Diesel 6V-53 6-cylinder diesel developing 215 bhp (160 kW)
Performance: maximum road speed 67 km/h (42 mph); maximum range 483 km (300 miles); gradient 60 per cent; vertical obstacle 0.61 m (2 ft 0 in); trench 1.68 m (5 ft 6 in)

The M163 consists of a 20-mm Gatling-type cannon mounted upon an M113 APC chassis. The gunner can select rates of fire of 1,000 or 3,000 rounds per minute for use with ground or airborne targets, and he can select bursts of 10, 30, 60 or 100 rounds. Maximum effective anti-aircraft range is 1600 m (1,750 yards).

USA
M247 Sgt York twin 40-mm self-propelled AA gun

Since the late 1960s the only self-propelled anti-aircraft gun system in front line service with the US Army has been the M163 20-mm Vulcan system, which has relatively short range and is not considered to be very accurate. In January 1978, after studying a number of proposals from industry, the United States Armament Research and Development Command issued two competitive contracts for the development of a self-propelled anti-aircraft gun system on a modified M48A5 tank chassis under the designation Division Air Defense Gun (DIVAD) system. General Dynamics, Pomona Division, entered a system that used twin 35-mm Oerlikon cannon while Ford Aerospace and Communications Corporation entered a system that used twin 40-mm L/70 Bofors guns. In the towed configuration some of the latter were already operated by a number of NATO countries. Both entries in the competition had a comprehensive fire-control system that included both surveillance and tracking radars designed to engage both aircraft and helicopter. Following evaluation of the two systems the Ford Aerospace and Communications model was selected for production in May 1981 and was later designated the **M247 Sgt York**. The US Army has a requirement for a total of 618 systems, which will be issued to anti-aircraft battalions at divisional level. The first production system was completed at the Ford Aerospace and Communications Corporation new DIVAD facility at Newport Beach, California, late in 1983.

As already mentioned the M247 is an M48A5 tank chassis with a new turret mounted in the centre of the hull. The driver is seated at the front of the hull, and the engine and transmission

are at the rear. Suspension is of the torsion-bar type, and consists of six dual tubber-tyred wheels, with the idler at the front and drive sprocket at the rear; there are five track-return rollers. Two radars are mounted on the turret, the circular tracking radar on the left and the flat search radar at the rear; both of these can be folded down to reduce the overall height of the

vehicle. The gunner is seated on the left of the turret and the commander on the right, each member being provided with a hatch cover. The gunner has a roof-mounted sight incorporating a laser rangefinder, while the commander has a panoramic roof-mounted periscope and fixed periscopes. The fire-control system of DIVAD is fully automatic with manual override.

The M247 Sgt York twin 40-mm self-propelled AA gun is to replace the M163 in service with the US Army. It is mounted on an M48 tank chassis, and so is more suitable for use with the M1 Abrams tank and M2 Bradley fighting vehicle now entering service.

Commando Vulcan 20-mm self-propelled AA gun

While the M163 self-propelled Vulcan air-defence system on the standard M113 chassis satisfied the US Army, it did not meet the requirements of the Saudi Arabian National Guard which operates a huge fleet of Cadillac Gage V-150 (4 x 4) armoured cars in a variety of versions. As it would create logistical, operational and training problems to integrate a tracked vehicle into a wheeled armoured battalion, General Electric and Cadillac Gage developed a version of the V-150 to meet the Saudi requirements and this Commando Vulcan system was taken into service. It consists of a standard V-150 (4 x 4) chassis fitted with the same turret, weapon and associated fire control systems of the M163, making training and the provision of spares easy. However, the Saudi National Guard purchased only 20 and no further sales were made.

The vehicle has a four-man crew consisting of the commander, gunner, radio operator and driver. The chassis is fitted with three hydraulic jacks. one at the front and one on each side of the hull at the rear, which can be lowered to the ground from within, providing a stable firing platform.

The system operates in four modes:

Radar: The most accurate system, this uses the radar to determine range and rate of change and supplies it to the fire control computer,

which then produces data for setting the gyro lead sight.

Manual: in which the gunner estimates target range and speed and enters them into the sight.

External: in which an external radar or hand-held remote control can be used to direct the gun at an approaching target.

Ground: in which the sights are locked at zero deflection and the gun is directed at ground targets by eye.

A typical radar engagement of the Commando Vulcan E system is as follows. The gunner observes the target visually or the system, tied into a radar that alerts the gunner to the appropriate heading and altitude of the target. The gunner then acquires the target in his sight and starts to track the target using the gyro lead-computing sight. The I-band pulse-Doppler radar mounted on the right side of the turret is servoed to the optical line of sight and provides target range and rate of change data to the sight generator. With other information the sight automatically computes the future position of the target and then adds the quadrant elevation required to hit the target.

When the target is within range a green light appears in the field of view of the sight. This informs the gunner that the radar has acquired the target and is performing its functions correctly, that the target is within the

effective range of the 20-mm cannon, so avoiding the waste of valuable ammunition, and that the firing circuits are completed so that the weapon may be fired.

The Commando Vulcan consists of an M163 gun, turret and fire control system mounted on a standard Cadillac Gage V-150 Commando armoured car chassis.

Specification:
Crew: 4
Weight: 10.2 tonnes
Dimensions: length 5.69 m; width 2.26 m; height 3.30 m
Engine: Cummins V-8 diesel, 202 bhp

at 3300 rpm
Performance: maximum road speed: 88 km/hr; operating range 640 km.
Ballistics: muzzle velocity 1030 m/sec; rate of fire 1000 or 3000 rds/min; effective range: approx. 2000 m.

Panhard M3 VDA twin 20-mm self-propelled AA gun

The Panhard AML (4×4) light armoured car has been one of the most successful vehicles of its type designed since World War II. To operate with this vehicle Panhard also developed a 4×4 armoured personnel carrier that uses 95 per cent of the automotive components (for example the engine, transmission and suspension) for the original armoured car. This vehicle, called the M3, has also proved to be highly successful and since production started in the early 1970s over 1,500 have been built for export to more than 30 countries. The anti-aircraft member of the M3 family is the **M3 VDA** (Véhicule de Defense Antiaérienne) and entered production in 1975.

The VDA is a standard M3 APC on top of which has been mounted a turret with twin 20-mm anti-aircraft cannon. The turret itself was designed by Hispano-Suiza with Galileo of Italy providing the sight, Oerlikon the 20-mm cannon and Electronique Serge Dassault the radar; the last is the prime contractor for the turret before it is delivered to Panhard for installation on the chassis. The M3 VDA is known to be in service with the Ivory Coast, Niger and Abu Dhabi, and the turret can also be fitted without difficulty to other tracked and wheeled chassis such as the Renault VAB (6×6), Simbas (6×6), Panhard ERC (6×6) and Eugesa EE-11 Urutu (6×6) wheeled vehicles and on the Alvis Spartan, Steyr and, most recently, AMX-13 VCI full-tracked vehicles.

The M3 VDA has a crew of three with the commander at the front, gunner in the turret (in the centre of the hull) and the commander at the rear. The turret has full powered traverse through 360° at a speed of 60° per

second, with the guns capable of elevation from −5° to +85° at a speed of 90° per second. Mounted on the turret rear is a radar scanner that rotates at a speed of 40 rpm; this carries out both surveillance and tracking functions, and can track up to four targets, information being relayed to a screen at the commander's position. The gunner has a P56T sight with magnifications of ×5 and ×12 for engaging aerial targets, a ground sight and six periscopes for all-round observation. The 20-mm cannon are mounted externally, one on each side of the turret, the gunner having the option of selecting either or both cannon. The gunner can also select single shots, bursts or full automatic fire. Two cyclic rates of fire are available, 200 or 1,000 rounds per minute. The latter is used for the anti-aircraft role. Each cannon is provided with 300 rounds of ready-use ammunition, and additional ammunition can be carried in the hull. A 7.62-mm (0.3-in) machine-gun is normally fitted for local protection, and two electrically-operated smoke dischargers are mounted on each side of the turret firing forwards. To provide a steadier firing platform, four stabilizers are lowered to the ground hydraulically before the equipment starts firing, although in an emergency the guns can be fired at the lower cyclic rate of fire without the stabilizers in position.

Specification
M3 VDA
Crew: 3
Weight: 7200 kg (15,873 lb)
Dimensions: length 4.45 m (17 ft 5 in); width 2.40 m (7 ft 11 in); height (excluding radar) 2.995 m (9 ft 11 in)
Powerplant: one Panhard Model 4 HD 4-cylinder air-cooled petrol engine

Above: The M3 VDA is a version of the successful Panhard M3 APC, armed with twin Oerlikon 20-mm cannon.

Below: Four stabilizers are lowered automatically before firing, although the guns can be fired at a low cyclic rate without them.

developing 90 hp (67 kW)
Performance: maximum road speed 90 km/h (56 mph); maximum range 1000 km (621 miles); gradient 60 per

cent; vertical obstacle 0.30 m (12 in); trench 0.80 m (2 ft 7 in) with one channel or 3.10 m (10 ft 2 in) with four channels

AMX-13 DCA twin 30-mm self-propelled AA gun

In the 1950s prototypes of a number of self-propelled anti-aircraft gun systems were designed and built to meet the requirements of the French army, but was not until the late 1960s that one of these was considered sufficiently developed to enter production. This was designated **AMX-13 DCA** (Défense Contre Avions) and was essentially an AMX-13 chassis fitted with a cast steel turret mounted on the hull at the rear. Prime contractor for the turret was SAMM, with CGT (now Thomson-CSF) responsible for the radar and its associated electronics, and with Hispano-Suiza of Switzerland (now taken over by Oerlikon-Bührle) responsible for the weapons and ammunition. Sixty AMX-13 DCA equipments were built for the French army, with final deliveries in 1969. In 1984 the AMX-13 DCA remains the only self-propelled anti-aircraft gun system in service with the French army. More recently the French army was to have received the VADAR twin 20-mm system on a VAB wheeled chassis, but this was cancelled on economy grounds several years ago.

Main armament of the AMX-13 DCA consists of twin HSS-831A 30-mm cannon with an elevation of +85° and a depression of −5° in a turret capable of traversing through 360°. Maximum rate of powered elevation is 45° per second, and of powered traverse 80° per second. Each cannon has 300 rounds of ready-use ammunition and the gunner can select single shots, 5- or 15-round bursts, or full automatic fire. The empty cartridge cases are ejected from the turret together with the links. In the anti-aircraft role the weapons have a maximum effective range of 3500 m (3828 yards), and also possess a very useful secondary capability against ground targets.

Mounted at the turret rear is the Oeil Noir 1 (black eye 1) radar scanner, which can be retracted into the turret bustle when not required. Although the cannon are normally aimed with the radar system and the anti-aircraft sights, sights are also provided for the engagement of ground targets. Mounted on each side of the turret is a bank of three electrically-operated smoke dischargers.

In the 1960s this DCA turret was also fitted to the chassis of the AMX-30 MBT, but the combination was not adopted by the French army as it was already ordering the Roland SAM system on the AMX-30 chassis. To provide close-in defence to its Thomson-CSF/MATRA Shahine mobile surface-to-air missile systems, Saudi Arabia ordered 53 examples of a more up-to-date version of this turret on the AMX-30 chassis, and by 1984 all of these equipments had been delivered. This is called the **AMX-30 SA**, and its turret is fitted with the more powerful Thomson-CSF Oeil Vert (green eye) radar as well as improved electronics. Thomson-CSF has also developed with SAMM the SABRE turret, which has for trials purposes already been installed on a number of other chassis such as the Chieftain MBT, Marder MICV and Steyr-Daimler-Puch APC. This also has twin 30-mm cannon but a different fire-control system.

Specification
AMX-13 DCA
Crew: 3
Weight: 17200 kg (37,919 lb)

Entering service with the French army in 1969, the AMX-13 DCA comprises a twin 30-mm Hispano (now Oerlikon) gun system mounted on an AMX-13 chassis with an Oeil Noir 1 (black eye 1) radar scanner mounted at the rear of the turret. A total of 60 AMX-13 DCAs were delivered to the French army.

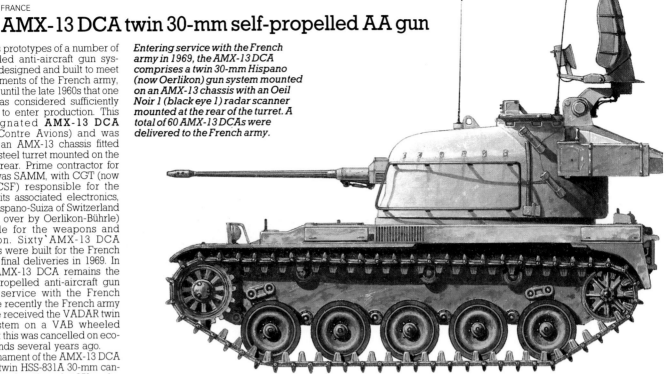

Dimensions: length 5.40 m (17 ft 11 in); width 2.50 m (8 ft 2 in); height (radar up) 3.80 m (12 ft 6 in); height (radar down) 3.00 m (9 ft 10 in)
Powerplant: one SOFAM Model 8Gxb 8-cylinder water-cooled petrol engine developing 250 hp (186 kW)
Performance: maximum road speed 60 km/h (37 mph); maximum range 300 km (186 miles); gradient 60 per cent; vertical obstacle 0.65 m (2 ft 2 in); trench 1.70 m (5 ft 7 in)

Below: Pursuing a line of development from the original DCA turret through the Saudi AMX-30 SA and the Dragon, Thomson-CSF have developed the Sabre. The twin 30-mm system has been mounted for trials purposes onto a Steyr APC, but has also been tested on the Chieftain MBT and the Marder.

Above: As a private venture, the DCA turret was mounted onto an AMX-30 MBT chassis, but found no buyers. A version with an improved turret was *sold to Saudi Arabia, and by 1984 the last of 53 examples ordered had been delivered.*

Dragon twin 30-mm self-propelled AA gun

Given the ever increasing cost of defence equipment, there has been an increasing trend since the 1960s, especially in Europe, for the co-operative development of weapon systems. For example, the 155-mm (6.1-in) FH-70 howitzer has been developed by West Germany, Italy and the United Kingdom, with production undertaken in all three countries. Private-venture development has also taken place along similar lines as in the case of the **Dragon** twin 30-mm SPAAG. The chassis has been developed by Thyssen-Henschel while the turret and its associated fire-control system have been developed by the Electronics Systems Division of Thomson-CSF. The chassis is similar to that of the Marder MICV and TAM medium tank, and is of all-welded steel construction which provides the crew with protection from small arms fire and shell splinters. The driver is seated at the front left with the engine to his right, the turret is in the centre and the reserve ammunition supply is at the rear of the hull. The Dragon retains the power-operated ramp in the hull rear allowing quick access to the reserve ammunition supply. The torsion-bar suspension consists of six dual rubber-tyred road wheels, with the drive sprocket at the front, and the idler at the rear; there are three track-return rollers. The upper part of the track is covered by a rubber skirt that helps to keep the dust down. Like the TAM tank, the Dragon can be fitted with additional fuel tanks at the rear of the hull to increase operating range from 600 km (373 miles) to 1000 km (621 miles).

The all-welded steel turret is in the centre of the hull, with the commander seated on the left and the gunner on the right. Mounted at the rear of the turret is the Oeil Vert (green eye) radar that carries out both tracking and surveillance functions; when not re-

quired the radar can be retracted into the turret bustle. Both the commander and gunner are provided with a sight for engaging ground targets, as well as periscopes for observation purposes.

The turret has full powered traverse through 360° at a speed of 35° per second, and the twin 30-mm cannon can be elevated from −8° to +85° at a speed of 30° per second. Turret traverse and weapon elevation are hydraulic, with manual controls for emergency use. The gunner can select bursts of one to five rounds, or a burst of 15 rounds. The weapons have a maximum effective range of 3000 m (3,280 yards), and can also be used against ground targets. In the latter role SAPHEI (semi-armour-piercing

high explosive incendiary) ammunition would be used to penetrate the thin armour of APCs before exploding inside the vehicle.

Dragon was one of a number of variation on the TAM/Marder chassis which were developed by Thyssen-Henschel in the 1980s, none of which ever got into production. Technically speaking, Dragon was a perfectly sound equipment, but the armies which believed in SPAA guns already had what they required, and the others didn't want to know.

Specification
Dragon
Crew: 3

Mounted on a Marder-type chassis, the new Dragon system is equipped with the Oeil Vert (green eye) radar used on the Saudi AMX-30.

Weight: 31000 kg (68,342 lb)
Dimensions: length 6.775 m (22 ft 3 in); width 3.12 m (10 ft 3 in); height (radar up) 4.195 m (13 ft 11 in)
Powerplant: one MTU 6-cylinder supercharged diesel developing 720 hp (536 kW)
Performance: maximum road speed 72 km/h (45 km/h); maximum range 600 km (373 miles); gradient 65 per cent; vertical obstacle 1.00 m (3 ft 3 in); trench 2.50 m (8 ft 2 in)

Gepard twin 35-mm self-propelled AA gun

When the West German army was formed in the 1950s it was supplied with some 500 M42 twin 40-mm self-propelled anti-aircraft gun systems by the United States. The M42 had quite a good range but lacked any kind of onboard fire-control system. From the late 1960s various projects were initiated for the development of a new SPAAG, but these all came to nothing. In 1966 contracts were issued for the development on a SPAAG based on the chassis of the Leopard 1 MBT which had recently entered production for the West Germany army, and after the completion of systems with twin 30-mm and twin 35-mm cannon the latter was selected for full-scale development. The prime contractor for the twin 35-mm system was Contraves of Switzerland and after the construction of additional prototypes this system was selected for service with the West German army as the **Flakpanzer Gepard**. The first production vehicle was completed in 1976 and

The Flakpanzer Gepard consists of a twin 35-mm Contraves turret mounted on a modified West German Leopard I MBT chassis.

final deliveries were made in 1970. Some 420 Gepards were built for the West German army, 55 for the Belgian army and 95 for the Dutch army. The last differed from the Belgian and West German vehicles in that the turret was fitted with a Dutch Hollandse Signaalapparaten surveillance and tracking radar with moving-target indication and other minor differences. The turret can also be installed on other chassis such as the Swiss Pz 68 MBT and Italian OTO Melara OF-40, and more recently Saudi Arabia has expressed an interest in acquiring up to 100 of a modernized version of this turret fitted to the chassis of the Leopard 2 MBT.

The chassis of the Gepard is similar to that of the Leopard 1 but with thinner armour protection for the hull. The driver is at the front of the hull on the right, with the auxiliary power unit to his left; the turret is in the centre; and the engine and transmission are at the rear. Suspension is of the torsion-bar type, and consists of seven dual rubber-tyred road wheels, with the idler at front and the drive sprocket at the rear; there are two track-return rollers. The search radar is mounted at the turret rear and can be folded down if required, while the tracking radar is on the front of the turret. Mounted externally on each side of the turret is a 35-mm Oerlikon KDA cannon with a cyclic rate of fire of 550 rounds per minute. This weapon is provided with 310 rounds of ready-use anti-aircraft ammunition and 20 rounds of APDS-T (armour piercing discarding sabot-tracer) for the engagement of ground

targets. In addition to the APDS-T ammunition, HEI (high explosive incendiary), HEI-T (high explosive incendiary-tracer), practice and SAPHEI-T (semi-armour-piercing high explosive incendiary tracer) ammunition is available. In addition to the tracking and surveillance radars the Gepard has a comprehensive fire-control system, onboard land navigation system, sights for engaging both aerial and ground targets, and an NBC system. Some of the West German Gepards have been fitted with a Siemens laser rangefinder.

Specification
Gepard
Crew: 3
Weight: 47300 kg (104,278 lb)
Dimensions: length (guns forward) 7.73 m (25 ft 4 in); length (hull) 6.85 m (22 ft 6 in); width 3.37 m (11 ft 1 in); height (radar elevated) 4.03 m (13 ft 3 in); height (periscopes) 3.01 m (9 ft 11 in)
Powerplant: one MTU MB 838 Ca M500 V-10 diesel developing 830 hp

Gepard is equipped with both tracking and surveillance radars, and onboard equipment includes computerized fire control and navigation equipment and an NBC system.

(619 kW)
Performance: maximum road speed 65 km/h (40 mph); maximum road range 550 km (342 miles); gradient 60 per cent; vertical obstacle 1.15 m (3 ft 9 in); trench 3.00 m (9 ft 10 in)

Wildcat twin 35-mm self-propelled AA gun

Krauss-Maffei of Munich built all of the Gepard twin 35-mm self-propelled anti-aircraft guns on a modified Leopard 1 chassis delivered to the Belgian, West German and Dutch armies. The company realized, however, that although this was a highly effective system for European armies it was too heavy, complicated and expensive for many countries overseas. With this in mind a decision was made to develop a complete family of self-propelled anti-aircraft gun systems that would be able to meet the requirements of almost every customer. Given Krauss-Maffei's experience with the Transportpanzer 1 (6×6) cross-country vehicle, already in production for the West German army, a decision was taken to use automotive components of this vehicle in a new hull which could be fitted with a turret armed with twin 30-mm cannon. Five different fire-control options are available, these ranging from the **V1** clear-weather system with optical tracking to the **V3** with radar target-detection and automatic target-tracking, up to the **V5** with an all-weather fire-control system and automatic target-tracking. As of early 1984 only one prototype had been built (to the **V3** configuration), although a decision had been taken to build another prototype to the **V4** configuration, and this is expected to be ready for trials in 1985.

The basic layout of the **Wildcat**, as the system is designated, is the same in all versions, with the driver and radio operator/gunner in the front, turret in the centre, and engine and transmission at the rear. The suspension consists of axles with coil springs and hydraulic shock absorbers to provide good cross-country ride. Steering is power-assisted on the front four wheels, and run-flat tyres can be fitted.

The turret is fitted with two externally-mounted 30-mm Mauser Mk 30-F cannon (one on each side), each with 250 rounds of ready-use ammunition. This cannon has a cyclic rate of fire of 800 rounds per minute and can fire three types of ammunition, namely APDS (armour-piercing discarding sabot), HEI (high explosive incendiary) and TP (target practice).

A typical target engagement could take place as follows. The radar operator/gunner monitors his radar scope on a constant basis, and once an aircraft has been spotted by the radar and appeared on his scope, the operator must then determine whether or not it is hostile. If the target is confirmed by IFF as hostile the periscope traverses onto the target's bearing and then searches for the target in elevation. The laser rangefinder then starts to feed information to the computer, whereupon the turret and guns are trained on the target, the cannon opening fire as soon as the target is in range. Krauss-Maffei, discovered the

Wildcat is based on a 6 × 6 cross-country chassis mounting a turret with twin Mauser 30-mm cannon. Modular design gives five alternative fire control systems, ranging from clear weather to all-weather automatic.

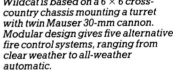

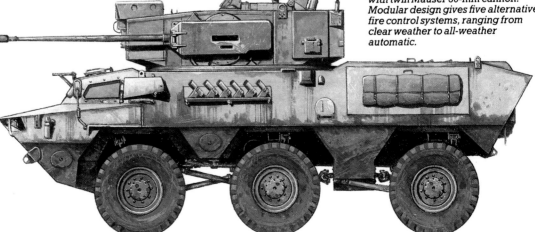

same problem that had defeated the Dragon SPAA gun. Although their intention was to make a practical weapon available at a reasonable price, those armies which believed in SPAA guns had already purchased what they wanted, whilst those who did not believe in them were not likely to be convinced on price alone. Even a proposal to use missiles instead of guns met with no success and the project was abandoned

Specification
Wildcat
Crew: 3
Weight: 18500 kg (40,785 lb)
Dimensions: length 6.88 m (22 ft 7 in); width 2.98 m (9 ft 9 in); height (radar down) 2.74 m (9 ft 0 in)
Powerplant: one Mercedes-Benz turbocharged 8-cylinder diesel developing 320 hp (239 kW)
Performance: maximum road speed 80 km/h (50 mph); maximum range 600 km (373 km); gradient 60 per cent

Wildcat is designed as an alternative to the capable but extremely costly systems such as Gepard and Sgt York, and is available with a range of capabilities. The automotive components are derived from the Transportpanzer.

SWITZERLAND

GDF-CO3 twin 35-mm self-propelled AA gun

For many years the Swiss-based company Oerlikon-Bührle, with subsidiaries in Italy and the United Kingdom, has produced the world's largest range of towed anti-aircraft guns including the highly successful GDF series of 35-mm weapons, of which more than 1,500 have been manufactured. It also designed the armament and weapons used in the West German Gepard twin 35-mm anti-aircraft gun system. The company also realized that there was a requirement for a highly mobile twin 35-mm system to defend rear-area targets such as airports, command centres and factories, and that such a system would not need to be based on an MBT chassis as was the Gepard. The result has been the GDF series of twin 35-mm anti-aircraft gun systems, which was announced several years ago. Two chassis are offered, one tracked and the other wheeled. The tracked chassis is a longer (by an additional road wheel on each side) version for the well known M548 tracked cargo carrier, itself a member of the M113 series of tracked armoured vehicle of which over 70,000 have been produced to date by the FMC Corporation of San Jose, California, for the home and export markets. The wheeled system is based on the chassis of the HYKA cross-country vehicle and offers a higher road speed and greater operational range than the tracked version, although it is some 3.5 tonnes heavier. In both cases two fire-control systems are offered, the **GDF-CO2** (tracked) and the **GDF-DO2** (wheeled) systems having a day/night fire-control system developed by Contraves and including a laser rangefinder; and the **GDF-CO3** (tracked) and **GDF-DO3** (wheeled) systems being similar apart from the addition of a Contraves (Italy) search radar that has a maximum range of some 23 km (14 miles). For most applications a customer would probably order one vehicle fitted with the radar to every three without the radar, the former then supplying target information to the others.

All versions are fitted with a power-operated turret armed with twin 35-mm KDF cannon and 430 rounds of ready-use ammunition. Each cannon

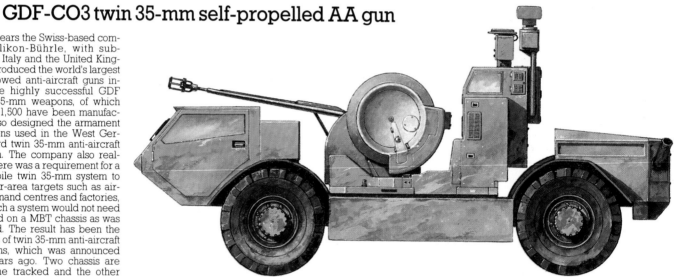

Above: Developed for the task of defending rear area targets such as airports, factories, ports and command centres, the GDF-DO3 has twin 35-mm KDF cannon mounted on the HYKA cross-country truck chassis, and is equipped with laser rangefinder and a Contraves (Italy) search radar.

Right: The GDF-CO2 has the same armament and fire control system as the wheeled version, but has no search radar. The vehicle is based on a derivative of the American M113.

has a cyclic rate of fire of 600 rounds per minute. Effective range of the 35-mm cannon is about 3500 m (3,830 yards), and type of ammunition that can be fired include HEI (high explosive incendiary), HEI-T (high explosive incendiary-tracer), SAPHEI-T (semi-armour-piercing high explosive incendiary-tracer), APDS-T (armour-piercing discarding sabot-tracer) and practice. The APDS-T round is used against ground targets such as light tanks and armoured personnel carriers, and will penetrate 40 mm (1.6 in) of armour at an angle of 60° at a range of 1000 m (1094 yards).

Although widely exhibited, the sys-

tem failed to arouse much interest and Oerlikon concentrated on ADATS (described elsewhere) as being more modern and versatile system.

Specification
GDF-CO3
Crew: 3
Weight: 18000 kg (39,683 lb)
Dimensions: length 6.70 m (22 ft 0 in);

width 2.813 m (9 ft 3 in); height 4.00 m (13 ft 2 in)
Powerplant: one GMC 6V-53T 6-cylinder diesel developing 215 hp (160 kW)
Performance: maximum road speed 45 km/h (28 mph); maximum road range 480 km (297 miles); gradient 60 per cent; vertical obstacle 0.609 m (2 ft 0 in); trench 1.80 m (5 ft 11 in)

M53/59 twin 30-mm self-propelled AA gun

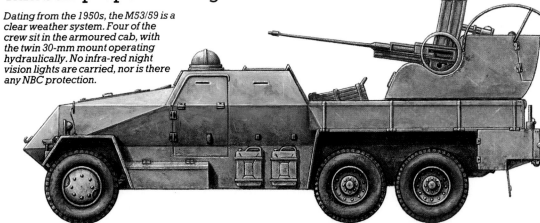

Dating from the 1950s, the M53/59 is a clear weather system. Four of the crew sit in the armoured cab, with the twin 30-mm mount operating hydraulically. No infra-red night vision lights are carried, nor is there any NBC protection.

It is widely believed that the Soviet Union forces its Warsaw Pact countries either to purchase Soviet equipment or manufacture it under licence. In fact some of the Warsaw Pact countries have their own flourishing defence industries, one such being Czechoslovakia, which has recently developed a 152-mm (6-in) self-propelled gun on an 8×8 Tatra truck chassis. In the 1950s Czechoslovakia developed and placed in production the **M53/59** twin 30-mm self-propelled anti-aircraft gun system, and this is known to be in service with Libya and Yugoslavia in addition to the Czech army itself. In some Czech units, however, the M53/59 has already been replaced by the ZSU-23-4 SPAAG which is a much more effective system.

The M53/59 was used by the Czech army in place of the Soviet ZSU-57-2 SPAAG, and consists essentially of the Praga V3S (6×6) 3-tonne truck chassis fitted with an armoured cab and a twin M53 30-mm anti-aircraft gun system at the rear.

The engine is at the front of the vehicle and provided with full armour protection from shell splinters and small arms fire. The cab is to the immediate rear of the engine, with the driver seated on the left and the commander on the right; the latter has a hemispherical Plexiglas cupola in the cab roof for all-round observation. Both crew members are provided with side door and vision slits while to their immediate front is a windscreen covered by an armoured shutter in combat. To the rear of the commander and driver are the two ammunition members, who sit facing the rear.

The twin 30-mm mount has hydraulic power traverse through 360°; the weapons elevate from −10° to +85°. Cyclic rate of fire is 450 to 500 rounds

per gun per minute, while the practical rate of fire (conditioned by ammunition resupply) is 150 rounds per minute per gun. The basic towed 30-mm M53 is fed with clips of 10 rounds whereas the M53/59 has a 50-round vertical magazine for each gas-operated cannon. It is estimated that between 600 and 800 rounds of 30-mm ammunition of two types (API and HEI) are carried. The API (armour-piercing incendiary) projectile will penetrate 55 mm (2.16 in) of armour at a range of 500 m (546 yards) and is used mainly against vehicles, while the HEI (high explosive incendiary) round is used against aerial targets. Both have a muzzle velocity of 1000 m (3,280 ft) per second. Effective anti-aircraft range of the system is estimated to be 3000 m (3,280 yards) and maximum vertical range is 6300 m (20,670 ft).

Apart from its obvious drawback of being a clear-weather anti-aircraft system, the M53/59 also lacks cross-country mobility when operating with

full-tracked vehicles such as tanks and armoured personnel carriers, and has neither NBC protection nor infra-red night-vision lights. An unusual feature of the M53/59 is that the complete mount can be removed from the chassis and placed on the ground.

Specification
M53/59
Crew: 6
Weight: 10300 kg (22,707 lb)
Dimensions: length 6.92 m (22 ft 8 in); width 2.35 m (7 ft 9 in); height (without magazines) 2.585 m (8 ft 6 in)

The age of the M53/59 is displayed by the lack of protection for the gunners, and its lack of cross-country mobility would hamper operations with tracked vehicles.

Powerplant: one Tatra T 912-2 6-cylinder diesel developing 110 hp (82 kW)
Performance: maximum road speed 60 km/h (37 mph); maximum range 500 km (311 miles); gradient 60 per cent; vertical obstacle 0.46 m (1 ft 6 in); trench 0.69 m (2 ft 3 in)

OTOMATIC 76-mm self-propelled AA gun

The **OTOMATIC 76-mm 76/62** self-propelled anti-aircraft/anti-helicopter system has been developed by OTO Melara of La Spezia as a private venture specifically for the export market. It consists basically of a modified OF-40 MBT chassis fitted with a new all-welded turret armed with a 76-mm (3-in) automatic gun that is a direct development of the same calibre naval weapon of the same calibre and used by many navies around the world and also manufactured in Japan, Spain and the USA. The unique feature of the OTOMATIC compared with the many other systems on the market today is that it is designed specifically to engage and destroy attack helicopters before they themselves can release their missiles at the tank. Most self-propelled anti-aircraft/helicopter systems are in the 30-mm to 40-mm cannon bracket and have a maximum effective range of between 3000 and 4000 m (3,280 and 4,375 yards), and can therefore just about engage attack helicopters before they launch their deadly missiles. New generations of air-launched missiles are now under advanced development or even entering service (an example is the American Hellfire) which have an even longer range as well as a fire-and-forget capability. Once these are in service in significant numbers the attack helicopter will be able to stand off and attack tank formations

without any danger of being destroyed by smaller-calibre self-propelled anti-aircraft gun systems.

The 76-mm (3-in) gun of the OTOMATIC is mounted in a turret with powered traverse, and the weapon has maximum elevation of +60° and a depression of −5°. Some 100 rounds of fixed ammunition are carried, of which 70 rounds are in the turret and the remaining 30 in the chassis; 25 of these rounds are in the automatic loading system for immediate use. For the engagement of aerial targets the weapon would fire high explosive or preformed fragmentation projectiles with either a point detonating or proximity fuse, while for the engagement of ground targets an APFSDS (armour-piercing discarding sabot) projectile is fired. According to the company, targets can be destroyed at a maximum range of at least 6000 m (6,560 yards), a six-round burst being considered sufficient for most targets. A comprehensive fire-control system is installed, and includes a search radar mounted on the rear of the turret and a tracking radar on the turret roof, both of which can be retracted if required. Mounted on each side of the turret is a bank of three electrically-operated smoke dischargers, while a 7.62-mm (0.3in) machine-gun can be mounted on the turret roof for local protection. Two prototypes were built, the sec-

ond on a Leopard 1 chassis, and were extensively tested by the Italian Army in the early 1990s. It is believed that the equipment will eventually be adopted by the Italians when finance is available.

A private venture by OTO-Melara, the OTOMATIC 76-mm self-propelled gun is designed to counter the threat of new-generation armoured helicopters with longer-ranged guided weapons.

Specification
OTOMATIC
Crew: 4
Weight: 46000 kg (101,411 lb)
Dimensions: length (gun forward) 9.635 m (31 ft 7 in); length (hull) 7.265 m (23 ft 10 in); width 3.35 m (11 ft 0 in); height (turret top) 3.152 m (10 ft 4 in)

Powerplant: one four-stroke supercharged diesel developing 1000 hp (746 kW)
Performance: maximum road speed 60 km/h (37 mph); maximum range (road) 500 km (311 miles); gradient 60 per cent; vertical obstacle 1.15 m (3 ft 9 in); trench 3.00 m (9 ft 10 in)

Modern Towed Artillery

Towed gun and howitzers still have a vital place in any army; the more so in the case of forces that are less likely to be confronted with a modern armoured force or threatened with nuclear weapons.

Towed artillery tended to be downgraded some years ago in favour of self-propelled (SP) guns and howitzers. This trend was most evident in the major Western armies which faced the threat of massed Soviet forces, and which therefore needed mobile, protected and self-sufficient artillery. But armies which were more likely to be facing insurgency or 'brush-fire wars' found that towed artillery was quite sufficient for their needs, and cheaper as well.

The technical improvements which we have seen applied to self-propelled weapons have also been made available to towed guns, giving them the same increase in range and effectiveness. The adoption of auxiliary propulsion – a small engine to provide sufficient power to the main gun wheels to allow the weapon to hide or find a fresh position without waiting for its tractor – has allowed a certain amount of dispersion to take place and has improved the gun's chances of survival.

The autonomy discussed under SP guns – the ability for guns to disperse across the countryside but concentrate their fire on to a specific target on demand – has been applied more slowly to towed guns. Various technical

Caesar is a French 155-mm howitzer mounted on a 6 x 6 truck to give an intermediary between towed and self-propelled artillery.

difficulties have been overcome – notably the provision of power for computing and position-finding – and it is now possible to disperse a troop of guns widely and still direct all their fire on to a single target.

The priority over the past decade has been the reduction in weight of the common 155-mm howitzer to provide air-

portability. Hitherto this capability had been restricted to the 105-mm group of weapons. Spurred on by specifications laid down by the US Army and Marine Corps, various manufacturers have put forward designs and tested them, and the most recent information indicates that a new weapon from Vickers is likely to be selected.

An interesting development, which is half-way between self-propelled and towed, is Caesar, developed for the French Army. This is simply a 155-mm howitzer mounted on the back of a 6 x 6 truck and provided with suitable stabilizing jacks. It may not be quite so good across country as a tracked SP, but its mobility is as good as any towed equipment.

CITEFA Model 77 155-mm howitzer

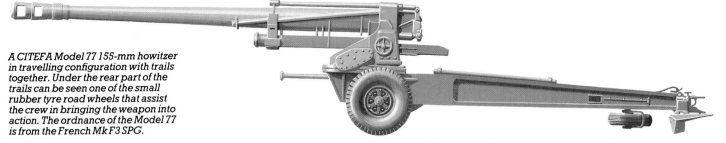

A CITEFA Model 77 155-mm howitzer in travelling configuration with trails together. Under the rear part of the trails can be seen one of the small rubber tyre road wheels that assist the crew in bringing the weapon into action. The ordnance of the Model 77 is from the French Mk F3 SPG.

Some years ago Argentina purchased a number of members of the AMX-13 family of light tracked vehicles from France as well as undertaking the assembly of a quantity of vehicles. These included the AMX-13 light tank with a 90-mm (3.54-in) gun, the AMX VCI armoured personnel carrier, and the 155-mm (6.1-in) Mk F3 self-propelled gun. At that time the standard 155-mm (6.1-in) towed howitzer of the Argentine army was the American M114, which dated back to World War II and had a maximum range of 14600 m (15,965 yards). To replace the M114 the Instituto de Investigaciones Cientificas y Tecnicas de las Fuerzas Armadas (CITEFA) designed a new bottom carriage that would take the complete top carriage (barrel, cradle, recoil system and equilibrators) of the Mk F3 self-propelled gun. After trials this was accepted for service with the Argentine army under the designation **155-mm Howitzer L33 X1415 CITEFA Model 77**, L33 referring to the length of the ordnance in calibres and Model 77 to the year of acceptance. A later model, the **Model 81**, differs in minor details and also has a barrel of Argentine rather than French manufacture. Together with the OTO Melara 105-mm (4.13-in) Model 56 pack howitzer the Model 77 was deployed to the Falklands, and all of these equipments were subsequently captured by the British, some of them being shipped to the UK for trial and display purposes.

The barrel of the Model 77 is 5.115 m (16 ft 9.4 in) long, and is provided with a double-baffle muzzle brake and a screw breech mechanism. The top carriage is of welded steel construction and contains the traverse mechanism and elevating brackets. The former is mounted inside the lower part

and forming the connection with the cradle trunnion attachment and the bottom carriage. The bottom carriage is of the split-trail type, and is also of welded construction. Each trail leg is provided with a small rubber-tyred road wheel to assist in bringing the weapon into and out of action, and at the end of each trail is a spade. When the equipment is in the firing position the carriage wheels are raised clear of the ground, support then being provided by a circular steel base attached to the carriage by a ball socket; the latter feature helps to compensate for rough ground. When the equipment is being towed, the support is raised, giving ground clearance of 0.3 m (12 in). Maximum rate of fire is four rounds per minute, and sustained rate one round per minute. The equipment fires an HE projectile weighing 43 kg (94.8 lb) with a maximum muzzle velocity of 765 m (2,510 ft) per second to a maximum range of 22000 m (24,060 yards); there are also illuminating and smoke projectiles. A rocket-assisted projectile has been developed for this weapon; full details have not been released, but the maximum range is 25,300m (27,670 yds).

Specification
Model 77 howitzer
Calibre: 155 mm (6.1 in)
Weight: travelling 8000 kg (17,637 lb)
Dimensions: length, travelling 10.15 m (33 ft 3.6 in); width, travelling 2.67 m (8 ft 9 in); height, travelling 2.20 m (7 ft 2.6 in)
Elevation: +67°/−0°
Traverse: total 70°
Maximum range: with normal ammunition 22000 m (24,060 yards) and with rocket-assisted projectile 23300 m (25,480 yards)

A CITEFA Model 77 155-mm howitzer in the firing position with ordnance at maximum elevation. Each trail is fitted with its spade, but as the weapon has yet to be fired they are not bedded in. The Model 77 was used against the British forces during the 1982 Falklands campaign.

GHN-45 155-mm gun/howitzer

In the 1970s PRB of Belgium, a well-known manufacturer of ammunition, and Space Research Corporation of Canada jointly established a company called SRC International with its headquarters in Brussels. This company developed a gun howitzer called the **GC 45**, of which 12 were subsequently ordered by the Royal Thai Marines, as well as a conversion kit for the standard 155-mm (6.1-in) M114 howitzer. The first two weapons were built in Canada while the remaining 10 were built in Canada but assembled in Austria by Voest-Alpine. Further de-

A Voest-Alpine GHN-45 155-mm gun/howitzer in the travelling position with ordnance locked over trails. This Austrian-produced weapon is in service with the Jordanian army, and some may have found their way to Iraq and seen recent use.

velopment by Voest-Alpine resulted in the **GHN-45** 155-mm (6.1-in) gun/howitzer, of which 200 were ordered by Jordan. Production of these weapons started in 1981, the first weapons being delivered during the following year. Unconfirmed reports have indicated that some of these weapons have already been transferred from Jordan to Iraq and used against Iran. The original weapons supplied to Thailand have been used in action on the Thai border against Kampuchea.

The basic version of the GHN-45 is normally towed by a standard 10-tonne (6×6) truck if required. More recently a model fitted with an auxiliary power unit on the front of the carriage has been developed. This enables the weapon to propel itself on roads at a maximum speed of 35 km/h (22 mph),

and the 80-litre (17.6-Imp gal) fuel tank provides a range of 150 km (93 miles). In normal practice the system is moved from one firing position to another by a truck with the ordnance traversed over the trails and locked in position to reduce its overall length, the APU then being used for final positioning and for bringing the weapon into and out of action more quickly.

The GHN-45 has a standard 45-calibre barrel fitted with a triple-baffle muzzle brake, and can fire a standard US M107 high explosive projectile to a maximum range of 17800 m (19,465 yards) or an M101 projectile to a maximum range of 24000 m (26,245 yards). With the Extended-Range Full Bore (ERFB) projectile manufactured by PRB, a range of 30000 m (32,810 yards) can be achieved, while the ERFB pro-

jectile with base bleed goes out to 39000 m (42,650 yards). With such long ranges, however, target-acquisition and projectile dispersion are major problems.

The ERFB projectile, developed from the earlier extended-range subbore and extended-range sub-calibre projectiles, is longer and more streamlined than a conventional projectile, and therefore has reduced aerodynamic drag and thus increased range. The ERFB base bleed is the basic projectile with a different boat tail containing the base bleed unit, which reduces drag at the rear of the projectile, which thus decelerates more slowly, so increasing range. The basic HE ERFB projectile weighs 45.54 kg (100.4 lb), of which 8.62 kg (19 lb) is the Composition B explosive. Other projectiles in-

clude smoke, illuminating, smoke base-ejection and a cargo round which carries 13 kg (28.7 lb) of M42 grenades, which would be highly effective against vehicles and personnel.

Specification
GHN-45 gun/howitzer
Calibre: 155 mm (6.1 in)
Weight: 8900 kg (19,621 lb)
Dimensions: length, travelling 9.068 m (29 ft 9 in); width, travelling 2.48 m (8 ft 1.6 in); height, travelling 2.089 m (6 ft 10.25 in)
Elevation: +72°/−5°
Traverse: total 70°
Maximum range: with ERFB ammunition 30000 m (32,810 yards) and with base-bleed ammunition 39000 m (42,650 yards)

Modèle 50 155-mm howitzer

For the last 30 years the **modèle 50** 155-mm (6.1-in) howitzer has been the standard towed howitzer of the French army, and has also been made under licence by Bofors of Sweden for the Swedish army under the designation **15.5-cm Field Howitzer Fr.** In the French army it will soon be replaced by the new 155-mm (6.1-in) TR towed gun, which has an integral auxiliary power unit and a much longer range, while in the Swedish army it is being replaced by the Bofors 155-mm (6.1-in) FH-77A. The modèle 50 howitzer, which is also called the **OB-155-50 BF** by the French army, was also exported to the Lebanon (where some were captured from the PLO during the fighting of the summer of 1982), Israel, Switzerland and Morocco.

The barrel of the modèle 50 is 4.41 (14 ft 5.6 in) long, and has an unusual multi-baffle muzzle brake, hydropneumatic recoil system that varies with elevation, and a screw breech mechanism. The carriage is of the split-trail type with two rubber-tyred road wheels located on each side of the forward part of the carriage. When being towed by a truck the ordnance is locked to the trails by a locking device which is situated in the rear part of the cradle. To enable the equipment to be towed at high speeds on roads, the modèle 50 has a brake system operated by compressed air from the towing vehicle.

When in the firing position the forward part of the carriage is supported by a circular pivot plate underneath and by the ends of each trail.

The modèle 50 is operated by an 11-man crew, and in the French army is normally towed by a Berliet GBU 15 (6+6) truck, which also carries the crew and ammunition. Ammunition is of the separate-loading type, the HE projectile weighing 43 kg (94.8 lb) and having a maximum muzzle velocity of 650 m (2,135 ft) per scond to give a range of 18000 m (19,685 yards). Illuminating and smoke projectiles can also be fired. More recently Brandt has developed a rocket-assisted HE projectile with a maximum range of 23300 m (25,480 yards). Maximum rate of fire is between three and four rounds per minute.

To meet the requirements of the Israeli army, the French Etablissement d'Etudes et Fabrications d'Armement de Bourges fitted the modèle 50 howit-

zer to a much modified Sherman chassis, and this entered service with the Israeli army in 1963 as the 155-mm (6.1-in) self-propelled howitzer **Model 50** (or **M-50**). The modifications to the chassis were extensive, and included moving the engine to the front of the vehicle on the right side with the driver being located to its left. The 155-mm (6.1-in) howitzer is mounted at the rear of the hull in an open-topped compartment, over which a tarpaulin cover can be fitted in wet weather. Stowage boxes are provided externally above the tracks. When the vehicle is in the firing position the rear of the hull folds

down and doors open on each side to reveal ammunition stowage. Loaded weight of the M-50 is 31 tonnes, and the crew consists of eight men including the driver. The Model 50 is still used by France, Sweden, Switzerland, Lebanon and Tunisia, mostly relegated to the reserve.

Specification
modèle 50 howitzer
Calibre: 155 m (6.1 in)
Weight: travelling 9000 kg (19,841 lb) and firing 8100 kg (17,857 lb)
Dimensions: length, travelling 7.80 m (25 ft 7.1 in); width, travelling 2.75 m

(9 ft 0 in); height, travelling 2.50 m (8 ft 2.4 in)
Elevation: +69°/−4°
Traverse: total 80°
Maximum range: with standard round 18000 m (19,685 yards) and with rocket-assisted projectile 23300 m (25,480 yards)

This Modèle 50 155-mm howitzer, captured by the Israeli army during the 1982 invasion of Lebanon, clearly shows the turntable in the raised position under the carriage. The weapon is still used by France, Morocco, Sweden and Switzerland.

TR 155-mm gun

While the United Kingdom, Italy and West Germany elected to develop a 155-mm (6.1-in) towed howitzer first (FH-70) and then a self-propelled model (SP-70), France decided to do the reverse. The 155-mm (6.1-in) GCT self-propelled gun on an AMX-30 MBT chassis entered production for Saudi Arabia in 1977, first production vehicles being completed during the following year, but the type was not formally adopted by the French army until 1979. Since then it has also been ordered by Iraq.

The prototype of the **TR** 155-mm (6.1-in) towed gun was shown for the first time at Satory in 1979 and following trials with eight prototypes production is expected to start in 1984. The French army has a requirement for 180 systems to replace the older towed 155-mm (6.1) modèle 50 howitzer.

The TR towed gun has a barrel 6.20 m (20 ft 4.1 in) long, a double-baffle muzzle brake, a hydropneumatic recoil system and horizontal-wedge breech mechanism. The carriage is of the split trail type, with an auxiliary power unit located on the forward part. The 39-hp (29-kW) engine drives three hydraulic pumps, one for each of the main road wheels and the third to provide power for elevation, traverse, raising the suspension, trail wheel jacks and projectile-loading mechanism. The APU enables the weapon to propel itself around the battery position or on the road at a maximum speed of 8 km/h (5 mph). When being towed or travelling under its own power, the TR has its barrel traversed 180° and locked in position over the closed trails. The projectile-loading system makes possible firing rates of three rounds in the first 18 seconds, six rounds per minute for the first two minutes, and 120 rounds per hour thereafter. On any future battlefield in Europe such a weapon would have to be redeployed in a very short time as its position would soon be determined by the enemy, resulting in counterbattery fire.

The TR can fire several types of ammunition: the older modèle 56/59 HE projectile to a range of 19250 m (21,050 yards), the more recent Cr TA 68 HE projectile weighing 43.2 kg (95.25 lb) to a range of 24000 m (26,245 yards), the 155-mm (6.1-in) illuminating projectile (providing 800000 candelas of light) to a range of 21500 m (22,515 yards), a smoke incendiary projectile to a range of 21300 m (23,295 yards), and a Brandt rocket-assisted projectile to a range of 30500 m (33,355 yards). GIAT has recently announced that it is developing three new projectiles for the TR and GCT. The first of these is the so-called cargo round, which carries six anti-tank mines dispensed over the target; each of these weighs 0.55 kg (1.2 lb) and will penetrate 50 mm (1.47 in) of armour steel. The HE base-bleed round is called the HE BB, has a maximum range of 29500 m (32,260 yards) and weighs 43.5 kg (95.9 lb) of which 10 kg (22.05 lb) is high explosive. The last is the rocket-assisted projectile, which has a range of 33000 m (36,090 yards).

The TR has an eight-man crew, and will be towed by the new TRM 10 000 (6×6) 10-tonne truck, which also carries 48 projectiles, charges and fuses.

Specification
TR gun
Calibre: 155 mm (6.1 in)
Weight: travelling and firing 10650 kg (23,479 lb)
Dimensions: length, travelling 8.25 m (27 ft 0.8 in); width, travelling 3.09 m (10 ft 1.65 in); height, firing 1.65 m (5 ft 5 in)
Elevation: +65°/−5°
Traverse: total 65°
Maximum range: with standard projectile 24000 m (26,245 yards) and with rocket-assisted projectile 33000 m (36,090 yards)

Above: One of the prototypes of the new French TR 155-mm gun in the firing position. The French army is to take delivery of 180 of these systems to replace the 155-mm Modèle 50 howitzer, which has been in service for some 30 years. Like most modern weapons of this type it is fitted with an auxiliary power unit.

Below: A TR 155-mm gun from the front, showing the auxiliary power unit on the front of the carriage. This not only provides the power required to propel the weapon around on its own, but also to bring the weapon into and out of action as well as running the projectile loading mechanism.

Soltam M-68 155-mm gun/howitzer

The only manufacturer of towed artillery in Israel is Soltam, which is believed to have close links with the Finnish company Tampella. The Soltam **M-68** 155-mm (6.1-in) gun/howitzer was developed as a private venture in the late 1960s, the first prototype being completed in 1968 and the first production models following two years later. As far as is known, the towed model is used only by Singapore and the Thai Marines, although the Soltam L-33 self-propelled gun/howitzer uses the ordnance, elevation and traverse system of the M-68. This entered service with the Israeli army in time to take part in the 1973 Middle East campaign.

The ordnance of the M-68 is 5.18 m (17 ft 0 in) long and fitted with a single-baffle muzzle brake, fume extractor and a horizontal breech mechanism. The recoil system is below the barrel and the counter recoil system above, the pneumatic equilibrators being located on side of the barrel. When travelling, the top carriage is traversed to the rear so that the ordnance is over the closed trails. The carriage is of the split-trail type. Two rubber-tyred road wheels are mounted on a bogie on each side; each wheel is fitted with a hydraulic brake, and a maximum tow-

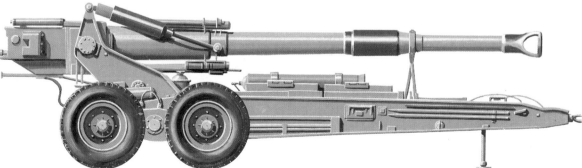

Above: The Soltam M-68 155-mm gun/howitzer in the travelling position with ordnance traversed to rear and locked in position over trails. The Israeli army uses this weapon mounted on a rebuilt Sherman tank chassis in the self-propelled role.

Right: The Soltam M-68 155-mm gun/howitzer in travelling configuration, being towed by a truck. More recently the company has developed a new long-barrelled howitzer.

155-mm Artillery Fire Control

In recent years many armies have not only introduced new types of towed and self-propelled weapons, but also complete artillery fire-control systems that make the maximum possible use of the artillery available. This is of considerable importance within NATO, whose forces are outnumbered by a factor of three to one in artillery systems. In the past, forward observers on the ground or air observation post (AOP) aircraft radioed the position of the target to the battery commander (or higher command authority), and once the target was engaged would watch the fall of shot and then correct aim. All this took time and often wasted valuable ammunition. This basic method of fire and correction is still employed, but a number of sophisticated devices are also now standard.

Today the forward observer is often mounted in a full-tracked armoured vehicle fitted with a land navigation system so that the observer can quickly determine his own position. He also has powerful binoculars, night observation equipment and a laser rangefinder; with the last he can determine the range to the target within just a few metres. The vehicle is also fitted with extensive communications equipment to relay this information to battery headquarters for immediate action. Not all forward observers are provided with armoured vehicles, however, many having jeeps in which the forward observer is provided with a hand-held laser rangefinder (the British use the Norwegian Simrad LP7) and a rapid-burst radio. With the latter the forward observer can enter all target information, which is then stored and sent in a very short burst of radio transmission, so making detection almost impossible.

In the past most NATO artillery regiments (towed and self-propelled) normally comprised three batteries each of six guns, but the trend is now to eight-gun batteries. A typical British army 105-mm (4.13-in) Light Gun battery has a headquarters battery and three EMI Cymbeline mortar-locating radars, three batteries each with six guns, and a light aid detachment (LAD). Each battery can be split into two troops each of three guns, each of the latter being towed by 1-tonne Land Rover. At battery headquarters is a Marconi Space and Defence Systems Field Artillery Computer Equipment (FACE). In the light regiments (with 105-mm/4.13-in guns) this is mounted in a long-wheelbase Land Rover, while in the self-propelled regiments a FV432 is used. FACE, which entered service in the early 1960s and is used by many other armies (including those of Australia, Canada and Egypt), can be used both in the survey and fire-calculation roles. In the latter role information such as a gun and target position, type of ammunition to be used (e.g. smoke or high explosive), muzzle velocity of each weapon, weather data (from AMETS), temperature and charge are entered; the computer then calculates the elevation and traverse of the gun to get the projectile onto the target; and this information is then passed to each gun by word of mouth, radio or the Artillery Weapons Data Transmission System (AWDATS), one of which can be positioned alongside each gun.

The British army also uses the Artillery Meteorological System (AMETS) at artillery division level. This equipment obtains information on atmospheric conditions, which is then passed down to the battery. With the increasing range of artillery weapons AMETS plays a vital role. For example, there may be little or no wind at the battery itself, but 20 km (12.4 miles) away at the target there could be a wind of 15 km/h (9.3 mph) or more, and this would obviously have an effect on the projectile.

A long-wheelbase Land Rover of the British Royal Artillery fitted with the Marconi Space and Defence System Field Artillery Computer Equipment (FACE), which is issued on the scale of one per command post.

The EMI Cymbeline radar is in service in two models, a trailer-mounted system towed by a long-wheelbase Land Rover and a self-propelled version mounted on the FV432 armoured personnel carrier. Cymbeline has a maximum range of 20 km (12.4 miles) and can determine the position of the enemy mortar in less than 30 seconds. The US Army has recently fielded the Firefinder system, a division normally having two AN/TPQ-36 mortar-locating radars and one larger AN/TPQ-37 artillery-locating radar, both developed by the Hughes Aircraft Company, Ground Systems Division. The AN/TPQ-36 is towed by a Gama Goat and can detect both artillery and mortars, whose exact position is plotted on a roller-type map display. The AN/TPQ-36 has also been ordered by a number of other countries including Jordan, Saudi Arabia, Thailand and Australia, and in 1983 was deployed to the Lebanon by the United States in an effort to pinpoint hostile mortars and artillery systems.

---

ing speed of 100 km/h (62 mph) is thus possible. When in the firing position the carriage is supported by a screw type firing jack. Four spades are carried, one of these being attached to the end of each trail for firing when the weapon is brought into action. The other two are carried to enable the eight-man crew to change direction and open fire again without taking out the original spdes.

The M-68 fires a standard NATO HE projectile weighing 43.7 kg (96.3 lb) to a maximum range of 21000 (22,965 yards), as well as smoke and illuminating projectiles. The weapon can also fire Soltam-designed projectiles with a higher muzzle velocity (820 m/2,690 ft per second compared with 725 m/2,380 ft per second) to a maximum range of 23500 m (25,700 yards).

The Soltam M-68 is no longer in volume production, although it could be placed back in production if sufficient numbers were ordered. The latest Soltam 155-mm (6.1-in) weapon is the **M-71** howitzer, which uses the same carriage, breech and recoil system as the M-68 but is fitted with a longer 39-calibre barrel. Mounted on the M-71 is a rammer powered by a compressed air cylinder on the right

trail, this enabling the weapon to be loaded at all angles of elevation and so making possible a short-period fire rate of four rounds per minute. The M-71 is known to be service with the Israeli army, and fires an HE projectile to a maximum range of 23500 m (25,700 yards). For trials purposes one M-71 has been fitted with an auxiliary power unit on the left trail and an ammunition-handling crane on the right trail, with elevation increased from 52° to 70°. The APU enables the weapon, called the **Model 839P**, to propel itself on roads at a maximum speed of 17 km/h (10.6 mph), sufficient fuel being carried for a range of at least 70 km (43.5 miles)

Specification
Soltam M-68 gun/howitzer
Calibre: 155 mm (6.1 in)
Weight: travelling 9500 kg (20,944 lb) and firing 8500 kg (18,739 lb)
Dimensions: length, travelling 7.20 m (23 ft 7.5 in); width, travelling 2.58 m (8 ft 5.6 in); height, travelling 2.00 m (6 ft 6.75 in)
Elevation: +52°/−5°
Traverse: total 90°
Maximum range: 21000 m (22,965 yards)

Israeli 155-mm M-68 gun/howitzer in the firing position with trails firmly staked to the ground. The split trail carriage is unusual in that it has a total of four rubber-tyred road wheels, each of which has a hydraulic brake operated from the towing vehicle.

OTO Melara modello 56 105-mm pack howitzer

The mountainous terrain of northern Italy is defended by five Alpine brigades, and these and the sole Italian airborne brigade required a 105-mm (4.13-in) howitzer that could be disassembled for easy transportation across the mountains and when assembled be light enough to be airdropped or carried slung underneath a helicopter. To meet this requirement the Italian armaments manufacturer OTO Melara at La Spezia designed a weapon that became known as the **modello 56** 105-mm (4.13-in) pack howitzer. This entered production in 1957, and was soon adopted by many countries all over the world. By 1984 some 2,400 weapons had been delivered, and the type has seen combat use in many areas. The British used it in the South Yemen and during the Borneo confrontation, while the Argentines used it in the Falklands campaign of 1982. By today's standards the modello 56 howitzer has a short range, and in the British Royal Artillery it has already been replaced by the Royal Ordnance Factory 105-mm (4.13-in) Light Gun, which has a maximum range of 17000 m (18590 yards) compared with only 10575 m (11,565 yards) for the modello 56, which is much lighter, however.

The modello 56 has a very short barrel with a multi-baffle muzzle brake, a hydraulic buffer and helical recuperator, and a vertical sliding wedge breech block. The carriage is of the split-trail type and fitted with rubber tyres for high-speed towing. An unusual feature of the modello 56 is that its wheels can be fitted in two different positions: in the normal field position the wheels are overslung, the weapon then having an elevation of +65° and a depression of −5°, and a total traverse of 36° (18° left and right); but for the anti-tank role the wheels are underslung and the weapon has an elevation of +25° and a depression of −5°, total traverse remaining 36°. The main advantage of having the wheels underslung is that the height is reduced from 1.93 m to 1.55 m (6 ft 4 in to 5 ft 1 in), so making the weapon much easier to conceal, a valuable asset in the anti-tank role.

The modello 56 can be dismantled into 11 sections for transport across rough country, and in peacetime the shield is often removed to save weight. The weapon is manned by a seven-man crew, and can be towed by a long-wheelbase Land Rover or similar vehicle. It can also be carried slung under a Bell UH-1 or Westland Wessex helicopter.

Another advantage of the modello 56 is that it fires the same ammunition as the American M101 or M102 105-mm (4.13-in) towed guns, and this ammunition is manufactured all over the world. Types of ammunition fired include an HE projectile weighing 21.06 kg (46.4 lb) with a maximum muzzle velocity of 472 m (1,550 ft) per second, as well as smoke, illuminating and HEAT (High Explosive Anti-Tank). The last weighs 16.7 kg (36.8 lb) and will penetrate 102 mm (4 in) of armour.

A Royal Artillery unit attached to the Royal Marine Commandos carry 105-mm pack howitzers in Norway. The normal towing vehicle is the Swedish BV 202, which was successfully used in the Falklands towing the more modern 105-mm Light Gun.

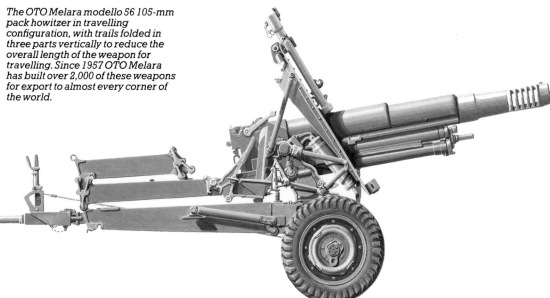

The OTO Melara modello 56 105-mm pack howitzer in travelling configuration, with trails folded in three parts vertically to reduce the overall length of the weapon for travelling. Since 1957 OTO Melara has built over 2,000 of these weapons for export to almost every corner of the world.

Specification
OTO Melara modello 56 howitzer
Calibre: 105 mm (4.13 in)
Weight: travelling 1290 kg (2,844 lb)
Dimensions: length, travelling 3.65 m (11 ft 11.7 in); width, travelling 1.50 m (4 ft 11 in); height, travelling 1.93 m (6 ft 4 in)
Elevation: +65°/−5°
Traverse: total 36°
Maximum range: 10575 m (11,565 yards)

Right: OTO Melara modello 56 105-mm pack howitzer of the Canadian Armed Forces, with its shield removed to reduce its weight. This photograph clearly shows the axle arrangement that allows the overall height to be dramatically reduced when being used in the anti-tank role.

155-mm Field Howitzer 70 (FH-70)

155-mm FH-70 in the firing position with ordnance horizontal. This weapon is now in service with West Germany, Italy, the UK and Saudi Arabia. The ordnance of FH-70 is also being used, suitably modified, for the SP-70 self-propelled howitzer, now undergoing user trials.

In 1968 a Memorandum of Understanding (MoU) was signed between the UK and West Germany for the joint development of a 155-mm (6.1-in) howitzer which would replace the 140-mm (5.5-in) gun for the former and the 155-mm (6.1-in) M114 howitzer for the latter. The main requirements of this weapon included a high rate of fire with a burst fire capability, increased range and lethality together with a new family of ammunition, high mobility and a minimum of effort for deployment. The UK was team leader for this weapon, which became known as the **FH-70**, while West Germany became team leader for the self-propelled equivalent, SP-70, which has still to enter service. Nineteen prototypes of the FH-70 were built, and in 1970 Italy joined the project as a full partner. In 1976 the FH-70 was accepted for service, the first production weapons being completed in 1978. Three production lines were established, one in the UK (Vickers Shipbuilding and Engineering Limited), one in West Germany (Rheinmetall) and one in Italy (OTO Melara). The UK ordered 71 equipments, West Germany 216 and Italy 164. The weapon has recently entered service with Saudi Arabia, and will be made under licence in Japan.

The barrel of the FH-70 is 6.022 m (19 ft 9 in) long, and has a double-baffle muzzle brake and a semi-automatic wedge-type breech mechanism. The carriage of the FH-70 is of the split-trail type, with an auxiliary power unit mounted on the forward part. This enables the FH-70 to propel itself on roads and across country at a maximum speed of 16 km/h (10 mph). In addition the APU provides power for steering, and for raising and lowering the main and trail wheels. When travelling, the ordnance is traversed to the rear and locked in position over the closed trails. To achieve the requirement for a burst-fire capability a semi-automatic loading system is fitted, and this operates at all angles of elevation. The loading system includes a loading tray that presents the projectile to the chamber. A burst rate of three rounds in 13 seconds can be achieved, while the normal rate of fire is six rounds per minute.

The FH-70 fires three main types of ammunition: HE with a weight of 43.5 kg (95.9 lb) smoke (base ejection), and illuminating. The last provides one million candelas for one minute. The FH-70 can also fire the Martin Marietta Cannon-Launched Guided Projectile (CLGP), although this has yet to be adopted by any European member of NATO, and the US M549A1 rocket-assisted projectile, which has a range of 30000 m (32,810 yards).

The FH-70 has an eight-man crew, and each country having a different towing vehicle: West Germany uses the MAN (6×6) 7-tonne truck, Italy the

Above: 155-mm FH-70s of the British Royal Artillery on the ranges. This weapon fires a high explosive projectile to a maximum range of 24000 m (26,245 yards), although a rocket assisted projectile can also be fired with a longer range.

Right: 155-mm FH-70 firing at high angle during trials in Sardinia some years ago. The UK is project leader for the FH-70, while West Germany is project leader for the SP-70. Each of the three producing countries do use different towing vehicles.

FIAT 66066 TM (6×6) truck, and the UK the Foden Medium Mobility Vehicle (6×6), which shares many common automotive components with the Low Mobility range of vehicles used in large numbers by the British army.

Specification
FH-70 field howitzer
Calibre: 155 mm (6.1 in)
Weight: travelling and firing 9300 kg (20,503 lb)
Dimensions: length, travelling 9.80 m (32 ft 1.8 in); width, travelling 2.204 m (7 ft 2.75 in); height, travelling 2.56 m (8 ft 4.8 in)
Elevation: +70°/−5°
Traverse: total 56°
Maximum range: with standard round 24000 m (26,245 yards) and with rocket-assisted projectile 30000 m (32,810 yards)

155-mm Ammunition

It is not always realized that today, as in the past, a gun or howitzer is normally designed and developed around the ammunition that it is to fire. An army issues a requirement for a weapon to fire a projectile of a specified weight to a determined range, an overall acceptable weight being placed on the complete weapon. The latter feature has become more important in recent years, as most medium-calibre weapons such as the US 155-mm (6.1-in) M198 have to be capable of being carried slung under helicopters or readily transported by air. During World War II medium-calibre weapons such as the US 155-mm (6.1-in) M114 towed howitzer fired only a small selection of ammunition including high explosives, smoke and chemical (with various fillings such as white phosphorus, mustard gas and titanium tetrachloride). Since then much development work has been carried out on ammunition, and the 155-mm (6.1-in) M198 of today can fire a wide range of ammunition to defeat a variety of battlefield targets, including armoured vehicles. Listed below are the types of ammunition fired by the M198.

RAAM (Remote Anti-Armor Mine System)
This has only recently entered service with the US Army, and is a projectile that carries nine anti-tank mines, each weighing 2.27 kg (5 lb) and ejected from the projectile as it passes over the target area. The **M741** projectile carries nine anti-tank mines which will self-destruct if they are not set off by a vehicle in 24 hours, while the **M718** projectile carries a similar number of mines with a longer period before they self-detruct.

HE (M107)
The high explosive M107 projectile weighs 42.91 kg (94.6 lb) and contains 6.62 kg (14.6 lb) of TNT or 6.98 kg (15.4 lb) of Composition B.

HE (M449)
This projectile weighs 43.09 kg (95 lb) and contains 60 M43 anti-personnel grenades dispensed over the target. This projectile is also effective against soft-skinned vehicles and troops in the open.

HE (M483)
This projectile weighs 46.53 kg (102.6 lb) and contains 88 (64 M42 and 24 M46) dual-purpose grenades for use against personnel and vehicles, the roof of the latter being one of their most vulnerable points.

ADAM (Area-Denial Artillery Munition)
This is in service only with the US Army and carries 36 anti-personnel mines. The **M692** projectile carries 36 mines that will self-destruct over a longer period than those of the M731 projectile, whose 36 mines self-destruct after a period of 24 hours if not activated.

Nuclear
The M198 can fire a nuclear projectile, the **M795** being used as a spotting round.

A 155-mm shell leaves the barrel of a US Army Sheridan light tank.

HERA (M549)
The High Explosive Rocket Assisted projectile weighs 43.54 kg (96 lb) and has a rocket motor at the rear that increases its range to 30000 m (33,810 yards) compared with the standard M107 projectile which has a maximum range of 18150 m (19,850 yards) when fired by the M198.

REMBASS
This projectile carries a number of sensors that drop to the ground and are difficult to detect. These relay information on vehicles and personnel in their immediate area, and this information is used both for surveillance and target-acquisition purposes.

Smoke
The white phosphorus projectile is called the **M110** while the smoke (base ejection) projectile is called the **M116**. There are also special projectiles for CS gas and chemical agents.

Jammer
Under development is a 155-mm (6.1-in) projectile that will drop expendable communications jammers well to the rear of the front line to disrupt enemy communications systems.

Illuminating
The M198 can fire two types of illuminating projectile, the **M118** and the **M485**, the latter being the more recent.

UK
105-mm Light Gun

In 1959 the Royal Artillery adopted the Italian OTO Melara 105-mm (4.13-in) pack howitzer as its standard weapon for employment with airborne and air-portable units, and this subsequently gave excellent service in such places as Aden and Borneo. The weapon's main drawback from the British point of view was its relatively short range of 10575 m (11,565 yards). So in 1965 the Royal Artillery issued a requirement for a replacement weapon with a longer range, ability to be towed across country at high speed and a more stable firing platform. Design work began at the Royal Armament Research and Development Establishment in 1966, and after the construction of prototypes, field tests and the resultant modifications the **105-mm Light Gun** was accepted for service in 1973. The first production weapons were completed at Royal Ordnance Factory Nottingham in 1974. In the Royal Artillery the weapon is issued on the scale of 18 guns per regiment, each battery having six guns. With the Royal Artillery the weapon is deployed only in the United Kingdom and Belize, and with the Gibraltar Regiment. So far over 400 Light Guns have been built, and sales have also been made to Australia (which is producing the weapon and its ammunition under licence), Brunei, Eire, Kenya, Malawi, Oman and the United Arab Emirates, and a number

of other undisclosed countries. In the British army the weapon is towed by a 1-tonne Land Rover. This is no longer produced, however, and the Light Gun can be towed by a number of other tracked and wheeled vehicles, including the Swedish Bv 202 all-terrain vehicle. The Light Gun can also be slung under a helicopter such as an Aérospatiale Puma, while the smaller Westland Wessex can take it in two loads.

Two types of barrel can be fitted. The standard barrel is the L19A1, which fires the Abbott range of ammunition out to 17200 m (18,810 yards), and there is also the shorter L20A1 barrel, which fires the standard American M1 series of ammunition out to 11000 m (12,030 yards). Many countries keep the Light Gun with the short barrel for training purposes as the ammunition is much cheaper and available from a variety of manufactur-

The Royal Ordnance Factory's 105-mm Light Gun fires at maximum elevation during demonstrations at the Royal School of Artillery at Larkhill, Wiltshire. The 105-mm Light Gun has now replaced the Model 56 Pack Howitzer in the Royal Artillery, and not only has a longer range but also fires the same highly lethal range of ammunition as the Abbot 105-mm self-propelled gun used by the British and Indian armies.

G5 155-mm gun/howitzer

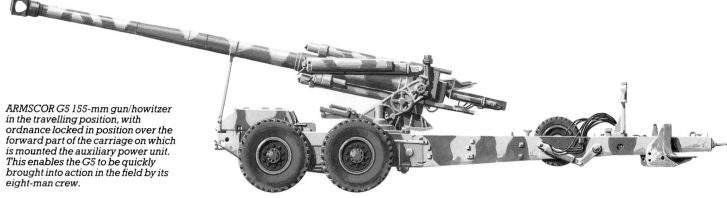

ARMSCOR G5 155-mm gun/howitzer in the travelling position, with ordnance locked in position over the forward part of the carriage on which is mounted the auxiliary power unit. This enables the G5 to be quickly brought into action in the field by its eight-man crew.

For many years after World War II the mainstay of the South African field artillery units were the British 140-mm (5.5-in) medium gun with a maximum range of 16460 m (18,000 yards) and the 25-pdr (88-mm) field gun with a maximum range of 12250 m (13,395 yards). During operations in Angola the South Africans found themselves outranged by enemy artillery and rocket fire and this led to the development of two indigenous systems as no Western country would supply South Africa with the arms it required. These systems, the **G5** 155-mm (6.1-in) gun/howitzer and the 127-mm (5-in) 24-round multiple rocket system, are now in production and service with the South African army and have seen combat during deep-penetration raids into Angola.

The G5 owes much to the Canadian Space Research Corporation GC 45 155-mm (6.1-in) weapon, of which 12 are in service with the Thai Marines, but so many additional features have been incorporated into the G5 that this now bears little resemblance to the original Canadian weapon.

The G5 has a 45-calibre barrel fitted with a single-baffle muzzle brake and an interrupted-thread breech mechanism. To the rear of the breech is a pneumatically-operated rammer to ram projectiles into the chamber at all angles of elevation; this is powered by an air bottle mounted on the right trail. The bagged charges are loaded by hand. On the forward part of the split trail carriage is the auxiliary power unit, which consists of a 68-hp (51-kW) diesel engine. In addition to providing power to the main driving wheels, the APU also supplies power for raising and lowering the circular firing platform under the carriage, for opening and closing the trails, and for

raising and lowering the trail wheels. To reduce the overall length of the G5 for travelling, the ordnance is normally traversed through 180° and locked in position over the trails. The ordnance has a total traverse of 84° and up to 15° of elevation, and 65° above 15° of elevation. Maximum rate of fire over a 15 minute period is three rounds per minute, with two rounds per minute possible in the sustained fire role. The weapon is operated by an eight-man crew, and is normally towed by a South African-built SAMIL 100 (6×6) 10-tonne truck which carries the crew, projectiles, charges and fuses.

The G5 can fire five types of ammunition, also manufactured in South Africa by ARMSCOR. The standard HE projectile weighs 45.5 kg (100.3 lb) and is of the Extended-Range Full Bore (ERFB) type. The HE

base-bleed (HE BB) type is slightly heavier because of the base-bleed attachment, but has a range of 37000 m (40,465 yards) at sea level, though greater ranges are attained when the G5 is fired at higher altitude. The other three projectiles are illuminating, smoke and white phosphorus. To operate with the G5 South Africa has developed a complete fire-control system including a muzzle-velocity measuring device, AS 80 artillery fire-control system with a 16-bit mini-computer, S700 meteorological ground station and a complete range of communications equipment. South Africa has also developed a 155-mm (6.1-in) self-propelled howitzer (6×6) called the **G6**, which has an ordnance based on the G5 and uses the same ammunition, but this has yet to enter production.

Three G5 155-mm gun/howitzers of the South African Army in the firing position. The G5 is normally towed by a SAMIL 100 (6×6) 10-tonne truck that also carries the gun crew and its ammunition. The G5 has an exceptionally long range.

Specification
G5 gun/howitzer
Calibre: 155 mm (6.1 in)
Weight: travelling 13500 kg (29,762 lb)
Dimensions: length, travelling 9.10 m (29 ft 10.25 in); width, travelling 2.50 m (8 ft 2.4 in); height, travelling 2.30 m (7 ft 6.55 in)
Elevation: +73°/−3°
Traverse: total 84° (see text)
Maximum range: with standard ammunition 30000 m (32,810 yards) and with base-bleed projectile 37000 m (40,465 yards)

Bofors FH-77A 155-mm field howitzer

In the late 1960s the Swedish army carried out a series of studies to determine its future artillery requirements, and finally decided to develop a new 155-mm (6.1-in) towed weapon that would have superior cross-country performance, a high rate of fire, good range and fire more effective ammunition. At that time Bofors was building the 155-mm (6.1-in) Bandkanon 1A self-propelled gun, which is fully armoured and has a high rate of fire as it is fitted with an automatic loader for 16 rounds of ready-use ammunition. Its main drawback, however, was and is its size and weight (53 tonnes), which limit its

movement in certain parts of Sweden as well as making it difficult to conceal.

Bofors was awarded the development contract for the new towed weapon, which subsequently became known as the **FH-77A** 155-mm (6.1-in) field howitzer, for which the first orders were placed by the Swedish army in 1975.

The FH-77A has a barrel 5.89 m (19 ft 3.9 in) long and fitted with a pepperpot muzzle brake and a vertical sliding breech mechanism. The split-trail carriage has an auxiliary power unit mounted on the front, enabling the FH-77A to propel itself on roads and across

country. The equipment is normally towed by a Saab-Scania SBAT 111S (6×6) truck, which also carries ammunition in pallets and the six man crew consisting of commander, gunner, two ammunition handlers, loader and crane handler. When the truck and the FH-77A encounter very rough country the main wheels of the howitzer can be engaged from the cab of the truck, so giving an 8×6 combination and a maximum speed of 8 km/h (5 mph). When this speed is exceeded the main wheels of the FH-77A are disengaged. Elevation and traverse of the FH-77A is hydraulic, though manual

controls are provided for emergency use. Mounted on the right side of FH-77A is the loading tray, on which clips of three projectiles can be placed. A typical firing sequence is that the cartridge case is placed on the loading tray followed by the projectile, which is fed from the loading table. When the projectile has slipped down into the neck of the cartridge case the projectile and charge are rammed, the breech is closed and the weapon is fired. Using this method three rounds can be fired in six to eight seconds. In the sustained-fire role six rounds can be fired every other minute for 20

Bofors FH-77A 155-mm field howitzer in the travelling position. The auxiliary power unit on the forward part of the carriage is used to propel the weapon across country without the aid of a truck, as well as assisting in bringing the weapon into action as quickly as possible.

minutes.

The Bofors-developed M/77 projectile weighs 42.4 kg (93.5 lb), has a muzzle velocity of 774 m (2,540 ft) per second and goes out to a maximum range of 22000 m (24,060 yards). It is believed that Bofors is currently developing a base-bleed projectile which will have a maximum range of between 27000 and 30000 m (29,530 and 32,810 yards). For the export market Bofors has developed the **FH-77B** with a slightly longer barrel, increased elevation of +70°, mechanized loading system and a number of other major improvements. The FH-77B has already been ordered by Nigeria. To meet the requirements of the Swedish coastal artillery Bofors has developed the **Karin**, which is essentially the carriage of the FH-77A fitted with a 120-mm (4.72-in) ordnance; this is now in series production.

Specification
Bofors FH-77A field howitzer
Calibre: 155 mm (6.1 in)
Weight: travelling 11500 kg (25,353 lb)
Dimensions: length, travelling 11.60 m (38 ft 0.7 in); width, travelling 2.64 m (8 ft 8 in); height, travelling 2.75 m (9 ft 0.25 in)
Elevation: +50°/+3°
Traverse: total 50°
Maximum range: 20000 m (21,870 yards)

Bofors FH-77A 155-mm field howitzer in the firing position with two ammunition members preparing to load charges. The first three projectiles can be fired in between six and eight seconds, with the loading tray on the right side of the carriage holding the three projectiles. The more recent FH-77B is now in production for Nigeria.

M102 105-mm howitzer

For many years the standard 105-mm (4.13-in) howitzer of the US Army was the M1, which was developed in the 1930s and finally standardized as the M2 in 1940. A total of 10,202 such weapons had been built by the time production ended in 1953. In the post-war period the weapon was re-designated the M101. The main drawback of the M101, which in 1948 was still in use in some 60 countries, was its weight of 2030 to 2258 kg (4,475 to 4,978 lb) depending on the model, and the lack of all-round traverse.

In 1955 a requirement was issued for a new 105-mm (4.13-in) howitzer which would fire the same range of ammunition and yet be lighter than the M101. Rock Island Arsenal designed a new weapon under the designation **XM102**, the first prototype being completed in 1962. Following trials the weapon was classified as standard A in the following year, and designated **M102**. First production M102s were completed in January 1964 and several months later the weapon was deployed to South Vietnam. After so short a development period problems were inevitably encountered with early M102s, but these were soon rectified. The M102 is issued on the scale of 18 per battalion, each battery having six weapons. Today the M102 is used mainly by air-borne and airmobile divisions, to whom weight rather than range is important. The M102 is also used by Brazil, Saudi Arabia, Kampuchea, South Korea and Vietnam.

The M102 consists of four main components, namely the M137 cannon, M37 recoil system, M31 carriage, and the fire-control equipment. The M137

cannon has a vertical sliding-wedge breech mechanism, but is not fitted with a muzzle brake. The recoil system is hydropneumatic and variable, so eliminating the need for a recoil pit. The most unusual feature of the M102 is the two-wheel box-type carriage, which is constructed of aluminium. When the weapon is deployed in the firing position, a circular baseplate is lowered to the ground under the forward part of the base and the two rubber-tyred road wheels are lifted clear of the ground. A roller located at the rear of the trial assembly allows the complete carriage to be traversed through 360°. This proved to be of considerable use in Vietnam, where M102s had to engage targets in different directions.

Specification
M102 howitzer
Calibre: 105 mm (4.13 in)
Weight: firing and travelling 1496 kg (3,300 lb)
Dimensions: length, travelling 5.182 m (17 ft 0 in); width, travelling 1.964 m (6 ft 5.25 in); height, travelling 1.594 m (5 ft 2.75 in)
Elevation: +75°/−5°
Traverse: total 360°
Maximum range: with M1 ammunition 11500 m (12,575 yards) or with M548 HERA 15100 m (16,515 yards)

An M102 105-mm light howitzer of the American 82nd Airborne Division in action during the invasion of Grenada in 1983.

M198 155-mm howitzer

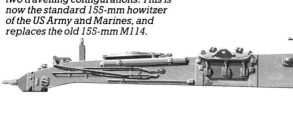

M198 155-mm howitzer in one of its two travelling configurations. This is now the standard 155-mm howitzer of the US Army and Marines, and replaces the old 155-mm M114.

For many years the standard 155-mm (6.1-in) towed howitzer of the US Army was the M114, which was developed in the 1930s and standardized as the M1 in 1941. By the end of World War II some 6,000 had been built, and in the post-war period the weapon was redesignated M114. Like the 105-mm (4.13-in) M101 towed howitzer, the M114 suffered the major drawback of having a limited range and traverse. Following the issue of a formal requirement for a new 155-mm (6.1-in) howitzer, Rock Island Arsenal started design work in 1968, its first development prototype being completed two years later. A total of 10 prototypes was built under the designation **XM198**, and after trials and the usual modifications it was adopted as the 155-mm (6.1-in) howitzer **M198**. Production started at Rock Island Arsenal in 1978, with the first battalion of 18 M198s forming at Fort Bragg in the following year. Each battalion has three batteries each with six M198s.

In addition to being used by the US Army and US Marine Corps, the M198 has also been ordered by Australia (36 to replace the British 140-mm/5.5-in gun) and a number of other countries, notably in the Middle East. In the US Army and US Marine Corps the M198 is towed by a 5-ton (6×6) truck which also carries the ammunition and 11-man crew, although the weapon can be towed by a variety of other tracked and wheeled vehicles. It is airportable, and can be carried slung underneath Boeing Vertol CH-47 and Sikorsky CH-53 helicopters. The M198 is normally issued to US infantry, airborne and air assault divisions, while the mechanized infantry and armoured divisions have the 155-mm (6.1-in) M109 self-propelled howitzer. The M198 was first used operationally by the US Marines in the Lebanon in 1983.

Main components of the M198 are the carriage, recoil system, fire-control equipment, and cannon (or ordnance, as the British prefer to call it). The carriage is of the split-trail type and fitted with a two-position rigid suspension. When the weapon is in the firing position, a firing platform is lowered to the ground under the forward part of the carriage and the wheels are raised clear of the ground. The cradle has the elevation and traverse system, while the top carriage has the assembly cradle, equilibrators and recoil guides. The recoil mechanism is of the hydropneumatic type with a variable recoil length. The M199 cannon has a double-baffle muzzle brake, thermal warning device and a screw-type breech mechanism. Fire-control equipment includes an M137 panoramic telescope, two elevation quadrants and an M138 elbow telescope.

When in the travelling position the ordnance is normally traversed to the rear and locked in position over the trails. Unlike the new French 155-mm (6.1-in) towed guns, British/West German/Italian FH-70 and the Swedish FH-77A, the M198 does not have an auxiliary power unit to enable it to be moved under its own power.

Ammunition is of the separate-loading type and includes Agent, anti-tank (carrying mines), Cannon-Launched Guided Projectile, high explosive, high explosive with various types of grenade including dual-purpose and anti-personnel, rocket assisted projectile, illumination, smoke, and tactical nuclear.

Specification
M198 howitzer
Calibre: 155 mm (6.1 in)
Weight: travelling 7076 kg (15,600 lb)
Dimensions: length, travelling 12.396 m (40 ft 8 in); width, travelling 2.794 m (9 ft 2 in); height, travelling 3.023 m (9 ft 11 in)
Elevation: +72°/−5°
Traverse: total 45°
Maximum range: with M107 projectile 18150 m (19,850 yards) and with rocket-assisted projectile 30000 m (32,810 yards)

M198 155-mm howitzer in static fire position, with sand bags providing some form of protection. This weapon was first used in combat during the recent fighting in Lebanon. It is also used by a number of other countries.

D-30 122-mm howitzer

The **D-30** 122-mm (4.8-in) howitzer was designed by the F.F. Petrov design bureau at Artillery Plant Number 9 at Sverdlovsk as the replacement for the 122-mm (4.8-in) M1938 (M-30)) howitzer which had been introduced into the Soviet army shortly before World War II. The D-30 entered service with the Soviet army in the early 1960s and has a number of significant advantages over the weapon it replaced, including a range of 15400 compared with 11800 m (16,840 compared with 12,905 yards) and a traverse of 360° compared with 49°. In addition to being used by the Soviet army, the weapon is in service with well over 30 countries, and has seen widespread use in the Middle East, Africa and the Far East. The more recent 122-mm (4.8-in) **M-1974** self-propelled howitzer has an ordnance based on the D-30. Another SP mounting was evolved some years ago, when Syria was short of self-propelled artillery and installed a number of D-30 ordnances on obsolete T-34/85 tank chassis. Under contract to the Egyptian government the Royal Ordnance Factory Leeds (where the Chieftain, Challenger and Khalid tanks are built) is fitting the D-30 howitzer onto the chassis of the Combat Engineer Tractor for the Egyptian army.

In the Soviet army the D-30 is issued on the scale of 36 per tank divisions (one artillery regiment with two battalions of 18 weapons, each battalion having three batteries of six D-30s), and each motorized rifle division has 72 D-30s (each motorized rifle regiment having a battalion of 18 D-30s and the artillery regiment two 18-gun battalions). More recently it is believed that the Soviets, like some members of NATO, are increasing the number of guns in the battery from six to eight: each battalion would thus now have 24 instead of 18 D-30s.

The D-30 has a 4.875-m (16-ft) barrel fitted with a multi-baffle muzzle brake and a semi-automatic vertical sliding-wedge breech mechanism, the recoil system being mounted over the ordnance. The weapon is towed muzzle first, the three trails being clamped in position under the ordnance. On arrival at the pre-determined firing position the crew must first unlock the barrel travel lock, which then folds back onto the central trail. The firing jack under

Three Soviet D-30 122-mm howitzers in the firing position. For many years the D-30 was the backbone of Soviet artillery regiments, but is now being replaced by the 122-mm M-1974 self-propelled howitzer. It has been supplied to almost every country receiving Soviet aid.

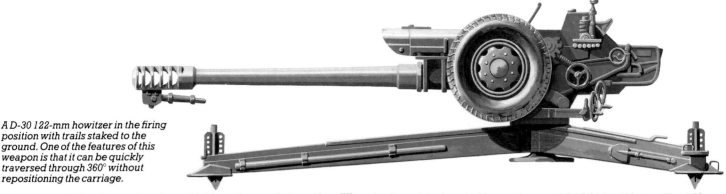

A D-30 122-mm howitzer in the firing position with trails staked to the ground. One of the features of this weapon is that it can be quickly traversed through 360° without repositioning the carriage.

the carriage is then lowered to the ground, so raising the wheels well clear of the ground, and the outer trails are each spread through 120°. The firing jack is then raised until the ends of each trail are on the ground to provide a stable firing platform, the ends of the trails being staked to the ground. The D-30 is provided with a small shield, and is normally towed by a ZIL-157 or Ural-375D (6×6) truck, or by an MT-LB multi-purpose tracked vehicle.

The D-30 fires case-type separate-loading ammunition including FRAG-HE, HEAT-FS (which will penetrate some 460 mm/18.1 in of armour), chemical, smoke and illuminating. More recently a rocket-assisted projectile has been introduced with a maximum range of 21000 m (22,965 yards).

Specification
D-30 howitzer
Calibre: 121.92 mm (4.8 in)
Weight: travelling 3210 kg (7,077 lb) and firing 3150 kg (6,944 lb)
Dimensions: length, travelling 5.40 m (17 ft 8.6 in); width, travelling 1.95 m (6 ft 4.75 in); height, travelling 1.66 m (5 ft 5.35 in)
Elevation: +70°/−7°
Traverse: 370°
Maximum range: with HE Projectile 15400 m (16,840 yards) and with HE rocket-assisted projectile 21000 m (22,965 yards)

Former USSR

M-46 130-mm field gun

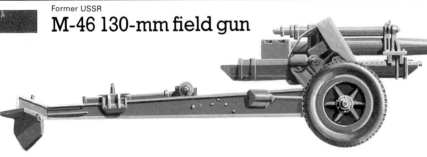

This M-46 130-mm field gun shows its long barrel with the pepperpot muzzle brake. It has been in service for some 30 years, and has a long range that has only recently been matched by the introduction of Western artillery weapons that fire a rocket-assisted projectile (RAP).

The **M-46** 130-mm (5.1-in) field gun is believed to be a development of a naval weapon, and was first seen in public during the 1954 May Day parade. For this reason the M-46 is sometimes designated **M-1954**. Although developed over 30 years ago, it still remains a highly effective weapon with its exceptional range. The weapon has been used in combat in both the Middle East and Vietnam, and in the latter conflict only the American 175-mm (6.89-in) M107 self-propelled gun (with a range of 32700 m/35,760 yards), could outrange the M-46.

In addition to being used by the Soviet Union, the M-46 is operated by more than 30 countries around the world. The Indians have taken the weapon off its normal carriage and installed it on the chassis of the Vickers Mk 1 main battle tank, which is built under the name of the Vijayanta as a self-propelled gun. There is also reason to believe that the Soviets have fitted the ordnance of the M-46 to a main battle tank chassis for use in the tank destroyer role. In the Soviet army the M-46 is deployed in the artillery regiment of an army, which includes two battalions each with 18 M-46s (three batteries each with six weapons). The artillery regiment also has an HQ and service battery, a target-acquisition battery and a battalion of 18 152-mm (6-in) D-20 gun/howitzers. The artillery division, deployed at front (army group) level also includes two regiments each with 54 M-46s, each regiment having three battalions of 18 weapons. The Chinese have a different model of the M-46 called the **Type 59** 130-mm (5.1-in) field gun.

The M-46 has a barrel 7.60 m (24 ft 11.2 in) and fitted with a very distinctive pepperpot muzzle brake and a horizontal sliding-wedge breech mechanism. The recoil system consists of a hydraulic buffer below the barrel and a hydropneumatic recuperator above the barrel. To reduce the overall length of the M-46 when travelling, the barrel is withdrawn out of battery to the rear and locked in position between the spades. The carriage is of the split-trail type and is provided with a two-wheel limber at the rear. For travelling the two spades are removed and carried on the tops of the trails. The M-46 has a nine-man crew, takes four minutes to bring into action and can be towed by a variety of vehicles including the AT-S, ATS-59 and M1972 unarmoured artillery tractors as well as the AT-P armoured tracked artillery tractor.

The ammunition fired by the M-46 is of the separate-loading type and includes FRAG-HE (fragmentation high-explosive) and APC-5 (armoured piercing capped tracer). The former weighs 33.4 kg (73.63 lb), of which 4.63 kg (10.2 lb) is the bursting charge; maximum muzzle velocity is 1050 m (3,445 ft) per second. The APC-T projectile also has a maximum muzzle velocity of 1050 m (3,445 ft) per second and will penetrate 230 mm (9.05 in) of armour at a range of 1000 m (1,095 yards). Other types of projectile available include illuminating and smoke, and a rocket-assisted projectile was introduced in the late 1960s. The RAP was first used by Syria during the 1973 Middle East war.

Specification
M-46 field gun
Calibre: 130 mm (5.12 in)
Weight: travelling 8450 kg (18,629 lb) and firing 7700 kg (16,975 lb)
Dimensions: length, travelling 11.73 m (38 ft 5.8 in); width, travelling 2.45 m (8 ft 0.5 in); height, travelling 2.55 m (8 ft 4.4 in)
Elevation: +45°/−2.5°
Traverse: total 50°
Maximum range: 27150 m (29,690 yards)

A battery of Soviet M-46 130-mm guns are camouflaged during training. When travelling the barrel is withdrawn out of battery to the rear to reduce its overall length and a two wheel dolly attached.

S-23 180-mm gun

For some 30 years this weapon has been able to outrange virtually all NATO towed and self-propelled artillery weapons. It was first seen in public during a 1955 Moscow parade, and for many years was known as the 203-mm (8-in) **M-1955** gun/howitzer in the West. It is believed to have entered service several years before 1955 and to be a development of a naval weapon. During the Middle East war of 1973 a number of these weapons were captured by Israel and then taken back to Israel for detailed evaluation by intelligence personnel. It was then discovered that the actual calibre of the weapon was 180 mm (7.09 in) and that its correct Soviet designation is **S-23**. In the Soviet army the S-23 is issued on the scale of 12 weapons in the heavy artillery brigade of every artillery division. More recent information has shown that the artillery division in the Soviet Union no longer has S-23s and now consists of a headquarters, anti-tank regiment with 36 T-12 or T-12A towed anti-tank guns, multiple rocket-launcher brigade with four battalions of BM-27 (8×8) multiple rocket-launchers (total of 72 launchers), target-acquisition battalion, signal company, motor transport battalion, two regiments of 130-mm (5.1-in) M-46 field guns (total of 108 equipments) and two regiments of 152-mm (6-in) D-20 gun/howitzers or the new M-1973 self-propelled gun/howitzer (total of 108 equipments).

The S-23 is known to be in service with a number of other countries including Egypt, India and Syria, and unconfirmed reports have added Cuba, Ethiopia, North Korea, Libya, Mongolia and Somalia. The weapon is normally towed by an AT-T heavy tracked artillery tractor, which also carries the 16-man crew and a small quantity of ammunition.

The S-23 has a barrel some 8.8 m (28 ft 10.46 in) long with a pepperpot muzzle brake, the recoil system under the barrel and a screw breech mechanism. To reduce the overall length of the weapon for travelling the barrel can be withdrawn out of battery to the rear and linked to the trails. The carriage is of the split-trail type, with to twin rubber-tyred road wheel units at the front and a two-wheel dolly at the rear.

The S-23 fires a bag-type variable-charge separate-loading HE projectile designated OF-43 (weighing some 84.09 kg/185.4 lb) with a maximum muzzle velocity of 790 m/2,590 ft per second) as well as a G-572 concrete-piercing projectile (weighing 97.7 kg/215.4 lb) and a 0.2-kiloton tactical nuclear projectile. After the weapon had been in service for some time an HE rocket-assisted projectile was introduced: with a muzzle velocity of 850 m (2,790 ft) per second this has a maximum range of 43800 m (47,900 yards) compared with 30400 m (33,245 yards) for the original projectile. Because of the heavy weight of the projectile the S-23 has a relative slow rate of fire (one round per minute), dropping to one round every two minutes in the sustained fire role.

Specification
S-23 gun
Calibre: 180 mm (7.09 in)

S-23 180-mm gun in travelling configuration with the dolly attached to the rear. For many years this was thought to be a 203-mm weapon, but examination of weapons captured by Israel showed that it was in fact 180 mm in calibre.

Weight: in action 21450 kg (47,288 lb)
Dimensions: length, travelling 10.485 m (34 ft 4.8 in); width, travelling 2.996 m (9 ft 9.95 in); height, travelling 2.621 m (8 ft 7.2 in)
Elevation: +50°/−2°
Traverse: 44°
Maximum range: with HE projectile 30400 m (33,245 yards) and with rocket-assisted projectile 43,800 m (47,900 yards)

M-56 105-mm howitzer

With the German surrender in Yugoslavia at the end of World War II, large quantities of German artillery were abandoned and much of this was taken over by the Yugoslav army. Even today, some 40 years later, numbers of German 88-mm (3.46-in) guns are still in service in the coastal-defence role, while the 105-mm (4.13-in) towed M18, M18M and M18/40 howitzers are known to be used by reserve units. In the immediate post-war period the United States supplied Yugoslavia with considerable amounts of towed artillery, including 155-mm (6.1-in) M114 and 105-mm (4.13-in) M101 howitzers, and 155-mm (6.1-in) M59 'Long Tom' guns. These remain in service today, as does a copy of the M114 called the M-65. More recently Yugoslavia has designed and built two weapons to meet her own requirements, these being the 105-mm (4.13-in) howitzer **M-56** and a 76-mm (3-in) mountain gun M-46, the latter developed to meet the specific requirements of Yugoslav mountain units.

The M-56 has a barrel 3.48 m (11 ft 5 in) long with a multi-baffle muzzle brake, a hydraulic recoil buffer and hydropneumatic recuperator above and below the barrel, and a horizontal sliding-wedge breech mechanism. The carriage is of the split-trail type, with a spade attached to each end of the pole-type trail. The M-56 has a split shield that slopes to the rear and sides. Some carriages have been observed with American type road wheels and tyres similar to that fitted to the M101, which allows the weapon to be towed up to 70 km/h (43.5 mph), while others have wheels with solid tyres similar to that fitted to the German 105-mm (4.13-in) howitzers of World War II. When the latter are fitted the weapon cannot be towed at high speed.

Fire-control equipment consists of a panoramic telescope with a magnification of ×4, a direct-fire anti-tank telescope with a magnification of ×2, and a gunner's quadrant.

Ammunition is of the semi-fixed type (e.g. projectile and a cartridge case containing the bagged charge). The following projectiles can be fired at a maximum rate of 16 rounds per minute for a short period: HE projectile weighing 15 kg (33.1 lb) with a muzzle velocity of 570 m (1,870 ft) per second, smoke projectile weighing 15.8 kg (34.8 lb), armour-piercing tracer, and high explosive squash head tracer (HESH-T). The HESH-T projectile weighs 10 kg (22.05 lb), and when it hits an enemy armoured vehicle the 2.2 kg (4.85 lb) of explosive flattens itself against the armour before exploding, when it can penetrate up to 100 mm (3.9 in) of armour plate at an angle of 30°.

An unusual feature of the M-56 is that in an emergency it can be fired before the trails are spread, although in this case total traverse is limited to 16° and elevation to +16°. The M-56 has a crew of 11 men and is normally towed by a TAM 1500 (4 x 4) truck. The M56 is currently in use by the various factions fighting in former Yugoslavia, and in Burma, Cyprus, El Salvador, Guatemala, Indonesia, Iran and Peru.

Specification
M-56 howitzer
Calibre: 105 mm (4.13 in)
Weight: travelling 2100 kg (4,630 lb) and firing 2060 kg (4,541 lb)
Dimensions: length, travelling 6.17 m (20 ft 3 in); width, travelling 2.15 m (7 ft 0.66 in); height, travelling 1.56 m (5 ft 1.4 in)
Elevation: +68°/−12°
Traverse: total 52°
Maximum range: 13000 m (14,215 yards)

A Yugoslav M-56 105-mm howitzer in its travelling configuration. This particular model has wheels with solid rubber tyres similar to those fitted to German 105-mm howitzers also used by the Yugoslav army since World War II.

Modern Towed Anti-Aircraft Weapons

The use of guns against attack from the air is now confined to low-level defence. But they are beginning to lose ground to hand-held missiles even in the low-level area, and it may be only their relative cheapness which keeps guns in the air defence business at all.

A remotely controlled Swiss Skyshield 35 Revolver gun shown firing AHEAD ammunition. The weapon has a rate of fire of 1000 rounds per minute.

The light air defence gun all but died out in the 1960s because of the difficulty of aiming at a fast and low target. But then came electro-optics and video cameras, devices which allowed the gunner to see the target in any conditions of light, and which could be harnessed to an electro-mechanical system to lock on and track the target faster and more reliably than a human operator. By the late 1970s 20-mm single and multiple guns were becoming standard across the world, and designers were working on heavier weapons.

The well-known Bofors 40-mm, which dates from 1929, was given a new, longer barrel and became the Bofors L/70; Oerlikon produced a two-barrel 35-mm weapon which has become almost as widespread and popular as the Bofors gun. The Russians produced a 57-mm gun of advanced design which appeared to have been based upon a never-completed German World War II project. Wherever the designs came from, once they were allied to modern image-intensifying sights or low-light-level video cameras and coupled to modern digital fire-control computers which could record the target's course and speed and calculate the amount of aim-off to be applied, the low-flying ground-attack aircraft found itself confronted with some very formidable defences.

In this field, though, the gun itself is only half the story. Much work has had to be done on ammunition, notably the shrinking of proximity fuses to fit into 40-mm and even 35-mm projectiles and still leave sufficient space for a worthwhile charge of explosive. Moreover, these fuses must be capable of reacting against helicopters as well as fixed-wing aircraft, targets which (so far as fuses are concerned) have very different echoing characteristics. Another step has been the development of pre-fragmented shells, so that the distribution and size of the fragments is pre-ordained and not left to chance.

The current tendency appears to be to mix ammunition, either within the same battery or on the same gun or missile launcher, so that by the turn of a switch the gunner can select whichever option he considers to be the most effective in the particular circumstances.

20-mm FK 20-2 light anti-aircraft gun

The 20-mm **FK 20-2** light anti-aircraft gun mounting was developed to meet the rather special requirements of the Norwegian armed forces and certain units of the West German army. The Rheinmetall twin 20-mm light anti-aircraft gun is widely used by the West German army, but its weight of 2160 kg (4,762 lb) is too great to permit the type's use by airborne and mountain units. The FK 20-2 weighs only 620 kg (1,367 lb) in its travelling configuration and can be quickly disassembled to allow transport by pack animals.

Companies involved in the design and development of the FK 20-2 included A/S Kongsberg Vappenfabrikk of Norway, Rheinmetall of West Germany, Hispano-Suiza of Switzerland (since taken over by Oerlikon-Bührle) and Kern, the last responsible for the sight.

The FK 20-2 is fitted with the Rheinmetall 20-mm MK 20 Rh 202 cannon as installed in the twin 20-mm mount used by the West German army and air force. The gunner can fire either single shots or bursts, the cannon having a cyclic rate of fire of 1,000 rounds per minute. A total of 160 rounds of ready-use ammunition is provided; of these, 150 are normally anti-aircraft ammunition and the remaining 10 armour-piercing for the engagement of armoured vehicles. On each side of the cannon is a box of 75 rounds of ammunition (high explosive incendiary/HEI or high explosive incendiary-tracer/HEI-T), while above the cannon is a box of 10 rounds of armour-piercing discarding sabot-tracer (APDS-T). Traverse and elevation are manual via two hand wheels, which

The 20-mm FK 20-2 anti-aircraft gun is a joint development between Norway and West Germany and uses the same 20-mm MK 20 Rh 202 cannon as the twin 20-mm Rheinmetall system used by the West German army and air force.

have the optical sight mounted between them. The latter has a magnification of ×1.5 for engaging aerial targets and ×5 for engaging ground targets. The sight has two eyepieces: the upper one is used when the gunner is seated while the lower one is used when the gunner is engaging ground targets from the much safer prone position. To the front of the gunner is a small shield, but in peace this is often removed to save weight.

The system is normally mounted on a two-wheeled carriage that can be towed by any light 4×4 cross-country vehicle, which also carries the three-man crew and a supply of ready-use ammunition.

In the firing position the weapon is supported on three outriggers, one at the rear and one on each side. The FK 20-2 is a clear-weather system only with no capability for radar control. Other anti-aircraft systems used by the Norwegian army include the American 12.7-mm (0.5-in) quadruple machine-gun, Bofors RBS-70 surface-to-air missile system and Bofors 40-mm L/60 and L/70 towed anti-aircraft guns.

The 20-mm Rheinmetall MK 20 Rh 202 cannon is also used by the Norwegian army, installed in a one-man Swedish turret mounted on M113 armoured personnel carriers.

Specification
FK 20-2
Calibre: 20 mm (0.79 in)
Weights: travelling 620 kg (1,367 lb); firing 440 kg (970 lb)

This 20-mm FK 20-2 anti-aircraft gun in the firing position clearly shows the two magazines, one each side of the barrel holding 75 rounds of ready-use ammunition. The gunner has a dual sight which enables him to track both aerial and ground targets easily.

Dimensions: length travelling 4.00 m (13 ft 1.5 in); width travelling 1.86 m (6 ft 1.2 in); height travelling 2.20 m (7 ft 2.6 in)
Elevation: +83°/−8°
Traverse: 360°
Ranges: maximum horizontal 6000 m (6,562 yards); maximum vertical 4500 m (14,764 ft); effective vertical 2000 m (6,562 ft)
Crew: 3 (1 on mount)

Breda 40-mm 40L70 anti-aircraft gun

For many years the Breda company of Brescia has been involved in the design and production of a wide range of weapons for both naval and ground forces. One of its most important naval weapons is the Compact Twin 40-mm L/70 Type 70 Naval Mount, which is already in service with over 20 navies and used in conjunction with an Orion radar to provide a close-defence system against both aircraft and air- or sea-launched anti-ship missiles. The company realized that this weapon also had an army application for the defence of high-value targets such as airfields, command posts, oil installations and so on. The 40-mm **Breda 40L70** mount is now in service with Venezuela, which already has the original naval installation in service on board its six 'Lupo' class frigates. The 40L70 cannot be used alone as it has no fire-control system, but a wide range of fire-control systems is available from a number of manufacturers, a typical equipment being the Dutch Hollandse Signaalappartean Flycatcher. When used in conjunction with the Flycatcher the complete system is known as the **Guardian**. A typical fire unit consists of two 40-mm 40L70s, one Flycatcher fire-control system, and generators.

The twin 40-mm 40L70 mount is essentially the standard naval turret installed on a four-wheeled carriage. In the firing position the system is supported on six jacks that are adjustable to suit the different ground conditions; one jack is located at each end of the carriage, and the other four are placed

Italian Breda 40L70 Field Mounting is essentially a naval anti-aircraft and anti-missile system, installed on a four-wheeled carriage for army use. Venezuela has recently taken delivery of 18 40L70 Field Mountings, which it uses in conjunction with the Dutch HSA Flycatcher radar.

two on each side on outriggers.

Turret traverse and weapon elevation are electric at a maximum traverse speed of 90° per second. The mount has two 40-mm 70-calibre Bofors guns which have a cyclic rate of fire of 300 rounds per barrel per minute. Ammunition is identical to that used in the famous Bofors L/70 anti-aircraft gun and includes proximity-fused pre-fragmented high explosive (PFHE),

high-capacity high explosive (HCHE), high explosive-tracer (HE-T), armour-piercing capped-tracer (APC-T) and target practice. To engage aerial targets such as helicopters, aircraft and missiles the PFHE round would be used as it produces over 2,400 fragments of which some 600 are tungsten pellets, which can penetrate 14 mm (0.55 in) of aluminium.

A total of 444 rounds of 40-mm

ammunition (in clips of four rounds) is provided under the turret, and the empty cartridge cases are ejected outside the forward part of the turret. When firing the turret is unmanned, being controlled by the operator in the fire-control centre.

For many years Breda has been producing the Bofors 40-mm L/70 anti-aircraft gun under licence, including the towed system. To increase the rate of fire of the latter weapon Breda has designed an automatic feeding device which increases cyclic rate of fire from 240 to 300 rounds per minute, with a total of 144 rounds carried for ready use.

More recently Breda has developed to the prototype stage a twin 30-mm towed anti-aircraft gun which uses the West German 30-mm Mauser Model F gun, which has a cyclic rate of fire of 800 rounds per gun per minute. Each barrel has 250 rounds of ready-use ammunition. The system is fitted with the Italian Galileo P75D optronic fire-control system and a on-carriage power unit.

Specification
Breda 40-mm 40L70
Calibre: 40 mm (1.57 in)
Weights: travelling without ammunition 9900 kg (21,826 lb); travelling with ammunition 10966 kg (24,176 lb)
Dimensions: length travelling 8.05 m (26 ft 4.9 in); width travelling 3.20 m (10 ft 6 in); height travelling 3.65 m (11 ft 11.7 in)
Elevation: +85°/–13°
Traverse: 360°
Ranges: maximum horizontal 12500 m (13,670 yards); maximum vertical 8700 m (28,543 ft); effective vertical 4000 m (13,123 ft)

The Breda 40-mm 40L70 Field Mounting has a total of 444 rounds of ammunition ready for immediate use. When the weapon is firing no crewmen are present as the guns are aimed and fired by remote control by the Flycatcher fire control system.

ISRAEL
20-mm TCM-20 light anti-aircraft gun

For some years Israel used the old American M55 trailer-mounted 12.7-mm (0.5-in) quadruple light anti-aircraft gun system, but they realized that it had a very short range. The RAMPTA Structures and Systems Division of Israel Aircraft Industries then modernized the system as the 20-mm **TCM-20** to meet the requirements of the Israeli Air Defence Command and, following trials with prototype systems, the type was accepted for service in time to be used in combat during the 1970 'War of Attrition', when it is claimed to have shot down 10 aircraft in 10 engagements. It was also used during the Yom Kippur War, when it is credited with shooting down some 60 per cent of enemy aircraft downed by air defences, the remaining 40 per cent being shot down by other anti-aircraft guns and HAWK surface-to-air missiles. In the 1982 invasion of the Lebanon the TCM-20 was used not only to shoot down Syrian aircraft and helicopters but also in urban fighting and to engage ground targets. The TCM-20 was offered on the export market at an early date and is now in service with at least six countries apart from Israel.

The TCM-20 is the M55 with the four 12.7-mm M2 HB Browning heavy machine-guns replaced by two Hispano-Suiza HS 404 cannon with a cyclic rate of fire of 650 to 700 rounds per minute, but a practical rate of fire of 150 rounds per minute. Each barrel has a quick-change drum magazine that holds 60 rounds of ready-use ammunition. The gunner aims the cannon with an M18 reflex sight. Turret traverse and weapon elevation are electric, with onboard power provided by two 12-volt batteries mounted at the rear of the carriage; the batteries are kept charged by an auxiliary power unit. In the firing position the wheels are normally removed and the carriage is supported on three levelling jacks.

The basic model is normally towed by any 4×4 light vehicle, although Israel also has in service a self-propelled model based on the M3 series halftrack. There is no provision for all-weather fire control, although warning of the exact direction of approach by enemy aircraft can be given by an Israeli-designed EL/M 2106 point-defence alerting radar.

More recently RAMPTA Structures

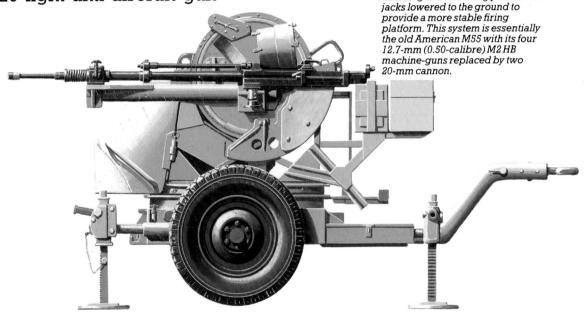

This TCM-20 twin 20-mm light anti-aircraft gun in the firing position has jacks lowered to the ground to provide a more stable firing platform. This system is essentially the old American M55 with its four 12.7-mm (0.50-calibre) M2 HB machine-guns replaced by two 20-mm cannon.

and Systems has developed a new system called the **TCM Mk 3**, which appears to be similar in concept to the original TCM but can be fitted with a variety of different weapons in the 20-mm to 25-mm class, the example shown in 1983 being fitted with 23-mm cannon as used in the Soviet ZU-23 towed anti-aircraft gun system. In addition to the same M18 optical sight as installed on the original TCM-20, the TCM Mk 3 is being offered with a Star-light sight with a magnification of ×4 for night operations and a fire-control system that includes a laser rangefinder and computerized sight.

Specification
TCM-20
Calibre: 20 mm (0.79 in)
Weights: travelling 1350 kg (2,976 lb)
Dimensions: length travelling 3.27 m (10 ft 8.7 in); width travelling 1.70 m (5 ft 6.9 in); height travelling 1.63 m (5 ft 4.2 in)
Elevation: +90°/–10°
Traverse: 360°
Ranges: maximum horizontal 5700 m (6,234 yards); maximum vertical 4500 m (14,764 ft); effective vertical 1200 m (3,937 ft)
Crew: 4

At present there are two versions of the Israeli TCM-20 twin 20 mm anti-aircraft gun system: towed and self-propelled, with the latter being mounted on the rear of an M3 halftracked vehicle. The system was used for the first time during the so-called War of Attrition in 1970.

20-mm Tarasque light anti-aircraft gun

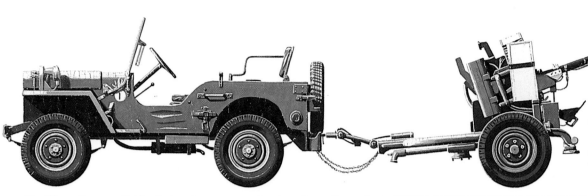

One of the features of the French 20-mm Tarasque light anti-aircraft gun is that it can be towed by a light vehicle such as the M201 (4×4). The 20-mm M693 cannon has dual feed, so enabling the gunner to change from one type of ammunition to another to engage different types of target.

The 20-mm **Tarasque** light anti-aircraft gun entered service with the French army several years ago under the designation **Type 53 T2**. It is armed with the 20-mm M693 cannon (the standard weapon of its type in the French army), which is also installed in the AMX-10P mechanized infantry combat vehicle and the AMX-30 main battle tank.

The Tarasque light anti-aircraft gun is carried on a two-wheeled carriage that can be towed by a light 4×4 vehicle such as the M201 or Land Rover. The weapon can be brought into action by two men in about 15 seconds: on arrival at the selected firing position the locking pin retaining the rear foot is removed and the mount slewed through 90° to place the other two feet in contact with the ground; the carriage is then removed and the mount supported on the three feet.

Only one man is required to operate the Tarasque gun, the other two men acting as ammunition handlers or aircraft spotters. The gunner is seated on the left side of the mount and moves in elevation with the 20-mm cannon. Elevation and traverse are hydraulic, though manual controls are provided for emergency use. Maximum traverse speed is 40° per second and maximum elevation speed is 80° per second.

The 20-mm M693 is a dual-feed cannon and has a cyclic rate of fire of 740 rounds per minute. The gunner fires the cannon by pressing down his right foot, and can fire single aimed shots or bursts. A total of 140 rounds of ready-use ammunition is carried, of which 100 are normally high explosive (HE) or high explosive incendiary (HEI) for engaging aerial targets, and 40 of

armour-piercing discarding sabot (APDS) for engaging armoured targets. The latter round will penetrate 20 mm (0.79 in) of armour at an incidence of 0° at a range of 1000 m (1,094 yards).

The gunner has an anti-aircraft sight with a magnification of ×1 and a ground-to-ground sight with a magnification of ×5.

The Tarasque can also be installed, less its carriage, in the rear of cross-country vehicles such as the TRM 2000 4×4 truck; this gives the weapon greater cross-country mobility as well as enabling it to open fire as soon as the vehicle comes to a halt.

The French air force uses the twin 20-mm **Cerbère** light anti-aircraft gun to provide close protection for the Crotale surface-to-air missile systems protecting its air bases. The Cerbère, also known as the **Type 76 T2**, is essentially the West German Rheinmetall twin 20-mm light anti-aircraft gun with its original MK 20 Rh 202 cannon replaced by the French GIAT M693 cannon. Currently being tested for use with the Cerbère is the DALDO target indicator helmet: in this system the gun commander, situated away from the Cerbère, constantly scans the sky for a target. Once a hostile target has been selected the commander presses a button and the Cerbère mount is automatically laid onto the target in elevation and traverse, thus saving valuable seconds in target acquisition.

More recently GIAT has developed a twin 20-mm light anti-aircraft gun system as a private venture. Designated **Type 53 T4** this weighs 2500 kg (5,512 lb), and is thus much heavier

The GIAT 20-mm Tarasque light anti-aircraft gun can also be carried in the rear of trucks such as this Renault TRM 2000 (4×4) for greater cross-

than the Cerbère or Tarasque. It has hydraulic elevation and traverse, and 150 rounds of ready-use ammunition for each of the 20-mm cannon.

Specification
Tarasque
Calibre: 20 mm (0.79 in)
Weights: travelling with ammunition 840 kg (1,852 lb); firing with ammunition 660 kg (1,455 lb)

country mobility. This gun is now in wide-scale use with the French army and is also offered for export, as are most French weapons today.

Dimensions: length travelling 4.15 m (13 ft 7.4 in); width travelling 1.90 m (6 ft 2.8 in); height travelling 1.70 m (5 ft 6.9 in)
Elevation: +83°/–8°
Traverse: 360°
Ranges: maximum horizontal 6000 m (6562 yards); maximum vertical 4500 m (14,764 ft); effective vertical 2000 m (6,562 ft)
Crew: 3 (1 on mount)

20-mm M55A2 light anti-aircraft gun

In recent years the Yugoslav defence industry has designed and placed in production a number of 20-mm light anti-aircraft guns, all of which use the same basic Hispano-Suiza 20-mm HSS-804 70-calibre barrel which is produced under licence in Yugoslavia.

The **20/1 mm M75** is the most unsophisticated weapon in the family, and has a single barrel with the gunner sitting on a seat at the rear of the mount. Elevation and traverse are manual, and the gunner aims the cannon at aircraft targets by means of an M73 reflex sight while a sight with a magnification of ×3.8 is used to engage ground targets. The cannon is normally fed from a drum holding 60 rounds of ammunition, but there is also a box type magazine that holds 10 rounds of ammunition; the latter is normally used for API, API-T and AP-T, while the

drum magazine is used for the anti-aircraft rounds (HEI and HEI-T). The ammunition used by this gun is identical to that used in other weapons of this family.

The **20/3 mm M55A4 B1** has a carriage and sighting system similar to that of the Oerlikon-Bührle GAI-DO1 light anti-aircraft gun, and each of the three barrels has a 60-round drum magazine. The gunner sits on a seat at the rear of the mount, and power for the hydraulic elevation and traverse system is provided by a Wankel engine mounted under the gunner's seat. Maximum traverse and elevation rates are 80° per second.

Sighting is effected by an Italian Galileo P56 sight with a magnification of ×1 for use against aircraft and ×4 for use against ground targets. Each of the 20-mm cannon has a cyclic rate of fire

of 700 rounds per minute, and the gunner fires the cannon by depressing a foot pedal. For transportation the mount is carried on a small two-wheel carriage, which in the firing position is supported on four outriggers.

The **20/3 mm M55A2** is very similar to the M55A4 B1 system, but has a different sight and manual elevation and traverse. The gunner is seated at the rear and has two handwheels (one for elevation and one for traverse), and fires the cannon by pressing a foot pedal. The gunner is provided with a sight for target tracking, but has to insert key data (for example target range and speed) manually to ensure a hit.

All of these 20-mm cannon are basically clear-weather systems with no provision for radar fire control. They are also offered for export, and sales

have been made to a number of countries including Cyprus and Mozambique.

Specification
M55A2
Calibre: 20 mm (0.79 in)
Weights: travelling (with ammunition) 1100 kg (2,425 lb); firing (without ammunition) 970 kg (2,138 lb)
Dimensions: length travelling 4.30 m (14 ft 1.3 in); width travelling 1.27 m (4 ft 2 in); height travelling 1.47 m (4 ft 9.9 in)
Elevation: +83°/–5°
Traverse: 360°
Ranges: maximum horizontal 5500 m (6,015 yards); effective horizontal 2500 m (2,734 yards); maximum vertical 4000 m (13,123 ft); effective vertical 2000 m (6,562 ft)
Crew: 6 (1 on mount)

30-mm M53 light anti-aircraft gun

Czechoslovakia had an excellent gun-making capability well before World War II, and this was subsequently taken over by the Germans. After the end of the war Czechoslovakia continued to design and build weapons such as the 30-mm **M53** light anti-aircraft gun, which it still uses in place of the Soviet 23-mm ZU-23. The Czech weapon is heavier and has a slower rate of fire, but it does have a more effective range than the ZU-23. In addition to being used by Czechoslovakia, it is also used by Cuba, Romania, Vietnam and Yugoslavia. There is also a self-propelled model called the **M53/59**, which is mounted on a modified and armoured Praga V3S 6×6 truck chassis. An unusual feature of the M53/59 is that the twin 30-mm weapons can be removed from the vehicle and placed on the ground for ease of concealment while the truck is driven away and camouflaged. The M53/59 is fed from vertical magazines holding 50 rounds, while the M53 is fed horizontally in 10-round clips.

The M53 system is mounted on a four-wheeled carriage, no shield being provided for the four man crew. To provide a more stable firing platform in action, the wheels are raised off the ground and the carriage is supported by four jacks, one on each side on outriggers and one at each end.

The weapons are gas-operated, each having a cyclic rate of fire of 450 to 500 rounds per minute though the practical rate of fire is only 100 rounds per minute. Ammunition is fed to each barrel in clips, and two types of ammunition are available, both having a muzzle velocity of 1000 m (3,281 ft) per second: these are high explosive incendiary (HEI) and armour-piercing incendiary (API) for use against armoured vehicles. The latter round will penetrate 55 mm (2.17 in) of

armour at a range of 500 m (547 yards).

The main drawback of the M53 light anti-aircraft gun is that, like the Soviet ZU-23, it is limited to clear-weather operations as there is no provision for radar or off-carriage fire-control.

Czechoslovakia developed two other anti-aircraft weapons in the period after World War II, although as far as it is known neither remains in front line service with the Czech forces. These are the 12.7-mm (0.5-in) M53 quadruple anti-aircraft machine-gun, and a 57-mm anti-aircraft gun. The M53 is a two-wheeled carriage fitted with four Soviet DShKM machine-guns, each fed from a drum holding 50 rounds of ammunition. This weapon has an effective anti-aircraft range of 1000 m (1,094 yards) and is normally towed by a GA-69 4×4 truck which also carries its crew and a small amount of ready-use ammunition. The 57-mm anti-aircraft gun was used by the Czech army in place of the Soviet 57-mm S-60 and has a higher rate of fire, being fed with three- rather than four-round clips of ammunition. It is reported that this weapon was exported to a few countries including Cuba, Guinea and Mali.

Specification
M53
Calibre: 30 mm (1.18 in)
Weights: travelling 2100 kg (4,630 lb); firing 1750 kg (3,858 lb)
Dimensions: length travelling 7.587 m (24 ft 10.7 in); width travelling 1.758 m (5 ft 9.2 in); height travelling 1.575 m (5 ft 2 in)
Elevation: +85°/–10°
Traverse: 360°
Ranges: maximum horizontal 9700 m (10,608 yards); maximum vertical 6300 m (20,669 ft); effective vertical 3000 m (9,843 ft)
Crew: 4

Twin 30-mm M53 weapons are towed by a Praga V3S 6×6 truck. Ammunition is fed to each of the 30-mm barrels in clips of 10 rounds, *with practical rate of fire being 100 rounds per barrel per minute. The M53 has no radar system, so is limited in its engagements.*

The Czech twin 30-mm M53 light anti-aircraft gun is used here to defend a 'Bar Lock' air defence radar installation against air attack. In *addition to this towed model there is also a self-propelled version called the M53/59, mounted on a 6×6 Praga V3S armoured truck chassis.*

23-mm ZU-23 light anti-aircraft gun

For many years after the end of World War II the standard light anti-aircraft gun of the Soviet army was the ZPU series of 14.5-mm (0.57-in) weapons using the Vladimirov KPV heavy machine-gun, which even today is installed in turrets mounted on a number of Soviet armoured vehicles including the BRDM-2, BTR-60PB and OT-64. There are three basic models of the ZPU, the ZPU-1, ZPU-2 and ZPU-4, the numeral referring to the number of barrels. Although withdrawn from front-line service with the Soviet army some years ago, the ZPU series remains in service with about 40 countries around the world.

In the 1960s the ZPU series was replaced in the Soviet army by the **ZU-23** twin 23-mm towed anti-aircraft gun system, which is no longer in front-line Soviet use, so far as is known, having been replaced by surface-to-air missiles. At divisional level the last users were the airborne or airborne rifle divisions which each had a total of 24 systems, four in each of the three airborne rifle regiments and 12 in the divisional artillery element. The weapon is still used by some 20 countries, however, and was even encountered by United States forces during their invasion of Grenada in October 1983, when ZU-23 and ZPU series light anti-aircraft guns downed a number of

American helicopters. In Afghanistan the Soviets have mounted a number of ZU-23s on the rear of trucks to provide suppressive ground-to-ground fire when convoys are attacked by guerrillas.

The ZU-23 is normally towed by a light vehicle such as the 4×4 GAZ-69,

the Soviet equivalent of the Land Rover. The carriage has two rubber-tyred road wheels: in the firing position these wheels are raised off the ground and the carriage is supported on three screw-type levelling jacks. Each of the 23-mm barrels is provided with a flash suppressor, and a handle is mounted

A Soviet-built 23-mm ZU-23 light anti-aircraft gun of the East German army is seen in the firing position, showing the box of 50 rounds of ready-use ammunition for each barrel. The ZU-23 has been seen in Afghanistan mounted on the rear of cross-country trucks.

on top of each barrel to enable it to be changed quickly. Each barrel has a box of 50 rounds of ready-use ammunition, and though a cyclic rate of fire of 800 to 1,000 rounds per minute is possible, the practical rate of fire is 200 rounds per minute. Two types of fixed ammunition are fired by the ZU-23: armour-piercing incendiary-tracer (API-T) and high explosive incendiary-tracer (HEI-T), the former being used to engage armoured vehicles and the latter to engage aircraft. Both projectiles have a muzzle velocity of 970 m (3,182 ft) per second, and the API-T projectile will penetrate 25 mm (0.98 in) of armour at a range of 500 m (547 yards). The mounting has no provision for off-carriage fire control. The 23-mm cannon of the ZU-23 are also used in the famous 23-mm ZSU-23-4 self-propelled anti-aircraft gun system, although in this application the weapons are water-cooled to enable a higher rate of fire to be achieved.

More recently Egypt has been testing two versions of the M113 armoured personnel carrier with twin 23-mm anti-aircraft guns mounted on the roof, while Israel has captured a number of BTR-152 6×6 armoured personnel carriers from the PLO with a ZU-23 mounted in the rear.

Specification
ZU-23
Calibre: 23 mm (0.91 in)
Weights: travelling 950 kg (2,094 lb); firing 950 kg (2,094 lb)
Dimensions: length travelling 4.57 m (15 ft 0 in); width travelling 1.83 m (6 ft 0 in); height travelling 1.87 m (6 ft 1.6 in)
Elevation: +90°/–10°
Traverse: 360°
Ranges: maximum horizontal 7000 m (7,655 yards); maximum vertical 5100 m (16,732 ft); effective vertical 2500 m (8,202 ft)
Crew: 5

Although no longer in large-scale use with the Soviet Union the twin 23-mm ZU-23 light anti-aircraft gun system is still highly effective, and a number were used against American forces during the invasion of Grenada.

Former USSR

57-mm S-60 anti-aircraft gun

The 57-mm (2.24-in) **S-60** anti-aircraft gun entered service with the Soviet army after the end of World War II as the replacement for the 37-mm M1939 light anti-aircraft gun; this was the Soviet equivalent of the famous Bofors 40-mm L/60 weapon used in large numbers by the American and British armies during the war. Until very recently each tank division and motorized rifle division in the Soviet army had an anti-aircraft regiment equipped with the S-60. Each regiment had four batteries each with six guns, each battery having two three-gun platoons. Each battery had a SON-9/SON-9A 'Fire Can' fire-control radar, while at regimental HQ were two 'Flat Face' target-acquisition radars. More recently the 'Flap Wheel' radar has been used with the S-60 system.

The S-60 is still used by some 30 countries, especially in Africa, the Middle East and the Far East, and features in the inventory of most Warsaw Pact countries. In the Soviet army it has been replaced in many front-line units by the SA-8 'Gecko' surface-to-air missile (SAM), which in addition to being a much more effective all-weather system can be ready for action within seconds. China has built a model of the S-60 under the designation **Type 59**, while the ZSU-57-2 self-propelled anti-aircraft gun system uses the same ammunition as the S-60.

The S-60 can be towed by a variety of vehicles including 6×6 trucks such as the Ural-375D or the AT-L light tracked artillery tractors. The weapon can engage anti-aircraft targets with its wheels in contact with the ground, but it is much more accurate with its wheels raised off the ground and the carriage supported by four screw jacks, one on each side on outriggers and one at each end. Optical sights are fitted for the engagement of both ground and aerial targets. Four modes of operation are available: firstly, manual with the crew operating handwheels for elevation and traverse; secondly, power-assisted with the handwheels operated by the crews but assisted by a servo motor; thirdly, remotely-controlled by a Puazo series director and zero indicator; and fourthly, fully automatic and remotely-

controlled by a director and zero indicator, plus radar. In each case ammunition is loaded in four-round clips by ammunition feeders, one clip being in the feed tray to the left of the breech and another clip on the mount itself. Three types of fixed ammunition can be fired by the S-60, all of which have a muzzle velocity of 1000 m (3,281 ft) per second: two types of fragmentation tracer (FRAG-T) and armour-piercing capped-tracers (APC-T). The latter will penetrate 96 mm (3.78 in) of armour at a range of 1000 m (1,094 yards). The S-60 has a cyclic rate of fire of 105 to 120 rounds per minute and a practical rate of fire of 70 rounds per minute.

Specification
S-60
Calibre: 57 mm (2.24 in)
Weights: travelling 4660 kg (10,274 lb); firing 4500 kg (9,921 lb)
Dimensions: length travelling 8.50 m (27 ft 10.6 in); width travelling 2.054 m (6 ft 8.9 in); height travelling 2.37 m (7 ft

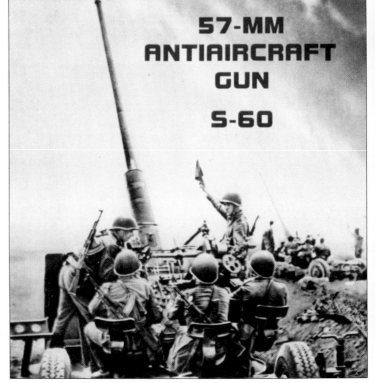

Right: The 57-mm S-60 anti-aircraft gun is highly effective when used together with the PUAZO-6/60 director and the SON-9/SON-9A radar, which is called 'Fire Can' by NATO. In 1985 Iraq was using the S-60 together with a low-light-level television system to engage Iranian aircraft.

9.3 in)
Elevation: +85°/–4°
Traverse: 360°
Ranges: maximum horizontal 12000 m (13,123 yards); maximum vertical 8800 m (28,871 ft); effective vertical with optical sights 4000 m (13,123 ft); effective vertical with off-carriage control 6000 m (19,685 ft)
Crew: 8

For many years the 57-mm S-60 was one of the standard towed anti-aircraft guns of the Soviet army and was issued on the scale of 24 guns per division. This S-60 is of the Egyptian army and is in the travelling position, being towed by a 6×6 truck. In the Soviet army its replacement is the SA-8.

100-mm KS-19 anti-aircraft gun

One of the standard anti-aircraft guns of the Soviet army during World War II was the 85-mm (3.35-in) M1939, replaced in production by the M1944 which had a longer barrel and fired ammunition with higher muzzle velocity for increased range. In 1985 the M1939 and M1944 are still used by almost 20 countries, although in the Warsaw Pact they have been replaced by surface-to-air missiles. After the end of the war the Soviet Union introduced two new towed anti-aircraft guns, the 100-mm (3.94-in) **KS-19** and the 130-mm (5.12-in) KS-30; by 1985 neither of these remained in front-line service with the Soviet Union, although some 20 countries still use the KS-19 and two or three the much heavier KS-30. China has built the KS-19 under the designation **Type 59**.

The KS-19 is normally towed by an AT-S medium or AT-T heavy full-tracked artillery tractor, which also carries the 15-man crew and a small quantity of ready-use ammunition. The weapon is mounted on a two-axle carriage, and in the firing position the axles are raised off the ground and the carriage is supported by four screw jacks, one on each side on outriggers and one at each end of the carriage. When travelling the mount is traversed to the rear and the barrel is held in position by a lock.

The KS-19 fires ammunition of the fixed type which is loaded in single rounds from the left; to increase its rate of fire, the weapon is fitted with a single-round loading tray, automatic fuse

The Soviet 100-mm KS-19 anti-aircraft gun was introduced some 40 years ago, but in Warsaw Pact countries has long been replaced in front-line service by missiles such as the SA-2 'Guideline'. The KS-19 is, however, still in widespread use in both the Middle and Far East.

setter and a power rammer. A well-trained crew can achieve a maximum rate of fire of 15 rounds per minute. Like most heavy-calibre anti-aircraft weapons, the KS-19 was designed as a dual-role (anti-aircraft and anti-tank) gun. Three types of ammunition, all with a muzzle velocity of 900 m (2,953 ft) per second, are available for the anti-aircraft role: high explosive, high explosive fragmentation and fragmentation. Two rounds are available for the anti-tank role: AP-T (armour-piercing tracer) and APC-T (armour-piercing capped tracer); the first of these has a muzzle velocity of 1,000 m (3,281 ft) per second and can penetrate 185 mm (7.28 in) of armour at a

range of 1000 m (1,094 yards).

Anti-aircraft targets can be engaged with the sights installed on the KS-19, but better results are obtained with the PUAZO-6/19 director and the SON-9/SON-9A (NATO reporting name 'Fire Can') fire-control radar system. In most countries the KS-19 is used to defend strategic rather than tactical targets, and the weapon can be tied into an overall air-defence system. Lighter anti-aircraft guns, such as the 57-mm S-60, are used by field armies as they are easier to move about. The KS-19 has been used in action during the Korean War, the many wars in the Middle East, and also by North Vietnam against American aircraft.

Specification
KS-19
Calibre: 100 mm (3.94 in)
Weight: travelling 9550 kg (21,054 lb)
Dimensions: length travelling 9.45 m (31 ft 0 in); width travelling 2.35 m (7 ft 8.5 in); height travelling 2.201 m (7 ft 2.7 in)
Elevation: +85°/−3°
Traverse: 360°
Ranges: maximum horizontal 21000 m (22,966 yards); maximum vertical with time fuse 12700 m (41,667 ft); maximum vertical with proximity fuse 15000 m (49,213 ft); effective vertical 13700 m (44,948 ft)
Crew: 15

12.7-mm M55 light anti-aircraft gun

The 12.7-mm (0.5-in) **M55** quadruple anti-aircraft gun system was developed in World War II by the Kimberly-Clark Corporation, and by the time production was completed in 1953 some 10,000 systems had been built. In addition to being used during World War II the M55 was used by the United States forces in both Korea and South Vietnam. In the latter conflict it was used in the ground fire-support role to break up mass attacks by Viet Cong on American supply bases and camps. Some M55 systems were also put on the rear of trucks and armour plated for use in the convoy escort role. In the US Army the M55 was replaced from the late 1960s by the 20-mm M167 Vulcan towed anti-aircraft gun system, but it is still used by almost 20 countries all over the world. More recently Israel has developed from the M55 the TCM-20 anti-aircraft gun system which has two 20-mm cannon in place of the four 12.7-mm (0.5-in) machine-guns of the original. The Brazilian company LYSAM has carried out a modernization of the M55 for the Brazilian army and has also fitted two 20-mm cannon in place of the four 12.7-mm machine-guns.

The M55 system consists essentially of two parts, the **M45C** mount and the **M20** trailer. The former is an armoured mount with a seat for the gunner and also contains an integral electric power unit which in turn is run from two 6-volt batteries. Mounted on each side of the mount are two 12.7-mm M2 HB machine-guns, each of which is fed from a belt containing 210 rounds of ready-use ammunition. The machine-guns are fully automatic and have a

cyclic rate of fire of 450 to 550 rounds per barrel per minute, though the practical rate of fire is 150 rounds per barrel per minute. Types of ammunition that can be fired by the M2 machine-guns include armour-piercing (AP), armour-piercing incendiary (API), armour-piercing incendiary-tracer (API-T), incendiary, standard ball and training.

Turret traverse and weapon elevation are electric at a rate of 60° per second, the gunner using a pair of control handles which also accommodate the triggers. The weapons continue to fire as long as there is sufficient ammunition left and the triggers are depressed. The M55 is a clear-weather system only, and the gunner has a standard M18 reflex sight to his front that projects a graticule image on an inclined glass plate. The graticule image consists of four concentric circles, each corresponding to various aircraft speeds, and three dots on a vertical line in the centre of the field of view that are used to determine line of sight and compensate for gravity pull on the projectile.

The M20 two-wheeled trailer can be towed by a light vehicle but not at speeds above 16 km/h (10 mph), and for this reason the M55 is normally carried in the rear of a 6×6 truck such as the American M35. The weapon can be fired from the truck or unloaded onto the ground with the aid of two channels, one of which is carried on each side of the truck. On the ground the M55 is supported by three jacks (one at the front and two at the rear) and the small road wheels are removed.

During World War II two self-propelled models of the M55 were built, and some of these still remain in service in South America and elsewhere. The M16 was based on the M3 halftrack, while the M17 was based on the M5 halftrack.

An American M55 quad 12.7-mm (0.50-calibre) anti-aircraft gun system is shown mounted in the rear of an M35 (6×6) truck. In addition to being used for the anti-aircraft role, it has also been used in the ground fire support role.

Specification
M55
Calibre: 12.7 mm (0.5 in)
Weights: travelling 1338 kg (2,950 lb); firing 975 kg (2,150 lb)
Dimensions: length travelling 2.89 m (9 ft 5.8 in); width travelling 2.09 m (6 ft 10.3 in); height travelling 1.606 m (5 ft 3.2 in)
Elevation: +90°/ 10°
Traverse: 360°
Ranges: effective horizontal 1500 m (1,640 yards); effective vertical 1000 m (3,281 ft)
Crew: 4

20-mm Vulcan light anti-aircraft gun

In the early 1960s the General Electric Company developed two anti-aircraft gun systems to meet the requirements of the US Army. Both of these used the same 20-mm cannon developed from the M61 series installed in high-speed fighter aircraft such as the Lockheed F-104 Starfighter. After trials with both systems at Fort Bliss, Texas (home of US Army air defence), both weapons were accepted for service. The self-propelled system, mounted on a modified M113 series armoured personnel carrier chassis, is called the M163 and was the replacement for the 40-mm M42 Duster self-propelled anti-aircraft gun. The towed model, called the **M167**, was the replacement for the 12.7-mm (0.5-in) M55 quadruple machine-gun system developed in World War II.

The M167 is still in front-line service with the US Army, where it is employed with airborne and airmobile divisions. Each of these formations has one air-defence battalion with a battalion headquarters and four batteries. Each of the latter has a battery headquarters and three firing platoons each with four M167 systems. Although the self-propelled M163 is to be replaced in the regular army by the twin 40-mm DIVAD, no decision has been taken on what will replace the M167, which has limited range and no all-weather capability.

The M167 low-level air-defence system consists of a two-wheeled carriage on which is mounted an electrically-powered turret containing the 20-mm **M168 Vulcan** cannon, the linked-feed ammunition system, and the fire controls.

The M168 Vulcan cannon has six barrels and two rates of fire, 1,000 and 3,000 rounds per minute. The slower rate is normally used against ground targets, while the higher rate is reserved for aerial targets. To conserve ammunition, the gunner can select bursts of 10, 30, 60 or 100 rounds from the total of 300 or 500 ready-use rounds provided. Ammunition is of the fixed type and includes armour-piercing-tracer (AP-T), high explosive incendiary (HEI) and high explosive incendiary-tracer (HEI-T), as well as the usual training rounds.

Turret traverse and weapon eleva-

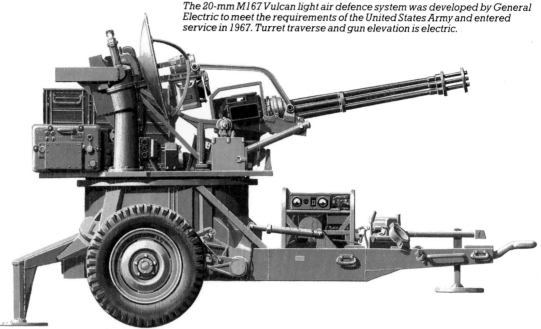

The 20-mm M167 Vulcan light air defence system was developed by General Electric to meet the requirements of the United States Army and entered service in 1967. Turret traverse and gun elevation is electric.

tion are electric, recharging being carried out by a generator installed on the forward part of the carriage. Turret traverse rate is 60° per second and weapon elevation rate is 45° per second.

The fire-control system on the M167 consists of a range-only radar on the right side of the mount, a sight current generator and a gyro lead-computing sight.

The M167 is normally towed by an M715 4×4 light truck and can also be slung under a helicopter. In addition to being used by the US Army, the M167 is also used by a number of other countries including Belgium, Ecuador, Israel, Jordan, Morocco, North Yemen, Saudi Arabia, Somalia, South Korea and Sudan.

Specification
Vulcan
Calibre: 20 mm (0.79 in)
Weights: travelling 1588 kg (3,501 lb); firing 1565 kg (3,450 lb)
Dimensions: length travelling 4.906 m (16 ft 1.1 in); width travelling 1.98 m

(6 ft 6 in); height travelling 2.038 m (6 ft 8.2 in)
Elevation: +80°/–5°
Traverse: 360°
Ranges: maximum horizontal 6000 m (6,562 yards); effective horizontal 2200 m (2,406 yards); maximum vertical 4500 m (14,764 ft); effective vertical 1200 m (3,937 ft)
Crew: 4-5 (1 on mount)

It is generally accepted that the 20-mm Vulcan anti-aircraft gun system has very limited capabilities. The M167 self-propelled model will be replaced by the 40-mm DIVAD, while the towed M163 will probably be replaced by a 25-mm gun or a new system combining a 25-mm gun and the Stinger missile.

Rheinmetall 20-mm twin light anti-aircraft gun

The **Rheinmetall 20-mm** light anti-aircraft gun was developed to meet the requirements of the West German ministry of defence by the Rheinmetall company of Düsseldorf. The mount is armed with two examples of the MK 20 Rh 202 20-mm cannon which is the standard weapon in its class in the West German army: it is also installed in the Marder mechanized infantry combat vehicle in a two-man power-operated turret; it arms the Wiesel light airportable armoured vehicle which has recently been ordered into production for West German airborne units; and it is fitted in a two-man turret on the Luchs 8×8 amphibious armoured car. The cannon is also installed on a single mount for various naval applications, and the Italians have installed the cannon in the FIAT/OTO Melara 6616 4×4 armoured car.

This 20-mm twin light anti-aircraft gun system is carried on a two-wheel

trailer that can be towed by a light vehicle such as a Mercedes-Benz Unimog 4×4 truck. The gunner is seated at the rear of the mount and aims the twin cannon using an Italian Galileo P56 computing sight which has an optical sight with a magnification of ×5, an electronic analogue computer for calculating the lead angles required to hit aerial targets, a joystick for elevation and traverse, and a panel for inserting target information.

A West German Rheinmetall twin 20-mm light anti-aircraft gun is seen in the firing position, showing the gunner's seat at the rear with the Italian Galileo P56 sight to his immediate front.

Elevation and traverse are hydraulic, maximum traverse speed being 80° per second and maximum elevation speed 48° per second, power for these functions being obtained from an air-cooled two-stroke petrol engine mounted under the gunner's seat.

The cannon are gas-operated and fully automatic, the gunner firing them via a foot-operated pedal that is fitted with a safety device. The gunner can select either single shots or full automatic with either barrel or both together. The cannon have a cyclic rate of fire of 2,000 rounds per barrel per minute and each cannon is provided with an ammunition box containing 270 rounds of fixed ammunition, another 10 rounds being in the flexible feed system that connects the ammunition boxes with the gun. Types of ammunition that can be fired include armour-piercing discarding sabot-tracer (APDS-T), armour-piercing incendiary-tracer (API-T), high explosive incendiary (HEI), high explosive incendiary-tracer (HEI-T), and various

training rounds. The APDS-T has a muzzle velocity of 1150 m (3,773 ft) per second.

In the firing position the weapon is supported on three outriggers. The system is essentially a clear-weather type, although it can be integrated into an overall defence system. In addition to being used by the West German armed forces it is also used by Argentina, Greece, Indonesia and Portugal. It was used by Argentina in the Falklands to defend Port Stanley airfield.

To meet the requirements of the Norwegian armed forces, Hispano-Suiza and A/S Kongsberg Vappenfabrikk designed and built a single-mount anti-aircraft gun called the **FK 20-2** which uses the same 20-mm cannon as the Rheinmetall twin 20-mm mount. This is used by the West German and Norwegian armies. In the future all of the 20-mm cannon of West Germany are expected to be replaced by the Mauser Model E 25-mm cannon, which was selected over the Rheinmetall Rh 205 25-mm cannon several years ago.

The Rheinmetall 20-mm MK 20 Rh 202 cannon is used in this twin anti-aircraft gun mount, the Marder MICV and the Luchs (8×8) reconnaissance vehicle. All of these guns will probably be replaced by the new Mauser Model E cannon, with longer range and improved ammunition.

Specification
Rheinmetall 20-mm mounting
Calibre: 20 mm (0.79 in)
Weights: travelling 2160 kg (4,762 lb); firing 1640 kg (3,616 lb)
Dimensions: length travelling 5.035 m (16 ft 6.2 in); width travelling 2.36 m (7 ft 8.9 in); height travelling 2.075 m (6 ft 9.7 in)
Elevation: +81.6°/−3.5°
Traverse: 360°
Ranges: maximum horizontal 6000 m (6,562 yards); maximum vertical 4500 m (14,764 ft); effective vertical 2000 m (6,562 ft)
Crew: 4-5 (but only 1 on mount)

Oerlikon 20-mm GAI-BO1 light anti-aircraft gun

The Oerlikon-Bührle 20-mm **GAI-BO1** light anti-aircraft gun was originally called the **10 ILa/5TG**, the 5TG standing for the actual cannon, which was subsequently called the KAB-001.

For many years Oerlikon-Bührle, now called Machine Tool Works Oerlikon-Bührle and based in Zurich, was in competition with Hispano-Suiza which also built an extensive range of light anti-aircraft weapons and their associated ammunition. In 1972 Hispano-Suiza was taken over by Oerlikon-Bührle and some of the former's weapons were subsequently integrated into the Oerlikon range. The HS-666A twin 20-mm weapon became the GAI-DO1, the 20-mm HS-639-B 3.1 became the GAI-CO1, the HS-639-B 4.1 became the GAI-CO3 while the HS-639-B5 became the GAI-CO4. By 1984 all of these had been phased out of production although they remained in service with many countries; for example, the GAI-CO1 is used by both Chile and South Africa.

The 20-mm GAI-BO1 was the lightest Oerlikon-Bührle weapon offered, although it too has now been phased out of service. It does, however, remain in use with many countries including Austria, South Africa, Spain and Switzerland. To provide greater mobility some countries have fitted the weapon in the rear of cross-country vehicles; for example, Austria has the weapon on the rear of the Steyr 6×6 vehicle with ready-use ammunition carried to the rear of the cab. The main drawback of systems such as the GAI-BO1 is that they rely on manual controls for elevation and traverse and therefore some operators find it difficult to track high-speed aircraft; no provision is made for radar fire control. Such systems do offer the advantage of being very light and can be disassembled into smaller parts for transportation in rough terrain where heavier weapons cannot be employed.

For travelling the GAI-BO1 is carried on a small two-wheeled carriage towed behind a light truck. The weapon can be brought into action in about 20 seconds, and is then supported on its outriggers.

For many years the 20-mm GAI-BO1 was the lightest in the extensive range of light anti-aircraft guns built by Oerlikon-Bührle. Traverse and elevation is manual, and drums of 20 or 50 rounds of ammunition can be fitted or a box holding just eight rounds.

An Oerlikon-Bührle 20-mm GAI-BO1 anti-aircraft gun is seen in the firing position. A key feature of this weapon is its very light weight, and it can be brought into action by its two-man crew in about 20 seconds.

The 20-mm cannon has a cyclic rate of fire of 1,000 rounds per minute, and the gunner can select either single shot or full automatic fire. Three types of magazine are available for this weapon: 50- and 30-round drums, and an eight-round box. The former two are normally used for anti-aircraft ammunition while the latter is for armour-piercing ammunition. The following types of ammunition can be fired by this cannon: armour-piercing-tracer (AP-T), high explosive incendiary-tracer (HEI-T), high explosive incendiary (HEI), semi-armour-piercing high explosive incendiary-tracer (SAPHEI-T), semi-armour-piercing high explosive incendiary (SAPHEI), and training.

The cannon is elevated by the gunner turning a handle, while traverse is obtained using the gunner's feet. An unusual feature of this weapon is that the gunner can also engage ground targets from the prone position; in this mode traverse is limited to 60° and elevation from −5° to +25°.

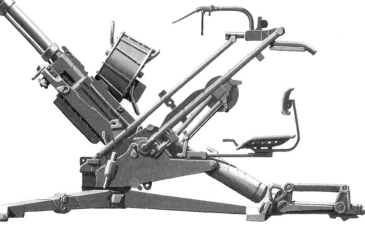

Specification
GAI-BO1
Calibre: 20 mm (0.79 in)
Weights: travelling 547 kg (1,206 lb); firing 405 kg (893 lb)
Dimensions: length travelling 3.85 m (12 ft 7.6 in); width travelling 1.55 m (5 ft 1 in); height travelling 2.50 m (8 ft 2.4 in)

Elevation: +85°/−5°
Traverse: 360°
Ranges: maximum horizontal 5700 m (6,234 yards); effective 2200 m (2,406 yards); maximum vertical 4500 m (14,764 ft); effective vertical 1500 m (4,921 ft)
Crew: 3 (1 on mount)

Oerlikon 20-mm GAI-DO1 light anti-aircraft gun

The Oerlikon-Bürhle twin 20-mm **GAI-DO1** light anti-aircraft gun was originally designed and built by Hispano-Suiza under the designation **HS-666A**, and was the most sophisticated 20-mm weapon in the company's range. The main advantages of the GAI-DO1 over the other 20-mm light anti-aircraft guns manufactured by the company were powered elevation and traverse, a new sight, and two rather than one 20-mm cannon.

The system is fitted with two 20-mm KAD series cannon with a cyclic rate of fire of 1,000 rounds per minute per barrel. Each barrel is provided with a box magazine that holds 120 rounds of fixed ammunition. The gunner can select either single shots, rapid single shot, bursts or full automatic fire. The ammunition fired by the GAI-CO1 is identical to that of the GAI-BO1.

The gunner is provided with a shield, and mounted under the gunner's seat is the Wankel engine which provides hydraulic power for cannon elevation and mount traverse, maximum elevation speed being 48° per second and maximum traverse speed 80° per second. As with all powered anti-aircraft guns, manual controls are provided for emergency use. The gunner also has an Italian Galileo P56 sight which is identical to that installed on the Rheinmetall twin 20-mm light anti-aircraft gun used by the West German armed forces. This allows the gunner to engage ground and aerial targets with a high hit probability.

In the firing configuration the GAI-DO1 is supported on three adjustable feet, and for transportation it is carried on a two-wheeled carriage towed by a light truck. From its travelling position the weapon can be brought into action by its crew in less than one minute.

The basic GAI-DO1 light anti-aircraft gun is a clear-weather system, and therefore limited to daylight use; in conditions of low cloud its effectiveness is much reduced. The weapon can, however, be used in conjunction with the Contraves (Italy) LPD-20 search radar, which would provide the gun with target information such as range and speed.

Oerlikon-Bürhle did offer a 25-mm anti-aircraft gun called the **GBI-AO1** with a single 25-mm KBA series cannon on a one-man mount with manual elevation and traverse. A feature of this weapon was that the dual-feed cannon was provided with two boxes of ammunition each containing 40 rounds, one holding armour-piercing discarding sabot-tracer (APDS-T) ammunition for engaging light armoured vehicles, and the other with high explosive incendiary-tracer (HEI-T) for engaging aerial targets. This weapon is no longer offered and is not known to have entered service in any quantity. In its place Oerlikon-Bürhle is now offering the much improved Diana twin 25-mm light anti-aircraft gun.

Specification
GAI-DO1
Calibre: 20 mm (0.79 in)
Weights: travelling with ammunition 1800 kg (3,968 lb); firing with ammunition 1330 kg (2,932 lb)
Dimensions: length travelling 4.59 m (15 ft 0.7 in); width travelling 1.86 m (6 ft 1.2 in); height travelling 2.34 m (7 ft 8.1 in)
Elevation: +81°/–3°
Traverse: 360°
Ranges: maximum horizontal 5700 m (6,234 yards); effective horizontal 2200 m (2,406 yards); maximum vertical 4500 m (14,764 ft); effective vertical 1500 m (4,921 ft)
Crew: 5 (1 on mount)

This Oerlikon-Bührle twin 20-mm GAI-DO1 light anti-aircraft gun in the firing position shows the Wankel engine under the gunner's seat. This is a clear-weather system, although a radar such as the Contraves LPD-20 could be used to provide early warning to a number of guns.

An Oerlikon-Bührle 20-mm GAI-DO1 twin light anti-aircraft gun in firing position. Mounted each side of the 20-mm cannon is a box of 120 rounds of ready-use ammunition. The gunner aims the weapon using an Italian Galileo P56 sighting and an aiming unit containing a computer.

Oerlikon 25-mm Diana light anti-aircraft gun

The Swiss company Oerlikon-Bürhle manufactures a wide range of 20-mm and 35-mm towed anti-aircraft gun systems, but some years ago realized that there was a gap between the most sophisticated 20-mm system (the twin GAI-DO1) and the twin 35-mm GDF series. To bridge this gap the company has developed the twin 25-mm **Diana** light anti-aircraft gun system, which has the company designation of the **GBF** series.

The Diana weighs only 2100 kg (4,630 lb) complete with ammunition, enabling it to be transported quickly by helicopters such as the Aérospatiale Puma or Sikorsky/Westland Sea King to where it is needed. The system is normally towed behind a light vehicle on its two-wheeled carriage. In the firing position the wheels are raised off the ground and the carriage is supported on three hydraulic jacks (one at the front and two at the rear) which can be adjusted to suit varying ground conditions.

So far two versions of the Diana are being offered, the **GBF-AOA** and the **GBF-BOB**. The first of these is armed with twin 25-mm KBA cannon, which is already used by four NATO countries installed in armoured vehicles and has a cyclic rate of fire of 570 rounds per barrel per minute. The 25-mm KBA fires five different types of ammunition: high explosive incendiary-tracer (HEI-T), semi-armour-piercing high explosive incendiary shell with tracer (SAPHEI-T), target practice with tracer (TP-T), armour-piercing discarding sabot-tracer (APDS-T), and armour-piercing practice-tracer (APP-T). The HEI-T is used to engage aerial targets while the APDS-T round is used against ground targets and will penetrate 25 mm (0.98 in) of armour at an angle of 30° at a range of 2000 m (2,187 yards). The GBF-AOA is fitted with the Italian P75 Galileo sight.

The GBF-BOB has the Oerlikon KBB cannon, which is also used on the Sea Zenith naval anti-missile defence system. The KBB has a longer barrel than the KBA, and fires ammunition with a

This Oerlikon-Bührle Diana twin 25-mm light anti-aircraft gun system in the firing position shows the wheels raised clear of the ground. Each cannon has a dual-feed system enabling the gunner to switch from one type of ammunition to another to engage either ground or air targets.

higher muzzle velocity and therefore greater target penetration. The GBF-BOB also has the Contraves Gun King sight which was first installed on the 35-mm GDF series of anti-aircraft gun. This features an optical sight with a magnification of ×5 and a 12° field of view, night sight, laser rangefinder with a range of 5000 m (5,468 yards) to an accuracy of ±5 m (5.46 yards), and a digital computer. Both the GBF-AOA and GBF-BOB have powered elevation and traverse to allow high-speed targets to be tracked: maximum traverse speed is 80° per second and maximum elevation speed is 48° per second.

The Diana can also be used in conjunction with the Contraves Sky Guard trailer-mounted fire-control system (originally designed for use with the Oerlikon GDF twin 35-mm cannon), which carries out both target surveillance and tracking. The Contraves Alerter radar can provide the gunner with the range and speed of the approaching target so the weapons are already laid in the general direction of the target as it appears.

As of early 1985 four prototypes of the Diana had been built with a turret suitable for installation on armoured vehicles.

The Oerlikon-Bührle Diana twin 25-mm light anti-aircraft gun has been introduced by the company to bridge the gap between its 20-mm and 35-mm weapons. Diana can be quickly brought into action and has rapid elevation and traverse, thanks to its on-board auxiliary power unit.

Specification
Diana
Calibre: 25 mm (0.98 in)
Weights: without ammunition 1725 kg (3,803 lb); with ammunition 2100 kg (4,630 lb)

Dimensions: length travelling 4.295 m (14 ft 1.1 in); width travelling 2.10 m (6 ft 10.7 in); height travelling 2.13 m (6 ft 11.9 in)
Elevation: +85°/–5°
Traverse: 360°

Ranges: maximum horizontal 6000 m (6,562 yards); effective horizontal 3000 m (3,281 yards); maximum vertical 5000 m (16,404 ft); effective vertical 2500 m (8,202 ft)
Crew: 4-5 (1 on mount)

Oerlikon 35-mm GDF anti-aircraft gun

In the late 1950s the Swiss company Oerlikon-Bührle developed a twin 35-mm towed anti-aircraft gun called the **1ZLA/353**, which today is more commonly known as the **GDF** series. Since this entered production in the early 1960s over 1,600 weapons have been built for sale to at least 20 countries. Known operators of the GDF series include Argentina, Austria, Brazil, Cameroun, Finland, Greece, Japan, South Africa, Spain and Switzerland. Early in 1985 it was announced that the British Royal Air Force Regiment was to form a new air-defence squadron equipped with the GDF twin 35-mm system to protect the Nimrod AEW base at Waddington, Lincolnshire. These GDF anti-aircraft guns were captured during 1982 in the Falklands, where they had been used by Argentina to defend Port Stanley airfield in conjunction with Rheinmetall twin 20-mm light anti-aircraft guns and Euromissile Roland surface-to-air missiles. It is believed that the Argentine GDFs shot down four British Aerospace Harrier aircraft and at least two Argentine aircraft as well.

The GDF twin 35-mm anti-aircraft gun system is mounted on a four-wheeled carriage. In the firing position the wheels are raised clear of the ground and supported on four jacks, one at each end and one on each side on outriggers. Weapon elevation and traverse are electro-hydraulic, traverse speed being a maximum of 112° per second and elevation a maximum of 56° per second.

Since its introduction the GDF has been constantly modernized and many of these modifications are now available in kit form to enable purchasers of older weapons to bring them up to the latest production standard. For example the basic weapon is fitted with a Ferranti sight but this can be replaced by the new Contraves Gun King mini-sight which also includes a

laser rangefinder.

The GDF series is armed with twin 35-mm KDB automatic cannon which have a cyclic rate of fire of 550 rounds per barrel per minute. The barrels are each fitted with a muzzle brake, and can be fitted with muzzle velocity-measuring equipment which feeds information to the fire-control system. A total of 112 rounds of ready-use ammunition is carried, with a further 126 rounds held in reserve on the mount. Each barrel has 56 rounds of ready-use ammunition in clips of seven rounds. Ammunition fired is of the fixed type and includes high explosive incendiary-tracer (HEI-T), high explosive incendiary (HEI), semi-armour-piercing high explosive incendiary-tracer (SAPHEI-T) and practice rounds.

The basic GDF is a clear-weather system only, but most countries prefer to use it in conjunction with a fire-control system. This was originally the Contraves Super Fledermaus, but this has been replaced in production by the much more effective Contraves Skyguard system. A typical GDF battery consists of two GDF twin 35-mm anti-aircraft guns, two generators and a single Skyguard fire-control system.

Twin 35-mm GDF anti-aircraft gun in travelling mode. When in firing position the carriage is raised clear of the ground and supported on four outriggers. This system is most effective when used with a fire control system such as the Swiss Contraves Skyguard.

Although designed primarily for use in the anti-aircraft role, the Oerlikon-Bührle twin 35-mm GDF anti-aircraft gun system is also highly effective in the ground role, and was thus used by the Argentine army against the British in the 1982 Falklands conflict.

Specification
GDF
Calibre: 35 mm (1.38 in)
Weights: travelling (with ammunition) 6700 kg (14,771 lb); travelling (without ammunition) 6300 kg (13,889 lb)
Dimensions: length travelling 7.80 m (25 ft 7.1 in); width travelling 2.26 m (7 ft 5 in); height travelling 2.60 m (8 ft 6.4 in)
Elevation: +92°/–5°

Traverse: 360°
Ranges: maximum horizontal 9500 m (10,389 yards); maximum vertical 6000 m (19,685 ft); effective vertical 4000 m (13,123 ft)
Crew: 3 (on mount)

40-mm Bofors L/70 anti-aircraft gun

The Swedish Bofors 40-mm L70 anti-aircraft gun is shown in the travelling position. This is the Model B with an auxiliary power unit mounted on the rear of the carriage, enabling the weapon to be run without any external power source and to be brought into action much faster.

Over 50 years ago the Bofors company developed a 40-mm towed anti-aircraft gun which within a few years became world famous. This had a 60-calibre barrel (resulting in the standard appellation Bofors 40 mm L/60) and had a cyclic rate of fire of 120 rounds per minute. This weapon was widely used during World War II and was manufactured under licence in many countries including the USA (as the M1), the UK (the Mk 1), Hungary, Italy and Poland. Even in 1985 the weapon remains in front-line service with more than 10 countries.

After the end of World War II a much-improved 40-mm light anti-aircraft gun was developed by Bofors, and this entered service in 1951 as the 40-mm **Bofors L/70**. In addition to having a longer 70-calibre barrel, the new weapon had a rate of fire increased to 300 rounds per minute (cyclic). This higher fire rate was achieved by ramming the new round during run-out and ejecting the empty cartridge cases forward of the mount towards the end of recoil. Initially two models of the Bofors 40-mm L/70 were offered, these being designated the **Bofors L/70 Model A** and **Bofors L/70 Model B**. The Model A relied on an external source for power while the Model B had its own generator mounted towards the front of the carriage.

The basic Bofors L/70 has a six-man crew, of whom four are on the carriage at all times: the elevation and traverse layers are seated one on each side of the mount, while two ammunition feeders are placed one on each side at the rear. Ammunition is fed to the weapon in clips of four rounds and an ammunition tray above the weapon can hold 26 rounds of ready-use ammunition. At the rear of the mount, one on each side, are ready-use racks that hold 96 rounds of ammunition.

Weapon elevation and mount traverse are electro-hydraulic, with manual controls for emergency use. Maximum elevation speed is 45° per second and maximum traverse speed is 85° per second.

Ammunition development is a continuous process at Bofors, and today five basic rounds are available for the Bofors L/70 anti-aircraft gun in its land and numerous naval applications. All ammunition fired by the gun is of the fixed type. The five types are pre-fragmented high explosive (PFHE), high-capacity high explosive (HCHE), high explosive-tracer (HE-T), armour-piercing capped-tracer (APC-T), and training. Additional details of the Bofors L/70 ammunition and its associated fire-control systems are given elsewhere.

In the firing position the wheels are raised clear of the ground and the carriage is supported on four jacks, one at each end of the carriage and one on each side on outriggers.

The Bofors L/70 has been made under licence in a number of countries including the UK, Italy, Spain, India, West Germany and the Netherlands. It is normally towed by a 4×4 or 6×6 truck, which also carries the crew and supply of ready-use ammunition. In some countries, for example the UK and West Germany, the Bofors L/70 has now been replaced by missiles such as Rapier or Roland. Nevertheless, with an up-to-date fire-control system, the Bofors L/70 remains a highly effective weapon system.

Specification
Bofors L/70

Calibre: 40 mm (1.57 in)
Weights: travelling (with generator) 5150 kg (11,354 lb); travelling (without generator) 4800 kg (10,582 lb)
Dimensions: length travelling 7.29 m (23 ft 11 in); width travelling 2.25 m (7 ft 4.6 in); height travelling 2.349 m (7 ft 8.5 in)
Elevation: +90°/−4°
Traverse: 360°
Ranges: maximum horizontal 12500 m (13,670 yards); maximum vertical 8700 m (28,543 ft); effective vertical 4000 m (13,123 ft)
Crew: 6 (4 on mount)

The Bofors gun has been primarily designed to engage aerial targets but can also be used with deadly effect against ground targets, including armoured personnel carriers with their thin armour. When engaging the latter an armour-piercing capped-tracer (APC-T) round is normally used.

Right: The 40-mm L70 Bofors gun has a cyclic rate of fire of 300 rounds per minute, but practical rate of fire is lower. The ammunition is fed to the gun in clips of four rounds, with the empty cartridge cases being ejected under the forward part of the mount. A maximum of 26 rounds of ammunition are for ready use.

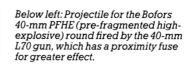

Below left: Projectile for the Bofors 40-mm PFHE (pre-fragmented high-explosive) round fired by the 40-mm L70 gun, which has a proximity fuse for greater effect.

Below: Cross-section of the new Bofors 40-mm PFHE (pre-fragmented high-explosive) round, with the fuse on the right and high-explosive content on left.

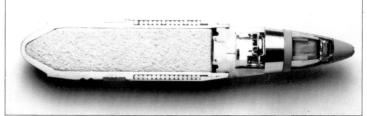

Anti-Tank Weapons

During the last 30 years of the Cold War, in no other class of weapon was there so much design and development activity as there was in anti-tank armaments. Scarcely a year passed without a new weapon being proposed, a course of events which reflected the major perceived threat of the time: the Soviet tank armies.

The group of weapons covered in this chapter illustrate the approaches which designers have taken in their search for a light, portable and accurate method of countering the main battle tank (MBT). The choice is whether to opt for a gun or a missile.

Since size and portability are paramount, an anti-tank gun has to be light and recoilless and capable of being carried by at most two men. These demands automatically condemn it to having a relatively low velocity, so that a shaped-charge projectile is the only possible type. The penetrative power that can be delivered from such a shoulder-fired weapon is astonishing. The gun is also, to a great degree, more versatile than a missile, since the operator can rapidly swing from target to target and engage other adversaries besides tanks if need be.

So, to some extent, can the missile operator, but the price of his missile is probably a few hundred times greater than the price of a round from a recoilless gun, and he is not encouraged to waste them on less vital targets. Two types of missile are shown here: first- and second-generation. The first generation was called MCLOS (Manual Command to Line of Sight). In other words, the

The next step? An artist's impression of LOSAT – the Line of Sight Anti-Tank missile, which will fly at hypersonic speeds and carry an armour-piercing warhead.

firer actually steered the missile by means of a joystick. This demanded great skill and long training. It was replaced by the second generation: SACLOS (Semi-Automatic Command to Line of Sight). In this system the missile carries a flare in its tail which is 'seen' by the firing post sight unit. The operator merely keeps his sight aligned with the target. If

the missile deviates from the line of sight the system automatically computes a correction and steers the missile back to the correct trajectory. As in the case of recoilless guns, the shaped charge is the preferred warhead, and most can penetrate almost one metre (39 in) of armour plate.

Now we are on the threshold of the third generation – the Fire

and Forget missile. With this, the operator will aim at a target and 'acquire' it. The missile is then fired and follows its lock to fly to its selected target. The operator, once he has fired, can turn his attention to another target. This type will appear in the 21st century as Trigat, a multi-national development which will outfit NATO in the future.

BAe Swingfire

Swingfire is the standard long-range ATGW of the British army, and is used from tracked vehicles. In its Beeswing guise the missile is produced under licence by Egypt to replace the obsolete Soviet AT-1 'Snapper' missile.

The **BAe Swingfire** is the British army's long-range wire-guided ATGW, and was designed originally for use on vehicles operating with armoured units. Allocated to the Royal Artillery, the Swingfire is mounted on the Striker (five with five reloads) and the FV438 (two with 14 reloads) armoured vehicles. Both can engage targets in either the direct or separated-fire modes. In the latter the controller can site himself up to 100 m (110 yards) from the launch point and up to 23 m (75 ft) higher, with the target up to 20° above or below the horizontal axis and up to 45° to each side of the concealed launcher's bearing. The Swingfire has now been adapted to fit on almost any vehicle and, in the **Beeswing** version, can be used from a removable crew-served launcher assembly. Once fired the missile is automatically gathered into the control sight's field of view, after which the operator flies the missile to the target by a joystick control. The warhead is able to defeat the armour of all known battle tanks. To improve the missile's combat capabilities a thermal-imaging sight has been developed for night engagements, and micro-miniaturized electronics have been introduced to increase reliability and maintainability. The Beeswing was made under licence in Egypt, who also supplied them to Syria. Swingfire is no longer used by the British Army but is still held by Belgium, Egypt and Kenya.

Specification
Swingfire
Type: anti-tank missile
Dimensions: length 1.07 m (3 ft 6 in); diameter 17.0 cm (6.7in); span 37.3 cm (1 ft 2.7 in)
Launch weight: 27 kg (60 lb)
Propulsion: two-stage solid-propellant booster/sustainer rocket
Performance: range 150-4000 m (165-4,375 yards)
Warhead: 7-kg (15.4-lb) hollow-charge HE
Armour penetration: 800 mm (31.5 in) or more

A British Army FV438 fires a Swingfire ATGW from its roof-mounted missile launcher rack assembly. The 4000-m (4,375-yard) range missile has a 7-kg (15.4-lb) hollow charge warhead capable of defeating the armour of all current main battle tanks.

Hunting LAW80

LAW 80 is a lightweight, one-shot, disposable anti-tank weapon developed to replace the 60-mm M72 LAW and supplement the Carl Gustav 84-mm gun in British army service. It was designed to defeat the frontal armour of the heaviest tank, and the rocket has a calibre of 94-mm. The shaped charge warhead can defeat 700-mm of homogeneous armour, though its chances in an attack against the current range of MBTs is marginal due to the compound and sloped armour.

LAW 80 has an extendible launching tube pre-loaded with a shaped-charge rocket. The launcher incorporates a 9-mm calibre aiming rifle firing a special cartridge which matches the trajectory of the rocket. The launcher is collapsed: when required to fire, the end caps are discarded, and the launch tube extended. The firer switches to 'Arm' and selects the aiming rifle on a trigger selector. Pressing the trigger fires the aiming rifle: the bullet has a tracer and an explosive head to indicate its strike. The aiming rifle is a self-loader with five rounds on its sealed magazine. The firer aims through a collimating sight, but the launcher also has a bracket to fit a night-sight.

The rocket motor is burnt before it leaves the launcher tube, but the signature of the weapon is a loud explosion and a bright flash. The warhead uses a double-skinned false nose to acts as a contact switch for the base fuse which detonates the charge.

Specification:
Type: shoulder-fired rocket
Dimensions: folded 1 m (39.37 in); extended 1.5 m (59 in). Calibre 94-mm (3.7-in)
Weight: In carry mode 10 kg (22 lb); firing mode: 9 kg (19.8 lb); rocket 4.6 kg (10.14 lb)
Effective range: 20 to 500 metres
Armour penetration: 700 mm (27.5 in).

Bofors Bantam

The **Bofors Bantam** is a small first-generation one-man portable manual command to line of sight wire-guided missile produced by AB Bofors. The missile container holds both the missile and a 20-m (66-ft) control cable which connects the missile to the control unit, which can take up to three missiles. Distribution boxes can be connected to each of the cables to boost this number to 18. To bring the Bantam into action the container is placed on the ground and the control unit is connected (if necessary extra cable can be used to displace the operator by up to 120 m/130 yards from the missile site). The operator then selects from between one and four of the tracking flares carried on the missile (according to the prevailing conditions of visibility) and launches the

The ground-launched version of the AB Bofors Bantam ATGW emerges from its container-launcher box under power from the booster. After 40 m (44 yards) of wire is reeled out, a micro-switch ignites the sustainer motor.

Right: The Swedish Bantam was one of the first generation wire-guided ATGWs, and was produced in large numbers until 1978 for the armies of Sweden and Switzerland. It is one of the smallest and lightest of the ATGWs and introduced into service the GRP airframe with folding wings.

The Bantam can also be used from fixed-wing light aircraft, or helicopters such as the Swedish army Agusta-Bell AB.204 Huey seen

here. The Swedes are already supplementing this old missile with quantities of the modern American TOW.

Bantam. The sustainer and flare are ignited after 40 m (130 ft) of guidance wire have been reeled out and the booster section has burnt out. The warhead is armed after 230 m (250 yards) and the operator manually guides the missile to the target. Only two countries, Sweden and Switzerland, adopted the Bantam, in 1963 and 1967 respectively, in a variety of launching modes including one from light fixed-wing aircraft. Production finished in the 1970s, and although the missile is considered to be obsolete it is still found in some numbers with those countries.

Specification
Bantam
Type: anti-tank missile
Dimensions: length 0.85 m (2 ft 9.46 in); diameter 11.0 cm (4.33 in); span 40.0 cm (15.75 in)
Launch weight: including the container 11.5 kg (25.35 lb)
Propulsion: two-stage solid-propellant booster/sustainer rocket
Performance: range 300-2000 m (330-2,190 yards)
Warhead: 1.9-kg (4.2-lb) hollow-charge HE
Armour penetration: 500 mm (19.68 in) or more

SWEDEN

FFV Ordnance Carl Gustav

Right: The Carl Gustav is normally fired by a two-man crew, one acting as the gunner and the other as the loader. A well-trained team can fire about six rounds per minute at moving or stationary armoured vehicles out to 400-500 m (437-547 yards) distance.

The 84-mm (3.31-in) calibre M2 Carl Gustav is seen here with the HEAT and HE rounds that it fires, together with the canisters in which they are carried.

The 84-mm (3.31-in) calibre **FFV Ordnance Carl Gustav** recoilless gun is intended for use by the infantry as a medium anti-armour weapon. It is normally crewed by two men, one acting as the firer and the other as the loader and ammunition carrier. A well-trained crew can sustain a rate of fire of six rounds per minute. The weapon is breech-loaded and can be fired from the shoulder, from the prone position, from the edge of a trench or from a mount on an APC. The usual sighting system on the **Carl Gustav M2** model is a ×2 telescope with a 17° field of view. The M2 can effectively engage a stationary armoured vehicle at 500-m (545-yard) range with the FFV551 HEAT round, and a moving target at ranges up to 400 m (435 yards) with a penetration of 400 mm (15.75 in). It is also a useful infantry support weapon in that it can fire the 3.1-kg (6.8-lb) spin-stabilized FFV545 illuminating round to 2300 m (2,515 yards), the 3.1-

kg (6.8-lb) FFV469 smoke round to 1300 m (1,420 yards) and the 3.1-kg (6.8-lb) FFV441 HE shrapnel round to an effective range of 1000 m (1,095 yards).

An improved version with a better sight, the **Carl Gustav M2-550**, has also been produced to fill the gap between close-range weapons and the ATGW. This uses a higher-velocity rocket-assisted HEAT round, the FFV551, which has a maximum effective engagement range of 700 m (765 yards) with the same armour-penetration capability as the FFV551 round, and can also fire the rounds mentioned above. A new 3.2-kg (7.1-lb) dual-purpose HE/HEAT FFV502 projectile is also under development for the Carl Gustav series, this being designed for use against light armoured vehicles (out to 250 m/275 yards with 200-mm/ 7.87 in armour penetration or more) as well as unprotected targets to 1000 m

(1,095 yards). In order to defeat the new composite-armour tanks, production is about to start of the FFV597 two-piece over-calibre rocket-assisted fin-stabilized HEAT round with a stand-off probe fuse to give optimum penetration effect. The FFV597 consists of a 4-kg (8.8-lb) warhead section, which is inserted into the muzzle of the gun, and a 3-kg (6.6-lb) propulsion cartridge which is loaded as normal. The 5.8-kg

(12.8-lb) projectile has a range in excess of 300 m (330 yards) and can penetrate over 900 mm (35.43 in) of frontal armour.

A lightweight version of the standard weapon, the **Carl Gustav M3**, entered production in 1984 and is able to fire all the existing types of ammunition. The Carl Gustav has seen extensive combat use throughout the world, including use with the British forces on

the Falklands in 1982. The basic Carl Gustav M2 is used by Australia, Austria, Canada, Denmark, Eire, Ghana, the Netherlands, Norway, Sweden, the United Arab Emirates, UK, East Germany and several other countries; the Carl Gustav M2-550 is operated by Japan, Sweden and other countries; and the Carl Gustav M3 is used only by Sweden.

Specification
Carl Gustav
Type: anti-tank rocket-launcher
Dimensions: length 1.13 m (3 ft 8.5 in); calibre 8.4 cm (3.31 in)
Weight: M2 14.2 kg (31.3 lb), M2-550 15 kg (33.1 lb) and M3 8 kg (17.6 lb)
Performance: range see text
Ammunition: see text
Armour penetration: see text

Aérospatiale SS.11

Originally developed by Nord-Aviation, the **Aérospatiale SS.11** started life in 1953 as the **Type 5210** and entered service with the French army in 1956. Apart from its normal ground- or vehicle-launched role, it can also be launched from a helicopter or ship. It is a manually-guided line-of-sight weapon, the operator acquiring the target by means of a telescopic sight. As soon as the missile enters his field of view after launch the operator commands it to his line of sight via a joystick control and wires, and then flies it to the target using tracking flares mounted on the rear of the missile for visual reference. From 1962 a modified **SS.11B1** variant was produced with transistorized firing equipment. This weapon can be fitted with a variety of warheads including the Type 140AC anti-tank, the Type 140AP02 semi-armour-piercing delay-action anti-personnel, and the Type 140AP59 anti-personnel fragmentation. Production ceased at the beginning of the 1980s after some 179,000 rounds of the SS.11 family had been built for more than 20 countries. A modified SS.11 derivative with a much improved semi-automatic guidance system, the **Harpon**, was

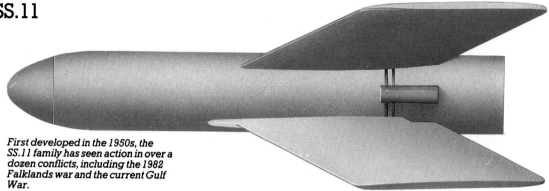

First developed in the 1950s, the SS.11 family has seen action in over a dozen conflicts, including the 1982 Falklands war and the current Gulf War.

produced in some numbers for the French West German and Saudi Arabian armies from 1967 onwards. The SSII was a pioneer; it was tested by almost every army in the world and influenced the design of many later missiles. It was used in several conflicts, including the Falklands campaign and the Iran/Iraq Gulf War,

and it was purchased by many countries, including Argentina, France, India, Iran, Iraq, Italy, Portugal, Tunisia, Turkey, the UK and Venezuela. It was, though, rapidly superseded by improved missiles using better guidance technology during the early 1980s and became obsolete in about 1985.

France used the SS.11 when it was amongst the earliest missiles to arm helicopters for the anti-tank role, as exemplified by the Aérospatiale Alouette III in action here.

Produced in large numbers since 1956, the SS.11 has served in many armies on a wide variety of vehicles. This triple launcher was photographed in Portugal.

Specification
SS.11B1
Type: anti-tank missile
Dimensions: length 1.20 m (3 ft 11.25 in); diameter 16.40 cm (6.46 in); span 50.00 cm (1 ft 7.7 in)
Launch weight: 29.9 kg (65.9 lb)
Propulsion: two-stage solid-propellant rocket
Performance: range 500-3000 m (545-3,280 yards)
Warhead: see text
Armour penetration: Type 140AC 600 mm (23.62 in) and Type 140AP02 10 mm (0.4 in)

Euromissile HOT

The **Euromissile HOT** is the heavyweight spin-stabilized tube-launched wire-guided counterpart to the MILAN for use from dug-out positions, vehicles and helicopters. Planned as the direct replacement for the SS.11, the HOT has automatic command to line of sight guidance with an IR tracking system. All the operator has to do is to keep his optical tracking sight on the target to ensure a hit. This guidance system allows a very rapid gathering of the missile to the line of sight after launch, thus enabling a very

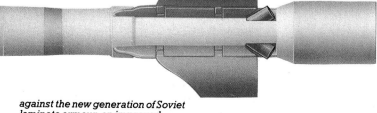

The long-range HOT is designed to be fired from vehicles, helicopters and fixed static positions against tanks, infantry combat vehicles and APC targets. To ensure its lethality

against the new generation of Soviet laminate armour, an improved hollow-charge warhead is under development.

good short-range engagement envelope. Vehicles which have been fitted with the system include the M113 APC (two launchers with 11 reloads), the AMX10P APC (four launchers with 16-20 reloads), the Panhard M3 APC (four launcher with 14 reloads), the Saviem VAB armoured vehicle (four launchers with eight reloads) and the Raketenjagdpanzer tank destroyer 3 (one launcher with 8 reloads). The helicopter types that have been fitted include the MBB PAH1 (six rounds), the Aérospatiale SA 341 and SA 342L Gazelle (four or six rounds), the Aérospatiale SA 361H Dauphin (eight rounds) and the Westland Lynx (eight rounds). The large hollow-charge warhead is detonated by distortion of the

A West German army Jagdpanzer Jaguar 1 tank destroyer fires a Euromissile HOT ATGW. The 316 Jaguars were rebuilt from Jagdpanzer Rakete vehicles equipped with two launchers for the less capable SS.11 ATGW during the period 1978-83.

nose skin to allow incidence attacks of up to 65°. The warhead is said to be capable of penetrating the armour of all known battle tanks in frontal attacks. The Syrians used HOT against the Israelis in the 1982 'Peace for Galilee' war from Gazelle helicopters on up to 100 occasions, and credit the system with destroying a sizable number of Israeli tanks and APCs. The Iraqis also

use it against the Iranians in the Gulf War from both vehicle and helicopter platforms. Euromissile, the manufacturer, states that as at early 1984 14 countries have ordered 52,907 missiles. Current operators of the HOT missile are Egypt, France, Iraq, Kuwait, Libya, Saudi Arabia, Spain, Syria, West Germany and five undisclosed countries.

Specification
HOT
Type: anti-tank missile
Dimensions: length 1.275 m (4 ft 2.2 in); diameter 16.5 cm (6.5 in); span 31.2 cm (12.28 in)
Launch weight: missile 23.5 kg (51.8 lb)

The Panhard 4×4 VCR APC, armed with the Euromissile Mephisto launcher system for the HOT long range ATGW. The UTM800 HOT turret variant of the 6×6 Panhard VCR/TT has already seen combat with the Iraqi army during the Gulf War.

and missile in launch tube 32 kg (70.55 lb)
Propulsion: solid-propellant booster/sustainer rocket
Performance: range 75-4250 m (82-4,650 yards)
Warhead: 6-kg (13.2-lb) hollow-charge HE
Armour penetration: 800 mm (31.5 in) or more

FRANCE/WEST GERMANY
Euromissile MILAN

The **Euromissile MILAN** is an advanced wire-guided second-generation man-portable spin-stabilized ATGW, and started life in 1962 as a design study between Nord-Aviation and Messerschmitt-Bölkow. It incorporates a semi-automatic guidance technique that requires the operator only to maintain the cross hairs of his guidance unit sight on the target during the engagement. The system comprises a launch-and-control unit and a missile in a container-launcher tube, which is mounted on the launcher/controller just before firing. The whole system can then be mounted on a tripod for ground launch or on a pivot for vehicle launch. Since it attained operational status the MILAN has had a night-firing capability developed for it in the form of the MIRA thermal imaging device for the French, West German and British armies. This consists of a 7-kg (15.4-lb) imaging sight which is mounted on the firing post to allow the detection of targets at over 3000 m (3,280 yards)

The MILAN has already seen combat service in a number of conflicts including Chad, where one was used to knock out a Panhard ERC armoured car that had been captured by the Libyan-backed rebels.

Above: The MILAN was used extensively in the 1982 Falklands war by the British army and Royal Marines, who fired several hundred

against well-prepared bunkers and emplacements in the hills and mountains barring the way to Port Stanley.

and their engagement at about 1500 m (1,640 yards). Once the missile has been launched, the forces inherent in the system throw the used container-launcher (which has been automatically disconnected) backwards from the firing post for reloading. The missile is automatically tracked in flight by an IR unit in the control unit, which monitors the radiation output from the tail-mounted flares on the missile. MILAN 2, introduced in 1984, had a warhead of 115 mm diameter to improve the frontal attack performance. The adoption of explosive reactive armour led to MILAN 2T in 1993, with a tandem warhea: two shaped charges designed so the first detonates the tank's explosive armour, and the second penetrates the exposed base armour. MILAN 3 appeared in 1995; this is MILAN 2T with an improved guidance system. Instead of a simple flare, it uses a xenon lamp flashing in a coded sequence. The firing post 'learns' this code when the missile is loaded, and during flight the guidance system responds only to that coded lamp,

ignoring flares, fires and other heat sources which could confuse it.

Specification
Type: anti-tank missile
Dimensions: length 0.769 m (2 ft 6.28 in); diameter 9.0 cm (3.54 in); span 26.5 cm (10.43 in)
Launch weight: missile 6.65 kg (14.66 lb) and complete launcher outfit (with control unit, launcher tube and tripod) 16.5 kg (36.38 lb)
Propulsion: solid-propellant booster/sustainer rocket
Performance: range 25-2000 m (27-2,190 yards)
Warhead: 2.98-kg (6.57-lb) hollow-charge HE
Armour penetration: 650 mm (25.6 in) or more

The man-portable Euromissile MILAN, mounted on the rear of a West German army Faun Kraka 4×2 light vehicle. The MILAN-equipped Kraka with six reload missiles has replaced the 106-mm recoilless rifle vehicles of the same type.

MBB Cobra and Mamba

The **MBB Cobra** started life in 1957 as a project by Bölkow GmbH, and went into service three years later in an initial 1600-m (1,750-yard) range form with the West German army. Since then some 170,000 or more rounds have been produced in both this form and the 2000-m (2,185-yard) range definitive **BO810 Cobra 2000** version for the armed forces of 18 countries. A first-generation ATGW, the Cobra is a one man line-of-sight wire-guided missile that is set up by being placed on the ground in a suitable space, with its nose preferably pointing in the required direction. The operator can deploy up to eight missiles in this fashion, the missiles being connected via 20-m (66-ft) cables to a junction box and thus to his control unit, which may itself be deployed up to a further 50 m (165 ft) away. The operator uses the controller to select and fire the round that is in the best position to engage the target. Once launched, the missile is given a vertical boost to rise into the air, where the limited-duration sustainer takes over. The operator then rapidly gathers the missile into his line of sight and flies the missile to the target with the aid of a joystick and tail-mounted flares.

In 1972 MBB announced a successor to the Cobra 2000 known as the **Mamba**. Of the same general appearance, this weapon system has a new and improved controller that can be attached to up to 12 missiles, and a new propulsion unit which allows jet lift throughout the flight at a higher maximum speed to give a shorter flight time. The Mamba is still in production and has replaced the Cobra in a number of armies with the added bonus that it can be fired from a five-round missile-launch frame mounted on a vehicle. The Cobra was used in combat during the Indo-Pakistan War of 1971 and by Israel against the Arabs in 1973. Like all first-generation missiles, both Cobra and Mamba are no longer in service, though some may still be used for training purposes. Almost all the countries who used them have

now re-equipped with second-generation missiles such as Milan and TOW.

Above: The first post-war German missile, the Cobra, achieved operational status with the West German army in 1960. Since then it has been superseded by the Mamba depicted here.

Below: Argentina took supplies of Cobras to the Falklands in their 1982 invasion, although none saw any use. Left-over stores were destroyed in controlled explosions.

Specification
Cobra

Type: anti-tank missile
Dimensions: length 0.95 m (3 ft 1.4 in); diameter 10.0 cm (3.93 in); span 48.0 cm (1 ft 6.6 in)
Launch weight: 10.3 kg (22.7 lb)
Propulsion: solid-propellant booster/sustainer rocket
Performance: range 400-2000 m (435-2,190 yards)
Warhead: 2.7-kg (5.95-lb) hollow-charge HE or anti-tank shrapnel
Armour penetration: hollow charge 500 mm (19.69 in) and shrapnel 350 mm (13.78 in)

Specification
Mamba

Type: anti-tank missile
Dimensions: length 0.955 m (3 ft 1.6 in); diameter 12.0 cm (4.72 in); span 40.0 cm (1 ft 3.75 in)
Launch weight: 11.2 kg (24.7 lb)
Propulsion: solid-propellant booster/sustainer rocket
Performance: range 300-2000 m (330-2,190 yards)
Warhead: 2.7-kg (5.95-lb) hollow-charge HE
Armour penetration: 500 m (19.69 in)

The Cobra ATGW was used in combat during the 1965 Indo-Pakistan war, with limited results. Despite this the missile is used by a number of armies in conjunction with other systems as a very useful man-portable unit.

Above: A Cobra sectioned to show the major internal subsystems. The booster rocket used to launch the missile can be seen between the lower pair of wings, its nozzle deflected downwards to give the sudden initial jump into the air on firing.

USA
Hughes BGM-71 TOW

The **Hughes BGM-71 TOW** (Tube-launched Optically-tracked Wire-guided) heavy anti-tank missile for helicopter- or vehicle-launch application entered the design phase in 1962, the first guided firings taking place in 1968. Two years later TOW entered service, and by the summer of 1972 had seen its first combat firings when it was used against North Vietnamese tank units. During the 1973 Yom Kippur War the Israelis had it delivered as part of the arms lift by the USA, and by 1984 the missile had been used in many conflicts all over the world. On the strength of its operational success the TOW has become the West's most numerous ATGW with over 350,000 units so far produced for more than 25 countries. As in most contemporary systems, all the operator has to do is keep the cross hairs of his optical sight on the target, an IR sensor tracking the signal from the missile to permit the calculation of correction commands which are automatically sent via the guidance wire link. In order to improve the lethality of the warhead of infantry units' TOW missiles, a two-stage upgrade programme was adopted: the first phase was marked by the procurement of a warhead of 127-mm (5-in) diameter fitted with a telescopic nose probe fuse that pops out when the missile is in flight to give an optimum stand-off penetration

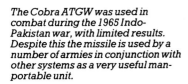

The TOW is now a standard Western ATGW system and has been produced in four versions: the basic TOW as shown, the enhanced-range TOW, the improved TOW and the TOW 2.

capability, the missile fitted with this warhead being known as the **Improved TOW**; the second stage saw the introduction of the **TOW 2** missile, which has a 152-mm (6-in) diameter warhead fitted with telescopic nose probe, improved digital guidance and a new propulsion system. All these improvements are also being retrofitted to the helicopter and armoured vehicle TOW launcher systems. TOW 2A adds a second shaped charge to the warhead so as to destroy explosive reactive armour and prepare the way for the main charge. TOW 2B is specifically designed to attack the upper surfaces of the tank by means of two special warheads aimed downwards and

firing explosively formed many fragments. The missile is programmed to fly over the top of the target and a dual-mode laser/magnetic sensor system detonates the two warheads at the appropriate point, maximising effectiveness, so as to strike downwards through the turret roof.

Specification
TOW

Type: anti-tank missile
Dimensions: length 1.174 m (3 ft 10.2 in) for basic model, 1.555 m (5 ft 1.2 in) for Improved TOW with probe, and 1.714 m (5 ft 7.5 in) for TOW 2 with probe; diameter 15.2 cm (6 in); span 34.3 cm (13.5 in)

Launch weight: 22.5 kg (49.6 lb) for basic model, 25.7 kg (56.65 lb) for Improved TOW, and 28.1 kg (61.95 lb) for TOW 2
Propulsion: two-stage solid-propellant rocket
Performance: range 65-3000 m (70-3,280 yards) for pre-1976 models, and 65-3750 m (70-4,100 yards) for post-1976 models
Warhead: 3.9-kg (8.6-lb) shaped-charge HE for basic and Improved TOW models, and 5.9-kg (13-lb) shaped-charge HE for TOW 2 model
Armour penetration: 600 mm (23.62 in) for basic model, 700 mm (27.56 in) for Improved TOW, and 800 mm (31.5 in) or more for TOW 2

173

McDonnell Douglas M47 Dragon

Above: Dragon has been supplied to a number of nations and is currently being used in combat by Iran against Iraq in the Gulf war. Propulsion is by 60 small rocket sustainers which fire in pairs and control attitude.

Right: The Dragon Medium Anti-tank/Assault Weapon is a tube-launched, optically tracked wire-guided missile operated by one man, who normally sits with his legs extended forward and the launcher resting on his shoulder, with the forward end of the smooth-bore glass fibre tube supported by a stand.

The manpack nature of Dragon is ideal for infantry units, as they can literally carry it on their backs around the battlefield. Further improvements to the missile to increase its range and lethality are under investigation in order to counter the current Soviet armour plate laminate types.

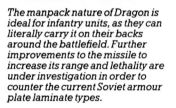

The **McDonnell Douglas M47 Dragon** (or **Medium Anti-tank/Assault Weapon**) was conceived in 1966 when an engineering development contract was awarded to the then McDonnell Aircraft Corporation. In 1972 the go-ahead was given to the follow-on McDonnell Douglas Corporation (MDC) for the first part of a multi-year procurement programme. From Fiscal Year 1975 onwards the procurement

was established initially on a two-source basis from MDC and Raytheon, though from 1975 the latter became sole source, with MDC as prime contractor. The Dragon is a one-man tube-launched optically-tracked wire-guided anti-tank weapon, with the front of the smooth-bore fibreglass tube supported on a stand and the firer normally seated with his legs extended forward with the mid-section of the tube resting on his shoulder. Once the missile has been fired the operator has no other task than keeping his cross hairs centred on the target. The missile is tracked in flight by a sensor that monitors the output from an infra-red transmitter on the missile's tail, and the displacement of this from the line of sight is measured. Any corrective commands are then sent via the wire.

Recently a 4.5 kg (9.9 lb) thermal imaging sight has been put into production to give the missile a night-firing capability. Superdragon, or Dragon II+, is a much improved model introduced in the early 1990s meant to serve until the introduction of the next generation of anti-tank system, expected in the early 2000s. The range is increased to 2000 m by using a heavier propulsion charge.

Dragon IIT is a special version requested by Turkey in 1993 and this model carries a tandem warhead fully capable of defeating explosive reactive armour.

Specification
M47 Dragon
Type: anti-tank missile

Dimensions: length 0.744 m (2 ft 5.3 in); diameter 12.7 cm (5 in); span 33.0 cm (1 ft 1 in)
Launch weight: missile 6.2 kg (13.66 lb) and whole system 13.8 kg (30.4 lb)
Propulsion: solid-propellant rocket after gas launch
Performance: range 75-1000 m (82-1,095 yards)
Warhead: 2.45-kg (5.4-lb) shaped-charge HE
Armour penetration: 600 mm (23.62 in)

The considerable debris and blast created by Dragon firing is evident in this photograph. Once fired, the fibreglass launcher is discarded and the tracking unit is clipped to a new launcher with its sealed-in missile.

ADATS

ADATS (Air Defence and Anti-Tank System) was developed by Oerlikon-Bührle of Switzerland as a private venture from 1979 onward and was envisaged as a single unit which could function equally well on the air defence or anti-tank roles. It was adopted by the Canadian Army as their Low Level Air Defence System in 1986. 36 equipments have been put into service by the Canadians, mounted on a modified M113A2 APC chassis, and eight were purchased by the USA, on modified M2 Bradley chassis, for extensive testing for their Forward Air Defense System requirement; in spite of successful tests, financial restraints have prevented much progress on this project.

The main part of the system is a power-operated turret that can be traversed through 360°, with the operator seated under cover between two banks of four missiles in launch containers. The latter can be elevated to +85° and depressed to −5°. The surveillance radar is mounted on the rear of the turret, the FLIR, TV tracker, laser rangefinder and missile guidance laser all being mounted in the forward part of the turret.

A typical aircraft target engagement would take place as follows. The airborne target is first detected by the Contraves Italiana surveillance radar (mounted on the turret rear), this being capable of detecting targets up to a maximum height of 5000 m (16,405 ft) and out to a maximum range of 20 km (12.4 miles). The radar first detects the target which, if confirmed as hostile, appears on the radar operator's PPI (plan position indicator) display. The radar operator is seated within the vehicle. The turret is then automatically traversed in bearing and search is initiated by the gunner to bring the target into the field of view of the FLIR or TV camera, the choice between the two sensors depending on the weather conditions at the time of the engagement; TV is used only in fair conditions. The sensor selected then locks onto the target and commences tracking. The target range is measured by the laser rangefinder to ensure that a missile is not launched if the target is not within range. Once the target is within range a missile is launched, riding along the missile-guidance radar beam until it impacts with the target.

The missile is carried in a launch/transport container which weighs 65 kg (143 lb) complete with missile. The latter has a Mach 3+ performance on its smokeless propellant motor, no wings and four control fins. It is fitted with a hollow-charge (HEAT) warhead that weighs 12 kg (26 lb) and gives a good fragmentation effect against aircraft. According to Oerlikon the missile's warhead will also penetrate over 900 mm (35.4 in) of armour. Two fuses are fitted, an impact type for ground targets and an electro-optical proximity type for aircraft targets. Engagement of ground targets is similar to that of aerial targets except that the target

Designed as a dual role air defence anti-tank missile system, ADATS consists of a 360° traversable turret with surveillance devices and eight ready-to-fire missile container-launchers that can be mounted on a variety of wheeled or tracked vehicles, such as the M113APC.

is first detected by FLIR or TV tracker with the laser rangefinder being used to determine target range. When being used against ground targets minimum and maximum ranges are 500 and 6000 m (545 and 6,560 yards) respectively.

Above: One of the two M113A2 ADATS prototypes launches a missile. The minimum and maximum ranges for an anti-tank engagement are 500 m (547 yards) and 6000 m (6562 yards) respectively.

Specification
ADATS missile
Length: 2.05 m (6 ft 8.7 in)
Diameter: 15.2 cm (5.98 in)
Launch weight: 51 kg (112 lb)
Range: 8000 m (8,750 yards)
Altitude: 5000 m (16,405 ft)

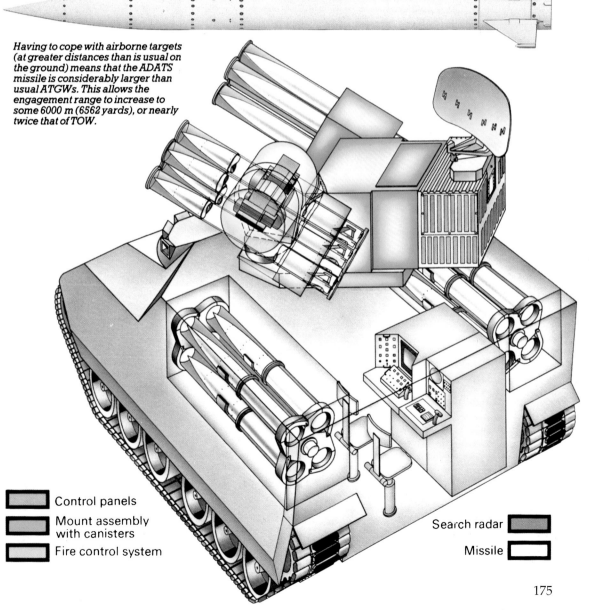

Having to cope with airborne targets (at greater distances than is usual on the ground) means that the ADATS missile is considerably larger than usual ATGWs. This allows the engagement range to increase to some 6000 m (6562 yards), or nearly twice that of TOW.

Control panels

Mount assembly with canisters

Fire control system

Search radar

Missile

Breda Folgore

The **Breda Folgore** is a modern recoil-less anti-tank rocket-launcher under advanced development by Breda Meccanica Bresciana for use in the shoulder-, tripod- or vehicle-mounted roles to a maximum range of 1000 m (1,095 yards) without too much effort in interchanging the systems. For the shoulder role it is normally operated by a two-man team, but can if required be used by one man only. A special lightweight optical sighting device and a bipod are used. In the case of the tripod mounting a larger optronic sight is provided in order to enable the aim-er to estimate within a few seconds the target's range, speed and angle of elevation. The vehicle mounting is nor-mally external to a small turret on a reconnaissance vehicle or APC with either of the sights mentioned above. The ammunition is the same in all three systems, and comprises a fin-stabilized hollow-charge rocket with a simple low pressure recoilless laun-ching cartridge that both fires the rocket clear of the tube and brings it up to a speed sufficient for its own dou-ble-base propellant motor to ignite and sustain the forward motion. The fusing utilizes an electrical double-safety system that is initially operated when the projectile attains a fixed acceleration rate and secondly when it strikes the target, thus considerably reducing the possibility of a prema-ture explosion. Folgore has been in service with the Italian Army since the late 1980s but no export interest appears to have arisen.

Specification
Folgore
Type: anti-tank rocket-launcher
Dimensions: length 1.85 m (6 ft 0.83 in); calibre 8.0 cm (3.15 in)
Weight: shoulder model 17 kg (37.5 lb) and tripod model 27 kg (59.5 lb)
Performance: effective range 50-700 m (55-765 yards)
Ammunition: 3 kg (6.6 lb) hollow charge rocket with 2.2 kg (4.85 lb) ejection round
Armour penetration: approx 450-mm. (17.71-in)

The Folgore shoulder-launch variant has an optical sighting device and is effective out to 700 m (766 yards).

Above: Apart from the shoulder-launch version, the Folgore will also be available in tripod ground mount and vehicle turret mount versions.

The heavier ground mount will use an optronic sighting device to target enemy vehicles.

AT-2 'Swatter'

The **AT-2 'Swatter'** was the second of the Soviet first-generation ATGWs to be identified. It is a manually-guided command to line of sight vehicle- and helicopter-mounted system known to the Soviets as the **PTUR-62 'Falanga'**. It is unusual among ATGWs in having a UHF radio command guidance link with three possible frequencies for ECCM purposes. It is at its most effec-tive when launched directly at the target but can, if required, be switched from one target to another as long as the new one is within the field of fire. The missile arms itself when it reaches 500 m (545 yards) from the launcher. In a later **'Swatter-B'** version the max-imum range was increased from the 3000 m (3,280 yards) of the original **'Swatter-A'** to 3500 m (3,830 yards). A **'Swatter-C'** version is now used on the Mil Mi-24 'Hind-A' and 'Hind-D' gunship helicopters (four rounds), with semi-automatic command to line of

sight guidance and a further increase in maximum range to 4000 m (4,375 yards). All three versions are used on BRDM-1 and BRDM-2 scout car con-versions in quadruple mounts. The 'Swatter' is now being replaced by more modern systems, and as far as it is known has never been used in com-bat, although 'Hind A' and 'Hind-D' helicopters have been seen carrying the type in Afghanistan. Countries that use the 'Swatter' are Bulgaria, Cuba, Czechoslovakia, East Germany, Egypt, Hungary, Libya, Poland, Romania, South Yemen, Syria and the USSR.

Specification
AT-2 'Swatter'
Type: anti-tank missile
Dimensions: length 1.14 m (3 ft 8.88 in); diameter 13.2 cm (5.2 in); span 66.0 cm (2 ft 2 in)
Launch weight: 'Swatter-A' 26.5 kg (58.4 lb), 'Swatter-B' 29.5 kg (65 lb) and 'Swatter-C' 32.5 kg (71.65 lb)
Propulsion: solid-propellant rocket
Performance: range 'Swatter-A' 500-3000 m (545-3,280 yards), 'Swatter-B' 500-3500 m (545-3,825 yards) and 'Swatter-C' 250-4000 m (275-4,375 yards)

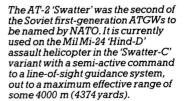

The AT-2 'Swatter' was the second of the Soviet first-generation ATGWs to be named by NATO. It is currently used on the Mil Mi-24 'Hind-D' assault helicopter in the 'Swatter-C' variant with a semi-active command to a line-of-sight guidance system, out to a maximum effective range of some 4000 m (4374 yards).

Warhead: hollow-charge HE
Armour penetration: 'Swatter-A' 480 mm (18.9 in) and 'Swatter-B/C' 510 mm (20.08 in)

AT-3 'Sagger'

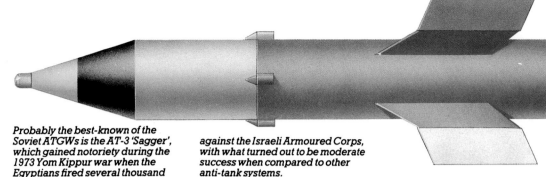

The **AT-3 'Sagger'** is known to the Soviets as the **PTUR-64 'Malatyuka'**, and until recently was their standard domestic and export ATGW. It was produced in three versions, the optically-tracked manually wire-guided **Sagger-A'**, the **'Sagger-B'** which came into service in late 1973 and has an improved propulsion motor to make it 25 per cent faster, and the **'Sagger-C'** which is the 'Sagger-B' with semi-automatic guidance and entered service in the late 1970s. The 'Sagger' is used in a number of ways, that most often encountered being the three-man team carrying two rounds and the control unit. The 'Sagger' is also used on sextuple launchers on the BRDM-1 (with no reloads) and the BRDM-2 (with eight reloads) tank destroyers. Single-rail launchers are fitted to the BMP-1 and BMD infantry combat vehicles (with four reloads each) for self-defence. The missile, believed to be the 'Sagger-B' and 'Sagger-C' versions, is also carried on the Mil Mi-2 'Hoplite', Mi-8 'Hip' and Mi-24 'Hind' helicopters of the Warsaw Pact and allies, whilst the Yugoslavs' have mated it to the Aérospatiale SA 342 Gazelle and their indigenous BOV-1 armoured vehicle on sextuple launcher (with six reloads). Other vehicle mounts include a modified East German BTR-40 APC and the Czech OT-64 APC. The missile has seen extensive combat service with many nations. The Arabs used it against the Israelis in the War of Attrition, the 1973 Yom Kippur War and the 1982 'Peace for Galilee' campaign. The North Vietnamese have used it against the South Vietnamese, Americans and Chinese in Indo-China, and the Iraqis have deployed the weapon extensively against Iranian targets in the Gulf War from the ground, vehicles and

Probably the best-known of the Soviet ATGWs is the AT-3 'Sagger', which gained notoriety during the 1973 Yom Kippur war when the Egyptians fired several thousand

against the Israeli Armoured Corps, with what turned out to be moderate success when compared to other anti-tank systems.

'Hind-D' helicopters. Although not given the missile before their ideological split with the Soviets, the Chinese have since copied the type, and the Taiwanese have used it as the basis of their **Kun Wu** ATGW. The AT-3 'Sagger' is widely employed, known operators being Algeria, Angola, Bulgaria, China (unlicensed copy), Cuba, Czechoslovakia, East Germany, Egypt, Ethiopia, Hungary, India, Iraq, Israel, Libya, Mozambique, North Korea, Poland, Romania, South Yemen, Syria, Taiwan (unlicensed copy), USSR, Vietnam and Yugoslavia.

Specification
AT-3 'Sagger'
Type: anti-tank missile
Dimensions: length 0.883 m (2 ft 10.76 in); diameter 11.9 cm (4.69 in); span not known
Launch weight: 11.29 kg (24.9 lb)
Propulsion: two-stage solid-propellant rocket
Performance: range 300-3000 m (330-3,280 yards)
Warhead: 3-kg (6.6-lb) hollow-charge HE
Armour penetration: 410 mm (16.14 in) or more

Above: A Soviet army AT-3 'Sagger-B' mounted on the launcher rail above the 73-mm gun of a BMP-1 infantry combat vehicle.

Below: A three-man infantry 'Sagger' team can deploy four missiles, checked and ready to fire, in between 12 and 15 minutes.

AT-4 'Spigot'

In the late 1970s persistent reports circulated about a new Soviet second-generation man-portable tripod-mounted ATGW with semi-automatic command to line of sight guidance. By 1980 the first photographs had appeared of the NATO-designated **AT-4 'Spigot'** system, which is believed to be called **'Faggot'** by the Soviets. The fact that in general appearance and operation the weapon is very similar to the Euromissile MILAN is more than coincidental, recent reports from the USA suggesting that the 'Spigot' is based on tech-

nology gained by spying and on the examination of actual specimens gained from third parties friendly to the Soviets. The main outward differences are that the AT-4's sight is smaller and that the guidance computer and goniometer are located in a box below the launch rail. By 1984 all of the most trusted Warsaw Pact Allies had been issued with the 'Spigot' to replace the 'Sagger' in the manpack role, the three-man team now carrying four rounds, sight and a tripod mount. More recently the 'Spigot' has been seen in East Germany on BRDM-2/'Spandrel'

vehicles on the two outermost (of five) launcher positions to give the vehicle a new missile load of six AT-5 'Spandrel' and eight 'Spigot' missiles. It has also been seen on some BMP-1 and BMD armoured vehicles replacing the 'Sagger' system; the same reload capacity is assumed. The 'Spigot' underwent its baptism of fire with the Syrians in 1982 against the Israelis, and several samples were said to have been captured. The AT-4 'Spigot' system is used by Czechoslovakia, East Germany, Hungary, Poland, Syria, USSR and several other countries.

Specification
AT-4 'Spigot'
Type: anti-tank missile
Dimensions: not known
Launch weight: total system 40 kg (88.2 lb)
Propulsion: solid-propellant rocket
Performance: range 25-2000 m (27-2,190 yards)
Warhead: shaped charge HE
Armour penetration: 600 m (23.62 in) or more

AT-5 'Spandrel'

The **AT-5 'Spandrel'** is a second-generation Soviet ATGW equivalent to the Euromissile HOT, and generally seen on BRDM-2 vehicles, on which the type is mounted in a quintuple launcher-tube assembly with a separate optical day and night tracking system on the vehicle's roof. A further five rounds are carried inside the vehicle as reloads. The BRDM-2 is replacing the older BRDM tank destroyer vehicles in the anti-tank companies of the Soviet units facing NATO and in Category 1 divisions within the USSR on a one-for-one basis. The missile is also to be found on the 30-mm gun-equipped BMP-2 as a roof installation in place of the 'Sagger' rail over the gun; a similar reload capacity is assumed. As far as it

can be ascertained, the Soviets have not yet exported or used the missile in combat. Further applications of the 'Spandrel' are expected over the next year or so.

Specification
AT-5 'Spandrel'
Type: anti-tank missile
Dimensions: length 1.30 m (4 ft 3.2 in); diameter 15.5 cm (6.1 in); span not known
Launch weight: 12 kg (26.45 lb)
Propulsion: solid-propellant rocket
Performance: range 100-4000 m (110-4,375 yards)
Warhead: hollow-charge HE
Armour penetration: 750 mm (29.53 in) or more

A close-up of the BRDM-2's quintuple launcher arrangement for the AT-5. The 'Spandrel' is very similar to

Euromissile's HOT in operation, and may be based on stolen technology.

AT-6 'Spiral'

The tube-launched **AT-6 'Spiral'** is believed to be the first third-generation Soviet ATGW. At present it is only deployed on the Mil Mi-24 'Hind-E' assault helicopter (four rounds) but its presence on the new Mi-28 'Havoc' attack helicopter as its standard ATGW payload is expected soon. Much conjecture has arisen over its guidance system, laser homing with a fire-and-forget capability being the most favoured suggestion. Recently, however, informed sources in the USA have indicated that the weapon has a much-improved radio command guidance unit with considerably enhanced ECCM capability than its predecessor, the AT-2 'Swatter'. This

would explain the apparent absence of a laser designator on the 'Hind-E'. No country other than the Soviet Union has fielded the AT-6, which indicates the importance of this missile in the Soviets' anti-armour force.

Specification
AT-6 'Spiral'
Type: anti-tank missile
Dimensions: length about 1.8 m (5 ft 10.86 in); diameter about 14.0 cm (5.5 in); span not known
Launch weight: 32 kg (70.55 lb)
Propulsion: dual-thrust solid-propellant rocket
Performance: range 100-7000 m (110-7,655 yards)

Warhead: 8-kg (17.6-lb) hollow-charge HE
Armour penetration: 800 mm (31.5 in) or more

A Mil Mi-24 'Hind' displays its empty AT-6 'Spiral' launch rails. No pictures have yet been released of the actual weapon.

RPG-7 family

The **RPG-7V** is the standard man-portable short-range anti-tank weapon of the Warsaw Pact and its allies. It is similar to the earlier RPG-2 in having a calibre of 40 mm (1.57 in), but its anti-tank rocket diameter is 85 mm (3.35 in) instead of 82 mm (3.23 in). The firer screws the cylinder containing the propellant into the warhead and then inserts the complete round into the muzzle of the launcher. The warhead nosecap is then removed and the safety pin extracted. A pull on the launcher's trigger then fires the round, which is reasonably accurate when there is no cross wind; if there is such a wind, the round becomes very erratic. The length of the launcher and noise are also significant operational problems. In 1968 a folding version of the RPG-7 was seen, this subsequently

RPG-7 ammunition has been upgraded to include a HE anti-personnel round and a new

being designated the **RPG-7D**, which is intended specifically for use by the airborne troops. The standard projectile is the 2.25-kg (4.96-lb) PGF-7 anti-tank round, which was supplemented in the late 1970s by the OG-7 anti-personnel fragmentation round and by the ballistically improved and penetration-superior PG-7M anti-tank round. A more modern rocket-

improved HEAT rocket. Ironically, it is the RPG-7 which is causing heavy losses to the Soviets in Afghanistan.

launcher, tentatively identified as the **RPG-16**, has also been seen in service with the Soviet army in Europe and Afghanistan. This is believed to rectify most of the problems found with the RPG-7. The RPG series has seen widespread combat service throughout the world with both regular and irregular troops, and has turned up in Northern Ireland in the hands of IRA terrorists.

Specification
RPG-7
Type: anti-tank rocket-launcher
Dimensions: length 0.99 m (3 ft 2.98 in); calibre 4.0 cm (1.57 in)
Weight: 7 kg (15.43 lb)
Performance: range 300 m (330 yards) against a moving target and 500 m (545 yards) against a stationary target
Ammunition: see text
Armour penetration: PG-7 round 320 mm (12.6 in) and PG-7M round 400 mm (15.75 in) or more

Surface-to-Air Missiles

Surface-to-air missiles were a growth industry from 1960 to 1990, but the limit now seems to have been reached and new designs are slow to appear. Targets also have ways of dealing with missiles, which has required the weapons engineers to develop counter-counter-measures in response.

The use of air defence missiles began in World War II and by the mid-1950s they were considered to be sufficiently accurate to replace heavy artillery as a means of dealing with high-flying aircraft. In fact the early missiles were not as accurate as had been hoped. It is known that during the Vietnam War the North Vietnamese Army fired 4,244 SA-2 Guideline missiles to bring down 76 American aircraft. In 1960 a total of 14 missiles were fired in the incident in which Gary Powers' U-2 aircraft was brought down over Sverdlovsk.

Matters have improved since then, but so also have the counter-measures which can be deployed against the missile. Depending upon the guidance system of the missile, its terminal homing system and other detectable and measurable characteristics, it becomes possible to devise radar and other decoys to confuse or misdirect the missile. This, of course, has led to counter-counter-measures being devised by the missile engineers, and so it goes on.

One-man missiles, such as Stinger and Grail, have become more reliable and very efficient. They are now being installed on

A British Army Rapier mobile surface-to-air missile launcher unit waits for customers. Rapier first entered service in 1971.

mobile mountings fitted with four or six launchers, radar and fire control systems to act as light air defence weapons. One drawback of the one-man missile was the very short time the operator had to see an approaching target, shoulder the missile, pick up the target in his sight, lock on to it and fire. The situation has now been eased by the development

of various simple radar warning devices which pick up the approaching aircraft, sound an alarm and indicate the direction of approach, ensuring the missile is shouldered and switched on when the target appears.

As the century draws to a close there are many plans stuck in the in the gestation stage, usually for financial reasons. The British

Bloodhound missile has gone, but there is, as yet, no sign of its replacement. Rapier 2000 is in service, and the Americans, having had some severe setbacks in the past in their selection of mobile air defence, are now putting their faith in the 'Light Armoured Vehicle Air Defence', an 8 x 8 APC with a Gatling cannon and pods carrying eight Stinger missiles.

Crotale surface-to-air missile system

In the early 1960s the South African government placed a contract with the French company of Thomson-Houston, which later became Thomson-CSF, for the development of a mobile all-weather SAM system. This became known as the **Cactus**, Thomson-CSF being responsible for the overall system, radar and electronics, and Engins Matra for the **R.440** missile as it had considerable experience in the development and production of air-to-air missiles. The first batteries were delivered to South Africa in 1971 with final deliveries in 1973. Since then the **Crotale**, this being its French name, has been ordered by Chile, Egypt, Libya, Pakistan, Saudi Arabia and the United Arab Emirates. Further development of the Crotale has resulted on the Shahine, SICA which is in service with Saudi Arabia. There is also a naval version of the Crotale.

A typical Crotale battery consists of one acquisition and two or three firing units, each of the latter having four missiles in the ready-to-launch position. Both units are based on a fully armoured 4×4 chassis whose wheels are raised off the ground by hydraulic jacks when the vehicle in the operating position. An unusual feature of the vehicle is that it is electrically propelled.

The acquisition unit carries out target surveillance, identification and designation and is fitted with a large radar with a maximum detection range of about 18 km (11.2 miles). It also has a real-time digital computer, display consoles, data links and is capable of handling up to 12 targets simultaneously.

A target engagement takes place as follows. The acquisition unit first locates the aircraft and, if this is confirmed as hostile, allocates it to one of the firing units, target information being transmitted via a data link. The radar on the firing unit can track one target and guide two missiles at the same time, there being a slight gap in launching. The firing unit also has the command transmitter, infra-red gathering system, digital computer, digital data link and a TV/optical tracking system for use in an ECM environment. Once the four missiles have been launched new missiles in the transport/launching containers have to be loaded with the aid of a crane. Four missiles can be loaded in about two minutes by a well trained crew.

The R.440 missile is 2.89 m (9 ft 5.75 in) long, 15.0 cm (5.9 in) in diameter and 54.0 cm (21.25 in) in span, and weighs 85 kg (187 lb) of which 15 kg (33 lb) is accounted for by the HE warhead, which is of the fragmentation

type to cause as much damage to the target as possible. The warhead is detonated by a proximity fuse which is not armed until after the missile is launched. The single-stage solid-propellant rocket motor gives the missile a top speed of about Mach 2.3. The effective range of the system depends on the speed of the target, but against an aircraft flying at a speed of Mach 1.2 a maximum range of 8500 m (9,295 yards) can be achieved with a maximum altitude of 3000 m (9,845 ft). Against slower aircraft and helicopters, the range is significantly greater.

The Crotale is normally used (for example by South Africa, Saudi Arabia and the French air force) for the defence of air bases and other strategic targets. Once halted, the Crotale/Cactus system takes about five minutes to become fully operational. Information from the acquisition unit can be passed to the firing unit by cable (maximum length of 800 m/875 yards) or a data link (maximum range 3000 m/3,280 yards).

Each Crotale launcher has four missiles. Three firing units are coupled to one acquisition unit to form a battery.

Specification
Matra R.440
Dimensions: length 2.89 m (9 ft 5 in); diameter 15 cm (5.9 in); span 54 cm (21.25 in)
Launch weight: 85 kg (187.4 lb)
Performance: speed Mach 2.3; maximum ceiling 3000 m (9842 ft); maximum range 12000 m (6.8 miles) against a 2000 m/sec (450 mph) target

Crotale missile being launched during trials in France. The missile itself is manufactured by Engins Matra with the overall system and electronics being the responsibility of Thomson-CSF. It was originally developed to meet the requirements of South Africa but has since been adopted by many other countries. Further development has resulted in the Shahine, SICA which has been produced specifically for Saudi Arabia.

Shahine, SICA surface-to-air missile system

The **Shahine, SICA** low-altitude SAM system was developed from 1975 specifically to meet the requirements of Saudi Arabia and is a logical development of the earlier Crotale. Prime contractor is the Electronics Systems Division of Thomson-CSF, which is responsible for the radars, electronics and systems integration; Engins Matra is responsible for the missiles. Following successful trials with prototype systems, production started in 1979, the first systems being delivered to Saudi Arabia in 1982 and final deliver-

ies being made in 1983. A total of 36 systems were delivered as were 53 AMX-30 DCA self-propelled 30-mm anti-aircraft guns to provide close in protection, especially when missiles are being reloaded.

The Shahine consists of a firing unit and an acquisition unit, each mounted on a modified AMX-30 MBT chassis which offers complete armour protection for the crew and electronics inside the vehicle as well as having much improved cross-country performance than the original Crotale wheeled sys-

tem.

The acquisition unit has a large pulse-Doppler surveillance radar with a range of some 18 km (11.2 miles) with a digital receiver for the MTI (moving target indication) function. The automatic information processing and threat evaluation system allows up to 40 targets to be registered on the computer and no less than 18 actual targets to be handled. One acquisition unit can control up to four firing units.

The firing unit has six missiles in the ready-to-launch position (the basic

Crotale has four); once these missiles have been launched replacement missiles in travelling/launch containers are loaded from a vehicle with the aid of a crane. Between the missile is a triple-channel fire-control radar that can simultaneously guide two missiles to a target. The radar tracks the missile and sends out guidance commands, acquisition of the missile during the early part of the flight being via an infra-red receiver sensitive to the wavelength of the missile exhaust. Another feature of this system is that a

TV system is integrated into the turret and this assumes target- and missile-tracking functions and also ensures a full back-up mode in case of enemy jamming.

The missile used by the Shahine is the **Matra R.460**, a longer and heavier version of the Matra R.440 used in the Crotale system, its SNPE double-stage rocket motor giving a burn of 4.5 seconds (compared with 2.5 seconds in the Crotale system) to produce a maximum speed of about Mach 2.

A major advantage of the Shahine over the original Crotale is that the firing units and acquisition unit can deploy over a much wider area as they do not have to stop and be coupled together by cables before target engagement. This is possible as the Shahine units are fitted with an automatic data transmission and reciprocal microwave system. This, coupled with the fact the missiles and radars have a longer range, makes the Shahine much more effective than the Crotale.

Specification
Matra R.460
Dimensions: length 3.15 m (10 ft 4 in); diameter 15.6 cm (6.14 in); span 59.0 cm (23.23 in)
Launch weight: 100 kg (220 lb)
Performance: maximum ceiling 6100 m (19,685 ft); maximum range 10000 to 13500 m (12,030 to 13,125 yards)

FRANCE/WEST GERMANY
Roland surface-to-air missile system

In the early 1960s Aérospatiale of France and Messerschmitt-Bölkow-Blohm of West Germany, working as Euromissile, began the development of a mobile low-altitude surface-to-air missile system which eventually became known as the **Roland**. France was responsible for the Roland clear-weather version while West Germany was design leader for the **Roland 2** all-weather version. As the Roland 2 is the current production model the description relates to this model. In the West German army Roland is based on the chassis of the Marder MICV while France uses an AMX-30 MBT chassis and the United States the M109 self-propelled howitzer chassis.

A typical target engagement of the Roland 2 takes place as follows. The pulse-Doppler radar, mounted on top of the turret rotating at 60 rpm, detects aircraft and helicopters at a range of between 15 and 18 km (9.3 and 11.2 miles). The target is then interrogated by the vehicle's own IFF system and, if confirmed as hostile, acquired and tracked. In normal engagements tracking is carried out by the tracking radar mounted on the forward part of the turret, but if enemy countermeasures are active an optical sight can also be used. In the radar mode the tracking radar has two channels, one of which tracks the target and the other the missile. The radar is slaved to follow the target by misalignment. Once a missile has been launched an infrared localizer on the antenna of the tracking radar is used to capture the missile between 500 and 700 m (545 and 765 yards) after launch as by this time the missile has entered the pencil of the tracking radar. Missile deviation is calculated from the angular deviation between target/antenna and antenna/missile, this information being supplied to the on-board computer which calculates the required gui-

dance commands which are then passed onto the missile via a radio command link. The missile receives the commands which are then converted into jet-deflection orders. With Roland it is possible for the operator to switch from the optical to the radar mode after the missile has been launched. The optical method is used whenever possible as it is more accurate, especially in a ECM environment.

The two-stage solid-propellant missile is 2.40 m (7 ft 10.5 in) long, with span and diameter of 50.0 and 16.0 cm (19.7 and 6.3 in respectively), and has a cruising speed of about Mach 1.6. Launch weight is 63 kg (139 lb), and the missile is provided with a high explosive warhead that is detonated either by impact or an electromagnetic (radar-type) proximity fuse.

In the case of the Marder and AMX-30 chassis versions of Roland, two missiles are carried in the ready-to-launch position, an additional eight missiles being carried inside the vehicle for automatic loading from two rotary-type magazines each holding four rounds.

In addition to being used by France and West Germany, the Roland is also used by Argentina (shelter version), Brazil (four only on Marder chassis), and the United States (27 systems only, built in the United States by Boeing and Hughes). The type has also been ordered by Iraq, Nigeria, Venezuela and Jordan via Iraq. There is also a shelter-mounted version of Roland

which can be carried on a 6×6 chassis or used in the static defence role.

Specification
Roland 2
Dimensions: length 2.4 m (7 ft 10½ in); diameter 16 cm (6.3 in); span 50 cm (19.7 in)
Launch weight: 63 kg (139 lb)
Performance: speed Mach 1.5; range 6000 m (3.73 miles); radar detection range 16 km (9.95 miles); minimum interception range about 500 m (1640 ft);

A West German army Roland SAM system, on Thyssen Henschel Marder chassis with two missiles in ready-to-launch position and eight missiles in reserve.

minimum interception height under 20 m (65.6 ft)

UK
Bloodhound Mk 2 surface-to-air missile system

The original **Bloodhound Mk 1** SAM system was developed from the late 1940s (to meet the requirements of the Royal Air Force) by the Bristol Aeroplane company (now British Aerospace Dynamics) and Ferranti, the first units becoming operational in 1958. Further development resulted in the much more effective **Bloodhound Mk 2**, which entered service in 1964. This was deployed by the RAF in the United Kingdom, West Germany and Singapore but by early 1983 those in West Germany had been redeployed to the United Kingdom and those in Singapore had been handed over to the Singapore Air Defence Command. The weapon is also used by Switzerland under the designation **BL-84** and was also used by Sweden as the **RB 68**,

but these were recently withdrawn from service. The British Army had a very similar missile system called the **Thunderbird**, but this has now been withdrawn from service without replacement, so leaving the army without any high-level air-defence system.

A typical Bloodhound missile section consists of four missiles on their individual launchers, target illuminating radar (TIR) and a launch control post (LCP). Two TIRs were developed, the air-transportable Ferranti Firelight and the semitransportable Ferranti Scorpion, the latter having a much longer range.

A Bloodhound target engagement takes place as follows. A target is first detected by surveillance radar, which may be part of the Bloodhound system or part of an overall air-defence system which would decide which particular weapon system would engage the target. Basic target information is then supplied to the TIR, which searches for the target, then tracks and illuminates it. At the same time the TIR

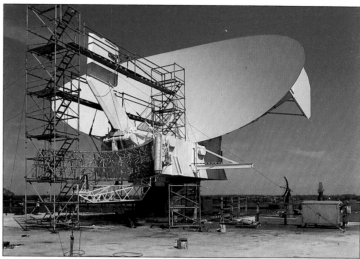

transmits this information to the launch control post. A computer in the latter then determines the optimum conditions for target engagement. When the target is within range a missile is launched, the receiver in the nose of the missile detecting and homing onto radiation reflected by the target. The warhead of the missile, which is in fact well to the rear of the nose, is high explosive and fitted with a proximity fuse developed by EMI Electronics.

The missile itself is launched by four solid-propellant boosters, which are mounted externally to take the missile to supersonic speed when the two Thor ramjets take over and the boos-

Bloodhound SAMs on their launchers at an RAF base. All these missiles have now been withdrawn from West Germany and concentrated along the east coast of England; no official announcement has so far been made concerning their replacement.

ters fall away. The ramjets are mounted above and below the missile and give the missile an exceptional range of some 80 km (50 miles) and a maximum speed of some 3860 km/h (2,400 mph). The control surfaces of the missile consist of two moving wings to provide the necessary manoeuvres and cruciform fixed tailplanes to pro-

The RAF also uses the Marconi Type 82 series radar for surveillance purposes with the Bloodhound SAM. In the background is a Plessey HF 200 height-finding radar. The Bloodhound is also used by Switzerland and Singapore.

vide pitch stability. The missile manoeuvres by means of twist and steer in the same way as a bird in flight: the wings are moved differentially so as to roll the missile into the vector direction in which the manoeuvre is required, and then moved in concert to pitch the missile in that direction to complete the manoeuvre.

Most of the guidance system is on easy-to-replace printed circuit cards, so repairs to faulty cards can be fast. Bloodhound 2 was taken out of Singapore service in 1990 and British in 1991; service in 1991: it is still in service in Switzerland.

Specification
Bloodhound Mk 2
Dimensions: length 7.75 m (25 ft 5 in); diameter 54.6 cm (21.5 in); wing span 2.83 m (9 ft 3½ in)
Weight: 2300 kg (5,070 lb)
Performance: operating altitude 100 to 23010 m (325 to 75,500 ft); range over 80 km (50 miles)

Blowpipe man-portable surface-to-air missile system

The **Blowpipe** missile was developed by the Missile Systems Division of Short Brothers to meet a British army requirement for a man-portable SAM missile system that could shoot down an attacking aircraft before it released its weapons. Other man-portable missiles, such as the American Stinger and the Soviet SA-7 home onto the exhaust of the attacking aircraft and can often only engage the attackers after they have released their weapons.

The Blowpipe system consists of two main components: the missile within its launching canister and the aiming unit. In the missile itself the forward part contains the guidance equipment, the HE warhead is in the centre and the rear part houses the rocket motors. There are four delta-shaped aerofoils on the nose for aerodynamic control and four at the tail to provide ballistic stability. The nose section of the missile is free to rotate independently of the main body, it being attached to the latter by a low-friction bearing. The missile is factory-sealed in a lightweight container which acts as a recoilless launcher. The container houses the firing sequence unit, thermal battery to power the aiming unit, guidance aerials and electrical connections. When the missile gyro is fired the front cap of the container is blown off by gas pressure while the laminated rear closure is ejected at launch.

The aiming unit is a self-contained firing and control pack with a pistol grip on the right side. The aiming unit contains a radio transmitter, auto-

gathering device, monocular sight and, if required an interrogator (IFF) system. The controls include a trigger, thumb-controlled joystick and switches for fuse option, auto-gather and guidance command frequency change.

Before use the aiming unit is clipped onto the canister containing the missile. The target is obtained visually in the monocular sight, which has a graticule to assist the operator in both range estimation and allowance for cross winds. The safety catch is then released and the trigger squeezed. The latter activates a generator which supplies firing current to the thermal batteries in the missile and canister. The missile is launched from the canister by a first-stage motor. Once the Blowpipe is a safe distance from the operator the second-stage motor ignites to accelerate the missile to supersonic (Mach 1.5) speed, the missile then cruising as a fully controlled dart. The Blowpipe is then automatically gathered into the centre of the operator's field of vision. He then guides the weapon onto the target by radio command produced by movements of the thumb-controlled joystick. The high explosive warhead is detonated by impact or a proximity fuse. Once the target has been destroyed the oper-

ator unclips the empty canister and replaces it with a fresh unit; he is then ready to commence another target engagement.

In the British Army Blowpipes are operated by the Royal Artillery. The weapon is also used by eight other countries including Argentina, Canada, Oman and Thailand. During the Falklands campaign of 1982 the Blowpipe is credited with shooting down at least nine Argentinian aircraft, with a further two claimed as probables.

Specification
Blowpipe
Dimensions: length of missile 1.39 m

A Shorts Blowpipe man-portable missile leaves its launcher tube. Unlike the Redeye, the Blowpipe does not home onto the exhaust of the attacking aircraft and is therefore able to engage the target before it releases its weapons.

(4 ft 4.7 in); length of canister 1.40 m (4 ft 7.1 in); diameter of missile 7.60 cm (3 in); span 27.5 cm (10.8 in)
Weights: complete system 21.9 kg (48.3 lb); missile and canister 13 kg (28.7 lb); missile 11 kg (24.5 lb)
Performance: effective ceiling 2000 m (6,560 ft); effective range about 3 to 4 km (1.86 to 2.5 miles)

Rapier surface-to-air missile system

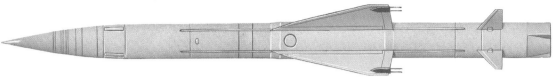

The **Rapier** low-level air defence missile system was developed by the British Aircraft Corporation (now British Aerospace) to meet the requirements of the British army and Royal Air Force for a mobile SAM system to replace the 40-mm Bofors guns then in service. Development started in the early 1960s, and the first production units were completed in 1971. In addition to being used by the United Kingdom, the Rapier has also been ordered by Abu Dhabi, Australia, Brunei, Iran, Oman, Qatar, Singapore, Switzerland, Turkey, Zambia and the United States. In the last case the weapon is used to protect USAF bases in the UK.

The basic clear-weather Rapier system consists of a fire unit, optical tracker and a generator. The former has four missiles in the ready-to-launch position, surveillance radar, IFF system, command transmitter and computer. The system is transported into action by two long wheelbase Land Rovers, one towing the missile launcher with its four missiles, generator, tracker and some reload missiles, and the second a trailer carrying additional missiles.

A typical target engagement takes place as follows. The target is first detected by the surveillance radar mounted on top of the launcher and is then automatically interrogated by the IFF system. If the target is friendly no action is taken but if hostile the tracker

operator is alerted. The operator then acquires the target in his optical sight and tracks it using a joystick control. The computer informs the operator when the target is within range, and a Rapier missile is then launched. Once the missile has been launched the operator continues to track the target using the joystick. A TV camera in the tracker, collimated to the tracking sight, watches the flares mounted in the tail of the missile and so measures a deviation from the sightline. The measurement is then fed to the computer which issues orders to the command transmitter for transmission to the missile. The missile itself is fitted with a high explosive warhead with an impact fuse. Once the four missiles have been launched new missiles can be quickly loaded by hand.

To give the system an all-weather capability Marconi Space and Defence Systems have developed the trailer-mounted DN181 Blindfire radar which can also be towed by a Land Rover or similar vehicle. In the **Blindfire Rapier** system the operator does not have to track the missile, this being fully automatic.

Early in 1983 the British army took delivery of the first of 62 **Tracked Rapier** systems. This was originally developed to meet the requirements of the Imperial Iranian Army but this contract was cancelled with the fall of the Shah. The Tracked Rapier consists of a modified M548 tracked cargo chassis, which itself is a member of the M113 family of vehicles, with a fully armoured cab. On the rear is a Rapier launcher with eight missiles (four on each side) in the ready-to-launch position, with additional missiles carried in reserve. The optical tracker is located in the cab and projects through the roof. In the future the Royal Artillery will have a mixture of towed and tracked Rapier systems.

At the 1983 Paris Air Show British Aerospace announced the **Rapier Laserfire**. This consists of a pallet which can be mounted on a variety of vehicles and has a surveillance radar, automatic laser tracker, crew cabin with system controls and displays, computer and other electronics, four ready-to-launch missiles, and a com-

mand link. The target is detected by the surveillance radar as in the basic Rapier system, but if deemed to be hostile the target is then acquired by the automatic laser tracker, which locks onto the target to provide the laser line of sight for the command to line of sight system. All the operator has to do is to fire when the indicators state that the target is in range. The Rapier missile is then commanded to fly along the laser sight line to impact with the target.

Rapier was first used operationally by Iran against Iraq during the 1970s, in the still-continuing Gulf War, and by the Royal Artillery in the Falklands campaign of 1982, when it is credited with shooting down some 20 aircraft.

Specification
Rapier
Dimensions: length 2.24 m (7 ft 4.2 in); diameter 13.30 cm (5.25 in); span 38.10 cm (15 in)
Launch weight: 42.6 kg (94 lb)
Performance: maximum ceiling 3000+ m (9,845+ ft); maximum range 6500+ m (7,100+ yards)

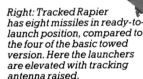

Above: One of the prototypes of the Tracked Rapier launching a missile during trials in the UK. The Royal Artillery will deploy a mix of towed and Tracked Rapiers in the British Army of the Rhine. The first system was delivered late in 1982.

Right: Tracked Rapier has eight missiles in ready-to-launch position, compared to the four of the basic towed version. Here the launchers are elevated with tracking antenna raised.

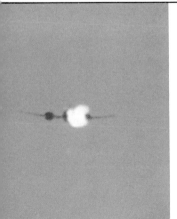
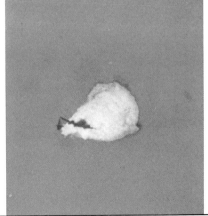

A Meteor target drone meets a fiery death as a highly effective Rapier missile strikes home.

RBS 70 man-portable surface-to-air missile system

The **RBS 70** SAM system was developed from the late 1960s by AB Bofors to meet the requirements of the Swedish army, although Switzerland did contribute some funds to its development. In addition to being used by Sweden it is now also used by Bahrain, Eire, Norway, Singapore and the United Arab Emirates.

The RBS 70 system consists of three main components, namely the stand, sight and missile in its launch tube, each of which can be transported by one man. The complete system can be assembled in about 30 seconds. If required the RBS 70 system can also be fitted with an IFF system; this has been developed for the Swedish army by SATT Elektronic AB.

The missile is an optical beam rider. The sight generates a modulated laser beam which coincides with the line of sight. Before firing, the operator aims coarsely the line of sight at the target with the whole sight. The missile is then launched from its container and comes into the guidance beam, which it follows until it hits the target. So all the operator has to do is to keep the sight on the target through the engagement, using a thumb lever to control the gyro-stabilized optics.

The missile is launched from the transport/launch tube by means of a booster which burns out in the tube and is then jettisoned. Once the missile has left the tube the fins and control surfaces are extended. The sustainer motor is ignited when the missile is a safe distance from the operator, and this accelerates the missile to supersonic speed. Once the sustainer motor has burned out the missile continues in free flight.

The pre-fragmented warhead contains a large number of heavy metal balls and is detonated either by a direct hit or by means of a proximity fuse when it passes close to the target. It can also be self-destructed by the operator simply by switching off the guidance beam.

The stand consists of a vertical tube, three legs which are folded up for transport, and the operator's seat. There are contacts on the central tube for the electrical connection of the sight, IFF equipment, target data receiver and the operator's headset. The sight consists of the guidance beam transmitter (with zoom optics) and an aiming telescope, all components being specially protected against rough handling.

The RBS 70 can also be used in conjunction with a central search radar which provides target information for a number of missile systems. The Swedish army uses the PS 70/R, or Giraffe, developed by L. M. Ericsson, although other radars can be used, for example the Dutch HSA Reporter. The PS 70/R is mounted on a container which is carried on a cross-country truck; the antenna is mounted on a folding mast which gives the former a height of 12 m (39 ft 4.5 in) above the ground. Each firing unit is then provided with a target data receiver so that it can receive target information (speed and direction) from the radar, the data being transmitted either by radio or land line.

Bofors has also developed a vehicle-mounted system of the RBS 70 which can be fitted on the rear of a Land Rover (4×4) or similar vehicle, and another version for installation on armoured vehicles such as the M113, although by early 1983 neither of these had been placed in production. A helicopter-mounted system is now being proposed to give the helicopter an air-to-air capability against other helicopters.

Bofors RBS 70 SAM being launched from a Land Rover, just one of the many launch platforms for this versatile missile system.

Specification
RBS 70 man-portable surface-to-air missile system
Dimensions: length 1.32 m (4 ft 4 in); diameter 10.6 cm (4.17 in); span 32.0 cm (12.6 in)
Weights: missile in container 24 kg (52.9 lb); stand 23.5 kg (51.8 lb); sight 35 kg (77.2 lb)
Performance: maximum ceiling 3000 m (9,845 ft); maximum range 5000 m (5,470 yards)

SA-4 'Ganef' surface-to-air missile system

The **SA-4 'Ganef'** (this being the American designation) medium-to-high altitude SAM system was developed in the late 1950s and was first seen in public during a parade held in Red Square, Moscow, in 1964. The only known operators apart from the Soviet Union are Czechoslovakia, East Germany and Poland. Several units were deployed to Egypt, but these were returned to the Soviet Union before the outbreak of the 1973 Middle East conflict.

The SA-4 system is organized into special brigades each of three battalions, each of the latter having three 'Ganef' batteries and eight ZSU-23-4 self-propelled anti-aircraft guns for close defence. Each battery has three SA-4 tracked launchers, plus one each of the 'Pat Hand' and 'Thin Skin' radars.

Known as Krug in the Soviet army, this is an SA-4 'Ganef' surface-to-air missile launcher in its travelling mode. The chassis is also used for the GMZ armoured minelayer and an SPG.

The SA-4 system is normally deployed well to the rear of the forward edge of the battle area, and forms an integral part of the Soviet concept of air defence in depth by a combination of gun and missile systems to cover all ranges and altitudes. The SA-4 system is believed to have a maximum horizontal range of 72 km (44.75 miles) and a

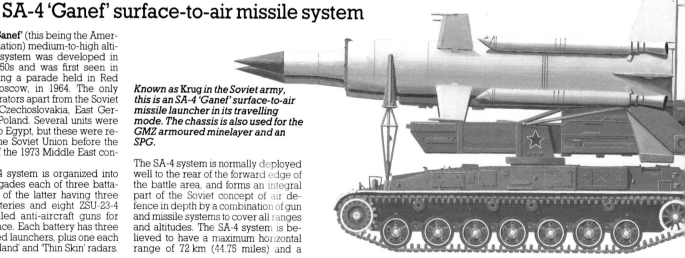

minimum horizontal range of 8 km (5 miles), the minimum effective engagement altitude being 1100 m (3,610 ft) and maximum altitude being 24000 m (78,740 ft).

The 'Ganef' transporter/launcher is a fully tracked vehicle based on the chassis of the GMZ armoured mine-layer, and this was subsequently adopted for the 152-mm M1973 self-propelled howitzer. Mounted on top of the vehicle is a hydraulically operated turntable carrying the two missiles, the left missile being carried slightly higher than the right one. Before the missiles can be launched they have to be released from their travelling locks, and the coverings over their inlets and nozzles have to be removed.

The missile itself weighs about 1800 kg (3,968 lb) and is fitted with an HE warhead detonated by a proximity fuse. The missile has a length of 9.0 m (29 ft 6.3 in), a diameter of 80.0 cm (31.5 in) and a span of 2.6 m (8 ft 6.4 in). It is launched by four solid-propellant booster rockets mounted externally around the body of the missiles, but once the integral ramjet sustainer ignites these fall away, the missile accelerating to Mach 2.5.

A typical target engagement takes place as follows. The 'Long Track' radar, which is mounted on a modified AT-T heavy artillery tractor, first detects the target and passes target information to the SA-4 battery (it can also pass target information to an SA-6 'Gainful' battery). The 'Pat Hand' fire-control and command guidance radar at the battery then takes over and acquires the target. Once the target is within range, with altitude confirmed by the 'Thin Skin' radar, a 'Ganef' missile is launched and guided to the target by command guidance with

semi-active terminal homing for the final stage. Mounted on one of the tail fins of the missile is a continuous-wave radar transponder beacon which enables the missile to be tracked in flight by the 'Pat Hand' radar.

More recently improved missiles have been produced that are more effective at lower altitudes. There are unconfirmed reports that the 'Ganef' has a secondary surface-to-surface capability.

Once the two missiles have been launched new missiles are loaded with the aid of a crane. A Ural-375 (6×6) 4-tonne truck carries one missile, which is so long that it protrudes over the cap of the vehicle. The 'Ganef' system apparently cannot achieve high rates of fire, as according to American sources the battery has only four re-load vehicles, each carrying only one missile.

Specification
SA-4 'Ganef'
Dimensions: length 8.8 m (28.87 ft); diameter 0.9 m (35.43 in); tailspan 2.6 m

(8.53 ft); wing span 2.3 m (7.54 m)
Launch weight: about 1800 kg (3968 lb)
Performance: speed Mach 2.5; range 72 km (44.74 miles); minimum engagement height 1100 m (3600 ft); ceiling 24000 m (78.74 ft)

Right: The SA-4 'Ganef' SAM system is used by Bulgaria, Czechoslovakia, East Germany, Poland and the USSR. It was also deployed to Egypt but withdrawn before the 1973 Middle East war. In wartime a fourth launcher is issued to each battery.

Below: SA-4 'Ganef' missiles being prepared for action shortly after coming to a halt. Before launching the intakes are uncovered, travel lock lowered to front of hull and target information received from the command post some way away.

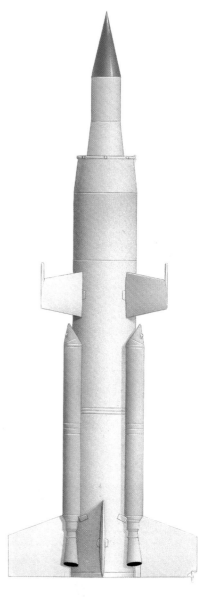

Former USSR

SA-6 'Gainful' surface-to-air missile system

The **SA-6**, which has been given the NATO reporting name 'Gainful', was first seen in Moscow in 1967 and was first used in action by the Egyptian and Syrian armies during the 1973 Middle East war. The SA-6 was one of the most successful air-defence systems of the campaign and forced Israeli aircraft to fly very low, where they could be engaged by SA-7 man-portable SAMs and the 23-mm ZSU-23-4 self-propelled anti-aircraft gun. The 'Gainful' has been exported on a large scale and in addition to the USSR it is also used by Algeria, Angola, Bulgaria, Cuba, Czechoslovakia, East Germany, Egypt, Ethiopia, Finland, Guinea-Bissau, Guyana, Hungary, India, Iraq, Kuwait, Libya, Mali, Mozambique, Peru, Poland, Romania, Somalia, Syria, Tanzania, Vietnam, Yemen Arab Republic (North Yemen), Yugoslavia and Zambia.

In the Soviet army SA-6s are deployed in regiments, each of these having a regimental HQ with one 'Thin Skin' height-finding and two 'Long Track' surveillance radars and five SA-6 batteries. Each SA-6 battery has one 'Straight Flush' fire-control radar vehicle, four SA-6 launchers and two ZIL-131 (6×6) missile resupply trucks, each carrying three missiles which are loaded with the aid of a crane.

The chassis of the SA-6 system is based on that of the ZSU-23-4, with the crew compartment at the front, the

missile-launcher in the centre, and the engine and transmission at the rear. Standard equipment includes an NBC system and night-vision equipment, but the system has no amphibious capability.

The three missiles are carried on a turntable that can be traversed through 360° and provide the missiles with an elevation of about +85°. For travelling the launcher is normally horizontal and traversed to the rear. The SA-6 missile itself is about 6.20 m (20 ft 4 in) long, 33.5 cm (13.2 in) in diameter and 1.52 m (5 ft 0 in) in span across the tail; the missile has a launch weight of about 550 kg (1,213 lb), of which the warhead weighs about 80 kg (176 lb). The missile's propulsion system consists of an integral ram/rocket, the latter being used to launch the missile. When a speed of about Mach 1.5 has been achieved the ramjet takes over and then increases speed to a maximum of Mach 2.8. The original version has a maximum range of about 22000 m (24,060 yards), and an en-

gagement altitude envelope between 100 to 9000 m (330 to 29,530 ft).

A target engagement takes place as follows. The 'Long Track' radar first detects the target and passes target information such as bearing, altitude and range to the SA-6 battery, where the 'Straight Flush' radar takes over. This is based on a similar chassis to that used by the SA-6 and carries out limited search, low-altitude detection/acquisition, target tracking and illumination, missile radar command guidance and secondary radar missile tracking functions. The 'Straight Flush' locates the target and, if this is confirmed as hostile, locks onto it using its tracking and illumination radars. Once this has been accomplished the radar changes to the continuous-wave mode and a missile is launched. The missile receives and transmits information back to the 'Straight Flush' radar, and terminal homing is of the semi-active radar type. The warhead is fitted with a radar proximity fuse as well as an impact fuse, and so does not have to

score a direct hit in order to destroy the target.

The basic SA-6 system is now some 20 years old and improved models have recently started to enter service, although the type's replacement could be on hand in the form of the SA-11. The Israelis captured many examples of this system in the 1973 Middle East war and were soon able to devise countermeasures to enable their aircraft to survive over the battlefield, and this information plus a number of complete SA-6 systems were supplied to the United States.

Specification
SA-6 'Gainful'
Dimensions: length 6.2 m (20 ft 4 in); diameter 33.5 m (13.2 in); span 1.52 m (5 ft 0 in)
Launch weight: about 550 kg (1212 lb)
Performance: speed Mach 2.8; maximum range 22-30 km (13.67 to 18.67 miles); range at low level about 60 km (37.34 miles); maximum ceiling up to 18000 m (59,000 ft) according to model

SA-7 'Grail' man-portable surface-to-air missile system

The **SA-7 'Grail'** man-portable SAM was developed in the early 1960s and is similar in concept to the US Redeye missile. It was first used in combat in the 1967 Middle East war, and has been issued to every member of the Warsaw Pact, most countries that have received Soviet aid and many guerrilla factions around the world. It is operated by a two-man team consisting of the gunner, who carries a gripstock and one missile in a canvas bag, and an assistant gunner who carries an additional missile.

The SA-7 system consists of the missile in its launcher, thermal battery and a reusable gripstock. The missile itself has an infra-red seeker head, two canard fins at the front and four spring loaded tail fins that stabilize the missile in flight. The gripstock assembly is attached to the underside of the forward part of the launcher, and contains the trigger mechanism, safety switch, locking pin and an audible alarm. The circular thermal battery is attached to the forward part of the gripstock assembly by a key slot which contains four locking pins.

A typical target engagement takes place as follows. Once the operator has sighted a target he removes the end cap of the launch tube and points the launcher at the target. The trigger has two stages of operation, the first stage switching on the thermal battery. When the missile has picked up sufficient infra-red radiation from the target an audible warning is given and a light also comes on. The trigger is then pulled right back and the missile is ejected from the launcher by a motor which burns out before the tail of the missile has left the launcher. A rocket booster then accelerates the missile to Mach 1.5 and the sustainer takes over. The infra-red seeker then homes onto the exhaust of the aircraft or helicopter. The missile is fitted with a direct-action and graze fuse, and therefore has to hit the target in order to detonate. The warhead contains RDX/AP explosive but from all accounts this will damage the aircraft rather than destroy it. If the missile has not hit its target after a period of 15 seconds or a range of about 6.5 km (4.04 miles) it will self-destruct. There are many accounts of Israeli aircraft, especially McDonnell Douglas A-4s, that returned with damaged tailpipes. Fresh missiles are delivered to the unit in wooden boxes which contain two missiles and four thermal batteries.

The SA-7 has a maximum speed of 1600 km/h (994 mph) and a maximum range and altitude of about 3.2 km (2 miles), while the later-production **SA-7B** has a maximum speed of 1930 km/h (1,200 mph) and a maximum altitude of about 4800 m (15,750 ft). When originally introduced the system was not fitted with an IFF system and the crew had therefore to make a positive identification before launching a missile, but later models were fitted with a IFF system. The SA-7B has a 28-pin connector between the gripstock and the launcher whereas the original model has a 24-pin connector.

The SA-7 missile has many limitations including its infra-red seeker, which tends to make it chase the aircraft, its relatively low speed and altitude, its limited manoeuvrability, its somewhat protracted warming-up period and its lack of an IFF system. All these make the SA-7 a somewhat ineffective weapon against combat aircraft moving at more than 925 km/h (575 mph). The threat of the SA-7 does, however, force pilots to fly at a higher altitude, where they can be engaged by other anti-aircraft systems.

Specification
SA-7 'Grail'
Dimensions: length of missile 1.30 m (4 ft 3.2 in); diameter about 7.0 cm (2.75 in); length of launcher 1.346 m (4 ft 5 in)
Weights: launcher 10.6 kg (23.4 lb); missile 9.2 kg (20.3 lb)
Performance: effective altitude between 45 and 1500 m (150 and 4,920 ft); range 3.2 km (2 miles)

SA-8 'Gecko' surface-to-air missile system

The **SA-8 'Gecko'** low-altitude surface-to-air missile system was first deployed in the early 1970s, and was first seen in public during a parade held in Red Square, Moscow, during 1975. Unlike earlier Soviet self-propelled air-defence missile systems, the SA-8 'Gecko' is completely self-contained in that it has its own tracking and surveillance radars and so can therefore operate on its own. In the Soviet army it is now rapidly replacing the 57-mm S-60 towed anti-aircraft gun, each division having five batteries each with four SA-8s and four missile resupply vehicles. At HQ level there is one 'Thin Skin' height-finding and two 'Long Track' surveillance radars for command and control. The system is also used by Jordan and Syria, and the latter country used the SA-8 operationally for the first time in the Bekaa Valley in the Lebanon during 1982.

The system is mounted on a 6×6 chassis which is believed to be a development of the ZIL-167 vehicle; this is fully amphibious, being propelled in the water by two waterjets at the rear of the hull. Steering is on the front and rear axles and a central tyre-pressure regulation system allows the driver to adjust the tyre pressures to suit the type of ground being crossed. The crew compartment, which is provided with an NBC system, is at the front of the hull, with the missile system in the centre, and the engine and transmission at the rear.

The missile system can be traversed through 360° and has two missiles in the ready-to-launch position on side at the rear, surveillance radar with a range of 30 km (18.6 miles) on top (when travelling this can be lowered horizontally to the rear), and the missile guidance group at the front. The last consists of the large central tracking radar with a smaller missile-guidance radar and a command-link

Left: The first version of the SA-8 'Gecko' (called Romb in the Soviet army) had four missiles in the ready-to-launch position but the production version is believed to have six missiles in launch/transport containers. It was first used in combat by Syria in mid-1982. On mobilization a further two launchers are issued to each battery.

horn for missile-gathering on each side. Mounted above each missile guidance radar is a low-light-level television/optical assistance system, which is believed to be used for tracking in conditions of either low visibility or heavy electronic countermeasures. Why the system has two tracking and two guidance radars is not completely clear, but it is probably to allow a salvo of two missiles to be launched at a target, with a gap between launchings, to give a higher kill probability. The missiles are believed to have infra-red and semi-active seekers.

The missile has a launch weight of 190 kg (419 lb) and is 3.20 m (10 ft 6 in) long, 21.0 cm (8.25 in) in diameter and 64.0 cm (25.2 in) in span. The solid-propellant single-stage rocket motor produces a maximum speed of Mach 2. Minimum and maximum target engagement altitudes are 50 m (165 ft) and 13000 m (42,650 ft), and maximum slant range is about 12 km (7.5 miles).

More recently an improved version of the SA-8 has been seen, and this has been given the Western designation **SA-8B.** This has six missiles in the ready-to-launch position, and these, which are possibly longer and have increased capabilities, are carried in fully enclosed containers. The latter provide the missile with increased environmental protection as well as giving the missile protection against rough handling in the field. The SA-8 launcher system has no integral reload capability.

Specification
SA-8 'Gecko'
Dimensions: length 3.2 m (10 ft 6 in); diameter 21.0 cm (8.25 in); span 64 cm (25.2 in)
Launch weight: 190 kg (419 lb)
Performance: speed Mach 2; range 12 km (7.5 miles); minimum engagement height 50 m (164 ft); maximum ceiling 13000 m (42,650 ft)

SA-9 'Gaskin' surface-to-air missile system

The **SA-9 'Gaskin'** low-altitude SAM system was developed in the 1960s and was first seen in public in the 1970s. It is deployed in the Soviet Army on the scale of 16 systems per division, with each regiment, be they tank or motorized rifle, having four systems. In addition to being used by the Soviet Union the SA-9 is also used by many other countries including Algeria, Egypt, East Germany, Hungary, India, Iraq, Libya, Poland, South Yemen, Syria, Vietnam and Yugoslavia. The first known operational use of the SA-9 system was in Lebanon in May 1981 when an SA-8 battery manned by Libyans engaged Israeli aircraft. The battery was subsequently destroyed by the Israeli air force without loss. The type has also been used operationally by Iraq against Iranian aircraft during the recent conflict.

The SA-9 'Gaskin' system is essentially the BRDM-2 (4×4) reconnaissance vehicle with its one-man machine-gun turret removed and replaced by a new power-operated turret. In the forward part of this is a seat for the operator, who is provided with a large transparent window to his front. To the rear of the operator is a pedestal and on each side of this are two missiles in their ready-to-launch containers. When the vehicle is travelling, the launcher and its associated missiles lie horizontally along the top of the hull. Once the four missiles have been launched the empty canisters have to be removed, and new missiles in their

containers are then loaded manually by the crew from outside the vehicle. As far as it is known the SA-9 retains the amphibious characteristics of the BRDM-2 and is fitted with two belly wheels between the front and rear axles, allowing it to cross trenches with ease.

It is believed that the missile is a further development of the SA-7 man-portable missile but fitted with a more powerful rocket motor for increased performance and a longer range. It is probable that target engagement is similar to that of the SA-7 but with two missiles launched at each target (with gap of five seconds) for a higher kill probability. The missile's infra-red seeker is set to operate against different target intensities in order to defeat flare-type decoys launched by the target aircraft.

The missile itself is carried and launched from a container that protects it during handling, and is about 1.829 m (6 ft 0 in) long, 11.0 cm (4.33 in) in diameter and 30.0 cm (11.8 in) in span. It has an effective range of 8000 m (8,750 yards) and a maximum engagement altitude of 4000 m (13,125 ft). The missile is believed to weigh about 30 kg (66 lb) and to have a maximum speed of more than Mach 1.5.

The SA-9 'Gaskin' has a number of major drawbacks in that it is a clear-weather system only and the gunner must traverse his turret continuously on the look out for targets, although initial target information such as direc-

tion, speed and altitude are probably provided from a central command post. The rate of fire is slow as the missiles have to be reloaded manually. For some years there have been unconfirmed reports that the SA-9 is being fitted with the 'Gun Dish' radar (as fitted to the ZSU-23-4 self-propelled anti-aircraft gun system) to give the system an all-weather capability. This radar, which is probably mounted above the turret, carries out target-acquisition and tracking functions to a maximum range of about 20 km (12.4 miles).

Because of its limitations the SA-9 is now being replaced by the SA-13 system, which has its own radars and carries four missiles in the ready-to-launch position.

An SA-9 'Gaskin' system, based on the BRDM-2 (4×4) amphibious scout car, parades through Red Square, Moscow.

Specification
SA-9 'Gaskin' launcher system
Crew: 3
Weight: 8000 kg (17,635 lb)
Dimensions: length 5.75 m (18 ft 10.4 in); width 2.35 m (7 ft 8.5 in); height (travelling) 2.35 m (7 ft 8.5 in)
Powerplant: one GAZ-41 V-8 water-cooled petrol engine developing 140 hp (104 kW)
Performance: maximum road speed 100 km/h (62 mph); maximum range 750 km (466 miles); fording amphibious; gradient 60 per cent; vertical obstacle 0.4 m (15.75 in); trench 1.25 m (4 ft 1 in)

SA-11 'Gadfly' surface-to-air missile

The **SA-11** is the replacement for the SA-6 'Gainful' SAM system, which has now been in service for almost 20 years. The chassis is similar to that of the SA-6 but carries four missiles on a turntable that can be traversed

through 360°. A second vehicle based on a similar chassis carries acquisition, guidance and tracking radars that provide information on the target's height, bearing and range. The missile, according to American sources, is ab-

out 5 m (16 ft 5 in) long and has a maximum effective altitude of 14000 m (45,930 ft) and a minimum altitude of less than 100 m (330 ft). Minimum range is about 3 km (1.86 miles) and maximum range is around 30 km (18.6

miles). Unconfirmed reports have stated that the SA-11 was introduced into the Soviet army in limited numbers in 1980 and that a small quantity have been deployed to Iraq and Syria for evaluation purposes.

SA-13 'Gopher' surface-to-air missile

The **SA-13** (an American designation in the absence of any known Soviet designation) was developed in the late 1970s and was first seen in the Group of Soviet Forces Germany (GSFG) in the spring of 1980. It is the replacement for the SA-9 Gaskin system on the BRDM-2 (4×4) chassis, and is issued on the scale of 16 systems per tank and motorized rifle division. Early in 1983 sever-

al SA-13 SAM systems were seen deployed around Kabul airport in Afghanistan.

The SA-13 is based on the chassis of the MT-LB multi-purpose tracked vehicle and has four missiles in the ready-to-launch position. The missiles are in containers of a type similar to those of the SA-9, and a version with six launch containers has also been

observed. Between the two banks of two missiles is a range-only radar, though passive radar emission detectors are also mounted. Most sources state that the seeker on the missile is cryogenically cooled and operates on two frequency bands. The latter factor gives a higher degree of resistance to infra-red countermeasures such as flares dropped or ejected from aircraft

and helicopters. Effective engagement altitude are a minimum of 50 m (165 ft) and a maximum of 10000 m (32,810 ft), and a slant range of 8 km (5 miles) is claimed. As far as it is known the SA-13 has no rapid reload system, although there is sufficient space inside of the vehicle to carry at least one complete reload of missiles. The system is believed to be in service with Syria.

M48 Chaparral surface-to-air missile system

The **M48 Chaparral** low-level self-propelled SAM system was developed some 20 years ago to meet a urgent US Army requirement. It consists essentially of a modified M548 tracked carrier, which is a member of the M113 family, with a missile launch station mounted on the rear. The latter consists of the base structure and turret with its four Chaparral missiles in the ready-to-launch position. The Chaparral is basically the Sidewinder air-to-air infra-red homing missile modified for the surface-to-air role. In the US Army a composite anti-aircraft battalion has 24 Chaparral SAM systems and 24 M163 20-mm Vulcan self-propelled anti-aircraft gun systems,

early warning for the battalion being provided by a number of truck-mounted AN/MPQ-49 Forward Area Alerting Radars.

The original missile used with the system was the **MIM-72A** which weighed 85 kg (187 lb) of which 11.2 kg (24.7 lb) was explosive; this

was replaced in production in the late 1970s by the much-improved MIM-72C which is slightly heavier at 86.3 kg (190 lb) but has a more powerful HE blast fragmentation warhead, new proximity fuse and a new seeker.

When travelling the launcher is normally covered by a tarpaulin cover

over metal frames, which can quickly be removed and stowed at the front of the vehicle. Reserve missiles are carried below and to each side of the launcher, and are reloaded manually.

The basic Chaparral is a day system, and a typical target engagement would take place as follows. The target aircraft would first be detected visually or by the AN/MPQ-49 radar. The gunner, who is seated under a transparent dome in the centre of the launcher, with two missiles to each side of his position, then acquires the target and continues tracking it using his power controls. Turret traverse is 360°, and the missiles on their launcher arms can be elevated to +90° and depressed to −5°. When the target is within the infra-red sensing range of the missile an audio tone is given in the gunner's headset. The missile is then launched and the gunner can then start tracking another target or keep tracking the original target in case the missile does not hit the target. Once the missile is launched it homes onto the hot exhaust of the target and the proximity fuse means that a direct hit is not required in order to destroy the target. The Chaparral system can engage targets flying at an altitude of between 350 and 3050 m (1,000 and 10,000 ft) and has a maximum range of 6000 m (6,560 yards).

The Chaparral was to have been replaced in the US Army by the Roland surface-to-air missile system manufactured in the United States by Boeing and Hughes Aircraft, but production of the Roland system was terminated in 1983 after only 27 systems, these being issued to the Texas National Guard. To keep the Chaparral system effective into the 1980s and beyond, several im-

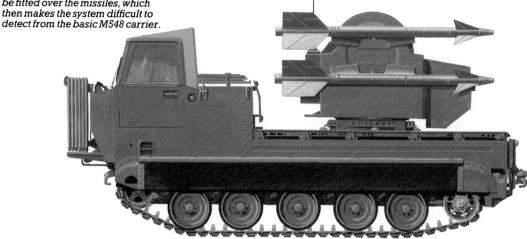

Chaparral SAM system in travelling configuration. If required the bows stowed on the front of the vehicle can be fitted over the missiles, which then makes the system difficult to detect from the basic M548 carrier.

provements are already being carried out to the system. These include a new smokeless motor for the missile, which makes detection of the launcher itself more difficult; a new seeker to reduce the effect of enemy countermeasures; and a forward-looking infra-red thermal imaging device. The latter will be mounted on the forward part of the launcher and will give the system a partial night and adverse-weather

capability as well as improving its performance under normal operating conditions.

Almost 700 of these systems have now been built by Ford Aerospace, and in addition to being used by the US Army they are also operated by Ecuador, Greece, Israel, Morocco, Taiwan and Tunisia; a naval version has also been developed and is used by Taiwan.

Specification
M48 Chaparral
Dimensions: length 2.91 m (9.54 ft); diameter 13 cm (5.12 in); span 64 cm (25.19 in)
Launch weight: 84 kg (185.18 lb)
Performance: speed, supersonic; range 6 km (3.72 miles); minimum engagement height 350 m (1,150 ft); maximum ceiling 3050 m (10,000 ft)

MIM-104 Patriot surface-to-air missile system

The **MIM-104 Patriot** tactical air-defence system has been developed from 1965 to meet the requirements of the US Army for a missile system to replace both the HAWK and Nike-Hercules. Prime contractor is the Raytheon Corporation, the principal sub-contractors being Martin-Marietta Aerospace for the missile airframe and launcher, and the Hazeltine Corporation for the IFF interrogator. First test launches took place in 1970 but for a variety of reasons, including both cost and design problems, limited production of the system was not authorized for some time, and the first operational Patriot battalion was not fielded until early 1983.

A typical Patriot fire unit consists of the radar set, engagement control system, electric powerplant, five launch stations (although a maximum of eight can be controlled by one radar set and engagement set), and supporting vehicles and equipment.

The AN/MPQ-53 radar set is a multi-function phased-array unit that provides for all of the functions of airspace surveillance, target detection and track, and support of missile guidance. The combination of computer control and phased-array technology permits the time-sharing of functions so that the performance workload of this radar is equal to that of the nine different radars used by present-day systems. The radar is on semi-trailer that is towed by a standard 5-ton (6×6) truck.

The AN/MSQ-104 engagement station is installed in a container carried on the rear of a standard M816 (6×6) long wheelbase truck, and houses the system's two operators, the weapons control computer and two tactical display consoles. The software-controlled computer exercizes author-

ity over all tactical operations from radar scheduling, weapon assignment, missile launch and intercept assessment. Several operating modes are available, including computer-aided manual mode, semi-automatic and full automatic, with the operator always retaining full override capability of computer decisions.

The M901 launch station is mounted on a semi-trailer which has its own generator and is also towed by a 5-ton 6×5 truck. Each of the four missiles is sealed into a canister which serves both as travelling and launcher tube. In a tactical situation the launchers are widely dispersed and communicate with the engagement control station via secure radio data links.

The missile itself is delivered to the unit as a certified round requiring no maintenance in the field. From the nose, the missile consists of the radome, semi-active radar (plus command) terminal guidance, high explosive warhead, propulsion system and control actuator section at the very rear. The missile has a five-year storage life and according to the manufacturer its high-g tail control outmanoeuvres any manned aircraft. The missile is powered by a single-stage solid-propellant Thiokol TX-486 motor which gives a maximum speed of Mach 3.

In 1979 the USA together with Belgium, Denmark, France, Germany,

Greece and the Netherlands signed a memorandum of understanding to study the most practical and economic ways for the European countries to procure the Patriot system. The system will be fully operational by the end of the 1980s, its high performance, powerful warhead and unique Track Via Missile (TVM, with a data downlink to upgrade the information in the digital computer in the engagement control station) guidance aspect ensuring the ability of the US Army to deal with targets of an air-breathing nature at all altitudes.

A Patriot SAM is launched from its canister during early trials. In the US Army this SAM will replace the HAWK and Nike Hercules and is expected to be made under licence in Europe.

Specification
MIM-104 Patriot
Dimensions: length 5.18 m (17 ft 0 in); diameter 40.6 cm (16 in); wing span 91.4 cm (36 in)
Launch weight: about 998 kg (2,200 lb)
Performance: maximum ceiling 24000 m (78,750 ft); range 60 km (37.3 miles)

MIM-23B Improved HAWK surface-to-air missile system

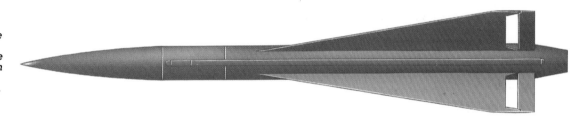

Above: Raytheon HAWK missile being launched. The HAWK is the most widely used SAM in the West and is also being built under licence by a European consortium headed by France and West Germany. Since being introduced in 1960 it has been constantly updated to enable it to remain an effective weapon system. The latest model is called the Improved HAWK.

The **HAWK** (Homing All the Way Killer) was developed by Raytheon to meet the requirements of the US Army. The first guided launch took place in June 1956 when a HAWK successfully shot down a QF-80 drone aircraft. The first US Army **MIM-23A HAWK** battalion was activated in August 1960, and since then the type has been purchased by some 20 countries and is also being built under licence in Europe and Japan. Since it was first introduced the HAWK has been constantly updated to meet the changing threat. The type was first used operationally in the 1973 Middle East war when Israeli HAWKs were credited with the destruction of at least 20 Egyptian and Syrian aircraft.

The latest model is the **MIM-23B Improved Hawk**, and this has a new guidance package, a larger and more effective warhead, improved motor propellant, and many smaller changes to the fire-control system. Mainte-

nance has also been much improved as electronics have not only become much smaller but also much more reliable since the missile was developed in the 1950s. The Improved HAWK entered service with the US Army in the 1970s, and most HAWK users are now bringing their older systems up to the improved standard.

Today an Improved HAWK battery consists of the Pulse Acquisition Radar, a new Continuous-Wave Acquisition Radar, the Range Only Radar, the Battery Control Centre, the high-power Continuous-Wave Illuminator, three launchers each with three missiles, plus tracked missile loaders/transporters. The launchers are mounted on a two-wheeled carriage that can be towed by a 2½-ton (6×6) truck or similar vehicles. A self-propelled version of the HAWK mounted on a modified M548 tracked carrier chassis designated the **M727 SP HAWK** was developed, but this was only used by

Israel and the United States, and is no longer in service with the former.

A typical Improved HAWK target engagement takes place as follows. The PAR and CWAR (the latter concerned with low-altitude threats) sweep the HAWK battery's area of defence, and when a target is detected and confirmed as hostile its position is relayed to the CWI radar. The latter illuminates the target with electromagnetic energy which is reflected back to the guidance system of the missile. The HAWK missile tracks the target by following the reflected electromagnetic energy. The missile itself is fitted with a high explosive blast-fragmentation warhead, and is powered by a dual-thrust solid-propellant motor.

A recent introduction into the US Army MIM-23B force is the Northrop-developed Tracking Adjunct System (TAS). This is a passive sensor system which tracks targets picked up by the

Improved HAWK radar and displays them on a television monitor. This increases the survivability of the HAWK battery as it enables operations to be carried out with a reduction of signals detectable by an enemy. It also permits the operator to discriminate between targets close together or near the horizon.

The nearest Soviet system to the Improved HAWK is the SA-6 'Gainful'; this is more mobile than the American system but it has a shorter operational range. In the US Army HAWK is to be replaced by the Raytheon Patriot.

Specification
MIM-23B Improved HAWK
Dimensions: length 5.12 m (16 ft 9½ in); diameter 35.6 cm (14 in); wing span 1.22 m (48 in)
Launch weight: 626 kg (1,380 lb)
Performance: effective ceiling 30 to 11580 m (100 to over 38,000 ft); range 40 km (25 miles)

FIM-92A Stinger man-portable surface-to-air missile system

The **Stinger** man-portable surface-to-air missile system, officially designated **FIM-92A**, was developed to meet the requirements of the US Army and US Marine Corps by the Pomona Division of General Dynamics, who had developed the earlier Redeye.

Main improvements over the Redeye may be summarized as an all-aspect engagement capability (it being possible for the operator to engage the aircraft while it is flying towards him), an IFF system, improved range and manoeuvrability, and much improved re-

sistance to enemy countermeasures. The Stinger can intercept and destroy hovering helicopters and high-speed manoeuvring targets. It became operational with the US Army in Germany during 1981, and with the 82nd Airborne Division in the continental USA

during 1982. It has also been ordered by Japan and will be built under licence in Europe.

A typical target engagement takes place as follows. The operator visually acquires the target and aligns this with the open sight on the launcher. He then

General Dynamics (Pomona Division) Stinger missile just coming out of its launcher tube. In September 1983 it was announced that this missile would be manufactured under licence in Europe for some NATO countries. A limited number of Stingers were used operationally by the SAS during the Falklands conflict; the missile is credited with destroying one Pucará ground-attack aircraft.

uses his belt-mounted IFF system, which is claimed to be the smallest of its type in the world, to identify the aircraft positively. If it is confirmed as hostile he actuates the missile functions and the missile is then launched and homes onto the enemy aircraft without any further action by the operator. The gripstock is then detached from the empty launcher, which is discarded to permit a fresh launcher/missile to be attached to the gripstock for the engagement of another target.

The missile has an HE warhead, electronic control system and a dual-thrust rocket motor, in which an ejector motor launches the missile before the flight motor boosts the missile to its Mach 2+ cruising speed once clear of the launcher. The Stinger uses a passive infra-red seeker and proportional navigation guidance.

For ease of transport the missile (in its launcher complete with gripstock, IFF system and battery coolant units) comes in a compact aluminium container which can be easily transported on the back of vehicles or in aircraft and helicopters without damage to the contents.

Currently under development by General Dynamics is the **Stinger-POST** (Passive Optical Seeker Technique) which has an advanced electro-optical seeker that uses a rosette scan to enable the missile to discriminate between targets and their background; this will be of particular use when engaging aircraft at very low level.

In addition to the air-defence version of Stinger two other versions have been proposed by General Dynamics. These are the **Multi-purpose Lightweight Missile System** (MLMS) and the **Air-Defence Suppression Missile** (ADSM), both of which are intended for use in helicopters. The MLMS would give helicopters an air-to-air capability against other helicopters, and a typical installation would consist of a pod of two missiles for the air-to-air role on one side of the helicopter and a pod of anti-tank missiles on the other side of the helicopter. As an alternative a small number of Stinger-armed helicopters would be dedicated to the air-to-air role. The ADSM would be similar to the Stinger but would be fitted with an anti-radiation seeker to enable it to home onto enemy radars, for example those of the 23-mm ZSU-23-4 self-propelled anti-aircraft gun system.

Specification
FIM-92A Stinger
Dimensions: length 1.52 m (5 ft 0 in); diameter 7.0 cm (2.75 in); span 9.14 cm (3.16 in)
Weights: missile 10.1 kg (22.3 lb); missile and launcher 13.6 kg (30 lb); complete system 15.1 kg (33.3 lb)
Performance: maximum ceiling 4800 m (15,750 ft); maximum range 5 km (3.1 miles)

JAPAN
Tan-SAM surface-to-air missile system

The **Tan-SAM** short range surface-to-air missile system has been developed by Toshiba from the mid-1960s as a replacement for the wide range of anti-aircraft guns at present used by the Japanese Ground Self-Defense Force, most of which date back to World War II. As a result of the usual shortage of funds, development of the Tan-SAM has been very slow, technical tests being carried out between 1972 and 1977 and operational tests in 1978 and 1979. Late in 1980 the weapon was finally standardized as the **Type 81** short-range SAM system, the first production units being delivered in 1982.

In the Japanese Ground Self-Defense Force the Tan-SAM will be deployed at division level, with each division allocated four sets, each of the latter comprising one fire-control vehicle and two launchers each mounted on an unarmoured Type 73 Truck (6×6), a type widely used by the Japanese Ground Self-Defense Force. The system will also be deployed by the Japanese Air Self-Defense Force for the defence of air bases.

The three main components of the system are the missile, the launcher and the fire-control system. The missile is powered by a single-stage solid-propellant rocket motor, which accelerates it to a maximum speed of about Mach 2.4. A major drawback is

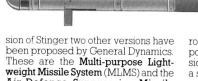

Tan-SAM is transported and launched from an unarmoured (6×6) truck and entered service with the Japanese Ground Self-Defense Forces in 1982.

that the rocket emits a considerable amount of smoke, which could lead to the launcher being detected and subsequently destroyed. The missile has an HE warhead and an infra-red passive homing/inflight lock-on guidance system; and in the centre of the missile are four wings, the four control fins being located at the rear.

The launcher is mounted on the rear of the Type 73 truck and once the four missiles have been launched new missiles are loaded hydraulically, although they have to be unpacked from the transit cases by hand. The launcher is stabilized by hydraulically operated legs.

The fire-control system consists of a phased-array search radar and a fire-control computer plus three cathode-ray tubes (CRTs) on which target information is displayed. The radar antenna rotates 10 times per minute

and sweeps through 360° in azimuth and 15° in elevation. In the sector-search mode it sweeps 110° in azimuth and 20° in elevation. The radar, which has an IFF system, has a range of 30 km (18.6 miles) and can handle a number of targets at the same time. The fire-control system has a four-man crew consisting of the commander, radar operator and two launch operators. To the rear of the cab is a generator.

Once the vehicles have halted it takes about 30 minutes for the system to become operational as the two launch vehicles have to be connected with the FCS; the vehicles can be up to 1000 m (1,095 yards) apart. Once operational the radar starts to search for targets with information (range, altitude and bearings) displayed on the CRT. The target is then selected by the commander and tracked by the radar. When the target is within range a mis-

sile is launched. For the first part of its flight the missile flies under command of the autopilot, but then the infra-red seeker takes over and locks onto the target and the target is destroyed. A Tan-SAM battery can handle up to four targets at once.

One of the major drawbacks of this system is the poor mobility of the Type 73 truck, the complete lack of any armour protection for the system and its crew, and the relatively low rate of fire.

Specification
Tan-SAM surface-to-air missile system
Dimensions: length 2.70 m (8 ft 10.3 in); diameter 16.0 cm (6.3 in); span 60.0 cm (23.6 in)
Launch weight: 100 kg (220 lb)
Performance: maximum ceiling (estimated) 3000 m (3,280 yards); maximum range (estimated) 7000 m (7,655 yards)

Assault Rifles

Today's assault rifle is more accurate than most soldiers can fire it. It has reached a level of performance which will be hard to improve upon. Where do we go from here?

The assault rifle – a light-weight rifle, firing a small-calibre cartridge and capable of single shots or automatic fire – has now become virtually the standard weapon in every army. Four cartridges feed assault rifles: the 7.62-mm x 51-mm NATO and 7.62 x 39-mm Soviet – both in decline in popularity – and the 5.56 x 45-mm NATO and 5.45 x 39-mm Soviet, both of which are in common use. The reasons for the move to a smaller round have little to do with the realities of warfare but a great deal to do with the realities of peacetime training. The small cartridges mean smaller and simpler rifles, lighter ammunition to carry, and reduced recoil when the rifle is fired, giving a less well-trained marksman a greater chance of hitting the target. Yesterday's soldier spent hours perfecting his marksmanship. Today's spends less time firing his rifle because he has a vast range of other equipment to master: surveillance radars, night vision equipment, infantry fighting vehicles to name but a few. Hence any design improvements which make a rifle easier to operate are welcomed.

We now have rifles which are as technically advanced as we can make them. In the 1980s the

Compact firepower: the Swiss SG551 SWAT assault rifle. Designed for civil defence forces it has a unique triple magazine to permit fast changes, and a telescopic sight for pinpoint accuracy.

US Army spent more than $300 million testing prototypes for their 'Advanced Combat Rifle'. They found none could provide sufficient improvement over the M16A2 service rifle to make worthwhile the huge cost that a switch would involve, so the US Army will start the 21st century with a version of a weapon that first entered service in 1960s.

The pointer to the future was the German G11 rifle, firing caseless ammunition, the development of which had taken some 15 years. A technical masterpiece, it failed at the last minute because of a cut in the defence budget in the wake of the collapse of the Soviet threat.

Designs for new assault rifles continue to appear, but in 99 cases out of every 100 they are simply reworked versions of existing designs – either Stoner's AR-15 or Kalashnikov's AK – with cosmetic changes or perhaps a new, exotic and totally impractical design of cartridge. As this chapter shows, anyone requiring an assault rifle has plenty of choice; there is little demand for anything new.

Steyr 5.56-mm AUG

The **Steyr AUG** (Armee Universal Gewehr, or army universal rifle or gun) is one of the most striking in appearance of all the modern assault rifles and it may almost be said to have a 'Star Wars' look about it. It is a 'bull-pup' design weapon, with the trigger group forward of the magazine, which makes it a short and compact weapon. The thoroughly modern appearance is enhanced by the liberal use of nylonite and other non-metallic materials in the construction. The only metal parts are the barrel and the receiver with the internal mechanism; even the receiver is an aluminium casting. All the materials are very high quality of their kind but the non-use of metal has been carried even as far as the magazine which is clear plastic so that the soldier can see at a glance how many rounds the magazine contains.

The Steyr AUG has been designed to be not only an assault rifle, for by varying the barrel length and the fittings on top of the receiver it can be easily produced as a carbine, or a specialist sniper, or a night-action rifle, or even a form of light machine-gun. By changing the fittings on the receiver the AUG can be fitted with a wide range of night sights or sighting telescopes, but the usual sight is a simple optical telescope with a graticule calibrated for normal combat ranges. Stripping the AUG for cleaning is rapid and simple, and cleaning is facilitated by the use of a chromed barrel interior. The AUG has been designed on a modular system so repairs can be easily effected by changing an entire module such as the trigger group, bolt group etc.

Production of the AUG began in 1978 for the Austrian Army after which it was purchased by Eire, Oman, Saudi Arabia, Morocco and other countries. It was then adopted by Australia and New Zealand in 1988, production taking place in Australia and it is also manufactured under licence in Malaysia.

Specification
Steyr AUG (assault rifle version)
Calibre: 5.56 mm (0.22 in)
Length: 790 mm (31.1 in)
Length of barrel: 508 mm (20.0 in)
Weight loaded: 4.09 kg (9.02 lb)
Magazine: 30-round box
Rate of fire, cyclic: 650 rpm

Above: The standard Steyr 5.56-mm AUG showing the overall 'bull-pup' layout and the optical sight over the receiver. The weapon has a 40-mm MECAR rifle grenade over the muzzle, which can be fired using normal ammunition to a range of about 100 m; HE, smoke and other grenades can be used.

Right: A Steyr 5.56-mm AUG in use by an Austrian soldier. Note the slender barrel with the flash-suppressor/grenade launcher, and how the folding foregrip is easy to hold and use to 'point' the weapon. The ×1 optical sight can be replaced by night sights or image intensifiers for use in poor light.

FA MAS

For some years before and just after World War II the French armaments industry lagged behind the rest of the world in small-arms design, but with the **FA MAS** assault rifle it has made up that leeway with a vengeance. The FA MAS is a thoroughly modern and effective little rifle, and yet another example of the overall compactness that can be achieved by using the unorthodox 'bull-pup' layout with the trigger group in front of the magazine. Even using this design the FA MAS is very short and handy, and must be one of the smallest in-service assault rifle designs of all.

The FA MAS has now been accepted as the standard service rifle for the French armed forces and this alone will keep the weapon coming off the production lines at St Etienne for at least the next 10 years. The first have already been issued to some paratroop and specialist units, and the type was used by French troops in Chad and the Lebanon in 1983. The FA MAS is easy to spot, for in appearance it is quite unlike any other assault rifle. It fires the American M193 5.56-mm cartridge and has over the top of the receiver a long handle that doubles as the rear- and fore-sight base. The butt is prominent and chunky, and from the front protrudes a short length of barrel with a grenade-launching attachment.

The French 5.56-mm FA MAS rifle, one of the smallest and most compact of the modern assault rifles. The magazine has been removed, but note that the carrying handle contains the sights and that the cocking lever is just underneath; note also the folded bipod legs.

There is provision for a small bayonet and bipod legs are provided as standard. The fire selector has three positions: single-shot, automatic and three-round burst. The mechanism to control this last feature is housed in the butt along with the rest of the rather complex trigger mechanism. The operation is a delayed blow-back system. Use is made of plastics where possible and no particular attention is paid to detail finish: for instance, the steel barrel is not chromed.

Despite its unusual appearance the FA MAS is comfortable to handle and fire, and presents no particular problems in use. Attention has been given to such features as grenade sights and generally easy sighting. In service the weapon has proved to be easy to handle, and training costs have been reduced by the introduction of a version that uses a small sparklet gas cylinder to propel inert pellets for target training; this version is identical to the full service version in every other respect.

The FA MAS F-1 has also been adopted by Djobouti, Gabon and Senegal but has been replaced on the export market by the FA MAS G2, a modified version which will fire any type of 5.46-mm ammunition accepts M16-type magazines and NATO-standard sights, and has a full-hand 'trigger-guard' similar to that of the Steyr AUG.

Specification
Calibre: 5.56 mm (0.22 in)
Length: 757 mm (29.80 in)
Length of barrel: 488 mm (19.21 in)
Weight loaded: 4.025 kg (8.87 lb)
Magazine: 25-round box
Rate of fire, cyclic: 900-1,000 rpm
Muzzle velocity: 960 m (3,150 ft) per second

An FA MAS fitted with a TN$_2$1 night sighting infra-red spotlight under the muzzle. This equipment has a useful range of 150 m, and the soldier picks up the infra-red reflections in the night vision binoculars held over his eyes. This equipment is in service with the French army.

BELGIUM/UK

FN FAL and L1A1

Produced by the Belgian concern of Fabrique Nationale, or FN, the rifle now known as the **Fusil Automatique Legère** (FAL, or light automatic rifle) was originally produced in 1948. At that time the prototypes fired the German 7.92-mm×33 *kurz* (short) cartridge but later attempts at NATO ammunition standardization meant that the FAL was eventually chambered for the standard 7.62-mm×51 cartridge. As such it has since been widely adopted, not only throughout NATO but in many other nations, and has even been licence-produced by nations as diverse as South Africa and Mexico. Many of these overseas production models differ in detail from the original FAL but the overall appearance is the same.

The FAL is a sturdy weapon which uses many of the manufacturing methods of a bygone era. High-grade materials are used throughout, and extensive use is made of machining and fine tolerances. The action is gas-operated, using a gas regulation system that taps off propellant gases from above the barrel to operate a piston that pushes back the bolt action for unlocking the breech. The unlocking system has a delay action built in for increased safety. Automatic fire is possible on most models by use of a selector mechanism located near the trigger group.

FAL models are many and various. Most have solid wooden or nylonite butts and other furniture but some models, usually issued to airborne forces, have folding butts that are far sturdier than many other folding butts in use. Overall, sturdiness is a feature of the FAL, for the high manufacturing standards have resulted in a weapon well able to withstand the rigours of service life.

One production version of the FAL that deserves further mention is the British version, known by its service designation **L1A1**. The L1A1 was adopted by the British armed forces only after a lengthy series of trials and modifications that resulted in the elimination of the automatic fire feature, the L1A1 thus firing single-shot only. There are some other differences as well, but the L1A1 itself has been adopted by many other nations, including India where the type is still in production. The Australians also adopted the type and even produced a shorter version, the **L1A1-F1**, to suit the stature of the New Guinea troops.

Both the FAL and the L1A1 are equipped to fire rifle grenades, but these grenades are now little used. Bayonets can also be fitted and some versions of the FAL have heavy barrels and bipods to enable them to be used as light machine-guns. Night sights are another optional fitting.

FN no longer manufacture the FAL but licensed versions are still in production by IMBEL of Brazil, including 5.56mm and .22 rimfire versions.

Specification
Calibre: 7.62 mm (0.3 in)

Top: A British L1A1, the standard British infantry weapon; centre: the FN FAL with a shortened barrel; bottom: an Argentinian FN FAL with folding butt. Note the overall similarity of all these weapons; the bottom two can fire on full automatic, unlike the L1A1.

Length: 1143 mm (45.0 in)
Length of barrel: 554 mm (21.81 in)
Weight loaded: 5 kg (11.0 lb)
Magazine: 20-round box
Rate of fire: 30-40 rpm (single shot) or 650-700 rpm (FAL, cyclic)
Muzzle velocity: 838 m (2,750 ft) per second

Australian infantrymen with their locally-produced version of the British L1A1; these rifles were produced at Lithgow in New South Wales. The Australians also produced a short version called the L1A1-F1 for use by local troops in New Guinea. They also use the M16A1.

5.56-mm Individual Weapon (IW) XL70E3

Immediately after the World War II the British army set about developing a new assault rifle chambered for a new 7-mm compact cartridge, a move which was doubtless inspired by the German development of the Sturmgewehr 44 and the short 7.92-mm cartridge. The rifle, known commonly as the EM2, passed its trials and was approved for service as the 'Rifle, 7-mm, No 9' in 1951. This, came into conflict with the principle of NATO standardisation. Members , free to use whatever rifle they wanted, had to use a cartridge acceptable to all. The Americans could not accept an 'intermediate' cartridge; it had to be their .30 or nothing. Eventually, they compromised on the 7.62 x 51-mm cartridge, which was simply their .30–.06 in a shorter case. Since the Rifle No 9 could not be re-designed to suit the 7.62 x 51-mm cartridge, that was the end of that.

Eventually, the Americans saw the sense of a smaller cartridge – less weight, smaller rifle, less recoil – and carried the thing to extremes by going for the 5.56-mm calibre. So, in the early 1970s small calibres were all the rage, and the British selected a 4.85-mm bullet using the 5.56-mm cartridge case.

The rifle developed for this cartridge was a gas-operated 'bull-pup' design: a rifle with the breech under the firer's chin so as to get the maximum length of barrel into the minimal overall length. It was submitted for the NATO trials of 1978–80, for selection of the next NATO standard cartridge and, as was predicted, the 4.85-mm cartridge was turned down and the 5.56-mm accepted as the future NATO standard, though using a heavier bullet than the American-developed M193 round.

This had been foreseen by the rifle's designers, who re-jigged their design to suit the 5.56-mm SS109 cartridge and submitted it to the army for trials. The design was approved as the 'Rifle, 5.56-mm L85A1' and production began at the Royal Small Arms Factory, Enfield Lock. Just at that time, too, (the early 1980s) the Royal Ordnance Factory organisation was 'privatised' and sold to British Aerospace. They sold the Enfield Lock factory and moved rifle production to the Royal Ordnance Factory at Nottingham, setting up new production machinery and a network of outside sub-contractors. This led to a sudden falling-off of quality and a rash of complaints from the troops about defective rifles. The rifle was introduced into service in 1986, but it took several years for all the defects to be tracked down and rectified. It has now become general issue throughout the British armed forces and is a reliable and well-liked weapon which has lived down its earlier reputation.

The L85 is a gas-operated selective-fire rifle, using a rotating bolt in a carrier. The infantry version is provided with an optical sight, whilst non-infantry troops are issued with an

The soldier on the right is holding the latest form of the 5.56-mm L85A1 Individual Weapon (IW), while the other holds the 5.56-mm Light Support Weapon (LSW) L86A1. Many components of the two weapons are interchangeable and both should soon be in British Army service.

Above: This is the original 4.85-mm XL65E3 Individual Weapon, from which the present 5.56-mm L85A1 has been developed. It differs from the current model in several ways, especially the shape of the forestock, and the magazine is now a slightly curved M16A1 item. Note the large optical sight, known as a SUSAT.

Right: The Light Support Weapon is the section support weapon version of the Individual Weapon. This model is the original version. the XL65E5, which has now been replaced by a 5.56-mm model: the L86A1, with a revised forestock shape and other modifications.

iron-sighted version. There is also a manually-operated single-shot model for Cadet training purposes. All types use the NATO-standard M16 magazine interface.

Specification:
L85A1
Calibre: 5.56-mm (.223-in)
Length: 785-mm (30.90-in)
Length of barrel: 518-mm (20.40-in)

Weight, loaded: 4.98 kg (10 lb 15 oz) with optical sight
Magazine: 30-round box
Rate of fire: 600–775 rds/min
Muzzle velocity: 940 m/sec

M16 family

Unlike so many rifles of its type, the rifle that is now the **M16A1** was a commercial design. It was a product of the prolific designer Eugene Stoner and first emerged as a product of the Armalite concern as its **AR-10** during the mid-1950s. The AR-10 used 7.62-mm ammunition, and with the advent of the 5.56-mm Fireball cartridge the AR-10 was redesigned to suit the new calibre. The result was the **Armalite AR-15.**

The AR-15 was submitted for a competition to decide the new standard rifle for the US armed forces. But before the competition was decided, commercial sales had already started: the British army took a batch of 10,000, making it one of the first customers to purchase significant quantities of the new design, and the US Air Force made another purchase soon afterwards. That was in 1961, and soon after this the AR-15 was selected by the US Army to become its new standard rifle as the **M16**. Production was then switched to the Colt Firearms Company, which took out a production and sales contract with Armalite. Since then Colt has kept its production contract, but somehow the name 'Armalite' still clings to the rifle that is now the M16A1.

The M16 became the M16A1 in 1966 with the addition of a bolt closure device fitted as the result of experiences in Vietnam. Since then the M16A1 can perhaps be regarded as the AK-47 of the Western world, for it has been produced in hundreds of thousands and has been widely issued and sold to nations all around the world. Numerous developments have been produced and tried, ranging from the usual light machine-gun variant with a heavy barrel and a bipod, down to short-barrel versions for special forces; there has even been a submachine gun variant. For all these changes the current M16A1 looks much like the first AR-15. Over the years there have been some changes as the rifling has been modified and more use is now made of internal chroming to aid cleaning. A recent introduction has been the **M16A2** which

has a heavier barrel that can be used with the new NATO 5.56-mm SS109 cartridge, demanding yet another change in rifling.

The M16A1 is a gas-operated weapon that uses the almost universally adopted locking system of the rotary bolt. A carrying handle over the receiver also acts as the rear-sight base, and nylonite is used for all the furniture. Although lending itself to mass production the M16A1 does not have the tinny appearance of many of its contemporaries, and has all the feel and finish of a high-quality weapon. In service it has become the carrier for a number of accessories which range from a blank adaptor to a special 40-mm grenade launcher mounted under the forestock (the M203).

The M16A2, adopted in 1985, uses a barrel with a rifling twist of one turn in 7 inches so that both US M193 and NATO SS109 ammunition can be fired. It also has a somewhat heavier barrel, a revised rear sight, an optional three-round burst facility and a circular handguard. A version of the rifle, with automatic fire instead of three-round bursts, was adopted by the Canadian Army in 1984.

An M16A3 rifle has been devel-

Above: Top: the original M16, recognized by the absence of the bolt-assist plunger of the M16A1 which is located above the trigger group. Below: the Colt Commando, a carbine version of the M16 and used in trials in Vietnam, where it was not a great success.

Right: M16A1 fitted with a 40-mm M203 grenade launcher under the barrel. This launcher can propel small spin-stabilized grenades to a range of about 350 m. Some of these grenades can be seen alongside the launcher and can be produced in a wide range of offensive loads, including HE and CS.

oped but not yet adopted. It is similar to the M16A2 but has removable carrying handle and rear sight unit, allowing electro-optical sights to fitted in their place.

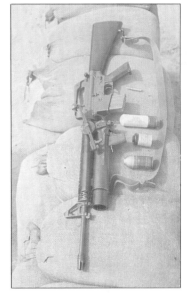

Specification
M16A1
Calibre: 5.56 mm (0.22 in)
Length: 990 mm (38.98 in)
Length of barrel: 508 mm (20.00 in)
Weight loaded: 3.64 kg (8.02 lb)
Magazine: 30-round box

Rate of fire, cyclic: 700-950 rpm
Muzzle velocity: 1000 m (3,280 ft) per seond

Armalite AR-18

Once the Armalite concern had cleared its design desks of the AR-15 with production under way by Colt Firearms of the M16/M16A1 series, it decided to look to the future for new products. With the 5.56-mm round well established, Armalite decided that what was needed was a simple weapon that could fire the cartridge. While the AR-15 was a sound weapon it was not easy to produce without sophisticated machine tools, and throughout much of the world these machine tools were not available. Thus the need for a weapon which could be simply produced by Third World nations was recognized, and a drastic revision of the AR-15 design was undertaken.

The result was the **AR-18**, which is very basically an AR-15 adapted for manufacture by the now-familiar production expedients of pressed steel, plastics and castings. For all these expedients the AR-18 is a sound design that is easy to produce, maintain and use. In general appearance and layout

it is similar to the AR-15 but the stamped steel receiver gives it a bulkier outline. The plastic butt is designed to fold alongside the receiver for stowage or firing from the hip.

Once the AR-18 design was complete Armalite attempted to find purchasers, but with the AK-47 and the M16A1 flooding the world markets there were few takers. An arrangement to produce the AR-18 in Japan fell through and for some years the design was in abeyance. Then the Sterling Armaments Company of the United Kingdom took out a licence, undertak-

ing some production and at one time moving production to Singapore. Some sales were then made locally but what was more important was that the local defence industry took the design as the basis for its own weapon designs, the AR-18 now living on disguised in many forms and under various labels.

Specification
Calibre: 5.56 mm (0.22 in)
Length: 940 mm (37.00 in) with stock extended or 737 mm (29.00 in) with stock folded

This AR-18 was originally manufactured in Japan but was captured from the IRA in Belfast. It is the standard production model with a butt that can be folded along the right-hand side of the receiver. The cocking handle can be seen poking upwards above the magazine.

Weight loaded: 3.48 kg (7.67 lb) with 20-round magazine
Magazine: 20-, 30- and 40-round box
Rate of fire, cyclic: 800 rpm
Muzzle velocity: 1000 m (3,280 ft) per second

Ruger Mini-14

When it was first produced in 1973, the **Ruger Mini-14** marked a significant turn away from the mass production methods introduced during World War II towards the fine finish and attention to detail that was formerly the hallmark of the gunsmith's art. The Mini-14 is an unashamed example of how guns used to be made before the steel stamping and the die-cast alloy came upon the scene.

From a design viewpoint the Ruger Mini-14 is a 5.56-mm version of the 7.62-mm (0.30-in) Garand M1 service rifle of World War II. By adopting the Garand action Ruger has managed to combine a sound and well-engineered design with the ammunition of a new technology. When this is allied to craftsmanship and a deliberate appeal to those who look for that something extra in a weapon the result is a remarkable little rifle.

In appearance the Mini-14 has the characteristics of a previous age. The materials used are all high quality and in an age where plastics have now taken over the furniture is all manufactured from high-grade walnut. But visual appeal has not been allowed to take precedence over functional safety, for the Mini-14 has been carefully engineered to prevent dust and debris entering the action. But some degree of eye appeal has been allowed to affect the finish, for the weapon has been carefully blued all over, and there is even a stainless steel version that sells very well in the Middle East.

The Mini-14 has not yet been adopted by any major armed forces but it has been sold to such establishments as police forces, personal bodyguard units and to many special forces who prefer a well-engineered and balanced weapon to the usual 'tinny' modern products. To suit the requirements of some armed forces Ruger has now developed a special version that should appeal to many soldiers. This is the **Mini-14/20GB**. Police forces have been catered for by the introduction of the **Ruger AC-556** with glassfibre furni-

ture, and another innovation is the **AC-556F** with a folding stock and a shorter barrel. The two AC-556 designs can be used to fire on full automatic for bursts, whereas the normal Mini-14 is a single-shot weapon only.

Specification
Mini-14
Calibre: 5.56 mm (0.22 in)
Length: 946 mm (37.24 in)
Length of barrel: 470 mm (18.50 in)
Weight loaded: 3.1 kg (6.83 lb) with 20-round magazine

Top: The attractive lines of the Ruger Mini-14 seen fitted with a 10-round box magazine. The bottom weapon is the Ruger AC-556F, which is intended for service as a purely military assault carbine. It has a folding metal butt and is seen here fitted with a 30-round box magazine.

Magazine: 10-, 20- or 30-round box
Rate of fire, cyclic: 40 rpm
Muzzle velocity: 1005 m (3,300 ft) per second

Vz.58

At first sight the Czech **vz.58** assault rifle looks very like the Soviet AK-47, but this resemblance is deceptive for the two designs are different mechanically. The vz.58 is a gas-operated weapon but the unlocking mechanism uses a pivoted locking piece in place of the rotating bolt of the AK-47 family. The trigger mechanism is also different and employs flat springs rather than coil springs. The overall result is an entirely different mechanism. Exactly why the Czechs felt it necessary to produce their own design in view of the availability of the AK-47 adopted by all other Warsaw Pact nations is uncertain, but one fact that has resulted from this 'go it alone' stance has been that the vz.58 has been sold on the open arms market with a facility that would not have been possible with the AK-47.

The vz.58 is very well made, with the receiver machined from solid metal.

Early versions used a wooden butt, with plastic for such items as the pistol grip and the forestock. More recent versions have used a form of plastic into which wooden chips and shavings have been compressed resulting in a characteristic appearance. Three basic models have been produced, one with a conventional butt, one with a folding butt and a version with the receiver fitted to take a variety of night sights. The last version may also be fitted with a light bipod and a prominent flash hider over the muzzle.

The facility with which the Czechs can market the vz.58 is such that the type can be purchased commercially 'over the counter' in many countries, but has still been used by armed forces as disparate as the Viet Cong and the IRA. One great attraction of the vz.58 is the price. Although this varies according to the quantity involved it is still relatively low compared with

many other weapons. The Czechs are very willing to supply the 7.62 mm×39 ammunition as well, again at a very attractive price.

Specification
Calibre: 7.62 mm (0.3 in)
Length: 820 mm (32.28 in)
Length of barrel: 401 mm (15.79 in)
Weight loaded: 3.28 kg (8.42 lb)
Magazine: 30-round box
Rate of fire, cyclic: 800 rpm
Muzzle velocity: 710 m (2,330 ft) per second

Seen here carried by a young Czech tank crewman, the Vz.58, also shown below, differs internally from the otherwise ubiquitous Kalashnikov. Also different is the compressed plastic/woodchip mixture which forms the butt and foregrip.

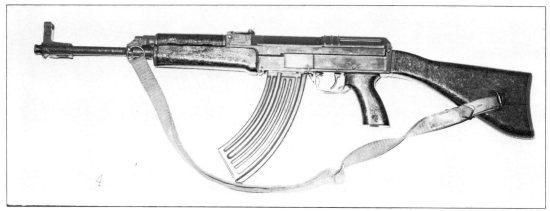

AK-47 and AKM

The **AK-47** must be rated as one of the most successful and widely-used of any type of small arm ever produced. Both it and its successor, the **AKM**, are now used all over the world by forces regular and irregular, and both types are still in production in one form or another in many countries.

The first AK-47 was designed around a short 7.62-mm calibre cartridge that owed much to the introduction of the German 7.92-mm *kurz* round. The Red Army was often on the receiving end of the German assault rifle family (the MP 43, MP 44 and StuG 44) and asked for their own counter. The result was the 7.62-mm×39 cartridge and the AK-47. The designer was Mikhail Kalashnikov and his design is often referred to by his surname. The first examples were issued for service during 1946 and the weapon gradually became the standard weapon of the Warsaw Pact forces. The production lines were huge and the numbers that rolled off them were vast, but such was the demand that most Warsaw Pact nations set up their own production facilities. From this sprang the large numbers of AK-47 sub-variants that continue to delight the gun research buff to this day.

The basic AK-47 is a sound and well-made weapon that carried over few of the mass production expedients employed by its German wartime equivalents. The AK-47 receiver is machined and good-quality steel is used throughout with wooden furniture as standard; the result is a weapon that can absorb any amount of hard use and mishandling. As there are few moving parts and stripping is very simple, maintenance is also simple and can be accomplished with even a minimum of training.

Before long different production versions of the basic AK-47 emerged, even within the Soviet Union, and a version with a folding steel butt was produced. All these different versions used the same mechanism, a simple rotary bolt that was cammed into corresponding grooves in the receiver by bolt cams. Operation is by gas tapped from the barrel via a gas port.

AK-47s were produced in China, Poland and East Germany and the basic design was copied by several designers abroad, including those of the Finnish **Valmet M60** and **M62**.

For all its huge success and accept-

ance, it was finally admitted during the late 1950s that production of the AK-47 was too involved in manufacturing facilities. A redesign produced the AKM, which outwardly resembles the earlier design but is generally revised to facilitate production. The most obvious external change is to the receiver, which is formed from a steel stamping in place of the former machined equivalent, but internally the locking system has been revised to make it more simple. There are numerous other differences but the overall changes are in manufacturing methods.

The AKM did not immediately take the place of the AK-47 but acted more as a supplement to numbers. The other Warsaw Pact production lines gradually switched to the AKM, some nations (such as Hungary) even going so far as to modify the basic design to

produce their own version, which often differs in many ways from the original (the Hungarian **AKM-63** even looks different but retains the basic mechanism of the AKM). A version with a folding steel butt is known as the **AKMS**.

The AKM is still being produced, and the AK-47 and AKM will remain in service until well into the next century, if not beyond. This longevity must be partially attributed to widespread availability and the numbers produced but the basic fact is that the AK-47 and AKM are both sound and tough weapons that are easy to use and simple to maintain.

Specification
AK-47
Calibre: 7.62 mm (0.3 in)
Length: 869 mm (34.21 in)
Length of barrel: 414 mm (16.30 in)
Weight loaded: 5.13 kg (11.31 lb)
Magazine: 30-round box
Rate of fire, cyclic: 600 rpm
Muzzle velocity: 710 m (2,330 ft) per second

Top: AK-47 with folding metal butt; centre: AKM identifiable by muzzle brake attachment and hand-grip on forestock, and bottom: Chinese Type 56 from Zimbabwe, the Chinese version of the AK-47 with its own integral bayonet seen folded under the forestock.

Specification
AKM
Calibre: 7.62 mm (0.3 in)
Length: 876 mm (34.49 in)
Length of barrel: 414 mm (16.30 in)
Weight loaded: 3.98 kg (8.77 lb)
Magazine: 30-round box
Rate of fire, cyclic: 600 rpm
Muzzle velocity: 710 m (2,330 ft) per second

Egyptian troops during the Yom Kippur War of 1973. Their weapons are AKMs with the characteristic angled muzzle attachments and the handgrip grooved into the forestock. The AKM is now the standard Egyptian service rifle.

The AK-47 has been manufactured throughout the Warsaw Pact countries, and this East German infantryman would be armed with the MPiKM version, made in the DDR.

Former USSR
AK-74

The Soviet Union was surprisingly slow in following the Western adoption of small-calibre cartridges for its future weapon designs. Perhaps the huge numbers of AK-47s and AKMs already in service made such a change a low priority, so it was not until the early 1970s that any intimation of a new Warsaw Pact cartridge was given. In time it emerged that the new cartridge had a calibre of 5.45-mm×39 and the first examples of a new weapon to fire it were noted. In time the weapon emerged as the **AK-74**, which is now in full-scale production to meet the requirements of the Red Army; in time it can be expected that the AK-74 will be issued to other Warsaw Pact armed forces.

The AK-74 is nothing more than an AKM revised to suit the new cartridge. It is almost identical to the AKM in appearance, weight and overall dimensions. Some changes, such as a plastic magazine, have been introduced and there is a prominent muzzle brake. There are versions with the usual wooden stock and with a folding metal stock.

One matter relating to the AK-74 that deserves special mention is the bullet used. To gain maximum effect from the 5.45-mm calibre bullet the designers have adopted a design that is very effective but outlawed by international convention, for the steel-cored projectile has a hollow tip and the centre of gravity far to the rear. This has the effect that when the nose strikes a target the nose deforms, allowing the weight towards the rear to maintain the forward impetus and so tumble the bullet. In this way the small-calibre bullet can have an effect on a target far in excess of its cross-sectional area. Some high-velocity projectiles can display this nasty effect, but on some, such as the M193 5.56-mm cartridge, it is an unintended by-product. On the Soviet 5.45-mm the effect has been deliberately designed into the projectile. International conventions have for many years outlawed such 'Dum-Dum' bullets and its various progeny, but to date no corresponding strictures appear to have been forthcoming regarding the 5.45-mm bullet.

Specification (provisional)
Calibre: 5.45 mm (0.215 in)
Length: 930 mm (36.61 in)
Length of barrel: 400 mm (15.75 in)
Weight unloaded: 3.6 kg (7.94 lb)
Magazine: 30-round box
Rate of fire: 650 rpm
Muzzle velocity: 900 m (2,955 ft) per second

Right: An AK-74 (top), with an AKM for comparison beneath. The AK-74 has a skeleton butt, but note the prominent muzzle brake and the brown plastic magazine. Note also the size difference between the 5.45-mm cartridges (top) and the 7.62-mm×39 cartridges.

The AK-74 is now in wide use in the Soviet armies, and has seen service in Afghanistan, where this example was captured. It is to all intents and purposes a small calibre AKM, with many parts seeming identical.

ISRAEL/SOUTH AFRICA
Galil and R4

The exact provenance of the **Galil** assault rifle is a trifle clouded, for although it is claimed that the design is an indigenous Israeli effort, there are some obvious likenesses to the Finnish Valmet assault rifles that were produced in a variety of models and calibres. Things are made more confused by the fact that the Valmet rifles were modelled on the Soviet AK-47. Though it would be an oversimplification to state that the Galil is an AK-47 derivative, there are some resemblances in operation (the usual rotating bolt) and general layout, but these are now common to many designs.

The Galil assault rifle has been produced in both 5.56-mm and 7.62-mm calibres, and is now one of the most widely used weapons issued to the various Israeli armed forces. It is produced in three forms: one is known as the **Galil ARM**, which has a bipod and a carrying handle and is the all-purpose weapon; another is the **Galil AR**, which lacks the bipod and handle; and the third is the **Galil SAR**, which has a shorter barrel and no bipod or carrying handle. All three have folding stocks. The bipod on the ARM can be used as a barbed wire cutter, and all three versions have a bottle cap opener fitted as standard to prevent soldiers using other parts of the weapon as bottle openers (eg the magazine lips). A fixture over the muzzle acts as a rifle grenade launcher.

In its full ARM version the Galil can be used as a form of light machine-gun and 35- and 50-round magazines are produced; there is also a special 10-round magazine used to contain the special cartridges for launching rifle grenades. As usual a bayonet can be fitted.

The Galil has proved to be very effective in action and has attracted a great deal of overseas attention. Some

The Israeli Galil ARM assault rifle with the metal stock folded forward to reduce the length. This version cannot be used to fire rifle grenades and does not have the bipod fitted to the longer models. It can be found calibrated for 5.56-mm and 7.62-mm ammunition.

have been exported and the design has also been copied – the Swedish 5.56-mm **FFV 890C** is obviously based on the Galil. One nation that negotiated licence production was South Africa, and its version is the **R4**, now the standard rifle for the front-line units of the South African defence forces. The R4 is produced in 5.56-mm calibre and differs in some details from the original, the changes resulting mainly from operational experience in the South African and Namibian bush. The R4 has also been exported to some unspecified countries.

Rate of fire, cyclic: 650 rpm
Muzzle velocity: 980 m (3,215 ft) per second

Specification
Galil 7.62-mm ARM
Calibre: 7.62 mm (0.3 in)
Length: 1050 mm (41.34 in)
Length of barrel: 533 mm (20.98 in)
Weight loaded: 4.67 kg (10.30 lb)
Magazine: 20-round box
Rate of fire, cyclic: 650 rpm
Muzzle velocity: 850 m (2,790 ft) per second

Specification
Galil 5.56-mm ARM
Calibre: 5.56 mm (0.22 in)
Length: 979 mm (38.54 in)
Length of barrel: 460 mm (18.1 in)
Weight loaded: 4.62 kg (10.19 lb) with 35-round magazine
Magazine: 35- or 50-round boxes

South Africa has adopted a modified form of the Galil as the new standard weapon of the Defence Forces: the R4 has been strengthened to withstand the rigours of the bush. The bipod is fitted as standard.

ITALY
Beretta AR70

The **Beretta AR70** was developed following a series of manufacturer's in-house trials involving several types of assault rifle designs, and from these evolved a gas-operated design using the rotary bolt locking principle but in a very simple form. For increased safety Beretta decided to strengthen the locking system with extra metal around the chamber area. The result is a functional and well-made weapon that can be stripped down into its few operating parts with ease.

There are three production versions of the AR70: one is the AR70 proper, which has a nylonite stock and furniture; another is the **SC70**, which has a folding butt constructed from shaped steel tubing; and the **SC70 Short** is a version of the SC70 with a shorter barrel for special troops. The AR70 and

SC70 can be used to fire 40-mm rifle grenades the SC70 Short cannot be used in this capacity.

Experience showed that the AR70 had some defects: the pressed steel receiver could deform under severe loads. When the Italian Army expressed a requirement for a 5.56-mm rifle, Beretta set about re-designing the AR70, adding some refinements. The receiver is stronger, has a different shape, with the bolt guides welded in place. The barrel is locked in place by a securing nut removing the need for headspace adjustment. The carrying handle supports are hollow to permit the line of

sight to pass through. It also acts as a mount for optical sights. Rifle and carbine versions were developed. The AS70/90 was adopted by the Italians in 1990.

Specification
AR70
Calibre: 5.56 mm (0.22 in)
Length: 955 mm (37.60 in)
Length of barrel: 450 mm (17.72 in)
Weight loaded: 4.15 kg (9.15 lb)
Magazine: 30-round box
Rate of fire, cyclic: 650 rpm
Muzzle velocity: 950 m (3,115 ft) per second

The Beretta AR70 assault rifle, fitted with a 20-round magazine showing the clean overall lines and good finish. It is used by some Italian anti-guerrilla special units and has been sold in Jordan and Malaysia, but large-scale sales have yet to be made.

The Beretta AR70 in service in the Malaysian jungles; note the applied camouflage paint scheme. The AR70 weighs only 4.15 kg loaded with 30 rounds and is thus a fairly handy weapon for the small-statured Asian races to handle, but they have begun to use the M16.

The AR70 has several equipment options, including the fitting of night sights, a bayonet or a MECAR rifle grenade. The butt is relatively easy to remove and replace with a skeleton butt to convert the rifle to SC70 standard.

Heckler und Koch G3

The **Heckler und Koch G3** assault rifle is a development of the CETME design and was adopted by the West German Bundeswehr during 1959. In many ways it has proved to be one of the most successful of all the post-war German weapon designs and it is still in production not only in West Germany but in numerous other countries which have produced their own weapons under licence.

Although the makers would not like it to be said, the Heckler und Koch G3 is the nearest that designers have come to the use-and-throw-away rifle. Despite the cost the G3 is a weapon designed from the outset for mass production using as much simple machinery as is possible. On the basis of the CETME design Heckler und Koch have developed the design so that plastics and pressed steel are used wherever possible. The ex-CETME locking roller system is retained to provide a form of delayed blow-back when firing.

There is a general resemblance to the FN FAL in the G3 but there are many differences. The G3 is a whole generation ahead of the FN FAL, and this is reflected not only in the general construction and materials but also in the development of a whole family of variants based on the basic G3. There are carbine versions, some with barrels so short they could qualify as submachine guns, sniper variants, light machine-gun versions with bipods and heavy barrels and so on. There is also a version for use with airborne or other such troops: this is the **G3A4**, which has a butt that telescopes onto either side of the receiver.

For all its overall simplicity the G3 has some unusual features. One is the bolt, which is so designed that it locks with the bulk of its mass forward and over the chamber to act as an extra mass to move when unlocking. Stripping is very simple and there are only a very few moving parts. With very few changes the basic G3 can be produced with a calibre of 5.56 mm and this version is already in production as the **Heckler und Koch HK 33**.

The success of the G3 can be seen in the number of nations that have

adopted the type. There are to date no fewer than 48, and of these 13 produce their own weapons under licence. The G3 was prominent in the overthrow of the Shah in Iran and was one of the weapons obtained despite sanctions by Rhodesia when defying the world before the establishment of Zimbabwe. Some nations find it profitable to produce the G3 under licence for further export sales. Into this category have come France and the United Kingdom. In many ways the G3 can be regarded as one of the most important of all modern assault rifles, but it uses the over-powerful NATO 7.62-mm×51 cartridge, in common with other de-

signs such as the FN FAL. Despite this it remains a popular assault rifle and one that will remain in production and service for years to come.

Specification
Heckler und Koch G3A3
Calibre: 7.62 mm (0.3 in)
Length: 1025 mm (40.35 in)
Length of barrel: 450 mm (17.72 in)
Weight loaded: 5.025 kg (11.08 lb)
Magazine: 20-round box
Rate of fire, cyclic: 500-600 rpm
Muzzle velocity: 780-800 m (2,560-2,625 ft) per second

The Heckler und Koch HK 21, a 7.62-mm light machine-gun version of the basic G3. This version uses a belt feed which can be altered to take a 20-round box magazine if required. This model is produced in Portugal and has been widely sold in Africa.

Using the same basic layout as the G3, this 5.56-mm version is known as the HK 33. It can take 20- or 40-round magazines and exists in several versions, including a special sniper's rifle and a version with a telescopic folding butt. Most versions can fire rifle grenades.

Heckler und Koch G11

The G11 rifle is one of the most revolutionary firearm of the 20th century, and the basis of the design is the cartridge it fires. Caseless cartridges have been designed in the past. But the difficulty lies in designing a weapon to use them, and here Tilo Moller, Heckler & Kochs designer, succeeded where others had failed.

It began in 1969 when the German Army asked for a rifle which would give a far higher first round hit probability than any previous weapon. Statistics showed that at 300 m range the dispersion of three shots would invariably result in a hit on the target; but the recoil forces of the 5.56-mm rifle were such that the movement of the barrel between shots would lead to excessive dispersion. Only if the rate of fire could be in excess of 2000 rounds per minute for those three shots, so that barrel movement would be nil, would the statistical theory hold good.

To Heckler & Koch this meant a caseless round; by doing away with the cartridge case two time-consuming phases of the firing cycle – extraction and ejection of the empty case – are also done away with. After much experiment, in conjunction with Dynamit-Nobel, the caseless round evolved as a block of propellant with the bullet embedded inside it, and a combustible cap at the rear end. The propellant is a special variant of Hexogen, designed to prevent ignition of the cartridge when loaded into a hot chamber.

The mechanism of the rifle is enclosed in a plastic casing with a carrying handle/optical sight on top and a pistol grip and trigger underneath. The magazine fits in above the barrel, the bullets pointing downward. By rotating a knob on the right side of the body, a disc, containing the chamber, is brought underneath the magazine; the first round drops

into the chamber, the disc revolves to align the bullet with the barrel, the trigger is pressed and the round is fired. Gas is tapped from the barrel into a conventional piston arrangement to operated the breech disc thereafter. The complete weapon mechanism, breech, barrel and magazine, recoil inside the rifle casing.

When set for automatic fire the same sequence takes place and continues to take place so long as the trigger is pressed, giving a rate of fire of about 600 rounds per minute. When set for a three-round burst, the sequence is entirely different. The first round fires as described above; during the recoil movement the second round is loaded and fired, and then the third. Only then does the recoil movement cease and the recoil force is felt by the firer on his shoulder, after all three bullets have been fired, at a rate slightly greater than 2000 rounds per minute. Since there is no upward

movement of the barrel between the three shots, the dispersion is in line with statistical theory and results in the desired hit probability.

The G11 was to be generally adopted by the German Army in 1990. But due to the re-unification of East and West the defence budget was severely cut and the G11 was among the first victims. About 1000 rifles were made and issued to German Special Forces, after which production ceased.

Specification
Calibre: 4.73-mm (0.186-in)
Length: 750-mm (29.52-in)
Length of barrel: 540-mm (21.26-in)
Weight loaded with 90 rounds: 4.30 kg (9 lb 8 oz)
Magazine: 45-round box
Rate of fire: 600 rds.min (auto fire); 2000 rds/min (3-rd burst)
Muzzle velocity: 930 m/sec (3050 ft/sec)

Machine Guns

The general-purpose machine-gun (GPMG) and the infantryman's rifle were linked through firing the same calibre of ammunition. As the size of rifle ammunition has diminished, so the calibre of machine-gun rounds has also shrunk to bring about a trend for lighter support weapons.

When the machine-gun first appeared it was a large, heavy, water-cooled, belt-fed affair which required two or three men to operate it. World War I brought the light machine-gun: air-cooled, magazine fed, carried by one man and served by two. This situation was standard in all armies at the outbreak of World War II. Germany, however, questioned the necessity for two different weapons to do the same job. Therefore they developed the concept of the 'general-purpose' machine-gun, a weapon which mounted on a tripod could deliver sustained fire for long periods but when fitted with a bipod and shoulder stock was a light machine-gun for the infantry squad.

This idea was a success, and it was widely adopted in the post-war years, with the FN MAG being the prime example. But the theory was based upon one simple premise: that the infantryman's rifle and his machine-guns all fired the same cartridge. Once the assault rifle and the small-calibre cartridge appeared, this relationship was upset. By that time, too, another shortcoming had begun to show itself: GP machine-guns were belt fed, and in the squad role this was inconvenient. Action heroes

The Belgian 5.56-mm FN Minimi machine-gun, using belt feed and with the belt carried inside a compact box beneath the weapon.

may look bold draped in belts of cartridges, but soldiers soon found that they impeded one's passage in most types of undergrowth, while putting belts into a box clamped to the gun usually resulted in bruises.

As a result of all this, 5.56-mm machine-guns have begun to make an impression. They use the same ammunition as the assault

rifle, some can be fed either by magazine or by belt, and most are little heavier than an assault rifle. Sadly some do not permit barrel changes, which is a serious drawback if sustained fire, is called for, although modern technology has produced 'Stellite' barrel linings which allow many thousands of rounds to be fired before a barrel exhibits any wear.

The selection covered in this chapter illustrates current trends: Heckler & Koch for rifle designs modified into machine-guns; the Bren as a long-lived example of 1920s engineering; the SIG and MAG as the epitome of general-purpose guns. The Ultimax and the Minimi represent the new breed of 5.56-mm weapon, and both have begun to appear.

7.62-mm FN MAG

World War II established the general-purpose machine-gun (GPMG) as a viable weapon with its ability to be fired from a light bipod in the assault role and from a heavy tripod in the defensive or sustained role. After 1945 many designers tried to produce their own version of the GPMG concept, and one of the best was produced in Belgium during the early 1950s. The company concerned was Fabrique Nationale or FN, based at Herstal, and its design became known as the **FN Mitrailleuse d'Appui Général** or **MAG**. It was not long before the MAG was adopted by many nations, and today it is one of the most widely-used of all modern machine-gun designs.

The MAG fires the standard NATO 7.62-mm (0.3-in) cartridge and uses a conventional gas-operated mechanism, in which gases tapped off from the barrel are used to drive the breech block and other components to the rear once a round has been fired. Where the FN MAG scores over many comparable designs is that the tapping-off point under the barrel incorporates a regulator device that allows the firer to control the amount of gas used and thus vary the fire rate to suit the ammunition and other variables. For the sustained-fire role the barrel can be changed easily and quickly.

In construction the MAG is very sturdy. Some use is made of steel pressings riveted together, but many components are machined from solid metal, making the weapon somewhat heavy for easy transport. But this structural strength enables the weapon to absorb all manner of rough use, and it can be used for long periods without maintenance other than changing the barrels when they get too hot. The ammunition is belt-fed, which can be awkward when the weapon has to be carried with lengths of ammunition belt left hanging from the feed and snagging on just about everything.

When used as an LMG the MAG uses a butt and simple bipod. When used as a sustained-fire weapon the butt is usually removed and the weapon is placed on a heavy tripod, usually with some form of buffering to absorb part of the recoil. However, the MAG can be adapted to a number of other mountings, and is often used as a co-axial weapon on armoured vehicles

or as a vehicle defence weapon in a ball mounting, and as an anti-aircraft weapon on a tripod or vehicle-hatch mounting. It is also used on many light naval vessels.

The MAG has been widely produced under licence. One of the better-known nations is the UK, where the MAG is known as the **L7A2**. The British introduced some modifications of their own, (and have produced the weapon for export), and there is no sign of it being replaced in the foreseeable future as far as the British armed forces are concerned. Other nations that produce the MAG for their own use include Israel, South Africa, Singapore and Argentina, and there are others. Even longer is the list of MAG users: a brief summary includes Sweden, Ireland, Greece, Canada, New Zealand, the Netherlands and so on. There is little chance of the MAG falling out of fashion, and production continues all over the world.

Specification
FN MAG

Calibre: 7.62 mm (0.3 in)
Weights: gun only 10.1 kg (22.27 lb); tripod 10.5 kg (23.15 lb); barrel 3 kg (6.6 lb)

The Belgian FN MAG is one of the most widely used of the post-World War II general-purpose machine-guns. Well made from what are usually solid metal billets machined to spec, the MAG is a very sturdy but heavy weapon that is still in production worldwide.

Lengths: gun 1260 mm (49.61 in); barrel 545 mm (21.46 in)
Muzzle velocity: 840 m (2,756 ft) per second
Rate of fire: (cyclic) 600-1000 rpm
Type of feed: 50-round belt

Below: The FN MAG is licence-produced in Israel by Israel Military Industries and is used by all branches of the Israeli armed forces.

Above: During the Falkland Islands campaign L7A1s were hastily pressed into use on improvised anti-aircraft mountings to provide some measure of defence against Argentine attacks on the shipping in San Carlos harbour.

Below: The FN MAG is fitted to the turrets of the German Leopard 2 tanks in service with the Dutch army. Pictured here in September 1984 on Exercise 'Lionheart', the MAG has been fitted with a blank firing adaptor.

FN 5.56-mm Minimi

With the turn away from the heavy NATO 7.62-mm (0.3-in) cartridge towards the smaller 5.56-mm (0.219-in) round for use by the standard rifles of most of the NATO nations (and many others), it followed that there was a need for a light machine-gun to use the new calibre. FN accordingly drew up the design of a new weapon that eventually became known as the **FN Minimi** and was first shown in 1974. The Minimi is intended for use only as a squad support weapon as there is no way that the light 5.56-mm cartridge can be used effectively for the heavy support or sustained-fire role, for it simply lacks the power to be effective at ranges much beyond 400 m (437 yards). Thus heavier-calibre weapons such as the FN MAG will still be retained for this role in the future.

The Minimi uses some design features from the earlier FN MAG, including the quick-change barrel and the gas regulator, but a new rotary locking device is used for the breech block which is guided inside the receiver by two guide rails to ensure a smooth travel. These latter innovations have made the Minimi into a remarkably reliable weapon, and further reliability has been introduced into the ammunition feed. This is one of the Minimi's major contributions to modern light machine-gun design as it does away with the long and awkward flapping ammunition belts used on many designs and which snag on everything when carried. The Minimi uses a simple box (under the gun body) which contains the neatly-folded belt. When the weapon is fired from a bipod, the box is so arranged that it will not interfere with normal use and on the move it is out of the way of the carrier. But the Minimi goes one step further: if required, the belt feed can be replaced by a magazine feed. FN has shrewdly guessed that the American M16A1 rifle would quickly become the standard weapon in its class, and has thus made provision for the Minimi to use the M16A1's 30-round magazine. This can clip into the receiver just under the belt feed guides after the belt has been removed.

The association with the American M16A1 rifle has turned out well for FN, for the Minimi has been adopted as the US Army's squad fire-support weapon, and is now known there as the **M249 Squad Automatic Weapon**, or **SAW**. This version will fire the new standard NATO SS109 5.56-mm cartridge rather than the earlier M193 cartridge. The SS109 has a longer and heavier bullet than the earlier cartridge and uses a different rifling in the barrel, but is otherwise similar to the American cartridge.

Two possible variants of the Minimi are a 'para' version which uses a shorter barrel and a sliding butt to make the weapon shorter overall, and a vehicle model with no butt at all for mounting in armoured vehicles. The Minimi itself has many ingenious detail points as well: the trigger guard may be removed to allow operation by a man wearing winter or NBC warfare gloves, the front handguard contains a cleaning kit, the ammunition feed box has a simple indicator to show how many rounds are left, and so on.

Overall the Minimi may be regarded as one of the best of the new family of 5.56-mm light machine-guns. It will be around for a very long time.

The FN Minimi has been adopted by the US Army for the Squad Automatic Weapon (SAW) as the M249. It is now entering service with the airborne divisions of the Rapid Deployment Joint Task Force (RDJTF).

Specification
FN Minimi
Calibre: 5.56 mm (0.219 in)
Weights: with bipod 6.5 kg (14.33 lb); with 200 rounds 9.7 kg (21.38 lb)
Lengths: weapon 1050 mm (41.34 in); barrel 465 mm (18.31 in)
Muzzle velocity: (SS 109) 915 m (3,002 ft) per second
Rate of fire: (cyclic) 750-1000 rpm
Type of feed: 100- or 200-round belt, or 30-round box magazine

---

7.62-mm vz 59

Czech machine-gun designers can trace their progeny back to the range of highly successful machine-guns started with the vz (*vzor*, or model) 26 in 1926 and which resulted in the famous Bren Guns. As successor to these designs the Czechs produced a new model during the early 1950s as the **vz 52**, which may be regarded as the old design updated to use an ammunition belt-feed system. This was not the success of the earlier weapons, and is now rarely encountered other than in the hands of 'freedom fighters' and the like, and the vz 52 has thus been superseded by the **vz 59**.

The vz 59 is much simpler than the earlier vz 52 but follows the same general lines in appearance and operation. In fact many of the operating principles of the vz 52 have been carried over, including the gas-operated mechanism. The ammunition feed system is also a carry-over from the vz 52, in which it was regarded by many as being the only successful feature. In this feed system the belt is carried into the receiver by guides where a cam system takes over and pushes the cartridge forward through the belt link into the weapon. This system was copied on the Soviet PK series, but on the vz 59 the belts are fed from metal boxes; for the light machine-gun role with the light barrel and designation **vz 59L**, one of these boxes can be hung from the right-hand side of the gun in a rather unbalanced fashion. The weapon may be used in the LMG role with bipod or tripod mountings.

For the heavy machine-gun role the vz 59 is fitted with a heavy barrel. In this form it is known merely as the vz 59. When fitted with a solenoid for firing in armoured vehicles on a co-axial or similar mount it is known as the **vz 59T**. This does not exhaust the variations of the vz 59 series for, no doubt with an eye to possible sales outside Czechoslovakia, there is a version that fires standard NATO 7.62-mm (0.3-in) ammunition and known as the **vz 59N**; the vz 59 series usually fires the Soviet 7.62-mm cartridge.

One rather unusual feature of the vz 59 is the telescopic sight, which can be used with the bipod and the tripod. This optical sight may be illuminated internally for use at night and is also used for anti-aircraft fire, for which role the vz 59 is placed on top of a tubular extension to the normal tripod.

To date the vz 59 is known to have been adopted only by the Czech army, although other nations may by now have the type in use. In the past Czech weapons have appeared wherever there has been a market for small arms, and Czech weapons have thus recently turned up in the Middle East, and especially in Lebanon; some vz 52s have certainly been seen there. To date there is no record of any nation purchasing the NATO-ammunition version, but no doubt that version will turn up in some unexpected trouble spot one day.

Specification
vz 59
Calibre: 7.62 mm (0.3 in)
Weights: with bipod and light barrel 8.67 kg (19.1 lb); with tripod and heavy barrel 19.24 kg (42.42 lb)
Lengths: with light barrel 1116 mm (43.94 in); with heavy barrel 1215 mm (47.84 in); light barrel 593 mm (23.35 in); heavy barrel 693 mm (27.28 in)
Muzzle velocity: with light barrel 810 m (2,657 ft) per second, and with heavy barrel 830 m (2,723 ft) per second
Rate of fire: (cyclic) 700-800 rpm
Type of feed: 50- or 250-round belts

The Czech 7.62-mm (0.30-in) vz 59 is a development of the earlier vz 52/57, but much easier to produce. Developed with an eye to the international export market, the vz 59 has been adopted by the Czech armed forces but others crop up in various corners of the world.

SWITZERLAND
7.62-mm SIG 710-3

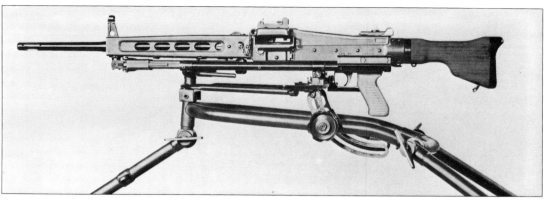

The Swiss 7.62-mm (0.3-in) SIG 710-3 is a weapon that on paper appears to be one of the finest of its class. The overall design, construction and reliability of the SIG design is such that it would appear to be a world leader. In fact nothing of the kind has occurred, for this most promising of machine-gun designs has now been taken out of production, and around the world it can be found in service with nations such as Brunei, Bolivia and Chile.

The reason for this strange state of affairs can perhaps be seen in the fact that when the Swiss produce any weapon design they do so in a manner that can only attract superlatives. The Swiss produce weapons with a magnificent degree of care and attention to finish, and while people may be willing to pay heavily for similarly-engineered Swiss watches, they are not willing to pay on the same scale for machine-guns. The SIG products tend to be expensive, and in a world where machine-guns can be produced on simple machine tools and metal stamping jigs the finely machined weapon has little chance of commercial success.

The SIG 710-3 is actually the third in a series of machine-guns, the first of which were produced during the early post-war years. In simple terms the first SIG 710 models were machine-gun versions of the Swiss Sturmgewehr Modell 57 (assault rifle model 1957), and the machine-gun employs the same delayed roller and block locking system as the CETME and the Heckler & Koch rifles. On the Swiss weapons

the system constitutes a form of delayed blowback, with the chamber fluted to prevent spent cases 'sticking'. The first SIG 710s were virtually hand-made weapons that attracted much attention (but few orders), so an increasing number of production expedients was incorporated into the design, to the point where the SIG 710-3 makes use of some stampings; needless to say, these are of very high quality. The machine-gun sports some features from German weapons. The Swiss were very influenced by the MG42 and in the years after the war produced several designs based on features of the model. The SIG 710-3 trigger mechanism is the same as that of the MG42, and so is the ammunition feed which is so efficient that it accommodates both American and German belt linkings without trouble.

The locking system is identical with that employed on the Sturmgewehr 45 which failed to reach service with the German army before the surrender of May 1945.

But the SIG 710-3 does have many original Swiss features, not the least of which is the type of rapid barrel change. Many extras were developed for these machine-guns, including one buffered tripod for sustained fire. Special features such as dial sights and telescopic sights were also produced, and in the end the SIG 710-3 could be regarded as one of the most advanced machine-guns available anywhere. But it was all for nothing as far as SIG was concerned, high development and production costs (combined with the strict rules of the Swiss government regarding arms sales) leading to an early exit from production.

The 7.62-mm (0.30-in) SIG 710-3 general-purpose machine-gun was based on German wartime design experience and should have emerged as one of the finest machine-gun designs ever, but in the event only small numbers were produced.

Specification
SIG 710-3
Calibre: 7.62 mm (0.3 in)
Weights: gun 9.25 kg (20.39 lb); heavy barrel 2.5 kg (5.51 lb); light barrel 2.04 kg (4.5 lb)
Lengths: gun 1143 mm (45 in); barrel 559 mm (22 in)
Muzzle velocity: 790 m (2,592 ft) per second
Rate of fire: (cyclic) 800-950 rpm
Type of feed: belt

USA
7.62-mm M60

The **M60** is a general-purpose machine-gun that can trace its origins back to the latter period of World War II, when it was known as the **T44**. The design was greatly influenced by the new German machine-gun designs: the ammunition feed is a direct lift from the MG42, and the piston and bolt assembly was copied from the revolutionary 7.92-mm (0.312-in) Fallschirmjägergewehr 42 (FG42). The T44 and its production version, the M60, made extensive use of steel stampings and plastics, and the first examples were issued for service with the US Army during the late 1950s.

These first examples were not a success. They handled badly and some of the detail design was such that changing a barrel involved taking half the weapon apart. These early difficulties were gradually eliminated, and the M60 is now as efficient a weapon as any, but many serving soldiers still profess not to like the weapon for its generally awkward handling properties. But the M60 is the US Army's first general-purpose machine-gun, and it now serves in a host of roles.

In its basic form as a squad support weapon, the M60 is fitted with a stamped steel bipod mounted just behind the muzzle. For this purpose it is carried by a small handle which is rather flimsy for the loads placed on it; moreover the point of balance of the handle is entirely wrong. Instead many soldiers prefer to use a sling, and the weapon is often fired on the move while being steadied by the sling.

Some special versions of the M60 have been produced. The **M60C** is a

remotely fitted version for external mounting on helicopters. The **M60D** is pintle mounted version, with no butt, for mounting in helicopter gunships and some vehicles. The **M60E2** is a much altered variant for use as a co-axial gun on armoured vehicles.

The M60 was not well adapted to the light role, and has now been more or less replaced by the M249 (the FN Minimi) as the squad automatic weapon. However, the Saco company, who manufactured most of the M60s, was aware of the weapon's shortcomings and has developed improved models. The **M60E3** is a lighter version of the M60, provided with a forward hand grip and generally considered as an 'assault' light machine gun. The **M60E4** has a shortened barrel, a bipod, a belt box and an optical sight, and is even heavier than the M60E3.

Although both these models have been taken into US service in small numbers (notably by Special Forces, who consider the heavier bullet to be worth the trouble), it seems unlikely that in the infantry squad they will supplant the M249, which is a far better weapon.

In the General Purpose role, the likely replacement for the M60 appears to be the M240G; this is simply the FN-MAG which was purchased several years ago for use as a co-axial tank and MICV machine gun. Its outstanding reliability caused the US Marines to adapt it to the ground role, and it has now been officially approved as a GPMG for ground use, thus returning it to the role for which it was originally designed.

The American M60 is a rather bulky and heavy weapon that is awkward to handle. First produced in the late 1940s, it underwent a protracted development programme before it entered service in the late 1950s, and has been widely used ever since. It is now a reliable and efficient weapon used by several armies.

Specification
M60
Calibre: 7.62 mm (0.3 in)
Weights: gun 10.51 kg (23.17 lb); barrel 3.74 kg (8.245 lb)
Lengths: gun overall 1105 mm (43.5 in); barrel 559 mm (22 in)
Muzzle velocity: 855 m (2,805 ft) per second
Rate of fire: (cyclic) 550 rpm
Type of feed: 50-round belt

5.56-mm CIS Ultimax 100

The relatively small nation of Singapore has in recent years become a major member of the international defence matériel market. Starting from virtually nothing, Singapore has rapidly built up a defence manufacturing industry and among recent products has been a light machine-gun called the **CIS Ultimax 100** or 3U-100.

The Ultimax 100 can trace its origins back to 1978. To provide a framework in which to work, the newly-formed Chartered Industries of Singapore (CIS) had obtained a licence to produce the 5.56-mm (0.219-in) Armalite AR-18 and also the Colt M16A1 rifles. Using these two weapons as a basis, CIS decided to build in some ideas of their own and the Ultimax 100 was the result. Some of the early prototypes were less than successful, but diligence and the application of some sound engineering removed the early problems, and the Ultimax 100 is now regarded as one of the best weapons in its class.

The Ultimax 100 fires the M193 5.56-mm cartridge, although there is no reason why it could not be converted to fire the new SS 109. It is a light machine-gun that is really light, for CIS was understandably keen to produce a weapon suited to the relatively light-statured personnel found in the Asian world. The result is that the Ultimax 100 handles very like an assault rifle. CIS has taken great pains to reduce recoil forces to a minimum, and has even introduced a feature it calls 'constant recoil'. With this feature the breech block does not use the back-plate of the receiver as a buffer, as is normal in many similar designs: instead a system of springs absorbs the forces and the result is a weapon that can be handled with ease and smoothness. The Ultimax 100 can be fired from the shoulder with no problems at all.

The likeness to an assault rifle is carried over to the ammunition feed. The Ultimax 100 uses a 100-round drum magazine under the body that can be changed with the same facility as a conventional box magazine. The drum magazines can be carried in a special webbing carrier. For firing on the move a forward grip is provided, and to make the weapon even handier the butt may be removed. For more accurate firing a bipod is a fixture and the barrel change is rapid and easy. If required normal M16A1 20- or 30-round

box magazines can be used in place of the drum.

Already accessories for the Ultimax 100 abound. Perhaps the most unusual of them is a silencer which is used in conjunction with a special barrel. More orthodox items include a special twin mounting in which two weapons are secured on their sides with the drum magazines pointing outwards. One very unusual extra is a bayonet, a feature which few similar weapons possess. Rifle grenades can be fired from the muzzle without preparation.

To date the Ultimax 100 is available in two versions; the **Ultimax 100 Mk 2** with a fixed barrel and the **Ultimax 100 Mk 3** with the easily-changed barrel. More versions are certain, for the Ultimax 100 has a most promising future. It is already in service with the Singapore armed forces and many more nations are showing a great interest in the weapon. It is certainly one of the handiest and most attractive of the 5.56-mm light machine-guns.

The Ultimax 100 Mark 3 light machine-gun is a small and light weapon that is ideally suited for many South East Asian armed forces. It is light and easy to handle and after a period of development is now a reliable and efficient weapon. It is now in full-scale production in Singapore.

Specification
Ultimax 100
Calibre: 5.56 mm (0.219 in)
Weights: gun empty 4.7 kg (10.36 lb); loaded with 100-round drum 6.5 kg (14.33 lb)
Lengths: overall 1030 mm (40.55 in); barrel 508 mm (20 in)
Muzzle velocity: (M193) 990 m (3,248 ft) per second
Rate of fire: (cyclic) 400-600 rpm
Type of feed: 100-round drum, or 20- or 30-round box magazine

Below: The Ultimax 100 uses a drum magazine holding 100 5.56-mm (0.219-in) rounds. It can also use 20- or 30-round box magazines. The full 100-round drum can be fitted in only 11.6 seconds, but more drums can be carried in the special carrier shown here. A bayonet can be fitted and a silencer is available.

7.62-mm PK

One very noticeable feature in Soviet small-arms design is the strange mixture of innovation and conservatism that seems to beset every generation of weapons. Despite the impact made by the then-novel 7.62-mm (0.3-in) × 39 cartridge used in the AK-47 assault rifle family, Soviet machine-guns have continued to use the much more powerful 7.62-mm × 54R cartridge, which retains a distinct rim at its base. This rim was originally used for extraction from the old Mosin-Nagant rifles that can be traced back to 1895, if not before, but the same round is used for the Red Army's current general-purpose machine-gun known as the **PK** series.

There are several members of the PK range. The PK is the basic gun with a heavy barrel marked by flutes along

its exterior. This was first seen in 1946, and since then the **IKM** has arrived on the scene; this is an improved version of the PK that is lighter and simpler in construction. The **PKS** is a PK mounted on a tripod which can be used for anti-aircraft as well as ground fire. The **PKT** is a version for use on armoured vehicles, while the **PKM** is a PK mounted on a bipod. When the PKM is mounted on a tripod it becomes the **PKMS**. The **PKB** has the usual butt and trigger mechanism replaced by spade grips and a 'butterfly' trigger arrangement.

The PK appears to be all things to all men, and as far as the Red Army is concerned it is a true multi-role type: the PK is used in roles ranging from infantry squad support to AFV use in special mountings. All the PK machine-guns operate on the same

principle, based on the Kalashnikov rotary-bolt system used in many other current Soviet weapons. The interior of the PK is populated by surprisingly few parts: there are just the bolt/breech block, a piston and a few springs. The ammunition feed makes up a few more parts, and that is about it. Thus the PK has few parts to break or jam and it is very reliable. When used in the light machine-gun role the ammunition is normally carried in a metal box slung under the gun. For tripod operation variable lengths of belt are used. In the sustained-fire role the barrel has to be changed at regular intervals even though it is chromium-plated to reduce wear (a common Soviet practice).

These PK weapons must rank among the most numerous of all mod-

ern machine-guns. They are used not only throughout the Red Army but also by many members of the Warsaw Pact. The Chinese produce a copy known as the **Type 80**. Both the PK and the Type 80 have been passed on to many nations in the third world and some are now in the hands of 'freedom fighters'.

The one odd thing regarding the PK series is the retention of the old rimmed 7.62-mm cartridge. Even the conservative British discarded their beloved 7.7-mm (0.303-in) cartridge decades ago, but the Soviets appear to be more conservative still. Thus there originated the odd alliance of the superb PK machine-gun with all its many fine points and a cartridge that was developed during the 1890s.

Specification
PK
Calibre: 7.62 mm (0.3 in)
Weights: gun empty 9 kg (19.84 lb);
tripod 7.5 kg (16.53 lb); 100-round belt
2.44 kg (5.38 lb)
Lengths: gun 1160 mm (45.67 in);
barrel 658 mm (25.91 in)
Muzzle velocity: 825 m (2,707 ft) per
second
Rate of fire: (cyclic) 690-720 rpm
Type of feed: 100-, 200- and 250-round
belts

*The Soviet 7.62-mm (0.30-in) PK
machine-gun is seen here in its light
machine-gun form as the PKM. It is a
simple and sturdy weapon with few
moving parts, and is widely used by
many Warsaw Pact armed forces and
other forces around the world.*

Former USSR

7.62-mm RPK

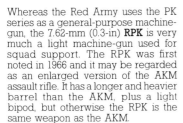

*Seen here in the hands of a Bulgarian
paratrooper, the RPK is used by
many Warsaw Pact armies as a
squad fire support weapon.
Developed from the AKM, it fires the
same 7.62-mm (0.30-in) ammunition
as the rifle but uses a larger 40-round
box magazine. The barrel cannot be
changed.*

Whereas the Red Army uses the PK
series as a general-purpose machine-
gun, the 7.62-mm (0.3-in) **RPK** is very
much a light machine-gun used for
squad support. The RPK was first
noted in 1966 and it may be regarded
as an enlarged version of the AKM
assault rifle. It has a longer and heavier
barrel than the AKM, plus a light
bipod, but otherwise the RPK is the
same weapon as the AKM.
This commonality of weapons
makes a great deal of sense. The AKM

fires exactly the same 7.62-mm×39
ammunition as the assault rifle, but the
commonality goes further. Some spare
parts can be interchanged between
the two weapons, and any soldier who
can use the AKM (and that means all of
them) can pick up and fire the RPK
with equal facility. If the special 75-
round drum magazine of the RPK is not
available any magazine from an AKM
can be fitted in its place. One thing the
Soviet soldier will miss if he ever has to
use the RPK in close action is that it

does not have a mounting bracket for a
bayonet.
Considering that the weapon is intended as a light machine-gun, it is
surprising that the RPK does not have
provision for changing the barrel when
it gets hot. In order to ensure the barrel
does not overheat, recruits are trained
to limit burst-firing to about 80 shots
per minute. For most tactical purposes
this will be more than adequate, but
there must be times when this fire rate
will have its disadvantages. Apart from
the 75-round drum already mentioned,
there are curved box magazines holding 30 or 40 rounds. Some RPKs have
been seen with infra-red night sights.
A copy produced by the Chinese is
known as the **Type 74**.
In recent years the Red Army has
changed its standard rifle calibre to
the new 5.45-mm (0.2146-in)×18 cartridge. For this round the AK-74 rifle
was developed, and it follows that a
new version of the RPK would follow. It
has now appeared as the **RPK-74**.
Apart from the scaling down of some
parts to suit the smaller calibre, the
RPK-74 is in overall terms identical
with the RPK.
The RPK appears to be a popular
weapon with the Red Army and the
many Warsaw Pact nations to which it
has been delivered. The type appears
to be produced in East Germany and
as far as can be determined the RPK is
still in production in the Soviet Union
(and China). It has been handed out to

some nations sympathetic to the Soviet
way of thinking, and needless to say
the RPK has found its way into the
hands of many 'freedom fighters'. RPKs
were observed during the recent
fighting in Lebanon and more have
been seen in action in Angola. Despite
its rate-of-fire limitations, the RPK will
no doubt be around for many years to
come, and the Red Army still retains
huge numbers of the type despite the
introduction of the RPK-74.

Specification
RPK
Calibre: 7.62 mm (0.3 in)
Weights: gun 5 kg (11.02 lb); 75-round
drum 2.1 kg (4.63 lb)
Lengths: gun 1035 mm (40.75 in);
barrel 591 mm (23.27 in)
Muzzle velocity: 732 m (2,402 ft) per
second
Rate of fire: (cyclic) 660 rpm and
(practical) 80 rpm
Type of feed: 75-round drum, or 30-
and 40-round box magazines

*The Soviet RPK is the standard
Warsaw Pact squad fire support
weapon. It does not have an
interchangeable barrel and so is not
capable of sustained fire. The design
may be regarded as a development
of the AKM assault rifle, and it fires
the same 7.62-mm (0.30-in)
ammunition. A Chinese version is
known as the Type 74.*

7.62-mm Bren Gun

When considering modern machine-guns, it seems something of a surprise that a weapon as old as the **Bren Gun** should be included, especially as this weapon can be traced back as far as the early 1930s. But the original Bren Guns were chambered for the 7.7-mm (0.303-in) rimmed cartridge, and when the decision was made to convert to the new standard NATO 7.62-mm (0.3-in) cartridge the British armed forces still had large stockpiles of the Bren Gun to hand. It made sound commercial sense to convert them for the new calibre, and such a programme was soon put into effect at the Royal Small Arms Factory at Enfield Lock in Middlesex.

The conversion to the new calibre entailed a complete overhaul, but the task was made easier by the fact that during World War II a Canadian company produced numbers of Bren Guns in 7.92-mm (0.312-in) calibre for China. As this round was rimless, it was found that the breechblocks intended for the 'China contract' were equally suitable for the new 7.62-mm cartridge and these were used in place of the originals. A new barrel was produced with a chromium-plated interior. This not only diminished wear on the barrel but also reduced the need for the frequent barrel-changes required on World War II versions. Thus the new gun was issued with only the one barrel.

The current version of the Bren Gun used by the British Army is the **L4A4**. This is not used as a front-line infantry weapon, but instead is issued to the many other arms of the service who require a machine-gun. Thus the L4A4 is used by the Royal Artillery for anti-aircraft and ground-defence of its bat-

teries, by the Royal Signals for the defence of its installations in the field, by units assigned for home defence, and so on. The L4A4 is also used by the Royal Air Force, and a version known as the **L4A5** is used by the Royal Navy. There is also a version known as the **L4A3** that is not often encountered as it is a conversion of the old Bren Mk 2 gun; the L4A4 is a conversion of the improved Bren Mk 3.

In all these versions the gas-operated mechanism of the original Bren Gun remains unchanged. So few are the changes involved in the change of calibre that the only points of note are that the 7.62-mm version uses a nearly-vertical magazine in place of the old curved equivalent, and the muzzle lacks the pronounced cone-

shape of the old weapon.

For the anti-aircraft role the L4A4 has been fitted with some fairly sophisticated sighting arrangements. The L4A4 does not use a tripod as did the old Bren Guns, but instead it can be mounted on the roof hatches of self-propelled guns and howitzers as well as on other armoured vehicles.

So the old Bren Gun soldiers on in a new form, and there seems to be no sign of its passing from use in the foreseeable future. Many of the Commonwealth nations still use the Bren, some in its original 7.7-mm form, so although the original design may be old the weapon is still regarded as effective and in its L4A4 form the old Bren Gun is as good as many far more modern designs.

The latest version of the venerable wartime Bren gun is the British L4A4, chambered for the NATO 7.62-mm (0.30-in) round. It has a new barrel, breech block and a new vertical 30-round box magazine and is now used by support and second-line British Army units.

Specification
L4A4
Calibre: 7.62 mm (0.3 in)
Weights: gun only 9.53 kg (21 lb); barrel 2.72 kg (6 lb)
Lengths: gun 1133 mm (44.6 in); barrel 536 mm (21.1 in)
Muzzle velocity: 823 m (2,700 ft) per second
Rate of fire: (cyclic) 500 rpm
Type of feed: 30-round box

5.56-mm Light Support Weapon (LSW)

Once the decision was taken to replace the British army's 7.62-mm rifle with one of smaller calibre, this automatically meant the development of a new light machine gun, since the squad automatic and the squad rifle must fire the same ammunition if logistic problems are to be avoided. As a result, parallel with the development of the 4.85-mm Individual Weapon (described elsewhere) a light machine gun, known as the Light Support Weapon (LSW) was also developed. Many of the components of the two weapons are the same, and, indeed, one could well say that the LSW is not much more than a heavy-barrelled version of the IW. It uses the same gas operating system with a rotating bolt and carrier, the same bullpup layout with the breech under the firer's chin, and the same 30-round magazine. One consequence of this is that the barrel can no longer be changed, so that the LSW is not really suited for sustained fire. It needs to be fired in short bursts with time for the barrel to cool between them.

However, on consequence of the longer and heavier barrel is that the LSW has proved to be remarkably accurate, good enough to be used in the single shot role as a sniping weapon. On the other hand, such accuracy is not generally considered to be a desirable feature in a light machine gun, which is intended to spread its bullets around the mean point of impact and thus have a better

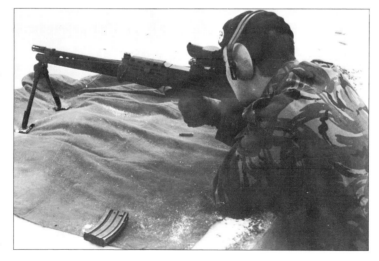

With the FN rifle about to be replaced by the 5.56-mm Individual Weapon, the British Army is adopting a squad support weapon of

the same calibre to replace the FN MAG general purpose machine-gun. The latter will be retained for the sustained fire role.

suppressive effect.

The LSW is fitted, as standard, with the SUSAT (Sight Unit, Small Arms, Trilux) optical sight, carried on a mount above the receiver. It also had a handgrip beneath the butt, for the firer's disengaged hand; hitherto, British practice has been to hold the top of the butt with the non-firing

hand, but the straight-line bullpup layout prevents this, and the handgrip is therefore provided.

The LSW was introduced into service in 1986, together with the rifle, and became the L86A1. It appears not to have suffered quality control problems to quite the same degree as the rifle, and a total of 22,391 weapons

Seen here in front of the GPMG is the 4.85-mm version of the Light Support Weapon, produced to complement the proposed 4.85-mm rifle. When NATO adopted the Belgian 5.56-mm round as standard, the 4.85-mm designs were abandoned despite their superior performance.

The Light Support Weapon shares many components with the 5.56-mm rifle; obvious differences are the heavy barrel, the bipod and the rear grip. The LSW uses the same magazine as the Individual Weapon – the 30-round M16A1 box.

were manufactured at the Royal Ordnance Factory, Nottingham, before production ceased. It is in use by British forces, but no other country has adopted it.

Specification
L85A1
Calibre: 5.56 mm (.223 in)
Weight, loaded: 6.58 kg (14 lb 8 oz) with optical sight
Length: 900 mm (35.43 in)
Barrel length: 646 mm (25.43 in)
Rate of fire: 600–775 rds/min
Muzzle velocity: 970 m/sec (3182 ft/sec)

7.5-mm AA 52

time the French army was equipped with a wide array of American, British and ex-German weapons, and the furnishing of support and spares for this array was too much for the army, which decided to adopt one standard general-purpose machine-gun. The result was the 7.5-mm (0.295-in) AA 52, a weapon designed from the outset for ease of production, and thus making much use of stampings and welded components.

The AA 52 is unusual among modern machine-guns in relying on a form of delayed-blowback operation, in which the force of the cartridge firing is employed to force back the breech block to the starting position, and also to power the feed mechanism. This system works very well with pistol cartridges in sub-machine guns, but using rifle cartridges in machine-guns demands something more positive if safety is to be regarded. On the AA 52 a two-part block is used: a lever device is so arranged that it holds the forward part of the block in position while the rear half starts to move to the rear; only when the lever has moved a predetermined distance does it allow the forward part of the block to move back. In order to make the spent cartridge easier to extract the chamber has

grooves that allow gas to enter between the chamber wall and the fired cartridge to prevent 'sticking', and a cartridge fired from an AA 52 can always be recognized by the fluted grooves around the case neck.

The AA 52 can be fired from a bipod or a tripod, but when a tripod is used for the sustained fire role a heavy barrel is fitted to the weapon. When used in the light machine-gun role the AA 52 is a rather clumsy weapon to carry, especially if a 50-round ammunition box is carried on the left-hand side. For this reason the box is often left off and the ammunition belt allowed to hang free. One unusual feature of the AA 52 is that for the light machine-gun role a monopod is fitted under the butt. This can be awkward at times, and another awkward point is the barrel change: the barrel can be removed readily enough, but the bipod is permanently attached to the barrel and in the light machine-gun role this can make barrel-changing very difficult, especially as the AA 52 barrels have no form of barrel plating that might reduce the temperature of the gun and barrel.

The AA 52 was originally intended to fire a 7.5-mm (0.295-in) cartridge first developed for use by the mle 1929 light machine-gun. This cartridge is powerful enough, but the switch to the NATO 7.62-mm (0.3 in) cartridge left the French army using a non-standard cartridge, and export prospects for the AA 52 were thus reduced. The basic

design has therefore been adapted to fire the NATO cartridge in a version known as the **NF-1**. Some of these have been issued to French army units, but exports have not materialized.

Overall the AA 52 is an adequate machine-gun, but it has many features (some of them regarded by some nations as inherently unsafe) that are at best undesirable. The weapon is no longer in production but is still offered for export.

Specification
AA 52
Calibre: 7.5 mm (0.295 in)
Weights: with bipod and light barrel 9.97 kg (21.98 lb); with bipod and heavy barrel 11.37 kg (25.07 lb); tripod 10.6 kg (23.37 lb)
Lengths: with butt extended (light barrel) 1145 mm (45.08 in) or (heavy barrel) 1245 mm (49.02 in); light barrel only 500 mm (19.69 in); heavy barrel only 600 mm (23.62 in)
Muzzle velocity: 840 m (2,756 ft) per second
Rate of fire: (cyclic) 700 rpm
Type of feed: 50-round belt

The French AA 52 uses a delayed blowback mechanism with a fluted chamber to ease extraction. A 7.62-mm (0.30-in) version known as the AA 7.62 NF-1 may also be encountered, but neither model is now in production. Bipod and tripod versions are in use, as are vehicle-mounted models.

Above: The French Foreign Legion use exactly the same weapons as the rest of the French army and so the AA 52 machine-gun, seen here in its light machine-gun form, is a familiar sight wherever the legion operates.

The machine-gun now known as the **AA 52** was designed and developed directly as a result of the Indo-China campaigns of the early 1950s. At that

Heckler & Koch machine-guns

The West German concern Heckler & Koch, based at Oberndorf-Neckar, is among the most prolific of all modern small-arms designers, and in addition to its successful range of assault rifles and sub-machine guns it also produces a wide variety of machine-guns. It may be an oversimplification, but Heckler & Koch machine-guns are basically modified versions of the company's G-3 and associated assault rifles. They all use the same delay-roller mechanism on their breech blocks, and some of the light machine-guns are simply rifles with heavier barrels and a bipod. To confuse the issue, Heckler & Koch produce virtually every model in belt- and magazine-fed versions, and some are produced in 7.62-mm (0.3-in) NATO or 5.56-mm (0.219-in) calibres, with the added variation in the latter for the new SS 109 cartridge or the older American M193.

One of the 'base' models in the range is the 7.62-mm **HK 21A1**, a development of the earlier **HK 21** which is no longer in production. The HK 21A1 uses a belt feed and may be used as a light machine-gun on a bipod or in the sustained-fire role on a tripod. For the latter, barrel changing is incorporated. Even in this version of the Heckler & Koch range the outline of the G-3 is apparent, and this is carried over to the latest versions of the HK 21, the **HK 21E**, which has a longer sight radius and a three-round burst selection feature. The barrel is longer, and changes have been made to the ammunition feed. There is also a 5.57-mm counterpart to this variant, and this is known as the **HK 23E**.

All the variants mentioned above are belt-fed weapons. There is also a magazine-fed version for every one of them: the **HK 11A1** is the magazine counterpart of the HK 21A1, while the **HK 11E** and **HK 13E** are the magazine counterparts of the HK 21E and HK 23E.

All this may sound rather confusing, but the basic factor that emerges is the ability of Heckler & Koch to produce a machine-gun suited to virtually any requirement. The belt-fed versions may be regarded as general-purpose machine-guns (although the 5.56-mm versions may really be too light for the sustained-fire role), and the magazine-fed versions as true light machine-guns. They offer a surprising amount of interchangeability of spare parts, and the magazines are usually the same as those used on their equivalent assault rifles, making the use of the automatic guns as squad support weapons even easier.

Specification
HK 21A1
Calibre: 7.62 mm (0.3 in)
Weights: gun with bipod 8.3 kg (18.3 lb); barrel 1.7 kg (3.75 lb); 100-round ammunition box 3.6 kg (7.94 lb)
Lengths: overall 1030 m (40.55 in); barrel 450 mm (17.72 in)
Muzzle velocity: 800 m (2,625 ft) per second
Rate of fire: (cyclic) 900 rpm
Type of feed: 100-round belt

The HK 21A1 is a development of the earlier HK 21. It uses a belt feed only, but the belt can be contained in a box slung under the receiver.

The Heckler & Koch HK 11 is the box magazine feed variant of the HK 21 and is a 7.62-mm (0.30-in) weapon.

The Heckler & Koch HK 13 is produced in several versions. This model accommodates a 40-round box magazine.

The Heckler & Koch HK 13E has a three-round burst capability as well as full automatic fire.

The Heckler & Koch HK 21 is no longer produced, but is still in use with nations such as Portugal.

7.62 mm MG3

One of the outstanding machine-gun designs of World War II was the MG42, a weapon that introduced the advantages of mass production to an area of weapon design that had for long clung to traditional methods of construction. With the MG42, the new era of steel pressings, welds and the elimination of many machining processes was allied to an excellent design that attracted widespread respect and attention. Thus, when the Federal Republic of Germany became a member of NATO and was once more allowed a measure of weapon production for rearmament, the MG42 was one of the first designs to be resurrected.

The original MG42 had a calibre of 7.92 mm (0.312 in), but with the adoption of the standard NATO 7.62-mm (0.3-in) round the old design was reworked to accommodate the new calibre. At first stockpiled MG42s were simply modified to this calibre with the designation **MG2**, but in parallel with this activity a production programme was under way by Rheinmetall to produce new weapons in 7.62-mm calibre. There were several variants of this production version, all having the designation **MG1**, although there were some minor changes to suit ammunition feed and so on. The current production version is the **MG3**, still manufactured by Rheinmetall.

In appearance, the war-time MG42 and the MG3 are identical apart from some minor details, few of which can be detected by the untrained eye, and there are more changes between the MG1 and MG3. Overall, however, the modern MG3 retains all the attributes of the original, and many of the mountings used with the MG3 are just adaptations or modifications of the World War II originals. Thus the MG3 can be used on a tripod that is virtually identical to the original, and the twin mounting for anti-aircraft use could still accommodate the MG42 without trouble. There are now available many mountings for the MG3.

The original MG42 was designed for ease of mass production, and this same feature makes the MG3 very suitable for manufacture in some of the less well-equipped arsenals that now abound in 'third-world' nations. The MG3 has proved to be relatively easy for such facilities and it is now licence-produced in nations such as Pakistan, Chile, Spain and Turkey; some of these nations fabricate versions of the MG1 rather than the MG3 proper. Yugoslavia also produces a version of this weapon, but the Yugoslav model is a direct copy of the MG42, still in 7.92-mm calibre and designated **SARAC M1953**.

Within NATO the MG3, or one or other of its variants, are used by the Bundeswehr, by the Italian armed forces, and by nations such as Denmark and Norway. Portugal makes the MG3 for use by the Portuguese armed forces, and is now offering the type for export. Thus from many sources the old MG42 design soldiers on. There is even talk of further development to produce a lighter version, but this is proceeding at a low priority, for the basic design of the MG3 is still as sound as it ever was, and any attempt to improve or modify the original appears to many to be an exercise about as fruitful as redesigning the wheel.

Specification
MG3
Calibre: 7.62 mm (0.3 in)
Weights: basic gun 10.5 kg (23.15 lb); bipod 0.55 kg (1.213 lb); barrel 1.8 kg (3.97 lb)
Lengths: gun with butt 1225 mm (48.23 in); gun less butt 1097 mm (43.19 in); barrel 531 mm (20.91 in)
Muzzle velocity: 820 m (2,690 ft) per second
Rate of fire: (cyclic) 700-1,300 rpm
Type of feed: 50-round belt

The West German MG3 is the modern version of the wartime MG42, and is currently rated as one of the best machine-guns of its type used by NATO. It has a high rate of fire and an easy and rapid barrel change, and can be fired from the bipod shown or from a heavy tripod for the sustained fire support role.

7.62-mm Uirapuru Mekanika

Over recent decades Brazil has changed from being a defence-equipment importer to a nation that exports over 95 per cent of its defence industry's produce. The nation has undoubted talent for the defence-based industries, and in an effort to harness some of this talent to producing small arms a design team was established in the early 1960s to develop a general-purpose machine-gun. This first design team was led by a team of three experts, but while its initial designs worked they had many inherent problems. These were too numerous for the possibility of acceptance by the Brazilian army, who turned the design problem over to a private concern. This fared no better than the original team, so one of the original triumvirate took over the project on his own.

Using the facilities of a design and research establishment, this individual approach worked. Thus there emerged a design now known as the **Uirapuru Mekanika** after a Brazilian jungle bird. The Uirapuru is a general-purpose machine-gun firing standard NATO 7.62-mm (0.3-in) ammunition. It can be used as a light machine-gun with a butt and bipod, or it can be fired from a heavy tripod for the heavy machine-gun role. It can also be fitted with a solenoid for use as a co-axial weapon on armoured vehicles, and it can be adapted to firing from a number of other mounts.

In appearance the Uirapuru is a rather long, ungainly-looking weapon, especially when fitted with a butt for the light machine-gun role. It uses a conventional gas-operated mechanism with an orthodox belt feed for the ammunition, and the barrel can be changed rapidly using a handle that also acts as a carrying handle for the weapon. The receiver of the weapon is very simple, being little more than a length of tube containing the breech block and its return spring. What appears to be a rectangular receiver is in fact the ammunition feed mechanism. The method of tapping off gas from the barrel is also simple. No gas regulating block or valve is used, the gas impingeing directly onto the return mechanism. No provision appears to have been made for firing single shots.

The barrel of the Uirapuru has a large pepperpot-type muzzle brake and it is recommended that the barrel is changed after every 400 rounds have been fired. Most of the parts appear to require some machining, which should ensure a rugged construction. The Brazilian army gave its approval to the Uirapuru after lengthy trials, and the type is now being prepared for full production at a factory near Rio de Janeiro. If past Brazilian salesmanship is any guide, it will not be long before the first examples are seen outside Brazil, for if the Uirapuru can withstand the varied combat conditions that can be encountered in Brazil it will put up with virtually anything, and the simple construction certainly should keep the price of a weapon down.

Specification
Uirapuru Mekanika
Calibre: 7.62 mm (0.3 in)

The Brazilian 7.62-mm (0.30-in) Uirapuru Mekanika is the first locally-produced machine-gun design to enter production, and although it appears at first sight to be rather long it is an efficient and basically simple weapon.

Weight: with butt and bipod 13 kg (28.66 lb)
Lengths: with butt 1300 mm (51.2 in); barrel 600 mm (23.62 in)
Muzzle velocity: 850 m (2,789 ft) per second
Rate of fire: (cyclic) 650-700 rpm
Type of feed: 50-round belt

Sub-machine Guns

Forty years ago the sub-machine gun seemed set to take over the world; today it is scarcely seen in military use. Yet new designs still appear every month. What happened?

The sub-machine gun, a child of World War I, came into its own during World War II, when whole Russian infantry divisions were armed with nothing more. They were cheaper than rifles, and quicker to produce, and they fitted in well with the Russian philosophy of war – to get to grips with the enemy at arm's length, not sit hundreds of metres away and snipe at him.

Other armies adopted sub-machine guns for different reasons: they were excellent for raiders and commandos, usefully compact for drivers and tank crews, a conveniently small weapon for officers and squad leaders. And in the post-war years, many designs appeared.

Some of the successful ones are still around: in the following pages you may find the Heckler & Koch MP5, the Uzi, the Sterling and the Beretta, all excellent weapons which replaced the hastily conceived wartime designs such as the Sten and the American 'Grease Gun'.

The reason for the decline in importance of the sub-machine gun was the rise of the small-calibre lightweight assault rifle. As small as many sub-machine guns, it could do much the same job, had a better range, better piercing ability against body

The FN P-90 Personal Defence Weapon (PDW) is compact and convenient to carry, but it can pierce a steel helmet at a 200-m (200-yard) range.

armour and helmets, and it meant one universal weapon for all soldiers. The sub-machine gun of the 1990s is more likely to be found in the hands of an anti-terrorist police officer than in the hands of an infantry soldier.

However, the situation appears to be changing, and by the first decade of the new century it may be different. The assault rifle is a

costly device, and really only the infantryman needs it. About two-thirds of any modern army has no requirement for an assault rifle and can be issued with something cheaper, more compact and with rather less performance. For example, a truck driver, liable to ambush, does not really need a weapon with 400-500-m (437-547-yard) range. Hence the

'Personal Defence Weapon' (PDW) has appeared. At the moment this can mean anything from an overgrown pistol to an underdeveloped machine-gun but seems to be settling down as a form of sub-machine gun firing a cartridge similar to a rifle round. There is talk of drawing up a NATO standard for the PDW in the next few years.

9-mm PA3-DM

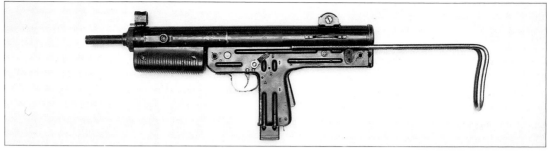

The Argentine **PA3-DM** is a typical example of modern sub-machine gun design in two respects; one is the use of the forward-mounted 'wrap-around' breech block and the other the ability of a relatively unsophisticated engineering industry to produce modern and viable weapons.

The 'wrap-around' bolt is now a virtual fixture on many modern sub-machine guns, for it provides two important functions. One is that the breech block is to a large extent forward of the chamber when the cartridge is fired, so providing extra mass for the recoil to overcome, thereby providing an increase in locking efficiency for what is otherwise a relatively effective but inefficient blowback system. The other advantage is that by placing much of the breech block around the barrel the weapon length can be much reduced, making the overall design shorter and handier for carriage and stowage. Nearly all these 'wrap-around' designs, and the PA3-DM is no exception, use the pistol grip as the magazine housing, and this has the advantage of allowing rapid aiming, for by holding the weapon with the 'master' hand, one-handed firing is possible as though the weapon is a pistol.

The first weapon to use this 'wrap-around' feature was the Czech vz 23 series, and it has appeared on many subsequent weapons. The Argentine design closely follows the Czech original in overall construction, for it relies on the use of simple stampings and has as its receiver housing nothing more than a section of steel tubing. The PA3-DM has its cocking handle on the left-hand side well forward so that it can be operated by either hand, and a hand grip is provided forward of the metal pistol group assembly. The PA3-DM may be found in two forms: one has a fixed plastic butt, while the other has a wire-form butt which telescopes forward on each side of the receiver. This latter is a direct copy of the wire butt used on the American M3 sub-machine gun. On both versions the barrel screws onto the front of the tubular receiver and the barrel can be adapted to mount a device for launching grenades.

The PA3-DM was used during the Falkland Islands campaign of 1982, though not in very great numbers. Some 'trophies' were returned to the United Kingdom and may be found in some regimental museums, but otherwise it is not a weapon that is likely to be encountered outside Argentina, where it is issued to the armed forces.

The PA3-DM is manufactured by the Fabrica Militar de Armas 'Domingo Matheu' at Rosario, from which the 'DM' of the designation is derived. It is only the latest model in a long string of sub-machine guns that have been designed and produced in Argentina since the period just after World War II. Many of these sub-machine guns were orthodox designs with little of note to mention, and not all of them reached the full production stage. Some were direct copies of successful designs elsewhere: for example, the **PAM 2** dating from the early 1950s was nothing more than a direct copy of the

Captured by British forces on the Falklands during the South Atlantic conflict, the PA3-DM exemplifies the modern sub-machine gun, being simply designed and easy to manufacture.

US M3A1 calibred in 9 mm (0.354 in). Some of the other designs, such as the **MEMS** series and the **Halcon** guns, were more adventurous designs that made little impact outside Argentina.

Specification
PA3-DM (fixed-butt version)
Calibre: 9 mm (0.354 in) Parabellum
Weight: loaded 3.9 kg (8.6 lb)
Length: 700 mm (27.56 in)
Length of barrel: 290 mm (11.4 in)
Muzzle velocity: 400 m (1,312 ft) per second
Cyclic rate of fire: 650 rpm
Magazine: 25-round box

9-mm L2A3 Sterling

The sub-machine gun that is now almost universally known as the **Sterling** entered British Army use in 1955 although an earlier form, known as the **Patchett**, underwent troop trials during the latter stages of World War II. It was intended that the Patchett would replace the Sten gun, but in the event the Sten lasted until well into the 1960s.

The British army model is designated the **L2A3** and equates to the **Sterling Mk 4** produced commercially by the Sterling Armament Company of Dagenham, Essex. This weapon is one of the major export successes of the post-war years, for to date it has been sold to over 90 countries and it is still in production in several forms. The basic service model is of simple design with the usual tubular receiver and a folding metal butt stock, but where the Sterling differs from many other designs is that it uses a curved box magazine that protrudes to the left. This arrangement has proved to be efficient in use and presents no problems. It has certainly created no problems for the army in India where the type is produced under licence, or in Canada where the design is produced as the **C1** with some slight modifications.

The Sterling is a simple blowback weapon with a heavy bolt, but this bolt incorporates one of the best features of the design in that it has raised and inclined splines that help to remove any internal dust or dirt and push it out of the way. This enables the Sterling to be used under the worst possible conditions. The usual magazine holds 34 rounds, but a 10-round magazine is available along with a string of accessories including a bayonet. The weapon can be fitted with any number of night vision devices or sighting systems, although these are not widely used.

Several variants of the Sterling exist. One is a silenced version known to the British army as the **L34A1**. This uses a fixed silencer system allied to a special barrel that allows the firing gases to leak through the sides of the barrel into a rotary baffle silencer that is remarkably efficient and almost silent in use. There is also a whole range of what are known as paratrooper's pistols that use only the pistol group and the receiver allied to a short magazine and a very short barrel. The Sterling L2A3 has now been phased out of British service, replaced by the L85 assault rifle, though it is still in extensive use on other countries, particularly as a police weapon. The sterling Armament Company ceased operations in 1987; in 1988 use in the company was bought by Royal Ordnance plc and the Dagenham factory closed. The production machinery was moved to ROF Nottingham, but no production has taken place under Royal Ordnance auspices.

Right: The Sterling saw considerable service in Malaya and Borneo, where the inherent inaccuracy of the sub-machine gun proved no handicap.

Below: The Sterling is seen on exercise in the UK, at Bassingbourn. It is being replaced by the new Enfield Individual Weapon.

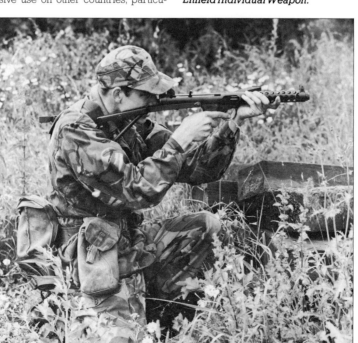

9-mm F1

During World War II a Lieutenant Owen invented the sub-machine gun that still bears his name, and this weapon was used by Australian soldiers during World War II and for many years after it. One of the most recognizable features of the **Owen** sub-machine gun was the vertical magazine, a feature with no particular merit or demerit but one that the Australians found very much to their liking. Thus when the Australian army began searching for a new design to replace the old and worn Owens, it was not averse to choosing a design with an overhead vertical magazine.

Before selecting the design now known as the **F1**, the Australians investigated a number of experimental weapons that rejoiced in such names as 'Kokoda' and the 'MCEM'. Some of these experimental designs had some advanced features but were generally regarded as not being 'soldier-proof' enough to suit Australian conditions. But in 1962 a design known as the **X3** was selected for production, and this became the F1. The predilections of the Australian military were very evident, for the F1 has a vertical magazine but in order to allow a certain amount of interchangeability with other weapons the magazine is now curved and identical to that of the British Sterling and the Canadian C1.

This interchangeability factor is also evident in several other features of the F1. The pistol grip is the same as that used on the L1A1 7.62-mm (0.3-in) NATO rifle, and the bayonet is another Sterling component. In fact it is tempting to regard the F1 as an Australian Sterling but there are too many differences to support such a claim. The F1 uses a simple 'straight-through' design with the butt fixed in line with the tubular receiver, and the pistol group is arranged differently from that of the Sterling. The overhead magazine does produce one difficulty, namely sighting. In action deliberate aiming is not common but has to be taken into account, so a form of offset sighting system had to be introduced. On the F1 this is done simply by using an offset leaf sight (folding down onto the tubular receiver) allied with a fixed offset foresight. The F1 does have one rather unusual safety built into the design

which is not common but yet is simple and effective: on a short-barrelled weapon it is often too easy to place the forward grip over the muzzle or too close to it for safety, but on the F1 a simple sling swivel bracket prevents the hand from getting too close to the muzzle.

The F1 has some other simple but effective design features. One is the cocking handle, which exactly duplicates the position and action of its counterpart on the L1A1 standard service rifle in use with the Australian forces; this handle has a cover which prevents dirt and debris getting into the action, though if enough dirt does get into the action to prevent the bolt closing the cocking handle can be latched to the bolt for the firer to force it closed in an emergency.

For all its many attributes the F1 has yet to be bought outside Australia and some of its associated territories. At one time there was talk of its being replaced by the American M16A1 rifle, but the F1 is still around and seems set for a long service career to come.

Above: Replacing the extremely popular Owen sub-machine gun in Australian service, the F1 retains the uniquely Australian feature of a vertical top-loading magazine. The F1 is otherwise similar to the Sterling.

Below: Simple and effective, the F1 in its prototype X3 form performed extremely well in the Mekong Delta during the Vietnam War. Modern construction made it almost 1 kg (2.2-lb) lighter than its World War II ancestor.

Specification
F1
Calibre: 9 mm (0.354 in) Parabellum
Weight: loaded 4.3 kg (9.48 lb) with bayonet
Length: 714 mm (28.1 in)
Length of barrel: 213 mm (8.386 in)
Muzzle velocity: 366 m (1,200 ft) per second
Cyclic rate of fire: 600-640 rpm
Magazine: 34-round curved box

9-mm Model 45

The 9-mm **Model 45** was produced originally by the Karl Gustav Stads Gevärsfaktori (now part of the FFV consortium) at Eskilstuna, and is thus widely known as the Carl Gustav sub-machine gun. The Model 45 is an entirely orthodox design with no frills, and uses a simple tubular receiver and barrel cover with a simple folding butt hinged onto the pistol grip assembly. The usual blowback operating principle is employed, and overall there is nothing remarkable about the Model 45.

But there is one interesting point regarding the Model 45, and that is the magazine. On many sub-machine guns the magazine is usually one of the most trouble-prone components, for the magazine relies upon simple spring pressure to push the rounds towards the receiver, whence they are fed into the firing system. It is all too easy for rounds to become misaligned or

forced together and the result is then a misfeed or jam, and these can happen at inopportune moments in combat. On the original Model 45 the magazine used was that once used on the pre-war Suomi Model 37-39, a 50-round magazine that was then considered to be one of the best in use anywhere. But in 1948 a new magazine was introduced that held 36 rounds in twin rows that were carefully tapered into a single row by the use of a wedge cross-section. This new magazine proved to be remarkably reliable and trouble-free in use, and was soon being widely copied elsewhere. Production Model 45s were soon being offered with a revised magazine housing to accommodate both the Suomi magazine and the new wedge-shaped magazine, and this version was known as the **Model 45/B**. Later production models made provision for the wedge-shaped magazine only.

The Model 45 and Model 45/B became one of Sweden's few major export weapons. Numbers were sold to Denmark and some other nations such as Eire. Egypt produced the Model 45/B as the **'Port Said'** under licence. Copies have also been produced in Indonesia. Perhaps the oddest service use of the Model 45/B was in Vietnam. Numbers of these weapons were obtained by the American CIA and converted in the United States to take a special barrel allied to a silencer. These were used in action in Vietnam by the US Special Forces on undercov-

The 9-mm Model 45 is generally known as the Carl Gustav, after its manufacturer. Conventional in design and operation, it has been in production since 1945 and has been exported widely.

er missions. According to most reports the silencers were not particularly effective and they were not retained in use for long.

Numerous accessories have been produced for the Model 45, one of the oddest being a special muzzle attachment that doubles as a blank firing device or a short-range target training device. The attachment is used together with special plastic bullets which are shredded into pieces as they leave the muzzle for safety. These bullets generate enough gas pressure to operate the mechanism and if required enough pressure is available to project a steel ball from the attachment itself. This reusable steel ball can thus be used for short-range target practice.

Specification
Model 45/B
Calibre: 9 mm (0.354 in) M39B Parabellum
Weight: loaded 4.2 kg (9.25 lb)
Length: with stock extended 808 mm (31.8 in) and with stock folded 551 mm (21.7 in)
Length of barrel: 213 mm (8.385 in)
Muzzle velocity: 365 m (1,198 ft) per second
Cyclic rate of fire: 550-600 rpm
Magazine: 36-round box

Used by many countries, including Egypt (in the 1967 war with Israel) and the USA (in a silenced version by special forces in Vietnam), the Carl Gustav remains in large-scale service with the Swedish forces.

9-mm MAT 49

Immediately after 1945 the French armed forces were armed with a variety of sub-machine guns, some of them dating from before the war and others were coming from the United States and the United Kingdom. While the weapons were serviceable enough, the range of ammunition calibres and types was considered to be too wide, and after a selection process it was decided to standardize on the 9-mm Parabellum round for future developments. A new sub-machine gun of French origins was requested, and three arsenals responded with new designs. That of the Manufacture d'Armes de Tulle (hence MAT) was selected, and the weapon went into production in 1949.

The **MAT 49** is still in widespread service, for it is a very well made weapon. Although it uses the now-commonplace method of fabricating parts and assemblies from stampings, those in the MAT 49 were made from heavy-duty steels and are thus very strong and capable of absorbing a great deal of hard use. The design uses the blowback principle but in place of what is now described as a 'wrap-around' breech block to reduce the

length of the receiver the MAT 49 has an arrangement in which a sizable portion of the breech block enters the barrel chamber to have much the same effect. No other design uses this feature, and there is another aspect of the MAT 49 which is typically French. This is the magazine housing, which can be folded forward with the magazine inserted to reduce the bulk of the weapon for stowage and transport. This feature is a carry-over from the pre-war MAS 38, and was considered so effective by the French army that it was retained in the MAT 49: a catch is depressed and the magazine housing (with a loaded magazine in place) is folded forward to lie under the barrel, while to use the weapon again the magazine is simply pulled back into place so that the housing acts as a foregrip. This foregrip is made all the more important by the fact that the MAT 49 can be fired on automatic only, so a firm grip is needed to keep the weapon under control when fired.

Considerable pains are taken on the MAT 49 to keep out dust and dirt, which is another historical carry-over from previous times as the MAT 49 was intended for use in the deserts of North

Africa. Even when the magazine is in the forward position a flap moves into position to keep out foreign matter. If repairs or cleaning are required the weapon can be easily stripped without tools. In action a grip safety locks both the trigger mechanism and any possible forward movement of the bolt.

Overall the MAT 49 is a sturdy and foolproof weapon. It has been superseded in French army first line use by the FA-MAS F-1 5.56mm assault rifle, tough it is probable that some may still be held in reserve stocks. It is still widely used by French police and para-military security forces, although even there the FA-MAS rifle is edging it out. Large numbers were handed over or sold to former French colonies and are still in use there by police and military forces.

Specification
MAT 49
Calibre: 9 mm (0.354 in) Parabellum
Weight: loaded 4.17 kg (9.19 lb)
Length: with butt extended 720 mm (28.34 in) and with butt closed 460 mm (18.1 in)
Length of barrel: 228 mm (8.97 in)
Muzzle velocity: 390 m (1,280 ft) per second
Cyclic rate of fire: 600 rpm
Magazine: 20- or 32-round box

Above: Entering French service in 1949, the 9-mm MAT 49 is an extremely rugged design, made from heavy-gauge steel stampings. The pistol grip/magazine housing hinges forward for stowage and transport.

Right: Designed with colonial service in mind, the MAT 49 was used extensively in Indo-China, as well as with the paratroops so notably involved in the bloody conflict in Algeria. It stood such stern tests successfully.

214

Heckler und Koch MP5

Since World War II the West German concern of Heckler und Koch has become one of Europe's largest and most important small-arms manufacturers with its success based soundly on the production of its G3 rifle, which has become a standard NATO weapon and is in use all over the world. Working from the G3 and employing its highly efficient breech-locking mechanism, the company has also produced the **Heckler und Koch MP5**, which may thus be regarded as the sub-machine gun version of the G3.

In appearance the MP5 looks very similar to the G3 although it is of course much shorter. It fires the usual 9-mm (0.354-in) × 19 Parabellum cartridge, and although this is relatively low-powered compared with the 7.62-mm (0.3-in) rifle cartridge the MP5 uses the same roller and inclined ramp locking mechanism as the G3. The complexity of this system is more than offset by its increased safety, and by the ability of the MP5 to be fired very accurately as it can fire from a closed bolt, i.e. the breech block is in the forward position when the trigger is pulled so there is no forward-moving mass to disturb the aim as there is with other sub-machine guns. The resemblance to the G3 is maintained by the use of many G3 components on the MP5.

There are six main versions of the MP5. The **MP5A2** has a fixed butt stock while the **MP5A3** has a metal strut stock that can be slid forward to reduce its length. There are no fewer than three differing versions of the **MP5 SD**, which is a silenced version of the basic model for use in special or anti-terrorist warfare. The **MP5 SD1** does not have a butt stock at all; the **MP5 SD2** has a fixed butt as on the MP5A2; and the **MP5 SD3** has the sliding metal butt stock used on the MP5A3. Then there is the **MP5K** which is a very short version of the basic MP5, only 325 mm (12.8 in) long and recognizable by a small foregrip under the almost non-existent muzzle. The **MP5K A1** is a special version of this variant with no protrusions so that it can be carried under clothing or in a special holster.

In all its forms the MP5 has proved to be an excellent and reliable sub-machine gun. It is in use with some of the various West German police agencies and border guards, and numbers have been purchased by Swiss police and the Netherlands armed forces. It is known to be one of the weapons most favoured by the British SAS for close-quarter combat.

Unfortunately some MP5s have fallen into the wrong hands, usually by theft from weapon stores. The MP5 was the main weapon of the Baader-Meinhoff gang and many similar groups are known to have used the MP5 at one time or another. The MP5 has been described by one counter-insurgency authority as 'the most efficient terrorist weapon now in production', and it will no doubt feature in many future terrorist or 'freedom fighter' outrages. This future use might well involve various forms of night sight, for the MP5 has been demonstrated on numerous occasions with such devices, along with other sighting devices such as telescopic sights and other rapid-aiming systems.

Top: The MP5A3 is fitted with a sliding metal strut stock which can allow a considerable reduction in overall length, from 660 mm (26 in) to 490 mm (19.3 in).

Above: The MP5A2 is fitted with fixed plastic butt stock. After 1978 the MP5 was fitted with a curved magazine to improve cartridge feed.

Below: The MP5SD3 is a silenced version of the MP5A3, all parts except barrel and silencer being the same. It is used by several military and police forces around the world.

Right: The extremely short MP5K was introduced for use by special police and anti-terrorist squads, where weapon concealment may be essential.

Specification
MP5A2
Calibre: 9 mm (0.354 in) Parabellum
Weight: loaded 2.97 kg (6.55 lb)
Length: 680 mm (26.77 in)
Length of barrel: 225 mm (8.86 in)
Muzzle velocity: 330 m (1,083 ft) per second
Cyclic rate of fire: 800 rpm
Magazine: 15- or 30-round box

Walther MP-K and MP-L

Walther has for long been in the forefront of small arms design and development, but the end of World War II saw most of its facilities taken over by the new East German government, so for many years the company was unable to re-enter its chosen market. But by the early 1960s Walther was back in business, and in 1963 introduced its 9-mm (0.354-in) **Walther MP-K** and **MP-L** sub-machine guns.

The MP-K and MP-L (MP standing for *Maschinenpistole*, K for *kurz* or short, and L for *lange* or long) differ only in their barrel length. They are both well-made sub-machine guns constructed in the usual manner from steel stampings, and both use the same blowback operating principle. The butt stock is a skeleton tube arrangement, and when not in use this can be folded along the right-hand side of the receiver. The box magazine is inserted into a housing under the receiver and just forward of the trigger group. This magazine is wedge-shaped in cross-section and contains 32 rounds. As one would expect with Walther products, the overall standard of manufacture is excellent.

From the side both models present a rather deep silhouette. This is because the main mass of the breech block is mounted over the barrel and guided throughout its backward and forward travel on a guide rod. Normally the bolt handle does not move with the breech block, but if required it can be latched into the block in order to clear a stoppage. There are all manner of small detail points on these two weapons. One is that when the stock is folded forward the butt portion can be used as a forward grip. Another is the rear sight, which is normally fixed for use at 100 m (109 yards) using conventional rear and fore sights. But for use in low visibility conditions the upper portion of the sight becomes an open rear sight and is used in conjunction with the top of the fore sight protector. There is a fire selector switch just behind the trigger, allowing rapid and easy selection of 'safe', single shot or full automatic.

The first Walther MP-Ks and MP-Ls were sold to the West German navy and to some German police forces. Since then more have been sold to Brazil, Colombia, the Mexican navy and Venezuela. The types are no longer in production, but both are still being offered for sale by Walther and could be placed back in production within a short time. Some accessories have been offered with these guns. At one point the MP-K was offered with a screw-on silencer, but this was apparently not long developed and there appear to have been few takers. All weapons have provision for sling swivels and these are so arranged that the sling can be used to stabilize the gun when firing bursts.

Specification
MP-K
Calibre: 9 mm (0.354 in)
Weight: loaded 3.425 kg (7.55 lb)
Length: with stock open 653 mm (25.7 in) and with stock folded 368 mm (14.49 in)
Length of barrel: 171 mm (6.73 in)
Muzzle velocity: 356 m (1,168 ft) per second
Cyclic rate of fire: 550 rpm
Magazine: 32-round box

Specification
MP-L
Calibre: 9 mm (0.354 in)
Weight: loaded 3.625 kg (7.99 lb)
Length: with stock open 737 mm (29 in) and with stock folded 455 mm (17.9 in)
Length of barrel: 257 mm (10.12 in)
Muzzle velocity: 396 m (1,299 ft) per second
Cyclic rate of fire: 550 rpm
Magazine: 32-round box

7.62-mm Type 64

The Chinese **Type 64** is one of the most unusual sub-machine guns in service today, for it has been designed and produced from the outset as a silenced weapon. During World War II several types of machine-gun were fitted with various types of suppressor for special missions (such as behind-the-lines and commando-type operations), but no country went to the extent of producing a special weapon for these roles. For reasons best known to themselves the Communist Chinese have done so.

The Type 64 fires the standard Soviet 7.62-mm (0.3-in) × 25 pistol round, but the use of a Maxim-type silencer arrangement makes this round effective only at short ranges. To make matters more complicated the Chinese use this pistol round fitted with a special bullet known as the Type P, which is slightly heavier than the normal bullet and is thus slightly more effective. As silenced weapons go the Type 64 has been tested to the point where it seems to be effective enough, but the time and trouble involved in the design and production of such a special weapon and cartridge seem wasteful to many Western experts.

The Type 64 is a mixture of various design features mainly lifted from other weapons. The basic overall design and bolt action resemble those of the Soviet PPS-43 of World War II, while the trigger mechanism is taken from the Bren Gun, many of which were used in China during and after World War II. The folding stock also comes from the Soviet PPS-43, while the silencer uses the well-established principles introduced by Hiram Maxim who was at one time as well known for his silencer designs as he was for his machine-guns. The barrel extends along only part of the silencer, and the last part of the barrel is perforated by a series of holes; the propellant gases exhaust through these and the muzzle into a series of baffles that continue until the muzzle of the silencer proper. This silencer also acts as a flash suppressor.

The exact operational role of this weapon with the ChiCom forces is not known with exactitude. The few examples seen in the West came mainly from Vietnam and other such Far East origins, and it is doubtful if the Type 64 was kept in production for very long or even if it was produced in any quantity. It remains an enigma.

The Type 64 uses a selective fire trigger mechanism derived from that of the Bren gun and a bolt action taken from the Type 43 – the Chinese copy of the Soviet PPS-43.

Specification
Type 64
Calibre: 7.62 mm (0.3 in) × 25 Type P
Weight: empty 3.4 kg (7.495 lb)
Length: with stock extended 843 mm (33.19 in)
Length of barrel: 244 mm (9.6 in)
Muzzle velocity: about 313 m (1,027 ft) per second
Cyclic rate of fire: uncertain
Magazine: 20- or 30-round box

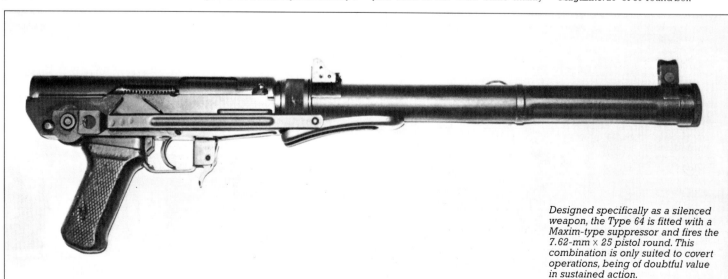

Designed specifically as a silenced weapon, the Type 64 is fitted with a Maxim-type suppressor and fires the 7.62-mm × 25 pistol round. This combination is only suited to covert operations, being of doubtful value in sustained action.

Model 61 Skorpion

The Czech **Model 61 Skorpion** lies in that small-arms no-man's-land where a weapon that is neither a pistol or a true sub-machine gun is described as a 'machine pistol': it is small enough to be carried and fired as a pistol, but it fires fully automatically when required. It has the advantages and disadvantages of both types of weapon and is perhaps below par as both a pistol and a sub-machine gun, but it is now one of the

The Model 61 Skorpion is a favourite weapon of the Palestine Liberation Organization, its small size making for easy concealment.

most feared of all 'underground' weapons, despite the fact that it was originally intended to be a standard service weapon for the Czech armed forces.

The Skorpion was designed for use by tank crews, signallers and other personnel who have no normal need for anything larger than a pistol. But since a pistol is essentially a short-range weapon, the introduction of a fully automatic feature provided this small weapon with a considerable short-range firepower potential. The Skorpion resembles a pistol, though the magazine is not in the butt but forward of the trigger assembly, and a folding wire butt is provided for aimed fire. The overall appearance is short and chunky, and the weapon is small enough to be carried in a rather over-sized belt holster. When fired on full automatic the weapon has a cyclic rate of about 840 rounds per minute, which

Above right: Stock fully extended, the Type 61 can shoot with reasonable accuracy at up to 200 m (220 yards). It uses a simple blowback operation, but the empty case is ejected directly upwards.

makes it a formidable weapon at short ranges, but this benefit is offset by two considerations. One is that using any machine pistol on full automatic makes the weapon almost impossible to aim accurately: the muzzle forces cause the muzzle to climb and judder to such an extent that it is virtually impossible to hold the weapon still for more than an instant. The other consideration is that the Skorpion uses magazines with only 10- or 20-round capacity, and on automatic either would soon be exhausted. But while the Skorpion fires it sprays bullets in an alarming swathe and this makes it a formidable close-quarter weapon.

The Skorpion operates on the blow-back principle. Single shots can be selected, and aiming is assisted by use of the folding wire butt. The basic

Model 61 Skorpion fires the American 0.32-in (actual 7.65-mm) cartridge, making it the only Warsaw Pact weapon to use this round, but the **Model 63** uses the 9-mm short (0.38-in) round and the **Model 68** the 9-mm (0.354-in) Parabellum. A silenced version of the Model 61 is available.

Apart from the Czech armed forces, the Skorpion has also been sold to some African nations, but its main impact has been in the hands of guerrillas and 'freedom fighters'. The firepower impact of the Skorpion is considerable at short ranges, which suits the requirements of assassination and terror squads, so the type is now much favoured by such groups. With them it has turned up in many parts of the world from Central America to the Middle East.

Specification
Model 61 Skorpion
Calibre: 0.32 in (actual 7.65 mm)
Weight: loaded 2 kg (4.4 lb)
Length: with butt extended 513 mm (20.2 in) and with butt folded 269 mm (10.6 in)

Length of barrel: 112 mm (4.4 in)
Muzzle velocity: 317 m (1,040 ft) per second
Cyclic rate of fire: 840 rpm
Magazine: 10- or 20-round box

9-mm wz 63 (PM-63)

The 9-mm **wz 63** (*wzor*, or model) is also known as the **PM-63**, and is one of those weapons that falls into the category of machine pistol. Although only slightly larger than an orthodox pistol, it can be fired fully automatic at a cyclic rate of 600 rounds per minute. It was designed by Piotr Wilniewicz, who led a design team to produce a weapon for those elements of the Polish forces who are unable to carry a conventional weapon during their combat duties. The wz 63 is thus used by Polish tank crews, signallers and other troops such as truck drivers.

The wz 63 is rather long for a conventional pistol and is fitted with a butt that can be folded forward to lie under the barrel. When folded forward the butt either lies under the forward grip, or the butt plate can be folded down to act as a forward grip. This forward grip is essential to hold the weapon steady on automatic fire, for the wz 63 suffers from the usual difficulty of rapid and erratic muzzle movement mainly caused by the cyclic rate of fire. Some of this muzzle movement is compensated by a simple fixture on the end of

the barrel which is little more than an open trough angled upwards at a slight angle to push the barrel downwards. In practice this device appears to be of marginal value. Accurate single-shot aiming is possible, but even when using the butt any deliberate aim is likely to be disturbed by the bolt moving forward as the trigger is pulled since, like most other blowback-operated weapons, the wz 63 operates from an open bolt. However its effective range using the stock extended into the shoulder is stated to be 200 m (219 yards); on automatic the range is much less.

The wz 63 may be used with either a 25- or a 40-round magazine, although some references also mention a 15-

Although classed as a machine pistol, the wz 63 is more complex than the Skorpion and it would require a firm hand indeed to fire 9-mm × 18 cartridges on full automatic. It is perhaps no accident that the handbook only shows it deployed for two-handed use.

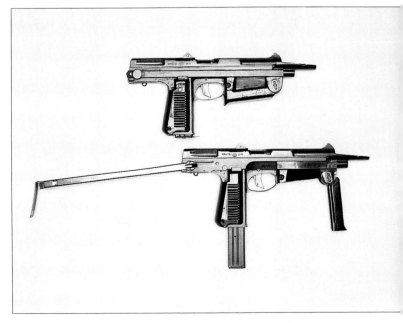

round magazine. It is normally issued together with a special holster and a pouch holding three magazines and a cleaning kit. A sling may also be supplied.

The round fired by the wz 63 is the 9-mm (0.354-in) × 18 Makarov cartridge, which differs in several ways from the usual 9-mm (0.354-in) × 19 Parabellum round. It provides the wz 63 with a considerable striking capability at short combat ranges but as stated before the ability of any machine pistol to remain on target for more than a fleeting second is unlikely. Instead the wz 63 produces a 'spray' effect which can be of considerable value in combat, but even this effect is reduced by the magazine capacity.

The wz 63 is still used by the Polish troops for which it was designed, and the type is now extensively used by Polish police and security units. Outside Poland the wz 63 appears to be little used, though numbers of these weapons have turned up in the Middle East and have been observed by several of the organizations involved in the civil war in Lebanon.

Specification
wz 63
Calibre: 9 mm (0.354 in) Makarov
Weight: with empty 32-round magazine 1.8 kg (3.97 lb)
Length: with stock retracted 333 mm (13.1 in)
Length of barrel: 152 mm (6 in)
Muzzle velocity: 323 m (1,060 ft) per second
Cyclic rate of fire: 600 rpm
Magazine: 25- or 40-round box; also references to 15-round box

---

Ingram Model 10

There have been few weapons in recent years that have 'enjoyed' the attentions of the Press and Hollywood to such an extent as that lavished on the Ingram sub-machine guns. Gordon B. Ingram had designed a whole string of sub-machine guns before he produced his **Ingram Model 10**, which was originally intended to be used with the Sionics Company suppressor. First produced during the mid-1960s, the little Ingram Model 10 soon attracted a great deal of public attention because of its rate of fire, supposedly high enough to 'saw a body in half', coupled with the highly efficient sound suppressor. Hollywood and television films added their dramatic commentaries and the Ingram Model 10 soon became as widely known as the old Thompson sub-machine guns of the 1920s.

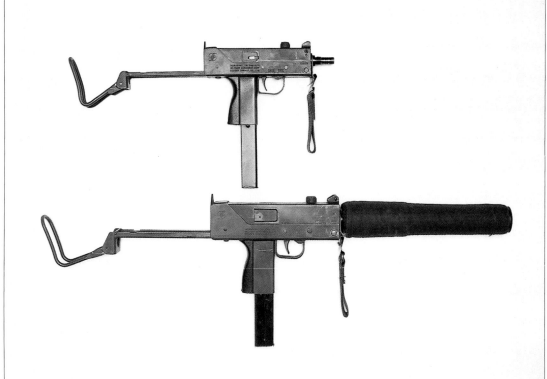

The Ingram Model 11 (top) is chambered for 9-mm Short (.380 ACP), while the Model 10 (below), fitted with a suppressor, can be chambered for either 9-mm Parabellum or .45 ACP. Both are relatively well balanced due to the bolt enveloping the breech.

The Ingram Model 10 is indeed a remarkable little weapon. It is constructed from sheet metal but manufactured to a very high standard and extremely robust. This has to be, for it fires at a cyclic rate of over 1,000 rounds per minute, yet control of the weapon is still relatively easy thanks to the good balance imparted by the centrally-placed pistol group through which the box magazine is inserted. Most versions have a folding metal butt

Its efficient suppressor makes the Ingram a handy weapon for the Special Forces. By reducing the escaping gas to subsonic speed and eliminating flash, the position of the firer can remain a mystery to the target, until hopefully it is too late.

but this may be removed, and many weapons not fitted with the long tubular suppressor use a forward webbing hand-strap as a rudimentary foregrip. The muzzle on most models is threaded to accommodate the suppressor, and when fitted this is covered with a heat-resistant canvas or plastic webbing to allow it to be used as a forward grip. The cocking handle is on top of the slab-sided receiver and when turned through 90° acts as a safety lock. As this handle is slotted for sighting purposes the firer can soon notice if this safety is applied, and there is a normal trigger safety as well.

The Model 10 may be encountered chambered for either the well-known 11.43-mm (0.45-in) cartridge or the more usual 9-mm (0.354-in) Parabellum. The latter round may also be used on the smaller **Model 11** which is normally chambered for the less powerful 9-mm Short (.380 ACP). In all these calibres the Ingram is a dreadfully efficient weapon and not surprisingly it has been sold widely to customers ranging from paramilitary forces to bodyguard and security agencies. Military sales on any large scale have been few but several nations have acquired numbers for 'testing and evaluation'. The British SAS is known to have obtained a small quantity for test-

ing. Sales were not helped by a series of insolvencies and personality clashes which ensured that the manufacture never stayed with one company for very long. Several variant models were produced in small numbers to tempt customers but in vain. In the early 1980s amid reports of worldwide sales enthusiasm, the last attempt to float the Ingram failed and the gun vanished into history. Some authorities claim that possibility 16,000 guns of all types were made during it short lifetime, others consider this far too high an estimate. The basic fact remains that the Ingram was never accepted in any quantity by any major military force.

Specification
Model 10 (0.45-in model)
Calibre: 11.43 mm (0.45 in)
Weight: loaded with 30-round magazine 3.818 kg (8.4 lb)
Length: with stock extended 548 mm (21.575 in) and with stock folded 269 mm (10.59 in)
Length of barrel: 146 mm (5.75 in)
Length of suppressor: 291 mm (11.46 in)
Muzzle velocity: 280 m (918 ft) per second
Cyclic rate of fire: 1,145 rpm
Magazine: 30-round box

9-mm UZI

Once Israel had fought its War of Independence in 1948 the new nation had some breathing space in which to arm itself for any future conflict. Submachine guns were high on the list of priorities, for the new Israeli army was then equipped with all manner of old weapons varying from Sten guns to Czech weapons. The Czech weapons attracted the close attention of one Lieutenant Uziel Gail, for they had the advantage that their breech blocks or bolts were 'wrapped around' the barrel, so placing the mass of the bolt well forward around the barrel on firing and allowing a short weapon to have a relatively long barrel. The Czech weapons concerned were of the vz 23 series, and using these Gail was able to design and develop his own design that was more suitable to the manufac-

turing methods then available in relatively undeveloped Israel. He came up with a weapon that is now universally known as the **UZI** after its designer.

The UZI is made largely from simple pressings held in place by spot welds or other welding. The main body is made from a single sheet of heavy gauge sheet steel with grooves pressed into the sides to take any dust, dirt or sand that might get into the works. This simple feature makes the UZI capable of operation under even the most arduous conditions, a fact that has been proved on many occasions. The overall cross-section of the main body is rectangular with the barrel secured to the body by a large nut just behind the muzzle. The trigger group is situated centrally, and the box magazine is inserted through the pistol grip, which

makes reloading very easy in the dark for 'hand will naturally find hand'. The normal combat magazine holds 32 rounds, but a common practice is to join two magazines together using a cross-over clip or even tape to allow rapid changing. A grip safety is incorporated into the pistol grip.

The UZI is now virtually one of the symbols of Israeli military prowess, but Israel is not the only nation to use the type. The West Germans also use the UZI, which they know as the **MP2**; this model was produced under licence by FN in Belgium. Numerous other nations also use the UZI. It is part of legend that the President of the United States is always accompanied by bodyguards carrying UZIs in specially fitted brief cases, and many other security agencies and police forces

use the UZI.

The UZI may be encountered with either a sturdy fixed wooden butt stock or a metal stock that can be folded forward under the main body with the butt plate still available to assist in steadying automatic fire. The UZI can be used to fire single-shot by use of a change lever just above the pistol butt.

Specification
UZI (with wooden stock)
Calibre: 9 mm (0.354 in) Parabellum
Weight: loaded with 32-round magazine 4.1 kg (9 lb)
Length: 650 mm (25.59 in)
Length of barrel: 260 mm (10.24 in)
Muzzle velocity: 400 m (1,312 ft) per second
Cyclic rate of fire: 600 rpm
Magazine: 25- or 32-round box

Right: The UZI (with wooden stock) and the Mini-UZI. The Mini-UZI is just 36-cm (14-in) long with its stock folded, making for easy concealment under ordinary clothing. The UZI is a design of great simplicity and is famous for reliability in awkward conditions.

Below: This Israeli carries the UZI fitted with metal folding stock. In addition to a grip safety, the UZI features a ratchet on the cocking handle to prevent accidental firing if the user's hand slips off the handle after the breech block has passed behind a round.

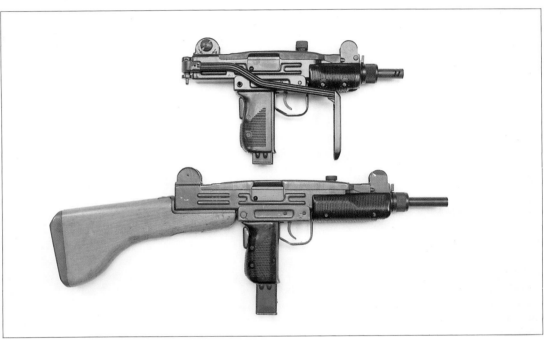

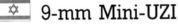

9-mm Mini-UZI

The **Mini-UZI** has been developed by Israel Military Industries from the full-scale UZI and differs from the original only in dimensions and weights. A few modifications have been introduced to the basic design, but these are only superficial while the operating system of the original has been retained unchanged.

The Mini-UZI has been developed as a weapon suitable for concealment by police and security personnel. This prompted an overall decrease in dimensions, and to improve this concealment a smaller 20-round magazine has been introduced, although the Mini-UZI can still use the existing 25- and 32-round magazines if required. The UZI parentage is immediately apparent but one change that can be noted is that the normal folding metal butt has been replaced by a single-strut butt stock that folds along the right-hand side of the body. When folded the butt plate acts as a rudimentary foregrip. but the normal foregrip is a plastic section just forward of the trigger group.

To date the Mini-UZI has been marketed as suitable for police and secur-

ity agencies but it is bound to attract the attentions of various military organizations for special missions. It would make an ideal commando-type weapon where light weight is required, and it must be stressed that although the Mini-UZI is a scaled-down version of the original it still uses the potent 9-mm (0.354-in) × 19 Parabellum round. As the weapon is lighter than the full-size version its breech block is lighter too, and this provides a cyclic rate of fire of 950 rounds per minute, which is much higher than on the original.

The Mini-UZI is being marketed in the United States carried in a specially-fitted brief case together with spare magazines and a small cleaning and spares kit. It has already been suggested that some form of silencer could be fitted to the muzzle.

There are also some UZIs other than the standard version and the Mini-UZI. One is the semi-automatic **Carbine UZI** which has been produced to conform with the legal requirements of some American states that require non-automatic weapons only to be held by their inhabitants. In order to prevent

the rapid conversion of semi-automatic versions of automatic weapons they call for such semi-automatic versions to have barrels at least 406 mm (16 in) long. Thus the standard UZI may be seen with a long barrel protruding from the body and this denotes that the weapon can be fired single-shot only.

Another UZI variant that has only recently been introduced is the UZI pistol. Although really outside the scope of this survey it is still recognizable as an UZI. It can be fired single-shot only and there is no form of butt stock.

Specification
UZI
Calibre: 9 mm (0.354 in) Parabellum
Weight: loaded with 20-round magazine 3.11 kg (6.85 lb)
Length: with stock extended 600 mm (23.62 in) and with stock folded 360 mm (14.17 in)
Length of barrel: 197 mm (7.75 in)
Muzzle velocity: 352 m (1.15 ft) per second
Cyclic rate of fire: 950 rpm
Magazine: 20-, 25- or 32-round box

9-mm Beretta Model 12s

During World War II the Beretta sub-machine guns were among the most highly-prized of all war trophies, and many remained for many years after the war in service with both military and paramilitary formations. The last of the 'war-time' Beretta variants was produced in 1949, and in 1958 an entirely new Beretta design was introduced. This owed nothing to previous designs and for the first time Beretta adopted the tubular receiver and stamped component construction that had for long been employed by many other manufacturers. The new design was the **Beretta Model 12**, but although it looked simple it was still a Beretta product, as was revealed by the overall high standard of finish and by its quality manufacture.

The Model 12 had an orthodox construction down to the 'wrap-around' bolt that was by then commonplace. This allowed it to be a short and handy weapon that as usual could be fitted with either a folding metal stock or a fixed wooden stock.

The Model 12 was sold extensively

The men of the Italian Parachute Brigade are mainly equipped with the BM59 rifle, but the Beretta 12S is better suited for close-range work. The 12S is designed to operate in harsh environments, having grooves along the sides of the receiver which catch any debris entering the weapon.

to such nations as Libya and Saudi Arabia, but only in small numbers to the Italian armed forces, who purchased the type for use only by special units. However, Beretta was able to negotiate licence production of the Model 12 in Indonesia and Brazil for local sales and export.

Beretta then decided to develop the basic design one stage further and produced the **Model 12S**. This is now the current Beretta sub-machine gun and production of the Model 12 has now ceased. Externally the Model 12S looks very like the Model 12 but there are some detail differences. One is the epoxy-resin finish, making the metal resistant to corrosion and wear. The fire selector mechanism on the Model 12 was of the 'push through' type, operated by pushing a button from either side of the receiver just over the pistol grip, but the Type 12S has a conventional single-lever mechanism with a safety that locks both the trigger and the grip safety. The folding butt, when fitted, now has a more positive lock for both the open and the closed positions, and some changes have been made to the sights. One laudable feature that has been carried over from the original Model 12 is the retention of the raised grooves that run along each side of the tubular receiver. These grooves act as catchers for any dirt or debris that find their way into the interior, and enable the Model 12S to operate under really muddy and arduous conditions.

To date the Model 12S has been

A dramatic break from pre-war Beretta designs, the Model 12 and 12S use heavy sheet metal stampings

to form the magazine housing and receiver, but retain the elegant simplicity associated with Beretta.

purchased by the Italian armed forces in small numbers and more were sold to Tunisia. For a short period in the 1980s FN Herstal held a licence to manufacture the Model 12S but its

doubtful if they made many. The general downturn in the employment of submachine guns by military forces that meant that foreign sales have been minimal.

The 12S can be distinguished from the earlier Model 12 by the single lever fire selector and safety. The white 'S' is for safe, the red 'I' for semi automatic and the 'R' for full automatic.

Specification
Model 12S (metal stock version)
Calibre: 9 mm (0.354 in) Parabellum
Weight: loaded with 32-round magazine 3.81 kg (8.4 lb)
Length: with stock extended 660 mm (26 in) and with stock folded 418 mm (16.45 in)
Length of barrel: 200 mm (7.87 in)
Muzzle velocity: 381 m (1,250 ft) per second
Cyclic rate of fire: 500-550 rpm
Magazine: 20-, 32- or 40-round box

Right: Although widely exported, the Model 12 is only issued to Special Troops of the Italian army, the rest having to content themselves with the MAB 38/49. The Model 12 is a very steady weapon with remarkably low muzzle climb while firing in full automatic.

Sniping Rifles

Sniping, as an anti-personnel activity, has a long history in warfare. Today, though, a new concept of sniping has arisen. Meet the anti-materiel rifle, with which snipers can take on new targets which can be just as vulnerable to a rifle round as a person is.

Sniping has always had an air of glamorous menace about it: the expert marksman concealing himself for hours or days to take one shot at some unfortunate person wandering along minding his own business. And sniping has always been a popular, if dangerous, job. The individual escapes the boring routine of day-to-day soldiering for a more independent existence. It is, above all, a job requiring the utmost discipline and skill, and because of that the sniper is given a superior tool with which to work.

Sniping rifles come in two types: either they are standard service rifles which have been picked out during their initial manufacture and test as being exceptionally accurate, or they are highly specialized rifles which have been specifically designed. Both extremes can be seen in this chapter. The British L42A1 was simply the old Lee-Enfield rifle given a better barrel, while the Walther WA2000 was a luxurious machine for delivering bullets with supreme accuracy at long ranges.

These two weapons also exhibit another division, which can still start an argument: bolt-action rifle or semi-automatic rifle, which is the more accurate?

Among the ultimate in anti-materiel rifles, the Steyr IWS2000 fires a 15-mm (0.59-in) tungsten dart which can penetrate 40 mm (1.57-in) of armour at a 1,000-m (1094-yard) range.

For many years the bolt-action rifle was considered the only option for sniping, since no semi-automatic weapon could approach it for accuracy. However, improvement in the standards of semi-automatics, plus careful selection and fitting of sniping versions has resulted in several semi-automatic sniping rifles of impeccable accuracy.

In the mid-1980s a new type of sniping rifle appeared, a heavy weapon built to fire the 0.5-in Browning machine-gun cartridge to ranges in excess of 910 m (1,000 yards). Reaction was mixed, most critics observing that the chance of a 0.5-in bullet being accurate enough to hit a man at that sort of range was fairly slim. The developers pointed out that

there were other objects which were vulnerable to a heavy bullet: radar sets, soft vehicles, helicopters and aircraft on the ground. Thus the 'anti-materiel' rifle is now gaining acceptance. For now its main use seems to be for disposing of explosive devices at long range – terrorist devices, for example – but in a future war it might fulfil its predicted role.

7.62-mm SSG 69

With this Austrian rifle the designation **SSG 69** stands for **Scharfschüt-zengewehr 69** (sharp-shooter rifle 69), 1969 being the year of the weapon's acceptance for service by the Austrian army. It is manufactured by the Steyr-Daimler-Puch AG concern at Steyr and was, in 1969, the latest in a long line of rifles produced by the concern.

The 7.62-mm (0.3-in) SSG 69 has some unusual design features, one of them being the use of a Männlicher bolt action with a form of rear locking instead of the far more common Mauser forward-lug locking. The bolt action is now uncommon, although it has been used on other recent Steyr rifles, and is so arranged that the entire action is very strong and the chamber is well

The Steyr SSG 69 rifle is the standard Austrian army sniper's rifle, and is used by mountain troops as it is possible for a single sniper to virtually seal a mountain pass against advancing troops for long periods. The SSG 69 is robust enough to survive in such conditions and retain its accuracy.

within the receiver for added rigidity. A safety catch locks both the bolt and firing pin when engaged. The barrel is cold-forged using a machine hammering process in which the barrel rifling is hammered into the bore using a mandrel. Another odd feature is the use of the Männlicher rotary magazine, a design feature that dates back to well before World War I. This rotary magazine holds five rounds but a more orthodox 10-round box magazine was available on early models.

The rifle stock is made of a synthetic material and is adjustable in length to suit the firer. The firer can also adjust the double-pull trigger pressure. It is also possible to make various adjustments to the standard Kahles ZF69 telescopic sight which has a magnification of ×6. Other forms of sight (including night sights) can be used on the SSG 69, the receiver having an overhead longitudinal rib that can accommodate a wide range of vision devices. 'Iron' sights are provided for emergency use only.

The SSG 69 is very accurate. Trials have shown that it is possible to fire 10-round groups no larger than 400 mm (15.75 in) at 800 m (875 yards), which is the maximum graduated range of the ZF69 sight; at shorter

ranges the groupings get much tighter.

Since the introduction of the SSG 69 Steyr has developed some more advanced sniper rifle models, but the SSG 69 remains in service with the Austrians for the simple reason that it is an excellent military sniper's rifle and far more practical than some of the more modern technical marvels now available. A target shooting version of the SSG 69 with a heavier barrel and match sights has been produced.

Specification
SSG 69
Calibre: 7.62 mm (0.3 in)
Lengths: overall 1140 mm (44.9 in); barrel 650 mm (25.6 in)
Weight: empty, with sight 4.6 kg (10.14 lb)
Muzzle velocity: 860 m (2,821 ft) per second
Magazine capacity: 5-round rotary

The Steyr SSG 69 rifle uses a Kahles ZF69 telescopic sight graduated up to 800 m (875 yards) – this example is not fitted with the usual 'iron' sights. The SSG 69 uses an unusual five-round rotary magazine, but can also be fitted with a 10-round box magazine.

Beretta Sniper

When the market for high-precision sniper's rifles expanded in the 1970s, virtually every major small-arms manufacturer in Europe and elsewhere started to design weapons they thought would meet international requirements. Some of these designs have fared better than others on the market, but one that does appear to have been overlooked by many is the **Beretta Sniper** 7.62-mm (0.3-in) sniping rifle. This design appears to have been given no numerical designation and it has only recently appeared on the scene, two factors that would normally indicate that the rifle is only just out of the development stage. But there are reports that it is already in use with some Italian paramilitary police units

for internal security duties.

Compared with many of the latest 'space-age' sniper rifle designs, the Beretta offering is almost completely orthodox but well up to the usual high standards of Beretta design and finish. The Sniper uses a manual rotary bolt action allied to the usual heavy barrel, and one of its most prominent features is the large and unusually-shaped hole carved into the high-quality wooden stock that forms a prominent pistol grip for the trigger.

Despite the overall conventional design there are one or two advanced features on the Sniper. The wooden forestock conceals a forward-pointing counterweight under the free-floating barrel that acts as a damper to reduce

the barrel vibrations produced on firing. At the front end of the forestock is a location point for securing a light adjustable bipod to assist aiming. The underside of the forestock contains a slot for an adjustable forward hand stop for the firer, and this forestop can also be used as the attachment point for a firing sling if one is required. The butt and cheek pads are adjustable and the muzzle has a flash hider.

Unlike many of its modern counterparts the Beretta Sniper is fully provided with a set of all-adjustable precision match sights, even though these would not normally be used for the sniping role. Over the receiver is a standard NATO optical or night sight mounting attachment to accommodate

virtually any military sighting system. The normal telescopic sight is the widely-used Zeiss Divari Z with a zoom capability from ×1.5 to ×6, but other types can be fitted.

Specification
Beretta Sniper
Calibre: 7.62 mm (0.3 in)
Lengths: overall 1165 mm (45.87 in); barrel 586 mm (23 in)
Weights: empty 5.55 kg (12.23 lb); complete 7.2 kg (15.87 lb)
Muzzle velocity: about 865 m (2,838 ft) per second
Magazine capacity: 5 rounds

FR-F1 and FR-F2

In this photograph the French sniper is using the telescopic sight of his FR-F1 as an observation aid, resting the barrel on a tree branch. He would never fire the weapon from such a stance, for accuracy would be minimal.

When the French army required a sniper's rifle to replace the varied selection of weapons which it had used since World War II, it decided that the easiest design course to follow was to modify its existing service rifle, the 7.5-mm (0.295-in) modèle 1936. This rifle had the dubious distinction of being one of the very last bolt-action rifles to be accepted as a standard service weapon by any of the major European powers, but it was not regarded as a very good design, even at the time, and was used mainly because of its French origins. Using this weapon as a starting point the resultant sniper's rifle, the **mle FR-F1**, emerged as not particularly brilliant.

The number of modifications involved in converting the modèle 1936 into the FR-F1 meant that very little of the original remained; it was just about discernible that the modèle 1936 had been used as the origin, but that was all. The main change was the introduction of a bipod, the addition of a pistol grip for the trigger, a longer barrel with a long flash hider, and a telescopic sight. The butt was provided with a cheek rest and the bolt action considerably altered.

Even with all these alterations the mle FR-F1 was not an immediate international success. For a start, the rifle fired the old French 7.5-mm standard cartridge at a time when other nations were changing to the new 7.62-mm (0.3-in) NATO round. This change to the new cartridge was so pronounced that eventually the French had to convert to it as well, and later-production mle FR-F1s were chambered for 7.62-mm ammunition; many of the older 7.5-mm rifles are still in use, however. The modèle 1936 bolt action was also retained, albeit in a much altered form. This action was regarded as an awkward one to use, and even in its revised form was little improved. The bipod was also rather flimsy and difficult to adjust. Also the weapon was considered by many to be too heavy.

The mle FR-F1 has now been replaced by the **mle FR-F2**. Basically this is much the same as the earlier weapon, but the long barrel is now encased in a thick black nylonite sleeve to reduce the heat haze from the barrel that might interfere with the performance of some night sights. The bipod has also been altered and relocated so that it is now secured directly to the barrel. The forestock has been changed from all-wood to all-metal, covered in a plastic coating. The mle FR-F2 has only been in production for a limited period so it is still too early to determine how it will fare in international esteem.

Specification
FR-F1
Calibre: 7.5 mm (0.295 in) or 7.62 mm (0.3 in)
Lengths: overall 1138 mm (44.8 in); barrel 552 mm (21.73 in)
Weight: empty 5.42 kg (11.95 kg)
Muzzle velocity: 852 m (2,795 ft) per second
Magazine capacity: 10 rounds

Rifle 7.62-mm L42A1

The Lee-Enfield rifle has had a long career with the British army reaching back to the 1890s, and throughout that time the basic Lee-Enfield manual bolt mechanism has remained little changed. It is still in service with the army to this day in the form of the **Rifle 7.62-mm L42A1**. These weapons are used only for sniping, and are conversions of 0.303-in (7.7-mm) No. 4 Mk 1(T) or Mk 1*(T) rifles, as used during World War II. The conversions involved new barrels, a new magazine, some changes to the trigger mechanism and fixed sights, and alterations to the forestock. The World War II No. 32 Mk 3 telescopic sight (renamed the L1A1) and its mounting over the receiver have been retained, and the result has for long been a good, rugged and serviceable sniping rifle, used not only by the army but also by the Royal Marines.

In modern terms the L42A1 is very much the product of a previous generation, but it can still give excellent first-shot results at ranges over 800 m (875 yards), although this depends very much on the skill of the firer and the type of ammunition used. Normally the ammunition is selected from special 'Green Spot' high-accuracy ammunition produced at the Royal Ordnance facility at Radway Green. The rifle itself is also the subject of a great deal of care, calibration and attention. When not in use it is stowed (and transported) in a special wooden chest that contains not only the rifle but the optical sight, cleaning gear, firing sling and perhaps a few spares such as extra magazines: the L42A1 retains the 10-round magazine of the 0.303-in version but with a revised outline to accommodate the new rimless ammunition. The often-overlooked weapon record books are also kept in the chest.

The L42A1 is not the only 7.62-mm Lee-Enfield rifle still around. A special match-shooting version known as the **L39A1** is still retained for competitive use, and there are two other models, the **Envoy** and the **Enforcer**. The former may be regarded as a civilian match version of the L39A1, while the Enforcer is a custom-built variant of the L42A1 with a heavier barrel and revised butt outline, produced specifically for police use. The L39A1 and Envoy are not normally fitted with optical sights but the basic information relating to the L42A1 applies to the three variants.

The L42A1 is now due to be replaced by a new sniper's rifle, a 7.62-mm design from Accuracy International.

Specification
L42A1
Calibre: 7.62 mm (0.3 in)
Lengths: overall 1181 mm (46.5 in); barrel 699 mm (27.5 in)
Weight: 4.43 kg (9.76 lb)
Muzzle velocity: 838 m (2,750 ft) per second
Magazine capacity: 10 rounds

Below: The L42A1 rifle is a 7.62-mm (0.30-in) conversion of an earlier 0.303-in (7.70-mm) Lee-Enfield rifle, and it has served the British Army well over the years. It was used by the Army and the Royal Marines during the Falklands war, usually in the form shown here with the weapon covered in camouflage scrim netting.

Changes to the old No. 4 Lee-Enfield rifle for the 7.62-mm (0.30-in) sniping role involved a new heavy barrel, a new 10-round box magazine, and cutting back the forestock over the barrel. A cheek rest was added to the butt and the rifle was virtually rebuilt. Changes were also made to the trigger, and a scope mount was added.

Parker-Hale Model 82

The Parker Hale Model 82 was selected by the Canadian Armed Forces as their sniper rifle, and is seen here in winter camouflage. It uses a Mauser-type bolt action and is fitted with a four-round box magazine.

Parker-Hale Limited of Birmingham has for many years been manufacturing match rifles and their associated sights, and also produces sniping rifles. The company's best-known product to date is the 7.62-mm (0.3-in) **Parker-Hale Model 82**, also known as the **Parker-Hale 1200TX**. The Model 82 has been accepted for military and police service by several nations.

In appearance and design terms the Model 82 is an entirely conventional sniping weapon. It uses a manual bolt action very similar to that used on the classic Mauser 98 rifle, allied to a heavy free-floating barrel; the barrel weighs 1.98 kg (4.365 lb) and is manufactured from chrome molybdenum steel. An integral four-round magazine is provided. The trigger mechanism is an entirely self-contained unit that can be adjusted as required.

The Model 82 is available in a number of forms to suit any particular customer requirements. Thus an adjustable cheek pad may be provided if wanted, and the butt lengths can be altered by adding or taking away butt pads of various thicknesses. The sights too are subject to several variations, but the Model 82 is one weapon that is normally supplied with 'iron' match-type sights. If an optical sight is fitted the rear-sights have to be removed to allow the same mounting block to be used. The forward mounting block is machined into the receiver. Various types of 'iron' foresight or optical night sights can be fitted.

The Australian army uses the Model 82 fitted with a Kahles Helia ZF 69 telescopic sight. The Canadian army uses a version of the Model 82/1200TX altered to meet local requirements; this service knows the Model 82 as the **Rifle 7.62-mm C3**. New Zealand also uses the Model 82.

Parker-Hale produces a special training version of the Model 82 known as the **Model 83**. This single-shot rifle is fitted with match sights only and there is no provision for a telescopic sight. It has been accepted by the British Ministry of Defence as the **Cadet Training Rifle L81A1**.

The Model 82 has now been updated to the **Model 85**. This has a revised butt outline compared with the Model 82, a 10-round box magazine and a bipod (optional on the Model 82) is fitted as standard. Parker-hale then sold their rifle designs and rights to the Gibbs Rifle Co of Martinsburg, WVa, USA who now produce the Model 85 and other Parke-Hale designs.

Specification
Model 82
Calibre: 7.62 mm (0.3 in)
Lengths: 1162 mm (45.75 in); barrel 660 mm (25.98 in)
Weight: unloaded 4.8 kg (10.58 lb)
Muzzle velocity: about 840 m (2,756 ft) per second
Magazine capacity: 4 rounds

Below: In service with the armed forces of Australia, New Zealand and Canada, the Parker Hale Model 82 is intended to hit point targets at up to 400 m in good light, or up to the maximum range of any sights fitted.

Mauser SP 66 and SP 86

The Mauser-Werke at Oberndorf in West Germany can lay claim to a long and distinguished design and production background for its manual bolt-action rifles that are now known under the blanket name of Mauser. The company's forward-locking bolt action is still widely used by designers who require maximum locking with accuracy, but the masters of its use are now undoubtedly the Mauser-Werke. The company has even introduced its own variations to the action, one of them being the relocation of the bolt handle from the rear of the bolt to the front.

On most rifles this would be of little account, but on a specialist sniper rifle it means that the firer can operate the bolt action without having to move his head out of the way as the bolt itself can be made relatively short; it also means the barrel can be made correspon-

This version of the SP 66, known as the Model 86 SR, is equipped with a set of target sights and a bipod for super-accurate competition shooting; the service version is basically the same weapon fitted with a telescopic sight but without the bipod.

dingly longer for enhanced accuracy. This has been done on a custom-built Mauser-Werke sniper's rifle known as the **Mauser SP 66**. The revised bolt action is but one instance of the care lavished on this weapon, for it also has a heavy barrel, a butt with a carefully contoured thumb aperture, provision for adjustable cheek and butt pads, and a special muzzle attachment. This last is so designed that on firing the great bulk of the resultant flash is

directed out of the firer's vision, and it also acts as a muzzle brake to reduce recoil. Reducing both these factors enables a user to fire second and subsequent shots more rapidly.

The standard of finish and careful design throughout the production of the SP 66 is very high. Even such details as roughening all surfaces likely to be handled to prevent slipping have been carried out with meticulous care, and the trigger is extra wide to allow it

to be used when gloves have to be worn.

The sights have been selected with equal attention. There are no fixed sights and the standard telescopic sight is a Zeiss-Divari ZA with zoom capability of from ×1.5 to ×6. Night sights can be fitted, though it is recommended that the manufacturer selects and calibrates them to an exact match for the rifle on which they are used. As is usual with such rifles the ammunition

fired from the SP 66 is taken from carefully-selected batches of 7.62-mm (0.3-in) NATO rounds produced specifically for use by snipers.

The SP 66 has been a considerable success even though it is manufactured virtually to order only. It is in service with the West German armed forces and more have been sold to a further 12 or so nations, most of which are unwilling to divulge their names for security reasons.

Specification
SP 66
Calibre: 7.62 mm (0.3 in)
Lengths: overall not divulged; barrel 680 mm (26.77 in)
Weight: not divulged
Muzzle velocity: about 860 m (2,821 ft) per second
Magazine capacity: 3 rounds

This Mauser SP 86 is fitted with a night vision device. It is recommended that the manufacturer selects and calibrates the sights of each individual weapon.

Long-range accuracy depends on good ammunition, and Mauser select theirs from batches of NATO 7.62-mm cartridges. This Mauser is fitted with a laser rangefinder.

A close-up of the double-row, detachable nine-round magazine of the Mauser SP 86, one of the improvements incorporated into this development of the SP 66.

Walther WA2000

With the **Walther WA2000** it would appear that small-arms design is already in the 'Star Wars' era, for this weapon has an appearance all of its own. The rifle was designed from the outset for the sniping role and the Walther approach has been to put aside all known small-arms design precepts and start from scratch after analysing the requirements.

The most important part of any rifle design is the barrel, for it alone imparts the required degree of accuracy. Walther decided to clamp the barrel at the front and rear to ensure that the torque imparted by a bullet passing through the bore would not lift the barrel away from the intended point of aim. The barrel is also fluted longitudinally over its entire length. This not only provides more cooling area but also reduces the vibrations imparted on firing, vibrations that can also cause a bullet to stray. The designers also decided to go for a gas-operated mechanism to reduce the need for bolt manipulation between shots, and to reduce recoil effects to a minimum the barrel is in direct line with the shoulder so that the muzzle will not be thrown upwards after every shot.

Thus the strange outline of the WA2000 begins to make sense, but there is more to come for the WA2000 is a 'bullpup' design with the gas-operated bolt mechanism behind the trigger group. Such an arrangement makes the overall design that much shorter and easier to handle without reducing the barrel length. It does mean that the ejection port is close to the firer, so special left- and right-hand versions have to be produced.

The overall standard of finish of the WA2000 is all that one would expect. The butt pad and cheek rests are adjustable, and there is a carefully-shaped pistol grip for added aiming stability. The normal telescopic sight is a Schmidt und Bender ×2.5 to ×10 zoom, but other types can be fitted.

Walther has decided that the best round for the sniping role is now the .300 (7.62-mm) Winchester Magnum cartridge, but while the WA2000 is chambered for this round others such as the 7.62-mm (0.3-in) NATO or much-favoured 7.5-mm (0.295-in) Swiss cartridge can be accommodated with the required alterations to the bolt and rifling.

Specification
WA2000
Calibre: see text
Lengths: overall 905 mm (35.63 in); barrel 650 mm (25.59 in)
Weights: empty, no sights 6.95 kg (15.32 lb); loaded, with sight, 8.31 kg (18.32 lb)
Magazine capacity: 6 rounds

Supplied with a Schmidt & Bender telescopic sight, the remarkable Walther WA2000 fires the 0.30-in Winchester magnum cartridge.

SVD

Anyone who reads accounts of the Great Patriotic War (World War II to the rest of the world) cannot but help note the emphasis given to sniping by the Soviet army. That emphasis remains undiminished, and to carry out the sniping role the Soviets have developed what is widely regarded as one of the best sniper's rifles around today; this is the **SVD**, sometimes known as the **Dragunov**.

The SVD (Samozariyadnyia Vintokvka Dragunova) first appeared in 1963, and ever since has been one of the most prized of infantry trophies. It is a semi-automatic weapon that uses the same operating principles as the AK-47 assault rifle but allied to a revised gas-operated system. Unlike the AK-47, which uses the short 7.62-mm (0.3-in)×39 cartridge, the SVD fires the older 7.62-mm×54R rimmed cartridge originally introduced during the 1890s for the Mosin-Nagant rifles. This remains a good round for the sniping role, and as it is still used on some Soviet machine-guns availability is no problem.

The SVD has a long barrel, but the weapon is so balanced that it handles well and recoil is not excessive. If the long barrel is not a decisive recognition point then the cut-away butt certainly is. The weapon is normally fired using a sling rather than the bipod favoured elsewhere, and to assist aiming a PSO-1 telescopic sight is provided. This is secured to the left-hand side of the receiver and has a magnification of ×4. The PSO-1 has an unusual feature in that it incorporates an infra-red detector element to enable it to be used as a passive night sight, although it is normally used in conjunction with an independent infra-red target-illumination source. Basic combat sights are fitted for use if the optical sight becomes defective.

Perhaps the oddest feature for a sniper rifle is that the SVD is provided with a bayonet, the rationale for this remaining uncertain. A 10-round box magazine is fitted.

Tests have demonstrated that the SVD can fire accurately to ranges of well over 800 m (875 yards). It is a pleasant weapon to handle and fire, despite the lengthy barrel. SVDs have been provided to many Warsaw Pact and other nations and it has been used in Afghanistan, some ending in the hands of the guerrillas, who are certainly no newcomers to sniping. The Chinese produce a direct copy of the SVD and offer this version for export, quoting an effective range of 1000 m (1,094 yards).

Specification
SVD
Calibre: 7.62 mm (0.3 in)
Lengths: overall less bayonet 1225 mm (48.23 in); barrel 547 mm (21.53 in)
Weight: complete, unloaded 4.385 kg (9.667 lb)
Muzzle velocity: 830 m (2,723 ft) per second
Magazine capacity: 10 rounds

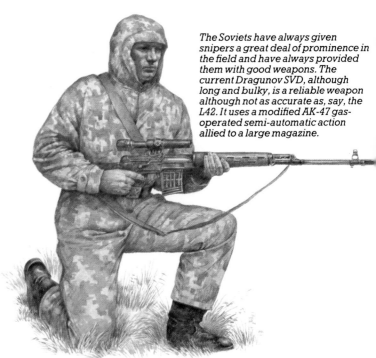

The Soviets have always given snipers a great deal of prominence in the field and have always provided them with good weapons. The current Dragunov SVD, although long and bulky, is a reliable weapon although not as accurate as, say, the L42. It uses a modified AK-47 gas-operated semi-automatic action allied to a large magazine.

Right: The Dragunov uses a bolt system similar to that of the AK-47 and its derivatives, but it is modified to suit the different characteristics of the rimmed 7.62 mm ×54 cartridge originally produced in 1908 for the Moisin-Nagant rifle.

The Dragunov has an excellent sight which displays a graduated range-finding scale, based on the height of the average man. By fitting the target into the grid, the firer gets an accurate idea of the range and aims accordingly. Simple, but effective.

China produces a direct copy of the SVD and is now offering it for export with various extras including this bayonet/wire-cutter.

Galil Sniping Rifle

Ever since Israel was formed in 1948 the role of the sniper within the Israeli armed forces has been an important one, but over the years snipers have usually been equipped with an array of weapons from all around the world. At one point attempts were made to produce sniper rifles locally, so for a period Israeli army snipers used an indigenous 7.62-mm (0.3-in) design known as the **M26**. This was virtually a hand-made weapon using design features from both the Soviet AKM and Belgian FAL rifles. But for various reasons the M26 was deemed not fully satisfactory, so work began on a sniping rifle based on the Israel Military Industries 7.62-mm Galil assault rifle, the standard Israeli service rifle.

The resultant **Galil Sniping Rifle** bears a resemblance to the original but it is virtually a new weapon. Almost every component has been redesigned and manufactured to very close tolerances. A new heavy barrel is fitted, as is an adjustable bipod. The solid butt (which can be folded forward to reduce carrying and stowage bulk) has an adjustable butt pad and cheek rest, while a Nimrod ×6 telescopic sight is mounted on a bracket offset to the left of the receiver. The mechanism is now single-shot only, the original Galil 20-round magazine being retained. The barrel is fitted with a muzzle brake/compensator to reduce recoil and barrel jump on firing. A silencer can be fitted to the muzzle, but subsonic ammunition must then be used. As would be expected, various night sights can be fitted.

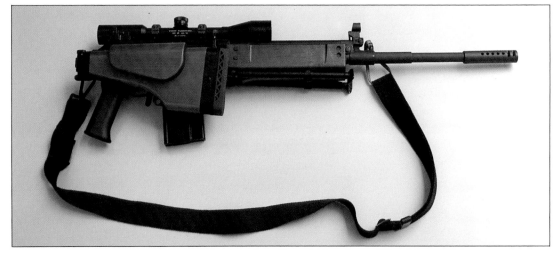

The Galil Sniping Rifle is now in production and has been offered for export. It is a very serviceable weapon that is far more suitable for the rigours of military life than many of the current crop of super-accuracy models. Despite its basic design approach it can still place groupings of less than 300 mm (11.8 in) at a range of 600 m (656 yards), which is more than adequate for most sniping purposes. Careful selection of the ammunition and use of the bipod ensures even better performances.

The Galil Sniping Rifle retains its 'iron' combat sights. When not in use the rifle is kept in a special case together with the telescopic sight, optical filters to reduce sun glare when using optical sights, a carrying and firing sling, two magazines and the all-important cleaning kit.

Specification
Galil Sniping Rifle
Calibre: 7.62 mm (0.3 in)
Lengths: overall 1115 mm (43.9 in); barrel 508 mm (20 in)
Weights: rifle only 6.4 kg (14.1 lb); complete 8.02 kg (17.68 lb)
Muzzle velocity: 815 m (2,674 ft) per second
Magazine capacity: 20 rounds

The design of the Galil sniper rifle was shaped by the IDF's extensive battlefield experience, and it is perhaps not surprising that the gun is built more for reliability in combat than exceptional accuracy in ideal conditions.

The semi-automatic Galil is a gas-operated weapon with a rotating bolt and a 20-round magazine. It fires standard NATO 7.62 mm ×51 and is built to hit the head at 300 m, half-body at 600 m and full figure at 800-900 m.

FN Model 30-11

Fabrique Nationale (FN) has for long kept an astute eye on the arms market from its Herstal headquarters, so when it noted an increased demand over recent years for highly accurate rifles for use against point targets the company came up with the **FN Model 30-11**. At first sight the Model 30-11 appears to be a highly conventional design. And so it is, though in order to make the weapon as accurate as possible it has been designed and manufactured with great care to obtain the best possible results.

The Model 30-11 fires carefully selected 7.62-mm (0.3-in) NATO

ammunition. The manual bolt action is the frequently used Mauser forward-locking action but manufactured using a very high standard of craftsmanship. The same can be said of the heavy barrel which is connected to the receiver with great care. A five-round

The Belgian FN Model 30-11 rifle was originally produced for police and para-military use, but many are in military hands. The example seen here is fitted with target sights. The odd butt shape is due to the degree of individual adjustment that can be incorporated.

box magazine is used, but normally single rounds only are loaded by hand direct into the chamber. The butt is adjustable in two planes (up and down/ forward and back) to suit the individual user's comfort. Swivels are provided for a shooting sling, and there is provision for mounting a bipod under the forestock; the same bipod is used on the FN MAG machine-gun.

This bipod is recommended for use when the Model 30-11 is employed with any of the larger sighting devices that can be fitted. Unlike many other sniper rifles the Model 30-11 can be used with precision-adjustable match-type 'iron' sights, but there is also a wide range of telescopic sights available. For use at night or in poor visibility conditions image intensifier or thermal imaging sights can be used. The sights selected are normally kept in a special protective carrying case together with the rifle when they are being transported or stored.

The Model 30-11 is used by the Belgian army, although most have been issued to Belgian paramilitary police units. Some sales have been made to other nations, but only in small numbers, for the degree of care lavished

on producing the Model 30-11 means that the weapon is not cheap. This has apparently prevented the usual appearance of high-class target shooting versions for commercial sales and as a result FN Herstal ceased production of the Model 30-11 in 1990.

Specification
Model 30-11
Calibre: 7.62 mm (0.3 in)
Lengths: overall 1117 mm (43.97 in); barrel 502 mm (19.76 in)
Weight: rifle only 4.85 kg (10.69 lb)
Muzzle velocity: 850 m (2,788 ft) per second
Magazine capacity: 5 rounds

The FN Model 30-11 can be fitted with a wide range of accessories. The large sight seen here is a standard NATO infra-red night vision sight, and the bipod fitted is that used on the FN MAG machine-gun. A range of other such items can be used with this weapon, which is supplied with a special carrying case.

USA
Rifle M21

When the US armed forces made the move from the 7.62-mm (0.3-in) NATO cartridge to the smaller 5.56-mm (0.223-in) round during the late 1960s they not surprisingly decided to retain the larger calibre for the sniping role. This was for the simple reason that the smaller round had been designed from the outset to impart its best performance at ranges much shorter than the usual sniping distances. This meant the retention of the then-current sniping rifle, at the time known as the **Rifle 7.62-mm M14 National Match (Accurised)**, but now known as the **Rifle M21**.

The M21 is a special version of the 7.62-mm M14, for many years the standard US service rifle. It retains the basic appearance and mechanism of the original, but some changes were introduced at the manufacturing stage. For a start the barrels were selected so that only those with the closest manufacturing tolerances were used. These barrels were left without their usual chromium plating inside the bore, again to reduce the possibility of manufacturing inaccuracies. A new muzzle supressor was fitted and reamed to the barrel to ensure correct alignment. The trigger mechanism was assembled by hand and adjusted to provide a crisp release action, and a new walnut stock was fitted, this latter being impregnated with an epoxy resin. The gas-operated mechanism was also the subject of attention to ensure smooth operation. The fully-automatic fire mode is retained on the M21 but normally the weapon is fired on semi-automatic (single shot) only.

The main change on assembly was the fitting of a ×3 magnification telescopic sight. As well as the usual aiming cross-hairs, this uses a system of graticules that allows the user to judge accurately the range of a man-sized target and automatically set the angle of elevation. Using this sight the M21 can place 10 rounds within a 152-mm (6-in) circle at 300 m (329 yards).

One piece of equipment that can be

fitted to the M21 is a sound suppressor. This is not a silencer in the usually accepted sense of the word, but a series of baffles that reduces the velocity of the gases produced on firing to below the speed of sound. This produces a muffled report with none of the usual firing signatures, and its use makes the source of the sound (and the firer) difficult to detect.

Specification
M21
Calibre: 7.62 mm (0.3 in)
Lengths: overall 1120 mm (44.09 in); barrel 559 mm (22 in)
Weight: loaded 5.55 kg (12.24 lb)
Muzzle velocity: 853 m (2,798 ft) per second
Magazine capacity: 20 rounds

This M14 is from the collection of the Weapons Museum at the School of Infantry, Warminster. The M21 is a special version of the M14, with all parts manufactured to the closest tolerances and with a muzzle suppressor and × 3 scope fitted.

Although many Israeli snipers use the Galil sniping rifle some still retain the American M21, the accurized version of the M14 rifle. They were observed in use during the early stages of the invasion of Lebanon, and many were used against the PLO in Beirut in August 1982.

Sniping Rifle M40A

The US Marine Corps has always been allowed its own equipment procurement system as it has long been accepted that its particular amphibious role requires equipment to match. Thus when the selection of a new sniping rifle to replace the M1C and M1D weapons based on the M1 Garand rifles came about, this service went its own way.

For the US Marines the sniper has always had a special role, often operating in advance of other supporting units to gain information as well as acting as a long-range killer. So when they contemplated weapons such as the

When the US Marine Corps decided to select their own sniping rifle they ordered numbers of commercial Remington Model 700 rifles, some still with 'iron' sights, as seen here. These became the M40 sniping rifle and many are still in use, despite the introduction of the later M40A1, but they are used only by the Marines.

M14/M21 sniper rifles they decided they wanted something better. They could not find exactly what they wanted on the open market but the design that came closest to their requirements was a commercial rifle known as the **Remington Model 700**. This became the **M40** in 1966.

The M40 has a Mauser-type manual bolt action and a heavy barrel. It is normally fitted with a Redfield telesopic sight with a zoom magnification of from ×3 to ×9. A five-round magazine is fitted, and the M40 is an entirely conventional but high-quality design. In service with the US Marines the M40 proved to be perfectly satisfactory, but experience gained with the basic design showed them that something better could be produced. They accordingly asked the Remington Arms Company to introduce a few modifications. These included the replacement of the barrel by a new stainless steel component, the replacement of the wooden furniture by fibreglass and the introduction of a new sight. This new telescopic sight has been produced entirely to demanding US Marine specifications and employs a fixed ×10 magnification. No iron sights are fitted in addittion to this optical sight.

With all these changes embodied the M40 is now the **M40A1**, and it is produced by Remington only for the US Marines. By all accounts it is one of the most accurate sniping rifles ever

The Marines adopted the Remington 700 in 1966 and have had the weapon modified to meet their requirements. The M40A1 rifle differs from the M40 in having a heavy stainless steel barrel, a fibreglass stock and a powerful telescopic sight.

produced, although exact figures are not available to confirm this assertion. The main reasons for this are the heavy stainless steel barrel and the superb optical sight. The magnification of this sight is much more than usual on such devices, but it produces a bright and clear image for the firer. All the usual windage and other adjustments can be introduced to the sight.

As always with a weapon of this type, the degree of accuracy is dependent on the skill of the user (the US Marines spend a great deal of time training their snipers) and the performance of the ammunition selected, but by all accounts the M40A1 is the rifle 'everyone else wants'.

Specification
M40A1
Calibre: 7.62 mm (0.3 in)
Lengths: overall 1117 mm (43.97 in); barrel 610 mm (24 in)
Weight: 6.57 kg (14.48 lb)
Muzzle velocity: 777 m (2,549 ft) per second
Magazine capacity: 5 rounds

Iver Johnson Model 300 Multi-Caliber Rifle

This weapon has undergone a few changes in name since it first emerged some years back from the drawing boards of the Research Armament Industries concern in Rogers, Arizona. Its full current title is the **Iver Johnson Model 300 Multi-Caliber Long-Range Rifle**, and it is marketed by Napco International Inc.

The Model 300 is another of the attempts to produce the perfect sniping rifle capable of being effective at ranges up to 1500 m (1,640 yards). On the Model 300 everything that can eliminate technical error has been incorporated, these features ranging from a fluted barrel with a counterweight beneath, to reduce vibrations and whip in the free-floating barrel, to an all-adjustable butt with a cheek pad. A ×9 Leupold telescopic sight is the only means of aiming the weapon and a bipod is provided for maximum aiming stability. A manual bolt action is used.

The designers also decided to provide what they regard as the optimum cartridge for long-range sniping. This was developed from an existing Rigby hunting cartridge by Research Arma-

ment Industries and has a calibre of 8.58 mm (0.338 in). Tables supplied to demonstrate the efficiency of this cartridge show that it has a much higher muzzle velocity than most comparable rounds and a considerably higher muzzle energy, giving the bullet a flatter ballistic path over longer ranges. However, the designers also realized that the acceptance of this new cartridge might be an uphill task, so they have also produced barrel and bolt head to enable existing 7.62-mm (0.3-in) NATO cartridges to be used; the calibres can be switched from one to the other as required. This provides the Model 300 with its 'Multi-Caliber' designation.

To date the Model 300 has had a mixed reception. It has attracted much attention by its very appearance but apparently hard orders have been slow in coming. Unconfirmed reports speak of some being used by US Special Forces, but that is all. The US Marines have procured trial numbers of the **Model 500**, a much larger and heavier version of the Model 300 that fires the 12.7-mm (0.5-in) machine-gun cartridge. The ballistic limitations of

this cartridge apparently ensured that the Model 500 was not a great success with the US Marines, and one feature of the Model 500 they did not accept is the fact that on this larger version the bolt has to be removed to load every round. After a few rounds the bolt often jammed and could not be removed without force, i.e. kicking it out.

Specification
Model 300
Calibre: 8.58 mm (0.338 in) or 7.62 mm (0.3 in)

Length: barrel only, both calibres 610 mm (24 in)
Weight: 5.67 kg (12.5 lb)
Muzzle velocity: 8.58-mm 915 m (3,002 ft) per second; 7.62-mm 800 m (2,625 ft) per second
Magazine capacity: 8.58-mm 4 rounds; 7.62-mm 5 rounds

The 'space age' Iver Johnson rifles are intended for super-long range use. The Model 300 (foreground) can fire either a 7.62-mm (0.30-in) or a special 8.58-mm cartridge.

7.92-mm M76

Yugoslavia is not one of the nations that automatically springs to mind when the international arms market is considered, but it is currently one of the nations most involved in the selling of arms to the Third World. Its small-arms industry is not particularly innovative, preferring to adapt or develop existing designs rather than branch out into startling new ventures. Thus when a requirement came to replace all the elderly World War II sniping weapons still in use by the Yugoslav armed forces it was again decided to adapt an existing design, in this case the M70B1 assault rifle, the Yugoslav derivative of the Soviet AKM.

Not surprisingly the resultant weapon, the **M76** semi-automatic sniping rifle, has much in common with the Soviet SVD. The main difference is the choice of cartridge, which on the M76 is a 7.92-mm (0.312-in) type, a left-over from the German World War II standard rifle calibre. Yugoslavia still uses this cartridge for some machine-guns, so its retention for the sniping role is understandable. For marketing purposes the Yugoslavs also offer the M76 chambered for the 7.62-mm (0.3-in) NATO cartridge and the elderly Soviet 7.62-mm (0.3-in) rimmed cartridge.

Having said that, the M76 resembles the original AKM design much more than does the Soviet SVD. The M76 is a semi-automatic weapon with a long barrel but much of the original M70B1/KM outline survives, including the solid wooden butt. The M76 uses a 10-round box magazine, and a telescopic sight with a ×4 magnification is mounted over the receiver. This sight has much in common with the Soviet

PSO-1, including the rubber eyepiece, and is stated to make the M76 effective at ranges of 800 m (875 yards) or more. A variety of night vision devices, usually passive infra-red sights, can be fitted in its place. The normal combat sights of the M70B1 are retained, but the bayonet feature of the SVD is not.

Although the M76 may be regarded as a derivative of a Soviet design there is nothing derivative in its production standards. In common with most other Yugoslav weapons, the M76 is well-made and rugged enough to withstand the hard knocks of service life. From this point of view it is a far more prac-

tical weapon than many of the 'super-accuracy' designs now likely to be encountered. The M76 is already in service with the Yugoslav armed forces, but it is difficult to determine exactly how export sales have fared.

Specification
M76
Calibre: 7.92 mm (0.312 in)
Lengths: overall 1135 mm (44.69 in); barrel 550 mm (21.65 in)
Weight: empty, complete 5.08 kg (11.2 lb)
Muzzle velocity: 720 m (2,362 ft) per second
Magazine capacity: 10 rounds

The Yugoslav M76 sniping rifle can be found chambered for 7.92-mm (0.312-in) and both Soviet and NATO 7.62-mm (0.30-in) ammunition. It is basically a specially produced variant of the Yugoslav M70 assault rifle based on the AKM and fitted with a longer barrel and an optical sight mounting.

The concealing face netting used by this Yugoslav army sniper is standard equipment for most snipers. In use here is an M76 rifle, noticeable by its long barrel, fitted with a standard ×4 magnification telescopic sight.

Combat Pistols

The pistols of today are a considerable improvement on those of World War II, yet none of the advances that have taken place were requested by the military. The military were, though, quick to take advantage of them.

Much of the improvement in pistols over the past 40 or so years has come about mainly because of police pressure. Faced with increasing violence from terrorists, European police forces, who were principally armed with 7.65-mm automatic pistols or 0.38-in revolvers, found themselves outgunned. Existing pistols showed the drawbacks. Principal among them was that two hands were needed to prepare an automatic for firing unless you were prepared to carry it cocked, with a cartridge in the chamber. In the early 1960s the German police drew up a specification calling for an automatic capable of stopping an opponent, but safe to carry and quick to bring into action.

All the subsequent pistol designs have stemmed from this initial demand, as various companies set about either answering the German request or, later on, developing weapons to compete against those who had answered. The principal mechanical change has been the near-universal adoption of a double-action trigger and hammer mechanism allied to a de-cocking lever and an automatic firing pin safety system. This has produced a weapon which can be loaded

The Heckler & Koch .45 Special Operations Command (SOCOM) pistol was developed for the US Army's Special Forces.

and cocked and the hammer then lowered safely on to the loaded chamber; the pistol can still be fired simply by pulling the trigger. Moreover, only deliberate operation of the trigger will cause the pistol to fire: it is impossible for it to go off from impact with the ground.

This description covers the majority of pistols shown here:

the Heckler & Koch P7 design led the way, although it uses an entirely unique system of cocking the firing pin, while the Beretta and SIG designs show hammer-fired systems at their best. The Heckler & Koch VP70 was a good idea which failed to catch on, while the Makarov is simply the 1929 Walther PP firing a different cartridge.

Revolvers in military use are now generally confined to military police, guards, aircraft crews and others who need a lightweight weapon which is simple to use but unlikely to be fired. Large-calibre revolvers and larger pistols such as the Desert Eagle will doubtless appear in the hands of individuals, but they are rarely authorized weapons.

French automatic pistols

The most important of the post-war French automatic pistols has been the **mle 1950 MAS** which was manufactured at both St Etienne and Chatellerault. It is no longer in production, but is still a standard pistol of the French armed forces and it has also been sold to many ex-French colonial forces.

The MAS uses a standard swinging-link locking mechanism and a virtually standard trigger system with all the usual safeties. The trigger mechanism uses an external hammer and the hammer can be lowered without firing if the safety catch is set to 'Safe'. When the pistol is in the firing condition a red dot appears next to the safety catch. Nine rounds can be loaded into the box magazine. All in all the MAS is a fairly straightforward pistol with few frills or items of particular note.

Another post-war French automatic pistol is the **Model D MAB**. Unlike the MAS, which fires the 9-mm (0.354-in) Parabellum cartridge, the Model D MAB fires either the 7.65-mm (0.301-in) or 9-mm Short (also known as 0.380-in Auto). These less powerful rounds are used as the Model D MAB was originally designed for police use where more powerful ammunition such as the 9-mm Parabellum is not normally needed. Some military sales of the Model D MAB have been made, however, as it is a handy little pistol with good accuracy. It has no external

hammer, and this allows the weapon to be carried in a pocket without any danger of the hammer catching in clothing. Despite its small size the Model D MAB still uses a nine-round box magazine, and a feature of this pistol is that it can be converted from 7.65-mm to 9-mm Short simply by changing the barrel, no other alterations being necessary. The cartridge fired by the Model D MAB is the 7.65-mm Longue, which is used only by the French.

The Model D MAB is still in production.

Specification
MAS
Calibre: 9 mm (0.354 in)
Weights: empty 0.86 kg (1.896 lb); loaded 1.04 kg (2.3 lb)
Lengths: overall 195 mm (7.677 in); barrel 112 mm (4.4 in)
Muzzle velocity: 354 m (1,161 ft) per second
Magazine capacity: 9 rounds

Model D MAB
Calibre: 7.65 mm (0.301 in)
Weights: empty 0.725 kg (1.6 lb); loaded 0.825 kg (1.82 lb)
Lengths: overall 176 mm (6.93 in); barrel 103 mm (4.05 in)
Muzzle velocity: 365 m (1,197 ft) per second
Magazine capacity: 9 rounds

The post-war 9-mm Model 1950 MAS self-loading pistol (made by Chatellerault as the MAC) used the basic M1911 Colt mechanism with modifications to its safety mechanism. It remains in French service.

The 9-mm PA15 MAB is the current service pistol of the French army, in production at Manufacture d'Armes Automatiques in Bayonne. The bulky grip of this delayed blowback design holds up to 15 Parabellum rounds.

SIG-Sauer P220

For very many years the Schweizerische Industrie-Gesellscahft (SIG) has been producing excellent weapons at its Neuhausen Rhinefalls factory, but has always been restricted by the strict Swiss laws governing military exports from making any significant overseas sales. By joining up with the West German J P Sauer und Sohn concern, SIG was able to transfer production to West Germany and gain access to more markets, and thus SIG-Sauer was formed.

One of the first military pistols developed by the new firm was the **SIG-Sauer P220**, a mechanically-locked single- or double-action automatic pistol. When dealing with the P220 it is difficult to avoid superlatives, for this is a truly magnificent pistol in many ways. Its standards of manufacture and finish are superb, despite the extensive use of metal stampings and an aluminium frame to keep down weight and cost. The pistol handles very well, being one of those weapons that immediately feels right as soon as it is picked up. It is accurate, and the overall design is such that it is difficult for dirt or dust to find its way into the interior and cause stoppages. Despite this the pistol is easy to strip and maintain, and has all the usual pistol safeties.

One design feature of the P220 is that it can be supplied in any one of four calibres. These are the usual 9-mm (0.354-in) Parabellum, 7.65-mm (0.301-in) Parabellum, 0.45-in ACP (11.27-mm, ACP standing for Automatic Colt Pistol) and 0.38-in Super (9-mm not to be confused with 9-mm Parabellum). It is possible to convert any pistol from one calibre to another and kits can be provided to convert any pistol to fire 0.22-in Long Rifle (5.59-mm) for training purposes. Using 9-mm Parabellum the magazine holds nine rounds, but when firing 0.45-in ACP only seven rounds can be accommodated.

The excellence of the P220 has rewarded SIG-Sauer with a stream of orders. To date well over 100,000 have been produced, one of the largest orders coming from the Swiss government who ordered a batch of 35,000 weapons. The P220 is now in service with the Swiss army, which knows it as the 9-mm **Pistole 75**, a designation which sometimes provides the P220 with the name **Model 75**.

There is a later version of the P220 known as the **P225** which is slightly smaller and chambered only for the 9-mm Parabellum cartridge. This version has been selected for Swiss and West German police use as the **P6**.

Specification
Pistole 75
Calibre: 9 mm (0.354 in)
Weight: empty 0.83 kg (1.83 lb)
Lengths: overall 198 mm (7.8 in); barrel 112 mm (4.4 in)
Muzzle velocity: 345 m (1,132 ft) per second
Magazine capacity: 9 rounds

The magnificent SIG-Sauer P220 resulted from a collaborative venture between the Swiss SIG company and JP Sauer und Sohn to produce a pistol for export, unfettered by Swiss government restrictions. It is available in 0.45 ACP, 9-mm Parabellum, 7.65-mm Parabellum and even .22 LR.

IMI Desert Eagle

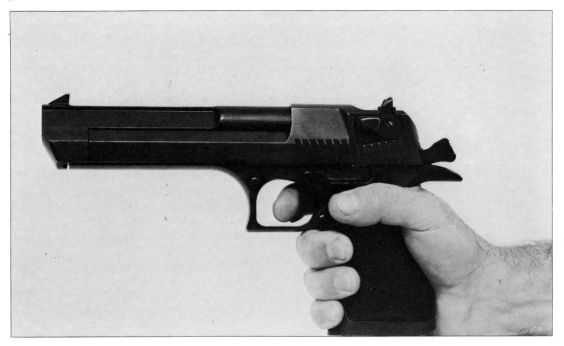

The automatic pistol produced by Israel Military Industries and known as the **IMI Desert Eagle** was originally an American design proposed by M.R.I. Limited of Minneapolis, Minnesota. The basic concept has been developed in Israel to the point where the Desert Eagle is an extremely advanced and powerful weapon.

The Desert Eagle can be converted to fire either the 0.357-in Magnum (9-mm) cartridge or the even more powerful 0.44-in Magnum (10.92-mm) round; the latter cartridge is one of the most powerful pistol rounds available. All that is required to convert the pistol from one calibre to the other is the replacement of a few parts. To ensure complete safety when using these large rounds the Desert Eagle uses a rotating bolt for a maximum locking action. The safety catch can be engaged by either the right or left hand, and when in position on 'Safe' the hammer is disconnected from the trigger and the firing pin is immobilized.

The pistol uses a 152-mm (6-in) barrel as standard, but this basic barrel is interchangeable with barrels 203 mm (8 in), 254 mm (10 in), and 356 mm (14 in) long. The extended barrels are intended for long-range target shooting and may be used with a telescopic sight fitted to a mounting on top of the receiver. No special tools are required to change the barrels.

Several other options are available for the Desert Eagle. The trigger can be made adjustable and several different types of fixed sight can be fitted. The trigger guard is shaped to be used with a two-handed grip, although special grips can be fitted if required. The normal construction is of high quality steels, but an aluminium frame can be supplied.

To date the Desert Eagle has been marketed with the civilian target shooter or enthusiast in mind, but it could also make a very powerful military or police weapon. However, most military authorities usually frown upon the use of Magnum cartridges as they are really too powerful for general military or police use and require a great deal of careful training for their best capabilities to be realised. Thus pistols such as the Desert Eagle seem destined to remain in the hands of special police units and enthusiast who simply want the best and most powerful hand-guns available.

Specification
Desert Eagle
Calibre: 0.357 in or 0.44 in Magnum
Weight: empty 1.701 kg (3.75 lb)
Lengths: overall with 6-in barrel

IMI have entered the pistol field with the 'Desert Eagle', an automatic chambered for the ever-popular 0.357 Magnum cartridge. Military interest remains speculative.

260 mm (10.25 in); barrel 152.4 m (6 in)
Muzzle velocity: 0.357 Magnum 436 m (1,430 ft) per second; 0.44 Magnum 448 m (1,470 ft) per second
Magazine capacity: 0.357 Magnum 9 rounds; 0.44 Magnum 7 rounds

Beretta Model 1951

Pietro Beretta SpA has been making high-quality automatic pistols at Brescia for decades, and as over the years it has made its mark on pistol development in a number of ways it came as something of a surprise when in 1951 Beretta developed a pistol that did away with the company's former use of a simple blowback mechanism in favour of a locked breech. In this system the breech and barrel are locked together for an instant after firing until they are unlocked by contact with the frame after a short recoil movement.

This pistol became known as the **Beretta Model 1951**, and it was also known at one time as the **Model 951** or **'Brigadier'**. It retained the usual Beretta trademark of an open-topped slide, but early hopes that this slide could be made from aluminium did not materialize and most production models use an all-steel unit. The first examples of the Model 1951 did not appear until 1957 as a result mainly of attempts to develop a satisfactory light slide. In more recent years the aluminium slide has become available as an option.

As always on Beretta weapons, the standard of finish of the Model 1951 was excellent and the pistol proved to be rugged and reliable. It was not long before overseas sales were made, and the Model 1951 became the standard service pistol of Israel and Egypt. In fact a production line was established in Egypt to manufacture the Model 1951: that was during the 1960s, and the Model 1951 is known in Egypt as the Helwan. The Model 1951 is also used in Nigeria and some other countries. The Italian armed forces also use large numbers of this pistol.

The Model 1951 continues to use the basic Beretta layout, despite the adoption of the locked breech system. The recoil rod and spring are still located under the largely open barrel, and the well-sloped butt holds the box magazine containing eight rounds. A very hard type of black nylon-based plastic is used for the butt grips. There is an external hammer and the safety catch engages the sear when in use. Both rear and fore sights are adjustable on most versions of the Model 1951.

Specification
Model 1951
Calibre: 9 mm (0.354 in)
Weight: empty 0.87 kg (1.918 lb)
Lengths: overall 203.2 mm (8 in); barrel 114.2 mm (4.45 in)

The Beretta Model 1951 is the standard pistol of the Italian armed forces and has been exported to a number of countries, including Israel and Egypt. This is an example manufactured in Egypt, where the locally produced model is called the Helwan.

Muzzle velocity: 350 m (1,148 ft) per second
Magazine capacity: 8 rounds

Beretta 9-mm Model 92 series

During 1976 Beretta placed in production two new families of automatic pistols, the Model 81 which used a blowback operating system and was chambered for calibres such as 7.65 mm (0.301 in), and the much larger **Beretta Model 92** which fires the usual 9-mm (0.354-in) Parabellum cartridge and accordingly uses a short recoil system very like that used on the earlier Model 1951. Since its introduction the Model 92 series has grown into a considerable range of weapons and it also seems certain to be one of Beretta's most successful designs for one of its variants, the **Model 92F**, has been selected as the US armed force's new standard automatic pistol.

Starting from the basic Model 92, the **Model 92 S** has a revised safety catch

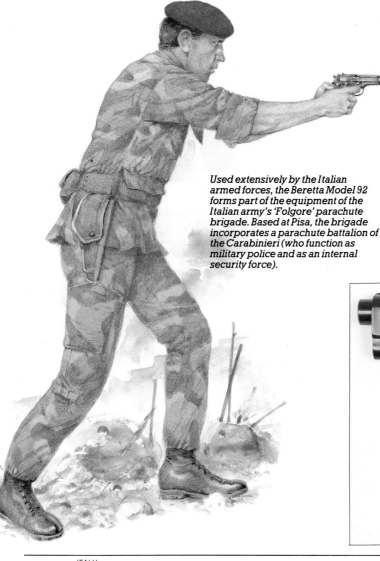

Used extensively by the Italian armed forces, the Beretta Model 92 forms part of the equipment of the Italian army's 'Folgore' parachute brigade. Based at Pisa, the brigade incorporates a parachute battalion of the Carabinieri (who function as military police and as an internal security force).

on the slide rather than below it as on the basic Model 92. This allows the hammer to be lowered onto a loaded chamber with complete safety as the firing pin is taken out of line with the hammer. The **Model 92 SB** is essentially similar to the Model 92 S, but the slide-mounted safety catch can be applied from each side of the slide. The **Model 92 SB-C** is a more compact and handier version of the Model 92 SB.

The Model 92F was a development of the Model 92 SB for the US Army pistol contest, which it won. The main changes from the Model 92 SB are a revised trigger guard outline to suit a two-handed grip (much favoured by the military), an extended magazine base, revised grips and a lanyard ring. The bore is chrome-plated and the exterior is coated in a Teflon-type material to resist wear and act as a non-glare surface.

Following on from the Model 92F there is a **Model 92F Compact** along the same lines as the Model 92 SB-C but using the features of the Model 92F, and also produced along the same lines is the **Model 92 SB-C Type M** which has an eight-round magazine instead of the 15-round magazine used on all the models mentioned above. To cap all these variants there are also two more models based on the Model 92 series but in a smaller calibre. They are the **Model 98** and **Model 99**, both in

7.65-mm calibre and based on the Model 92 SB-C and Model 92 SB-C Type M respectively.

This array of Model 92 pistols should be enough to satisfy just about every military or police requirement likely to arise. The selection of the Model 92F for the American armed forces has already led to a number of orders from other sources, including one from a police force in the UK, and more such orders can be expected. The original Model 92 is now no longer in production, but the Model 92 S still is and all the other variants are available. Apart from the American order various forms of the Model 92 are in service with the Italian armed forces and some of the 'compact' versions are used by various police forces in Italy and elsewhere.

Specification
Model 92F
Calibre: 9 mm (0.354 in)
Weight: loaded 1.145 kg (2.524 lb)
Lengths: overall 217 mm (8.54 in); barrel 125 mm (4.92 in)
Muzzle velocity: about 390 m (1,280 ft) per second
Magazine capacity: 15 rounds

Introduced in 1976, the Model 92 has proved a logical successor to the Modello 1951. This has a frame-mounted safety catch (later models have the catch on the slide).

Beretta 9-mm Model 93R

With the **Beretta Model 93R** one is back in that no-man's land between true machine pistols and selective-fire pistols, for the Model 93R is another modern pistol design intended to fire three-round bursts. Derived from the Beretta Model 92, the Model 93R can be handled and fired as a normal automatic pistol, but when the three-round burst mode is selected the firer has to use both hands to hold the pistol reasonably steady during the burst. To do this Beretta has designed a simple and compact grip system on which the right hand carries out its normal function of operating the trigger and grasping the butt. For the left hand a small forehand grip is folded down from in front of the elongated trigger guard. The left thumb is inserted into the front of the trigger guard and the rest of the

fingers grasp the forehand grip. For additional assistance in holding the pistol steady during firing the end of the protruding barrel is equipped with a muzzle brake that also acts as a flash hider.

To provide even more firing stability it is possible to fix a metal folding stock to the butt. When not in use this can be carried in a special holster, and when mounted on the pistol can be extended to two lengths to suit the firer.

Two type of box magazine can be used with the Model 93F, one holding 15 rounds and the other holding 20. The usual 9-mm (0.354-in) Parabellum cartridge is used.

The design detail incorporated into the Model 93R is considerable and one item that will no doubt be seen on future designs is the use of the foregrip in

front of the trigger guard. This is so arranged tht the two-handed grip derived from its use is much steadier than the usual two-handed grip with both hands wrapped around what is often a bulky pistol butt. Using this foregrip it is quite possible to provide reasonably accurate burst fire as both hands are 'spaced' to produce a longer holding base and yet are close enough to prevent either hand wavering. It is possible to fire bursts without using the metal extending stock, but for really accurate fire (even with single shots) its use is recommended.

As yet the Model 93R is not on the open market and is still under development. One problem seems to be that the three-round burst mechanism is rather complicated and at present requires the services of a trained tech-

nician to carry out maintenance and repairs. Once this difficulty has been ironed out the Model 93R will no doubt attract a great deal of attention from many sources. It would certainly make a formidable close-quarter self-defence weapon.

Specification
Model 93R
Calibre: 9 mm (0.354 in)
Weights: loaded with 15-round magazine 1.12 kg (2.47 lb); loaded with 20-round magazine 1.17 kg (2.58 lb)
Lengths: pistol 240 mm (9.45 in); barrel 156 mm (6.14 in)
Muzzle velocity: 375 m (1,230 ft) per second
Magazine capacity: 15 or 29 rounds

Smith and Wesson revolvers

Smith and Wesson has been making revolvers for well over 100 years, and during that time it has produced just about every type of revolver it is possible to make. Among the company's prolific output have been many military revolvers, but today Smith and Wesson do not make any revolver specifically for military use. This does not prevent many armed forces from using Smith and Wesson revolvers for many roles, but from the outset it has to be said that it is unlikely that any armed forces are likely to use Smith and Wesson revolvers in a front-line capacity. Instead they are to be found with military and security police and other such military agencies.

Top of the current list come the Magnums. For reasons explained elsewhere in this study such weapons are usually confined to special purpose units, one of them being very special for it is one of the most powerful revolvers available today. This is the **No. 29** 0.44-in Magnum (10.92-mm) which was first introduced in 1955. The No. 29 is too much of a handful for most users since its recoil is prodigious, so the **No. 57** was introduced in 1964 to use the less potent 0.41-in Magnum (10.41-mm). This has the same overall dimensions as the No. 29, is rather more manageable yet still retains its massive striking power.

But to most observers of the pistol scene Smith and Wesson means 0.38-in (9-mm) revolvers. There are many of these still on the Smith and Wesson marketing lists, a typical example being the **No. 38 Bodyguard**. This small snub-nosed revolver has a shrouded hammer to allow it to be concealed on

the person without too much danger, but a stud over the hidden hammer allows the pistol to be cocked for single-action shooting. The cylinder holds only five rounds, and the No. 38 uses an aluminium body; the otherwise similar No. 49 uses an all-steel body.

Pistols such as the No. 38 and No. 49 are not likely to be used in front-line combat, but they can still be found on the inventories of many armed forces. Pilots carry them (or pistols very similar to them) on missions over enemy territory, and the weapons are often issued to military personnel operating in plain clothes in areas where the local population is hostile to their presence. It seems that there will always be a need for weapons such as the small Smith and Wesson revolvers.

Specification
No. 38 Bodyguard
Calibre: 0.38 in (9 mm)
Weight: 0.411 kg (0.9 lb)
Lengths: overall 165 mm (6.5 in); barrel 51 mm (2 in)
Muzzle velocity: 260 m (853 ft) per second
Chamber capacity: 5 rounds

Smith and Wesson 0.38-in (9-mm) revolvers are in common use with police and military forces worldwide. The typical snub-nosed, double-action weapon (top) is most widely seen, but the more specialized No. 38 Bodyguard has no external hammer and can be brought rapidly into action from a pocket or holster without danger of snagging.

Colt revolvers

To many the very name Colt means revolvers since it was the Colt's Firearms Company that produced the first successful commercial revolvers, including the famous single-action Colts such as the 'Peacemaker', the gun enshrined in the legends of the Old West. Gradually Colt moved away from producing revolvers (to leave the field open to others, as it was to learn to its cost) and concentrated on automatics. But Colt still continued to make some revolver designs apart from its various well-known and attractive commemorative models.

The modern Colt military revolvers are now all double-action designs, and although most models are produced with police use in mind many are still used by various military agencies in the USA and elsewhere. Many are used by military police units who can obtain the special training needed to handle the powerful Magnum rounds now in use. Thus although many present-day Colt revolvers have names such as **Trooper, Lawman, Police Positive** and so on, they may well be used in military hands.

One particular Colt revolver that comes into this category is the **Python**. First introduced in 1955, this weapon has a shrouded barrel with a distinctive appearance and is chambered for one cartridge only, the 0.357-in Magnum (9-mm). The Python is a very powerful weapon, but to absorb some of the effects of the heavy cartridge load it has to be constructed in an equally heavy fashion. It is thus very

heavy (1.16 kg/2.56 lb) but this weight makes the revolver a very steady weapon to aim and fire, and also makes it very strong, so strong in fact that it can withstand the very worst rigours of a long military life. The Python is available in two barrel lengths, 102 mm (4 in) and 152 mm (6 in).

One advantage of the revolver is its capacity to remain in operation after harsh treatment. Powerful weapons such as the Colt Python would be extremely valuable to a Central American guerrilla, with guns, rounds and spares provided in many cases by interested parties in the USA.

Another Colt revolver is the Trooper. Although no longer available, the Trooper first appeared in 1953, again in a variety of barrel lengths and in various calibres, most of them tending to the heavy side, and with many ending up in military use, although mostly in security rather than combat roles. The Trooper has now been replaced by the **Lawman Mark III**, which is produced only in 0.357-in Magnum and with barrels as short as 51 mm (2 in). Again, many of these are in military use all over the world.

Specification
Lawman Mark III
Calibre: 0.357-in Magnum (9-mm)
Weight: 1.022 kg (2.253 lb)
Lengths: overall 235 mm (9.25 in); barrel 2 or 4 in (51 or 102 mm)
Muzzle velocity: about 436 m (1,430 ft) per second
Chamber capacity: 6 rounds

Colt revolvers are available in a number of calibres, with the .357 Magnum round (actually of 9-mm calibre) being used in the powerful Lawman Mk III. The Colt Cobra (bottom) is similar to the Python, but is chambered for the 0.38 Special round instead of the Magnum.

USA
Ruger revolvers

The armaments concern of Sturm, Ruger and Company Inc. of Southport, Connecticut, produced its first pistol, an automatic, in 1949 and thereafter has never looked back. The company owe a great deal of its success to the astute observation that there was still a large market for single-action revolvers in the USA but that Colt, the obvious choice for such a weapon, was no longer interested in making them. Sturm, Ruger and Co. decided to fill the gap and have been making revolvers (among other types of weapon) ever since.

Before simply copying the old Colt designs, William B. Ruger decided to examine the fundamental design aspects of the revolver in all its forms and soon came up with what was a very modern version of a weapon that had been around for nearly a century. New types of steel and other materials (especially springs) were introduced and the manufacture was gradually developed into a modular system where components could be added or subtracted to form any particular model. The point has now been reached where Sturm, Ruger and Co. produces a very wide range of modern revolvers to meet just about any requirement, military or civil.

Ruger revolvers are today produced in various barrel lengths and in varying finishes, including stainless steel. The revolvers are also available in a wide range of calibres from 0.38-in Special (9-mm) up to the Magnums, although the Magnums are not usually selected for ordinary military use. Typical of the service revolvers currently on offer is the **Service-Six** chambered for either the 0.38 Special or 0.357-in Magnum (again 9-mm) cartridges. The Service-Six can be fitted with either a 70-mm (2.75-in) or 102-mm (4-in) barrel, while the generally similar **Security-Six**, intended for police use, can have even longer bar-

rels. The trigger actions of both are single- and double-action. Some Ruger revolvers fire rimless 9-mm Parabellum ammunition, so for loading these rounds special 'half moon' clips, each holding three rounds, have to be used.

One particular Ruger revolver caused quite a stir when it was first introduced in 1955. This was the famous **Ruger Blackhawk** that could fire the very powerful 0.44-in Magnum (10.92-mm) round, making the Blackhawk one of the most powerful revolvers obtainable. This was too much of a handful for most users, so the Blackhawk range has now been extended to include other less potent cartridges and it is still in great demand by many pistol enthusiasts.

Specification
0.38-in Service-Six
Calibre: 0.38-in Special (9 mm)

Above: Ruger's Speed-Six is known to the US Army as the GS-32N. It is made in two versions: one for 0.357 Magnum/0.38 Special and one for 9-mm Parabellum. The 9-mm is rimless so three round half-moon clips are used to ensure ejection.

Weight: 0.935 kg (2.06 lb)
Lengths: overall 235 mm (9.25 in); barrel 102 mm (4 in)
Muzzle velocity: 260 m (853 ft) per second
Chamber capacity: 6 rounds

Most Ruger pistols in US military use are in the hands of military police or security forces. These roles require familiarity with and training in handling powerful handguns so that the capability of Magnum or Special calibre pistols is not wasted.

9-mm FN High-power

The Browning High-Power design was begun by John M.Browning, and completed after his death by Dieudonne Saive, Chief Designer of FN Herstal. In essence it was Browning's Colt M1911 brought up to date, with a large capacity magazine and a modified breech locking system. It appeared in 1935 and has been in continuous production ever since, though various improvements have been made from time to time.

The original model was a single-action automatic with a 13-round magazine, firing the 9-mm Parabellum cartridge. This was adopted by 70 countries as their military pistol and continued in production until the 1970s. It was then slightly improved into the 'Mark 2' and shortly after that a new version with double-action trigger was developed. These, however, ran into quality control problems and were also subject to fierce competition by newer designs of pistol which came on to the market at that time. FN Herstal therefore closed down their production lines, installed new modern computer-controlled machinery, re-designed the pistol to suit the new methods, and started again; the results fully justified their actions.

The current version is the Mark 3, which is simply the 1935 pattern but with strengthened frame and slide, new grips and improved sights. The Mark 3S, for police, also has an automatic firing pin safety system which prevents the firing pin moving except when the trigger is correctly pulled.

An improved version is the BDA-9 which is the High-Power but with a new double-action trigger mechanism and a de-cocking lever. The pistol can be loaded, de-cocked, and the fired by simply pulling the trigger. It also has the automatic firing pin safety system, and the controls can be operated by either hand. A modified version is the BDAO, (for Double Action Only) in which the hammer always follows the slide down after each shot and is always fired by pulling through on the trigger to cock and drop the hammer.

In 1997 FN Herstal SA introduced the FN FiveSeveN, a delayed blow-back pistol firing the 5.7-mm car-

Above: Many of the great J.M. Browning's designs have proven exceptionally long-lived, with the Browning High-power pistol being no exception. This example has an advanced 'red spot' sighting device, and custom non-slip grips.

tridge introduced with the FN P90 personal defence weapon. This has a 20-round magazine, immense penetrative power, and might be considered as the 'New Generation' Browning pistol.

Specification
BDA-9
Calibre: 9-mm Parabellum
Length overall: 200-mm (7.87-in)
Barrel length: 118.5mm (4.66in)
Weight: empty 915 g (2 lb 0 oz)
Magazine capacity 14 rounds
Muzzle velocity: 350 m/sec (1148 ft/sec)

Above: Developed from the High-power to provide a genuine pocket pistol capable of firing full-power rounds, the Browning Compact has a very short butt, although the shortened slide is less obvious.

Left: Latest development from FN is the 7.65-mm or 9-mm short DA 140. Years of experience with the High-power and a collaboration with Beretta of Italy have produced a light, effective pistol.

Above: The 'Grande Puissance' remains in production after 45 years, and is in use in 55 countries. It was the first of the large-capacity pistols, and remains one of the most popular.

Heckler & Koch pistols

Since the early 1950s Heckler & Koch GmbH of Oberndorf-Neckar has been one of the major European small-arms manufacturers, and although best known for its range of rifles and sub-machine guns the firm has also produced a range of advanced automatic pistol designs.

One of the first of these was the **Heckler & Koch HK4** intended as a small pistol firing a variety of light ammunition varying from 9-mm Short (0.380-in), through 7.65-mm (0.301-in) to 6.35-mm (0.25-in) and even 0.22-in Long Rifle (5.59-mm). All that has to be done to change the ammunition fired is the replacement of the barrel, the springs and the magazine. The HK4 is no longer in production.

The much larger **P7 K3** pistol uses 9-mm Parabellum ammunition and is one of the West German 'super safety' pistols with various built-in safety features to meet police requirements. It uses a prominent grip safety to prevent firing if the pistol is dropped accidentally and the same grip safety also acts as a cocking device for complete one-handed operation. Locking is carried out using a gas-operated delayed-blowback method similar to that used on the Steyr GB pistol and the German Volkspistole of World War II. The P7 K3 has been adopted by the West German army and many police forces.

By contrast a third Heckler & Koch pistol, the **P9S**, uses a small version of the roller and block delay locking device used on the Heckler & Koch G3 assault rifle. This system uses the recoil forces to force the bolt-body to the rear but at the same time two rollers are forced into barrel extensions to prevent further movement until the pressure on the bolt body has dropped to a safe level. This safe locking system allows the 9-mm Parabellum cartridge to be fired from a relatively light pistol, and to add to the locking safety there are numerous others including the usual feature that allows the pistol to be carried safely with a round already in the chamber; this safety can be released by operating a small cocking lever. The P9S has been sold to many armed and police forces worldwide. At one time an 11.43-mm (0.45-in) version was produced for the American market, and a special version with a magazine holding 13 rounds, the **P7M13**, can be supplied. The P9S is licence-manufactured in Greece as the **EP9S**.

Specification
HK4
Calibre: 9 mm Short*
Weight: loaded 0.6 kg (1.32 lb)
Lengths: overall 157 mm (6.18 in); barrel 85 mm (3.35 in)
Muzzle velocity: 299 m (981 ft) per second
Magazine capacity: 7 or 8 rounds*
(* also other smaller calibres, all using an 8-round magazine)

P9S
Calibre: 9 mm (0.354 in)
Weight: loaded 1.065 kg (2.348 lb)
Lengths: overall 192 mm (7.56 in); barrel 102 mm (4.015 in)
Muzzle velocity: 351 m (1,152 ft) per second
Magazine capacity: 9 rounds

P7 K3
Calibre: 9 mm (0.354 in)
Weight: loaded 0.95 kg (2.09 lb)
Lengths: overall 171 mm (6.73 in); barrel 105 mm (4.13 in)
Muzzle velocity: 351 m (1,152 ft) per second
Magazine capacity: 8 or 13 rounds

Above: Conceived as a military pistol, the Heckler & Koch P9 is unusual in that it employs a version of the roller and block delayed-locking system (as used in the well-known Heckler & Koch family of rifles).

Below: Of rugged and simple construction, the Heckler & Koch P7 (PSP) self-loading pistol has been adopted as standard by the West German police and army. It has been designed as a police pistol.

An increasingly important element in any nation's armed forces is that of counter-terrorist warfare. Many nations have formed paramilitary units within the police forces; amongst the most effective of such groups is West Germany's GSG-9, ostensibly a branch of the Border Police.

Heckler & Koch 9-mm VP70M

The 9-mm (0.354-in) **Heckler & Koch VP70M** is a rather unusual pistol that at one time might have been placed in the machine pistol category, but for various reasons it cannot be called that for it has only a limited automatic-fire capability. A true machine pistol can fire in fully automatic mode, but the VP70M can fire only three-round bursts and then only when the carrying holster is attached to the butt to form a shoulder stock.

As a conventional pistol the VP70M uses a blowback action allied to an unusual trigger design. It uses a double-action mechanism and requires a pronounced first pressure when pulled back. Further pressure causes the trigger bar to slip off a spring-loaded firing pin to fire the loaded cartridge. There is thus no additional safety catch as it requires a definite pressure to fire the weapon.

Much of the receiver is made from hard plastics and there are only four moving parts, a number that has been kept to a minimum, for when the pistol is firing three-round bursts the cyclic rate of fire is equivalent to 2,200 rounds per minute which sets up considerable internal forces. The three-round bursts can only be fired when the holster/shoulder stock is fitted as the selector for the burst mode is in the holster. The stock engages in grooves on the pistol receiver and butt, and to take full advantage of the burst mode the magazine holds 18 rounds. Single shots can still be selected when the stock is attached.

A special version of the VP70M known as the **VP70Z** was produced. This version did not have the holster/

shoulder stock capability and could not be used to fire bursts. It was produced for civilian sales only.

The VP70M caused quite a stir when it first appeared, and sales were made to several police and armed forces in Asia and Africa. But both the VP70M and VP70Z are now no longer manufactured. The VP70M in particular was viewed with deep suspicion by security forces in several European nations who had visions of these pistols falling

into the wrong hands, but for all that the design features of the VP70M are almost certain to reappear in future pistols.

Specification
VP70M
Calibre: 9 mm (0.354 in)
Weights: empty 0.823 kg (1.814 lb); pistol loaded 1.14 kg (2.5 lb); pistol and stock loaded 1.6 kg (3.53 lb)
Lengths: pistol 204 mm (8.03 in); barrel

Heckler & Koch's VP-70 represents one of the most successful compromises between handling and rate of fire.

116 m (4.57 in); pistol and stock 545 mm (21.45 in)
Muzzle velocity: 360 m (1,181 ft) per second
Magazine capacity: 18 rounds
Rate of fire: 3-round burst (cyclic) 2,200 rpm

Walther P1 and P5

One of the most widely-admired and respected pistol designs that emerged from World War II was the 9-mm (0.354-in) **Walther Pistole 38**, or **P38**. This is still in production to this day at the Carl Walther Waffenfabrik at Ulm, but is now known as the **Walther P1**, though versions produced for civilian sales are still marked as the P38.

The main change in the P1 from the wartime version is that the modern weapon uses a lighter frame rather than the all-steel frame of World War II. Otherwise the only differences are the markings. The P1 remains an excellent combat pistol and it is still used by the West German armed forces and by those of a number of other nations,

including Portugal and Chile.

The **Walther P5** is a much more modern design that was originally produced to meet a West German police specification that called for a double-action trigger mechanism combined with a high standard of safety. The resultant weapon emerged as a very compact and neat design with the required double action but with no less than four inherent safety features. The first is that the firing pin is kept out of line with the hammer unless the trig-

Walther's P5 pistol has been adopted by several European police forces, and has been built to a very high safety specification.

ger is physically pulled. Another is that even if the hammer is released by any other means than the trigger the firing pin will not be struck. The hammer itself has a safety notch to form the third safety feature, and to top it all the pistol will not fire unless the slide is fully closed with the barrel locked to it.

Getting all these safeties into a pistol as small as the P5 has been a major design accomplishment, but the P5 is an easy weapon to use and fire, and as far as the user is concerned there are no extra features to worry about. The P5 is easy to aim and shoot, and its smooth lines ensure that it is unlikely to be caught on clothing when being handled. It continues to use the same

well-tried 9-mm Parabellum ammunition as the P1 and many other pistols. To date some West German regional police forces have adopted the P5 and it has been adopted as the standard police pistol for the Netherlands police force.

Specification
P1
Calibre: 9 mm (0.354 in)
Weight: loaded 0.96 kg (2.11 lb)
Lengths: overall 218 mm (8.58 in);

The Walther P1 is still produced commercially as the P.38. This is the P.38K, or short version of the pistol.

barrel 124 mm (4.88 in)
Muzzle velocity: 350 m (1,148 ft) per second
Magazine capacity: 8 rounds

P5
Calibre: 9 mm (0.354 in)
Weight: loaded 0.885 kg (1,95 lb)
Lengths: overall 180 mm (7.09 in); barrel 90 mm (3.54 in)
Muzzle velocity: 350 m (1,148 ft) per second
Magazine capacity: 8 rounds

Weapons fitted with suppressors are much in demand for clandestine purposes. This version of the P1, known as the P4, was among a batch seized by Customs to forestall an attempt to export them illegally to Libya.

9-mm Makarov

The **Makarov** automatic pistol was developed in the USSR during the late 1950s and was first noticed by various Western intelligence agencies during the early 1960s. In design terms it is an enlarged version of the German Walther PP, a pistol first introduced in 1929 and ever since acknowledged to be one of the best of its type. However, the Makarov uses a different 9-mm (0.354-in) cartridge to any other in use, for it is intermediate in power between the 9-mm Parabellum and the 9-mm Short. This allows the Makarov to use a straightforward blowback operating mechanism without the complications that would be needed with a more powerful cartridge. The Makarov cartridge appears to have been based on a World War II design known as the Ultra which was not accepted for German war-time service, but which attracted some attention in the West for a while. The Ultra has not been produced in the West in any form, but the Soviets took to it and also use the Makarov round in the Stechkin machine pistol.

The Soviets know the Makarov as the **PM (Pistole Makarov)**. As well as being used by the Soviet armed forces

the Makarov is also used by virtually all other Warsaw Pact forces and by a great many of the Eastern bloc police forces as well. It is a sound, rugged and simple weapon that can be relied upon to operate even under severe conditions. Most accounts state that the pistol is rather awkward to handle as the butt is rather thick, but this is presumably no problem for Eastern bloc soldiers, many of whom have to wear heavy gloves during most of the year.

The Makarov has been manufactured outside the USSR. One of the largest producers is China, where it is known as the **Type 59** and from where it is being offered for export in opposition to the Soviets who often hand out Makarovs as part of their military aid packages. The East Germans produce a pistol almost identical to the Makarov known as the **Pistole M**, while the Poles turn out yet another Makarov 'lookalike' known as the **P-64**. The special Makarov ammunition is also manufactured in all three of these countries.

Below: The Makarov is a straightforward blowback pistol apparently derived from the pre-war Walther PP and PPK designs.

Specification
Makarov
Calibre: 9 mm (0.354 in)
Weight: empty 0.663 kg (1.46 lb)
Lengths: overall 160 mm (6.3 in); barrel

91 mm (3.58 in)
Muzzle velocity: 315 m (1,033 ft) per second
Magazine capacity: 8 rounds

An officer of the Soviet Naval Infantry prepares to fire his Makarov 9-mm pistol. The Naval Infantry is small in comparison with most Soviet arms, but for its size is regarded as one of the most effective fighting forces possessed by the Soviet Union.

The World's Modern Fighters

The modern fighter is a marvel of state-of-the-art structural, propulsion and electronic technologies packaged into the smallest possible volume to create a platform offering high performance and agility. At the same time it has the operational flexibility to function successfully in a number of related fighter roles.

Some aircraft are designed for a specific role, others are extremely versatile. Traditionally the fighter is an interceptor: a light and agile combat machine dedicated to the evasion and defeat of any opponent with cannon fire or air-to-air missiles.

New technology has enabled designers to develop single-seater fighters with many of the capabilities of their weightier companions. The General Dynamics (now Lockheed Martin) F-16 Fighting Falcon can outstrip any opponent. Unlike the heavier Panavia Tornado F.Mk 3, it is able to loiter at great distances from its base, then shoot down an intruder 40 km (25 miles) distant even after a low-level pursuit at speed.

Many fighters now in service were conceived as dual-role aircraft. With advanced multi-function avionics, fighters of the kind typified by the McDonnell Douglas (now Boeing) F/A-18 Hornet are equally in their element in combat or delivering ordnance with pinpoint accuracy. Such versatility is difficult to achieve without compromises, but the dividends of success are in terms of cost-effectiveness. This is particularly true of naval aircraft, where numbers are limited by space restrictions. In

The Eurofighter 2000 development aircraft DA5 in flight bearing Luftwaffe serial number 9830. Eurofighter comes in a single-seater version and a two-seater combat capable trainer.

an overland battle, though, it is clearly beneficial to possess a fighter which can repel an attack and turn for the counter-thrust.

Increasingly the fighter is both interceptor and ground-attack/strike aircraft, in equal proportions so far as technology allows. Technology is the main driving force of aircraft and avionics development, as

engineers strive for extra speed, the tighter turning circle and the lighter yet stronger airframe.

The most recent aircraft of this basic type have exploited the agility advantages of relaxed static stability and a computer-directed 'fly-by-wire' control system in combination with the canard configuration, with foreplanes in place of the traditional tailplane.

Examples of this type are the Eurofighter EF2000, the French Dassault Rafale and the Swedish Saab 39 Gripen. Other fighters that have entered service recently are the MiG-29 'Fulcrum', the heavier Su-27 'Flanker' and the Mitsubishi F-2 (a major development of the F-16 Fighting Falcon). Forthcoming is the Lockheed Martin F-22 Raptor.

Panavia Tornado ADV

At the start of the Tornado programme it was expected that air-combat fighting would be a role, but the dominant requirement of the customers was long-range interdiction and other surface-directed roles (though with Radpac software and changed weapons fighter capability is considerable). The RAF alone raised a requirement for a long-range all-weather interceptor to patrol the vast airspace for which the UK is responsible (from Iceland to the Baltic), replacing the Lightning and later the Phantom, and 165 are being bought for RAF Strike Command. First flown on 27 October 1979 the **Panavia Tornado ADV** (Air-Defence Version), designated **Tornado F.Mk 2** by the RAF, has proved to have performance beyond prediction. The new Marconi/Ferranti Foxhunter radar can pick individual targets at over 185 km (115 miles) and track several targets simultaneously, and the longer radome gives enhanced transonic acceleration. The fuselage was lengthened to accommodate tandem pairs of recessed missiles (the BAe Sky Flash, with a range of more than 40 km/25 miles and the ability to snap down on targets as

Designated Tornado F.Mk 2 in service with the RAF, the ADV had to be made longer than the original IDS version to accommodate the new Foxhunter radar and four Sky Flash missiles.

low as 75 m/245 ft despite ground clutter and electronic countermeasures), and this also increases internal fuel so that in a demonstration an unrefuelled sortie was flown lasting 4 hours 30 minutes, with 2 hours 20 minutes patrol at a radius of 374 miles (602 km) with full armament. Other avionics features of the Tornado F.Mk 2 are ESM (electronic surveillance measures), ECCM (electronic counter-countermeasures) and an ECM-resistant data link. The definitive model is the Tornado F.Mk 3 with improvements such as a more advanced cockpit, longer afterburners and more capable elec-

tronics. The UK bought 170 Tornado ADVs (including 18 interim F.Mk 2s with 24 leased to Italy) for service from 1985, and another 24 were delivered to Saudi Arabia.

Specification
Tornado F.Mk 3
Type: long-range all-weather interceptor
Armament: one 27-mm Mauser gun; four Sky Flash or AIM-120 AMRAAM medium-range AAMs plus four AIM-9L Sidewinder or ASRAAM short-range AAMs

Powerplant: two 7493-kg (16,520-lb) afterburning thrust Turbo-Union RB.199 Mk 104 turbofans
Performance: maximum speed 2338 km/h (1,453 mph) or Mach 2.2 at 10,975 m (36,000 ft); service ceiling about 21,335 m (70,000 ft); patrol radius 740 km (460 miles) for a 2 hour CAP
Weights: empty 14,502 kg (31,970 lb); maximum take-off 27,986 kg (61,700 lb)
Dimensions: span (swept) 8.60 m (28 ft 2½ in); length 18.68 m (61 ft 3½ in); height 5.95 m (19 ft 6¼ in); wing area 26.60 m² (286.33 sq ft)

Saab JA37 Viggen

When Sweden planned its next-generation combat aircraft, System 37, in the early 1960s the most urgent need was for attack and multi-sensor reconnaissance versions to replace types such as the Saab 32 Lansen, Saab 35 Draken and Saab 105. A total of 180 of these models, the AJ37 attack aircraft, SF37 and SH37 overland and overwater reconnaissance platforms, and SK37 trainer, were delivered by 1981. By this time production was centred on the **Saab JA37 Viggen** interceptor, which uses the same airframe (except for having the extra swept tip to the fin first seen on the SK) but has totally new sensors (including L.M. Ericsson UAP-1023 pulse-Doppler high-performance long-range radar feeding information to a Singer-Kearfott SKC-2037 digital central computer, which in turn keeps the pilot in the picture by means of a Smiths head-up display) and weapons, including the high-velocity Oerlikon KCA 30-mm cannon, whose shell has a very flat trajectory and a kinetic energy after a flight of 1500 m (1,640 yards) equivalent to that of a DEFA or Aden cannon (of the same calibre) at the muzzle. Even the engine has different fan/compressor blading and other changes to increase thrust, and like other versions has a giant afterburner and thrust reverser for pulling the aircraft up quickly. STOL operations, facilitated by the canard configuration, are routinely made from straight stretches of country highway, with no-flare landings on the tandem-wheel main gears, in order to prevent the squadrons being destroyed on their fixed air bases. The Swedish Flygvapen (air force) ordered 149 to equip eight squadrons over the period 1979-85. The JA37 was the first fighter in any part of Europe to enter service with an advanced pulse-Doppler radar, and its

avionics and displays are representative of the very latest practice and are also compatible with the delivery of air-to-surface weapons, giving the type a very useful secondary attack capability.

Specification:
Saab JA37 Viggen
Type: interceptor and multi-role fighter
Armament: one fixed 30-mm Oerlikon cannon with 150 rounds, and provision for stores carried on three underfuselage and four underwing hardpoints; these stores can include up to six RB71 (Sky Flash) medium-range and RB24

(Sidewinder) short-range air-to-air missiles; maximum stores weight is 7000 kg (15,432 lb)
Powerplant: one 12,750-kg (28,108-lb) afterburning thrust Volvo Flygmotor RM8B turbofan
Performance: maximum speed more than 2125 km/h (1,320 mph) or Mach 2 at high altitude; hi-lo-hi combat radius with external stores more than 1000 km (621 miles)
Weight: normal take-off 17000 kg (37,478 lb) with stores.
Dimensions: span 10.60 m (34 ft 9¼ in); length including probe 16.40 m (53 ft 9¾ in); height 5.90 m (19 ft 4¼ in); wing area (including canard foreplanes) 52.20 m² (561.9 sq ft)

The JA37 Viggen in its new air superiority grey scheme, carrying a full complement of BAe Sky flash air-to-air missiles, AIM-9L Sidewinders and ventral fuel tank. The JA37 was the last version of the Viggen to be manufactured, and was by far the most costly of the model.

JA37 Viggen of the Swedish air force. This model has a completely new set of avionics and weapons, and will fulfil Sweden's air defence capability until at least the mid-1990s.

Dassault-Breguet Mirage III/5/50 series

One of the most famous fighters in history, the basic **Dassault Mirage** delta stemmed from Dassault's disbelief in the French official light-fighter concept, and his decision at company expense to build a larger tailless delta Mirage powered by an Atar engine. The Mirage III-001 prototype flew on 17 November 1956 and the first production **Mirage IIIC** fighter for l'Armée de l'Air flew in 1960, to be followed by more than 1,400 basically similar machines for 21 countries. Early models could have a booster rocket engine under the rear in place of gun ammunition and a fuel tank. The large main wheels were sized for rough-field operation, though this is nullified by the very high take-off and landing speeds giving field lengths over 1800 m (6,000 ft) on attack missions. The **Mirage IIIB** and **Mirage IIID** are tandem dual versions, the **Mirage IIIE** series are fighter-bombers with extra weapon-delivery systems (French Mirage IIIEs carry the AN52 nuclear bomb) and **Mirage IIIR** reconnaissance aircraft have a distinctive camera nose replacing the Cyrano II radar. The **Mirage IIIO** is the Australian version of the Mirage IIIE. South African **Mirage III CZ, DZ** and **RZ** Mirages have the 7200-kg (15,873-lb) thrust Atar 9K50 engine which is standard in the **Mirage 50** first flown in 1979 and with upgraded avionics (so far bought by Chile). In contrast the popular **Mirage 5** is a clear-weather day attack aircraft with extra fuel and weapons replacing the radar and other avionics (various radar and laser/HUD options are available). Mirage 5 variants are the **Mirage 5A** single-seater, **Mirage 5D** tandem two seater trainer and **Mirage 5R** reconnaissance aircraft. The final standard, with features intended for retrofit, was the 'fly-by-wire' Mirage IIING with canard foreplanes, uprated Atar 9K engine and advanced avionics.

Mirage IIIE of the the French Armée de l'Air Escadre de Chasse 2/4 'La Fayette'.

Mirage IIIEE of the Egyptian Arab air force.

A Royal Australian Air Force Mirage IIIO of No. 75 Sqn.

Mirage IIICZ of No. 2 Sqn, South African Air Force.

Specification:
Mirage IIIE
Type: fighter-bomber
Armament: two 30-mm cannon each with 125 rounds (no rocket); three external pylons for 454-kg (1,000-lb) bombs or equivalent stores including pods, tanks, AS.30 missiles or, for air-to-air role, an R.530 or Super 530 AAM plus two Sidewinder or Magic AAMs.
Powerplant: one 6200-kg (13,670-lb) afterburning thrust SNECMA Atar 9C turbojet

Two-seat Mirage trainers of the Escadre de Chasse de Transformation 2/2 'Côte d'Or' based at Dijon.

Performance: maximum speed, clean at 12000 m (39,370 ft) 2350 km/h (1,460 mph) Mach 2.2, or clean at sea level 1390 km/h (863 mph); service ceiling 17000 m (55,775 ft); radius on a hi-lo-hi attack mission with one or two tanks 1200 km (745 miles)
Weights: empty 7050 kg (15,540 lb); maximum take-off 13700 kg (30,200 lb)

Dimensions: span 8.22 m (26 ft 11½ in); length 15.03 m (49 ft 3½ in); height 4.5 m (14 ft 9 in); wing area 34.85 m² (374.6 sq ft)

A Mirage of the Argentine air force prior to the Falklands war of 1982. Most were held back for air defence of the Argentine mainland.

Dassault-Breguet Mirage F.1

Not believing in the enduring appeal of the Mirage III, Dassault sought a successor from 1961 and settled on a much larger type powered by the big TF306 augmented turbofan and flown with a delta wing, a high wing and tail (Mirage F.2) and even VTOL lift jets. The Mirage F.2 was a good aircraft but Dassault eventually, in 1965, persuaded l'Armée de l'Air to buy a similar aircraft scaled back to Atar size, and this, the **Dassault Mirage F.1**, first flew in 1966. Though the wing is much smaller than the delta, it is so much more efficient (with double-slotted trailing-edge flaps and a drooping leading edge) that, combined with 40 per cent more internal fuel in a smaller airframe, the Mirage F.1 has a much shorter field length, three times the supersonic endurance, twice the tactical radius at low level and all-round better manoeuvrability. The avionics core of the series is the Thomson-CSF Cyrano IV fire-control radar, which in the Mirage F.1E version has modifications for air-to-surface ranging and to permit low-altitude penetration of enemy air space under any weather conditions. More advanced radar was developed. The **Mirage F.1C** all-weather interceptor reached l'Armée de l'Air squadrons in 1973, and by 1983 total Mirage F.1 orders reached over 700, almost 500 of them for export. Variants include the **Mirage F.1A** simplified attack aircraft, **Mirage F.1B** dual trainer, **Mirage F.1E** comprehensive all-weather attack aircraft and **Mirage F.1R** multi-sensor reconnaissance platform. The **Mirage F.1C-200** is a French variant with an inflight-refuelling probe for overseas deployment. Quick scramble is enhanced by a ground truck which cools the missile seekers, radar and cockpit, heats navigation and weapon-aiming systems and shields the cockpit with a sunshade! Production was shared with other companies as with other Mirages

with SABCA/Sonaca of Belgium, who built the rear fuselage. Armaments Development and Production corporation of South Africa holds a manufacturing licence, and its models are indicated by a Z suffix to the basic designation. French Mirage F.1C interceptors have by 1983 been updated to carry the R.530F radar-homing air-to-air missile.

Specification:
Mirage F.1C
Type: fighter-bomber
Armament: two 30-mm DEFA cannon each with 125 rounds; AAM (Sidewinder/Magic rails at wingtips, plus five Alkan universal pylons for 4000 kg (8,818 lb) of external stores including tanks, bombs, pods, launchers or R.530 or Super 530 AAMs, AS.30 or reconnaissance pod with cameras, EMI SLAR and Cyclope IR system
Powerplant: one 7200-kg (15,873-lb) afterburning thrust SNECMA Atar 9K-50 turbojet
Performance: maximum speed, clean at high altitude 2350 km/h (1,460 mph) or Mach 2.2, or clean at sea level 1450 km/h (900 mph) or Mach 1.2; ser-

Mirage F.1C of the Armée de l'Air's Escadron de Chasse EC 2/5 'Ile de France' based at Orange-Caritat.

vice ceiling 20000 m (65,600 ft) radius on a lo-lo mission with 1600 kg (3,527 lb) of weapons 644 km (400 miles)
Weights: empty 7400 kg (16,314 lb); maximum take-off 15200 kg (33,510 lb)
Dimensions: span 8.40 m (27 ft 6¾ in); length 15.0 m (49 ft 2½ in); height 4.50 m (14 ft 9 in); wing area 25.0 m² (269.1 sq ft)

Libya is just one of the dozen nations that fly the commercially very successful and capable Mirage F.1.

Dassault-Breguet Mirage 2000

After the Mirage F.1 was ordered, Dassault spent much effort on the large variable-sweep Mirage G series. This led to the ACF (Avion de Combat Futur) with a wing fixed at 55°, but in December 1975 this too was cancelled. In its place came another of the small single-Atar machines, and it marked a return to the tailless delta configuration. It was, however, a totally different aircraft, designed to CCV (control-configured vehicle) technology with variable camber wings having hinged leading and trailing edges, electrically signalled controls and artificial stability. Structure was entirely new, as was the engine whose extremely low bypass ratio was designed for Mach 2 at high altitudes, calling for small frontal area, rather than for subsonic fuel economy. Choice of a single-shaft engine also greatly increased weight; the basic engine weighing 1450 kg (3,195 lb).

The very pretty but very expensive Mirage 2000 chalked up an impressive export sales total even prior to the type entering service with the French air force. Egypt, India and Peru were among the early buyers.

The prototype **Dassault-Breguet Mirage 2000** flew on 10 March 1978 and the first production fighter flew in December 1982, with 1983 production including tandem-seat **Mirage 2000B** trainers. The early aircraft were all completed in air-defence configuration with the RDM multi- mode radar that was replaced from the 51st

machine by the considerably more capable RDI air interception radar, which is a pulse-Doppler equipment designed to detect a target of 5 m² (54 sq ft) at a range of 100 km (62 miles). By mid-1998 sales of the Mirage 2000 had reached 639 (36 for Abu Dhabi, 20 for Egypt, 380 for France, 40 for Greece, 49 for India,

12 for Peru, 12 for Qatar, 60 for Taiwan and 30 for the UAE), and the type was developed. Complementing the original **Mirage 2000B/C**, these variants are: the **Mirage 2000D** low-level interdictor with advanced conventional weapons; **Mirage 2000E** multi-role export variant of the **Mirage 2000C**; **Mirage 2000ED**

Though similar to the earlier Mirage III, the Mirage 2000 is a completely new aircraft, equipped with 1980s style, structure and aerodynamics.

export counterpart of the Mirage 2000B; two-seat **Mirage 2000N** low-level interdictor with nuclear weapons; **Mirage 2000R** reconnaissance variant of the Mirage 2000E; **Mirage 2000-5** multi-role export type with RDY multi-function radar and **Mirage 2000-9**, improved version of the Mirage 2000-5.

Specification
Mirage 2000C
Type: fighter
Armament: two 30-mm cannon each with 125 rounds; up to 6300 kg (13,889 lb) of disposable stores on nine hardpoints
Powerplant: one 9700-kg (21,384-lb)

afterburning thrust SNECMA M53-P2 turbofan
Performance: maximum speed 2338 km/h (1,453 mph) or Mach 2.20 at 11,000 m (36,090 ft); service ceiling 16,450 m (53,970 ft); range more than 1850 km (1,150 miles) with two drop tanks

Weights: empty 7500 kg (16,534 lb); maximum take-off 17000 kg (37,478 lb)
Dimensions: span 9.13 m (29 ft 11½ in); length 14.36 m (47 ft 1¼ in); height 5.20 m (17 ft ¾ in); wing area 41 m² (441.33 sq ft)

ISRAEL

IAI Kfir

When the French cut off military supplies to Israel in June 1967, the decision was taken for Israel to become self-sufficient in Mirage-type aircraft. A near-copy with the Atar engine was built as the **IAI Nesher** (available Neshers were bought secondhand by Argentina and named **Dagger**, being very active in the Falklands campaign). Israel Aircraft Industries then tackled the much greater task of building a development with the more powerful and also shorter J79 engine. A J79, similar to those in Israeli Phantoms, was flown in a two-seat Mirage IIIB in September 1971. A prototype **IAI Kfir** (Lion Cub) was flown in 1973 and publicly revealed in April 1975. In July 1976 the definitive **Kfir-C2** was shown, with fixed canard foreplanes on the inlets, small strakes along the redesigned nose and a new dogtooth leading edge to the wing. The object of the exercise (achieved most successfully) was improvement in field performance coupled with a great increase in combat capability (especially at the lower end of the speed range to which dogfights almost invariably descend) by bettering the sustained turn rate; collateral benefits are re-

The orange triangles disrupting the effective desert camouflage of this Kfir is to ensure visual recognition by other Israeli pilots – although the Egyptians have adopted the same device!

duced gust response at low altitude and better handling at high angles of attack. The different engine installation had previously required total redesign of the rear fuselage and a cooling inlet in the dorsal fin. The new forward fuselage is extended to house various avionic items including the Elta 2001B target-acquisition and tracking air-to-air and air-to-ground pulse-Doppler radar, and extremely comprehensive navigation/communication identification, navigation and weapon-delivery systems are installed, as well as a Martin-Baker Mk 10 seat. In early 1981 IAI revealed the tandem-seat **Kfir-TC2** with longer and down-sloping nose; this is a weapon-system trainer and EW (electronic warfare) platform. About 250 were estimated to have been delivered by late 1982,

Ecuador being the first export customer. In 1982 Kfirs saw extensive action over Lebanon. The final conversions, produced as upgrades, are the **Kfir-C7** with improved weapons capability and the **Kfir-C10** with EL/M-2032 radar.

Specification:
Kfir-C2
Type: multi-role fighter and attack aircraft
Armament: two 30-mm IAI-built DEFA 552 cannon each with 140 rounds; up to 4295 kg (9,468 lb) of stores on seven hardpoints including bombs, rockets, Maverick/Hobos/Durandal ASMs, Shrike anti-radar missiles, Shafrir 2 AAMs (or Sidewinders), ECM pods and tanks
Powerplant: one 8119-kg (17,900-lb)

thrust General Electric J79-J1E afterburning turbojet
Performance: maximum speed, clean at high altitude 2440 km/h (1,516 mph); climb to 15250 m (50,000 ft) in 5-17 minutes; service ceiling 17680 m (58,000 ft); radius on hi-lo-hi mission with seven 227-kg (500-lb) bombs, two AAMs and two tanks 768 km (477 miles)
Weights: empty 7285 kg (16,060 lb); maximum take-off 14700 kg (32,408 lb)
Dimensions: span 8.22 m (26 ft 11½ in); length 15.65 m (51 ft 4¼ in); height 4.55 m (14 ft 11¼ in); wing area 34.8m² (374.6 sq ft)

A capable all-rounder, the Kfir is seen here in low-visibility fighter markings, though it is being bombed up for an attack mission.

McDonnell Douglas F-15 Eagle

Like its predecessor in the St Louis factory (the F-4), the **McDonnell Douglas F-15 Eagle** is widely regarded as the best fighter in the world, though it has the disadvantages of great size and high operating cost. It was developed to rival the MiG-25, but unlike the Soviet aircraft it is not a stand-off interceptor but a close-combat dogfighter with a vast wing area and two extremely powerful engines. The four Sparrow AAMs are carried against the square corner edge along the bottom of the large inlet ducts, and the gun is mounted in the right inboard wing, drawing ammunition from a large 940-round drum in the fuselage. Hughes provide the AN/APG-63 pulse-Doppler radar, with computerized data-processing to leave nothing on the pilot's head-up or head-down displays except the vital items of real interest. All-round view is superb, and the F-15 pioneered the HOTAS (hands on throttle and stick) concept to ease the pilot's task in combat. Very heavy attack weapon loads can be carried, and the original **F-15A** and tandem-seat **F-15B** have been followed by the **F-15C** and two seat **F-15D** in which internal fuel is increased, CFT

A newly-delivered F-15 of the Israeli air force (Heyl Ha'Avir).

(Conformal Fuel Tank) pallets fitting against the sides of the fuselage give 4423 kg (9,750 lb) of extra fuel with no additional drag, and avionics are updated. Updates of the US aircraft are in progress, the most important being the APG-63(V)1 radar and a modernised cockpit. By mid-1998 deliveries (now by Boeing after its takeover of McDonnell Douglas) amounted to 894 aircraft including 52 and 74 for Israel and Saudi Arabia respectively but excluding 213 **F-15J** and **F-15DJ** single- and two-seat aircraft being produced by Mitsubishi for the Japanese air force. The most advanced version is the **F-15E** strike fighter with more capable electronics and the ability to carry a heavier weight of drop loads. The USAF

ordered 233 of this model, of which 25 and 72 were also delivered to Israel and Saudi Arabia with the designations **F-15I** Thunder and **F-15S** respectively.

Specification:
F-15C Eagle
Type: fighter with secondary attack role
Armament: one 20-mm M61A-1 cannon; four Sparrow (latter AMRAAM) AAMs plus four Sidewinder (later ASRAAM) AAMs; option of 7258 kg (16,000 lb) attack weapon load on five pylons
Powerplant: two 10855-kg (23,930-lb) thrust Pratt & Whitney F100-100 aug-

mented turbofans
Performance: maximum speed, clean except AAMs at high altitude 2660 km/h (1,650 mph) or Mach 2.5; absolute ceiling 30500 m (100,000 ft); ferry range with maximum fuel 5560 km (3,450 miles)
Weights: empty 14334 kg (31,600 lb); loaded, clean 20185 kg (44,500 lb); maximum take-off 30845 kg (68,000 lb)
Dimensions: span 13.05 m (42 ft 9¾ in); length 19.43 m (63 ft 9 in); height 5.63 m (18 ft 5½ in); wing area 56.5 m² (608.0 sq ft)

An F-15 of the 49th Tactical Fighter Wing displays its potent weapon load: four Sidewinders, four Sparrows and the 20-mm cannon housed in the wing root.

General Dynamics F-16 Fighting Falcon

Initiated as an LWF (Light Weight Fighter) demonstrator in 1972, to see whether or not a fighter smaller and less costly than the F-15 could have any value, the YF-16 flew in February 1974, won over a Northrop rival and was then developed into the larger and immensely more capable **General Dynamics F-16A Fighting Falcon**, which was not only ordered in large numbers (650, later increased to 1,388 against a planned total of 2,333) by the USAF but also by Belgium, Denmark, the Netherlands and Norway to replace the F-104. Other buyers are Israel, South Korea, Egypt, Pakistan and Venezuela. In structure, aerodynamics, avionics and systems the F-16 is outstandingly well engineered, combining CCV (control-configured vehicle) technology and fly-by-wire signalling with an unprecedented thrust/weight ratio using a single F-15 type engine fed by a fixed ventral inlet upstream of the nose gear. The overall

effect is a magnificent air-combat platform with adequate performance but phenomenally good agility, roll, climb and acceleration. Important contributory factors are the unswept wing with automatically variable camber, and the pilot reclining in an Aces II seat under a frameless canopy with his right hand grasping a small stick which senses any applied forces with near-zero movement. All combat controls for the aircraft, weapons, Westinghouse APG-66 radar and Marconi HUD (head-up display) are on the stick or throttle. The APG-66 radar is a highly capable equipment: the look-up range is 74 km (46 miles) while the look-down range, even against ground clutter, is 56 km (35 miles). The set is of the pulse-Doppler type and has range and angle track modes, with information fed to the pilot via a Marconi head-up display and Kaiser radar electro-optical display. Other key avionics are the Delco fire-control computer, ALR-

69 radar warning receiver and Sperry air-data computer. The USAF buy includes 204 **F-16B** combat-capable two-seaters with reduced fuel. The equivalent **F-16C** and **F-16D** single- and two-seaters have progressively updated and augmented avionics including AMRAAM missiles, LANTIRN night/all-weather pods and new cockpit displays. Now a product of Lockheed Martin since its purchase of General Dynamics' fighter division, the **F-16** is the Western world's most successful warplane since World War II, sales by mid-1998 totalling some 3,970 aircraft to 18 customer nations. Numerous upgrades and updates keep the **F-16** abreast of the latest developments.

Specification:
F-16A Fighting Falcon
Type: multi-role fighter
Armament: one 20-mm M61 cannon with 515 rounds; nine hardpoints for

normal maximum load of 7802 kg (17,200 lb), with theoretical limit of 9276 kg (20,450 lb) including all available tactical stores, 'Pave Penny' laser tracker, ECM—EW pods (usually ALQ-131) and special stores including ARMs in 'Wild Weasel' role
Powerplant: one 10814-kg (23,840-lb) afterburning thrust Pratt & Whitney F100-200 turbofan
Performance: maximum speed, clean except AAMs at 12190 m (40,000 ft) 2173 km/h (1,350 mph) or Mach 2.05; service ceiling more than 15240 m (50,000 ft); radius on a hi-lo-hi mission with six Mk 82 bombs and no tanks 547 km (340 miles)
Weights: empty 6866 kg (15,137 lb); maximum take-off 17010 kg (37,500 lb)
Dimensions: span 9.5 m (31 ft 0 in); length 14.52 m (47 ft 7¾ in); height 5.09 m (16 ft 8½ in); wing area 27.87 m² (300.0 sq ft)

Northrop F-5E/F Tiger II

Northrop's F-5 family of lightweight fighters has racked up a remarkable sales total of more than 2,700 aircraft to 30 countries in spite of the fact that it was never adopted (or even marketed) as a major type in its own country! The original **Northrop N-156F Freedom Fighter** flew on 30 July 1959, with two 1850-kg (4,080-lb) thrust J85 engines and armed with two 20-mm cannon and two Sidewinder AAMs. After development, 1,040 were sold of the single-seat **F-5A** and two-seat **F-5B** version (plus a few of the **RF-5A** reconnaissance version), and others were built by Canadair, CASA and Fokker. The **F-5E Tiger II**, flown on 11 August 1972, has uprated engines fed via improved inlets, a wider fuselage housing more fuel, longer wing-root strakes and much better avionics including a small X-band radar. The tandem-seat **F-5F** flew on 25 September 1974. Sales of the F-5E/F have been even brisker than those of the F-5A/B, and 1,400 had been bought by 19 air forces by 1983. These are still rather limited aircraft, without all-weather intercept or attack capability, but they are tough, simple, cheap, beautiful to fly, extremely agile and not only useful as advanced trainers (the F-5E is used by the USAF and US Navy for Aggressors/Top Gun fighter pilot training) but also quite effective in simple wars in visual conditions. There is an **RF-5E Tigereye** with quick-change day/night reconnaissnce equipment and Northrop is offering such extras as a 30-mm underbelly gun pod, inertial navigation and various tactical sensors. The last development of the series, not produced, was the much more advanced **F-20** (originally **F-5G**) **Tigershark**. This switched to a single-engined powerplant (a single afterburning General Electric F404 turbofan rated at 7257-kg (16,000-lb thrust) and offers far more comprehensive avionics. These latter include General Electric AN/APG-67 look-up/look-down multi-mode radar, Teledyne solid-state digital mission computer, AN/ALR-46 radar warning receiver and AN/ALE-40 countermeasures dispenser. More than 3630 kg (8,000 lb) of weapons can be carried, these including four AGM-65 Maverick missiles or three 30-mm cannon pods.

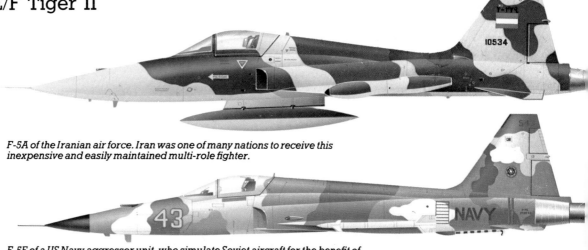

F-5A of the Iranian air force. Iran was one of many nations to receive this inexpensive and easily maintained multi-role fighter.

F-5E of a US Navy aggressor unit, who simulate Soviet aircraft for the benefit of Navy pilot training.

Specification:
F-5E Tiger II
Type: light tactical fighter
Armament: two 20-mm M39A-2 cannon each with 280 rounds; up to 3175 kg (7,000 lb) of external weapons including numerous bombs, rockets, Maverick ASMs, clusters, pods and tanks
Powerplant: two 2268-kg (5,000-lb) thrust General Electric J85-21A afterburning turbojets
Performance: maximum speed, clean at high altitude 1734 km/h (1,077 mph) or Mach 1.63; initial climb rate 10515 m (34,500 ft) per minute; service ceiling 15790 m (51,800 ft); radius on a lo-lo-lo mission with maximum weapons and reserves 222 km (138 miles)
Weights: empty 4392 kg (9,683 lb); maximum take-off 11193 kg (24,676 lb)
Dimensions: span 8.13 m (26 ft 8 in); length 14.68 m (48 ft 2 in); height 4.06 m (13 ft 4 in); wing area 17.3 m² (186.0 sq ft)

Above: Touching down at Dübendorf, this Northrop F-5E is operated by the armed forces of Switzerland. The original order in 1976 called for 66 F-5Es and six F-5Fs.

Below: The F-20 Tigershark is the third major stage of F-5 development. Unlike its predecessors, it has a single engine, with rear fuselage width maintained by lateral 'shelves'.

McDonnell Douglas F-4 Phantom II

Planned as a multi-role attack aircraft, the **McDonnell Douglas F-4 Phantom II** eventually reached the US Navy as a fleet defence fighter with no weapons except AAMs (carried in a novel way, with four large Sparrows recessed under the broad fuselage for minimum drag) and just one pylon for a single drop tank. Soon world records were being set for speed, climb and ceiling, and when bombs were carried it was clear the Phantom was a world-beater. The USAF bought the AN/APG-100 radared **F-4C** minimum-change version of the US Navy's **F-4B** (AN/APG-72 radar), and then the **F-4D** more closely tailored (particularly in avionics, with AN/APG-109A radar) to its own needs which were biased towards ground attack. The RF-4 family emerged as the world's fastest and most fully equipped unarmed tactical reconnaissance aircraft, in the form of the **RF-4B** for the US Marine Corps, **RF-4C** for the US Air Force and **RF-4E** for export. Vietnam experience led to the final and most important fighter model, the **F-4E** with improved radar (AN/APG-120 solid-state set in a smaller radome), more power, more internal fuel, an internal 20-mm rotary-barrel gun and a slatted wing for better manoeuvrability at high weights. The UK bought a largely redesigned version (the **F-4K** for the Fleet Air Arm and **F-4M** for the RAF, designated **Phantom FG.Mk 1** and **Phantom FGR.Mk 2** respectively) with Rolls-Royce Spey turbofan engines, whose great power was largely dissipated in increased aircraft drag. Germany's Luftwaffe is modifying its slatted **F-4F** fleet to carry the advanced AMRAAM missile, with a new radar, and its RF-4E fleet to drop bombs. Japan built its own **F-4EJ** model. The last sub-type to emerge is the **F-4G** dedicated EW (electronic-warfare) aircraft, used by the USAF Tactical Air Command and USAF Europe, and produced by conversion of F-4Es. It combines complex AN/APR-38 sensor, analyser and jammer systems with special air-to-ground weapons including Shrike, Standard ARM, Maverick and HARM. The **F-4J** was the ultimate new-build version for the US Navy and US Marine Corps, based on the F-4B but fitted with more

RAF Phantom FGR.Mk 2 (F-4M) of No. 92 Sqn based in Germany. All RAF air-defence Phantoms are now painted in low-visibility grey. They usually fly with AIM-9L Sidewinders and BAe Sky Flash missiles.

powerful engines, a slotted tailplane, drooping ailerons and improved avionics, including AN/AWG-10 fire-control radar and an AN/AJB-7 bombing system. F-4Js were later upgraded to **F-4S** standard with avionics improvements and leading-edge slats. The **F-4N** was an upgraded F-4B.

Specification:
F-4E Phantom II
Type: multi-role fighter
Armament: one 20-mm M61 gun under nose; four Sparrow (later AMRAAM) AAMs recessed under fuselage (one may be replaced by ECM pod), and up to 7258 kg (16,000 lb) of assorted stores on wing pylons including air-to-ground weapons, tanks, two more Sparrows or four Sidewinder AAMs
Powerplant: two 8120-kg (17,900-lb) thrust General Electric J79-17 afterburning turbojets
Performance: maximum speed, clean plus Sparrow AAMs 2414 km/h (1,500 mph) or Mach 2.27 at high altitude; initial climb rate 18715 m (61,400 ft) per minute; service ceiling 18975 m (62,250 ft); range on internal fuel only without weapons 2817 km (1,750 miles)
Weights: empty 13757 kg (30,328 lb); maximum take-off 27500 kg (60,360 lb)
Dimensions: span 11.71 m (38 ft 5 in); length 19.20 m (63 ft 0 in); height 4.96 m (16 ft 3⅓ in); wing area 49.24 m² (530.0 sq ft)

A trio of F-4D Phantoms line up to take on fuel from a Boeing KC-135 tanker before a strike into North Vietnam. The F-4 proved its worth in Vietnam, emerging as a genuine multi-role fighter.

The F-4C was the original 'minimum change' model for the US Air Force. This 1963 example, with infra-red seeker under the nose, was serving with the 171st FIS of the Michigan ANG in 1980.

Final model of fighter Phantom, the F-4E introduced more power and fuel, and was later given an internal gun and slats. This F-4E was assigned to the 32nd TFS at Camp Amsterdan (Soesterberg), Netherlands.

Phantom FGR.Mk 2 (F-4M) of No. 23 Sqn, RAF, based at Wattisham in 1976. This unit has now also adopted the air superiority grey. They are now the Falklands air defence unit, renumbered from No. 29 Sqn.

Mikoyan-Gurevich MiG-21 'Fishbed'

In 1954 the MiG and Sukhoi design teams each went ahead with prototypes to test two new configurations for supersonic combat aircraft. Eventually the acutely swept wing plus swept tail was judged best for attack aircraft, resulting in the Sukhoi Su-7, while the tailed delta gave highest performance for a fighter and was adopted for what became the **Mikoyan-Gurevich MiG-21 'Fishbed'**. Early MiG-21s reached the Soviet Frontal Aviation and PVO defence force in 1959, and were very simple aircraft just able to carry two cannon (sometimes only one, to save weight) and two small AA-2 missiles. Powered by the R-11 rated at 5750-kg (12,676-lb) thrust with afterburner, the MiG-21 reached Mach 2 and was a joy to fly. Over the next quarter-century the MiG-21 became the most prolific fighter in the world, with about 15,000 built in 15 major and over 100 minor versions, plus corresponding two-seat trainers. Each successive major model has featured more thrust or better avionics or a greater or better spectrum of weapons. All the later versions have the R-11-300, or R-11F2S-300, or R-13-300 or R-25 engine fed by an enlarged duct with an all-weather radar in the centrebody cone. Drag is reduced by progressively larger dorsal

fairings which in some models contain fuel, and there are numerous options of reconnaissance sensors and EW (electronic warfare) systems. Large numbers continue to be built in India and China; the latter designates the type the **Xian J-7** for indigenous use and **F-7** for export. Some of the major versions of the Soviet 'Fishbed' series are the **MiG-21PF 'Fishbed-D'** limited all-weather fighter with R1L radar; **MiG-21FL** export versions of the MiG-21PF with R2L radar and provision for a gun pod; **MiG-21PFM 'Fishbed-F'** improved version of the MiG-21PF with forward- rather than side-hingeing canopy and R2L radar; **MiG-21PFMA 'Fishbed-J'** multi-role version of the MiG-21PFM with four hardpoints and provision for a GSh-23 cannon pack; **MiG-21R 'Fishbed-H'** tactical reconnaissance version of the MiG-21PFMA;

MiG-21MF 'Fishbed-J' upengined version of the MiG-21PFMA; **MiG-21bis 'Fishbed-L'** third-generation fighter with much improved avionics and structure; **MiG-21bis 'Fishbed-N'** definitive third-generation fighter with more powerful R-25 engine; and **MiG-21U 'Mongol'** tandem two-seat trainer in several variants.

Specification:
MiG-21bis 'Fishbed-N'
Type: multi-role fighter
Armament: one 23-mm GSh-23 twin-barrel gun with 200 rounds; maximum of 1500 kg (3,307 lb) of ordnance carried on four wing pylons, including two 500-kg (1,102-lb) and two 250-kg (551-lb) bombs or other stores in attack missions, or four AA-2-2 'Advanced Atoll' AAMs or two AA-2-2 and two AA-8 'Aphid' AAMs in air-to-air role

Powerplant: one 7500-kg (16,535-lb) thrust Tumansky R-25 afterburning turbojet
Performance: maximum speed, clean at high altitude 2285 km/h (1,420 mph) or Mach 2.15; initial climb rate 17700 m (58,070 ft) per minute; service ceiling 15000 m (49,210 ft); range at high altitude (with internal fuel only) 1100 km (683 miles)
Weights: empty about 5715 kg (12,600 lb); maximum take-off 9400 kg (20,725 lb)
Dimensions: span 7.15 m (23 ft 5½ in); length, excluding probe typically 15.10 m (49 ft 7 in); height 4.10 m (13 ft 5½ in); wing area 23.0 m² (247.6 sq ft)

Still in limited front-line service with the CIS air forces, the MiG-21 was in its time a versatile and relatively potent weapon. About 15,000 were built.

Yugoslavia operated about 200 MiG-21s, of which this MiG-21MF complete with AA-2 'Atoll' air-to-air missiles is an example.

Mikoyan-Gurevich MiG-23 'Flogger'

The Soviet Union's standard shape for an optimized swing-wing aircraft was perfected in 1964 and assigned to Sukhoi for a large twin-engine aircraft and to the MiG OKB (design bureau) for a smaller aircraft with one engine. The MiG prototype (designated E-231) was publicly flown in 1967, but considerable redesign was needed and production of the **Mikoyan-Gurevich MiG-23 'Flogger'** series did not start until 1970, with a different engine. Since then the rate of delivery has surpassed that of all other combat aircraft, and 10 basic sub-families have been identified, all named 'Flogger' by NATO but divided by the Soviets into MiG-23 and MiG-27 families. Both the FA (Frontal Aviation) and IA-PVO (Air-Defence Forces) of the Soviet Union

use MiG-23 interceptor variants with large multi-mode nose radar ('High Lark' with a search range of 85 km/53 miles and a tracking range of 54 km/34 miles), fully variable engine inlets and AAM armament. The FA also uses the **MiG-27** attack aircraft (**'Flogger-D'** and **'Flogger-J'**) with a tapered downslop-

ing nose packed with air-to-ground sensors, large armour plates round the cockpit and fixed inlets. All have full-span flaps, outboard leading-edge flaps, roll control by spoilers and tailerons, rough-field main gear folding into the fuselage, and a large ventral fin which folds sideways for take-off and

landing. Deliveries to 17 air forces exceeded 2,600 by the spring of 1983, and the main operational variants of the MiG-23 series are the **MiG-23MF 'Flogger-B'** single-seat air-combat fighter, with limited look down/shoot down capability; the **MiG-23U 'Flogger-C'** two-seat combat-capable con-

MiG-23MF 'Flogger-B' in the standard air superiority overall light grey. Note the rocket pods and AAM launching shoes.

version trainer; the **MiG-23 'Flogger-E'** export version of the 'Flogger-B' with less capable avionics including 'Jay Bird' radar matched to AA-2 'Atoll' air-to-air missiles; the **MiG-23BN 'Flogger-F'** export close-support and interdictor aircraft combining the nose section of the 'Flogger-D' with the powerplant, variable-geometry inlets and GSh-23 twin-barrel 23-mm cannon of the MiG-23 series; the **MiG-23MF 'Flogger-G'** variant of the 'Flogger-B' with a smaller

dorsal extension to the fin; and the **MiG-23BN 'Flogger-H'** variant of the 'Flogger-F' with extra avionics.

Specification:
MiG-23MF 'Flogger-B'
Type: variable-geometry air-combat fighter
Armament: one GSh-23 twin-barrel 23-mm cannon, and up to 2000 kg (4,409 lb) of stores on five hardpoints; the most common air-to-air weapons

are the AA-7 'Apex' and AA-8 'Aphid' air-to-air missiles
Powerplant: one 12,475-kg (27,502-lb) afterburning thrust Tumansky R-29B turbojet
Performance: maximum speed about 2,500 km/h (1,553 mph) or Mach 2.35 at altitude; service ceiling 18600 m (61,025 ft); combat radius about 1200 km (746 miles)
Weight: maximum take-off 16000 kg (35,273 lb)

The MiG-23 was by far the most important aircraft in the Soviet inventory. Capable of a variety of missions, it appears in many versions, of which this is the 'Flogger-G'.

Dimensions: span spread 14.25 m (46 ft 9 in) and swept 8.17 m (26 ft 9½ in); length 16.80 m (55 ft 1½ in); wing area about 37.0 m² (398.3 sq ft)

Former USSR

Mikoyan-Gurevich MiG-25 'Foxbat'

Libya reportedly acquired 55 MiG-25s of various types, probably flown initially by Soviet pilots. This is an interceptor armed with four advanced AA-6 'Acrid' radar missiles.

Designed specifically to intercept the B-70 Mach 3 bomber (which never went into service) the **Mikoyan-Gurevich MiG-25 'Foxbat'** was designed for speed at the expense of such other attributes as short field-length, combat manoeuvrability, modest weight and economic cost. The E-266 prototypes were displayed in 1967 and caused a great stir among Western observers, a stir heightened by a string of world records for speed (often over long ranges with heavy payloads) and astonishing rate of climb and high altitude, such as a climb from rest to 35000 m (114,829 ft) in 4 minutes 11 seconds. The basic **MiG-25 'Foxbat-A'** interceptor, an example of which was flown to Japan by a defector in September 1976, is made mainly of steel, with titanium or its alloys around the engines and on leading edges. The unswept wing is thin and sharp-edged, and has a fixed leading edge and plain flaps and ailerons. Large fuel tankage is provided in 11 welded steel tanks built into the airframe, and the low-pressure turbojets have giant afterburners and fully variable inlets with water/alcohol sprays. The giant radar is typical of 1959 technology and is associated with comprehensive EW systems and va-

rious AAMs. At least two types of **MiG-25R** (identified by NATO as **'Foxbat-B'** and **'Foxbat-D'**) carry large cameras, infra-red and radar reconnaissance systems, and the **MiG-25U 'Foxbat-C'** trainer has a second cockpit replacing the radar. The latest version of the MiG-25 (possibly the MiG-25M) is the **'Foxbat-E'**, which is the 'Foxbat-A' converted with a look-down/shoot-down radar/weapon fit of limited capability, possibly comparable with that of the 'Flogger'. The **MiG-31 'Foxhound'** is a replacement with more thrust from Tumansky R-15 engines and later weapons and radar (and possibly with a gun and second seat); the missile fit comprises four radar-homing AA-9 weapons under the wings and four shorter-range AA-8 'Aphid' weapons for self-defence.

Specification:
MiG-25 'Foxbat-A'
Type: all-weather stand-off interceptor
Armament: four AAMs (usually AA-6 'Acrid')
Powerplant: two 11000-kg (24,250-lb) thrust Tumansky R-31 afterburning turbojets
Performance: maximum speed, clean at high altitude (dash) 3400 km/h (2,115 mph) or Mach 3.2, or (sustained)

2978 km/h (1,850 mph) or Mach 2.8; initial climb rate 12480 m (40,950 ft) per minute; service ceiling 24400 m (80,000 ft); radius at high altitude 1125 km (700 miles)
Weights: empty 20095 kg (44,300 lb); maximum take-off 36200 kg (79,800 lb)
Dimensions: span 13.95 m (45 ft 9 in);

Early exposure to the MiG-25 caused grave consternation to Western defence analysts.

length 23.82 m (78 ft 1¾ in); height 6.10 m (20 ft 0¼ in); wing area 56.83 m² (611.7 sq ft)

Sukhoi Su-15 'Flagon'

The final operational variant of the Su-15 was the 'Flagon-F'. Immediately distinguishable by its more aesthetically pleasing ogival radome, this version also incorporated uprated Tumansky R-13F-300 engines, giving extremely high performance.

With a Soviet requirement for a Mach 2.5 interceptor in the 1960s, the Sukhoi design bureau adapted the existing **Su-11** to take twin Tumansky R-11 afterburning turbojets and a large radar nose. The result was the **Su-15 'Flagon'**, the first prototype of which flew in 1965. The original R11 engines were later replaced by somewhat more powerful R-13s, making these aircraft among the world's fastest fighters.

The Su-15's original armament of two AA-8 'Aphid' close-range and two or four AA-3 'Anab' longer range missiles were replaced by longer-range versions of the same weapon. Despite some reports to the contrary there is no evidence that the aircraft carries an internal cannon, though this could be fitted as an external pod. Unlike Frontal Aviation aircraft, which regularly use roads as strips, the Su-15 needs a long paved runway of 2000-3000 m (6560-9840 ft), and streams its drag chute on landing. The Su-15 carries a comprehensive internal fit of highly capable electronic warfare systems. The last service versions of the Su-15 were the **'Flagon-E'** and **'Flagon F'** single-seat interceptors made notorious in the shooting down of a South Korean Boeing 747 airliner. Also operated were **'Flagon-C'** two-seat trainers.

About 700 Su-15 aircraft were in service in the mid-1980s, but the type was then supplanted in the all-weather interception role by the MiG-23 'Flogger-G' and MiG-25 'Foxbat'.

Specification:
Sukhoi Su-15 'Flagon-F'
Type: all-weather interceptor
Armament: two AA-3 'Anab' missiles; body pylons could carry two more but are usually empty or used for tanks
Powerplant: two 6600-kg (14,550-lb) thrust Tumansky R-13F-300 afterburning turbojets
Performance: maximum speed, clean at high altitude 2660 km/h (1,653 mph) or Mach 2.5; combat radius at high altitude with two AAMs 725 km (450 miles)
Weights: empty probably about 10000 kg (22,046 lb); maximum take-off estimated at 16000 kg (35,274 lb)
Dimensions: (estimated) span 10.53 m (34 ft 6 in); length 20.5 m (68 ft 0 in); height 5.0 m (16 ft 6 in); wing area about 35.7 m² (384.3 sq ft)

The prototype Su-15 'Flagon-B', with lift-jets incorporated in the fuselage (used only on this variant), but also showing the distinctive kinked delta planform of subsequent models.

Tupolev Tu-128 'Fiddler'

Tupolev Tu-128 of the Soviet air force with four AA-3 'Ash' anti-aircraft missiles.

When first seen in 1961, this large supersonic twin-jet was thought by Western observers to be a Yakovlev design. In fact it was the **Tupolev Tu-28** long-range surveillance fighter, from which was derived the **Tu-28P 'Fiddler'** interceptor. The Tupolev bureau numbers for these two types were Tu-102 and **Tu-128**. In many respects the largest fighter in the world and certainly the most powerful fighter put into service, the Tu-128 had a long fuselage with a fuel capacity to handle PVO (air defence force) missions covering vast areas of the Soviet frontier. The original Tu-28 was intended to operate almost without ground

help, but the Tu-128 was assisted by ground radars and defence systems that guided it to its target. Then the extremely large 'Big Nose' I/J-band radar took over until either a radar- or IR-homing AA-5 missile could be fired. A pair of each type of missile was carried, and no other interceptor

was ever seen with these large weapons. The Tu-128's considerable weight was spread by bogie landing gear units that in flight were retracted into fairings typical of the Tupolev aircraft of the period. Capability against low-flying aircraft was probably enhanced in the 1980s because

even the new Su-27 'Flanker' could not offer an equal area defence capability. The 100 or so in service were axed from the middle of the decade.

Specification:
Tu-128 'Fiddler'
Type: long-range interceptor
Armament: four AA-3 'Ash' AAMs, two radar-guided and two IR-homing
Powerplant: two afterburning turbojets, almost certainly Lyulka AL-21F-3 each rated at 11000-kg (24,250-lb) thrust
Performance: maximum speed at high altitude 1900 km/h (1,200 mph) or Mach 1.8; service ceiling 20000 m (65,615 ft); radius at high altitude with four AAMs 1250 km (777 miles)
Weights: (estimated) empty 24500 kg (54,012 lb); maximum take-off 40000 kg (88,183 lb)
Dimensions: span 18.10 m (60 ft 0 in); length 27.20 m (89 ft 3 in); height 7.0 m (23 ft 0 in); wing area 80.0 m² (860 sq ft)

The world's biggest fighter, the Tupolev Tu-128, served only with the Soviet air force. Deployed in remote areas, the type had an incredible endurance or eight hours.

The First Supersonic Fighters

The technological developments of the late 1940s opened the way for sustained supersonic performance in the 1950s, and designers jumped at the opportunity to create a new breed of fighters that would, they hoped, give their crews a decided performance advantage over their adversaries.

The Phantom was originally designed as a naval warplane, and the F-4B (shown here) was the first major production model. Land-based variants followed.

By the start of the 1950s, fighter designers had their sights set on supersonic flight. When the designs reached fruition, the course of air warfare changed. Aircrart could now intercept each other at greater distances and in shorter times than had been previously possible. Dogfights, however, were not fought at supersonic speeds, a situation that has lasted to this day.

A whole new era of military aircraft opened up, with the North American F-100 and Mikoyan-Gurevich MiG-19 paving the way for the classic Dassault Mirage III, McDonnell F-4 Phantom II and MiG-21. Alongside the Lockheed F-104 Starfighter, these aircraft equipped the air forces of most of the major nations. They soon found themselves ever more involved in action, mostly against each other. The wars in the Middle East in 1967, 1973 and 1982 and the protracted air war over Vietnam forged tactics for air combat between supersonic aircraft that lasted into the 1980s. The air battles that took place in these wars were different from those of Korea, as the air-to-air missile, had largely replaced the cannon as the main armament. Some of the abovementioned aircraft are still in service in modernized forms as the front-line equipment of many nations. However, they were largely overtaken during the 1980s by types such as the General Dynamics F-16 and Mikoyan-Gurevich MiG-23.

In the later years of World War II fighters performed ground-attack missions as well as air-to-air tasks. This capability was developed in the first jet fighters, and when the supersonic age arrived these aircraft were often used more as bombers than as fighters. Once again, the Vietnam War illustrated the new brand of air war, with only a handful of F-4s carrying air-to-air missiles while the rest of the Phantoms, the F-105 Thunderchiefs and the F-100 Super Sabres carried only bombs and air-to-ground loads.

Together with the F-4, the aircraft covered in this chapter shaped the modern fighter, and their influence has lasted beyond the 1980s. The lessons learned from their experiences in battle have provided current military strategists with all the air combat input they need to plan future defence.

BAC Lightning

Attaining operational service during the course of 1960, the **BAC Lightning** holds the distinction of being the first British aircraft to exceed Mach 2 in level flight, and has been an integral part of the UK's aerial defences for the past 24 years.

Development of what eventually became the Lightning can be traced back to 1947 when the English Electric Company was awarded a study contract for a supersonic research aircraft. Known as the **P.1**, this made its maiden flight in early August 1954 and subsequently demonstrated Mach 1+ performance, serving as a starting point for the **P.1B** which far more closely approached the requirements needed by an operational aircraft. Flight trials with the P.1B began in April 1957 and showed sufficient promise to warrant a contract for 20 pre-production test specimens of the Lightning, as the type had by then been named.

The first squadron to equip was No. 74 at Coltishall, this receiving the **Lightning F.Mk 1** variant which also served with Nos 56 and 111 Squadrons. Production then switched to the **Lightning F.Mk 2**, which offered better performance and was armed with Red Top missiles in place of the Lightning F.Mk 1's Firestreaks. Two squadrons received this model, both being quickly moved to West Germany, whilst the much improved **Lightning F.Mk 3** eventually equipped five home-based squadrons from mid-1964 onwards. The final single-seat Lightning to see service with the RAF was **Lightning F.MK 6** with a greatly modified and much improved fuel capacity and this model remained in active service with the RAF up to 1988.

In addition to single-seaters, two two-seat variants were also built for training duty, these being the **Lightning T.Mk 4** and **Lightning T.Mk 5**, and

Above: Lightnings flew for many years with the RAF in natural metal finish and vivid paint schemes. This F.Mk 3 served with No. 56 Sqn at Wattisham in 1965, when the type was the UK's main air defence fighter.

a few of the latter mark are also still airworthy.

Modest success was also achieved on the export front, Saudi Arabia and Kuwait purchasing close to 50 aircraft between them. These were retired in 1985 and 1977 respectively, and were re-placed by the McDonnell Douglas F-15 and Dassault Breguet Mirage F 1 respectively.

Specification
BAC Lightning F.Mk 6
Type: single-seat all-weather interceptor
Powerplant: two Rolls-Royce Avon Mk 302 turbojets, each rated at 7112-kg (15,680-lb) afterburning thrust
Performance: maximum speed 2414 km/h (1,500 mph) at 12190 m (40,000 ft); initial climb rate 15240 m (50,000 ft) per minute; service ceiling 16765 m (55,000 ft); range 1287 km (800 miles) on internal fuel

Weights: empty about 12701 kg (28,000 lb); normal loaded 19047 kg (42,000 lb); maximum take-off about 22680 kg (50,000 lb)
Dimensions: span 10.62 m (34 ft 10 in); length 16.84 m (55 ft 3 in) including probe; height 5.97 m (19 ft 7 in); wing area 35.31 m^2 (380.1 sq ft)
Armament: two 30-mm Aden cannon, plus two Firestreak or Red Top infra-red homing air-to-air missiles

The export derivative of the Lightning F.Mk 6 was the F.Mk 53, supplied to Kuwait and Saudi Arabia; one of the latter's aircraft is seen here. Two-seat trainers were also supplied with the designation T.Mk 55.

A Lightning F.Mk 3 of the No. 75 Sqn displays the carriage of the Firestreak missiles and the original wing with straight leading edges.

Dassault Super Mystère

Unique in being the first Western European aircraft capable of supersonic speed in level flight, the **Dassault Super Mystère** has virtually disappeared from the scene although a few are understood still to be active with the Honduran air force.

A logical development of the earlier Mystère, the Super Mystère first flew in prototype form on 2 March 1955, although this aircraft was powered by a Rolls-Royce Avon rather than the SNECMA Atar 101G which was fitted to production-configured machines. Five pre-production test specimens followed the prototype down the assembly line, the first of these getting airborne on 15 May 1956, whilst production **Super Mystère B-2** aircraft began to enter service with the 10e Escadre de Chasse during 1957, other operational units being the 5e Escadre at Orange and the 12² Escadre at Cambrai. Production terminated during 1959, by which time some 180 Super Mystères had been built, this total including 24 for service with the Israeli air force, with which they saw combat action on several occasions.

Development of the type did not cease with the Super Mystère B-2 model, for Dassault also completed two prototypes of the **Super Mystère B-4**. Powered by a single SNECMA Atar 09C engine, this flew for the first time on 9 February 1958 and eventually achieved a top speed of Mach 1.4 in level flight at 11000 m (36,090 ft). In the event, however, the even more promising Dassault Mirage III was coming along and the Super Mystère B-4 eventually slipped quietly into obscurity.

The only Super Mystères now flying are those of the Honduran air force, this

Above: Israel was a major operator of the Super Mystère and her aircraft saw much action, especially in the Six Day War of 1967, where it was employed in the ground-attack role using iron bombs.

air arm having received 12 from Israel during the 1970s. These aircraft provide further evidence of Israeli ingenuity, for they were all modified to take a non-afterburning Pratt & Whitney J52 turbojet.

Specification
Dassault Super Mystère B-2
Type: single-seat fighter-bomber
Powerplant: one SNECMA Atar 101G-2 or Atar 101G-3 turbojet rated at 3400-kg (7,495-lb) dry thrust and 4460-kg (9,833-lb) afterburning thrust
Performance: maximum speed 1195 km/h (743 mph) at altitude; initial climb rate 5335 m (17,500 ft) per minute; service ceiling 17000 m (55,775 ft); range (clean) 870 km (540 miles)
Weights: empty 6930 kg (15,278 lb); normal loaded 9000 kg (19,842 lb); maximum take-off 10000 kg (22,046 lb)

Dimensions: span 10.52 m (34 ft 6 in); length 14.13 m (46 ft 4¼ in); height 4.55 m (14 ft 11 in); wing area 35.00 m² (376.75 sq ft)
Armament: two 30-mm DEFA cannon and 35 68-mm (2.68-in) unguided rockets (the latter in a belly pack), plus up to 1000 kg (2,205 lb) of external ordnance including bombs and rockets

The Super Mystère was employed by France from 1957 until the late 1970s. This Armée de l'Air example shows the dogtooth in the leading edge, which improved high-altitude manoeuvrability. Armament consisted of two 30-mm cannon and internal rockets, with pylons for external stores. Most aircraft carried long-range fuel tanks under the wings

---

Dassault Mirage III and Mirage 5

By far the most successful post-war European fighter aircraft, the **Dassault Mirage III** and **Mirage 5** remained in production in late 1984, albeit in a very small way.

Developed in response to a French air force requirement of the early 1950s, the Mirage was one of three submissions put forward, all of which were intended to use dual turbojet/rocket power in order to gain altitude rapidly in fulfilling the primary task of interception. Subsequently, it became clear that this unusual concept significantly impaired endurance and Dassault returned to the drawing board, coming up with the now familiar tailless delta which relied on a single SNECMA Atar 101G turbojet for propulsion, plus an optional boost rocket.

Construction of a private-venture prototype forged ahead rapidly, this eventually taking to the air for the first time during November 1956 and very quickly vindicating Dassault's theories, whilst at the same time providing valuable data which could be incorporated in any future production variant.

Official interest, initially lukewarm, was quickly confirmed by an order for 10 pre-production specimens just six months after the maiden flight. Testing and evaluation of these began in May 1958 and quickly led to the first major production order for a variant known as the **Mirage IIIC**, this duly entering service at Dijon during 1961.

From then on, the Mirage never looked back, successive develop-

Above: The major aircraft of Israel's lightning victory over its Arab neighbours in 1967 was the Mirage III. This was used for both air-to-air and air-to-ground missions.

ments including the **Mirage IIIB** two-seat pilot training version, the **Mirage IIIE** for tactical nuclear strike and conventional attack, and the **Mirage IIIR** for reconnaissance. In addition to the large numbers built for service with the French air force, versions of all four basic types have been exported throughout the world.

Specification
Dassault Mirage IIIE
Type: single-seat all-weather fighter-bomber
Powerplant: one SNECMA Atar 9C turbojet rated at 6205-kg (13,680-lb) afterburning thrust, plus one optional SEPR 844 rocket rated at 1500-kg (3,307-lb) thrust
Performance: maximum speed 2350 km/h (1,460 mph) at 12200 m (40,025 ft); climb to 11000 m (36,090 ft) in 3 minutes; service ceiling (without

rocket) 17000 m (55,775 ft); combat radius 1200 km (746 miles) on a ground-attack mission
Weights: empty 7200 kg (15,875 lb); normal loaded (clean) 9800 kg (21,605 lb); maximum take-off 13500 kg (29,762 lb)
Dimensions: span 8.22 m (26 ft 11½ in); length 15.03 m (49 ft 3½ in); height 4.50 m (14 ft 9 in); wing area 35.00 m² (376.75 sq ft)

Dassault's remarkable Mirage III has served with the Armée de l'Air since 1961, and still flies in large numbers. These early Mirage IIICs are receiving pre-flight preparations.

Armament: two 30-mm DEFA cannon, plus up to 2270 kg (5,004 lb) of external ordnance including air-to-air missiles, air-to-surface missiles, bombs, rockets and napalm

Mikoyan-Gurevich MiG-19/Shenyang J-6

Europe's first truly supersonic production jet fighter traces its lineage back to the late 1940s and was initially conceived around the newly-developed Lyulka AL-5 axial-flow jet engine. However, slow progress with this powerplant prompted a change to a twin-engine design with a pair of Mikulin AM-5s. In its earliest form, as the I-350, the **Mikoyan-Gurevich MiG-19** featured a T-tail layout but this was quickly revised following the loss of the prototype as a result of flutter, a low-set tailplane being adopted and successfully flown on the I-350(M) during late 1952.

Production-configured **MiG-19F** fighters began to appear soon afterwards, but these were destined to enjoy only short service careers, high attrition rates bringing about the model's forced retirement.

The second version to make its debut was the slab-tailplane **MiG-19S** which began to enter service in 1955, and this proved to be much more reliable although it was quickly supplanted by the **MiG-19PF**, which introduced *Izumrud* radar and which ultimately provided the basis for the first supersonic Soviet missile-armed fighter, the **MiG-19PM**, backbone of Soviet air defences for a number of

Pakistan has been a major recipient of the Shenyang J-6 and this country has appreciated the type's toughness and agility. The Pakistani J-6s are fitted with Martin-Baker ejection seats and are Sidewinder-capable.

Carrying four AA-1 'Alkali' missiles and featuring Izumrud radar, the MiG-19PM was one of the Warsaw Pact's first missile fighters. This example served with Poland, who retained these fighters until about 1970.

The State Aircraft Factory at Shenyang began producing copies of the MiG-19 for the Chinese air force under the designation J-6. These appeared mainly in natural metal but a few were camouflaged in the 1960s.

years. The MiG-19 has the NATO reporting name **'Farmer'**.

Soviet manufacture of the MiG-19 is understood to have ceased during 1958 but the type remained in production in Czechoslovakia until at least 1961, whilst a copy, known as the J-6, has been built by China's Shenyang factory for many years.

Examples of the J-6 have also been supplied to a number of friendly nations including Albania, Pakistan, Tanzania and Vietnam, the Pakistani machines being particularly unusual in that they are fitted with British Martin-Baker ejection seats and have provision for carriage of the American AIM-9 Sidewinder air-to-air missile.

Although now rather dated, the MiG-19/J-6 is still a most potent warplane if flown by an experienced pilot, possessing great agility and devastating guns.

Specification
Mikoyan-Gurevich MiG-19/Shenyang J-6C
Type: single-seat fighter
Powerplant: two Wopen-6 (Tumansky R-9BF-811) turbojets, each rated at 3250-kg (7,165-lb) afterburning thrust
Performance: maximum speed 1540 km/h (957 mph) at 11000 m (36,090 ft); initial climb rate more than

9145 m (30,000 ft) per minute; service ceiling 17900 m (58,725 ft); tactical radius 685 km (425 miles) with two drop tanks; ferry range 2200 km (1,365 miles) with maximum internal and external fuel
Weights: empty 5670 kg (12,700 lb); normal loaded 7545 kg (16,634 lb); maximum take-off 8965 kg (19,764 lb)
Dimensions: span 9.20 m (30 ft 2¼ in); length 12.60 m (41 ft 4 in) excluding probe; height 3.88 m (12 ft 8¾ in); wing area 25.00 m² (269.1 sq ft)
Armament: two or three 30-mm NR-30 cannon, plus up to 500 kg (1,102 lb) of external ordnance including four air-to-air missiles, rockets and bombs

Mikoyan-Gurevich MiG-21

Continuing in production and development more than 25 years after its maiden flight, the **Mikoyan-Gurevich MiG-21** looks set fair to establish a longevity record which is unlikely to be equalled and provides perhaps the classic example of how an aircraft can 'grow' in service.

Development of the MiG-21 began during the mid-1950s and was in large part predicated upon the experience gained in the Korean War, which indicated a need for an uncompromised air superiority fighter. A series of prototypes was constructed and flown in 1955-6, and after detailed study it was decided to adopt the tailed-delta **Ye-5** as the basis for a new fighter, a few examples of the pre-series **Ye-6** entering service with a trials unit in 1957, but it was not until 1959 that the first definitive variant became available. This was the **MiG-21F**, essentially a fine-weather interceptor possessing 'short legs' and only marginal payload capability.

Subsequent redesign has seen the MiG-21 assume a multitude of functions from interception through reconnaissance to strike and close air support and in its most recent guise, as the **MiG-21bis**, it is considered to possess genuine multi-role capability although range and payload potential are still somewhat limited. Nevertheless, the MiG-21bis is now the principal export variant and could conceivably be encountered anywhere where Soviet influence is strong. The NATO reporting name for the series is **'Fishbed'**.

Currently in service with more than 30 air arms throughout the world, variants of the MiG-21 have engaged in combat on numerous occasions, from Israel to India and from Afghanistan to Vietnam, with varying degree of success, but there can be little doubt that in the hands of a skilled pilot it is still a most capable opponent.

Specification
Mikoyan-Gurevich MiG-21bis
Type: single-seat multi-role fighter
Powerplant: one Tumansky R-25 turbojet rated at 5800-kg (12,790-lb) dry thrust and 7500-kg (16,535-lb) afterburning thrust
Performance: maximum speed 2,230 km/h (1,386 mph) at altitude; initial climb rate 17675 m (57,990 ft) per minute; service ceiling about 17500 m (57,415 ft); ferry range about 1590 km (988 miles)
Weights: empty 6200 kg (13,670 lb); normal loaded 7960 kg (17,550 lb);

The first version in service with the enlarged nose cone, necessitated by the larger R1L radar, was the MiG-21PF, built in vast numbers in the 1960s to equip the air defence regiments of the Soviet Union.

maximum take-off about 10000 kg (22,046 lb)
Dimensions: span 7.15 m (23 ft 5½ in); length about 17.56 m (51 ft 8½ in) including probe; height 4.50 m (14 ft 9 in); wing area 23.00 m² (247.6 sq ft)
Armament: one 23-mm GSh-23L twin-barrel cannon plus up to 1500 kg (3,307 lb) of external ordnance including air-to-air missiles, air-to-surface missiles, bombs and rockets

The MiG-21 was sold to several countries including Finland, and India

Sukhoi Su-9/11

Never as widely used or as well known as the contemporary Mikoyan-Gurevich MiG-21 'Fishbed' or Su-7 'Fitter-A', the Sukhoi bureau's delta-wing prototype of 1955-6 nevertheless led to the Su-9 'Fishpot-B', the most numerous supersonic interceptor in the PVO (Air Defence Forces) fleet for many years. The type was supplanted by the Su-15 'Flagon' on the production lines in the late 1960s, but some 600 remained in service throughout the 1970s.

The Su-9 was designed as an all-weather fighter based on the same tailed-delta configuration as the MiG-21. Entering service in 1958-59, it typified Soviet practice in that it combined a new engine and airframe with an existing weapon, the K-5M 'Alkali' air-to-air missile already in service on the MiG-19PFM 'Farmer'. The small radar fitted quite simply into the nose of the Su-9, which was closely similar to that of the Su-7. However, the all-weather capability of the Su-9 was fairly limited, as this radar lacks search range. In practice, the type certainly operated in close co-operation with ground control.

The 1961 Tushino air display, however, saw the appearance of a new derivative of the basic type, featuring a longer and less tapered nose. The inlet diameter was considerably larger, and there was a proportionate increase in the size of the centre-body radome to accommodate a new and more powerful radar known to NATO as 'Skip Spin'. The new type replaced the Su-9 on the production lines, and was designated Su-11, with the code-

name 'Fishpot-C'; it appears to be Soviet practice to apply new designations to reflect relatively minor changes, the Su-11 being no more different from its predecessor than some MiG-21 versions differ from others.

A measure of the comparative worth of the 'Alkali' and later 'Anab' missiles is the fact that the Soviet air force was prepared to accept two of the more potent later weapons on the Su-11 in place of four 'Alkalis' on the Su-9. It is probable that, like many first-generation missile systems, the performance of the K-5M *Izumrud* system was barely good enough for operational clearance. The 'Anab' has clearly

been more successful, and has remained in service and under development for many years.

Like most Soviet interceptors the Su-9 and Su-11 were never exported, even to the Warsaw Pact.

Specification
Type: all-weather interceptor
Powerplant: one 10000-kg (22,046-lb) afterburning Lyulka AL-7F turbojet
Performance: maximum (clean) 2250 km/h (1,398 mph), or Mach 2.1; maximum speed with two AAMs and external fuel tanks 1600 km/h (994 mph) or Mach 1.5; service ceiling 20000 m (65,615 ft); range about 1125 km (699 miles)

First supersonic interceptor in the Soviet inventory with limited all-weather capability, the Sukhoi Su-9 served in large numbers. It is now out of service, along with the Su-11 improved model.

Weights: empty 9000 kg (19,842 lb); maximum loaded 13500 kg (29,873 lb)
Dimensions: span 8.43 m (27 ft 8 in); length (including instrument boom) 18.3 m (60 ft); height 4.9 m (15 ft); wing area 26.2 m² (282 sq ft)
Armament: (Su-9) four K-5M (AA-1 'Alkali') beam-riding air-to-air missiles on wing pylons; (Su-11) two AA-3 'Anab' semi-active homing (almost certainly) AAMs

---

Yakovlev Yak-28P

Alexander Yakovlev's Yak-28 family of combat aircraft, similar in concept and performance to the French Sud-Ouest Vautour series, continue to fill an important role in the Soviet air arm, although the numbers in service are declining. The last to be retired will be the 'Brewer-E' ECM aircraft, with some Yak-28P 'Firebar-Es' carrying on in less strategically important areas of the Soviet periphery.

The current Yak-28s are direct descendants of the original Yak-25, developed from 1950 as the Soviet Union's first all-weather jet fighter. The layout of the Yak-25, with engines under the swept wings, was most unusual and followed wartime German studies; it was one of the first aircraft to feature a 'zero-track tricycle' undercarriage, with a single twin-wheel main unit on the centre of gravity and

Yakovlev Yak-28P 'Firebar' of the IA-PVO Strany. Possessing long range the Yak-28P was used for long-range interception, and modest numbers of the type survived in this role into the late 1980s.

single nose and outrigger wheels. Like the Mikoyan-Gurevich MiG-19, the Yak-25 was powered by Mikulin AM-5 engines, which eventually were manufactured by Tumansky and became the RD-9. Developments of the Yak-25 included the Yak-25RD 'Mandrake', Yak-26 and Yak-27 'Mangrove'.

The Yak-28 series bears little relationship to these earlier aircraft, beyond a general similarity in configuration. Initially, the Yak-28 seems to have been developed as a transonic all-weather fighter using two of the Tumansky R-11 turbojets developed for the MiG-21. The Yak-28's wing is more sharply swept than that of its predecessors and is raised from the mid to the shoulder position. The landing gear has a true bicycle layout, leaving

space for a large weapons bay between the main units. On the Yak-28P interceptor this space is used for fuel;

Below: Displaying its futuristic layout, this Yak-28P prepares to land. The bicycle main undercarriage with wingtip outriggers was a notable feature of the type. The missiles are AA-3 'Anabs'.

the strike version carries stores in the internal bay and drop tanks on underwing stations.

Deliveries of the Yak-28P Firebar started in 1962, and the type became widely used by the PVO air defence force. It offers slightly better endurance than the Sukhoi Su-15, which has similar engines but is lighter and much faster. Later Yak-28Ps, seen from 1967, have sharper and much longer nose radomes and provision for AA-2 'Atoll' short-range missiles on additional underwing pylons.

Developed in parallel with the Yak 28P was a glazed-nose strike version with a second crew member seated ahead of the pilot and a bombing-navigation radar aft of the nose landing gear. Originally codenamed 'Firebar' by NATO, the type was re-christened 'Brassard' when its bomber role became obvious, and the reporting name was then changed to 'Brewer' to avoid confusion with the French Holste Broussard. Because the designations

'Firebar-A' and 'Firebar-B' had already been allotted, the 'Brewer' series appears to have started as 'Brewer-C'.

Specification
Type: Yak-28P 'Firebar' all-weather interceptor; Yak-28U 'Maestro' two-seat conversion trainer
Powerplant: two 6000-kg (13,228-lb) Tumansky R-11 afterburning turbojets
Performance: maximum speed at medium altitude 1200 km/h (746 mph) or Mach 1.13; maximum speed at sea

level Mach 0.85; service ceiling 17000 m (55,775) ft
Weights: empty 13600 kg (29,982 lb); maximum loaded 20000-22000 kg (44,092-48,502 lb)
Dimensions: span 12.95 m (42 ft 6 in); length (except late 'Firebar') 21.65 m (71 ft); length (late 'Firebar') 23.17 m (76 ft); height 3.95 m (13 ft)
Armament: ('Firebar C') two AA-3 'Anab' air-to-air missiles and, on some aircraft, two AA-2 'Atoll' air-to-air missiles

Saab 35 Draken

One of several classic fighters which originated in Europe at around the same time, the highly distinctive double-delta **Saab 35 Draken** (dragon) is still extensively used by the Swedish air force (Flygvapen) and also serves with Finland and Denmark in some numbers.

Arising in response to a 1949 specification calling for a single-seat all-weather interceptor capable of operation from relatively short and austere airstrips, the Draken prototype flew for the first time on 25 October 1955, this event having preceded by a series of trials with the much smaller Saab-210 in order to explore handling characteristics of what was then a unique wing planform.

Several pre-production aircraft also took part in the flight test programme from early 1958 but by this time the Draken was well established in production, an initial order for the **J35A** being placed during the summer of 1956. Deliveries to the Flygvapen got under way on 8 March 1960, Flygflottilj 13 at Norrköping being the first unit to

The first production version of the Draken was the J35A, shown here in the markings of F13 wing based at Norrköping. It features the early Swedish striped camouflage.

convert from the J29, and this was quickly followed by F16 at Uppsala.

Refinement of the fire control system resulted in the appearance of the **J35B** (many of the original J35As being progressively modified to this standard), deliveries taking place from 1961. The next single-seat variant was the **J35D** which was essentially similar to the J35B apart from incorporating a rather more powerful version of the licence-built Rolls-Royce Avon engine, and this was followed by the **S35E** for reconnaissance duties. Fitted with a battery of cameras in an extensively redesigned nose, the S35E first flew on 27 June 1963 but has now been replaced

by the SF37 and SH 37 Viggen.

The most capable variant of the Draken, and incidentally the most numerous, was the **J35F** which entered service during 1965-6, relying on licence-built radar and infra-red homing versions of the Hughes Falcon.

In addition to the single-seaters already described, one two-seat model also attained quantity production for the Flygvapen, this being the **Sk35C** used for operational training.

Although Saab made repeated strenuous attempts to find export customers, it was not until shortly before production was due to cease that the company succeeded in securing over-

seas orders, Denmark purchasing fighter-bomber, reconnaissance and trainer versions of the **Saab-35X** export variant. Finland also opted to buy the Draken, acquiring 12 **J35Xs** interceptors which it presently operates alongside a number of former Swedish air force J35Bs, J35Fs and Sk35Cs.

A pair of J35Ds from F13 wing display the distinctive lines of this fine aircraft. The dark smudges on the leading edges of the wings mark the position of the two internal cannon. The missiles carried are licence-built Sidewinders.

Specification
Saab J35F Draken
Type: single-seat all-weather interceptor
Powerplant: one Svenska Flygmotor RM6C turbojet rated at 8000-kg (17,637-lb) afterburning thrust
Performance: maximum speed 2125 km/h (1,320 mph) at 12200 m (40,025 ft); initial climb rate 10500 m (34,450 ft) per minute; service ceiling about 19800 m (64,960 ft); ferry range 3250 km (2,020 miles) with maximum external fuel
Weights: empty 8245 kg (18,177 lb); maximum take-off 12270 kg (27,050 lb)
Dimensions: span 9.40 m (30 ft 10 in);

length 15.35 m (50 ft 4 in) including probe; height 3.89 m (12 ft 9 in); wing area 49.20 m^2 (529.6 sq ft)
Armament: one 30-mm Aden cannon and two RB27 Falcon radar-homing

air-to-air missiles plus two RB28 Falcon infra-red homing air-to-air missiles, or a combination of these missile type with the RB24 Sidewinder infra-red homing air-to-air missile

The final interceptor version of the Draken is the J35F, which features much improved avionics. It is easily distinguished from earlier marks by the infra-red seeker under the nose.

USA

North American F-100 Super Sabre

The first example of the classic 'Century-series' of fighters to attain operational status, the **North American F-100 Super Sabre** is perhaps most noteworthy for being the first fighter in the world after the MiG-1G to possess genuine supersonic performance. Providing the backbone of US tactical air power for several years during the late 1950s and early 1960s, it is now used by the US Air Force only as the **QF-100** target drone, although a number of F-100s remain operational with the air arms of Taiwan and Turkey.

Begun as a development of North American's highly successful F-86, the F-100 was initially known by that company as the Sabre-45, this appellation referring to the degree of wing sweep, and development of the type began in early February 1949. North American's enterprise was rewarded with a contract for a pair of prototypes and 110 production specimens in November

Assigned to the 127th TFS, Kansas ANG at McConnell AFB, this F-100C was one of the oldest Super Sabres left in service at the end of the 1970s. The rear fuselage was left unpainted due to the high temperatures.

1951, and the first **YF-100A** made a successful maiden flight on 25 May 1953. Production-configured **F-100A** aircraft began to join the test programme in mid-October of the same year, and the Super Sabre subsequently entered service less than a year later, on 27 September 1954, when the 479th Fighter Day Wing at George AFB, California, received its first aircraft.

Thus far, development had progressed smoothly, but then a series of mysterious crashes occurred during 1954, these eventually leading to the F-100 being grounded during November whilst investigations were made into the cause of the accidents. It later became clear that under certain conditions roll-coupling was taking place, and the main cure was the fitting of

extended wingtips; this and other changes were retrospectively applied to the first 70 F-100As.

An F-100D drops a bomb on a Viet Cong target in South Vietnam. As well as South East Asia, the 'Hun' also saw combat with the Turkish forces over Cyprus.

Production then switched to the **F-100C** model, which made its first flight in January 1955 and which had greater payload capability. Entering service first with the 450th Fighter Day Wing in July 1955, 476 F-100Cs were completed, these being followed by the definitive **F-100D** which featured a number of detail design improvements, including inboard landing flaps and modified vertical tail surfaces. No less than 1,274 F-100Ds were built between 1955 and 1959, and this model

subsequently saw extensive service as a fighter-bomber in Vietnam.

The only other significant variant to appear was the two-seat **F-100F** combat proficiency trainer, first flown on 7 March 1957 and of which no less than 339 had been built by the time production ceased in 1959. A small number later served as 'Wild Weasel' SAM-a suppression aircraft in South East Asia although they were soon replaced by Republic F-105F Thunderchiefs.

Specification
North American F-100D Super Sabre
Type: single-seat fighter bomber
Powerplant: one Pratt & Whitney J57-P-21A turbojet rated at 5307-kg (11,700-lb) dry thrust and 7689-kg (16,950-lb) afterburning thrust
Performance: maximum speed 1390 km/h (864 mph) at 10970 m (36,000 ft); initial climb rate 4875 m (16,000 ft) per minute; service ceiling 13715 m (45,000 ft); combat radius (clean) 885 km (550 miles); ferry range

2415 km (1,500 miles) with drop tanks
Weights: empty 9526 kg (21,000 lb); normal loaded 13500 kg (29,762 lb); maximum take-off 15800 kg (34,832 lb)
Dimensions: span 11.81 m (38 ft 9 in); length 16.54 m (54 ft 3 in) including probe; height 4.96 m (16 ft 2¾ in); wing area 35.77 m² (385 sq ft)
Armament: four 20-mm Pontiac M39E cannon, plus up to 3193 kg (7,040 lb) of external ordnance including bombs, rockets and napalm

---

USA
McDonnell F-101 Voodoo

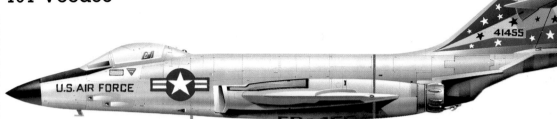

Although its designation indicates that the **McDonnell F-101 Voodoo** was the second of the 'Century-series' fighters to make an appearance, development of this type in fact predated that of the F-100 and can be traced back to the summer of 1946, when McDonnell began work on a strategic penetration fighter to escort bomber aircraft of the Strategic Air Command. Initially known as the **XF-88** and first flown in prototype form during October 1948, McDonnell's original proposal was cancelled in August 1950 only to be reborn in the following year as the F-101.

Again, it was intended to serve as a strategic fighter, a batch of 29 pre-production machines being ordered in May 1953, but SAC soon lost interest in the requirement and subsequently cancelled it at the end of September 1954. By then, however, Tactical Air Command had begun to show interest and development was allowed to continue, the first pre-production **F-101A** flying on 29 September 1954.

At this time, the type was intended as a fighter-bomber, but early flight trials revealed numerous deficiencies including a serious tendency to 'pitch up' and enter an uncontrollable spin. Work on eradicating these failings eventually achieved the desired result, but it was not until May 1957 that the F-101A entered service with the 27th Fighter-Bomber Wing at Bergstrom AFB. Ultimately, the F-101A and the basically similar **F-101C** joined USAFE's 81st Tactical Fighter Wing, remaining in use until about 1965 when the survivors were modified to reconnaissance configuration as the **RF-101G** and **RF-101H** respectively and issued to the Air National Guard.

In addition to fighter-bomber models, a substantial number of Voodoos were built from the outset for reconnaissance tasks, 35 **RF-101A** aircraft being followed by 166 **RF-101C**

Originally planned as an escort fighter for Strategic Air Command, the F-101A soon passed to TAC and then to Europe, where this aircraft is seen in the colours of the 81st TFW based at Bentwaters and Woodbridge in England.

machines, and these two variants enjoyed a lengthy operational career, seeing extensive combat duty in Vietnam. The RF-101 airframe was basically similar to that of the earlier fighter-bomber apart from the modified nose section which housed a battery of cameras.

The most numerous variant of the Voodoo was the two-seat **F-101B** interceptor, which made its maiden flight on 27 March 1957, a total of 480 eventually being built for service with Air Defense Command although 66 of these were transferred in 1961 to what was then the Royal Canadian Air Force. Retired from the operational USAF inventory in the early 1970s, some F-101Bs remained active with the Air National Guard until 1982, whilst the Canadian Armed Forces have replaced their CF-101Bs with CF-18s.

Specification
McDonnell F-101B Voodoo
Type: two-seat all-weather interceptor
Powerplant: two Pratt & Whitney J57-P-55 turbojets, each rated at 5439-kg (11,990-lb) dry thrust and 6799-kg (14,990-lb) afterburning thrust
Performance: maximum speed 1963 km/h (1,220 mph) at 12190 m (40,000 ft); initial climb rate 5180 m (17,000 ft) per minute; service ceiling 15545 m (51,000 ft); maximum range

2495 km (1,550 miles)
Weights: empty 13141 kg (28,970 lb); normal loaded 18099 kg (39,900 lb); maximum take-off 23462 kg (51,724 lb) on an area interception mission
Dimensions: span 12.09 m (39 ft 8 in); length 20.55 m (67 ft 4¾ in); height 5.49 m (18 ft 0 in); wing area 34.19 m² (368 sq ft)
Armament: two AIR-2A nuclear-

One of the first US jet aircraft to go to Vietnam was the RF-101C, the only Voodoo model to serve in that theatre. These were the prime reconnaissance platforms for the USAF in the early years.

tipped unguided air-to-air rockets and two AIM-4C infra-red homing air-to-air missiles

---

USA
Convair F-102 Delta Dagger

Capitalizing to a great degree on wartime German research and early postwar experience gained with the experimental XF-92A, the **Convair F-102 Delta Dagger** was unique in being the first supersonic delta-winged aircraft to enter operational service.

This was an ambitious project from the outset, and development which began in earnest in 1950 was plagued by numerous problems, not least of which was the fact that in its original form it was clear that the type would never exceed Mach 1, one of the prime features of the requirement.

The type was first flown on 24 October 1953 in prototype form as the **YF-102**, but early trials were marred by the loss of the initial machine and by the realization that drastic redesign would be necessary, the parent company eventually having no option but to return to the drawing board and incorporate the then-new concept of area rule which seemed to offer the best chance of reducing unacceptably high transonic drag. In the event, adoption of the so-called 'coke bottle' fuselage lines satisfactorily resolved the performance question although

further major redesign was necessary with regard to the vertical tail and air inlet ducting, so it was not until April 1956 that the type entered service with Air Defense Command.

Subsequently, the **F-102A** enjoyed a lengthy operational career, serving as an interceptor with ADC, Pacific Air Forces and United States Air Forces in Europe, 875 of the 889 single-seaters built eventually joining the active inventory. In addition, 111 examples of the two-seat **TF-102A** combat proficiency trainer were also completed, this rather unusually adopting side-by-

side seating arrangement in a completely new forward fuselage section.

Retired from service as an interceptor with the Air National Guard during the latter half of the 1970s, the Delta Dagger gained a new lease of life as the **PQM-102** target drone, several hundred being converted for use in weapons training and trials programmes.

Specification
Convair F-102A Delta Dagger
Type: single-seat all-weather interceptor

Powerplant: one Pratt & Whitney J57-P-23 turbojet rated at 5307-kg (11,700-lb) dry thrust and 7802-kg (17,200-lb) afterburning thrust
Performance: maximum speed (clean) 1328 km/h (825 mph) at 12190 m (40,000 ft); initial climb rate 5305 m (17,400 ft) per minute; service ceiling 16460 m (54,000 ft) tactical radius 805 km (500 miles) with external fuel and full armament
Weights: empty 8641 kg (19,050 lb); normal loaded 12565 kg (27,700 lb); maximum take-off 14288 kg (31,500 lb)
Dimensions: span 11.62 m (38 ft 1½ in); length 20.84 m (68 ft 4⅔ in) including probe; height 6.46 m (21 ft 2½ in); wing area 61.45 m² (661.5 sq ft)
Armament: various combinations of AIM-4C Falcon infra-red homing air-to-air missiles, AIM-4A/AIM-4E Falcon radar homing air-to-air missiles, and AIM-26A Falcon nuclear-tipped air-to-air missiles in an internal weapons bay

These two F-102As are typical of the aircraft which defended the continental United States for several years. Later these were converted to drones.

Lockheed F-104 Starfighter

The most widely used, and possibly best-known, member of the 'Century series', the diminutive **Lockheed F-104 Starfighter** is still in service today with several air arms throughout the world, although its days as an operational fighter are now clearly numbered.

Intended initially to serve purely as a day superiority fighter, the type first flew in prototype form on 7 February 1954 and like most of its contemporaries it suffered from numerous teething troubles, no less than 52 Starfighters being involved in the test programme at one time. In the event, most of these difficulties were overcome and the **F-104A** entered service with the USAF's 83rd Fighter Interceptor Squadron shortly before the end of January 1958, only to be grounded in April following a series of engine-related accidents. Re-engining with the J79-GE-3B went some way towards resolving these problems, but the type's generally poor safety record and short range resulted in it disappearing from the US front-line inventory in 1960, most surviving F-104As being issued to the Air National Guard.

The first multi-mission model was the **F-104C**, which served with Tactical Air Command for several years and which incorporated inflight-refuelling equipment as well as the ability to carry a range of stores on two underwing stations. In the event only 77 F-104Cs were built, these being the last Starfighters to be used operationally by the USAF; some undertook combat in South East Asia, although their contribution was small. Two-seat equivalents of the F-104A and F-104C were the **F-104B** and **F-104D** respectively, a combined total of 47 being produced.

The definitive Starfighter was the **F-104G**, which is a true multi-mission machine with sophisticated radar optimized for air-to-air and air-to-ground modes. Development of this variant began in 1958 and it subsequently secured substantial orders from European members of the NATO alliance

as well as from Canada (as the **CF-104**) and Japan (as the **F-104J**), eventually becoming one of the most important fighters of the 1960s and the centrepiece of a bribery scandal which emerged in the 1970s. A two-seat derivative intended for training duties is known as the **TF-104G** (**CF-104D** for Canada), this retaining partial weapons capability. Two other trainer variations, both based essentially on the earlier F-104D, are the **F-104DJ** for Japan and the **F-104F** for West Germany. The **RF-104G** is the dedicated reconnaissance version of the F-104G.

Specification
Lockheed F-104G Starfighter
Type: single-seat multi-role fighter
Powerplant: one General Electric J79-GE-11A turbojet rated at 4536-kg (10,000-lb) dry thrust and 7167-kg (15,800-lb) afterburning thrust
Performance: maximum speed 2092 km/h (1,300 mph) at 12190 m (40,000 ft); initial climb rate 12495 m (41,000 ft) per minute; service ceiling 16765 m (55,000 ft); tactical radius 1110 km (690 miles); ferry range 3200 km (1,988 miles) with maximum external fuel
Weights: empty 6388 kg (14,082 lb); maximum take-off 13054 kg (28,779 lb)
Dimensions: span 6.68 m (21 ft 11 in); length 16.69 m (54 ft 9 in); height 4.11 m (13 ft 6 in); wing area 18.22 m² (196.1 sq ft)
Armament: one 20-mm M61A1 Vulcan rotary-barrel cannon and two tip-mounted AIM-9 Sidewinder infra-red homing air-to-air missiles, plus up to 1814 kg (4,000 lb) of external ordnance

Assigned primarily to the tactical reconnaissance role, the F-104G Starfighters of the Netherlands' No. 306 Sqn carry optical cameras and Oude Delft infra-red linescan systems.

In order to train pilots for this tricky fighter, Lockheed developed a two-seat trainer version, the TF-104G.

This retains the NASARR radar and weapon delivery boxes but the internal rotary cannon was deleted.

On patrol over Vietnam: the F-104 served in a minor role in South East Asia on both air-to-air sorties and on

low-level, high-speed strikes. It was not too successful at either and was quickly replaced.

Republic F-105 Thunderchief

USA

Arguably the greatest of the 'Century series' by virtue of its exploits in combat over South East Asia, the **Republic F-105 Thunderchief** also suffered its fair share of development headaches and teething troubles during its early service career. Like the F-102, it was largely redesigned in detail to take advantage of the benefits bestowed by area rule, and this resulted in performance figures which handsomely exceeded those originally envisaged and which were to prove of inestimable value to the pilots who later flew it in combat.

The F-105 originated as a private-venture successor to the highly successful Republic F-84 Thunderstreak, and was rewarded with a development contract in 1954, the type being intended at that time to fulfil the nuclear strike role. Non-availability of the planned J75 engine meant that the prototype **YF-105A** entered flight test on 22 October 1955 with the J57-P-25 powerplant, and it was not until May 1956 that the definitive engine/airframe pairing took to the air for the first time, this ending in near disaster when the landing gear failed to lower satisfactorily, test pilot Hank Beaird experiencing the ignominy of a wheels-up landing on the dry lake bed at Edwards AFB, California.

Following the completion of flight trials, the **F-105B** variant began to enter service with the 335th Tactical Fighter Squadron in August 1958, but its early career was marred by poor serviceability rates, most of the problems encountered being allied to the highly sophisticated fire-control system. In the event, only 75 F-105Bs were built, production switching to the even more

advanced **F-105D** in 1958, and this eventually became the definitive variant, 610 being completed by January 1964, just a few months before the type began to fly combat missions in Vietnam.

Although attempts to produce a two-seat model for training duties had been made in the 1950s it was not until the advent of the **F-105F** that these succeeded, the 143 aircraft of this subtype that were manufactured having been ordered originally as F-105D single-seaters. Retaining full operational capability, the F-105F also saw extensive combat action and provided the basis for the 'Wild Weasel' surface-to-air missile suppression modification, specially configured F-105Fs undertaking this hazardous duty for much of the Vietnam War. At a later date, approximately 60 were fitted out with an internally mounted jamming system and other mission-related equipment, these being known as **F-105G** aircraft.

After a service career spanning some 25 years, the last airworthy Thunderchiefs were retired by the Air Force Reserve during February 1984.

Specification
Republic F-105D Thunderchief
Type: single-seat strike fighter

The original F-105 production version was the F-105B, seen here in the markings of the 335th TFS, 4th TFW at Seymour-Johnson AFB. This was the only front-line wing to operate this model.

Powerplant: one Pratt & Whitney J75-P-19W turbojet rated at 7802-kg (17,200-lb) dry thrust and 11113-kg (24,500-lb) afterburning thrust; thrust could be increased to 12020 kg (26,500 lb) for 60 seconds by the use of water injection
Performance: maximum speed 2237 km/h (1,390 mph) at 10970 m (36,000 ft); initial climb rate (clean) 10485 m (34,400 ft) per minute; service ceiling 15850 m (52,000 ft); tactical radius 1480 km (920 miles) with two Bullpup missiles and three drop tanks; ferry range 3845 km (2,390 miles)
Weights: empty 12701 kg (28,000 lb); normal loaded (clean) 17252 kg (38,034 lb); maximum take-off 23835 kg (52,546 lb)

Bombed-up and headed for Vietnam, this F-105D carries conventional bombs, some fitted with fuse extenders which ensured the bomb exploded before it buried itself in the mud. These were commonly referred to as 'daisy-cutters'.

Dimensions: span 10.65 m (34 ft 11¼ in); length 19.51 m (64 ft 0 in); height 5.99 m (19 ft 8 in); wing area 35.77 m² (385 sq ft)
Armament: one 20-mm M61A1 Vulcan rotary-barrel cannon, plus up to 5443 kg (12,000 lb) of external ordnance including AIM-9 Sidewinder air-to-air missiles, AGM-12 Bullpup air-to-surface missiles, conventional bombs, napalm and rockets

---

Convair F-106 Delta Dart

USA

A substantially improved development of the F-102A Delta Dagger, the **Convair F-106 Delta Dart** began life as the **F-102B** and was intended to fulfil the 1954 'Ultimate Interceptor' requirement. Work on the F-102B got under way during the early 1950s, the first formal contract being awarded in November 1955 and calling for an initial batch of 17 aircraft. But by June 1956 it was fast becoming apparent that the proposed F-102B would differ significantly from its predecessor and it was therefore decided to redesignate it F-106.

Flight testing of the new interceptor began on 26 December 1956, and while early USAF trials revealed great promise subsequent evaluation revealed deficiencies in the areas of acceleration and maximum speed; Convair therefore incorporated a few modifications to achieve the desired objectives. Inevitably this resulted in delay which, coupled with the USAF decision also to purchase the McDonnell F-101B, almost brought about cancellation in 1957. Finally, it was decided to continue with both types but this in turn greatly reduced planned acquisition, total production of the Delta Dart being just 340 instead of the 1,000 originally envisaged.

Of this figure, 277 emerged as single-seat **F-106A** interceptors, this variant entering service with the 498th Fighter Interceptor Squadron at Geiger AFB, Washington, in 1959, whilst the remaining 63 were tandem two-

seat **F-106B** aircraft for training tasks with effect from July 1960.

Despite the numerous problems encountered in development and early service, the Delta Dart proved to be a fine interceptor and progressive modification enabled it to keep pace with improvements being made in the field of air defence. Today, it still equips three front-line units as well as four Air National Guard squadrons, but the phase-out process has begun and it now seems likely that the Delta Dart will disappear from the active inventory in about 1987-8.

Specification
Convair F-106A Delta Dart
Type: single-seat all-weather interceptor
Powerplant: one Pratt & Whitney J75-P-17 turbojet rated at 7802-kg (17,200-lb) dry thrust and 11113-kg (24,500-lb) afterburning thrust
Performance: maximum speed 2454 km/h (1,525 mph) at 12190 m

Delta Darts flew in colourful markings, and this F-106A of the 49th Fighter Interceptor Squadron is no exception. This unit was based at Griffiss AFB, near Rome, New York.

(40,000 ft); initial climb rate 12130 m (39,800 ft) per minute; service ceiling 17375 m (57,000 ft); combat radius 925 km (575 miles) on internal fuel
Weights: empty 10726 kg (23,646 lb); maximum take-off 17554 kg (38,700 lb)
Dimensions: span 11.67 m (38 ft 1½ in); length 21.56 m (70 ft 8¾ in); height 6.18 m (20 ft 3¼ in); wing area 58.65 m² (631.3 sq ft)
Armament: various combinations of AIR-2A Genie, AIR-2B Super Genie,

The Delta Dart soldiered on in the defence of the United States, slowly being replaced by the F-15 Eagle. Several others serve on test units, such as this Weapons Development F-106A.

AIM-4F Falcon and AIM-4G Falcon air-to-air weapons carried internally; aircraft with the 'Sixshooter' modification can carry one 20-mm M61A1 Vulcan rotary-barrel cannon

Modern Strike Aircraft

A new breed of strike aircraft emerged in the 1950s, capable of delivering nuclear as well as conventional weapons over considerable range at high subsonic speeds and increasingly low altitudes. These warplanes were amongst the classics of their breed, and many served long and fruitfully, being capable of constant upgrade.

By the late 1940s several countries recognized that penetration of defended airspace would require attack aircraft capable of flying low and fast over long distances so they could pass under the lower edge of an enemy's surveillance radar and its associated anti-aircraft weapons. Many forces set their sights on Mach 2 performance, a speed reached only at great cost and at great height where no manned aircraft can survive except in airspace devoid of modern defences.

From the mid-1960s the conventional attack and nuclear strike aircraft that entered service generally had maximum speeds below that of sound, especially when encumbered with external bomb loads. Ironically, the Royal Navy's Blackburn Buccaneer, which was scorned for its low maximum speed but had a capacious internal weapon bay, could fly with a 1,814 kg (4,000 lb) bomb-load for long distances at treetop height faster than its supersonic rivals, and using less than half the fuel!

The Vought A-7 Corsair II, McDonnell Douglas A-4 Skyhawk and Grumman A-6 Intruder were all important attack types that served in large numbers despite the fact that they found it hard to

The F-117 Nighthawk was the first operational aircraft to employ 'stealthiness'. An attack type rather than a true strike aircraft, it is used for high-precision bombing operations.

deliver ordnance at speeds much beyond 740 km/h (460 mph). At the upper end of the scale of size and cost, however, was the monster Rockwell (now Boeing) B-1A, which was designed for Mach 2 at high altitude. It was hopelessly vulnerable there, though, and was slowly transmogrified into the slower, low-level B-1B Lancer.

Today's attack aircraft needs stealth quality, for if its presence is not detected it will not be shot down; conversely, if it is detected, it will be shot down no matter how fast it flies. In the absence of stealth, a comprehensive electronic system for detecting hostile threats is essential, as are fast-reacting countermeasure systems. The quality of

'stealthiness' was evident in the Lockheed (now Lockheed Martin) F-117 Nighthawk 'stealth fighter', an airplane of very low observability designed for attacks on high-value targets with precision weapons. Since the early 1980s stealthiness has been a key requisite of all new combat aircraft, and is reflected in the new designs.

Dassault Mirage IVA

When France decided to create its nuclear deterrent in 1954 the size of aircraft needed was almost that of the B-58, with two afterburning J75 engines. Finally the bold decision was taken to build a smaller supersonic bomber, unable to fly a return trip but relying heavily on inflight-refuelling from a force of 14 Boeing C-135F tankers. The **Dassault Mirage IVA** was thus designed around two of the existing Atar engines, with an airframe derived from an unbuilt night-fighter similar to a scaled-up Mirage III. The slim fuselage has a refuelling probe in the nose, pilot and navigator/systems operator in tandem Martin-Baker BM4 seats, a mapping radar with a circular radome bulge just ahead of the recess for the bomb, and engine ducts with inlets similar to the half-cone centrebody type of the Mirage III. Bogie main gears with non-skid brakes and large tail parachutes assist recovery at short airbases in friendly territory. Dassault built 62 from 1963, a 1970s modification being addition of wing hardpoints for heavy conventional bomb loads. In the late 1990s the Armée de l'Air still flew five **Mirage IVP** aircraft for the combined strike and reconnaissance roles. These are **Mirage IVP** conversions with updated electronics and the ability to carry and launch the ASMP nuclear-armed stand-off missile. Another 12 aircraft, were Mirage IVA conversions to the **Mirage IVR** standard for operational and strategic reconnaissance.

Specification
Dassault Mirage IVA
Type: supersonic bomber
Powerplant: two 7000-kg (15,432-lb) thrust SNECMA Atar 9K afterburning turbojets
Performance: maximum speed (brief dash at high altitude) 2340 km/h (1,454 mph); sustained speed 1966 km/h (1,222 mph) at 18290 m (60,000 ft); radius in the nuclear role with 12190 m (40,000 ft) cruise 1240 km (770 miles); ferry range 4000 km (2,485 miles)
Weights: empty 14500 kg (31,967 lb); maximum take-off 33475 kg (73,800 lb)
Dimensions: span 11.85 m (38 ft 10.5 in); length 23.5 m (77 ft 1 in); height 5.40 m (17 ft 8.5 in); wing area 78.0 m² (839.6 sq ft)

Above: The original weapon of the IVA was the 65-kilotonne AN 22 nuclear bomb seen here recessed into the belly. Some IVAs retain this weapon, but with a quick-retard system added for use in the low-level role. Other aircraft have been equipped to carry HE bombs.

Below: All Mirage IVA bombers are camouflaged. Some 19 aircraft were later rebuilt for service until 1996 carrying the long range ASMP nuclear missile of 100,150 kilotonnes yield.

Dassault-Breguet Mirage 2000N

Though externally similar in appearance to the original Mirage III of 1956, the **Dassault-Breguet Mirage 2000** is a totally new aircraft. In structure, aerodynamic design, flight-control system, radar, engine, cockpit and weapons it represents an enormous advance over all previous Mirages, and in particular marks a rejection of the costly multi-role formula previously attempted in Dassault's ACF (Avion de Combat Futur). The ACF was abandoned in 1975, when work on the Mirage 2000 began, and the first Mirage 2000 flew on 10 March 1978. Initial production was of the basic Mirage 2000C1 fighter which entered service at Creil in June 1984.

Subsequently Dassault-Breguet was given a contract to develop the **Mirage 2000N** (N for *nucléaire*) to replace the Mirage IIIE in air-to-surface attack roles. Though inevitably a fixed-geometry aircraft with a large delta wing is the wrong shape for full-throttle attack at sea level, the Mirage 2000N is restressed to fly at speeds up to 1110 km/h (690 mph) at treetop height, though the rough ride would certainly affect crew efficiency. Two crew are carried, cutting slightly into fuselage tankage, the navigator having extra displays fed by the new Thomson-CSF/ESD Antilope V radar which has a terrain-following mode. Other new equipment includes twin inertial platforms and augmented ECM installations. The first prototype Mirage 2000N flew on 3 February 1983. In service with the Armée de l'Air from early 1987, this version will normally fly with two 1700-litre (374-Imp gal) drop tanks, carrying the ASMP standoff nuclear missile. Other loads are possible for tactical use, as listed below.

Specification
Dassault-Breguet Mirage 2000N
Type: two-seat attack bomber
Powerplant: one SNECMA M53-5 afterburning bypass turbojet rated at 9000-kg (19,842-lb) thrust with maximum afterburner
Performance: maximum speed at low level, with eight bombs plus two AAMs 1110 km/h (690 mph); service ceiling 18000 m (59,055 ft), where speed can easily exceed Mach 2 (clean); range with two tanks more than 1850 km (1,150 miles)

The prototype Mirage 2000N is seen here turning to begin its take-off, carrying two tanks and two self-defence Matra Magic AAMs. The two-seat 2000N is strengthened to fly at 600 kts at low level (Tornados are cleared to 800 kts).

Weights: empty (basic Mirage 2000 fighter) 7400 kg (16,314 lb); maximum take-off (fighter) 16500 kg (36,376 lb)
Dimensions: span 9.00 m (29 ft 6.3 in); length 14.55 m (47 ft 9 in); height not stated; wing area 41.0 m² (441.3 sq ft)
Armament: pylons under fuselage and wings for theoretical maximum load of 6000 kg (13,228 lb) of various bombs, rockets or missiles including Exocet, AS.30 Laser, Durandal or Belouga; primary weapon will be a single ASMP ramjet-propelled standoff nuclear attack missile; in all cases two Magic AAMs can be carried on the outer wing pylons for self-defence

A Mirage 2000N prototype carries a dummy ASMP as well as two tanks and Magic AAMs. With a yield of 100-150 kilotonnes, ASMP will fly up to 62 miles (100 km) lifted by the projecting inlet ducts to its ramjet engine.

  UK/FRANCE

SEPECAT Jaguar

Developed jointly by BAC (now BAe) and Breguet (now Dassault-Breguet), who formed the consortium to manage the programme, the **SEPECAT Jaguar** was created to meet a need by the RAF and Armée de l'Air for a low-level all-weather attack aircraft and, especially for the latter buyer, advanced jet and weapons training. Slightly different versions were produced, with one or two seats, for the two original customers, and 403 aircraft of these basic four sub-types were delivered. Export sales have been the responsibility of the UK partner (often in head-on competition with the French partner) and have so far taken sales beyond 550. The **Jaguar International** has more powerful engines and is available with radar and other sensors, Magic AAMs and certain aerodynamic improvements which enhance air-to-air and anti-ship capability as well as giving true all-weather avionics. Orders

A Jaguar GR.Mk 1 of RAF No. 54 Sqn, normally based at Coltishall, Norfolk.

worth £108 million were flown out to Oman and Ecuador, and Oman has placed a repeat order. India placed an order which in full will be worth over £1 billion. A substantial sale has been made to Nigeria. All versions have complete ability to operate from short grass airstrips or any good section of highway. Not least of the good results achieved has been a level of maintenance man-hours roughly one-third that demanded by previous combat aircraft.

Specification
SEPECAT Jaguar International
Type: multi-role tactical attack fighter
Powerplant: two 3810-kg (8,400-lb) thrust Rolls-Royce Turboméca Adour Mk 811 afterburning turbofans
Performance: maximum speed at high altitude 1750 km/h (1,087 mph), and at low altitude 1350 km/h (839 mph); attack radius on a lo-lo-lo mission 917 km (570 miles)
Weights: empty 7000 kg (15,432 lb); maximum take-off 15700 kg (34,612 lb)

Dimensions: span 8.69 m (28 ft 6 in); length excluding probe 15.52 m (50 ft 11 in); height 4.89 m (16 ft 0.5 in); wing area 24.18 m² (260.27 sq ft)
Armament: two 30-mm Aden or DEFA cannon; seven hardpoints plus two overwing AAM pylons for total of 4763 kg (10,500 lb) of varied stores

French Jaguars have a different equipment fit from those of the RAF; this example comes from EC 11 at Toul-Rosières.

Hawker Siddeley Buccaneer

For many years derided (because it was not supersonic) by the RAF and Fleet Street, the **Hawker Siddeley Buccaneer** is one of the best attack aircraft of its era, and it was designed to a far-seeing Admiralty requirement. The latter laid stress on the ability to attack at very low level to evade detection by enemy radars, and the 1953-4 design eventually used extraordinarily advanced boundary-layer control, ejecting engine bleed air through slits ahead of the flaps, ailerons and tailplane. This enabled all aerodynamic surfaces to be made markedly smaller, in turn increasing sea-level speed and greatly reducing buffet. Another good feature was a substantial internal weapon bay, so that with a 4,000-lb (1814-kg) bombload the derided Buccaneer is faster than a Phantom or Mirage with the same load (and, without afterburner, far more fuel efficient). The Gyron Junior-powered **Buccaneer S.Mk 1** (60) was succeeded by the much better **Buccaneer S.Mk 2** with more powerful fan engines, the first production example flying on 5 June 1964. Originally all went to the Fleet Air Arm, apart from 16 **Buccaneer Mk 50** aircraft for the SAAF with boost rocket packs and AS.30 missiles, but survivors were transferred to the RAF (70 out of 84) being designated **Buccaneer S.Mk 2A** with RAF avionics and Martel equipment. A further 43 **Buccaneer S.Mk 2B** aircraft were built to RAF specification, the first flying in January 1970. Immensely capable and popular, the Buccaneer had unique qualities and remained in service in the maritime attack and laser designation roles, up to 1994.

Above: A Buccaneer of No. 16 Sqn, which re-formed on the type at Laarbruch, Germany, in 1972. This squadron has since converted to the Tornado GR.Mk 1.

Right: in the 1980s the Buccaneer sported B-class red/blue national insignia, but this aircraft was engaged on Ministry trials with various external loads.

Below: The Buccaneer S.Mk 2s of the RAF's No.208 Squadron based at Honington operated in the maritime attack role with bombs and missiles.

Specification
Hawker Siddeley Buccaneer S.Mk 2B
Type: low-level attack aircraft
Powerplant: two 5103-kg (11,250-lb) thrust Rolls-Royce Spey Mk 101 turbofans
Performance: maximum speed at low altitude with full internal bombload 1110 km/h (690 mph); tactical radius with internal fuel on a hi-lo-hi mission 998 km (620 miles)
Weights: empty 13540 kg (29,850 lb); maximum take-off 28123 kg (62,000 lb)
Dimensions: span 13.41 m (44 ft 0 in); length 19.33 m (63 ft 5 in); height 4.95 m (16 ft 3 in); wing area 47.82 m^2 (514.7 sq ft)
Armament: internal bay for four 454-kg (1,000-lb) bombs, reconnaissance pod or LR tank; four wing pylons each for triple 454-kg (1,000-lb) bombs or various other stores

---

Panavia Tornado IDS

Bearing its nationality code letter and unit aircraft number at the top of the fin, this Tornado belongs to the AMI (Italian air force) but is on the strength of the Trinational Tornado Training Unit at RAF Cottesmore.

The world's first combat aircraft to be developed by three nations jointly, to meet the requirements of four national customers (RAF, Luftwaffe, Marineflieger and Italian AMI), the **Panavia Tornado** is the world's best long-range low-level interdiction aircraft. No other aircraft combines two small and fuel-efficient engines, a crew of two with an outstandingly modern low-drag tandem cockpit, swing-wings for efficient subsonic loiter but treetop-height dash at 1483 km/h (921 mph) and the ability to carry every tactical store in the European NATO armoury. Despite this, the Tornado is a relatively small aircraft, with a shorter body than the F/A-18 and a wing so much smaller that the gust response in the low high-speed attack role (at speeds 35 per cent higher than the limit for the US aircraft) is more than 10 times better. Including four of the six pre-series aircraft, the initial customer procurement by 1998 totalled 322 for Germany, 99 for Italy and 228 for the UK, supplemented by 96 aircraft for Saudi Arabia. In 1998 the UK received 142 aircraft upgraded from Tornado GR.Mk 1 to Tornado GR.Mk 4 standard with enhanced 'stealthiness' and improved nav/attack systems as well as the ability to carry a wider assortment of external loads. Germany and Italy are pursuing similar upgrades.

Specification
Panavia Tornado IDS (RAF Tornado GR.Mk 1)
Type: All-weather multi-role attack and reconnaissance aircraft
Powerplant: two 7167-kg (15,800-lb) thrust Turbo-Union RB.199 Mk 101 (from 1983, uprated Mk 103) augmented turbofans
Performance: maximum speed, clean at high altitude 2414 km/h (1,500 mph); radius (on a hi-lo-lo-hi mission with 3628 kg/8,000 lb of bombs) 1390 km (863 miles)
Weights: empty about 14000 kg (30,865 lb); maximum over 26490 kg (58,400 lb)
Dimensions: span (swept) 8.60 m (28 ft 2.5 in); length 16.70 m (54 ft 9.5 in); height 5.70 m (18ft 8.5 in); wing area not stated
Armament: two 27-mm Mauser cannon; total of 8165 kg (18,000 lb) of disposable stores on two tandem fuselage pylons plus four swivelling wing pylons, plus centreline for multi-sensor reconnaissance pod

Below: Another Italian AMI Tornado, this time based in Italy, showing a typical conventional attack load of eight BL.755 cluster bombs, two self-defence Sidewinders and two Elettronica ECM pods. Britain, Germany and Italy all use different ECM jammer pods.

Aeritalia/EMBRAER AMX

This extremely attractive light attack aircraft was launched to meet a need of the Aeronautica Militare Italiana to replace the Fiat G91 and Lockheed F-104G. The Brazilian air staff decided they had a need for a similar aircraft, mainly to replace the EMBRAER AT-26 Xavante (itself a licensed Italian design, the Aermacchi M.B. 326GB). The eventual airframe team comprises Aeritalia in partnership with Aermacchi in Italy and EMBRAER in Brazil, the latter having a 30 per cent share by value made up of the complete wing, air inlets, tailplane and pylons. Aeritalia has 46 per cent, comprising the centre fuselage, wing movables, vertical tail, elevators and radome. Aermacchi has 24 per cent, comprising the nose fuselage (with cockpit and avionics integration), tailcone and canopy.

The emphasis of the **AMX** has wisely been on simplicity and affordability. Useful short-field ability has been achieved by a good thrust/weight ratio and excellent high-lift devices. The AMI ordered 187 AMX aircraft, while the Brazilian air force is receiving 64 with different avionics and guns. Both versions have a fuselage bay which can hold three different types of reconnaissance pallet or other mission avionics. The first prototype flew on 15 May 1984. Other variants are the AMX(T) two-seat trainer (51 aircraft for Italy and 15 for Brazil respectively) and the AMX(ATA) combined light attack and trainer variant (24 for Venezuela). A number of upgrade programmes are being implemented.

Specification
Aeritalia/Aermacchi/EMBRAER AMX
Type: single-seat tactical attack and reconnaissance aircraft
Powerplant: one 5000-kg (11,032-lb) thrust Italian-built Rolls-Royce Spey 807 turbofan
Performance: maximum speed not disclosed but about 1130 km/h (700 mph) clean at sea level; attack radius with full allowances (2722-kg/6,000-lb bombs on a hi-lo-hi mission)

520 km (321 miles)
Weights: empty 6000 kg (13,228 lb); maximum take-off 11500 kg (25,353 lb)
Dimensions: span (over AAMs) 10.00 m (32 ft 9.7 in); length 13.575 m (44 ft 6.5 in); height 4.576 m (15 ft 0.2 in); wing area 21.0 m² (226 sq ft)
Armament: (Italian) one 20-mm M61A1 multi-barrel cannon with 350 rounds, (Brazilian) two 30-mm DEFA 553 cannon each with 130 rounds, plus a total of 3500 kg (7,716 lb) of ordnance

The first prototype AMX was tragically lost early in its test programme, test pilot Quarantelli succumbing to the injuries he sustained. The second aircraft took over flight development at once, after its roll-out on 5 July 1984.

hung on five external pylons, not including two Sidewinder self-defence air-combat AAMs on wingtip rails

---

Sukhoi Su-24 'Fencer'

Just as TsAGI produced the shapes adopted by all the major constructors of supersonic aircraft of the 1955-80 era, so did it develop both an interim swing-wing scheme for modifying existing aircraft (applied to the Su-7 and Tu-22) and also an ideal shape for new designs. The latter was adopted by the MiG bureau for the MiG-23/27 and also by Sukhoi for its **Sukhoi Su-24**, the latter having exactly twice the power of the MiG aircraft. Unlike the MiG the new Sukhoi has been developed purely for long-range all-weather attack, and there is no known fighter version (though parts may be used in the Su-27 'Ram-K'). In many respects the Su-24 is similar to the American F-111, though it is smaller, lighter, much more powerful and has a belly that can be festooned with weapons. Features include a large forward-looking radar, side-by-side seats, twin guns with bulged ventral fairings partly formed by the twin airbrakes, variable lateral inlets and twin ventral fins on the flanks of the wide fuselage. A very heavy load of at least 25 different types of external store can be carried, and missions can be flown to the tip of Brittany, Scotland or as far as Spain. Called 'Fencer' by NATO, this efficient and well-equipped aircraft has given the Soviet FA (Frontal Aviation) a quantita-

Frontal Aviation attack aircraft have recently been seen in various colours, and though this Su-24 shows a commonly used camouflage, some aircraft of this type have even been seen unpainted in bright polished metal!

Looking up at an Su-24 with the wings at minimum sweep. In the landing pattern, this aircraft has the twin speed brakes part-open. NATO codenames have been applied to three positively identified variants of this formidable aircraft, but details are unknown.

tive edge over the West and also a large qualitative one. The Tornado is a Western counterpart, but it is smaller and later in timing, and is being produced at a slower rate.

Specification
Sukhoi Su-24M 'Fencer-D'
Type: all-weather attack aircraft
Powerplant: two 11,200-kg (24,691-lb) afterburning thrust NPO Saturn (Lyul'ka) AL-21F-3A turbojets
Performance: maximum speed 1435 km/h (892 mph) or Mach 1.35 at 11,000 m (36,090 ft); service ceiling 17,500 kg (57,415 ft); radius 1050 km (652 miles) on a hi-lo-hi attack mission with a 3000-kg (6,614-lb) warload and two drop tanks
Weights: empty 22,300 kg (49,163 lb); max. take-off 39,570 kg (87,235 lb)
Dimensions: span 17.6 m (57 ft 10 in) spread, 10.37 m (34 ft) swept;

length 24.6 m (80 ft 8¼ in) including probe; height 6.19 m (20 ft 3½ in); wing area 55.17 m² (594 sqft) spread, 51. m² (549 sq ft) swept
Armament: one 30-mm Gryazev-Shipunov GSh-23-6M cannon; up to 8,100 kg (17,857 lb) of disposable stores carried on nine hardpoints, comprising most types of Soviet nuclear and conventional weapons.

Another 'Fencer' in the circuit at an airfield of the GSFG (Group of Soviet Forces in Germany). In this case the twin airbrakes – which cover a gun and (it is believed)a weapon-aiming sensor – are closed. Some of the nine pylons, which give the aircraft an 8000-kg (17,637-lb) ordnance capacity, are visible.

Former USSR

Tupolev Tu-22 'Blinder'

Displayed publicly in 1961, the **Tupolev Tu-22** was larger and more powerful than previous Soviet supersonic bombers, and though it still lacked the range for many missions, it was put into production and about 250 were built in four versions, all equipped with an inflight-refuelling probe. The basic free-fall bomber, named **'Blinder-A'** by NATO, was deployed in limited numbers from 1965, but the main production centred on the **'Blinder-B'** missile-carrier and various **'Blinder-C'** reconnaissance and electronic-warfare platforms, as well as a few **'Blinder-D'** dual trainers with the instructor in a second cockpit above and behind that for the original pilot. Most versions have a large mapping and navigation radar in the pointed nose, followed by a navigator/bombardier compartment with glazed downlook windows. Aft of the pressurized cockpit section is an enormous fuselage tank, behind which is the unique engine installation on each side of the fin, with the nozzles close to the rear warning radar, ECM aerials and remote-control tail cannon. In 1983 about 125 of the 'Blinder-A' and 'Blinder-B' versions remained operational, as well as a squadron in Libya and a few in Iraq. The most active version is 'Blinder-C', of which about 40 continue to fly intensively with the AV-MF (Soviet naval air force) on maritime reconnaissance and electronic-warfare duties with various fits of cameras, IR linescan, passive receivers and, in some aircraft, ECM jammers and dis-

pensers. The free-fall bomber version has been used in action over Iran, Iraq (against Kurds), Tanzania (by Libya) and most recently against Afghan rebels by the Soviet air force.

Specification
Tupolev Tu-22 'Blinder-A/B'
Type: bomber and missile-carrier
Powerplant: believed to be two 14000-kg (30,864-lb) thrust Kolesov VD-7 afterburning turbojets
Performance: maximum speed at high altitude about 1480 km/h (920 mph) or Mach 1.4; radius on a hi-lo-hi mission with maximum bombload 3100 km (1,926 miles)
Weights: empty about 40800 kg (89,949 lb); maximum take-off 84000 kg (185,188 lb)
Dimensions: span 27.7 m (90 ft 10.5 in); length 40.53 m (132 ft 11.5 in); height 10.67 m (35 ft 0 in); wing area 145.0 m² (1,560.8 sq ft)
Armament: (A) up to 10000 kg (22,046 lb) of bombs or (B) one AS-4 'Kitchen' missile; two 23-mm tail cannon in remote-control barbette

First foreign client to be supplied with the enormous Tu-22 was Libya, which used one in anger to drop bombs during a conflict with Tanzania. Others have been used 'for real' by Iraq.

Above: Taken when Tu-22s were being delivered to Libya in April 1977, this photograph shows the original national insignia used by that country. The escorting US Navy F-4N came from VF-111 'The Sundowners'. Inflight refuelling is not fitted to Libyan Tu-22 bombers.

Below: Take-off by one of the first production Tu-22s, showing the socket above the nose for the inflight-refuelling probe (which is not fitted). The fuselage, vertical tail and inner wing survive basically unchanged in today's 'Backfire'.

Tupolev Tu-22M/Tu-26 'Backfire'

A 'Backfire-B' of the naval AVMF which had about 120 of the 255 in service in late 1984. This example is shown carrying an AS4 'Kitchen' supersonic cruise missile.

Thought for some time to be the Tu-26, the **Tupolev Tu-22M** is a powerful bombing, missile-launching and reconnaissance warplane derived from the Tu-22 with a wing with pivoting outer panels and two conventionally installed turbofans. Only nine Tu-22M-1 were built entering service in 1973. Superseded by the **Tu-22M-2 'Backfire-B'**, it was revised for better performance and offensive capability. New features were longer-span wings without the rearward-protruding pods, two 22,000-kg (48,501-lb) afterburning thrust NK-22 turbofans and revised landing gear. The Tu-22 M-2 was armed with a single Kh-22 ASM

in the lower fuselage. Later revised with two underwing missiles of the same type, increasing the max. weapons load to 21,000 kg (46,296-lb). 211 Tu-22M-2 were produced. The **Tu-22M-2 'Backfire-C'** was introduced in 1984 with an uprated powerplant, an upturned nose radome with different nav/attack radar, more versatile offensive armament, and the defensive armament reduced to one 23-mm GSh-23L cannon in the tail barbette. The Tu-22M is used by the bomber force for strategic operations and by the naval air force for electronic reconnaissance. Production ended in 1993.

Specification
Tupolev Tu-22M-3 'Backfire-C'
Type: variable-geometry strategic bomber/reconnaissance warplane
Powerplant: two 25,000-kg (55,115-lb) afterburning thrust KKBM (Kuznetsov) NK-25 turbofans
Performance: max speed 2000 km/h (1,242 mph), Mach 1.88 at 11,000 m (36,090 ft); service ceiling 13,300 m (43,635 ft); radius 2200 km (1,365 miles) on a hi-hi-hi with max warload
Weights: empty 54,000 kg (119,048 lb); max. take-off 124,400 kg (278,660 lb)
Dimensions: span 34 m (112ft 5 in) spread, 23 m (76 ft 5 in) swept; length 42.5 m (139 ft 3in); height 11 m (36ft

3 in); wing area 183.6 m² (1976 sqft) spread, 175.8 m² (1,892 sq ft) swept
Armament: one 23-mm Gryazev-Shipunov GSh-23L two-barrel cannon in a radar-controlled rear barbette; max 24,000 kg (52,910 lb) disposable stores in a lower-fuselage weapons bay and on four hardpoints.

Taken by a Swedish fighter, for which the 'Backfire' was deliberately posed, this photograph shows the highly loaded wings spread out in the cruise position. The twin 23-mm tail cannon are remotely directed by radar, and extremely comprehensive ECM is installed.

Tupolev (?) 'Blackjack'

The **Tupolev Tu-160** is the heaviest and largest bomber in the world. Tu-160 made its maiden flight on 19 December 1981 at Zhukhovskii, (Ramenskoye). Spotted by a US reconnaissance satellite before its first flight, it received the temporary designation 'Ram-P' before being redesignated as the 'Blackjack'. A combination of a variable-geometry wing planform and extensive high-lift devices provided good low-speed handling and the required field performance with the wing in the minimum-sweep position of 20°, excellent payload/range performance with the wing at 35°, and very high speed with the wing in the maximum-sweep

position of 65°. The wing sweep angle is selected manually, and the high-lift devises include full-span slats on the leading edges and double- slotted flaps on the trailing edges.

A crew of four sit side-by-side pairs. Tricycle landing gear with main units each carrying a six-wheel bogie, a 'fly-by-wire' control system, analogue cock-pit instrumentation, and a long pointed nose radome for the terrain-following and attack radar, with a fairing below it for the forward-looking TV camera used for visual weapon aiming. Intercontinental range is assured by a fully retractable inflight-refuelling probe. The warload is carried in a tandem arrangement of

two weapons bay, each 12.80 m (42 ft) long and located in the lower fuselage. Each bay houses a rotary launcher which can carry either six Kh-55M (AS-15 'Kent') cruise missiles or 12 Kh-15P (AS-16 'Kickback') 'SRAMski' defence-suppression missiles. Production continued until 1992.

Specification
Tupolev Tu-160 'Blackjack-A'
Type: variable-geometry supersonic strategic bomber and missile-launcher
Powerplant: four 25,000-kg (55,115-lb) afterburning thrust SSPE Trud (Kuznetsov) NK-321 turbofans
Performance: maximum speed

2,220 km/h (1,379.5 mph) or Mach 2,05 at 12,000 m (39,370 ft); service ceiling 15,000 m (49,215 ft); range 12,300 km (7,643 miles) with standard fuel
Weights: empty 118,000 kg (260,140 lb); maximum take-off 275,000 kg (606,261 lb)
Dimensions: span 55.70 m (182 ft 9 in) spread and 35.60 m (116 ft 9¾ in) swept; length 54.10 m (177 ft 6 in); height 13.10 m (43 ft 0 in); wing area 360.00 m²(3,875.13 sq ft)
Armament: up to 40,000 kg (88,183 lb) of nuclear and conventional weapons carried in two lower-fuselage weapons bays and on hardpoints under the wing gloves.

General Dynamics F-111

The specification by the US Air Force for a TFX (tactical fighter experimental) in 1960 demanded such long range that the final aircraft came out far too large to be effective as a fighter, but it found its true role as the world's first attack aircraft with both supersonic speed and avionics for blind first-pass attack on a point target. Winning over a Boeing-Wichita rival, the **General Dynamics F-111** flew on 21 December 1964, featuring for the first time in a production type variable-sweep 'swing wings', augmented turbofan engines and terrain-following radar. Pilot and navigator are side-by-side in a jettisonable capsule which can serve as a boat or survival shelter. The large main-gear tyres are suited to rough strips but are so located that fuselage stores are limited to an ECM pod, apart from a small weapon bay which can carry a gun. In the **F-111C** for the RAAF and **FB-111A** for SAC the wings have greater span and the gear is strengthened for greater gross weights. Thanks to enormous internal fuel (usually 19010 litres/4,182 Imp gal) range exceeds that of any other TAC type, but problems with engines, inlet ducts and avionics resulted in successive sub-types such as the **F-111A** (141 built), **F-111D** (96, advanced but costly avionics), **F-111E** (94) and **F-111F** (106, greater power and optimized avionics). SAC received 76 FB-111s, serving in two wings with normal load of two B43 bombs or two SRAM missiles internally plus up to four SRAMs externally. Grumman later rebuilt 42 F-111As as **EF-111A Raven** electronic warfare platforms, and the USAF retired its last F-111 series warplanes in 1998.

The F-111C version for the RAAF has low-thrust TF30 engines but the long-span wing as fitted to the FB-111A. Four of them have been modified to carry a multi-sensor reconnaissance pack, though they would not normally fly both reconnaissance and attack in the same mission.

Specification
General Dynamics F-111F
Type: all-weather interdiction aircraft
Powerplant: two 11385 kg (25,100 lb) thrust Pratt & Whitney TF30-100 augmented turbofans
Performance: maximum speed, clean at 12190 m (40,000 ft) 2655 km/h (1,650 mph) or Mach 2.5; range at high altitude, clean with maximum internal fuel 4707 km (2,925 miles)

Weights: empty 21537 kg; (47,481 lb); maximum take-off 45359 kg (100,000 lb)
Dimensions: span (wings spread) 19.20 m (63 ft 0 in); length 22.40 m (73 ft 6 in); height 5.22 m (17 ft 1.5 in); wing area 48.77 m^2 (525.0 sq ft)
Armament: internal bay for two B43 or other bombs or one bomb and one 20-mm M61 gun; six wing pylons for theoretical conventional load of 14288 kg (31,500 lb)

Afterburner take-off by a USAF F-111 carrying four empty MERs (multiple ejector racks). The only stores carried on the fuselage are ECM pods.

View from the right seat of an FB-111A of USAF Strategic Air Command as a companion takes on fuel from a KC-135 tanker. The technique is vital to FB-111As.

USA
Rockwell International B-1B

No aircraft in history took as long to mature as the **Rockwell (now Boeing) B-1B Lancer,** which entered USAF service in 1985 reaching operational capability in July 1986 as replacement for the Boeing B-52. The latter has already had to soldier on several times longer than planned, and is costing increasingly more to update and still falling short on penetrative capability. The original **B-1A,** first flown in December 1974, was a Mach-2 high-altitude nuclear bomber, with limited low-level conventional-warfare capability. The B-1B, which looks much the same, is designed to fly at low level on terrain-following radar, with extremely heavy loads of varied weapons, and to use the world's most comprehensive avionic systems for navigation, weapon delivery and, in particular, protection against hostile defence systems. Unlike the original four prototypes it will have plain fixed engine inlets, four ordinary ejection seats and no special provision for supersonic flight. Fuel capacity is greatly increased for global range even without

refuelling, the weapon-bay bulkhead is movable for carriage of such long stores as the ALCM, and the structure is strengthened and specially designed and coated to reduce radar cross-section (apparent size on enemy radars) to one-tenth that of the B-1A, which itself was one-tenth that of a B-52H. Production totalled 100 aircraft, of which 95 remained in service late in 1998. The aircraft are currently being upgraded in their electronics and in the variety of weapons they can carry.

Specification
Rockwell International B-1B
Type: strategic bomber

This B-1A prototype is shown with conventional ejection seats instead of a capsule, fixed inlets and other updates, but retains the dorsal spine and long pointed tailcone.

Powerplant: four 13563-kg (29,900-lb) thrust General Electric F101-102 augmented turbofans
Performance: maximum speed, clean at 152 m (500 ft) 1207 km/h (750 mph) or Mach 0.99; range with maximum internal fuel, maximum missile load and unrefuelled over 11265 km (7,000 miles)
Weights: empty 72575 kg (160,000 lb); maximum take-off 216364 kg (477,000 lb)
Dimensions: span variable 23.84 to 41.67 m (78 ft 2.5 in to 136 ft 8.5 in); length 45.78 m (150 ft 2.5 in); height 10.24 m (33 ft 7.25 in); wing area 181.2 m² (1,950.0 sq ft)

Armament: eight ALCM internally plus 14 externally, or 24 SRAM internally plus 14 externally, or 12 B28 or B43 nuclear bombs internally plus 8/14 externally, or 24 internal and 14 external B61 or B83 nuclear bombs, or 36287 kg (80,000 lb) of conventional bombs

The fourth B-1A prototype is air-refuelled by an Air National Guard KC-135A. In fact it was the second B-1A that was brought up most closely to B-1B standard, the most externally obvious change being removal of the long dorsal spine.

ISRAEL
IAI Lavi

Fortified by the success of the Nesher and the Kfir, Israel Aircraft Industries (IAI) agreed in 1976 to create a completely new multi-role combat aircraft for service from the 1990s. The resulting **IAI Lavi** programme was launched in 1980 with full-scale development by 1982, and was specifically designed to meet the requirements of the Israeli air force for a new-technology warplane configured primarily for the tactical air combat and attack roles in succession initially to the McDonnell Douglas A-4 Skyhawk and the Kfir. At first it was expected that collaborative deal would be reached. While Pratt & Whitney had an interest in collaboration in the propulsion aspect, the only major subcontract was placed with

Grumman, whose great experience in advanced composite structures was exploited in the design and manufacture of the wing.
Like most agile air combat warplanes the Lavi had a canard foreplane, swept back and close-coupled to the wing and located, in line with the cockpit. A ventral air inlet was adopted, ahead of the nose unit of the tricycle landing gear whose main units retracted into the fuselage. A turbojet engine was selected. A very significant spin-off of the engine choice was that Israel was one of the largest operators of the McDonnell Douglas F-4 Phantom, for which the PW1120 engine (a turbojet derivative of the F100 turbofan) was the favoured unit The first two-seater prototypes made their maiden flights

in December 1986 and March 1987. Political opposition in the USA, which was funding the programme, cancelled the Lavi in favour of the purchase of GD F-16 Fighting Falcon multi-role fighters. Elements of the prototypes were used in the third Lavi, which first flew in September 1989 as a demonstrator for the advanced technologies which Israel has marketed to China.

Specification
IAI Lavi
Type: tactical fighter
Powerplant: one 20,620-lb (9353-kg) afterburning thrust Pratt & Whitney PW1120 turbojet

Performance: max speed 1965 km/h (1,22 mph) or Mach 1.85 at 10,975 m (36,000 ft); range 213 km (1,324 miles) on a hi-lo-hi attack mission with two 454-kg (1,000-lb) or six 113-kg (250-lb) bombs
Weights: empty about 703 kg (15,500 lb); maximum take-off 19,277 kg (42.500 lb)
Dimensions: span 8.78 m (47 ft 9⅔ in); length 14.57 m (47 ft 9⅔ in); height 4.78 m (15 ft 8 1/4 in); wing area 33.05 m² (355.76 sq ft)
Armament: hardpoints under the fuselage and wing for a wide assortment of air-to-air and air-to-surface missiles, 'dumb' and 'smart' bombs, multiple rocket launchers and drop tanks

271

Saab 37 Viggen

A Saab SF37 reconnaissance Viggen from wing F21, which also uses another multi-sensor version, the SH37. The latter has nose radar, like the attack AJ37 but unlike this chisel-nose machine, which is depicted with a Red Baron recon pod.

By 1960 the Swedish air board had once again taken the bold decision to procure a new-generation combat aeroplane from Sweden's own industry. As before it was agreed the same basic type should be developed for multiple roles, and on this occasion particular emphasis was wisely placed on the ability to operate away from known airfields. STOL capability was demanded, for safe operation from country roads, and this was achieved by selecting a giant rear wing and a large flapped canard, tandem-wheel main gears strong enough for no-flare landings, and a thrust reverser. The first **Saab 37** prototype flew on 8 February 1967, and the System 37 was subsequently developed as an integral part of Sweden's Stril 60 electronic defence system.

Several versions were subsequently produced for the Swedish air force (Flygvapen). First, and most numerous, was the **AJ37** attack variant. Even this initial model contains some 600 kg (1,323 lb) of special avionics, including a large Ericsson radar, comprehensive navaids, two quite different aids to blind landing and very advanced weapon-delivery systems and ECM, some of the latter being housed in external pods. Closely related versions were the SF37 and SH37 reconnaissance aircraft and SK37 dual trainer, production of these four sub-types

together totalling 180. Since 1979 deliveries have continued of the completely revised JA37 interceptor, which also has considerable attack potential as a secondary role.

Specification
Saab AJ37 Viggen
Type: single-seat attack aircraft
Powerplant: one Volvo Flygmotor RM8A augmented turbofan rated with maximum afterburner at 11800-kg (26,015-lb) thrust
Performance: maximum speed, clean Mach 1.2 at low level, and over Mach 2 (2130 km/h/1,323 mph) at high altitude; tactical radius with external weapons on a hi-lo-hi mission 1000 km (621 miles)
Weights: empty 11700 kg (25,794 lb); maximum take-off 20500 kg (45,195 lb)
Dimensions: span 10.60 m (34 ft 9.5 in); length 16.30 m (53 ft 5.7 in); height 5.80 m (19 ft 0.2 in); wing area (main wing) 46.0 m² (495.2 sq ft)
Armament: seven pylons (two more optional) for all types of bomb, rocket-launcher, gun pod and various missiles including Saab RB04E or RB05A, RB75 (Maverick) or RB24 Sidewinder or RB28 Falcon AAMs

Above: Head-on aspect of an AJ37 attack Viggen over the Baltic islands with two of the big RB04E anti-ship cruise missiles. The usual centreline store is a long-range fuel tank, which is also carried by reconnaissance Viggens.

Below: An AJ37 attack Viggen from wing F7, armed with four pods each housing six formidable 135-mm air/surface rockets. The curved grey rectangle on the side of the rear fuselage is a thrust-reverser outlet.

Modern Attack Aircraft

The modern attack warplane is optimized for operation over the battlefield and is capable of lifting an assortment of conventional weapons and delivering them accurately. The nature of the attack task demands considerable ability to survive combat damage, and also at times the ability to loiter over the battlefield.

The modern attack aircraft occupies an ill-defined area between the bomber and the COIN (counter-insurgency) aircraft. It represents an attempt to combine the heavy weapons load and comprehensive nav/attack and self-protection systems of the former with the light weight and agility of the latter. Of course, there must be compromises, for this idea is unattainable in the fullest sense despite recent advances in aerodynamics and electronics, so each new aircraft type is designed to fulfil a specific need or adapted from a fighter with certain roles in mind.

A study of attack aircraft reveals a diversity of design philosophies from the slow but well-protected Fairchild Republic A-10 Thunderbolt II to the dedicated attack version of the sleek, Mach 2 Saab 37 Viggen, with every degree of sophistication or simplicity in between. The majority of these aircraft perform solely in the close-support or attack roles: that is to say, they carry only conventional weaponry. The aircraft are often optimized for short-range operations over the battlefield or as far as the enemy's forward airfields and supply dumps, and therefore fly in the dedicated

A McDonnell Douglas F-4G 'Wild Weasel' aircraft carrying (front to back) AGM-88A HARM, AGM-65D Maverick, ALQ-119 jammer pod, AGM-78 ARM and AGM-45 Shrike.

tactical role. Close air support, to which the BAe Harrier was ideally suited, sometimes involves attacks under the supervision of a forward air controller to take out targets possibly only a short distance from friendly troops in the field.

Faster, larger, more advanced types, normally equipped with radar and other aids to all-weather operation, have the option of carrying nuclear weapons, and as such are classified as strike aircraft. The definitions 'strike' and 'attack' are often confused, since some aircraft fall into both categories. The Viggen would make an excellent strike aircraft but is in the attack category because Sweden does not possess nuclear weapons. Many attack types are employed in the tactical reconnaissance role, while the USAF modified some of its McDonnell Douglas F-4 Phantom II aircraft to the highly specialized 'Wild Weasel' task of detecting, then knocking out enemy radars. Finally retired only in 1998, these merit inclusion in this overview of the battlefield work-horses of the air war.

Mikoyan-Gurevich MiG-23BN/MiG-27

Mikoyan-Gurevich MiG-23BN 'Flogger-F' of the Czech air force based at Pardubice, east of Prague.

MiG-23BN of the Algerian air force, one of 40 delivered.

A specialized ground-attack version of the MiG-23 fighter, with which it shares the NATO reporting name 'Flogger', the **Mikoyan-Gurevich MiG-27** differs from its companion in some respects. The most significant of these are the fixed-geometry air inlets and afterburner nozzles, which indicate a simplicity of design permitted by the mission requirement of only transonic speed, compared with Mach 2.35 attainable by the MiG-23. First of the MiG-27 variants, the **MiG-27 'Flogger-D'** features a nose sharply tapered from the windscreen and containing a laser ranger and marked-target seeker, whilst a six-barrel 23-mm gun is positioned beneath the belly. Pilot vision is improved for attack missions by a raised seat and canopy, and low-pressure tyres are compatible with rough-field operation. Issued in quantity to the Soviet tactical air force, Frontal Aviation, the 'Flogger-D' has an export counterpart in the **MiG-23BN 'Flogger-F'**, which retains the original 125070-kg (27,557-lb) R-29 afterburning turbojet (plus variable inlets and nozzle) and twin-barrel cannon. The similar **MiG-23BN 'Flogger-H'**, another 'high-speed'

variant, is distinguished by two avionics pods astride the lower fuselage, forward of the nosewheel doors. In 1981, the **MiG-27 'Flogger-J'** was first noted, this differing from the 'Flogger-D' in further nose revision, with a lip on the top and a blister fairing beneath. Podded guns on two wing pylons have

barrels which can be depressed for attacking ground targets without recourse to a steep dive. India began licensed manufacture of the 'Flogger-J' in 1985. The last Russian 'Floggers' were retired in the mid-1990s.

Specification
MiG-27 'Flogger-D'

Type: single-seat variable-geometry ground attack and tactical nuclear strike aircraft

Armament: one fixed six-barrel 23-mm gun; five weapon pylons and two rear-fuselage racks for stores including AS-7 'Kerry' ASMs and self-defence AA-2 'Atoll' AAMs up to a maximum weight of at least 4000 kg (8,820 lb)

Powerplant: one 11500-kg (25,353-lb) thrust Tumansky R-29B afterburning turbojet

Performance: maximum speed Mach 1.5 at altitude; maximum speed Mach 1.1 at sea level; service ceiling 16000 m (52,495 ft); combat radius on a lo-lo-lo mission 390 km (242 miles) with four 500-kg (1,102-lb) bombs and two AA-2s

Weight: maximum take-off 18000 kg (39,863 lb)

Dimensions: span, full extension (16° sweep) 14.25 m (46 ft 9 in), fully swept (72°) 8.17 m (26 ft 9½ in); length 16.00 m (52 ft 6 in); height 4.35 m (14 ft 4 in) wing area, spread 27.26 m² (293.4 sq ft)

AS-7 'Kerry' missiles can be carried by the MiG-27 on fuselage and glove pylons. The protrusion on the wing leading edge above the pylon is believed to be connected with this air-to-surface missile.

Sukhoi Su-7

Egyptian air force Su-7BMK strike aircraft have been refitted with a British nav/attack system. The aircraft is very popular with its pilots but is hampered by extremely short range.

Though criticized for its poor payload/range capabilities, the obsolescent **Sukhoi Su-7** possesses the saving graces of excellent handling qualities, good low-level gust response and manoeuvrability. Remaining in service with 15 air arms, although almost re-

placed within Soviet front-line units, it has seen action on several occasions during wars in the Middle East and Indian sub-continent. First flown in 1955, the aircraft entered service four years later in its **Su-7B** form, under the NATO reporting name **'Fitter-A'**, and rapidly established itself as the standard fighter-bomber of the Soviet air force and some Warsaw Pact allies. Three progressively improved models followed, but featured insufficient changes to warrant a change of Western designation. In the **Su-7BM**, underwing stores pylons were doubled to

four; the muzzle velocity of the internal cannon was increased; and an uprated engine was fitted, take-off power being further boosted, if required, by two JATO bottles. The aircraft also introduced a radar warning receiver in the tail and two duct fairings running long the spine. Rough-field operation was provided in the **Su-7BKL**, whose

large, low-pressure nosewheel tyre is betrayed by a blistered floor to its bay. Further changes of detail were incorporated in the later **Su-7BMK**, but little could be done to moderate the demands of the thirsty AL-7F engine, which on full afterburner at sea level would consume the entire 2940 litres (647 Imp gal) of internal fuel in a little

over eight minutes. Even so, fuel capacity is reduced in the operational trainer versions (**Su-7UM** and **Su-7UMK**, known to NATO as **'Moujik'**) to make way for a second seat, despite a slight lengthening of the fuselage.

Specification
Su-7BMK 'Fitter-A'

Type: single-seat ground-attack fighter

Armament: two 30-mm NR-30 cannon (with 70 rpg) in wing roots; six weapon pylons: two under fuselage and two under the inner wings, each carrying up to 500 kg (1,102 lb) of stores, plus two under the outer wings each carrying up to 250 kg (551 lb); weapon load reduced to 1000 kg (2,205 lb)

when two 600-litre (132-Imp gal) drop-tanks are carried on fuselage pylons
Powerplant: one 10000-kg (22,046-lb) thrust Lyulka AL-7F-1 afterburning turbojet
Performance: maximum speed at sea level 850 km/h (528 mph) without afterburning, or 1350 km/h (839 mph)

with afterburning; initial climb rate 9120 m (29,920 ft) per minute; service ceiling 15150 m (49,705 ft)
Weights: empty 8620 kg (19,004 lb); normal take-off 12000 kg (26,455 lb); maximum take-off 13500 kg (29,762 lb)
Dimensions: span 8.93 m (29 ft 3½ in); length, including probe 17.37 m (57 ft

These Su-7BMs are parked outside the flight office of No. 122 Sqn, Indian Air Force. Seventy-five are still used in the strike role, but Jaguars are replacing them.

0 in); height 4.57 m (15 ft 0 in); wing area 27.60 m² (297 sq ft)

Former USSR

Sukhoi Su-17/20/22

Sukhoi Su-20 'Fitter-C' of the Egyptian air force. The Su-20 was the export model of the Su-17 with reduced avionics. Egypt operates 30 in the strike role.

When a version of the Su-7 'Fitter-A' with variable-geometry outer wing sections was first revealed in 1967 it was labelled **'Fitter-B'** by NATO and dismissed as a research version of an unimpressive ground-attack fighter.

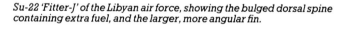

Not until the mid-1970s did it dawn on the West that the modification, together with a more powerful but fuel-efficient engine and new avionics, had resulted in a vastly improved aircraft with doubled weapon load, 30 per cent greater range and substantially better short-field take-off characteristics. So successful has been the aircraft that numerous versions are in service with Frontal Aviation, the Soviet naval air arm, Warsaw Pact and left-leaning

Su-22 'Fitter-J' of the Libyan air force, showing the bulged dorsal spine containing extra fuel, and the larger, more angular fin.

countries abroad. **Sukhoi Su-17** variants based in eastern Europe and the USSR have been progressively improved from the basic **'Fitter-C'** initial-production model, firstly to the **'Fitter-D'** with its undernose terrain-avoidance radar and a marked-target seeker in the inlet centrebody. A conversion trainer, the **'Fitter-E'**, parallels the 'Fitter-C' except for a slightly drooped forward fuselage and lack of a port wing root gun, whilst the **'Fitter-G'** operational trainer has a taller, straight-topped fin and a marked-target seeker. Newest of the single-seat variants is the **'Fitter-H'** which has the revised fin and a deep dorsal fairing behind the canopy, presumably for extra fuel tanks. Export versions of the 'Fitter-C' have a reduced avionics fit and are designated **Su-20**, but when the **Su-22 'Fitter-F'** appeared as a 'Fitter-D' counterpart, its bulged rear fuselage revealed a change of engine to the 11500-kg (25,353-lb) thrust Tumansky R-29B afterburning turbojet for even better performance. A 'Fitter-

H' counterpart, the **Su-22 'Fitter-J'**, is similarly powered and identified by a more angular dorsal fin. Su-22s are also employed as interceptors with AA-2 'Atoll' AAMs. A Tumansky-powered two-seater has been noted in Soviet service.

Specification
Su-17 'Fitter-C'
Type: single-seat variable-geometry ground-attack fighter
Armament: two 30-mm NR-30 cannon (with 70 rpg) in wing roots; four underwing and four underfuselage weapon pylons for up to 4000 kg (8,818 lb) of ordnance including

Exported in 1976, this Egyptian Su-20 was refurbished in 1982 and brought back to operational status. Egypt was a major user of Soviet equipment but has bought F-16s and Mirage 2000s.

tactical nuclear weapons and AS-7 'Kerry' ASMs
Powerplant: one 11200-kg (24,691-lb) thrust Lyulka AL-21F-3 afterburning turbojet
Performance: maximum speed 2300 km/h (1,429 mph) or Mach 2.17 at altitude; maximum speed 1285 km/h (798 mph) or Mach 1.05 at sea level; initial climb rate 13,800 m (45,275 ft per

minute); service ceiling 18000 m (59,055 ft); combat radius with 2000 kg (4,409 lb) of stores 630 km (391 miles) on a hi-lo-hi mission, or 360 km (224 miles) on a lo-lo-lo mission
Dimensions: span, extended (28° sweep) 14.00 m (45 ft 11 in), fully-swept (62°) 10.60 m (34 ft 9½ in); length 18.75 m (61 ft 6¼ in); height 4.75 m (15 ft 7 in); wing area, extended 40.1 m² (432 sq ft)

Sukhoi Su-25

Expansion of Soviet tactical air strength during the 1970s kept the West on the lookout for new combat aircraft, satellite reconnaissance of the Ramenskoye test centre revealing a number of designs in the early stages of flight development. Amongst these was an aircraft resembling the Northrop A-9, and as the A-9 was an unsuccessful contender in the competition which brought the Fairchild A-10 Thunderbolt II into USAF service, the Soviet machine's close-support role was readily apparent. Originally known to NATO as the **Ram-J** (tenth new type seen at Ramenskoye), it was identified subsequently as the **Sukhoi Su-25** and issued with the fighter-classification reporting name 'Frogfoot'. By 1982, a trials squadron was operating in Afghanistan against tribesmen opposing the Soviet occupation. This opportunity has been taken to develop operational techniques, including co-ordinated low-level attacks by Mil Mi-24 Hind helicopter

gunships and Su-25s in support of ground troops. Smaller than the Thunderbolt, and perhaps with engines of lower thrust, the Su-25 appears to carry less weight of ordnance than its American counterpart, although performance is probably better. Deliveries to operational units of Frontal Aviation in the western USSR and eastern Europe began in the mid-1980s, and 330 aircraft were built up to 1989.

Specification
Sukhoi Su-25K 'Frogfoot-A'
Type: close-support/anti-tank aircraft
Powerplant: two 4500-kg (9,921-lb) thrust MNPK 'Soyuz' (Tumansky) R195 turbojets
Performance: max speed 950 km/h (590 mph) at sea level; service ceiling 7,000 m (22,965 ft); radius 495 km (308 miles) on a hi-lo-hi attack mission with 4000-kg (8,818-lb) warload
Weights: empty 9,800 kg (21.605 lb); max take-off 18,600 kg (41,005 lb)
Dimensions: span 14.4m (47 ft 1½ in)

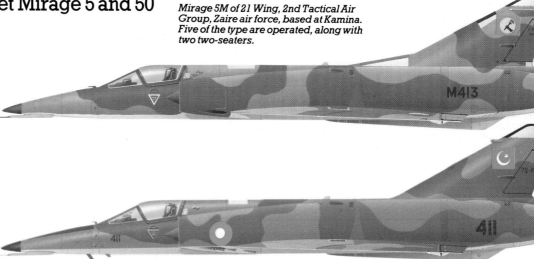

length 15 m (50 ft11 in); height 4.8 m (15 ft 9 in); wing area 30 m² (324 sqft)
Armament: max 4000 kg (8,818 lb) disposable stores on 10 underwing hardpoints

This early general arrangement drawing reveals the Western world's early and not too inaccurate thinking about the Su-25 in the early 1980s.

Dassault-Breguet Mirage 5 and 50

Mirage 5M of 21 Wing, 2nd Tactical Air Group, Zaire air force, based at Kamina. Five of the type are operated, along with two two-seaters.

Responding to Israeli suggestions, Dassault-Breguet produced a simplified (and thus cheaper) version of its highly successful Mirage III, the new variant, designated **Dassault-Breguet Mirage 5**, making its first flight on 19 May 1967. Optimized for visual ground attack and interception, the aircraft lacked several features of its Mirage IIIE progenitor, notably the Cyrano II nose-mounted radar (replaced by a simple radar rangefinder) and other avionics. Retaining Mach 2 performance and the ability to operate from semi-prepared strips, the Mirage 5 emerged with certain enhancement, such as greater range, easier maintenance and no less than seven weapon attachment points beneath its fuselage and wings. No sooner had this simplification been achieved, and the first of many orders booked, than the process began of developing a family of aircraft based on the Mirage 5 and incorporating various degrees of sophistication according to customer preference. After the camera-nosed **Mirage 5R** and two-seat **Mirage 5D** trainer came versions equipped with SAGEM inertial navigation and nav/attack systems incorporating a head-up display and the choice of Aïda II radar and an air-to-surface laser ranger or Agave multi-purpose radar. These options produced a plethora of sub-marks, some of which were almost indistinguishable from the Mirage III, such as the Egyptian **Mirage 5E2** which in-

corporate the nav/attack system of the Alpha Jet MS2. The next evolutionary step was to replace the 6200-kg (13,668-lb) thrust Atar 9C afterburning turbojet by a more powerful Atar 9K-50 to produce the **Mirage 50**, first flown on 15 April 1979 and exemplified by the non-radar **Mirage 50FC** and radar-equipped **Mirage 50C** delivered to Chile. The Mirage 50's usual radar fit is Agave or Cyrano IV, allowing the aircraft to operate in the attack or interceptor modes. Current models offered by Dassault are the **Mirage 3-50** and **Mirage 5-50** versions of the Mirage III

and Mirage 5, both of which are powered by Atar 9K-50 engines.

Specification
Mirage 5-50
Type: single-seat multi-mission fighter
Armament: two 30-mm DEFA cannon (with 125 rpg) in fuselage; five weapon pylons for ASMs, rocket pods and various bombs to a weight of 4000 kg (8,818 lb) or more
Powerplant: one 7200-kg (15,873-lb) thrust SNECMA Atar 9K-50 afterburning turbojet
Performance: maximum speed

2350 km/h (1,460 mph) or Mach 2.2 at altitude; maximum speed 1390 km/h (863 mph) or Mach 1.13 at sea level; initial climb rate 11100 m (36,415 ft) per minute; service ceiling 18000 m (59,055 ft); combat radius on a lo-lo-lo mission with 800 kg (1,764 lb) of bombs

South America has been a good market for Dassault-Breguet to sell their Mirage range, whose relatively low price and high performance combines with France's competitiveness. Venezuela operates seven Mirage 5s.

630 km (391 miles)
Weights: empty 7150 kg (15,763 lb);
normal take-off, clean 9900 kg
(21,825 lb); maximum take-off 13700 kg
(30,203 lb)
Dimensions: span 8.22 m (27 ft 0 in);
length 15.56 m (51 ft 0½ in); height
4.50 m (14 ft 9 in); wing area 35.00 m²
(376.7 sq ft)

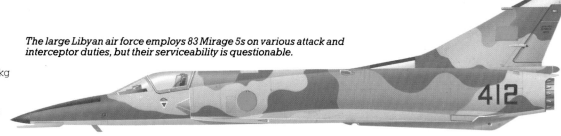

*The large Libyan air force employs 83 Mirage 5s on various attack and
interceptor duties, but their serviceability is questionable.*

FRANCE

Dassault-Breguet Mirage F.1

*Although strictly interceptors, the Fuerza Aérea Ecuatoriana (Ecuador) can
use its Mirage F.1JAs in the attack role.*

When Dassault-Breguet Aviation was
commissioned to produce a successor
to its versatile Mirage III, doubts with
regard to the viability of the air force
specification were resolved by building two designs: the private-venture
Dassault-Breguet Mirage F.1 and the
officially-inspired Mirage F.2. The larger, heavier Mirage F.2 was con-
signed to posterity once the Mirage
F.1 (first flown on 23 December 1966)
had proved itself to be an agile and
capable interceptor well suited to
additional employment in the attack
role. Naturally, the home air force is
the major operator of the Mirage F.1,
almost 700 of which have been
ordered by a total of 11 countries. The
Mirage F.1C entered service with
France's air defence command (CAF-
DA) in 1973, equipped with Thomson-
CSF Cyrano IV all-sector fire-control
radar. Production of 81 of this variant
was followed by 89 **Mirage F.1C-200**
fighters fitted with a fixed inflight-
refuelling probe at the base of the
windscreen, whilst 20 **Mirage F.1B**
conversion trainers (based on the Mirage F.1C but lacking its internal cannon) have also been received. The tactical reconnaissance **Mirage F.1CR**,
which entered service in 1983, is
based on the Mirage F.1C-200 and has
a secondary attack capability, its
prime sensors being three internal
cameras (including one panoramic
and one infra-red linescan) and a
range of specialized pods attached to
the centreline pylon. Mirage F.1C
variants serve with the air forces of
Ecuador, Greece, Jordan, Kuwait,
Morocco, South Africa and Spain. A
simplified version, lacking certain
avionics such as the Cyrano radar, was
produced for South Africa and Libya as
the **Mirage F.1A**, although the latter
country, together with Iraq, Jordan,
Morocco, Qatar and Spain, also bought

*Morocco's Mirage F.1CHs have seen strike action against the Polisario
guerillas in the Spanish Sahara alongside the force's Mirage F.1EHs. Eighteen
of the former and 20 of the latter have been supplied by France.*

the multi-role **Mirage F.1E**. This carries a wide variety of underwing stores
as an alternative to AAMs and features
inertial navigation, a central nav/attack
computer, and additional air-ground
modes for its Cyrano IV radar for low-
altitude penetration and accurate
target ranging.

Specification
Mirage F.1E
Type: single-seat multi-role fighter
Armament: two 30-mm DEFA 553
cannon (with 125 rpg) in front fuselage;
wingtip rails for Magic or Sidewinder
AAMs; four wing pylons and one

centreline pylon for up to 4000 kg
(8,818 lb) or ordnance including
Martel and AS.30/AS.30L ASMs
Powerplant: one 7200-kg (15,873-lb)
thrust SNECMA Atar 9K-50
afterburning turbojet
Performance: maximum speed, clean
Mach 2.2 at high altitude; service

ceiling 20000 m (65,615 ft); endurance
3 hours 45 minutes
Weights: empty 7400 kg (16,314 lb);
maximum take-off 16200 kg (35,714 lb)
Dimensions: span 8.40 m (27 ft 6¾ in);
length 15.00 m (49 ft 2½ in); height
4.50 m (14 ft 9 in); wing area 25.00 m²
(269.1 sq ft)

*In common with most Mirage F.1
users, Greece flies its aircraft mainly
in the interceptor role, but they have
secondary attack capabilities. This is
one of 39 F.1CGs flying from Tanagra
with 114 Pterix (wing).*

SWEDEN

Saab AJ37 Viggen

Sweden, a country which takes its
neutrality seriously, has a long tradition
of producing effective fighters to defend its territory. Epitomizing these is
the **Saab 37 Viggen** (thunderbolt) multi-role combat aircraft of advanced design, whose canard delta configuration
derives from the requirement for
STOL performance to permit operation from short roadway dispersal
airfields. In addition, it is powered by
an economical US-designed JT8D turbofan engine which has a powerful
Swedish-produced afterburner, thereby combining the qualities of long
range or protracted loiter with swift
acceleration when needed. Short-field
ability is enhanced by an automatic
speed control and a thrust reverser, so
that with its numerous aerodynamic

aids the Viggen can take off in 400 m
(1,310 ft) and land in 500 m (1,640 ft),
coming 'over the fence' at a remarkably docile 220 km/h (137 mph) for
such a high-performance aircraft. First
flown on 8 February 1967, the Viggen
entered service four years later in its

AJ37 form, the prefix letter indicating
primary attack and secondary interceptor roles. Production of the AJ37
totalled 110 aircraft, but three basically
similar models were produced in parallel, conforming to the Swedish practice of producing a single airframe
capable of adaptation to specialist
roles. Associated models were 26
SH37 maritime radar-surveillance

variants; 26 **SF37** overland photo-
reconnaissance aircraft; and 18 **Sk37**
two-seat trainers with taller fins. All
have secondary attack duties with
weaponry similar to that of the AJ37.
The more advanced, higher-powered
JA37, which was issued to squadrons

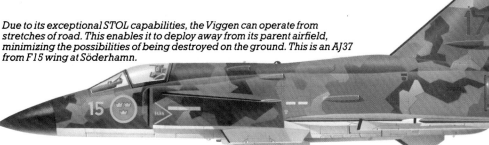

*Due to its exceptional STOL capabilities, the Viggen can operate from
stretches of road. This enables it to deploy away from its parent airfield,
minimizing the possibilities of being destroyed on the ground. This is an AJ37
from F15 wing at Söderhamn.*

from 1979 onwards, is optimized for interception yet may also be used for attack. Orders for this variant total 149.

Specification
AJ37 Viggen
Type: single-seat all-weather attack aircraft with secondary interceptor capability

Armament: seven attachment points (four wing and three fuselage) for bombs, rocket pods, 30-mm Aden cannon pods, Rb04, Rb05 and Maverick ASMs, plus (interception mission) Rb24 Sidewinder and Rb28 Falcon AAMs

Powerplant: one 11800 kg (26,014-lb) thrust Volvo Flygmotor RM8A (Pratt & Whitney JT8D-22) afterburning turbofan

Performance: maximum speed Mach 2+ at altitude; maximum speed Mach 1.2 at 100 m (330 ft); climb to 10000 m (32,810 ft) in under 100 seconds; tactical radius, armed 1000+ km (621+ miles) on a hi-lo-hi mission, 500+ km (310+ miles) on a lo-lo-lo mission

Weights: empty about 11800 kg (26,015 lb); maximum take-off 20500 kg (45,194 lb)

Dimensions: span 10.60 m (34 ft 9¼ in); length 16.30 m (53 ft 5¾ in); height 5.80 m (19 ft 0¼ in); wing area 46.00 m² (495.1 sq ft)

Flying from Satenas, F7 wing operates the AJ37 Viggen as a dedicated attack aircraft. The camouflage is one of the most complicated in the world, with four colours applied with precision. Seven hardpoints are available for a wide range of stores.

YUGOSLAVIA/ROMANIA
Soko/CNIAR Orao/IAR-93

The Romanian prototype of the CNIAR IAR-93, known in Yugoslavia as the Orao. Pre-production examples have non-afterburning engines.

A unique example of co-operation in military aircraft design by countries on opposite sides of the Iron Curtain, the Orao was made possible by the unusual latitude allowed to Romania by its Soviet ally in the Warsaw Pact, and the Communist persuasion of non-aligned Yugoslavia. Built in the latter country as the **Soko Orao** (eagle) and in Romania as the **CNIAR** (Centrul National al Industriei Aeronautica Române) **IAR-93**, the aircraft was designed by a joint team and developed under a programme known as YuRom, the name indicating the partner countries. Prototypes assembled by Soko and CNIAR made their first flights within minutes of each other on 31 October 1974, and these were followed by a pair of two-seat variants, both of which flew on 29 January 1977. During 1978, deliveries began of a pre-production batch of 15 to each country, after which the initial series model, known in Romania as the **IAR-93A**, entered service. This is fitted with a pair of non-afterburning Viper Mk 632 engines, but after a short run of single-and two-seat aircraft to this standard (20 of them for Romania) manufacture began of the definitive **IAR-93B** which features a licence-built afterburner and structural changes such as integral wing fuel tanks and a honeycomb rudder and tailplane. Romania requires 165 IAR-93Bs, including some two-seat models, with similar operational capability to the main version, for advanced training and weapons instruction. Yugoslav plans are believed to be similar. The Orao/IAR-93 is limited to the close support role by its lack of radar or inertial navigation, but low-level interception is a secondary duty.

Specification
IAR-93B
Type: single-seat close-support fighter with two-seat derivative

Armament: two 23-mm GSh-23L twin-barrel cannon (with 200 rpg) in front fuselage; four wing pylons and one centreline pylon carrying five 250-kg (551-lb) bombs or equivalent loads including rocket pods

Powerplant: two 2268-kg (5,000-lb) Rolls-Royce Viper Mk 633-47 afterburning turbojets

Performance: maximum speed 1160 km/h (721 mph) at sea level; service ceiling 12500 m (41,010 ft); initial climb rate 3960 m (12,990 ft) per minute

Weights: empty equipped 5900 kg (13,007 lb); maximum take-off 10097 kg (22,260 lb)

Dimensions: span 9.62 m (31 ft 6¾ in); length, excluding probe 13.96 m (45 ft 9½ in); height 4.45 m (14 ft 7¼ in); wing area 26.00 m² (279.86 sq ft)

A Romanian Orao undergoes maintenance. The two underfuselage dive-brakes are open and the port 23-mm twin-barrel cannon is visible under the air intake.

British Aerospace Harrier

Evolved from the **Hawker P.1127** vertical take-off technology demonstrator, whose intended supersonic development (the P.1154), was cancelled, the **BAe Harrier** remains the only Western combat aircraft in the world powered by a vectored-thrust engine. Originally regarded as an impractical novelty, it confounded its critics by giving sterling service during the Falklands war of 1982, combining technical reliability with accuracy in attack and resistance to heavy defensive fire, while its naval cousin achieved undisputed air superiority over the islands. Though the P.1127 first flew in September 1960, it was not until exactly nine years later that the RAF's first squadron was formed with **Harrier GR.Mk 1** aircraft, the designation subsequently changing to **Harrier GR.Mk 1A** and then **Harrier GR.Mk 3** as the Pegasus progressed from the 8709-kg (19,200-lb) Mk 101 through Mk 102 to the present Mk 103. The two-seat trainer, with longer fuselage and taller fin, was similarly designated **Harrier T.Mk 2**, **Harrier T.Mk 2A** and **Harrier T.Mk 4**. Despite power increases, the Harrier is unable to take off vertically with a full weapon load, but can take off from a short length of road or semi-prepared strip.

Two T.Mk.4 and two GR.Mk.3 Harriers of No. 233 OCU at Wittering on a summer's morning. Training is vitally important, for the Harrier is like no other aircraft. In times of war, the OCU would become operational and carry weapons.

in the STOVL (short take-off, vertical landing) mode for tactical concealment. Equipped from the outset with a Ferranti FE541 inertial navigation system with head-up display, the RAF aircraft were fitted from 1976 with a Marconi LRMTS (laser ranger and marked-target seeker) resulting in a much extended profile to the nose. A Marconi ARI 18223 E-J band radar warning receiver was added to the fin and extreme rear fuselage at the same time. The Harrier carries a single oblique camera in the port side of the nose, but may be equipped with a sensor pod beneath the fuselage for more extensive reconnaissance. Following the production of six pre-production aircraft, the RAF received 114 single-seat Harriers and has ordered four more for replacement of Falklands losses. US Marine Corps contracts covered 102 **AV-8A** aircraft (now converted to **AV-8C** standard), and the Spanish navy acquired 11 **VA.1 Matador** aircraft. Two-seat trainer orders cover 23 for the RAF (those not fitted with LRMTS being Harrier **T.Mk 4A** aircraft), eight **TAV-8A** aircraft, two **VAE.1 Matador** aircraft, a Harrier T.Mk 4 and three navalized **Harrier T.Mk 4M** aircraft for the Royal Navy, plus a company demonstrator.

Specification
Harrier GR.Mk 3
Type: single-seat close-support and reconnaissance fighter
Armament: two 30-mm Aden cannon (with 130 rpg) on fuselage

strongpoints; four wing pylons carrying up to 2268 kg (5,000 lb) of ordnance (or 455-litre/100-Imp gal tanks, inboard only), including 454-kg (1,000-lb) free-fall or retarded bombs, 68-mm (2.68-in) SNEB rocket pods, BL755 cluster bombs, AIM-9L Sidewinder AAMs (single round each outer pylon), or optionally, Paveway laser-guided bombs and (Royal Navy aircraft) 51-mm (2-in) rocket pods
Powerplant: one 9752-kg (21,500-lb) thrust Rolls-Royce Pegasus 103 vectored-thrust turbofan
Performance: maximum speed, clean 1159 km/h (720 mph) at 305 m (1,000 ft) or Mach 0.95; tactical radius on a hi-lo-hi mission 418 km (260 miles)

The Harrier gains its remarkable performance from the four swivelling thrust nozzles which can provide both lift for VTOL and forward thrust by rotating through 90°. This aircraft is from No. 4 Sqn, one of the two squadrons maintained in Germany.

Weights: empty 5425 kg (11,960 lb); maximum for vertical take-off 8165 kg (18,000 lb); maximum for short-take-off 11340+ kg (25,000+ lb)
Dimensions: span 7.09 m (23 ft 3 in); length 14.27 m (46 ft 10 in); height 3.45 m (11 ft 4 in); wing area 18.67 m² (201.0 sq ft)

CHINA

Nanchang Q-5

Known in the West as the **Nanchang A-5 'Fantan-A'** and to the People's Liberation Army Air Force as the **Qiang-jiji 5** (Attack Aircraft Type 5), the Q-5 was revealed in limited detail only during 1980 although conceived about a decade before as China's first 'almost indigenous' jet fighter-bomber and limited-capability strike aircraft. Detailed examination justifies the qualification, for the Q-5 (particularly its wing) is based on the Mikoyan-Gurevich MiG-19, already built in the People's Republic under the designation Shenyang J-6. Slightly longer than its ancestor, the Q-5 differs considerably in profile by reasons of a 'solid' nose and cheek air inlets made necessary by transfer of some avionics from the centre fuselage to make way for an internal weapons bay (now used for additional fuel), although the MiG's four wing strongpoints and root-mounted cannon are retained for close-support work. Powered by the same Soviet-designed, Chinese-built engines as the J-6, this considerably modified variant has a taller fin and a narrower centre fuselage, the latter an aerodynamic improvement conforming to area-rule. A camera mounted on the starboard side of the nose is for gunnery recording only. The revised nose shape has led to speculation that a radar-equipped version is (or was) planned, but no evidence has emerged to support this suggestion, even though such equipment would improve capabilities as a tactical nuc-

lear bomber, in the apparent absence of an inertial navigation system. Interceptor Q-5s are reported to be in operation with the People's Navy, any differences in equipment being unknown. The Q-5 remains in production at the Nanchang State Aircraft Factory in Jiangxi province, where more than 800 have been built including 60 delivered to Pakistan in 1982–83, as well as 40 to North Korea and 20 aircraft delivered to Bangladesh.

Specification
Nanchang Q-5
Type: single-seat ground-attack aircraft with interceptor capability
Armament: two 23-mm Type 23-2 cannon (with 100 rpg) in wing roots; four wing and four fuselage pylons carrying (normally) 1000 kg (2,205 lb) or (maximum) 2000 kg (4,409 lb) of ordnance, including AAMs, or a tactical nuclear weapon
Powerplant: two 3250-kg (7,165-lb) thrust Shenyang Wopen-6 (Tumansky R-9BF-811) afterburning turbojets
Performance: maximum speed 1190 km/h (739 mph) or Mach 1.12 at

11000 m (36,090 ft) and 1210 km/h (752 mph) at sea level; service ceiling 16000 m (52,495 ft); combat radius with maximum load 400 km (249 miles) on a lo-lo-lo mission or 600 km (373 miles) on a hi-lo-hi mission
Weights: empty 6494 kg (14,317 lb); maximum take-off 12000 kg (26,455 lb)

Nanchang Q-5 of the Chinese air force. The Chinese hope to import Western avionics to improve the Q-5's capabilities.

Chinese Q-5 pilots pose for the camera with model aircraft simulating combat manoeuvres. The Q-5 is China's most potent attack aircraft.

Dimensions: span 9.70 m (31 ft 10 in); length 16.73 m (54 ft 10½ in); height 4.51 m (14 ft 9½ in)

CHINA

Shenyang J-6

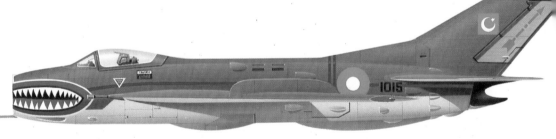

Phased out of production in the Soviet Union during the late 1950s, the Mikoyan-Gurevich MiG-19 continues to be built in China under a licence agreement of January 1958. The J-6 (Jianjiji 6, or Fighter Aircraft Type 6) is normally credited to the Shenyang production facility, although a second assembly line is located at Tianjin. First of the Chinese production models was the J-6 equivalent of the MiG-19S/SF day fighter, this giving way to the **J-6A**/MiG-19PF limited all-weather interceptor and the later **J-6B**/MiG-19PM, the latter augmenting gun and rocket armament by AA-1 'Alkali' AAMs. An improved MiG-19SF, known as the **J-6C** and identified by a brake parachute housing at the base of the fin, is currently in production, as is the **J-6Xin** ('New J-6') which features a sharply-pointed radome in the engine air intake for a Chinese-developed airborne gun-ranging radar. The **JZ-6** (Jianjiji Zhenchaji 6) is a MiG-19R reconnaissance version equivalent with the forward fuselage cannon replaced by a camera array. Despite limited Soviet production of a MiG-19UTI, Chinese requirements for a dual-control trainer were met by a local redesign to produce the **JJ-6** (Jianjiji Jiaolianji 6), with its 0.84 m (2 ft 9 in) fuselage extension. Several thousand J-6s have been built for the Chinese army and navy air forces since 1961, whilst export variants (known as the **F-6** and trainer **FT-6**) serve in Albania,

Bangladesh, Egypt, Iraq, Pakistan, Tanzania and Vietnam as interceptors and close-support aircraft. Despite its age and short range, the J-6 is well liked by its pilots as a manoeuvrable fighter and stable weapons platform, Pakistan's aircraft having been improved by the addition of a third (underfuselage) fuel tank, US-designed AIM-9B/J Sidewinder AAMs and Martin-Baker PKD Mk 10 automatic zero-zero ejection seats.

Specification
Shenyang/Tianjin J-6C
Type: single-seat close-support fighter

and day interceptor
Armament: three internal 30-mm NR-30 cannon (one on starboard side of nose, two in wing roots); wing pylons for two 250-kg (551-lb) bombs or four rocket packs, plus fuel tanks
Powerplant: two 3250-kg (7,165-lb) Shenyang Wopen-6 (Tumansky R-9BF-811) afterburning turbojets
Performance: maximum speed, clean 1540 km/h (957 mph) or Mach 1.45 at 11000 m (36,090 ft); maximum speed 1340 km/h (833 mph) or Mach 1.09 at low level; service ceiling 17900 m (58,725 ft)
Weights: empty 5760 kg (12,698 lb);

A Pakistan air force J-6 equipped with reconnaissance pack under the fuselage, and two guns only.

normal take-off, clean 7545 kg (16,634 lb); maximum take-off with external stores about 10000 kg (22,046 lb)
Dimensions: span 9.20 m (30 ft 2¼ in); length, excluding probe 12.60 m (41 ft 4 in); height 3.88 m (12 ft 8¾ in); wing area 25.00 m² (269 sq ft)

The Shenyang J-6 was a direct Chinese copy of the MiG-19, but later versions have local improvements such as AI radar and extra cannon.

McDonnell Douglas F-4G 'Wild Weasel'

USA

During its bombing attacks on North Vietnam, the USAF proved the effectiveness of the 'Wild Weasel' concept; that is the use of specially-equipped aircraft flying with, or slightly in advance of, the main attack and tasked with destruction or suppression of hostile radars, particularly those associated with SAM and AA gun guidance. Republic F-105G Thunderchiefs performed well in this role in the early 1970s and 35 F-4C Phantoms were similarly converted in 1968-9, but when the specification for an Advanced 'Wild Weasel' aircraft was drawn up in 1975 the F-4E variant of the Phantom was selected as the basis for modification. Already established as one of the world's most effective interceptor and fighter-bomber aircraft, the Phantom took to the mission with ease, becoming the **McDonnell Douglas F-4G** in the process. First require-

Also based at Spangdahlem with the 81st TFS is this F-4G, identified by the antennae pod on the top of the fin and the receiver and computer pod replacing the gun under the nose. Its role is that of radar suppression, and it uses radar-homing missiles to destroy its targets.

ment of a 'Wild Weasel' is to locate and classify enemy radars. This is undertaken by a McDonnell Douglas AN/APR-38 radar homing and warning system (RHAWS), the principal external features of which are a receiver and computer pod beneath the nose (replacing the Vulcan rotary cannon) and 56 antennae in a small fintip pod, on the fin sides, upper fuselage and other locations. Three cathode-ray tube displays in the rear cockpit (backed by digital readouts, aural warning system and indicator lights) provide the electronic warfare officer with a detailed picture of the tactical situation and automatically allocate attack priorities to the 15 most pressing threats in order of the danger which they represent. Weapons delivery is also aided by computer, allowing the F-4G to attack its target 'blind' with bombs, anti-radiation missiles and the

latest AGM-65D Maverick which has infra-red TV-type guidance. There were 116 conversions to F-4G, these aircraft entering service in 1978 and including 24 based at Spangdahlem, Germany, with the 81st RFS/52nd TFW for operations on the NATO Central Front. The F-4G was retired in 1998.

McDonnell Douglas F-4G 'Wild Weasel' Phantom II of the 81st TFS, 52nd TFW, based at Spangdahlem in West Germany.

Specification
F-4G 'Wild Weasel' Phantom
Type: two-seat defence-suppression aircraft
Armament: up to 7258 kg (16,000 lb) of ordnance on seven external mountings, including AGM-45 Shrike, AGM-78 Standard and AGM-88 HARM ARMs and AGM-65 Maverick ASMs;

up to four AIM-7F Sparrow and four AIM-9L Sidewinder AAMs for self-defence
Powerplant: two 8119-kg (17,900-lb) thrust General Electric J79-GE-17A afterburning turbojets
Performance: maximum speed with external stores Mach 2+; initial climb rate at maximum take-off weight 2003 m (6,570 ft per minute); service ceiling 16580 m (54,400 ft); combat radius 1145 km (712 miles)
Weights: empty 13757 kg (30,328 lb); maximum take-off 28030 kg (61,795 lb)
Dimensions: span 11.77 m (38 ft 7½ in); length 19.20 m (63 ft 0 in); height 5.02 m (16 ft 5½ in); wing area 49.2 m² (530 sq ft)

USA

McDonnell Douglas F-15E Enhanced Eagle

Renowned as an extremely capable interceptor, the F-15 Eagle was modified in 1980 to perform in the all-weather interdictor role whilst still retaining the ability to operate as an air superiority aircraft. This private venture, first known as the **Strike Eagle**, was redesignated **McDonnell Douglas F-15E Enhanced Eagle** when the USAF expressed interest in the concept and conducted an evaluation between November 1982 and April 1983. Together with the delta-winged General Dynamics F-16E, the Enhanced Eagle was competing for selection in the USAF's Derivative Fighter Program as a supplement and eventual replacement for the General Dynamics F-111. Funding shortages delayed the decision, but the USAF eventually received 233 F-15E Eagle aircraft that were built with a very considerably improved air-to-surface weapon-delivery systems and navigation aids. McDonnell Douglas has moved in two directions to enhance the Eagle, concentrating on avionics

and weapon-carrying ability. The rear cockpit of the prototype (a converted F-15B trainer) has been fitted with four multi-purpose cathode ray tubes (CRTs) for information display to the systems operator and three more CRTs are to be installed for the pilot in production versions. Beneath the nose-cone, high resolution radar provides long-range ground-mapping of remarkable clarity, whilst forward-looking infra-red (FLIR) gives close-range images of similar quality. In combination, these systems allow rapid target identification in all weath-

McDonnell Douglas F-15E Enhanced Eagle carrying bombs and Sidewinders whilst on test for the USAF.

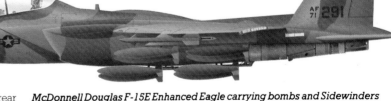

ers and ensure accurate weapon delivery. Ordnance carriage has been improved by addition of bomb attachment points on the 'conformal' wing-root fuel and sensor packs, resulting in less drag and freeing wing pylons for additional fuel tanks. Called Tangential Carriage, the modification extends the Eagle's endurance by 40 per cent in some cases. During proving trials, the F-15E demonstrated an ability to take off at a weight of 34020 kg

(75,000 lb), some 3175 kg (7,000 lb) above the present maximum.

Specification
F-15E Enhanced Eagle
Type: two-seat multi-role fighter
Armament: one M61A1 Vulcan 20-mm gun (with 940 rounds); up to 10866 kg (24,000 lb) of ordnance on three airframe and/or six fuel-pack attachment points; four AIM-9 Sidewinder and four AIM-7 Sparrow

AAMs
Powerplant: two 10855-kg (23,930-lb)
thrust Pratt & Whitney F100-PW-100
afterburning turbofans
Performance: maximum speed Mach
2.5+ at altitude; maximum speed
1481 km/h (920 mph) at sea level;
ceiling 20000 m (65,610 ft); endurance
5 hours 15 minutes with conformal
tanks
Weights: not released
Dimensions: span 13.05 m (42 ft 9¾ in);
length 19.43 m (63 ft 9 in); height 5.63 m
(18 ft 5½ in); wing area 56.5 m²
(608 sq ft)

*Up to 10866-kg (24,000-lb) of
ordnance can be carried by the
F-15E. This view shows the
'conformal' wing root fuel tanks and
the position of the bomb load. Four
Sidewinder AAMs are still carried to
augment the gun in self-defence.*

USA
Vought A-7 Corsair II

Produced to a US Navy specification
for a carrier-based light attack aircraft,
the **Vought Corsair II** was based on the
earlier F-8 Crusader interceptor and
first flew on 27 September 1965. Required to operate with a larger load of
conventional ordnance than the standard naval fighter-bomber of the day
the Douglas A-4 Skyhawk, it enjoyed a
rapid development period, and by December 1967 was in operational service over Vietnam. Three naval Corsair variants were produced before
the USAF commissioned a new model,
designated **A-7D**. This was an extensively improved variant with a far more
capable nav/attack system, as part of a
completely revised avionics fit, and a
licence-built Rolls-Royce Spey turbofan providing more power than the
Pratt & Whitney TF30 installed in earlier aircraft. Such were the changes
that the A-7D had only 25 per cent
commonality with the original **A-7A**.
Production of the A-7D totalled 459 between 1968 and 1976, the survivors currently operating with 13 Air National
Guard (ANG) units, some aircraft having seen service in Vietnam during
1972, flying from Thailand. Deliveries
of a combat-capable trainer, the **A-7K**,
involved 32 aircraft (31 new and a converted A-7D which acted as prototype)
between 1980 and 1983, one being
issued to each ANG squadron and the
rest to a training group. Land-based
export versions comprised 60 **A-7H**
aircraft for Greece, a version similar to
the naval **A-7E**, itself an A-7D development; six (five new) **TA-7H** trainers for
Greece; and 44 **A-7P** plus six **TA-7P**
aircraft for Portugal. The latter variants
are TF30-engined A-7As rebuilt with
more capable A-7E avionics.

Specification
A-7D Corsair II
Type: single-seat close-support and
interdictor aircraft
Armament: one internal M61A1 20-mm
rotary cannon (with 1,000 rounds); six
underwing and two fuselage pylons for

*Now retired from ANG as well as
USAF service, the A7 set new standards of bombing accuracy when it
appeared in 1967. This A-7D from
Davis-Monthan AFB fires rockets at
the ground target.*

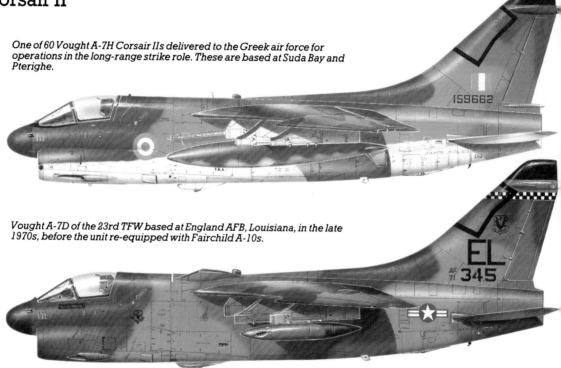

*One of 60 Vought A-7H Corsair IIs delivered to the Greek air force for
operations in the long-range strike role. These are based at Suda Bay and
Pterighe.*

*Vought A-7D of the 23rd TFW based at England AFB, Louisiana, in the late
1970s, before the unit re-equipped with Fairchild A-10s.*

over 6804 kg (15,000 lb) of stores,
including AIM-9 Sidewinder AAMs on
fuselage attachments
Powerplant: one 6804-kg (15,000-lb)
thrust Allison TF41-A-2 (Rolls-Royce
Spey) turbofan

Performance: maximum speed
1110 km/h (690 mph) at sea level, or
1040 km/h (646 mph) at 1525 m
(5,000 ft) with 12 227-kg (500-lb)
bombs; ferry range 3670 km (2,280
miles) on internal fuel

Weights: empty 8676 kg (19,127 lb);
maximum take-off 19051 kg (42,000 lb)
Dimensions: span 11.80 m (38 ft 9 in);
length 14.06 m (46 ft 1½ in); height
4.90 m (16 ft 0¾ in); wing area 34.83 m²
(375 sq ft)

Fairchild A-10A Thunderbolt II

Produced in reply to an exacting specification of 1967 which called for a hard-hitting close-support aircraft, the **Fairchild A-10A Thunderbolt II** first flew on 10 May 1972 and was selected by the USAF in preference to the Northrop A-9 after a competitive fly-off. The Thunderbolt's unusual appearance derives from the care taken to enhance its survival prospects over the battlefield and incorporate maximum fire-power. Absorbing much of the centre fuselage is a potent GAU-8/A Avenger seven-barrel 30-mm cannon, the muzzle protruding slightly beneath the nose, which can be fired at the rates of 2,100 or 4,200 rounds per minute. Although unconventional, the engine location is considered optimum for minimizing hits by ground-fire, and has the additional advantage that the wing and tail mask the infra-red emissions of exhaust gases and therefore affords some protection against heat-seeking SAMs. A robust airframe, which includes an armoured 'bathtub' surrounding the pilot, has numerous constructional features resistant to battle-damage or conducive to swift repair, such as interchangeable (left or right) flaps, fuselage components, rudders, elevators and main landing gear legs. There are two primary hydraulic systems, each with manual back-up,

Fairchild A-10A Thunderbolt II of the 23rd Tactical Fighter Wing, based at England AFB, Louisiana.

and the landing gear can be extended under gravity if necessary. Well protected electronically by AN/ALQ-119 jamming pods, plus an AN/ALE-40 chaff and flare dispenser, the Thunderbolt carries a Pave Penny laser designation pod on a pylon to the right of the forward fuselage for accurate marking. In prospect is the far more advanced LANTIRN (Low-Altitude Navigation Targeting Infra-Red for Night) pod. Altogether the USAF has received over 700 aircraft, including **A-10B** dual control-trainers, whilst a private-venture two-seat **Thunderbolt N/AW** (Night/Adverse Weather) has been offered, as yet without success.

Below: Ground crew reload the A-10's GAU-8/A ammunition tank,

which can hold 1,350 rounds of 30-mm depleted uranium ammunition, enough for 10 two-second bursts. The tank is extremely well protected as a hit in this area would destroy the aircraft.

Specification
A-10A Thunderbolt II
Type: single-seat close-support aircraft
Armament: one internal General Electric GAU-8/A Avenger 30-mm seven-barrel cannon with 1,174 rounds; eight wing and three fuselage pylons for up to 7258 kg (16,000 lb) or ordnance, including laser-guided bombs and AGM-65 Maverick ASMs
Powerplant: two 4112-kg (9,065-lb) thrust General Electric TF34-GE-100 high-bypass turbofans
Performance: maximum speed, clean 706 km/h (439 mph) at sea level at maximum weight; combat limit 704 km/h (438 mph) at 1525 m (5,000 ft) with six 227-kg (500-lb) bombs; initial climb rate 1829 m (6,000 ft) per minute;

operational radius 460 km (285 miles) with 1.7 hours over target
Weights: empty operating 11321 kg (24,959 lb); maximum take-off 22680 kg (50,000 lb)
Dimensions: span 17.53 m (57 ft 6 in); length 16.26 m (53 ft 4 in); height 4.47 m (14 ft 8 in); wing area 47.01 m^2 (506.0 sq ft)

Fairchild A-10 N/AW (night/adverse weather) evaluator. Modelled on this aircraft, the A-10B is in production as a trainer, featuring a second cockpit and taller fins.

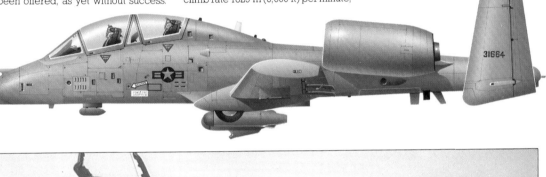

Airborne Early Warning Aircraft

Airborne early warning (AEW) aircraft are genuine 'force multipliers'. Their huge development and production costs make procurement impossible in all but small numbers, while their capabilities radically enhance the ability of other warplanes to undertake their tasks with success.

A Grumman E-2 Hawkeye aboard the USS *Constellation*. Its primary mission is the detection of hostile aircraft and cruise missiles and the direction of friendly fire against them.

Aviation's first military role was to look down on a battlefield and report on the enemy's movements, and the first aircraft used for this purpose were balloons and man-lifting kites. Today large aircraft also have the ability to view the whole battlefield and to control a complete war situation in a way that was previously impossible.

Aircraft that perform this task are AEW (Airborne Early Warning) aircraft, which carry a large surveillance radar to a height of 8,000–10,000 m (26,245–32,810 ft) above the ground, from which vantage point its line-of-sight horizon is opened out from the 32 km (20 miles) or so at sea level to a distance of 395 km (245 miles). Such a view can take

in an entire theatre of war and enable a commander to take in the whole situation in incredible detail. Objects can be seen far beyond the sea-level horizon. For example, hostile aircraft or missiles can be seen as they are launched. The sensors aboard the AEW platform can include an ESM (Electronic Support Measures) system, which operates passively,

identifying all signals beyond the visual horizon, without the platform itself making any telltale transmissions. Today AEW aircraft have extra capability with the addition of communications systems and computers, which enable the crew to exert a direct control function and also allow them to communicate with friendly forces on the ground.

Externally AEW aircraft look strikingly different from anything else in the sky. The antenna is usually on top of the fuselage in a rotating radome, or divided into parts mounted on the nose, sides and tail of the airplane. Many AEW platforms look like passenger aircraft, their only visible differences being their aerials.

Now the AEW airplane is more affordable, it is found in many countries. The USA has led the way with the Boeing E-3 Sentry and Grumman E-2 Hawkeye, with comparable systems installed on airframes based on the Boeing Model 767 airliner and Lockheed P-3 Orion, as well as on conversions of the Lockheed C-130 Hercules. Electronic and computing advances have made smaller AEW radars possible. As a result surveillance radars can be mounted on aircraft as small as twin-engined commuter and regional transports.

British Aerospace (Avro) Shackleton AEW.Mk 2

It is typical of the RAF that, perhaps through plain shortage of money, it was unable to provide itself with any AEW aircraft until the 1970s. Even then the radars were taken from defunct carrier-based Fairey Gannet AEW.Mk 3s, though with a major overhaul and update. The radar is, in fact, a direct descendant of the original APS-20 of 1946, and not all the skill and dedication of its operators could make up for its basically prehistoric design, absence of modern solid-state flexible memory, need for constant manual control and interpretation, and range limit of some 129 km (80 miles). To put such a set, and second-hand at that, into service with the RAF in 1972 is a sad reflection on the British planners and Treasury.

Even the aircraft were already well worn when, from 1970, they were channelled through RAF Kemble to be rebuilt by what was then Hawker Siddeley Aviation at Woodford and Bitteswell. Altogether 12 Shackleton MR.Mk 2 aircraft were rebuilt, the first flying at Woodford in **Shackleton AEW.Mk 2** form on 30 September 1971. Almost all the original maritime patrol and ASW (anti-submarine warfare) equipment was removed, and replaced by the APS-20F radar mounted mainly under the floor of the pilots' cockpit, with the 'guppy' radome in line with the contra-rotating propellers. All 12 aircraft were assigned to No. 8 Squadron at Kinloss, where they have been lovingly maintained and operated, mainly over sea areas around the UK and usually on practice missions in partnership with friendly combat aircraft. From 1973 improved AMTI (airborne moving-target indication) was added, with range increased slightly to about 185 km (115 miles). In 1981 budget cuts forced withdrawal of half the force, which was to have been replaced by the BAe Nimrod AEW.Mk 3, which was in the event not built, and finally superseded in 1991 by the Boeing Sentry AEW.Mk 1.

Seen over the coast of Grampian (formerly Morayshire) this Shackleton AEW. Mk 2 still soldiers on with RAF No.8 Sqn, though the unit then relocated to RAF Waddington, where it was to have worked up on the new-generation but ultimately abortive Nimrod AEW.Mk 3.

Specification
BAe (Avro) Shackleton AEW.Mk 2
Type: land-based AEW aircraft
Powerplant: four 2,455-hp (1831-kW) Rolls-Royce Griffon 57A Vee-12 piston engines
Performance: maximum speed 439 km/h (272 mph); operating ceiling about 6095 m (20,000 ft); endurance normally 14 hours; range limit 6440 km (4,000 miles)
Weights: empty 25855 kg (57,000 lb); maximum take-off 44453 kg (98,000 lb)
Dimensions: span 36.58 m (120 ft 0 in); length 26.59 m (87 ft 3 in); height 5.1 m (16 ft 9 in); wing area 132.01 m^2 (1,421 sq ft)

The faithful old AEW Shackletons were given names from The Magic Roundabout *TV series, this example being WR960 Dougal. They survived thanks to the skill of their crews, but had a poor ceiling and electronically they were archaic. Their operational life was prolonged by the failure of the Nimrod AEW.Mk 3.*

Westland Sea King AEW

In the early 1950s the development of AEW radar triggered the introduction of many types of what were called 'radar picket' aircraft to perform a surveillance function. Among them was the big Sikorsky S-56 helicopter, the HR2S-1W version of 1957 being equipped with an APS-20E radar in a giant swollen chin radome. In 1966 the impoverished UK was forced to look at the same idea of a surveillance helicopter when the government of the day terminated all future Royal Navy carriers and announced fixed-wing

An airborne early warning version of the Sea King naval helicopter was proposed in the 1970s but refused funding. After the Falkland Islands were seized in 1982 a programme was launched, an initial pair of Sea King HAS.Mk 2 naval helicopters being adapted to carry the Thorn-EMI Searchwater surveillance radar.

airpower at sea would be run down to nothing. AEW protection of the fleet was a blindingly obvious requirement, but the planners decided the Royal Navy would never have to operate outside the range of the old Kinloss-based Shackletons or the helpful US Navy's carriers. The carefully studied proposal for an AEW version of the Westland Sea King was thus rejected. The crass shortsightedness of this decision was obvious even to the officials when British ships began to be sunk in the South Atlantic in April 1982. A crash programme was organised. In 11 weeks Westland and their suppliers produced the **Westland Sea King**

AEW.Mk 2, converted from a surplus Sea King HAS.Mk 2 airframe with the Thorn-EMI Searchwater radar, similar to that in the BAe Nimrod MR.Mk 2, is installed in the centre fuselage with the aerial in a kettledrum radome kept in shape by internal inflation. This radome is normally aligned towards the rear fuselage on the right side, but for use it is swung down through 90° to have a clear view below the helicopter. The radar required modification to provide reliable indication of waveskimming aircraft, but is now believed to provide good protection out to a radius of about 96 km (60 miles). The first two urgently modified AEW heli-

copters were former Sea King HAS.Mk 2 ASW machines XV650 and 651, and they went out to the South Atlantic aboard HMS *Illustrious* in August 1982. In 1983 trials began with an improved installation incorporating a Cossor Type 3570 IFF interrogator, and in 1984 a further six helicopters, previously of the Sea King HAR.Mk 3 search and rescue type, were reported to be undergoing conversion to this standard for deployment aboard RN ships.

Specification
Westland Sea King AEW
Type: shipboard AEW helicopter
Powerplant: two 1,660-shp (1238-kW)

Rolls-Royce Gnome H.1400-1 turboshafts
Performance: normal transit speed about 201 km/h (125 mph); hovering ceiling 975 m (3,200 ft); range with standard fuel 1230 km (764 miles); endurance 3 hours 45 minutes on station at 370-km (230-miles) radius
Weights: empty about 6124 kg (13,500 lb); maximum take-off 9525 kg (21,000 lb)
Dimensions: main rotor diameter 18.90 m (62 ft 0 in); length, excluding rotors 17.01 m (55 ft 9¾ in); height overall 5.13 m (16 ft 10 in); main rotor disc area 280.47 m² (3,019 sq ft)

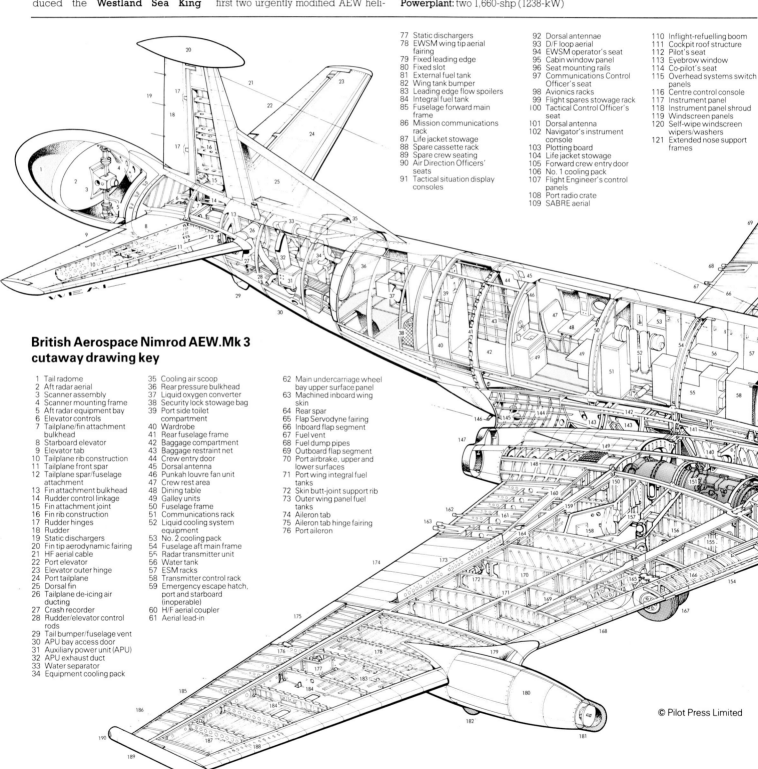

British Aerospace Nimrod AEW.Mk 3 cutaway drawing key

1. Tail radome
2. Aft radar aerial
3. Scanner assembly
4. Scanner mounting frame
5. Aft radar equipment bay
6. Elevator controls
7. Tailplane/fin attachment bulkhead
8. Starboard elevator
9. Elevator tab
10. Tailplane rib construction
11. Tailplane front spar
12. Tailplane spar/fuselage attachment
13. Fin attachment bulkhead
14. Rudder control linkage
15. Fin attachment joint
16. Fin rib construction
17. Rudder hinges
18. Rudder
19. Static dischargers
20. Fin tip aerodynamic fairing
21. HF aerial cable
22. Port elevator
23. Elevator outer hinge
24. Port tailplane
25. Dorsal fin
26. Tailplane de-icing air ducting
27. Crash recorder
28. Rudder/elevator control rods
29. Tail bumper/fuselage vent
30. APU bay access door
31. Auxiliary power unit (APU)
32. APU exhaust duct
33. Water separator
34. Equipment cooling pack
35. Cooling air scoop
36. Rear pressure bulkhead
37. Liquid oxygen converter
38. Security lock stowage bag
39. Port side toilet compartment
40. Wardrobe
41. Rear fuselage frame
42. Baggage compartment
43. Baggage restraint net
44. Crew entry door
45. Dorsal antenna
46. Punkah louvre fan unit
47. Crew rest area
48. Dining table
49. Galley units
50. Fuselage frame
51. Communications rack
52. Liquid cooling system equipment
53. No. 2 cooling pack
54. Fuselage aft main frame
55. Radar transmitter unit
56. Water tank
57. ESM racks
58. Transmitter control rack
59. Emergency escape hatch, port and starboard (inoperable)
60. H/F aerial coupler
61. Aerial lead-in
62. Main undercarriage wheel bay upper surface panel
63. Machined inboard wing skin
64. Rear spar
65. Flap Servodyne fairing
66. Inboard flap segment
67. Fuel vent
68. Fuel dump pipes
69. Outboard flap segment
70. Port airbrake, upper and lower surfaces
71. Port wing integral fuel tanks
72. Skin butt-joint support rib
73. Outer wing panel fuel tanks
74. Aileron tab
75. Aileron tab hinge fairing
76. Port aileron
77. Static dischargers
78. EWSM wing tip aerial fairing
79. Fixed leading edge
80. Fixed slot
81. External fuel tank
82. Wing tank bumper
83. Leading edge flow spoilers
84. Integral fuel tank
85. Fuselage forward main frame
86. Mission communications rack
87. Life jacket stowage
88. Spare cassette rack
89. Spare crew seating
90. Air Direction Officers' seats
91. Tactical situation display consoles
92. Dorsal antennae
93. D/F loop aerial
94. EWSM operator's seat
95. Cabin window panel
96. Seat mounting rails
97. Communications Control Officer's seat
98. Avionics racks
99. Flight spares stowage rack
100. Tactical Control Officer's seat
101. Dorsal antenna
102. Navigator's instrument console
103. Plotting board
104. Life jacket stowage
105. Forward crew entry door
106. No. 1 cooling pack
107. Flight Engineer's control panels
108. Port radio crate
109. SABRE aerial
110. Inflight-refuelling boom
111. Cockpit roof structure
112. Pilot's seat
113. Eyebrow window
114. Co-pilot's seat
115. Overhead systems switch panels
116. Centre control console
117. Instrument panel
118. Instrument panel shroud
119. Windscreen panels
120. Self-wipe windscreen wipers/washers
121. Extended nose support frames

© Pilot Press Limited

286

British Aerospace Nimrod AEW.Mk 3

Intended to fulfil the same function as the Boeing E-3 Sentry, the **BAe Nimrod AEW.Mk 3** was instantly recognisable by the bulbous radomes at the nose and tail to carry the antennae for the Marconi pulse-Doppler radar that provided coverage through 360° in azimuth. The type was based on the airframe of Nimrod MR.Mk 1 aircraft, and the RAF planned the receipt of 11 such aircraft as 'production line' conversions. The project suffered technical problems and delays, and was finally cancelled in favour of a British purchase of the E-3 as the Sentry AEW.Mk 1.

The sophistication of the Nimrod

AEW.Mk 3's electronics was the cause of the development problems and delays. The surveillance radar was first air-tested in a specially adapted de Havilland Comet 4C airframe, in this revised form, in June 1977. This machine was later supplemented by three Nimrod AEW.Mk 3s converted from Nimrod AEW.Mk 1` standard, of which the second was assigned to the testing of the complete radar IFF (Identification Friend or Foe) and passive Elint (Electronic intelligence) receiver equipment with effect from July 1980.

It had originally been hoped that the first delivery of a 'production stan-

dard' conversion could begin in mid-1983 to allow the start of crew training but this date was missed marking the beginning of the end for the Nimrod AEW.Mk 3 programme. In service it was to have been operated by a crew of nine, comprising the pilot, co-pilot and flight engineer on the flightdeck as well as one communications officer and five AEW operators in the cabin. In addition to its radar, it would have featured an extensive collection of communications equipment including LF, HF and UHF radio as well as VHF/UHF secure voice-links and secure digital data links.

Specification
BAe Nimrod AEW.Mk 3
Type: airborne warning and control system platform
Powerplant: four 5507-kg (12,140-lb) thrust Rolls-Royce RB.168-20 Spey Mk 250 turbofans
Performance: maximum speed about 925 km/h (575 mph) at altitude; service ceiling about 12800 m (42,000 ft); endurance about 12 hours
Weight: maximum take-off about 80287 kg (177,000 lb)
Dimensions: span 35.08 m (115 ft 1 in); length 41.90 m (137 ft 5.5 in); height 10.06 m (33 ft 0 in); wing area 197.04 m² (2,121 sq ft)

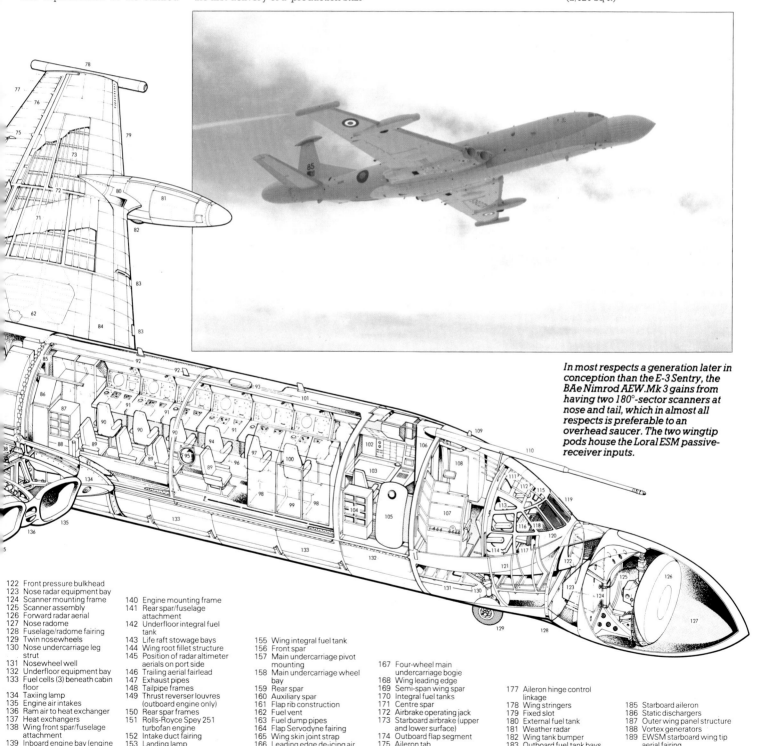

In most respects a generation later in conception than the E-3 Sentry, the BAe Nimrod AEW.Mk 3 gains from having two 180°-sector scanners at nose and tail, which in almost all respects is preferable to an overhead saucer. The two wingtip pods house the Loral ESM passive-receiver inputs.

122 Front pressure bulkhead
123 Nose radar equipment bay
124 Scanner mounting frame
125 Scanner assembly
126 Forward radar aerial
127 Nose radome
128 Fuselage/radome fairing
129 Twin nosewheels
130 Nose undercarriage leg strut
131 Nosewheel well
132 Underfloor equipment bay
133 Fuel cells (3) beneath cabin floor
134 Taxiing lamp
135 Engine air intakes
136 Ram air to heat exchanger
137 Heat exchangers
138 Wing front spar/fuselage attachment
139 Inboard engine bay (engine omitted)

140 Engine mounting frame
141 Rear spar/fuselage attachment
142 Underfloor integral fuel tank
143 Life raft stowage bays
144 Wing root fillet structure
145 Position of radar altimeter aerials on port side
146 Trailing aerial fairlead
147 Exhaust pipes
148 Tailpipe frames
149 Thrust reverser louvres (outboard engine only)
150 Rear spar frames
151 Rolls-Royce Spey 251 turbofan engine
152 Intake duct fairing
153 Landing lamp
154 Leading edge flow spoilers

155 Wing integral fuel tank
156 Front spar
157 Main undercarriage pivot mounting
158 Main undercarriage wheel bay
159 Rear spar
160 Auxiliary spar
161 Flap rib construction
162 Fuel vent
163 Fuel dump pipes
164 Flap Servodyne fairing
165 Wing skin joint strap
166 Leading edge de-icing air ducting

167 Four-wheel main undercarriage bogie
168 Wing leading edge
169 Semi-span wing spar
170 Integral fuel tanks
171 Centre spar
172 Airbrake operating jack
173 Starboard airbrake (upper and lower surface)
174 Outboard flap segment
175 Aileron tab
176 Aileron hinge fairing

177 Aileron hinge control linkage
178 Wing stringers
179 Fixed slot
180 External fuel tank
181 Weather radar
182 Wing tank bumper
183 Outboard fuel tank bays
184 Fuel tank access panels

185 Starboard aileron
186 Static dischargers
187 Outer wing panel structure
188 Vortex generators
189 EWSM starboard wing tip aerial fairing
190 EWSM aerials

Lockheed EC-130 Hercules

In the number of derivatives which have seen service with the US armed forces, the **Lockheed C-130 Hercules** is almost as prolific as the Boeing C-135. Almost inevitably, the multiplicity of variants has included a number of electronic specialists, some being engaged on the acquisition of intelligence whilst others have undertaken C^3 (Command, Control and Communications) tasks in the vicinity of the battlefield, suitably modified machines seeing extensive service during the course of the Vietnam War.

ELINT variants comprise the **C-130A-II** and the **C-130B-II**, which operated in Europe and South East Asia for many years although all of the survivors are known to have reverted to standard cargo configuration during the early or mid-1970s. More recently, the **EC-130H** electronic warfare version has appeared, this model entering service with the 41st Electronic Countermeasures Squadron at Davis-Monthan AFB, Arizona in April 1982 although relatively little is known about the precise nature of the work undertaken.

As far as the C^3 mission is concerned, the first aircraft to be associated with this was the **C-130E-II** (later redesignated as the **EC-130E**) which was used from Thailand for airborne control of tactical fighter/strike aircraft. At least nine examples of the Hercules were so modified to take the USC-15 C^3 system, but these should not be confused with yet another sub-type which, rather confusingly, uses the same EC-130E designation. The 'second-generation' EC-130E is in fact a most distinctive machine, being instantly identifiable by prominent

blade antenna fairings at the forward edge of the fin and beneath each wing. It also carries the modular USC-15 system in the cargo hold, and eight aircraft have been modified to this configuration for service with the Air National Guard.

Two other 'electronic' Hercules subtypes serve with the US Navy, these being the **EC-130G** and **EC-130Q** which are assigned to the mission of maintaining VLF radio contact with the US Navy's large fleet of nuclear-powered and nuclear-armed submarines. Consequently, they feature

comprehensive communications equipment, and these were superseded by the Boeing E-6A Hermes. The two latest versions are the USAF's **EC-130H** stand-off jammer and the US Coast Guard's **EC-130V** AEW platform.

Specification
Lockheed EC-130E Hercules
Type: C^3 platform
Powerplant: four 4,050-shp (3020-ekW) Allison T56-A-7 turboprops
Performance: maximum cruising speed 592 km/h (368 mph); range 3895 km (2,420 miles) with 20412 kg

Totally unlike other EC-130E versions, the Coronet Solo II EC-130E variant has replaced various EC-121 models as a dedicated USAF surveillance platform. The longest wavelengths are received by miles of wire rolled out from the pods.

(45,000 lb) maximum payload
Weights: empty 33064 kg (72,892 lb); maximum take-off not known
Dimensions: span 40.41 m (132 ft 7 in); length 29.79 m (97 ft 9 in); height 11.66 m (38 ft 3 in); wing area 162.12 m² (1,745 sq ft)

Boeing EC-135

Though its variants are physically smaller and much lighter than the Boeing 707-320 family, the Boeing C-135 series has proved to be capable of development for a multitude of uses which include an extraordinary variety of missions concerned with reconnaissance and electronic warfare, as well as for operational use as command post and special communications aircraft. Many other members of the C-135 family have been used for research, and the situation has been complicated as there are two basic types of aircraft (one with J57 turbojets and the other with TF33 turbofans). While some have been modified for electronic duties, often several times in succession, others have been built as such from the outset.

In numerical order, the **EC-135A** designation identified six KC-135A tankers rebuilt as radio relay platforms for use in the SAC PACCS (Post Attack Command/Control System), operating from Ellsworth AFB, South Dakota. The TF33-engined **EC-135C** carries a mass of special communications served by various wire, trailing-wire, blade, saddle and pole antennae; 14 were assigned to the 2nd Airborne Command and Control Squadron at Offutt AFB, and to the 4th ACCS at Ellsworth. Four **EC-135G** aircraft, covered in special communications, serve SAC as airborne ICBM launch control centres. They fly with the 4th ACCS, and with the 305th ARW at Grissom AFB. The five **EC-135H** aircraft are part of the

Most EC-135s are communications relay and command-post aircraft. This profile shows one of the five EC-135H aircraft used by C-in-C Europe and C-in-C Atlantic. Note the saddle aerial and the HF radio probes projecting ahead of each wingtip; these installations are common to several variants.

national control system, one flying with the 6th ACCS from Langley AFB for the Commander-in-Chief Atlantic and the other four with the 10th ACCS from RAF Mildenhall and other European bases for the US Commander-in-Chief Europe. Likewise the ABNCP (airborne national command post) version for the PACAF (Pacific Air Forces) is the **EC-135J**, four being based at Hickam AFB, Hawaii, with the 9th ACCS. Three basically similar **EC-135K** aircraft serve as the national command posts with TAC (USAF Tactical Air Command) flying with the 8th TDCS from Tinker AFB. Five **EC-135L** aircraft form part of the SAC PACCS global network, identified by red/white radiation hazard striping round the rear fuselage to keep personnel away from their super-powerful radio relay systems. Another five tankers were rebuilt as **EC-135P** command posts to serve with the 6th ACCS in the ABNCP network. Among the many other mod-

els are the **EC-135B** and **EC-135N** used for range instrumentation and spacecraft tracking. Reconnaissance sub-types, which include the most grotesquely modified of all, are outside the scope of this survey.

Specification
Boeing EC-135 (baseline figures for J57 aircraft)
Type: various (see above)
Powerplant: four 13,750-lb (6237-kg) thrust Pratt & Whitney J57-59W turbojets
Performance: typical operating speed 800 km/h (497 mph); typical ceiling 11900 m (39,000 ft); range about 8850 km (5,500 miles)
Weights: empty 47000-57000 kg (103,615-125,661 lb); maximum take-off 143338 kg (316,000 lb)
Dimensions: span 39.88 m (130 ft 10 in); length about 40.5 m (133 ft); height (tall fin) 12.69 m (41 ft 8 in); wing area 226 m² (2,433 sq ft)

Another view of a regular EC-135H, operated by the USAF 10th Airborne Command and Control Squadron normally based at RAF Mildenhall. All retain their old J57 engines, which smoke profusely on water-injection departures. They retain the air-to-air refuelling receptacle and Flying Boom installation.

Boeing E-3A Sentry

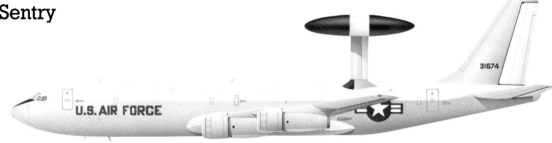

Originally known by the designation **EC-137D**, the **Boeing E-3 Sentry** is based essentially on the Boeing 707-320B airframe, being instantly identifiable by virtue of the massive rotodome carried on top of two support members above the aft fuselage section. Flown for the first time during 1972, the two prototypes were fitted with different AWACS (Airborne Warning and Control Systems) radars (one by Hughes and the other by Westinghouse), and after competitive evaluation, the latter company's APY-1 radar was selected as being more suitable.

Production specimens of the basic **E-3A** began to enter service with the US Air Force in March 1977, but a further 13 months were to pass before operational status was attained. Since then, the USAF continued to purchase the Sentry in modest numbers: production reached 34 out of a planned 46 aircraft completed for use by the 552nd Airborne Warning and Control Wing at Tinker AFB, Oklahoma.

Progressive updating of those aircraft in USAF service will eventually bring about the disappearance of the E-3A, at least as far as the USAF is concerned, the two primary models then being the **E-3B**, which will in fact

be a modernized E-3A, and the **E-3C**. In both cases, the main difference concerns provision of JTIDS (Joint Tactical Information Distribution System), which offers greater security with regard to communications and thus limits the chances of eavesdropping by an enemy. (NATO Sentries will retain the E-3A designation even though they are also to be fitted with JTIDS.)

In addition to those for the USAF, a total of 18 Sentries have been ordered for service with a unique NATO unit at Geilenkirchen in Germany. These aircraft have been upgraded to a standard approximating the most modern US standard with a host of improvements, especially to the radar. The other three customers for the Sentry have been Saudi Arabia, which received five electronically downgraded aircraft, and the UK and France, which took

delivery of seven E-3D (Sentry AEW. Mk 1) and four E-3F aircraft respectively.

Specification
Boeing E-3A Sentry
Type: airborne warning and control system aircraft
Powerplant: four 9526-kg (21,000-lb) thrust Pratt & Whitney TF33-PW-100/100A turbofans
Performance: maximum speed 853 km/h (530 mph); service ceiling more than 8850 m (29,000 ft); endurance on station 6 hours at a radius of 1610 km (1,000 miles)
Weights: empty about 78019 kg (172,000 lb); maximum take-off 147417 kg (325,000 lb)
Dimensions: span 44.42 m (145 ft 9 in); length 46.61 m (152 ft 11 in); height 12.93 m (42 ft 5 in); wing area 283.35 m² (3,050 sq ft)

USAF no. 73-1674 was the first E-3A Sentry (apart from the EC-137D test aircraft), and is today known as a Core E-3A because it has the initial form or core without all the later additions.

Right: New Core E-3As at Boeing Aerospace. All these early production aircraft (nos 1-24) entered service with the 552nd AWAC Wing at Tinker AFB, becoming operational in April 1978.

NATO E-3A Sentries have USAF numbers but NATO insignia and official ownership by the Grand Duchy of Luxembourg! What has yet to be fully worked out is the extent to which C-in-C Europe can interoperate them with the RAF Nimrods.

Tupolev Tu-126 'Moss'

A derivative of the Soviet Tu-114D airliner the **Tupolev Tu-126 'Moss'** is optimised for airborne early warning and control tasks and was first identified in 1969. Operational from 1971 to the early 1990s, the Tu-126 featured a voguish dorsal rotodome, this being similar although, with an 11.0-m (36-ft) diameter, much larger than that of the American E-3 Sentry.

Containing 'Flat Jack' radar in the forward half, the rotodome in its rear houses an IFF array and may also contain data-link equipment, while passive and active electronic warfare antennae are located in four blister fairings on the rear fuselage sides and bottom. Installation of the rotodome has also necessitated a number of aerodynamic improvements, the most visible of which is the addition of a

In the opinion of the Americans the Soviet Tupolev Tu-126 (called 'Moss' by NATO) has a generally poor radar performance and is 'ineffective' over land. The Indian Air Force, however, found it a most valuable aircraft during the 1971 war with Pakistan, and praised it highly.

large ventral strake which offers improved longitudinal stability.

From an operational standpoint, the Tu-126's performance with regard to detection and tracking capability almost certainly leaves a great deal to be desired, a conclusion which would seem to be confirmed by recent estimates which indicate that only about a dozen aircraft are in service; that the Soviets are now working on an Ilyushin Il-76 AWACS aircraft also seems to bear witness to the Tu-126's less than satisfactory performance. Be that as it may, the 'Moss' is believed to possess powerful jamming equipment and may well have an offensive application in the stand-off jamming role.

With regard to operational use, the 'Moss' is thought to be mainly employed in augmenting Soviet ground-based radars, filling such gaps as exist in coverage and working in fairly close conjunction with interceptors to counter the threat posed by enemy strike aircraft operating at low level.

Specification
Tupolev Tu-126 'Moss'
Type: airborne warning and control system platform
Powerplant: four 14,795-eshp (11033-ekW) Kuznetsov NK-12MV turboprops
Performance: maximum speed 740 km/h (460 mph) at altitude; service ceiling 10000 m (32,820 ft); endurance

Derived from the Tupolev Tu-114, the Tu-126 'Moss' is thought to augment Soviet ground-based air defence radars. The front of the rotodome contains a 'Flat Jack' surveillance radar, with the rear half thought to be devoted to IFF, data link and EW antennae.

more than 20 hours.
Weights: empty 90720 kg (200,000 lb); maximum take-off 165550 kg (364,969 lb)
Dimensions: span 51.20 m (168 ft 0 in); length 57.30 m (188 ft 0 in) including inflight-refuelling probe; height 11.58 m (38 ft 0 in); wing area 311.2 m² (3,350 sq ft)

Ilyushin A-50 'Mainstay'

First flown in March 1971, the Ilyushin Il-76 'Candid' turbofan-powered tactical transport bears a distinct similarity to the Lockheed C-141 StarLifter. From this the Soviets developed the A-50 'Mainstay' as successor to the Tupolev Tu-126 'Moss', the leading role in the development programme being taken by the Beriev rather than Ilyushin experimental design bureau. Developed in the 1970s, production of 20 aircraft began in the 1980s.

The adaptation process was based on the reconfiguration of the hold for specialist electronics for the type's airborne early warning and control function, requiring the introduction of situation display consoles for the tactical crew within the mission complement of the A-50's normal crew of 15. Its role is indicated by the large rotodome added above the fuselage in line with the trailing edge of the wing's centre section, the forward part of this

rotodome accommodating the antenna for the advanced look-up/look-down air surveillance radar, and the rear part the antennae associated with IFF and secure data-link systems. A canoe fairing farther forward on the fuselage carries a satellite communications antenna. It also has defensive capability in the form of a radar warning receiver and two packs of flares on the sides of the rear fuselage, and electronic warfare pods are under

development for wing- tip installation. The A-50U improved version was first revealed in 1995.

Specification
Ilyushin A-50 'Mainstay'
Details are similar to the Il-76. Height of 14.8 m (48 ft 5 in) and an operating altitude of 10,000 m (32,810 ft) for a figure-eight track with 100 km (62 miles) between the centres of the lobes' orbits.

Strategic and Tactical Reconnaissance Aircraft

Reconnaissance platforms never carry offensive weapons and seldom take off with defensive weapons. Even so, their operations are crucial to the successful planning of any air, land or sea campaign by providing planners and commanders with information about the enemy's disposition and strength.

Operational from 1967 and shrouded in secrecy throughout its long career, the high-flying, long-range, supersonic Lockheed SR-71 'Blackbird' has now been placed in store.

One of the prime requisites in waging war successfully is knowing the intentions of one's opponent, what forces he has deployed and how they are disposed. This 'intelligence' can be obtained in a variety of ways but one effective method is aerial reconnaissance.

Aerial reconnaissance falls into two areas of activity, strategic and tactical, and can be carried out in any one of several ways using a variety of tools. More concerned with the long-term picture, strategic reconnaissance is now very much the preserve of 'spy satellites', and there is as yet no effective means of countering these although the US Air Force and, one must assume, the former Soviet air forces have worked on

the development of anti-satellite missiles. Strategic reconnaissance can also be, and is being, carried out by manned aircraft.

Few of the types engaged in such duty are examined here. Much of their mission entails collecting Elint (Electronic intelligence) and Sigint (Signals intelligence). The United States accomplishes this task mainly

with variants of the Boeing RC-135. The Soviet successors generally employ converted bomber types such as the Tupolev Tu-16 'Badger' and Tu-95 'Bear'. The UK meanwhile operates the BAe Nimrod R.Mk 1, and Germany has converted Dassault Atlantic maritime patrollers to the Elint task. The most impressive strategic reconnaissance tool up to 1998, though, was the Lockheed SR-71A 'Blackbird'. It was able to contribute significantly to the near-term view, which is more generally the domain of tactical reconnaissance aircraft, many of which are variants of combat types.

Improvements in aircraft performance have been matched by those in reconnaissance systems, although the camera, shooting black-and-white film is still the most used tool for providing information about the battlefield. Current efforts are directed towards finding alternative methods of obtaining data, such as video, and then downloading it to a ground station in as near as possible to real time.

Strategic and tactical reconnaissance aircraft complement each other in ascertaining the 'big picture', and should not be neglected.

FRANCE
Dassault-Breguet Mirage IIIR

Evolved from the definitive Mirage IIIE tactical strike fighter, the **Dassault-Breguet Mirage IIIR** first flew in prototype form on 31 October 1961, with production aircraft beginning to replace the Republic RF-84F Thunderflash in Armée de l'Air service at Strasbourg during the course of 1963, all three *escadrons* of the parent wing eventually converting by the mid-1960s. An initial batch of 50 aircraft was acquired by the French air force, these subsequently being joined by 20 examples of the **Mirage IIIRD**, this latter variant featuring a number of detail changes over the original production model, such as an improved navigation radar. These aircraft are now being progressively replaced by the newer Mirage F.1CR.

Like most photographic-reconnaissance derivatives of fighter aircraft, the Mirage IIIR has a redesigned nose section, deletion of the Cyrano II fire-control radar permitting the installation of up to five cameras for day or night operation. To permit armed reconnaissance missions to be undertaken, the Mirage IIIR can be equipped with two 30-mm DEFA can-

As well as receiving Mirage III interceptors, Pakistan also purchased 13 Mirage IIIRP reconnaissance variants, distinguished by the redesigned nose housing various forward, downward and sideways-looking cameras.

Dassault Mirage IIIR of 33ᵉ Escadre, Armée de l'Air, based at Strasbourg. This unit has now re-equipped with F.1CRs.

non, and it is also able to carry various types of ordnance underwing, the pilot being provided with a reflector gun sight and low-altitude bombing system equipment to assist in weapons delivery.

In addition to those aircraft acquired for service with the French air force, reconnaissance models of the Mirage have found favour overseas, close to 100 being built for the export market. These include variants of the Mirage IIIR for Pakistan (13 **Mirage IIIRP** aircraft), South Africa (eight **Mirage IIIRZ** aircraft) and Switzerland (18 **Mirage IIIRS** aircraft) plus numerous examples of reconnaissance-configured Mirage 5s, the latter being a simplified Mirage intended specifically for export. Customers for the **Mirage 5R** include Abu Dhabi, Belgium, Colombia, Egypt, Gabon and Libya which between them have taken delivery of approximately 50 aircraft, most of which are still in use today.

Specification
Mirage IIIR
Type: single-seat tactical reconnaissance aircraft
Powerplant: one SNECMA Atar 9C turbojet rated at 6200-kg (13,670-lb) afterburning thrust
Performance: maximum speed at sea level 1390 km/h (863 mph) or Mach 1.14; maximum speed at altitude 2350 km/h (1,460 mph) or Mach 2.2; range in clean condition about 1600 km (1,000 miles); ferry range with full external fuel 4000 km (2,485 miles)
Weights: empty 6600 kg (14,550 lb); maximum take-off 13500 kg (29,760 lb)
Dimensions: span 8.22 m (27 ft 0 in); length 15.50 m (50 ft 10¼ in); height 4.25 m (13 ft 11½ in); wing area 35.00 m² (377 sq ft)

This is the development aircraft for the Mirage IIIR programme, involving removing the nose fire control radar (Cyrano II) and replacing this with cameras. The airframe was the same as the standard model, and weapons can be carried.

FRANCE
Dassault-Breguet Mirage F.1CR

Flown for the first time in prototype form shortly before Christmas Day 1966, the **Dassault-Breguet Mirage F.1** has proved to be almost as versatile as the Mirage III which preceded it, being able to undertake a multiplicity of missions including air superiority, tactical strike, ground-attack and, more recently, tactical reconnaissance.

Initial production examples of the basic F.1C all-weather interceptor model entered service with the French air force during the course of 1973 and this type has also met with considerable success on the export

market, customers including Ecuador, Greece, Iraq, Jordan, Kuwait, Libya, Morocco, South Africa and Spain. It seems likely that manufacture of variants of the Mirage F.1 will continue until at least 1987, several hundred now being on order or in service throughout the world.

The specialized reconnaissance model is the **Mirage F.1CR**, and this is now in process of replacing the 50 or so Mirage IIIR/RD aircraft which equip the 33ᵉ Escadre at Strasbourg, the French air force's sole tactical reconnaissance unit. Selected in February 1979, two Mirage F.1CR prototypes

were produced for test duties, the first making its maiden flight on 20 November 1981. These two machines are being followed by 62 production examples, deliveries of the first to the 33ᵉ Escadre having begun fairly recently.

Mission-related equipment includes OMERA cameras carried internally together with an infra-red sensor, while additional electromagnetic or optical sensors can be housed in an external pod fitted beneath the aircraft's belly. Air-to-air missiles can also be carried for defensive purposes, while inflight-refuelling gear is also fitted as standard.

Thus far, the reconnaissance variant has not been ordered for export but, in view of past sales successes, it would seem reasonable to assume that some overseas customers will acquire this model in due course.

Specification
Mirage F.1CR
Type: single-seat tactical reconnaissance aircraft
Powerplant: one SNECMA Atar 9K-50 turbojet rated at 7200-kg (15,873-lb) afterburning thrust
Performance: maximum speed at sea level 1475 km/h (917 mph) or Mach 1.2;

maximum speed at altitude 2335 km/h (1,450 mph) or Mach 2.2; ferry range 3300 km (2,050 miles)
Weights: empty 7400 kg (16,314 lb); maximum take-off 16200 kg (35,715 lb)

Dimensions: span 8.40 m (27 ft 6¾ in); length 15.00 m (49 ft 2½ in); height 4.50 m (14 ft 9 in); wing area 25.00 m² (269.1 sq ft)

Now replacing the Mirage IIIs of the 33ᵉ Escadre at Strasbourg, the Mirage F.1CR can carry external reconnaissance pods as well as its internal cameras. Aircraft can carry

Matra Magic air-to-air missiles for self-defence and this example is carrying practice missiles. Inflight-refuelling equipment is standard.

SEPECAT Jaguar

Resulting from a collaborative venture between France and the United Kingdom, the **SEPECAT Jaguar** is primarily a single-seat strike/tactical support aircraft, and it is only the Royal Air Force which employs the type in the reconnaissance role, a task far removed from that originally envisaged when development work began in the mid-1960s.

At that time, the UK was searching for an advanced trainer aircraft whilst France was on the look-out for an inexpensive strike aircraft, and it seemed for a time that both of these requirements could be satisfied by a single design. In the event, the Jaguar metamorphosed into a somewhat more sophisticated machine than either nation originally planned, and there are significant differences between the French and British aircraft with regard to avionics fit.

Tactical reconnaissance is undertaken by two RAF units (No. 2 Squadron at Laarbruch in West Germany and No. 41 Squadron at Coltishall in the UK), each equipped with **Jaguar GR.Mk 1** machines identical to those aircraft assigned to the six squadrons engaged in strike duties. For the units' designated reconnaissance role, however, their Jaguars each carry a large pod on the centreline stores station, containing cameras and infra-red linescan equipment. Reconnaissance cameras are located in a pair of rotating drums within the pod, swivelling to expose the camera ports during photography. Two side-mounted and one forward-looking camera are positioned in the forward drum whilst the

second can contain a pair of oblique cameras for low-level work or a solitary vertical camera best suited for photography from medium altitudes. This combination offers quite comprehensive coverage, one particularly useful facility being a data conversion unit which automatically annotates the aircraft's position on the film, details of this being obtained from the onboard navigation computer. IR-linescan film is similarly marked.

In addition to serving with France and the United Kingdom, strike versions of the Jaguar have been supplied to India, Oman and Ecuador, the latest order coming from Nigeria.

Specification
Jaguar GR.Mk 1 .
Type: single-seat tactical reconnaissance/strike fighter
Powerplant: two Rolls-Royce/ Turboméca Adour Mk 104 turbofans

each rated at 3647-kg (8,040-lb) afterburning thrust
Performance: maximum speed at altitude 1700 km/h (1,055 mph) or Mach 1.6; ferry range 4205 km (2,614 miles)
Weights: empty about 7000 kg (15,432 lb); maximum take-off 15700 kg (34,612 lb)
Dimensions: span 8.69 m (28 ft 6 in); length 15.52 m (50 ft 11 in); height 4.89 m (16 ft 0½ in); wing area 24.18 m² (260.27 sq ft)

Jaguar GR.Mk 1s fly in the reconnaissance role with No. 2 Sqn in Germany, carrying a pod under the fuselage containing cameras and infra-red equipment. These form RAFG's tactical reconnaissance element and will eventually be replaced by Tornados.

🇬🇧 BAC Canberra

Although the basic design dates back to the late 1940s, the **BAC Canberra** is still in fairly widespread service, several specialized photographic-reconnaissance specimens being numbered amongst those aircraft that are still in use. In the United Kingdom a handful of **Canberra PR.Mk 9** aircraft equip No. 1 Photographic Reconnaissance Unit at Wyton but the main force of PR.Mk 9s are being completely rebuilt by Shorts (the original manufacturer) to carry CASTOR (Corps Air-

borne Stand-Off Radar), a giant SAR (Synthetic Aperture Radar) for surveillance over Germany from heights over 18.3 km (60,000 ft) exactly similar to that done by the TR-1A. India's air force is believed still to use a small number of **Canberra PR.Mk 57** aircraft on operational reconnaissance tasks. Finally, the Venezuelan air force still has a solitary example of the **Canberra PR.Mk 83** which serves alongside about a dozen Canberra B.Mk 82s and B(I).Mk 82s with Grupo de Bombardeo

13 at Barcelona.

Specification
Canberra PR.Mk 9
Type: two-seat tactical photographic reconnaissance aircraft
Powerplant: two Rolls-Royce Avon 206 turbojets each rated at 4559-kg (10,050-lb) thrust
Performance: maximum speed 998 km/h (620 mph) or Mach 0.94; service ceiling about 18290 m (60,000 ft); maximum range 7240 km

(4,500 miles)
Weight: normal take-off 22680 kg (50,000 lb)
Dimensions: span 20.68 m (67 ft 10 in); length 20.32 m (66 ft 8 in); height 4.75 m (15 ft 7 in)

Alongside target tugs and ECM trainers, No. 1 Photographic Reconnaissance Unit operates Canberra PR.Mk 9 aircraft in a limited role.

 ITALY

Aeritalia G91R

The winning contender of a NATO design contest to find a lightweight reconnaissance/strike fighter in the early 1950s, the **Aeritalia G91** flew for the first time on 9 August 1956 but failed to achieve widespread adoption by the nations which comprise the NATO alliance. Originally ordered for service with Greece, Turkey, Italy and West Germany, the type eventually achieved operational status only with the latter two nations, more than 700 being built. The majority were of **G91R** configuration featuring a modified nose installation containing three Vinten cameras for forward and lateral oblique photography.

The initial production variant was the **G91R-1** which entered service with the Italian air force at the beginning of the 1960s, this air arm eventually acquiring over 100 similar aircraft. However, it was West Germany which proved to be the major customer, receiving a sizeable batch of Fiat-built **G91R-3** aircraft plus a substantial number built under licence by a consortium comprising Dornier, Messerschmitt and Heinkel. The first German-built example of the G91R-3 made its maiden flight from Oberpfaffenhofen during July 1961, and the type entered service with Aufklärungsgeschwader 53 at Leipheim during 1962.

In the event, Germany's Luftwaffe also operated some 50 or so **G91R-4** aircraft, originally being earmarked for equal distribution between Greece

and Turkey, which eventually rejected them. After a fairly short career with the Luftwaffe, 40 of these aircraft were transferred to Portugal and the survivors remain in service today alongside a number of G91R-3s made redundant when the Luftwaffe re-equipped its light attack units with Dassault-Breguet/Dornier Alpha Jets in the late 1970s and early 1980s.

Italy also acquired a variant which was known as the **G91Y** and differed significantly, being larger all round

and employing two General Electric J85-GE-13A afterburning turbojets in place of the G91R's single Orpheus. Like the G91R, this features a reconnaissance nose, the two prototypes being followed by 66 production specimens, most of which are still in service today. In addition, about 160

Ex-Luftwaffe Aeritalia G91R-4 of Escuadra 121 'Tigres' when based in Portuguese Guinea (Guinea-Bissau) in 1967.

Aeritalia G91R-1A of the 51st Aerobrigata, 14th Gruppo, part of No. 2 Stormo Tattici Ricognitori Leggeri based at Istrana.

examples of the two-seat G91T trainer variant were also completed and this has also seen service with Italy, Portugal and West Germany.

Specification
G91Y
Type: single-seat tactical reconnaissance/strike fighter
Powerplant: two General Electric J85-GE-13A turbojets each rated at 1851-kg (4,080-lb) afterburning thrust
Performance: maximum speed 1110 km/h (690 mph); service ceiling 12500 m (41,000 ft); combat radius at sea level 600 km (372 miles); ferry range 3500 km (2,175 miles)
Weights: empty 3900 kg (8,598 lb); maximum take-off 8700 kg (19,180 lb)
Dimensions: span 9.01 m (29 ft 6½ in); length 11.67 m (38 ft 3½ in); height 4.43 m (14 ft 6 in); wing area 16.42 m² (176.74 sq ft)

Aircraft of the Italian air force's 32° Stormo overfly Brindisi. These are G91Ys, differing from the earlier version by having two engines for greater payload and safety, and a redesigned nose.

USA
Grumman OV-1 Mohawk

Grumman OV-1D Mohawk of the US Army. This example was originally an OV-1B, serving in Vietnam, but has since been updated.

Intended primarily for battlefield reconnaissance duties, the somewhat bug-eyed **Grumman OV-1 Mohawk** dates back to the late 1950s, but despite its age and considerable vulnerability it remains in widespread service with the United States Army, which received close to 400 examples during the course of the 1960s.

Initial variants were reasonably unsophisticated but progressive modification efforts over the years have brought about a significant improvement in its sensor systems. The first production model to see service was the **OV-1A**, essentially intended to fulfil photographic reconnaissance duties by day or night, being fitted with cameras, flares and advanced navigation equipment. It was succeeded by the **OV-1B** which was the first model to incorporate SLAR (Side-Looking Airborne Radar), this AN/APS-94 equipment being housed in a prominent pod carried externally under the lower starboard forward fuselage. The next derivative was the **OV-1C**, which utilised the AN/AAS-24 infra-red sensor in place of the SLAR gear, while the final new-build member of the family was the **OV-1D**, basically a quick-change aircraft capable of operating with either infra-red or SLAR sensors. Deliveries of the OV-1D terminated in 1970, bringing total production to 375. Additional OV-1Ds were made available by the relatively simple expedient of converting most of the 100-plus OV-1Bs and OV-1Cs which remained.

More recently, a number of other derivatives have appeared, including the **RV-1D** and the **EV-1E**. The former version is a conversion of the OV-1B specifically intended for Elint (electronic intelligence) duty, the dozen or so aircraft known to exist being fitted with a multiplicity of passive receivers, analysers and recorders to gather unknown or 'hostile' signals. The EV-1E, again a rebuilt OV-1B, is fitted with AN/ALQ-133 'Quick Look II' surveillance radar, additional Elint equipment and electronic warfare pods. At least 16 conversions have been produced. Israel's air force has received two OV-1Ds, and continued updating effort should result in updated or converted OV-Ds for various customers including Pakistan and the US Army. The JOV-1B was an armed version used in Vietnam. The last of the OV-1 series have been retired.

The Grumman OV-1D can carry the AN/AAS-24 infra-red surveillance system or, as here, the AN/APS-94 side-looking airborne radar (SLAR) package.

Specification
OV-1D
Type: two-seat battlefield surveillance/reconnaissance aircraft
Powerplant: two Avco Lycoming T53-L-701 turboprops each rated at 1,400 hp (1044 kW)
Performance: maximum speed 465 km/h (289 mph); range 1520 km (944 miles)
Weights: empty 5467 kg (12,053 lb); maximum take-off 8214 kg (18,109 lb)
Dimensions: span 14.63 m (48 ft 0 in); length (with SLAR) 13.69 m (44 ft 11 in);

An excellent portrait of a JOV-1B Mohawk carrying the SLAR pod, long range fuel tanks and bombs. These aircraft saw much service in Vietnam and all have now been converted to OV-1D or RV-1D standard.

height 3.86 m (12 ft 8 in); wing area 30.66 m² (330 sq ft)

USA

Lockheed F-104 Starfighter

Winner of a previous so-called 'sale of the century' and used by several NATO air arms for many years, the **Lockheed F-104G** variant of the Starfighter is now fast disappearing from service within central Europe as more and more General Dynamics F-16 Fighting Falcons and Panavia Tornados become available.

During its heyday, however, the Starfighter formed the backbone of the NATO alliance's air power and a number of reconnaissance-configured aircraft were produced, sensor packages varying considerably according to the specialized requirements of the parent air arm. The most widespread variant, and the one which remains in service today in modest numbers, was the **RF-104G**, which featured a belly fairing containing cameras, installation of these necessitating the removal of the M61 Vulcan rotary cannon armament. West Germany, Italy and the Netherlands all operated this variant of the Starfighter for a time, but today only Italy retains this type in its original configuration although the Netherlands does still use the standard F-104G for reconnaissance tasks, using the Orpheus pod to accomplish this mission. The German Luftwaffe and Marineflieger used the RTF-104G two-seater.

In addition to those aircraft manufactured in Europe during the early 1960s, the parent company also completed a number of RF-104Gs for export under the Military Assistance Program to friendly nations. These were essentially similar in appearance to their Euro-pean counterparts and were fitted with three Hycon KS-67A cameras, examples being delivered to Norway and Taiwan, a small group still being in front-line service with the latter nation today whilst most of the Norwegian specimens have been passed on to Turkey.

Canada's **CF-104** was also originally engaged in reconnaissance duty, aircraft assigned to this task being fitted with a prominent belly-mounted pod containing a battery of Vinten cameras. This is no longer operational.

Specification
RF-104G
Type: single-seat all-weather tactical reconnaissance aircraft
Powerplant: one General Electric J79-GE-11A turbojet rated at 7167-kg (15,800-lb) afterburning thrust
Performance: maximum low level speed 1473 km/h (915 mph) or Mach 1.2; maximum stabilized speed at 12190 m (40,000 ft) 2124 km/h (1,320 mph) or Mach 2.0; tactical radius with external fuel 1110 km (690 miles)
Weights: empty 6486 kg (14,300 lb); maximum take-off 11352 kg (25,027 lb)
Dimensions: span 6.68 m (21 ft 11 in); length 16.69 m (54 ft 9 in); height 4.11 m (13 ft 6 in); wing area 18.22 m² (196.1 sq ft)

Lockheed CF-104G of No. 441 Sqn CAF at Marville, France, carrying the Vicom camera pod under the fuselage.

Although no longer used, the RF-104G Starfighter was an important reconnaissance type in the NATO inventory, carrying its cameras in the fuselage after the removal of the Vulcan cannon pod. The Dutch still fly F-104s in the recce role with Orpheus camera pods.

Lockheed U-2/TR-1

Lockheed TR-1 tactical reconnaissance platform.

Colloquially known as 'the black lady of espionage', in a reference to earlier exploits on behalf of the Central Intelligence Agency, the **Lockheed U-2** family of reconnaissance aircraft is now somewhat overshadowed by this company's rather more spectacular SR-71 but it still has a valid role to play, this being reflected by the remarkable fact that, as the **TR-1**, it has recently been reinstated in production for the second time, a unique distinction indeed.

Conceived originally to meet a CIA requirement for an aircraft with the potential of operating at extreme altitude and first flown in the mid-1950s, the U-2's unique capabilities rendered it virtually immune from interception and made possible repeated overflights of the Soviet Union as part of the intelligence-gathering efforts of that era. The destruction of the aircraft being flown by Francis 'Gary' Powers in May 1960 brought an abrupt halt to this phase of activities, CIA attentions then focussing on the People's Republic of China which in the early 1960s was fast emerging as a major nuclear power.

Today, U-2 and TR-1 operations are usually conducted in what is best described as a 'permissive' environment on the friendly side of important frontiers. With the exception of a couple of aircraft assigned to NASA, none of the original production examples remain active, the principal model now used by Strategic Air Command being the **U-2R** which entered service in the late 1960s and which differs from its predecessors by virtue of greatly increased length and wing span. The U-2R is in the process of being joined by an in-

creasing number of TR-1s, these externally being very similar although they are intended for tactical rather than strategic missions. Current USAF planning envisages basing about 18 **TR-1A** aircraft at Alconbury in the United Kingdom, these being tasked with surveillance of the battle area or potential battle area by day or night and in all kinds of weather. Flown for the first time in August 1981, the TR-1A will rely on a sophisticated array of electronic sensors to accomplish the reconnaissance mission. Currently carried is the UPD-X side-looking airborne radar and the Lockheed PLSS (Precision Location Strike System).

The three **TR-1B/U-2RT** two-seat trainers are now TU-2 machines, while the TR-1As have become **U-2R** aircraft that were upgraded to **U-2S** standard with General Electric F118 turbofans.

Specification
TR-1A
Type: single-seat all-weather tactical/strategic reconnaissance aircraft
Powerplant: one Pratt & Whitney J75-PW-13B turbojet rated at 7711-kg (17,000-lb) thrust
Performance: estimated maximum cruise speed at over 21335 m (70,000 ft) 692 km/h (430 mph); operational ceiling estimated at 27430 m (90,000 ft); maximum range more than 4825 km (3,000 miles)
Weights: empty about 7258 kg (16,000 lb); maximum take-off 18144 kg (40,000 lb)
Dimensions: span 31.39 m (103 ft 0 in); length 19.20 m (63 ft 0 in); height 4.88 m (16 ft 0 in); wing area about 92.90 m² (1,000 sq ft)

Predecessor of the TR-1 was the U-2R, which in turn was a larger version of the earlier U-2. The utility 'U' designation veiled a more sinister role, and the U-2 aroused much controversy.

Below: The second test TR-1A aircraft seen over California, devoid of mission pods. All the early deliveries have come to Europe, notably the 17th Reconnaissance Wing at Alconbury.

Lockheed SR-71A

Developed from the A-12 and flown for the first time during December 1964, the **Lockheed SR-71A** is still the world's fastest operational aircraft, approximately a dozen examples of this outstanding machine being active with the 9th Strategic Reconnaissance Wing at any given time. Possessing the ability to survey 260000 km² (100,000 sq miles) of the Earth's surface in just one hour, the SR-71A routinely cruises at Mach 3 at altitudes in excess of 24385 m (80,000 ft) during the course of its duties, and is able to gather a variety of data by virtue of highly classified but interchangeable photographic and electronic sensors which are installed to meet specific mission objectives.

Deliveries to Strategic Air Command began in January 1966, and it is believed that a total of 32 aircraft was built, this figure including two examples of the two-seat **SR-71B** plus a single **SR-71C**, the latter model also being a two-seater for pilot training, built of components taken from crashed aircraft and a structural test specimen.

Specific details of the work undertaken by the SR-71A remain shrouded in secrecy, but it is known that operations are routinely conducted from two forward operating locations by aircraft detached from the wing's headquarters at Beale AFB, California. The first of these, at Kadena in Okinawa, normally has three aircraft attached at any time, whilst Mildenhall in the United Kingdom is the location of the second SR-71 detachment which usually controls the activities of two aircraft. In addition, Beale serves as the centre for crew training and may well also support operational flights using inflight-refuelling to extend the range of the SR-71.

The rigours of high-speed flight at extreme altitude are such that the two crew members, comprising a pilot and a reconnaissance systems operator, both wear full pressure suits similar to those of astronauts, and indeed selection procedures are identical to those originally used in choosing trainee astronauts. The SR-71 was retired in 1998.

Specification
SR-71A
Type: two-seat all-weather strategic reconnaissance
Powerplant: two Pratt & Whitney J58 turbo-ramjet engines each rated at 14742-kg (32,500-lb) afterburning thrust
Performance: maximum speed at 24385 m (80,000 ft) 3661 km/h (2,275 mph) or Mach 3.35; operational ceiling 26060 m (85,500 ft); maximum unrefuelled range at Mach 3 5230 km (3,250 miles)
Weights: empty 27216 kg (60,000 lb); maximum take-off 78019 kg (172,000 lb)
Dimensions: span 16.94 m (55 ft 7 in); length 32.74 m (107 ft 5 in); height 5.64 m (18 ft 6 in); wing area 166.76 m² (1,795 sq ft)

Seen banking over its home base at Beale AFB, California, this SR-71A is from the 1st Strategic Reconnaissance Squadron, 9th SRW.

A Lockheed SR-71 going through training

USA
Northrop RF-5

The diminutive but highly successful **Northrop F-5 Freedom Fighter/Tiger** family has also been developed to perform photographic reconnaissance duties; approximately 100 examples of the **RF-5A** and **RF-5E Tigereye** have been built to date.

The first and thus far most numerous reconnaissance model to appear was the RF-5A, 89 examples of which were constructed by the parent company between 1967-72. Featuring a nose-mounted battery of four KS-92A cameras, the RF-5A entered development in October 1963 in response to a US Air Force directive calling for a daylight tactical reconnaissance model of the Freedom Fighter for supply to friendly nations as part of military assistance and foreign military sales programmes.

The RF-5A flew for the first time during May 1968, deliveries beginning during the following month with the initial aircraft going to Iran, which received 13 production examples as part of the military aid programme then in being. Subsequent customers comprised Turkey (20 aircraft), South Vietnam (10), Thailand (4), Greece (16), South Korea (8), Morocco (2) and Norway (16) before production of this model ceased in June 1972.

In addition to those aircraft produced by the parent company, the Freedom Fighter was also built under licence in Spain, 17 examples of the reconnaissance model known locally as the **SRF-5A** being completed by CASA whilst many of the 89 **CF-5As** and **75 NF-5As** completed by Canadair for service with the armed forces of Canada, the Netherlands and Venezuela also featured latent reconnaissance capability, being fitted with camera noses.

More recently, Northrop has developed the **RF-5E Tigereye** for reconnaissance duties and this is a rather more sophisticated machine based on the F-5E Tiger II and using up to six cameras or infra-red scanners on quick-change pallets which can be inserted into the extended nose. Making its maiden flight on 29 January 1979, the RF-5E has thus far failed to find a ready market, the only customers being Malaysia, which took delivery of two during 1983, and Saudi Arabia, which has ordered 10.

Specification
RF-5A
Type: single-seat tactical reconnaissance aircraft
Powerplant: two General Electric J85-GE-13 turbojets each rated at 1851-kg (4,080-lb) afterburning thrust
Performance: maximum speed at 10975 m (36,000 ft) 1489 km/h (925 mph) or Mach 1.4; combat ceiling 15240 m (50,000 ft); range 2595 km (1,612 miles)
Weights: empty 3667 kg (8,085 lb); maximum take-off 8952 kg (19,736 lb)
Dimensions: span 7.70 m (25 ft 3 in); length 14.38 m (47 ft 2 in); height 4.01 m (13 ft 2 in); wing area 15.79 m² (170 sq ft)

Malaysia operates two Northrop RF-5E Tigereyes on reconnaissance duties, equipped with Sidewinder air-to-air missiles on the wingtips for protection. The type features a redesigned nose and an arrester hook in common with most US fighters.

SWEDEN
Saab 35 Draken

Flying for the first time on 27 June 1963, the **Saab S35E** is a variant of the distinctive double-delta Draken (dragon) interceptor, optimized for the tactical reconnaissance role and able satisfactorily to perform low-, medium- or high-altitude reconnaissance by day or night. Essentially similar to the J35D fighter, the S35E features a battery of forward-facing, vertical and oblique cameras in a redesigned nose section, the entire outer shell of which slides forward to permit rapid access and thus facilitate removal and replacement of camera magazines.

Entering service with the Swedish air force's Flygflottilj 11 in the mid-1960s, the S35E served as the Flyg-vapen reconnaissance workhorse for many years, although it has now been largely supplanted by a version of the Viggen. Some 60 examples of the S35E were produced, this figure being fairly evenly split between new-build airframes and reconfigured J35Ds, whilst a further 20 reconnaissance Drakens were produced for the Royal Danish air force (forming part of the total of 52 Drakens acquired by Denmark in the early 1970s) and being known by the designation **RF35** in that country's service. With the exception of a handful of attrition losses, all are still in service today, equipping Eskadrille 729 at Karup. In company parlance, the machines are known as the **S35SD**, the basic Saab 35X being a derivative of the definitive J35F interceptor earmarked for the export market.

Specification
S35E/RF35
Type: single-seat tactical reconnaissance aircraft
Powerplant: one Svenska Flygmotor RM6C turbojet rated at 7760-kg (17,108-lb) afterburning thrust.

Danish Drakens are used in the tactical reconnaissance role when fitted with external pods. Another version, the S35E (RF-35 in Denmark), has a full camera nose with provision for up to five OMERA cameras.

Performance: maximum speed 2125 km/h (1,320 mph) or Mach 2.0; range on internal fuel about 1290 km (800 miles); maximum range 3250 km (2,020 miles)
Weights: empty 8245 kg (18,180 lb); maximum take-off 16000 kg (35,275 lb)
Dimensions: span 9.40 m (30 ft 10 in); length 15.85 m (52 ft 0 in); height 3.89 m (12 ft 9 in); wing area 49.20 m^2 (529.6 sq ft)

Saab-Scania Viggen

Undoubtedly one of the most impressive and capable combat aircraft to emerge in the past couple of decades, the **Saab-Scania 37 Viggen** (thunderbolt) is available in several different sub-types, two of which are principally engaged in reconnaissance duties.

To fulfil Flygvapen (Swedish air force) requirements in the tactical reconnaissance area, the SF37 was developed, and this features the almost obligatory camera nose in place of the radar doppler fitted to other members of the Viggen family. An impressive array of cameras (totalling seven in all) is provided, comprising four vertical or oblique units for low-level photography, two vertical cameras for medium- to high-altitude tasks, and a solitary infra-red camera. Additional capability is provided by pod-mounted systems as and when required, such facilities enhancing both day and night reconnaissance potential and including additional specialized cameras and Red Baron infra-red linescan equipment. Ordered into production early in 1973, the SF37 variant flew for the first time on 21 May of the same year, with deliveries to the first operational unit, F21 at Lulea, beginning during April 1977. This model replaced the same company's S35E Draken in Swedish air force service.

The other reconnaissance derivative of the Viggen is the SH37 which is optimized for maritime applications. Featuring a special long-range, forward-facing camera contained in a fairing located beneath and slightly aft of the starboard engine air inlet, this model unlike the SF37 retains a nose-mounted radar for surveillance purposes and it can also operate with additional sensors or weaponry. Replacing the S32C Lansen, the SH37 prototype made its maiden flight on 10 December 1973, production specimens being delivered from June 1975. This sub-type is now active with at least two Flygvapen units.

In May 1991, Saab converted 115 AJ37, SF37 and SH37 aircraft to AJS37 standard for service as air-defence, attack and reconnaissance fighters.

Specification
SF37/SH37
Type: single-seat tactical reconnaissance/maritime surveillance aircraft

Saab SF37 Viggen of F21 based at Lulea with centreline drop tank and Red Baron multi-sensor pod.

Powerplant: one Volvo Flygmotor RM8A turbofan rated at 11800-kg (26,015-lb) afterburning thrust
Performance: maximum speed at altitude 2125 km/h (1,320 mph) or Mach 2.0; tactical radius more than 1000 km (621 miles)
Weights: empty 9000 kg (19,840 lb);

Deleting the radar of earlier models, the SF37 carries four low-level, two high-altitude and an infra-red camera in its nose. It can also carry

maximum take-off 20500 kg (45,195 lb)
Dimensions: span 10.60 m (34 ft 9¼ in); length 16.30 m (53 ft 5¼ in); height

ECM pods, Red Baron pods and attack weaponry. This example is from F13 at Norrköping.

5.80 m (19 ft 0¼ in); wing area 46.00 m^2 (495.1 sq ft)

Mikoyan-Gurevich MiG-21R 'Fishbed'

Without doubt the most widely used and prolific fighter aircraft of the post-World War II era, the **Mikoyan-Gurevich MiG-21 'Fishbed'** remains in quantity production today, albeit in a very different form from that of its debut during the mid-1950s, and it has almost inevitably spawned a number of reconnaissance derivatives which feature varying sensor packages.

The original reconnaissance model was the **MiG-21R** (based on the MiG-21PFMA which introduced the large dorsal spine, now a common feature of

Mikoyan-Gurevich MiG-21R (sub-model unknown) of the Czech air force, carrying a centreline reconnaissance pod.

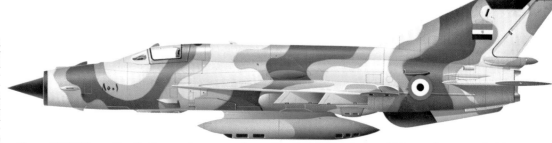

the 'Fishbed'), produced in several sub-types with equipment ranging from basic internally-mounted optical cameras (occupying the area previously used to accommodate the integral twin-barrelled GSh-23 23-mm cannon armament) to an external pod system known to house forward and oblique cameras plus infra-red line-scan apparatus. Powered by a single Tumansky R-11 turbojet, all variants of the MiG-21R can also operate with wingtip-mounted electronic countermeasures pods and it would seem reasonable to assume that K-13A 'Atoll' or AA-8 'Aphid' air-to-air missiles can also be carried to provide a measure of self-defence capability where the threat from hostile fighters is high.

More recently, the principal 'Fishbed' reconnaissance derivative has been the **MiG-21RF** which is essentially similar to the MiG-21MF in relying on the Tumansky R-13-300 engine offering greater power and featuring increased airflow despite being no larger. Sensor packages and equipment are probably the same as those incorporated in the earlier MiG-21R variant.

Above: MiG-21R sporting the three-colour camouflage of the Egyptian air force, with internal cameras (behind the nosewheel) as well as the underfuselage pod.

Mikoyan-Gurevich MiG-21R 'Fishbed-H' of the Polish air force. This model is based on the MiG-21MF with the addition of a centreline sensor pod and the replacement of the cannon pack with a further three cameras.

Specification
MiG-21RF
Type: single-seat tactical reconnaissance aircraft
Powerplant: one Tumansky R-13-300 turbojet rated at 6600-kg (14,550-lb) afterburning thrust
Performance: maximum speed at sea level 1300 km/h (810 mph) or Mach 1.06; maximum speed at altitude 2230 km/h (1,385 mph) or Mach 2.1; service ceiling 17500 m (57,400 ft); range with maximum fuel 1670 km (1,038 miles)
Weight: maximum take-off 9400 kg (20,723 lb)
Dimensions: span 7.15 m (23 ft 5½ in); length 15.76 m (51 ft 8½ in); height about 4.06 m (13 ft 4 in); wing area 23.00 m² (247.6 sq ft)

Former USSR

Mikoyan-Gurevich MiG-25R 'Foxbat'

Evolution of the **Mikoyan-Gurevich MiG-25 'Foxbat'** began in about 1958, initially in response to the anticipated threat represented by the North American B-70 Valkyrie strategic bomber. Despite the 1961 Presidential decision to employ the latter type only for research duties, work on the 'Foxbat' continued, though greater emphasis was then placed upon reconnaissance potential. Accordingly, to date, two of the five variants which have been identified are primarily intended for reconnaissance duties.

Flown in prototype form in about 1964, the 'Foxbat' is believed to have entered operational service during 1970 and, despite the fact that much of the avionics equipment is typical of the era when it was designed, it is nevertheless a most potent interceptor and over 300 examples of the 'Foxbat-A' interceptor are now in service with home defence elements of the Voyska PVO while others have been exported to Algeria, Libya and Syria.

The first reconnaissance derivative to appear was the **MiG-25R 'Foxbat-B'**, which features a total of five vertical/oblique cameras in the nose section ahead of the cockpit. SLAR (Side-Looking Airborne Radar) apparatus is also installed in the forward fuselage, whilst this model and the later '**Foxbat-D**' both employ a different wing of shorter span than that of the interceptor.

The 'Foxbat-B' is also thought to have entered service in 1970, and it is known that four Soviet air force aircraft of this type were deployed to Egypt in the spring of 1971, making a number of forays from Cairo West to conduct reconnaissance sorties over the Israeli-occupied Sinai peninsula and down Israel's coast. Israeli attempts to intercept these with McDonnell Douglas F-4E Phantoms met with no success, and the MiG-25Rs remained in Egypt until the autumn of 1975.

The 'Foxbat-B' was followed in due course by the 'Foxbat-D', the latter being generally similar in appearance although it lacks the camera installation and also incorporates a somewhat larger SLAR, this being located slightly farther aft and much closer to the cockpit. Recent estimates indicate that a combined total of about 160 examples of the 'Foxbat-B' and 'Foxbat-D' models are at present active with Soviet tactical air forces, further machines having been supplied to Algeria, India, Libya and Syria since 1979.

Specification
MiG-25R
Type: single-seat all-weather tactical/strategic reconnaissance aircraft
Powerplant: two Tumansky R-31 turbojets each rated at 11000-kg (24,250-lb) afterburning thrust
Performance: maximum speed 3400 km/h (2,115 mph) or Mach 3.2; service ceiling 27000 m (88,580 ft); normal operational radius 1095 km (690 miles); ferry range 2575 km (1,600 miles)
Weights: empty 19595 kg (43,200 lb); maximum take-off 33400 kg (73,635 lb)
Dimensions: span 13.40 m (44 ft 0 in); length 23.82 m (78 ft 1¾ in); height 6.10 m (20 ft 0¼ in); wing area 56.00 m² (603 sq ft)

Two reconnaissance versions of the MiG-25 together: on the left is a 'Foxbat-D' and on the right a 'Foxbat-B' with smaller SLAR. The 'D' model does not carry cameras but houses electronic sensors as well as its radar.

Post-War Helicopters

The helicopters that entered service after World War II were limited by their piston-engined powerplants. Even so, many military services were able to start the process of developing effective tactical roles that would become really practical only after the introduction of the turbine engine.

Although the concept of rotary-wing flight has exercised man's ingenuity for centuries, it was not until the 20th century and the advent of the internal combustion engine that such aircraft could become a reality. Even so, the challenge presented by the complex technical problems encountered dictated that the development of the helicopter as an effective and practical flying machine would be a long process.

The first helicopters suitable for military use made their appearance during World War II, with Germany producing both small observation machines and larger multi-purpose aircraft in some numbers. At the same time in the United States, Igor Sikorsky was the leading light in helicopter development, and I. P. Bratukhin was head of a Soviet design team producing larger and more powerful machines.

To the military, the prospect of being able to move men and equipment by air into areas unsuitable for the landing of conventional aircraft was very attractive. Trials were arranged during the last year of World War II,

A Bristol Type 192 tandem-rotor helicopter airlifts a Bristol/ Ferranti Bloodhound surface-to-air guided weapon on its trolley. The Type 192 later became the HC.Mk 1 Belvedere.

and helicopters operated off ships and flew in climatic conditions ranging from an Alaskan winter to the Burmese monsoon. By the outbreak of war in Korea in 1950, the military helicopter was being adapted to tasks ranging from seaborne search and rescue, through battlefield casualty evacuation, to the rapid

movement of generals about their commands.

It was not until the mid-1950s that the change came about that was to make the helicopter an essential feature of the modern battlefield. Up to that time power had been provided by the piston engine, which was heavy, prone to failure and rattled the airframe

unmercifully. Piston engines also gave a poor power-to-weight ratio, limiting payload and performance. However, 1955 saw the first flight of the turbine-powered Aérospatiale Alouette II, whose light and smooth-running powerplant opened the way to higher speeds and payloads together with much increased safety.

Aérospatiale SE 313B Alouette II

Of conventional configuration but sturdy design, the **Aérospatiale Alouette II** was one of the first true light multi-purpose helicopters and excelled in a variety of roles. This adaptability was facilitated by its reliable turboshaft engine, easy maintenance, and landing gear which could be either of wheel or skid type, or floats, with provision for emergency flotation gear.

The Alouette II originated as the **Sud-Est SE 3120 Alouette** (lark), a three-seat light helicopter designed mainly for agricultural purposes. The first SE 3120 prototype was flown on 31 July 1952, powered by a 149.1-kW (200-hp) Salmson 9NH radial engine, and a year later established a new international helicopter closed-circuit duration record of 13 hours 56 minutes. The basic airframe was then completely redesigned to take the 268.5-kW (360-shp) Turboméca Artouste I turboshaft, and the first of two prototypes, designated **SE 3130**, was flown on 12 March 1955, followed by three pre-production aircraft in 1956. The Alouette II was granted a French certificate of airworthiness on 2 May 1956, and was soon in demand on the international market. In 1957 Sud-Est merged with Sud-Aviation, at which time the designation of the Alouette II was altered to SE 313 B, remaining unchanged after Sud's take-over by Aérospatiale.

From the beginning, the Alouette II proved a most successful design and was found particularly suitable for operations in higher altitudes. Thus, during the period 9-13 June 1958, an Artouste-powered Alouette II set up a helicopter altitude record of 10981 m (36,027 ft) for all classes, and a height record of 9583 m (31,440 ft) in the 1000/1750-kg (2,205/3,858-lb) category. By September 1960 no less than 598

Alouette IIs had been ordered by customers in 22 different countries and the type was being assembled by Republic in the USA and Saab in Sweden. It also became the first French aircraft of any kind, and the first helicopter in the world, to be granted an American certification.

In the military role, the Alouette II can be fitted with a wide variety of rockets, missiles and guns.

Specification
Aérospatiale SE 313B Alouette II
Type: light general-purpose helicopter
Powerplant: one 395.2-kW (530-shp)

Turboméca Artouste II C6 turboshaft, derated to 268.5 kW (360 shp)
Performance: (at maximum take-off weight) maximum speed at sea level 185 km/h (115 mph); maximum cruising speed at sea level 165 km/h (103 mph); rate of climb at sea level 282 m (925 ft) per minute; service ceiling 2150 m (7,055 ft); hovering ceiling in ground effect 1650 m (5,415 ft); hovering ceiling out of ground effect 920 m (3,020 ft); range with maximum fuel at sea level 565 km (351 miles); range with 545-kg (1,202-lb) payload at sea level 100 km (62 miles); range with 390-kg (860-lb) payload at sea level 300 km (186

French commanders were the first to see the potential of light helicopters such as these Alouettes as mobile HQs, and it was while leading his men from an Alouette that Colonel Jeanpierre of the 1st REP was killed.

miles); flight endurance with maximum fuel at sea level 4 hours 6 minutes
Weights: empty 895 kg (1,973 lb); maximum take-off 1600 kg (3,527 lb)
Dimensions: main rotor diameter 10.20 m (33 ft 5.6 in); diameter of tail rotor 1.81 m (5 ft 11.3 in); length (rotor blades folded) 9.70 m (31 ft 9.9 in); height 2.75 m (9 ft 0.3 in); main rotor disc area 81.70 m² (879.4 sq ft)

Vought-Sikorsky R-4 and R-6

Deriving its place in history from the fact that it was the first helicopter ordered in quantity for service with the US forces, Sikorsky's initial production helicopter was based on the VS-300 of 1939. A prototype of the two-seat **XR-4** conducted its maiden flight on 13 January 1942, followed by three pre-series **YR-4A** (134.2-kW/180-hp Warner R-550-1) and 41 **YR-4B** (with a larger cabin) helicopters. Seven of the latter went to the US Navy as **HNS-1** machines. All bore the company designation **Vought-Sikorsky VS-316A**, and as a result of their gross weight increasing from the prototype's 1111 kg (2,450 lb) to 1315 kg (2,900 lb) they suffered a drastic fall of top speed from 164 km/h (102 mph) to 121 km/h (75 mph). Nevertheless the early R-4s undertook valuable trials work, including deployments in Burma and Alaska and the first US helicopter landing aboard a ship, in May 1943, preparing the way for 100 **R-4B** models (149.1-kW/200-hp R-550-3), 22 of which became HNS-1s with the US Navy and US Coast Guard. Diversions were made to the UK of two YR-4As, five YR-4Bs and 45 R-4Bs, these mainly serving the Royal Navy as the **Hoverfly Mk I**, apart from one forwarded to the Royal Canadian Air Force. The sole **XR-4C** was the original prototype modified in 1943 with an R-550-1 in place of its 123-kW (165-hp) R-500-3 and its 10.97-m (36-ft)

main rotor replaced by the larger unit introduced from the YR-4A onwards.

Metal skinning replaced fabric on the more streamlined **VS-316B** or **R-6**, a prototype of which flew on 15 October 1943, powered by a 167.8-kW (225-hp) Franklin O-437-7. Five pre-series XR-6A helicopters with the 179-kW (240-hp) O-435-9 included three passed to the US Navy as the **XHOS-1**, although main production was by Nash-Kelvinator Corp of 26 **YR-6A** and 193 **R-6A** helicopters. Of the 193, the US Navy absorbed 38 as the **HOS-1**, while the UK received only 43 of a planned 150 **Hoverfly Mk II** helicopters mainly for the RAF, and supplied one of these

to Canada. Problems with the R-6A's engine shortened service life and led to plans for an **R-6B** powered by a Lycoming O-435-7 of 167.8-kW (225 hp), but this failed to emerge, as did the **R-7**, which would have had a 179-kW (240-hp) O-405-9.

Specification
Vought-Sikorsky YR-4B
Type: two-seat general-purpose helicopter
Powerplant: one 134.2-kW (180-hp) Warner R-550-1 radial piston engine
Performance: maximum speed 121 km/h (75 mph); climb to 2438 m (8,000 ft) in 45 minutes; service ceiling

A Vought Sikorsky R-4 comes in to land by the side of a B-29 Superfortress on the Marianas Islands a few weeks after the end of the war.

2438 m (8,000 ft); range 209 km (130 miles)
Weights: empty 916 kg (2,202 lb); maximum take-off 1150 kg (2,535 lb)
Dimensions: main rotor diameter 11.58 m (38 ft 0 in); fuselage length 10.79 m (35 ft 5 in); height 3.78 m (12 ft 5 in); main rotor disc area 105.36 m² (1,134.1 sq ft)
Armament: none

Vought-Sikorsky R-5

Known to its manufacturer as the **Vought-Sikorsky VS-327**, the **R-5** derived from earlier demonstrations of helicopter viability by the R-4 and a USAF requirement issued in 1943 for an observation helicopter. Five **XR-5** prototypes were acquired and flew from 18 August 1943 onwards, two of them later being fitted with British equipment and redesignated **XR-5A**. A pre-production series of 26 **YR-5A** helicopters, two of them transferred to the US Navy (and later to the US Coast Guard) as the **HO2S-1**, was followed by only 34 of a planned 100 **R-5A** SAR models which saw operational use with the Air Rescue Service as its first helicopter. The type had provision for a stretcher mounted externally on each side of the fuselage, and 20 (plus a single YR-5A) were converted to **R-5D** standard with a nosewheel landing gear, a rescue hoist and provision for a second internal passenger. The **YR-5E** was a dual-control trainer conversion of five YR-5As. The nosewheel, an extra 30.5 cm (12 in) of rotor span, four seats and a maximum weight of 2812 kg (6,200 lb) characterized the civil **Sikorsky S-51** of 1946, 11 of which entered USAAF service in 1947, designated **R-5F**, followed by 19 hoist-equipped **H-5G** helicopters in 1948 (the earlier aircraft also adopting 'H' in place of 'R'). Finally, 16 **H-5H** models were ordered in 1949 with interchangeable wheel or pontoon landing gear and a 2948-kg (6,500-lb) gross weight. The US Navy cancelled 34 more HO2S-1 helicopters, but bought 88 H-5F variants known as the **HO3S-1**, for duties including aircraft carrier plane-guard, while the US Coast Guard obtained nine similar **HO3S-1G** helicopters. The designation **XHO3S-3** was used by a rotor test-bed modification, and **HO3S-2** was the unadopted naval H-5H. In the UK Westland began licensed manufacture of the **Westland WS-51 Dragonfly** during 1948 and pro-

duced 137, mostly for the RAF and Royal Navy, followed by 12 mainly civil **Widgeon** helicopters featuring a redesigned five-seat cabin. Dragonflies undertook experimental helicopter passenger and mail services, and pioneered SAR and casualty evacuation with the armed forces. Military models comprised the Royal Navy **Dragonfly HR.Mk 1** and **Dragonfly HR.Mk 3**; and the **Dragonfly HC.Mk 2** and VIP **Dragonfly HC.Mk 4** of the RAF. Dragonfly export customers included Ceylon, Egypt, France, Iraq, Italy, Thailand and Yugoslavia, plus Brazil and Jordan with Widgeons.

Specification
Vought-Sikorsky R-5B
Type: SAR/general-purpose helicopter
Powerplant: one 335.6-kW (450-hp) Pratt & Whitney R-985-AN-5 radial piston engine
Performance: maximum speed 171 km/h (106 mph); climb to 3048 m (10,000 ft) in 15 minutes; service ceiling 4389 m (14,400 ft); range 579 km (360 miles)
Weights: empty 1715 kg (3,780 lb);

maximum take-off 2189 kg (4,825 lb)
Dimensions: main rotor diameter 14.63 m (48 ft 0 in); fuselage length 12.45 m (40 ft 10 in); height 3.96 m (13 ft 0 in); main rotor disc area 168.11 m² (1,809.56 sq ft)
Armament: none

Designed concurrently with the XR-6, the R-5 was a tandem two-seater helicopter powered by a 335.6-kW (450-hp) Pratt & Whitney engine and was used by the US Navy, US Coast Guard and the Air Rescue Service.

The US Navy version of the S-51 was designated HO3S-1 and a total of 88 was ordered for the fleet and nine of the similar HO3S-1G for the US Coast Guard. Westland built the S-51 under licence in the UK as the Westland Dragonfly with Leonides engine.

Bell Model 47

On 8 December 1945 Bell flew the prototype of a classic helicopter design, the **Bell Model 47**. On 8 March 1946 this was awarded the first approved type certificate issued for a civil helicopter anywhere in the world. The Model 47 remained in continuous production by Bell into 1973, and was also built under licence by Agusta in Italy from 1954 to 1976. The Model 47 has been used on a large scale by armed forces all over the world, its simplicity and low cost more than outweighing its limited capabilities.

In 1947 the USAF (then USAAF) procured 28 of the improved **Model 47A**, powered by 117.1-kW (157-hp) Franklin O-335-1 piston engines, for service evaluation: 15 were designated **YR-13**, three **YR-13A**s were winterized for cold-weather trials in Alaska, and the balance of 10 went to the US Navy for evaluation as **HTL-1** trainers. Little time was lost by either service in deciding that the Model 47 was an excellent machine, and the orders began to flow in.

The US Army's first order was issued in 1948, 65 being accepted under the designation **H-13B**; all US Army versions were later named **Sioux**.

US Navy procurement began with 12 **HTL-2** and nine **HTL-3** helicopters, but

the first major version was the **HTL-4**.

The Model 47 has been built under licence by Agusta in Italy, Kawasaki in Japan, and Westland in the UK (the **Model 47G-2** for the British army, with the name Sioux), and in various roles Model 47s have served with more than 30 armed services.

Experimental versions have been numerous. Perhaps the two most important were the **Model 201** (service designation **XH-13F**) and the **Model 207 Sioux Scout**. The Model 201 was powered by a Continental XT51-T-3 (licence-built Turboméca Artouste) turboshaft. The Model 207 was the first true armed helicopter: powered by the 193.9-kW (260-hp) turbocharged Avco Lycoming TVO-435-A1A piston engine, the Sioux Scout featured a revised cabin seating two in tandem, small stub wings containing additional fuel and helping to offload the main rotor in forward flight, and a remotely controlled chin barbette, containing two 7.62-mm (0.3-in) M60 machine-guns, and movable 200° in azimuth, with elevation from −45° to +15°.

Bell's production of Model 47s eventually came to an end in late 1973, versions of the **Model 47G-5** being the last to be built.

Specification
Bell Model 47G-5A
Type: general utility helicopter
Powerplant: one 197.6-kW (265-hp) Avco Lycoming VO-435-B1A flat-six piston engine
Performance: maximum speed at sea level 169 km/h (105 mph); cruising speed 137 km/h (85 mph) at 5,000 ft (1525 m); service ceiling 3200 m (10,500 ft); range with maximum fuel 412 km (256 miles)
Weights: empty equipped 786 kg (1,732 lb); maximum take-off 1293 kg (2,850 lb)
Dimensions: main rotor diameter

11.32 m (37 ft 1.5 in); tail rotor diameter 1.78 m (5 ft 10 in); length 13.30 m (43 ft 7.5 in); height 2.84 m (9 ft 3.75 in); main rotor disc area 100.61 m² (1,083.0 sq ft)

Simple, cheap and reliable, the Bell Model 47 first flew in 1945 and remained in production until 1976. Seen here before its debut in Korea, a US Army H-13 passes over a mixed column of M4 (Sherman-derived) battle tanks including an M4A3E8 'Easy Eight'.

Piasecki H-21

Developed from the US Navy's HRP-2, the **Piasecki PD-22** tandem-rotor helicopter prototype (US Air Force designation **XH-21**) was first flown on 11 April 1952. Eighteen **YH-21** helicopters had been ordered in 1949 for USAF evaluation, these being followed by an initial production batch of 32 **H-21A** helicopters, named **Workhorse** in USAF service. For use by the Military Air Transport Service Air Rescue Service, the H-21As were each powered by a derated 932.1-kW (1,250-hp) Wright R-1820-103 engine; the first flew in October 1953. Six more were built to USAF contract but supplied to Canada under the Military Assistance Program.

The second production variant was the **H-21B**, which used the full power of the 1062.6-kW (1,425-hp) R-1820-103 to cover an increase in maximum take-off weight from 5216 kg (11,500 lb) to 6804 kg (15,000 lb). Some 163 were built, mainly for Troop Carrier Command, and these had autopilots, could carry external auxiliary fuel tanks, and were provided with some protective armour. They could carry 20 troops in the assault role.

The US Army's equivalent was the **H-21C Shawnee**, of which 334 were built. This total included 98 for the French army, 10 for the French navy and six for Canada; 32 Shawnees were

The Air Rescue Service took the initial production batch of 34 H-21s and christened the type 'Workhorse'. The H-21As were powered by a 932-kW (1,250-hp) engine, giving a maximum take-off weight of over 5000 kg (11,500 lb).

supplied to West Germany, serving with the army's Heeresfliegerbataillon 300. The H-21C, redesignated **CH-21C** in July 1962, had an underfuselage sling hook for loads of up to 1814 kg (4,000 lb). Production deliveries were made between September 1954 and March 1959, later helicopters acquiring the company designation **Model 43** when the Piasecki Helicopter Corporation became the Vertol Aircraft Corporation in 1956. The H-21A and H-21B retrospectively became the **Model 42**.

Two turboshaft conversions of H-21C airframes were the **Model 71 (H-21D)**, with two General Electric T58 engines first flown in September 1957, and the **Model 105** which had two Avco Lycoming T53s. From the latter was designed the Vertol 107 (Boeing Vertol H-46 series).

Specification
Piasecki H-21C Shawnee
Type: troop/cargo transport

Powerplant: one 1062.6-kW (1,425-hp) Wright R-1820-103 Cyclone radial piston engine
Performance: maximum speed 211 km/h (131 mph) at sea level; service ceiling 2362 m (7,750 ft); range 644 km (400 miles)

Weights: empty 3629 kg (8,000 lb); maximum take-off 6668 kg (14,700 lb)
Dimensions: rotor diameter, each 13.41 m (44 ft 0 in); length, rotors turning 26.31 m (86 ft 4 in); height 4.70 m (15 ft 5 in); rotor disc area, total 282.52 m² (3,041.07 sq ft)

Piasecki HUP Retriever

Left: After the Sperry autopilot trials fulfilled every expectation, the HUP-2 was developed and 193 supplied to the US Navy. The significantly improved directional stability of the HUP-2 enabled the designers to dispense with the endplate fins.

Below: A Piasecki HUP-2 Retriever lands on the fantail of the US Navy cruiser USS Helena (CA-75). Although most HUPs were assigned to search and rescue missions, a number were fitted with dunking sonar equipment for anti-submarine warfare.

The 'flying banana' shape of the HRP-1 was discarded in the **Piasecki Model PV-14**, of which two **XHJP-1** prototypes were ordered for evaluation in the rescue and aircraft-carrier planeguard roles. This model was developed into the **PV-18**, US Navy designation **HUP-1 Retriever**, which featured angled endplate fins on the horizontal tail surfaces mounted to the rear rotor pylon. Some 32 HUP-1s, each powered by a single 391.5-kW (525-hp) Continental R-975-34 engine, were built for the US Navy between February 1949 and 1952; the first squadron, HU-2, took delivery of its initial aircraft in February 1951.

Successful Sperry autopilot trials in an XHJP-1 led to development of the **HUP-2**, whose improved directional stability allowed the endplate fins to be deleted, and the more powerful 410.1-kW (550-hp) R-975-46 engine was fitted. A total of 339 was built, including 193 for the US Navy. A number of these were designated **HUP-2S** when fitted with dunking sonar equipment for anti-submarine operations. Some 15 HUP-2s were also supplied to

the French navy. The US Army ordered an initial batch of an improved version in 1951, this being known as the **H-25A Army Mule**. Powered by the R-975-46A engine, the H-25A introduced power-boosted controls, strengthened floors and enlarged cargo doors. Fifty similar machines were transferred to the US Navy under the designation **HUP-3**, three serving with the Royal Canadian Navy's Squadron VH-21. Under the unified designation system introduced in September 1962, the HUP-2 and HUP-3 were redesignated **UH-25B** and **UH-25C**.

Specification
Piasecki HUP-3
Type: utility/cargo helicopter
Powerplant: one 410.1-kW (550-hp) Continental R-975-46A radial piston engine
Performance: maximum speed 169 km/h (105 mph); service ceiling 3048 m (10,000 ft); maximum range

547 km (340 miles)
Weights: empty 1782 kg (3,928 lb); maximum take-off 2767 kg (6,100 lb)
Dimensions: rotor diameter, each

10.67 m (35 ft 0 in); length, rotors turning 17.35 m (56 ft 11 in); height 3.81 m (12 ft 6 in); rotor disc area, total 178.76 m² (1,924.23 sq ft)

Hiller Model 360, UH-12 and OH-23 Raven

Hiller Helicopters Inc. was formed in 1942 for the development and production of rotary-wing aircraft. Early work on the **Hiller Model XH-44, UH-4 Commuter**, and the **UH-5** which introduced a newly-developed 'Rotor-Matic' rotor control system, led to the **Hiller Model 360** prototype. The company's first production helicopter followed and this, known as the **Hiller UH-12** since Hiller had become part of United Helicopters, was of simple construction, incorporating a two-blade main rotor and a two-blade tail rotor on an upswept boom. The design was highly successful, being built extensively in two- and three-seat configurations for both civil and military use, and an early Model 12 was the first commercial helicopter to record a transcontinental flight across the United States. More than 2,000 were built before production ended in 1965, some 300 of this total being exported, and throughout this period the power and capability of the helicopter was steadily improved.

The commercial **UH-12A** to **UH-12D** became the **OH-23A** to **OH-23D Raven** respectively for service with the US Army, and the US Navy acquired UH-12As as **HTE-1** and **HTE-2**. The **UH-12E** was basically a three-seat dual control version of the OH-23D and was built also as the military **OH-23G**. A lengthened-fuselage four-seat civil **UH-12E4** was produced as the military **OH-23F**, and later civil versions with uprated powerplant included the UH-12E variants suffixed **L3, L4, SL3** and **SL4**. OH-23s were exported to Argentina, Bolivia, Colombia, Chile, Cuba, Dominica, Guatemala, Guyana, Mexico, Morocco, the Netherlands, Paraguay, Switzerland, Thailand and Uruguay. The Canadian army acquired OH-23Gs which it operated with the designation **CH-112 Nomad**, and the Royal Navy used a number of ex-US Navy HTE-2s under the designation **Hiller HT.Mk2**.

At the height of UH-12/OH-23 production Hiller was acquired by the Fairchild Stratos Corporation to form Fairchild Corporation, but in 1973 a new Hiller Aviation company was formed, acquiring from Fairchild design rights and production tooling for the UH-12E, and initially continued to provide support for the worldwide fleet of UH-12 helicopters. In the mid-1970s production of the UH-12E was restarted, and versions available currently from this company include the UH-12E, a four-seat **UH-12E4**, and turbine-powered equivalents designated **UH-12ET** and **UH-12E4T** respectively. These have as powerplant a 313.2-kW (420-shp) Allison 250-C20B turboshaft which is derated to 224.5 kW (301 shp) in this application.

Specification
Hiller OH-23D Raven
Type: three-seat military helicopter
Powerplant: one 240.9-kW (232-hp) Avco Lycoming VO-540-A1B flat-six piston engine
Performance: maximum speed 153 km/h (95 mph); cruising speed

Overshadowed to some extent by the Bell and Sikorsky designs, the Hiller H-23 made a significant contribution to helicopter operations in the Korean war. This example has just collected casualties from Yoju for evacuation to a casualty station.

132 km/h (82 mph); service ceiling 4025 m (13,200 ft); range 330 km (205 miles)
Weights: empty 824 kg (1,816 lb); maximum take-off 1225 kg (2,700 lb)
Dimensions: main rotor diameter 10.82 m (35 ft 6 in); length 8.53 m (28 ft 0 in); height 2.97 m (9 ft 9 in); main rotor disc area 92.47 m² (995.38 sq ft)

Sikorsky S-55

Known to the US Army as the H-19 Chickasaw, the Sikorsky S-55 was generally similar in layout to the later models of the H-5 series but had a novel engine arrangement, mounting the powerplant in the nose. This provided maximum cabin space, the long extension shaft being carried diagonally up to the main rotor gear drive.

Expanding its horizons with ever larger and more operationally useful helicopters, Sikorsky flew the prototype **YH-19** (company designation **Sikorsky S-55**) on 10 November 1949 with the 410.1 kW (550 hp) of a Wright R-1340-57 piston engine. This was located in the nose for ground-level access and to provide maximum cabin space for up to 10 passengers. The USAF followed five trials YH-19s by a contract for 50 **H-19A** helicopters, some of which were converted for SAR as the **SH-19A** (later re-designated **HH-19A**). The US Army bought 72 of the H-19C (later **UH-19C**) type and named it **Chickasaw**. These had 447.4-kW (600-hp) R-1340 engines. Naval equivalents were the **HRS-1** and **HRS-2**, 60 and 101 of which, respectively, were used for US Marines transport. Ten of the latter were diverted to the Royal Navy and named **Whirlwind HAR.Mk 21**. Ten observation model **HO4S-1** helicopters also joined the US Navy, although the US Coast Guard failed to adopt the planned **HO4S-2**. There followed a series of models powered by a 522.0-kW (700 hp) Wright R-1300-3, comprising 105 US Marine **HRS-3** (later **CH-19E**) helicopters; 79 ASW **HO4S-3** (UH-19F) aircraft, including 15 supplied to the Royal Navy as **Whirlwind HAS.Mk 22**; 30 US Coast Guard **HO4S-3G** (HH-19G); 264 USAF **H-19B** (UH-19B), of which some became SAR **SH-19B** (HH-19B) models; and 301 US Army **H-19D** (**UH-19D**) transports. There was only civil production of the **S-55A**, with its 596.6-kW (800-hp) R-1300 engine, and the **S-55C**, which combined R-1340 power with the downward-canted tail-boom (or 'broken back') introduced with the H-19B. The proposed **HRS-4** with a 764.3-kW (1,025-hp) Wright R-1820 did not materialize. Sikorsky built almost 1,300 S-55 series helicopters for civil and military use at home and abroad, but this total was swelled by licensed manufacture in Japan of 44 by Mitsubishi; in France by Sud-Est; and in the UK by Westland. The last-mentioned began with Wright R-1340 engines with the **Westland Whirlwind** Srs 1, but progressed to a 633.8-kW (850-hp) Alvis Leonides Major for the **Whirlwind Srs 2** and a 783.0-kW (1,050-hp) Bristol Siddeley Gnome H.1000 turboshaft for **Whirlwind Srs 3** aircraft. In total, Westland built 437 Whirlwinds for civil and export customers and the UK forces. Rescue and transport versions were designated **Whirlwind HAR.Mks 1, 2, 3, 4, 5, 9**, and **10**; the **Whirlwind HAS.Mk 7** was assigned to anti-submarine work; and the **Whirlwind HCC.Mk 8** and **HCC.Mk 12** served The Queen's Flight. Odd mark numbers were Royal Navy and even RAF; the Gnome was fitted in the Mks 9 to 12. Others throughout the world have modernized their aircraft with turbine power, typically the **Sikorsky S-55T** with a 626.4-kW (840-hp) AiResearch TSE-331.

Specification
Sikorsky H-19B
Type: 10-passenger utility helicopter
Powerplant: one 596.6-kW (800-hp) Wright R-1300-3 radial piston engine
Performance: maximum speed 180 km/h (112 mph); cruising speed 146 km/h (91 mph); initial climb rate 311 m (1,020 ft) per minute; range 579 km (360 miles)
Weights: empty 2381 kg (5,250 lb); maximum take-off 3583 kg (7,900 lb)

Dimensions: main rotor diameter 16.15 m (53 ft 0 in); fuselage length 12.88 m (42 ft 3 in); height 4.06 m (13 ft 4 in); main rotor disc area 204.95 m^2 (2,206.19 sq ft)
Armament: none

Settling down on to the surface of Long Island Sound near Bridgeport, Connecticut, this USAF H-19 shows off its amphibious landing gear during a test flight. In the medical evacuation role the H-19 could carry eight litter patients and one attendant.

USA
Sikorsky S-56

The ungainly **Sikorsky S-56** was produced in response to a 1950 requirement of the US Marine Corps for a transport helicopter capable of airlifting 20 troops or the equivalent in cargo, such as two jeeps. Four prototypes, designated **XHR2S-1**, made their initial flights from 18 December 1953 onwards, proving the manufacturer's first twin-engine helicopter to be one of the fastest (and largest) in the West at that time. Further claims to distinction by the aircraft were its rare employment of a retractable landing gear, and equipment with night flying aids. Installation of engines in outboard pods provided stowage for the main wheels, kept drive shafts short and reduced obstructions in the 53.8-m^3 (1,900-cu ft) cargo hold to a minimum. Entered via hydraulically-powered clamshell doors or a smaller side door, the hold included a winch hoist with monorail. Deliveries of 55 **HR2S-1** helicopters (36 more were cancelled) to the US Marines began in 1956 for equipment of three helicopter transport (medium) squadrons, and these aircraft were redesignated **CH-37C** in 1962. Two more were produced as the **HR2S-1W** airborne early warning model with a belly-mounted AN/APS-20E radar scanner and additional operating crew, but failed to stimulate a production order. More successful was the aircraft

loaned to the US Army in 1954 for trials under the designation **YH-37**, as this was followed between 1956 and May 1960 by 94 production **H-37A Mojave** helicopters. All except four were modified from June 1961 onwards to **H-37B** standard, with Lear automatic stabilization equipment (to permit loading and unloading at the hover), a redesigned cargo door and crashproof fuel tanks. These were known as **CH-37B** from 1962, and the programme naturally included those based in Germany from 1959 onwards. Commercial success eluded the S-56, even though its dynamic and control systems were adopted by the later S-60, S-64, S-65 and the abortive Westland Westminster.

Specification
Sikorsky CH-37B Mojave
Type: transport helicopter
Powerplant: two Pratt & Whitney R-2800 Double Wasp piston engines each rated at 1416.8 kW (1,900 hp) for normal, or 1566.0 kW (2,100 hp) for emergency running
Performance: maximum speed 209 km/h (130 mph) at sea level; initial climb rate 277 m (910 ft) per minute; hovering ceiling 335 m (1,100 ft) out of ground effect; service ceiling 2652 m (8,700 ft); range 233 km (145 miles)
Weights: empty 9385 kg (20,690 lb);

normal take-off 14061 kg (31,000 lb)
Dimensions: main rotor diameter 21.95 m (72 ft 0 in); fuselage length 19.76 m (64 ft 10 in); height 6.71 m (22 ft 0 in); main rotor disc area 378.24 m^2 (4,071.5 sq ft)
Armament: none

The Sikorsky S-56 was the largest helicopter to become operational with US forces up to the end of 1961. Unusually the HR2S-1, as it was known to the USMC, featured retractable landing gear and night-flying aids.

The S-56 was primarily designed as a transport helicopter to USMC specifications, but Sikorsky also produced two HR2S-1W early warning models fitted with AP/APS-20E radar in a massive bulbous nose. Although a useful concept, the AEW model failed to attract any orders.

Above: Equipping three USMC transport squadrons from 1956, the S-56 was subsequently evaluated by the US Army, which then ordered 94 machines, designated H-37 Mojave. From 1961 the army modified their H-37s by fitting Lear automatic stabilization equipment.

Former USSR
Mil Mi-1 'Hare'

By 1947 it had become clear to the Soviet leadership that helicopters would be necessary for many military and civil tasks, and a specification for a three-seat general-purpose helicopter was issued. One of three design bureaux asked to produce helicopter designs was that of Mikhail L. Mil, whose last previous design had been the A-15 autogyro of 1938. The first prototype, designated **GM-1**, flew in autumn 1948 and was the first Soviet production helicopter of the classic single-rotor layout. It was selected for production over the twin-rotor Bratukhin competitor and single-rotor Yakovlev Yak-100. The Soviet air force demonstrated the type for the first time in 1951 as the **Mil Mi-1T**, given the NATO reporting name **'Hare'**.

Float-equipped (**Mi-1P**) and trainer (**Mi-1U**) versions of the basic Mi-1T were produced in quantity, in addition to Soviet air force and navy co-operation and liaison aircraft. The overhaul life of critical components such as the transmission and rotor head was substantially improved dur-

A semi-derelict example of the Mil Mi-1 'Hare' is shown in Finnish markings. The 'Hare' was a very good first-generation helicopter but cried out for further development and a turbine powerplant. The design was updated to become the Mil Mi-2.

ing the production run, from 100 hours in 1951, to 500-600 hours in 1956, and to 1,000 hours in 1960.

The Mi-1 also started the record-breaking tradition which has typified Soviet helicopter development, setting up a variety of class records in the late 1950s. Long-distance records of up to 1224 km (761 miles) were set, as well as a speed of 141.2 km/h (87.7 mph) in a 1000-km (621-mile) closed circuit.

Production of the Mi-1 in the Soviet Union tailed off in 1956-8, being gradually transferred to the Polish state aircraft factory WSK-Swidnik. Both the airframe and engine were licence-built in Poland, WSK-manufactured aircraft being designated **SM-1**. About 150 SM-1s were deliverd to the Soviet

Union, and manufacture of the type paved the way for Polish production of the later Mi-2.

Specification
Mil Mi-1
Type: utility and training helicopter
Powerplant: one 428.8-kW (575-hp) Ivchenko AI-26V radial piston engine
Performance: maximum speed 205 km/h (127 mph); cruising speed 140 km/h (87 mph); hovering ceiling 2000 m (6,562 ft); range 590 km (367 miles)
Weights: empty 1760 kg (3,880 lb); normal loaded 2400 kg (5,291 lb); maximum take-off 2550 kg (5,622 lb)
Dimensions: main rotor diameter 14.346 m (47 ft 0.8 in); fuselage length 12.00 m (39 ft 4.4 in); height 3.30 m (10 ft 9.9 in); main rotor disc area 161.64 m² (1,739.9 sq ft)

Former USSR
Mil Mi-2 'Hoplite'

The Poles played an important part in the evolution of the early Mil helicopters, building them under licence and developing improved versions. This Mil Mi-2 is carrying rocket pods and wears current Polish air force insignia.

The **Mil Mi-2 'Hoplite'** was developed in the early 1960s by the Mil bureau as a straightforward turbine-powered version of the Mi-1, the availability of the shaft-turbine engine having revolutionized the design of the helicopter. The twin turbines develop 50 per cent more power than the Mi-1's piston engine for barely half the dry weight, more than doubling the payload. The fuselage of the Mi-2 is completely different from that of its progenitor, carrying the engines above the cabin. Although some of the points of commonality between the Mi-1 and the Mi-2 were eliminated during development, the overall dimensions of the two types remain closely similar.

The Mi-2 was flown in 1962, but never put into production in the Soviet Union. Instead responsibility for the type was assigned to PZL-WSK-Swidnik now in Poland as part of a Comecon rationalization programme, becoming the only Soviet-designed helicopter to be built solely outside the Soviet Union. Production in Poland started in 1965, and continues in the mid-1980s.

The Mi-2 is now the standard training helicopter of the Soviet Union, and has also been seen armed with anti-tank guided weapons. Its role, however, may be as a weapons trainer rather than an attack helicopter, as its slow speed and relatively old-technology rotor system (which limits its manoeuvrability for low-level 'nap-of-the-earth' flying) would render it vulnerable to

NATO defences. It is therefore more likely that pilots and weapon operators learn their skills on the Mi-2 before proceeding to the Mi-24 'Hind'.

PZL has developed a slightly enlarged version of the Mi-2, designated **Mi-2M**, but this 10-seat aircraft appears to be aimed mainly at the civil market. A reported version with a lighter skid landing gear (the only use of such a feature on a recent Warsaw Pact helicopter) has not been proceeded with, but efforts have been made to sell a US-engined version of the Mi-2 in the United States.

Specification
Mil Mi-2
Type: eight-passenger transport, attack and training helicopter
Powerplant: two 321.4-kW (431-shp) Isotov GTD-350 turboshafts
Performance: maximum speed at sea level 210 km/h (130 mph); cruising speed 190 km/h (118 mph); service ceiling 4000 m (13,123 ft); maximum range 590 km (367 miles); range with eight passengers 240 km (149 miles)
Weights: empty 2402 kg (5,296 lb); maximum take-off 3700 kg (8,157 lb)
Dimensions: main rotor diameter 14.56 m (47 ft 9.2 in); fuselage length 11.94 m (39 ft 2.1 in); height 3.75 m (12 ft 3.6 in); main rotor disc area 166.5 m² (1,792.25 sq ft)
Armament: up to four AT-3 'Sagger' (possibly AT-6) anti tank guided weapons or a combination of rocket pods and gun pods

Former USSR
Mil Mi-4 'Hound'

Developed to flight-test status in only seven months following a personal edict from Stalin, the **Mil Mi-4 'Hound'** was at first considered to be a Soviet copy of the Sikorsky S-55 until it was realized that it was considerably larger than the later S-58. It was thus the first of a long line of large Mil helicopters.

The first prototype Mi-4 was completed in April 1952. It shared the basic layout of the S-55, with the powerful radial engine in the nose and quad-

ricycle landing gear, but added a pair of clamshell loading doors capable of admitting a small military vehicle or most light infantry weapons such as anti-tank guns. It was thus a far more capable military transport than its Western contemporaries, and several thousand of the type were built.

The Mi-4 entered service in 1953. Early production aircraft had wooden-skinned rotor blades of very short life, but later aircraft had all-metal blades. Special versions include an amphi-

bious development, tested in 1959, and the **Mi-4V** for high-altitude operations with a two-stage supercharger fitted to the ASh-82FN engine. The Mi-4 was also put into production at the Shenyang plant in China, as the **H-5**.

The Mi-4 has been one of the most important helicopters in service with the Soviet armed forces. At the 1956 Tushino air display, a formation of 36 Mi-4s demonstrated their ability to land a sizeable and well-equipped infantry force; later, the type became the

Soviet Union's first armed helicopter, with a machine-gun in the nose of the navigator's gondola and rocket pods on outriggers from the fuselage. This version was introduced as an interim armed helicopter with the expansion of the Soviet tactical air forces in the late 1960s. More recently, Mi-4s have been equipped with prominent aerials for communications jamming equipment.

With the rise of the Soviet navy, the Mi-4 found another new role: a number

The Mil Mi-4, dubbed 'Hound' by NATO, was one of the world's largest helicopters when it entered service. It was built in enormous numbers and formed the backbone of the Warsaw Pact's helicopter forces for many years. It still serves in a number of roles with a variety of operators.

of the type were fitted with search radar beneath the nose and used as anti-submarine warfare aircraft in the Black Sea and Baltic areas. Other ASW equipment includes a magnetic anomaly detector (MAD) installed in a 'bird' towed behind the helicopter, and the type presumably also carries dunking sonar. The Mi-4 ASW variant paved the way for the later introduction of the Mi-14 'Haze'.

Specification
Mil Mi-4
Type: 12-seat transport and anti-submarine warfare helicopter
Powerplant: one 1267.7-kW (1,700-hp) Shvetsov ASh-82V two-row radial piston engine
Performance: maximum speed 210 km/h (130 mph); cruising speed 160 km/h (99 mph); service ceiling 6000 m (19,685 ft); hovering ceiling 2000 m (6,562 ft); normal range 590 km (367 miles)
Weights: empty 5390 kg (11,883 lb); maximum take-off 7800 kg (17,196 lb)
Dimensions: main rotor diameter 21.00 m (68 ft 10.8 in); fuselage length 16.79 m (55 ft 1 in); height 5.18 m (17 ft 0 in); main rotor disc area 346.36 m^2 (3,728.3 sq ft)
Armament: 7.62-mm (0.3-in) machine-gun in ventral gondola, and rocket or gun pods; (ASW) depth charges or torpedoes

The Mil Mi-4 has been produced as the Whirlwind H-25 or H-5. One has been fitted with a Pratt & Whitney Canada PT6 engine, but this version has not entered service. Chinese Mil Mi-4s are believed to have been used in action recently against Vietnam.

 UK
Bristol Type 171 Sycamore

Late in 1944 the Bristol Aeroplane Company formed a Helicopter Department at Filton and recruited Raoul Hafner from the Airborne Forces Experimental Establishment, where he had been leading a British rotorcraft development team. Drawing on pre-war experience with his A.R.III Gyroplane, Hafner started work on a single-engine four-seat helicopter for both civil and military applications. The lack of a sufficiently developed British engine of the required power led to selection of the widely-used 335.6-kW (450-hp) Pratt & Whitney Wasp Junior for the first two **Bristol Type 171 Mk 1** prototypes, developed to Ministry of Supply Specification E.20/45.

The design featured a light alloy cabin section and a stressed-skin tail-boom attached to a central engine and gearbox mounting, the rotor head being fitted with three wooden monocoque blades. After extensive component testing, ground running of the completed airframe began on 9 May 1947, and the first flight was made by H.A. Marsh on 27 July. The second air-

craft joined the test programme in February 1948 and on 25 April 1949, to facilitate its flight to the Paris Salon, it became the first British helicopter to be granted a civil certificate of airworthiness. An Alvis Leonides radial was installed in the third airframe which appeared in the static park at the 1948 SBAC exhibition at Farnborough. Designated **Type 171 Mk 2**, this helicopter made a successful first flight on 3 September 1949, although a second take-off attempt ended abruptly when the rotor disintegrated. With a strengthened rotor, development flying was resumed while work continued on the assembly of 15 production **Type 171 Mk 3** helicopters.

The Bristol Sycamore was underpowered, but its superbly-designed and well-balanced rotor system made it efficient and a joy to fly, despite its lack of autostabilization.

In these, airframe changes included a shortened nose and a 0.20-m (8-in) increase in cabin width to accommodate three passengers on the rear seat. In order to maintain essential systems in the event of engine failure, the accessory drive was transferred from the engine to the rotor gearbox. The initial production batch included one **Sycamore HC.Mk 10** and four **Sycamore HC.Mk 11** ambulance and communications machines for evaluation by the Army Air Corps, and four **Sycamore HR.Mk 12** helicopters for rescue duties with RAF Coastal Command. Two **Sycamore Mk 3A** helicopters, with a freight hold behind the engine bay, were built for British European Airways.

The main production was the **Type 177 Sycamore Mk 4**, incorporating modifications evolved from Mk 3 experience; these included taller landing gear, four cabin doors and the pilot's position moved from port to starboard. Deliveries included three **Sycamore HR.Mk 50** and seven **Sycamore HC.Mk 51** helicopters for the Royal Australian Navy, three **Sycamore Mk 14** aircraft for Belgian air force use in the Congo, and 50 **Sycamore Mk 52** helicopters for the Federal German army and navy; the Royal Air Force received two **Sycamore HR.Mk 13** and

A Bristol Sycamore HR.Mk 14 of No. 118 Squadron, a search and rescue and communications unit based in Northern Ireland. Unusually the aircraft carries squadron markings – black and white wavy lines inherited from the squadron's Hunters.

more than 80 **Sycamore HR.Mk 14** helicopters equipped with winches for air-sea rescue duties, initially with No. 275 Squadron, Fighter Command, which received its first helicopter on 13 April 1953. Sycamores also operated in the light assault and reconnaissance roles in Malaya, Cyprus and Borneo.

Specification
Sycamore HR.Mk 14
Type: five-seat communications/SAR/light troop-carrying helicopter

Powerplant: one 410.1-kW (550-hp) Alvis Leonides 73 radial piston engine
Performance: maximum speed 204 km/h (127 mph) at sea level; cruising speed 169 km/h (105 mph); endurance 3 hours
Weights: empty 1728 kg (3,810 lb); maximum take-off 2540 kg (5,600 lb)
Dimensions: main rotor diameter 14.81 m (48 ft 7 in); length, rotors folded 14.07 m (46 ft 2 in); height 3.71 m (12 ft 2 in); main rotor disc area 172.22 m² (1,853.8 sq ft)

Bristol Types 173 and 192 Belvedere

The first British tandem-rotor helicopter, the **Bristol Type 173** combined two sets of Sycamore rotors and control systems, each powered by a 428.8-kW (575-hp) Alvis Leonides engine. These were each arranged to drive through a freewheel clutch so that, with both rotor gearboxes interconnected by a shaft, either engine could drive both rotors in the event of an engine failure.

The first of two prototypes, developed to Ministry of Supply Specification E.4/47, made its first hovering flight on 3 January 1952, flown by C.T.D. Hosegood, but ground resonance problems delayed further progress until July. The first flight from the airfield at Filton took place on 24 August, and this **Type 173 Mk 1** helicopter appeared at the SBAC show in September. RAF evaluation followed, and in 1953 naval trials were undertaken aboard the aircraft-carrier HMS *Eagle*.

The second prototype, designated **Type 173 Mk 2**, was first flown on 31 August 1953 and was transferred to the Royal Air Force in August 1954 for further naval trials.

Three more prototypes, designated **Type 173 Mk 3**, were built for the Ministry of Supply, having 633.8-kW (850-hp) Leonides Major engines, four-blade metal rotors and a taller rear pylon. Only the first progressed beyond the ground-running stage, beginning hovering trials on 9 November 1956. The third had the shortened fuselage and long-stroke landing gear of the **Type 191** version.

The Royal Air Force had a requirement for a personnel and paratroop transport and casevac helicopter, also capable of lifting bulky loads on an external sling. An order for 22 of the **Type 192** version was placed in April 1956, later increased to 26, all to be Napier Gazelle-powered. The prototype, first flown at Weston-super-Mare on 5 July 1958, was joined in the development programme by nine preproduction aircraft. These originally had wooden rotor blades, and tailplanes with anhedral and end-plate fins; they were later brought up to production standard for delivery to the RAF. Modifications included the substitution of metal rotor blades and compound anhedral tailplanes, the provision of powered flying controls, sliding doors, improved air inlets and enlarged low-pressure tyres. The eleventh aircraft was completed by Westland as the first **Belvedere HC.Mk 1**, delivered to No. 66 Squadron at RAF Odiham in August 1961. This unit was also the last to operate Belvederes, disbanding at RAF Seletar in March 1969.

Specification
Bristol (Westland) Belvedere HC.Mk 1
Type: short-range tactical transport
Powerplant: two 1092.5-kW (1,465-shp) Napier Gazelle NGa.2 turboshafts
Performance: maximum cruising speed 222 km/h (138 mph); service ceiling 5275 m (17,300 ft); range with payload of 2722 kg (6,000 lb) 121 km (75 miles); ferry range 740 km (460 miles)
Weights: empty 5277 kg (11,634 lb); maximum overload take-off 9072 kg (20,000 lb)
Dimensions: rotor diameter, each 14.91 m (48 ft 11 in); length, rotors turning 27.36 m (89 ft 9 in); height 5.26 m (17 ft 3 in); rotor disc area, total 349.18 m² (3,758.7 sq ft)

The Bristol Belvedere was originally designed as a naval helicopter, with little need for a capacious fuselage and with a high nose-up sit to allow for easy loading of a torpedo. The Navy requirement was met by the Wessex.

The Belvedere had a superbly designed rotor system, and the prototypes could be flown without autostabilization. The engine and gearbox arrangement allowed for a safe landing to be made in the event of either engine or synchronizing

shaft failure and the aircraft proved pleasant to fly. It was maintenance-intensive and performed poorly in Aden with No. 26 Squadron, although their record in Malaya was good due to better maintenance.

Armed Combat Helicopters

In tactical terms, the helicopter's role in the support of troops on the battlefield has become increasingly important. This is true not only of the transportation of soldiers around the battlefield, but also of the anti-tank role when armed with anti-tank guided missiles.

Although helicopters are slower than non-rotary-wing aircraft, they offer a unique combination of agility and hovering efficiency, which has gradually opened up a range of applications in warfare. The first armed helicopters of the immediate post-war period were used for simple experiments with machine-guns, air-to-surface rockets and anti-submarine weapons. The payload was limited by the piston engine, so it was impossible to carry much in the way of weapons and still have a worthwhile mission radius or endurance.

The turning point for the helicopter was the switch to gas turbine propulsion from the mid-1950s. This slashed the helicopter's empty weight, increased available power and improved both safety and reliability. The failure of either engine in a twin-engined helicopter results in only a slight reduction in flight performance.

Continued improvement in turbine engines, structural materials, avionics and new design techniques have led to breeds of helicopter which can fly reliably in all weathers, deal devastating blows against hostile armour or warships, and yet remain either hidden from or surprisingly

A US Army AH-64D Longbow prototype undergoes flight testing near the McDonnell Douglas test facility at Mesa, Arizona.

immune to return fire. From being the most vulnerable aircraft in the sky, the armed helicopter has become extremely difficult to shoot down.

There are obvious advantages in being small and agile. Battlefield helicopters can be very elusive targets, none more so than the Hughes Defender, which has a main rotor with a diameter of only

just over 8 m (26 ft). The later Defenders have an MMS (Mast-Mounted Sight), which enables the helicopter to engage targets while still remaining hull-down behind natural cover. The MMS system has become increasingly popular for battlefield helicopters.

Maritime helicopters range from compact types for use from small warships to larger ASW machines

with the flight crew separate from the mission crew. In a tactical cabin, the mission crew monitors input from sensors such as sonobuoys, radar and MAD gear, and computers to manage the overall attack, which may be co-ordinated with friendly warships. Most naval helicopters need to be compact enough to operate from ships other than carriers. It is noteworthy that the newest large multi-role machine in this class, the European Helicopter Industries (Westland/Agusta) EH.101, is the same size as a Sea King despite the fact that it is 50 per cent heavier and 50 per cent more powerful.

Among the latest entrants into the armed combat helicopter field is the Boeing/Sikorsky RAH-66 Comanche from the United States. Only slightly smaller but much lighter than the AH-64 Apache, the Comanche is armed with a nose-mounted Lockheed Martin three-barrel 20-mm cannon. Other new helicopters include the Denel CSH-2 Rooivalk from South Africa; the Eurocopter Tiger and Tigre from Germany and France; the Eurocopter Fennec and Panther from France; the Kamov Ka-50, Ka-52 and Mil Mi-28 from Russia; and the NH Industries NH90 from France, Germany, Italy and the Netherlands.

Aérospatiale Alouette III

The **Aérospatiale Alouette III** is in reality an enlarged and aerodynamically refined version of the Alouette II, using the same basic dynamic system with a more powerful engine to provide increased performance despite the greater payload. The prototype, designated **SE 3160**, first flew on 28 February 1959, and was followed by the initial production version, the **SA 316A Alouette III**, which remained available until the end of the 1960s. This version was chosen for licence-production in India under the designation **HAL Chetak** for general military purposes. From 1970s the standard model was the **SA 316B Alouette III**, which retained the 570-shp (525-kW) Turboméca Artouste IIIB turboshaft of its predecessor, but combined in this application with a strengthened transmission to permit greater weights. The SA 316A had proved moderately popular with military air arms, but the SA 316B was immensely popular for its increased payload, greater reliability and excellent high-altitude performance. This last the SA 316B had inherited from the SA 316A, which had set several helicopter records for altitude and payload-to-altitude. Small numbers of the **SA 316C Alouette III** were also built, this version having the Artouste IIID turboshaft. The enlarged cabin of the Alouette III series can accommodate a pilot and up to six passengers, or a slung load of 750 kg (1,653 lb) can be carried as an alternative. In military service, however, the Alouette III is used mostly as a two-seat light attack helicopter, with a variety of guns, rocket pods and missiles carried externally on the sides of the cabin for close support and anti-tank operations.

In 1967 there flew the prototype **SA 319B Alouette III Astazou** derived from the SA 316B but using the considerably more efficient Astazou XIV for greater performance combined with a fuel burn reduced by some 25 per cent. This model entered production in 1973, and immediately proved the most successful variant of the series, offering military operators improved attack capability (thanks to the type's ability to lift more weapons, or to carry the same weapons load as the SA 316 series at higher performance) and greater economy. Though more modern types have generally replaced the Alouette III as a front-line helicopter in the world's more advanced air arms, the type still plays a significant part in the inventories of many smaller air arms.

Specification
Aérospatiale SA 319B Alouette III Astazou
Type: general-purpose military helicopter
Powerplant: one 870-shp (649-kW) Turboméca Astazou XIV turboshaft derated to 600 shp (448 kW)
Armament: a wide assortment of weapons can be carried, these including a 20-mm cannon, various types of machine-gun, rocket pods and AS.11 or AS.12 air-to-surface missiles
Performance: maximum speed 220 km/h (136 mph) at sea level; range

Now being replaced by the SA 342M Gazelle with HOT missiles, the Alouette III is still widely used by the French army light aviation as an anti-tank machine.

605 km (375 miles) with maximum internal load
Weights: empty 1146 kg (2,527 lb); maximum take-off 2250 kg (4,960 lb)
Dimensions: main rotor diameter 11.02 m (36 ft 1¾ in); fuselage length 10.03 m (32 ft 10¾ in); height 3.00 m (9 ft 10 in); main rotor disc area 95.38 m² (1,026.5 sq ft)

One of the 52 foreign military customers for the Aérospatiale SA 316C Alouette III is South Africa, which uses at least 40 and possibly as many as 70 for training, liaison, COIN assault and utility duties. Alouette III units are at Durban, Ysterplaat, Port Elizabeth, Bloemspruit and Zwartkop.

Aérospatiale Gazelle

Though distantly derived from the Alouette, the Aérospatiale **Gazelle** was designed as a more capable military and civil helicopter embodying an advanced rotor system (including a *fenestron* anti-torque rotor buried in a low-drag installation within the fin) and streamlined contours to improve performance. This means that in comparison with the Alouette, the Gazelle differs in having a completely streamlined stressed-skin fuselage and cabin for side-by-side pilots with dual controls. The first prototype flew on 7 April 1967, and the first production SA 341 flew on 6 August 1971, and featured the Bölkow-developed rigid main rotor and Aérospatiale *fenestron* shrouded tail rotor in a duct built into the fin. As part of the 1967 agreement with the UK many early Gazelles were assembled and partly built by Westland for the British army (**Gazelle AH.Mk 1**), RN (**Gazelle HT.Mk 2**) and RAF (**Gazelle HT.Mk 3**). The Gazelle AH.Mk 1 has Doppler, auto-chart display and (optionally) TOW missiles and roof sight; the HT variants have a stability-augmentation system, the naval Gazelle HT.2 also having a rescue hoist. Powerplant of the Gazelle AH.Mk 1 is the 600-shp (448-kW) Astazou IIIN turboshaft. The **SAL 341F** is the basic ALAT (French Army light aviation) model, with the Astazou IIIC turboshaft and intended for utility purposes. The **SA 341H** military export version is powered by the Astazou IIIB turboshaft and licence-built by Soko of Yugoslavia. The **SA 342** introduced an Astazou engine uprated from 590 to 859 shp (440 to 641 kW) and an improved *fenestron* permitting weight to be increased, and resulted from a Kuwaiti requirement. Of several military SA 342 versions, ALAT is buying 120 of the **SA 342M** model with advanced avionics and four HOT missile tubes with a stabilized sight on the roof, this type providing the French army with very effective anti-tank defence. Total sales of all versions reached 1,000 by 1983, including deliveries to 14 military customers worldwide. The type has also been produced for the civil market in **SA 341G** and **SA 342J** forms. The SA 342 variants generally have slightly better overall performance than the

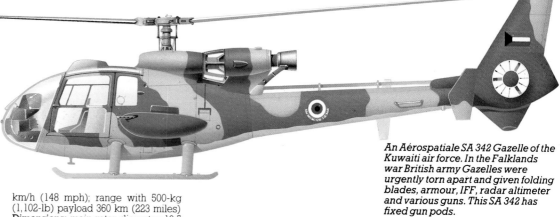

SA 341 models, but have greater payload and superior 'hot-and-high' capabilities.

Specification:
Aérospatiale SA 342M
Type: military utility helicopter
Accommodation: two pilots in front with optional bench seat behind for three which folds down for cargo carrying; sling for 700-kg (1,543-lb) freight load and hoist for 300 lb (135 kg)
Armament: option for two machine-guns or 20-mm cannon, two pods of 2.75-in or 68-mm rockets, four/six HOT missiles, or four AS.11 or two AS.12 missiles
Powerplant: one 859-shp (641-kW) Turboméca Astazou XIV turboshaft
Performance: maximum speed 310 km/h (193 mph); cruising speed 238 km/h (148 mph); range with 500-kg (1,102-lb) payload 360 km (223 miles)
Dimensions: main rotor diameter 10.5 m (34 ft 5½ in); fuselage length 9.53 m (31 ft 3¼ in); height 3.18 m (10 ft 5¼ in); main rotor disc area 86.5 m² (931 sq ft)

An Aérospatiale SA 342 Gazelle of the Kuwaiti air force. In the Falklands war British army Gazelles were urgently torn apart and given folding blades, armour, IFF, radar altimeter and various guns. This SA 342 has fixed gun pods.

Firing a HOT anti-tank missile from an Aérospatiale Gazelle. This light helicopter carries four such missiles, the SA 342M version being fitted with a roof-mounted sight.

Agusta A 109A

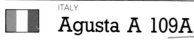

One of the most aesthetically attractive helicopters, the **Agusta A 109A** was planned as a streamlined twin-turbine machine for a pilot and seven passengers, with all-weather avionics and a cabin easily adaptable for a variety of other civil and military applications. The main rotor has an articulated hub and aluminium honeycomb blades, and the tricycle landing gear is fully retractable. The first example flew on 4 August 1971 and soon ambulance, cargo and SAR (search and rescue)

One of the spoils of the Falklands war was this Agusta A 109A multi-role helicopter captured by the 3rd Commando Brigade Air Sqn.

versions were on order, with deliveries beginning early in 1976. In 1975 development began of armed versions, and by 1983 Agusta offered an **A 109A Aerial Scout** with machine-gun, rockets, stabilized sight and special communications; an **A 109A Light Attack**, in various sub-types with rockets and machine-guns for soft targets or the Hughes TSU (telescope sight unit) on the nose and tubes for up to eight TOW missiles; an **A 109A Command and Control** for target designation and direction of attack helicopters, and with the armament options of the A 109A Light Attack; an **A 109A Utility** for cargo or casevac patients, and provision for a slung load of 907 kg (2,000 lb); an **A 109A ESM/ECM** with comprehensive electronic warfare systems including passive receivers, active jammers and dispensed payloads; and an **A 109A Naval** for ASW, anti-ship, stand-off missile guidance, SAR, patrol, EW and many other duties. The proposed armament for the A 109A Naval is a pair of AS.12 or AM-10 wire-guided missiles, and the type can also be fitted to provide guidance correction for the Otomat ship-launched anti-ship missile. Various sensors are available as custom-er options. In 1981 production began to switch to the **A 109A Mk II** with an uprated transmission for greater weights and speeds.

Specification
Agusta A 109A Mk II
Type: multi-role helicopter
Accommodation: up to eight seats of which front two may both be pilots, plus provision for 907-kg (2,000-lb) slung load, 150-kg (331-lb) hoist, two stretchers and two attendants or more than 60 special role fits including wide range of weapon schemes
Powerplant: two 420-shp (313-kW) Allison 250-C20B turboshafts
Performance: maximum speed at maximum weight 269 km/h (184 mph); cruising speed 230 km/h (143 mph); range, not stated except with maximum fuel and no reserves 548 km (341 miles)
Weights: empty, depending on equipment from 1551 kg (3,419 lb) to 1889 kg (4,164 lb); maximum take-off 2600 kg (5,732 lb)
Dimensions: main rotor diameter 11.0 m (36 ft 1 in); fuselage length 10.7 m (35 ft 1½ in); height 3.3 m (10 ft 10 in); main rotor disc area 95.03 m² (1,023.0 sq ft)

Agusta A 129

Now an effective anti-tank and armed scout helicopter, the **Agusta A 129** Mangusta (mongoose) was conceived in 1978 as a special variant of the A 109, but during its design and development period he machine grew in weight and capability to an extent that it is today a completely different helicopter in the class of medium-weight helicopter gunships. It is being designed both for the Italian army and for export. The deep but slim fuselage has cockpits for the pilot, high at the rear, and for the co-pilot/gunner, low in the nose, both with flat glazed panels to avoid glint and with the side panels explosively jettisoned for emergency escape. A Harris digital integrated multiplex data system links every part of the A 129 to manage propulsion, navigation, systems and utilities, communications, power distribution and fire control with various weapons. The nose is occupied by the stabilized night/all-weather night sytem, which in the initial production A 129 is the Hughes TOW sight unit, with a FLIR (forward-looking infra-red) sensor for target acquisition and designation and with a laser for precise ranging. Alternatives include a Martin Marietta mast-mounted sight and pilot's helmet sight/ display and night-vision equipment. The first of five A129 prototypes flew in September 1983, but deliveries did not start until 1990, the Italian army's air corps received 60 of these small but capable battlefield helicopters.

Specification
Agusta A 129
Type: anti-armour and armed scout helicopter
Armament: Italian version has four pylons for eight (two quadruple units) TOW missiles plus either two 12.7-mm (0.5-in) guns or two pods each with seven or 19 70-mm (2.75 in) rockets
Powerplant: two Rolls-Royce Gem 2-2 turboshafts each with an emergency rating of 1,035 shp (772 kW)
Performance: maximum speed 270 km/h (168 mph); range with weapons 574 km/h (357 miles)
Weights: empty 2530 kg (5,575 lb); maximum take-off 3655 kg (8,058 lb)
Dimensions: main rotor diameter

Many nations are considering buying the Agusta A 129, shown here as a full-scale mock-up with eight Hughes TOW guided missiles.

11.9 m (39 ft 0½ in); fuselage length 12.275 m (40 ft 3¼ in); height 3.35 m (11 ft 0 in); main rotor disc area 111.2 m² (1,197.0 sq ft)

Messerschmitt-Bölkow-Blohm BO 105

Though it is expensive for its size, the **MBB BO 105** has matured as a small helicopter of exceptional performance, agility, capability and safety. Construction of three prototypes (the first with two Allison 250-C18 turboshafts and a conventional hinged rotor, and the other two with Allison or MAN-Turbo 6022 turboshafts and hingeless main rotor units) began in 1964, the prototypes all flying in 1967 and being followed by two pre-production helicopters with uprated Allison 250-C20 turboshafts. The first of these flew on 11 January 1971 and was followed by production BO 105C helicopters. The **BO 105** was the first small helicopter to offer full twin-engine safety, and all versions are available with all-weather avionics and very comprehensive equipment. A particular feature of all versions is the rigid main rotor with a hingeless (except for the feathering hinge) hub of forged titanium carrying efficient blades of glassfibre-reinforced plastics. In the passenger role most versions seat five, though there is a lengthened six-seater and MBB in partnership with Kawasaki of Japan is also producing the 8/10-seat **BK 117**. Versions are being assembled in the Philippines, Indonesia and Spain, but the biggest military customer has been Federal Germany itself. The Heer (army) has **227 BO 105M**

The German MBB company has been successful in marketing many military and paramilitary versions of its agile BO 105 twin-turbine helicopter. The Royal Netherlands army uses the BO 105C in various utility roles typically with four passengers.

(VBH) observation machines with many advanced features. A prototype is investigating further types of all-weather sights and displays. The Heer has also deployed a further 212 of the **BO 105P** type as the **PAH-1** (anti-armour helicopter No. 1). These have six HOT anti-tank missiles, a stabilized all-weather sight above the cabin, Doppler navigation and numerous items for battlefield protection. Each army corps has an anti-tank PAH regiment with two squadrons of 28 helicopters operating in four flights of seven. A further 21 are reserved for special duties with the 6th Panzergrenadier Division. The type is also the basis of the BO 105/Ophelia (Optique Platforme HELIcoptère Allemande) advanced experimental model. This has a mast-mounted sight (forward-looking infra-red and TV sensors and a laser rangefinder) in a spherical mounting above the rotor head, and head-up/head-down displays in the cabin. The type also has provision for helmet-mounted sights and displays, and began flight trials in 1981.

Specification
MBB BO 105P (PAH-1)
Type: anti-tank helicopter
Armament: normally six HOT missiles on lateral outriggers, with quick-reload of launch tubes
Powerplant: two 420-hp (313-kW) Allison C20B turboshafts
Performance: maximum continuous speed 210 km/h (130 mph); mission endurance with 20-minute reserve 1 hour 30 minutes
Weights: empty 1322 kg (2,915 lb); maximum take-off 2400 kg (5,291 lb)
Dimensions: main rotor diameter 9.84 m (32 ft 3⅓ in); fuselage length (plus tail rotor) 8.56 m (28 ft 1 in); height 3.0 m (9 ft 10 in); main rotor disc area 78.65 m² (846.6 sq ft)

The BO 105P, selected as PAH-1 (anti-tank helicopter type 1) by the West German army. Six HOT missiles are carried in their sealed tubes on outrigger pylons, the stabilized sight being mounted in the cabin roof.

Westland Scout

One of the few helicopters of exclusively British design to have been built in quantity, the **Westland Scout** was developed from the **Saunders-Roe P.531**, which was taken over when the parent company was absorbed by Westland in 1959. The first P.531 was flown on 20 July 1958 on the power of a 400-shp (298-kW) Blackburn (Turboméca) Turmo 603 turboshaft, derated in this application to 325 shp (242 kW). The Royal Navy showed an immediate interest in the type, and this was instrumental in the development of the type as an operational helicopter. The British army was also interested in the type as a light battlefield helicopter, and the chosen powerplant was the 710-shp (529-kW) Turboméca A.129, derated to 635 shp (474 kW) and developed in the UK by Bristol Siddeley as the Nimbus. The first version of the British army was the **P.531-2 Mk 1**, essentially a pre-production and development variant which first flew in August 1960. This proved so successful that only one month later the British Army placed its initial production contract for the **Scout AH.Mk 1**, which differed from earlier models only in having powered controls. The first Scout AH.Mk 1 flew in March 1961, and the type began to enter service early in 1963 as a replacement for the Saunders-Roe Skeeter, which it clearly outmoded by its combination of greater reliability, substantially improved payload and general operating superiority. Production amounted to 160 Scout AH.Mk 1 helicopters, and these have since 1963 been standard multirole tactical aircraft with skid landing gear, a five/six-seat cabin and the Nimbus 101 or 102 turboshaft. External loads can include two litters in side-

mounted pods, and a variety of weapons. The rear bench seat, which normally accommodates three passengers, can be removed to provide space for two more litters. The type has proved its operational versatility, operating in the close-support, liaison, light freighting, medevac, communication, reconnaissance, SAR and training roles. Small numbers of the Scout were exported, mainly to Jordan, Australia, Bahrain and Uganda. The last Scouts, then used only for secondary roles, were retired from British service in 1994.

Specification
Westland Scout AH.Mk 1
Type: multi-role tactical helicopter
Armament: this can include various combinations of guns up to 20-mm calibre and rocket pods, or AS.11 anti-tank missiles
Powerplant: one Rolls-Royce (Bristol) Nimbus Mk 101 or Mk 102 turboshaft derated from 1,050 shp (783 kW) to 685 shp (511 kW)
Performance: maximum speed 211 km/h (131 mph) at sea level; range 505 km (314 miles) with maximum fuel

An ATGW Scout helicopter from No. 652 Aviation Squadron, Army Air Corps, is seen firing an AS-11 anti-tank guided weapon, live, at tank targets.

and five persons
Weights: empty 1465 kg (3,232 lb); maximum take-off 2405 kg (5,300 lb)
Dimensions: main rotor diameter 9.83 m (32 ft 3 in); fuselage length 9.24 m (30 ft 4 in); height 2.72 m (8 ft 11 in); main rotor disc area 75.9 m² (16.9 sq ft)

Westland Lynx (Army)

Launched as part of the Anglo-French helicopter agreement of February 1967, the **Westland Lynx** is an extremely modern and versatile machine. Its design is wholly of Westland origin, but the production of the type is shared in the ratio of 70/30 between the UK and France, in the form of the nationalized Aérospatiale concern. One of the primary French responsibilities is the forged titanium hub, a one-piece structure for the four-blade semi-rigid main rotor which is one of the most important features of the design. All versions of the Lynx have advanced digital flight controls plus all-weather avionics, and no previous helicopter can equal the type for agility and all-weather one-man operation. The origins of the design lie with the **WG.13** proposal, which was schemed in general-purpose naval and civilian applications. But so versatile did the design appear that the concept was expanded to land-based tactical operations, in which the type's agility and performance would prove a very considerable asset. The first prototype of the Lynx flew on 21 March 1971, and the six prototypes were used exhaustively for all aspects of the certification programme, for trials and for record-breaking. The second production model was the **Lynx AH.Mk 1** battlefield helicopter for the British army. This first flew on 11 February 1977, and the type was cleared for service introduction at the end of 1977. Since that

Capable of being armed with a wide assortment of weapons, the Lynx is also tasked with carrying MILAN armed anti-tank teams.

time the Lynx has built up an enviable reputation as a versatile battlefield helicopter, being able to carry up to 12 troops in addition to a crew of two, or 907 kg (2,000 lb) of internal freight, or a slung load of 1361 kg (3,000 lb), or a wide assortment of weapons including eight TOW anti-tank missiles aimed with a stabilized sight mounted in the flightdeck roof. The chief distinguishing feature of the land-based Lynx is its skid landing gear, the naval Lynx having wheeled tricycle landing gear.

Later types have included the **Lynx AH.Mk 5** of which only three were completed, with two Gem Mk 41-1 turboshafts, upgraded to Gem Mk 42-1 standard; **Lynx AH.Mk 7** (11 helicopters) with upgraded systems, Gem Mk 42-1 engines, an IR suppres-

system, swept-tip BERP composite main rotor blades and a tail rotor rotating in the opposite direction to that of the Lynx AH.Mk 1; Lynx AH. Mk 1GT (104 AH.Mk 1 conversions) with the TITOW (Thermal Imaging TOW) anti-tank missile sight system, the M65 unit fitted with a GEC Sensors, thermal imaging sensor for better nocturnal capability; and **Lynx AH.Mk 9** (16 new and eight AH.Mk 7 conversions) with upgraded avionics, composite BERP rotor blades, Gem Mk 42-1 engines, tricycle landing gear, secure radio, a Decca Tactical Air Navigation System, and a tele-briefing system.

The **Lynx Mk 28** is a version of the AH.MK 1 for the Qatari police, and the privately developed **Lynx-3** is yet to secure a production order.

Specification
Westland Lynx AH.Mk 1
Armament: weapons can include a 20-mm cannon, a 7.62-mm (0.3-in) Mini-gun, rocket pods, or various types of air-to-surface missile including HOT, TOW and AS.11
Powerplant: two 900-shp (671-kW) Rolls-Royce Gem 41 turboshafts, each flat-rated to 750 shp (559 kW)
Performance: maximum speed 259 km/h (171 mph); range 540 km (336 miles) with a full load of troops
Weights: empty, equipped for anti-tank strike 3072 kg (6,772 lb); maximum take-off 4,536 kg (10,000 lb)
Dimensions: main rotor diameter 12,802 m (42 ft 0 in); length overall, rotors turning 15.163 m (49 ft 9 in); height 3.66 m (12 ft 0 in); main rotor disc area 128.69 m² (1,385.35 sq ft)

Taken in 1977, this picture shows the second production Lynx AH.Mk 1 for the British army. Since then over 100 have been delivered, of which 60 in Germany are being equipped with the Hughes TOW, with a stabilized roof-mounted sight. Westland is now developing the Lynx 3 as a dedicated armed helicopter.

Mil Mi-24 'Hind'

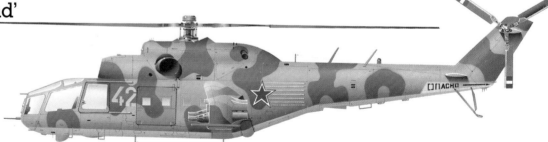

The first version of the Mi-24 to be built in large numbers was 'Hind-A', with four weapon pylons, two twin 'Swatter' missile rails and a heavy machine-gun.

The **Mil Mi-24 'Hind'** is a most important combat helicopter family, and has dynamic parts (engines and rotors) bearing close kinship with those of the Mi-8, yet while the main rotor is considerably smaller in diameter the engines are much more powerful! The series was designed to be able to assault-land a squad of infantry and support the squad from the air with gunfire, rockets and missiles. The Mi-24 is thus a massive helicopter but agile for the bulk, and probably flew in prototype form in the early 1970s, entering service in 1973. The first Mi-24 version, called **'Hind-A'** by NATO, was initially seen in large numbers in East Germany in 1974, and so is thought to have flown as a prototype in about 1968. Its fuselage is divided into a large cockpit area for a normal flight crew of four (pilot, co-pilot, gunner/navigator with heavy machine-gun, and forward observer) and an unobstructed main cabin for eight fully equipped troops. On each side large wing-like weapon arms (which do in fact give lift in forward flight) slope sharply downwards and support six pylons, four of them for rocket pods, bombs or other heavy stores and the outermost carrying twin rails for a total of four AT-2 'Swatter' guided missiles for use against armour or other hard targets. The 'Hind-A' was in fact preceded into service by the 'Hind-B', with straight wings lacking the tip stations for missiles. The **Hind-C** is similar to the 'Hind-A' but lacks the nose gun and tip stations for missiles. Relatively few were built. Larger numbers have been built of another model, **'Hind-D'**, which has a revised airframe with the tail rotor moved from the right to the left of the swept fin, and a new nose equipped for a pilot at the upper level and a weapon operator lower down in the extreme nose, and with the greatest array of tactical sensors, weapon-aiming systems, communications, EW devices and all-weather avionics ever seen on a helicopter. This is a true gunship helicopter with a rotary-barrel heavy machine-gun under the nose. By the late 1990s, 2,500 of these helicopters had been built in several sub-types, many being exported to 19 other countries. The latest armed variants are the **'Hind-E'** with improved sensors and up to eight AT-6 'Spiral' anti-tank missiles, and the **'Hind-F'** with a two-barrel 30-mm cannon on the starboard side.

Specification
Mil Mi-24 'Hind-D'
Type: tactical gunship helicopter
Armament: one 12.7-mm (0.5-in) four-barrel gun in remote-control turret under nose for use against ground or aerial targets; four inboard weapon pylons for various loads (usually 32-tube 57-mm/2.24-in rocket pods) and two outboard pylons for twin launch rails for AT-2 'Swatter' or AT-6 'Spiral' laser-homing anti-armour missiles
Powerplant: two 2,200-hp (1641-kW) Isotov TV3-117 turboshafts
Performance: maximum speed 346 km/h (215 mph); range with maximum weapon load 900 km (559 miles)
Weights: empty about 6500 kg (14,300 lb); maximum take-off 11500 kg (25,400 lb)
Dimensions: main rotor diameter about 17.0 m (55 ft 9 in); fuselage length 17.0 m (55 ft 9 in); height 4.25 m (14 ft 0 in); main rotor disc area 227.0 m² (2,443.5 sq ft)

Bell 209 HueyCobra

The **Bell Model 209** was developed as an urgent company-funded programme to provide a cheaper alternative to the problem-ridden Lockheed AH-56A, and once the prototype had flown on 7 September 1965 its future was assured. The project arose from the US Army's experience in Vietnam during the first half of the 1960s. Experience had shown both the utility and the vulnerability of the conventional helicopter for tactical transport, and it was rapidly appreciated that the optimum means of escorting and supporting such helicopters was with an agile, armoured and armed helicopter, in fact a gunship helicopter. Based on the Model 204, the Model 209 had a new slim fuselage with a fighter-type cockpit for the pilot high in the rear and a co-pilot/gunner lower in the front directing the fire of a wide range of weapons mounted on lateral stub wings or under the nose. The **AH-1G HueyCobra** went into production in 1966 and over 1,000 were delivered in the first four years. Powered by a 1,400-shp (1044-kW) T53, the AH-1G saw extensive service in Vietnam. Many were converted as **TH-1G** dual-control trainers. The **AH-1J SeaCobra** was the first twin-engine version, for the US Marine Corps, with an 1,800-shp (1343-kW) T400 installation; in 1974-5 a batch of 202 with TOW missiles was supplied to Iran. The **AH-1Q** was an interim US Army version adapted from AH-1G helicopters with TOW missiles, while the **AH-1R** has the 1,800-shp (1343-kW) T53-703 engine, but no provision for the TOW missile. The current US Army model is the **AH-1S**, produced in four successively improved

This was the original configuration of the AH-1G HueyCobra, with a single T53 engine, curved canopy and M28 armament subsystem with a Minigun and 40-mm grenades.

stages: (the **Modified AH-1S** produced by conversion of AH-1Gs with the 1,800-shp/1342-kW T53-703, TOW missiles and an upgraded rotor system; the **Production AH-1S** similar to the Modified AH-1S but with flat-plate canopy and improved avionics/instrumentation; the **Up-gun AH-1S** based on the Production AH-1S but with superior stores-management system and provision for a universal turret capable of accepting a variety of 20-mm and 30-mm cannon; and the **Modernized AH-1S** with all the previous improvements and IR suppression of the exhausts (to reduce the type's vulnerability to IR-homing missiles) ending with flat-plate canopies. TOW missiles and over 80 new or improved items of avionics and equipment for all-weather flying at almost ground level. The current USMC model is the **AH-1T Improved SeaCobra** with longer fuselage, TOW missiles and 1,970-shp

(1470-kW) T400 engine group. The latest development of the SeaCobra is the AH-1W **SuperCobra** with a four-blade main rotor driven by two 1,723-shp (1285-kW) General Electric T700-GE-401 engines.

Specification
Bell AH-1S
Type: anti-armour attack helicopter
Accommodation: pilot and co-pilot/gunner
Armament: eight TOW missiles on outboard wing points, with pods inboard housing groups of 7 or 19 of any of five types of 69.9-mm (2.75-in) rocket; General Electric turret under nose with M197 20-mm three-barrel gun (alternatives are 30-mm gun or combined 7.62-mm/0.3-in Minigun plus 40-mm grenade-launcher)
Powerplant: one 1,800-shp (1343-kW) Avco Lycoming T53-703 turboshaft
Performance: maximum speed varies

from 333 km/h (207 mph) to 227 km/h (141 mph) depending on equipment fit; range at sea level with maximum fuel and 8 per cent reserves 507 km (315 miles)
Weights: empty 2939 kg (6,479 lb); maximum take-off 4535 kg (10,000 lb)
Dimensions: main rotor diameter 13.41 m (44 ft 0 in) or, in AH-1T family, 14.63 m (48 ft 0 in); fuselage length 13.59 m (44 ft 7 in) or, in AH-1T, 14.68 m (48 ft 2 in); height over tail rotor 4.12 m (13 ft 6¼ in); main rotor disc area 141.26 m² (1,520.5 sq ft) or, in AH-1T, 168.1 m² (1,809.6 sq ft)

Rotor downwash breaks up the motor smoke trail of a missile fired by one of a formation of US Marine Corps AH-1T SeaCobras on an assault exercise. These are twin-engined and have the triple-barrel GE M197 cannon in an under-nose turret.

Hughes Model 500 Defender

In 1965 the US Army held an LOH (Light Observation Helicopter) contest, with potential production for a four-figure total. When the **Hughes OH-6A Cayuse** won there was a storm of protest, it being claimed the company was selling below cost. Despite this, 1,415 OH-6s gave splendid service in Vietnam, and as its tadpole shape was extremely compact, and performance on a 317 shp (236-kW) Allison engine the highest in its class, the OH-6 was most popular. From it the company developed the **Hughes Model 500** family, the company astutely seeing the considerable market for a versatile, high-performance military helicopter of low cost and proven reliability. The basic **Model 500M** with improved 317-shp (236-kW) engine was sold to nine countries and licence-made in Argentina and Japan. Operated by Spain as a light anti-submarine platform, the Model 500M has AN/ASQ-81 magnetic anomaly detection (MAD) gear with a towed 'bird', and provision for two Mk 44 torpedoes. The **Model 500MD Defender** has the more powerful Allison 250-C20B engine and can have self-sealing tanks, inlet particle filter, IR-suppressing exhausts, and many role fits including seven seats, or two stretchers and two attendants, or various weapons, including the TOW anti-tank missile and nose-mounted sight. Licensed production proceeds at BredaNardi (Italy) and KAL (South Korea), and the type is in worldwide service for training, command and control, light attack, observation, logistic support, troop transport and ASW. The **Model 500MD Scout Defender** is the basic armed version (with a base-

line fit of 14 2.75-in/70-mm rockets plus one 7.62-mm/0.3 in Minigun with 2,000 rounds, or one 7.62-mm/0.3-in EX-34 Chain Gun with 2,000 rounds, or one 30-mm Chain Gun with 600 rounds, or one 40-mm grenade-launcher) and a sub-type (**Model 500MD Quiet Advanced Scout Defender**) has the MMS (mast-mounted sight) for 'hull-down' surveillance or missile guidance, and quiet-running features. The **Model 500MD/TOW Defender** has four TOW missiles, original deliveries having a stabilized nose sight. The **Model 500MD Defender II** is an updated multi-role model now being delivered with quiet rotors (including a five-rather than four-blade main unit), MMS, IR suppression, FLIR (forward-

looking IR) night vision and many other devices including APR-39 passive radar warning. This model can carry two Stinger air-to-air missiles, indicating the way in which the helicopter is becoming an air-to-air weapon, and that the company is keeping more than abreast of developments with this classic light helicopter.

Specification
Hughes Model 500MD Defender
Type: multi-role combat helicopter
Accommodation: two
Armament: options include Hughes 30-mm Chain Gun (firing rate reduced to 350 rounds per minute), four TOW missiles and two Stinger MLMS AAMs
Powerplant: one 420-shp (313-kW)

Originally built in the 1960s as one of 1,434 'Loach' (OH-6A Cayuse) light observation helicopters, this machine is civil-registered and used by Hughes as a development vehicle, with MMS, ADSM (Stinger) missiles and IR-suppressed exhausts.

Allison 250-C20B turboshaft
Performance: maximum speed 217 km/h (152 mph); range 509 km (366 miles)
Weights: empty typically 572 kg (1,260 lb); maximum take-off 1361 kg (3,000 lb)
Dimensions: main rotor diameter 8.05 m (26 ft 4¾ in); fuselage length 7.01 m (23 ft 0 in); height 2.71 m (8 ft 10¾ in); main rotor disc area 50.7² (546.0 sq ft)

Kenya is one of many customers worldwide for the Hughes 500MD Defender family, this example having a nose-mounted sight installation to direct the fire of four TOW anti-tank guided missiles.

Hughes AH-64 Apache

Designed in 1972-3 to meet the US Army's need for an AAH (Advanced Attack Helicopter), the **Hughes AH-64A** beat a Bell competitor which had reversed the traditional Cobra arrangement of seating the pilot above and behind the co-pilot/gunner, an arrangement maintained by Hughes. Features include two T700 engines flat-rated to provide high emergency power and with large IR-suppressing exhaust systems to reduce the chances of a hit by an IR-homing missile, a large flat-plate canopy with boron armour, multi-spar stainless steel and glass-fibre rotor blades designed to withstand 23-mm hits, extremely comprehensive avionics and weapon fits, and numerous crash-resistant features to protect the crew. All these features are vital in a combat helicopter designed to undertake the most arduous of battlefield roles by day and night, and even under the most adverse of weather conditions. Development was unfortunately prolonged, the first prototype flying on 30 September 1975 and the programme being hard hit by modification. The type's appearance changed during its development, especially at the nose and tail. The nose carries the Martin Marietta TADS/PNVS (Target Acquisition and

The Hughes AH-64 Apache, certainly the most expensive vehicle ever proposed for use in a land battle.

Designation sight/ Pilot's Night Vision system). The type carries the AGM-114 Hellfire as its primary anti-tank missile type, and the IHADSS (Integrated Helmet And Display Sighting System) is fitted, both crew members being able to acquire targets by head movements.

The **AH-64A** entered service in 1984. The US Army acquired 827 with another 200 ordered by export customers excluding the UK. The US Army is currently receiving 232 **AH-64D Longbow Apaches** with the Longbow target acquisition and fire-control radar added at the head of a mast above the main rotor. Other helicopters will be revised to AH-64C standard with provision for the rapid

retrofit of this radar. The Apache is now built by Boeing since its acquisition of McDonnell Douglas, which bought Hughes Helicopters in 1984.

Specification
Hughes AH-64A Apache
Type: armed battlefield helicopter
Accommodation: pilot and co-pilot/gunner
Armament: one 30-mm Hughes Chain Gun with 1,200 rounds and remote aiming; four stub-wing hardpoints for normal anti-armour load of 16 Hellfire missiles (initially with laser guidance); other loads can include four 18-round pods of 2.75-in (70-mm) rockets
Powerplant: two 1,536-shp (1146-kW) General Electric T700-700 turboshafts

Performance: maximum speed (at 6316 kg/13,925 lb) 309 km/h (192 mph); range (internal fuel) 611 km (380 miles), and (ferry) 1804 km (1,121 miles)
Weights: empty 4657 kg (10,268 lb); maximum take-off 8006 kg (17,650 lb)
Dimensions: main rotor diameter 14.63 m (48 ft 0 in); fuselage length 14.97 m (49 ft 1½ in); height 4.22 m (13 ft 10 in); main rotor disc area 168.11^2 (1,809.5 sq ft)

Air Vehicle 06, last of the development prototypes, hovering practically at ground level. The AH-64 is the most sophisticated of all battlefield helicopters, and probably the most survivable.

Assault Helicopters

One of the most important assignments now performed by the helicopter on the battlefield is that of assault transport. This task is undertaken by helicopters able to carry anything from a squad to a platoon and gives commanders the maximum possible battlefield mobility.

The unarmed Sikorsky CH-53E Super Stallion is the largest and most powerful helicopter produced in the West. A prototype once flew with an all-up weight of 33,793 kg (74,500 lb).

Only since the early 1950s has the helicopter gained widespread acceptance as a weapon of war. Capable of operating virtually anywhere in the world, it is a truly remarkable machine, and its impact on the conduct of war has been no less dramatic than that of fixed-wing aircraft. But it was not always so, and there were many who questioned the very validity of the concept. From the early 1960s, the Vietnam War, the availability of turbine power, and the immortal 'Huey' changed all that, and no self-respecting air force, navy or army would now be without a complement of these highly versatile machines.

Today helicopters routinely undertake a multiplicity of missions, ranging from anti-submarine warfare through airborne early warning to electronic combat. Perhaps the most important single mission is that of assault and assault support. No longer is it necessary for the humble 'grunt' to march for days before taking up arms: today he can travel rapidly by helicopter to the combat zone, arriving ready to do battle. Similarly, artillery support can be deployed rapidly by helicopter to virtually any location. In this way, artillery can take over the support of the ground troops from assault helicopters armed with cannon, machine guns and air-to-surface rockets. It is also possible to evacuate personnel and equipment quickly using helicopters, thus enabling them to fight another battle another day. To use the modern military vernacular, the helicopter, be it large like the Sikorsky CH-53E Super Stallion or small like the Bell OH-58 Kiowa, can thus be said to be a genuine 'force multiplier'.

Many older helicopters survive in the assault transport role, but recently these have been supplemented by updated or new aircraft. Among the new arrivals are the Bell and Agusta descendants of the twin-engined UH-1N with greater power and a four-blade main rotor. Others include the European Helicopter Industries EH.101, the Eurocopter AS 532 Cougar renamed version of the AS 332 Super Puma and AS 555 Fennec renamed version of the Dauphin, the Mil Mi-17 updated version of the Mi-8, the Mil Mi-26, the NH Industries NH90, and the Sikorsky S-72.

Aérospatiale SA 321 Super Frelon

A development of the original **Sud-Aviation SA 3200 Frelon** (hornet) medium-transport helicopter which flew for the first time during June 1959, the **Aérospatiale SA 321 Super Frelon** holds the distinction of being the largest European-designed helicopter yet to attain quantity production, and is presently in service with several of the world's air arms.

A number of variants have appeared to date, optimized for a variety of missions ranging from anti-submarine warfare through conventional transport to assault duty, and the type has seen some combat action, most notably with Israel's Heyl Ha'Avir which employed the type in the commando raid on Beirut airport several years ago.

Initially designated **SA 3210**, two prototypes were built (one troop transport model and one for maritime applications), these making their respective maiden flights in December 1962 and May 1963. Four pre-production **SA 321** helicopters followed them down the Marignane line before examples of the **SA 321G** ASW model for France's Aéronavale began to appear in the last quarter of 1965, these subsequently entering service during the course of 1966. Designed for operation from the

often cramped confines of aircraft-carriers, the SA 321G has a folding tail section to assist in stowage and incorporates Sylphe panoramic radar in the outrigger floats, dunking sonar equipment and provision for the carriage of up to four homing torpedoes.

In addition to the maritime version produced for France, the Super Frelon has also appeared in civil guise but failed to secure any substantial orders. However, it has achieved some success in the export market, Israel being one of the first customers when it ordered the **SA 321K** for military transport duties. Delivery of these began in 1967, and the type has since proved its worth in airborne assault missions on

several occasions. Lacking the amphibious qualities of the SA 321G, the SA 321K is essentially a military variant of the SA 321J; another derivative of this type is the **SA 321L**, which is in widespread service with the South African Air Force, another air arm which has used the Super Frelon in combat on numerous occasions. Another subtype is the **SA 321M** operated by Libya in dual ASW/search-and-rescue tasks, whilst further customers include China and Iran.

Specification
Aérospatiale SA 321G Super Frelon
Type: ASW helicopter
Armament: four homing torpedoes

An Aérospatiale Super Frelon in the colours of the Libyan air force before the introduction of a plain green Islamic flag in the mid 1970s. Libyan Super Frelons are used mainly for search and rescue.

Powerplant: three Turboméca IIIC-6 turboshafts each rated at 1,550 shp (1156 kW); (SA 321K) 1,870 shp (1394 kW) GE T58-10 engines
Performance: maximum speed at sea level 275 km/h (171 mph); cruising speed at sea level 250 km/h (155 mph); service ceiling 3150 m (10,325 ft); normal range at sea level 820 km (509 miles)
Weights: empty 670 kg (14,771 lb); maximum take-off 13000 kg (28,660 lb)
Dimensions: main rotor diameter 18.90 (62 ft 0 in); length of fuselage 19.40 m (63 ft 7¾ in); height at tail rotor 6.65 m (21 ft 10 in); main rotor disc area 280.55 m² (3,020 sq ft)

Aérospatiale/Westland SA 330 Puma

A Puma of the Royal Moroccan Gendarmerie Air Squadron, a paramilitary force organized along the same lines as the French Gendarmerie. The Puma has been widely exported and over 600 have been built.

A Puma of No. 230 Sqn RAF garishly painted with 'Tiger Stripes' for a NATO Tiger Meet. The RAF's Pumas were used extensively in Rhodesia during Britain's monitoring of the elections and the ceasefire.

Without doubt one of the more successful examples of Anglo-French collaboration, the **Aérospatiale/Westland SA 330 Puma** has been in quantity production for more than 15 years and is in widespread use throughout the world, serving with close to 40 air arms plus many civilian concerns.

Originally conceived by Sud-Aviation in response to a French army (ALAT) requirement for an all-weather/all-climate medium tactical helicopter capable of carrying 16 troops or freight, the SA 330 prototype was still in the process of manufacture when, in 1967, it was selected to fulfil

the Royal Air Force's Tactical Transport Programme, subsequently becoming the subject of a joint production agreement between Aérospatiale in France in Westland Helicopters in the United Kingdom. Coincidental with this decision, an order was placed for 40 **Puma HC.Mk 1** helicopters for the RAF.

Two prototypes and six pre-production specimens were built in all, the first of these making a succesful maiden flight in mid-April 1968. The first production example of the **SA 330B** for ALAT took to the air in September 1968, with deliveries beginning fairly soon after that, in March 1969, although the variant did not attain full operational status until June 1970. By then, the last pre-production machine had been modified to RAF configuration and this was joined by the first Westland-built **SA 330E** in the trials programme on 25 November 1970. Deliveries to the RAF got under way in 1971, initially to No. 240 Operational Conversion Unit and later in the year to No. 33 Squadron, both being based at Odiham.

In addition to these two customers, the Puma soon found favour overseas, the initial export model being the **SA 330C**. Based on the SA 330B, this

achieved considerable success although it is no longer in production, having been supplanted by later models such as the **SA 330H** and **SA 330L**, both of which incorporate improvements arising from early operational experience, which indicated a need for additional power.

Production of the Puma was originally centred on Yeovil and Marignane, but licence production and assembly agreements have since been reached with ICA in Romania, with Nurtanio in Indonesia and with Helibras in Brazil, while a more recent development, the **AS 332 Super Puma**, first flew in September 1978, this featuring different and more powerful engines, composite rotor blades, single-wheel main landing gear units and full de-icing equipment.

Specification

Aérospatiale/Westland SA 330L Puma

Type: medium transport/assault helicopter

Armament: a wide diversity of cannon, machine-guns, rockets and missiles can be carried

Powerplant: two Turboméca Turmo IVC turboshafts each rated at 1,575 shp (1174 kW)

Performance: maximum permissible speed 293 km/h (182 mph); maximum cruising speed 271 km/h (168 mph); service ceiling 6000 m (19,685 ft); maximum range at normal cruise speed 572 km (355 miles)

Weights: empty 3615 kg (7970 lb); maximum take-off 7400 kg (16,315 lb)

Dimensions: diameter of main rotor 15.00 m (49 ft 2½ in); length 18.15 m (59 ft 6½ in); height 5.14 m (16 ft 10½ in); main rotor disc area 176.71 m² (1,902.2 sq ft)

The pilot of this No. 33 Sqn Puma indulges in some low flying along a river in Belize. The squadron, normally based at Odiham, keeps a detachment in Belize in support of British ground forces who deter expansion by neighbouring Guatemala.

 UK
Westland Wessex

Despite the fact that it is essentially based upon the early 1950s vintage Sikorsky S-58, the **Westland Wessex** is still extensively used by the British armed forces, examples serving with the Royal Air Force and the Fleet Air Arm on a variety of tasks which encompass air-sea rescue, commando assault and logistical support.

Initially acquired to fulfil the Royal Navy's need for a modern and relatively sophisticated anti-submarine warfare helicopter, the Wessex has demonstrated considerable versatility and durability since then. Built under licence and developed by Westland, the Wessex enjoyed the benefits bestowed by turbine power and entered service with the Fleet Air Arm as the **Wessex HAS.Mk 1** during 1960. The next major variant to appear was the **Wessex HC.Mk 2** for the RAF, this being able to carry a payload of 16 troops or seven stretchers when operating in the casevac (casualty evacuation) role.

Further refinement of the specialized ASW equipment brought about the **Wessex HAS.Mk 3** version, which was instantly identifiable by virtue of the distinctive dorsal radome, many of the original Wessex HAS.Mk 1s being retrofitted with this equipment. Two **Wessex HCC.Mk 4** helicopters for The Queen's Flight followed, the final version being the **Wessex HU.Mk 5**. Used solely by the Fleet Air Arm, the Wessex HU.Mk 5 was earmarked principally for assault duties and was the logical replacement for those Westland Whirlwinds which had performed this function for several years. Payload capability of the Wessex HU.Mk 5 was essentially identical to that of the RAF's Wessex HC.Mk 2 and, indeed, both variants are able to carry underslung loads, a valuable option when speed is of paramount concern, as is often the case in combat.

Although less capable than the Sea King HC.Mk 4 with regard to payload, the Wessex HU.Mk 5 was extensively

used during the Falklands conflict, taking part in operations on East Falkland and also being involved in lesser actions at South Georgia. Losses were fairly high, largely as a result of the sinking of the *Atlantic Conveyor*, which was carrying a number of Wessex reinforcements when it was struck by an Exocet missile.

Specification

Westland Wessex HU.Mk 5

Type: tactical transport and assault helicopter

Armament: provision for machine-guns and anti-tank missiles

Powerplant: one Rolls-Royce Coupled Gnome 101/111 limited to total combined power of 1,350 shp (1007 kW)

Performance: maximum speed 212 km/h (132 mph); cruising speed 195 km/h (121 mph); service ceiling 4300 m (14,100 ft); range with standard fuel 628 km (390 miles)

Weights: empty 3927 lb (8,657 lb); maximum take-off 6120 kg (13,500 lb)

Dimensions: main rotor diameter 17.07 m (56 ft 0 in); length of fuselage 14.74 m (48 ft 4½ in); height 4.93 m (16 ft 2 in); main rotor disc area 228.82 m² (2,463 sq ft)

A Wessex HC.Mk 2 of No. 28 Sqn based at Kai Tak, Hong Kong. The squadron's role is mainly one of supporting the Hong Kong police and British Army in anti-illegal immigration operations.

A Royal Navy Wessex HU.Mk 5 disembarks a group of Royal Marines on an exercise in Norway. British Wessex helicopters have been used operationally in the Middle East and in the Falklands conflict of 1982. Older Wessex are single-engined.

Westland Commando

Optimized for tactical military duties, the **Westland Commando** evolved from the Westland Sea King anti-submarine warfare helicopter, itself a development of the original Sikorsky SH-3 Sea King which is widely used by the US Navy.

Lacking specialized ASW equipment, the Commando was originally conceived mainly for the export market and has achieved some success in this field, examples being purchased by Egypt and Qatar. A basically similar machine, known as the **Sea King HC.Mk 4**, has also been acquired by the Royal Navy and this presently serves with two Commando squadrons, being employed purely in the assault role.

Featuring a fixed tail-wheel landing gear and lacking the sponsons of the Sea King, the Commando can carry up to 28 fully-armed troops as well as a crew of two. In addition, it possesses the ability to carry underslung loads of up to 3629 kg (8,000 lb), whilst provision for fitment of armament also exists, the parent company having evaluated a variety of weapons including guns, rocket pods and missiles. A particularly versatile helicopter, the Commando is equally adept at assault, casualty evacuation, logistical support, combat

search and rescue and strike tasks.

Unlike the Commando, which is principally intended for use from land bases, the Sea King HC.Mk 4 is frequently deployed aboard aircraft-carriers and thus possesses folding main rotor blades and tail unit to facilitate stowage aboard ship. Airlift capability is slightly less than that of the Commando, at 27 troops or 3402 kg (7,500 lb) of cargo slung externally, but the type more than proved its value in the Falklands during the 1982 campaign, playing a major part in supporting the rapid advance of British troops on Port Stanley. A total of 15 Sea King

The Westland Commando is a dedicated assault version of the naval Sea King helicopter, and has been widely exported. This example is one of 28 operated by the Egyptian air force.

HC.Mk 4s was obtained, these routinely being used to airlift Royal Marines and possessing the ability to operate in all kinds of environment, ranging from the heat and humidity of the tropics to the bitter cold of the Arctic circle.

Specification
Westland Sea King HC.Mk 4
Type: tactical transport/assault helicopter
Armament: a wide variety of cannon, machine-guns, rockets and missiles can be carried
Powerplant: two Rolls-Royce Gnome H.1400-1 turboshafts each rated at

1,660 shp (1238 kW)
Performance: cruising speed at sea level 208 km/h (129 mph); range with maximum payload and reserves 444 km (276 miles); ferry range with maximum fuel 1460 km (907 miles)
Weights: empty 5,544 kg (12,222 lb); maximum take-off 9525 kg (21,000 lb)
Dimensions: main rotor diameter 18.90 m (62 ft 0 in); length, rotors turning 22.15 m (72 ft 8 in); height 5.13 m (16 ft 10 in); main rotor disc area 280.47 m² (3,019 sq ft)

An Egyptian Commando on test in Britain before delivery. The Commando is not used by Britain's armed forces, but the generally similar Sea King HC.Mk 4 was used intensively in the Falklands.

USA
Sikorsky CH-3 and HH-3

A variant of the highly successful **Sikorsky S-61** series which was originally conceived in response to a US Navy requirement, the **CH-3** was intended for service with the US Air Force purely in the transport role, and came about in the early 1960s when the USAF identified a need for a long-range helicopter to resupply the 'Texas Tower' radar facilities situated in the offshore water in the southern USA.

This task was first performed with a trio of **CH-3B** helicopters, these being simply HSS-2s obtained on loan from the USS Navy, and their success soon led to a formal USAF decision to acquire the **CH-3C**. To enable the US Air Force mission to be performed satisfactorily several design changes were recommended, the most obvious of these concerning the aft fuselage which was modified to incorporate a hydraulically-powered rear door and loading ramp, whilst the landing gear was also changed in favour of a more conventional tricycle layout with twin wheels on each unit. In addition, a high degree of self-sufficiency was required for operation at remote sites

where ground facilities were lacking, and this necessitated provision of an auxiliary power unit.

Known in company parlance as the **S-61R**, this model made its maiden flight in June 1963, entering service at Tyndall AFB, Florida, just before the end of the same year. A total of 50 helicopters of this type was built for the USAF, production switching in 1966 to the more powerful **CH-3E**, of which 77 were produced although many appeared as (or were later modified to) **HH-3E Jolly Green Giant** standard for service with the Aerospace Rescue and Recovery Service in the combat search and rescue role, in which the type performed many heroic rescue actions in both North and South Vietnam.

Best known for its exploits in the rescue role, the CH-3 is also employed in drone recovery, whilst a handful of examples has seen service with the USAF's small force of special operations squadrons in support of US Army special forces units engaged in clandestine operations. These have now largely given way to the CH-53C.

An essentially similar version, the

HH-3F Pelican, is widely used by the US Coast Guard on search and rescue duties of a humanitarian nature.

Specification
Sikorsky CH-3E
Type: transport helicopter
Armament: none
Powerplant: two General Electric T58-GE-5 turboshafts each rated at 1,500 shp (1119 kW)
Performance: maximum speed 261 km/h (162 mph); service ceiling 3385 m (11,100 ft); range with maximum fuel and reserves 748 km

A Sikorsky HH-3E Jolly Green Giant recovers a downed pilot in Vietnam. The HH-3 was used extensively in Vietnam, some in the assault role.

(465 miles)
Weights: empty 6010 kg (13,255 lb); normal take-off 9635 kg (21,247 lb); maximum take-off 10000 kg (22,050 lb)
Dimensions: main rotor diameter 18.90 m (62 ft 0 in); length, rotors turning 22.25 m (73 ft 0 in); height 5.51 m (18 ft 1 in); main rotor disc area 280.5 m² (3,019 sq ft)

USA
Sikorsky CH-53 Sea Stallion

In its present production form as the **CH-53E Sea Stallion**, the Sikorsky S-65 is easily the largest and most powerful helicopter to emerge in the West, prototype examples demonstrating impressive lift capability on numerous occasions in recent years. Design of the basic Sea Stallion in fact dates back to 1960, when the US Marine Corps requested industry to submit proposals for a new type to replace the Sikorsky CH-37 Mojave, a piston-engine type which was then rapidly approaching obsolescence.

Sikorsky responded with the S-65, a quite massive machine with a number of interesting features and with heavy emphasis placed on payload capability and ease of operation in the field. Flown for the first time in prototype form during October 1964, the type was ordered into production with deliveries of the initial variant, the **CH-53A**, beginning in September 1966. Deployment to Vietnam followed swiftly, examples being active from the US Marine Corps facility at Marble Mountain near Da Nang at the beginning of 1967, and thereafter the Sea Stallion played a major part in the remainder of the war, its all-weather capability significantly enhancing heavy-lift resources in that theatre.

The second major production model to see service with the US Marines was the **CH-53D** which was introduced in March 1969 and fitted with more powerful engines a well as a special internal cargo-handling system capable of operation by just one man. Up to 55 fully-armed troops could be carried by the CH-53D, and this derivative

still equips several USMC squadrons today.

Other variants which have appeared include the **HH-53B** and **HH-53C**, both for service with the Aerospace Rescue and Recovery Service on combat search and rescue duties, and the **CH-53C** which is employed by the USAF in support of special forces units and to move ground-based tactical radars.

Yet another derivative is the **RH-53D** minesweeper, this using towed sweeping equipment in clearance operations. Currently equipping three US Navy squadrons, the RH-53D was also the model which took part in the disastrous attempt to free the American hostages held in Tehran.

The most recent addition to the Sea Stallion range is the **CH-53E Super Stallion** mentioned above. This is a radically different machine which arose from the realization in the early 1970s that even greater heavy-lift potential would be needed in future by the US Marine Corps. Although its airframe is basically similar to that of earlier models, the CH-53E has three engines driving a seven-bladed main rotor and also incorporates a greatly uprated transmission. The type has recently been introduced to operational service, production is continuing for the US Marines, and the US Navy has plans to obtain the **MH-53E** mine counter-

measures model in the fairly near future to replace the RH-53D.

Specification
Sikorsky CH-53E Super Stallion
Type: heavy-lift transport/assault helicopter
Armament: none
Powerplant: three General Electric T64-GE-415 turboshafts each rated at 3,670 shp (2737 kW)
Performance: maximum speed at sea level 315 km/h (196 mph); maximum cruising speed at sea level 278 km/h (173 mph); range at optimum cruise condition with reserves 492 km (306

miles)
Weights: empty 14537 kg (32,048 lb); maximum take-off 31369 kg (69,750 lb)
Dimensions: main rotor diameter 24.08 m (79 ft 0 in); length, rotors turning 22.48 m (73 ft 9 in); height 8.46 m (27 ft 9 in); main rotor disc area 455.36 m² (4,901.66 sq ft)

A Sikorsky RH-53D Sea Stallion in the markings of Marine Helicopter Mine Countermeasures Squadron 16. Helicopters from this unit made the ill-fated attempt to rescue America's Embassy hostages in Tehran.

About 25 S-65 helicopters were purchased by the Heyl Ha'Avir (Israel air force). They are basically CH-53Ds with inflight-refuelling probes and desert equipment.

USA

Sikorsky CH-54 Tarhe

No longer operating even with the US Army, the **Sikorsky CH-54 Tarhe** evolved in response to a late 1950s requirement for a heavy-lift helicopter. Although the use of cargo hooks to lift heavy and bulky loads was a feature of the design, the Tarhe was also intended to straddle interchangeable pods in much the same way as the Mil Mi-10 does, and the resulting helicopter was particularly bizarre in appearance.

First flown in prototype form in May 1962, the type was evaluated by the US Army at Fort Benning in Georgia and proved sufficiently promising to warrant the placing of a production order for what was, by US Army standards, a relatively small quantity. Against this background, the parent company went ahead with the design of external containers for troop transport, field

hospital support, anti-submarine warfare, mine-sweeping and heavy-lift operations, but these ambitious concepts met with little success, the only such pod being built taking the form of a universal type which could be employed in some of the aforementioned functions.

Almost inevitably, the type was deployed to Vietnam and it did perform well there, being instrumental in the recovery of no less than 380 aircraft and helicopters as well as facilitating rapid movement of bulldozers, graders and, on occasion, armoured fighting vehicles.

The evolutionary process eventually resulted in the appearance of the **CH-54B** derivative, this being fitted with more powerful engines, an uprated gearbox, a high-lift rotor blade, twin mainwheel landing gear members

and an improved flight-control system, whilst the opportunity was also taken to strengthen the basic structure. Once again, the quantity acquired was small, deliveries beginning in 1969, most of those produced being deployed to Europe.

As far as is known, no example of the CH-54 remains in front-line service with the US Army today, those that were operated having given way to the Chinook several years ago.

Specification
Sikorsky CH-54A Tarhe
Type: heavy-lift 'flying crane' helicopter
Armament: none
Powerplant: two Pratt & Whitney T73-P-1 turboshafts each rated at 4,500 shp (3357 kW)

Performance: maximum speed at sea level 203 km/h (126 mph); maximum cruising speed 169 km/h (105 mph); service ceiling 2475 m (9,000 ft); range with maximum fuel and reserves 370 km (230 miles)
Weights: empty 8724 kg (19,234 lb); maximum take-off 19050 kg (42,000 lb)
Dimensions: main rotor diameter 21.95 m (72 ft 0 in); length, rotors turning 26.98 m (88 ft 6 in); height 7.75 m (25 ft 5 in)

The Sikorsky CH-54 Tarhe has now been largely replaced in service by the CH-47 Chinook. It was designed as a flying crane and to carry large, special-purpose pods under its fuselage, but these were never widely used.

USA

Sikorsky UH-60 Black Hawk

Although the Bell UH-1 Iroquois was and still is a fine helicopter, US Army requirements for the 1980s and beyond were such that it became clear at the start of the 1970s that the 'Huey' would eventually need replacement. So, in August 1972, after studying several proposals from industry, the US Army chose the Boeing Vertol and Sikorsky candidates for a competitive evaluation, a project which was undertaken during 1976 and which resulted in the **Sikorsky UH-60A Black Hawk** being adjudged the winner. An announcement to this effect was made on 23 December 1976, production of an initial batch of 15 getting under way in late 1977, and these were just the first of well over 1,000 machines operated by the US Army in many important roles.

Deliveries to the US Army began late in 1978 and the type has since

been widely deployed with US Army combat formations in both the USA and, more recently, Europe. Although originally conceived under the generic title UTTAS (Utility Tactical Transport Aircraft System), the UH-60A is in fact seen primarily as an assault helicopter and is therefore an extremely rugged machine, being able to withstand direct hits of armour-piercing rounds up to 7.62 mm (0.3 in) calibre in the fuselage. With accommodation for a crew of three and 11 fully-equipped troops, the Black Hawk is fitted with an external cargo hook with a capacity of 3629 kg (8,000 lb), whilst it can also operate in the casualty evacuation role, removal of cabin seats permitting up to four stretchers to be carried. Armament capability is at present limited to a pair of 7.62-mm (0.3-in) machine-guns firing from opened side

doors, but provision also exists for chaff and flares to be dispensed.

Other proposals for the US Army have included the **EH-60A** electronic countermeasures variant and the **EH-60B** SOTAS (Stand-Off Target Acquisition System) model, both of which have flown in prototype form although there is some doubt as to whether they will be proceeded with, the latter apparently being plagued by numerous problems.

Somewhat more successful is the **SH-60B Seahawk** for the US Navy, this arising from that service's LAMPS (Light Airborne Multi-Purpose System) Mk III requirement for a seagoing helicopter to serve aboard surface combatant vessels in the anti-submarine warfare/anti-ship missile defence roles. The SH-60B entered service in 1984, and was complemented by the carrier borne SH-60F Ocean Hawk replacement for the SH-3. Surviving SH-60B and SH-60F

helicopters have been upgraded to a SH-60R standard.

Specification
Sikorsky UH-60A Black Hawk
Type: assault helicopter
Armament: two 7.62-mm (0.3-in) machine-guns
Powerplant: two General Electric T700-GE-700 turboshafts each rated at 1,543 shp (1150 kW)
Performance: maximum speed at sea level 296 km/h (184 mph); maximum cruising speed 272 km/h (169 mph); service ceiling 5790 m (19,000 ft); range at maximum take-off weight with 30-minute reserves 600 km (373 miles)
Weights: empty 4944 kg (10,900 lb); mission take-off 7462 kg (16,450 lb); maximum take-off 9185 kg (20,250 lb)
Dimensions: main rotor diameter 16.36 m (53 ft 8 in); length, rotors turning 19.76 m (64 ft 10 in); height 5.13 m (16 ft 10 in); main rotor disc area 210.05 m² (2,261 sq ft)

Bell UH-1 Iroquois

Probably best known for its exploits during the Vietnam War, the **Bell Model 204/205** series earned a justifiable reputation as a true workhorse in that conflict, being employed in a multiplicity of missions ranging from troop transport through casualty evacuation and liaison to more offensive applications as a gunship in search-and-destroy and riverine operations. As a by-product of its extensive use by all elements of the US armed forces, it became the most successful turbine-powered helicopter of its day and, indeed, subsequent derivatives based on the original **XH-40** prototype and **UH-1 Iroquois** production model are still in quantity production today, almost 30 years after it first flew in prototype form.

In service with approximately 60 air arms throughout the world, variants of the 'Huey' have been produced by the parent company at Fort Worth, by Agusta in Italy, by Fuji in Japan, by AIDC in Taiwan, by Dornier in West Germany and, most recently, by the People's Republic of China. Over the same period, the gross operating weight has virtually trebled although overall size and appearance has changed relatively little.

Major production variants for the US armed forces include the **UH-1B, UH-1D** and **UH-1H** of the US Army; the

UH-1F, HH-1H and **UH-1N** for the US Air Force; and the **UH-1E, HH-1K, TH/UH-1L** and **UH-1N** for the US Navy and US Marine Corps. Examples of most of these models were also produced in substantial amounts for export markets.

Armament and payload capability varied considerably between early- and late-production machines, but the UH-1H model of the US Army usually carries a couple of 7.62-mm (0.3-in) machine-guns adjacent to and fired from the main cabin. In addition to the pilot, up to 14 troops could also be accommodated, alternative configurations permitting carriage of up to six stretchers or 1814 kg (4,000 lb) of cargo. In later variants this figure is almost doubled.

Although now being supplanted in US Army service by the Sikorsky UH-60A, there is little doubt that the UH-1 will contine to form an important part of the US Army's aviation components for many years to come, whilst with later variants still in quantity production it is clear that the saga of the 'Huey' still has a long time to run.

Specification
Bell UH-1H
Type: utility helicopter
Armament: usually two 7.62-mm (0.3-in) machine-guns

A Bell UH-1 over Vietnam. This one is armed with rocket pods and has had its doors removed to allow a greater

Powerplant: one Avco Lycoming T53-L-13 turboshaft rated at 1,400 shp (1044 kW)
Performance: maximum and cruising speeds 204 km/h (127 mph); range with maximum fuel 512 km (318 miles)

American infantrymen leap from a hovering Bell UH-1 during the Vietnam war. The assault helicopter

field of fire for its two 7.62-mm (0.3-in) machine-guns.

Weights: empty 2362 kg (5,210 lb); maximum take-off 4309 kg (9,500 lb)
Dimensions: main rotor diameter 14.63 m (48 ft 0 in); length, rotor stowed fore and aft, 17.61 m (57 ft 9½ in); height 4.42 in (14 ft 6 in); main rotor disc area 168.1 m² (1,809.6 sq ft)

won its spurs in Vietnam, giving ordinary soldiers a previously undreamed-of degree of mobility.

Bell OH-58 Kiowa

Arising from a 1962 requirement for a new US Army LOH (Light Observation Helicopter), the type which eventually became the **Bell OH-58 Kiowa** in fact enjoyed a rather chequered early development history, losing out in the competition to the Hughes OH-6A Cayuse in a quite intense evaluation programme which also involved a Hiller submission.

Although the **Model 206** was not selected by the US Army, company confidence in the machine was particularly high and the design was quickly evolved into the **Model 206A JetRanger**, a type which went on to achieve considerable success in the civilian and export military markets and which is still being built today, albeit in much improved form.

The failure by Hughes in the mid-1960s to contain OH-6 costs and achieve the desired production rate eventually led to the LOH contest being re-opened during 1967, and it was a case of second time lucky for Bell, whose Model 206A emerged as the winner during March 1968. The reward was a contract for no less than 2,200 examples, all of which were delivered by 1973.

Differing from its civilian counterpart by virtue of a larger-diameter main rotor, military avionics and a few detail changes, the OH-58A Kiowa, as the type became known, began to enter service with US Army units in May 1969 and was quickly deployed operationally, reaching combat units in South Vietnam within four months. Since then, it has seen service with US Army elements throughout the world and it is still a most important asset, normally operating in conjunction with AH-1 HueyCobra gunships as a scout helicopter.

Although not normally armed, the Kiowa has been tested with a variety of weapons and US Army examples can carry the XM27 Minigun. More recently, a substantial number have been re-engined and brought to **OH-58C** standard, other more visible indications of this change being the provision of infra red-suppressed exhaust nozzles, flat glass canopies to cut down reflection and wire cutters above and below the cockpit canopy.

The OH-58D Kiowa is an armed scout/attack version with an uprated powerplant driving a four-blade main rotor, and the US Army has received some 335 earlier helicopters upgraded to this standard. The Bell 206 has also secured useful orders from a number of export military customers.

Specification
Bell OH-58A Kiowa

The Bell Kiowa is used by the US Army as an unarmed light observation and scout helicopter, although it does have an assault role in some smaller air forces.

Type: light observation/scout helicopter
Armament: none usually
Powerplant: one Allison T63-A-700 turboshaft rated at 317 shp (237 kW)
Performance: maximum speed at sea level 222 km/h (138 mph); cruising speed 188 km/h (117 mph); maximum range at sea level with 10 per cent reserves 481 km (299 miles)
Weights: empty 664 kg (1,464 lb); maximum take-off 1361 kg (3,000 lb)
Dimensions: main rotor diameter 10.7 mm (35 ft 4 in); length, rotors turning 12.47 m (40 ft 11 in); height 2.91 m (9 ft 6½ in); main rotor disc area 91.1 m² (980.5 sq ft)

Boeing Vertol CH-47 Chinook

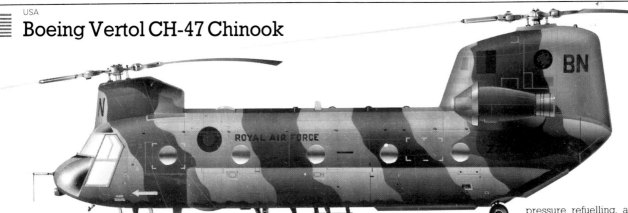

A CH-47 Chinook of No. 18 Sqn, RAF. The one RAF Chinook not destroyed in the sinking of the Atlantic Conveyor *proved to be of immense value during the Falklands war.*

Evolution of the **Boeing Vertol CH-47 Chinook** can be traced back to the late 1950s, when the US Army began to search for a turbine-powered medium transport helicopter capable of all-weather operation in virtually all types of climatic conditions. Of the several proposals submitted in response, the **Boeing Vertol Model 114** was adjudged most suitable, and this led to a contract for five prototype specimens in mid-1959.

First flown in prototype form on 21 September 1961, the Chinook began to enter service with the US Army just over a year later and quickly began to compile an impressive record, being deployed to Vietnam soon after US involvement in that conflict began to escalate. Capable of airlifting up to 40 troops, the CH-47 also proved of great value in airlifting supplies to the numerous garrisons which lay dotted around South Vietnam, whilst it was also frequently used to recover downed aircraft and helicopters and for the evacuation of casualties and refugees.

The initial **CH-47A** model was soon replaced in production by the rather more powerful **CH-47B**, but it was the **CH-47C** which was the definitive Chinook, this flying for the first time in October 1967 and entering service early in the following year. Once again, considerably more powerful engines were fitted, this model also having a strengthened transmission system and additional fuel capacity.

Further studies aimed at improving the Chinook's already impressive capabilities still further led eventually to the **CH-47D**, this incorporating revised electrical systems, glassfibre rotor blades, modular hydraulic systems, triple cargo hook, advanced flight-control systems, single-point pressure refuelling, auxiliary power unit and revised avionics. However, this version is being produced by the simple expedient of a modernization programme involving surviving CH-47As, CH-47Bs and CH-47Cs, a programme which began in 1979 with the conversion of three **YCH-47D** prototypes for trials work. Production-configured CH-47Ds began to join the US Army during 1983.

Variants of the Chinook have also met with some success on the export market, other operators including Argentina, Australia, Canada, Iran, Italy, Libya, Spain, Thailand and the United Kingdom, whilst it should also be noted that the type is produced under licence by Elicotteri Meridionali in Italy.

Specification
Boeing Vertol CH-47C Chinook
Type: medium transport/assault
helicopter
Armament: none
Powerplant: two Avco Lycoming T55-
L-11A turboshafts each rated at
3,750 shp (2796 kW)

Performance: maximum speed
304 km/h (189 mph); service ceiling
4570 m (15,000 ft); mission radius with
3294-kg (7,262-lb) payload 185 km (115
miles)
Weights: empty 9351 kg (20,616 lb);
loaded 14,969 kg (33,000 lb); maximum
take-off 20,866 kg (46,000 lb)

Dimensions: rotor diameter, each
18.29 m (60 ft 0 in); length, rotors
turning 30.18 m (99 ft 0 in); fuselage
length 15.54 m (50 ft 0 in); height 5.66 m
(18 ft 7 in); rotor disc area, total
525.34 m² (5,654.9 sq ft)

*One of 12 Boeing Vertol Chinooks of
the Spanish army. The Chinook has
been widely exported and is built
under licence in Italy. It also saw
service in Vietnam.*

Former USSR

Mil Mi-6 'Hook' and Mi-10 'Harke'

First flown during September 1957, the
Mil Mi-6 'Hook' was the first Soviet helicopter to rely on turbine power and is
still one of the largest flying machines
of this type in the world. Arising from a
joint civil/military need for a heavy lift
helicopter, the Mi-6 possesses the
ability to carry light armoured vehicles
in its capacious cabin (direct access
being provided by means of clam-
shell-type loading doors at the rear)
whilst it also employs large fixed stub
wings to alleviate loads on the rotor to a
quite substantial degree when cruising. A further benefit bestowed by
these wings is the fact that the Mi-6
may employ STOL techniques, permitting it to get airborne with a greater
payload than it can lift vertically. As far
as payload is concerned, the normal
load is limited to around 12000 kg
(26,455 lb) but, like most modern heli-

copters, it can also carry external cargo although in such instances the limit
imposed is about 9000 kg (19,840 lb).
Alternatively, approximately 70 troops
can be carried, but it is unlikely that
the type would be employed near the
forward battle zones, its large size and
limited manoeuvrability being likely to
make it an attractive and vulnerable
target.

In addition to the basic Mi-6, two
flying crane derivatives are known to
have appeared, these being the **Mi-10**
and the **Mi-10K**. Both are known by the
NATO reporting name **'Harke'** although there are a number of notewor-

thy differences, the Mi-10 having a
massive quadricycle landing gear
which enables it to straddle and lift
bulky loads of the order of 15000 kg
(33,069 lb) while the Mi-10K has a
much shorter and more conventional
landing gear with an aft-facing crew
station beneath the nose, from which a
member of the crew monitors loading
and unloading operations. Both the Mi-
10 and Mi-10K can carry up to 28 passengers internally.

Specification
Mil Mi-6 'Hook'
Type: heavy transport helicopter
Armament: none
Powerplant: two Soloviev D-25V
turboshafts each rated at 5,500 shp

(4101 kW)
Performance: maximum speed
300 km/h (186 mph); cruising sped
250 km/h (155 mph); service ceiling at
maximum take-off weight 4400 m
(14,435 ft); range with 12000-kg
(26,455-lb) payload 200 km (124 miles);
range with 4000-kg (8,818-lb) payload
1000 km (621 miles)
Weights: empty 27240 kg (60,055 lb);
normal take-off 40500 kg (89,286 lb);
maximum vertical take-off 42500 kg
(93,700 lb)
Dimensions: main rotor diameter
35.00 m (114 ft 10 in); fuselage length
33.18 m (108 ft 10½ in); wing span
15.30 m (50 ft 2½ in); height 9.17 m
(30 ft 1 in); main rotor disc area
962.1 m² (10,356.4 sq ft)

*A Mil Mi-6 'Hook' of the Egyptian air force. The Mi-6 was the Soviet Union's first
turbine-engined helicopter, and is one of the world's largest military helicopters.*

Mil Mi-8 'Hip'

A Mil Mi-8 'Hip' of No. 121 Sqn, Indian Air Force. Indian Mi-8s are frequently armed with rocket pods and have largely replaced the fixed-wing C-47 Dakota in Indian service, as well as being used for offshore oil support missions.

Widely used by the Soviet air force and its Warsaw Pact allies, the **Mil Mi-8 'Hip'** began life as a logical turbine-powered adaptation of the earlier Mi-4 'Hound' although the degree of commonality which exists between the production configured 'Hip' and its predecessors is virtually non-existent.

First flown in prototype form during 1961, the Mi-8 initially appeared with a four-bladed rotor driven by a single Soloviev turboshaft engine, this being superseded on the second prototype by the now-standard twin-engine installation. About two years later, the original rotor assembly was supplanted by a five-bladed type and it

was in this guise that the 'Hip' eventually entered production in about 1967.

Since then, well over 7,000 examples have been built and, in addition to Warsaw Pact nations, the 'Hip' also serves with the air arms of Afghanistan, Bangladesh, Egypt, Ethiopia, Finland, Iraq, North Korea, Pakistan, Peru, Somalia, South Yemen, Syria and Vietnam. In Soviet service the type is thought to be mainly assigned to tactical helicopter formations, and it can be assumed that it would therefore be mainly employed in assault-type operations.

Including the prototypes, at least six variants are known to have been built, those intended for assault and utility operations being the **'Hip-C'**, **'Hip-E'** and **'Hip-F'**. All feature rear-loading doors which permit carriage of 32 troops or 4000 kg (8,818 lb) of bulky or awkward items of cargo in the cabin, and all possess the ability to carry armament, the 'Hip-E' being particu-

larly noteworthy in that it can operate with a 12.7-mm (0.5-in) nose-mounted gun, up to 192 rockets carried in no less than 12 external pods and four AT-2 'Swatter' anti-tank missiles. The latest assault version to be identified is the **'Hip-F'**, which appears to be aimed mainly at export markets and incorporates different armament in the shape of six AT-3 'Sagger' missiles. The **'Hip-D'** is yet another model in the family, this being optimized for electronic warfare tasks with extra aerials and large rectangular containers on external pylons. The **'Hip-G'**, **'Hip-J'** and **'Hip-K'** are communication-relay, ECM and advanced ECM versions respectively. The latest the MiG-17 models use 1,950-shp (1454-kW) TV3117MT engines. The tail rotor is on the port side of the tail pylon, a combination offering improved performance.

A Mi-8 in Afghan air force markings.

Specification
Mil Mi-8 'Hip-C'
Type: medium transport/assault helicopter
Armament: up to four rocket pods each with 32 57-mm (2.24 in) rockets and four AT-2 'Swatter' anti-tank missiles, plus one 12.7-mm (0.5-in) machine-gun
Powerplant: two Isotov TV-2-117A turboshafts each rated at 1,700 shp (1267 kW)
Performance: maximum speed 260 km/h (161 mph); cruising speed 200 km/h (124 mph); hover ceiling 4500 km (14,765 ft); range with 2950-kg (6,504-lb) payload 425 km (264 miles)
Weights: empty 7160 kg (15,785 lb); maximum take-off (VTO mode) 12020 kg (26,499 lb)
Dimensions: main rotor diameter 21.29 m (69 ft 10½ in); fuselage length 18.31 m (60 ft 1 in); height 5.60 m (18 ft 4½ in); main rotor disc area 356.000 m² (3,832 sq ft)

Post-War Carrier Aircraft

Following the triumph of the aircraft carrier during World War II, naval aviation continued throughout the 1950s as a major component of Western military power. Carrier aircraft advanced in technology as quickly as their land-based counterparts, and were soon in action over Korea (1950–53) and Suez (1956).

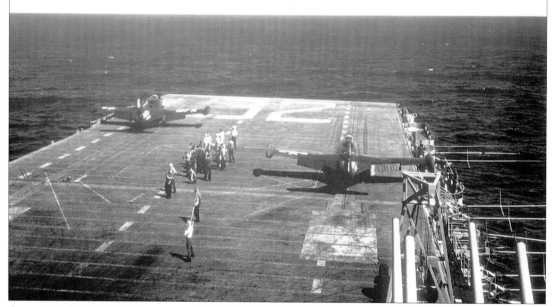

Grumman P9F Panthers sit on the deck of the US 'Essex' class carrier *Leyte*. In July 1950, F9Fs from USS *Valley Forge* carried out the first carrier jet fighter sortie of the Korean War.

Seaborne aviation probably reached its zenith in the 1950s. Nations such as Australia, Canada, France, the Netherlands, the UK and the United States operated aircraft carriers, and used them on several occasions to project air power across distances of several thousand miles: Korea and Suez were just two examples of carrier air power at work.

The decade was also a time of great innovation as far as equipment embarked on carriers was concerned, with jet-powered aircraft beginning to take the place of such war-weary veterans as the Vought Corsair and Supermarine Seafire. The decade witnessed a remarkable transformation in terms of performance. Nowhere was this change more evident than in the US Navy, which pioneered jet operations at sea. At the start of the 1950s the performance of jet aircraft was only marginally better than that of the warplanes of the piston-engined era, but by the end of the decade the US Navy had introduced an aircraft capable of sustained supersonic speed in level flight (the Vought F-8U Crusader) and was looking ahead to Mach 2 performance with the truly remarkable McDonnell F4 Phantom II.

No less significant were the changes embodied in the aircraft-carriers themselves, Foremost amongst these was the widespread introduction of the steam catapult and the angled deck, both features which greatly contributed to improved safety. In addition, the size of carriers also grew remarkably. Again, the United States was largely responsible, with four examples of the truly massive 'Forrestal' class of aircraft carrier in commission by the end of 1959.

Perhaps the most significant feature of the aircraft carrier (and one which was clearly displayed in the South Atlantic campaign during 1982) is that its ability to range the world's oceans means that air power can quickly be brought to bear at the point where it is most needed for the protection of national interests. Paradoxically, though, the constraints placed on defence expenditure throughout the world have witnessed the disappearance of the carrier from all but a handful of navies, an occurrence which certainly gives one pause for thought.

de Havilland Sea Hornet

Although bearing a strong family resemblance to the highly successful and versatile Mosquito, the **de Havilland Hornet** was in fact a new design and came about as a private-venture response to the need for a long-range single-seat escort fighter for service in the Pacific. Development began in 1942, the prototype making its maiden flight on 28 July 1944, but like many aircraft which appeared late in World War II the Hornet suffered heavily through post VJ-Day cancellations. Nevertheless, the Hornet's outstanding performance (it was the fastest twin-engine piston-powered fighter to serve with any air arm in the world) saved it from total oblivion, the type being employed by the Royal Air Force in some numbers between 1946 and 1956.

Consideration of the possibility of acquiring a carrier-based variant resulted in the testing of three **Hornet F.Mk 1** aircraft in 1944-5, the third of these being a fully navalized specimen and such was the success of these trials that a production order for 79 **Sea Hornet F.Mk 20** fighters soon followed, deliveries getting under way to No. 801 Squadron in June 1947. Armament was basically similar to that of the RAF Hornet, and this model remained in service until 1951 in a front-line capacity. The next version was the **Sea Hornet NF.Mk 21** night-fighter, whose development began in 1946 although it was not until January 1949 that this attained operational status with the Fleet Air Arm, equipping No. 809 Squadron at Culdrose until 1954, when

it finally gave way to jet-powered equipment in the shape of the de Havilland Sea Venom. Subsequently, the Sea Hornet NF.Mk 21 was reassigned to the training of night-fighter radar operators, a task it performed until 1956 when the handful of remaining aircraft were scrapped.

Production of the Sea Hornet was completed with the **Sea Hornet PR.Mk 22** for photographic reconnaissance, about two dozen examples being completed, all of which employed a pair of F52 cameras for use by day and a single K19B camera for night work. In order to undertake the reconnaissance mission, the cannon armament was deleted, its place being filled by cameras.

Specification
de Havilland Sea Hornet F.Mk 20
Type: carrierborne escort and strike fighter
Powerplant: two 2,030-hp (1514-kW) Rolls-Royce Merlin 133/134 inline piston engines
Performance: maximum speed 748 km/h (465 mph) at 6705 m (22,000 ft); service ceiling 10,670 m (35,000 ft); range 2414 km (1,500 miles) with auxiliary fuel

Used as a long-range fighter and strike aircraft, the de Havilland Sea Hornet F.Mk 20 served aboard the Royal Navy's carriers from 1947 to 1951, when it was replaced by the Sea Venom.

Weights: empty 6033 kg (13,300 lb); maximum take-off 8405 kg (18,530 lb)
Dimensions: span 13.72 m (45 ft 0 in); length 11.18 m (36 ft 8 in); height 4.32 m (14 ft 2 in); wing area 33.54 m² (361 sq ft)
Armament: four 20-mm cannon, plus eight 27-kg (60-lb) rockets or two 454-kg (1,000-lb) bombs

---

de Havilland Sea Venom

Following the evaluation of a standard RAF Venom NF.Mk 2 night-fighter during the course of 1950, the Royal Navy ordered three fully navalized prototype aircraft as the **de Havilland Sea Venom NF.Mk 20**, the first of which made its maiden flight on 19 April 1951. Subsequent carrier compatibility trials conducted aboard HMS *Illustrious* showed that the type possessed considerable promise, and an initial batch of 50 production Sea Venom NF.Mk 20s was contracted, deliveries getting under way during the mid-1950s.

Attaining operational status with No. 890 Squadron aboard HMS *Albion* in July 1955, the Sea Venom NF.Mk 20 was quickly followed by the **Sea Venom FAW.Mk 21**, which used the more powerful Ghost 104 turbojet engine and which was also fitted with American APS-57 airborne interception radar. Deliveries of the Sea Venom FAW.Mk 21 began before the Sea Venom NF.Mk 20 became operational, the delivery beginning in May 1955 of what eventually became the most widely used version, a total of 167 being built for service with the Fleet Air Arm. Production of the Sea Venom was completed with 39 examples of the **Sea Venom FAW.Mk 22**, which differed mainly by virtue of being powered by the Ghost 105 turbojet.

Like other Fleet Air Arm aircraft of this era, the Sea Venom was in action in the Suez Crisis, being employed against targets in the Canal Zone, but its combat swan-song came in 1960 when No. 891 Squadron's Sea Venom FAW.Mk 22s flew a number of missions against Yemeni rebels in Aden.

Shortly afterwards the Sea Venom was retired from the front-line inventory, although some continued to fly with second-line elements until 1970.

In addition to service with the Fleet Air Arm, 39 **Sea Venom FAW.Mk 53** aircraft were exported to Australia in 1955 whilst about 80 aircraft were built under licence by Sud-Est in France, where the type was known as the **Aquilon**. Based on the Sea Venom NF.Mk 20, the Aquilon served with the Aéronavale from 1955 to 1965, some aircraft being configured to carry the Nord 5103 air-to-air missile. Following delivery of the Vought F-8E(FN) Crusader, surviving Aquilons were relegated to secondary duties.

Specification
de Havilland Sea Venom FAW.Mk 21
Type: carrierborne all-weather fighter
Powerplant: one 2245-kg (4,950-lb) thrust de Havilland Ghost 104 turbojet
Performance: maximum speed 1014 km/h (630 mph) at sea level; service ceiling 14995 m (49,200 ft); range 1609 km (1,000 miles)
Weight: maximum take-off 7212 kg

(15,900 lb)
Dimensions: span 13.08 m (42 ft 11 in); length 11.15 m (36 ft 7 in); height 2.59 m (8 ft 6 in); wing area 25.99 m² (279.75 sq ft)
Armament: four 20-mm cannon, plus up to 907 kg (2,000 lb) of external ordnance including bombs and rockets

De Havilland's Sea Venom was widely employed by the Royal Navy for six or seven years. Its most important combat was during the Suez crisis, when this FAW.Mk 21 was pictured after a wheels-up landing. The fairing over the hook is clearly visible.

Fastest of all the naval Venoms was the French Sud-Est Aquilon 203. This example served with Aéronavale Flottille 16F and was later armed with the Nord 5103 command-guidance air-to-air missile.

Fairey Firefly

One of the most successful World War II designs to originate in the UK, the **Fairey Firefly** initially entered service in 1943 and racked up an impressive combat record in World War II. Notable highlights included the attack on the German battleship *Tirpitz* and a series of strikes on mainland Japan shortly before VJ-Day brought hostilities to a conclusion. In the post-war era, the Firefly demonstrated a considerable degree of versatility, turning its hand to other duties such as target towing and anti-submarine warfare as well as continuing in its primary function of fighter-bomber. By the time production ceased 1,702 had been built, some remaining active with the Fleet Air Arm 'until as late as 1957 whilst others served with Australia, Canada, Denmark, Ethiopia, India, the Netherlands, Sweden and Thailand.

Post-war production initially involved the **Firefly FR.Mk 4** reconnaissance fighter, which flew for the first time on 25 May 1945. Incorporating a number of new features such as clipped wingtips and redesigned tail surfaces, 160 were completed by early 1948, and these saw service with several Fleet Air Arm squadrons, some later being modified to **Firefly TT.Mk 4** standard for target-towing duty. The next basic model to appear was the Mk 5, variants including the **Firefly NF.Mk 5** night-fighter, the **Firefly FR.Mk 5** day reconnaissance fighter and the **Firefly AS.Mk 5** anti-submarine patrol aircraft; the last eventually became the most numerous post-war version, over 300 being produced between 1947 and 1950. Production then switched to the three-seat **Firefly AS.Mk 6**, which entered service in 1951, the 149 aircraft built eventually equipping six front-line and six

reserve squadrons, and these were followed in 1952 by the **Firefly FR.Mk 7**. Only 36 were completed to this standard, the remaining 160 Mk 7s all being **Firefly T.Mk 7** trainers. Firefly production eventually terminated in March 1956 with the delivery of the last of 24 new-build **Firefly U.Mk 8** target drones, but 54 Mk 5s were also converted to this mission, these being known as **Firefly U.Mk 9** aircraft.

Operationally, British Fireflies of various marks saw considerable post-war action, taking part in the Malayan confrontation between 1949 and 1954 as well as the Korean War, whilst the

Dutch **Firefly FR.Mk 1** aircraft undertook combat duty against rebel forces in the Dutch East Indies.

Specification
Fairey Firefly FR.Mk 4
Type: carrierborne reconnaissance fighter
Powerplant: one 2,245-hp (1674-kW) Rolls-Royce Griffon 74 inline piston engine
Performance: maximum speed 591 km/h (367 mph) at 4265 m (14,000 ft); service ceiling 9725 m (31,900 ft); range 2148 km (1,335 miles)
Weights: empty 4388 kg (9,674 lb);

After serving with distinction in the closing months of World War II, the Fairey Firefly continued to give valuable service for several years. These Firefly FR.Mk 4s are seen in company with a trio of Sea Furies.

maximum take-off 7083 kg (15,615 lb)
Dimensions: span 12.55 m (41 ft 2 in); length 11.58 m (38 ft 0 in); height 4.24 m (13 ft 11 in); wing area 30.66 m² (330 sq ft)
Armament: four 20-mm cannon, plus 16 27-kg (60-lb) rockets or two 454-kg (1,000-lb) bombs

---

Hawker Sea Fury

First conceived as a long-range fighter for use by the Royal Air Force in the Pacific against the Japanese, Hawker's initial design was known originally as the Tempest Light Fighter. It very quickly generated considerable Royal Navy interest which led to the issue of a formal specification in February 1943, this being followed in April 1944 by an order for 400 aircraft to be shared equally by the RAF and the Fleet Air Arm.

The first example to fly was the RAF's Fury Mk 1 on 1 September 1944, whilst the **Hawker Sea Fury** prototype took to the air for its maiden flight on 21 February 1945. However, the return of peace led to large-scale defence cutbacks, Hawker's newest fighter suffering badly with all the RAF examples and half of the Royal Navy aircraft being cancelled, although the manufacturer did ultimately achieve modest export sales of the land-based Fury, customers including Egypt, Iraq and Pakistan.

As far as the Royal Navy's aircraft was concerned, this first flew in production form as the **Sea Fury F.Mk 10** on 7 September 1946, duly entering service with No. 807 Squadron in July 1947. Manufacture of the Sea Fury as a pure fighter was, however, destined to be short-lived and only 50 were completed, production thereafter switching to the **Sea Fury FB.Mk 11** fighter-bomber derivative which could carry

up to 907 kg (2,000 lb) of external ordnance and which also featured a lengthened arrester hook plus provision for rocket-assisted take-off gear. This variant became the definitive Sea Fury, deliveries beginning in May 1948, and by the time the line closed in the early 1950s some 515 had been completed, as well as 60 examples of the **Sea Fury T.Mk 20** two-seat trainer. By then the Sea Fury had also been engaged in combat in Korea, where it proved to be an excellent ground-attack platform as well as no mean performer in air-to-air combat, emerging victorious over the jet-powered MiG-15 on at least two occasions.

By the mid-1950s the Sea Fury had been supplanted by more modern types with the Fleet Air Arm, but some export Sea Furies continued to fly with the air arms of Australia, Burma, Canada, Cuba and the Netherlands for a few more years.

Specification
Hawker Sea Fury FB.Mk 11
Type: carrierborne fighter-bomber
Powerplant: one 2,480-hp (1849-kW) Bristol Centaurus 18 radial piston engine
Performance: maximum speed 740 km/h (460 mph) at 5485 m (18,000 ft); service ceiling 10910 m (35,800 ft); range 1127 km (700 miles) on internal fuel

Weights: empty 4191 kg (9,240 lb); maximum take-off 5670 kg (12,500 lb)
Dimensions: span 11.70 m (38 ft 4.75 in); length 10.57 m (34 ft 8 in); height 4.84 m (15 ft 10.5 in); wing area

26.0 m² (280 sq ft)
Armament: four 20-mm cannon, plus up to 907 kg (2,000 lb) of external ordnance including bombs, rockets and mines

Representing the pinnacle of piston-engined fighter design, the Hawker Sea Fury FB.Mk 11 was powered by an 18-cylinder two-row radial which gave the aircraft a top speed of over 700 km/h (435 mph). It saw much action in Korea and claimed a few MiG victories.

Supermarine Attacker

After World War II the UK's hectic pace of aircraft development slowed almost to a halt, as the government invoked a 'ten-year rule' which stated there would be a 10-year warning of any emergency, so new equipment was not urgent. This philosophy was dented by the Berlin Airlift and shattered by Korea in June 1950, and by this time the Fleet Air Arm's first jet fighter had been in the air two months. The **Supermarine Attacker** prototype had been built to a 1944 specification, using a new Nene-engined fuselage mounted on the wings of the Spiteful with radiators removed. The result was the **Attacker F.Mk 1**, a mediocre fighter whose main advantages were cheapness and easy handling at low level. The latter was put to use by adding bombs in the **Attacker FB.Mk 1** version, and the **Attacker FB.Mk 2** had powered ailerons and a stronger metal-framed canopy. The last of 145 of the three marks was delivered in 1953,

and these served with No. 736 training and Nos 800, 803 and 890 first-line squadrons from late 1951 until 1955, thereafter continuing with the RNVR until that force was disbanded in 1957.

Specification
Supermarine Attacker FB.Mk 2
Type: single-seat carrier-based fighter-bomber
Powerplant: one 2313-kg (5,100-lb) thrust Rolls-Royce Nene Mk 102 turbojet
Performance: maximum speed 950 km/h (590 mph) at sea level; initial climb (light weight 5216 kg/11,500 lb) 1935 m (6,350 ft) per minute; service ceiling (maximum weight) 11890 m (39,000 ft); range (with 1137-litre/250-Imp gal belly tank) 1700 km (1,060 miles)
Weights: empty 4495 kg (9,910 lb); maximum take-off 7938 kg (17,500 lb)

Dimensions: span 11.26 m (36 ft 11 in); length 11.43 m (37 ft 6 in); height 3.03 m (9 ft 11 in); wing area 21 m² (226 sq ft)
Armament: four 20-mm Hispano Mk 5 cannon, plus provision for two 454-kg (1,000-lb) bombs or eight rockets

Britain's first naval jet to reach a squadron, the Supermarine Attacker was also exported to Pakistan. The wing was developed from that flown on the Spiteful, which had in turn been developed from the Spitfire.

Westland Wyvern

Unique in being the only turboprop-powered naval strike fighter to attain operational status, the **Westland Wyvern** came about in response to a 1944 specification, but was plagued by numerous developmental problems that conspired to delay the type's introduction for several years and eventually limited production in favour of more reliable jets such as the Hawker Sea Hawk.

Early Wyverns were fitted with Rolls-Royce Eagle piston engines, but following the RAF's decision to proceed no further with this project the Royal Navy opted to concentrate all future development around the Armstrong Siddeley Python turboprop engine, the first of two prototypes with this powerplant taking to the air on 22 March 1949. Subsequent testing was drawn out, with the result that some three years passed before examples of the Wyvern reached Fleet Air Arm trials squadrons, and it was not until September 1953 that the type became operational with No. 813 Squadron. Even then, more time seems to have been spent ashore than at sea although operations were conducted from HMS *Albion* and HMS *Eagle* during the first year of service.

The principal production model was the **Wyvern S.Mk 4**, 94 being built in the early to mid-1950s, and these were augmented by a number of **Wyvern TF.Mk 2** aircraft modified to Wyvern S.Mk 4 standard. In addition, a solitary **Wyvern T.Mk 3** trainer was also completed although no production orders were forthcoming from the Fleet Air Arm which, one suspects, rather regretted proceeding with the Wyvern in the first place.

By the spring of 1958 the Wyvern had all but disappeared from the scene, but not before gaining its brief moment of glory in the Suez crisis of 1956 when No. 830 Squadron flew many strikes against targets in Egypt, losing two aircraft to ground fire in the process.

A formation of Westland Wyvern S.Mk 4 strike fighters. The Wyvern was the Fleet Air Arm's first turboprop type to see service. The first Wyvern unit formed at RNAS Ford in May 1953 and embarked on HMS Albion in April 1954.

Powerplant: one 4,110-eshp (3065-ekW) Armstrong Siddeley Python ASP3 turboprop
Performance: maximum speed 616 km/h (383 mph) at sea level; service ceiling 8535 m (28,000 ft); range 1455 km (904 miles) with auxiliary fuel
Weights: empty 7080 kg (15,608 lb); maximum take-off 11113 kg (24,500 lb)
Dimensions: span 13.41 m (44 ft 0 in); length 12.88 m (42 ft 3 in); height 4.80 m (15 ft 9 in); wing area 32.98 m² (355 sq ft)
Armament: four 20-mm cannon, plus up to 1361 kg (3,000 lb) of external ordnance including bombs and rockets

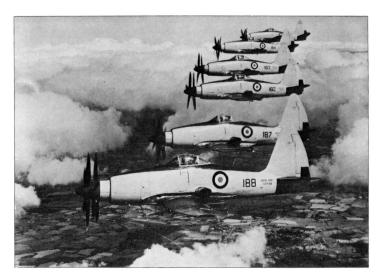

Below: A Westland Wyvern S.Mk 4 landing on HMS Eagle. During 1956 No. 830 Sqn, aboard HMS Eagle, *became the only Wyvern unit to see operational service when it was involved at Suez.*

Specification
Westland Wyvern S.Mk 4
Type: carrierborne strike fighter

Douglas AD Skyraider

USA

No survey of carrier aircraft of the 1950s would be complete without some reference to the **Douglas AD Skyraider**, a type which was conceived during World War II. Arriving on the scene too late to participate in that conflict, the Skyraider underwent its combat baptism of fire over Korea and was still very much a part of the US Navy's front-line inventory more than 10 years later when the Vietnam War began, surpassing earlier achievements by being responsible for the destruction of two MiGs in air-to-air combat.

Originally conceived in 1944 as a replacement for the tried and tested Douglas SBD Dauntless dive-bomber, the Skyraider entered service with Attack Squadron VA-1B in 1947, this marking the start of a career spanning some 23 years during which it demonstrated an as-yet unparalleled versatility. Equally adept at airborne early warning, electronic countermeasures, bombing, close air support, target towing, troop carrying and even VIP transport, no less than 3,180 Skyraiders were completed between 1945 and February 1957, when the assembly line finally closed. These aircraft saw service with the US Air Force, the US Navy and the US Marine Corps as well as overseas air arms including those of France, South Vietnam and the UK.

Flown for the first time in prototype form as the **XBT2D-1** on 18 March 1945, the type was ordered into production

just one month later but soon suffered from VJ-Day cutbacks which at one time seemed likely to threaten the future of the whole project. Fortunately, it survived early vicissitudes and by the end of the Korean War had, in the words of Rear Admiral John Hoskins, commanding Task Force 77, become 'the best and most effective close support aircraft in the World'.

Space does not permit close examination of individual variants (there were at least 28) but in addition to single-seat attack aircraft such as the **AD-1**, **AD-6** and **AD-7**, there was also the multi-place **AD-5** which was perhaps the most interesting Skyraider of all in that it could by means of packaged

conversion kits be reconfigured for different missions within just a matter of hours. Flown for the first time in August 1951, variants of the AD-5 subsequently performed AEW (**AD-5W**), ECM (**AD-5Q**), day attack (**AD-5**) and night attack (**AD-5N**) missions amongst other tasks, making it easily the most versatile model of this remarkable warplane. In 1962 the type was redesignated **A-1**.

Specification
Douglas AD-7 Skyraider
Type: carrierborne attack aircraft
Powerplant: one 3,050-hp (2274-kW) Wright R-3350-26WB radial piston engine

Performance: maximum speed 552 km/h (343 mph) at 6095 m (20,000 ft); service ceiling 7740 m (25,400 ft); range 2092 km (1,300 miles)
Weights: empty 5486 kg (12,094 lb); maximum take-off 11340 kg (25,000 lb)
Dimensions: span 15.25 m (50 ft 0.25 in); length 11.84 m (38 ft 10 in); height 4.78 m (15 ft 8.25 in); wing area 37.2 m² (400.33 sq ft)
Armament: four 20-mm cannon, plus up to 3629 kg (8,000 lb) of external ordnance on 15 hardpoints

The Douglas AD was the main US Navy attack aircraft during the 1950s and 1960s. This example is an AD-7 (A-1J).

BuAer No. 134589 was a straightforward AD-6 which was redesignated A-1H in 1962. It served until 1965 with VA-145 from USS Constellation *off the coast of Vietnam.*

Douglas F3D Skyknight

Although produced in only fairly limited numbers, the **Douglas F3D Skyknight** enjoyed a lengthy career by the standards of the day, remaining in front-line service with the US Marine Corps as an electronic countermeasures platform until 1969. During the course of its 18-year career the Skyknight also undertook combat duty in both the Korean and Vietnamese conflicts, and it is probably not widely known that the Skyknight secured a permanent niche in aviation history when, on the night of 2 November 1952, it succeeded in downing a North Korean Yakovlev Yak-15, this marking the first recorded kill in a jet-versus-jet combat at night. Even more remarkable is the fact that the F3D ended the Korean War as the most successful naval fighter type in terms of aircraft destroyed in air combat. Today, despite its age, two examples of the Skyknight still provide valuable service to the US armed forces, these being used by the US Army in support of air defence missile testing at White Sands, New Mexico.

Unique in being the US Navy's first jet-powered night-fighter, the Skyknight began development in 1945, Douglas being awarded a contract for three XF3D-1 prototypes in April 1946, and the first of these made its maiden flight from Muroc (now Edwards AFB) on 23 March 1948, this event being followed in June by an order for 28 production F3D-1 (later redesignated F-10A) fighters. Service acceptance trials were conducted by VC-3 at Moffett Field from December 1950, the type then being handed over to Marine Night Fighter Squadron VMF(N)-542. In the event, the F3D-1 did not see action, being quickly supplanted by the upengined **F3D-2 (F-10B)**, 237 of which were completed in the early 1950s. It was this model which made the Skyknight's combat debut with VMF(N)-513 in June 1952.

In US Navy service, the F3D enjoyed

only a brief front-line career, being quickly relegated to radar intercept training duties as the **F3D-2T** and **F3D-2T2 (TF-10B)**, the last example being retired in the early 1960s. US Marine Corps composite squadrons continued to use the **F3D-2Q (EF-10B)** type in ECM duties, however, and the type again saw action in Vietnam with VMCJ-1 until 1969 when it was finally replaced by the Grumman EA-6A Intruder.

A proposed swept-wing version known as the **F3D-3** was cancelled in 1952, but other service variants were the missile-armed **F3D-1M** and **F3D-2M (MF-10B)**.

Specification
Douglas F3D-2 Skyknight
Type: carrierborne night and all-weather fighter
Powerplant: two 1542-kg (3,400-lb) thrust Westinghouse J34-WE-36 turbojets
Performance: maximum speed 909 km/h (565 mph) at 6095 m (20,000 ft); service ceiling 11645 m (38,200 ft); range 2478 km (1,540 miles)
Weights: empty 8237 kg (18,160 lb);

The most successful naval type in air-to-air combat over Korea, the Douglas F3D Skyknight was flown by both Marines and Navy. This example is a Marines F3D-2. These continued in service until 1969 in the electronic counter-measures role.

maximum take-off 12556 kg (27,681 lb)
Dimensions: span 15.24 m (50 ft 0 in); length 13.84 m (45 ft 5 in); height 4.90 m (16 ft 1 in); wing area 37.16 m² (400 sq ft)
Armament: four 20-mm cannon, plus provision for two 907-kg (2,000-lb) bombs

---

Grumman AF-2 Guardian

In 1944 Grumman set out to produce a successor to the war-winning TBF Avenger torpedo bomber, and the first result was the **XTBF-1**, first flown on 19 December 1945. Looking like a slimmer and neater TBF, this machine had a Westinghouse J30 (later an Allis-Chalmers J36, otherwise de Havilland Goblin) turbojet in the tail for high-speed boost propulsion. This was later omitted, and at last the first **Grumman AF-2 Guardian** flew in November 1949. It was put into production in two versions, which operated from US Navy carriers in the ASW (anti-submarine warfare) role in pairs, known as hunter/killers. The hunter was the **AF-2W**, distinguished by its big 'guppy' APS-20A search radar, the displays and controls for which were in a two-seat rear compartment as in radar-equipped Skyraiders. The killer was the **AF-2S**, which took over when its companion had obtained a sure 'contact'. First it used its smaller APS-30 radar under the right outer wing to pinpoint its target, using a searchlight in an identical pod under the left wing to illuminate it if necessary. Then it would attack using any of its assortment of weapons. The Guardians were among the largest single-engine military

ary aircraft, heavier than a Douglas DC-3 and with a roomy side-by-side cockpit, the AF-2S having a third rear-compartment seat for the single radar operator. Grumman delivered 193 of the AF-2S attack version and 153 of its companion AF-2W model in 1950-3. The company then followed with 40 **AF-3S** machines, which were the first aircraft in service with MAD (magnetic-anomaly detection) gear in a retractable tail-boom mounting.

Specification
Grumman AF-2S Guardian
Type: three-seat carrier-based ASW and attack aircraft
Powerplant: one 2,400-hp (1790-kW) Pratt & Whitney R-2800-48W 18-cylinder radial piston engine
Performance: maximum speed 510 km/h (317 mph) at medium/high altitude; service ceiling 9910 m (32,500 ft); range 2415 km (1,500 miles)
Weights: empty 6632 kg (14,620 lb); maximum take-off 11567 kg (25,500 lb)
Dimensions: span 18.49 m (60 ft 8 in); length 13.21 m (43 ft 4 in); height 4.93 m (16 ft 2 in); wing area 52 m² (560.0 sq ft)
Armament: internal bay for 1814 kg (4,000 lb) o torpedoes, bombs, depth charges, mines or other stores, with

additional wing racks for similar weapons

The Grumman Guardian was designed to carry out its anti-submarine role in pairs, with a 'hunter-killer' arrangement. The nearest aircraft, an AF-2W, carries powerful search radar whilst the further aircraft, an AF-2S, carries the stores to dispatch any submarines.

Grumman F7F Tigercat

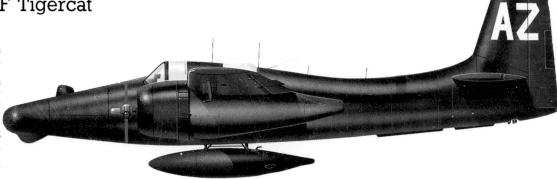

Aesthetically perhaps the most pleasing of Grumman's World War II designs, the **Grumman F7F Tigercat** was intended primarily for service aboard the 45,000-ton 'Midway' class aircraft-carriers, although in the event it was mainly employed by the US Marine Corps as a land-based fighter, largely as a result of its weight and size. Unique in being the first fighter with tricycle landing gear to be accepted for US Navy service, the Tigercat suffered badly from post VJ-Day cancellations, production terminating with the delivery of the 364th example.

Based on experience gained with the earlier and unsuccessful XF5F Skyrocket design, the initial contract awarded to Grumman in June 1941 covered the construction of two **XF7F-1** prototypes, both of which flew from Bethpage, Long Island, during November 1943. Subsequent testing revealed considerable promise and the type was ordered into production as the **F7F-1**, deliveries to the US Marine Corps getting under way during April 1944 when VMF-911 became the first squadron to receive the Tigercat.

By this time it had been decided to use the type mainly as a night-fighter, and this policy decision quickly led to the appearance of the **F7F-2N**, a fuel tank being removed to provide room for a radar operator. In addition, the four nose-mounted machine-guns were also deleted in favour of radar but the F7F-2N was still heavily armed, possessing four 20-mm cannon buried in the wing leading edges. A total of 45 F7F-2Ns was built.

The next version to appear was the **F7F-3**, and this was without a doubt the best-performing Tigercat. Some 189 were built, a few being fitted with cameras for reconnaissance as the **F7F-3P**, whilst 60 two-seat **F6F-3N** night-fighters were also completed before production came to a close in November 1946 with 13 **F7F-4N** aircraft featuring an enlarged vertical tail, improved radar and other refinements.

Although too late for World War II, the Tigercat did see action in Korea, VMF(N)-542's F7F-3Ns entering combat in October 1950 and performing well by both day and night in the interdiction task.

Used in small numbers during the Korean campaign, the Grumman F7F-3N night fighter proved to be an extremely effective aircraft. This aircraft served with a Marines Headquarters flight.

Specification
Grumman F7F-3 Tigercat
Type: carrierborne fighter
Powerplant: two 2,100-hp (1566-kW) Pratt & Whitney R-2800-34W radial piston engines
Performance: maximum speed 700 km/h (435 mph) at 6705 m (22,000 ft); service ceiling 12405 m (40,700 ft); range 1931 km (1,200 miles)
Weights: empty 7380 kg (16,270 lb); maximum take-off 11667 kg (25,720 lb)
Dimensions: span 15.70 m (51 ft 6 in); length 13.83 m (45 ft 4.5 in); height 5.05 m (16 ft 7 in); wing area 42.27 m² (455 sq ft)
Armament: four 12.7-mm (0.5-in) machine-guns and four 20-mm cannon

Grumman's Tigercat only ever saw action with the Marine Corps, despite being designed as a carrier fighter. Several aircraft were handed over to the Navy and converted into drone directors with an extra cockpit for the drone pilot. Drones were mostly F6F Hellcats.

Grumman F8F Bearcat

Conceived as a replacement for the earlier Grumman F6F Hellcat, the **Grumman F8F Bearcat** was also intended to surpass the Japanese Mitsubishi A6M 'Zeke' (itself no mean performer), and later fighters. But although deliveries began before VJ-Day the Bearcat played no part in World War 2, most of the 8,000 or so examples on order being cancelled following the return of peace. Despite being overtaken by events, the Bearcat did see service with the US Navy in substantial numbers, a total of 1,263 eventually being completed for this service, and many of these were later passed on to the air arms of France, Thailand and South Vietnam.

Optimized for interception tasks, which dictated a lightweight airframe possessing a good rate of climb, the Bearcat was probably Grumman's finest propeller-driven fighter, and had the war continued there is little doubt that it would have given a good

This Grumman F8F-1 was flown by Armée de l'Air squadron GC II/21 from Tan Son Nhut during the Indo-China campaign, where its firepower proved useful to the French, although it was hampered by limited range.

account of itself. Standard production machines were capable of speeds well in excess of 644 km/h (400 mph), whilst the specially modified aircraft flown by stunt pilot Al Williams actually achieved a speed of 805 km/h (500 mph) at 5790 m (19,000 ft). Even more startling, however, was the rate of climb, one F8F-1 reaching 3050 m (10,000 ft) in just 94 seconds from brakes-off during November 1946 and setting a national record in the process.

Initial production involved the **F8F-1** variant, 770 of which were built, and these were followed by 126 **F8F-1B** fighters which had four 20-mm cannon in place of the more usual quartet of 12.7-mm (0.5-in) machine-guns. Refinement of the basic design resulted in the **F8F-2** which had taller vertical tail surfaces and a revised engine cowling, some 365 being completed in the early post-war years before the jet era arrived and revolutionized carrierborne aviation.

In addition to these new-build aircraft, close to 50 Bearcats were later retrofitted with APS-19 radar for nightfighter tasks as the **F8F-1N** and **F8F-2N**, whilst 60 more acquired cameras and became **F8F-2P** photographic reconnaissance aircraft, these having only two cannon installed.

Specification
Grumman F8F-1 Bearcat
Type: carrierborne interceptor fighter
Powerplant: one 2,100-hp (1566-kW) Pratt & Whitney R-2800-34W radial piston engine
Performance: maximum speed 678 km/h (421 mph) at 6005 m

(19,700 ft); service ceiling 11795 m (38,700 ft); range 1778 km (1,105 miles)
Weights: empty 3207 kg (7,070 lb); maximum take-off 5873 kg (12,946 lb)
Dimensions: span 10.92 m (35 ft 10 in);

length 8.61 m (28 ft 3 in); height 4.22 m (13 ft 10 in); wing area 22.67 m² (244 sq ft)
Armament: four 12.7-mm (0.5-in) machine-guns

Grumman F8F-1 Bearcats began replacing the F6F Hellcat as the US Navy's main fighter. Here aircraft from VF-15A and VF-16A prepare for launch from USS Tarawa.

Grumman F9F Panther

The first jet-powered 'cat' to be produced by the company, the **Grumman F9F Panther** seems to have lacked the charisma of the earlier F8F Bearcat but nevertheless acquired a welldeserved reputation as a rugged and reliable machine. Historically significant by virtue of the fact that it was the first carrier borne jet to get into combat, the Panther performed well in Korea where it constituted the backbone of US Navy and US Marine Corps air power, and by the time production ceased in late 1952 close to 1,400 had been built.

The initial F9F proposal was for a four-engine two-seat night-fighter, but this was subsequently abandoned before design work was complete, Grumman then turning its attentions to a single-seat single engine jet day fighter, two prototypes duly being ordered with the designation **XF9F-2**. Powered by an imported Rolls-Royce Nene engine, the first of these made its maiden flight on 24 November 1947 and such was the promise shown that substantial orders were soon forthcoming for production-configured **F9F-2** aircraft fitted with the licencebuilt Pratt & Whitney J42 copy of the Nene turbojet.

Although the F9F-2 was the initial production model, the honour of being the first variant to enter service fell to the **F9F-3**, which used the slightly less powerful Allison J33 engine. This joined US Navy Fighter Squadron VF-51 during May 1949 but in the event

VF-781 flew the Grumman F9F-2 Panther in the Korean campaign. The aircraft was the mainstay of the fighter squadrons throughout the war alongside the F2H Banshee and F3D Skyknight.

only 54 F9F-3s were completed, most being modified later to F9F-2 standard. The next version to appear was the **F9F-4** with the Allison J33-A-16, deliveries of this variant beginning in November 1949, about a month before the maiden flight of what became the most prolific and, incidentally, the last member of the Panther family. This was the **F9F-5** which was powered by the Pratt & Whitney J48, a licence-built Rolls-Royce Tay, and over 600 were completed by the time production ceased at the end of 1952, this total including a small number of **F9F-5P** aircraft for photo reconnaissance duties.

The F9F-5 was the last version to see squadron service, being finally retired by VAH-7 in October 1958, although many Panthers continued to fly after that date with training units, and as **F9F-5KD** (from 1962 **DF-9E**) drone targets and controllers for missile trials.

Specification
Grumman F9F-5 Panther
Type: carrierborne day fighter
Powerplant: one 3175-kg (7,000-lb) thrust Pratt & Whitney J48-P-6 turbojet
Performance: maximum speed 932 km/h (579 mph) at 1525 m (5,000 ft); service ceiling 13380 m (43,900 ft); range 2092 km (1,300 miles)
Weights: empty 4603 kg (10,147 lb); maximum take-off 8492 kg (18,721 lb)
Dimensions: span 11.58 m (38 ft 0 in);

length 11.58 m (38 ft 0 in); height 3.73 m (12 ft 3 in); wing area 23.23 m² (250 sq ft)
Armament: four 20-mm cannon, plus up to 1361 kg (3,000 lb) of external ordnance

Seen over Korea, this F9F-2 Panther of VF-721 is typical of the Panthers serving in that war. Internal fuel tankage was almost double that of the similarly powered Sea Hawk.

Grumman F9F Cougar

First flown in prototype form as the **XF9F-6** on 20 September 1951, the **Grumman F9F Cougar** evolved from the earlier F9F Panther series of fighter aircraft. It differed mainly from its predecessors by virtue of possessing swept wings and tailplane, thus earning the distinction of being the first swept-wing carrierborne type to enter service. Apart from this, changes were kept to a minimum to facilitate rapid production. Indeed, the new Cougar entered service just 14 months after its maiden flight took place, initial examples of the Pratt & Whitney J48-engined **F9F-6** (later designated **F-9F**) joining VF-32 of the Atlantic Fleet naval air force during November 1951. Shortly after this deliveries to Pacific Fleet units got under way, and the type was very soon introduced to combat in Korea.

Production of the F9F-6 totalled 706 aircraft, 60 of which were completed as **F9F-6P** machines for reconnaissance duties, and these were followed by the **F9F-7 (F-9H)** which was powered by an Allison J33 turbojet. This proved to be only a temporary change, and after completing 168 F9F-7s Grumman reverted to the Pratt & Whitney J48 engine for the **F9F-8 (F-9J)**, which became the definitive Cougar, well over 1,000 being completed in three basic variants. First to appear was the F9F-8 (601 built) which possessed increased fuel capacity and also introduced a modified 'saw-tooth' leading edge to the wing; and large numbers were later modified to **F9F-8B (AF-9J)** standard with provision for air-to-surface guided missiles. Some 110 specimens of a photo-reconnaissance version designated **F9F-8P (RF-9J)** appeared, whilst the Cougar also lent itself to the training of future naval aviators; a prototype two-seat **YF9F-8T** was followed by no less than 400 **F9F-8T (TF-9J)** production examples, some of which remained in use with Naval Air Training Command until well into the 1970s.

As far as front-line units were concerned, the Cougar disappeared from the scene early in 1960, the last operational version being the F9F-8P, but many continued to fly long after that date with the Reserve Force and with Air Training Command. Surplus aircraft became **F9F-6K (QF-9F)** and **F9F-6K2 (QF-9G)** target drones or **F9F-6D (DF-9F)** drone directors.

Specification
Grumman F9F-8 Cougar
Type: carrierborne fighter and attack aircraft
Powerplant: one 3289-kg (7,250-lb) thrust Pratt & Whitney J48-P-8A turbojet
Performance: maximum speed 1033 km/h (642 mph) at sea level; service ceiling 12800 m (42,000 ft); range 1931 km (1,200 miles)
Weights: empty 5382 kg (11,866 lb); maximum take-off 11232 kg (24,763 lb)
Dimensions: span 10.52 m (34 ft 6 in); length 12.85 m (42 ft 2 in); height 3.72 m (12 ft 2.5 in); wing area 31.31 m² (337 sq ft)
Armament: four 20-mm cannon, plus up to 1814 kg (4,000 lb) of external ordnance including bombs, rockets and napalm tanks

Grumman's F9F-8 Cougar was distinguished from other marks by the large nose blister and redesigned wing. This example served with VF-61.

The earlier Cougars, in this case an F9F-6, featured slimmer wings, evident in this photograph. This aircraft is seen on the lift of USS Hornet whilst the carrier was part of the 7th Fleet sailing in the Far East.

Illustrating the broad stubby wings of the F9F-8, this Cougar carries four of the new Sidewinder air-to-air missiles and two fuel tanks on its underwing pylons. The F9F-8 was also built in a reconnaissance version (F9F-8P).

North American FJ Fury

A navalized variant of the remarkably successful North American F-86 Sabre, the swept-wing **North American FJ-2 Fury** brought the clock full circle, for the Sabre itself evolved from the original straight-wing **FJ-1 Fury**, this being the first US jet fighter to operate from an aircraft-carrier in squadron strength, an event which took place in early 1948 with VF-51 as the unit concerned.

The FJ-1's operational career was very short (it very quickly giving way to the rather more advanced Grumman Panther), and it was not until 1951 that the name Fury reappeared, when the US Navy requested North American to convert a pair of F-86Es for carrier trials. The first of these, designated **XFJ-2**, took to the air for its maiden flight on 19 February 1952, and with the successful conclusion of initial carrier qualification trials aboard the USS *Midway* in that summer, this type was ordered into quantity production.

Deliveries to fleet units got under way in January 1954 when Marine Fighter Squadron VMF-122 at Cherry Point began to convert from the F9F-5 Panther, but only 200 General Electric J47-powered FJ-2s had been completed by the spring of 1954 when production switched to the J65-powered **FJ-3**, which eventually became the most widely used version, no less than 538 rolling from the assembly line. By

A North American FJ-3M Fury of Navy Squadron Fighting 142 displaying the type's obvious descent from the F-86 Sabre. The FJ-3M was Sidewinder-capable, and earlier machines were upgraded to this standard.

far the majority (458 in all) were completed as FJ-3s, but the advent of efficient missiles resulted in the final 80 appearing as **FJ-3M** fighters with provision for two heat-seeking AIM-9A Sidewinders; a substantial number of early production FJ-3s was later upgraded to this configuration.

The penultimate variant, the **FJ-4**, was in many ways virtually a new aircraft, featuring a much deeper fuselage and revised wing planform, and this was first flown in prototype form during October 1954, 150 production machines being followed by 222 ex-

amples of the more capable **FJ-4B**. This was optimized for close support tasks and incorporated a strengthened airframe, additional underwing hardpoints and a low-altitude bombing system. Introduced to service in 1957, the FJ-4B was finally retired from the frontline inventory in late 1962 although it continued to fly with second-line squadrons and Reserve units for several more years, the post-1962 designations being **F-1C** (FJ-3), **MF-1C** (FJ-3M), **F-1E** (FJ-4) and **AF-1E** (FJ-4B). Lesser-used variants were the **FJ-3D** and **FJ-3D2** (**DF-1C** and **DF-1D**) drone-

director conversions.

Specification
North American FJ-4B Fury
Type: carrierborne fighter-bomber
Powerplant: one 3493-kg (7,700-lb) thrust Wright J65-W-16A turbojet
Performance: maximum speed 1094 km/h (680 mph) at sea level; service ceiling 14265 m (46,800 ft); range 4458 km (2,770 miles) with maximum external fuel
Weights: empty 6250 kg (13,778 lb); maximum take-off 12701 kg (28,000 lb)
Dimensions: span 11.91 m (39 ft 1 in);

A FJ-3 Fury from a test squadron completes a trap with the aid of arrester gear and the aircraft's divebrakes mounted on the rear fuselage. The Fury lasted on into the 1960s in a variety of roles, including that of drone-director.

length 11.07 m (36 ft 4 in); height 4.24 m (13 ft 11 in); wing area 31.46 m² (338.66 sq ft)
Armament: four 20-mm cannon, plus up to 2722 kg (6,000 lb) of external ordnance including bombs, rockets and air-to-surface missiles

USA
North American AJ Savage

The first heavy attack type to see service from aircraft-carriers of the US Navy, the **North American AJ Savage** used a novel method of propulsion, two Pratt & Whitney radial engines being augmented by a tail-mounted Allison J33 turbojet. In practice the type saw only limited use in the strategic bombing role for which it had been designed, being replaced from the mid-1950s onwards by the Douglas A3D Skywarrior, but several were subsequently modified to serve as inflight-refuelling tankers with a hose-and-reel unit in place of the turbojet.

Development began soon after World War II came to an end. An initial contract for three prototype **XAJ-1** aircraft was awarded to North American in late June 1946, and construction of these got under way almost immediately although more than two years were to elapse before the Savage took to the air for the first time on 3 July 1948. In its original guise the Savage was manned by a crew of three and was intended to carry a 4536-kg (10,000-lb) weapon load in an internal bomb bay in the aircraft's belly.

Production-configured aircraft began to enter service with Composite Squadron VC-5 in mid-September 1949, but it was not until the end of August 1950 that this unit was consi-

dered operationally ready, this marking the climax of several months of seaborne trials aboard the USS *Coral Sea*. The first variant to see service with the US Navy was the **AJ-1**, of which 40 were built, and these were followed by 70 examples of the **AJ-2** which featured slightly more powerful radial engines as well as increased fuel capacity, a slightly longer fuselage and a taller fin and rudder to improve handling qualities. The final new-build version was the **AJ-2P**, which was intended for photographic reconnaissance and thus incorporated nose radar and a battery of no less than 18 cameras for use by day and night. A total of 30 AJ-2Ps was

built, this being the last model to see squadron service, not being retired from the active inventory until the beginning of 1960. In 1962 surviving AJ-1 and AJ-2 aircraft were redesignated **A-2A** and **A-2B** respectively.

Specification
North American AJ-2 Savage
Type: carrierborne nuclear strike aircraft
Powerplant: two 2,500-hp (1864-kW) Pratt & Whitney R-2800-48 radial piston engines and one 4,600-lb (2087-kg) thrust Allison J33-A-10 turbojet
Performance: maximum speed 628 km/h (390 mph); service ceiling

Of mixed propulsion, the North American AJ Savage was designed for the delivery of nuclear weapons from a carrier. Although replaced quickly in this role by the Skywarrior, Savages continued in the role of tanker.

12190 m (40,000 ft); range 3540 km (2,200 miles)
Weights: empty 12247 lb (27,000 lb); maximum take-off 23396 kg (51,580 lb)
Dimensions: span 21.77 m (71 ft 5 in); length 19.23 m (63 ft 1 in); height 6.22 m (20 ft 5 in); wing area 77.62 m² (835.5 sq ft)
Armament: up to 4536 kg (10,000 lb) of bombs carried internally

McDonnell FH-1 Phantom

First production aircraft designed by the company, the **McDonnell FH-1 Phantom** was notable in being also the first jet designed to operate from an aircraft-carrier. The US Navy placed the original letter of intent on 30 August 1943, and the first prototype made its initial flight from St Louis airport, Lambert Field, on 26 January 1945. The type was certainly not over-powered, because the final propulsion system, adopted after many studies of alternatives, was two slim Westinghouse 19B engines buried in the wing roots. Later produced in small numbers as the J30, these were hardly enough for adequate performance. The first flight is thus all the more remarkable in that, at that time, Westinghouse had been able to deliver only one engine, and one of the wing-root engine bays was empty! At that time McDonnell's US Navy designator letter was D, the prototype being the **XFD-1**, but because of confusion with Douglas (which also used letter D) McDonnell was assigned letter H, so that the 60 production Phantoms were designated FH-1. They were gentle and easy to fly, and on 21 July 1946 a prototype landed on and took off from USS *Franklin D. Roosevelt* (a British de Havilland Sea Vampire had made carrier trials the previous year). The production aircraft were delivered from December 1946

served mainly with US Marine fighter squadron VMF-122. Their fault was lack of performance and lack of firepower, and the next-generation F2H Banshee was a vast improvement on both counts.

Specification
McDonnell FH-1 Phantom
Type: single-seat carrier-based fighter

Powerplant: two 726-kg (1,600-lb) thrust Westinghouse J30-20 turbojets
Performance: maximum speed 771 km/h (479 mph) at sea level and 813 km/h (505 mph) at high altitude; service ceiling 13000 m (43,000 ft); range 1110 km (690 miles) without belly drop tank
Weights: empty 3031 kg (6,683 lb); maximum take-off 5459 kg (12,035 lb)
Dimensions: span 12.42 m (40 ft 9 in);

Possessing only marginal performance, the McDonnell FH (FD) Phantom was quickly replaced by more sophisticated jets. However, it was the US Navy's first jet fighter.

length 11.81 m (38 ft 9 in); height 4.32 m (14 ft 2 in); wing area 25.64 m^2 (276 sq ft)
Armament: four 12.7 mm (0.5-in) machine-guns in upper part of nose

---

McDonnell F2H Banshee

Another early jet-powered type to see service with the US Navy, the **McDonnell F2H Banshee** began life even before the end of World War II when the US Navy requested an improved version of the FH-1 Phantom. Bearing a strong resemblance to the earlier type, the Banshee was rather larger and more powerful, flying in prototype form for the first time as the **XF2D-1** from St Louis, Missouri, on 11 January 1947. Initial trials were successfully accomplished, McDonnell being rewarded in May 1947 by a contract for 56 production **F2H-1** fighters, which began to enter service with VF-171 of the Atlantic Fleet during March 1949.

Like the later Phantom II, the Banshee proved to be a most versatile machine, satisfactorily undertaking day and night fighter tasks, all-weather interception, close air support and photographic reconnaissance with seemingly equal facility in the course of the next 10 years. Following on from the original F2H-1 came the **F2H-2**, which had slightly more powerful engines and a longer fuselage. Production of the basic F2H-2 totalled 364, some of which were later modified to **F2H-2B** standard for close support tasks whilst 14 examples of the **F2H-2N** specialized night-fighter derivative were also completed, these incorporating airborne interception radar. For reconnaissance, 58 **F2H-2P** aircraft were completed as new, these being unarmed and featuring a battery of cameras in an elongated nose section.

Production then switched to the **F2H-3** (in 1962 redesignated **F-2C**), which was optimized for all-weather fighter duties, the first of 250 entering service during April 1952 and being easily recognizable by virtue of a fuselage- rather than fin-mounted tailplane, but plans to acquire the **F2H-3P** for reconnaissance were abandoned. The

final production model was the **F2H-4 (F-2D)**, which introduced improved APG-41 radar and more powerful engines, the 150th and last bringing production of the trusty 'Banjo' to a close in August 1953.

Apart from serving with the US Navy and US Marine Corps, 39 F2H-3s were supplied to Canada in 1955, these operating from HMCS *Bonaventure* until September 1962, when the last examples were retired from service.

Specification
McDonnell F2H-3 Banshee
Type: carrierborne all-weather interceptor
Powerplant: two 1633-kg (3,600-lb) thrust Westinghouse J34-WE-36 turbojets
Performance: maximum speed 933 km/h (580 mph) at sea level; service ceiling 14205 m (46,600 ft); range 1883 km (1,170 miles)
Weights: empty 5980 kg (13,183 lb); maximum take-off 11437 kg (25,214 lb)
Dimensions: span 12.73 m (41 ft 9 in); length 14.68 m (48 ft 2 in); height 4.42 m (14 ft 6 in); wing area 27.31 m^2 (294 sq ft)
Armament: four 20-mm cannon, plus (Canadian aircraft only) two AIM-9 Sidewinder air-to-air missiles

Above: Flying for the first time as the F2D, the McDonnell Banshee was soon redesignated F2H and was first delivered to a squadron in March 1949. This example is an F2H-2 which featured more powerful engines and longer fuselage than the first model.

Below: An F2H-3 Banshee about to make a text-book trap. The aircraft saw much service in Korea, where both the Navy and the Marine Corps used the aircraft for air combat and ground attack. In its F2H-2P version, the Banshee was one of the most important reconnaissance aircraft of the war.

Carrierborne Aircraft

No war machine embodies greater power than the modern carrier aircraft. Concentrated into a tight airframe are powerful engines, sophisticated avionics, the very best weapon systems and highly professional aircrews, combining to produce an awesome military asset.

There can be few sights more impressive than that of a giant aircraft carrier at full speed with up to 80 aircraft ranged on its acres of deck in closely spaced lines, wings and rotors folded. It is the epitome of power at sea, and a daunting challenge to the air forces of nations which border the world's oceans. The significance of the aircraft carrier, both as an escort for shipping and as an instrument of attack, was illustrated in World War II, and the lesson has been driven home since in operations off the coasts of Korea, Vietnam and the Falkland Islands.

That two-thirds of the modern carrierborne aircraft described here are of American origin is not a result of bias. It is simply a confirmation of the fact that the US Navy possesses by far the most powerful seagoing air arm – in fact the US Navy has in its own right the world's third-largest air force. It is based on a dozen or so major vessels and a similar number of smaller 'flat-tops' including those of the US Marine Corps. Although its specifications for new aircraft invariably demand multiple capabilities, the US Navy can boast a separate type for almost every role demanded of embarked aviation.

France and the UK, whilst

The BAe Sea Harrier F/A2 is a modified and updated version of the FRS1 fighter, reconnaissance and strike aircraft. It can operate with AMRAAM, the Advanced Medium Range Air-to-Air Missile.

eclipsed as naval powers, continue development of carrier-based fixed-wing aircraft, but in contrast with US counterparts, both the Dassault Super Etendard and the BAe Sea Harrier are tasked with both air defence and strike missions for reasons of economy and available stowage. Specialized early-warning, ECM and modern patrol aircraft are absent from the decks of these navies, and as the UK found in 1982, this omission can impinge on the effectiveness of surface combatants and their aircraft.

Russia (former the Soviet Union) is represented by just a single, rudimentary VTOL carrier-based aircraft, indicating a belated recognition of the potentialities of a sea-going air force. The form of the aircraft that follow the Yakovlev Yak-38 remained a matter of conjecture in the West until the 1990s when the Russians revealed a penchant for 'navalized' land-based aircraft. Despite the origins of the aircraft, thinking is abundantly clear: naval power, meaning naval air power, is the key to control of large portions of the globe.

Breguet Alizé

Principal anti-submarine patrol aircraft of the French and Indian navies for more than two decades, the **Breguet Br.1150 Alizé** evolved from a late-1940s design for a carrier-based attack aircraft, the **Br.960 Vultur**, in which a turboprop engine was augmented by a jet to give sprint performance during critical phases of its mission. The Vultur failed to proceed beyond the prototype stage, but l'Aéronavale ordered the similar, though much slower, Alizé for ASW duties. With a larger fuselage, accommodating three crew, and a smaller wing, the prototype flew in 1956.

Carrying a search radar in a ventral 'dustbin' which retracts into the rear fuselage when not in use, the Alizé may be armed with depth charges, rockets or air-to-surface missiles. Sonobuoy stowage is in the large wing fairings which also house the main landing gear units. Series production amounted to 87 aircraft, of which 12 were ordered by the Indian Navy for service aboard the carrier *Vikrant* and at shore bases, these seeing heavy utilization during the 1971 war with Pakistan.

To some extent, the Alizé's duties

with l'Aéronavale have been assumed by the Aérospatiale Super Frelon helicopter, but two operational squadrons continue to fly the type, and deployments are regularly undertaken aboard the carriers *Foch* and *Clemenceau*. From 1980 28 aircraft were upgraded to Alizé NG standard for service into the 1990s, then the early 2000s after the 1990 addition of a datalink. Among the new systems were a Thomson-CSF Iguane radar, SERCEL-Crouzet VLF Omega inertial navigation system, electronic support measures (ESM) equipment, new communications systems and other improved avionics. Under original plans the Alizé would now be extinct in Europe, but now both its operators plan to keep the aircraft in service until their present carriers are withdrawn.

Specification
Dassault-Breguet Br.1050 Alizé
Type: three-seat carrier-based anti-submarine aircraft
Powerplant: one 1,975-shp (1,473-kW) Rolls-Royce Dart RDa.7 Mk 21 turboprop
Performance: maximum speed 518 km/h (322 mph) at 3050 m

(10,000 ft); patrol speed 240-370 km/h (149-230 mph); service ceiling 8000 m (26,245 ft); normal range 2500 km (1,553 miles); maximum endurance 7 hours 40 minutes
Weights: empty equipped 5700 kg (12,566 lb); maximum take-off 8200 kg (18,078 lb)
Dimensions: span 15.60 m (51 ft 2 in); length 13.86 m (45 ft 6 in); height 5.00 m (16 ft 4¾ in); wing area 36.00 m² (387.51 sq ft)
Armament: underfuselage weapons bay accommodating one torpedo or

The Breguet Alizé has been in operation with the French navy (Aéronavale) for many years. It has a retractable ventral radome for its role of anti-submarine warfare.

three 160-kg (353-lb) depth charges; racks under inner wings for two 160-kg (353-lb) or 175-kg (386-lb) depth charges; racks beneath outer wings for six 12.7-cm (5-in) rockets or two Nord AS.12 air-to-surface missiles; and sonobuoys in underwing weapon/wheel nacelles

---

Dassault-Breguet Super Etendard

Super Etendards gained fame during the Falklands campaign due to their use against British shipping; Argentinian Super Etendards sank HMS Sheffield *with Exocet sea-skimming missiles.*

Principal front-line aircraft of the French navy's air arm (Aéronavale), the **Dassault-Breguet Super Etendard** serves with three squadrons and is regularly deployed aboard the carriers *Foch* and *Clemenceau*. The original **Etendard** shipboard strike-fighter evolved from a mid-1950s NATO requirement for a land-based aircraft, but when its replacement received consideration, an improved version was ordered in place of the originally-proposed navalized Jaguar.

The exacting French specification called for the standard aircraft to incorporate the strike and reconnaissance roles previously undertaken by two Etendard variants (**Etendard IVM** and **Etendard IVP** respectively), and combine this with a new air-defence capability. Accordingly, the Super Etendard was produced with Agave radar for attack as well as intercept duties, an inertial navigation system (SKN 2602) with head-up display and

provision for a wide range of underwing stores, including Matra R 550 Magic infra-red AAMs and hose-equipped tanks for 'buddy' refuelling. Aerodynamic improvements concerned a revised wing with drooped leading edges and double-slotted flaps, whilst a new (8K50) version of the well-tried Atar engine gives additional thrust; no afterburner is fitted.

Having entered service in 1978, the Super Etendard was supplied to Argentina from 1981 onwards, the first

five of 14 on order seeing operational use from land bases in the Falklands war, destroying two British ships with their potent AM.39 Exocet missiles. The single Argentine squadron achieved carrier qualification aboard the *Veinticinco de Mayo* early in 1983. At the same time, production was completed of 71 Super Etendards for l'Aéronavale, but in response to an Iraqi request, five of these (together with 20 Exocets) were lent to the air force for operations in the Gulf against Ira-

nian targets, particularly offshore oil installations. Delivery took place in October 1983.

Specification
Dassault-Breguet Super Etendard
Type: single-seat carrier-based attack aircraft
Powerplant: one 5000-kg (11,025-lb) thrust SNECMA Atar 8K50 turbojet
Performance: maximum speed at low altitude, clean 1200 km/h (748 mph); initial climb rate 6000 m (19,685 ft) per minute; service ceiling 13700 m (44,950 ft); radius on a hi-lo-hi mission with one AM39 and one tank 650 km (403 miles)
Weights: empty 6450 kg (14,220 lb); maximum take-off (allows maximum weapons or maximum fuel, but not both) 11500 kg (25,350 lb)
Dimensions: span 9.6 m (31 ft 6 in); length 14.31 m (46 ft 11½ in); height 3.86 m (12 ft 8 in); wing area 28.4 m² (305.7 sq ft)
Armament: two 30-mm DEFA cannon each with 125 rounds; fuselge pylons for two 551-lb (250-kg) bombs, four wing hardpoints for 882-lb (400-kg) bombs, rocket pods or Magic AAMs; alternatively one AM39 Exocet ASM under the right wing and one 242-Imp gal (1100-litre) tank under the left wing

The third Super Etendard seen during carrier trials; the double slotted flaps are depressed for maximum lift. They are deployed aboard the carriers Foch *and* Clemenceau.

BAe AV-8A/C

A Harrier which regularly goes to sea but is not a Sea Harrier, the **BAe AV-8A** is the US Marines' version of the Harrier GR.Mk 1, in service with three operational squadrons and a training unit. As such it is principally a ground-attack aircraft, lacking the laser nose retrospectively fitted to British variants but ideally suited to the US Marines' requirements for a high-performance close-support aircraft which can operate at sea from comparatively small assault carriers and then redeploy to the beach-head to work beside the disembarked troops. On one occasion, AV-8As have formed part of a Navy Carrier Air Wing aboard the USS *Franklin D. Roosevelt*, whilst the type has occasionally been deployed from its base at Cherry Point to a forward station at Iwakuni, Japan.

Although American personnel flew a military evaluation version of the original P.1127, known as the Kestrel, USMC interest in the Harrier's unique capabilities did not develop into a production order until some years later. The first of an eventual 102 AV-8As and eight two-seat **TAV-8A** trainers was delivered in 1971, but because several small batches were ordered, plans for US manufacture could not be implemented, and all AV-8As were built in the UK. Power was provided by the Pegasus 11 engine, although the first 10 had Pegasus 10s when delivered. Six AV-8As and two TAV-8As were ordered through US channels by Spain for use aboard the carrier *Dédalo*, followed by a further five direct from

With the Spanish navy designation VA.1, BAe Harriers fly from the carrier Dédalo. *These are similar to the US Marines' AV-8A and are known as Matadors.*

Below: US Marines AV-8A as flown by VMA-231. These can be flown from assault carriers for support of ground forces.

BAe. These have the local designations **VA.1** for the single-seaters and **VAE.1** for the trainers.

AV-8As surviving in USMC service were upgraded to **AV-8C** standard by addition of new avionics and systems as well as some features of the AV-8B, including the retractable dam near the gun ports and larger gunpod strakes to boost take-off lift by forming a cushion of trapped exhaust gases. The only operator of this first-generation carrier borne Harrier in 1999 was the Thai navy, with nine ex-Spanish aircraft.

Specification
BAe AV-8C
Type: single-seat ship- or land-based light attack fighter
Powerplant: one 9752-kg (21,500-lb) thrust Rolls-Royce Pegasus Mk 103 vectoring-thrust turbofan
Performance: maximum speed over 1186 km/h (737 mph) or Mach 0.97 at low altitude; climb to 12190 m (40,000 ft) in 2 minutes 22 seconds; service ceiling more than 15240 m (50,000 ft); combat radius with 1361-lb (3,000-lb) external stores load 95 km

(59 miles) after VTO or 705 km (438 miles) after a 365-m (1,200-ft) run
Weights: empty 5529 kg (12,190 lb); maximum take-off 7734 kg (17,050 lb) for VTO or 10115 kg (22,300 lb) for STO
Dimensions: span 7.70 m (25 ft 3 in); length 13.87 m (45 ft 6 in); height 3.45 m (11 ft 4 in); wing area 18.68 m^2 (201.1 sq ft)
Armament: two 30-mm cannon, plus up to 2404 kg (5,300 lb) of disposable ordnance on five hardpoints, plus two AIM-9 Sidewinder air-to-air missiles

---

BAe Sea Harrier

During the Falklands war, Sea Harriers were painted in low visibility grey.

Derived from the RAF Harrier, which preceded it in squadron service by a full 10 years, the **BAe Sea Harrier** was ordered into production in 1975 by the Royal Navy for service aboard the three 'Invincible' class ASW carriers, or 'through-deck' cruisers. Prime requirement was for a multi-role aircraft, and thus the Sea Harrier added a nose radome for Ferranti Blue Fox air-intercept radar and two (later increased to four) AIM-9L Sidewinder AAMs on wing pylons to give fleet-defence capability. Retaining, in addition, the Harrier's ground-attack and tactical reconnaissance roles, the navalized variant is equipped to carry Sea Eagle anti-ship missiles when these enter service in the mid-1980s.

Sea Harriers became operational in April 1980 and performed with distinction during the Falklands war of April-June 1982, when they destroyed 20 Argentine aircraft without loss. Only two Sea Harriers were shot down by ground fire in over 1,100 combat air patrol missions and 90 offensive support operations, undertaken by a force of 28 aircraft during hostilities, Sea Harriers returning a remarkable 95 per cent serviceability and flying 99 per cent of all sorties planned. For take-off at maximum weight, the aircraft uses a short run terminating in a ramp, or 'ski jump' but employs vertical thrust for landing, even when poor weather prohibits flying by other fixed-wing carrier aircraft. Royal Navy **Sea Harrier FRS.Mk 1** orders currently total 48, whilst a further six **Sea Harrier FRS.Mk 51** fighters and two **Sea Harrier T.Mk 60** trainers were delivered to the Indian Navy for operation from the carrier

Vikrant.

The Sea Harrier's considerable capabilities were expanded in the late 1980s by the conversion of 31 FRS.Mk 1s and manufacture of 18 new aircraft to Sea Harrier F/A.Mk 2 standard with Blue Vixen pulse-Doppler radar and AIM-120 AMRAAM missiles for a look-down/shoot-down capability, relocation of the Sidewinder AAMs to the wingtips, and addition of LERXes (Leading-Edge Root eXtensions) for enhanced agility.

Specification
BAe Sea Harrier FRS.Mk 1
Type: single-seat V/STOL ship-based multi-role combat aircraft
Powerplant: one 9752-kg (21,500-lb) thrust Rolls-Royce Pegasus Mk 104 vectored-thrust turbofan
Performance: maximum speed 'over 1185 km/h (736 mph)' at sea level; dive limit Mach 1.25; climb to 12190 m (40,000 ft) in 2 minutes 20 seconds;

'Black Death' became the Sea Harrier's name amongst Argentinian pilots who tried to attack the British task force. This example is from No. 899 Sqn, Royal Navy.

service ceiling more than 15240 m (50,000 ft); radius without inflight-refuelling (high-altitude interception) 750 km (460 miles), or (low-level strike) 463 km (288 miles)
Weights: empty 5670 kg (12,500 lb); maximum take-off more than 11794 kg (26,000 lb)

Dimensions: span 7.70 m (25 ft 3 in); length 14.50 m (47 ft 7 in); height 3.71 m (12 ft 2 in); wing area 18.68 m^2 (201.1 sq ft)
Armament: two 30-mm Aden cannon each with 125 rounds (optional); underwing loads can include all weapons of Harrier plus AIM-9L or (India) Magic AAMs and Sea Eagle, Harpoon or other anti-ship missiles

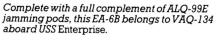

Grumman A-6 Intruder

USA

A-6E of the Marines' all-weather attack squadron VMA(AW)-121, known as the 'Green Knights'.

Carrier Air Wing CVW-7 aboard USS Independence flies this A-6E of VA-65 'Tigers'.

Visually one of the less inspiring aircraft of the US Navy and US Marine Corps, the **Grumman A-6 Intruder** is nevertheless a versatile and effective all-weather attack aircraft bearing a most appropriate name. Designed in the mid-1950s primarly for nuclear attack, it was transformed in the trials stage and entered service in 1963 carrying a broad spectrum of conventional weaponry (both free-fall bombs and air-to-surface missiles), which has expanded still further with the advent of more advanced equipment.

Employed on combat missions over Vietnam, the Intruder was the sole embarked strike aircraft of its day to possess full all-weather capability and the potential for a single-pass attack, despite early unserviceability problems with its avionics. The initial models were fitted with APQ-92 search radar and APQ-88 track radar linked, with other equipment, to a Litton computer and providing the two-man crew with a picture of the scene ahead with tactical information superimposed. Basic production was of the **A-6A** variant, a few of which were modified to **A-6B** aircraft with AGM-78 Standard anti-radar missiles for defence suppression; the **A-6C** carrying a TRIM (Trails, Roads Interdiction Multi-sensor) pack for detection of small targets by forward-looking infra-red (FLIR) and low-level-level TV; **EA-6A** aircraft for electronic jamming; and **KA-6D** inflight-refuelling tankers. The last-mentioned has an internal hose

drum unit, but retains the normal Intruder tankage and a limited (daylight) attack capability.

The current version of the Intruder, known as the **A-6E**, features an extensive avionics refit, some of the principal changes being an APQ-148 multimode radar (in place of the two earlier units) and an ASQ-133 solid-state computer. In an undernose turret is TRAM (Target Recognition Attack Multi-sensor) including FLIR and a laser ranger, which permits study of land surfaces and acquisition of targets marked by the aircraft's or other lasers, leading to pinpoint delivery of

ordnance, whether ballistic or 'smart'. Most surviving A-6A/B/Cs have been converted to A-6Es augmenting new production of this variant, and TRAM was retrofitted to earlier A-6E aircraft. The last Intruders were retired in 1998.

Specification
Grumman A-6E Intruder
Type: two-seat carrier- or shore-based all-weather attack aircraft
Powerplant: two 4218-kg (9,300-lb) thrust Pratt & Whitney J52-P-8B turbojets
Performance: maximum speed 1036 km/h (644 mph) at sea level;

cruising speed 763 km/h (474 mph); service ceiling 12925 m (42,400 ft); range with maximum military load 1627 km (1,011 miles)
Weights: empty 12093 kg (26,660 lb); maximum take-off, catapult 26581 kg (58,600 lb); field 27397 kg (60,400 lb)
Dimensions: span 16.15 m (53 ft 0 in); length 16.69 m (54 ft 9 in); height 4.93 m (16 ft 2 in); wing area 49.13 m² (528.9 sq ft)
Armament: one underfuselage and four underwing attachment points for maximum external load of 8165 kg (18,000 lb), including a wide variety of nuclear or conventional weapons, air-launched missiles and fuel drop tanks

---

Grumman EA-6B Prowler

USA

Complete with a full complement of ALQ-99E jamming pods, this EA-6B belongs to VAQ-134 aboard USS Enterprise.

Obviously derived from the Intruder, as evidenced by retention of the basic A-6 designation, the **Grumman EA-6B Prowler** qualified for a new name by reason of its highly specialized role: electronic warfare (EW). Having identified the need for such an aircraft in the early 1960s, the US Navy and US Marine Corps took the interim step of converting a dozen A-6As to **EA-6A Intruder** standard before the prototype Prowler, with much increased capability, made its first flight in 1968.

Intended to precede or accompany naval aircraft making forays into hostile airspace and to provide them with protection against radars associated with enemy SAMs, interceptors and surveillance units, the Prowler is equipped with the powerful Cutler-Hammer ALQ-99 active jamming system. Recognition features include the fin-tip pod (containing the ALQ-99's receiver aerials) and the additional glazing for two EW operators positioned in Martin-Baker GRU-7 ejection seats immediately behind the flight crew. The active jammers are carried in up to five external pods, which may be replaced by fuel tanks when the aircraft is engaged on passive intelligence-gathering.

Sole shipboard EW aircraft of the United States, the Prowler remains in production against a requirement for 132 aircraft to be operated by 12 four-aircraft squadrons for a similar number of Naval air wings, plus 18 for the US Marines. Intended to remain in service well into the 21st century, the Prowler has already been subject to three modification programmes to extend its jamming repertoire and improve receivers, displays and software, the

most recent being known as ADVCAP (ADVanced CAPability). The Prowler can provide active jamming in Bands 1-2 and 4-9, covering the full range of Soviet radars, including those used in conjunction with some surface-to-surface missiles.

Specification
Grumman EA-6B Prowler
Type: four-seat carrier- or land-based advanced ECM aircraft
Powerplant: two 5080-kg (11,200-lb) thrust Pratt & Whitney J52-P-408 turbojets
Performance: (with five external pods) maximum speed 1003 km/h (623 mph); cruising speed at optimum altitude 774 km/h (481 mph); service ceiling 11580 m (38,000 ft); ferry range 3254 km (2,022 miles)
Weights: empty 14588 kg (32,162 lb); stand-off jamming configuration take-off 24703 kg (54,461 lb); ferry range configuration take-off 27492 kg (60,610 lb); maximum take-off 29484 kg (65,000 lb)
Dimensions: span 16.15 m (53 ft 0 in); length 18.11 m (59 ft 5 in). height 4.93 m (16 ft 2 in); wing area 49.13 m² (528.9 sq ft)

This EA-6B amply shows the modifications to the basic A-6 airframe. The lengthened nose houses an extra cockpit for the ECM operators and the tail radome contains the receiver aerials.

Grumman E-2 Hawkeye

First line of defence from air attack for the US Navy, the **Grumman E-2 Hawkeye** is a carrier-operated airborne early warning system which has been in service since 1964 and now flies with 13 seagoing squadrons. Patrolling at 9145 m (30,000 ft) in all weathers with a crew of five (including three systems operators), the Hawkeye's principal sensor is the APA-171 antenna which is housed in a distinctive rotodome. In conjunction with the APS-125 ARPS (Advanced Radar Processing System) and an ALR-59 passive detection system, the discus-shaped scanner, turning six times each minute, can locate aircraft up to 480 km (300 miles) distant, its main concern being those attempting to infiltrate beneath the coverage of ships' radars.

Highly automated systems aboard the Hawkeye enable the aircraft to track more than 250 targets and simultaneously to control in excess of 30 interceptions by friendly fighters. It can identify an object the size of a cruise missile 185 km (115 miles) distant, but is also capable of monitoring shipping and movements of vehicles on land.

Production of the **E-2A** version totalled 56, all survivors of which became **E-2B** aircraft with addition of enhanced computing facilities, whilst the present **E-2C**, which has more reliable and easily maintained radar (originally the APS-125 was replaced by the more capable and flexible APS-138, APS-139 and APS-145 equipments), is to be manufactured until the US Navy

The US Navy's principal AEW platform is the Grumman E-2 Hawkeye. This is an E-2C of VAW-126, forming part of CVW-9 aboard USS Constellation.

has received a total of 146 examples in a programme also notable for the incorporation and retrofit of steadily improved electronic features (computing power and enhanced ESM systems).

The French navy also fly the Hawkeye (two aircraft with options on another two), but 31 land-based E-2C aircraft have been ordered by Egypt (6), Israel (4), Japan (13), Singapore (4) and Taiwan (4) for the control of attack missions as well as the co-ordination of defence operations.

Specification
Grumman E-2C Hawkeye
Type: five-seat airborne early warning and control aircraft
Powerplant: two 4,910-eshp (3661-kW) Allison T56-A-425 turboprops
Performance: maximum speed 602 km/h (374 mph); long-range cruising speed 499 km/h (310 mph); service ceiling 9390 m (30,800 ft); endurance with maximum fuel 6 hours

6 minutes
Weights: empty 17211 kg (37,945 lb); maximum take-off 23503 kg (51,817 lb)
Dimensions: span 24.56 m (80 ft 7 in); length 17.54 m (57 ft 6¾ in); height 5.58 m (18 ft 3 in); wing area 65.03 m² (700.0 sq ft)

Evident in this photograph of an E-2C is the radome, housing the APA-171 radar. The unusual four-fin tail enables the height to be kept down to that of the hangar interiors.

Grumman F-14 Tomcat

VF-32 on USS John F. Kennedy was one of the first units to receive the F-14A Tomcat.

Undoubtedly the most potent interceptor to operate from an aircraft-carrier, and an equal to the best of its land-based compatriots, the **Grumman F-14 Tomcat** has the further distinction of being the only variable-geometry (VG) aircraft in naval service. Produced to an exacting specification as a substitute for the ill-fated General Dynamics/Grumman F-111B fleet-defence fighter, the Tomcat numbers among its aerodynamic refinements a unique foreplane which extends from the fixed portion of the wing leading edge to regulate changes in centre of pressure and thus obviate pitching as the wings are moved from the fully-extended 20° of sweepback to the maximum 68°.

Ordered in quantity for the US Navy which hoped to acquire 845, the Tomcat has a remarkable differential in armament range, beginning with the M61A1 rotary cannon and progressing via the infra-red AIM-9 Sidewinder and radar-guided AIM-7 Sparrow AAMs to the 200-km (125-mile) range AIM-54A Phoenix. In conjunction with the powerful Hughes AWG-9 radar, the Phoenix has the longest 'reach' of any AAM, although the Tomcat may

also operate in the attack role with a useful 6577 kg (14,500 lb) of ordnance. The **F-14A** entered service in 1972 and recently acquired a further capability through the TARPS (Tactical Air Reconnaissance Pod System), which is carried beneath the fuselage.

The aircraft's first air-to-air combat took place in August 1981 when two Libyan Sukhoi Su-22 'Fitter-Js' were shot-down by Sidewinders after they had attacked a pair of Tomcats over the Mediterranean, but it appears that the 80 aircraft supplied to Iran have seen little service in the Gulf war with Iraq. Only a few of the Iranian Tomcats are serviceable, and their AIM-54s are inoperative.

The survivors of the 478 F-14A fighters built for the US Navy are now complemented by smaller numbers of two more advanced models,

namely 56 converted to F-14B standard with General Electric F110-GE-400 turbofans and upgraded electronics, and 37 new-build F-14D fighters with F110 engines and digital avionics.

Specification
Grumman F-14A Tomcat
Type: two-seat carrier-based air-superiority fighter
Powerplant: two 9480-kg (20,900-lb) afterburning thrust Pratt & Whitney TF30-P-412 turbofans
Performance: maximum speed at height 2517 km/h (1,564 mph) or Mach 2.34; maximum speed at sea level 1470 km/h (910 mph) or Mach 1.2; initial climb rate over 9145 m (30,000 ft) per minute; service ceiling over 17070 m (56,000 ft); range (interceptor, with external fuel) about 2,000 miles (3200 km)

Weights: empty 8036 kg (39,762 lb); normal take-off 26553 kg (58,539 lb); take-off with four Sparrow AAMs 26718 kg (58,904 lb); take-off with six Phoenix AAMs 31656 kg (69,790 lb); maximum take-off 33724 kg (74,348 lb)
Dimensions: span, unswept 19.45 m (64 ft 1½ in) and swept 11.65 m (38 ft 2½ in); length 19.10 m (62 ft 8 in); height 4.88 m (16 ft 0 in); wing area 52.49 m² (565.0 sq ft)
Armament: one M61A1 Vulcan 20-mm multi-barrel cannon in forward fuselage with 675 rounds, four AIM-7 Sparrow or AIM-54 Phoenix air-to-air missiles under fuselage, two AIM-9 Sidewinder air-to-air missiles (or one Sidewinder plus one Phoenix or Sparrow) under each wing glove box, tactical reconnaissance pod containing cameras and electro-optical sensors, or up to 6577 kg (14,500 lb) of bombs, missiles or other weapons.

A Tomcat about to 'trap' aboard its 'homeplate'. The striped arrester hook is ready to engage no. 1 wire and the wings are set in the minimum sweep position of 20° at the leading edge. The wide-track undercarriage makes carrier landings easier.

Grumman C-2 Greyhound

COD (carrier on-board delivery) is the prime function of the **Grumman C-2A Greyhound**, and only the US Navy possesses a specially-built aircraft for this role. Typical COD missions between distant carriers (or more likely from shore to ship) involve transfer of personnel and urgently-needed equipment and supplies, ensuring maximum operability of embarked combat forces. With the Greyhound, the cargo can be up to 28 passengers; 12 stretchers and attendants; or 4536 kg (10,000 lb) of freight, increasing to 6804 kg (15,000 lb) for land operation. As such, the aircraft represents a faster, more efficient method of transport than the commando-type helicopter which most navies have to use for this work.

Obviously a close relation to the Hawkeye, the Greyhound entered service in 1966, differing from their early-warning compatriots in having a bigger fuselage with rear-loading doors and, of course, no rotodome. Production totalled 19 aircraft based on the E-2A, of which most remain in use with land-based squadrons at locations as far apart as Japan and Italy. The C-2A has all-weather capability and provision for catapult take-offs and arrested landings.

Considerable expansion of the COD force, involving replacement of the veteran Grumman C-1 Trader, began with the delivery in 1985 of the first of 39 Greyhounds from relaunched production. Though still known by the C-2A designation, the new aircraft parallel the E-2C through the installation of uprated engines and more modern avionics, plus improved protection against corrosion. Passenger comfort was also improved, while an APU (Auxiliary Power Unit) gives a measure of autonomy when operating into poorly-equipped airfields.

Specification
Grumman C-2A Greyhound
Type: two-crew on-board delivery aircraft

The lifeline of the fleet are the 'CODfish'. This duty is performed almost exclusively by the Greyhound, being able to carry substantial loads from the deck of a carrier.

The C-2 Greyhound has operated in the COD (carrier onboard delivery) role since 1966. Originally developed from the E-2 Hawkeye, the C-2 features a much deeper fuselage for cargo.

Powerplant: two 4,912-ehp (3663-kW) Allison T56-A-425 turboprops
Performance: maximum speed at optimum altitude 636 km/h (395 mph); cruising speed 482 km/h (299 mph); service ceiling 10210 m (33,500 ft); ferry range 2889 km (1,795 miles)

Weights: empty 14131 kg (31,154 lb); maximum take-off 24654 kg (54,354 lb)
Dimensions: span 24.56 m (80 ft 7 in); length 17.27 m (56 ft 8 in); height 5.16 m (16 ft 11 in); wing area 65.03 m² (700.0 sq ft)

Lockheed S-3 Viking

An airborne exercise in squeezing a quart into a pint pot (as emphasized by its dumpy appearance) the **Lockheed S-3A Viking** undertakes from aircraft-carriers the tasks performed by much larger land-based aircraft such as the Lockheed P-3 Orion and BAe Nimrod MR.Mk 2. Tightly packed with sophisticated electronics and their associated sensors, the Viking is the sole fixed-wing ASW (anti-submarine warfare) patroller of the US Navy's embarked air fleet, and though some allied navies have cast covetous glances in its direction, none has been able to afford its high cost.

Though bearing a Lockheed nametag, the Viking was produced in close collaboration with LTV which, in view of its greater experience with carrier-based aircraft, undertook design and construction of several major components. At the heart of the Viking is a Sperry-Univac digital computer for high-speed processing of information from radar, forward-looking infra-red (FLIR), the retractable MAD (magnetic anomaly detector) tailboom and ESM. With four crew, including two operators in the fuselage, Vikings carry a wide range of offensive armament, both internally and externally. The 166 production aircraft delivered from 1974 onwards equip 11 front-line squadrons, plus a training unit.

An updating and modification procedure known as WSIP (Weapon System Improvement Program) saw 121 of these converted to S-3B standard from 1987 onwards, with better acoustic processing, expanded ESM coverage, increased radar processing capability, new sonobuoy receiver system and provision for Harpoon anti-ship missiles. A further 16 S-3A aircraft were adapted as ES-3A Shadow machines for the Elint and electronic warfare roles, but have now been withdrawn, and only demonstration numbers of the US-3A carrier transport (six) and KS-3A inflight-refuelling tanker (one) models were completed.

Specification
Lockheed S-3A Viking
Type: four-seat carrier-based patrol/attack aircraft
Powerplant: two 4207-kg (9,275-lb) thrust General Electric TF34-GE-2 turbofans
Performance: maximum cruising speed 686 km/h (426 mph); loiter speed 296 km/h (184 mph); service ceiling more than 10670 m (35,000 ft); combat range more than 3701 km (2,300 miles)
Weights: empty 12088 kg (26,650 lb); normal ASW mission take-off 19278 kg (42,500 lb)
Dimensions: span 20.93 m (68 ft 8 in); length 16.26 m (53 ft 4 in); height 6.93 m (22 ft 9 in); wing area 55.55 m² (598.0 sq ft)
Armament: weapons including bombs, depth-bombs, mines or torpedoes up to 907 kg (2,000 lb) in internal weapons bay, plus cluster-bombs, flare-launchers or auxiliary fuel tanks on underwing pylons

Seen on the lift of USS Enterprise, *this S-3A belongs to anti-submarine squadron VS-29, one of the early recipients of the Viking.*

With its home base at Oceana, Virginia, this S-3A is seen as deployed on board the nuclear carrier USS Nimitz with VS-24, air wing CVW-8. These aircraft are currently undergoing a refit of weapon systems, including provision for Harpoon missiles, after which they will be designated S-3B.

McDonnell Douglas/BAe AV-8B Harrier II

For all its remarkable attributes, the original BAe Harrier was no more than a re-engineered version of a technology demonstrator which was to have led to a far more advanced combat aircraft. However, when the British government failed to fund an improved design, McDonnell Douglas and BAe decided to proceed with an improved Harrier, the US firm having acquired development rights for the aircraft as part of the agreement under which AV-8As were bought by the US Marine Corps. Well pleased with their aircraft, the US Marines supported work on an upgraded aircraft, and the resultant **McDonnell Douglas/BAe Y AV-8B** prototype made its first flight at St Louis in 1978.

Featuring a completely new supercritical-section wing (produced to a large extent of carbonfibre) with slotted trailing-edge flaps, an uprated Pegasus 11-21E engine of 9979-kg (23,000-lb) thrust, and a raised cockpit for improved vision, what is now termed the **AV-8B Harrier II** can carry twice the weapon load of the Harrier GR.Mk 3. Totally new gun and ammunition pods are installed, and the wing pylons have been increased in number from four to six to accommo-

date a large armoury of bombs and rockets plus Sidewinder AAMs.

In 1983, 286 Harrier II aircraft (including TAV-8B two-seat trainers) for the USMC entered service with the F402-RR-406 engine, replaced from the 197th machine by the F402-RR-408 engine. From the 167th machine they were Night Attack AV-8B standard, with a FLIR, moving map display and head-down display, the last 27 are to the AV-8B Harrier II Plus standard (supplemented by 73 conversions) with nose-mounted radar. BAe completed 96 Harrier GR.Mk 5, for the RAF later converted to the Harrier GR.Mk 7 night attack standard, and the RAF's counterpart to the TAV-8B is the Harrier T.Mk 10. The Harrier II has also been exported to Italy and Spain, which received 18 and 30 aircraft

Chosen for the US Marine Corps, the McDonnell Douglas AV-8B is a natural development from the AV-8A Harrier.

respectively.

Specification
AV-8B Harrier II
Type: single-seat close-support ship- or land-based attack aircraft
Powerplant: one 9979-kg (22,000-lb) thrust Rolls-Royce F402-RR-406 (Pegasus 11-21E) vectored-thrust turbofan
Performance: maximum speed, clean at low altitude 1113 km/h (690 mph); initial climb rate 4485 m (14,715 ft) per minute; service ceiling more than 15240 m (50,000 ft); combat radius on a hi-lo-hi mission with seven bombs plus tanks and after a 300-m (1,000-ft) run 1204 km (748 miles)

Weights: empty 5783 kg (12,750 lb); maximum take-off 13494 kg (29,750 lb)
Dimensions: span 9.25 m (30 ft 4 in); length 14.12 m (46 ft 4 in); height 3.56 m (11 ft 8 in); wing area 21.37 m² (230.0 sq ft)
Armament: two cannon pods (USMC, one 25-mm GAU-12/U in one pod with ammunition in the other; RAF, not yet decided) plus seven pylons for total weapon load of 7711 kg (17,000 lb)

This pre-production AV-8B shows the new supercritical wing, LERXs (leading edge root extensions) and reshaped nose that distinguish it from the earlier Harrier.

McDonnell Douglas F/A-18 Hornet

One of the development aircraft assigned to the fleet trials squadron VFA-125, carrying two dummy Sidewinder AAMs.

Designed as successor to the McDonnell F-4 Phantom II multi-role fighter and Vought A-7 Corsair II attack warplane, the **McDonnell Douglas F/A-18 Hornet** was delivered from 1980 for carrier borne service with the US Navy and US Marine Corps, which ordered 1,366. Development problems, included a shortfall in payload/range performance and higher costs, but the type has matured to an exceptional warplane in fighter and attack tasks.

The Hornet traces its origins to the **Northrop YF-17**, which was beaten by the General Dynamics YF-16 in the US Air Force's Light Weight Fighter competition. Northrop then teamed

with McDonnell Douglas (now part of Boeing) to offer further development of the **YF-17** to the US Navy. The airframe makes extensive use of graphite/epoxy composites, and the Hornet is optimised for high agility, with LERXes (Leading-Edge Root eXtensions),leading edge flaps and drooping ailerons as well as a 'fly-by-

wire' control system. The avionics include a head-up display and an inertial navigation system, and with additional sensors, such as a FLIR and advanced nav/attack packages, as well as the majority of current and projected weapons of both the 'dumb' and 'smart' types.

Production of 770 of the F/A-18A single- and F/A-18B two-seat variants, the latter a combat-capable type with only a modest reduction in fuel capacity to allow enlargement of the cockpit, included Australia 75, Canada 138 and Spain 72. From 1986 more than 585 examples of the F/A-18C and

F/A-18D models with advanced weapons and upgraded nav/attack avionics, have followed. This includes 64, 40 and 34 aircraft for Finland, Kuwait and Switzerland respectively.

The USN and USMC are acquiring more than 500 examples of the latest variants, which are the F/A-18E single- and F/A-18F two-seat variants of the somewhat revised Super Hornet with more capable electronics and its linear dimensions increased by 25% for the carriage of a heavier weapons load over a longer range with the aid of 33% more fuel and the uprated powerplant of two 9979-kg (22,000lb) afterburning thrust General Electric F414-GE-400 turbofans.

Specification
McDonnell Douglas F/A-18A Hornet
Type: single-seat carrier-based combat/strike aircraft
Powerplant: two 7257-kg (16,000-lb) afterburning thrust General Electric F404-GE-400 turbofans
Performance: maximum speed (clean) Mach 1.8; maximum speed at intermediate power Mach 1.0; combat ceiling about 15240 m (50,000 ft); combat radius (fighter mission, unrefuelled) more than 740 km (460 miles); ferry range (unrefuelled) more than 3700 km (2,300 miles)
Weights: take-off, fighter 15234 kg (33,585 lb); take-off, fighter escort 15875 kg (35,000 lb); maximum take-off 21319 kg (47,000 lb)
Dimensions: span 11.43 m (37 ft 6 in); length 17.07 m (56 ft 0 in); height 4.66 m (15 ft 3½ in); wing area 37.16 m² (400 sq ft)
Armament: carried on nine external weapon stations up to a maximum capacity of 7711 kg (17,000 lb) or 6214 kg (13,700 lb) for high-g missions; weapons can include Sidewinder, Sparrow or AIM-120 air-to-air missiles, bombs, air-to-surface missiles and rockets; sensor pods and fuel tanks can also be carried on these weapons stations; inbuilt armament comprises one M61 20-mm six-barrel cannon in the nose

One of the development aircraft assigned to the fleet trials squadron VFA-125 shows the low-visibility scheme carried by all Navy and Marines aircraft. The missiles are Sidewinders.

Vought A-7 Corsair II

Sluf (Short, Little Ugly Fellah) as it is affectionately known by its crews, the **Vought A-7 Corsair II** does, indeed, appear to be a stunted version of Vought's earlier creation, the Crusader supersonic naval interceptor. This was not accidental, for when the US Navy called for a Douglas Skyhawk replacement in 1963, it specified a variant of an existing design to ensure speedy and inexpensive development. The aim was achieved handsomely, and after a contract had been placed in March 1964, the prototype flew in September 1965 and production aircraft were bombing targets in Vietnam by December 1967, flying from the USS *Ranger*.

That the Corsair failed to replace the Skyhawk completely was more a result of the latter's remarkable versatility than any deficiency on the part of the former. Corsairs rapidly established for themselves a reputation for weapon carrying and technical reliability, the US Navy accepting 196 each of the **A-7A** and **A-7B** models, both powered by a non-afterburning version of the TF30 turbofan. A more profound change came after the USAF had ordered a land-based version known as the **A-7D**, this featuring completely revised avionics including a greatly improved nav/attack system, and considerably more thrust from the TF41, a US-built enlarged development of the Rolls-Royce Spey.

The naval version of the USAF model became the **A-7E** and proved to be the definitive carrierborne Corsair,

The Vought A-7 has been in service since 1967 aboard US carriers. This early A-7B of VA-113 'Stingers' is being loaded with Snakeye retarded bombs.

with production totalling 551 (plus 67 examples of the TF30-powered **A-7C**). Also blooded in Vietnam, the A-7E has even higher engine power than its US Air Force predecessor. It eventually served with 12 shipboard squadrons of the Atlantic Fleet and a similar number of units of the Pacific Fleet, together with training squadrons and those of the US Navy Reserve. Many aircraft were retrofitted with automatic manoeuvring flaps and an upgraded nav/attack system, but the Corsair II now serves only with Greece, Portugal and Thailand, which received 102, 56 and 18 aircraft respectively.

Specification
Vought A-7E Corsair II
Type: single-seat all-weather strike aircraft
Powerplant: one 6804-kg (15,000-lb)

One of several low-visibility schemes tested by the US Navy is seen on this A-7E. An all-over blue-grey was eventually adopted.

thrust Allison Rolls-Royce TF41-A-2 turbofan
Performance: maximum speed 1112 km/h (691 mph) at sea level; maximum speed clean 1102 km/h (685 mph) at 1525 m (5,000 ft); ferry range with maximum fuel 4604 km (2,861 miles)

Weights: empty 8669 kg (19,111 lb); maximum take-off 19051 kg (42,000 lb)
Dimensions: span 11.81 m (38 ft 9 in); length 14.06 m (46 ft 1½ in); height 4.90 m (16 ft 0¾ in); wing area 34.84 m² (375 sq ft)
Armament: a wide range of stores totalling more than 6804 kg (15,000 lb)

can be carried on two fuselage stations and six underwing pylons, and these can include air-to-air and air-to-surface missiles, TV and laser-guided weapons, general-purpose bombs, rockets and gun pods; inbuilt armament comprises one M61 Vulcan 20-mm six-barrel cannon.

Former USSR

Yakovlev Yak-36MP 'Forger'

Always regarded as an interim type, the Yak-36MP has the drawback of having to take off vertically, so limiting the useful load able to be carried.

Operated from the three ASW carriers *Kiev, Minsk* and *Novorossisk*, the **Yakovlev Yak-36MP 'Forger'** is the Soviet Union's equivalent of the BAe Sea Harrier, although only in the most general of terms. From the 1917 revolution until recent times, the Soviet navy remained a small force with purely local-defence responsibilities, but efforts are currently being made to develop a 'blue-water navy' which already rivals the United States' previously undisputed mastery of the seas. As evidenced by the Yak-36 'Forger-A' and its two seat trainer version the Yak-36U 'Forger-B' the USSR still had a long way to go in seagoing air power.

First seen in July 1976, when the class-name ship *Kiev* sailed into the Mediterranean, the aircraft appears to be intended more for operational development than for combat use, although its four underwing pylons in-

This picture of Yak-36MPs on the Russian carrier Kiev shows the intakes open for the two lift jets mounted in the front of the fuselage. These become deadweight when the aircraft attains level flight.

dicate some ground-attack potential, and visual air defence will be possible by mounting infra-red AAMs. Unlike the Sea Harrier, the Yak-36MP has no radar except a ranging unit, but most remarkable of all is its employment of two lift engines (dead weight for most of a mission). The almost vertical turbojets are mounted forward and enclosed by doors when not in use, whilst two rear nozzles of the horizontal (main) engine turn downwards for hovering. There is a small toe-in on all four jet pipes.

Restricted by its 1960s technology, the Yak-36MP is incapable of a Harrier-type short take-off to maximize weapon loads. When seen in operation, the aircraft take-off and land verti-

cally, the latter with a degree of precision which suggests some form of shipboard guidance. About 12 'Forgers' are based on each 'Kiev' class vessel, but larger carriers meant that conventional aircraft could be carried, and the Sukhoi Su-33 was developed from the land-based Su-27 'Flanker'.

Specification
Yakovlev Yak-36MP 'Forger-A'
Type: single-seat light VTOL shipboard strike fighter
Powerplant: one 7950-kg (17,526-lb) thrust vectoring turbojet in the rear fuselage, and two 3625-kg (7,992-lb) thrust Kolesov lift turbojets in the forward fuselage
Performance: maximum speed

1170 km/h (725 mph) or Mach 1.1 at high altitude; maximum speed 1125 km/h (700 mph) or Mach 0.8 at sea level; initial climb rate 4500 m (14,765 ft) per minute; service ceiling 12000 m (39,370 ft); combat radius 250 km (150 miles) on a lo-lo-lo mission with maximum stores
Weights: empty 7485 kg (16,500 lb); maximum take off 11565 kg (35,275 lb)
Dimensions: span 7.32 m (24 ft 0 in); length 15.25 m (50 ft 0 in); height 4.37 m (14 ft 4 in); wing area 16.0 m² (172.22 sq ft)
Armament: four underwing pylons for up to 1360 kg (3,000 lb) of stores, including AA-8 'Aphid' air-to-air missiles, air-to-surface missiles, gun pods, rocket pods and bombs

Carrier Aircraft of the 1960s

Carrierborne aircraft continued to develop throughout the 1960s, and the aircraft of the new generation were more capable than ever. Leading the way in the field were the Americans, who had the chance of putting their carrierborne air power to the test in the skies over Southeast Asia.

A Grumman S-2 Tracker ASW aircraft in flight. Operating from a carrier, the S-2 could both find and kill submarines; previously two aircraft had been required, one assigned to each task.

Well before the 1950s came to an end, the frantic pace of aircraft technical development during the decade had resulted in several major advances in shipboard aircraft. One was the emergence of the helicopter as a useful weapon and transport vehicle. Another was the mating of the supersonic jet with the carrier deck, a synthesis that was assisted by growth in the size of those decks, but which was later accomplished by the British and French using decks no larger than those of World War II. The gas turbine engine played a central role in many of the new developments, one obvious advantage being the elimination from the scene of high-octane petrol (gasoline). The gas turbine's power transformed the capabilities of shipboard attack aircraft, and two of the bombers discussed in this chapter could take off at a weight of more than 40 tons.

Another new development, which in fact was first achieved with piston engines, was the combination in one aircraft of the ability to search for submerged submarines and the ability then to attack them: previously these tasks had demanded a team of two aircraft, one the hunter and the other the killer.

It is well known that carrier aircraft have a harsher life than those based on land, and that their design has to be more complex. For example, they almost invariably have to fold up to fit in small hangars below decks. Less obvious is how tough the aircraft have to be. The pull of the modern catapult is nothing short of brutal: even if the aircraft had its engine off and the wheel brakes locked, the 'cat' would fling the aircraft off the deck at 241 km/h (150 mph). Each one-ton store hung under the aircraft slams back with the force of five tons, and even the fuel exerts a two-ton force on every square foot of tank rear wall! Landing is roughly like dropping from the roof of a two-storey building, often over a deck that is rolling or pitching. At the instant of impact the pilot slams the throttle wide open in case the arresting cables are missed. The hook then snatches a cable, and the colossal pull brings the screaming mass to a stop in just two seconds. Modern aircraft are designed to suffer this treatment – and remain serviceable – 6,000 times.

Douglas F-6 (F4D) Skyray

USA

Douglas F4Ds of Marine squadron VMF-531 formate for the camera showing the distinctive lines of this aircraft. Bestowed with astonishing vertical climb, the Skyray served with the Marines until 1964, in both interceptor and ground-attack roles.

Yet another of Ed Heinemann's designs for the US Navy, the prototype **Douglas XF4D-1 Skyray** flew on 23 January 1951. Inspired by the German Lippisch designs, it was almost a tailless delta, the wing actually being a curved swept wing of low aspect ratio with remarkable drooping slats and with elevons and outboard ailerons on the trailing edge. Another unusual feature was that the skin was composed of inner and outer layers of thin aluminium joined at a series of dimples on the inner skin to give stability. Yet another unusual choice was that the flight controls were fully powered, almost for the first time on a fighter, but in the event of failure the pilot could extend his telescopic control column to give increased leverage in the manual mode.

Designed to climb fast and steeply to intercept bombers attacking the fleet, the **F4D-1** (from its designation popularly called the 'Ford') was another US Navy type that began life with the Westinghouse J40 engine. This succeeded in setting a world speed record at 1211.5 km/h (752.8 mph) in 1953 but was actually a failure, and the J57 was fitted to the 420 production 'Fords' delivered in 1956-8. Thanks to its early inception the Skyray did not dispense with guns, and in service with US Navy and US Marine Corps squadrons it quickly established itself as a highly agile and popu-

lar aircraft. It was one of the first single-seaters to be equipped with a large all-weather interception radar fire-control system, the Westinghouse APQ-50/Aero 13. In two successive years the Skyray won the premier trophy awarded to the best of all fighter squadrons based in the USA, despite the fact it equipped the only non-USAF unit to compete.

In 1962 the Skyray was redesignated **F-6A**. By this time it was being replaced in first-line service by the F-4 and F-8, but a few survived with US Marine units in both intercept and ground attack missions until 1964.

Specification
Douglas F-6A Skyray
Type: single-seat carrier-based interceptor
Powerplant: one 6804-kg (15,000-lb) afterburning thrust Pratt & Whitney J57-8 turbojet
Performance: maximum speed 1162 km/h (722 mph) at sea level; range on internal fuel 1931 km (1,200 miles); service ceiling 16765 m (55,000 ft)
Weights: empty 7268 kg (16,024 lb); maximum take-off 12701 kg (28,000 lb)
Dimensions: span 10.21 m (33 ft 6 in); length 13.79 m (45 ft 3 in); height 3.96 m (13 ft 0 in); wing area 51.75 m^2 (557 sq ft)
Armament: four 20-mm Mk 12 cannon each with 70 rounds, plus seven external pylons for 1814 kg (4,000 lb) of bombs, rocket pods or four Sidewinder AAMs

The Skyray could carry bombs or unguided rockets (illustrated) in the ground attack role, as well as the four wing-mounted 20-mm cannon. For interception duties, AIM-9 Sidewinders were usually carried. This example is from VFAW-3.

Douglas A-3 (A3D) Skywarrior

USA

Representing a fantastic quantum jump in the capability of carrier-based attack aircraft, the prototype **Douglas XA3D-1 Skywarrior** flew in 1952, yet many of these great machines soldier on in the mid-1980s. Planned to fit the giant new 'Forrestal' class carrier, the A3D was almost a seagoing Boeing B-47, and it gave the US Navy nuclear retaliation capability all over the world. Ed Heinemann's design team at first said 'This is a Westinghouse airplane built by Douglas', because that supplier was responsible for the big podded engines, the defensive tail turret, the giant nose nav/bombing radar, the electrical system and many other items. But the engine was a failure and the A3D-1 entered service in 1956 with the reliable J57, thereafter being standard equipment in the US Navy VAH heavy attack wings.

A three-seater, the A3D (redesignated **A-3** in 1962) has swept folding wings and folding vertical tail, giant fuselage airbrakes and a capacious weapons bay. Variants included the **RA-3B** five-seat reconnaissance aircraft with an impressive fit of cameras (12) and other sensors, the **EA-3B** seven-seat EW (electronic warfare) and ECM (electronic countermeasures) models with great electronic reconnaissance capability, the **TA-3B** eight-seat crew trainer, and the **KA-3B** tanker. Disappearing in the early 1990s, the last service variant was the tanker, though some were **EKA-3B** air-

craft with various EW systems. Despite use of the Grumman KA-6D Intruder, the KA-3D was still found on US Navy carriers, as well as being the standard heavy tanker for use from shore bases. As it was designed to a 1949 requirement, the Skywarrior had an amazingly long innings, and in its five major versions proved an ideal aircraft for many of the US Navy's most challenging missions throughout the 1960s.

Specification
Douglas A-3B Skywarrior
Type: three-seat carrier-based bomber
Powerplant: two 5625-kg (12,400-lb) thrust (wet rating) Pratt & Whitney J57-10 turbojets
Performance: maximum speed 982 km/h (610 mph) at 3050 m (10,000 ft); range on internal standard fuel 4667 km (2,900 miles); service ceiling 12500 m (41,000 ft)
Weights: empty 17876 kg (39,409 lb); maximum take-off 37195 kg (82,000 lb)
Dimensions: span 22.10 m (72 ft 6 in); length (excluding probe) 23.27 m (76 ft 4 in); height 6.95 m (22 ft 9.5 in); wing area 75.43 m^2 (812 sq ft)
Armament: typically 5443 kg (12,000 lb) of various bombs, including nuclear, plus two 20-mm cannon in radar-directed tail turret

The immense size of the Skywarrior is evident in this picture of USS Nimitz crewmen moving a VQ-1 EA-3B prior to launch. The Skywarrior was used in the operational and training eletronic warfare roles for more than 25 years.

This Douglas A3D-2T (TA-3B after 1962) crew/radar trainer is attached to reconnaissance squadron RVAH-3. These aircraft had a pressurized fuselage for six pupils, and retained the original remotely-controlled tail gun barbette, although the actual guns were removed.

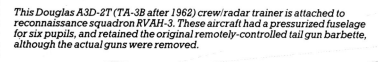

Douglas (McDonnell Douglas) A-4 (A4D) Skyhawk

Another of the brilliant designs of Ed Heinemann at the El Segundo plant, the **Douglas A4D Skyhawk** jet attack aircraft came out at just half the weight the US Navy predicted, and was also dramatically faster. The engine chosen was the British Armstrong Siddeley Sapphire (licence-built as the Wright J65), which was placed above a wing made in the form of an integral tank from tip to tip and so small it did not have to fold. The long main gears were arranged to retract forwards without cutting into the wing except for the wheel bay ahead of the front spar. Everything possible was done to simplify the design. The prototype flew on 22 June 1954, and soon set a world 500-km (311-mile) circuit speed record. The **A4D-1** (later **A-4A**) entered service, in 1956.

So good was the Skyhawk that termination of production was postponed until 1979, when the 2,960th and last example came off the line. There were 14 basic variants, some purely for export, and many later sub-types produced by conversions. The chief alteration during production was the switch to the J52 engine in the **A-4E** of 1961, giving more thrust and slightly better range. Throughout the early 1960s the J65-engined **A-4C** was the main version, serving with 23 US Navy and US Marine attack squadrons, but this gave way to the A-4E and the

This A-4 Skyhawk was employed by VX-5 at the Navy's test centre at China Lake on aerodynamic tests for airborne nuclear weapons.

greatly updated **A-4F** which was the first with a 'camel hump' fairing for Bullpup guidance and other extra avionics. All models from the A-4E have five pylons, as well as provision for an in-flight-refuelling probe on the right side of the nose. The **TA-4F** and simplified **TA-4J** are major tandem dual trainer versions, and the ultimate new-build single-seater was the **A-4M Skyhawk II** with a square-tip fin (later fitted with an ECM pod), new windshield and canopy, drag chute and many other updates. The **OA-4M** is a rebuilt two-seat TA-4F for forward air control duties with very comprehensive avionics. Among the many export versions Israel's completely rebuilt **A-4N** is distinguished by long anti-missile jetpipes, while Singapore's **TA-4S** has two separate cockpit windshields and canopies.

Specification
Douglas A-4M Skyhawk II
Type: single-seat carrier-based attack aircraft
Powerplant: one 5080-kg (11,200-lb) thrust Pratt & Whitney J52-408A turbojet

Performance: maximum speed, clean at sea level 1078 km/h (670 mph); combat radius with external weapons on a hi-lo-hi mission 620 km (385 miles); service ceiling 12880 m (42,250 ft)
Weights: empty 4899 kg (10,800 lb); maximum take-off 11113 kg (24,500 lb)
Dimensions: span 8.38 m (27 ft 6 in); length (with or without probe) 12.29 m (40 ft 4 in); height 4.57 m (15 ft 0 in); wing area 24.15 m² (260 sq ft)

Armament: two 20-mm Mk 12 cannon each with 200 rounds, plus one centreline pylon rated at 1587 kg (3,500 lb), two inboard wing pylons each rated at 1021 kg (2,250 lb) and two outboard wing pylons each rated at 454 kg (1,000 lb)

A late-model A-4M of Marines squadron VMA-324 fires a Zuni air-to-ground unguided rocket at a range in California.

Grumman S-2 (S2F) Tracker

First flown on 4 December 1952, the **Grumman XS2F-1** prototype had its genesis in a US Navy specification two years earlier demanding the previously unattainable quality of being able to operate from a small (i.e. not a giant 'Forrestal' class) carrier whilst carrying both ASW (anti-submarine warfare) sensors and weapons to effect the kill. Previously the task had demanded two aircraft operating in a hunter/killer team. Grumman's G-89 design was a basically conventional aircraft with a high wing of long span, two piston engines and a cabin ahead of the wing for two pilots and two radar and sensor

operators.

It was no easy job to package all the required items into a compact airframe. The APS-38 radar was put in the rear fuselage, the radome being winched down for use. A searchlight was installed on the outer right wing, and the MAD (magnetic anomaly detector) was mounted on a tube which could be extended from the rear fuselage well aft of the tail. Sonobuoys could be ejected from the rear of the engine nacelles, and weapons were carried in an internal bay and also on six wing pylons.

From the start of operational service

in February 1954 the **S2F-1**, named **Tracker**, did all that was asked. Production continued until after 1960 and there were many conversions and rebuilds, the later models having APS-88 radar, twice as many sonobuoys (32),

These two Grumman C-1 Traders are seen on a regular supply mission to a US Navy carrier. The Trader could carry up to nine passengers as well as cargo in the fully-equipped hold.

This VS-31 S-2 Tracker displays the main sensor used by the aircraft for detecting submarines, the magnetic anomaly detector. This retracts back into the fuselage when not in use. The idea of the extendable sting is to take the detector gear as far away from the metal aircraft as possible.

Julie/Jezebel detection gear, increased wing span and tail area and numerous improved avionics systems. The last major addition was the AQA-7 Difar sonobuoy processing system. Over 1,170 Trackers were built, not including 100 **CS2F-1 Tracker** aircraft built at Toronto by DH Canada. From 1962 the designation was changed to **S-2A** to **S-2G**, depending on model.

Many S-2 Tracker ASW aircraft were later converted into **US-2C** aircraft and various other utility versions used as hacks and for general trucking duties. In addition Grumman was con-

tracted to supply the US Navy with a specially designed transport for COD (carrier on-board delivery) missions, which involves supplying a carrier at sea with personnel, mail and all urgently needed stores. The requirement dated from 1950, but pressure of other work delayed the G-96, which appeared in 1955 as the **Grumman TF-1 Trader**, the designation actually meaning trainer (a secondary role). In the rationalized USAF/US Navy scheme of 1962 the Trader was redesignated **C-1A**.

Using the wing, engines and many

other parts of the S-2 Tracker, its tail being of the enlarged type introduced with the S-2D, the C-1A was given a new fuselage with increased volume, providing sufficient room for nine strong 9g aft-facing passenger seats, or a cargo load of 1587 kg (3,500 lb). All loads go on board via side doors, large items and small vehicles not being compatible. Of course full carrier compatibility is retained, the fully loaded aircraft making arrested landings and catapult take-offs.

Grumman delivered 87 production C-1A Traders, as well as four of the

G-125 version which entered Navy service in 1957 as the **TF-1Q** specialized ECM (electronic countermeasures) platform with the main cabin taken over by high-power receivers and jamming systems. In 1962 these little-publicized machines were redesignated as **EC-1A**.

Eventually, from 1965, the Trader began to be replaced by the much more powerful Grumman C-2A Greyhound, but a few continued in second-line service until the end of the decade.

Specification
Grumman S-2E Tracker
Type: four-seat carrier-based ASW aircraft
Powerplant: two 1,525-hp (1137-kW) Wright R-1820-82WA Cyclone piston engines
Performance: maximum speed 426 km/h (265 mph) at sea level; patrol speed 240 km/h (149 mph); range 1850 km (1,150 miles); endurance 9 hours
Weights: empty 8633 kg (19,033 lb); maximum take-off 12187 kg (26,867 lb)
Dimensions: span 22.12 m (72 ft 7 in); length 13.26 m (43 ft 6 in); height 5.05 m (16 ft 7 in); wing area 46.08 m² (496 sq ft)
Armament: internal bay and six pylons for total load up to 2182 kg (4,810 lb) including AS torpedoes, depth bombs and rockets

USA

Grumman E-1 (WF-2) Tracer

In 1954 the success of Lockheed Super Constellations and other US Navy aircraft tested in the high-flying AEW (airborne early warning) role, which then was called radar picket duty, caused Grumman to receive a contract for a development of the S2F-1 Tracker specially configured to carry a large surveillance radar. This aircraft, the **WF-1**, never flew; instead the company type number G-117 was carried over to a radar-carrying development of the more capacious C-1A Trader, the **Grumman WF-2**, with the bigger wing and tail. The C-1A (then TF-1) BuNo 136792 was fitted with a mock-up of the proposed radome and tail to serve as the aerodynamic prototype. This flew on 1 March 1957 and the first of 88 production machines, named **Tracer** and after 1962 redesignated as **E-1B**, flew on 2 February 1958. (The new designation arrived too late to prevent the unofficial name, from the WF designation, becoming 'Willy Fudd'.)

The radar used in the Tracer was the AN/APS-82, with the main racking filling the centre and rear fuselage and the rotating aerial (antenna) housed inside an unusual aerofoil-profile radome like a vast teardrop saucer carried on struts above the fuselage. The front of this fixed radome had a de-icer boot larger than any previously made, while at the rear it was extended to join the centre fin of the com-

pletely redesigned three-fin tail. The two operators amidships worked at identical consoles but with different duties, managing not only the main radar but also extensive IFF and communications systems, the two pilots handling navigation. In service as detachments of VAW-11 and VAW-12 the Tracer pioneered shipboard early-warning and fighter direction, being replaced by the much more powerful E-2A Hawkeye from 1964.

Specification
Grumman E-1B Tracer
Type: four-seat AEW surveillance and control aircraft
Powerplant: two 1,525-hp (1137-kW) Wright Cyclone R-1820-82WA piston engines
Performance: maximum speed 402 km/h (250 mph) at medium altitudes; operating height 6095 m (20,000 ft); maximum endurance 8 hours
Weights: empty 9536 kg (21,024 lb);

Seen with its predecessor, the Douglas EA-1 Skyraider, this Grumman E-1B Tracer prepares for launch from the wooden decks of USS Oriskany. The radical carriage of the radar antenna is clearly visible.

maximum take-off 12232 kg (26,966 lb)
Dimensions: span 22.05 m (72 ft 4 in); length 13.82 m (45 ft 4 in); height 5.13 m (16 ft 10 in); wing area 47.0 m² (506 sq ft)
Armament: none

McDonnell F3H (F-3) Demon

Like the contemporary Supermarine Swift in the UK, the **McDonnell F3H Demon** was sustaining a big production programme when it was belatedly recognized that the aircraft pouring off the line were unacceptable; a great outcry ensued as dozens of aircraft were scrapped or put aside for later rework. McDonnell knew the fault lay solely with the J40 engine, and after years of trauma got a redesigned F3H into US Navy service where it proved a fine aircraft.

When the **XF3H-1** prototype flew on 7 August 1951, it was structurally and aerodynamically the most advanced navy aircraft in the world. All wing and tail surfaces were acutely swept, the wing having fully variable camber and the tailplane being a slab. During flight testing the US Navy demanded extra fuel and all-weather radar, and the J40 engine proved totally unable to cope with the increased weight. McDonnell eventually, in 1954, redesigned the aircraft with the J71 engine, with still more fuel and a bigger wing. Production at last went ahead with 519 in three main models. The **F3H-2** (**F-3B** after 1962) was the basic strike fighter, 239 being delivered. These had the new air-

frame and engine but retained the original Hughes APG-51 radar matched with gun armament, four wing pylons being added for attack loads. McDonnell delivered 80 **F3H-2M** (later called **MF-3B**) aircraft which had augmented avionics for all-weather interception and a CW (continuous-wave) target illuminator for use with the primary air-to-air armament of four AIM-7C Sparrow III missiles, the first time these entered service. The **F3H-2N** (**F-3C**), of which 144 were delivered, was a limited all-weather fighter with basic APG-51 radar and four Sidewinder AAMs of the radar-guided AIM-9C variety.

Demons had a very active career, seeing combat duty around Quemoy

and off the Lebanon in 1958. Last deliveries took place in 1959 and replacement by the McDonnell F-4 was complete by August 1964 (first line) and February 1965 (reserve).

Specification
McDonnell F-3C Demon (F3H-2N)
Type: single-seat carrier-based fighter
Powerplant: one 6350-kg (14,000-lb) afterburning thrust Allison J71-2 or -2E turbojet
Performance: maximum speed, clean at sea level 1170 km/h (727 mph); range 2205 km (1,370 miles); service ceiling 13000 m (42,650 ft)
Weights: empty 9656 kg (21,287 lb); maximum take-off 15161 kg (33,424 lb)

McDonnell F3H-2 Demon of VF-131 based on the USS Constellation in the early 1960s.

Dimensions: span 10.77 m (35 ft 4 in); length 17.98 m (59 ft 0 in); height 4.44 m (14 ft 7 in); wing area 48.22 m^2 (519 sq ft)
Armament: four 20-mm Mk 12 cannon, plus four wing pylons for AIM-9C Sidewinder AAMs or up to 2722 kg (6,000 lb) of various attack weapons

A Demon of VF-61 'Jolly Rogers' launches. The severe delay in development meant that the F3H-2 had to compete with the F8U Crusader, but the Sparrow III did much to redress the balance.

McDonnell F-4 Phantom II

Produced as a private company venture in the mid-1950s, the **McDonnell Phantom II** was first ordered as the **AH-1** attack aircraft but then became the **F4H** interceptor with only a single centreline pylon for a giant drop tank. Guns were deleted, four Sparrow III AAMs were recessed under the broad flat belly, a powerful Westinghouse AN/APQ-50 Mod radar was added along with a radar operator in the back seat, and the first of 23 test aircraft flew on 27 May 1958. Though large, their splendid propulsion system, installed between fully variable inlets and nozzles with carefully arranged secondary flow, gave all-round flight performance never attained by any fighter. Early F4H (**F-4A**) aircraft captured almost every world record for speed at low and high altitudes, time to height and other parameters, so that it

was also bought in vast numbers as a land-based fighter for air forces.

The initial carrier-based model was the **F-4B**, of which 649 were built (including 12 **F-4G** aircraft with different radio). This had a bulged nose to house the 810 mm (32-in) dish of the AN/APQ-72 radar and a raised rear seat. It went to sea in August 1962 and became the standard all-weather fighter with the US Navy and US Marines, the latter service also buying 46 unarmed **RF-4B** multi-sensor reconnaissance aircraft. Service experience led to the **F-4J** of 1965, with the AWG-10 fire-control system, an extra tank, slotted tailplane, drooping ailerons, bigger wheels and brakes and (as a modification) ECM fin cap. This replaced the F-4B model in the US Navy and US Marines, 522 being built, and the survivors were later updated and also fitted with slatted

wings as the **F-4S**.

The UK's Royal Navy bought 24 **F-4K** aircraft similar to the F-4J but with Rolls-Royce Spey engines, AWG-11 with radar in a hinged nose, double-extension nose leg and other changes, another 28 going to the RAF (designation **Phantom FG.Mk 1**) which later had all surviving **Phantom FG.Mk 1** aircraft. The RAF and many other air forces purchased land-based versions.

The F-4 was the world's premier fighter of the 1960s. It saw extensive combat duty in Vietnam and has also been much used by Israel, Iran and other countries. Total production was 5,177.

Specification
McDonnell F-4B Phantom II
Type: two-seat carrier-based all-weather fighter

Powerplant: two 7711-kg (17,000-lb) afterburning thrust General Electric J79-8B turbojets
Performance: maximum speed, clean at 14630 m (48,000 ft) 2390 km/h (1,485 mph); combat radius interceptor with tanks, over 1448 km (900 miles); ferry range 3701 km (2,300 miles); service ceiling 18900 m (62,000 ft)
Weights: empty 12700 kg (28,000 lb); maximum take-off 24766 kg (54,600 lb)
Dimensions: span 11.71 m (38 ft 5 in); length 17.75 m (58 ft 3 in); height 4.95 m (16 ft 3 in); wing area 49.2 m^2 (530 sq ft)
Armament: four AIM-7 Sparrow III AAMs, up to four AIM-9B or 9D Sidewinder AAMs, and up to 7257 kg (16,000 lb) of attack weapons

North American (Rockwell) A-5 (A3J) Vigilante

North American RA-5C of RVAH-5 based on USS Constellation during the Vietnam war.

Though it never made the limelight, the **North American A3J Vigilante** probably introduced more design innovations than any other aircraft in history, including fully variable inlets and nozzles, a one-piece moving fin, slab tailerons used for roll in conjunction with roll-control spoilers, variable-camber blown wings, complete inertial navigation with autopilot coupling, automatic bad-weather carrier approach, drogue-stabilized rocket-augmented seats, and extensive titanium structure with gold coating in high-temperature areas. The prototype was a tandem-seat carrier-based bomber flown in August 1958. Yet another advanced feature was the large tunnel between the engines along the centreline. This housed two large fuel tanks and a nuclear weapon, all joined together and released as one unit over the target (the tanks then being empty and stabilizing the fall of the bomb); the assembly was ejected to the rear by gas pressure.

By early 1962 the first combat unit, VAH-7, was operating from USS *Enterprise*, the original **A3J-1** designation becoming **A-5A**. NAA delivered 57, followed by six **A-5B** aircraft with a giant humped fuselage housing extra fuel, and with still further high-lift wing systems. By far the most important model was the **RA-5C** long-range multi-sensor reconnaissance platform, which formed the airborne part of the US Navy Integrated Operational Intelligence System with automatic real-time information processing on the carrier or at a shore base. The RA-5C replaced the bomb tunnel by extra fuel, and a giant SLAR (side-looking airborne radar) was housed in a fairing along the belly. An impressive array of cameras and Elint (electronic intelligence) sensors made up the most comprehensive reconnaissance system of its day. NAA delivered 55 RA-5Cs, plus 59 converted from previous models. RVAH-5 equipped with this fine aircraft in June 1964, operating from the USS *Ranger* in South East Asia. Not until 1980 did the Vigilante begin to be replaced by the F-14 with a TARPS reconnaissance pallet.

The attack version of the Vigilante was the A3J-1 (A-5A after 1962) which featured a tunnel bomb-bay between the two engines. The bomb was released backwards during a climb over the target. This proved slightly dangerous in practice as leaking fuel in the tunnel often ignited.

Specification
North American RA-5C Vigilante
Type: two-seat multi-sensor reconnaissance aircraft
Powerplant: two 7711-kg (17,000-lb) afterburning thrust General Electric J79-8A/8B turbojets
Performance: maximum speed, clean at high altitude 2229 km/h (1,385 mph); range 4828 km (3,000 miles); service ceiling 19505 m (64,000 ft)
Weights: empty 17009 kg (37,498 lb); maximum take-off 36100 kg (79,588 lb)
Dimensions: span 16.15 m (53 ft 0 in); length 23.32 m (76 ft 6 in); height 5.91 m (19 ft 4.8 in); wing area 70.0 m² (754 sq ft)
Armament: none

The most important version of the Vigilante was the RA-5C. Its main sensor was an enormous side-looking airborne radar (SLAR) mounted under the fuselage along with other cameras. RA-5s were usually escorted by F-4s over Vietnam to protect them from MiGs.

Vought F-8 (F8U) Crusader

It is a remarkable fact that, powered by the near-identical J57 engine, the carrier-based **Vought F8U Crusader** came out faster, much longer-ranged, more manoeuvrable, much slower landing and in almost every other way superior to the famed North American F-100 Super Sabre, even though it had all the penalties of carrier operation! By the 1960s it was distinctly long in the tooth and being replaced by the F-4, yet in Vietnam it not only gained more air-combat victories than any other type but was so popular it was commonly said that 'When you're out of F-8s, you're out of fighters'.

The requirement was issued in September 1952, calling for a supersonic air-superiority fighter. The most unusual feature was that the wing was placed above the fuselage and hinged so that, by varying its angle of incidence, the fuselage could be tilted nose-down to give the pilot a perfect forward view on the approach to the carrier. This also enabled the landing gears to be short, folding into the belly of the fuselage which also carried a giant door-type airbrake which, in turn, mounted the large tray of unguided air-to-air rockets forming the main armament. Four cannon were also installed, in the sides of the nose beside the engine air duct. The slab tailplane was mounted low, and another advanced feature was that the entire wing inboard of the fold axis on each side formed an integral tank.

The **XF8U-1** prototype flew on 25 March 1955, and after most rapid development the first US Navy squadron, VF-32, completed conversion in March 1957. Their **F8U-1** aircraft (later restyled **F-8A**) had a Martin-Baker F5 seat, neat folding inflight-refuelling probe in the left side of the fuselage and launch rails for Sidewinder on each side of the fuselage. Vought built 318 of this model before following with 130 **F-8B** aircraft with radar, 187 of an upgraded all-weather model, the **F-8C**, 152 of the **F-8D** with more power (fastest version, at Mach 1.86 or

1975 km/h/1,227 mph) and new avionics, and 286 **F-8E** multi-role attack machines with new radar, an IR seeker and various external weapons. The final 42 were **F-8E(FN)** fighters for the French Aéronavale with French R530 missiles and modified high-lift wing to suit small flight decks. By 1970 a total of 446 US Navy and US Marine F-8s had been completely rebuilt into new versions (**F-8H** to **F-8M**). Many of the unarmed **RF-8A** photo aircraft were rebuilt as **RF-8G** platforms, and these were the last to remain in US service.

Specification
Vought F-8E Crusader
Type: single-seat carrier-based attack fighter

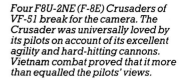

Four F8U-2NE (F-8E) Crusaders of VF-51 break for the camera. The Crusader was universally loved by its pilots on account of its excellent agility and hard-hitting cannons. Vietnam combat proved that it more than equalled the pilots' views.

Powerplant: one 8165-kg (18,000-lb) afterburning thrust Pratt & Whitney J57-20A or -420 turbojet
Performance: maximum speed 1859 km/h (1,155 mph); range 2253 km (1,400 miles)
Weights: empty 8935 kg (19,700 lb); maximum take-off 15422 kg (34,000 lb)
Dimensions: span 10.72 m (35 ft 2 in); length 16.61 m (54 ft 6 in); height 4.8 m (15 ft 9 in); wing area 34.84 m² (375 sq ft)
Armament: four 20-mm Mk 12 cannon each with 84 or 125 rounds and two/four Sidewinder AAMs, plus up to 1814 kg (4,000 lb) of bombs, rockets or Bullpup missiles on four wing pylons

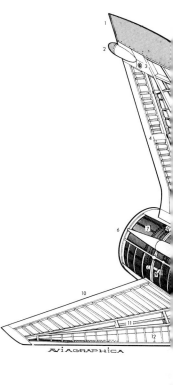

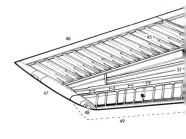

The variable-incidence wing was an ingenious answer to the problem of excessive angle of attack during landing and take-off, which severely restricted pilot vision. The principle worked well on the Crusader and no major problems were ever uncovered.

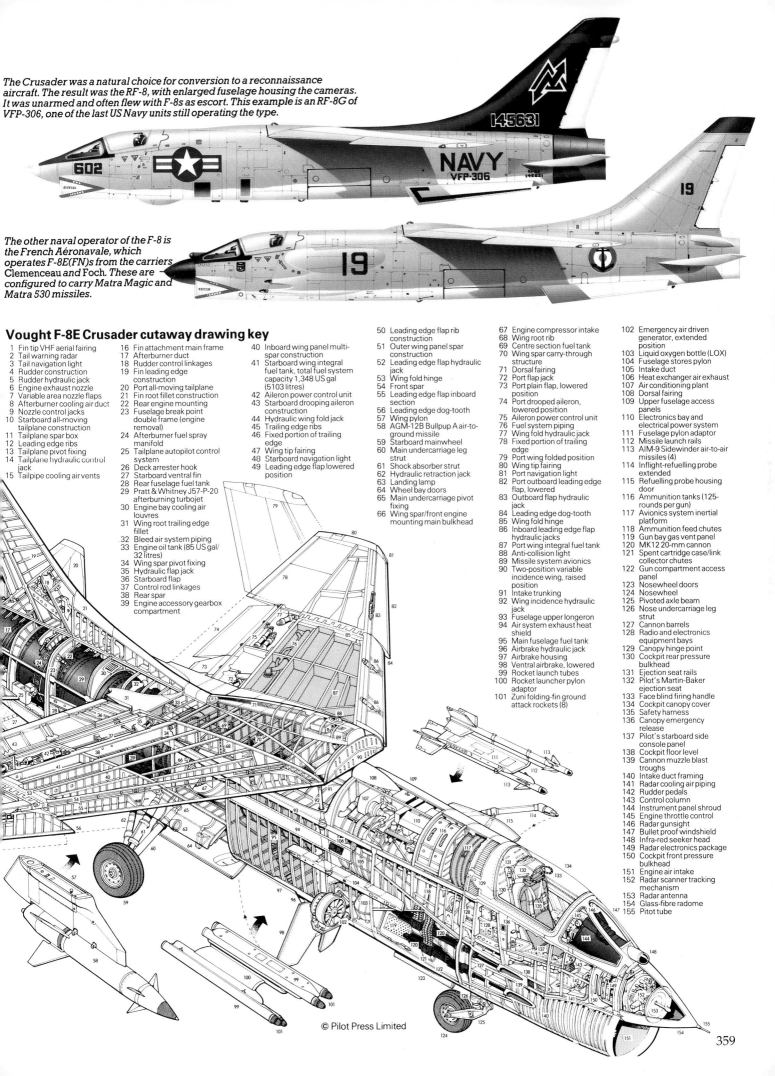

The Crusader was a natural choice for conversion to a reconnaissance aircraft. The result was the RF-8, with enlarged fuselage housing the cameras. It was unarmed and often flew with F-8s as escort. This example is an RF-8G of VFP-306, one of the last US Navy units still operating the type.

The other naval operator of the F-8 is the French Aéronavale, which operates F-8E(FN)s from the carriers Clemenceau and Foch. These are configured to carry Matra Magic and Matra 530 missiles.

Vought F-8E Crusader cutaway drawing key

1 Fin tip VHF aerial fairing
2 Tail warning radar
3 Tail navigation light
4 Rudder construction
5 Rudder hydraulic jack
6 Engine exhaust nozzle
7 Variable area nozzle flaps
8 Afterburner cooling air duct
9 Nozzle control jacks
10 Starboard all-moving tailplane construction
11 Tailplane spar box
12 Leading edge ribs
13 Tailplane pivot fixing
14 Tailplane hydraulic control jack
15 Tailpipe cooling air vents
16 Fin attachment main frame
17 Afterburner duct
18 Rudder control linkages
19 Fin leading edge construction
20 Port all-moving tailplane
21 Fin root fillet construction
22 Rear engine mounting
23 Fuselage break point double frame (engine removal)
24 Afterburner fuel spray manifold
25 Tailplane autopilot control system
26 Deck arrester hook
27 Starboard ventral fin
28 Rear fuselage fuel tank
29 Pratt & Whitney J57-P-20 afterburning turbojet
30 Engine bay cooling air louvres
31 Wing root trailing edge fillet
32 Bleed air system piping
33 Engine oil tank (85 US gal/32 litres)
34 Wing spar pivot fixing
35 Hydraulic flap jack
36 Starboard flap
37 Control rod linkages
38 Rear spar
39 Engine accessory gearbox compartment

40 Inboard wing panel multi-spar construction
41 Starboard wing integral fuel tank, total fuel system capacity 1,348 US gal (5103 litres)
42 Aileron power control unit
43 Starboard drooping aileron construction
44 Hydraulic wing fold jack
45 Trailing edge ribs
46 Fixed portion of trailing edge
47 Wing tip fairing
48 Starboard navigation light
49 Leading edge flap lowered position
50 Leading edge flap rib construction
51 Outer wing panel spar construction
52 Leading edge flap hydraulic jack
53 Wing fold hinge
54 Front spar
55 Leading edge flap inboard section
56 Leading edge dog-tooth
57 Wing pylon
58 AGM-12B Bullpup A air-to-ground missile
59 Starboard mainwheel
60 Main undercarriage leg strut
61 Shock absorber strut
62 Hydraulic retraction jack
63 Landing lamp
64 Wheel bay doors
65 Main undercarriage pivot fixing
66 Wing spar/front engine mounting main bulkhead

67 Engine compressor intake
68 Wing root rib
69 Centre section fuel tank
70 Wing spar carry-through structure
71 Dorsal fairing
72 Port flap jack
73 Port plain flap, lowered position
74 Port drooped aileron, lowered position
75 Aileron power control unit
76 Fuel system piping
77 Wing fold hydraulic jack
78 Fixed portion of trailing edge
79 Port wing folded position
80 Wing tip fairing
81 Port navigation light
82 Port outboard leading edge flap, lowered
83 Outboard flap hydraulic jack
84 Leading edge dog-tooth
85 Wing fold hinge
86 Inboard leading edge flap hydraulic jacks
87 Port wing integral fuel tank
88 Anti-collision light
89 Missile system avionics
90 Two-position variable incidence wing, raised position
91 Intake trunking
92 Wing incidence hydraulic jack
93 Fuselage upper longeron
94 Air system exhaust heat shield
95 Main fuselage fuel tank
96 Airbrake hydraulic jack
97 Airbrake housing
98 Ventral airbrake, lowered
99 Rocket launch tubes
100 Rocket launcher pylon adaptor
101 Zuni folding-fin ground attack rockets (8)

102 Emergency air driven generator, extended position
103 Liquid oxygen bottle (LOX)
104 Fuselage stores pylon
105 Intake duct
106 Heat exchanger air exhaust
107 Air conditioning plant
108 Dorsal fairing
109 Upper fuselage access panels
110 Electronics bay and electrical power system
111 Fuselage pylon adaptor
112 Missile launch rails
113 AIM-9 Sidewinder air-to-air missiles (4)
114 Inflight-refuelling probe extended
115 Refuelling probe housing door
116 Ammunition tanks (125-rounds per gun)
117 Avionics system inertial platform
118 Ammunition feed chutes
119 Gun bay gas vent panel
120 MK12 20-mm cannon
121 Spent cartridge case/link collector chutes
122 Gun compartment access panel
123 Nosewheel doors
124 Nosewheel
125 Pivoted axle beam
126 Nose undercarriage leg strut
127 Cannon barrels
128 Radio and electronics equipment bays
129 Canopy hinge point
130 Cockpit rear pressure bulkhead
131 Ejection seat rails
132 Pilot's Martin-Baker ejection seat
133 Face blind firing handle
134 Cockpit canopy cover
135 Safety harness
136 Canopy emergency release
137 Pilot's starboard side console panel
138 Cockpit floor level
139 Cannon muzzle blast troughs
140 Intake duct framing
141 Radar cooling air piping
142 Rudder pedals
143 Control column
144 Instrument panel shroud
145 Engine throttle control
146 Radar gunsight
147 Bullet proof windshield
148 Infra-red seeker head
149 Radar electronics package
150 Cockpit front pressure bulkhead
151 Engine air intake
152 Radar scanner tracking mechanism
153 Radar antenna
154 Glass-fibre radome
155 Pitot tube

© Pilot Press Limited

Fairey (Westland) Gannet

Unique in many ways, this distinctive machine began life as the **Fairey GR.17** (from the specification, GR.17/45), the first prototype flying on 19 September 1949. It was designed as an ASW (anti-submarine warfare) hunter-killer able to operate from small carriers yet carry radar and sonobuoys to detect submarines, as well as weapons in an internal bay to kill such submarines as were found. Delay was caused by a sudden decision to add a third crew-member, but eventually the **Gannet AS.Mk 1** entered service with No. 826 Squadron in January 1955.

Propulsion was provided by a turboprop with two independent power sections each driving one half of a double co-axial propeller. Thus, without affecting the handling, either half-engine and its propeller could be shut down in flight to extend mission endurance. Another advantage was that the engine could operate on ship's diesel oil. The large wing folded in four places to reduce span and height without interfering with access to the rear cockpits or the twin jetpipes, and other features included steerable twin-wheel nose gears, a very large

Providing the Fleet Air Arm's airborne early warning throughout the 1960s was the Westland Gannet AEW.Mk 3, which replaced the Douglas Skyraider in this role. This aircraft served on board HMS Ark Royal with No. 849 Sqn.

weapon bay and a radar extended from below the rear fuselage. **Gannet AS.Mk 1**, **Gannet AS.Mk 4**, **Gannet AS.Mk 6** and **Gannet AS.Mk 7** aircraft served with the Royal and some other navies, surviving into the early 1960s in West Germany, Australia and Indonesia. The **Gannet T.Mk 2** and **Gannet T.Mk 5** were trainers.

Most important in the 1960s was the **Westland Gannet AEW.Mk 3**, the airborne early-warning version built to replace the Skyraider in the Royal Navy's No. 849 Squadron. Powered by an uprated engine, this had a new fuselage with no weapon bay, a single pilot cockpit at the front and a cabin for two radar observers aft of the wing, the tail also being enlarged to balance the big radome of the APS-20A radar, and the landing gear being lengthened. The last was delivered in 1961, and

when the RN fixed-wing force was run down and 'B' Flight of No. 849 Squadron left HMS Ark Royal in 1978 the UK had no seaborne AEW capability, something bitterly regretted just four years later in the South Atlantic.

Specification
Westland Gannet AEW.Mk 3
Type: three-seat carrier-based AEW aircraft
Powerplant: one 3,875-hp (2890 kW) Bristol Siddeley (previously Armstrong Siddeley, later Rolls-Royce) Double Mamba 102 coupled turboprop
Performance: maximum speed 417 km/h (259 mph); range 1127 km (700 miles); patrol height 7770 m (25,500 ft)
Weights: empty 7421 kg (16,360 lb); maximum take-off 11340 kg (25,000 lb)
Dimensions: span 16.61 m (54 ft 6 in); length 13.41 m (44 ft 0 in); height 5.13 m (16 ft 10 in); wing area 44.9 m^2 (483 sq ft)
Armament: none

The Fairey Gannet was developed as an anti-submarine aircraft and served in this role for many years until superseded by the Westland Sea King helicopter. This example is a T.Mk 5 trainer. An unusual feature of the Gannet was the four-folding wing.

Hawker Siddeley (Blackburn/BAe) Buccaneer

Designed as a strike aircraft for the Royal Navy, the **Hawker Siddley Buccaneer** first flew in April 1958. Latterly it served in the maritime attack role with the RAF's Nos 12 and 208 Squadrons based at Lossiemouth. Seating the pilot and navigator in tandem, the **Buccaneer S.Mk 2** is a large aircraft distinguished by its capacious internal bomb bay, whose rotary door incorporated a large fuel tank, with a load of 1814 kg (4,000 lb) inside the bay. This subsonic aircraft was faster than any supersonic warplane with the same load carried externally, and its fuel consumption was modest because the efficient turbofan engines had no afterburners. An inflight-refuelling probe could be attached above the nose but was seldom needed.

Sidewinder AAMs were later added for self-defence and the ECM fit was also considerably enhanced for the same reason. Though a few aircraft were lost to the service in 1982 as a result of structural problems, which required the implemen-

The initial colour scheme for the Buccaneer was overall 'anti-flash' white, as carried by the 18th pre-production aircraft, bearing the marking of Fleet Air Arm trials unit No. 700Z Sqn based at Lossiemouth.

The first operational user of the Buccaneer S.Mk 2 was No. 801 Sqn, which formed in 1965 for service on board HMS Victorious. Early S.Mk 2s had extra-dark sea grey upper sides with anti-flash white underneath.

tation of a major anti-fatigue modification programme. Replacement of the aircraft in some squadrons by the Panavia Tornado meant that there was no shortage of these popular long-range attack aircraft up to their retirement from British service in 1991 after service as laser designation machines in the Gulf War of the same year.

Sixteen Buccaneer S.Mk 50 aircraft served with the South African Air Force up to 1990. These aircraft carried the AS.30 air-to-surface missile amongst other weapons, and had an inbuilt BS.605 rocket motor to boost 'hot-and-high' take-offs.

Specification
Hawker Siddeley Buccaneer S.Mk 2B
Type: two-seat attack aircraft
Powerplant: two 5003-kg (11,030-lb) thrust Rolls-Royce Spey 101 turbofans
Performance: maximum speed, clean at sea level 1110 km/h (690 mph); range with internal bombs and maximum fuel on a hi-lo-hi mission 3701 km (2,300 miles)
Weights: empty 13608 kg (30,000 lb); maximum take-off 28123 kg (62,000 lb)
Dimensions: span 13.41 m (44 ft 0 in); length 19.33 m (63 ft 5 in); height 4.95 m (16 ft 3 in); wing area 47.82 m^2 (514.7 sq ft)
Armament: maximum bombload of 1814 kg (4,000 lb) in internal bay plus

A Blackburn Buccaneer S.Mk 1 lands on HMS Eagle while a 'plane-guard' Wessex waits, ready to pick up any aircrew unfortunate enough to ditch. The Buccaneer S.Mk 1 was powered by two 3,220-kg (7,100-lb) DH Gyron Junior engines.

5443 kg (12,000 lb) on four wing pylons; loads can include Sea Eagle, Martel, Harpoon, Shrike, Alarm and Sidewinder missiles

---

UK
Hawker Siddeley (DH/BAe) Sea Vixen

This impressive two-seat all-weather interceptor began life in 1946 and might have been in service in 1951, but thanks to a succession of indecisions and a horrific crash of a prototype, the de Havilland Sea Vixen languished until the Royal Navy renewed interest in 1954. Eventually a fully navalized prototype flew in 1957 and the first **Sea Vixen FAW.Mk 1** squadron was commissioned on 2 July 1959.

Retaining the company's twin-boom layout, the Vixen was unique in seating the pilot high on the left, with the radar observer inside what was called 'the coal hole' low down on the right, with a roof hatch and small window. Immediately beside were the inlet ducts from the wing roots leading to the two turbojets in the rear of the nacelle. The nose was filled by the big GEC AI.Mk 18 radar. No guns were fitted, their place being occupied by two hinged packs each housing a battery of 14 air-to-air rockets. Wing pylons carried up to four Blue Jay (Firestreak) IR-homing AAMs, and the Vixen was also cleared to operate in the attack role with a wide range of bombs and air-to-surface missiles such as Bullpup. In

practice these fine aircraft were used mainly as interceptors.

The 92nd aircraft was modified on the production line as the first **Sea Vixen FAW.Mk 2**, with swollen tail booms housing more fuel, and with a modified fire-control system compatible with the much more formidable Red Top AAM. As on the Mk 1 aircraft, an in-flight-refuelling probe could be attached in the wing leading edge outboard of the left boom, and there were additional avionic items. Total production of both marks was 148, many Mk 1s

being converted after delivery to Mk 2 standard. After replacement by McDonnell Douglas Phantoms from 1970, many Sea Vixens were rebuilt as **Sea Vixen D.Mk 3** pilotless RPV targets.

Specification
de Havilland Sea Vixen FAW.Mk 2
Type: two-seat carrier-based all-weather fighter
Powerplant: two 5094-kg (11,230-lb) thrust Rolls-Royce Avon 208 turbojets
Performance: maximum speed 1110 km/h (690 mph) at sea level; range at high altitude on internal fuel 1931 km (1,200 miles); service ceiling 14630 m (48,000 ft)
Weights: empty 11793 kg (26,000 lb); maximum take-off 18858 kg (41,575 lb)
Dimensions: span 15.54 m (51 ft 0 in); length 16.94 m (55 ft 7 in); height 3.28 m (10 ft 9 in); wing area 60.2 m^2 (648 sq ft)
Armament: four Red Top AAMs and 28 Microcell 2-in (51-mm) rockets, plus provision for very varied offensive loads up to 1361 kg (3,000 lb) in weight on four or six wing pylons

Part of the Sea Vixen's repertoire was buddy-buddy refuelling, here demonstrated by two FAW.Mk 1s from No. 899 Sqn. The missiles carried are de Havilland Firestreak infra-red homing. The FAW.Mk 2 featured enlarged tail booms which extended forward of the leading edge, and was equipped to fire the more advanced Red Top missile.

Supermarine Scimitar

In the UK the process of introducing transonic swept-wing fighters into the Fleet Air Arm was painfully slow. Virtually nothing was done in the first five years after World War II; then, apparently unexpectedly, the carrier trials of the swept-wing Supermarine Type 510 in November 1950 showed that there need not be any problem. Even then it was to be almost another 10 years before anything reached the squadrons. Via the butterfly-tailed Supermarine Type 508 and Type 529 and all-swept Type 525 the halting progress led to the Type 544, or N.113D, of January 1956. This was fitted with 200-series Avons, large flaps intended to be blown from the engines, folding wings, perforated airbrakes on the rear fuselage and a slab tailplane. It led directly to the first of 76 **Supermarine Scimitar F.Mk 1** aircraft built in 1957-60.

A big and tough machine, the Scimitar had been planned as a carrier-based interceptor, though nobody thought of giving it any radar. By the mid-1950s it seemed that the need was for a low-level bomber and in service the Scimitar, though designated as a fighter, spent most of its brief life in vague attack roles. Its four wing pylons were each rated at 907 kg (2,000 lb), though no squadron machine ever carried external loads of weapons greater than 1814 kg (4,000 lb). Nuclear capability was announced, though the Fleet Air Arm did not possess such weapons. It was also announced that the Scimitars would carry 'missiles', but the only offensive type carried (very briefly, on trials) was the command-guidance Bullpup. There was never any proper air/surface weapon-aiming system, and the lone pilot in any case had his hands full trying to navigate at sea without any modern navaids. At least the squadron aircraft had a nose-mounted inflight-refuelling probe, and the Scimitar's last combat role was carrying a buddy pack to refuel Hawker Siddeley Buccaneers of No. 800 Squadron in 1965-6. With proper avionics these basically capable aircraft might have had long careers.

Specification
Supermarine Scimitar F.Mk 1
Type: single-seat attack fighter
Powerplant: two 5103-kg (11,250-lb) thrust Rolls-Royce Avon 202 turbojets, with bleed for flap-blowing
Performance: maximum speed, clean at sea level 1143 km/h (710 mph); combat radius on a hi-lo-hi mission with internal fuel 579 km (360 miles); ferry range 3380 km (2,100 miles); service ceiling 14020 m (46,000 ft)
Weights: empty 11295 kg (24,900 lb); maximum take-off 18144 kg (40,000 lb)
Dimensions: span 11.33 m (37 ft 2 in); length (excluding probe) 16.87 m (55 ft 4 in); height 4.65 m (15 ft 3 in); wing area 45.0 m² (484.9 sq ft)
Armament: four 30-mm Aden cannon each with 100 rounds, plus four wing pylons each rated at 907 kg (2,000 lb) for Sidewinder AAMs, bombs, rocket

Seen with AEW Skyraiders and Sea Venoms, this Scimitar F.Mk 1 is being prepared for a mission. The Scimitar was never successful in its intended role and was retired in favour of the two-seat Buccaneer early in its expected life, as the extra crew member made life much easier.

pods, buddy packs or 909-litre (200-Imp gal) drop tanks

Dassault Etendard

Designed at the same time as the Mirage, in 1954-5, the **Dassault Etendard** was intended as a NATO light attack aircraft but eventually, in 1962, entered service with the French Aéronavale as a carrier-based attack aircraft (**Etendard IVM**) or photo-reconnaissance aircraft (**Etendard IVP**). The engine selected, after flight testing various other arrangements of single and twin engines, was the Atar 8B, basically a Mirage III engine without the afterburner (because there was no requirement for supersonic performance). An extremely conventional aircraft, the Etendard seated its pilot in a Martin-Baker N4A seat, had long-stroke main gears, small flaps and ailerons all inboard of the wing fold (which folded only the tips) and a horizontal tail pivoted well up the large fin. The leading edges had a marked dogtooth inboard of hinged flaps depressed at low speeds for flight at high angles of attack.

A total of 69 Etendard IVM attack aircraft was delivered, equipping squadrons 11F and 17F and often operating from the carriers *Foch* or *Clemenceau*. A refuelling probe can be attached above the slim nose, which houses a small Aïda ranging radar (which has no search or bad-weather capability), and the only aid to weapon delivery is a Saab toss-bombing computer. The unique fin under the nose housed the guidance transmitter aerial for the Nord AS.20 or AS.30 missiles. The Etendard IVP replaces the radar by a fixed probe and the guns by five OMERA cameras.

Another modification in the Etendard IVP is an indepeddnet navigation system. This model, of which 21 were ordered, equips a single squadron and has no visible replacement.

The Etendard has served with the French Aéronavale since 1962 as both a light strike aircraft and a photo-reconnaissance aircraft. The Etendard IVP carries out the latter function and carries cameras in a redesigned nose. These are still in service and there is no likely replacement yet.

Specification
Dassault Etendard IVM
Type: single-seat carrier-based attack aircraft
Powerplant: one 4400-kg (9,700-lb) thrust SNECMA Atar 8B turbojet
Performance: maximum speed, clean at sea level 1099 km/h (683 mph); tactical radius on a lo attack mission with maximum internal fuel 300 km (186 miles)
Weights: empty 6123 kg (13,500 lb); maximum take-off 10275 kg (22,650 lb)
Dimensions: span 9.60 m (31 ft 6 in); length 14.40 m (47 ft 3 in); height 4.30 m (14 ft 1.3 in); wing area 29.0 m² (312.2 sq ft)
Armament: two 30-mm DEFA cannon each with 100 rounds, plus four wing pylons for a maximum total load of 1361 kg (3,000 lb) of bombs or other stores including AS.30 attack missiles or Sidewinder self-defence AAMs

Maritime Aircraft

From the oilfields of the North Sea to the myriad islands of the Philippines and Indonesia, the maritime regions of the modern world have assumed an ever-increasing economic importance in recent years. The vast areas involved must be guarded, and by far the most effective and far-reaching method is from the air.

One of the most oft-repeated statistics concerning the Earth is that two-thirds of its surface is covered with water. A further fact worthy of mention is that many who live on the land have a keen interest in what happens on and under that water. Other countries' warships, illegal fishermen, smugglers and several sources of pollution are to be found on the high seas, and it is an unwise government that takes an interest only when such problems come within sight of the coast.

Aircraft represent a highly effective method of locating, identifying and on occasion dealing with these potential problems far out at sea. Most but not all such aircraft are land-based types. The larger of these aircraft, which possess considerable range, are designated maritime patrol or maritime reconnaissance aircraft, and are exemplified by the US Navy's Lockheed Martin P-3 Orion patroller and the RAF's BAe Nimrod MR.Mk 2 reconnaissance platform. These aircraft are extensively equipped with complex avionics for the difficult task of locating submarines and surface vessels, and their armament includes depth charges and torpedoes as well as anti-ship missiles.

Most Lockheed P-3 Orions are maritime patrol and ASW aircraft, but electronic warfare (EP-3), reconnaissance (RP-3) and weather-mission (WP-3) variants have also been produced.

Of lesser sophistication are the maritime surveillance aircraft, usually equipped with radar, but lacking anti-submarine warfare (ASW) equipment except of the simplest kind. These machines are most often adaptations of transport aircraft or business jets and are employed on protection of economic zones. In several cases they carry little or no weaponry. However, recent models of the Fokker F.27 Maritime, with their missile armament, have clearly moved into a higher bracket and are to be regarded as front-line equipment.

An almost universal feature of maritime aircraft is that they are equipped for search-and-rescue (SAR) missions. Among the stores usually carried are emergency kits (containing an inflatable boat, food, water etc.) and the appropriate radios for direct contact with other emergency services. It is in this role that maritime aircraft often make the news, but to seagoing nations their principal task is to act as the fast, long-range 'eyes and ears' of the navy.

EMBRAER EMB-110 and EMB-111

EMBRAER of Sao José dos Campos, Brazil, came into operation only in 1970 but has already built more than 3,000 aircraft and has made Brazil a leading aircraft producer. Its wide range includes the best-selling **EMBRAER EMB-110 Bandeirante** (pioneer), sold in numbers as a light twin-turboprop airliner even to the UK, the USA and France. The **EMB-110S1** is a remote-sensor geophysical model with MAD tailboom, the **EMB-110P1K** is a mass-produced military transport (called **C-95A** by the Brazilian air force) and among many other offshoots is the short-body pressurized **EMB-121 Xingu** family called **VU-9** by the Brazilian air force and bought as the stan-

dard aircrew trainer and liaison transport for the French Armée de l'Air (25) and Aéronavale (16). The **EMB-111** is a comprehensively equipped maritime surveillance aircraft, with a mainly Collins avionics fit but including AIL nose radar, Bendix autopilot, Thomson-CSF passive ECM and optional Omega receiver. The normal crew numbers 3-7 and the interior is equipped not only with displays and observation stations but also for cargo and paratrooping or equipment dropping. The **EMB-111** first flew on 15 August 1977, and 12 were sold to the Brazilian air force coastal command with designation **P-95**. The first of a growing list of export customers was Chile, whose aircraft

have full de-icing and passive ECM under the nose.

Specification
EMB-111
Type: maritime surveillance aircraft
Powerplant: two 559.3-kW (750-shp) Pratt & Whitney of Canada PT6A-34 turboprops
Performance: (at maximum weight, ISA + 15°C, a severe criterion) maximum cruising speed 385 km/h (239 mph); range at 3048 m (10,000 ft) with 45-minute reserves 2945 km (1,830 miles)
Weights: empty 3760 kg (8,289 lb); maximum take-off 7000 kg (15,432 lb)
Dimensions: span 15.95 m (52 ft 4 in);

length 14.91 m (48 ft 11 in); height 4.91 m (16 ft 1.3 m); wing area 29.1 m² (313.24 sq ft)
Armament: four wing pylons for four pairs of 12.7-cm (5-in) HVAR rockets or launchers each with seven 69.9-mm (2.75-in) FFAR rockets, or three stores pylons plus 50 million candlepower searchlight; other gear includes smoke bombs, markers, flares, chaff dispenser and loud hailer

Entering service with the Forca Aérea Brasileira in April 1978, the EMB-111 carries pairs of 12.7-cm (5-in) HVAR rockets together with a searchlight of 50 million candlepower on the starboard wing.

Grumman HU-16 Albatross

Although no longer operational with any element of the US Armed forces, the distinctive **Grumman Albatoss** amphibian is still in service with a few other air arms in a variety of roles ranging from air-sea rescue through liaison and communications to anti-submarine warfare. It also holds the distinction of being the last amphibian to see service with the US armed forces and in its heyday established a number of world records for aircraft in its class.

A logical outgrowth of earlier Grumman amphibians such as the Goose and Widgeon, the Albatross began development in the closing stages of World War II, the aircraft which eventually emerged being significantly larger than its predecessors although it bore a strong family resemblance. Initially ordered by the US Navy, the prototype **XRJ2F-1** made its maiden flight on 24 October 1947, subsequently entering service as the **UF-1** in July 1949. Originally intended to fulfil mainly utility functions, the Albatross soon

proved to be a most versatile machine, and another notable early customer was the US Air Force which acquired a large number of **SA-16A** aircraft for the Military Air Transport Service's air rescue organization, these machines soon proving their worth in this demanding task.

Refinement of the design led to the appearance in the mid-1950s of the **SA-16B** and **UF-2**, both of which featured

increased wing span and larger tail surfaces as well as more effective de-icing equipment. Many earlier aircraft were eventually brought to this later standard and the type also found favour overseas, customers including Canada, Indonesia, Italy, Japan, Mexico, Norway, the Philippines, Spain, Taiwan and West Germany.

In addition to the basic utility and

The ASW version of the Grumman HU-16 is distinguishable by the larger search radar in the nose together with a retractable magnetic anomaly detector (MAD) boom in the tail. Greece is the last country to use this model.

rescue versions, an ASW-capable Albatross was also conceived by Grumman, this featuring such familiar items as nose-mounted radar, a searchlight, a MAD (Magnetic Anomaly Detector) boom and specialized ordnance including torpedoes and depth charges. Most, if not all, ASW-configured aircraft were simply conversions of HU-16Bs, and they retained the same designation following conversion, examples of the type being known to have served with the air arms of Greece, Spain and Turkey, although only the first is believed still to use the Albatross for ASW duties.

Specification
HU-16B Albatross
Type: anti-submarine warfare, utility and rescue amphibian
Powerplant: two 1062.6-kW (1,425-hp) Wright R-1820-76A/76B Cyclone radial piston engines
Performance: maximum speed 380 km/h (236 mph) at sea level; cruising speed 241 km/h (150 mph); range with 4826 litres (1,275 US gal) of fuel 4345 km (2,700 miles); maximum endurance 22 hours 54 minutes

Dimensions: span 29.46 m (96 ft 8 in); length 18.67 m (61 ft 3 in); height 7.87 m (25 ft 10 in); wing area 96.15 m² (1,035 sq ft)
Armament: four underwing hardpoints capable of carrying depth bombs, mines, unguided air-to-surface rockets and torpedoes; in addition, depth charges and sonobuoys are carried internally

---

Fokker F.27 Maritime

The **Fokker F.27 Maritime** is an adaptation of the Friendship turboprop transport, which first flew in 1955 and remains in production to this day. Foreseeing a market for a medium-range maritime patrol aircraft to replace such stalwarts as the Lockheed Neptune and the Grumman Tracker and Albatross, Fokker began conversion of a prototype **F.27MPA** (Maritime Patrol Aircraft) in 1975, this making its initial flight during February 1976. Unarmed in its initial form, the aircraft is suitable for sealane and fishery patrol, offshore oilfield policing, SAR and pollution control, its prime sensor being a Litton AN/APS-504(V)2 360° radar scanner mounted in a ventral radome. Up to six crew members are carried. Peru's navy received the first two F.27 Maritimes in September 1977 and February 1978, whilst other customers have comprised the Spanish air force, with three supplied in 1979 for patrol and SAR missions from the Canary Islands (Spanish military designation **D.2**); the Philippine navy which received three in 1981-2; the Angolan air force with one; the Dutch air force (mixed air force and navy crews) with two delivered in 1981-2 for missions in the Antilles; and the Nigerian air force with two supplied in 1984.

A major upgrading of the design came in 1984 when the **Maritime Enforcer** was revealed, three examples for Thailand's navy being the first order. The Enforcer is an ASW aircraft equipped with Marconi central tactical and sonobuoy processing systems, plus an Alkan stores-management system. It can locate submarines and all classes of surface vessels using not only search radar, but also passive and active acoustic equipment (via sonobuoys launched from bays in the rear fuselage) and an electronic surveillance and monitoring system. Inputs from these sensors, together with visual observations, are fed into a central display controlled by the tactical co-ordinator. Most importantly, however, the Maritime Enforcer has provision for armament; up to six torpedoes, or depth charges for ASW, or up to four anti-ship missiles on a new stores position at the lower sides of the centre fuselage.

Specification
F.27 Maritime Enforcer
Type: maritime patrol aircraft
Powerplant: two 1,730-kW (2,320-shp) Rolls-Royce Dart Mk 536-7R turboprops
Performance: cruising speed 463 km/h (288 mph); patrol speed 277-333 km/h (172-207 mph) at 457 m (1,500 ft); initial climb rate 442 m (1,450 ft) per minute; service ceiling 8990 m (29,495 ft); range 5000 km (3,107 miles) with wing pylon tanks
Weights: empty 12519 kg (27,600 lb);

The three Spanish F.27 Maritimes operate out of the Canaries on general unarmed patrol and SAR missions. An armed, ASW-dedicated version is available, the Maritime Enforcer.

maximum take-off 20412 kg (45,000 lb)
Dimensions: span 29.00 m (95 ft 1.7 in); length 23.56 m (77 ft 3.6 in); height 8.50 m (27 ft 10.6 in); wing area 70.00 m² (753.5 sq ft)
Armament: up to four Aérospatiale AM.39 Exocet or McDonnell Douglas AGM-84A Harpoon ASMs, or six bombs/depth charges/torpedoes

---

Grumman S-2 Tracker

Still in modest service more than 45 years after first flight (on 4 December 1952), the **Grumman G-89 Tracker** was the first successful carrier-based ASW aircraft, containing the search and attack capability in one aircraft. Piston engines were chosen for sea-level endurance of 9 hours, and the crew of four were seated in a single nose compartment. Weapons were housed internally and under the high-mounted folding wing, and after entering US Navy service in 1954 with the basic designation **S-2** production reached a total of 1,181 in five major versions, not including the **C-1 Trader** COD (Carrier On-board Delivery) transport and **E-1 Tracer** surveillance versions. DH Canada built 100 in two versions, and though many **S-2A** aircraft and other variants were progressively updated, the chief type today is the **S-2E** (245 built) with the longer span, bigger cockpit and bigger tail of the **S-2D** plus a range of improved sensors. The last recipient was the Royal Australian Navy, which lost all but three of its S-2Es in a hangar fire in December 1976; the USN quickly provided 16 replacement aircraft. Several countries use the **TS-2** (usually **TS-2A** conversion) as a trainer; others use **US-2** utility and **RS-2** photographic aircraft.

Specfication
S-2E Tracker
Type: ASW aircraft
Powerplant: two 1137.2-kW (1,525-hp) Wright R-1820-82WA Cyclone piston engines
Performance: maximum speed 426 km/h (265 mph); range with 10 per cent reserve 2092 km (1,300 miles)
Weights: empty 8505 kg (18,750 lb); maximum take-off 13222 kg (29,150 lb)
Dimensions: span 22.12 m (72 ft 7 in); length 13.26 m (43 ft 6 in); height 5.05 m (16 ft 7 in); wing area 46.08 m² (496 sq ft)
Armament: one Mk 47 or Mk 101 nuclear depth bomb (USN only, no longer active) or wide range of conventional depth bombs or AS torpedoes, plus torpedoes, mines, rockets or bombs on wing pylons

Primarily a carrierbased ASW aircraft, the Grumman S-2 Tracker no longer serves aboard the carriers of the US Navy, but is still in widespread use worldwide. Japan used the aircraft for many years.

Lockheed P-2 Neptune

In terms of numbers built arguably the most successful post-war maritime aircraft, the **Lockheed Neptune** can in fact be traced as a development back to September 1941, when work began on the company's **Model 26**. However, the more urgent considerations of World War II dictated a very leisurely rate of progress, and it was not until April 1944 that Lockheed received a contract covering the construction of a pair of **XP2V-1** prototypes and an initial production batch of just 15 **P2V-1** aircraft. Subsequent developments of the Neptune enabled the type to remain in continuous production for close to 35 years, thus establishing an exceptional longevity record.

Flown for the first time in prototype form on 17 May 1945, the Neptune duly entered service with the US Navy in March 1947, shortly after the **P2V-2** variant made its maiden flight. Some 81 examples of this sub-type were completed, these being followed by 53 **P2V-3** and 30 **P2V-3W** aircraft, the latter model introducing the ventral radome which was to become such a

characteristic feature of the Neptune. Production then switched to the **P2V-4** (later designated **P-2D**), but only 52 were completed before the **P2V-5** (later **P-2E**) made its debut, this eventually becoming the most numerous version, some 424 being produced for service with the US Navy and a number of other countries including Argentina, Australia, Brazil, the Netherlands, Portugal and the UK.

Further refinements to the basic design led to the appearance of the **P2V-6** (later **P-2F**) in late 1952, 67 standard aircraft being followed by 16 specially-configured **P2V-6M** aircraft which were compatible with the Fairchild AUM-N-2 Petrel air-to-surface missile. Lockheed production of the Neptune terminated with the **P2V-7** (later **P-2H**) version, which was the only model to feature auxiliary jet engines from the outset although this feature was later retrofitted to the earlier P2V-5 and P2V-6. The **P2V-7S** (later **SP-2H**) was a conversion with Julie and Jezebel submarine detection equipment. A total of 311 P2V-7s was completed by the pa-

rent company, these being supplemented by 48 Japanese-built examples, and it was Japan which was the source of the final production version, namely the **P2V-7KAI** which benefitted from the adoption of turboprop engines, a pair of General Electric-IHI T64s replacing the Wright R-3350 radial engines of earlier Neptunes. Production of the P2V-7KAI (later **P-2J**) eventually ceased with the completion of the 82nd example, this bringing the total number of Neptunes built to 1,133.

Specification
SP-2H Neptune
Type: maritime patrol and anti-submarine warfare aircraft
Powerplant: two Wright R-3350-32W Turbo-Compound 18-cylinder radial piston engines, each rated at 2610 kW (3,500 hp) and two Westinghouse J34-WE-36 turbojets, each rated at 1542-kg (3,400-lb)
Performance: maximum speed

649 km/h (403 mph) at 3048 m (10,000 ft); patrol cruising speed 333 km/h (207 mph) at 2591 m (8,500 ft); ferry range 5930 km (3,685 miles)
Weights: empty 22650 kg (49,935 lb); maximum take-off 36240 kg (79,895 lb)
Dimensions: span 31.65 m (103 ft 10 in); length 27.84 m (91 ft 4 in); height 8.94 m (29 ft 4 in); wing area 92.90 m² (1,000 sq ft)
Armament: assortment of mines, depth charges, bombs and torpedoes can be housed in an internal weapons bay; underwing stores stations can accommodate additional ordnance including bombs and high-velocity aerial rockets

Serving finally with the air arm of the Japanese Maritime Self-Defence Force into the 1990s, the Lockheed P-2 was in service for more than four decades.

Lockheed P-3 Orion

By August 1957 it appeared the Lockheed P-2 Neptune was coming to the end of its development, and the US Navy invited submissions for a replacement. Lockheed won with a patrol/ASW derivative of its **L-188 Electra** civil transport, the **Lockheed P-3 Orion** with airframe almost unchanged except for the addition of an unpressurized weapon bay ahead of the wing in a shortened fuselage, pylons for external stores and a MAD boom behind the tail. An aerodynamic prototype with these changes flew on 19 August 1958. The first production **P-3A** flew on 15 April 1961 and by 1983 Lockheed-California had delivered almost 600 P-3s of successively improved models. Most are regular maritime patrol aircraft but the US Navy uses **EP-3B** and **EP-3E** electronic-warfare platforms with giant canoe radars, **RP-3A** machines are special reconnaissance aircraft and four **WP-3A** aircraft fly weather missions. The standard 1985 model is the **P-3C Update III**, the various Update programmes having contributed improved sensors, data-processing, nav/com and other avionic systems. The Canadian Armed Forces bought 18 **CP-140 Aurora** aircraft which packaged the Lockheed S-3A sensors, avionics and data-processing systems into the P-3 airframe. Japan's 109 P-3C aircraft (including subvariants) comprise three Lockheed-built aircraft and 106 assembled or wholly built under license by Kawasaki.

Norway's No. 332 Sqn flies the P-3B Orion on maritime duties around the long coastline. These are unusual in being painted dark grey.

Specification
P-3C Orion
Type: maritime patrol and ASW aircraft
Powerplant: four 3661.4-ekW (4,910-ehp) Allison T56-14 turboprops
Performance: maximum speed at a weight of 47628 kg (105,000 lb) 761 km/h (473 mph); maximum radius with no time on station 3835 km (2,383 miles)
Weights: empty 27891 kg (61,491 lb); maximum take-off 64410 kg (142,000 lb)
Dimensions: span 30.38 m (99 ft 8 in); length 35.61 m (116 ft 10 in); height 10.27 m (33 ft 8.5 in); wing area 120.77 m² (1,300 sq ft)
Armament: total expendable load 9072 kg (20,000 lb) comprising up to 3289 kg (7,252 lb) in internal bay (made up typically of two Mk 101 depth bombs, four Mk 44 torpedoes and numerous sensors/signals) plus underwing load on 10 pylons (maximum six 907-kg/2,000-lb mines)

The Canadian Armed Forces have bought 18 Lockheed CP-140 Auroras, these being standard P-3 airframes but with the electronic and sensor package found in the same company's S-3 Viking.

Lockheed C-130 Hercules

Undoubtedly one of the most successful Western military aircraft of the post-war era, the **Lockheed Hercules** has been in continuous production since 1955 and the number built is now creeping up towards the 2,000 mark. Although designed primarily to fulfil airlift-type duties, the Hercules has proved to be a most versatile machine and presently undertakes such diverse tasks as inflight-refuelling, support of Antarctic exploration, weather reconnaissance, satellite capsule recovery, drone launch and control, airborne command post and search and rescue.

In addition to these missions, the Hercules has also proved to be well-suited for maritime applications. For the most part these are confined to surveillance and, indeed, the maritime Hercules lacks offensive capability although it is by no means beyond the realms of possibility that it could eventually be reconfigured in order to permit the carriage of dedicated anti-submarine warfare weaponry such as depth charges.

Based on the **C-130H**, which is the current production model of the Hercules, those aircraft intended for maritime tasks incorporate a number of detail changes, but the basic design can be more or less tailored to meet customer requirements. Optional equipment available includes a crew rest/galley module; a ramp equipment pallet containing rescue kit, a loudspeaker, flare launchers and an aft-facing observation platform; specialized sea search radar; advanced navigation equipment; searchlights; system interfaces for camera and data annotation gear; and observation stations in the cabin area. In addition, of course, the Hercules can also undertake airlift-type duties with equal facility, a factor which must be particularly attractive to those nations which have only limited funds available for the purchase of new equipment.

Specification
C-130H (maritime configuration)
Type: medium/long-range cargo/maritime surveillance aircraft
Powerplant: four 3361.6-kW (4,508-shp) Allison T56-A-15 turboprop engines
Performance: maximum cruising speed 621 km/h (386 mph); patrol range with auxiliary fuel at surveillance altitude of 1524 m (5,000 m) 4661 km (2,896 miles)
Weights: zero fuel in typical maritime

configuration 39945 kg (88,064 lb); maximum normal take-off 70307 kg (155,000 lb); maximum overload take-off 79379 kg (175,000 lb)
Dimensions: span 40.41 m (132 ft 7 in); length 29.79 m (97 ft 9 in); height 11.66 m (38 ft 3 in); wing area 162.11 m² (1,745 sq ft)
Armament: none

Above: Given the astonishing range of tasks it has performed in its 30-year career, it is hardly surprising that there should be a maritime surveillance version of the Lockheed Hercules. Used by Indonesia, the C-130H-MP can patrol for up to 16 hours at an altitude of 1525 m (5,000 ft).

Below: The US Coast Guard has more than 20 HC-130 Hercules, although some of the earlier models are in storage. The HC-130H is an extended range model originally used by the Air Force Aerospace Rescue & Recovery Service, with 12 subsequently produced for the US Coast Guard.

Dassault-Breguet Atlantic

The **Dassault-Breguet Atlantic** stemmed from the **Breguet Br 1150**, the winning design in a 1958 NATO contest for a new maritime patrol aircraft to succeed the Lockheed Neptune. Though the choice was approved by all 15 NATO members in December 1958, and ordered into production by a multinational consortium called SECBAT,

Manufactured by an international consortium to a French design, the Atlantic is only operated in any quantity by France, Germany and Italy. Germany operates 14 Atlantics in the maritime role, with five more aircraft being dedicated to Elint.

the Atlantic was bought by only a few countries, notably excluding the UK and the USA, and Belgium whose industry had a major share in SECBAT. Other partners, apart from the parent firm, were Sud-Aviation, Dornier and Fokker. Italy joined after placing an order, and the British engines and propellers were likewise shared out among participating nations. The prototype flew on 21 October 1961 and deliveries began in December 1965, totalling 87 for France (37), West Germany (20), Italy (18), Netherlands (9) and Pakistan (3). Skinned largely with aluminium honeycomb sandwich, the Atlantic has a capacious double-bubble fuselage, an efficient long-span wing, and comprehensive avionics managed by a crew of 12. Five German machines are ECM platforms. On 8 May 1981 Dassault-Breguet flew the first **ANG (Atlantic Nouvelle Génération)** with completely updated avionics and improved structure. France expects to buy 42 ANGs (now known as the **Atlantique**) made by the same SECBAT consortium, and other orders are being sought.

The 27 Atlantics currently in service form the backbone of France's maritime reconnaissance strength. The new Atlantique was first flown in May 1981, and 42 have been ordered by the Aéronavale. The new model features a strengthened structure and new avionics.

Specification
Atlantique
Type: maritime patrol and ASW aircraft
Powerplant: two 4638.3-ekW (6,220-ehp) Rolls-Royce Tyne 21 turboprops made by multinational group
Performance: maximum speed at sea level 592 km/h (368 mph), and at 6096 m (20,000 ft) 658 km/h (409 mph);

range 8150 km (5,065 miles); endurance 18 hours
Weights: empty 25300 kg (55,777 lb); maximum take-off 46200 kg (101,854 lb)
Dimensions: span (over ESM pods) 37.30 m (122 ft 4.5 in); length 32.62 m (107 ft 0.25 in); height 11.35 m (37 ft 2.9 in); wing area 120.34 m^2 (1,295.3 sq ft)

Armament: unpressurized weapon bay houses all NATO bombs, torpedoes (8), depth charges, mines and missiles, a typical load being one AM39 Exocet plus three AS torpedoes; four wing pylons for 3500 kg (7,716 lb) of stores including pods, containers, rockets or ASMs

---

Shin Meiwa PS-1 and US-1

Today the great fleets of military flying-boats and amphibians have all but vanished, and the only type recently in production is the **Shin Meiwa SS-2** family which was produced as the **PS-1** and **US-1** for the JMSDF (Japan Maritime Self-Defence Force). The company was famed as that wartime builder of marine aircraft, Kawanishi, and when it received a 1966 contract for an ASW (anti-submarine warfare) flying-boat it produced a very advanced design with four turboprops for propulsion and a fifth gas turbine to provide high-pressure air for boundary-layer control blowing over the flaps, rudder and elevators. This enables the aircraft to fly extremely slowly under full control and also greatly reduces take-off and alighting distances. The first SS-2 (PS-1) flew in October 1967, and eventually 23 production machines were delivered, 19 remaining in service with the JMSDF's 31st Wing at Iwakuni to 1989. The PS-1 had a crew of 10 comprising two pilots, flight engineer, navigator, two sonar operators (sonar can be repeatedly dipped in rough seas after alighting), MAD operator, radar and radio operators and tactical co-ordinator. A beaching chassis is permanently attached and PS-1 can taxi ashore under its own power. The **SS-2A** amphibian, on the other hand, has full tricycle landing gear, and 17 were delivered as US-1 and upgraded US-1A search/rescue aircraft with a crew of nine and room for either 20 seated survivors or 12 litters, or 69 ordinary passengers.

Whilst on patrol the PS-1 made repeated alightings and take-offs, dunking its sonar after alighting. This process could be accomplished in seas with waves up to 3 m (10 ft) high.

Specification
PS-1
Type: ASW flying-boat
Powerplant: four 2281.8-ekW (3,060-ehp) General Electric T64-IHI-10 turboprops (made under licence by IHI)
Performance: maximum speed 547 km/h (340 mph); range at low altitude with maximum weapons 2168 km (1,347 miles)
Weights: empty 26300 kg (57,982 lb); maximum 43000 kg (94,799 lb)

Dimensions: span 33.14 m (108 ft 8.7 in); length 33.50 m (109 ft 10.9 in); height 9.71 m (31 ft 10.3 in); wing area 135.82 m^2 (1,462 sq ft)
Armament: internal weapon bay for

four 149-kg (328-lb) AS bombs and extensive search gear, two underwing pods for four Mk 44 or 46 homing AS torpedoes and triple launcher under each wingtip for 127-mm (5-in) rockets

A highly advanced wing and engine combination gives the Shin Meiwa PS-1 and the amphibious US-1 very good STOL and low speed handling capabilities.

British Aerospace Nimrod

After many years studying other ideas, the RAF picked the **British Aerospace Nimrod** as its replacement for the Avro Shackleton in the maritime patrol role, and the first production **Nimrod MR.Mk 1** flew on 28 June 1968. Features include an enormously capacious fuselage with a very large unpressurized lower lobe housing the radar, weapon bays and much systems equipment. Flight is possible on any one of the four fuel-efficient turbofan engines, the outers having reversers to back up the anti-skid brakes on the bogie main gears and enormous plain flaps. The normal crew comprise 12, who have an outstandingly complete and well integrated array of sensors, data processing and navigation/communication/identification systems for ASW, SAR, Elint, reconnaissance and other tasks for surface forces and even transport with accommodation for 45 passengers in the rear compartment. The 43 Nimrod MR.Mk 1 aircraft established an outstanding record, only one being lost in 10 years of intensive operation, mainly in extremely adverse conditions and at very low levels.

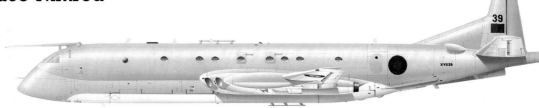

Nimrod's latest MR.Mk 2P guise has a hemp colour scheme and an inflight-refuelling probe added.

Three **Nimrod R.Mk 1** aircraft serve in the dedicated Elint role. From 1979 a total of 32 Nimrod MR.Mk 1s were rebuilt to **Nimrod MR.Mk 2** standard with upgraded avionics, sensors and data-processing equipment. Eleven further aircraft were to have been rebuilt as **Nimrod AEW.Mk 3s** but were then cancelled. From 2002 the RAF should receive the first of 21 Nimrod 2000 aircraft, which are wholly revitalized Nimrod MR.Mk 2 machines that will serve with the designation **Nimrod MRA.Mk 4**. The Nimrod 2000 standard includes a new Boeing mission system and BMW/Rolls-Royce BR710 turbofan engines.

Specification
Nimrod MR.Mk 2
Type: maritime patrol aircraft
Powerplant: four 5507-kg (12,140-lb) thrust Rolls-Royce Spey 250 turbofans
Performance: maximum speed 926 km/h (575 mph); patrol speed on two engines 370 km/h (230 mph); range 9262 km (5,755 miles); endurance 18 hours
Weights: empty 39009 kg (86,000 lb); maximum take-off 87090 kg (192,000 lb)
Dimensions: span 35.0 m (114 ft 10 in); length 38.63 m (126 ft 9 in); height 9.06 m (29 ft 8.5 in); wing area 197 m² (2,121 sq ft)

Armament: 14.78 m (48 ft 6 in) weapon bay carries six lateral rows of stores including nine torpedoes as well as bombs; provision for wing pylons for ASMs or other stores; very comprehensive ASW sensor systems

Nimrods were given a limited self-defence capability during the Falklands campaign by the addition of AIM-9L Sidewinders under the wings; these were also to be used against Argentine Boeing 707s which were patrolling the same oceans. This aircraft is an MR.Mk 2P with inflight-refuelling probe.

Pilatus Britten-Norman Maritime Defender

The British firm Britten-Norman flew a prototype of the highly successful **Britten-Norman BN-2 Islander** nine-passenger light transport in 1965. A rugged aircraft with fixed landing gear, it has also been produced in the Philippines, Romania and Belgium, although the parent company at Bembridge, Isle of Wight, is now Swiss-owned. Several air arms adopted the Islander for personnel and freight transport, including five delivered to the Indian Navy in 1976. Later, these aircraft were modified with a nose-mounted radar for maritime patrol duties, being augmented in 1981-3 by a further dozen to the same standard. Similarly, the Philippine navy operates five locally-built Islanders in the surveillance role.

The next stage in development was the **Defender**, built to military standards and with optional fitments including four underwing weapon pylons and a weather radar in the nose to provide a simple maritime-search capability. Low cost has resulted in considerable sales, especially to Third World countries. To meet the specialized maritime requirement more fully, the manufacturer has introduced the **Maritime Defender**, the main feature of which is a Bendix RDR 1400 radar providing an enhanced search range: 67 km (41.5 miles) for a 100-m² (1,076-sq ft) object in sea state 4-5. The nose radome increases fuselage length from the standard 10.86 m (35 ft 7.75 in), and the antenna scans 60° to

each side, giving a search band of 111 km (69 miles) at optimum altitude. For day or night operations in coastal patrol, fishery protection and SAR roles, the aircraft carries a pilot, a co-pilot, a radar operator and two observers, together with such aids as Omega navigation, a radio altimeter and a transponder. Wing pylons are retained for SAR kits as well as more warlike loads such as BAe Sea Skua anti-ship missiles, Marconi Stingray homing torpedoes, self-defence AIM-9 Sidewinder AAMs and a range of ECM/ESM pods. An optional searchlight and hand-held camera are available for fishery and other policing tasks. Customers may opt for the **Turbine Defender** version, powered by two 238.6-kW (320-shp) Allison 250-B17C turboprop engines.

Specification
Maritime Defender
Type: armed maritime surveillance aircraft
Powerplant: two 193.9-kW (260-hp) Avco Lycoming O-540-E4C5 flat-six piston engines
Performance: maximum speed, clean 280 km/h (174 mph); initial climb rate 396 m (1,300 ft) per minute; service ceiling 5182 m (17,000 ft); range with maximum payload 673 km (418 miles)
Weights: empty 1823 kg (4,020 lb); maximum take-off 2994 kg (6,600 lb)
Dimensions: span 14.94 m (49 ft 0 in) standard, or 16.15 m (53 ft 0 in)

optional; length 11.07 m (36 ft 3.75 in); height 4.18 m (13 ft 8.75 in); wing area 30.19 m² (325.0 sq ft) or 31.31 m² (337.0 sq ft)
Armament: various missiles and bombs on four underwing pylons

Pilatus Britten-Norman's Defender provides a low-cost alternative for a maritime aircraft. This example flies with the Benin Defence Force on maritime duties, armed with torpedoes under the wings.

Former USSR

Myasishchev M-4 'Bison'

Now just past the end of its operational career, the **Myasishchev M4 'Bison'** entered the design stage in 1951 and was first seen airborne in a May Day flypast over Moscow in 1954. Service deliveries began in 1956, and with the nickname **'Molot'** (hammer) it gained the distinction of being the USSR's first operational four-jet strategic bomber. V.M. Myasishchev had previously been a leading light in the Tupolev bureau, and this product emerged as a robust, yet innovative aircraft which met most aspects of an extremely demanding strategic bomber specification. Similar in many respects to early models of the Boeing B-52, the **'Bison-A'** numbered among its achievements a world record speed 1028 km/h (639 mph) in a 1000-km (621-mile) closed circuit carrying a 27000-kg (59,525-lb) payload. Perhaps 200 of the type were built, of which 40 remain as bombers and 30 have been fitted as inflight-refuelling tankers.

A maritime version, the **'Bison-B'** was first observed in 1964, being distinguished by a solid nose radome with attached inflight-refuelling probe, a bulge in the forward portion of the centre bomb bay doors, and a comprehensive sensor fit betrayed by several blister fairings beneath the fuselage. The original upper and lower rear fuselage gun turrets were removed, leaving six NR-23 cannon for self-defence. The improved **'Bison-C'** continued the MR theme, but its improved search radar was contained in a new, longer nose and a prone bombing position with an optically flat windscreen was added in the floor of the cockpit. In addition, more small windows and a domed observation and

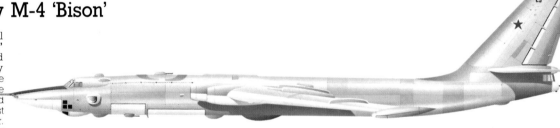

'Bison-C' is the main maritime version of the M-4, which features an elongated nose containing more capable radar. 'Bison-B' was the earlier maritime version.

gun-aiming position were added to each side of the fuselage, although the belly retained the same modification as the 'Bison-B'. As such, the 'Bison-C' version was available for reconnaissance, Elint, electronic warfare and mid-course guidance of large anti-ship missiles. The 'Bison-A', and a few 'Bison-B' and 'Bison-C' aircraft were in use with the Soviet (finally Russian) naval air force to the early 1990s.

Specification
M-4 'Bison-C'
Type: maritime reconnaissance bomber
Powerplant: four 13000-kg (28,660-lb) thrust Soloviev D-15 turbojets
Performance: maximum speed 1005 km/h (624 mph) or Mach 0.945 at 11000 m (36,089 ft); unrefuelled radius of action 5600 km (3,480 miles)
Weights: empty about 83900 kg (184,968 lb); maximum take-off 210000 kg (462,971 lb)
Dimensions: span 52.50 m (172 ft 2.9 in); length excluding probe 49.38 m (162 ft 0 in); height 14.24 m (46 ft 8.7 in); wing area 320.0 m² (3,444.6 sq ft)
Armament: six NR-23 23-mm cannon in dorsal, tail and ventral barbettes

The Mysasishchev M-4 heavy bomber, known by the NATO reporting name 'Bison', was the first Soviet four-jet operational heavy bomber. With an unrefuelled combat radius of over 5600 km (3,480 miles), it proved suitable for the maritime reconnaissance and attack roles, and two dedicated MR versions were produced.

Tupolev Tu-16 'Badger'

Bearing the Tupolev designation Tu-88, this strategic jet bomber first flew in late 1952. **'Badger-A'** bomber versions were in service by 1954 and these were followed by **'Badger-B'** and **'Badger-G'**, which could carry two stand-off air-to-surface missiles under the wings. **'Badger-C'** is an anti-shipping version with a 'Kipper' missile carried in a recess under the fuselage (some now have pylons for 'Kingfish' missiles under the wings). There have been many maritime reconnaissance, Elint and ECM variants: the **'Badger-D'** maritime reconnaissance platform with large undernose radar, **'Badger-E'** with cameras in bomb bay, **'Badger-F'** with Elint pods carried under the wings, **'Badger-H'** specialist ECM air-

craft with primary chaff-dispensing function, **'Badger-J'** specialist electronic jamming aircraft and **'Badger-K'** electronic reconnaissance aircraft. All these versions are widely seen around Western naval forces, and also make electronic intelligence flights around the coasts of NATO countries, eavesdropping on communications. Support is provided by Tu-16 tankers, which refuel other 'Badgers' by the wingtip-to-wingtip method. About 400 Tu-16s remained in service with the naval air force until retirement during the 1990s.

Specification

Type: strategic bomber, missile platform, maritime reconnaissance, ECM and Elint aircraft

Powerplant: two 8700-kg (19,200-lb) Mikulin AM-3M turbojets
Performance: maximum speed 1000 km/h (620 mph); cruising speed 850 km/h (530 mph); service ceiling 14000 m (46,000 ft); maximum range 6400 km (4,000 miles)
Weights: empty 3600 kg (80,000 lb); maximum take-off 72000 kg (158,500 lb)
Dimensions: wing span 34.54 m (113 ft 3 in); length 36.5 m (120 ft); height 10.8 m (35 ft 6 in); wing area 170 m^2 (1,820 sq ft)
Armament: all versions have seven 23-mm NR-23 cannon: one fixed in forward fuselage, two in tail turret and two each in ventral and dorsal barbettes; ('Badger-C') one AS-2

'Kipper', ('Badger-G') two AS-5 'Kelt' or one AS-6 'Kingfish' air-to-surface missiles; bomber versions have provision for 6000 kg (13,000 lb) of internal stores

Anti-shipping and reconnaissance versions of the Tu-16 were widely seen around NATO ships and coastlines. This 'Badger-C' carries a larger radar under the nose, and has pylons under the wings for anti-ship missiles.

Tupolev Tu-95 and Tu-142 'Bear'

'Bear-F' is the specialist anti-submarine version of the Tu-142. Most examples lack the nose radar of the 'Bear-D' but sport a magnetic anomaly detector (MAD) boom projecting from the top of the fin.

Designed as a strategic nuclear bomber, the **Tupolev Tu-20** first flew in 1954 and was initially regarded in the West as an aircraft of little promise. Having the design bureau project number **Tu-95**, it was essentially a swept-wing version of the Tu-85 with four turboprop engines driving contra-rotating four-blade propellers of massive 5.6 m (18 ft 4.5 in) diameter. At a time when turbojet bombers were proliferating, the engine configuration caused the design to be assessed as obsolescent, and not until later did the West appreciate the remarkable range and bombload capabilities of the aircraft. Accommodating up to 16 personnel, comprising two crews, the Tu-20 received the NATO reporting name **'Bear'** and was found to be capable of flying over 160 km/h (99 mph) faster than the supposed maximum speed for

a propeller driven aircraft of its size.
Main production of the 'Bear' ended in 1961-2 after approximately 300 aircraft, although a dozen or so were produced annually for the next 20 years to maintain force levels. Currently, the Soviet air force (V-VS) has about 115 Tu-20s (a little more than half the remaining aircraft) of the **'Bear-A'**, **'Bear-B'**, **'Bear-C'** and **'Bear-G'** variants for free-fall bombing or carrying cruise missiles. Production of new **'Bear-H'** aircraft at the Taganrog plant began recently in order to provide a carrier for the AS-15 cruise missile.
Maritime reconnaissance versions of the 'Bear' have the bureau designation **Tu-142**, this number having been revived and used in preference to Tu-20 in order to identify naval models exempt from the 1979 SALT-2 arms-control talks. These comprise 45 **'Bear-**

D' aircraft with a large I-band radome under the belly; a small number of **'Bear-E'** aircraft equipped with cameras in the bomb bay; and 50 **'Bear-F'** aircraft for anti-submarine duties. The last-mentioned is a revised design with changes including a 2.00 m (6 ft 6.75 in) fuselage extension forward of the wings. Other 'Bears' have been noted with a variety of special sensor equipment fitments and 11, designated Tu-142M, were delivered to the Indian naval air arm from 1985 for ASW duties as the sole exports of the Tu-20 series. Despite its age, the 'Bear' remains an effective reconnaissance aircraft and will continue to serve Soviet naval aviation (AV-MF) for some time to come. Western observers speculate that its 'replacement' could prove to be a prop-fan version of the same basic design.

Specification
Tu-20 (Tu-142) 'Bear-F'
Type: long-range maritime reconnaissance aircraft
Powerplant: four 11032.6-kW (14,795-shp) Kuznetsov NK-12MV turboprops
Performance: maximum speed 925 km/h (575 mph) at 12500 m (41,010 ft); maximum unrefuelled range (bomber) 12550 km (7,798 miles)
Weight: maximum take-off about 188000 kg (414,469 lb)
Dimensions: span 51.10 m (167 ft 7.8 in); length 49.50 m (162 ft 4.8 in); height 12.12 m (39 ft 9.2 in); wing area 310.5 m^2 (3,342.3 sq ft)
Armament: two NR-23 23-mm self-defence cannon in tail turret, plus depth charges, bombs and torpedoes.

Beriev Be-12 Tchaika 'Mail'

One of the world's few remaining amphibious aircraft, the **Beriev Be-12** medium-range patroller is a record-holder par excellence, having swept the board of all 22 distinctions in FAI Class C2 (turboprop flying-boats) and another 22 in Class C3 (turboprop amphibians). Despite these achievements, the aircraft is not a special trials model, but in regular service with the Soviet Northern and Black Sea Fleets, being responsible for anti-submarine and surveillance duties out to some 370 km (230 miles) from shore. An ungainly aircraft, the Be-12 was appropriately named **Tchaika** (seagull) by reason of its gull wing, mounting the engines at the highest point to keep the propellers clear of spray at take-off and landing.

Developments took place during the late 1950s with the intention of replacing the Be-6, and the NATO name 'Mail' was bestowed following the type's debut at the 1961 Aviation Day display at Tushino, Moscow. Service entry took place around 1965, and at least 100 were delivered before production ended in the early 1970s, about 80 of them continuing to provide naval

aviation with a valuable asset. Prominent equipment for the main anti-submarine role are the 'Short Horn' J-band radar in the nose for long-range search and bombing, and a tail-mounted MAD boom. Depth charges and other stores can be released through a hatch in the lower hull, behind the step. Other equipment, such as torpedoes, may be attached externally on two pylons outboard of each engine. At least five crew members are carried, comprising a pilot, co-pilot, engineer, radar/ESM operator and ASW operator (and up to nine when a visual search is to be undertaken). The aircraft also appears to be used for electronic intelligence missions, particularly over the Baltic. Operating from coastal bases, the Be-12 uses a tailwheel landing gear, the

main units of which fold upwards into the hull, although the tips of the wheels remain visible. Stabilizing floats mounted close to the wing tips are fixed. Be-12s ceased operation from Egypt in EAF insignia when that country distanced itself from the USSR, but since 1981 up to a dozen have been delivered to Vietnam (apparently still Soviet-crewed) for missions over the South China Sea. The type is also known as the **M-12**.

Specification
Be-12 'Mail'
Type: amphibious maritime patrol aircraft
Powerplant: two 3124.8-ekW (4,190-ehp) Ivchenko AI-20D turboprops
Performance: maximum speed 608 km/h (378 mph); initial climb rate

Known to the Soviets as the M-12, the Beriev Tchaika (Seagull) is one of the last amphibians to see large-scale military use, for purposes from ASW to electronic intelligence.

910 m (2,986 ft) per minute; service ceiling 11280 m (37,008 ft); maximum range 4000 km (2,485 miles)
Weights: empty about 20000 kg (44,092 lb); maximum take-off about 29450 kg (64,926 lb)
Dimensions: span 29.71 m (97 ft 5.7 in); length 30.17 m (98 ft 11.8 in); height 7.00 m (22 ft 11.6 in); wing area 105.0 m^2 (1,130.2 sq ft)
Armament depth charges, torpedoes and bombs carried internally or on four wing pylons.

Ilyushin Il-38 'May'

Ilyushin's Il-18 turboprop was one of the most successful Soviet passenger liners, with enormous production and exports, including many used by air forces. In about 1967 his design bureau flew the first **Il-38** ASW conversion, very similar to that effected by Lockheed to produce the P-3 Orion, though in Ilyushin's case the internal equipment resulted in a remarkable forward shift of the wing. The original circular-section pressurized fuselage is slightly lengthened and the windows replaced by a few small ports, and shallow weapon bays are added ahead of and behind the low-mounted wing. The forward shift of the wing may have

been in order to leave the long rear fuselage devoid of metal to improve performance of the MAD stinger in the extended tailcone. It cannot be accounted for merely by the weight, under the forward fuselage, of the surveillance radar, which resembles that of some Ka-25 helicopters. The absence of wing pylons is noteworthy. Crew is reported to number 12, eight being mission operators in the main tactical compartment. Production was probably about 100, completed in the early 1970s. In 1972 several operated from Egypt, and in 1979 Il-38s (called 'May' by NATO) operated from the Yemen. India bought three ex-AV-MF

(Soviet navy) aircraft, which fly from Goa with No. 315 Sqn.

Specification
Il-38 'May'
Type: maritime patrol and ASW aircraft
Powerplant: four 3169.2-ekW (4,250-ehp) Ivchenko AI-20M turboprops
Performance: (estimated) cruising speed 645 km/h (401 mph); range 7250 km (4,505 miles)
Weights: (estimated) empty 36300 kg (80,028 lb); maximum take-off 64000 kg (141,096 lb)
Dimensions: 37.40 m (122 ft 8.4 in); length 39.60 m (129 ft 11.1 in); height

10.17 m (33 ft 4.4 in); wing area 140.0 m^2 (1,507.0 sq ft)
Armament: not known, but certainly includes numerous sonobuoys and AS torpedoes housed internally; wing hardpoints have been reported but remain unconfirmed

Like its slightly earlier contemporary, the Orion, the Il-38 was evolved from a civilian airliner. Some 60 are believed to be operational with the Soviet navy and can be found over the Atlantic, Mediterranean and increasingly, over the Indian Ocean. Eight such aircraft are in Indian naval service.

Naval Helicopters

Today, the helicopter is one of the true work-horses of a modern navy. Its assignments include anti-submarine warfare, reconnaissance, assault, transport, search and rescue. In its combat role, it carries a formidable array of weaponry and will continue to be an increasingly vital component of a carrier air group.

The world's first operational helicopters, America's Sikorsky YR-4 and Germany's Flettner Fl 282, were both designed as flying observation posts; it was not envisaged that either might be turned into a combat machine, despite early experiments showing that a satisfactory degree of accuracy could be obtained in dropping bombs from a helicopter, particularly in forward flight. Nevertheless, a bomb-carrying version of the Fl 282 was on the drawing board before the end of World War II, and it was then that the Americans and Germans alike realized that the armed helicopter could prove invaluable in at least one operational role: anti-submarine warfare.

It was not until the advent of the Sikorsky S-55 that the Americans had a helicopter with a payload big enough to make it suitable for conversion to the ASW role. Even then, the payload of the S-55 (or HO4S-1, as it was called in the US Navy) was not big enough to allow it to undertake the dual role of hunter-killer, so the US Navy operated its HO4S-1s in pairs, one carrying detection gear and the other torpedoes. The system worked fairly well, but was overtaken in 1954 by the Sikorsky S-58, which

A Royal Navy Sea King helicopter hoists a crewman from the deck of a surfaced submarine. Sea King helicopters were used extensively in the Falklands campaign of 1982.

was capable of lifting two homing torpedoes as well as the necessary detection gear. The S-58 – or Westland Wessex, as the British version was known – was the true progenitor of the modern ASW helicopter.

In recent years there has been high demand for compact ASW helicopters designed to operate from cruisers, destroyers and frigates. Such helicopters, which can carry homing torpedoes and other weapons but are not necessarily fitted with search equipment, form a vital extension of the warship's fixed armament. One of the most effective small helicopters in this category was Britain's Westland Wasp, which operated from frigates and carried two homing torpedoes.

An interesting development in the field was the rotary-wing drone, typified by the US Navy's Gyrodyne QH-50. This little unmanned rotorcraft, which carried two acoustic torpedoes and was guided to its target by remote control, operated from more than 50 American destroyers at the height of the Cold War.

FRANCE

Aérospatiale Dauphin

The **Aérospatiale Dauphin** was originally planned as a modern replacement for the mass-produced Alouette III, but it quickly diversified into a large family with different fuselages, landing gears (fixed tailwheel type with forward spatted mainwheels or retractable tricycle gear, for example) and various single or twin engines. The original **SA 360C Dauphin** introduced the four-blade 'Starflex' main rotor of 11.50 m (37 ft 8¾ in) diameter, driven by a Turboméca Astazou XVIIIA turboshaft rated at 783 kW (1,050 shp). The first flew on 2 June 1972, and it was followed on 24 January 1975 by the first **SA 365C** powered by two 492-kW (660-shp) Turboméca Arriel engines. These earlier versions were superseded by the **SA 365N Dauphin 2** and its derivatives, which have a new structure making extensive use of composite materials such as glass-fibre, Nomex, Kevlar and Rohacell, and with carbon-fibre composite in the spars of the rotor blades. The SA 365N also features fully retractable tricycle landing gear, and is one of the fastest of all current helicopters, having set many world point-to-point speed records including Paris-London in 63 minutes at an average of just over 322 km/h (200 mph). In 1979 Aérospatiale beat strong US competition with a derived model, the **SA 366G**, powered by two Avco Lycoming LTS101 engines of 507 kW (680 shp) each; an initial order of 90 was placed by the US Coast Guard which calls its very fully equipped offshore patrol model the **HH-65A Dolphin**. An even bigger contract gained in 1980 by France was the vast 'Sawari' order for military equipment for Saudi Arabia. Part of this comprised 24 **SA 365F Dauphin 2** helicopters of a new type, the final 20 being equipped with four AS.15TT anti-ship missiles. This anti-ship Dauphin which competes with the existing Lynx with Sea Skua missiles was developed with Saudi funds and has a Thomson-CSF Agrion radar providing guidance for the AS.15TT which itself was financed by this contract. This missile is effective over ranges up to 15 km (9.3 miles). Aerospatiale sell Dauphin 2 helicopters for ASW SAR missions flown with sonobuoys (with provision for sonar) MAD and two homing torpedoes, and other naval duties. The Saudis used Dauphin 2 with AS.15TT during the 1990 Gulf War.

Specification:
Aérospatiale SA 365F Dauphin 2
Type: anti-ship attack helicopter
Powerplant: two 710-shp (529-kW) Turboméca Arriel turboshafts
Armament: four Aérospatiale AS.15TT radar-guided missiles
Performance: maximum cruising speed (clean) 252 km/h (156 mph) at sea level and 259 km/h (161 mph) at medium height; range (maximum fuel, sea level) 898 km (558 miles); endurance (with maximum fuel) 4 hours 25 minutes, or (two missiles) 3 hours 45 minutes, or (four missiles) 2 hours 45 minutes
Weights: empty 2141 kg (4,720 lb); maximum take-off 3900 kg (8,598 lb)
Dimensions: main rotor diameter 11.93 m (39 ft 1¾ in); fuselage length 12.11 m (39 ft 8¾ in); height 3.99 m (13 ft 1 in); main rotor disc area 111.7 m² (1,202.4 sq ft)

The Dauphin 2 displays its four AS.15TT anti-ship missiles and bulbous radome housing the Agrion 15 radar system. This highly effective kit enables the aircraft to detect at long ranges and track 10 surface targets.

Above: The US Coast Guard operates 90 HH-65A Dauphins for short range recovery tasks which though not requiring offensive capabilities, *means the aircraft must have the latest maritime search and surveillance equipment.*

FRANCE

Aérospatiale Super Frelon

The largest helicopter to be produced in quantity in Western Europe, the **Aérospatiale Super Frelon** was built mainly for air force, army and commercial customers, with regular land-type landing gear. The first production model, however, was the **SA 321G**, of which 24 were supplied to the French Aéronavale in 1966-70. They are used by Flottille 32F based at Lanvéoc-Poulmic in Brittany, where among other duties they have the vital task of supporting the French national deterrent by shadowing each 'Redoutable' class strategic missile submarine as it departs from its base at the Île Longue on combat patrol. The whole point of the submarine-based deterrent is that its location should be unknown to a potential enemy, and should a submarine be followed by another submarine belonging to a potentially hostile power its future position would clearly always be known. Thus the SA 321G helicopters of 32F make certain that there is no other submarine anywhere in the vicinity as each French missile submarine goes on patrol. To be effective the friendly vessel should be accompanied for the greatest possible distance, and here the large size and long range of the Super Frelon is an advantage. All Super Frelons have a six-blade main rotor in order to absorb the power of the three engines within the same diameter as the much lighter twin-engined S-61 Sea King. The cockpit is occupied by the pilot and co-pilot, who have the services of comprehensive navaids and communications systems including Doppler, while in the main tactical compartment is the mission crew of three

The primary mission of the Aéronavale's Super Frelon is the prevention of Soviet submarines shadowing French missile-carrying submarines as they leave port. This model has also fired Exocet missiles in anti-ship trials, but the helicopter does not normally carry these weapons.

who manage the detection, tracking and attack equipment. When delivered the SA 321G helicopters were fitted with ORB 31 Héraclès I radar in the nose, but since 1981 they have been converted to take the ORB 32

One useful attribute of the Super Frelon is its ability to put down at sea. The sealed hull is a feature borrowed from the Sikorsky S-61.

Héraclès II which has 360° all-round coverage and twice the operating power. There is a main tactical display on which the returns from a dipping sonar can also be presented, and other equipment includes towing and MCM (mine countermeasures) gear and a rescue hoist of 275 kg (606 lb) capacity. Frequently these large machines operate in groups of three or even four, to make certain no submarine could

escape detection.

Specification
Type: ASW and ASV shore-based helicopter
Powerplant: three 1,570-shp (1171-kW) Turboméca Turmo IIIC6 turboshafts
Armament: up to four homing anti-submarine torpedoes or two AS.39 Exocet anti-ship missiles

Performance: cruising speed 248 km/h (154 mph); range with 3500-kg (7,716-lb) mission load 1020 km (633 miles); endurance in ASW role 4 hours
Weights: empty 6863 kg (15,130 lb); maximum take-off 13000 kg (28,660 lb)
Dimensions: main rotor diameter 18.90 m (62 ft 0 in); length overall 23.0 m (75 ft 6½ in); height 6.76 m (22 ft 2¼ in); main rotor disc area 280.5 m² (3,019.0 sq ft)

ITALY
Agusta-Bell AB.204, AB.205 and AB.212

The Italian company Costruzione Aeronautiche Giovanni Agusta has built Bell helicopters under licence since 1952. Large numbers of the Model 204, the first and smallest member of the 'Huey' family, were built under the designation **Agusta AB.204** for many customers, some of them (including the Swedish navy version) being powered by a Rolls-Royce Gnome turboshaft in place of the usual T53. Production switched in 1966 to the larger multi-role **AB.205**, and went on in 1971 to include the twin-engined **AB.212**. In contrast to Bell Helicopter Textron, which has concentrated on 'Huey' models for army and air force customers, Agusta has placed much emphasis on a special **AB.212ASW** version, extensively redesigned and fully equipped for anti-submarine warfare, with secondary roles which include anti-ship missile attack and SAR (search and rescue). The basic ASW role equipment includes a search radar specially designed for good discrimination in rough seas, with the rotating scanner above the cockpit. The radar is automatically linked to the AB.212ASW navigation system (Tacan, Doppler radar, UHF homer and navigation computer) to give a continuously updated picture of the overall tactical situation. There is an ad-

vanced flight-control and auto-stabilization system, one of its modes being auto-approach to hover at a chosen spot and at a height set by the radar altimeter. An IFF/SIF transponder is fitted, and various advanced ECM systems can be installed. The basic ASW sensor is a low-frequency variable-depth sonar usable down to a depth of 137 m (450 ft). The auto flight control can hold the helicopter stationary over any chosen 'dip point' in a complex sonar search pattern. ASW weapons are listed separately. In the anti-ship mission guided missiles of various kinds may be carried, though the usual pattern on most existing machines is the AS.12. These wire-guided weapons are steered by the

co-pilot using the XM-58 gyro-stabilized sight system. Clearly the obsolescent missile will soon be replaced by AB.212ASW operators with a more modern weapon. This helicopter can also serve in the role of stand-off guidance platform for anti-ship missiles fired by other friendly launchers, in particular the ship-fired Otomat 2 cruise missile. In this role the helicopter is fitted with the search radar and a TG-2 real-time target data transmission system.

Specification
AB.212ASW
Type: multi-role helicopter for shipboard operation
Powerplant: one 1,875-shp (1398-kW)

The Marinavia (Italian naval air arm) deploys 28 AB.212 ASWs aboard its surface warships for both anti-submarine and anti-ship work.

Pratt & Whitney Canada T400 (PT6T-6) Turbo Twin Pac with two gas-turbine power sections
Armament: two Mk 46 AS torpedoes, or two depth charges or two anti-ship missiles (typically AS.12)
Performance: maximum speed 196 km/h (122 mph); cruising speed 185 km/h (115 mph); search endurance 3 hours 12 minutes; maximum range with auxiliary tanks (no reserve) 667 km (414 miles)
Weights: empty 3420 kg (7,540 lb); maximum 5070 kg (11,176 lb);
Dimensions: main rotor diameter 14.63 m (48 ft 0 in); length overall 17.40 m (57 ft 1 in); height 4.53 m (14 ft 10¼ in); main rotor disc area 173.9 m² (1,872.0 sq ft)

EH Industries EH 101

The most powerful helicopter ever designed in Western Europe, the **EH 101** has its genesis in an SKR (Sea King Replacement) study by the British MoD (Navy) in 1977. Westland responded with a proposal designated WG.34, but meanwhile the Italian navy had come up with a similar requirement, though one with the accent on shore basing rather than operations from warships. Westland and Agusta decided to collaborate, formed EHI (Elicotteri Helicopter Industries Ltd) and, with extreme care and underpinned by much research, drew up the design for the EH 101 as the next-generation helicopter for the British and Italian navies. The same basic machine is also being developed as a civil passenger and utility cargo transport whose engines, rotor systems, airframe and main systems are common

with those of the naval variant. The latter is very like a scaled-down CH-53E in configuration, though the three engines are arranged symmetrically around the main rotor. The main cabin is 6.5 m (21 ft 4 in) long, 2.5 m (8 ft 2½ in) wide and, allowing for interior soundproofing, 1.82 m (5 ft 11½ in) high, all dimensions exactly tailored to the missions, as are the folded dimensions for easy shipboard stowage. The maritime roles for which the EH 101 has been designed are ASW, anti-ship surveillance, anti-surface vessel strike, amphibious operations, SAR, AEW and vertrep (vertical replenishment). An unusual feature is that, despite the striking differences between these missions (for example, between cargo vertrep, ASW, and AEW with a giant radar) all role changes can be carried out on board ship. The main five-blade

rotor has composite blades with extended-chord tips of the BERP type as fitted to the latest Lynx and Westland 30, while the tail carries a four-blade rotor and can be power-folded, like the main rotor blades, for reduced overall dimensions. Use of three engines confers outstanding safety for flight at maximum weight in all weathers, and General Electric expect the same basic engine to mature at powers some 50 per cent greater than that given in the specification. First flight has been set for early 1985, with production machines following in 1988. The EH 101 will equip the Royal Navy Type 23 frigates and the extensive flying trials unit was commissioned in December 1998.

Specification
EH 101 Naval

Type: multi-role maritime helicopter
Powerplant: three 1,600-shp (1198-kW) General Electric T700-401 turboshafts
Armament: enclosed weapons bay able to accommodate wide range of torpedoes (Marconi Stingray for RN version) and other stores; total disposable load 6085 kg (13,411 lb)
Performance: maximum cruising speed 278 km/h (173 mph); endurance at distant station with full weapon load (dunking ASW role) 5 hours
Weights: maximum take-off 13000 kg (28,660 lb)
Dimensions: main rotor diameter 18.59 m (61 ft 0 in); length overall 22.90 m (75 ft 1½ in), and folded 15.85 m (52 ft 0 in); height 6.50 m (21 ft 4 in); main rotor disc area 271.72 m² (2,925.0 sq ft)

Westland Wasp

Though its development can be traced back to the **Saro P.531**, flown in 1958, the **Westland Wasp HAS.Mk 1** emerged in October 1962 as a highly specialized machine for flying useful missions from small ships, such as frigates and destroyers with limited deck pad area. The missions were ASW (anti-submarine warfare) and general utility, but the Wasp was not sufficiently powerful to carry a full kit of ASW sensors as well as weapons, and thus in this role relies on the sensors of its parent vessel and other friendly naval forces, which tell it where to drop its homing torpedoes. In the anti-surface vessel role the Wasp is autonomous, and though it has no radar it can steer the AS.12 wire-guided missile under visual conditions over ranges up to 8 km (5 miles). Other duties include SAR (search and rescue), liaison, VIP ferrying, casualty evacuation with two internally carried stretchers, ice reconnaissance and photography/survey. The cockpit is quite well equipped for bad-weather operation with auto-stabilization, radar altimeter, beacon receivers, UHF radio and UHF homer, and in RN service limited EW provisions. The stalky quadricycle landing gear has wheels that castor so that, while the machine can be rotated on deck, it cannot roll in any direction even in a rough sea. Sprag (locking)

brakes are fitted to arrest all movement. Provision was made for various hauldown systems such as Beartrap to facilitate alighting on small pads in severe weather. Deliveries to the Royal Navy began in 1963, and a few were active in Operation 'Corporate' in the South Atlantic right at the end of their active lives when most had been replaced in RN service by the Lynx. Wasp HAS.Mk 1s operated from eight ships in that campaign, all assigned to RN No. 829 Squadron. They flew almost 1,000 hours in 912 combat sorties during which they made no fewer than 3,627 deck landings. Most were used in reconnaissance and utility missions, though several operated in the casevac role. Three, two from HMS *Endurance* and one from the frigate HMS *Plymouth*, engaged the Argentine submarine *Santa Fe* and holed its conning tower with AS.12 missiles which passed clean through before exploding. Other Wasps serve with the Royal Australian, Brazilian, Malaysian and South African navies

Specification
Type: light multi-role ship-based helicopter
Powerplant: one 710-shp (529-kW) Rolls-Royce Nimbus 503 turboshaft
Armament: two Mk 44 AS torpedoes or two AS.12 anti-ship missiles

Performance: maximum speed with weapons 193 km/h (120 mph); cruising speed 177 km/h (110 mph); range 435 km (270 miles)
Weights: empty 1566 kg (3,452 lb); maximum take-off 2495 kg (5,500 lb)
Dimensions: main rotor diameter 9.83 m (32 ft 3 in); length overall 12.29 m (40 ft 4 in); height 3.56 m (11 ft 8 in); main rotor disc area 75.90 m² (816.86 sq ft)

The Westland Wasp took a long time to see action. In service with the Royal Navy for nearly 20 years, Wasps were very active during the Falklands war, just in the twilight of their careers.

Westland Wessex

The **Westland Wessex** is an excellent helicopter very quickly derived by Westland from the American Sikorsky S-58, to replace the all-British Bristol 192 as the Royal Navy's first dedicated ASW helicopter. The original version was the **Wessex HAS.Mk 1**, powered by a Napier (today Rolls-Royce) Gazelle of 1,450 shp (1081 kW), and this was supplanted by the **Wessex HAS.Mk 3** version popularly called the Camel because of its humpbacked search radar above the rear fuselage. These ASW versions had almost been replaced by Sea Kings at the start of Operation 'Corporate' in April 1982, just two being sent to the war zone, XM837 aboard HMS *Glasgow* and XP142 aboard *Antrim*, both assigned to No. 737 Squadron. The latter caught the Argentine submarine *Santa Fe* and

crippled it with depth charges and machine-gun fire; the helicopter returned to the UK peppered with splinter holes and was retired to the FAA Museum. Its sister was the last aircraft lost to enemy action when, on 12 June, it was destroyed by a shore-fired Exocet which passed through its hangar. Much more important numerically is the **Wessex HU.Mk 5** version, the Royal Marine Commando assault version, to which the specification refers. These twin-engine machines once numbered almost 100. Virtually all those in the naval inventory accompanied the Task Force, No. 845 Squadron aboard RFAs (Royal Fleet Auxiliaries) and other ships being backed up by two new squadrons (nos 847 and 848) hurriedly formed from second-line units and stored Wessexes. The latter lost

half its aircraft aboard *Atlantic Conveyor*, so most of the action fell to No. 847 Squadron, one of whose Wessex HU.Mk 5s knocked out the Argentine HQ in the Port Stanley police station using a newly installed AS.12 missile. Another important operator of the maritime Wessex is the Royal Australian Navy, which still has 10 **Wessex HAS.Mk 31B** (basically similar to the Wessex HAS.Mk 3) helicopters, usually based at Nowra, having previously been embarked aboard HMAS *Melbourne*. Another nine are in storage. They operate chiefly in the SAR role, and like their British counterparts have been progressively updated with improved avionics and role equipment. Their place was taken in the ASW role by the Sea King MK 50. Other Wessex may still be in use in Brunei, Ghana and Iraq, though not in maritime roles.

Specification
Wessex HU.Mk 5
Type: commando assault helicopter
Powerplant: one Rolls-Royce Coupled Gnome twin-turboshaft with two power sections each rated at 1,350 shp (1007 kW), but with combined output limited to 1,550 shp (1156 kW)
Armament: role kit can include two 7.62-mm (0.3-in) GPMGs firing ahead, one or two 20-mm cannon, two or four AS.11 wire-guided missiles, or rocket pods
Performance: maximum speed 214 km/h (133 mph); cruising speed 195 km/h (121 mph); range 769 km (478 miles)
Weights: empty 3927 kg (8,657 lb); maximum take-off 6120 kg (13,500 lb)
Dimensions: main rotor diameter 17.07 m (56 ft 0 in); length overall 20.03 m (65 ft 9 in); height 4.93 m (16 ft 2 in); main rotor disc area 228.81 m² (2,463.0 sq ft)

Westland Sea King

UK

In 1959, the year in which the Sikorsky S-61 helicopter first flew, Westland of the UK concluded a licence agreement, and the company developed the **Westland Sea King HAS.Mk 1** as the new ASW (anti-submarine warfare) helicopter of the Royal Navy, delivering 56 in 1969-72. Compared with the US Navy HSS-2 (SH-3), the Sea King HAS.Mk 1 has equipment for completely autonomous operation with no help from the parent warship, including AW 391 dorsal radar, Plessey Type 195 dunking sonar and a fully fitted tactical compartment for managing a whole ASW operation. These machines have been modified to **Sea King HAS.Mk 2** standard with more powerful Rolls-Royce Gnome engines and improved equipment; 21 Sea King HAS.Mk 2 helicopters also being built new. The **Sea King HAS.Mk 3** is the RAF search-and-rescue model with very complete equipment and great versatility (SAR models carry up to 22 rescuees including stretcher casualties). The **Sea King HC.Mk 4** is the version of the Command for the Royal Navy (used for Royal Marine assault transport) with the shipboard features (such as folding blades and tail) but simple fixed landing gear and fitted for 27 troops or 6,000 lb (2722 kg) of cargo. The **Sea King HAS.Mk 5** is the current RN ASW model with dramatically uprated avionics, all Sea King HAS.Mk 2s were converted to this standard; 17 were built new after the Falklands (when Sea Kings flew almost non-stop in terrible weather) nine more were ordered. The Royal Navy operates a small number of Sea King.

AEW helicopters in response to a need appreciated in the Falklands war of 1982. This model has Thorn-EMI Searchwater radar with its antenna in an inflated and swivelling radome projecting from the right side of the fuselage. Key items in the Sea King HAS.Mk 5's avionics suite are the MEL Sea Searcher surveillance radar with a radome of considerably different shape and size, provision for the launch of passive sonobuoys, LAPADS (Lightweight Acoustic Processing and Display System) by Marconi for the quicker and more precise handling of acoustic data, and a better display system. To permit the installation of the extra equipment, the cabin has been extended aft by 1.83 m (6 ft). Westland have exported ASW and SAR Sea Kings (including the upgraded **Sea King Mk 50** with Bendix sonar for Australia) to eight countries. The **Commando**, which first flew on 12 September 1973, is a tactical transport similar to the Sea King HC.Mk 4.

Specification
Type: ASW and multi-role helicopter
Armament: extremely comprehensive ASW sensors and systems plus up to four Mk 46 torpedoes or Mk 11 depth charges
Powerplant: two 1,660-shp (1238-kW) Rolls-Royce Gnome H.1400-1 turboshafts
Performance: cruising speed at maximum weight 208 km/h (129 mph); range on standard fuel 1230 km (764 miles)
Weights: empty 6201 kg (13,672 lb); maximum take-off 9525 kg (21,000 lb)
Dimensions: main rotor diameter 18.9 m (62 ft 0 in); fuselage length 17.01 m (55 ft 9¾ in); height 5.13 m (16 ft 10 in); main rotor disc area 280.5 m² (3,019.1 sq ft)

Above: Following the Falklands conflict, Westland Sea King HAS.Mk 2s and HAR.Mk 3s were hastily converted to the AEW role by the addition of Thorn-EMI Searchwater radar in rotating 'kettledrums' on the side of the fuselage.

Left: Known as the 'Grey Whales', the Sea King HAR.Mk 3 detachment from No. 202 Sqn RAF based at Port Stanley in the Falklands has provided sterling service in the SAR role, whilst also giving much help with transport duties around the islands and surrounding ocean.

Right: Another operator of the SAR (search and rescue) Westland Sea King is the Norwegian air force, which has 11 of this Mk 43 version serving with No. 330 Sqn. Pairs are detached around the coast but home base is Bodö. Westland also supplied an uprated Sea King Mk 42A.

Left: The Westland Sea King Mk 50 is the standard anti-submarine helicopter of the Royal Australian Navy's Fleet Air Arm group serving with HS-817 squadron. The Mk 50 improved on earlier models and led to the HAS.Mk 2 for the Royal Navy.

Westland Lynx

On technical grounds the **Westland Lynx** is the best medium shipboard helicopter in the world, and from the original **WG.13** concept which formed part of the Anglo-French helicopter agreement of 1967 has been derived a series of uprated versions which not only bring in additional missions but also greatly enhanced capabilities. Though all are similar in terms of overall dimensions, the later versions have increased power for operation at greater weights, and the recent development of upgraded models of **Westland 30** (the large-fuselage variant) has opened the way to machines which completely equal the mission capability of the Sikorsky SH-60B but in a smaller and more compact helicopter. The original naval model, the **Lynx HAS.Mk 2** for the Royal Navy, was actually the first production variant to fly, in February 1976. Powered by two 750-shp (559-kW) Gem 2 engines, this has a gross weight of 4309 kg (9,500 lb), yet carries a crew of two (three in the ASW or SAR roles) plus all equipment for a wide range of shipboard missions including ASW, SAR, ASV (anti-surface vessel) search and strike, reconnaissance, troop transport (typically 10 troops), fire support, communication

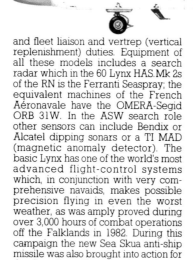

The Westland Lynx Mk 21 for the Brazilian navy is based on the Royal Navy HAS.Mk 2 with Seaspray surveillance radar, various anti-submarine devices and Sea Skua anti-ship missiles.

and fleet liaison and vertrep (vertical replenishment) duties. Equipment of all these models includes a search radar which in the 60 Lynx HAS.Mk 2s of the RN is the Ferranti Seaspray; the equivalent machines of the French Aéronavale have the OMERA-Segid ORB 31W. In the ASW search role other sensors can include Bendix or Alcatel dipping sonars or a TI MAD (magnetic anomaly detector). The basic Lynx has one of the world's most advanced flight-control systems which, in conjunction with very comprehensive navaids, makes possible precision flying in even the worst weather, as was amply proved during over 3,000 hours of combat operations off the Falklands in 1982. During this campaign the new Sea Skua anti-ship missile was also brought into action for the first time. Though other missiles

can be carried the Sea Skua was used also effectively in the Gulf War. In 1979 the Royal Netherlands navy received the upgraded **Lynx Mk 27**, first of a Mk 2 family with Gem41-1 engines and weights ranging from 4736–4990- kg (10,500–11,000-lb). The most recent batches for the RN and Aéornavale are of this new standard which offers greater capability. **Lynx 3** development to 5443-kg (12,000-lb) has been completed and **Lynx 4** will take the weight to 6577-kg (14,500-lb) using a five blade rotor. The Royal Navy uses the Mk 8 and the safer Lynx is in service with Malaysia and South Korea.

Specification
Lynx HAS.Mk 2
Type: multi-role shipboard helicopter
Powerplant: two 750/900-shp (559/671-

kW) Rolls-Royce Gem 2 turboshafts
Armament: two Mk 44, Mk 46 or Sting Ray homing AS torpedoes, or four BAe Sea Skua anti-ship missiles, or two Mk 11 depth charges, in each case with full mission equipment
Performance: maximum cruising speed 232 km/h (144 mph); time on ASW hover at 93 km (58 miles) 2 hours; ferry range 1046 km (650 miles)
Weights: empty 2740 kg (6,040 lb); maximum take-off (early machines) 4309 kg (9,500 lb) or (later machines) 4763 kg (10,500 lb)
Dimensions: main rotor diameter 12.80 m (42 ft 0 in); length overall 15.16 m (49 ft 9 in); height 3.60 m (11 ft 9¾ in); main rotor disc area 128.71 m² (1,385.4 sq ft)

One of the most important combinations of missile and helicopter in the western world is the lynx and the Sea Skua. These proved deadly in the South Atlantic in 1982.

USA/JAPAN
Boeing Vertol 107

First flown on 22 April 1958, the **Boeing Vertol Model 107** twin-turbine tandem-rotor helicopter was built by the company in large numbers as the **H-46** series for the US Navy and US Marine Corps, plus other customers. The same basic design remains in production in various versions in Japan, as the **Kawasaki KV-107** family. The original production model was ordered in 1961 after winning a US Marine Corps competition for an assault troop transport. This basic model, in service as various forms of **CH-46 Sea Knight**, accommodates a typical total of 26 troops or 15 casualty litters. The US Navy bought the **UH-46** model, with the same accommodation but also able to carry 3175 kg (7,000 lb) of cargo, including vehicles loaded through the full-section rear ramp door, for use in the vertrep (vertical replenishment) of ships at sea. Both Sea Knight families can have rescue hoists and are equipped for limited amphibious operation, though they are not intended for sustained alighting on rough seas. A total of 624 of both models was delivered by 1971, and in recent years most surviving examples have been subjected to major update programmes which include fitting glassfibre rotor blades. The best 273 Sea Knights in US Marine

Corps service were gradually rebuilt and **CH-46E** helicopters with more powerful engine listed in the data, replacing the 1250- or 14,00-shp (932- or 1044-kW) T58 engines originally fitted as well as numerous improvements to improve reliability, rescue capability and ability to survive a crash on land or on water. From 1981 a total of 368 kits were supplied to provide further modifications to improve safety and reduce costs. Sweden uses the Gnome-engined **HKP-7** version for ASW and minesweeping duties, while the major licence-production by Kawasaki has resulted in 12 new versions which include several for naval use. Most are long-range SAR (search and rescue) and cargo/troop transports, but the naval **KV-107II-3** is a specialized MCM (mine countermeasures) helicopter, of which nine serve with the JMSDF's 111th Air Wing. This version has uprated engines (1,400 shp/1044 kW) instead of 1,250 shp/932 kW) and comprehensive equipment for minesweeping and retrieval, as well as long-range tanks, cargo hook and towing gear. Another operator is Canada, whose **CH-113** versions are being updated to an improved maritime SAR standard with extra fuel, weather

radar, a water dam for use of the rear ramp at sea and an APU (auxiliary power unit).

Specification
CH-46E Sea Knight
Type: multi-role transport helicopter
Powerplant: two 1,870-shp (1394-kW) General Electric T58-16 turboshafts
Armament: none in most versions (Sweden uses AS torpedoes)
Performance: maximum speed 267 km/h (166 mph); cruising speed 193 km/h (120 mph); range (3000-kg/

Workhorse of the US Navy for nearly 20 years, the UH-46 Sea Knight serves as a ship replenishment helicopter. Japan builds the type under licence.

6,614-lb payload) 175 km (109 miles)
Weights: empty 5240 kg (11,585 lb); maximum take-off 9706 kg (21,400 lb)
Dimensions: main rotor diameter 15.24 m (50 ft 0 in); length overall 25.70 m (84 ft 4 in); height 5.09 m (16 ft 8½ in); rotor disc area 364.8 m² (3,927.0 sq ft)

USA
Kaman SH-2 Seasprite

The original prototype **Kaman HU-2K** (later styled **UH-2A Seasprite**) utility helicopter flew on 2 July 1959, and from 1962 Kaman delivered 190 of these very attractive machines each powered by a T58 engine and with fully retractable forward-mounted main landing gears. The **UH-2A** and **UH-2B** could each carry a 1814-kg (4,000-lb) slung load or 11 passengers, and did sterling work in planeguard, SAR, fleet reconnaissance, vertrep (vertical replenishment) and utility transport duties, operating from many surface warships as well as at shore bases. From 1967 all available Seasprites have been converted to twin-T58 helicopters with full engine-out safety and generally improved performance plus better weight-carrying capabilities. Among many other models the most important current variant is the **SH-2F** (Mk 1 LAMPS, for Light Airborne Multi-purpose System) for shipbased ASW and anti-ship missile defence with secondary SAR, observation and utility capability, in all weather conditions.

With a crew of pilot, co-pilot, ad sensor operator, the SH-2F can carry full ASW gear including LN-66HP surveillance radar, AN/ASQ-18 MAD, AN/ALR-54 passive detection receiver, sonobuoys and comprehensive nav/com and display systems. A 1814-kg (4,000-lb) cargo ability remains and a 272-kg (600-lb) rescue hoist. From 1973 Kaman delivered conversions of

Anti-submarine warfare is just one of the Seasprite's tasks. The type is a multi-purpose machine, taking in

earlier models and 88 new SH-2Fs, followed in 1983–4 by 18 additional machines. The Seasprite LAMPS MK 1 was supplemented by Sikorsky SH-60 LAMPS Mk III in the 1980s and remained in service in the 1990s in

observation, missile defence and general utility work.

the US navy's older surface vessels. The new SH-2G Super Seasprite has given the design a new lease of life in export markets. Operators include Egypt, Australia and New Zealand.

Specification
Kaman SH-2F Seasprite
Type: shipboard helicopter (see text)
Armament: one or two AS torpedoes (usually Mk 46)
Powerplant: two 1,350-shp (1007-kW) General Electric T58-8F turboshafts
Performance: maximum speed 265 km/h (165 mph); range with maximum internal fuel 679 km (422 miles)
Weights: empty 3193 kg (7,040 lb); maximum take-off 6033 kg (13,300 lb)
Dimensions: main rotor diameter 13.41 m (44 ft 0 in); fuselage length 12.3 m (40 ft 6 in); height 4.72 m (15 ft 6 in); main rotor disc area 141.25 m² (1,521.0 sq ft)

The Seasprite is a neat, ship-based utility and rescue helicopter. Here it has dropped marker dye in the water prior to lifting the 'victim' to safety.

Anti-Ship Helicopters

The anti-ship helicopter is as a species relatively young. This is mainly because its principal weapon, the sea-skimming missile, did not exist until after 1960, and did not become effective and common until the late 1970s. Now that the two have been brought together the result is a singularly potent combination which is especially effective against small but important naval vessels such as missile-armed FPBs (fast patrol boats). Helicopters are already widely used for coastal patrol (catching blockade-runners, drug smugglers and the like), and larger machines can carry missiles powerful enough to disable major warships.

Naval helicopters were armed with wire-guided anti-tank missiles such as the French SS.12 weapon to allow them to support amphibious landings. Even this puny weapon was also deadly against small ships. The anti-ship helicopter had to wait for the anti-ship missile which flies just above the ocean surface.

Anti-ship missiles for launch from aeroplanes date from the immediate post-war period, but helicopter-launched versions almost all date from after 1967, when the destruction of an Israeli destroyer by missiles stirred naval staffs from lethargy. Italy's Sistel Marte (Sea Killer 2) France's AM.39 Exocet, the USA's Harpoon, Japans ASM-1 and Germany's Kormoran all date from this period, though the last two have not been adapted for use from helicopters. Much more recently the British Sea Skua and French A-15 have triggered off a new family of smaller anti-ship missiles specifically designed to be launched from helicopters. The Sea Skua was developed to deal with the Soviet Nanuchka type corvette, which was armed with SA.N.4. short-range missiles. The specification called for longer range than SA.N.4 and sufficient warhead to disable corvettes and fast attack craft.

In virtually every case the helicopter or a co-operating aircraft has to use surveillance radar to detect and identify the hostile ship(s). This is one of the weak links in the procedure, in that the helicopter has to be well above the horizon as seen from the ship, and then illuminate the ship with radar signals which trigger the ship's own ESM (electronic support measures) warning systems. The missile is then released towards the target, and under its rocket, turbojet or ramjet propulsion accelerates to high subsonic speed and drops to a very low altitude (typically 33 ft/10 m). Most of its flight is made under self-contained autopilot or inertial guidance; when it is within a few miles of the target the missile activates its own seeker (homing head). Again, this is almost always a radar, which again alerts the ship by illuminating it with radar signals so that the missile can home on the reflections. The ship will probably turn stern-on to reduce its apparent size, and fire clouds of chaff and decoys to try to cause the missile's radar to 'break lock' and instead aim for the chaff or decoys.

Requirements of any ship-based helicopter include small overall size, complete all-weather and night capability, advanced flight-control and autostabilization, and the ability to land on a small steel deck that is pitching and rolling to the extent that most people could not stand upright on it. Various haul-down systems have been developed in which the helicopter lowers a grapnel on a cable to catch a grid on the deck, thus enabling a winch (usually in the helicopter) to pull the machine down with improved security until the wheels touch. Special landing gear is needed, with sprag (pawl/ratchet) locking brakes and wheels that can be locked in offset (castored) positions so that the helicopter cannot roll off the deck into the sea. Although Sea Skua was used to disable an Argentine patrol ship its great success was the Battle of Bubiyan Channel, when three Lynxes knocked out the majority of the Iraqi fleet in a few minutes.

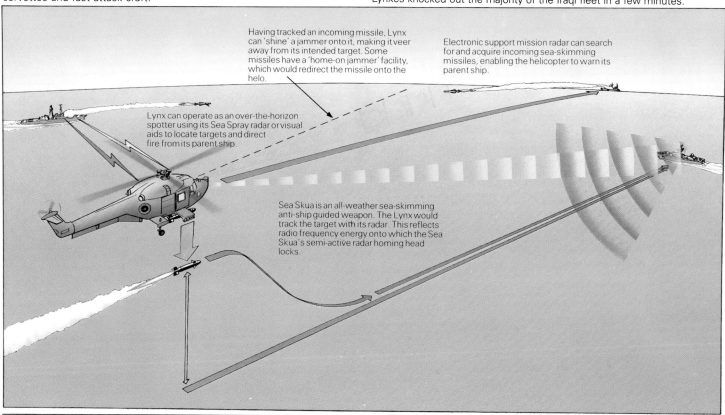

Having tracked an incoming missile, Lynx can 'shine' a jammer onto it, making it veer away from its intended target. Some missiles have a 'home-on jammer' facility, which would redirect the missile onto the helo.

Electronic support mission radar can search for and acquire incoming sea-skimming missiles, enabling the helicopter to warn its parent ship.

Lynx can operate as an over-the-horizon spotter using its Sea Spray radar or visual aids to locate targets and direct fire from its parent ship.

Sea Skua is an all-weather sea-skimming anti-ship guided weapon. The Lynx would track the target with its radar. This reflects radio frequency energy onto which the Sea Skua's semi-active radar homing head locks.

USA
Sikorsky S-61/H-3 Sea King

One of the most important helicopter families yet developed, and a mainstay of the Western world's shipborne anti-submarine, forces, the **Sikorsky SH-3 Sea King** series began life as the **HSS-2** anti-submarine helicopter for the US Navy. The prototype of this helicopter first flew on 11 March 1959, and the helicopter, which has the company designation Sikorsky S-61B, was the first which could carry all the sensors and weapons needed for ASW missions without external help (though the US Navy policy has been to regard the aircraft as an extension of the ASW surface vessel from which it operates, so that helicopter-carried sensors detect the hostile submarine before the warship is called in for the 'kill'). New

features included an amphibious boat hull with retractable tailwheel landing gear, twin turboshaft engines (for power, lightness, reliability and single-engine flight capability) above the cabin and an unobstructed tactical compartment for two sonar operators whose sensors include a dipping sono-buoy lowered through a keel hatch. Above the extensive avionic systems is an attitude-hold autopilot and a sonar coupler which maintains exact height and station in conjunction with a radar

The reliability and versatility of the SH-3 family have put it at the forefront of naval helicopters since it entered service with the US Navy in 1961.

altimeter and Doppler radar. Over 1,100 H-3 type helicopters have been built, the ASW models being SH-3s in four basic models. The SH-3A was the original model with 1,250-shp (933-kW) General Electric T58-8B turboshafts, the SH-3D is the upgraded version described below; the SH-3G is the utility version; and the SH-3H is the multi-role model fitted with dipping sonar and MAD gear for ASW and search radar for the detection of incoming anti-ship missiles. Agusta makes versions in Italy, some with Marte anti-ship missile armament, and Westland's Sea King is described separately. The S-61R, first flown in 1963, led to a new CH-3 family of multi-role land-based transports with tricycle landing gear and a rear ramp for loading vehicles or bulky cargo. One model, the HH-3E of the USAF Aerospace Rescue and Recovery Service, is famed under the name Jolly Green Giant. It has an in-flight-refuelling probe, hoist and much special role gear, and has also been

developed into the radar-equipped HH-3F Pelican advanced search-and-rescue helicopter for the US Coast Guard. Export models have included the S-61A utility transport based on the S-61B, and the S-61D anti-submarine model based on the SH-3D. SH-3s are in Canadian service under the designation CH-124, and American variants are RH-3 minesweeping and VH-3 executive transport helicopters.

Specification
Sikorsky SH-3D Sea King
Type: ASW helicopter
Armament: external hardpoints for total of 381 kg (840 lb) of weapons, normally comprising two Mk 46 torpedoes
Powerplant: two 1,400-shp (1044-kW) General Electric T58-10 turboshafts
Performance: maximum speed 267 km/h (166 mph); range with maximum fuel and 10 per cent reserves 1005 km (625 miles)
Weights: empty 5382 kg (11,865 lb); maximum take-off 9752 kg (21,500 lb)

Dimensions: main rotor diameter 18.9 m (62 ft 0 in); fuselage length 16.69 m (54 ft 9 in); height 5.13 m (16 ft 10 in); main rotor disc area 280.5 m² (3,019.1 sq ft)

The highly successful S-61/H-3 Sea King has been built under license by Agusta in Italy. This SH-3D operates primarily in the anti-submarine role.

USA

Sikorsky S-70/SH-60B Seahawk

To meet the severe demands of the US Navy, the SH-60B Seahawk is by far the largest, most powerful and most costly helicopter designed for normal operation from such ships as frigates and destroyers.

A derivative of the US Army's UH-60 Black Hawk, now entering widespread service with combat formations as a successor to the venerable Bell UH-1 series, the Sikorsky SH-60B Seahawk (produced under the company designation S-70L) won the US Navy's LAMPS III (Light Airborne Multi-Purpose System) competition in September 1977, and will be deployed aboard all the newest USN destroyers and frigates. A large, complex and extremely expensive machine, the SH-60B has two main missions: ASW and ASST, the latter meaning anti-ship surveillance and targeting (the aerial detection of incoming sea-skimming anti-ship missiles, and the provision of radar-derived data for similar weapons launched from US warships. Secondary missions include SAR, medevac (casualty evacuation) and vertrep (vertical replenishment, ie bringing supplies to warships at sea). The basic airframe differs from that of the UH-60 in being marinized, with a sealed tailboom, tailwheel moved forward quite considerably and inflatable bags for emergency buoyancy, and with an electrically folding main rotor and pneumatically folding tail (including upward-hinged tailplanes). Other modifications are greater fuel capacity and the removal of armour for the pilot and co-pilot, and the type is also fitted with haul-down equipment to facilitate recovery onto small platforms when ships are pitching and rolling in heavy seas. Under the nose is the large APS-

124 radar, on the left side of the fuselage is a large vertical panel with 25 tubes for launching sonobuoys, low on the right of the rear fuselage is the pylon from which the MAD bird can be towed and there is extensive EW, navigation (including Doppler) and data processing equipment. The first prototype flew on 12 December 1979. By 1983 deliveries were beginning of a planned total of 204 for the US Navy, which became operational in 1984 and several navies have bought the S-70B1 variant.

Specification
Sikorsky SH-60B Seahawk
Type: multi-role shipboard helicopter
Armament: normally two Mk 46 anti-submarine torpedoes, but planned to include anti-ship missiles
Powerplant: two 1,690-shp (1261-kW) General Electric T700-401 turboshafts
Performance: maximum speed 234 km/h (145 mph); range about 373 km (500 miles)
Weights: empty 6300 kg (13,889 lb); maximum take-off 9926 kg (21,884 lb)
Dimensions: main rotor diameter

16.36 m (53 ft 8 in); fuselage length 15.26 m (50 ft 0¾ in); height 3.63 m (11 ft 11 in); main rotor disc area 210.05 m² (2,261 sq ft)

In common with most US Navy aircraft, the SH-60B Seahawk flies in low-visibility grey, with toned-down national markings. The machine carries an impressive array of radar and sensors to enable it to detect submarines and hostile sea skimming missiles, and to direct missiles from its mother ship.

Sikorsky S-65/H-53

Though the original **Sikorsky S-65** production model, the **CH-53A** assault transport of the US Marine Corps, has only two engines each of 2,850 shp (2125 kW), today's **CH-53E** has three engines each of 4,380 shp (3266 kW) and is the most powerful helicopter ever built outside the Soviet Union. Of the early versions, all are transports (139 CH-53As and 126 of the more powerful **CH-53D**, all for the US Marines) except for 15 transferred to the US Navy as **RH-53A** minesweeping machines, used to explore the possibilities of this new technique which had previously been tried only with machines of inadequate power, and the 20 **RH-53D** special-purpose machines with droptanks and inflight-refuelling probes, some of which were used in the unsuccessful mission to rescue Americans from imprisonment in Iran in April 1980. Today the chief versions are based on the CH-53D, which though hardly any larger has far greater power, a greatly modified airframe which folds for shipboard use, and the first seven-blade main rotor to be used (the even larger Soviet Mi-26 has an eight-blade rotor). The CH-53E was developed to meet a 1973 demand for an upgraded heavy-lift transport for the US Navy and US Marine Corps. With three much more powerful engines driving into a new transmission rated at 13,140 hp (9798 kW), the new

machine can carry payloads almost equal to the laden weight of the first version, though the main cabin is almost unchanged in dimensions and still seats a maximum of 55 troops. The CH-53E scores in its vastly increased lifting ability, without occupying significantly more deck space yet retaining compatibility with existing ships. The first production CH-53E flew on 13 December 1980, and by mid-1983 more than 40 had been delivered out of 72 ordered. In addition Sikorsky developed the derived **MH-53E** Sea Dragon as a MCM (mine countermeasures) helicopter, with very comprehensive minesweeping gear using all existing MCM devices. Enormously enlarged side sponsors accommodate extra 3785 litres (833 Imp gal) of fuel, for extended sweeping missions with the engines at sustained high power. The MH-53 E is also used around the

vertrep (vertical replenishment of ships) role, and has been made compatible with the cargo hold of the Lockheed C-5 Galaxy in order that it can be deployed rapidly anywhere in the world. The production prototype MH-53E in September 1983 and deliveries started in late 1986.

Specification
CH-53E
Type: heavy shipboard assault transport
Powerplant: three 4,380-shp (3266-kW) General Electric T64-416 turboshafts
Armament: normally none
Performance: maximum speed 315 km/h (196 mph); cruising speed at sea level 278 km/h (173 mph); ferry range 2075 km (1,290 miles)

The United States Marine Corps have ordered 72 of the Sikorsky CH-53E for rapid deployment of troops from ship to shore. These massive machines are the largest helicopters outside the USSR, with a lift capability of 14515 kg (32,000 lb).

Weights: empty 15071 kg (33,226 lb); maximum take-off 33339 kg (73,500 lb)
Dimensions: main rotor diameter 24.08 m (79 ft 0 in); length overall 30.19 m (99 ft 0½ in); height 8.66 m (28 ft 5 in); main rotor disc area 455.38 m² (4,902.0 sq ft)

Seven rotor blades are needed to transmit the colossal power of the CH-53E. This model is easily distinguished by a smooth rear fuselage and larger fin which is inclined to the left. The tailplane has to be gull-winged to bring the outboard portion horizontal.

Kamov Ka-25 'Hormone'

Called '**Hormone**' by NATO, the compact **Kamov Ka-25** helicopter has appeared in various sub-types which have since 1965 been the standard type carried aboard Soviet surface warships for defensive and offensive roles. The traditional Kamov layout with superimposed coaxial rotors reduces disc diameter, and in any case automatic blade folding is provided for stowage in small hangars. The four-legged landing gear is specially tailored to operation from pitching decks, each leg having an optional quick-inflating flotation bag which gives the 'Hormone' a distinctly unusual appearance. The rear legs can be raised vertically, on their pivoted bracing struts, to lift the wheels out of the vision of the search radar always fitted under the nose. Two radars have been identified. The smaller type is carried by the '**Hormone-A**' variant on ASW missions; this model also has a towed MAD bird, dipping sonar, electro-optical sensor (and possibly others), and an optional right-side box of sonobuoys. A larger radar is fitted to the '**Hormone-B**', which is believed to be able to guide the SS-N-12 'Sandbox' cruise missile fired from friendly surface ships and, especially, submarines. Many other equipment items include a cylindrical container under the rear of the cabin and a streamlined pod under the tail. In 1982 Ka-25s were seen without flotation gear but with a long ventral box housing (it is believed) a long wire-guided torpedo. All Ka-25s have

a large cabin normally provided with 12 folding seats additional to those for the crew of two pilots plus three systems operators. Some 460 of all variants were built by 1975, and the type continues to play an important part in Soviet naval operations, operating from destroyers, cruisers, helicopter carriers (18 are believed to be carried on each of the two ships *Moskva* and *Leningrad*) and aircraft carriers (*Kiev* and *Minsk* each accommodate 16 'Hormone-A' and three 'Hormone-B' helicopters). The type has also been exported for ship- and land-based operations. The last variant is the '**Hormone-C**' search-and-rescue helicop-

ter based on the 'Hormone-A' without mission equipment. This has been replaced by the KA-32 'Helix' as the Russian navy's shipboard helicopter.

Specification
Kamov Ka-25 'Hormone'
Type: multi-role shipboard helicopter
Armament: normally equipped with ventral bay or external box for two AS torpedoes, nuclear or conventional depth charges and other stores
Powerplant: two 990-shp (739-ekW) Glushenkov GTD-3BM turboshafts
Performance: maximum speed 209 km/h (130 mph); range with external tanks 650 km (405 miles)

The 'Hormone-C' general-purpose version of the Ka-25.

Weights: empty about 4765 kg (10,500 lb); maximum 7500 kg (16,500 lb)
Dimensions: main rotor diameter (both) 15.74 m (51 ft 8 in); fuselage length 9.75 m (32 ft 0 in); height 5.37 m (17 ft 7½ in); main rotor disc area (combined) 389.7 m² (4,193.0 sq ft)

Ka-25 'Hormone-C', used for utility duties such as light transport and SAR. The ungainly four-leg undercarriage is extremely stable on deck, and has rapidly inflating flotation bags on each leg in case of ditching.

Kamov Ka-27 'Helix'

Early publicity of the **Kamov Ka-27 'Helix'** was associated with civil applications, including reconnaissance from the nuclear-powered icebreakers *Arktika, Lenin, Rossiva* and *Sibir,* and all forms of transport and agricultural flying. Photographs were first taken of an Aeroflot (civil) and AVMF (naval air force) examples at sea aboard the new destroyer *Udaloy* in September 1981, and NATO allocated the reporting name 'Helix'. Clearly an enlarged successor to the familiar Ka-25, the Ka-27 has similar three-blade co-axial rotors (each negating the torque of the other and so removing the need for an anti-torque tail rotor, with consequent advantages in the designers' ability to reduce overall dimensions) but the blades are of different shape and increased diameter. All fold to the rear for stowage in ship hangars. The fuselage is considerably more capacious than that of the Ka-25, and it is estimated that in a utility role the Ka-27 could carry 14 troops or substantial quantities of cargo: the civil version is described as able to lift slung loads up to 5000 kg (11,023 lb), and carry such a load over a range of 185 km (115 miles). The ASW version, known in the West as **'Helix-A'**, has a large box on each side (probably for sonobuoys), a box under the tail boom (probably for a MAD), a large chin radar and extremely comprehensive avionics including EW installations. **'Helix-B'** is a targeting aircraft for anti-ship missiles, intended as a replacement for the Ka-25 'Hormone-B'. From the Soviet navy's point of view, the real advantage of the Ka-27 series is that while the overall dimensions are little altered from those of the Ka-25, permitting the type to use existing platforms and hangars, payload and general utility have been enhanced considerably.

Specification
Kamov Ka-27 'Helix-A'
Type: ASW and multi-role naval helicopter
Armament: includes AS torpedoes
Powerplant: two turboshafts, probably uprated Glushenkov GTD-3BM type of about 1,200 shp (895 kW) each
Performance: not yet known, but range with 5-tonne payload said to be 185 km (115 miles)

Weights: empty about 5750 kg (12,680 lb); maximum take-off probably about 9000 kg (19,840 lb)
Dimensions: (estimated) main rotor diameter 16.75 m (54 ft 11½ in); fuselage length 11.0 m (36 ft 1 in); height 5.5 m (18 ft 0½ in); main rotor disc area 440.0 m² (4,736 sq ft)

The Kamov KA-32 'Helix' only entered service in late 1981. This 'Helix-a' anti-submarine helicopter is seen on the deck of the guided-missile destroyer Udaloy.

Mil Mi-14 'Haze'

Also known to the design bureau as the **V-14,** the **Mil Mi-14 'Haze'** is a large twin-turbine helicopter and has some kinship with the mass-produced Mi-8 but has the more powerful TV3 type engines of the Mi-17 and Mi-24. The fuselage is totally different from any other Mil helicopter, and has much in common with the Sikorsky S-61R, the boat-hulled transport version of the Sea King, in that it is fitted with nose-wheel type landing gear with the main units retracting into rear sponsons which also incorporate water keels. The Mi-14 was designed in the 1960s as the replacement for the piston-engine Mi-4 'Hound' as the Soviet AV-MF (naval air force) shore-based ASW and multi-mission helicopter. It is too large for convenient operation from ships, where the Ka-25 'Hormone' and Ka-32 'Helix' are used. The numbers deployed are small, the estimate in mid-1983 being only 65 for the AV-MF and 12 for Bulgaria. The cockpit houses the pilot and co-pilot, who have comprehensive navaids including Doppler, search radar with 360° surveillance, a radar altimeter and full de-icing equipment, though there are no inlet screens on the engines. In the

large main cabin, which in transport versions can be equipped with 32 seats, a mission crew of three or four sit round a tactical display served by the radar, a towed MAD (magnetic anomaly detection) 'bird' and dipping sonar. The hull is watertight and has limited amphibious capability, but the Mi-14 is not intended for sustained operations from the open sea. Some examples have additional radio aerials and a few have a rescue hoist above the large sliding door on the left side. Fuel is housed in large tanks along the sides under the main floor, and possibly also in the rear sponsons, leaving the central compartment free for use as a weapon bay, with belly doors. De-

tails of what can be carried are not yet known, and no Mi-14 has been seen with externally mounted weapons. In addition to the basic ASW version, a transport version exists for utility and SAR roles. Because of its size, this model is probably not suitable for vertrep (vertical replenishment of ships) roles.

Specification
Type: shore-based ASW (possibly also anti-ship) helicopter
Powerplant: two 2,200-shp (1641-kW) Isotov TV3-117A turboshafts
Armament: certainly includes AS homing torpedoes and/or depth charges; may also include anti-ship missiles

The USSR's main shore-based ASW platform is the Mil Mi-14, complete with search radar under the nose, towed MAD bird (stowed behind the rear fuselage), and dipping sonar.

Performance: maximum speed probably same as Mi-8 at 260 km/h (161 mph); maximum cruising speed probably 240 km/h (149 mph); range with full mission load probably about 500 km (311 miles)
Weights: empty about 8000 kg (17,650 lb); loaded probably 12000 kg (26,455 lb)
Dimensions: main rotor diameter assumed to be 21.29 m (69 ft 10½ in); length overall about 25.30 m (83 ft 0 in); height on ground 5.65 m (18 ft 6½ in); main rotor disc area 355.0 m² (3,828.0 sq ft)

Aircraft Carriers

Used by the Royal Navy as early as World War I, the aircraft carrier eclipsed the battleship in World War II to become the new capital ship. Modern carriers, like the giant US 'Nimitz' class vessels, are now used for power projection, armed as they are with the strike power of a small air force.

By the end of World War I, the aircraft carrier was a fact of naval life, and in the summer of 1918 British carrier-based aircraft were regularly operating against enemy targets. The British continued to develop aircraft carriers in the years between the wars, conscious that in the carrier they had an ideal means of policing their far-flung empire, and led the field until they were outstripped by the Americans.

During World War II, it was the small escort carriers – converted American merchantmen, for the most part – that helped to turn the tide in the Battle of the Atlantic; while on the other side of the world, aircraft carriers like the *Enterprise* and the numerous and long-serving 'Essex' class vessels proved decisive in the destruction of Japan's naval power in the Pacific.

In the limited wars since 1945, aircraft carriers have continued to play their part. In Korea, carrier-borne fighter-bombers waged a non-stop interdiction campaign, cutting rail and road communications as fast as the enemy could repair them; and in Vietnam, it was the US Navy that bore the brunt of operations against the North, the carrier pilots flying sortie after sortie into the most heavily defended air

A 'Nimitz' class carrier, the USS *Dwight D Eisenhower* (CVAN 69), at sea. This huge carrier, the size of a floating city, was completed in 1977 and will be in service for some time to come.

space in the world.

During the Cold War, the American carrier task groups, with their nuclear-capable strike aircraft, presented a serious threat to the Soviet Union, which developed the concept of long-range maritime aircraft armed with cruise missiles to deal with it. In a nuclear exchange, it is certain that the carriers would

have been early victims.

In more recent times, carrier aircraft have played a key part in spearheading task forces operating under the auspices of the United Nations, as in the Arabian Gulf during the 1991 conflict with Iraq, or under the orders of a national government, as was the case in 1982 when the carriers HMS *Hermes* and HMS

Invincible led the task force that sailed south to recapture the Falkland Islands from Argentina.

In today's highly unpredictable world, the mere appearance of a massive nuclear-powered aircraft carrier off the coast of some trouble spot can have a sobering effect on an unstable regime. The carrier has therefore become a powerful political tool.

'Kiev' class

Planning for a class of hybrid cruiser-carriers probably started in the Soviet Union in the early 1960s, when the need was seen for a small number of ships suitable for carrying interceptor aircraft capable of providing the air defence necessary for Soviet submarine-hunting forces and submarines operating in hostile sea areas. Although the 'Moskva' class of helicopter-cruisers was meant to be in series production, with a total of 12 planned, the units of the class could operate only ASW helicopters, and so did not meet the new requirement. Thus the yard building the 'Moskva' class, Black Sea Shipyard No. 444 at Nikolayev, was switched to building the new design after only two 'Moskva' class ships had been completed. The first of the new four-ship class, the *Kiev*, was laid down in September 1970, launched in December 1972 and commissioned in October 1976 after extensive trials. The second ship, the *Minsk*, followed in December 1972, was launched in August 1975 and commissioned in July 1979. The third ship, the *Novorossiysk* (to a modified design) was laid down in September 1975, launched in December 1978 and entered service in June 1983. The final vessel, *Kharkov* (later *Admiral Gorshkov*) was laid down in January 1979, launched in April 1982 and entered service in 1987. A nuclear powered conventional fixed-wing carrier followed on from the 'Kiev' class. This vessel was not completed due to the Soviet Union collapse.

The *Kiev* and her sisterships are basically the same in physical appearance but differ in equipment fits. All have seven take-off and landing spots marked on their angled flightdecks on the port side: six (marked with the letter C and the numbers 1 to 6) are for helicopters, whilst the Yakovlev Yak-36MP 'Forger-A' VTOL fighters take off from position 6 and land on the 189-m (620-ft) long, 20.7-m (68-ft) wide asbestos tile-coated flightdeck near position 5 on a specially designated spot, marked with an E on the *Kiev* and an M on the *Minsk* and *Novorossiysk*. Each of the first two ships have seven deck lifts, a 7-m (23-ft) square unit for cargo on the port side of the island forward, a 19.2 m (63 ft) by 10.35 m (34 ft) unit for helicopters close to the island midpoint, an 18.5 m (60 ft 8 in) by 4.7 m (15 ft 5 in) unit aft of the island for the 'Forgers', three 6.5 m (21 ft 4 in) by 1.5 m (5 ft) weapons lifts in line astern next to the helicopter lift, and a similarly-sized personnel lift on the port side. The third ship does not have the cargo lift and has only two ammunition lifts. In addition she has a test area for running up the 'Forger' engines on the starboard side of the flight deck. The air wing for the 'Kiev' class comprises 12 Yak-36s (including one 'Forger-B' unarmed conversion trainer), 18 Kamov

Ka-25 'Hormone-A' ASW helicopters, three 'Hormone-B' midcourse missile-guidance correction/target designator/ELINT helicopters and one 'Hormone-C' SAR plane-guard helicopter. The *Novorossiysk* has also been seen with a number of Kamov Ka-27 'Helix-A' ASW helicopters for carrier evaluation trials. All the embarked aircraft can be carried in the hangar. The *Novorossiysk* is fitted with space for the new SA-N-8 SAM vertical launch system in place of the SA-N-4 'Gecko' bin launchers carried by her sisters. On the electronics side the *Novorossiysk* does not carry the characteristic 'Side Globe' ESM domes on each side of the island superstructure, but has instead two as yet unidentified radars and four 'Bell Crown' electro-optical targeting systems that were first seen on the nuclear powered battle cruiser *Kirov*. There were to be two 'Kievs' each with the Pacific and Northern fleets for surface action/ASW group command and controls roles with at least one operating on an out-of-the-area politico-military mission at any one time. The 'Kievs' carry nuclear-armed SS-N-12s FRAC-1s and depth bombs in their magazines. The first three were scrapped in the 1990s, and *Admiral Gorshkov* is to be sold to India.

Specification

Displacement: 36,000 tons standard, 44,000 tons full load
Dimensions: length 275 m (902 ft 3 in); beam 50 m (164 ft) including flightdeck and sponsons; draught 9.5 m (31 ft 2 in)
Machinery: four-shaft geared steam turbines delivering 180,000 shp (134225 kW)
Speed: 32 kts
Armament: four twin SS-N-12 'Sandbox' SSM launchers (16 missiles), two twin SA-N-3 'Goblet' area-defence SAM launchers (72 missiles), two twin SA-N-4 'Gecko' short-range SAM launchers (36 missiles, not in third vessel), two twin 76-mm (3-in) DP, eight 30-mm ADG-630 six-barrel 'Gatling' CIWS, two 12-barrel 250-mm (9.84-in) MBU 600 ASW rocket-launchers, one twin SUW-N-1 ASW launcher (20 FRAS-1 and SS-N-14 'Silex' carried) and two quintuple 533-mm (21-in) ASW torpedo tubes
Electronics: one 'Top Knot' TACAN system, one 'Top Sail' and one 'Top Steer' 3D radar, one 'Don Kay' and two 'Palm Frond' navigation and surface-search radars (three 'Palm Frond' and two unidentified in *Novorossiysk*), one 'Bob Tail' and two 'Punch Bowl' satellite navigation systems, one 'Trap Door' SS-N-12 guidance radar, two 'Head Light' SA-N-3 guidance radars, two 'Pop Group' SA-N-4 guidance radars

(not in third vessel), two 'Owl Screech' fire-control radars for 76-mm (3-in) guns, four 'Bass Tilt' fire-control radars for ADG-630 guns, most Soviet naval ESM systems including 'Side Globe', 'Rum Tub', 'Top Hat' and 'Bell' series, one low-frequency bow-array sonar, and one medium-frequency variable-depth towed sonar
Complement: 1,200 excluding air wing

Kiev seen during a Soviet Fleet exercise in 1978 south of Iceland. Four Kamov Ka-25 'Hormone' helicopters are ready for flight, with another eight on deck with rotors folded. Used primarily for ASW, they carry a surface search radar, dunking sonar, sonobuoys and ASW weapons.

Below: Destined to be a class of four, there are already several variations in the 'Kiev' ships as to weapon and electronic fits. The third and fourth units will probably carry the new SA-N-8 vertical launch SAM system as soon as this has finished trials.

Above: Deployed on several occasions to the Mediterranean, Kiev uses her Yak-36MP 'Forger-A' VTOL fighters as maritime patrol aircraft interceptors under strict GCI conditions.

Vikrant

Formerly the British 'Majestic' class carrier, **HMS Hercules** that had been laid up in an incomplete state since May 1946, **Vikrant** as she was later re-named) was purchased by India in January 1957, and taken in hand by the Belfast shipyard Harland & Wolff in April 1957 for completion with a single hangar, two electrically-operated air-craft lifts, an angled flight deck and steam catapult. She was also partially fitted with an air conditioning system for tropical service, and commissioned in March 1961. During the 1971 Indo-Pakistan War the *Vikrant* operated a mixed air group of 16 Hawker/Arm-strong Whitworth Sea Hawk fighter-bombers and four Breguet Alizé ASW aircraft off East Pakistan (now called Bangladesh), the elderly Sea Hawks attacking many coastal ports, airfields and small craft in a successful opera-tion to prevent the movement of Pakis-tani men and supplies during Indian army operations to 'liberate' that coun-try. In January 1979 the *Vikrant* com-menced a major refit that ended in January 1982 to enable her to operate BAe Sea Harrier FRS.Mk 1 aircraft. In-cluded in the refit was the construction of a ski-jump ramp, the fitting of new boilers and engines, the provision of new Dutch radars and the fitting of a new operations control systems. Interestingly enough the steam cata-pult was retained in order that the carrier could still operate the Alizé ASW aircraft, a number of which were refurbished at the same time for con-tinued effective service up to the early 1990s. The *Vikrant* was laid up in the 1990s when her machinery wore

out and she has since been scrapped. The Indian naval air arm has been planning replacements for the *Vikrant* and *Viraat* since 1987. However up until 1998 negotiations were still to be completed to take over the *Admiral Gorchkov* from the Russian Navy.

Specification
Displacement: 15,700 tons standard, 19,500 tons full load
Dimensions: length 213.4 m (700 ft); beam 24.4 m (80 ft); draught 7.3 m (24 ft); flightdeck width 39.0 m (128 ft)
Machinery: two-shaft geared steam turbines delivering 40,000 shp (29,830 kW)
Speed: 24.5 kts
Armament: nine single 40-mm AA
Aircraft: see text
Electronics: one LW-05 air-search radar, one ZW-06 surface-search radar, one LW-10 tactical search radar, one LW-11 tactical search radar, one Type 963 carrier controlled approach radar
Complement: 1,075 (including air group) in peace, 1,345 (including air group) in war

Used extensively in the 1971 Indo-Pakistan war, INS Vikrant was the major Indian Navy unit responsible for the blockade of East Pakistan. Her air group of Breguet Alizé ASW aircraft and Sea Hawk fighter-bombers sank a number of Pakistani naval and merchant craft.

'Hancock' and 'Intrepid' class

Originally part of the six-strong 'Essex' class, these two sub-classes were extensively modernised in the 1950s with enclosed bows, armoured and angled lightdeck, improved air-craft elevators, increased aircraft fuel storage and new steam catapults. The 'Essex' design can claim to be the most effective carriers to serve the Pacific, and arguably the most effec-tive warships of their generation. The *Lexington* (commissioned in 1943) was in active service with the Atlantic fleet as the US Navy's sole deck land-ing training career. As such the *Lexington* had no aircraft support facilities aboard. Two other ships in the class, USS *Bonne Homme Richard* and the USS *Oriskany*, commissioned in 1944 and 1950 respectively, both saw active service in the Pacific fleet.

The *Lexington* ran on in to the 1980s in the training role until

replaced by the *Forrestal* when the ship was phased out. The last of the class never saw front line service. The actual aviation ordnance load was believed to have been in the order of 750 tons and that of aviation fuel about 1.35 million litres (300,000 US gal).

Specification
'Hancock' and 'Intrepid' classes
Displacement: (first two) 29,660 tons standard, 41,900 tons full load; (third) 28,200 tons standard, 40,600 tons full load
Dimensions: length (first) 270.9 m (889 ft) and (other two) 274 m (899 ft); beam (first two) 31.4 m (103 ft) and (third) 32.5 m (106 ft 6 in); draught 9.5 m (31 ft); flightdeck width (first) 58.5 m (192 ft), (second) 52.4 m (172 ft) and (third) 59.5 m (195 ft)
Machinery: four-shaft geared steam turbines delivering 150,000 shp (111855 kW)
Speed: 29.1 kts
Aircraft: 60-70 (none in *Lexington*)

Armament: two (*Oriskany*) or four (*Bonne Homme Richard*) 127-mm (5-in) DP
Electronics: one SPS-10 surface-search and navigation radar, one SPS-30 air-search radar (one SPS-12 in *Lexington*), one SPS-43A air-search radar (one SPS-37 in *Oriskany*), one SPN-10 and one SPN-43 aircraft landing aids, several Mk 25/35 fire-control radars (none in *Lexington*), one URN-20 TACAN system
Complement: 2,090 plus 1,185 air group (*Lexington* 1,440)

Now stricken from service, USS Intrepid *served as an ASW carrier during her later years. Her only active sister is USS* Lexington, *serving as a training carrier into the late 1980s.*

'Midway' class

Originally from a class of three the *Midway, Coral Sea* (commissioned 1945 and 1947) and *Franklin D. Roosevelt* were the largest carriers to be constructed during World War II and the only ones capable, in unmodified form, of operating the post-war generation of heavy nuclear-armed attack aircraft. All three eventually underwent modernization programmes which, because they occurred over a long time span, differed considerably in detail. Only the *Midway* and *Coral Sea* remain in service, the former being attached to the Pacific Fleet and homeported in Yokosuka, Japan, and the latter serving as a front-line carrier on the strength of the Atlantic Fleet with reduced air groups from carriers that are in refit. The third vessel, the USS *Franklin D. Roosevelt*, was struck off in 1977, her name subsequently being assigned to a new 'Nimitz' class carrier. Because of their smaller size the 'Midway' class carry the McDonnell Douglas F4N/S Phantom in place of the Grumman F-14A Tomcat, and do not embark the Lockheed S-3A Viking or Sikorsky SH-3 Sea King helicopter. Both ships are fitted with three deck-edge aircraft elevators, but while the *Midway* has only two steam catapults the *Coral Sea* has three. A total of 1,210 tons of aviation ordnance and 4.49 million litres (1.186 million US gal) of JP5 aircraft fuel are carried for the air wing. Of the two ships the *Midway* is the more capable as she underwent an extensive refit in 1966, but both ships will be phased out by the late 1980s, the *Coral Sea* in 1988 and the *Midway* in the following year.

A stern view of USS Midway, *considered to be the more capable of the two 'Midway' class vessels left in service. It is planned that she will be run on until 1989 as a front-line carrier whilst her sister, USS* Coral Sea, *will be phased out in 1988.*

Specification
Displacement: *Midway* 51,000 tons standard, 64,000 tons full load; *Coral Sea* 52,500 tons standard, 63,800 tons full load
Dimensions: length 298.4 m (979 ft); beam 36.9 m (121 ft); draught 10.8 m (35.3 ft); flightdeck width 72.5 m (238 ft)
Machinery: four-shaft geared steam turbines delivering 212,000 shp (158090 kW)
Speed: 30.6 kts
Aircraft: see text
Armament: two octuple Sea Sparrow SAM launchers (no reloads) in *Midway* only, three 20-mm Phalanx CIWS in both
Electronics: (*Midway*) one LN-66 navigation radar, one SPS-65V air/surface-search radar, one SPS-43C air-search radar, one SPS-49 air-search radar, one SPS-48C 3D radar, one SPN035A, two SPN-42 and one SPN-44 aircraft landing aids, two Mk 115 fire-control radars, one URN-29 TACAN system, one SLQ-29 ESM suite, four Mk 36 Super RBOC chaff launchers
Electronics: (*Coral Sea*) one LN-66 navigation radar, one SPS-10 surface-search and navigation radar, one SPS-43C air-search radar, one SPS-30 air-search radar, one SPN-43A aircraft landing aid, one URN-20 TACAN

system, one SLQ-29 ESM suite, four Mk 36 Super RBOC chaff launchers
Complement: *Midway* 2,615 plus 1,800 air group; *Coral Sea* 2,710 plus 1,800 air group

Below: Because of their smaller size, the two 'Midway' class ships have to operate with reduced air groups. These contain no ASW aircraft or helicopters and use the McDonnell Douglas F-4 Phantom as their main interceptor in place of the larger and much heavier Grumman F-14 Tomcat.

'Forrestal' class

The four ships of the 'Forrestal' class were originally conceived as smaller versions of the ill-fated strategic carrier design, the USS *United States*, with four aircraft catapults and a flush flightdeck with no island. However, following a complete redesign they were actually completed as the first carriers designed and built specifically for jet aircraft operations with a conventional island and an angled flight deck to allow the four catapults to be retained. The ships are the USS **Forrestal**, USS **Saratoga**, USS **Ranger** and USS **Independence**, and were commissioned in October 1955, April 1956, August 1957

and January 1959 respectively. Their aviation ordnance load is 1,650 tons; and 2.84 million litres (750,000 US gal) of AVGAS aviation fuel, 2.99 million litres (789,000 US gal) of JP5 aviation fuel are carried for the air wing embarked. The air group is similar to those of the larger carriers, but McDonnell Douglas F-4N6S Phantoms are carried in place of Grumman F-14A Tomcats. The ships have the standard four aircraft elevators to service the flightdeck, and are due to undergo the SLEP refit (in the order *Saratoga, Forrestal, Independence* and *Ranger*) to extend their service lives up to

around the year 2000. During the Grenada landings of November 1983 *Constellation* provided the air cover and strike support to the US Marine Corps and US Army Ranger assaults whilst maintaining ASW cover against any possible incursions by the two Cuban 'Foxtrot' class conventional attack submarines. In order to rectify some of the deficiencies encountered in combat operations, the SLEP refits will improve the habitability, add Kevlar armour to enclose the vital machinery and electronics spaces, improve the NTDS fitted, add TFCC facility and replace the catapults. The radar outfit

was also upgraded and the air defence armament strengthened with the addition of the Phalanx 'Gatling' gun for anti missile use. In early 1998 only *Ranger* and *Independence* were still in service. *Forrestal* was redesignated AVT-59 as a training carrier, but her conversion was cut at short notice and she was decommissioned in 1993.

Specification
Displacement: (first two) 59,060 tons standard, 75,900 tons full load; (second two) 60,000 tons standard, 79,300 tons full load

Forming a class of four, the Forrestal ships exchanged their F-4 Phantoms for the more capable F-14 Tomcat. They also operated the new F/A-18 Hornet multi-role fighter.

Dimensions: length (first) 331 m (1,086 ft), (second) 324 m (1,063 ft), (third) 326.4 m (1,071 ft) and (fourth) 326.1 m (1,070 ft); beam 39.5 m (129 ft 6 in); draught 11.3 m (37 ft); flightdeck width 76.8 m (252 ft)

Machinery: four-shaft geared steam turbines delivering 260,000 shp (193880 kW) in *Forrestal* and 280,000 shp (208795 kW) in others

Speed: 33 kts (*Forrestal*) or 34 kts (others)

Aircraft: as for 'Nimitz' class but Phantoms instead of Tomcats

Armament: three octuple Sea Sparrow SAM launchers (no reloads), three 20-mm Phalanx CIWS

Electronics: one LN-66 navigation radar, one SPS-10 surface-search radar, one SPS-48C 3D radar, one SPS-58 low-level air-search (except *Ranger*), two SPN-42 and one SPN-43A aircraft landing aids, two Mk 91 fire-control radars (three in first two), one URN-20 TACAN system, one SLQ-29 ESM suite and three Mk 36 Super RBOC chaff launchers

Complement: 2,790 plus 2,150 air group

Seen here in 1975, USS Independence *was used to provide the air cover for the Grenada landings. She has also seen extensive combat service in the Vietnam war off both the North and South coasts.*

The US Carrier Battle Groups

The US Navy allocates its main strike potential to a number of Carrier Battle Groups (CBG), each of which comprises a single multi-mission aircraft-carrier (with composite interceptor/strike/ASW air wings) and a six-ship escort. The latter generally consists of one or two Standard ER missile-equipped cruisers, one Standard MR missile-equipped destroyer and two or three 'Spruance' class ASW destroyers and/or 'Knox' class ASW frigates. If the carrier is nuclear-powered then the cruisers will also be nuclear-powered wherever possible.

In late 1983 there are 14 front-line carriers available, of which one is assigned to the Service Life Extension Program (SLEP) at any time. The 14 vessels consist of 12 post-war construction (including four nuclear-powered) and two modified World War II-built carriers; two nuclear-powered replacements for the two 'Midway' class carriers have been ordered. There is also a 15th carrier, an obsolete ship which is being run on till the late 1980s solely as a carrier deck landing training ship and as such has no combat capability.

Thus the effective operational strength of the US fleet is 13 carriers, which is a sufficient number to provide for a minimum of four carrier battle groups to be deployed in forward areas on a continuous basis whilst the remaining nine are in short-period overhaul, on working up exercises or in transit to and from the operational areas. The Pacific Fleet operates four CBGs with its 3rd Fleet and two with its 7th Fleet in the operational North West Pacific and South East Asia areas. One of the carrier battle groups attached to the 7th Fleet is deployed to the Indian Ocean on a regular basis. In the Atlantic Fleet area of operations the US 2nd Fleet has four CBGs available whilst the strategically important 6th Fleet in the Mediterranean has two. Again one of these is occasionally deployed to the Indian Ocean.

The basic role of the CBG is to provide for its parent fleet both offensive power projection and defensive sea control capabilities in its area of responsibility. For this the embarked carrier air wing has available a wide variety of aviation ordnance to meet most conventional and nuclear war requirements. It is not widely known that for the latter contingency each carrier includes in its weapon inventory over 100 nuclear gravity bombs of the B43, B57 and B61 types (with yields varying from 5 kt up to 900 kt) and nuclear-armed Walleye air-to-surface missiles (with 100-kt yield warheads). To deliver these and other weapons the carrier has available 34 Vought A-7 Corsair and Grumman A-6 Intruder aircraft for strike missions and 16 Lockheed S-3A Viking aircraft and Sikorsky SH-3H Sea King helicopters for anti-submarine operations. Of these the most deadly are the 10 Intruders, which are proven and very accurate all-weather day and night attack aircraft. The presence of a limited number of air-laid ground mines within the weapons load also allows the possibility of a blockade to become part of the carrier's offensive options.

In addition to the CBG, an Underway Replenishment Group (URG) has to be formed to support it with food, fuel, spares, ammunition and other sundry items. The oiler attached to this URG normally carries enough fuel to replenish the entire CBG twice over before it has itself to be refuelled. It is this component of the CBG concept which is the most vulnerable because if an enemy can detect and destroy the URG either before or during an operation then the CBG runs the risk of running out of the supplies essential to its operations and will not be able to complete its assigned mission.

A US Carrier Battle Group in the Indian Ocean centred on USS Midway, *also showing USS* Bainbridge, *a missile cruiser, and the oiler* Navasota.

'Kitty Hawk', 'America' and 'John F. Kennedy' classes

Built to an improved 'Forrestal' class design, these four carriers in reality constitute three sub-classes that are easily distinguished from their predecessors by the fact that their island superstructures are set farther aft. In addition two of their four aircraft elevators are forward of the island, the 'Forrestals' having only one in this location. A lattice radar mast is also carried abaft of the island. The USS **America** (commissioned in January 1965) is very similar to the first two ships (USS **Kitty Hawk** and USS **Constellation**, commissioned in April 1961 and October 1961), and was built in preference to an austere-version nuclear-powered carrier. She is, however, the only US carrier of post-war construction to be fitted with a sonar system. The last unit, the USS **John F. Kennedy**, was built to a revised design incorporating an underwater protection system developed originally for the nuclear carrier programme, and was commis-

sioned in September 1968. All have four steam catapults and carry some 2,150 tons of aviation ordnance plus about 7.38 million litres (1.95 million US gal) of aviation fuel for their air groups. These are again similar in size and composition to those of the 'Nimitz' class. The tactical reconnaissance element in each of the air wings is provided by three Grumman F-14s equipped with a TARPS reconnaissance pod. Both these aircraft and the Vought A-7 Corsairs will eventually be replaced by the McDonnell Douglas F/A-18A Hornet multi-role fighter and strike aircraft. The ships are already fitted with or will shortly have the full ASCAC, NTDS and TFCC facilities, the America being the first carrier to be fitted the with NTDS. The ships have the OE-82 satellite communications system, and were the first carriers able simultaneously to launch and recover aircraft easily; on previous carrier classes this was considered a difficult

operation. Their SLEP refits ran from 1988–93. The Kennedy had 'complex overhaul' and is planned to serve until 2018. The Constellation will serve until 2003, the Kitty Hawk until 2008. America was laid up in 1996.

Specification
'Kitty Hawk', 'America' and 'John F. Kennedy' classes
Displacement: first two 60,100 tons standard, 80,800 tons full load; third 60,300 tons standard, 81,500 tons full load; fourth 61,000 tons standard, 82,561 tons full load
Dimensions: length (first two) 318.8 m (1,046 ft), (third) 319.3 m (1,047 ft 6 in) and (fourth) 320.7 m (1,052 ft); beam 39.6 m (130 ft); draught (first three) 11.3 m (37 ft) or (fourth) 10.9 m (35 ft 11 in)
Machinery: four-shaft geared steam turbines delivering 280,000 shp (208795 kW)
Speed: 33.6 kts

Aircraft: see 'Nimitz' class
Armament: three octuple Sea Sparrow SAM launchers (no reloads), three 20-mm Phalanx CIWS
Electronics: (first three) one SPS-10F navigation radar, one SPS-43A air-search radar, one SPS-48C 3D radar, one SPN-35A, two SPN-42 and one SPN-43A aircraft landing aids, one URN-20 TACAN system, three Mk 91 fire-control radars, one SLQ-29 ESM suite, four Mk 36 Super RBOC chaff launchers (America only), one SQS-23 sonar
Electronics: (fourth) one SPS-10F navigation radar, one SPS-49 air-search radar, one SPS-48C 3D radar, one SPN-35A and two SPN-42 aircraft landing aids, one URN-20 TACAN system, three Mk 91 fire-control radars, one SLQ-29 ESM suite, four Mk 36 Super RBOC chaff launchers, fitted for but not with sonar
Complement: 2,900 plus 2,500 air group

Above: USS Constellation *and the guided missile cruiser* Leahy *undergo underway replenishment in the South China Sea from the fast combat support ship* Niagara Falls *whilst part of Carrier Task Force 77.7 during a deployment in 1979.*

Below: Essentially built to a improved 'Forrestal' design, these carriers carry an air group similar in size and composition to the 'Nimitz'

class but with less fuel and ordnance due to the necessity of carrying their own bunkerage.

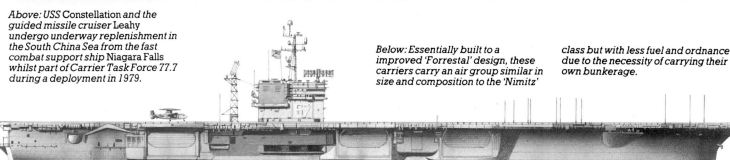

Enterprise

The world's first nuclear-powered aircraft-carrier, the **Enterprise** was laid down in 1958 and commissioned in November 1961 as what was then the largest warship ever built. Since exceeded in size by the 'Nimitz' class ships, the *Enterprise* was built to a modified 'Forrestal' class design with her larger dimensions dictated by the powerplant of eight A2W pressurized-water enriched uranium fuelled nuclear reactors. The high cost of her construction prevented five other vessels in the naval building programme from being built. From January 1979 to March 1982 the *Enterprise* underwent an extensive refit which included the rebuilding of her island superstructure and the fitting of new radar systems and mast to replace the characteristic ECM dome and billboard radar antenna that had been used since she was built. The *Enterprise* is equipped with four steam catapults, four deck-edge aircraft elevators and carries 2,520 tons of aviation ordnance plus 10.3 million litres (2.72 million US gal) of aircraft fuel, sufficient for 12 days of sustained air operations before replenishment. Like that of other US carriers the *Enterprise*'s ordnance includes 10-kt B61, 20-kt B57, 60-kt B43, 100-kt B61, 200-kt B43, 330-kt B61, 400-kt B43, 600-kt B43 and 900-kt B61 tactical nuclear gravity bombs, 100-kt Walleye air-to-surface missiles and 10-kt B57 depth bombs, while 1.4-mt B43 and 1.2-mt B28 strategic bombs can be carried as and when required. The air group is simi-

The first nuclear-powered aircraft carrier, USS Enterprise, is seen here on sea trials after the major drydocking that included the rebuilding of her island superstructure and the replacement of her old ECM and radar systems.

lar in size and configuration to that carried by the 'Nimitz' class carriers, and the *Enterprise* is fitted with the same ASCAC, NTDS and Tactical Flag Command Center (TFCC) facilities. In addition to her OE-82 satellite system she also carries two British SCOT satellite communications antenna units for use with British fleet units and NATO. These two systems were fitted in 1976. The Enterprise is currently deployed with the Pacific Fleet and was overhauled twice between 1979 and 1994. It is estimated that she will eventually be paid off in about 2013.

Specification
Displacement: 75,700 tons standard, 89,600 tons full load
Dimensions: length 335.9 m (1,102 ft); beam 40.5 m (133 ft); draught 10.9 m (35 ft 9 in); flightdeck width 76.8 m

(252 ft)
Machinery: four-shaft geared steam turbines (eight A2W nuclear reactors) delivering 280,000 shp (208795 kW)
Speed: 32 kts
Aircraft: see 'Nimitz' class
Armament: three octuple Sea Sparrow SAM launchers (no reloads), three 20-mm Phalanx CIWS
Electronics: one SPS-48C 3D radar, one SPS-49 air-search radar, one SPS-

65 air/surface-search radar, one SPS-58 low-level air-search radar, one SPS-10 surface-search and navigation radar, one SPN-41, one SPN-35A and one SPN-44 aircraft landing aids, one URN-26 TACAN system, three Mk 91 fire-control radars, one SLQ-29 ESM suite, four Mk 36 Super RBOC chaff launchers
Complement: 3,395 plus 1,891 air group

The use of nuclear power as the propulsion plant allows USS Enterprise to carry sufficient aircraft fuel and ordnance for 12 days of sustained air operations before having to undergo underway replenishment.

'Nimitz' class

The first three 'Nimitz' class carriers were originally designed as replacements for the elderly 'Midway' class carriers. They differ from the earlier nuclear-powered USS *Enterprise* in having a new two-reactor powerplant design in two separate compartments with ordnance magazines between and forward of them. This increases the internal space available to allow some 2,570 tons of aviation weapons and 10.6 million litres (2.8 million US gal) of aircraft fuel to be carried. These totals are sufficient for 16 days of continuous flight operations before the stocks have to be replenished. The class is also fitted with the same torpedo protection arrangement as carried by the USS *John F. Kennedy*, and is laid out with the same general arrangement and electronic fit as the 'JFK'.

Under the present multi-mission designations of the USS carrier force the class is being fitted with an ASW Classification and Analysis Center (ASCAC) for data sharing of subsurface operations between the carrier, her escorts, their airborne ASW aircraft and supporting long-range maritime ASW and patrol aircraft. The ships also have the Naval Tactical Data System (NTDS) with intership and aircraft data links 11 and 14, and are fitted with the OE-82 satellite communications outfit. A Tactical Flag Command Center is also being fitted for use by the fleet command officers normally

embarked. Four deck-edge aircraft elevators are available, two forward and one aft of the island on the starboard side and one aft on the port side. The hangar is 7.8 m (25 ft 7 in) high, and like those of other US carriers can accommodate at most only 40-50 per cent of the aircraft embarked at any one time, the remainder being spotted on the flightdeck in aircraft parks. The angled flight deck is 237.7 m (780 ft) long and is fitted with three arrester wires and an arrester net for recovering aircraft. Four steam catapults are carried, two on the bow launch position and two on the angled flightdeck. A typical 'Nimitz' class air group comprises two squadrons of Grumman F-14A interceptors, two squadrons of Vought A-7E Corsair light attack aircraft and one squadron of Grumman A-6E Intruder all-weather attack aircraft, plus Grumman KA-6D Intruder tankers, Grumman E-2C Hawkeye airborne early warning, Grumman EA-6B Prowler electronic countermeasures, Lockheed S-3A Viking ASW and Sikorsky SH-3H Sea King ASW units. There are also facilities for a Grumman C-2A Greyhound carrier on-board delivery aircraft.

In 1981 the first of at least three improved 'Nimitz' class carriers was ordered after much discussion both within the Congress and the Pentagon. These vessels will have Kevlar armour (being retrofitted in the other ships)

over their vital areas and have improved hull protection arrangements in addition to those already fitted. The core life of the A4W reactors fitted is under normal usage expected to provide a cruising distance of some 1287440 to 1609300 km (800,000 to 1,000,000 miles) and last for 13 or so years before the cores have to be replaced. The three original ships were expected to last until 2025, 2037 and 2032 respectively but this has been reduced to 2015, 2017 and 2022 because of their intensive service. The first two units (USS *Nimitz* commissioned in May 1975, and the USS *Dwight E. Eisenhower* commissioned in 1977 were assigned to the Atlantic Fleet while the USS *Carl Vinson*, commissioned in February 1982, was assigned to the Pacific Fleet. Five more have been built since 1981; the *Theodore Roosevelt* (CVN 71), *Abraham Lincoln* (CVN 72), *George Washington* (CVN 73), *John C Stennis* (CVN 74), and *Harry S Truman* (CVN 75). The *Ronald Reagan* (CVN 76) will be commissioned in 2002.

Specification
Displacement: 81,600 tons standard, 91,487 tons full load or (*Theodore Roosevelt* onwards) 96,351 tons full load
Dimensions: length 332.9 m (1,092 ft); beam 40.8 m (134 ft); draught 11.3 m

(37 ft); flightdeck width 76.8 m (252 ft) or (*Theodore Roosevelt* onwards) 78.4 m (257 ft)
Machinery: four-shaft geared steam turbines (two A4W/A1G nuclear reactors) delivering 280,000 shp (208795 kW)
Speed: 35 kts
Aircraft: 24 F-14A Tomcat, 24 A-7E Corsair, 10 A-6E Intruder, 4 KA-6D Intruder, 4 EA-6B, 4 E-2C, 10 S-3A, 6-8 SH-3H and provision for 1 C-2A
Armament: three octuple Sea Sparrow SAM launchers (no reloads) in first two, or four 20-mm Phalanx close-in weapon systems (CIWS) in others
Electronics: (first three) one SPS-48B 3D radar, one SPS-43A air-search radar, one SPS-10F surface-search radar, one LN-66 navigation radar, two SPN-42, one SPN-43A and one SPN-44 aircraft landing aids, one URN-20 TACAN system, one SPN-43A and one SPN-44 aircraft landing aids, one URN-20 TACAN system, one SLQ-29 ESM suite, four Mk 36 Super RBOC chaff launchers
Electronics: (second three) one SPS-53 navigation radar, one SPS-55 surface-search radar, one SPS-48C 3D radar, one SPS-65 air-search radar, one SPN-44 aircraft landing aids, one TACAN system, three Mk 91 fire-control radars, one SLQ-29 ESM suite and four Mk 36 Super RBOC chaff launchers
Complement: 3,300 plus 3,000 air group

Hermes

The original post-war HMS *Hermes* was the sixth vessel of the 'Centaur' class, but in October 1945 she was cancelled and the name given to the *Elephant* of the same class. As very little work had been done on this hull the vessel was able to benefit from a complete redesign and was thus commissioned in November 1959 with a 6½° angled flightdeck, a deck-edge aircraft lift as one of the two lifts fitted, and a 3D radar system. In 1964-6 the new HMS **Hermes** was refitted with two quadruple Seacat SAM systems in place of her original AA armament of five twin 40-mm Bofors mountings, and access to the seaward side of the island was constructed. In 1971 in a further refit the Type 984 3D radar was replaced by a Type 965 'bedstead' system, and a comprehensive deck landing light system was fitted after the ship had been paid off for conversion to a commando assault carrier, as she could operate only a 28-aircraft group of de Havilland Sea Vixen, Blackburn Buccaneer and Fairey Gannet fixed-wing aircraft but not the modern McDonnell Douglas Phantoms. During this conversion the *Hermes* also lost her arrester wires and catapult, and was converted to carry a complete Marine Commando unit with its associated squadron of Westland Wessex assault helicopters. By 1977 the

Hermes was again in refit to become an ASW carrier, though she retained the Commando carrying ability. As such she carried nine Westland Sea King ASW and four Wessex HU.Mk 5 utility helicopters. In 1980 the *Hermes* began her third major conversion to change her role yet again, this involving a strengthening of the flight deck and the provision of a 7½° ski-jump ramp overhanging the bow to allow the operation of five BAe Sea Harriers in place of the Wessexes. In 1982, because of her more extensive communications fit and greater aircraft-carrying ability, the *Hermes* was made the flagship of the task force sent to recover the Falklands. During this operation she initially operated an air group of 12 Sea Harriers, nine Sea King HAS.Mk 5s and nine Sea King HC.Mk 4s. However, as the campaign progressed this was modified to 15 Sea Harriers, six Harrier GR.Mk 3s, five ASW Sea Kings and two Westland Lynxes. Following her success in the Falklands it was announced that the *Hermes*, after a series of deployments in 1983 would be sold to India. She was refitted in 1986-7 and recommissioned as INS *Viraat* in May 1987. She suffered flooding of the engine in 1993. Although no longer in the prime of life the India plans to keep her in service until 2010 or 2012.

HMS **Hermes** *with her goalkeeper, a Type 22 Frigate, steaming in heavy weather. The Type 22 provides the necessary close-in anti-aircraft and anti-missile defence with the Sea Wolf SAM system that the carrier lacks;* Hermes *had two Seact laucnhers.*

Specification
Displacement: 23,900 tons standard, 28,700 tons full load
Dimensions: length 226.9 m (744 ft 4 in); beam 27.4 m (90 ft); draught 8.7 m (28 ft 6 in); flightdeck width 48.8 m (160 ft)
Machinery: two-shaft geared steam turbine delivering 76,000 shp (56675 kW)
Speed: 28 kts
Armament: two quadruple Seacat SAM launchers (estimated 40 missiles carried)
Aircraft: normal five (to be increased to six) Sea Harriers and nine Sea King ASW helicopters; maximum see text
Electronics: one Type 965 air-search radar, one Type 993 surface-search radar, one Type 1006 navigation radar, two GWS22 Seacat guidance systems, one TACAN system, one Type 184 sonar, several passive and active ECM systems, two Corvus chaff launchers
Complement: 1,350 including air group (plus provision for a complete 750-man Marine Commando unit for which four LCVPs are carried)

Having recently completed her last operational voyage, Hermes *is going to Devonport Naval Base for a short refit before ending up at Portsmouth as a training ship. Because of manning problems, she will be maintained at 30 days' notice for sea.*

'Invincible' class

The demise of the British fixed-wing aircraft-carrier, when the CVA01 fleet carrier replacement programme was cancelled in 1966, resulted in the issue during the following year of a Staff Requirement for a 12,500-ton command cruiser equipped with six Westland Sea King ASW helicopters. A redesign of this basic concept to give more deck space (and the results from several operational analysis studies) showed that a nine-helicopter air group was much more effective. These new specifications resulted in a design draft which became known as the 19,500-ton 'through deck cruiser' (TDC) design, the term TDC being used for what was essentially a light carrier design because of the political sensitivity with which politicians viewed the possibility of a carrier resurrection at the time. Despite this the designers showed initiative in allow-

HMS Invincible *with several Sea Harriers on the flight deck. The slant of the forward ski-jump can readily be seen; this enables the V/STOL fighters to take off with larger fuel and ordnance loads than they could normally carry, a factor which was very useful during the Falklands war.*

ing sufficient space and facilities to be incorporated from the outset for a naval version of the RAF's V/STOL fighter programme that might surface. The designers were duly awarded for such foresight in May 1975 when it was announced officially that the TDC would carry the BAe Sea Harrier. Thus the first of the class, HMS **Invincible**, which had been laid down in July 1973 at the Vickers shipyard at Barrow-in-Furness, was not delayed during building. In May 1976 the second ship, HMS **Illustrious**, was ordered, and in December 1978 the third, HMS **Indomitable** was contracted. However as a result of public disquiet the Admiralty in placatory mood, renamed her **Ark Royal.** The ships were commissioned in July 1982 and November 1985.

The ships of the class are the largest gas turbine-powered warships in the world, with virtually every piece of equipment below decks, including the engine modules, suitable for maintenance by exchange. During building both the *Invincible* and the *Illustrious* were fitted with 7° ski-jump ramps, whilst the *Ark Royal* will be completed with a 15° ramp. In February 1982 in what can only be classed as one of the classic defence disaster statements of all time, it was announced that the *Invincible* was to be sold to Australia as a helicopter carrier to replace the *Melbourne* so that only two carriers would remain in British service. However,

this deal was cancelled after the Falklands campaign, to the relief of the naval high command, as it was realized by the government that three carriers ought to be available to ensure two in service at any one time. During Operation 'Corporate' the *Invincible* started with an air group of eight Sea Harriers and nine Sea King HAS.Mk 5 ASW helicopters. However, as a result of losses and replacements this was modified to a group of 11 Sea Harriers, eight ASW Sea Kings and two Lynx helicopters configured for Exocet decoy duties. One of the problems was that most of the extra aircraft had to be accommodated on the deck as there was insufficient rooom for them in the hangar. The *Illustrious* was hurried through to completion in time to relieve the *Invincible* after the war, and she went south with 10 Sea Harriers, nine ASW Sea Kings and two AEW Sea King conversions. She and her sisterships were also fitted with two American 20-mm Phalanx Gatling gun CIWS for anti-missile defence and two single 20-mm AA guns to improve on the previous nonexistent close-in air defences. The normal air group consisted of five Sea Harriers and eight ASW Sea Kings and two AEW Sea Kings.

Since the 1980s the British Royal navy has run two ships with the third undergoing a refit. HMS **Invincible** was brought to the standard of the Ark Royal, then HMS **Illustrious** followed.

HMS *Ark Royal* will start a two-year refit in 1999.

All three carriers had nuclear weapons for their air groups. According to official sources the Sea Kings can carry US nuclear depth bombs and the Sea Harriers are beleived to be capable of carrying tactical nuclear gravity bombs. The former were probably the same type as carried on RAF Nimrods: the 227 kg (500 lb) American B57 type with 10 kt yield.

In recent years six RAFGR.7 Hermes have been regularly embanked for ground-attack missions. *Illustrious* has had her sea-dog missile launcher removed to allow space for a flight extension and a new ordnance magazine. In the Gulf HMS *Invincible* operates ASW helicopters such as the Lynx and Westland Wasp. In addition the lower yield (by a factor of 10) weapon would be particularly useful in combat scenarios where the use of the higher yield weapon would cause considerable operational problems to friendly units such as submarines.

Specification
Displacement: 16,000 tons standard, 19,500 tons full load
Dimensions: length 206.6 m (677 ft); beam 27.5 m (90 ft); draught 7.3 m (24 ft); flightdeck width 31.9 m (105 ft)

Although more flexible in operations than fixed-wing carriers, 'Invincible' class ships suffer from inadequate numbers of fighters and have no fixed wing AEW aircraft, though the new Sea King AEW helicopter may help.

Machinery: two-shaft gas turbine (4 Rolls-Royce Olympus TM3B) delivering 112,000 shp (83,520 kW)
Speed: 28 kts
Armament: one twin GWD30 Sea Dart area-defence SAM launcher (22 missiles), two 20-mm Phalanx CIWS and two single 20-mm AA
Aircraft: see text
Electronics: one Type 1022 air-search radar, one Type 002R air search radar, two Type 909 Sea Dart guidance radars, two Type 1006 navigation and helicopter direction radars, one Type 184 or Type 2016 bow-mounted sonar, one Type 762 echo sounder, one Type 2008 underwater telephone, one ADAWS 5 action information data-processing system, one UAA1 Abbey Hill ESM suite, two Corvus chaff launchers
Complement: 1,000 plus 320 air group (with provision for a Marine Commando in extreme circumstances)

 ARGENTINA

Veinticinco de Mayo

The **Vienticinco de Mayo** (25 May) was originally a 'Colossus' class carrier purchased from the UK by the Dutch and commissioned into the Royal Netherlands navy on 28 May 1948. In April 1968 the ship suffered a serious boiler room fire, and was subsequently judged to be uneconomical to repair. In the following October Argentina bought the vessel, which was refitted and commissioned into the Argentinian navy in the Netherlands. She sailed for Argentina on 1 September 1969. The vessel is fitted with a modified Ferranti CAAIS data-processing system and Plessey Super CAAIS console displays. This system allows the ship to control her carrier-based aircraft and to communicate via data links with the two Type 42 destroyers of the Argentinian navy and their ASAWS 4 action information systems. Her modified superstructure differs considerably from those of other ex-British carriers in service with other navies. In 1980-1 she underwent a further refit to

increase the strength of the flightdeck and add extra deck space to allow two extra aircraft to be parked in readiness for the Dassault-Breguet Super Etendards that Argentina was acquiring. Luckily for the UK none of these strike aircraft had qualified to land on the carrier by the time of the Falklands war, and the carrier's air group consisted of eight McDonnell Douglas A-4Q Skyhawks, six Grumman S-2E Trackers and four Sikorsky SH-3D Sea Kings. The *Veinticinco de Mayo* played a major part in the initial landings on the Falklands and was ready to launch a strike against the British task force on 2 May 1982 when fate intervened in the

form of poor flying conditions. The subsequent sinking of the *Belgrano* then forced the Argentine carrier to retire to the relative safety of Argentina's coastal waters, where she played no further part in the proceedings and landed her air group for land-based operations. After the Argentine loss of the Falklands the remaining Super Etendards were delivered. These were rapidly deck-qualified but the planned modernisation was never completed and the gutted hulk was ordered to be scrapped in 1998.

Specification
Displacement: 15,892 tons standard, 19,896 tons full load
Dimensions: length 211.3 m (693 ft 3 in); beam 24.4 m (80 ft 0 in); draught 7.6 m (25 ft 0 in); flight deck width 42.4 m (138 ft 5 in)
Machinery: two-shaft geared steam turbines delivering 40,000 shp (29830 kW)
Speed: 24.25 kts
Armament: nine single 40-mm AA
Aircraft: see text
Electronics: one LW-01 air-search radar, one LW-02 air-search radar, one SGR-109 height-finder radar, one DA-02 target-indicator radar, one ZW-01 navigation/surface-search radar, one URN-20 TACAN system, and one CAAIS action information system
Complement: 1,000 plus 500 air group

The main target for the British SSN force during the Falklands was **Vienticinco de Mayo,** *the flagship of the original task force that invaded the islands. The sinking of the* **Belgrano** *caused her to return to port without taking part in a battle.*

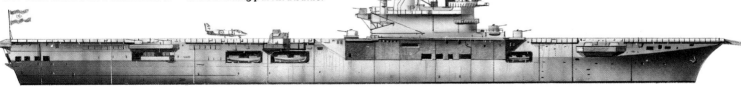

Minas Gerais

A sistership of the Argentinian *Veinticinco de Mayo*, the ex-*Vengeance* started life in the Royal Navy in 1945. Three years later she was fitted out for an experimental cruise to the Arctic and was then lent to the Royal Australian Navy in 1953. She was returned to the Royal Navy in 1955 and was purchased by Brazil in December 1956 as the ***Minas Gerais.*** She was transferred to the Netherlands, where she was comprehensively refitted between 1957 and 1960 with new weapons, a 13365-kg (29,465-lb) capacity steam catapult, an 8½° angled flight deck, a mirror sight deck landing system, a new island superstructure, new US radars and two centreline aircraft elevators. The hanger is 135.6 m (445 ft) long by 15.8 m (52 ft) wide and 5.3 m (17 ft 6 in) high. In 1976-81 the carrier underwent another refit to allow her to operate through to the 1990s. A data link system was installed so that the carrier can co-operate with the 'Niteroi' class of frigates in service with the Brazilian navy, and the obsolete American SPS-12 radar was replaced

with a modern SPS-40B two dimensional air-search system. The role of the *Minas Gerais* throughout her service with the Brazilian navy has been anti-submarine warfare with an air group (since the late 1970s) of eight Grumman S-2E Trackers of the Brazilian air force (the Brazilian navy is not allowed to operate fixed-wing aircraft) plus four navy Sikorsky SH-3D Sea King ASW helicopters, two Aérospatiale SA530 Ecureuils and two Bell 206 Jet-Ranger utility helicopters. She was modernised in 1991–93 with a Ferranti system 500 Combat System and is now expected to serve until at least the end of 2010. It is hoped to operate A-4 Skyhawks from her if funds permit.

Specification
Displacement: 15,890 tons standard, 19,890 tons full load
Dimensions: length 211.8 m (695 ft); beam 24.4 m (80 ft); draught 7.5 m (24.5 ft); flightdeck width 37.0 m (121 ft)
Machinery: two-shaft geared steam

turbines delivering 40,000 shp (29830 kW)
Speed: 25.3 kts
Armament: two quadruple 40-mm AA, and one twin 40-mm AA
Aircraft: see text
Electronics: one SPS-40B air-search radar, one SPS-4 surface-search radar, one SPS-8B fighter direction radar, one SPS-8A air control radar, one Raytheon 1402 navigation radar and two SPG-34

A recent view of Minas Gerais *with four S-2E Trackers, four SH-3D Sea Kings, two Lynx and an Ecureuil ranged on the flight deck. A more modern V/STOL carrier design is currently under study to replace her in the late 1980s/early 1990s.*

fire-control radars
Complement: 1,000 plus 300 air group

'Clemenceau' class

The ***Clemenceau*** was the first carrier designed as such to be completed in France. Built in the late 1950s and commissioned in November 1961, she incorporated all the advances made in carrier design during the early 1950s, namely a fully angled flight deck, mirror landing sight and a fully comprehensive set of air-search, tracking and air-control radars. The flight deck is 165.5 m (543 ft) in length and 29.5 m (96 ft 9 in) in width, and is angled at 8° to the ship's centreline. Two aircraft lifts, each rated at 2036 kg (44,895 lb) are provided, one abaft the island on the deck edge and the other offset to starboard and just forward of the island. Two steam catapults are fitted, one on the port side of the bow and the other on the angled flight deck. The hangar has a usable area of 152 m (499 ft) by 24 m (78 ft 9 in) by 7 m (23 ft). The fuel capacity of the *Clemenceau* is 1200 m³ of JP5 aircraft fuel and 400 m³ of AVGAS whilst her sistership, the *Foch* (commissioned in July 1983), carries 1800 m³ and 109 m³ respectively. During the period September 1977 to November 1978 the *Clemenceau* underwent a major refit, the *Foch* following between July 1980 and August 1981. During these refits both ships were converted to operate the Dassault-Breguet Super Etendard strike fighter, for which they carry AN52 15-kt tactical nuclear gravity bombs in their magazines. They also receive SENIT 2 automated tactical information-processing systems as part of their command, control and communication suites. Following the refits the two carriers' air groups now each comprise 16 Super Etendard strike fighters, three Dassault-Breguet Etendard IVP photographic reconnaissance fighters, 10 Vought F-8E Crusader interceptors

and seven Breguet Alizé ASW aircraft, plus two Aérospatiale Super Frelon ASW and two Aérospatiale Alouette III utility helicopters. The carriers can also act, if required, as helicopter carriers with an air group of 30-40 helicopters depending upon the types embarked. During the Lebanon crisis of 1983 France used one of the carriers in support of her peace-keeping force, Super Etendards being used to attack several gun positions that had engaged French troops. The *Clemenceau* was paid off in 1997 and the *Foch* will be paid off in 2000 when replaced by the 400,000 tonne *Charles de Gaulle*, but a second CVN may be replaced by a conventionally powered ship built to joint Anglo-French design.

Specification
Displacement: 22,000 tons standard, 32,185 tons full load (*Clemenceau*) or 32,780 tons full load (*Foch*)
Dimensions: length 265 m (869 ft 5 in); beam 31.7 m (104 ft) with bulges; draught 8.6 m (28 ft 3 in)
Machinery: two-shaft geared steam turbines delivering 126,000 shp (93960 kW)
Speed: 33 kts
Armament: eight 100-mm (3.9-in) DP
Aircraft: see text
Electronics: one DRBV 50 surveillance radar, one DERBV 23B air-search radar, one DRBV 20C air-warning radar, two DRB 31 fire-control radars, two DRBC 32 fire-control radars, two DRBI 10 height-finding radars, one Decca 1226 navigation radar, one NRBA aircraft landing radar, one URN-6 TACAN system, one SENIT 2 data-processing system, various ESM systems and one SQS-503 sonar
Complement: 1,338

Above: Seen entering Nice, Clemenceau *and her sister provided air support to the French contingent in Lebanon in 1983.*

Left: The 'Clemenceau' class were the first French vessels to be designed from the outset as aircraft carriers, incorporating all the design lessons learned in the 1950s.

After recent modification the two 'Clemenceau' class carriers will serve on until the 1990s. Their replacements will be two 34600-ton nuclear-powered vessels, the first to be laid down in 1986 at Brest and to be named Charles De Gaulle.

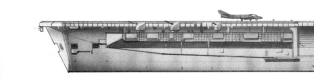

Dédalo and Príncipe de Asturias

The **Dédalo** is an ex-US 'Independence' class carrier built during World War II that ended her days in the US Navy as an aviation transport. She was reactivated and modernized as a carrier at the Philadelphia Naval Shipyard before being transferred to Spain on a five-year loan from 30 August 1967. In December 1975 the Dédalo was purchased outright and now acts as the Spanish navy's fleet flagship. Her flight deck is 166.1 m (545 ft) long and 32.9 m (108 ft) wide, and the hangar can accommodate 18 Sikorsky Sea King type helicopters with another six on the flight deck. The Dédalo's normal air wing comprises four air groups with at least one with eight BAe Matador V/STOL fighters, one with four SH-3D/G Sea King ASW helicopters, one with four Agusta (Bell) AB.212 ASW anti-submarine and electronic warfare helicopters, and one of four helicopters as required by the mission assigned to the carrier (these could, for example, be four Bell AH-1G Cobra attack helicopters to support an amphibious landing). A maximum of seven four-aircraft groups can be handled aboard.

To replace the Dédalo in 1986, the Spanish ordered on 29 June 1977 a gas turbine-powered vessel based on the final design variant of the abortive US Navy's Sea Control Ship. Named **Príncipe de Asturias**, the new ship has a flightdeck measuring 175 m (574 ft) in length and 30 m (98 ft 6 in) in width, fitted with a 12° ski-jump ramp blended into the bow. Two aircraft lifts are fitted, one of them at the extreme stern. For the Príncipe de Asturias' air wing Spain has ordered the McDonnell Douglas AV-8B Harrier II V/STOL fighter and the Sikorsky SH-60B Seahawk ASW helicopter. The complement of aircraft and helicopters will be 20, made up of six to eight AV-8Bs, six to eight SH-3s or SH-60s, and four to eight AB.212s, the actual mix depending upon the operational requirement.

A fully digital command and control system is fitted with a LINK 11 intership data transmission terminal. It is expected that a second vessel of this type will be ordered later.

Specification
Dédalo
Displacement: 13,000 tons standard, 16,416 tons full load
Dimensions: length 189.9 m (623 ft); beam 21.8 m (71 ft 6 in); draught 7.9 m (25 ft)
Machinery: four-shaft geared steam turbines delivering 100,000 shp (74570 kW)
Speed: 24 kts
Aircraft: see text
Armament: one quadruple 40-mm AA, and nine twin 40-mm AA
Electronics: one SPS-8 3D radar, one SPS-6 air-search radar, one SPS-40 air-search radar, one SPS-10 surface-search and tactical radar, two Mk 29 fire-control systems, two Mk 28 fire-control systems, two navigation radars, one URN-22 TACAN system, one WLR-1 electronic countermeasures system
Complement: 1,112 without air group

Specification
Príncipe de Asturias
Displacement: 14,700 tons full load
Dimensions: length 195.1 m (640 ft); beam 24.4 m (80 ft); draught 9.1 m (29 ft 10 in)
Machinery: one-shaft gas turbine (two GE LM 2500) delivering 46,000 shp (34300 kW)
Speed: 26 kts
Aircraft: see text
Armament: four Meroka 20-mm CIWS
Electronics: one SPS-55 surface-search radar, one SPS-52 3D radar, four Meroka fire-control radars, one SPN-35A air control radar, one URN-22 TACAN system, four Mk 36 Super RBOC chaff launchers
Complement: 790 without air group

Above: The elderly Spanish carrier Dédalo *was converted from an ex-US World War II carrier of the 'Independence' class. Currently the flagship of the Spanish fleet, she is due to be replaced by an indigenous-built version of the US Sea Control Ship design.*

Below: As USS Cabot, *Dédalo survived a kamikaze attack during the Battle of Leyte Gulf. Spanning naval generations, she is today one of the few ships to operate V/STOL aircraft on a regular basis.*

Giuseppe Garibaldi

Essentially designed as a gas turbine-powered carrier for helicopters the *Giuseppe Garibaldi* also incorporates features suiting her for the carriage and operation of V/STOL fighters. The flight deck is 173.8 m (570 ft 2 in) long and 21 m (68 ft 11 in) wide, and is fitted with a ski-jump ramp. The hangar is 110 m (360 ft 11 in) long, 15 m (49 ft 3 in) wide and 6 m (19 ft 8 in) high, and is built to accommodate 12 Agusta (Sikorsky) Sea King ASW helicopters, or 10 V/STOL aircraft and one Sea King, although the available height will permit the embarkation of heavy-lift Meridionali (Boeing Vertol) CH-47 Chinook helicopters if required. Two aircraft lifts are fitted (one forward and one abaft the island), and there are six marked flightdeck spaces for helicopter operations. The *Giuseppe Garibaldi* was designed specifically to provide ASW support for naval task forces and merchant convoys, and as such is fitted with full flagship facilities plus command, control and communication systems for both naval and air force operations. In emergencies she can also carry up to 600 troops for short periods. The extensive weaponry fitted also allows her to operate as an independent surface unit. To permit

helicopter operations in heavy weather she has been fitted out with two pairs of fin stabilizers, and her aircraft maintenance facilities are sufficient not only to service her own air group but also the light ASW helicopters of any escorting warships she was commissioned in 1985 to replace both the 6,500 ton 'Andrea Doria' class helicopter-cruiser. The AV-8B Harrier plus STOVL aircraft was acquired in 1989 with ten allocated to the air group. The SH-3D helicopters will be replaced by the EH101 from 2000 onwards.

Specification
Displacement: 10,100 tons standard, 13,139 full load
Dimensions: length 179 m (587 ft 3 in); beam 30.4 m (99 ft 9 in); draught 6.7 m (22 ft)
Machinery: two-shaft gas turbine (four Fiat/GE LM2 500) delivering 80,000 hp (59655 kW)
Speed: 30 kts
Aircraft: 12 SH-3D Sea King helicopters with space on flight deck for six more
Armament: six Teseo Otomat Mk 2 SSM launchers (12 missiles), two

octuple Albatros short-range SAM systems (56 missiles), three twin 40-mm Dardo CIWS, two triple 325-mm (12.75-in) ASW torpedo tubes for Mk 46 and Whitehead AS244/S torpedoes
Electronics: one RAN 3L 3D radar, one RAT 31 air-search radar, one RAN 10S air-search radar, one SPS 702 surface-search radar, three RTN 20X Dardo

tracking radars, two RTN 30X Albatros fire-control radars, one SPS 703 navigation radar, one TACAN system, one IPN 10 data-processing system, various passive ESM systems, two SCLAR chaff launchers and one DE 1160 sonar
Complement: 550 normal, 825 maximum including air group

The first Italian aircraft-carrier to actually see service, the Giuseppe Garibaldi *is designed to carry V/STOL fighters, although her air group will*

actually consist of Sea King ASW helicopters for the foreseeable future as the Italian navy is short of funds.

Modern Cruisers

During World War II cruisers were essential for the protection of convoys crossing any sea. Modern cruisers are conventionally or nuclear powered SAM-armed warships used only by larger navies. The main roles for today's cruisers are convoy and battlegroup escort and surface action with anti-ship missiles.

The USS *Vincennes* (CG 49), an early 'Ticonderoga' class cruiser, unleashes an anti-submarine missile. These vessels also carry Standard SM-1s SAMs and Harpoon anti-ship missiles.

During World War II the role of the cruiser was vital, and varied from commerce protection, convoy raiding and offensive operations to fleet reconnaissance. Fast vessels, usually with a main armament of 152-mm (6-in) or 203-mm (8-in) guns, ranged the oceans in the service of all major combatants and proved extremely effective.

The modern cruiser is a luxury item in the world's navies because of its immense cost. Only the Superpowers continue to produce them, and they have eliminated virtually all gun armament, replacing it with powerful surface-to-air and surface-to-surface missile systems considered more suitable for the vagaries of modern warfare.

Since World War II the cruiser has evolved into an expensive SAM-armed warship capable of operating in the highest-threat areas as a vital part of a task force unit. In the US Navy the cruiser has become both conventionally powered and nuclear-powered, and is tasked primarily with the area SAM defence of fast carrier battle groups.

The Russian Navy's cruisers, on the other hand, are purpose-built anti-ship or anti-submarine vessels. The traditional fire-support gun cruisers in most other navies have been paid off, sold or converted to hybrid helicopter carriers or SAM ships as the rush for missile-armed ships in the 1960s gained momentum.

With their 'Kirov' class nuclear-powered vessel, commissioned in 1980, the Russians produced the nearest thing to the obsolete battlecruiser category of modern times. It came as a surprise to the Americans, and to match it they started a reactivation programme for their 'Iowa' class battleships, laid up since the Vietnam War.

It is interesting to note that if the Royal Navy had been able to deploy the cruisers HMS *Tiger* or HMS *Blake* (both hybrid helicopter carrier conversions armed with a twin 152-mm (6-in) turret forward) for the Falklands campaign in 1982, the task of bombarding Argentine shore positions – particularly Port Stanley airfield – might have been made a lot easier than was the case. It would also have enabled the Task Force Commander to release his small Sea Harrier force for vital missions elsewhere, or for extra combat air patrols.

'Colbert' class

A development of the pre-war 'De Grasse' design, the post-war Brest-built **Colbert** (C 611) was commissioned in 1959, and incorporated a number of modifications such as an increase in beam, different armour protection and a shortened transom stern that improved her stability and allowed for a helicopter landing pad to be carried aft.

From April 1970 until October 1972 the *Colbert* underwent a major refit to equip her with the Masurca area-defence SAM system for fleet-defence duties. As a result of financial restraints the original refit plan had to be modified to include the retention of some of her original AA armament. The bridge structure was rebuilt and air-conditioning was installed throughout. In order to cope with the increased power requirements thus needed, the electrical generator system was uprated to give a 5000-kW output. A modernized electronics suite was also installed, and a SENIT-1 action information system was fitted in the operations room to enable the *Colbert* to act as a flagship for the French Mediterranean fleet, a role in which she has served since the end of the 1970 refit. From August 1981 to November 1982 she underwent a second major refit to extend her operational life to 1991. During this a satellite communications system was fitted and improvements made to extend the range of Masurca Mk 2 Mod 3 semi-active hom-

ing missiles beyond their normal 60 km (37 miles); the altitude engagement limits of the missile are between 30 and 22500 m (100 and 73,820 ft).

Specification
'Colbert' class
Displacement: 8,500 tons standard and 11,300 tons full load
Dimensions: length 180.0 m (590.55 ft); beam 20.2 m (66.27 ft); draught 7.9 m (25.9 ft)
Propulsion: geared steam turbines delivering 86,000 shp (64130 kW) to two shafts

Speed: 31.5 kts
Complement: 562
Aircraft: none embarked, though a helicopter platform is provided
Armament: four MM.38 Exocet SSM launchers with four missiles, one twin Masurca SAM launcher with 48 missiles, two 100-mm (3.9-in) DP guns and six twin 57-mm AA guns
Electronics: one DRBV 23C air-search radar, one DRBI 10D height-finder radar, one DRBV 50 tactical radar, one Decca RM 416 navigation radar, one DRBV 20 air-search radar, two DRBR 51 SAM fire-control radar, one DRBR

Serving as the flagship of the French Mediterranean Fleet, the Colbert underwent a refit to extend her operational life to 1991. Included in it was the upgrading of her Masurca SAM system to meet the threat of Soviet bombers and anti-ship missiles.

32C gun fire-control radar, two DRBC 31 100-mm (3.9-in) fire-control radars, one URN-20 TACAN, one SENIT-1 action information system, one passive ECM suite, and two Syllex chaff launchers.

'Vittorio Veneto' class

Originally to have been a third 'Andrea Doria' class ship, the **Vittorio Veneto** (C 550) was radically altered in design on several occasions when it was realized that these earlier ships were too small. The *Vittorio Veneto* is thus half as large again as an 'Andrea Doria', with a raised 40 m (131.2 ft) by 18.5 m (60.7 ft) flight deck aft with a two-decks deep 27.5 m (90.2 ft) by 15.3 m (50.2 ft) hangar below it. This allows up to nine AB.204As or AB.212ASW or six SH-3D Sea King ASW helicopters to be carried, although the two 18 m (59.1 ft) by 5.3 m (17.4 ft) aircraft lifts preclude the Sea Kings from being struck down into the hangar. The extra space forward allows the fitting of an American Mk 20 Aster SAM/ASW launcher system in place of the Mk 10 used on the 'Andrea Doria' class. The new launcher has three rotary drums loaded with 40 SAMs and 20 ASROC ASW missiles so that the operations centre can choose the missile type to be fired according

to the nature of the threat detected. During her latest refit (1981-3) the *Veneto* was modified to fire the Standard SM1-ER SAM. She also had fitted four Teseo launchers for Otomat SSMs, and two Dardo close-in weapon system mountings with three twin 40-mm Breda gun turrets. The *Veneto*, which was originally commissioned in 1969, is currently used as the Italian navy's flagship, but she will hand this role over to the carrier *Guiseppe Garibaldi* when it commissions. Her replacement is *Nuova Unita Maggiore* (NUM).

Specification
'Vittorio Veneto' class
Displacement: 7,500 tons standard and 8,870 tons full load
Dimensions: length 179.6 m (589.25 ft); beam 19.4 m (63.6 ft); draught 6.0 m (19.7 ft)
Propulsion: geared steam turbines delivering 73,000 shp (54435 kW) to two shafts

Speed: 30.5 kts
Complement: 565
Aircraft: nine Agusta (Bell) AB.212ASW or six Agusta (Sikorsky) SH-3D Sea King anti-submarine and anti-ship helicopters
Armament: one twin Standard SM1-ER/ASROC SAM6 ASW launcher with 40 Standard and 20 ASROC missiles, four Teseo SSM launchers with four Otomat missiles, eight 76-mm (3-in) DP guns, three twin 35-mm CIWS mountings, and two triple 324-mm (12.75-in) ASW torpedo tube mountings for Mk 44, Mk 46 and A244 torpedoes
Electronics: one SPS-52C 3D radar, one SPS-40 air-search radar, one SPS-70 surface-search radar, two SPG 55C SAM fire-control radars, four RTN10X 76-mm (3-in) fire-control radars, two Dardo CIWS fire-control radars, three RM7 navigation radars, one Abbey Hill passive ESM suite, two SCLAR flare/chaff launchers, and one SQS-23 sonar

Above: The Vittorio Veneto (C550) the Italian Flagship until replaced by the carrier Guiseppe Garibaldi when that ship commissions. The Veneto operated up to nine AB.212 ASW or six SH-3D Sea King ASW Helicopters from her flight deck.

Originally to have been a third 'Andrea Doria' class hybrid cruiser/helicopter carrier, the Vittorio Veneto was radically altered in design when it became apparent to the Italian navy that the earlier ships were much too small for their assigned tasks.

USA

'Long Beach' class

The first US surface warship to have nuclear power, the USS *Long Beach* (CGN 9) was to have originally been frigate-sized but grew rapidly during design to the dimensions of a heavy cruiser. As built she had two twin long-range Talos SAM missile systems (with 52 missiles), two Terrier medium-range SAM systems (with 120 missiles) and what was then the revolutionary SPS-32/33 fixed-array air-search radar system with an early version of the NTDS data system. During the Vietnam War the *Long Beach* used her Talos missiles to attack MiGs on seven occasions during 1967-8 whilst they flew deep within North Vietnamese territory, shooting down two (in May and June 1968) at ranges of more than 120 km (75 miles). As a result of experiences in the Vietnam War the *Long Beach* had a conventional SPS-12 air-search radar fitted in 1968 to supplement the fixed arrays, and an integral IFF and digital Talos fire-control system were added in 1970. By 1979 the Talos system was becoming obsolete, so the launchers and radars were removed, two quadruple Harpoon SSM launchers being added. In the following year the inadequate fixed-array systems were removed and replaced by SPS-48 and SPS-49 radars, the original planar array panels being replaced on the superstructure by armour plate. Two 20-mm Phalanx CIWS mountings were also added, and the sonar was modified to improve its passive capabilities (without the need to add a second dome). In 1981 the Standard SM2-ER replaced the SM1-ER model that had been used since the late 1970s. During her next major refit in 1984-5 the *Long Beach* will have a Tactical Flag Command center and additional Kevlar armour fitted. The *Long Beach* was decommissioned in 1994.

Specification
'Long Beach' class
Displacement: 15,540 tons standard and 17,525 tons full load
Dimensions: length 219.8 m (721.2 ft); beam 22.3 m (73.2 ft); draught 9.5 m (31.2 ft)
Propulsion: two Westinghouse C1W pressurized-water cooled reactors powering geared steam turbines delivering 80,000 shp (59655 kW) to two shafts
Speed: 36 kts
Complement: 1,160 plus flag accommodation of 68
Aircraft: none embarked, though a helicopter platform is provided
Armament: two quadruple Harpoon SSM launchers with eight missiles, two twin Standard SM2-ER SAM launchers with 120 missiles, one octuple ASROC ASW launcher with 20 missiles, two 127-mm (5-in) DP guns, two 20-mm Phalanx CIWS mountings, and two triple 324-mm (12.75-in) Mk 22 ASW torpedo tube mountings with six Mk 46 torpedoes
Electronics: one SPS-48C 3D radar, one SPS-10 surface-search radar, one SPS-49B air-search radar, four SPG-55A Standard fire-control radars, two SPG-49 gun fire-control radars, two SPW-2 fire-control radars, one NTDS equipment, one ESM suite, Mk 36 Super RBOC chaff launchers, and one SQQPAIR-23 sonar

USS Long Beach *(CGN 9) was the first US surface warship to have nuclear power. During the Vietnam War in 1967-8 her long range Talos SAM systems engaged North Vietnamese MiGs on seven occasions, shooting down two at ranges in excess of 120 km (75 miles).*

USA

'Leahy' and 'Bainbridge' classes

The 'Leahy' class was the first American warship design with the SAM missile as primary armament, with two twin 76-mm (3-in) guns added almost as an afterthought. The SAM launchers are two twin Mk 10 Terrier launchers fore and aft, the former being protected in heavy seas by the knuckling of the hull (a feature previously unseen in US ships). The ASW outfit was limited as the ships' primary mission is anti-war warfare defence. The nine ships are the USS *Leahy* (CG 16), USS *Harry E. Yarnell* (CG 17), USS *Worden* (CG 18), USS *Dale* (CG 19), USS *Richmond K. Turner* (CG 20), USS *Gridley* (CG 21), USS *England* (CG 22), USS *Halsey* (CG 23) and USS *Reeves* (CG 24), all commissioned between 1962 and 1964 and in their careers these have all undergone extensive modernization, an NTDS data system being fitted, the missile fire-control systems being upgraded for the Standard SM1-ER (later SM2-ER) missile, two quadru-

The lead ship of the class, USS Leahy *(CG 16). In the latter part of the Vietnam war her sister ship, USS* Worden, *was hit accidentally by Shrike ARMs (Anti-Radiation Missiles) fired from US Navy planes. The missiles destroyed her fighting capability without damaging her sailing abilities.*

ple Harpoon launchers being fitted, and the 76-mm (3-in) mountings being replaced by two 20-mm Phalanx CIWS mountings.

At the same time as the 'Leahy' class cruisers were built a single nuclear-powered variant was also constructed in the form of the USS *Bainbridge* (CGN 25). She is essentially similar, but larger in dimensions and tonnage to accommodate the nuclear power-plant. The 'Leahy' class were all disposed of in 1993–4 while the *Bainbridge* went in 1995.

Specification
'Leahy' class
Displacement: 5,670 tons standard and 8,203 tons full load
Dimensions: length 162.5 m (533.0 ft); beam 16.7 m (54.8 ft); draught 7.9 m (24.9 ft)

Propulsion: geared steam turbines delivering 85,000 shp (63385 kW) to two shafts
Speed: 32.7 kts
Complement: 431
Aircraft: none embarked, though a helicopter platform is provided
Armament: two quadruple Harpoon SSM launchers with eight missiles, two twin Standard SM2-ER SAM launchers with 80 missiles, one octuple ASROC ASW launcher with eight missiles, two 20-mm Phalanx CIWS mountings, and two 324-mm (12.75-in) Mk 32 ASW torpedo tube mountings with 12 Mk 46 torpedoes
Electronics: one SPS-48A 3D radar, one SPS-49 air-search radar, one SPS-10F surface-search radar, four SPG-55B Standard fire-control radars, one URN-20 TACAN, one SLQ-32(V)2 ESM suite, four Mk 36 Super RBOC chaff

launchers, and one SQS-23B PAIR sonar

Specification
'Bainbridge' class
Displacement: 7,804 tons standard and 8,592 tons full load
Dimensions: length 172.2 m (565.0 ft); beam 17.6 m (57.75 ft); draught 7.7 m (25.25 ft)
Propulsion: two General Electric D2G pressurized-water cooled reactors powering geared steam turbines delivering 60,000 shp (44740 kW) to two shafts
Speed: 38 kts
Complement: 488
Aircraft: none embarked, though a helicopter platform is provided
Armament: two quadruple Harpoon SSM launchers with eight missiles, two twin Standard SM2-ER SAM launchers

The nuclear-powered cruiser USS Bainbridge (CGN25) executes a high-speed turn to port. Bainbridge is essentially similar to the 'Leahy' class cruisers, but has larger dimensions and tonnage to accommodate the two D2G pressurized-water cooled reactors that give her a 38 kts speed.

with 80 missiles, one octuple ASROC ASW launcher with eight missiles, two 20-mm Phalanx CIWS mountings, and two 324-mm (12.75-in) Mk 32 ASW torpedo tube mountings with 12 Mk 46 torpedoes
Electronics: one SPS-52 3D radar, one SPS-49 air-search radar, one SPS-10F surface-search radar, four SPG-55B Standard fire-control radars, one URN-20 TACAN, one SLQ-32(V)2 ESM suite, four Mk 36 Super RBOC chaff launchers, and one SQS-23 sonar

The 'Leahy' class cruiser USS Harry E. Yarnell (CG17). The primary mission of these ships is anti-air warfare, for which they carry two twin Standard SM2-ER SAM launchers that can engage targets out to over 140 km (87.5 miles) at altitudes up to 24390 m (80000 ft).

'Belknap' and 'Truxtun' classes

The 'Belknap' class suffered a very long and tortuous development history even by American standards, being redesigned on a number of occasions as the costs gradually increased. The design eventually stabilized as a single-ended missile ship with facilities for the DASH ASW drone anti-submarine helicopter hangar and a single 127-mm (5-in) DP gun at the other end. The nine ships are the USS *Belknap* (CG 26), USS *Josephus Daniels* (CG 27), USS *Wainwright* (CG 28), USS *Jouett* (CG 29), USS *Horne* (CG 30), USS *Sterett* (CG 31), USS *William H. Standley* (CG 32), USS *Fox* (CG 33) and USS *Biddle* (CG 34). Since completion between 1964 and 1967 the class has been used as trials ships for a number of new systems: for example, the *Wainwright* was the test ship for the first NTDS data system integrated into a fire-control system and for the Standard SM2-ER missile, whilst the *Fox* evaluated the Tomahawk cruise missile box-launcher arrangement. On 22 November 1975 the *Belknap* suffered very severe fire damage following collision with the carrier USS *John F. Kennedy* in the Mediterranean, and had to be towed back to the USA for rebuilding. Before that time several of the *Belknap*'s sister ships had accumulated great combat experience in the Vietnam War both as combat air patrol fighter-guidance controllers and as air-defence ships. The 1972 North Vietnamese invasion of South Vietnam and the subsequent American bombing, mining and naval bombardment of North Vietnam coastal areas resulted in two air attacks on the American fleet that involved 'Belknap' class ships. The first, on 19 April 1972, saw the *Sterret* fighting off a combined air and surface attack on a gunfire support group, her Terrier missiles destroying a 'Styx' SSM (the first occasion on which a SAM was used to destroy an anti-ship cruise missile in combat) and two MiGs (one at 9-km/5.6-mile range and the other at 27.5-km/17-mile range). Later, on 19 July, the *Biddle* engaged an incoming raid of five MiGs attempting a night attack on Task Force 77 off the North

Vietnamese coast, her Terriers shooting down two MiGs at about 32 km (20 miles) and driving the rest off. As had occurred with the 'Leahy' class, a larger and nuclear-powered version of the 'Belknap' class ships was constructed, the USS *Truxtun* (CGN 35), basically similar in weapon and electronic equipments. All six were deleted in 1993–5 while the *Truxtun* was decommissioned in 1995.

Specification
'Belknap' class
Displacement: 6,570 tons standard and 8,200 tons full load (CG 27, CG 28 and CG 29) or 8,065 tons full load (others)
Dimensions: length 166.7 m (547.0 ft); beam 16.7 m (54.8 ft); draught 8.8 m (28.8 ft)
Propulsion: geared steam turbines delivering 85,000 shp (63385 kW) to two shafts
Speed: 32.5 kts
Complement: 511 (CG 26) or 443 (others)
Aircraft: one Kaman SH-2D Seasprite multi-role helicopter
Armament: two quadruple Harpoon SSM launchers with eight missiles, one twin Standard SM2-ER/ASROC SAM/ASW launcher with 40 Standard and 20 ASROC missiles, one 127-mm (5-in) DP gun, two 20-mm Phalanx CIWS mountings, and two triple 324-mm (12.75-in) Mk 32 ASW torpedo tube mountings with 12 Mk 46 torpedoes
Electronics: one SPS-48A or SPS-48C 3D radar, one SPS-40 or SPS-49 air-search radar, one SPS-10 surface-search radar, one LN66 navigation

radar, two SPG-55D Standard fire-control radars, one SPG-53A 127-mm (5-in) fire-control radar, one URN-20 TACAN, one NTDS equipment, one SLQ-32(V)2 ESM suite, four Mk 36 Super RBOC chaff launchers, and one SQS-26BX sonar (except CG 26, which has SQS-53)

Specification
'Truxtun' class
Displacement: 8,200 tons standard and 9,127 tons full load
Dimensions: length 171.9 m (564.0 ft); beam 17.7 m (58.0 ft); draught 9.5 m (31.2 ft)
Propulsion: two General Electric D2G pressurized-water cooled reactors powering geared steam turbines delivering 60,000 shp (44740 kW) to two shafts
Speed: 38 kts
Complement: 528
Aircraft: one Kaman SH-2D Seasprite multi-role helicopter
Armament: two quadruple Harpoon

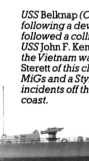

The sole nuclear powered version of the 'Belknap' class is USS Truxtun *(CGN35). She normally operates in the American Pacific Fleet as the partner to USS* Bainbridge *escorting a nuclear-powered carrier.*

SSM launchers with eight missiles, one twin Standard SM2-ER/ASROC SAM/ASW launcher with 40 Standard and 20 ASROC missiles, one 127-mm (5-in) DP gun, two 20-mm Phalanx CIWS mountings, and two triple 324-mm (12.75-in) Mk 32 ASW torpedo tube mountings with 12 Mk 46 torpedoes
Electronics: one SPS-48 3D radar, one SPS-40 air-search radar, one SPS-10 surface-search radar, one LN66 navigation radar, two SPG-55B Standard fire-control radars, one SPG-53F 127-mm (5-in) fire-control radar, one URN-20 TACAN, one NTDS equipment, one SLQ-32(V)3 ESM suite, four Mk 36 Super RBOC chaff launchers, and one SQS-26BX sonar

USS Belknap *(CG26) had to be rebuilt following a devastating fire that followed a collision with the carrier USS* John F. Kennedy *in 1975. During the Vietnam war USS* Biddle *and USS* Sterett *of this class shot down four MiGs and a Styx SSM in two separate incidents off the North Vietnamese coast.*

'California' class

Intended originally to have been a five-ship nuclear-powered guided-missile frigate version of the ill-fated Fiscal Year 1966 conventionally-powered guided-missile destroyer design, the 'California' class was cut back to only two vessels, the USS *California* (CGN 36) and USS *South Carolina* (CGN 37), the money for the other going towards the follow-on 'Virginia' class. The 'California' class ships were commissioned in 1974 and 1975, and were the first to have the improved D2G reactor systems with three times the core life of the original plant fitted in the USS *Bainbridge* and USS *Truxtun*. A helicopter landing pad is provided, but no hangar or maintenance facilities are fitted. Two torpedo tubes for the Mk 48 heavyweight ASW torpedo were also fitted in the transom, but

these were discarded together with the original heavy Mk 42 127-mm (5-in) gun mounts, the latter being replaced by a pair of Mk 45 lightweight 127-mm (5-in) mountings. Under modernization plans two Phalanx CIWS mountings will be fitted, together with Kevlar plastic armour and Tomahawk SSM. Both ships were completely refitted between 1992 and 1993, but were scheduled to be decommissioned in the period 1998–9.

The main SAM battery comprised two single-rail Mk 13 launchers with SPG-51 D digital fire-control radars. The missile is the standard SM1-MR, harpoon SSM launchers were fitted and the main ASW armament was provided by a reloadable eight-round Mk 16 ASROC launcher.

Specification
'California' class (as modified)
Displacement: 9,561 tons standard and 11,100 tons full load (CGN 36) or 10,473 tons full load (CGN 37)
Dimensions: length 181.7 m (596.0 ft); beam 18.6 m (61.0 ft); draught 9.6 m (31.5 ft)
Propulsion: two General Electric D2G pressurized-water cooled rectors powering geared steam turbines delivering 60,000 shp (44740 kW) to two shafts
Speed: 39 kts
Complement: 563
Aircraft: none embarked, though a helicopter platform is provided
Armament: two quadruple Tomahawk SSM launchers with eight missiles, two

quadruple Harpoon SSM launchers with eight missiles, two single Standard SM2-MR SAM launchers with 80 missiles, one octuple ASROC ASW launcher with 24 missiles, two 127-mm (5-in) DP guns, two 20-mm Phalanx CIWS mountings, and four single 324-mm (12.75-in) Mk 32 ASW torpedo tubes with 16 Mk 46 torpedoes
Electronics: one SPS-48A 3D radar, one SPS-40B air-search radar, one SPS-10 surface-search radar, four SPG-51D Standard fire-control radars, one SPQ-9A fire-control radar, one SPG-60 127-mm (5-in) fire-control radars, one URN-20 TACAN, one SLQ-32(V)3 ESM suite, one NTDS equipment, four Mk 36 Super RBOC chaff launcher, one SQS-26CX sonar, and one SATCOMM system

'Virginia' class

Initially intended as nuclear counterparts of the 'Spruance' class guided-missile destroyer design, the USS *Virginia* (CGN 38), USS *Texas* (CGN 39), USS *Mississippi* (CGN 40) and USS *Arkansas* (CGN 41) eventually evolved into a slightly improved 'California' sub-class derivative, the 'Virginia' class. Like most guided-missile frigates (DLG or DLGN) they were re-designated as nuclear-powered guided-missile cruisers (CGN) during 1975, the ships commissioning between 1976 and 1980. A fifth unit was projected but not funded by the US Congress. Compared with the 'California' class ships they are some 3.35 m (11 ft) shorter, are fitted with two Mk 26 launcher systems for Standard SM1-ER SAMs, ASROC ASW missiles and, if required, Harpoon SSMs. They also have a hangar with telescoping hatch cover beneath the fantail flight deck and this is said to leak badly in heavy weather; the helicopter carried is a Kaman SH-2D Seasprite ASW type, and the ships will not be fitted for the Sikorsky SH-60B Seahawk follow-on ASW helicopter. The forthcoming SQR-19 tactical towed sonar array will not be fitted because of the ships' inherently noisy reactor machinery systems.

The normal role of the 'Virginia class' ships was deployment in pairs to act as fast area defence SAM escorts to nuclear powered aircraft carriers. They were to have been modernised with plans for two Phalanx CIWS mountings, the SAM system adapted to fire standard SM2-ER missiles, Kevlar plastic armour fitted in vulnerable command and machinery space, and eight Tomahawk cruise missiles launcher boxes added to supplement the harpoon SSMs already carried.

Despite their impressive statistics the design was not as successful as the California class. Modernisation was stopped and all four were decommissioned between 1994 and 1997.

Above: Last of the 'Virginia' class to be completed was USS Arkansas *(CGN41). The 'Virginias' are smaller than the 'Californias' but have a much improved layout, including the provision of a hangar below decks for two LAMPS ASW helicopters.*

pressurized-water cooled reactors powering geared steam turbines delivering 70,000 shp (52,200 kW) to two shafts
Speed: 40 kts
Complement: 519
Aircraft: one Kaman SH-2D Seasprite multi-role helicopter (a second can be carried in emergencies)
Armament: two quadruple Harpoon SSM launchers with eight missiles, two quadruple Tomahawk SSM launchers with eight missiles, two twin Standard SM2-ER/ASROC SAM/ASW launchers with 50 Standard, 20 ASROC and two test missiles, two 127-mm (5-in) DP guns, two 20-mm Phalanx CIWS mountings, and two triple 324-mm (12.75-in) Mk 32 ASW torpedo tube mountings with 14 Mk 46 torpedoes
Electronics: one SPS-51D surface-search radar, one SPS-40B air-search radar, one SPS-48A or SPS-48C 3D

Specification

'Virginia' class (as modified)
Displacement: 8,623 tons standard and 10,420 tons full load
Dimensions: length 177.3 m (581.7 ft); beam 19.2 m (63.0 ft); draught 9.5 m (31.2 ft)
Propulsion: two General Electric D2G

radar, two SPG-51D Standard fire-control radars, one SPQ-9A fire-control system. one SPG-60D gun fire-control system, one URN-20 TACAN, one SLQ-32(V)3 ESM suite, four Mk 36 Super RBOC chaff launchers, one NTDS equipment, one SATCOMM system, and one SQS-53A sonar

USS Texas *(CGN39) on constructor's trials. The fantail flight deck and rear Mk 26 SAM launcher are clearly seen. The 127 mm (5 in) gun mount is of the Mk 45 dual-purpose type, firing 31.8 kg (70-lb) rounds in the surface bombardment and anti-aircraft roles.*

'Ticonderoga' class

Evolved as minimum-cost aegis SAM area-defence platform for construction in large numbers the 'Ticonderoga' class is based on the hull of the largest existing destroyer design available, the 'Spruance' class. The original force level to be constructed was 30 but this was cut back to 27. The basic Spruance class hull and machinery layout was used but the larger displacement resulted in a noticeable reduction in speed. Some criticism of the amount of top weight carried was voiced but trials of the lead ship *Ticonderoga* (CG-47) in 1983 showed that stability was sufficient.

The heart of the ship is the com-

puterised aegis area defence system which has two paired SPY-1A fixed antenna, electronic scanning radar capable of control friendly aircraft as well as providing simul-

The first of the aegis-equipped cruisers, USS Ticonderoga *(CG47) saw action off Lebanon during 1983 when she engaged shore targets with her 127-mm (5-in) guns. She provided much needed air defence for American task forces against threats from both aircraft and missile attacks.*

The heart of the AEGIS system is the two paired SPY-1A fixed-antenna S-band electronic scanning radars that provide simultaneous surveillance, target-detection, and target-tracking in a hemisphere over and around the ship out to well over 160 km (100 miles) distance. They can also control friendly aircraft flying on combat air patrols.

taneous surveillance, target-detection and target-tracking in a hemisphere over and around the ship. The missiles used are Standard SM2-ERs on two twin Mk 26 launcher, which can deal with saturation attacks by high-performance aircraft in combination with low-level and high-level air, surface and sub-surface launched anti-ship missiles in very heavy ECM environments. From the sixth ship onwards the two Mk 26 launchers and their magazines will be replaced by two Mk 41 vertical launchers for a total

of 122 Harpoon. Standard ASW and Tomahawk missiles instead of the 104 carried in the older ships. The last of the class, USS *Shiloh* was commissioned in 1994. The *Princeton* was badly damaged by an Iraqi mine during the Gulf War in 1991.

Specification
'Ticonderoga' class
Displacement: 9,600 tons full load
Dimensions: length 172.8 m (566.8 ft); beam 16.8 m (55.0 ft); draught 9.5 m (31.0 ft)

Propulsion: four General Electric LM 2500 gas turbines delivering 80,000 shp (59655 kW) to two shafts
Speed: 30 kts
Complement: 360
Aircraft: two Kaman SH-2D Seasprite or Sikorsky SH-60B Seahawk multi-role helicopters
Armament: two octuple Harpoon SSM launchers with 16 missiles, two twin Standard SM2-ER/ASROC SAM/ASW launchers with 68 Standard and 20 ASROC missiles, two 127-mm (5-in) DP guns, two 20-mm Phalanx CIWS

mountings, and two triple 324-mm (12.75-in) Mk 32 ASW torpedo tube mountings with 14 Mk 46 torpedoes
Electronics: two paired SPY-1A AEGIS radar arrays, one SPS-49 air-search radar, one SPS-10 surface-search radar, one SPQ-9A gun fire-control system, four SPG-62 Standard fire-control radars, one SLQ-32 ESM suite, four Mk 36 Super RBOC chaff launchers, one NAVSAT system, one SATCOMM system, one SQS-23 sonar, and one SQR-19 tactical towed-array sonar system

 USA
'Iowa' class

Although constructed (1940-4) during World War II as the largest examples of their type ever built apart from the Japanese *Yamato* and *Musashi*, the US battleships of the 'Iowa' class, USS *Iowa* (BB 61), USS *New Jersey* (BB 62), USS *Missouri* (BB 63) and USS *Wisconsin* (BB 64), saw considerable service after the war on various duties. In the immediate post-war period three were mothballed, whilst the *Missouri* served as a training ship. However, the Korean War (1950-3) saw all four again in active service for use as naval gunfire support vessels off the North and South Korean coastlines. They then reverted to reserve status during 1954-8 and were again mothballed. On 6 April 1967 the *New Jersey* began her second reactivation refit for active service off South Vietnam and the North Vietnamese panhandle region as a floating battery. During this deployment she spent 120 days on the 'gun line', firing 5,688 406-mm (16-in) rounds and 14,891 127-mm (5-in) rounds at targets; she then fell foul of economy cuts in 1969, when she decommissioned for her third period of mothballing.

By the 1970s the four battleships were considered as little more than relics from a bygone age, but in 1980 the need to augment the US surface combat fleet and match new Soviet warship classes resulted in the US Congress authorizing funds to reacti-

Below: Although considered for many years to be relics from a bygone ages the four 'Iowa' class battleships became the most powerful surface combatants afloat following refitting with new weapon systems and electronics. Their last bow was in the Gulf War of 1991.

Above: The first of the reactivated battleships USS New Jersey (BB62). Her 406-mm (16-in) main guns gave much needed artillery support to the beleaguered US Marine Corps force located near Lebanon's international airport in Beirut.

vate the battleship force. After much heated debate the initial vessel chosen, the *New Jersey*, recommissioned after modernization on 27 December 1982, beginning her first operational deployment with the Pacific Fleet in March 1983. By the end of that year she had served as part of the task forces deployed off the Nicaraguan coasts and, in December off Lebanon, had used her main armament to bombard Syrian AA positions that had fired on US Navy reconnaissance aircraft that were supporting the US Marine Corps units ashore. Eventually all four ships are to be in fleet service to operate with battle groups in the highest-threat areas with or without organic air cover and to provide US amphibious units with much-needed heavy gun fire support.

The initial modernization programme included the upgrading of the electronics, conversion of the propulsion plant to burn Navy distillate fuel, the fitting of a Combat Engagement Cen-

ter, and the addition of new weapons systems. at the expense of four twin 127-mm (5-in) mountings. The fantail was also reshaped to accommodate up to three Kaman SH-2D Seasprite ASW helicopters in open stowage with a fourth on the helicopter landing pad located there. A second major modernization refit is planned for the class during the ships' service lives, but its actual configuration is still under consideration. The last two units to be reactivated may be rebuilt in this configuration from scratch. The main battery of 406-mm (16-in) guns fires both 862-kg (1,900-lb) HE and 1225-kg (2,700-lb) AP shells out to 38000 m (41,560 yards) and 36750 m (40,190 yards) respectively. The Iowa and Missouri fired 16-in shells and Tomahawk missiles at Kuwait City in 1991, but manpower shortages forced the US Navy to decommission all four in 1995.

Specification
'Iowa' class
Displacement: 45,000 tons standard and 57,450 tons full load (BB 61 and 63), or 59,000 tons full load (BB 62) or 57,216 tons full load (BB 64)
Dimensions: length 270.4 m (887.2 ft) except BB 62 270.5 m (887.6 ft); beam 33.0 m (108.2 ft); draught 11.6 m (38 ft)
Propulsion: geared steam turbines delivering 212,000 shp (158090 kW) to four shafts
Speed: 32.5 kts, except BB 63 27.5 kts as a result of a grounding accident
Complement: BB 61 and 62 1,571, and BB 63 and 64 2,365
Aircraft: two or four Kaman SH-2D Seasprite multi-role helicopters on the fantail landing pad (BB 61 and 62 only)
Armament: (BB 61 and 62) eight quadruple Tomahawk SSM launchers with 32 missiles, four quadruple Harpoon SSM launchers with 16 missiles, three triple 406-mm (16-in) guns, six twin 127-mm (5-in) DP guns, and four 20-mm Phalanx CIWS

mountings
Armament: (BB 63 and 64) nine 406-mm (16-in) guns, and 10 twin 127-mm (5-in) DP guns
Electronics: (BB 61 and 62) one SPS-10F surface-search radar, one SPS-49 air-search radar, one LN66 navigation radar, two Mk 38 guns fire-control systems, four Mk 37 gun fire-control systems, one Mk 40 gun director, one Mk 51 gun director, one SLQ-32 ESM suite, eight Mk 36 Super RBOC chaff launchers, one NAVSAT system, and one SATCOMM system
Electronics: (BB 63 and 64) one SPS-10 surface-search radar, one SPS-6C air-search radar, one SPS-8A height-finder radar, four Mk 37 gun fire-control systems, two Mk 38 gun fire-control systems, one Mk 40 gun director, four Mk 51 gun directors, six Mk 56 and two Mk 53 gun fire-control system (BB 63 only)

USSR
'Sverdlov' class

Destined originally to be a 24-ship programme in Stalin's post-war Soviet navy plan, the 'Sverdlov' class finally consisted of 20 hulls laid down, of which only 17 were launched; three of these latter were never completed and were laid up in the Neva river at Leningrad for a number of years before being scrapped. The remaining 14 were completed during the period 1951-5 in two slightly different forms, but all were essentially an improved version of the pre-war designed but post-war completed 'Chapayev' cruiser class. One, the *Ordzhonikidze*, was transferred to Indonesia in 1962 as the *Irian* (and scrapped in 1972 in Taiwan following a chronic spares problem), whilst in the late 1950s the *Dzerzhinsky* was converted into an experimental SAM cruiser with a navalized version of the Soviet army's SA-2 'Guideline' fitted in place of the X 152-mm (6-in) gun turret. This proved to be unsuccessful in service and the vessel had by the late 1970s been placed in reserve with the Black Sea Fleet. The *Admiral Nakhimov* was also converted around the same time to a trials ship for the SS-N-1 'Scrubber' anti-ship missile system, but was subsequently scrapped in 1961 without ever having left Soviet waters. Of the remaining ships two (the *Admiral Senyavin* and *Zhdanov*) were converted to the KU (*Korabl' Upravleuiye*, or command ship) role in 1971-2; the former serves as the Pacific Fleet flagship for special deployments and the latter with the Black Sea Fleet for the same purposes. The other nine *Admiral Lazarev, Admiral Ushakov, Aleksander Nevsky, Aleksandr Suvorov, Dmitri Pozharsky, Mikhail Kutzov, Murmansk, Oktyabskaya Revolutsiya* and *Zhdanov*) are conventional cruisers (Soviet designation KR, *Kreyser*). The primary use for these vessels lay with their main and secondary armaments for the support of Soviet and Warsaw pact army units and Naval infantry in amphibious assaults on NATO and other Western targets. This capability was unmatched in all NATO navies other than American which had the reactivated Iowa class battleships with

heavier armaments.

The first Russian unit to be scrapped was the *Admiral Lazarev* (1986) followed by the *Admiral Ushakov* and *Dimitri Pojharski* in 1987, the *Sverdlov, Aleksander Nevski* and *Dzerzhinski* in 1989 and the rest in 1990-91.

Specification
'Sverdlov' class
Displacement: 12,900 tons standard and 17,000 tons full load
Dimensions: length 210.0 m (689.0 ft); beam 22.0 m (72.2 ft); draught 7.2 m (23.6 ft)
Propulsion: geared steam turbines delivering 110,000 shp (82025 kW) to two shafts
Speed: 32.5 kts
Complement: 1,000
Aircraft: one Kamov Ka-25 'Hormone-

C' utility helicopter (in *Admiral Senyavin* only)
Armament: one twin SA-N-2 'Guideline' SAM launcher with eight missiles (in *Dzerzhinsky* only) or one twin SA-N-4 'Gecko' SAM launcher with 18 missiles (in *Admiral Senyavin* and *Zhdanov* only), four triple 152-mm (6-in) DP guns (three triple mountings in *Dzerzhinsky* and *Zhadanov*, and two triple mountings in *Admiral Senyavin*), six twin 100-mm (3.9-in) DP guns, 16 twin 37-mm AA guns (14 twin mounting in 1977-9 modifications, and eight twin mountings in the *Dzerzhinsky, Admiral Senyavin* and *Zhdanov*), four twin 30-mm AA (in *Zhdanov* only, while the *Admiral Senyavin* and 1977-9 modifications have eight twin mountings), and up to 200 mines (none in *Admiral Senyavin* and *Zhdanov*)
Electronics: (*Dzerzhinsky*) one 'Big Net' air-search radar, one 'Low Sieve' air-search radar, one 'Slim Net' air-search radar, one 'Fan Song-E' SA-N-2 fire-control radar, two 'Sun Visor' 152-mm (6-in) fire-control radar, one 'Top Bow' gun fire-control radar, and one 'Neptune' navigation radar

Electronics: (*Admiral Senyavin* and *Zhdanov*) one 'Top Trough' air-search radar, one 'Pop Group' SA-N-4 fire-control radar, one 'Sun Visor' 152-mm (6-in) fire-control radar, two 'Top Bow' 152-mm (6-in) fire-control radars, four 'Drum Tilt' 30-mm fire-control radars (only two in *Zhdanov*), and six 'Egg Cup' gun fire-control radars
Electronics: (others) one 'Big Net' or 'Top Trough' air-search radar, one 'High Sieve' or 'Low Sieve' air search radar, one 'Knife Rest' air-search radar (in some ships only), one 'Slim Net' air-search radar, one 'Don-2' or 'Neptune' navigation radar, two 'Sun Visor' gun fire-control radars, two 'Top Bow' 152-mm (6-in) fire-control radars, eight 'Egg Cup' gun fire-control radars, and one 'Watch Dog' ECM system

The experimental SAM missile cruiser Dzerzhinsky, fitted with a navalized version of the Soviet army's SA-2 'Guideline' missile, which proved unsuccessful in service. The vessel was placed in the reserve category with the Black Sea Fleet in the late 1970s.

'Kynda' class

Launched at the Zhdanov Shipyard in Leningrad between 1961 and 1964, in a programme that was curtailed after only four ships had been built, the 'Kynda' class cruisers *Grozny, Admiral Fokin, Admiral Golovko* and *Varyag* were the first ships in the Soviet navy to introduce a pyramid superstructure supporting the type's numerous radar and ESM systems. Classed as RKR units by the Soviets, these are dedicated anti-surface ship warfare vessels tasked with countering the American carriers. For this role the main armament comprises two trainable four-round launcher banks of SS-N-3B 'Shaddock' cruise missiles, one reload for each tube located within magazines in the superstructure immediately behind each launcher unit. The reloading operation is a slow and difficult process, however, requiring a relatively calm sea. The ships have no organic air component other than a simple helicopter landing pad aft, and thus have to rely on third-party targeting sources such as naval air force Tupolev Tu-95 'Bear-D' aircraft for over-the-horizon missile engagements.

Propulsion is provided by a set of pressure-fired geared steam turbines that exhaust through large twin funnels. The air-defence armament is limited to a single SA-N-1 'Goa' twin launcher forward and two twin 76-mm (3-in) DP gun turrets aft, whilst the ASW armament is limited to a pair of RBU 6000 ASW rocket-launchers and two triple ASW torpedo tube banks. The RBU 6000 fires a 75-kg (165-lb) HE projectile with optional depth or magnetic proximity fusing. The 12 barrels are fired in a paired sequence after the launcher has been trained in azimuth and elevation by a dedicated fire-control console. The launcher is reloaded automatically when it is trained to the vertical, the magazine being directly beneath the launcher. The 533-mm (21-in) torpedoes are

acoustic-homing types optimized for ASW role. The *Varyag* was decommissioned in 1990, followed by the *Grozny* and *Admiral Fokin* in 1993. *Admiral Golovko* returned to service as Black Sea Flagships 1995–97.

Specification
'Kynda' class
Displacement: 4,400 tons standard and 5,600 tons full load
Dimensions: length 141.7 m (464.9 ft); beam 16.0 m (52.5 ft); draught 5.3 m (17.4 ft)
Propulsion: geared steam turbines delivering 100,000 shp (74570 kW) to two shafts

Speed: 35 kts
Complement: 375
Aircraft: none embarked, though a helicopter platform is provided
Armament: two quadruple SS-N-3B 'Shaddock' SSM launchers with 16 missiles, one twin SA-N-1 'Goa' SAM launcher with 16 missiles, two twin 76-mm (3-in) DP guns, four 30-mm ADG6-30 CIWS mountings (in *Varyag* only), two 12-barrel RBU 6000 ASW rocket-launchers, and two triple 533-mm (21-in) ASW torpedo tube mountings
Electronics: two 'Head Net-A' air-search radars (in *Grozny* and *Admiral Golovko*), or one 'Head Net-A' and one 'Head Net-C' air-search radars (in *Admiral Fokin* only) or two 'Head Net-C' air-search radars (in *Varyag* only),

One of the Soviet Pacific Fleet's two 'Kynda' class rocket cruisers' (RKR) with a Lockheed P-3B Orion maritime patrol aircraft in attendance. Then 'Kyndas' relied on over the horizon targeting data to use their main armament effectively.

two 'Plinth Net' surface-search radars (none in *Admiral Golovko*), two 'Don-2' navigation radars, one 'Owl Screech' 76-mm (3-in) fire-control radar, one 'Peel Group' SAM fire-control radar, two 'Scoop Pair' SSM fire-control radars, two 'Bass Tilt' CIWS fire-control radars (in *Varyag* only), 'Bell Clout', 'Bell Slam' and 'Bell Tap' ECM systems, one 'Top Hat' ECM system, and one high-frequency hull sonar

'Kresta I' and 'Kresta II' classes

Built at the Zhdanov Shipyard in Leningrad, the first 'Kresta I' class BPK (later changed by the Soviets to RKR) was completed in 1967. Only four ships were built (*Admiral Zozulya, Vladivostok, Vitse-Admiral Drozd* and *Sevastopol*, commissioned 1967-9), and it is likely that they were an interim design between the anti-ship 'Kynda' and the ASW 'Kresta II' classes. The 'Kresta I' class ships are larger than the former class with a different hull form, half the SS-N-3B 'Shaddock' SSM battery (but with no reloads) and increased anti-air warfare capabilities. The ships were also the first Soviet surface combatants to have a helicopter hangar, for a single Kamov Ka-25 'Hormone-B' missile-targeting helicopter. Two of the ships underwent additions to their super structure, but all four were decommissioned in

1991-4 and scrapped.

The SA-N-1 'Goa' systems carried in this class have a secondary anti-ship capability with an alternative 10-kiloton yield nuclear warhead in place of the usual 60-kg (132-lb) HE type.

Following the last Kresta I on the slipway came the first of the 10 Kresta II BPK hulls (the *Kronshtadt, Admiral Isakov, Admiral Nakhimov, Admiral Makarov, Marshal Voroshilov,*

Admiral Oktyabrisky, Admiral Isachenkov, Vasily Chapayev and *Admiral Yumashev*), all commissioned between 1970 and 1978. These are similar in design but have significantly different SAM, ASW and electronic outfits. The 'Shaddock' launchers were replaced by two quadruple SS-N-14 'Silex' ASW missile-launcher boxes (although the first mis-

siles were not actually carried for several years, hence the incorrect NATO designation of the SS-N-10 anti-ship missile assigned to these launchers), whilst the SA-N-1 SAM system was replaced by the SA-N-3 'Goblet' system. For operation in heavy weather fin stabilizers were fitted. The same hangar arrangement was adopted, but with a Kamov Ka-25 'Hormone-A' ASW

A Soviet 'Kresta II' class BPK, armed with SS-N-14 'Silex' ASW missiles in two quadruple launcher boxes either side of the bridge. The class also has a useful anti-ship capability in its 'Silexes' and SA-N-3 'Goblet' SAM missiles. The latter can be fitted with a 25 kt nuclear warhead in place of its HE warhead.

Helicopter. All nine 'Kresta Is' were decommissioned in 1991–4 and scrapped.

Specification
'Kresta I' class
Displacement: 6,000 standard and 7,600 tons full load
Dimensions: length 155.5 m (510.2 ft); beam 17.0 m (55.75 m) draught 6.0 m (19.7 ft)
Propulsion: geared steam turbines delivering 100,000 shp (74570 kW) to two shafts
Speed: 34 kts
Complement: 380
Aircraft: one Kamov Ka-25 'Hormone-B' missile-guidance helicopter
Armament: two twin SS-N-3B 'Shaddock' SSM launchers with four missiles, two SA-N-1 'Goa' SAM launchers with 32 missiles, two twin 57-mm DP guns, four 30-mm ADG6-30 CIWS mountings (in *Vitse-Admiral Drozd* only), two 12-barrel RBU 6000 ASW rocket-launcher, two six-barrel RBU 1000 ASW rocket-launchers, and two quintuple 533-mm (21-in) ASW torpedo tube mountings
Electronics: one 'Big Net' air-search radar, one 'Head Net' 3D radar, two 'Peel Group' SAM fire-control radars, two 'Muff Cob' 57-mm fire-control radars, two 'Bass Tilt' CIWS fire-control radars (in *Vitse-Admiral Drozd* only), two 'Plinth Net' surface-search radar, two 'Don-2' navigation radars, one 'Scoop Pair' SSM-guidance radar, one 'Side Globe' ESM suite, 'Bell Clout', 'Bell Tap' and 'Bell Slam' ECM systems, and one high-frequency hull sonar

Specification
'Kresta II' class
Displacement: 6,000 standard and 7,600 tons full load
Dimensions: length 158.5 m (520.0 ft); beam 17.0 m (55.75 m) draught 6.0 m (19.7 ft)
Propulsion: geared steam turbines delivering 100,000 shp (74570 kW) to two shafts
Speed: 34 kts
Complement: 400
Aircraft: one Kamov Ka-25 'Hormone-A' ASW helicopter
Armament: two quadruple SS-N-14 'Silex' ASW launchers with eight missiles, two twin SA-N-3 'Goblet' SAM launchers with 48 missiles, two twin 57-mm DP guns, four 30-mm ADG6-30 CIWS mounting, two 12-barrel RBU 6000 ASW rocket-launchers, two six-barrel RBU 1000 ASW rocket-launchers, and two quintuple 533-mm (21-in) ASW torpedo tube mountings
Electronics: one 'Head Net-C' 3D radar, one 'Top Sail' 3D radar, two 'Head Light' SAM fire-control radars, two 'Muff Cob' 57-mm fire-control radars, two 'Bass Tilt' CIWS fire-control radars, two 'Don Kay' navigation

Almost certainly an interim class between the 'Kynda' and 'Kresta II' designs, the anti-ship RKR 'Kresta I' class carries two twin launchers for the SS-N-3B 'Shaddock' SSM either side of the bridge. To target the missiles they carry their own Kamov Ka-25 'Hormone-B' helicopter in a stern-mounted hangar.

radars, two 'Don-2' navigation radars, one 'Side Globe' ESM suite, 'Bell Clout', 'Bell Tap' and 'Bell Slam' ECM systems, and one medium-frequency bow sonar

'Kara' and 'Krasina' classes
Former USSR

Built at the 61 Kommuna, Nikolayev North Shipyard between 1971 and 1977, the seven units of the 'Kara' class (*Nikolayev, Ochakov, Kerch, Azov, Petropavlovsk, Tashkent* and *Tallinn*) are rated by the Soviets as BPKs (*Bolshoy Protivolodochnyy Korabl'*, or large anti-submarine ship). They are an enlarged COGAG gas turbine-powered refinement of the steam-powered 'Kresta II' design with improved anti-air warfare and ASW warfare systems, commissioned between 1973 and 1980 for service in the Mediterranean and Pacific Fleet theatres of operations. They also have extensive command and control facilities and can act as hunter-killer task group leaders. The SA-N-3 'Goblet' and SS-N-14 'Silex' ASW missiles carried have secondary anti-ship capabilities, the former missile having a 25-kiloton nuclear warhead available in place of the normal 150-kg (331-lb) HE type. All Soviet ships with dual-capable weapon systems have at least 25 per cent of their missiles equipped

with nuclear warheads whilst at sea. The 'Kara' class design's large super-structure is dominated by a single low gas turbine exhaust funnel. On the ship's stern is a helicopter landing pad with a hangar partially recessed below the flight deck, and to stow the Kamov Ka-25 'Hormone-A' ASW helicopter the hanger roof hatch and doors have to be opened before the helicopter is pushed in and then lowered to the deck via an elevator. The fourth ship completed, the *Azov*, was the trials ship for the new generation SA-N-6 vertical SAM and 'Top Dome' fire-control radar in the Black Sea after her aft SA-N-3 'Goblet' and 'Headlight' fire-control radar combination had been replaced by the new systems.

By 1998 only four survived three unmodified and the trials ship 'Azov' (project 1134,7BF).

Fitted to act as ASW hunter-killer task group leaders, the 'Kara' class are essentially COGAG gas-turbine-powered refinements of the 'Kresta II' design, with considerably improved defensive anti-air warfare systems.

A total of seven 'Kara' class were built at the 61 Kommuna, Nikolayev North Shipyard. One, the Azov, acted as trials vessel for the SA-N-6 vertical launch SAM system in the Black Sea, where she has remained since being built.

The 'Krasina' class of RKR is the follow-on to the 'Kara' class. Powered by gas turbines, they can manage 36 kts at full power and have a main battery of eight twin SS-N-12 'Sandbox' SSM missile launchers, augmented by a SAM defence which includes both the SA-N-6 and SA-N-4 systems.

Four 'Kara' class ships were previously deployed with the Black Sea Fleet, frequently in the Mediterranean, and the rest were in the pacific Fleet. Only two remain in commission.

In 1983 the first of the 'Kara' follow-on class, the 'Krasina' class RKR missile cruiser, was seen outside the Black Sea. The lead ship, the **Slava**, was laid down at the same Nikolayev Shipyard in 1976 after the last 'Kara' hull, and launched in 1979 with completion in 1983 after extensive trials. The hull appears to be an improved 'Kara' type with increased beam and length to accommodate new weapon systems, enhance stability and allow the radar mast height to be increased. Twin funnel exhausts are fitted, indicating gas turbine propulsion. The primary role is anti-ship warfare for which two rows of four paired SS-N-12 'Sandbox' SSMs are carried on each side of the forward superstructure. Aft of the funnels are eight eight-round vertical-launch SA-N-6 bin launchers and a 'Top Dome' fire-control radar. All other available details are given in the specification. By 1998 only three 'Slavas' were in service. The fourth, the *Admiral Lobov* was still incomplete.

Specification
'Kara' class
Displacement: 8,200 tons standard and 9,700 tons full load
Dimensions: length 173.0 m (567.6 ft); beam 18.6 m (61.0 ft); draught 6.7 m (22.0 ft)
Propulsion: COGAG gas turbine

arrangement delivering 120,000 shp (89485 kW) to two shafts
Speed: 34 kts
Complement: 525
Aircraft: one Kamov Ka-25 'Hormone-A' anti-submarine helicopter
Armament: two twin SA-N-3 'Goblet' SAM launchers with 72 missiles (except in *Azov* which has only one SA-N-3 system plus one SA-N-6 SAM system), two twin SA-N-4 'Gecko' SAM launchers with 36 missiles, two quadruple SS-N-14 'Silex' ASW launchers with eight missiles, two twin 76-mm (3-in) DP guns, four 30-mm ADG6-30 CIWS mountings, two 12-barrel RBU 6000 ASW rocket-launchers, two (none in *Petropavlovsk*) RBU 1000 ASW rocket-launchers, and two quintuple 533-mm (21-in) ASW torpedo tube mountings.
Electronics: one 'Top Sail' 3D radar, one 'Head Net-C' 3D radar, two 'Pop Group' SA-N-4 fire-control radars, two 'Head Light' SA-N-3 fire-control radars (except in *Azov*, which has one 'Head Light' plus one 'Top Dome' SA-N-6 fire-control radar), two 'Owl Screech' 76-mm (3-in) fire-control radars, two 'Bass Tilt' CIWS fire-control radars, two 'Don Kay' navigation radars, one 'Don-2' or 'Palm Frond' navigation radar, one 'Side Globe' ESM suite, 'Bell' series ECM systems (in *Nikolayev* and *Ochakov* only) or 'Rum Tub' ECM systems (except in *Nikolayev* and *Ochakov*), two 'Round House; TACAN (in *Petropavlovsk* only), one low-frequency bow sonar, and one medium-frequency variable-depth sonar

Specification (provisional)
'Krasina' class
Displacement: 11,550 tons standard and 13,000 tons full load
Dimensions: length 187.0 m (613.5 ft); beam 22.3 m (73.2 ft); draught 7.6 m (24.9 ft)
Propulsion: gas turbines
Speed: 36 kts
Complement: 650
Aircraft: two Kamov Ka-27 helicopters (one 'Helix-A' anti-submarine helicopter and one 'Helix-B' missile-guidance helicopter)
Armament: eight twin SS-N-12 'Sandbox' SSM launchers with 16 missiles, eight SA-N-6 SAM launchers with 64 missiles, two twin SA-N-4 'Gecko' SAM launchers with 36 missiles, one twin 130-mm (5.12-in) DP gun, six 30-mm ADG6-30 CIWS mountings, two 12-barrel RBU 6000

The first 'Krasina' class cruiser, the Slava, *pictured at anchor off Solum, Libya during her first out-of-area deployment in late 1983. She later sailed to join the Soviet Northern Fleet, passing the United Kingdom on the way. Only the USA has ships that can match her.*

ASW rocket-launchers, and two quadruple 533-mm (21-in) ASW torpedo tube mountings
Electronics: one 'Top Pair' 3D radar, one 'Trap Door' SS-N-12 guidance radar, one 'Kite Screech' 130-mm (5.12-in) fire-control radar, one 'Top Dome' SA-N-6 fire-control radar, two 'Pop Group' SA-N-4 fire-control radars, three 'Bass Tilt' CIWS fire-control radars, one 'Side Globe' ESM suite, one 'Rum Tub' ECM suite, and one low-frequency bow sonar

Former USSR
'Kirov' class

In December 1977 at the Baltic Shipyard in Leningrad the Soviet Union launched the largest warship built by any nation since World War II except for aircraft-carriers. Commissioned into Soviet fleet service in 1980, the **Kirov** was assigned the RKR (*Raketnyy Kreyser*, or missile cruiser) designation by the Soviets and a CGN designation by the Americans. However, in appearance and firepower the *Kirov* is more akin to the obsolete battle-cruiser category. Her powerplant is unique in being a combined nuclear and steam propulsion system with two reactors coupled to oil-fired boilers

that superheat the steam produced in the reactor plant to increase the power output available during high-speed running. The massive superstructure has most of the weapons systems located forward of it, the after end thus being available for machinery and a below-decks helicopter hangar. Up to

five Kamov Ka-25 'Hormone' or Ka-27 'Helix' helicopters can be accommodated in the hangar, with access to the flight deck by a deck lift. The helicopters are a mix of the ASW and missile-guidance/ELINT variants, the latter providing target data for the main battery of 20 SS-N-19 Mach-2.5 anti-ship cruise missiles located forward in 45°

recessed launch tubes.

The area-defence SAM is the vertical launch SA-N-6 system, which has 12 below-decks eight-round rotary launchers forward of the SS-N-19 bins. The SA-N-6 is some 7 m (23 ft) long with a 10/100-km (6.2/62-mile) range envelope, and can engage sea-skimming cruise missiles if required. The maxi-

The Soviet warship Kirov *built in the late 1970s is the closest thing to a modern version of battle cruiser. She and her sisters carried the heaviest armament seen to date on a Soviet surface combatant.*

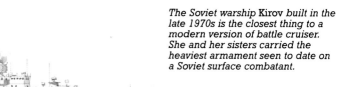

mum target engagement height is around 30000 m (98,425 ft), and with the two 'Top Dome' missile-control radars up to 12 missiles can be controlled at any one time. Close-in air defence is handled by a mix of SA-N-4 'Gecko' missiles, 30-mm CIWS mountings and 100-mm (3.9-in) DP guns.

The ASW armament is unique in being based on a reloadable twin SS-N-14 'Silex' missile-launcher with associated variable-depth low-frequency sonar aft and a low-frequency bow sonar. The usual ASW rocket-launchers and 533-mm (21-in) ASW torpedoes complement the SS-N-14 system.

The *Kirov* is fitted with an extensive command, control and communications outfit, suiting the ship to act as a task group command escort to the future nuclear-powered carrier or to operate on its own. Four ships were laid down, *Kirov* (renamed *Admiral Ushakov*) the *Frunze* (renamed

Admiral Lazarev) *Kalinin* (renamed *Admiral Nakhimov*) and *Yuri Andropov* (renamed *Petr Velikiy*). All four were redesignated after the fall of the Soviet Union but the *Petr Velikiy* is incomplete because of lack of funds.

Specification
'Kirov' class
Displacement: 22,000 tons standard and 28,000 tons full load
Dimensions: length 248.0 m (813.65 ft); beam 28.0 m (91.86 ft); draught 8.8 m (28.87 ft)
Propulsion: two pressurized-water cooled reactors with combined superheating boilers delivering 150,000 shp (111855 kW) to two shafts
Speed: 36 kts
Complement: 800
Aircraft: five Kamov Ka-25 'Hormone' or Ka-27 'Helix' anti-submarine and missile-guidance helicopters
Armament: 20 SS-N-19 SSM launchers

each with one missile, 12 SA-N-6 SAM launchers with 96 missiles, two twin SA-N-4 'Gecko' SAM launchers with 36 missiles, two 100-mm (3.9-in) DP guns, eight 30-mm ADG6-30 CIWS mountings, one twin SS-N-14 'Silex' ASW launcher with 16 missiles, one 12-barrel RBU 6000 ASW rocket-launcher, two six-barrel ASW rocket-launchers, and two quadruple 533-mm (21-in) ASW torpedo tubes
Electronics: one 'Top Pair' 3D radar, one 'Top Steer' 3D radar, two 'Top Dome' SA-N-6 fire-control radars, two 'Pop Group' SA-N-4 fire-control radars, three 'Palm Front' navigation radars, one 'Kite Screech' 100-mm (3.9-in) fire-control radar, two 'Eye Bowl' SS-N-14 fire-control radars, four 'Bass Tilt' CIWS fire-control radars, one 'Side Globe' ESM suite, 10 'Bell' series ECM systems, four 'Rum Tub' ECM systems, two twin chaff/flare launchers, one low-frequency bow sonar, and one low-frequency variable-depth sonar

The Kirov *under way. Recent intelligence reports indicate that the second vessel of the class is undergoing final acceptance trials in the Baltic. Named* Leonid Brezhnev, *she differs in detail in the weapons and sensors from her sister ship and may carry an operational laser defence system.*

Former USSR
'Moskva' class

Classified by the Soviets as PKRs (*Protivolodochnyy Kreyser*, or anti-submarine cruiser), the two 'Moskva' class ships are in fact hybrid helicopter-carriers and missile cruisers, and were developed to counter the Western strategic missile submarines in the regional seas adjacent to the Soviet Union. However, by the time the first two vessels, the *Moskva* and the *Leningrad*, had been completed at the Nikolayev South Shipyard in 1967 and 1968, it was found that they were incapable of coping with both the numbers of submarines and their capabilities, so the programme was terminated. The 'Moskva' class ships are deployed primarily to the Mediterranean as part of the Soviet 5th Eskadara. They have also on occasion appeared in the North Atlantic, North Sea, Baltic and Indian Ocean as part of deployed task forces or on transit.

In appearance the two ships are missile cruisers forward with extensive anti-air warfare and ASW systems located step-wise on the forward superstructure arrangement, which then ends abruptly in a large steam turbine exhaust stack and main radar mast assembly. A 15-m (49.2-ft) long hangar suitable for two helicopters side by side is located within this structure between the stack uptakes. The after end of the ship is taken up by an 86 m (282.2 ft) by 34 m (111.5 ft) flight deck with four mesh-covered helicopter take-off and landing spots marked out with the numbers 1 to 4. A fifth spot, marked with the letter P, is located centrally. Two 16.5 m (54.1 ft) by 4.5 m (14.8 ft) aircraft lifts serve the flight deck from the 65 m (213.25 ft) by 24 m (78.75 ft) hangar deck below. The han-

gar space can accommodate a maximum of 18 Kamov Ka-25 'Hormone-A' ASW helicopters, although 14 is the number usually carried. The *Leningrad* has been seen with two Mil Mi-8 'Hip-C' helicopters stowed on her flight deck for minesweeping duties when she assisted in the clearing of the southern end of the Suez Canal zone following the Yom Kippur War of 1973.

The quintuple 533-mm (21-in) ASW torpedo tubes originally carried behind the accommodation ladders in the ship's sides have been removed. The ASW armament relies on two 6000-m (6,500-yard) range 250-mm (9.84-in) calibre automatically reloaded rocket-launchers and a twin SU-W-N1 unguided ballistic missile-launcher firing the 30-km (18.6-mile) range FRAS-1 (Free Rocket Anti-Submarine) rocket fitted with a 15-kiloton nuclear depth bomb as the warhead. The target data for the FRAS-1 is generated by the low-frequency bow sonar and medium-frequency variable-depth sonar carried. The 'Hormone-A' helicopters provide the ASW screen at medium ranges (between 55 and 74 km/34 and 46 miles from the ship) using dipping sonar, sonobuoys, 450-mm (17.7-in) ASW torpedoes, and conventional and nuclear depth bombs. The 'Moskva' class ships were fitted to serve as command ships for ASW hunter-killer groups with maritime

patrol ASW aircraft in support. Both Ships were decommissioned in 1991–96.

Specification
'Moskva' class
Displacement: 14,500 tons standard and 17,000 tons full load
Dimensions: length 189.0 m (620.1 ft); beam 26.0 m (85.3 ft); draught 7.7 m (25.25 ft)
Propulsion: geared steam turbines delivering 100,000 shp (74570 kW) to two shafts
Speed: 30 kts
Complement: 850
Aircraft: 18 Kamov Ka-25 'Hormone-A' anti-submarine helicopters

Armament: eight twin SA-N-3 'Goblet' SAM launchers with 48 missiles, two twin 57-mm DP guns, one twin SU-W-N1 ASW launcher with 20 FRAS-1 rockets, and two 12-barrel RBU 6000 ASW rocket-launchers
Electronics: one 'Top Sail' 3D radar, one 'Head Net-C' 3D radar, two 'Head Light' SAM fire-control radars, two 'Muff Cob' 57-mm fire-control radars, three 'Don-2' navigation radars, one 'Side Globe' ESM suite, two 'Bell Clout' ECM systems, two 'Bell Slam' ECM systems, two 'Bell Tap' ECM systems, two twin-barrel flare/chaff launchers, one low-frequency bow sonar, and one medium-frequency variable-depth sonar

Above: the PKR Moskva *is a hybrid helicopter-carrier and missile cruiser designed originally to counter the Western SSBNs in seas close to the Soviet homeland. An air group of 14 Kamov Ka-25 'Hormone-A' helicopters is normally carried, which work in four aircraft flights to form medium range ASW screens.*

Below: The 'Moskva' class have full command and control facilities to co-ordinate both hunter-killer task groups and maritime patrol aircraft, including their own ASW helicopters, to 'sanitize' areas of ocean.

Destroyers

Originally developed as an antidote to fast torpedo boats late in the 19th century, the destroyer is now fitted with an array of missiles, making it a specialist craft suitable for either anti-submarine warfare or the anti-aircraft role. It is in the latter area that it is likely to make its mark in any future conflict.

HMS *Glasgow,* a 'Type 42' destroyer commissioned in 1979. Its armament includes a 114-mm (4.5-in) gun, two 20-mm Oerlikons, six anti-submarine torpedo tubes and four Mk 46 torpedoes.

The modern destroyer would hardly be recognizable to one familiar with the classic gun-and-torpedo-armed vessels of World War II. They were the most active surface units in World War II: this was especially notable in the Japanese fleet in the Pacific, the German fleet preying on Soviet convoys, and the Italian anti-submarine attacks in the Mediterranean.

Even the term 'destroyer' is somewhat loose, covering as it does vessels ranging from the small, gun-armed 'Kotlin' class of the former Soviet navy up to the Russian 'Sovremenny' and American 'Spruance' and 'Kidd' classes, each as large as light cruisers of the 1940s.

Since World War II the destroyer has evolved from a torpedo-armed, all-gun surface warfare vessel into a highly specialized anti-air or anti-submarine ship capable either of independent operations for a short time or of operating as an escort in a task force.

The losses suffered by the Royal Navy's destroyers during the Falklands war was a wake-up call to others. It proved to NATO that the UK's minimally armed warships, which had been so constructed to satisfy restraints imposed by the UK Treasury, were extremely vulnerable in a conventional war, let alone the nuclear scenarios proposed for the North Atlantic theatre of operations. Short-term action was taken to rectify some of the faults, and plans were made to update the vessels as they became due for a refit, with the installation of close-range weapons a high priority.

Probably the most capable modern destroyer design is the 'Spruance' class, optimized for ASW. Modifying the design for the anti-air role produced the 'Kidd' class, which at the time of their commissioning were the most powerfully armed general-purpose destroyers in the world. Some of the 'Spruance' class vessels were retrofitted with the Tomahawk cruise missile, which they can discharge from vertical launchers, but not all the ships received the necessary modifications. This decision was taken on the grounds that it would be too expensive to modify all 31 vessels in service.

'Haruna' and 'Shirane' classes

The **'Haruna' class** and follow-on improved **'Shirane' class** are the only destroyer-sized ships in the world which can carry and operate three large Sea King ASW helicopters. Both ship classes were built with strong ASW armaments and are weaker than most Western designs in both anti-air and anti-surface warfare systems, although they are to be modernized within the next few years with systems such as the Harpoon SSM and the 20-mm Phalanx CIWS to help rectify these shortcomings. The 'Haruna' class, *Haruna* (DDH141) and *Hiei* (DDH142), have continuous superstructures with their single combined radar mast and funnel (known as a 'mack') offset to port to allow space for the third helicopter in the hangar. The later 'Shirane' class units, *Shirane* (DDH143) and *Kurama* (DDH144) have a broken superstructure with two 'macks', one offset to port atop the main superstructure forward and the other atop the detached hangar aft. For landing the helicopters in most weather conditions they are fitted with the Canadian Bear Trap hauldown system, whilst to reduce their underwater radiated noise levels from the main propulsion machinery they adopted the 'Masker' bubble-generating system: this forms a continuous curtain of minute air bubbles over the parts of the hull beneath the machinery spaces with the bubbles acting as a sound-damping layer. A further class of large helicopter-

Hiei (DDH 142) executes a turn to port at high speed. The lack of any air defence systems, apart from the 127-mm (5-in) dual-purpose gun mounts, is readily apparent, although it is hoped that a Sea Sparrow SAM system will be fitted in the future.

carrying destroyers is expected within the next few years.

Specification
'Haruna' class
Displacement: 4,700 tons standard and 6,300 tons full load
Dimensions: length 153.0 m (502 ft); beam 17.5 m (57 ft 5 in); draught 5.1 m (16 ft 9 in)
Machinery: geared steam turbines delivering 70,000 shp (52,200 kW) to two shafts
Speed: 32 kts
Aircraft: three Mitsubishi-Sikorsky SH-3 Sea King ASW helicopters
Armament: two quadruple Harpoon SSM launchers (no reloads, to be fitted), one octuple Sea Sparrow SAM launcher (no reloads, being fitted), two single 127-mm (5-in) DP guns, two 20-mm Phalanx CIWS (being fitted), one octuple ASROC ASW missile launcher (16 missiles), and two triple 324-mm (12.75-in) Type 68 ASW torpedo tubes (6 Mk 46 torpedoes)
Electronics: one SPS-52B 3D radar, one OPS-17 surface-search radar, two

Type 72 gun fire-control radars, one WM-25 missile fire-control radar (being fitted), one URN-20 TACAN, one ESM suite, one OQS-3 hull sonar, and one SQS-35(J) variable-depth sonar
Complement: 340

Specification
'Shirane' class
Displacement: 5,200 tons standard and 6,800 tons full load
Dimensions: length 158.8 m (521 ft); beam 17.5 m (57 ft 5 in); draught 5.3 m (17 ft 5 in)
Machinery: geared steam turbines

delivering 70,000 shp (52200 kW) to two shafts
Speed: 32 kts
Aircraft: as 'Haruna' class
Armament: as Modernized 'Haruna' class
Electronics: one OPS-12 3D radar, one OPS-28 surface-search radar, one OPS-22 navigation radar, one WM-25 missile fire-control radar, two Type 72 gun fire-control radars, one URN-20A TACAN, one ESM suite, one OQS-101 hull sonar, one SQR-18A towed-array sonar, and one SQS-35(J) variable-depth sonar
Complement: 370

The 'Haruna' class and the follow-on 'Shirane' design are the only destroyer-size ships in the world to carry three large ASW helicopters as part of their armament. Although very capable ASW platforms, they are very weak in anti-air and surface ship weapons.

'Tachikaze', 'Takatsuki' and 'Hatsuyuki' classes

In order of building, the **'Takatsuki' class** was the first of these three classes to be constructed. Comprising the *Takatsuki* (DD164), *Kikuzuki* (DD165), *Mochizuki* (DD166) and *Nagatsuki* (DD167), the class has a typical American appearance in having two single 127-mm (5-in) guns and an ASROC ASW missile launcher. They originally carried and operated the American ASW DASH system for which they carried a hangar aft for three QH-50 drones. Although DASH was unsuccessful in American service, it proved successful in the Japanese navy, and was retired from service with this class only in 1977. Major refits in the 1990s improved their impressive ASW armaments. The *Mochizuki* was relegated to training duties as ASU-7019 in 1995 and *Nagatsuki* was stricken in 1996.

During the early 1970s the Japanese Maritime Self-Defense Force needed to improve its medium-range area-defence SAM capabilities and thus laid down the three 'Tachikaze' class ships at three-yearly intervals from

1973. These vessels are the *Tachikaze* (DDG168), *Asakaze* (DDG169) and *Sawakaze* (DDG170) and commissioned in 1976, 1979 and 1982 respectively. They each carry a single-rail Mk 13 launcher for the Standard SM-1MR missile. No helicopter facilities are provided, and the ASW armament is confined to ASROC missiles and Mk 46 self-defence torpedoes. In order to save on construction costs the class adopted the propulsion plant and machinery of the 'Haruna' class of helicopter-carrying ASW destroyers.

The **'Hatsuyuki' class** was ordered in the mid-1970s as a gas turbine-powered multi-purpose design with a balanced anti-air, anti-ship and anti-submarine sensor and armament fit from the outset. An aluminium-alloy superstructure is used. Five ships from an eventual 12-ship class were in service by 1983, namely the *Hatsuyuki* (DD122), *Shirayuki* (DD123), *Mineyuki* (DD124), *Sawayuki* (DD125) and *Hamayuki* (DD126), with the remainder due to commission at regular intervals up to 1987. A slightly larger 'Im-

proved Hatsuyuki' class with steel superstructure is due for the late 1980s.

Specification
'Takatsuki' class
Displacement: (DD164-165) 3,050 tons standard and 4,500 tons full load;

Designed to enhance the Japanese Maritime Self-Defense Forces anti-aircraft defences, the guided-missile destroyer Tachikaze (DDG 168) and her two sisters carry a single-rail Mk 13 Standard MR-1 SAM system aft to provide area defence.

(DD166-167) 3,100 tons standard and 4,500 tons full load
Dimensions: length 136.0 m (446 ft 2 in); beam 13.4 m (44 ft); draught 4.4 m (14 ft 5 in)
Machinery: geared steam turbines delivering 60,000 shp (44740 kW) to two shafts
Speed: 32 kts
Aircraft: helicopter landing platform (DD166-167 only)
Armament: (DD164-165) two quadruple Harpoon SSM launchers (no reloads), one octuple Sea Sparrow SAM launcher (no reloads), one single 127-mm (5-in) DP gun, provision for two 20-mm Phalanx CIWS mountings, one octuple ASROC ASW missile launcher (16 missiles), one Type 71 375-mm (14.76-in) Bofors ASW rocket launcher (36 rockets), and two triple Type 68 324-mm (12.75-in) ASW torpedo tubes (6 Mk 46 torpedoes)
Armament: (DD166-167) two single 127-mm (5-in) DP guns, one octuple ASROC ASW missile launcher (16 missiles), one Type 71 375-mm (14.76-in) Bofors ASW rocket launcher (36

rockets), and two triple Type 68 324-mm (12.75-in) ASW torpedo tubes (6 Mk 46 torpedoes)
Electronics: one OPS-11B air-search radar, one OPS-17 surface-search radar, two Mk 56 fire-control radars (Type 72 in DD167), one URN-20 TACAN (not in DD165), one NOLR-1B ECM system (NOLQ-1 in DD165-166 with Mk 36 Super RBOC chaff launchers), one OQS-3 hull sonar, one SQS-35(J) variable-depth sonar (DD166-167 only) and one SQR-18A towed-array sonar (DD164-165 only)
Complement: 270

Specification
'Tachikaze' class
Displacement: (DD168-169) 3,850 tons standard and 4,800 tons full load; (DD170) 3,950 tons standard and 4,800 tons full load
Dimensions: length 143.0 m (469 ft 2 in); beam 14.3 m (46 ft 11 in); draught 4.6 m (15 ft 1 in)
Machinery: geared steam turbines delivering 70,000 shp (52200 kW) to two shafts

Speed: 32 kts
Armament: two quadruple Harpoon SSM launchers (no reloads, in DD170 only), one single-rail Mk 13 Standard SM-1MR launcher (40 missiles), two single 127-mm (5-in) DP guns, one 20-mm Phalanx CIWS mounting (being fitted), one octuple ASROC ASW missile launcher (16 missiles), and two triple Type 68 324-mm (12.75-in) ASW torpedo tubes (6 Mk 46 torpedoes)
Electronics: one SPS-52B 3D radar, one OPS-11B (OPS-28 in DD170) air-search radar, one OPS-17 surface-search radar, two SPG-51C Standard fire-control radars, two Type 72 gun fire-control radars, two SATCOMM communications systems, one OLT-3 ESM suite, four Mk 36 Super RBOC chaff launchers, and one OQS-3 (OQS-4 in DD170) hull sonar
Complement: 260 in DD168, 250 in DD169 and 270 in DD170

Specification
'Hatsuyuki' class
Displacement: 2,950 tons standard and 3,700 tons full load

Dimensions: length 131.7 m (432 ft 1 in); beam 13.7 m (45 ft); draught 4.3 m (14 ft 2 in)
Machinery: two Rolls-Royce Olympus TM3B gas turbines delivering 45,000 shp (3355 kW) and two Rolls-Royce Tyne RM1C gas turbines delivering 10,680 shp (7965 kW) in a COGOG arrangement to two shafts
Speed: 30 kts
Aircraft: one Mitsubishi-Sikorsky SH-3 Sea King ASW helicopter
Armament: two quadruple Harpoon SSM launchers (no reloads), one octuple Sea Sparrow SAM launcher (no reloads), one single 76-mm (3-in) DP gun, two 20-mm Phalanx CIWS mountings, one octuple ASROC ASW missile launcher (16 missiles), and two triple Type 68 324-mm (12.75-in) ASW torpedo tubes (6 Mk 46 torpedoes)
Electronics: one OPS-14B air-search radar, one OPS-18 surface-search radar, one FCS2 missile fire-control radar, one GFCS2 gun fire-control radar, one ECM suite, and one OQS-4 hull sonar
Complement: 190

ITALY
'Audace' class

Essentially an enlarged version of the 'Impavido' class hull design with greatly improved armament and an increased freeboard, the *Audace* (D551) and *Ardito* (D550) have proved to be excellent ships in terms of habitability and seaworthiness, so much so that two further units of an 'Improved Audace' class design were built between 1986 and 1993 to replace the 'Impetuoso' class destroyers. In terms of capabilities the two **'Audace'** class units are an improvement on the 'Andrea Doria' class of helicopter carriers in almost every respect save the number of helicopters carried. They received the Otomat Mk 2 SSM system in 1988–91 and are relatively area in NATO service in having four stern-mounted 533-mm (21-in) torpedo tubes for dual-role long-range wire-guided active/passive acoustic-homing A184 torpedoes as well as self-defence 324-mm (12.75-in) tubes for American Mk 46 ASW torpedoes. The Whitehead A184 is a dual-role 1300-kg (2866-lb) weapon with a range of around 14 km (8.7 miles). The two embarked ASW helicopters carry both Mk 44 and Mk 46 torpedoes, American Mk 54 depth bombs, dipping sonar and sonobuoys for use against sub-surface targets, and the French AS.12 missile for use against surface targets. The

helicopters are also being provided with the capability to provide midcourse guidance for the Otomat missiles during 'over-the-horizon' missile engagements.

Specification
'Audace' class
Displacement: 3,950 tons standard and 4,559 tons full load
Dimensions: length 136.6 m (448 ft); beam 14.23 m (46 ft 8 in); draught 4.6 m (15 ft)
Machinery: geared steam turbines delivering 73,000 shp (54,435 kW) to

two shafts
Speed: 33 kts
Aircraft: two Agusta-Bell AB.212ASW helicopters or one Agusta-Sikorsky SH-3D Sea King ASW helicopter
Armament: one single-rail Mk 13 Standard SM-1MR SAM launcher (40 missiles), two single 127-mm (5-in) DP guns, four single 76-mm (3-in) AA guns, two triple 324-mm (12.75-in) ILAS-3 ASW torpedo tubes (12 Mk 46 torpedoes), and two twin 533-mm (21-in) torpedo tubes (12 A184 torpedoes)
Electronics: one SPS-52 3D radar, one RAN20S air-search radar, one SPQ2

The 'Audace' class, by use of modern lightweight weapon systems and the mounting of a Mk 13 SAM launcher atop the hangar, has greater capabilities in almost every respect (save the number of helicopters carried) than the 'Andrea Doria' class.

air- and surface-search radar, two SPG-51B Standard fire-control radars, one 3RM20 navigation radar, one ESM suite, two 20-barrel SCLAR chaff and IR decoy launchers, and one CWE610 hull sonar
Complement: 380

The Audace (D551) uses an enlarged version of the 'Impavido' class hull design with increased freeboard. A vastly improved armament fit includes a hangar and flight deck suitable for operating either two Agusta-Bell AB.212ASW or one Agusta-Sikorsky SH-3D Sea King ASW helicopters.

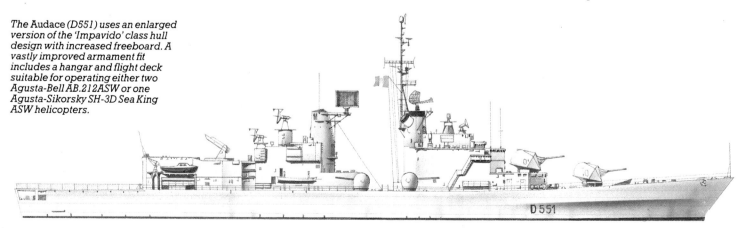

FRANCE
'Suffren' class

Originally classed as light cruisers, the **Suffren** (D602) and the **Duquesne** (D603) were reclassed as 'Suffren' class destroyers. In actual fact they are guided-missile destroyers designed to give area anti-air warfare and ASW protection to the 'Clemenceau' class aircraft-carriers. Initial plans called for three ships to be built as a start, with more planned, but in practice only two were laid down. Built almost exclusively with French weapons and sensors, they were the first French naval vessels to be designed to carry SAM missiles, and with three pairs of gyro-controlled non-retractable stabilizers are very stable missile platforms. They are distinguishable in French service by the isolated tall central 'mack' and the distinctive DRBI 23 radome forward, the radome being unique to this class. In the mid-1970s both vessels underwent modifications to fit new weapons and to upgrade the area-defence SAM system to fire only the Masurca Mk 2 Model 3 semi-active radar homing missile. Both ships are now serving with the French Mediterranean Fleet as escorts to the carriers, being transferred there in 1975. The area-defence ASW missile carried is the Malafon, a 1500-kg (3,307-lb) 13-km (8.1-mile) range command-guided glider. This is launched with the aid of a double booster and has as payload a 30-kt 533-mm (21-in) L4 active/passive acoustic-homing ASW torpedo weighing 540 kg (1,190 lb) and having a range of around 5.5 km (3.4 miles). The vessels use the 35-kt 1000-kg (2,205-lb) L5 Model 4 active/passive acoustic-homing torpedo in their self-defence tubes. These have a 150-kg (331-lb) HE warhead compared with the 104-kg (229-lb) warhead of the L4, and a range in the order of 7 km (4.35 miles).

Specification
'Suffren' class
Displacement: 5,090 tons standard and 6,090 tons full load
Dimensions: length 157.6 m (517 ft); beam 15.54 m (51 ft); draught 7.25 m (23 ft 9 in)
Machinery: geared steam turbines delivering 72,500 hp (54065 kW) to two shafts
Speed: 34 kts
Aircraft: none
Armament: four single MM.38 Exocet launchers (no reloads), one twin Masurca SAM launcher (48 missiles), two single 100-mm (3.9-in) DP guns, four single 20-mm AA guns, one single Malafon ASW missile launcher (13 missiles), and four single fixed ASW 533-mm (21-in) torpedo tubes (10 L5 torpedoes)
Electronics: one DRBI 23 air-search and target-designation radar, one DRBV 50 surface-search radar, two DRBR 51 Masurca fire-control radars, one DRBC 32A fire-control radar, one DRBN 32 navigation radar, one URN-20 TACAN, one SENIT 1 action information system, one ESM suite, two Dagaie chaff/decoy launchers, one DUBV 23 hull sonar, and one DUBV 43 variable-depth sonar
Complement: 355

Above: Classed initially as a missile cruiser and then as a frégate, the Suffren (D602) was the first French warship designed from the outset to carry surface-to-air missiles in order to act as an ASW and anti-air warfare escort for the two French fixed-wing aircraft carriers, Clemenceau and Foch.

The two 'Suffren' class vessels are characterized in French navy service by the very distinctive radome covering the DRBI-23 3D radar system, which provides target data for the stern mounted twin-rail Masurca semi-active radar homing area defence SAM launcher. The main ASW defence is the amidships Malafon ASW missile launcher.

FRANCE
'Type C70' class

The 'Type C70' class is designed to replace both the 'Type T47' and 'Type T53' class destroyers built in the 1950s, and as such is divided into two groups, one specifically for the ASW task and the other for anti-air warfare duties.

The eight 'Type C70/ASW' vessels, the **George Leygues** (D640), **Dupleix** (D641), **Montcalm** (D642), **Jean de Vienne** (D643) plus four others as yet unnamed, incorporate many of the features employed in the three 'Type F677' frigates but on a smaller displacement. The first four 'Type C70/1' ships have the same hangar and facilities for the two embarked Westland Lynx helicopters, one of which is equipped for the localization, classification and attack of sub-surface targets with dipping sonar, Mk 44 and Mk 46 torpedoes, and 161-kg (350-lb) depth bombs, whilst the other is configured for the detection, identification and attack of small lightly-defended surface targets with AS.12 wire-guided and AS.15TT command-guided missiles. The last four ships form a separate sub-class ('Type C70/2') and will incorporate several modifications to the basic design, including a longer-range anti-missile capable Crotale SAM system, a towed-array sonar and a raised bridge structure. No Malafon ASW missile system could be carried by either sub-class because of the space required for the gas-turbine propulsion system and its exhaust outlets.

The same hull is used for the 'Type C70/AA' anti-air warfare version, but the armament and propulsion fits are completely different. Only the first two ships have been ordered as yet for completion in 1987-8, the final two units being scheduled for commissioning in 1990. The Mk 13 Standard missile launchers used will be refurbished units taken from 'Type T47' destroyers as

they pay off for replacement by the 'Type C70s'. The single Aérospatiale SA 365F Dauphin helicopter carried by each ship will be used primarily in the anti-surface ship role with AS.15TT missiles, and will also be capable of providing mid-course guidance of the MM.40 Exocets.

Specification
'Type C70/ASW' class
Displacement: 3,830 tons standard and 4,170 tons full load
Dimensions: length 139.0 m (456 ft); beam 14.0 m (45 ft 11 in); draught 5.7 m (18 ft 8 in)
Machinery: CODOG arrangement with two Rolls-Royce Olympus gas turbines delivering 52,000 shp (38775 kW) and two SEMT-Pielstick 16PA6 CV280 diesels delivering 10,400 shp (7755 kW) each to two shafts

Speed: 30 kts
Aircraft: two Westland Lynx anti-submarine and anti-ship helicopters
Armament: up to eight single MM.38 Exocet (MM.40 Exocet from *Montcalm* onwards) anti-ship missile launchers (no reloads), one octuple Crotale Naval SAM launcher (26 missiles), one single 100-mm (3.9-in) DP gun, two single 20-mm AA guns, and two single fixed 533-mm (21-in) ASW torpedo tubes (10 L5 torpedoes)
Electronics: one DRBV 26 air-search radar, one DRBV 51C air- and surface-search radar, one DRBC 32D fire-control radar, two Decca 1226 navigation radars, one SPG-51C missile fire-control radar, one SENIT 4 action information system, one ARBR 17 passive ESM system, two Sagaie and two Dagaie chaff/decoy launchers, one DUBV 23 hull sonar, one DUBV 43 variable-depth sonar and (last four only) one EBTF passive towed-array

sonar
Complement: 216

Specification
'Type C70/AA' class
Displacement: 4,000 tons standard and 4,340 tons full load
Dimensions: length 139.0 m (456 ft); beam 14.0 m (45 ft 11 in); draught 5.5 m (18 ft)
Machinery: four SEMT-Pielstick 18PAG BTC diesels delivering 42,300 shp (31545 kW) to two shafts
Speed: 29.6 kts
Aircraft: one Aérospatiale SA 365F Dauphin anti-ship helicopter
Armament: four twin MM.40 Exocet anti-ship missile launchers (no reloads), one Mk 13 single-rail Standard SM-1MR SAM launcher (40 missiles), two single 100-mm (3.9-in) DP guns, two single 20-mm AA guns,

and two single fixed 533-mm (21-in) ASW torpedo tubes (10 L5 torpedoes)
Electronics: one DRBJ 11B 3D radar, one DRBV 26 air-search radar, two SPG-51C SAM missile-control radars, one DRBC 32D fire-control radar, one SENIT 6 action information system, one ARBR 17 and one ARBB 33 ESM systems, two Dagaie and two Sagaie chaff/decoy launchers, one DUBA 25 hull sonar, and one EBTF passive towed-array sonar
Complement: 241

Designed to replace the 'Type T47' and 'Type T53' classes of destroyers, the 'Type C70' is to be built in two sub-classes for ASW and anti-air warfare purposes. The lead ship of the ASW group is the Georges Leygues (D640)*, and she will be joined by seven sister ships.*

Former USSR

'Kashin' and 'Kashin (Mod)' classes

Built as the world's first major class of warships powered by gas turbines, the 20-ship **'Kashin' class** was produced from 1963 onwards at the Zhdanov Shipyard, Leningrad (four units 1964-6), and at the 61 Kommuna (North) Shipyard, Hikolayev (16 units 1963-72). The last ship, *Sderzhanny*, was completed to a revised design subsequently designated **'Kashin (Mod)' class** by NATO. This involved lengthening the hull, modernizing the electronics and fitting four SS-N-2c 'Styx' SSM launchers, ADG6-30 CIWS mountings and a variable-depth sonar. Since the *Sderzhanny* was completed five other ships (the *Ognevoy, Slavny, Smely, Smyshlenny* and *Stroyny*) have undergone conversion to this configuration between 1973 and 1980. In 1974 the *Otvzhny* of the standard type foundered in the Black Sea following a catastrophic explosion and fire that lasted for five hours. Over 200 of her crew were killed, making this the worst peacetime naval disaster since World War II. In 1981 the *Provorny* re-entered service with the Black Sea Fleet following conversion to the trials ship for the SA-N-7 SAM system. Apart from the previously mentioned units the other units of this *bolshoy protivo-lodochny korabl'* (large ASW ship) type are the *Komsomolets Ukrainy, Krasny-Kavkaz, Krasny-Krim, Obraztsovy, Odarenny, Reshitelny, Skory, Smetlivy, Soobratzitelny, Sposobny, Steregushchy* and *Strogy*. Most are expected to serve on into the 1990s, although a new missile-armed destroyer class is expected to enter service as their eventual replacements. Three further units, designated **'Kashin II'** by NATO, were built at

Nikolayev in the late 1970s for India; named *Rajput* (D51), *Rana* (D52) and *Ranjit* (D53) these are considerably modified in comparison with the Soviet ships, having only a single 76-mm (3-in) gun mount, four SS-N-2b 'Styx' SSM launchers in pairs on each side of the bridge, and a helicopter flight deck and hangar aft for one Kamov Ka-25 'Hormone-A' ASW helicopter in place of the after 76-mm (3-in) gun mount. A further three ships were believed to have been ordered by India in 1982.

Specification
'Kashin' class
Displacement: 3,750 tons standard and 4,500 tons full load
Dimensions: length 144.0 m (472 ft 5 in); beam 15.8 m (51 ft 10 in); draught 4.8 m (15 ft 9 in)
Machinery: four gas turbines delivering 96,000 shp (71585 kW) to two shafts
Speed: 36 kts
Aircraft: helicopter landing pad only
Armament: two twin SA-N-1 'Goa' SAM launchers (32 missiles) except *Provorny* one SA-N-7 single-rail SAM launcher (24 missiles), two twin 76-mm (3-in) DP guns, two 250-mm (9.84-in) RBU600 ASW rocket launchers, one quintuple 533-mm (21-in) ASW torpedo tube mounting (except *Provorny* none), and 20-40 mines (according to type)
Electronics: (*Provorny*) one 'Head Net-C' 3D radar, one 'Top Steer' 3D radar, two 'Don Kay' navigation radars, eight 'Front Dome' SA-N-7 fire-control radars, two 'Watch Dog' ECM systems, one 'High Pole-B' IFF system, two 'Owl Screech' 76-mm (3-in) fire-control radars, and one high-frequency hull

sonar
Electronics: (rest) eight ships one 'Big Net' air-search and one 'Head Net-C' 3D radars, or three ships two 'Head Net-A' air-search radars, or *Soobrazitelny* two 'Head Net-C' 3D radars, two 'Peel Group' SA-N-1 fire-control radar, two 'Don Kay' or 'Don 2' navigation radars, two 'Owl Screech' 76-mm (3-in) fire-control radars, two 'Watch Dog' ECM systems, two 'High Pole-B' IFF systems, and one high-frequency hull sonar
Complement: 280

Specification
'Kashin (Mod)' class
Displacement: 3,950 tons standard and 4,650 tons full load
Dimensions: length 147.0 m (482 ft 3 in); beam 15.8 m (51 ft 10 in); draught 4.8 m (15 ft 9 in)
Machinery: as 'Kashin' class
Speed: 35 kts
Aircraft: helicopter landing pad only
Armament: four single SS-N-2c 'Styx' SSM launchers (no reloads), two twin

Although construction of the 'Kashin' class has long since halted for the Soviet navy, the class in a heavily modified form has been reintroduced specifically for export to India.

SA-N-1 'Goa' SAM launchers (32 missiles), four 30-mm ADG6-30 CIWS mountings, two 250-mm (9.84-in) RBU6000 ASW rocket launchers, and one quintuple 533-mm (21-in) ASW torpedo tube mounting
Electronics: one 'Big Net' aft-search radar, one 'Head Net-C' 3D radar, (except *Ognevoy* two 'Head Net-A' air-search radars), two 'Don Kay' navigation radars, two 'Owl Screech' 76-mm (3-in) fire-control radars, two 'Bass Tilt' CIWS fire-control radars, two 'Peel Group' SA-N-1 fire-control radars, two 'Bell Shroud' and two 'Bell Squat' ECM systems, four 16-barrel chaff and IR decoy launchers, one medium-frequency hull sonar, and one low-frequency variable-depth sonar
Complement: 300

The 'Kashin' class first entered service in the early 1960s with the last of 20 units commissioning in 1972. Surprisingly, only six have undergone extensive modifications during that time to form the 'Kashin Mod' sub-class, whilst the others have undergone only normal refits.

'Udaloy' class

The 'Udaloy' class (Soviet designation *bolshoy protivolodochny korabl'*, or large ASW ship) was originally given the provisional NATO codename Bal-Com 3. The two ships operational in early 1984, the *Udaloy* and *Vitse Admiral Kulakov*, are similar in concept to the American 'Spruance' class ASW destroyers, even to the use of gas turbine propulsion. The class is under construction at the Yantar Shipyard (Kaliningrad) and the Zhdanvo Shipyard (Leningrad), and it is estimated that around a dozen will be in service by the end of the decade. The class has four funnels in an arrangement similar to that of the 'Kashin' class missile destroyers, and carries two quadruple launchers for the SS-N-14 'Silex' missile as the main armament. A unique twin hangar system with associated helicopter flight deck is located aft for two Kamov Ka-27 'Helix-A' ASW helicopters. These carry dipping sonar, sonobuoys, a surface-search radar, nuclear or conventional depth charges, and 450-mm (17.7-in) ASW torpedoes for their anti-submarine role, and can be used in all-weather and night dipping sonar operations. It is probable that the 'Helix-A' also car-

ries a targeting and mid-course guidance unit for the 'Silex' missiles, so making it possible for the missile's 55-km (34.1-mile) maximum range to be exploited fully. If this is correct, the capability of the 'Udaloys' is considerably enhanced over that of other Soviet ASW ships, it being thought previously that only suitably equipped surface ships could guide the 'Silex'. The self-defence SAM carried is the vertical-launch SA-N-8 system, with an as-yet unidentified missile in eight six-round launch bins.

Specification
'Udaloy' class
Displacement: 6,700 tons standard and 8,200 tons full load
Dimensions: length 162.0 m (531 ft 6 in); beam 19.3 m (63 ft 4 in); draught 6.2 m (20 ft 4 in)
Machinery: four gas turbines in a COGOG arrangement delivering 120,000 shp (89485 kW) to two shafts
Speed: 34 kts
Aircraft: two Kamov Ka-27 'Helix-A' ASW helicopters
Armament: two quadruple SS-N-14 'Silex' ASW missile launchers (no reloads), eight SA-N-8 SAM launchers

(48 missiles), two single 100-mm (3.9-in) DP guns, four 30-mm ADG6-30 CIWS mountings, two 250-mm (9.84-in) RBU6000 ASW rocket launchers, two quadruple 533-mm (21-in) ASW torpedo tubes, and 30-50 mines (depending on type)
Electronics: two 'Strut Pair' air- and surface-search radars, three 'Palm Frond' navigation and helicopter-control radars, two unoccupied positions or missile fire-control radars, two 'Eye Bowl' SS-N-14 fire-control radars, one 'Kite Screech' 100-mm (3.9-in) fire-control radars, two 'Bass Tilt' CIWS fire-control radars, two 'Round House' TACAN, two 'High Pole-B' IFF, one 'Fly Screen-B' aircraft landing aid, two 'Bell Shroud' and two 'Bell Squat' ECM systems, two twin-barrel chaff and IR decoy launchers, one low-frequency bow sonar, and one low-frequency variable-depth sonar
Complement: 300

Right: Fitted with eight launchers for a new vertical launch point defence SAM system plus the usual variety of Soviet ASW weapon systems, the 'Udaloy' class of ASW destroyer is well capable of taking care of itself in unfriendly waters whilst prosecuting a submarine contact.

Below: The 'Udaloy' class, according to the latest American intelligence reports, is being constructed at a very fast rate with up to six units operational and another five either being built or fitted out at two different shipyards. This building of specialist surface ship classes follows the doctrine laid down by Admiral Gorshkov in the 1960s.

'Sovremenny' class

Known originally as **BalCom 2** (Baltic Combatant no. 2) by NATO, the 'Sovremenny' class took over the construction slipway at the Zhdanov Shipyard, Leningrad, that had been used by the 'Kresta II' ASW cruiser class. Two units, the *Sovremenny* and *Otchyanny*, are currently in service with additional units joining at yearly intervals from 1983 onwards. Designated by the Soviets as *eskadrenny minonosets* (destroyer), the class is devoted to surface strike warfare with a self-defence SAM system and a limited ASW capability. The propulsion plant is of the pressurized geared steam turbine type, and the design is the first Soviet warship type to be fitted with a telescoping helicopter hangar amidships next to the helicopter landing platform. The main armament comprises two quadruple SSM launchers for the new SS-N-22 (an improved and higher-speed version of the SS-N-9 'Siren') fitted with either a 500-kg (1,102-lb) HE or 200-kiloton nuclear warhead. Two twin 130-mm (5.12-in) fully automatic water-cooled gun mounts are also fitted fore and aft: controlled by a 'Kite Screech' H-band fire-control radar, these can engage surface targets out to 28000-m (30,600-yard) range. The SAM system fitted is the SA-N-7, which uses two single-rail launchers and six 'Front Dome' radar directors. The Mach 3 SA-N-7 is a navalized version of the Soviet

army's solid-fuel SA-11 missile and will eventually replace the SA-N-1 'Goa' as the navy's medium-range SAM system. Target engagement altitudes are between 300 m (100 ft) and 14000 m (45,930 ft), with a minimum range of 3 km (1.86 miles) and a maximum range of 28 km (17.4 miles). It is estimated that by the late 1980s 10 'Sovremenny' class will be in service.

Specification
'Sovremenny' class
Displacement: 6,200 tons standard and 7,800 tons full load
Dimensions: length 155.6 m (510 ft 6 in); beam 17.3 m (56 ft 9 in); draught 6.5 m (21 ft 4 in)
Machinery: geared turbo-pressurized steam turbines delivering 100,000 shp (74570 kW) to two shafts
Speed: 36 kts
Aircraft: one Kamov Ka-25 'Hormone-B' missile-guidance/Elint helicopter
Armament: two quadruple SS-N-22 SSM launchers (no reloads), two single SA-N-7 SAM launchers (48 missiles), two twin 130-mm (5.12-in) DP guns, four 30-mm ADG6-30 CIWS mountings, two RBU1000 300-mm (11.8-in) ASW rocket launchers, two twin 533-mm (21-in) ASW torpedo tubes, and 30-50 mines (according to type)
Electronics: one 'Top Steer' 3D radar, three 'Palm Frond' navigation and helicopter-control radars, one 'Band

The 'Sovremenny' class introduced a new fully-automatic water-cooled 130-mm (5.12-in) dual-purpose gun

Stand' SS-N-22 fire-control radar, two 'Bass Tilt' CIWS fire-control radars, one 'Kite Screech' 130-mm (5.12-in) fire-control radar, six 'Front Dome' SA-N-7 fire-control radars, two 'Bell

into service, as well as a telescopic helicopter hangar forward of the landing pad.

Shroud' and two 'Bell Squat' ECM systems, two twin-barrel chaff/IR decoy launchers, and one medium-frequency hull sonar
Complement: 350

'Iroquois' class

Ordered in 1968 as anti-submarine destroyers, the four **'DDH 280' class** destroyers HMCS *Iroquois* (280), HMCS *Huron* (281), HMCS *Athabaskan* (282) and HMCS *Algonquin* (283) are a revised version of the eight Tartar SAM-equipped 'Tribal' class of general-purpose frigates cancelled in 1963. They have the same hull design, dimensions and basic characteristics as the 'Tribals' but have enhanced ASW features such as three sonars, a helicopter flight deck and twin hangar for two licence-built Sikorsky CH-124 Sea King ASW helicopters. The weapons and sensor fit is a mixed bag with an Italian 127-mm (5-in) OTO-Melara Compact gun, two four-rail launchers for the American Sea Sparrow SAM system that retract into a deckhouse in the forward part of the superstructure, Dutch and American electronics, and a British ASW mortar. The last is the ubiquitous triple-barrelled Mk 10 Limbo that fires 175-kg (385-lb) hydrostatic or proximity fused HE projectiles to a maximum range of 900 m (985 yards) and down to depth of 375 m (1,230 ft). The Sea Sparrow system uses a ship-launched version of the AIM-7E Sparrow air-to-air missile, and is reputed to be able to engage targets flying between 15 and 15240 m (50 and 50,000 ft) at ranges from 14.9 km (9.25 miles) to 22.2 km (13.86 miles) depending upon target height. For a new class of helicopter-carrying destroyers due shortly, the *Huron* tested a vertical-launch Sparrow system in 1982. For the embarked helicopters the ships carry both the active acoustic-homing 30 kt Mk 44 5.5 km (3.44-mile) range torpedo with a 34-kg (75-lb) HE warhead for use in shallow waters, and the active/passive acoustic-homing 45-kt 11-km (6.84-mile range) Mk 46 torpedo with a 43.5-kg (96-lb) HE warhead for deep-water work. It is expected that all four ships

will be modernized for service into the 1990s.

Specification
'Iroquois' class
Displacement: 3,551 tons standard and 4,700 tons full load
Dimensions: length 129.8 m (426 ft); beam 15.2 m (50 ft); draught 4.4 m (14 ft 6 in)
Machinery: two Pratt & Whitney FT4A gas turbines delivering 50,000 shp (37285 kW) and two Pratt & Whitney FT12AH3 cruising gas turbines delivering 7,400 shp (5520 kW), both to

two shafts
Speed: 29 kts
Aircraft: two Sikorsky CH-124 Sea King ASW helicopters
Armament: two quadruple Sea Sparrow SAM launchers (32 missiles), one single 127-mm (5-in) DP gun, one triple-barrel Mk 10 ASW mortar, and two triple Mk 32 324-mm (12.75-in) ASW torpedo tubes (12 Mk 46 torpedoes)
Electronics: one SPS-501 air-search radar, one SPQ2D surface-search and navigation radar, two WM-22 weapon-control radar systems, one URN-20

The 'Iroquois' class destroyer HMCS Huron (281) launches a Sea Sparrow SAM missile from her starboard side missile rack just forward of the bridge. The design allows for the carriage and operation of two licence-built CH-124 Sea Kings.

TACAN, one WLR-1 ECM system, ULQ-6 ECM system, two Corvus chaff launchers, one SQS-505 bow sonar, one SQS-505 variable-depth sonar, and one SQS-501 target-classification hull sonar
Complement: 285

The Iroquois (280) was commissioned in July 1972 and with her three sister ships is destined to serve on into the late 1990s as the major ASW platform of the Canadian Navy. A new class will supplement them from the late 1980s onwards to replace the older frigates now approaching the end of their operational lives.

ARGENTINA

'Meko 360H2' class

Originally to have been a class of six, with four to have been built in Argentina, the **'Meko 360H2' class** design is based on the modularized systems concept whereby each of the weapons and sensor systems carried form a separate modular unit and can be interchanged with a replacement or newer system without the usual reconstruction that otherwise accompanies the modernization of a ship. The final

agreement signed with the West German firms of Thyssen Rheinstahl and Blohm und Voss in December 1978 was for four ships to be built in West Germany. All four, the **Almirante Brown** (D10), **La Argentina** (D11), **Heroina** (D5) and **Sarandis** (D13), will commission in 1983-4, the first pair having done so in 1983. During the Falklands war the ships were under construction, and the British Rolls-Royce

Olympus and Tyne gas turbines which propel them were embargoed for a short time. They are officially classed as frigates, and their near sister is the Nigerian navy's **Aradu** (F89), which was ordered in November 1977 as the first warship in the world to use extensive modular prefabrication and containerized weapons in building. She differs from the Argentine vessels in having Otomat Mk 2 SSMs, a single

helicopter and a combined diesel or gas turbine (CODOG) propulsion system. The Meko modular building technique has since been extended to smaller frigate designs.

Specification
'Meko 360H2' class
Displacement: 3,360 tons full load
Dimensions: length 125.9 m (413 ft

1 in); beam 14.0 m (46 ft); draught 5.8 m (19 ft)
Machinery: four Rolls-Royce gas turbines (two Olympus TM3B and two Tyne RM1C) in COGOG arrangement delivering 51,800 shp (38625 kW) to two shafts
Speed: 30.5 kts
Aircraft: two light ASW type (still to be chosen)
Armament: two twin MM.40 Exocet launcher (no reloads), one octuple Albatross SAM launcher (24 missiles),

one single 127-mm (5-in) DP gun, two twin 40-mm AA guns, and two triple 324-mm (12.75-in) ILAS-3 ASW torpedo tubes (18 Whitehead A244/S torpedoes)
Electronics: one DA-08A air- and surface-search, one ZW-06 navigation radar, one WM-25 fire-control system with STIR facilities, one AEG-Telefunken ECM suite, two 20-barrel SCLAR chaff and IR decoy launchers, and one Atlas 80 hull sonar
Complement: 198

Initially to have been a class of six, with four to have been built in Argentina, that country's order was subsequently changed to four 'Meko 360H2' destroyers to be built by Blohm und Voss at Hamburg and six 'Meko 140A16' class corvettes to be built by AFNE at Rio Santiago in Argentina.

Right: The first two of the 'Meko 360' destroyers, Almirante Brown (D10) and La Argentina (D11) undergo sea trials off West Germany. The commissioning of these vessels and their sister ships into the Argentine navy represents a significant increase in its capabilities that will tax the Royal Navy heavily in any future conflict that may break out over the Falkland Islands.

 UK
'County' class

The title 'destroyer' was applied to the **'County' class** ships in order to obtain Treasury approval for their construction, but they are little short of guided-missile cruisers. Built around the British first-generation Seaslug beam-riding area-defence SAM system, the 'County' class was ordered in two batches. Of the four **'County Batch 1'** class ships the *Devonshire, Hampshire* and *Kent* have been deleted from Royal Navy service, whilst the *London* was sold to the Pakistani navy as the light cruiser *Babur* (C84) without the Seaslug system. The **'County Batch 2'** ships *Fife, Glamorgan, Antrim* and *Norfolk* were modernized with Exocet missiles in place of one of their two 114-mm (4.5-in) gun mounts and carried the Seaslug Mk 2 SAM with limited SSM capability. All four ships were scheduled to remain in service until the late 1980s because of their extensive command and control facilities, which made them good flagships. HMS *Glamorgan* (D19) and HMS *Antrim* (D18) served with distinction in the Falklands war, the former surviving a direct hit from an MM.38 Exocet and the latter a hit from a bomb which failed to explode. As a result of the 1981 British defence cuts, however, the *Norfolk* had been sold to the Chilean navy as the missile destroyer *Prat* (03) whilst the *Fife* (D20) underwent a major refit which kept her out of the war. In February 1984 it was announced that the *Antrim* was to be decommissioned

and sold to Chile. The Chileans retain the vessels' Seaslug capabilities and will probably buy up the remaining Seaslug stocks from the UK as the other two 'County' class ships pay off to release trained personnel for new-build ships.

Specification
'County Batch 2' class
Displacement: 6,200 tons standard and 6,800 tons full load
Dimensions: length 158.7 m (520 ft 6 in); beam 16.5 m (54 ft); draught 6.3 m (20 ft 6 in)
Machinery: COSAG arrangement with two geared steam turbines delivering 30,000 shp (22370 kW) and four G.6 gas turbines delivering 30,000 shp (22370 kW) to two shafts
Speed: 32.5 kts
Aircraft: one Westland Lynx HAS.Mk 2 or 3 ASW and surface strike helicopter
Armament: four single GWS Mk 50 MM.38 Exocet SSM launchers (no reloads), one twin Seaslug Mk 2 SAM launcher (30 missiles), one twin 114-mm (4.5-in) DP gun, two quadruple GWS Mk 22 Sea Cat SAM launchers (32 missiles), two single 20-mm AA guns, and two triple 324-mm (12.75-in) STWS1 ASW torpedo tubes (12 Mk 46 torpedoes, only in *Fife* and *Glamorgan*)
Electronics: one Type 965M air-search radar, one Type 992Q air-search and target-designation radar, one Type 901 Seaslug fire-control radar, one

Type 278M height-finder radar, two Type 904 Sea Cat fire-control radars, one MRS3 114-mm (4.5-in) fire-control system, one Type 1006 navigation and helicopter-control radar, one ADAWS 1 action information system, one ESM suite, two Corvus chaff launchers, one Type 184 hull sonar, one Type 170B attack sonar, one Type 182 torpedo decoy system, and one Type 185 underwater telephone
Complement: 472

Above: HMS Glamorgan (D19) following a refit to repair the damage suffered during the Falklands war. Second of the four Batch 2 'County' class destroyers, she now carries a Westland Lynx HAS.Mk 2 helicopter in place of the original Westland Wessex HAS.Mk 3.

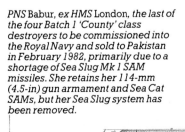

PNS Babur, ex HMS London, the last of the four Batch 1 'County' class destroyers to be commissioned into the Royal Navy and sold to Pakistan in February 1982, primarily due to a shortage of Sea Slug Mk 1 SAM missiles. She retains her 114-mm (4.5-in) gun armament and Sea Cat SAMs, but her Sea Slug system has been removed.

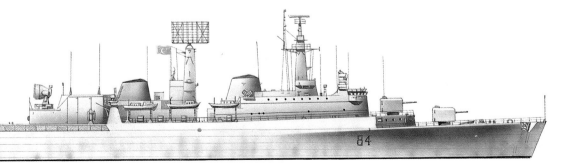

UK
'Type 82' and 'Type 42' classes

Used during the Falklands war, the solitary **'Type 82' class** destroyer HMS *Bristol* (D23) was originally to have been the lead ship of a class of four vessels designed for the ASW and area-defence SAM escorts to the 'CVA-01' class aircraft-carriers. With the demise of the carrier project in 1966 the class was cut back to one unit for specific deployment as a trials vessel for the new generation of weapons systems entering British service. The ship has a unique three-funnel configuration for her combined steam and gas turbine propulsion system, and superficially resembles a cleaned-up 'County' class destroyer. The main weapons systems are a twin GWS Mk 30 zero-length Sea Dart SAM launcher and an Ikara ASW missile launcher. The 549-kg (1,210-lb) semi-active radar homing ramjet-powered Sea Dart is an area-defence weapon with a maximum range of 65 km (40 miles) and engagement altitude limits of 30 m (100 ft) and 18290 m (60,000 ft). Although considered by many to be a white elephant, the *Bristol* is in fact a very valuable member of the Royal Navy's surface forces, having the necessary command and control facilities required to act as a flagship and the communications and data links necessary to act as a 'gateway' ship for other RN vessels to communicate through her with NATO ships possessing incompatible communications systems.

With the cancellation of the carriers, a Naval Staff Requirement was issued for a small fleet escort capable of providing area defence. This resulted in the **'Type 42' class** design, which suffered considerably during gestation from constraints that were placed on the dimensions by the Controller of the Navy as a result of Treasury pressure to minimize costs. As built, the ships lacked any significant close-range air-defence systems, had reduced endurance on full power output from their gas turbines (necessitating regular replenishments at sea on operations), and a short forecastle which resulted in a very wet forward section. The main armament comprised the Sea Dart system, but with only half the missile outfit of the *Bristol* and 1950s-technology main radars, which did not exactly enhance their air-defence capabilities. The class was subsequently built in three batches: the **'Type 42 Batch 1'** comprised HMS *Sheffield*, HMS *Birmingham* (D86), HMS *Cardiff* (D108), HMS *Coventry*, HMS *Newcastle* (D87) and HMS *Glasgow* (D88); the **'Type 42 Batch 2'** consisted of HMS *Exeter* (D89), HMS *Southampton* (D90), HMS *Nottingham* (D91) and HMS *Liverpool* (D92);

and the **'Type 42 Batch 3'** was made up of HMS *Manchester* (D95), HMS *Gloucester* (D96), HMS *York* (D98) and HMS *Edinburgh* (D97). The Batch 3 vessels were lengthened and broadened in an effort to remedy some of the problems encountered in the first two batches.

During the Falklands war four Batch 1 ships (*Sheffield*, *Cardiff*, *Coventry* and *Glasgow*) saw action, together with the *Exeter* from Batch 2. Of these the *Sheffield* was hit by an AM.39 Exocet on 4 May 1982 and later sank, the *Glasgow* narrowly missed being blown apart on 12 May by a bomb which passed through her hull amidships from one side to the other without exploding, whilst the *Coventry* sustained three bomb hits on 25 May and sank within forty-five minutes. The lack of any close-range air-defence systems was a significant factor in each case. On the credit side the ships' Sea Dart missiles are officially credited with eight aircraft shot down, although seven seems to be the actual figure secured by some 18 Sea Darts launched from the *Bristol* and the 'Type 42s'. The *Coventry* shot down two McDonnell Douglas A-4 Skyhawks and an Aérospatiale SA 330 Puma helicopter in the days before she was sunk, whilst the *Exeter* was the most successful with two Skyhawks, an English Electric Canberra and a Learjet 35A. The Argentines knew all about the 'Type 42' and its Sea Dart missile system because their navy had bought two vessels of this class from the UK,

namely the *Hercules* (D1) and the *Santissima Trinidad* (D2).

Following the war considerable modifications were made to the British 'Type 42s', with respect particularly to the armament.

HMS Bristol was to have been one of a class of four cruiser-size carrier escorts, but the cancellation of the carrier project in 1966 meant that the other 'Type 82s' were not built.

Specification
'Type 82' class
Displacement: 6,100 tons standard and 7,100 tons full load
Dimensions: length 154.5 m (507 ft); beam 16.8 m (55 ft); draught 7.0 m (23 ft)
Machinery: COSAG arrangement with two geared steam turbines delivering 30,000 shp (22370 kW) and two Rolls-Royce Olympus TM1A gas turbines delivering 30,000 shp (22370 kW) to

The first of the stretched 'Type 42s', HMS Manchester (D95). These vessels are designed to remedy the shortcomings of the original class by restoring the length cut-off and increasing the beam slightly. However, as originally conceived they would have suffered from the same lack of armament as HMS Sheffield.

HMS Nottingham (D91), built with the Type 1022 radar in place of the outdated Type 965 that proved to be of limited value in the Falklands war. The main weakness of the original 'Type 42s' lies in the constraints placed on their dimensions by Treasury pressure during the design phase.

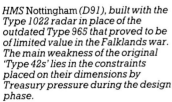

two shafts
Speed: 28 kts
Aircraft: helicopter landing pad only
Armament: one twin GWS Mk 30 Sea Dart SAM launcher (40 missiles), one single 114-mm (4.5-in) DP gun, two single 20-mm AA guns, one GWS Mk 40 Ikara ASW missile system (20 missiles), and one triple Mk 10 Limbo ASW mortar
Electronics: one Type 965 air-search radar, one Type 992Q air-search and target-designation radar, two Type 909 Sea Dart fire-control radars, one Type 1006 navigation and helicopter-control radar, two Ikara fire-control radars, one ADAWS 2 action information system, one Abbey Hill ESM suite, two Corvus chaff launchers, two SCOTT satellite communications systems, one Type 184 medium-frequency hull sonar, one Type 162 classification sonar, one Type 182 torpedo decoy system, one Type 185 underwater telephone, and one Type 170 Limbo attack sonar
Complement: 407

Specification
'Type 42 Batch 1' and 'Type 42 Batch 2' classes
Displacement: 3,850 tons standard and 4,350 tons full load
Dimensions: length 125.6 m (412 ft); beam 14.3 m (47 ft); draught 5.8 m (19 ft)
Machinery: COGOG arrangement with two Rolls-Royce Olympus TM3B gas turbines delivering 56,000 shp (41760 kW) and two Rolls-Royce Tyne RM1A gas turbines delivering 8,500 shp (6340 kW) to two shafts
Speed: 30 kts
Aircraft: one Westland Lynx HAS.Mk 2 or 3 ASW and surface strike helicopter
Armament: one twin GWS Mk 30 Sea Dart SAM launcher (20 missiles), one

single 114-mm (4.5-in) DP gun, two twin 30-mm AA guns, four single 20-mm AA guns, and two triple 324-mm (12.75-in) STWS 1 ASW torpedo tubes (12 Mk 46 torpedoes)
Electronics: one Type 965R air-search radar (Type 1022 in Batch 2 and being retrofitted to Batch 1), one Type 992Q or Type 992R air-search and target-designation radar, two Type 909 Sea Dart fire-control radars, one Type 1006 navigation and helicopter-control radar, one ADAWS 4 action information system (ADAWS 7 in Batch 2), one UAA1 Abbey Hill ESM suite, two Corvus chaff launchers, two SCOTT satellite communications systems, one Type 184M medium-frequency hull sonar, one Type 162M classification sonar, one Type 182 torpedo decoy system, and one Type 185 underwater telephone
Complement: 301

Specification
'Type 42 Batch 3' class
Displacement: 4,775 tons standard and 5,350 tons full load
Dimensions: length 141.1 m (462 ft 9 in); beam 14.9 m (49 ft); draught 5.8 m (19 ft)
Machinery: as 'Type 42 Batches 1 and 2'
Speed: 31.5 kts
Aircraft: as 'Type 42 Batches 1 and 2'
Armament: as 'Type 42 Batches 1 and 2' except 40 missiles for Sea Dart system, and the possibility of fitting Lightweight Sea Wolf SAM system in place of one Type 909 radar is being explored
Electronics: as 'Type 42 Batches 1 and 2' except one Type 1022 air-search radar, one ADAWS 8 action information system, and one Type 2016 multi-frequency hull sonar
Complement: 312

HMS *Southampton (D90) in June 1983. Since the Falklands war most 'Type 42s' have had additional close-range air defence guns fitted, and augment* these with at least four General Purpose Machine Guns fitted to the bridge wings for use in high-threat areas.

'Charles F. Adams' class

Guided-missile destroyers of the 'Charles F. Adams' class are currently in service with the Australian navy in the form of HMAS *Perth* (D38), HMAS *Hobart* (D39) and HMAS *Brisbane* (D41) and the West German navy in the form of the *Lütjens* (D185), *Mölders* (D186) and *Rommel* (D187), and with the US Navy (23 ships). Each version differs from the others, the Australian ships having two single-rail Ikara ASW missile launchers amidships with 32 missiles in place of the ASROC launcher, and the German vessels having combined funnel and radar mast layout. They are excellent sea boats and are considered to be very capable

multi-purpose vessels. All 23 American ships were due to receive extensive midlife refits but due to massive cost increases this has had to be limited to six ships, the USS *Conyngham* (DDG 17), USS *Tattnall* (DDG 19), USS *Goldsborough* (DDG 20), USS *Benjamin Stoddart* (DDG 22), USS *Richard E. Byrd* (DDG 23) and *Waddell* (DDG 24), with the other 17 due for

One of the best of the earlier missile ship designs, the 'Charles F. Adams' class were at first equipped with a twin Mk 11 Tartar SAM system, as seen here on USS John King *(DDG3) here.*

deletion from the late 1980s onwards. the 'Charles F. Adams' class was built to a revised 'Forrest Sherman/Hull' design to accommodate either a single- or twin-rail Tartar SAM launcher system. Since completion some units have been fitted with a four-round ASROC reload magazine on the starboard side alongside the forward funnel. The modernized vessels will have a three-computer NTDS action data system, an integrated combat system, more modern sensors and countermeasures equipment, and the Standard SM-2MR missile. The ships which are not being modernized are the USS *Charles F. Adams* (DDG 2), USS *John King* (DDG

3), USS *Lawrence* (DDG 4), USS *Claude V. Ricketts* (DDG 5), USS *Barney* (DDG 6), USS *Henry B. Wilson* (DDG 7), USS *Lynde McCormick* (DDG 8), USS *Towers* (DDG 9), USS *Sampson* (DDG 10), USS *Sellers* (DDG 11), USS *Robison* (DDG 12), USS *Hoel* (DDG 13), USS *Buchanan* (DDG 14), USS *Berkeley* (DDG 15), USS *Joseph*

The last 10 'Charles F. Adams' class vessels, including USS Semmes *(DDG 18), were equipped with the single-rail Mk 13 Tartar SAM launcher. It was this sub-class that attracted the attention of the Australian and West German navies.*

417

Strauss (DDG 16), USS *Semmes* (DDG 18), and USS *Cochrane* (DDG 21). The vessels in the other two navies have already been modernized for service into the 1990s.

Specification
'Charles F. Adams' class (US Navy)
Displacement: 3,370 tons standard and 4,526 tons full load
Dimensions: length 133.2 m (437 ft);

beam 14.3 m (47 ft); draught 6.1 m (20 ft)
Machinery: two geared steam turbines delivering 70,000 shp (52200 kW) to two shafts
Speed: 31.5 kts
Aircraft: none
Armament: one twin Mk 11 Tartar SAM/Harpoon SSM launcher (36 Tartar and 6 Harpoon, in DDG 2-14 only) or one single Mk 13 Tartar SAM/

Harpoon SSM launcher (36 Tartar and 4 Harpoon, in DDG 15-24 only), two single 127-mm (5-in) DP guns, one octuple ASROC ASW missile launcher (4 reloads in some ships), and two triple Mk 32 324-mm (12.75-in) ASW torpedo tubes (6 Mk 46 torpedoes)
Electronics: one SPS-39A 3 D radar, one SPS-40B (DDG 2-14) or SPS-37 (DDG 15-24) air-search radar, one SPS-10F surface-search radar, two

SPG-51C Tartar fire-control radars, one SPG-53A 127-mm (5-in) fire-control radar, one URN-20 (URN-25 in DDG 11-16) TACAN, one WLR-6 ECM system, one ULQ-6B ECM system, two Mk 36 Super RBOC chaff launchers, one SQS-23A bow sonar (DDG 20-24), one SQQ-23 PAIR hull sonar (DDG 2-19), and one Fanfare torpedo decoy system
Complement: 354

USS Farragut, *a 'Coontz' class destroyer, was originally classed as a frigate (as were the guided missile cruisers of the same vintage). While looking similar to the 'Charles F. Adams' class, USS* Farragut *is larger, and is almost as capable as a cruiser.*

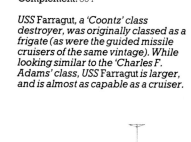

USA
'Arleigh Burke' class

Designed as the gas turbine-powered replacement for the 'Coontz' guided-missile destroyer class and the 'Leahy' and 'Belknap' classes of missile cruisers from the early 1990s, the **'Arleigh Burke' class** will be less capable than the contemporary 'Ticonderoga' class missile cruisers in the anti-air warfare role but will also have a secondary anti-surface ship role assigned to them. Apart from aluminium funnels each ship will be constructed from steel to prevent any recurrence of the USS *Belknap's* fire damage when she collided with the carrier USS *John F. Kennedy*. Plastic Kevlar armour will be fitted over all vital machinery and operations room spaces whilst, surprisingly enough, the class will also be the first US warship class to be equipped fully for warfare in a nuclear, chemical or biological (NBC) environment with the crew confined in a citadel located within the hull and superstructure. The main sensors will be a pair of the reduced-capability SPY-1D AEGIS radars, with the new Seafire fire-control system to provide laser designator facilities for the guidance of 127-mm (5-in) shells fired from the single lightweight 127-mm (5-in) gun mount.

The Mk 32 self-defence torpedo tubes will be the first to employ the Mk 50 Barracuda Advanced Lightweight Torpedo now under development. At least 60 vessels (DDG 51 onwards) are planned, the lead ship taking the name USS *Arleigh Burke*, although the final number will be subject to much Congressional debate as costs rise. One point of criticism already raised is that no hangar has been provided for a helicopter although a flightdeck for a Sikorsky SH-60B Seahawk ASW helicopter is part of the design.

Specification (provisional)
'Arleigh Burke' class
Displacement: 8,200 tons standard and 8,500 tons full load
Dimensions: length 142.1 m (466 ft); beam 18.3 m (60 ft); draught 7.6 m (25 ft)
Machinery: four General Electric LM2500 gas turbines delivering 100,000 shp (74570 kW) to two shafts
Speed: 32 kts
Aircraft: helicopter landing pad only
Armament: two quadruple Harpoon SSM launchers (no reloads), two vertical-launch missile systems (90 Standard SM-2MR SAM, ASROC ASW and Tomahawk SSM missiles), one 127-mm (5-in) DP gun, two 20-mm Phalanx CIWS mountings, and two triple 324-mm (12.75-in) Mk 32 ASW

torpedo tubes (14 Mk 50 torpedoes)
Electronics: two SPY-1D paired AEGIS radars, one SPS-10 surface-search radar, three SPG-62 Standard fire-control radars, one Seafire fire-control system, one Mk 99 fire control system, one SLQ-32(V)2 ESM suite, two Mk 36 Super RBOC chaff launchers, one SQS-53C bow sonar, and SQR-19 towed-array sonar
Complement: 307

Artist's impression of the new 'Arleigh Burke' (DDG51) class of destroyers. To be armed with vertical-launch SAM systems, they will use the AN/SPY-1D version of AEGIS, and are expected to supplement the 'Ticonderoga' class of missile cruisers in the anti-air warfare role as replacements for the 'Coontz/Leahy/Belknap' classes.

The entire 'Arleigh Burke' ship, except for aluminium funnels, will be made of steel, and will be the first US warship class to have a collective protection system for defence against nuclear fallout and biological and chemical weapons, with the crew being encased in a citadel-type structure with double airlock doors.

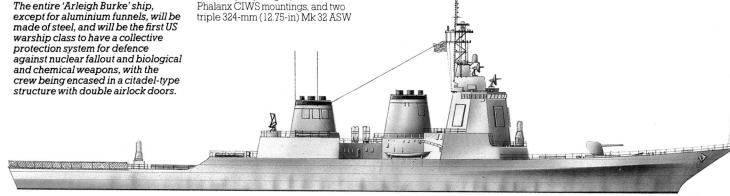

'Spruance' and 'Kidd' classes

Built as the replacements for the many 'Gearing (FRAM I)' class destroyers, the 31-strong **'Spruance' class** is the most capable ASW surface ship class yet built, so much so that construction of the class is to resume in the late 1980s to replace the 'Forrest Sherman' and 'Hull' classes in the early 1990s. Constructed by the modular assembly technique, whereby large sections of the hull are built in various parts of the shipyard then welded together on the slipway, these were the first large US warships to employ all gas-turbine propulsion. The ships are due to be refitted with 61-round vertical launch missile units from 1985 onwards. The active/passive SQS-53 low-frequency sonar carried in the large bow dome is capable of operating in both the short-range direct-path and the long-range bottom-bounce and convergence-zone modes, targets at long ranges being engaged by the ASW helicopters carried aboard. The current units of the 'Spruance' class are the USS *Spruance* (DD 963), USS *Paul F. Foster* (DD 964), USS *Kinkaid* (DD 965), USS *Hewitt* (DD 966), USS *Elliott* (DD 967), USS *Arthur W. Radford* (DD 968), USS *Peterson* (DD 969), USS *Caron* (DD 970), USS *David R. Ray* (DD 971), USS *Oldendorf* (DD 972), USS *John Young* (DD 973), USS *Comte de Grasse* (DD 974), USS *O'Brien* (DD 975), USS *Merrill* (DD 976), USS *Briscoe* (DD 977), USS *Stump* (DD 978), USS *Conolly* (DD 979), USS *Moosbruger* (DD 980), USS *John Hancock* (DD 981), USS *Nicholson* (DD 982), USS *John Rodgers* (DD 983), USS *Leftwich* (DD 984), USS *Cushing* (DD 985), USS *Harry W. Hill* (DD 986), USS *O'Bannon* (DD 987), USS *Thorn* (DD 988), USS *Deyo* (DD 989), USS *Ingersoll* (DD 990), USS *Fife* (DD 991), USS *Fletcher* (DD 992), and USS *Hayler* (DD 997).

In 1974 the government of Iran ordered six SAM-equipped versions of the 'Spruances' for service in the Persian Gulf and Indian Ocean. However, following the revolution in that country two were cancelled in 1979 whilst the remaining four under construction were taken over by the US Navy as the **'Kidd' class**. These are the world's most powerfully armed general-purpose destroyers, and are unofficially known in the US Navy as the **'Ayatollah' class**. The four ships were commissioned as the USS *Kidd* (DDG 993), USS *Callaghan* (DDG 994), USS *Scott* (DDG 995) and USS *Chandler* (DDG 996).

Lead ship of the 31-strong 'Spruance' class is USS Spruance (DD963). She is first large US warship to be fitted with an all-gas turbine propulsion system. The class was built by Ingalls Shipbuilding Corporation under the modular assembly technique, and has proved to be the best ASW destroyer type yet built.

Specification
'Spruance' class
Displacement: 5,826 tons standard and 7,800 tons full load
Dimensions: length 171.7 m (563 ft 3 in); beam 16.8 m (55 ft 2 in); draught 8.8 m (29 ft)
Machinery: four General Electric LM2500 gas turbines delivering 80,000 shp (59655 kW) to two shafts
Speed: 33 kts
Aircraft: two Kaman SH-2D/F Seasprite LAMPS Mk I helicopter or one Sikorsky SH-3H Sea King ASW helicopter
Armament: two quadruple Harpoon SSM launchers (no reloads, and not in DD 964 and DD 965), two quadruple Tomahawk SSM launchers (no reloads, and for DD 963, DD 964, DD 969, DD 972, DD 979, DD 984, DD 985, DD 988, DD 989 and DD 993 only), one octuple Sea Sparrow SAM launcher (24 missiles), one octuple ASROC ASW missile launcher (24 missiles), two single 127-mm (5-in) DP guns, two 20-mm Phalanx CIWS mountings (being fitted), and two triple 324-mm (12.75-mm) Mk 32 ASW torpedo tubes (14 Mk 46 torpedoes)
Electronics: one SPS-40B air-search radar, one SPS-55 surface-search radar, one SPG-60 fire-control radar, one SPQ-9A fire-control radar, one Mk 91 Sea Sparrow fire-control system, one Mk 86 gun fire-control system, one Mk 116 ASW fire-control system, one SLQ-32(V)2 ESM suite, two Mk 36 Super RBOC chaff launchers, one SQS-53 bow sonar, one SQR-19 towed-array sonar, one SATCOMM communications system, and one Fanfare torpedo decoy system
Complement: 296

Specification
'Kidd' class
Displacement: 6,210 tons standard and 9,200 tons full load
Dimensions: length 171.6 m (563 ft); beam 16.8 m (55 ft); draught 9.1 m (30 ft)
Machinery: as 'Spruance' class
Speed: 32 kts
Aircraft: two Kaman SH-2D/F Seasprite LAMPS Mk I or two Sikorsky SH-60B Seahawk LAMPS Mk III helicopters
Armament: two quadruple Harpoon SSM launchers (no reloads), two twin Mk 26 Standard SM-1ER SAM/ASROC ASW missile launchers (50 Standard, 16 ASROC and 2 test missiles), two single 127-mm (5-in) DP guns, two 20-mm Phalanx CIWS mountings, two triple 324-mm (12.75-mm) Mk 32 ASW torpedo tubes (14 Mk 46 torpedoes)
Electronics: one SPS-48C 3D radar, one SPS-55 surface-search radar, two SPG-51D Standard fire-control radars, one SPG-60 fire-control radar, one SPQ-9 fire-control radar, two Mk 86 gun fire-control systems, one Mk 116 ASW fire-control system, one URN-20 TACAN, one SLQ-32(V)2 ESM suite, two Mk 36 Super RBOC chaff launchers, one SQS-53 bow sonar, one SQR-19 towed-array sonar, and one Fanfare torpedo decoy system
Complement: 338

USS Comte de Grasse (DD974). Although carrying the Kaman SH-2D LAMPS I ASW helicopter at present, the 'Spruances' will eventually carry the Sikorsky SH-3H Sea King, from which the B57 nuclear depth bomb is to be used as well as conventional ASW weapons.

Modern Western Frigates 1

Developed during the 18th century as a forerunner of the cruiser and revived in World War II as an ocean-going escort, the frigate today is a highly adaptable, dependable vessel, which may be designed for an anti-submarine warfare role or as an escort for convoys or amphibious warfare task groups.

The USS *Oliver Hazard Perry* (FFG 7) under way. Launched in 1976, this vessel is the leader of a large class of frigates armed with guided missiles and two ASW helicopters.

Ever since it was conceived in the 18th century, when it was used mainly for reconnaissance and commerce raiding, the frigate has played a very important part in the navies of the world. Today, the name is applied to a wide variety of vessels, ranging from very expensive and highly specialized anti-submarine warfare (ASW) ships, like the Royal Navy's 'Type 22', to cheaper vessels such as the US Navy's 'Knox' class, designed to escort convoys and amphibious warfare task groups.

The frigate was an important part of the warship inventories of both East and West during the years of the Cold War. The British 'Leander' class of general-purpose frigate, for example, which entered service in the 1960s, served the Royal Navy well for many years; 26 were built. The 'Leanders' were to have been succeeded by 26 examples of the 'Type 22' 'Broadsword' class, conceived as ASW ships for use in the Greenland-Iceland-UK gap against Soviet nuclear submarines. In the event only 14 were built. The other principal class of British frigate was the 'Type 21' 'Amazon' class, of which eight were constructed.

Together with the 'Type 42' destroyers, such as HMS *Glasgow*, the 'Type 22' frigates are the 'goalkeepers' of the Royal Navy; the former with the long-range British Aerospace Sea Dart defence SAM and the latter with close-range Seawolf. Both weapons were used effectively in the Falklands conflict, where Seawolf proved to be a formidable deterrent to low-flying aircraft.

France rates her frigates as sloops and uses them mainly as 'gunboats' to protect her interests overseas; they play a vital part in guarding the approaches to the French nuclear test centre at Mururoa Atoll in the Pacific. During the Cold War, some European nations – the Netherlands and what was then the Federal German Republic, for example – co-operated in frigate design and construction, producing two vessels that satisfied a common requirement. At the turn of the 21st century Britain, France and Italy were studying a joint proposal for an anti-aircraft frigate, the 'Horizon' class.

NORWAY
'Oslo' class

Based on the US 'Dealey' class destroyer escorts, the **'Oslo' class** frigates have a higher freeboard forward (to suit the sea conditions off Norway) and many European-built subsystems. They were built under the 1960 five-year naval plan, with half the cost borne by the USA. The class underwent modernization refits in the late 1970s, these including the fitting of Penguin Mk 2 SSMs, a NATO Sea Sparrow SAM launcher and Mk 32 ASW self-defence torpedo tubes. A replacement class is being designed for possible construction in the 1990s.

Currently the largest surface combatants in the Norwegian navy, the 'Oslos' provide the only major ASW force in the region. For this role they carry a forward-mounted sextuple rocket-launcher with a rapid reload capability for the 370 to 825-m (405 to 900-yard) range Terne III ASW rocket. This is a 120-kg (265-lb) weapon fitted with a combination depth and proximity Doppler fuse for its 6.1-m (20-ft) lethal radius 48-kg (105.8-lb) HE warhead; the target depth can be between 15 and 215 m (50 and 705 ft). Once fired the launcher is automatically trained to the vertical and reloaded within 40 seconds. The ships' SQS-36 sonar acts as the search unit whilst the Terne Mk 3 attack sonar is used for target range and depth determinations. For self defence the ships have the American 45-kt 11-km (6.8-mile) range Mk 46 acoustic-homing torpedo fired from the Mk 32 torpedo tubes. The five ships in service are the *Oslo* (F300), *Bergen* (F301), *Trondheim* (F302), *Stavanger* (F303) and *Narvik* (F304).

Specification
'Oslo' class
Displacement: 1,450 tons standard and 1,850 tons full load
Dimensions: length 96.6 m (316.9 ft); beam 11.2 m (36.7 ft); draught 4.4 m (14.4 ft)
Propulsion: geared steam turbines delivering 20,000 hp (14914 kW) to one shaft
Speed: 25 kts

The 'Oslo' class frigate Bergen (F301) *is seen firing a Penguin surface-to-surface missile.*

Armament: six single Penguin Mk 2 surface-to-surface missile launchers with six missiles, one octuple NATO

Sea Sparrow surface-to-air missile launcher with 24 missiles, two twin 76-mm (3-in) Mk 33 DP guns, one sextuple Terne ASW rocket launcher, and two triple 324-mm (12.75-in) Mk 32 ASW torpedo tubes with Mk 46 torpedoes
Aircraft: none
Electronics: one DRBV 22 air- and surface-search radar, one WM-22 fire-control radar, one Decca 1226 navigation radar, one Terne Mk 3 sonar, and one SQS-36 hull sonar
Complement: 150

'Oslo' class frigates are a modification of the 'Dealey' class of destroyer escort (DE) built in the USA in the 1950s Oslo sank while under tow on 24 January 1994 after running aground following a complete engine failure.

WEST GERMANY
'Bremen' (Type 122) class

A Germanized modification of the gas turbine-powered Dutch 'Kortenaer' design the eight-ship 'Bremen class' replaced the deleted 'Fletcher' (type 119) class destroyers and the elderly 'Köln' (Type 120) class frigates. The hulls are mated with the propulsion plant in the building yards, and are then towed to Bremer Vulkan, where the weapon systems and electronics are fitted. The first order was placed in 1977, and the ship eventually commissioned in May 1982 after government approval had been given further for the construction in 1976. A further two units Augsburg (F213) and Lübeck (F214) were built later. The ships were subsequently fitted with fin stabilizers and the American Praerie/Masker bubble system on the hull and propellers to reduce radiated noise levels from the machinery spaces. A complete NBC defence

Bremen (F207) is the first of a class of six frigates for the Bundesmarine. These general-purpose vessels carry their main anti-submarine punch in the two Lynx helicopters with which each ship is equipped.

citadel system is also fitted. Two of the new passive radar/infra-red terminal homing 24-round RAM point defence SAM launches were installed atop the hanger in the mid-1990s. The ASW helicopters carried are Westland Lynx HAS MK 88s which differ from Royal Navy machines in having an active Bendix DASQ-18 dunking sonar for use with the Mk 46 homing torpedoes and Mk 54 depth charges they carry. For firing in rough weather the ships are armed with the Canadian Bear Trap landing systems.

The eight ships are the *Bremen* (F207), *Niedersachsen* (F208) *Rheinland-Pfalz* (F209), *Emden* (F210), *Köln* (F211), *Karlsruhe* (F212), *Augsburg* (F213) and *Lübeck* (F214). All have received an updated EW fit since 1994.

Specification
'Bremen' class
Displacement: 2,900 tons standard and 3,750 tons full load
Dimensions: length 130.5 m (428.1 ft); beam 14.4 m (47.25 ft); draught 6.0 m (19.7 ft)
Propulsion: CODOG arrangement with two General Electric/FIAT LM2500 gas turbines delivering 51,600 hp (38478 kW) and two MTU 2OV TB92 diesels delivering 10,400 hp (7755 kW)

to two shafts
Speed: 32 kts
Armament: two quadruple Harpoon surface-to-surface missile launchers with eight missiles, one octuple NATO Sea Sparrow surface-to-air missile launcher with 24 RIM-7M missiles, two 24-round RAM point-defence surface-to-air missile launchers with 48 missiles (being fitted), one 76-mm (3-in) DP gun, and four single Mk 32 324-mm (12.75-in) ASW torpedo tubes for Mk 46 torpedoes
Aircraft: two Westland Lynx HAS.Mk 88 ASW helicopters
Electronics: one DA-08 air- and surface-search radar, one WM-25 fire-

control radar, one STIR fire-control radar, one 3RM20 navigation radar, one SATIR tactical data system, one FL1800S ESM intercept system, four Mk 36 Super RBOC chaff launchers, and one DSQS-21B(Z) bow sonar
Complement: 204 normal and 225 maximum

Developed from the Dutch 'Kortenaer' class of frigate, the 'Bremen' class has the same hull form and minor differences in armament. The major alteration is in the provision of diesel cruising engines in place of the turbines of the 'Kortenaer' class.

FRANCE

'D'Estienne d'Orves' (A-69) class

Designed for coastal ASW, the **'D'Estienne d'Orves' class** can also be used for scouting missions, training and for 'showing the flag' overseas, for which role a total of one officer and 17 men from the naval infantry can be accommodated. Since entering service in the mid-1970s the design has been sold to the Argentine navy, whose three ships the *Drummond* (P1), *Guerrico* (P2) and *Granville* (P3) saw service in the 1982 Falklands war. In this campaign the *Guerrico* suffered the ignominy of being damaged by shore fire from small arms and anti-tank rocket-launchers during the Argentine seizure of South Georgia on 3 April; this required her to be dry-docked for three days for repairs to the hull and armament.

Rated as *avisos* by the French, the first of the class was laid down at Lorient Naval Dockyard in 1972 and commissioned into service in 1976. Under present French navy plans the first three vessels built will be paid off in 1996, the other 14 units being decommissioned at regular intervals until 2004. All 17 vessels were built at Lorient, but at present ship a number of armament fits. Six vessels serve in the Mediterranean, eight in the Atlantic and three with the Channel squadron.

The class consists of the *D'Estienne d'Orves* (F781), *Amyot D'Inville* (F782), *Drogou* (F783), *Détroyat* (F784), *Jean Moulin* (F785), *Quartier*

The 'D'Estienne D'Orves' class are austere, simple vessels, designed with economy of operation very much in mind. Not suitable for deep water ASW, they are used around the coast, with secondary colonial patrol duties.

Maître Anquetil (F786), *Commandant de Pimodan* (F787), *Second Maître de Bihan* (F788), *Lieutenant de Vaisseau Le Henaff* (F789), *Lieutenant de Vaisseau Lavalle* (F790), *Commandant l'Herminier* (F791), *Premier Maître l'Her* (F792), *Commandant Blaison* (F793), *Enseigne de Vaisseau Jacoubet* (F794), *Commandant Ducuing* (F795), *Commandant Birot* (F796) and *Commandant Bouan* (F797).

Specification
'D'Estienne d'Orves' class
Displacement: 1,100 tons standard and 1,250 tons full load
Dimensions: length 80.0 m (262.5 ft); beam 10.3 m (33.8 ft); draught 5.3 m (17.4 ft)
Propulsion: two SEMT-Pielstick 12PC2 diesels delivering 11,000 hp (8203 kW) to two shafts; in F791 two SEMT-Pielstick 12PA6BTC diesels delivering 14,400 hp (10738 kW)
Speed: 24 kts
Armament: (F781, F78, F786, and F787) two single MM40 Exocet surface-to-surface missile launchers with two missiles (replacing earlier MM38 Exocet missiles) of (F792, F797) four single MM.40 Exocet surface-to-surface missiles, one 100-mm (3.9-in)

Classed as an aviso, or coastal escort, Commandant Blaison is one of the most recent of the A-69 series to enter service. All the class have Exocet capacity, though the weapons are not always shipped.

DP gun, two single 20-mm AA guns, one sextuple 375-mm (14.76-in) Creusot Loire ASW rocket-launcher, and four single ASW torpedo launchers with four L3 or L5 torpedoes
Aircraft: none
Electronics: one DRBV 51A air- and surface-search radar, one DRBC 32E 10-mm (3.9-in) gun-control radar, one DRBN 32 navigation radar, and one DUBA 25 hull sonar; all vessels are to be fitted with one ARBR 16 passive ESM system and two Dagaie decoy launchers
Complement: 79, plus 17 naval infantry on overseas deployments

Type 22 'Broadsword' class

Originally to have been a class of 26 to follow the 'Leanders' the **Type 22** or **'Broadsword' class** design was conceived as an ASW ship for use in the Greenland-Iceland-UK gap against modern high-performance nuclear submarines. However, as has happened to most modern British naval programmes, the 'chop' fell during defence cuts and the procurement schedule has been changed somewhat. The original four **'Broadsword Batch 1'** vessels ordered were HMS **Broadsword** (F88), HMS **Battleaxe** (F89), HMS **Brilliant** (F90) and HMS **Brazen** (F91). Although rated as frigates, these are in fact larger than the contemporary Type 42 destroyers, and were designated frigates for purely political reasons. The hull, with greater freeboard than that of the destroyers is an improved Type 12 design for use in rough weather without a significant reduction in speed.

Unfortunately, because of design shortcomings they cannot be fitted with the definitive Type 2031(Z) towed-array sonar at the stern, so a lengthened **'Broadsword Batch 2'** ver-sion had to be authorized. The six Batch 2s subsequently ordered to rectify the problem were HMS **Boxer** (F92), HMS **Beaver** (F93). HMS **Brave** (F94), HMS **London** (F95), HMS **Sheffield** (F96) and HMS **Coventry** (F97), and these will also differ amongst themselves as from the *Brave* onwards the propulsion plant will be two Rolls-Royce Spey SM1A and two Rolls-Royce Tyne RM1A gas turbines in a COGAG arrangement. The *Brave* will also be the first Type 22 unit to have an enlarged flight deck to take a Sea King or EH101 ASW helicopter.

Following the 1982 Falklands war a 'Broadsword Batch 3' was ordered. The four units HMS **Cornwall**, **Cumberland**, **Campbeltown** and **Chatham**, all have the same basic hull as the Batch 2s but with eight Harpoon SSMs, a single 114-mm (4.5-in) DP gun and two CIWS. All three batches will eventually have the new Type 2050 fleet sonar to replace the Type 2016.

During the Falklands war the *Brilliant* and *Broadsword* distinguished themselves in combat, the former being the first vessel to fire the Sea Wolf SAM in anger.

Specification
'Broadsword Batch 1' class
Displacement: 3,500 tons standard and 4,400 tons full load
Dimensions: length 131.1 m (430.0 ft); beam 14.8 m (48.5 ft); draught 6.1 m (19.9 ft)
Propulsion: COGOG arrangement with two Rolls-Royce Olympus TM3B gas turbines delivering 50,000 hp (37285 kW) and two Rolls-Royce Tyne RM1A gas turbines delivering 8,500 hp (6338 kW) to two shafts
Speed: 29 kts
Armament: four single MM.38 Exocet surface-to-surface missile launchers with four missiles, two sextuple GWS25 Sea Wolf surface-to-air missile launchers with 60 missiles, two single 40-mm AA guns, two single 20-mm AA guns, and (F90 and F91) two triple 324-mm (12.75-in) STWS1 ASW torpedo tubes with Mk 46 and Stingray torpedoes
Aircraft: one or two Westland Lynx HAS.Mk 2/3 ASW/anti-ship helicopters

Batch 3 variants of the 'Broadsword' class will be highly capable ships, although the frigate description may seem odd for a vessel nearing 5000 tonnes and with significant air, surface and anti-submarine capabilities.

Electronics: one Type 967/968 air- and surface-search radar, two Type 910 Sea Wolf fire-control radars, one Type 1006 navigation radar, one CAAIS combat data system, one UAA-1 ESM system, two Corvus chaff launchers, two Mk 36 Super RBOC chaff launchers, one Type 2016 hull sonar, and one Type 2008 underwater telephone
Complement: 223 normal and 248 maximum

A high-speed turn is made by HMS Broadsword (F88), first of the Type 22 class. These vessels, with their twin Lynx helicopters, were designed to counter modern high-performance nuclear submarines. All the Batch 1 vessels were sold to Brazil in the period 1995-97.

Type 12 'Modified Leander' class

A total of 26 general-purpose 'Leander' class frigates were built for the Royal Navy in three sub-groups: eight 'Leander Batch 1', eight 'Leander Batch 2' and 10 broad-beam 'Leander Batch 3' ships. Since the first unit entered service in 1963 underwent numerous refits and modernisations so that eventually it was divided into six separate sub-classes. The five Batch 3 ships HMS *Andromeda* (F57), HMS *Hermione* (F58), HMS *Jupiter* (F60), HMS *Scylla* (F71) and HMS *Charybdis* (F75) have undergone conversion by the addition of a GWS25 Sea Wolf automatic point-defence missile system plus numerous new sensor systems to give the most capable of the sub-classes. The conversion of the remaining five Batch 2 units to this configuration was shelved because of the usual economic reasons. One of them, the ex-*Bacchante*, has since been sold to New Zealand as HMNZS *Wellington* (F69) to join an existing 'broad-beam' HMNZS *Canterbury* (F421) and the standard version HMNZS *Waikato* (F55). The remaining four units are HMS *Achilles* (F12), HMS *Diomede* (F16), HMS *Apollo* (F70) and HMS *Ariadne* (F72), which still retain their 114-mm (4.5-in) gun and Sea Cat SAM armament. The Batch 2 units were due to form a single Exocet-armed class, but this has now changed to three different types. The first comprises HMS *Cleopatra* (F28), HMS *Sirius* (F40), HMS *Phoebe* (F42) and HMS *Minerva* (F45), and is known as the 'Batch 2 Towed Array Exocet Group' as the ships have been fitted with the Type 2031(I) general-purpose surveillance and tactical towed-array sonar on the starboard side of the stern. Three of the remaining Batch 2 vessels are HMS *Danae* (F47), HMS *Argonaut* (F56) and HMS *Penelope* (F127) which now form the original Exocet conversion group with the twin Mk 6 114-mm (4.5-in) gun mount replaced by four MM.38 Exocet launchers and a third GWS22 Sea Cat SAM launcher. The last Batch 2 ship, HMS *Juno* (F52), had her Exocet conversion halted and is now converting to serve as the fleet's navigation training ship.

The eight Batch 1 vessels were converted to ASW ships by the fitting of a GWS40 Ikara ASW missile installation in place of the gun mount. To compensate for the loss in AA capability a second GWS22 Sea Cat launcher was added aft atop the hangar. One vessel, the ex-*Dido* was sold to New Zealand as HMNZS *Southland* (F104) whilst the other seven remained in RN service: these were HMS *Aurora* (F10) HMS *Euryalus* (F15), HMS *Galatea* (F18), HMS *Arethusa* (F38), HMS *Naiad* (F39), HMS *Ajax* (F114) and HMS *Leander* (F109). The remaining service life of these vessels was limited, as the decision was taken to phase out the Ikara system.

In addition to the vessels for the Royal Navy, a number of other nations have either purchased British-built 'Leanders' or constructed their own under licence. These latter include the Australian HMAS *Swan* (D50) and HMAS *Torrens* (D53), the Indian navy *Nilgiri* (F33), *Himgiri* (F34), *Udaygiri* (F35), *Dunagiri* (F36), *Taragiri* (F41) and *Vindhygiri* (F42), and the Dutch *Van Speijk* (F802), *Van Galen* (F803), *Tjerk Hiddes* (F804), *Van Nes* (F805), *Isaac Sweers* (F814) and *Evertsen* (F815). The former vessels are the Chilean *Condell* (06) and *Almirante*

Lynch (07). In all cases the countries obtained 'Leanders' with better armament and sensor fits than Royal Navy vessels, apart from the latest Sea Wolf conversions. The Dutch managed to double the surface-to-surface missile armament to eight by using the Harpoon, and the Indians managed to fit the last two of their vessels to carry Westland Sea King ASW helicopters.

Specification
'Leander' class (RN Sea Wolf conversion)
Displacement: 2,500 tons standard and 2,962 tons full load
Dimensions: length 113.4 m (372.0 ft); beam 13.1 m (43.0 ft); draught 4.5 m (14.8 ft)
Propulsion: geared steam turbines delivering 30,000 hp (22371 kW) to two shafts
Speed: 27 kts
Armament: four single MM.38 Exocet surface-to-surface missile launchers with four missiles, one sextuple GWS25 Sea Wolf surface-to-air missile launcher with 30 missiles, two single 20-mm AA guns, and two triple 324-mm (12.75-in) STWS1 ASW torpedo tubes with Mk 46 and Stingray torpedoes
Aircraft: one Westland Lynx HAS.Mk 2 ASW helicopter

Completed in 1965, HMS Arethusa was converted to carry Ikara ASW rocket-launcher during a major refit completed in 1977. All RN Leanders had been placed in reserve pending disposal by 1990.

Electronics: one Type 967/978 air- and surface-search radar, one Type 910 Sea Wolf fire-control radar, one Type 1006 navigation radar, one CAAIS combat data system, one UAA-1 ESM system, two Corvus chaff launchers, one Type 2016 hull sonar, and one Type 2008 underwater telephone
Complement: 260

Specification
'Van Speijk' class
Displacement: 2,255 tons standard and 2,835 tons full load
Dimensions: length 113.4 m (372.0 ft); beam 12.5 m (41.0 ft); draught 4.2 m (13.8 ft)
Propulsion: as 'Leander' class
Speed: 28.5 kts
Armament: two quadruple Harpoon surface-to-surface missile launchers

---

HMS Andromeda 'Leander' class frigate cutaway drawing key

1 Flagstaff
2 Variable depth sonar
3 Crane for sonar
4 Screw guard
5 Twin balanced rudder
6 Support
7 Twin screws
8 Shaft
9 Stores
10 Capstan
11 Three-barrel Mk 10 anti-submarine mortar
12 ASM local command post
13 Winch
14 Sonar and mortar control position
15 Mortar ammunition
16 Flight deck
17 Junior ratings' hall
18 Junior ratings' mess hall
19 Deck landing lights
20 Hangar
21 Aviation stores
22 Westland Lynx Mk II helicopter
23 Sea Cat director
24 Sea Cat missile launcher
25 Mainmast
26 Type 965 long-range air search radar and IFF
27 Receiving wireless aerials
28 Aft radar plotting room
29 Corvus chaff launcher
30 Air operation control room
31 Galley
32 Launch
33 Funnel casing
34 Funnel
35 Central control station
36 Boiler room
37 Boilers
38 Blower
39 Reserve feed tank
40 Engine room control panel
41 Diesel filling tank
42 Double bottom
43 Engine room
44 Wheel house
45 Stokers' mess
46 Wing tanks
47 Fuel

Type 21 'Amazon' class

UK

The **Type 21** or **'Amazon' class** general-purpose frigate was a private ship-builder's design to replace the obsolete Type 41 or 'Leopard' and Type 61 or 'Salisbury' class frigates. Because of numerous bureaucratic problems, private and official ship designers were not brought together on the project, resulting in a class which handles well and is well liked by crews, but lacks sufficient 'growth' potential to take the new generation of sensor and weapon fits. Thus the vessels will not receive new equipment as such during their refit cycles. During the 1982 Falklands war HMS **Avenger** (F185), HMS **Ardent** (F184), HMS **Antelope** (F170), HMS **Arrow** (F173), and HMS **Alacrity** (F174) served in the main combat zone, whilst HMS **Active** (F171) and

HMS **Ambuscade** (F172) assisted in supporting operations and the occasional shore bombardment. Only the lead ship, HMS **Amazon** (F169), missed the war as she was in the Far East. On 21 May 1982 the *Ardent* was so badly damaged in bomb attacks that she sank, whilst two days later the *Antelope* caught fire and exploded when an unexploded bomb that was being defused detonated aboard her. After the war the remaining class members were found to have suffered severe hull cracking; indeed one unit, *Arrow*, had to limp precariously home from the Falklands to enter emergency refit. Further hull modifications to reduce noise and vibration were begun in 1988 and finally completed in 1992.

Specification
'Amazon' class
Displacement: 2,750 tons standard and 3,250 tons full load
Dimensions: length 117.0 m (384.0 ft); beam 12.7 m (41.7 ft); draught 5.9 m (19.5 ft)
Propulsion: COGOG arrangement with two Rolls-Royce Olympus TM3B gas turbines delivering 50,000 hp (37285 kW) and two Rolls-Royce Tyne RM1A gas turbines delivering 8,500 hp (6338 kW) to two shafts
Speed: 32 kts
Armament: four single MM.38 Exocet surface-to-surface missile launchers with four missiles (not in F169 and F172), one quadruple GWS24 Sea Cat surface-to-air missile launcher with 20 missiles, one 114-mm (4.5-in) DP gun,

four single 20-mm AA guns, and two triple 324-mm (12.75-in) STWS1 ASW torpedo tubes with Mk 46 and Stingray torpedoes
Aircraft: one Westland Lynx HAS.Mk 2 ASW helicopter
Electronics: one Type 978 navigation radar, one Type 992Q air- and surface-search radar, two RTN10X fire-control radars, one CAAIS combat data system, one UAA-1 ESM system (only in some), two Corvus chaff launchers, one Type 162M hull sonar, and one Type 184M hull sonar
Complement: 177 normal and 192 maximum

Below: After refitting, HMS Andromeda and the other four Batch 3 'Leanders' are the most powerful of the 'Leander' variants. The planned conversion of the other five Batch 3s has fallen victim to cuts in the defence budget.

with eight missiles, two quadruple Sea Cat surface-to-air missile launchers with 32 missiles, one 76-mm (3-in) DP gun, and two triple 324-mm (12.75-in) Mk 32 ASW torpedo tubes with Mk 46 torpedoes
Aircraft: one Westland SH-14B/C Lynx ASW helicopter
Electronics: one LW-03 air-search radar, one DA-05/2 target-indicator radar, one Decca TM1229C navigation radar, two WM-44 Sea Cat fire-control radars, one WM-45 gun fire-control

radar, one SEWACO II data information system, one passive ESM system, two Corvus chaff launchers, one CWE610 hull sonar, and one SQR-18A towed-array sonar
Complement: 180

From the 17th 'Leander' the design was amended by increasing the beam. HMS Andromeda was the first of five broad-beamed 'Leanders' to be fitted with Sea Wolf and Exocet missiles, re-commissioning in 1980.

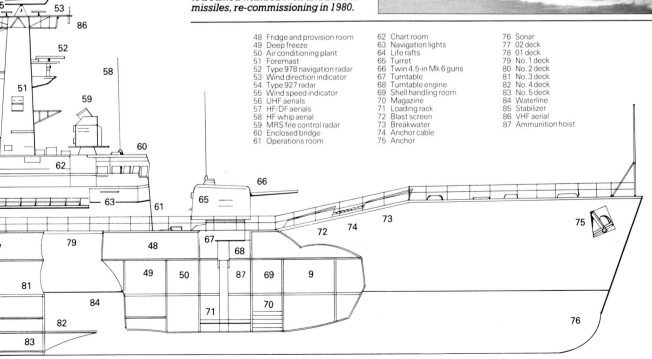

48 Fridge and provision room	62 Chart room	76 Sonar
49 Deep freeze	63 Navigation lights	77 02 deck
50 Air conditioning plant	64 Life rafts	78 01 deck
51 Foremast	65 Turret	79 No. 1 deck
52 Type 978 navigation radar	66 Twin 4.5-in Mk 6 guns	80 No. 2 deck
53 Wind direction indicator	67 Turntable	81 No. 3 deck
54 Type 927 radar	68 Turntable engine	82 No. 4 deck
55 Wind speed indicator	69 Shell handling room	83 No. 5 deck
56 UHF aerials	70 Magazine	84 Waterline
57 HF/DF aerials	71 Loading rack	85 Stabilizer
58 HF whip aerial	72 Blast screen	86 VHF aerial
59 MRS fire control radar	73 Breakwater	87 Ammunition hoist
60 Enclosed bridge	74 Anchor cable	
61 Operations room	75 Anchor	

'Chikugo' class

Designed and built with structural features to reduce noise and vibration, the 'Chikugo' class ships were used primarily for coastal ASW missions around the Japanese home islands. To facilitate their use in this role they were equipped to carry and operate the SQS35(J) variable-depth sonar from an open well offset to starboard at the stern. They were also the smallest warships ever to carry the octuple ASROC ASW missile-launcher system, though no reloads were carried; the amidships launcher was trained to the bearing and then elevated to fire two-round salvo of the solid-fuel RUR-5A rockets with their MK 46 parachute-retarded homing torpedo payloads out to a maximum range of 9.2 km (5.7 miles). The Japanese vessels did not carry the alternative payload of a one kiloton Mk 17 nuclear depth charge carried by American ships. The propulsion plant comprised either four Mitsubishi-Burmeister & Wan UEV30/40 (in DE 215, 217, -219, 221, 225) or four Mitsui 28VBC-38 diesels (in the remainder) A Mk 51 fire-control

director with no radar controls the twin 40-mm mount aft. The hull-mounted OQS3 sonar is a licence-built version of the American SQS-23 set, a variant of which is used on the 'Spruance' class ASW destroyers. The 11 vessels in service are the *Chikugo* (DE215), *Ayase* (DE216), *Mikumo* (DE217), *Tokachi* (DE218), *Iwase* (DE219), *Chitose* (DE220), *Niyoda* (DE221), *Teshio* (DE222), *Yoshino* (DE223), *Kumano* (DE224) and *Noshiro* (DE225).

Specification
'Chikugo' class
Displacement: (DE215 and DE220) 1,480 tons standard, (DE216-DE219 and DE221) 1,470 tons standard or (DE222-DE225) 1,500 tons standard and 1,700-1,800 tons full load
Dimensions: length 93.1 m (305.5 ft); beam 10.8 m (35.5 ft); draught 3.5 m (11.5 ft)
Propulsion: four diesels delivering 16,000 hp (11931 kW) to two shafts
Speed: 25 kts
Armament: one twin 76-mm (3-in) Mk 33 DP gun, one twin 40-mm AA gun,

one octuple ASROC ASW missile launcher with eight missiles, and two triple 324-mm (12.75-in) Mk 68 ASW torpedo tubes with Mk 46 torpedoes
Aircraft: none
Electronics: one OPS-14 air-search radar, one OPS-28 surface-search radar, one GCFS-1B fire-control radar, one OPS-19 navigation radar, one NORL-5 ESM system, one OQS-3 hull sonar, and one SQS-35(J) variable-

Tokachi (DE218) pays a courtesy visit to Hawaii. As in all except the most recent Japanese designs, the 'Chikugo' class has significant ASW capability but little in the way of surface-to-surface or AAW equipment.

depth sonar
Complement: 165

'Yubari' class

The **'Yubari' class** is basically an improved and enlarged variant of the 'Ishakiri' design authorized in 1977-8. The greater length and beam improved the seaworthiness and reduced the internal space constrictions of the earlier design. The original number of units to be built was three, but this was reduced by one when the Japanese government deleted funds from the naval budget in the early 1980s. A new three-vessel 'Improved Yubari' class is to be constructed in the 1983-7 five-year plan.

Although not heavily armed and having no helicopter facilities in comparison with contemporary European designs, the 'Yubaris' are ideal for use in the waters around Japan, where they would operate under shore-based air cover. Most of the weapons, machinery and sensors have been built under licence from foreign manufacturers. The propulsion plant is a CODOG arrangement with a licence-built Kawasaki/Rolls-Royce Olympus TM3B gas turbine and a Mitsubishi 6DRV 35/44 diesel. Extensive automation of the machinery has reduced the crew total to below 100, which is extremely good for a warship of this size. The vessels which comprise the class are the *Yubari* (DE227) and *Yubetsu* (DE228).

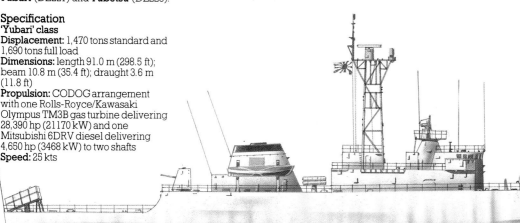

Specification
'Yubari' class
Displacement: 1,470 tons standard and 1,690 tons full load
Dimensions: length 91.0 m (298.5 ft); beam 10.8 m (35.4 ft); draught 3.6 m (11.8 ft)
Propulsion: CODOG arrangement with one Rolls-Royce/Kawasaki Olympus TM3B gas turbine delivering 28,390 hp (21170 kW) and one Mitsubishi 6DRV diesel delivering 4,650 hp (3468 kW) to two shafts
Speed: 25 kts

Armament: two quadruple Harpoon surface-to-surface missile launchers with eight missiles, one 76-mm (3-in) DP gun, one 20-mm Phalanx CIWS (being fitted), one quadruple 375-mm (14.76-in) Bofors ASW rocket launcher, and two triple 324-mm (12.75-in) Mk 68 ASW torpedo tubes with Mk 46 torpedoes

Aircraft: none
Electronics: one OPS-28 surface-search radar, one OPS-19 navigation radar, one GFCS-1 fire-control radar, one NOLQ-6 ESM system, one OLT-3 ECM jammer, two Mk 36 Super RBOC chaff launchers, and one OQS-1 hull sonar
Complement: 98

Smaller than the preceding 'Chikugo' class, the 'Yubari' class is highly automated, with a crew of under 100. Designed to operate under land-based air cover, the design has little AAW capability. The vessels were paid off at the rate of one a year from 1990.

Developed from the interim 'Ishakiri' design, Yubari and Yubetsu have been enlarged in both length and beam, the better to handle the armament mounted. Two quadruple Harpoon launchers give the class considerable anti-ship capability.

'Lupo' class

Built and designed by CN Riuniti naval shipbuilders, the four vessels of the 'Lupo' class in the Italian navy are the *Lupo* (F564), *Sagittario* (F565), *Perseo* (F566) and *Orsa* (F567). These were designed primarily for the convoy escort role, with a capability for anti-surface warfare using SSMs if required. The hull is based on 14 water-tight compartments and has fixed-fin stabilizers. To reduce the ship's complement the machinery plant has been highly automated and divided into four separate compartments housing the auxiliaries, gas turbine modules, reduction gearbox and the diesel alternator sets. A telescopic hangar has also been fitted to accommodate a light ASW helicopter that can also double in the missile-armed surface strike role.

The 'Lupos' have proved very popular in Italian navy service, and the type has been exported to Venezuela, Peru and Iraq in a modified form that has a fixed-hangar structure and no reloads for the SAM launcher. The six Venezuelan ships are the *Mariscal Sucre* (F21), *Almirante Brion* (F22), *General Urdaneta* (F23), *General Soublette* (F24), *General Salom* (F25) and *Almirante José de Garcia* (F26). The four Peruvian ships are the *Meliton Carvajal* (F51), *Manuel Villavicienco* (F52), *Montero* (F53) and an as yet unnamed unit. The four Iraqi units are the *Hittin*, *Thi Qar*, *Al Yarmook* and *Al Qadisyaa*, which are in various stages of construction with the first to be delivered next year.

The main anti-ship weapon carried on the Italian ships is the Otomat Mk 2 Teseo missile, which has an Italian SMA active radar-homing seeker and a sea-skimming flight profile. To utilize the missile's over-the-horizon capabilities fully, the embarked helicopter is used for mid-course guidance. Export ships carry the less capable Otomat

Mk 1 missile that has a pop-up terminal attack manoeuvre.

Specification
'Lupo' class (Italian navy)
Displacement: 2,208 tons standard and 2,525 tons full load
Dimensions: length 113.2 m (371.3 ft); beam 11.3 m (37.1 ft); draught 3.7 m (12.1 ft)
Propulsion: CODOG arrangement with two General Electric/FIAT LM2500 gas turbines delivering 51,600 hp (38478 kW) and two GMT A230 diesels delivering 7,900 hp (5891 kW) to two shafts

Speed: 35 kts
Armament: eight single Otomat Mk 2 surface-to-surface missile launchers with eight missiles, one octuple NATO Sea Sparrow surface-to-air missile launcher with 24 Aspide missiles, one 127-mm (5-in) DP gun, two twin 40-mm Dardo CIWS, and two triple Mk 32 324-mm (12.75-in) ASW torpedo tubes with Mk 46 torpedoes
Aircraft: one Agusta-Bell AB.212ASW helicopter
Electronics: one RAN10S air- and surface-search radar, one SPQ2F surface-search radar, one RAN11/LX air- and surface-search radar, one

Perseo, the third 'Lupo' class frigate to enter service with the Italian navy, is seen with her forward OTO-Melara 76-mm gun at high elevation. The Lupos' are being progressively replaced by the 'Maestrale' class.

RTN10X fire-control radar, two RTN20X Dardo fire-control radars, one SPN703 navigation radar, one IPN10 command and control system, active and passive ESM systems, two SCLAR chaff launchers, and one DE1160B hull sonar
Complement: 186

'Maestrale' class

The **'Maestrale' class** is essentially a stretched version of the 'Lupo' design with less weapons and a greater emphasis on ASW. The increase in length and beam over the earlier 'Lupos' was to provide for a fixed hangar installation and a variable-depth sonar (VDS) housing at the stern. The improvements have resulted in better seaworthiness and habitability, plus the room required to carry and operate a second light helicopter. However, to compensate for this the class carries four less SSMs, and because of the extra tonnage has suffered a speed reduction of around 3 kts. The Raytheon VDS operates on the same frequencies as the hull sonar set and gives the vessels a valuable below-the-thermal-layer capability for use in the very difficult ASW conditions met in the Mediterranean. To enhance the ships' ASW operations further, the Agusta-Bell AB.212 helicopters carried are fitted with Bendix ASQ-13B active dunking sonars. The armament they carry is either the American Mk 46 homing torpedo or Mk 54 depth charge. The ship uses the A244/S torpedo as well. It is also fitted with two fixed tubes for the 36-kt 25-km (15.5-mile) range Whitehead Motofides A184 533-mm (21-in) wire-guided torpedo beneath the helicopter pad aft.

The A184 can be used against surface and sub-surface targets. A towed-array system that can use the existing VDS installation is currently under development. The helicopters can also carry AS.12 wire-guided anti-ship missiles and will eventually be converted

to the Marte ASM system.

The eight ships are the *Maestrale* (F570), *Grecale* (F571), *Libeccio* (F572), *Scirocco* (F573), *Aliseo* (F574), *Euro* (F575), *Espero* (F576) and *Zeffiro* (F575), and all are now in service with the Italian navy.

Comparable to the Dutch 'Kortenaer' or German 'Bremen' classes, the 'Maestrale' class is somewhat faster, Largely a stretched version of the preceding 'Lupo' class, Maestrale and her seven sisterships possess enhanced ASW abilities.

Faster than most Western frigates (although slower than the 'Lupo' class), Maestrale is comprehensively equipped with modern ASW technology, including both a hull sonar and towed variable-depth sonar.

Specification
'Maestrale' class
Displacement: 3,040 tons standard and 3,200 tons full load
Dimensions: length 122.7 m (402.6 ft); beam 12.9 m (42.3 ft); draught 8.4 m (27.6 ft)
Propulsion: CODOG arrangement with two General Electric/FIAT LM2500 gas turbines delivering 51,600 hp (38478 kW) and two GMT B230 diesels delivering 10,146 hp (7566 kW) to two shafts
Speed: 32 kts
Armament: four single Otomat Mk 2 surface-to-surface missile launchers with four missiles, one octuple Albatros surface-to-air missile system with 24 Aspide missiles, one 127-mm (5-in) DP gun, two twin 40-mm Dardo CIWS, two single 533-mm (21-in) torpedo tubes for A184 torpedoes, and two triple 324-mm (12.75-in) ILAS-3 ASW torpedo tubes for Mk 46 and A244/S torpedoes
Aircraft: two Agusta-Bell AB.212 ASW helicopters
Electronics: one RAN10S air- and surface-search radar, one SPQ2F surface-search radar, one RTN30X Albatros acquisition radar, two RTN20X Dardo fire-control radars, one RTN10X fire-control radar, one SPN703 navigation radar, one IPN10 command and control system, active and passive ESM systems, two SCLAR D chaff launchers, one DE1160B hull sonar, and one DE1164 variable-depth sonar
Complement: 213

USA

'Garcia' and 'Brooke' classes

Designed in the late 1950s as replacements for World War II destroyers, the 'Garcia' class ASW escort and 'Brooke' class SAM ship were ordered by the US Navy to the extent of 10 and six units respectively. Further production of the latter ended during Fiscal Year 1963 because of their high cost and limited capability. Although they are relatively modern, there are no plans to modernize the ASW ships USS *Garcia* (FF1040), USS *Bradley* (FF1041), USS *Edward McDonnell* (FF1043), USS *Brumby* (FF1044), USS *Davidson* (FF1045), USS *Voge* (FF1047), USS *Sample* (FF1048), USS *Koelsch* (FF1049), USS *Albert David* (FF1050) and USS *O'Callahan* (FF1051) with new guns, Harpoon SSM and modern ESM equipment. Over the years the class has been used to test a number of prototype systems including the SQR-15 linear towed-array sonar which is now fitted to FF1040 and FF1043 in place of a LAMPS I ASW helicopter. An automated ASW tactical data system (TDS) is carried by FF1047 and FF1049, whilst from FF1047 onwards an ASROC reload magazine has been fitted within the superstructure.

The SAM ships USS *Brooke* (FFG1), USS *Ramsey* (FFG2), USS *Schofield* (FFG3), USS *Talbot* (FFG4), USS *Richard L. Page* (FFG5) and USS *Julius F. Furer* (FFG6) are identical to the 'Garcias' except that a single-rail Mk 22 launcher, originally for Tarter and later for Standard SM-1MR missiles, replaced the aft 127-mm (5-in) gun mount. From FFG4 onwards an ASROC reload magazine was also incorporated into the superstructure. The Talbot was used as the test ship for the weapons and sensor fit for the 'Oliver Hazard Perry' class but was later returned to normal appearance. Eight units were transferred to Pakistan; the remainder were placed in reserve pending disposal.

Specification
'Garcia' class
Displacement: 2,620 tons standard and 3,560 tons full load
Dimensions: length 126.3 m (414.5 ft); beam 13.5 m (44.2 ft); draught 4.4 m (14.5 ft)
Propulsion: geared steam turbines delivering 35,000 hp (26100 kW) to two shafts
Speed: 27.5 kts
Armament: two single 127-mm (5-in) DP guns, one octuple ASROC anti-submarine missile launcher with eight (first five ships) or 16 (other ships) missiles, and two triple 324-mm (12.75-in) Mk 32 ASW torpedo tubes with Mk 46 torpedoes
Aircraft: one Kaman SH-2F Seasprite LAMPS I helicopter (not in FF1040 and FF1043)
Electronics: one SPS-40 air-search radar, one SPS-10 surface-search radar, one SPG-35 fire-control radar, one LN66 navigation radar, one WLR-1 ECM system, one WLR-3 ECM system, one ULQ-6 ECM system, one SRN-15 TACAN (not in FF1040 and FF1043), one SQS-26 bow sonar, and (FF1040 and FF1043 only) one BQR-15 towed sonar
Complement: 247 except FF1040, FF1041, FF1043 and FF1044 239

Specification
'Brooke' class
Displacement: 2,643 tons standard and 3,426 tons full load
Dimensions: length 126.3 m (414.5 ft); beam 13.5 m (44.2 ft); draught 4.6 m (15.0 ft)
Propulsion: as 'Garcia' class
Speed: 27.2 kts
Armament: one single-rail Mk 22 Standard surface-to-air missile launcher with 16 SM-1MR missiles, one 127-mm (5-in) DP gun, one octuple ASROC anti-submarine missile launcher with eight (first three ships) or 16 (other ships) missiles, and two triple 324-mm (12.75-in) Mk 32 ASW torpedo tubes with Mk 46 torpedoes
Aircraft: one Kaman SH-2F Seasprite LAMPS I helicopter
Electronics: one SPS-52B 3D radar, one SPS-10F surface-search radar, one LN66 navigation radar, one SPG-51C Standard fire-control radar, one SPG-35 gun fire-control radar, one SRN-15 TACAN, one SLQ-32(V)2 ESM system, two Mk 36 Super RBOC chaff launchers, and one SQS-26 bow sonar
Complement: 248

USS Edward McDonnell (FF1043) of the 'Garcia' class plunges through a heavy sea. Unlike later US frigate classes, the 'Garcias' are ASW-dedicated, and have little or no modern anti-aircraft capability.

USS Brooke (FFG1) is name ship of a six-vessel class built to a modified 'Garcia' design. The difference lies in the fitting of a Mk 22 single-rail missile launcher in place of the aft 5-in (127-mm) gun. The standard SM-1MR missiles now carried give the class considerable anti-aircraft potential.

USA
'Knox' class

The '**Knox' class** is similar to the 'Garcia' and 'Brooke' designs, but is slightly larger because of the use of non-pressure fired boilers, and was designed in the early 1960s. The first vessels entered US Navy service in 1969, the last units of the 46-strong class being delivered in 1974. They are specialized ASW ships and have been heavily criticized because of their single propeller and solitary 127-mm (5-in) gun armament.

A five-ship class based on the design but with a Mk 22 missile launcher for 13 Standard SM-1MR and three Harpoon missiles was constructed in Spain for the Spanish navy. Built with American aid, the *Baleares* (F71), *Andalucia* (F72), *Cataluna* (F73), *Asturias* (F74) and *Extremadura* (F75) also carry two Mk 25 ASW torpedo tubes as well as the two triple Mk 32 systems, for which a total of 22 Mk 44/46 and 19 Mk 37 ASW torpedoes are stored in each ship's magazines.

From 1980 onwards the American 'Knoxes' were taken in hand to receive raised bulwarks and spray stakes forward to improve their seakeeping in heavy weather. Like the 'Garcia' class, numerous 'Knoxes' have been used over the years to test individual prototype weapon and sensor systems. A total of 32 (FF1052-1083) were equipped with an octuple Sea Sparrow launcher, and this was replaced by 20-mm Phalanx CIWS of the type fitted to all 46 ships. The port pair of four twin cells of the SROC launcher were retrofitted to fire Harpoon surface-to-surface missiles while all vessels were fitted to carry the SQR-18A TACTASS towed array sonar. In 34 ships it replaced the SQS-35A VDS system carried in a stern well. For helicopter operations and SRN-15 TACAN was carried and the SLQ-32(V)1 ESM system was upgrade to the SLQ-32(V)2 configuration. To reduce

USS Knox *(FF1052) was the first of its class. Evolved from the preceding 'Garcia' and 'Brooke' classes, the 'Knox' class vessels are to be fitted with Harpoon SSMs and the 20-mm Phalanx close-in weapon system (CIWS).*

underwater radiated noise the Prairie/Masker bubble system has been used on the hull and propeller. The ASW TDS first evaluated in the 'Garcia' class were installed as ships entered refit. By 1986 eight units had been assigned to the Naval Reserve Force as replacements for old World War II destroyers. The class comprised the USS *Knox* (FF1052), USS *Roark* (FF1053), USS *Gray* (FF1054), USS *Hepburn* (FF1055), USS *Connole* (FF1056), USS *Rathburne* (FF1057), USS *Meyerkord* (FF1058), USS *W.S. Sims* (FF1059), USS *Lang* (FF1060), USS *Patterson* (FF1061), USS *Whipple* (FF1062), USS *Reasoner* (FF1063), USS *Lockwood* (FF1064), USS *Stein* (FF1065), USS *Marvin Shields* (FF1066), USS *Francis Hammond* (FF1067), USS *Vreeland* (FF1068), USS *Bagley* (FF1069), USS *Downes* (FF1070), USS *Badger* (FF1071), USS *Blakely* (FF1072), USS *Robert E. Peary* (FF1073), USS *Harold E. Holt* (FF1074), USS *Trippe* (FF1075), USS *Fanning* (FF1076), USS *Ouellet* (FF1077), USS

Joseph Hewes (FF1078), USS *Bowen* (FF1079), USS *Paul* (FF1080), USS *Aylwin* (FF1081), USS *Elmer Montgomery* (FF1082), USS *Cook* (FF1083), USS *McCandless* (FF1084), USS *Donald B. Beary* (FF1085), USS *Brewton* (FF1086), USS *Kirk* (FF1087), USS *Barbey* (FF1088), USS *Jesse L. Brown* (FF1089), USS *Ainsworth* (FF1090), USS *Miller* (FF1091), USS *Thomas C. Hart* (FF1092), USS *Capodanno* (FF1093), USS *Pharris* (FF1094), USS *Truett* (FF1095), USS *Valdez* (FF1096) and USS *Moinester* (FF1097).

Specification
'Knox' class
Displacement: 3,011 tons standard and 3,877 tons (FF1052-FF1077) or 4,250 tons (other ships) full load
Dimensions: length 133.5 m (438.0 ft); beam 14.3 m (46.8 ft); draught 4.6 m (15.0 ft)

USS Pharris *(FF1094) seen during an exercise of the South American coast. The 46 'Knox' class vessels were progressively transferred to the Naval Reserve Force from 1989.*

Propulsion: geared steam turbines delivering 35,000 hp (26100 kW) to one shaft
Speed: 27 kts
Armament: one 127-mm (5-in) DP gun, one 20-mm Phalanx CIWS (being fitted), one octuple Sea Sparrow surface-to-air missile launcher with eight missiles (being replaced), one octuple ASROC anti-submarine and Harpoon surface-to-surface missile launcher with 12 ASROC and four Harpoon missiles, and two twin 324-mm (12.75-in) Mk 32 ASW torpedo tubes with 22 Mk 46 torpedoes
Aircraft: one Kaman SH-2F Seasprite LAMPS I helicopter
Electronics: one SPS-40B air-search radar, one SPS-10 surface-search radar, one SPG-53 fire-control radar, one LN66 navigation radar, one ASW tactical data system, one SRN-15 TACAN, one SQS-26 bow sonar, and one SQS-35 variable-depth sonar (in 34 ships); all are to have SQR-18A towed sonar
Complement: 283

USA
'Oliver Hazard Perry' class

Destined to be numerically the largest warship class in the US Navy, the '**Oliver Hazard Perry' class** was designed for anti-air warfare with ASW and anti-surface warfare as its secondary roles. Because of cost considerations the first 26 were not fitted to carry two LAMPS III ASW helicopters, but retained the two LAMPS machines. The LAMPS facilities included the Recovery Assistance Security and Traversing (RAST) system which allowed the launch and recovery of the Sikorsky SH-60 Seahawk helicopters with the ship rolling through 28° and pitching up to 5°. All have aluminium alloy armour over

their magazine spaces and Kevlar plastic armour over vital electronics and communications facilities.

A further four ships are HMAS *Adelaide* (F01), HMAS *Canberra* (F02), HMAS *Sydney* (F03) and HMAS *Darwin* (F04) for Australia, which may also construct up to another six under licence. Spain is also building under licence three vessels of the type for her navy: these are the *Navarra* (F81), *Murcia* (F82) and *Leon* (F83).

The magazine for the single-rail Mk 13 SAM launcher can take only Standard and Harpoon missiles, so the shipboard ASW weapons are Mk 46 torpedoes and the LAMPS helicopters.

Eighteen of the US class have been assigned to the Naval Force Reserve as training ships along with several 'Knox' class ASW frigates. Two ships, the *Stark* and the *Samuel B. Roberts*, were hit by missiles in the Arabian Gulf during the Iraq-Iran war. The class consists of the USS *Oliver Hazard Perry* (FFG7), USS *McInerney* (FFG8), USS *Wadsworth* (FFG9), USS *Duncan* (FFG10), USS *Clark* (FFG11), USS *George Philip* (FFG12), USS *Samuel Eliot Morison* (FFG13), USS *John H. Sides* (FFG14), USS *Estocin* (FFG15), USS *Clifton Sprague* (FFG16), USS *John A. Moore* (FFG19), USS *Antrim* (FFG20), USS *Flatley* (FFG21), USS

Fahrion (FFG22), USS *Lewis B. Puller* (FFG23), USS *Jack Williams* (FFG24), USS *Copeland* (FFG25), USS *Gallery* (FFG26), USS *Mahlon S. Tisdale* (FFG27), USS *Boone* (FFG28), USS *Stephen W. Groves* (FFG29), USS *Reid* (FFG30), USS *Stark* (FFG31), USS *John L. Hall* (FFG32), USS *Jarret* (FFG33), USS *Aubrey Fitch* (FFG34), USS *Underwood* (FFG36), USS *Crommelin* (FFG37), USS *Curts* (FFG38), USS *Doyle* (FFG39), USS *Halyburton* (FFG40), USS *McClusky* (FFG41), USS *Klakring* (FFG42), USS *Thach* (FFG43), USS *De Wert* (FFG45), USS *Rentz* (FFG46), USS *Nicholas* (FFG47), USS *Vandergrift* (FFG48), USS *Robert*

USS Oliver Hazard Perry *(FFG1) is the first of a class of over 50 general-purpose vessels designed to escort merchant convoys or amphibious squadrons. ASW is handled by the two LAMPS helicopters embarked, and the class can also fire Harpoon and Standard missiles.*

G. Bradley (FFG49), USS *Taylor* (FFG50), USS *Gary* (FFG51), USS *Carr* (FFG52), USS *Hawes* (FFG53), USS *Ford* (FFG54), USS *Elrod* (FFG55), USS *Simpson* (FFG56), USS *Reuben James* (FFG57), USS *Samuel B. Roberts* (FFG58), USS *Rodney M. Davis* (FFG60) and two unnamed (FFG59 and FFG61).

Specification
'Oliver Hazard Perry' class
Displacement: 2,769 tons standard and 3,658 tons full load
Dimensions: length 135.6 m (445.0 ft) in LAMPS I ships or 138.1 m (453.0 ft) in LAMPS III ships (FFG8, FFG36-FFG43 and FFG45-FFG61); beam 13.7 m (45.0 ft); draught 4.5 m (14.8 ft)
Propulsion: two General Electric LM2500 gas turbines delivering 40,000 hp (29828 kW) to one shaft
Speed: 29 kts
Armament: one single-rail Mk 13 Standard/Harpoon missile launcher with 36 SM-1MR surface-to-air and four Harpoon surface-to-surface missiles, one 76-mm (3-in) DP gun, one 20-mm Phalanx CIWS, and two triple 324-mm (12.75-in) Mk 32 ASW torpedo tubes with 24 Mk 46 torpedoes
Aircraft: two Kaman SH-2F Seasprite

LAMPS I or two Sikorsky SH-60B Sea Hawk LAMPS III helicopters
Electronics: one SPS-49 air-search radar, one SPS-55 surface-search radar, one STIR fire-control radar, one

URN-25 TACAN, one SLQ-32(V)2 ESM system, two Mk 36 Super RBOC chaff launchers, one SQS-56 hull sonar, and (in FFG36-FFG43 and FFG45-FFG61 only) one SQR-19A towed sonar
Complement: 215

USS Oliver Hazard Perry *is seen together with USS* Antrim *(FFG20) and USS* Jack Williams *(FFG24). Each is armed with an OTO-Melara 76-mm (3-in) quick-firing gun and a Phalanx 20-mm CIWS.*

'Tromp' class

Although designated by the Dutch as frigates, the **'Tromp' class** vessels *Tromp* (F801) and *De Ruyter* (F802) are, by virtue of their armament and size, more akin to guided-missile destroyers. They are equipped with an admiral's cabin and supporting command and control facilities to serve as the flagships of the two Dutch navy ASW hunter-killer groups assigned to EASTLANT control during wartime. Fitted with fin stabilizers, they are excellent seaboats and weapons platforms in most types of weather. The propulsion is of the COGOG type with pairs of Rolls-Royce Olympus and Tyne gas turbines that have been downrated to improve gas generator life and ease of maintenance. A full

NBC citadel defence is built into the hull.

The primary role assigned to the ships is the provision of area SAM defence against aircraft and missiles to the hunter-killer group or convoy it may be escorting. They also have a secondary ASW and anti-surface vessel role. The main armament is a single-rail Mk 13 Standard SM-1MR SAM launcher, backed up by an octuple NATO Sea Sparrow SAM launcher with a large reload magazine. The appearance of the vessels is characterized by the large plastic radome fitted over the forward SPS-01 3D radar. A new multi-beam target-acquisition radar, SMART, is under development to replace the SPS-01.

Specification
'Tromp' class
Displacement: 3,665 tons standard and 4,308 tons full load
Dimensions: length 138.4 m (454.0 ft) beam 14.8 m (48.6 ft); draught 4.6 m (15.1 ft)
Propulsion: COGOG arrangement with two Rolls-Royce Olympus TM3B gas turbines delivering 50,000 hp (37285 kW) and two Rolls-Royce Tyne RM1C gas turbines delivering 8,200 hp (6115 kW) to two shafts
Speed: 28 kts
Armament: two quadruple Harpoon surface-to-surface missile launchers with eight missiles, one single-rail Mk 13 Standard surface-to-air missile launcher with 40 SM-1MR missiles, one

octuple NATO Sea Sparrow surface-to-air missile launcher with 60 missiles, one twin 120-mm (4.72-in) Bofors DP gun, and two triple 324-mm (12.75-in) Mk 32 ASW torpedo tubes with Mk 46 torpedoes
Aircraft: one Westland SH-14B/C Lynx ASW helicopter
Electronics: one SPS-01/D radar, two ZW-05 surface-search radars, one WM-25 fire-control radar, two SPG-51C fire-control radars, one SEWACO I data information system, one Sphinx ESM system, two Corvus chaff launchers, one Type 162 hull sonar, and one CWE610 hull sonar
Complement: 306

Replacing two cruisers in service with the Royal Netherlands navy, HNLMS Tromp *and* De Ruyter *are among the largest and most capable of frigates afloat. They will be replaced in 2002–4 by De Zeven Provincien class.*

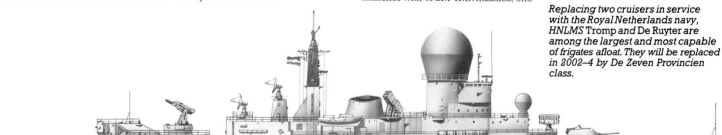

'Kortenaer' and 'Jacob van Heemskerck' classes

The **'Kortenaer'** or 'Standard' class frigate design was authorized in the late 1960s as the replacement for the 12 ASW destroyers of the 'Holland' and 'Friesland' classes. The propulsion plant and machinery layout was taken from the 'Tromp' design, the power of the gas turbines being kept normal to give higher maximum and cruising speeds in order to permit operations against nuclear submarines. A single pair of fin stabilizers is fitted, and as far as possible internal systems have been automated to reduce crew numbers. Eight ships were ordered in 1974, and a further four in 1976. In 1982, however, two newly completed units were purchased by Greece as the *Elli* (F450) and *Limnos* (F451). These were replaced in the Dutch order by two vessels to be constructed to an air-defence variant design known as the **'Jacob van Heemskerck' class**. The two ships are the *Jacob van Heemskerck* (F812) and *Witte de With* (F813), and were planned to alternate as the flagship of the Dutch navy's third ASW hunter-killer group, assigned to NATO's Channel Command in wartime. The helicopter facilities of the 'Kortenaers' has been replaced by a Mk 13 Standard SAM missile launcher. The two vessels were both commissioned in 1986. The ten vessels of the ASW class are the *Kortenaer* (F807), *Callenburgh* (F808), *Van Kingsbergen* (F809), *Banckert* (F810), *Piet Hein* (F811), *Abraham Crijnssen* (F816), *Philips van Almonde* (F823), *Bloys van Treslong* (F824),

HNLMS Banckert (F810) was the fourth 'Kortenaer' class frigate to enter service with the Royal Netherlands navy. The 'Kortenaers' have a well-balanced armament fit, primary ASW weapons being the two Westland Lynx helicopters carried.

Jacob van Brakel (F825) and *Pieter Florisz* (F826).

Specification
'Kortenaer' class
Displacement: 3,050 tons standard and 3,786 tons full load
Dimensions: length 130.5 m (428.1 ft); beam 14.6 m (47.9 ft); draught 4.3 m (14.1 ft)
Propulsion: COGOG arrangement with two Rolls-Royce Olympus TM3B gas turbines delivering 51,600 hp (38478 kW) and two Rolls-Royce Tyne RM1C gas turbines delivering 9,800 hp (7308 kW) to two shafts
Speed: 30 kts
Armament: two quadruple Harpoon surface-to-surface missile launchers with eight missiles, one octuple NATO Sea Sparrow surface-to-air missile launcher with 24 missiles, one 76-mm (3-in) DP gun, one 30-mm Goalkeeper CIWS, and two twin 324-mm (12.75-in) Mk 32 ASW torpedo tubes with Mk 46 torpedoes
Aircraft: two Westland SH-14B/C Lynx ASW helicopters
Electronics: one LW-08 air-search radar, one ZW-06 navigation radar, one WM-25 fire-control radar, one STIR fire-control radar, one SEWACO

II data information system, one Sphinx (F807-F811) or Ramses (others) ESM system, two Corvus chaff launchers, and one SQS-505 bow sonar
Complement: 176 normal and 200 maximum

Specification
'Jacob van Heemskerck' class
Displacement: 3,000 tons standard and 3,750 tons full load
Dimensions: as 'Kortenaer' class
Propulsion: as 'Kortenaer' class
Speed: as 'Kortenaer' class

Armament: as 'Kortenaer' class without 76-mm (3-in) DP gun but with one single-rail Mk 13 Standard surface-to-air missile launcher with 40 SM-1MR missiles
Aircraft: none
Electronics: one SMART 3D radar, one ZW-06 navigation radar, one STIR fire-control radar, two Mod STIR fire-control radars, one SEWACO II data information system, one Ramses ESM system, four Mk 36 Super RBOC chaff launchers, and one PHS36 bow sonar
Complement: 176 plus 20 flag staff

'Wielingen' (E-71) class

The **'Wielingen' class** is the first postwar warship type to be completely designed and built in Belgium. The programme was approved in June 1971, the final studies being completed in July 1973. The order for the first two ships was placed in October of that year, and the hulls were laid down in 1974. The remaining two were laid down in 1975, all four units commissioning into the Belgian navy in 1978.

Based at Zeebrugge, the four vessels are the largest surface warships in the Belgian navy and form its only seagoing escort ship element. They are fully air conditioned, and are fitted with Vosper fin stabilizers and a Westinghouse hull sonar. The armament and sensor fit is from a wide variety of NATO countries and was chosen to make the class as well-armed as possible for so compact a size. For economy a combined diesel or gas turbine (CODOG) machinery outfit was installed using a single Rolls-Royce TM3B Olympus gas turbine and two Cock-

erill CO-240V-12 diesels to drive two shafts fitted with controllable-pitch propellers. The four vessels built are the **Wielingen** (F910), **Westdiep** (F911), **Wandelaar** (F912) and **Westhinder** (F913), and these will remain in operational service until the early years of the next century.

Specification
'Wielingen' class
Displacement: 1,880 tons standard and 2,283 tons full load
Dimensions: length 106.4 m (349.1 ft); beam 12.3 m (40.4 ft); draught 5.6 m (18.4 ft)
Propulsion: CODOG arrangement with one Rolls-Royce Olympus TM3B gas turbine delivering 28,000 shp (20880 kW) and two diesels delivering 6,000 hp (4474 kW) to two shafts
Speed: 29 kts
Armament: four single MM.38 Exocet surface-to-surface missile launchers with four missiles, one octuple NATO

Sea Sparrow surface-to-air missile launcher with eight missiles, one 100-mm (3.9-in) DP gun, two single 20-mm AA guns (to be replaced by one 30-mm Goalkeeper CIWS), one sextuple 375-mm (14.76-in) Creusot Loire ASW rocket-launcher, and two single ASW torpedo catapults with 10 L5 torpedoes
Electronics: one DA-05 air- and

surface-search radar, one WM-25 fire-control radar, one TM1645/9X navigation radar, one SEWACO IV tactical data system, two Mk 36 Super RBOC chaff launchers, one SLQ-25 NIXIE ASW decoy system, and one SQS-505A hull sonar
Aircraft: none
Complement: 160

Above: Of the three remaining ships in the Weilingen class two are operational at all times, the third being laid up on a rotational basis. They provide Belgium's only ocean-going escort capability.

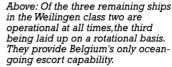

Distinguished by their low superstructure and relatively massive funnel, the 'Wielingens' are the first post-war Belgian-designed and -built vessels. Gun armament includes a 100-mm dual purpose weapon, together with a Goalkeeper 30-mm CIWS soon to be installed.

Modern Western Frigates 2

Whereas the frigate may be designed and fitted out for a specific task in the world's wealthier navies, in smaller maritime forces it often serves as the work-horse. Yet whether in the specialized or in the general-purpose role, the modern frigate bristles with the most up-to-date technology and weapon systems.

The 'Type 23' 'Duke' class frigate HMS *Norfolk* on sea trials. Developed as a cheaper version of the expensive 'Type 22', the 'Type 23' is nevertheless one of the quietest ASW vessels in service.

To counter the modern nuclear-powered submarine with its high underwater speed and advanced electronics and missiles, most modern frigates are fitted with twin-shaft gas turbine engines with controllable-pitch propellers, and the most up-to-date weapons systems. The fact that frigates must be at the cutting edge of naval technology makes their design and construction prohibitively costly for smaller navies, which usually prefer to buy them 'off the shelf' from the principal maritime powers.

The Royal Navy's 'Type 23' frigates, the first of which was completed in 1990, were the first to be fitted with GWS26 Mod 1 Vertical-Launch Seawolf, which combines a Type 911 tracker with 32 canister-mounted missiles, featuring a tandem booster with thrust-vector control. A further version of the Seawolf, the GWS27, is an advanced fire-and-forget weapon against all-aspect targets.

Although ideally optimized for anti-submarine warfare in the world's leading navies, frigates tend to be used as general purpose work-horse vessels in smaller navies; only the navies of wealthier countries have the benefit of custom-built ships out-fitted for a specific maritime role.

A good example of this is Saudi Arabia, which purchased 'Type F2000' class frigates from France in the 1980s. In terms of capability and equipment, these vessels, at the time of delivery, could out-perform many of the frigates in service with NATO and the Warsaw Pact, with particular regard to their state-of-the-art electronic equipment.

Some small navies, on the other hand, opt for small, light frigates armed with missiles. The former Soviet Union specialized in building this type of vessel and since the end of the Cold War many have been offered for sale on the international arms market. Although Russian maritime technology in many areas is less sophisticated than that of the West, it is entirely adequate for Third World nations eager to establish naval superiority in their particular spheres.

'Parchim' class

Previously known to NATO as the 'BAL-COM-4' class (Baltic Combatant No. 4) and to the technical press as the 'Koralle' class, the 'Parchim' class of light frigates was believed to be based on the Soviet 'Grisha' design with local modifications to suit its use by the East Germany navy. Built as the Peenewurft shipyard at Wolgast from the late 1970s onwards, the 'Parchims replaced the very unsatisfactory 'Hai III' class of large patrol craft that was constructed in the mid to late 1960s. The new class was designed primarily for coastal ASW operations but carried the heavy AA armament characteristic of Warsaw

Pact naval units operating in the Baltic Sea area. In total sixteen Parchim I ships were built, including the *Wismar*, *Parchim*, *Bad Doberan*, *Buetzow*, *Perelberg*, *Lübz*, *Teterow Purna*, and *Anlam*. They were followed by the improved Parchim IIs, of which there were twelve, all operating in the Baltic. A number of these served under the command of the Coastal Frontier Brigade at Rostock, which performed duties similar to those of the Soviet KGB. For this role the vessels armaments were modified to include additional guns at the expense of some ASW capability.

Specification
'Parchim' class
Displacement: 960 tons standard and 1,200 tons full load
Dimensions: length 72.5 m (237.9 ft); beam 9.4 m (30.8 ft); draught 3.5 m (11.5 ft)
Propulsion: two diesels delivering 8948 kW (12,000 hp) to two shafts
Speed: 25 kts
Armament: two quadruple launchers for 32 SA-N-5 'Grail' SAMs, one twin 57-mm AA and one twin 30-mm AA guns, four single 406-mm (16-in) tubes for anti-submarine torpedoes, two 12-barrel RBU6000 250-mm (9.84-in) ASW rocket-launchers with 120 rockets, two

racks for 24 depth charges, and between 20 and 30 mines according to type
Aircraft: none
Electronics: one 'Strut Curve' air-search radar, one 'Muff Cob' fire-control radar, one TSR333 navigation radar, one 'High Pole-B' IFF, two 'Watch Dog' ECM systems, two 16-barrel chaff launchers, one medium-frequency hull-mounted sonar, and (in some on starboard side of the main superstructure) one high-frequency dipping sonar
Complement: 60

'Grisha' class

Built as a *malyy protivolodochnyy korabl'* (MPK, or small anti-submarine ship) between 1968 and 1974 the 'Grisha I' class production run ended after only 16 units. These provided a more specialized ASW capability than the earlier 'Mirka' and 'Petya' classes. They were followed during 1974 and 1976 by eight 'Grisha II' class *pogranichnyy storozhevoy korabl'* (PSKR, or border patrol ship) units for the Maritime Border Directorate of the KGB. These differed from the 'Grisha Is' in having a second twin 57-mm AA mount substituted for the SA-N-4 'Gecko' SAM launcher forward and in having no 'Pop Group' fire-control radar. From 1975 onwards to the present the 'Grisha III' class has been the Soviet navy's production model. A 'Bass Tilt' gun fire-control radar (atop a small deckhouse to port on the aft super-structure) has replaced the 'Muff Cob' system on the earlier versions, whilst the space previously occupied by this radar has been taken up by a single 30-mm CIWS. To date 32 'Grisha III' units have been built with a construction rate of about three per year. Two Grisha IIs went to Lithuania in 1992, and four were transferred to the Ukraine in 994. Latest variant is the Grisha V, one of which was also delivered to the Ukraine in 1996.

Specification
'Grisha' classes
Displacement: 950 tons standard and 1,200 tons full load
Dimensions: length 72.0 m (236.2 ft) beam 10.0 m (32.8 ft) draught 3.7 m (12.1 ft)
Propulsion: CODAG arrangement with one gas turbine and four diesels delivering power to two shafts
Speed: 30 kts
Armament: one twin launcher for 18 SA-N-4 'Gecko' SAMs, one twin 57-mm AA and ('Grisha III' only) one 30-mm AA CIWS gun, two 12-barrel RBU6000 250-mm (9.84-in) ASW rocket-launchers with 120 rockets, two twin 533-mm (21-in) tubes for anti-

submarine torpedoes, two rails for 12 depth charges, and between 20 and 30 mines according to type
Aircraft: none
Electronics: one 'Strut Curve' air-search radar, one 'Pop Group' SAM fire-control radar, one 'Muff Cob' or ('Grisha III' only) 'Bass Tilt ' gun fire-control radar, two 'Watch Dog' ECM systems, one 'High Pole-B' IFF, one medium-frequency hull-mounted sonar, and one high-frequency dipping sonar
Complement: 80

Right: A 'Grisha I' unit in heavy weather shows that there is no bow sonar dome. There is a hull set and a dipping sonar which is housed in the deckhouse aft beneath the hump-shaped superstructure.

The 'Grisha II' class light frigate is used solely by the maritime element of the KGB for protecting Soviet territorial waters and to prevent people escaping to the West by boat.

'Riga' class

Built at the Kaliningrad, Nikolayev and Komsomolsk shipyards in the Soviet Union, the 64 units (including eight for export) of the **'Riga' class** were the design successors to the six slightly older 'Kola' class escorts. Always designated *storozhevoy korabl'* (SKR, or patrol ship) by the Soviets, the class has proved to be an excellent coastal-defence design and followed the Soviet practice in the 1950s of building flushdecked hulls with a sharply raised forecastle. Over the years the 'Rigas' have become one of the larger Soviet ship classes, and have been exported in some numbers. In all, 17 were transferred; two to Bulgaria, five to East Germany (of which one was burnt out in an accident soon after being taken over), two to Finland and eight to Indonesia. Most of these units have now been either scrapped or placed in reserve, and China built four further units in her shipyards from components supplied by the Soviets. All Riga class units still on the Russian inventory are now permanently laid up.

A small number of the operational vessels were modified during the 1970s, a twin 25-mm AA gun being added on each side of the funnel and a dipping sonar fitted abreast of the bridge. Before this, however, all units were fitted with two hand-loaded 16-barrel RBU2500 ASW rocket-launchers forward to replace the original ASW armament of a single MBU600 'Hedgehog' and four aft-mounted BMB-2 depth-charge throwers. One of the active units was also fitted with a taller stack cap and several 'Bell' series ECM systems, possibly as a trials ship.

Now obsolete, the 'Riga' class remains in service with the Soviet navy in relatively large numbers for second-line duties and as training vessels.

Specification
'Riga' class
Displacement: 1,260 tons standard and 1,510 tons full load
Dimensions: length 91.5 m (300.2 ft); beam 10.1 m (33.1 ft); draught 3.2 m (10.5 ft)
Propulsion: geared steam turbines delivering power to two shafts
Speed: 28 kts

Armament: three single 100-mm (3.9-in) DP, two twin 37-mm AA and (some units) two twin 25-mm AA guns, two 16-barrel RBU2500 250-mm (9.84-in) ASW rocket-launchers with 160 rockets, two racks for 24 depth charges, and one twin or triple 533-mm (21-in) tube mounting for two or three anti-ship torpedoes
Aircraft: none

One of the most popular pastimes practised by the Soviets in warm climates is relaxing on deck away from their spartan living conditions, as the majority of the crew of this 'Riga' class frigate is doing.

Electronics: one 'Slim Net' air-search radar, one 'Sun Visor-B' fire-control radar, one 'Wasp Head' fire-control radar, one 'Don-2' or 'Neptune' navigation radar, one 'High Pole-B' IFF, two 'Square Head' IFF, two 'Watch Dog' ECM systems, and one high-frequency hull-mounted sonar
Complement: 175

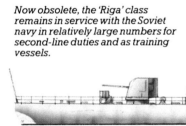

Seen during the 'Okean '70' exercise off the Philippines, this 'Riga' class frigate of the Pacific Fleet is still useful in that area because one of the potential adversaries is the similarly equipped navy of the People's Republic of China.

The two Finnish navy 'Riga' class frigates Hameenmaa and Uusimaa lead a group of patrol boats. In 1980 the latter was stricken to provide spares for her sister ship, which was redesignated as a minelayer.

'Petya' classes

Former USSR

The 18 units of the **'Petya I' class** were constructed at the Kaliningrad and Komsomolsk shipyards between 1961 and 1964. From the latter year until 1969 both shipyards switched to building a total of 27 **'Petya II' class** units, which differed from their predecessors in having an extra quintuple 406-mm (16-in) ASW torpedo tube mounting in place of the two aft ASW rocket-launchers. The two forward-mounted RBU2500 rocket-launchers were also exchanged for the RBU6000 system with automatic loading facilities. Both variants also had mine rails.

From 1973 onwards eight 'Petya I' vessels were modified to give the **'Petya I (Mod)' class**. The conversion involved the addition of a medium-frequency variable-depth sonar (VDS) system in a new raised stern deckhouse, which necessitated the removal of the mine rails. A further three units were then converted as trials vessels and given the same sub-group designation: one was fitted with a larger VDS system with no deckhouse at the stern; the second had a deckhouse installed abaft the stack (following the removal of the torpedo tubes) and fitted with a complex reel/winch installation for what may be either a towed non-acoustic ASW sensor or a towed surface-ship sonar array; the third vessel had a small box-like structure built at the stern for a towed sensor deployed from a hole in the stern. In 1978 a single unit of the Petya II type was also converted to a trial vessel and given the title **'Petya II (Mod)' class**. The conversion was along the lines of the 'Petya I (Mod)' but with a slimmer VDS deckhouse which allowed retention of the minelaying capability.

In late 1984 the Soviet navy had a total of seven 'Petya I', 11 'Petya I (Mod)' including three trials vessels, 23 'Petya II' and one 'Petya II (Mod)' (for trials) in service with all four fleets. A further three 'Petya II' of the Soviet navy were transferred to Vietnam (two ships) and Ethiopia (one ship), whilst another 18 export ships were speci-

fically built with a triple 533-mm (21-in) torpedo tube mounting and RBU2500 ASW rocket-launchers for the navies of India (12 ships), Vietnam (four ships) and Syria (two ships). The 'Petyas' were rated by the Russians as 'stororzhevoy korabi' (SKR, or patrol ship).

Specification
'Petya' classes
Displacement: 950 tons standard and 1,150 tons or ('Petya II') 1,160 tons full load
Dimensions: length 81.8 m (268.4 ft) or ('Petya II') 82.5 m (270.7 ft); beam 9.1 m (29.9 ft); draught 2.9 m (9.5 ft)
Propulsion: CODAG arrangement with two diesels and two gas turbines delivering power to three shafts
Speed: 33 kts
Armament: two ('Petya I (Mod)' towed-array trials ship one) twin 76-mm (3-in) DP guns, four 16-barrel RBU 2500 250-mm (9.84-in) ASW rocket-launchers with 320 rockets or ('Petya II' and 'Petya II (Mod)' only) two 12-barrel RBU6000 250-mm (9.84-in) ASW rocket-launchers with 120 rockets or ('Petya I (Mod)' only) two 16-barrel RBU2500 launchers with 160 rockets, two ('Petya I (Mod)' only one) racks for 24 or 12 depth charges, one ('Petya II (Mod)' two and 'Petya I (Mod)' towed-array trials ship none) 533-mm (21-in) quintuple tube mounting for five or 10 anti-submarine torpedoes, and between 20 and 30 mines (none in 'Petya I (Mod)') according to type
Aircraft: none
Electronics: one 'Slim Net' or 'Strut Curve' air-search radar, one 'Hawk Screech' 76-mm gun fire-control radar, one 'Don-2' navigation radar, one 'High Pole-B' and (only in 'Petya I') two 'Square Head' IFF, two 'Watch Dog' ECM systems one high-frequency hull-mounted sonar, one high-frequency dipping sonar, and (in some, see text) one variable-depth sonar
Complement: 98

This unmodified member of the 'Petya I' class of light frigates is easily identified by the presence of the RBU2500 ASW rocket-launchers in front of the bridge and the lack of any stern superstructure for a variable-depth sonar system.

Above: One task sometimes undertaken by the 'Petyas' in the absence of any larger units is that of the 'Tattle-tale'; here a 'Petya II' shadows the carrier HMS Eagle in 1975 while the latter was on an exercise.

The 'Petya II' differs from the earlier 'Petya I' in having a heavier ASW armament in the form of RBU6000 automatic rocket-launchers and extra torpedo tubes.

'Mirka' classes

Former USSR

Built between 1964 and 1965 at the Kaliningrad shipyard, the nine **'Mirka I' class** vessels were followed on the stocks during the latter half of 1965 and 1966 by nine **'Mirka II' class** units. They were constructed as a more specialized variation of the early 'Petya' design and were initially rated by the Soviets as *malyy protivolodochnyy korabl* (MPK, or small anti-submarine ship). As with some other ASW-oriented ship classes, this was changed in 1978 to *stororzhevoy korabl* (SKR, or patrol ship).

The various vessels of the two 'Mirka' classes served only with the Soviet baltic and Black Sea fleets. The prop-

ulsion plant is similar in concept to the combined diesel and gas turbine plant of the 'Petyas', with a high maximum speed for use in attacks on submerged submarines. The basic difference in the two variants is that the 'Mirka IIs' lack the two aft 250-mm (9.84-in) RBU6000 ASW rocket-launchers of the

The 'Mirka I' and 'Mirka II' units of the Black Sea Fleet were regularly deployed to the Mediterranean squadron to provide ASW protection to higher-value surface units and the many deep water anchorages that the Soviet navy had in the region.

'Mirka I' but have instead an additional quintuple ASW torpedo tube mounting for the bridge and the mast. Also, the later 'Mirka II' units have a 'Strut Curve' air-search radar in place of the earlier ships' 'Slim Net' set. Almost all units of both classes have now been fitted with a dipping sonar either instead of the internal depth-charge rack in the port side of the stern or abreast the bridge. This is intended for use in areas like the Baltic where oceanographic conditions for ASW operations are notoriously difficult. The Mirkas had been reduced to five units by 1990, and all had been laid up or scrapped by 1998.

Specification
'Mirka' classes
Displacement: 950 tons standard and 1,150 tons full load
Dimensions: 82.4 m (270.3 ft); beam 9.1 m (29.9 ft); draught 3.0 m (9.8 ft)
Propulsion: CODAG arrangement with two diesels and two gas turbines delivering power to two shafts
Speed: 35 kts

Armament: two twin 76-mm (3-in) DP guns, four ('Mirka I') or two ('Mirka II') 12-barrel RBU6000 250-mm (9.84-in) ASW rocket-launchers with 240 or 120 rockets, and one ('Mirka I') or two ('Mirka II') 533-mm (21-in) quintuple tube mountings for five or 10 anti-submarine torpedoes
Aircraft: none

Electronics: one 'Slim Net' or (some 'Mirka II' only) 'Strut Curve' air-search radar, one 'Hawk Screech' 76-mm gun fire-control radar, one 'Dan-2' navigation radar, two 'High Pole-B' IFF, two 'Square Head' IFF, two 'Watch Dog' ECM systems, one medium-frequency hull-mounted sonar, and (in most units) one high-frequency dipping sonar
Complement: 98

All the nine 'Mirka II' class frigates built have now been fitted with a new type of dipping sonar in place of the internal depth charge rack on the port side of the stern to improve their ASW capabilities in the Mediterranean and Baltic.

Former USSR

'Koni' class

Although constructed in the Soviet Union at the Zelenodolsk Shipyard on the Black Sea, the **'Koni' class** of *storozhevoy korabl* (SKR, or patrol ship) is intended only for export, a mere one unit, the *Timofey Ul'yantsev*, being retained by the Soviets as a crew training ship for the naval personnel from those countries which have bought vessels of this class. There are two distinct subclasses, the **'Koni Type II' class** differing from the **'Koni Type I' class** in having the space between the funnel and the aft superstructure occupied by an extra deckhouse believed to contain air-conditioning units for use in tropical climates.

The countries which have taken delivery of 'Koni' class units are East Germany (the two Type Is *Rostock* (141) and *Berlin* (142)), Yugoslavia (the two Type Is *Split* (31) and *Koper* (32)), Algeria (the two Type IIs *Murat Reis* (901) and *Ras Kellich* (902)), and Cuba (the two Type IIs *Mariel* (350) and unnamed (356)). The two Yugoslav units have been further modified by the Yugoslavs themselves to carry two single aft-firing container-launchers for SS-N-2B 'Styx' anti-ship cruise missiles on each side of the superstructure which houses the SA-N-4 'Gecko' SAM launcher-bin assembly. A tenth unit is known to be under construction for export, with more planned. The Type IIs have also had two 16-barrel chaff launchers added to their equipment fit.

Specification
'Koni' class
Displacement: 1,700 tons standard and 1,900 tons full load
Dimensions: length 95.0 m (311.7 ft);

The Type I 'Koni' class frigate was built in the Soviet Union primarily for export. The Type II differed in having additional super structure which housed air conditioning system.

beam 12.8 m (42.0 ft); draught 4.2 m (13.8 ft)
Propulsion: CODAG arrangement with one diesel and two gas turbines delivering power to three shafts
Speed: 27 kts
Armament: one twin launcher for 18 SA-N-4 'Gecko' SAMs, two twin 76-mm

(3-in) DP and two twin 30-mm AA guns, two 12-barrel RBU600 250-mm (9.84-in) ASW rocket-launchers with 120 rockets, two racks for 24 depth charges, and between 20 and 30 mines according to type
Aircraft: none
Electronics: one 'Strut Curve' air-

search radar, one 'Pop Group' SAM fire-control radar, one 'Hawk Screech' 76-mm fire-control radar, one 'Drum Tilt' 30-mm gun fire-control radar, one 'High Pole-B' IFF, two 'Watch Dog' ECM systems, and one medium-frequency hull-mounted sonar
Complement: 110

The East German navy had two Type I 'Koni' class frigates, the Rostock *(141) and the* Berlin *(142). They differed from other 'Koni' class units, not having chaff launchers and carried East German built TSR 333 navigation radars in place of the more unusual Don-2 sets.*

'Nanuchka' classes

Classed by the Soviets as a *malyy raketnyy korabl'* (MRK, or small rocket ship), the 17 units of the **'Nanuchka I' class** were built between 1969 and 1974 at Petrovsky, Leningrad with a modified variant, the **'Nanuchka II' class**, following at that yard and at an as yet unnamed Pacific coast shipyard from 1977. Now in slow series construction (one per year) the 'Nanuchkas' are considered by Western observers to be coastal missile corvettes, although the fact that they are very often seen quite far from home waters (on deployment to such areas as the North Sea, the Mediterranean and the Pacific) tends to put them more in the very light frigate category, especially when the firepower of the class is considered. The anti-ship missile carried is the Mach 0.9 SS-N-9 'Siren', which can be fitted to carry either a 500-kg (1,102-lb) HE or 200-kiloton nuclear warhead over a range of 110 km (68 miles). The SS-N-9 uses a dual active radar and infra-red terminal homing system, with third-party targeting and mid-course corrections to guide it in over the horizon engagements.

In 1977 an export version, the **'Nanuchka II' class** was delivered to India. This differs from the standard Soviet models in having twin SS-N-2B 'Styx' SSM launchers in place of the triple SS-N-9 'Siren' launcher systems. Nanuchkas were exported to several of the Soviet Union's regular customers, including India, Libya and Algeria. The Libyan vessels have occasionally been in confrontation with US naval units in the Mediterranean.

Specification
'Nanuchka' classes
Displacement: 780 tons standard and 900 tons full load
Dimensions: length 59.3 m (194.6 ft); beam 12.6 m (41.3 ft); draught 2.4 m (7.9 ft)

The 'Nanuchka I' class of small missile ship carries the SS-N-9 'Siren' anti-ship missile as its main armament. For maximum range a third-party over-the-horizon targeting source is required.

A 'Nanuchka I' small missile ship underway. The export 'Nanuchka II' class differs mainly in carrying SS-N-2B 'Styx' missile launchers, whilst the latest Soviet variant, the 'Nanuchka III', has a different gun armament.

Propulsion: three paired diesels delivering power to three shafts
Speed: 32 kts
Armament: two triple container-launchers for SS-N-9 'Siren' anti-ship missiles, one twin launcher for 18 SA-N-4 'Gecko' SAMs, one twin 57-mm AA gun or ('Nanuchka III' only) one 76-mm (3-in) DP and one 30-mm CIWS guns
Aircraft: none
Electronics: one 'Band Stand' air- and surface-search radar, one 'Peel Pair' surface-search and navigation radar, one 'Spar Stump' surface-search and navigation radar, two 'Fish Bowl' SAM fire-control radars, one 'Muff Cob' or ('Nanuchka III' only) 'Bass Tilt' fire-control radar, one 'High Pole-B' IFF, two passive ECM systems, and two 16-barrel chaff launchers
Complement: 70

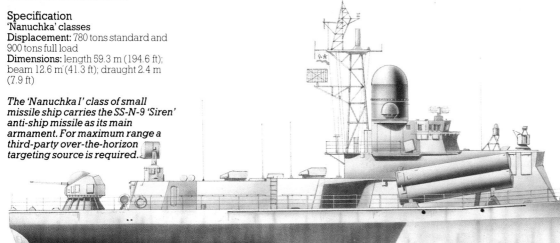

'Tarantul' class

Built at Petrovsky, Leningrad, the first **'Tarantul I' class** unit was completed in 1978. Like the 'Nanuchka', the class is designated a *malyy raketnyy korabl'* (MRK, or small rocket ship), but its exact place in Soviet naval plans is not yet clear, since in many respects it is not as modern as the 'Nanuchka' class. However, seven 'Tarantul I' units are in service at present, and a production rate of some three ships per year is being sustained. In order to rectify some of the shortcomings of the design the later units of the class have possibly been fitted while building with updated electronics whilst a further unit was completed in 1981 to the **'Tarantul II' class** configuration with two twin

over-and-under missile container-launchers for the long-range supersonic SS-N-22 derivative of the SS-N-9 'Siren' in place of the original SS-N-2C 'Styx' system.

One possible explanation for the existence of this design is that it is intended for export, and in fact during 1983 a 'Tarantul I' was transferred to the Polish navy, with more to follow. It is not certain at present whether this first vessel was an ex-Soviet navy unit or new build specifically for transfer. The 'Tarantuls' deploy a modified version of the Soviet navy's small ship armament of a fully automatic 76-mm (3-in) DP gun, capable of 120 rounds per minute, and two 30-mm 6-barrel

Gatling gun mounts that in the Soviet navy have the designation AK-630 (the ADG630 designation often used being a NATO nickname).

Specification
'Tarantul' classes
Displacement: 480 tons standard and 580 tons full load
Dimensions: length 56.0 m (183.7 ft); beam 10.5 m (34.4 ft); draught 2.5 m (8.2 ft)
Propulsion: CODOG arrangements with two diesels and two gas turbines delivering power to two shafts
Speed: 36 kts

Armament: two twin container-launchers for SS-N-2C 'Styx' anti-ship missiles, one quadruple launcher for 16 SA-N-5 'Grail' SAMs, one 76-mm (3-in) DP and two 30-mm CIWS guns
Aircraft: none
Electronics: one 'Band Stand' air- and surface-search radar or 'Plank Shave' surface-search radar, one (not in early units) 'Light Bulb' targeting data system, one 'Spin Trough' navigation radar, one 'Bass Tilt' gun fire-control radar, one 'High Pole-B' IFF, one 'Square Head' IFF, four passive ECM systems, and two 16-barrel chaff launchers
Complement: 50

'Krivak' classes

In 1970 the first unit of the gas turbine-powered **'Krivak I' class** of *bol'shoy protivolodochnyy korabl'* (BPK, or large anti-submarine ship) entered service with the Soviet navy. Built at the Zhdanov Shipyard in Leningrad, the Kaliningrad Shipyard and the Kamish-Burun Shipyard in Kerch between 1970 and 1982, 21 units of this variant were constructed. In 1976 the **'Krivak II' class**, of which 11 were built at Kaliningrad between that year and 1981, was first seen. This differed from the previous class in having single 100-mm (3.9-in) guns substituted for the twin 76-mm (3-in) turrets of the earlier version, and a larger variable-depth sonar housing at the stern. Both classes were re-rated to *storozhevoy korabl'* (SKR, or patrol ship) status in the late 1970s, possibly in view of what some Western observers considered to be the type's deficiencies in terms of size and limited endurance for ASW operations in open waters.

The first unit of the **'Krivak III' class**, designed to remedy some of the probable defects, appeared in mid-1984. This has a helicopter hangar and flight deck in place of the aft gun turrets and SA-N-4 'Gecko' SAM launcher, and the forward quadruple SS-N-14 'Silex' ASW missile-launcher is replaced by a single 100-mm DP gun turret. The variable-depth sonar system is retained beneath the flight deck at the stern, whilst single 30-mm ADG630 CIWS are located on each side of the hangar. The other ASW armament of the 'Krivak I/II' classes and the forward SA-N-4 launchers are also retained. 19 Krivak Is, IIs and IIIs are still in Russian service, although the Is and IIs are to be scrapped.

Specification
'Krivak' classes
Displacement: 3,000 tons standard and 3,700 tons ('Krivak I') or 3,800 tons ('Krivak II') full load
Dimensions: length 123.5 m (405.2 ft); beam 14.0 m (45.9 ft); draught 4.7 m (15.4 ft)
Propulsion: COGAG arrangement with four gas turbines delivering power to two shafts
Speed: 32 kts
Armament: one quadruple launcher for SS-N-14 'Silex' anti-submarine missiles, two twin launchers for 36 SA-N-4 'Gecko' SAMs, two twin 76-mm (3-in) DP ('Krivak I') or two single 100-mm (3.9-in) DP ('Krivak II') guns, two 12-barrel RBU6000 250-mm (9.84-in) ASW rocket-launchers with 120 rockets, two quadruple 533-mm (21-in) tube mountings for anti-submarine torpedoes, and between 20 and 40 mines according to type
Aircraft: none
Electronics: one 'Head Net-C' air-search radar, two 'Pop Group' SAM fire-control radars, two 'Eye Bowl' 'Silex' fire-control radars, one 'Owl Screech' ('Krivak I') or 'Kite Screech' ('Krivak II') gun fire-control radar, one 'Don Kay' or 'Palm Frond' navigation radar, two 'Bell Shroud' ECM systems, two 'Bell Squat' ECM systems, four 16-barrel chaff launchers, one 'High Pole-B' or 'Salt Pot' IFF, one medium-frequency hull-mounted sonar, and one medium-frequency variable-depth sonar
Complement: 220

The long rack of the bow with the anchor well forward betrays the presence of a large bow sonar dome for a medium frequency active sonar. For underlayer searching a variable-depth low-frequency sonar system is fitted aft.

Soviet frigate 'Krivak Class II' cutaway drawing key

1. VDS handling area
2. VDS protective door in raised position
3. Control centre for VDS
4. Torpedo decoys
5. Mine rails set in deck
6. Balanced rudder
7. Screw support
8. Double screw
9. Shaft
10. 100-mm gun
11. Turntable/ammunition hoist
12. SA-N-4
13. Missile stowage
14. Stores
15. Turbine reduction gear
16. Engine room
17. COGAG gas turbines
18. Funnel casing
19. Funnel uptakes
20. Ventilators
21. Launch
22. Radar control centre
23. 'Kite Screech' radar
24. 'Pop Group' radar
25. Air command guidance
26. Turntable
27. 533-mm quad torpedo tubes
28. Boat crane
29. Turntable and machine room for torpedo tubes
30. Bilge keels
31. Radio direction finder
32. 'Head-Net-C' radar
33. 'Eye Bowl' radar
34. Bridge
35. Navigation bridge
36. Life-saving equipment
37. Control centre
38. Gangway
39. Officers' quarters
40. 'Bell Stroud' ECM
41. RBU 6000 launcher
42. Blast screen between RBU 6000 launchers
43. Reload chamber for SA-N-4
44. Crew
45. SS-N-14 quad launcher
46. Blast screen
47. Waterline
48. Anchor
49. Sonar
50. Magazine
51. Fuel tanks
52. Magazine and hoist to RBU launcher
53. Whip aerials

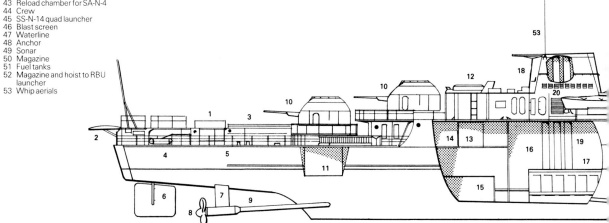

'Krivak' in Action

Designed to hunt and kill nuclear submarines in the deep waters of the world's oceans, the 'Krivak' class of frigate is faster and much more heavily armed than Western contemporaries.

When the first 'Krivak I' *bolshoy protivolodochnyy korabl'* (large anti-submarine ship) entered service with the Soviet navy during 1970 it made an immediate impression with Western naval powers, who generally saw the design in a highly impressive light, especially when compared with contemporary Western missile destroyer and frigate designs. Despite the Soviet description of ASW ship, Western observers mistook the type's actual role to be surface strike, with anti-air and anti-submarine weapons embarked only for self-protection. The reason for this misassessment was that the class shipped in a forward position a quadruple container-launcher missile assembly for the same supersonic derivative of the SS-N-2 'Styx' as supposedly carried by the contemporary 'Kresta II' class cruisers and initially allocated the NATO designation SS-N-10. The mistake was finally resolved during the 1970s by Western naval intelligence agencies: the revised designation SS-N-14 'Silex' was adopted as the original and the incorrect SS-N-10 label was simultaneously dropped. One apparent reason for all the confusion was reportedly the result of the Soviets actually sending the 'Kresta II' class to sea without any missiles aboard for several years as the system was undergoing final testing, a brilliant piece of deception which led intelligence services to the wrong conclusions.

No confirmed picture of an SS-N-14 has ever been released to the technical press, but reliable reports indicate that it is in fact a solid-propellant rocket-powered winged cruise missile that conceptually resembles the Australian Ikara ASW missile in dropping a parachute-retarded acoustic-homing torpedo. The maximum and minimum ranges are 55.5 km (34.5 miles) and 7.4 km (4.6 miles) respectively. The maximum range figure means that to ensure the missile's terminal accuracy dependence is placed not on the ship's own sensors but on a third-party source. This is a capability which fits in well with known Soviet ASW practices: for long-range targets the 'Krivak' is supplied with target position data from other surface ships or airborne platforms via a data-link system after missile launch and early control by the vessel's own 'Eye Bowl' missile tracking and command guidance link radars. The presence of a pair of these radars aboard a 'Krivak' suggests that a salvo of two SS-N-14 missiles can be used during an engagement to increase the kill probability.

To aid in the high-speed manoeuvring associated with some aspects of ASW opera-

The 'Krivak I' class Soviet frigate Storozhevoy *is seen in the English Channel. By the stern housing for the variable depth sonar can be seen the towed decoys that make up part of the BAT-1 acoustic noise making system used against homing torpedoes.*

tions the class is fitted with a four-engine gas turbine COGAG arrangement, the two smaller units being coupled up with the two larger units for full-power operations. The exaggerated overhang of the bow is a good indication of a bow-mounted sonar, probably of the medium-frequency type. For operations against submarines operating below the thermal layer a variable-depth sonar system is located aft, inside a prominent housing on the quarterdeck. The model carried is the same low-frequency set that is fitted to most contemporary Soviet ship designs, and may be used to target the 'Silex' missiles in close-range attacks.

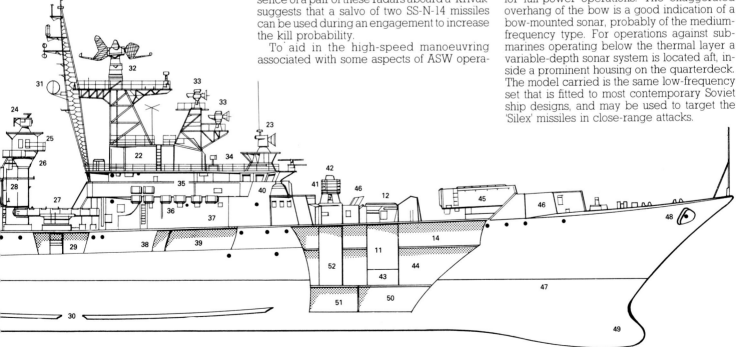

'Esmeraldas' class

Although strictly speaking rated as missile corvettes rather than small light frigates, the units of the '**Esmeraldas**' class must, because of their multi-purpose capabilities, be ranked with the latter. Ordered in 1978 from the Italian firm CNR del Tirreno, the design is based on the '**Wadi M'ragh** (now '**Assad**') class for Libya but with more powerful diesel engines, the addition of a helicopter landing platform amidships and a SAM launcher aft of the bridge. All six units of the class, the *Esmeraldas* (CM11), *Manabi* (CM12), *Los Rios* (CM13), *El Oro* (CM14), *Galapagos* (CM15) and *Laja* (CM16) are now in service with the Ecuadorean navy as the country's primary antiship surface strike force. The helicopter platform is used to operate one of the navy's three Aérospatiale Alouette III light helicopters in the surface-search and air-sea-rescue roles as circumstances dictate. The anti-ship missile system fitted is the 65-km (40.4-mile) range MM.40 Exocet, with two banks (each of three single container-launchers, firing outwards) located between the landing platform and the bridge. The SAM system fitted is the lightweight four-round launcher version of the Italian Albatros weapon system which uses the Aspide multi-role missile. Only self-defence ASW torpedo tubes are fitted, together with a hull mounted sonar set, for sub-surface warfare operations.

Although more correctly classed as a missile corvette, the Ecuadorian navy's 'Esmeraldas' class has more firepower per ship than a number of light frigate classes. They are armed with six MM.40 Exocets, a quadruple Albatros SAM launcher, guns and torpedoes.

Specifications
'Esmeraldas' class
Displacement: 620 tons standard and 685 tons full load
Dimensions: length 62.3 m (204.4 ft); beam 9.3 m (30.5 ft); draught 2.5 (8.2 ft)
Propulsion: four MTU diesels delivering 18195 kW (24,400 hp) to four shafts
Speed: 37 kts
Armament: six single container-launchers for MM.40 Exocet anti-ship missiles, one Albatros quadruple launcher for four Aspide SAMs, one 76 mm (3-in) DP and one twin 40-mm AA gun, and two triple 324-mm (12.76-in) ILAS-3 tube mountings for six

The Galapagos *(CM15) is the fifth unit of the 'Esmeraldas' class, built in Italy for Ecuador. The quadruple Albatros SAM launcher behind the bridge superstructure and mast fires the multi-role Aspide missile.*

Whitehead A244/S anti-submarine torpedoes
Aircraft: provision for one light helicopter on a landing pad
Electronics: one RAN10S air- and surface-search radar, one Orion 1OX fire-control radar, one Orion 2OX fire-control radar, one Decca TM1226 navigation radar, one IPN20 data information system, one Gamma ESM system, and one Diodon hull-mounted sonar
Complement: 51

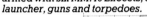

'MEKO 140A16' class

As part of the Argentine navy's modernization plans, a contract was signed in October 1980 with the West German firm of Blohm und Voss for six '**MEKO 140A16**' class ships, to be built (to a light frigate design based on the Portuguese 'João Coutinho' class) under licence at the AFNE shipyard in Rio Santiago, Ensenada and known locally as the '**Espora**' class. The lead ship *Espora* (P4) was commissioned into the Argentine navy in 1983, a trio comprising the *Rosales* (P5), *Spiro* (P6) and *Parker* (P7) following in 1985, with a final pair, the *Robinson* (P8) and *Seaver* (P9), in 1986 and 1987 respectively. The first three differ from the last three units in initially having only a helicopter landing platform amidships,

As part of the Argentine navy's modernization programme in the 1970s, six West German 'MEKO 140' class light frigates were ordered to be licence-built in Argentina. All will eventually be fitted with a hangar facility.

whereas the others are being constructed with a telescopic hangar to allow the permanent carriage of a light helicopter. The earlier units will be retrofitted at the first available opportunity if finances allow.

The Argentines are currently studying a plan whereby in order to cut military expenditure they might well have to sell off some of their new ships. Among the ships being considered is an 'Espora' class unit. The 'Espora' class is replacing some of Argentina's obsolete ex-American World War II destroyers, and its members are equipped predominantly with ASW and anti-surface warfare weapon systems. The four MM.38 Exocet container-launchers shipped aft could be replaced by eight canisters for the lighter but longer-range MM.40 Exocet

which the Argentines use on their 'MEKO 360' type destroyers. Although designed for use primarily on coastal operations, the class forms a potent offensive force for use in any future naval operations against the Falkland islands.

Specification
'MEKO 140A16' class
Displacement: 1,470 tons standard and 1,700 tons full load
Dimensions: length 91.2 m (299.2 ft); beam 12.2 m (40.0 ft); draught 3.3 m (10.8 ft)

Propulsion: two diesels delivering 16853 kW (22,600 hp) to two shafts
Speed: 27 kts
Armament: four single container-launchers for MM.38 Exocet anti-ship missiles, one 76-mm (3-in) DP and two twin 40-mm AA guns, two single 12.7-mm (0.5-in) machine-guns, and two triple 324-mm (12.76-in) tube mountings for 12 Whitehead A244/S anti-submarine torpedoes
Aircraft: one Aérospatiale Alouette III or Westland Lynx HAS.Mk 23 light helicopter
Electronics: one DA-05/2 air-search radar, one WM-28 fire-control radar, one Decca TM1226 navigation radar, two LIROD optronic fire-control systems, one Daisy automatic action information system, one RDC-2ABC ESM system, one RCM-2 ESM system, two Dagaie chaff launchers, and one ASO-4 hull-mounted sonar
Complement: 93

'Fatahillah' class

The 'Fatahillah' class of Dutch-designed and -built light ASW frigate was ordered in August 1975 as the first major new-build warship type for the Indonesian navy since the acceptance of Soviet ships in the 1950s and 1960s. The class numbers only three, the last unit, the *Nala* (363), differing from her two sisterships, the *Fatahillah* (361) and *Malahayati* (362), in having a new type of helicopter landing deck aft which folds around the MBB BO105 light helicopter carried to form a hangar structure; the other ships have no helicopter facilities at all. The armament and electronics fit was procured from a variety of NATO countries, whilst for service in the hot climates of the Far East the ships are fitted with air-conditioned living spaces. They also have a full nuclear-biological-chemical (NBC) warfare citadel, and have fin stabilizers and a combined diesel or gas turbine (CODOG) propulsion plant arrangement for 'quick-start' operations. The magazines fitted can carry a total of 400 120-mm (4.7-in) and 3,000 40-mm rounds. The main radar fire-control system for the guns is backed by a single LIROD television/laser/infra-red optronic fire-control unit.

If present plans are continued, an additional two or three frigates will be bought for the Indonesian navy, but it is not known if these will be of the 'Fatahillah' class. Moreover, it is not known if they will be procured at all as the Indonesians have bought three reconditioned ex-Royal Navy 'Tribal' class frigates.

The anti-ship missile armament fitted to the 'Fatahillahs' is two pairs of container-launchers for the 42 km (26-mile) range MM.38 Exocet, and this primary armament allows the ships to operate as effective supports for the growing force of missile- and gun-armed attack units which are being procured for use among the myriad islands which make up the Indonesian republic.

Specification
'Fatahillah' class
Displacement: 1,160 tons standard and 1,450 tons full load
Dimensions: length 84.0 m (275.6 ft); beam 11.1 m (36.4 ft); draught 3.3 m (10.8 ft)
Propulsion; CODOG arrangement with one Rolls-Royce Olympus TM3B gas turbine delivering 16674 kW (22,360 shp) and two MTU diesels delivering 5966 kW (8,000 hp) to two shafts
Speed: 30 kts
Armament: four single container-launchers for MM.38 Exocet anti-ship

The Indonesian navy 'Fatahillah' class frigate Malahayati (362). If money can be found it is possible that a further batch of these frigates

missiles, one 120-mm (4.7-in) DP, one (two in *Nala*) 40-mm AA and two single 20-mm AA guns, one twin Bofors 375-mm (14.76-in) ASW rocket-launcher with 54 rockets, and (except in *Nala*) two triple 324-mm (12.76-in) Mk 32 tube mountings for 12 Whitehead A244/S or Mk 44 anti-submarine torpedoes

may be built to replace ex-American and Soviet frigate classes which are still in service after some 25 years of use.

Aircraft: (*Nala* only) one MBB BO105 light helicopter
Electronics: one DA-05 air- and surface-search radar, one Decca AC1229 navigation radar, one WM-28 fire-control radar, one LIROD optronic fire-control system, one Daisy automatic action information system, one SUSIE I ESM system, two Corvus chaff launchers, one T Mk 6 torpedo decoy system, and one PHS-32 hull-mounted sonar
Complement: 89

The Dutch-built 'Fatahillah' class for the Indonesian navy has proved a success in service. The general-purpose version armed with MM.38 Exocet missiles is shown here.

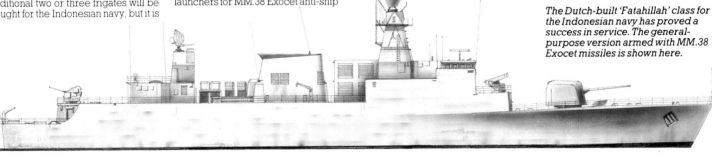

'Type F2000' class

Ordered from France in October 1980 as a major part of the 14,000 million franc Sawari weapons supply contract, the first of a total of four 'Type F2000' class frigates was laid down in the Arsenal de Lorient shipyard in 1981 and launched in 1983 for commissioning in 1984 as the *Madina* (702). The remaining three vessels are the *Hofuf* (704), *Abha* (706) and *Taif* (708), and were laid down at the CNIM shipyard at Seyne-sur-Mer in 1982-3 for delivery during 1985-6.

The class is a very complex design and uses much untried state-of-the-art electronics technology, and may well be too sophisticated for so young a navy as that of Saudi Arabia. The weapon systems are predominantly French in origin, although the surface-to-surface missiles are the Franco-Italian Otomat Mk 2 rather than the more usual member of the Exocet family, which indicates a long-range anti-ship strike role, especially as the Aérospatiale SA365 Dauphin 2

embarked helicopter will be able to carry out targeting functions.

The presence of the class, in an area of particularly sensitive strategic importance to both major power blocs, will be of considerable interest to all the Arabian Gulf oil states, and the 'Type F2000s' will be matched only by Iraq's Italian 'Lupo' class frigates. A further two large frigates armed with an area-defence surface-to-air missile system was under consideration at one point.

In the late1990s the Type F2000s

A 'Type F2000' frigate of the Saudi Arabian navy. The purchase of this sophisticated class from France is typical of oil-rich Arab nations buying weapons with more capacity than is necessary.

underwent an extensive upgrade programme. Three Type 3000 (*La Fayette* class) frigates were also on order, for delivery in 2002–2004.

Specification
'Type F2000' class
Displacement: 2,250 tons standard and 2,610 tons full load
Dimensions: length 115.0 m (377.3 ft); beam 12.5 m (41.0 ft); draught 4.7 m (15.4 ft)
Propulsion: four SEMT-Pielstick

diesels delivering 24235 kW (32,500 hp) to two shafts
Speed: 30 kts
Armament: eight single container-launchers for Otomat Mk 2 anti-ship missiles, one octuple launcher for 26 Crotale Naval SAMs, one 100-mm (3.9-in) DP and two twin 40-mm AA guns, four single 533-mm (21-in) tubes for F17P wire-guided anti-ship and anti-submarine torpedoes, and two single 324-mm (12.76-in, Mk 32 tubes for Mk 46 anti-submarine torpedoes
Aircraft: one Aérospatiale SA 365 Dauphin 2 light strike helicopter
Electronics: one DRBV 15 air- and surface-search radar, one Castor II fire-control radar, two Decca 1226 navigation radars, one DRBC 32E SAM fire-control radar, one SENIT VI action information system, one DR4000 ESM system, two Dagaie chaff launchers, one Diodon TSM2630 hull-mounted sonar, and one Sorel variable-depth sonar
Complement: 179

'Niteroi' class

Ordered in September 1970 from the English shipyard Vosper-Thornycroft in ASW and general-purpose versions, the 'Niteroi' class ships were based on the company's Mk 10 frigate design and were constructed both in the UK and Brazil. The four ASW ships are the *Niteroi* (F40), *Defensor* (F41), *Independencia* (F44) and *União* (F45), and are fitted with the Branik missile-launcher system derived specifically for the Brazilians from the Australian Ikara ASW missile system. The two general-purpose units are the *Constitucão* (F42) and *Liberal* (F43), and these are similar to the ASW ships though instead of the Branik system they have a second 114-mm (4.5-in) Mk 8 DP gun mount aft (in the place occupied by the Branik system in the ASW ships) and two pairs of container-launchers for MM.38 Exocet SSM missiles located between the bridge and the funnel. Fitted with a combined diesel or gas turbine (CODOG) propulsion plant, the design is considered to be exceptionally economical in terms of manpower when compared with previous warships of this size. A CAAIS action information system is fitted to allow co-ordinated surface-ship ASW and surface strike operations with other vessels of the Brazilian

navy, including the aircraft-carrier **Minas Gerais**.

In June 1981 a modified 'Niteroi' class frigate, the **Brasil** (U27), was ordered for commissioning in 1985 from a local firm as a training ship for the naval and merchant marine academies. Fitted with a light AA armament, the vessel is fitted with a hangar and landing deck aft for two Westland Lynx HAS.Mk 21 helicopters.

Specification
'Niteroi' class
Displacement: 3,200 tons standard and 3,800 tons full load
Dimensions: length 129.2 m (423.9 ft); beam 13.5 m (44.3 ft); draught 5.5 m (18.0 ft)
Propulsion: CODOG arrangement with two Rolls-Royce Olympus TM3B gas turbines delivering 41759 kW (56,000 shp) and four MTU diesels delivering 11752 kW (15,760 hp) to two shafts
Speed: 30.5 kts
Armament: (F40, F41, F44 and F45) one Branik ASW missile launcher with 10 Ikara missiles, two triple launchers for 60 Seacat SAMs, one 114-mm (4.5-in) DP and three single 40-mm AA guns, one twin Bofors 375-mm (14.76-in) ASW rocket-launcher with 54 rockets,

The 'Niteroi' class ASW vessel Uniao (F45) has a Branik missile launcher system aft which fires the Australian Mk 44/46 torpedo-equipped Ikara

two triple 324-mm (12.76-in) STWS-1 tube mountings for six Mk 44 or Mk 46 anti-submarine torpedoes, and one rail for five depth charges
Armament: (F42 and F43) four single container-launchers for MM.38 Exocet anti-ship missiles, two 114-mm (4.5-in) DP and three single 40-mm AA guns, one twin Bofors 375-mm (14.76-in) ASW rocket-launcher with 54 rockets, two triple 324-mm (12.76-in) STWS-1 tube mountings for 12 Mk 44 or Mk 46 anti-submarine torpedoes, and one rail

ASW missile. The magazine carries a total of 10 such missiles, which are targeted by both the bow sonar and the VDS system.

for five depth charges
Aircraft: one Westland Lynx HAS.Mk 21 light helicopter
Electronics: one AWS 2 air-search radar, one ZW-06 surface-search radar, two RTN1OX fire-control radars, one Ikara tracking radar (not in F42 and F43), one CAAIS action information system, one RDL-2/3 ESM system, one EDO 610E hull-mounted sonar, and (not in F42 and F43) one EDO 700E variable depth sonar
Complement: 201

'Jiangnan' and 'Jianghu' classes

In the late 1950s the Chinese assembled in their Hutung shipyard at Shanghai four frigates of the Soviet 'Riga' class from components supplied by the USSR. Known locally as the **'Chengdu' class**, these ships were followed in 1965 by the laying down of the first hull of an indigenous enlarged and modified variant at the Jiangnan shipyard in Shanghai, resulting in the designation **'Jiangnan' class**. Four further units were completed at the Tung Lang shipyard, Guangzhou (Canton) between 1967 and 1969. Four of the class, together with the four 'Chengdu' class ships, serve with the Chinese navy's South Sea Fleet, whilst the 'Jiangnan' class lead ship serves with the East Sea Fleet. At least one of the 'Jiangnans' took part in the combat operations against South Vietnamese naval vessels during the January 1974 occupation of the Paracel Islands. Apart from being larger than the 'Chengdus', the 'Jiangnans' have the major differences of a diesel propulsion plant (instead of geared steam turbines) and that they have not been refitted to carry the Shanghou-Yihou 1 (the Chinese copy of the Soviet SS-N-2 'Styx') anti-ship cruise missile.

Following the political upheaval of the Cultural Revolution the first frigate design to emerge was the **'Jiangdong' class**, two units of which were constructed at the Hutung shipyard between 1970 and 1978. The long building and commissioning times were caused by the fact that the ships were due to carry the first Chinese-designed and -built naval SAM system,

which is still not operational although one of the units has now been seen with missile mountings. The class also introduced into service the first Chinese twin 100-mm (3.9-in) gun mount.

While the 'Jiangdongs' were under construction, a new design for greater anti-ship engagement capability was being formulated. The first three or four units of what became known as the **'Jianghu I' class** were laid down in 1973-4 at Hutung, launched in 1975 and commissioned in 1976. A second shipyard, the Tungmang at Shanghai, is since believed to have joined the programme. An estimated 15 units are in commission with another three at the fitting-out stage and three more under construction. Apart from the 'Jianghu I' series (with a rounded stack for venting the diesel exhaust fumes from its propulsion plant), at least three of those built so far were constructed to the **'Jianghu II' class** design with a squared stack thought to be for a locally-designed and -built combined diesel or gas turbine (CODOG) powerplant. There is also a single example of the **'Jianghu III' class**, which reverts to the rounded stack of the first subgroup but has twin 100-mm (3.9-in) gun mounts (fore and aft) of the type fitted to the 'Jiangdongs'. An eventual total of some 25-30 'Jianghu' class vessels is expected.

Specification
'Jiangnan' class
Displacement: 1,150 tons standard and 1,500 tons full load
Dimensions: length 90.8 m (297.9 ft); beam 10.0 m (32.8 ft); draught 3.9 m (12.8 ft)
Propulsion: four diesels delivering power to two shafts
Speed: 28 kts
Armament: three single 100-mm (3.9-in) DP, four twin 37-mm AA and two twin 14.5-mm AA guns, two 12-barrel RBU1200 ASW rocket-launchers with 120 rockets, four BMB-2 depth-charge throwers and two depth-charge rails with a total of 60 depth charges, and between 40 and 60 mines according to type
Aircraft: none
Electronics: one 'Ball End' surface-search radar, one 'Wok Won' fire-control radar, one 'Fin Curve' navigation radar, one 'High Pole-A' IFF, and one high-frequency hull-mounted sonar
Complement: 185

Specification
'Jianghu' classes
Displacement: 1,568 tons standard and 1,900 tons full load
Dimensions: length 103.2 m (338.6 ft); beam 10.2 m (33.5 ft); draught 3.1 m (10.2 ft)
Propulsion: ('Jianghu I' and 'Jianghu III') two diesels delivering power to two shafts
Propulsion: ('Jianghu II') probably a CODOG arrangement delivering power to two shafts
Speed: 26.5 kts for 'Jianghu I' and 'Jianghu III', and 30 kts for 'Jianghu II'
Armament: two twin container-launchers for Shanghou-Yihou 1 anti-ship missiles, two single (or twin in 'Jianghou III') 100-mm (3.9-0in) DP and six twin 37-mm AA guns, two or four 12-barrel RBU1200 250-mm (9.84-in) ASW rocket-launchers with 100 or 200 rockets, two racks for 60 depth charges, and between 40 and 60 mines according to type
Aircraft: none
Electronics: one 'Eye Shield' air-search radar (being fitted), one 'Square Tie' missile fire-control radar, one 'Sun Visor-B' fire-control radar (in some), one 'Fin Curve' and/or one 'Don-2' navigation radar, one 'High Pole-B' IFF, one 'Yard Rake' IFF (being fitted), and one high-frequency hull-mounted sonar
Complement: 195

The People's Republic of China has built the 'Jianghu' frigate in three different versions. Still in production, the Egyptian navy has recently bought two 'Jianghu I' units with revised gun armaments.

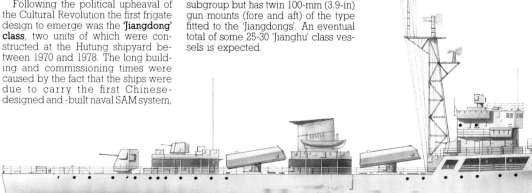

Modern Patrol Craft

Reminiscent in many cases of the motor gunboats and motor torpedo boats of World War II and after, the modern patrol craft has proved its capability in recent conflicts. Armed with a variety of weapons and often capable of great speeds, patrol craft can pose a genuine threat to larger vessels.

Fast, versatile, and highly manoeuvrable, the patrol craft is a major asset to all modern navies. Armed with a wide array of weaponry and equipped with the latest technology, these small, often elusive, craft are capable of causing immense destruction among vessels many times their size.

During World War II, torpedo attack craft were the principal surface threat to coastal shipping. Their development continued afterwards, and they were progressively armed with longer-range torpedoes and heavier weaponry. But it was the Soviet Union that first saw a deadly new application: the combination of fast attack craft and anti-ship missiles. This concept was ignored by the West until 1967, when a Russian-built 'Komar' class missile boat of the Egyptian Navy sank the Israeli destroyer *Eilat*.

The capability of the fast attack craft was further proved in the Indo-Pakistan War of 1971, when Indian 'Osa' class missile boats attacked Karachi harbour, sinking and damaging a number of Pakistani vessels. In

An 'Osa II' missile boat armed with SS-N-2 missiles. 'Osa II' class boats were produced solely for the Soviet Navy from 1966-70, and then built for export.

the Arab-Israeli Yom Kippur War of 1973, duels were fought between missile-armed attack craft of both sides.

In the 1991 Gulf War the Iraqis made extensive use of patrol craft to ferry troops and to attempt attacks on coalition warships. American and British aircraft and helicopters destroyed them in

considerable numbers; on the evening of 29 January 1991, for example, Lynx helicopters from HMS *Gloucester* and HMS *Brazen* engaged a flotilla of 17 Iraqi craft and sank four of them with their Sea Skua missiles. Twelve more were damaged by further attacks by US Marine Corps AH-1 Cobra helicopters and AE-6 Prowler

carrier aircraft.

Patrol craft, despite being vulnerable to air attack, are unlikely to disappear from the world's navel inventories. They will remain a definite asset to navies operating on limited budgets. In modern war, the threat posed to major surface units by such craft is not taken lightly.

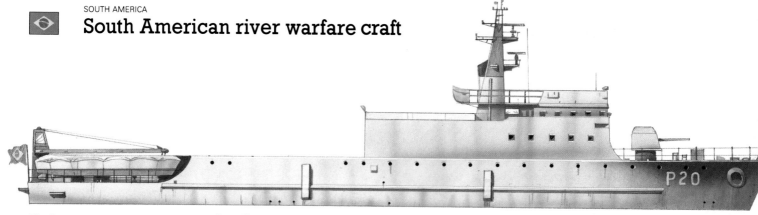

South American river warfare craft

The Amazon and the other large rivers of South America provide one of the last havens for the river gunboat and its modern day counterparts. Brazil, Colombia, Peru and landlocked Paraguay all have such craft in service. The Brazilians have the largest fleet with five vessels (two 'Pedro Teixeira' class and three 'Roraima' class patrol ships) in the Amazon flotilla and one 'Thornycroft' type river monitor in the Matto Grosso flotilla. The latter dates from the 1930s. Colombia utilizes two 'Arauca' class patrol craft dating from the 1950s and a 'Barranquilla' class river gunboat built in 1930. Peru has four purpose-built (two 'Maranon' class and two 'Loreto' class) gunboats for use on the upper Amazon. Paraguay has two purpose-built 'Humaita' class river-defence ships, three 'Bouchard' class converted ex-Argentinian mine-sweepers, and a 1908-vintage converted tug for use on its internal river systems.

Recently Brazil has built a new gunboat based on one of its designs for Paraguay. The five Brazilian vessels belonging to its Amazon flotilla are by far the most modern with the two 'Pedro Teixeira' craft carrying a light helicopter in a hangar and two LCVPs to land troops if required. The smaller 'Roraimas' carry only a single LCVP and no helicopter. Brief characteristics of all the purpose-built craft are given in the accompanying specifications. Colombia also has a third 'Arauca' class vessel which has been disarmed and equipped as a floating hospital for use on the country's rivers. Brazil is known to be interested in building further craft for use on its rivers; a design between the 'Pedros Teixeira' and 'Roraima' classes in size is believed to be under construction.

The Brazilian Parnaiba, dating from 1937, is one of the oldest naval vessels serving anywhere in the world. Armed with one 76-mm (3-in) gun and 20-mm, 40-mm and 47-mm cannon, Parnaiba serves in the Matto Grosso.

Specification
'Pedro Teixeira' class
Names: *Pedro Teixeira* and *Raposo Tavares*
Displacement: 700 tons full load
Dimensions: length 62.0 m (203.4 ft); beam 9.35 m (30.7 ft); draught 1.65 m (5.4 ft)
Propulsion: two diesels delivering 3,840 hp (2865 kW) to two shafts
Maximum speed: 16 kts
Complement: 78
Armament: one 40-mm AA gun, two single 81-mm mortars, six single 12.7-mm (0.5-in) heavy machine-guns, one helicopter and two LCVPs
Electronics: two navigational radars
Built: 1972-3

Specification
'Thornycroft' type
Name: *Parnaiba*
Displacement: 720 tons full load
Dimensions: length 55.0 m (180.5 ft); beam 10.1 m (33.3 ft); draught 1.6 m (5.1 ft)
Propulsion: two Thornycroft triple-expansion steam engines delivering 1,300 hp (970 kW) to two shafts
Maximum speed: 12 kts
Complement: 90
Armament: one 76-mm (3-in) dual-purpose, two single 47-mm, two six 40-mm AA and six single 20-mm AA guns
Electronics: none
Built: 1937

Specification
'Roraima' class
Names: *Roraima, Rondonia* and *Amapa*
Displacement: 365 tons full load
Dimensions: length 45.0 m (147.6 ft); beam 8.45 m (27.7 ft); draught 1.37 m (4.5 ft)
Propulsion: two diesels delivering 912 hp (680 kW) to two shafts
Maximum speed: 14.5 kts
Complement: 63

Armament: one 40-mm AA gun, two single 81-mm mortars, six single 12.7-mm (0.5-in) heavy machine-guns and one LCVP
Electronics: three navigational radars
Built: 1975-6

Specification
'Arauca' class
Names: *Rio Hacha* and *Arauca*
Displacement: 184 tons full load
Dimensions: length 47.25 m (155 ft); beam 8.23 m (27 ft); draught 1.0 m (3.3 ft)
Propulsion: two Caterpillar diesels delivering 800 hp (597 kW) to two shafts
Maximum speed: 13 kts
Complement: 43
Armament: two single 76-mm (3-in) dual-purpose and four single 20-mm AA guns
Electronics: none
Built: 1955

Specification
'Barranquilla' class
Name: *Cartagena*
Displacement: 142 tons full load
Dimensions: length 41.9 m (137.5 ft); beam 7.16 m (24.5 ft); draught 0.8 m (2.6 ft)
Propulsion: two Gardner diesels delivering 600 hp (448 kW) to two shafts
Maximum speed: 15.5 kts
Complement: 39
Armament: two single 76-mm (3-in) and one 20-mm AA guns, and four single 7.7-mm (0.3-in) machine-guns
Electronics: none
Built: 1930

Specification
'Humaita' class
Names: *Paraguay* and Humaita
Displacement: 865 tons full load
Dimensions: length 70.15 m (230.2 ft); beam 10.7 m (35.1 ft); draught 1.65 m (5.4 ft)

Pedro Teixeira, one of the Brazilian vessels designed for use on the Amazon. It can carry a light Bell JetRanger helicopter and two armed LCVPs for use in the region. This large, corvette-sized vessel forms part of the Amazon Flotilla.

Propulsion: two Parsons geared steam turbines delivering 3,800 hp (2835 kW) to two shafts
Maximum speed: 17.5 kts
Complement: 86
Armament: two twin 120-mm (4.7-in), three single 76-mm (3-in) AA and two single 40-mm AA guns, plus six mines
Electronics: none
Built: 1931

Specification
'Maranon' class
Names: *Maranon* and *Ucayali*
Displacement: 365 tons full load
Dimensions: length 47.22 m (154.8 ft); beam 9.75 m (32 ft); draught 1.22 m (4 ft)
Propulsion: two British Polar diesels delivering 800 hp (597 kW) to two shafts
Maximum speed: 12 kts
Complement: 40
Armament: two single 76-mm (3-in) dual-purpose and two twin 20-mm AA guns
Electronics: none
Built: 1951

Specification
'Loreto' class
Names: *Amazonas* and *Loreto*
Displacement: 250 tons full load
Dimensions: length 46.7 m (153.2 ft); beam 6.7 m (22 ft); draught 1.2 m (4 ft)
Propulsion: two diesels delivering 750 hp (560 kW) to two shafts
Maximum speed: 15 kts
Complement: 25
Armament: two single 76-mm (3-in) dual-purpose, two single 40-mm AA and two single 20-mm AA guns
Electronics: none
Built: 1934

'Spica' class fast attack craft (torpedo and missile)

Because of Sweden's close proximity to the Soviet Union and that nation's extensive Baltic Fleet, which includes large numbers of small combatants, the Swedish navy has gradually paid off most of its large surface combatants and replaced them by a surface fleet of fast torpedo and missile attack craft, the largest component of which is and will continue to be provided by the 'Spica I' class, 'Spica II' class and 'Spica III' class. The six 'Spica Is' were commissioned between 1966 and 1968, and are currently armed with a single 57-mm dual-purpose Bofors gun and six 533-mm (21-in) torpedo tubes for the High-Test Peroxide-powered Tp61 anti-ship wire-guided torpedo. By 1985 two to four of the tubes will be replaced by four to eight Bofors RBS15 SSMs. On each side of the bridge are rails for a total of four 103-mm and six 57-mm rocket flare launchers. If necessary the torpedo tubes and missile launcher-containers can be replaced by mines. For fire-control purposes the 'Spica Is' have an M22 system with co-mounted radars in a single radome.

Between 1973 and 1976 a further 12 vessels were commissioned to the improved 'Spica II' design. These have an armament similar to the 'Spica I' but carry only eight 57-mm flare-launcher rails on each side of the forward gun turret. Their armament will also be modified in the same way as that of the 'Spica I' but with the addition of an LM Ericsson Giraffe low-level air-search radar. They have the earlier PEAB 9LV200 Mk 1 analog version of the digital fire-control system that is fitted to the latter 'Hugin' class. Both the classes have to have the two foremost torpedo tubes swung out through several degrees before they can be fired.

In 1981, as a direct response to the latest build-up of the Soviet Baltic Fleet, the Swedish navy ordered from Karlskrona Varvet, the main builder of the 'Spicas', two vessels of the 'Spica III' or 'Stockholm' class. These 320-ton full load craft will act as flotilla leaders for the fast attack units, with the first due to commission in 1984. The 58-m (190-ft) long design has a maximum speed of over 30 kts and will be armed with a single 57-mm dual-purpose gun forward, a single 40-mm AA gun aft, two 533-mm (21-in) tubes for the Tp61 tor-

Above: The 'Spica' classes form the backbone of the Swedish navy's fast attack craft forces. They are designed as multi-role vessels with the capability of switching armament fits to suit the assigned mission.

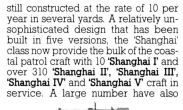

Right: A 'Spica II' class vessel carries four container-launcher boxes for the new Bofors RBS-15 surface-to-surface anti-ship missile. The 'Spica II' class are all due to convert to RBS-15 carriers by the end of 1984.

pedo, and eight RBS15 SSMs. In addition they will carry an ASW outfit comprising variable-depth sonar, Tp42 400-mm (15.75-in) ASW torpedoes and depth charges. Mine rails will also be fitted. The same fire-control system as fitted to the 'Hugin' class, an EWS905 passive ECM suite and an Ericsson Giraffe radar will be the electronics fit carried.

Specification
'Spica I' class
Names: *Spica, Sirius, Capella, Castor, Vega* and *Virgo*
Displacement: 215 tons full load

Dimensions: length 42.7 m (140.1 ft); beam 7.1 m (23.3 ft); draught 2.6 m (8.5 ft)
Propulsion: three Rolls-Royce Proteus gas turbines delivering 12,720 hp (9490 kW) to three shafts
Maximum speed: 40 kts
Complement: 28
Armament: see text
Electronics: one Scanter 009 search radar and one HSA M22 fire-control system

Specification
'Spica II' class
Names: *Norrköping, Nynäshamn,*

Norrtälje, Varberg, Västerås, Västervik, Umeå, Piteå, Luleå, Halmstad, Strömstad and *Ystad*
Displacement: 215 tons full load
Dimensions: length 43.6 m (143 ft); beam 7.1 m (23.3 ft); draught 2.4 m (7.4 ft)
Propulsion: three Rolls-Royce Proteus gas turbines delivering 12,900 hp (9623 kW) to three shafts
Maximum speed: 40.5 kts
Armament: see text
Electronics: one Scanter 009 search radar and one PEAB 9LV200 Mk 1 fire-control system

---

'Huchuan' and 'Shanghai' class fast attack craft (gun and torpedo)

For many years the Chinese navy relied on vessels given to it by the Soviet Union or on building basic copies of Soviet designs in their shipyards. In 1959 the first prototypes of what has become the major construction programme in the coastal forces build-up were seen. These were of the 'Shanghai' class motor gunboats, which are

still constructed at the rate of 10 per year in several yards. A relatively unsophisticated design that has been built in five versions, the 'Shanghai' class now provide the bulk of the coastal patrol craft with 10 'Shanghai I' and over 310 'Shanghai II', 'Shanghai III', 'Shanghai IV' and 'Shanghai V' craft in service. A large number have also

been exported to Albania (6), Bangladesh (8), Cameroun (2), Congo (3), Guinea (6), North Korea (8), Pakistan (12), Sri Lanka (7), Sierra Leone (3), Tanzania (7), Vietnam (8) and Romania

The 'Huchuan I' class of torpedo-equipped hydrofoil as used by the People's Republic of China, which has some 140 in service.

445

(20+ built locally in three variants). The last is particularly intriguing as Romania is a member of the Soviet Warsaw Pact alliance.

Around 1966 the first of an indigenously designed and built hydrofoil torpedo attack craft was seen. Constructed by the Hudung shipyard in Shanghai, this 'Huchuan' class has subsequently been identified in two versions. The first, the 'Huchuan I', has a twin 14.5-mm (0.51-in) heavy machine-gun mounting amidships with a second twin mounting aft of it, whilst the bridge is placed forward of the torpedo tube mouths. The second, the 'Huchuan II', has the bridge placed farther aft, in line with the tubes, and the amidships mounting moved to the forecastle. The hull is of all-metal construction and the forward pair of foils can be withdrawn into recesses in the hull when the craft is hullborne. At present there are some 140 in service with China and the class has been exported to Albania (32), Pakistan (4), Tanzania (4) and Romania (3 plus 17+ as part of the local construction programme). The torpedoes carried are Chinese-built copies of Soviet 533-mm (21-in) anti-ship designs.

Specification
'Huchuan' class
Displacement: 39 tons full load
Dimensions: length 21.8 m (71.5 ft); beam 4.9 m (16.1 ft) or 7.5 m (24.6 ft) when foilborne; draught 1.0 m (3.3 ft) or 0.31 m (1.0 ft) when foilborne
Propulsion: three M50 diesels delivering 3,600 hp (2685 kW) to three shafts
Maximum speed: 54 kts

Complement: 12-15
Armament: two 533-mm (21-in) anti-ship torpedo tubes and two twin 12.7-mm (0.5-in) heavy machine-guns
Electronics: one 'Skin Head' radar

Specification
'Shanghai I' class
Displacement: 100 tons full load
Dimensions: length 35.1 m (115 ft); beam 5.5 m (18 ft); draught 1.7 m (5.5 ft)
Propulsion: four diesels delivering 4,220 hp (3148 kW) to four shafts
Maximum speed: 28 kts
Complement: 25
Armament: one twin 57-mm AA and one twin 37-mm guns, eight depth charges and up to 10 mines
Electronics: one 'Skin Head' radar and one hull-mounted sonar

Specification
'Shanghai II, III, IV and V' classes
Displacement: 155 tons full load
Dimensions: length 38.8 m (127.3 ft); beam 5.4 m (17.7 ft); draught 1.5 m (4.9 ft)
Propulsion: four diesels delivering 4,800 hp (3580 kW) to four shafts
Maximum speed: 30 kts
Complement: 38
Armament: (Type II) two twin 37-mm AA and two twin 25-mm AA guns; (Types III and IV) one twin 57-mm AA and one twin 25-mm AA guns; some boats carry a twin 75-mm recoilless rifle mounting in the bows, and all types carry eight depth charges and have provision for up to 10 mines
Electronics: one 'Pot Head' or 'Skin Head' radar and provision for hull-mounted sonar

USA
'Pegasus' class patrol combatant hydrofoil (missile)

Hydrofoils were the only exception to the United States Navy's lack of interest in fast attack craft during the 1950s. The first such unit launched was the USS *High Point,* in 1962, for ASW Trials work. Interest then shifted to fast gunboats during the mid-1960s, when the USS *Flagstaff* and USS *Tucumcari* were tested. The final shift was when it was decided to develop a missile-armed patrol hydrofoil (PHM) successor to the missile-armed 'Asheville' class patrol gunboat variant that had been used in the Mediterranean. The US Navy combined with West Germany and Italy on the project to make a NATO design. However, as costs rose only the USA, which planned 30 units, remained in the programme. The numbers to be built were cut back to six, and then, only after *Pegasus* (PHM1) had been launched in 1974, the Department of Defense decided in April 1977 to cancel the remaining five units. However, in August 1977 these five 'Pegasus' class craft were reinstated to the building programme at the request of the Congress. By 1982 the last unit, USS *Gemini,* had been commissioned into service with the deliveries of the craft from the builders (the Boeing Company in Seattle) running seven months late and 26 per cent over cost estimates. All six craft will form a unit to be based at Key West, Florida, for tests and the evaluation of systems and tactics, and for surveillance duties in the Caribbean area. As the US Navy believes that the class requires too specialized a logistic support network for forward deployment to the Mediterranean and similar front line areas, the craft will only have a limited role within the fleet. No further missile or gunboat classes are planned at present.

Above: USS Pegasus *off San Diego, California. The foils can clearly be seen beneath the surface of the water. Considered too specialized for forward deployment, the six 'Pegasus' class are based in Florida.*

10 Windscreen wiper control box
11 Magazine
12 OTO Melara Mk 75 76-mm/72 cal automatic gun
13 Forward foil machinery room
14 Forward foil in retracted position
15 Displacement water line (DWL)

30 Propulsor gearbox
31 Diesel and pump machinery room
32 Foilborne propulsor
33 Hullborne diesel engine, 800-hp Mercedes-Benz 8V331 and C80
34 Foilborne propulsion waterjet inlet
35 Rear foil in down position

USS *Taurus*

1 Masthead navigation lights
2 Main mast
3 Fire control antenna structure/dome
4 Radar
5 Radio mast
6 Radio antenna
7 Pilot house
8 Pilot's seat
9 Instrument panel

16 Forward foil in down position
17 Normal foilborne water line
18 Bow thruster
19 Companionway ladder
20 Communication room
21 Passageway

22 Electronics equipment room
23 Gas turbine air intake
24 Gas turbine machinery room door
25 Auxiliary machinery room no. 1

26 Marine gas turbine, General Electric LM 2500
27 Fuel tank (aft)
28 Gas turbine machinery room
29 Auxiliary machinery room no. 2

36 Hullborne water jet nozzle
37 SSPU no. 2 (Ship Service Power Unit)
38 Rear foil in retracted position
39 Auxiliary machinery room no. 3

The *Pegasus* itself is fitted with the Mk 94 fire-control system, which is the US designation for the Hollandse Signaalapparaten WM28 system; the remaining five craft are fitted with the Mk 92 Model 1 system, which is a modified WM28 built by the Sperry Company of the USA. The single 76-mm (3-in) Mk 75 licence-built OTO-Melara automatic gun carried has a total of 330 rounds in its ready-use magazine and main below-deck magazine. There is also additional space abaft the mast for mounting two single 20-mm Mk 20 AA guns if required. However, the main armament is a pair of quadruple Harpoon SSM container-launcher canister groupings fitted on the stern. The Harpoon is a 695.5-kg (1,533-lb), 110-km (68-mile) range active-radar terminal homing missile of the 'fire and forget' type.

Specification
Names: *Pegasus, Hercules, Taurus, Aquila, Aires* and *Gemini*
Displacement: 240 tons full load
Dimensions: hull length 44.3 m (145.3 ft), beam 8.6 m (28.2 ft) and draught 2.3 m (7.5 ft); foilborne length 40.5 m (132.9 ft) and beam 14.5 m (47.5 ft)
Propulsion: foilborne one General Electric gas turbine delivering 18,000 shp (13428 kW) to two waterjets, and hullborne two MTU diesels delivering 3,200 hp (2387 kW) to two waterjets
Maximum speed: 11 kts hullborne and 48 kts foilborne
Complement: 22
Armament: one 76-mm (3-in) Mk 75 dual-purpose gun and eight Harpoon SSMs in two quadruple launchers
Electronics: one SPS-63 search radar, one Mk 92 fire-control system (Mk 94 in *Pegasus*), one SLR-20 ECM system and two Mk 35 SRBoc Chaff launchers

Right: USS Pegasus *in company with a USN VC-1 composite squadron Sikorsky SH-3G Sea King helicopter and McDonnell Douglas TA-4J Skyhawk two-seat operational attack trainer jet off Hawaii. It is envisaged that the 'Pegasus' class will have only a limited role within the US Fleet.*

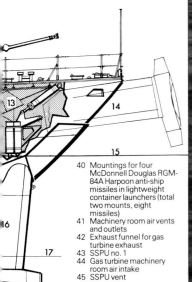

40 Mountings for four McDonnell Douglas RGM-84A Harpoon anti-ship missiles in lightweight container launchers (total two mounts, eight missiles)
41 Machinery room air vents and outlets
42 Exhaust funnel for gas turbine exhaust
43 SSPU no. 1
44 Gas turbine machinery room air intake
45 SSPU vent

'Asheville' class patrol combatant

Seventeen 'Asheville' class patrol gunboats were built by Tacoma Boatbuilding and Peterson Builders in the period between 1966 and 1971 out of a planned 22 for coastal patrol and blockade duties, the gas-turbine craft having been developed in the Kennedy era as a response to the Cuban crisis of the early 1960s. Subsequently craft were used extensively in the riverine warfare operations conducted in Vietnam and, in the mid-1970s, four were modified to carry Standard anti-radiation homing SSM to act as anti-tattletale escorts against Soviet warships in the Mediterranean. The hulls are of aluminium, and with superstructures of aluminium and fibreglass construction. Currently only two of the 'Ashevilles' remain in the US Navy at Norfolk, Virginia, to train Saudi Arabian naval personnel. The remaining vessels have either been transferred (two in a disarmed state to the US Government Environmental Protection Agency, one to South Korea, two to Turkey, two to Taiwan, three to US Navy research and development centres and two to Colombia) or placed in storage awaiting transfer. Eventually all 17 will be transferred.

One major task that the vessels undertook as training units in the US Navy for several years was the simulation of Soviet small missile craft during US and NATO naval exercises. Although considered to be reasonably good seaboats (they can ride out very severe storms), the craft have also acquired a bad reputation for discomfort in seaways. They also have a cavitation problem associated with the type of propeller used, which prevents them achieving their maximum design speed of over 40 kts. Two of the units, USS *Antelope* and USS *Ready*, tested the Dutch-designed Mk 87 fire-control system, a near relative to the Mk 92 used on the later PHM and FFG classes, in place of their standard-fit Mk 63 system.

A multi-mission variant of the 'Asheville' class produced by Tacoma Boatbuilding is the **PSMM 5'** class, which is operated by the Philippines (three South Korean-built craft), South Korea (four plus four locally-built craft) and Taiwan (one plus three locally-built craft).

Specification
'Asheville' class
Displacement: 245 tons full load
Dimensions: length 50.1 m (164.5 ft); beam 7.3 m (23.8 ft); draught 2.9 m (9.5 ft)
Propulsion: CODOG (COmbined Diesel Or Gas turbine) two Cummins diesels delivering 3,500 hp (2611 kW) or one General Electric gas turbine delivering 13,300 shp (9922 kW) to two shafts
Maximum speed: 38 kts
Complement: 28
Armament: one 76-mm (3-in) Mk 34 AA guns, one 40-mm Mk 3 AA gun and twin 12.7-mm (0.5-in) heavy machine-guns
Electronics: one Raytheon Pathfinder navigation radar, one SPG-50 fire-control radar and one Mk 63 fire-control system

Although 17 'Asheville' class patrol gunboats were built, only four remain in US Naval Reserve service. These are scheduled for transfer to other nations in the near future. Many of the class served off the coast of Vietnam, including USS Gallup, *seen here in June 1967.*

'PCF', 'PBR' and 'PB' series patrol craft

The two principal coastal warfare craft used by the Americans in the Vietnam War were the **PCF** (or **'Swift' class**) and the **PBR** (or **Plastic**) type. The Patrol Craft, Fast design was adopted from that of a standard commercial work boat used for oil rig support work in the Gulf of Mexico. The 200 or so PCFs were all constructed by Sewart Seacraft of Berwick, Louisiana in 1965-6. The first 104 were of the **PCF Mk I** design, whilst the remainder (with less sheer, the pilot house located farther aft and a broken deck line) were built to the improved **PCF Mk II** design. Currently three Mk I and two Mk II craft remain in service with the US Navy. A total of 104 was transferred to South Vietnam in 1968-70, 12 to the Philippines in 1966, nine to Cambodia in 1972-3 and seven to Zaire. Additional units were constructed for the Philippines (14), South Korea and Thailand (12). Others were lost during the Vietnam War.

The Patrol Boat, River, of which some 500 were constructed in **PBR Mk I** and **PBR Mk II** variants between 1966 and 1973, is smaller than the PCF, with a fibreglass-reinforced plastic hull, ceramic armour and an open-topped conning bridge. Propulsion and steering are by means of a waterjet system. For work in the narrow and shallow inland waterways of Vietnam these boats were designed with a draught of less than 1 m (3.3 ft). Some 160 PBR Mk Is were constructed, the rest being PBR Mk IIs. Only 22 of the latter remain in service with the US Naval Reserve for training purposes. Most (293) of the remainder were transferred to South Vietnam, with others going to Cambodia (25), Thailand (37) and Israel (28, the majority of which were built locally).

The Patrol Boat was conceived of as the successor to the PCF. The first two, of the **PB Mk I** variant, were built by Sewart Seacraft in 1972 for delivery in 1973. An alternative design, the **PB Mk III**, was then tested in competition with the PB Mk I to meet the US Navy requirement for a multi-mission inshore warfare craft. The PB Mk III won, and 17 were built by Paterson Shipbuilders of Sturgeon Bay, Wisconsin. Like the PCF, the PB was derived from a Gulf of Mexico oil rig work boat design. The wheel house is offset to starboard to allow maximum weapon space, and the boats can be rigged to carry a wide variety of armament including Penguin Mk 2 SSMs, mines, torpedoes or minesweeping equipment. The engines are quietened to allow the boats to be used in clandestine operations. The missing PB Mk II design was not built.

Specification
PCF Mk I
Displacement: 19 tons full load
Dimensions: length 15.3 m (50.2 ft); beam 4.0 m (13.1 ft); draught 1.1 m (3.6 ft)
Propulsion: two General Motors diesels delivering 850 hp (634 kW) to two shafts
Maximum speed: 28 kts
Complement: 6
Armament: two single 12.7-mm (0.5 in) heavy machine-guns and one combined 8 mm mortar and 12.7-mm (0.5 in) heavy machine-gun mounting
Electronics: one LN66 navigation radar

Specification
PCF Mk II
Displacement: 19.2 tons full load
Dimensions: length 15.6 m (51.2 ft); beam 4.1 m (13.5 ft); draught 1.1 m (3.6 ft)
Propulsion: two General Motors diesels delivering 850 hp (634 kW) to two shafts
Maximum speed: 28 kts
Complement: 6

Armament: as for PCF Mk I
Electronics: one LN66 navigation radar

Specification
PBR Mk I
Displacement: 6.5 tons full load
Dimensions: length 9.5 m (31.2 ft); beam 3.2 m (10.5 ft); draught 0.6 m (2 ft)
Propulsion: two General Motors diesels delivering 430 hp (321 kW) to two pumpjets
Maximum speed: 25 kts
Complement: 4-5
Armament: one twin 12.7-mm (0.5-in) heavy machine-gun, one 7.62-mm (0.3-in) medium machine-gun and one 40-mm grenade-launcher
Electronics: one Raytheon 1900 search radar

Specification
PBR Mk II
Displacement: 7.2 tons full load
Dimensions: length 9.7 m (31.8 ft);

Above: A PB Mk III patrol craft under way. Known as the 'Sea Spectre' class, this design was derived from a Gulf of Mexico oil rig work boat.

Seen during the Vietnam war, this PCF is returning to base after a mission with a US Navy Underwater Demolition Team embarked. The armament has been modified to include a twin 12.7-mm (0.5-in) heavy machine-gun mounting.

beam 3.6 m (11.8 ft); draught 0.8 m (2.6 ft)
Propulsion: two General Motors diesels delivering 430 hp (321 kW) to two pumpjets
Maximum speed: 25 kts
Complement: 4-5
Armament: as for PBR Mk I plus one 60-mm mortar in some boats
Electronics: one Raytheon 1900 search radar

Specification
PB Mk I
Displacement: 36.3 tons full load
Dimensions: length 19.8 m (65 ft); beam 4.9 m (16.1 ft); draught 1.5 m (4.9 ft)
Propulsion: two General Motors diesels delivering power to two shafts
Maximum speed: 26 kts

Complement: 5
Armament: one twin and four single 12.7-mm (0.5-in) heavy machine-guns or 20-mm cannon
Electronics: one LN66 navigation radar

Specification
PB Mk II
Displacement: 41.3 tons full load
Dimensions: length 19.8 m (65 ft); beam 5.5 m (18 ft); draught 1.8 m (5.9 ft)
Propulsion: three General Motors diesels delivering 950 hp (709 kW) to three shafts
Maximum speed: 26 kts
Complement: 5
Armament: four single 12.7-mm (0.5-in) heavy machine-guns
Electronics: one LN66 navigation radar

A PBR Mk II craft on a high-speed patrol in the Long Tau river, South Vietnam. The PBR was especially *useful in patrolling the rivers and canals to prevent movement of enemy forces and supplies.*

Riverine warfare classes

For war in the Mekong Delta and other river systems in Vietnam, the US Navy and the US Army developed joint task forces. To outfit these the US Navy had to organize river assault squadrons with specially designed types of assault craft. These were mainly based on modifications of the 'LCM6' landing craft. The squadrons were deployed with complements of 52 **Armoured Troop Carrier (ATC)**, five **Command and Control Boat (CCB)**, 10 fire-support **Monitor (MON)** and two ATC refuelling craft. They also had 32 **Assault Support Patrol Boat (ASPB)** craft assigned, and these last were of the only type specifically built for riverine warfare.

Two versions of the ASPB were built in 1967-8. Both had welded steel hulls, aluminium superstructures and an engine silencing system fitted with underwater exhaust outlets. The boats were usually used as the leading units of assault forces, sweeping ahead with a chain drag to counter command-detonated river mines. They also acted as escorts, patrol craft and counter-ambush vessels. The ASPB hull was also converted to a riverine minesweeper variant, the **MSR** patrol minesweeper, and as a command and control craft. Armament was usually a single 20-mm gun in a forward turret, a twin 12.7-mm (0.5-in) heavy machine-gun (HMG) in an aft turret atop the conning position, two 7.62-mm (0.3-in) medium machine-guns (MMGs) in two further turrets just forward of the HMG turret, and two 40-mm fully automatic grenade-launchers. A dual 81-mm/ 12.7-mm (0.5-in) mortar/HMG mount was also carried on some boats in an open well aft. The alternate fit most frequently adopted was the replacement of the aft 12.7-mm guns by another single 20-mm gun.

The monitors were either converted 'LCM6' craft or specially constructed **MON Mk V** craft that differed primarily in having rounded bows instead of the landing craft bow door arrangement of the 'LCM6'. A typical armament of the conversions was a single 40-mm gun in an armoured turret forward, a single 20-mm gun in a small turret aft on top of the conning position, two single 12.7-mm (0.5-in) HMGs in similar turrets just forward of this to port and starboard, an 81-mm mortar or two army M10-8 flamethrower units in a well located between the control position and the forward turret, plus various small arms mounted along the craft's sides. The later MON Mk Vs had a twin 20-mm bow turret, an 81-mm mortar in the well, the two 12.7-mm (0.5-in) HMG turrets and four 7.62-mm (0.3-in) MMGs. A few of them had the forward turret and the mortar well replaced by an armoured turret containing an army M101 105-mm howitzer for direct-fire missions against riverside bunker complexes. Both types had screen and bar armour fitted to defend against hollow-charge rocket-projectile and recoilless-rifle fire.

The CCB was similar to the MON types except that the mortar well was covered over by a command and communications facility module. The armament was the bow turret with either a single 20-mm or 40-mm gun, the aft turret with a 12.7-mm (0.5-in) HMG and the two other turrets with 7.62-mm (0.3-in) MMGs. A 60-mm mortar was also carried by some craft. An alternative weapon fit was three single 20-mm guns in turrets, two single 7.62-mm (0.3-in) MMGs and two 40-mm automatic grenade-launchers. Both the MON and CCB could tow disabled craft via a towing rig located on their sterns.

The ATCs were converted 'LCM6' craft with bar armour on the hull and superstructure, bulletproof awnings over the troop and cargo deck and space for up to one platoon of 40 fully-

equipped infantrymen. A few were also fitted with a helicopter pad in place of the awnings to act as battalion medical aid stations for casualty evacuation during operations. Others had a 4500-litre (990-Imp gal) diesel fuel tank fitted to the cargo deck so that they could act as refuelling craft. A **Combat Salvage Boat (CSB)** was also produced as an 'LCM6' conversion.

Precise numbers of the various riverine types built or converted have never been revealed, although it is known that at least nine CCBs, 84 ASPBs, 42 MON Mk Vs, 22 MON conversions, 100 ATCs and four CSBs were transferred to South Vietnam in the 1960s and early 1970s. The remainder were discarded, although unknown numbers were also lost in combat during the war.

Specification
'CCB' class
Displacement: 75.5 tons full load
Dimensions: length 18.3 m (60 ft); beam 5.3 m (17.4 ft); draught 1.0 m (3.3 ft)
Propulsion: two diesels delivering 330 hp (246 kW) to two shafts
Maximum speed: 8.5 kts
Complement: 11
Armament: see text
Cargo: none

Specification
Monitor (converted type)
Displacement: 75 tons full load
Dimensions: length 18.3 m (60 ft); beam 5.2 m (17 ft); draught 1.0 m (3.3 ft)
Propulsion: two diesels delivering 330 hp (246 kW) to two shafts

Maximum speed: 8 kts
Complement: 10
Armament: see text
Cargo: none

Specification
Monitor Mk V type
Displacement: 75.5 tons full load
Dimensions: length 18.3 m (60 ft); beam 5.3 m (17.4 ft); draught 1.0 m (3.3 ft)
Propulsion: two diesels delivering 330 hp (246 kW) to two shafts
Maximum speed: 8.5 kts
Complement: 11
Armament: see text
Cargo: none

Specification
'ATC' class
Displacement: 70 tons full load
Dimensions: length 17.1 m (56.1 ft); beam 5.3 m (17.4 ft); draught 1.0 m (3.3 ft)
Propulsion: two diesels delivering 330 hp (246 kW) to two shafts
Maximum speed: 8.5 kts
Complement: 7
Armament: see text
Cargo: 40 fully-equipped troops

Specification
'ASPB' class
Displacement: 38 tons full load
Dimensions: length 15.3 m (50.2 ft); beam 5.3 m (17.4 ft); draught 1.2 m (3.9 ft)
Propulsion: two diesels delivering 880 hp (656 kW) to two shafts
Maximum speed: 14 kts
Complement: 5
Armament: see text
Cargo: none

The self-propelled auxiliary barracks ship USS Benewah lie in the Soil Rap river, acting as mother ship to the riverine warfare assault craft alongside.

'Sparviero' class fast attack hydrofoil (missile)

Together with the United States Navy, Italy is unique among NATO navies in having missile-armed hydrofoils as part of its operational surface fleet. The prototype of the 'Sparviero' class was based on the Boeing Tucumcari design and assessed in detail by the Alinavi Society, which was formed in 1964 by the Italian government's IRI, Carlo Rodriguez (a builder of commercial hydrofoils) of Messina and the US Boeing Company. Built between 1971 and 1974, the original craft was followed by six others between 1980 and 1983. They use the Boeing jetfoil system, with one foil forward and two aft.

Power for the foilborne mode comes from a gas turbine driving a waterjet system, whilst hullborne power comes from a single diesel. The hull is made entirely of aluminium, and it has been found that the craft have a relatively short range and limited armament for combat operations. However, the Italian navy is willing to accept this as Italy is surrounded by restricted waters ideal for such craft.

The six later vessels have a more modern surface search radar than the *Sparviero*, and also carry the later 150-km (93-mile) range Teseo Mk 2 SSM variant of the Otomat SSM, though use of this extra range capability requires a helicopter for mid-course guidance and targeting. The radar is fitted with an IFF interrogator unit, and the gun armament is a single OTO-Melara 76-mm (3-in) dual-purpose gun forward.

Specification
Names: *Sparviero, Nibbio, Falcone,* *Astore, Grifone, Gheppio* and *Condore*
Displacement: 62.5 tons full load
Dimensions: hull length 23.0 m (75.4 ft), beam 7.0 m (22.9 ft) and draught 1.6 m (5.2 ft); foilborne length 24.6 m (80.7 ft) and beam 12.1 m (39.7 ft)
Propulsion: CODOG (COmbined Diesel Or Gas turbine), foilborne one Rolls-Royce Proteus gas turbine delivering 4,500 hp (3357 kW) to waterjet, and hullborne one diesel delivering 180 hp 9134 kW) to one shaft
Maximum speed: foilborne 50 kts and hullborne 8 kts
Armament: one 76-mm (3-in) dual-purpose gun and two Otomat Mk 1 (Teseo Mk II in last six) SSMs
Electronics: one 3RM-7 radar, one RTN-10X fire-control radar and one NA10 fire-control system

Italy is unique in European NATO navies in having missile-armed hydrofoils in Fleet sevice.

'Combattante II' and 'Combattante III' class fast attack craft (missile)

Surprisingly enough, the French navy has not adopted either the **'Combattante II' class** or the **'Combattante III' class** for its own use. The 'Combattante II' class is reported to be derived from a West German Lürssen design and, together with its larger version, has proved very popular with a number of navies. The hull is made of steel whilst the superstructure is made of light alloys. The versatility in the design allows the operator country to choose its own electronics and weapon fits, although the French tend to be a lot happier if its Thomson-CSF fire-control systems and radars with Aérospatiale MM38 or MM40 Exocet SSMs are selected. At present the following countries have the 'Combattante II' in

service: Greece (four with MM38s), Iran (12 with Harpoon SSMs), Libya (10 with Otomat SSMs) and Malaysia (four with MM38s). The Iranian craft, known as the **'Kamam' class** saw extensive service in the 1980s Iran-Iraq conflict, at least two and a 1,135-ton frigate having been lost to AM39 Exocets air-launched from Aérospatiale Super Frelon helicopters flown by the Iraqi air force. The craft have apparently launched several Harpoons against Iraqi naval ships, with at least one 'Polnocny' LSM and several 'P6' MTBs being sunk by them.

Both the 'Combattante II' and the larger steel-hulled 'Combattante III' have excellent habitability, the latter being designed for longer endurance and to act as command ships for smaller craft. The 'Combattante III' has been adopted by Greece (four with MM38s plus six locally built with cheaper machinery, electronics and missile fit of Penguin Mk II SSMs), Nigeria (three with MM38s) and Tunisia (three with MM40s). Typical class characteristics are given in the accompanying specifications. The builder for both versions is CNM at Cherbourg. The Greek 'Combattante IIIs' of the first type differ from the rest in having two rearward-

firing 533-mm (21-in) torpedo tubes. These carry the West German SST4 wire-guided anti-ship active/passive acoustic homing torpedo with a warhead of 260 kg (573 lb) and maximum range of about 20 km (12.4 miles).

Specification
'Combattante II' or 'Kaman' class
Names: *Kaman, Zoubin, Khadang, Peykan, Joshan, Falakhon, Shamshir, Gorz, Gardouneh, Khanjar, Heyzeh* and *Tabarzin* (minus at least one craft reported sunk)
Displacement: 275 tons full load
Dimensions: length 47.0 m (154.2 ft); beam 7.1 m (23.3 ft); draught 1.9 m (6.2 ft)
Propulsion: four MTU diesels deliver-

A Type I Greek navy 'Combattante III' class missile boat with four MM38 Exocet container-launchers, two 76-mm (3-in) guns and two torpedo tubes.

ing 14,400 hp (10740 kW) to four shafts
Maximum speed: 36 kts
Complement: 31
Armament: four single Harpoon SSM container-launchers, one 76-mm (3-in) dual-purpose gun and one 40-mm AA gun
Electronics: one WM28 radar fire-control system

Specification
'Combattante III' class (Greek version)
Names: *Antiploiarhos Laskos, Plotarhis Blessas, Ipoploiarhos Mikonios* and *Ipoploiarhos Troupakis* (Type I); *Simeoforos Kavaloudis, Anthipoploiarhos Kostakos, Ipoploiarhos Deyiannis, Simeoforos Xenos, Simeoforos Simitzopoulos* and *Simeoforos Starakis* (Type II)

Displacement: 425 tons full load
Dimensions: length 56.15 m (184.2 ft); beam 8.0 m (26.2 ft); draught 2.5 m (8.2 ft)
Propulsion: (Type I) four MTU diesels delivering 18,000 hp (13425 kW) to four shafts; (Type II) four MTU diesels delivering 15,000 hp (11190 kW) to four shafts
Maximum speed: (Type I) 36.5 kts and (Type II) 32.5 kts
Complement: 42
Armament: (Type I) two single 76-mm (3-in) 76-mm (3-in) dual-purpose guns, two twin 30-mm AA guns, four single MM38 Exocet SSM launcher-containers and two 533-mm (21-in) torpedo tubes; (Type II) two single 76-mm (3-in) dual-purpose guns, two twin 30-mm AA guns and six Penguin Mk 2 SSM launcher-containers

Electronics: (Type I) one Thomson-CSF fire-control system, one Castor radar, one Pollux radar and one Triton radar; (Type II) one Thomson-CSF fire-control system, one Decca TM1226 radar and one D1280 radar

The first of the Type II Greek navy 'Combattante III' class, Simeoforos Kavaloudis, equipped with six container-launchers for the cheaper Penguin Mk II surface-to-surface missile system in place of Exocet.

'Ramadan' class fast attack craft (missile)

As a direct result of the break with the Soviet Union in the early 1970s, and to make good the war losses from the 1973 'Yom Kippur' War with Israel, Egypt turned to the British shipbuilders Vosper Thornycroft in 1977 with a £150 million contract to complement its ageing missile craft force of six 'Osa I', four 'Komar' and six 'October' class craft, of which the last is a locally built variant of the 'Komar' with two Otomat SSMs). Vosper came up with a 52-m (170.6-ft) design that was subsequently designated the **'Ramadan' class** by the Egyptians. The first was launched in 1979 and the last in 1980, and all were in service by 1982. Capable of facing the Israeli missile craft classes on equal terms the boats have an opera-

tions room equipped with a Marconi Sapphire fire-control system with two radar and TV gun directors for the weapons aboard. Two alternative optical fire-control directors are also carried. A Decca-Racal Cutlass ECM outfit is also fitted for electronic warfare purposes. The main gun armament comprises a single Italian-built 76-mm (3-in) OTO-Melara dual-

The Vosper Thornycroft-built Ramadan missile boat, lead vessel of a six-vessel class that has given the Egyptian navy a quantum leap in its missile boat capabilities.

purpose gun forward. The gun is effective up to 7000 m (7,655 yards) for anti-aircraft fire and to 15000 m (16,405 yards) in the surface-to-surface role. Ordered by some 20 nations, the gun is used extensively on larger missile and patrol craft. Aft is a twin Breda 40-mm AA mounting, whilst the missile armament comprises four launcher-containers for Otomat Mk I SSMs. To

back up the 'Ramadans' the older missile boats are gradually being put through modernization programmes.

Specification
Names: *Ramadan, Khyber, El Kadesseya, El Yarmouk, Hettein* and *Badr*
Displacement: 312 tons full load
Dimensions: length 52.0 m (170.6 ft); beam 7.6 m (25 ft); draught 2.0 m (6.6 ft)
Propulsion: four MTU diesels delivering 17,150 hp (12795 kW) to four shafts
Maximum speed: 40 kts
Complement: 40
Armament: see text
Electronics: one S820 radar, one S810 radar, two ST802 radars, one Sapphire fire-control system and one Cutlass ECM suite

'Saar', 'Reshef' and 'Alia' class fast attack craft (missile)

After the USSR, and hastened in its plans by the loss of the *Eilat* to an Egyptian missile attack in 1967, the Israeli navy was the first of the 'European' powers to realize the importance of the missile craft. The first class that Israel ordered was the **'Saar' class**, built by the French CMN shipyard in Cherbourg between 1967 and 1969 to a West German Lürssen design with steel hulls and light alloy superstructures. The first six units were originally built as the **'Saar I' class** with an all-gun armament of three single 40-mm AA guns. The second six were constructed as the **'Saar II' class** with a single 76-mm (3-in) OTO-Melara gun

forward, two single 12.7-mm (0.5-in) heavy machine-guns and two triple mountings for the Gabriel Mk I SSM. Currently all the 'Saars' have been modified to carry new armament. Four of the original 'Saar I' have been modified as ASW units with EDO 780 variable-depth sonar aft and two to four Mk 32 tubes for 324-mm (12.75-in) Mk 46 45-kt, 11-km (6.8-mile) range active/passive acoustic-homing ASW torpedoes. The gun fit is two single 40-mm AA and two single 12.7-mm (0.5-in) heavy machine-guns. The remaining

An Israeli 'Reshef' class missile boat. Equipped with a cocktail of missile types, the vessels of this class are amongst the most capable missile boats in service.

two units have been given the same gun armament plus one triple and two single launchers for Gabriel Mk I and Mk II missiles. They have been redesignated 'Saar II', while the original six 'Saar II' craft have been re-equipped with a pair of Harpoon SSM launchers in place of one of the triple Gabriel mountings and redesignated the **'Saar III' class**. The remaining Gabriel launcher has been equipped to fire Mk I and Mk II missiles.

For longer-range missions in the Mediterranean and the Red Sea Israel required a new design, so the locally designed and built **'Reshef' (or 'Saar IV') class** of steel-hulled craft was pro-

duced. The first two of these, *Reshef* and *Keshet*, were involved in the 1973 Arab-Israeli war. These craft have air-conditioned quarters, a combat operations centre, and Italian- and Israeli-built ESM/ECM systems. A total of 10 was constructed (two subsequently being transferrd to Chile), whilst three others were built in Israel 'for South Africa with another six built at Durban under licence. Currently the Israeli 'Reshefs' carry an armament formed from the following: two or four Harpoon SSMs, four or five Gabriel Mk II or Mk III SSMs, one or two single 76-mm (3-in) dual-purpose guns or one 76-mm (3-in) dual-purpose gun and one 40-mm AA gun plus, in all craft, two single 20-mm AA cannon and three twin 12.7-mm (0.5-in) heavy machine-guns. An EDO sonar is fitted in some craft.

Following the testing of the 'Reshef' class *Nitzhon* with a temporary helicopter landing pad aft, and to meet a requirement for a missile craft group leader, the **'Alia' (or 'Saar 4.5') class** was designed and built. Using the successful 'Reshef' class hull as the basis the 'Alias' have a helicopter hangar and landing platform aft for a Bell Model 206 ASW and target-spotting helicopter. The latter is particularly useful for over-the-horizon targetting of the Harpoon SSMs carried on one quadruple or two twin launchers. The other armament is four single Gabriel Mk II and Mk III SSMs, a twin 30-mm AA gun mounting, two single 20-mm AA guns and four single 12.7-mm (0.5-in) machine-guns. Provision is also made on the hangar roof for a Barak short-range air-defence missile system when it comes into service. Further missile boat designs are believed to be under consideration.

Specification
'Saar II and III' classes
Names: *Mivtach, Miznag, Mifgav, Eilath, Haifa* and *Akko* ('Saar II'); *Saar, Soufa, Gaash, Herev, Hanit* and *Hetz* ('Saar III')
Displacement: 250 tons full load
Dimensions: length 45.0 m (147.6 ft); beam 7.0 m (23 ft); draught 2.5 m (8.2 ft)
Propulsion: four Maybach (MTU) diesels delivering 14,000 hp (10440 kW) to four shafts
Maximum speed: 40 kts
Complement: 35-40
Armament: see text
Electronics: one Thomson-CSF Neptune TH-D1040 radar, one Selenia Orion RTN-10X radar, ECM equipment and EDO 780 variable-depth sonar

Specification
'Reshef' class
Names: *Reshef, Kidon, Tarshish, Yaffo, Nitzhon, Komemuit, Atsmout* and *Moledet*
Displacement: 450 tons full load
Dimensions: length 58.1 m (190.6 ft); beam 7.6 m (24.9 ft); draught 2.4 m (8 ft)
Propulsion: four Maybach (MTU)

diesels delivering 14,000 hp (10440 kW) to four shafts
Maximum speed: 32 kts
Complement: 45
Armament: see text
Electronics: one Thomson-CSF Neptune TH-D1040 radar, one Selenia Orion RTN-10X radar, one Elta MN-53 ECM system, chaff launchers and (in some craft) ELAC sonar

Specification
'Alia' class
Names: *Alia, Geoula, Romat, Keshet* and two more
Displacement: 500 tons full load
Dimensions: length 61.7 m (202.4 ft);

A 'Reshef' class vessel, used as the testbed for the IAI Barak short-range point-defence missile system. This will take the place of the SA-7 'Grail' and the Redeye shoulder-launched missiles currently used.

beam 7.6 m (24.9 ft); draught 2.4 m (7.9 ft)
Propulsion: four Maybach (MTU) diesels delivering 14,000 hp (10440 kW) to four shafts
Maximum speed: 31 kts
Complement: 53
Armament: see text
Electronics: as on the 'Reshef' class craft

'Komar', 'Osa' and 'Matka' class fast attack craft (missile)

The **'Komar' class** of missile craft (Soviet designation RKA, or *raketnyy kater*) was built between 1959 and 1961. Heralding an entirely new concept in coastal forces, the first of the Komars were converted from newly completed 'P6' motor torpedo boat hulls. About 100 were built of the wooden-hulled design. The 'Komar' carries one fixed forward-firing open-ended missile-launcher bin aimed at about 1.5° outboard and elevated at about 12°, on each side of the deck aft. The missiles carried are the specially designed SS-N-2A 'Styx', a liquid-fuel rocket-engined type with a solid-fuel jettisonable booster motor. The 6.3-m (20.66-ft) long SS-N-2A has fixed wings, and is fitted with an autopilot and an I-band active-radar terminal-homing seeker. The warhead is HE and weighs 500 kg (1,102 lb) and maximum range is 46 km (29 miles). To decrease the load placed on the bow of the modified 'P6' design, the single 25-mm mount and the bridge were moved aft. Wedge-shaped sponsons were also fitted at deck level aft as the missile installation was wider than the boat it-self. Struts were fitted to protect the launchers from spray. No 'Komars' remain in service with the Soviet navy, but several still serve in other navies. The Chinese still build a steel-hulled variant, the **'Hegu' class** with two 25-mm AA mountings. The 'Komar' was the world's first missile boat to be used in action when in October 1967 two Egyptian boats sank the Israeli destroyer *Eilat*. In April 1972 a North Vietnamese 'Komar' launched a 'Styx' SSM at three American warships bombarding coastal targets in North Vietnam.

The USS *Sterett*, a guided-missile cruiser, engaged the missile with a Terrier SAM and shot it down, this being the first time an anti-ship missile was destroyed by another missile in combat.

From 1961 onwards to 1966 the replacement for the 'Komars' was built, this being the steel-hulled **'Osa I' class.** The design carried four completely enclosed launcher bins for the SS-N-2A, two on each side of the superstructure and arranged so that the aft launchers, elevated to 15°, fire over the forward pair, elevated to 12°. From 1966 to 1970 the **'Osa II' class** was produced for the Soviet navy, and then subsequently for export. This version has four cylindrical launcher-containers for the SS-N-2B 'Styx', which differs from the SS-N-2A variant in having infra-red terminal homing and folding wings. The 'Osa' class has an NBC citadel for nuclear and chemical warfare environments. Many of the 'Osa II' craft have now been fitted with a quadruple launcher for the SA-N-5 SAM system (the navalized version of the SA-7 'Grail' man portable infra-red homing missile). Osa class missile boats were sunk by US Navy fighter-bombers during the 1991 Gulf War . 'Osa I' has seen combat service with four navies: those of Egypt (1973), India (1971), Iraq (current Gulf War) and Syria (1973). The 'Osa II' has seen combat with Iraq. The type has been exported widely, and the Chinese also produce their own variant.

In 1978 the first of the 'Osa' replacement class was seen. This is the **'Matka' class**, which utilizes the 'Osa' hull but has a hydrofoil system similar to that of the 'Turya' class of torpedo hydrofoil in order to improve seaworthiness. The missile armament is reduced to two single cylindrical container-launchers for the much improved SS-N-2C variants of the 'Styx', this having a 74-km (46-mile) range and the choice of either infra-red or active-radar terminal homing. The gun armament is considerably enhanced with a new model of single-barrel 76-mm (3-in) dual-purpose turret forward and an ADG6-30 Gatling-type close-in defence sys-

The 'Komar class' was the first small coastal craft to be armed with missiles. It is no longer in service with the Russian Navy but is in use in several Soviet client states.

tem aft. Current building rate of the 'Matka' class is three per year.

Specification
'Komar' class
Operators: Algeria (6), China (2 plus 96 of locally-built variants), Cuba (10), Egypt (4 plus 6 of a locally-built variant), North Korea (6 plus 4 of a locally-built variant) and Vietnam (3).
Displacement: 80 tons full load
Dimensions: length 26.8 m (87.9 ft); beam 6.4 m (21 ft); draught 1.8 m (5.9 ft)
Propulsion: four diesels delivering 4,800 hp (3580 kW) to four shafts
Maximum speed: 40 kts
Complement: 11
Armament: two SS-N-2A 'Styx' SSM launchers and one twin 25-mm AA gun
Electronics: one 'Square Tie' search radar, one 'high Pole-A' IFF and one 'Dead Duck' IFF

Specification
'Osa I' class
Operators: Algeria (3), Bulgaria (3), China (115), Cuba (5), East Germany (15), Egypt (8), India (6), Iraq (4), Libya (12), North Korea (8), Poland (14), Romania (5), Syria (6), USSR (70), Yugoslavia (10)
Displacement: 210 tons full load
Dimensions: length 39.0 m (128 ft); beam 7.7 m (25.3 ft); draught 1.8 m (5.9 ft)

Propulsion: three diesels delivering 12,000 hp (8950 kW) to three shafts
Maximum speed: 38 kts
Complement: 30
Armament: four SS-N-2A 'Styx' SSM launchers and two twin 30-mm AA guns
Electronics: one 'Square Tie' search radar, one 'High Pole-B' IFF, one 'Drum Tilt' fire-control radar and two 'Square Head' IFF interrogators

Specification
'Osa II' class
Operators; Algeria (9), Angola (4), Bulgaria (2), Cuba (13), Ethiopia (4), Finland (4), India (8), Iraq (8), Libya (12), Somalia (2), South Yemen (6), Syria (8), USSR (50), North Yemen (2), South Yemen (7) and Vietnam (8)

Displacement: 245 tons full load
Dimensions: 39.0 m (128 ft); beam 7.7 m (25.3 ft); draught 1.9 m (6.2 ft)
Propulsion: three diesels delivering 15,000 hp (11190 kW) to three shafts
Maximum speed: 40 kts
Complement: 30
Armament: four SS-N-2B 'Styx' SSM launchers, one quadruple SA-N-5 SAM launchers and two twin 30-mm AA guns
Electronics: as on 'Osa I' class

Specification
'Matka' class
Operator: USSR (17+)
Displacement: 260 tons full load
Dimensions: length 40.0 m (131.2 ft); beam 7.7 m (25.3 ft) for the hull and 12.0 m (39.4 ft) for the foil; hull draught

An Egyptian 'Osa I' missile boat. Most Egyptian Soviet-built missile boats have undergone refits with Western electronic equipment in place of the Soviet systems. They also carry SA-N-5 SAMs.

1.9 m (6.2 ft)
Propulsion: three diesels delivering 15,000 hp (11190 kW) to three shafts
Maximum speed: 42 kts
Complement: 30
Armament: two SS-N-2C 'Styx' SSM launchers, one 76-mm (3-in) dual-purpose gun and one ADG6-30 AA 'Gatling' gun
Electronics: one 'Cheese Cake' search radar, one 'Bass Tilt' fire-control radar, one 'High Pole-B' IFF and one 'Square Head' IFF interrogator

Former USSR

'P4', 'P6', 'Shershen', 'Mol' and 'Turya' class fast attack craft (torpedo)

The **'P4' class** was the second Soviet post-war torpedo boat class. Built with aluminium hulls from around 1952 to 1958, their small size restricted employment to inshore waters. Armed with two 457-mm (18-in) anti-ship torpedo tubes, a twin heavy machine-gun mounting and between four and eight depth charges, the 'P4' has long been struck from Soviet navy service, although it still can be found with other navies.

The successor to the 'P4' was the wooden-hull **'P6' class**, built from 1953 to 1960. This was the standard Soviet torpedo attack craft until the mid-1970s, over 500 hulls being constructed. The basic hulls were also converted to other types, such as the 'Komar' (about 100), the 'MO-VI' patrol craft (50), the 'P8' and 'P10' experimental torpedo attack craft (20) and as target and KGB border surveillance patrol craft. Large numbers were exported, whilst the last versions in Soviet service have now been retired.

The largest conventional torpedo attack craft built was the **'Shershen' class** from 1962 to 1974. This design was based on a smaller version of the 'Osa I' hull with the same powerplant and four 533-mm (21-in) tubes for long-range anti-ship torpedoes instead of missiles. Fitted with an NBC citadel, the class is intended to work with the 'Osa' missile boats in mixed brigades of coastal craft. The **'Mol' class** is a

modified version for export and based on the standard 'Osa' hull. These carry shorter-range torpedoes than those carried on Soviet navy torpedo craft. The Soviets have built some 85 'Shershens' and seven 'Mols', but have only some 30 'Shershens' in service at present. These are slowly being phased out.

In 1971 the 'Shershen' was joined in production by the **'Turya' class** torpedo-armed fast attack hydrofoil. This has the 'Osa II' hull and machinery with a single foil system forward. The class is usually stated to be for anti-ship attacks, but the four 533-mm (21-in) torpedo tubes fitted actually carry acoustic-homing anti-submarine torpedoes. The vessels act as fast-reaction ASW units and work in conjunction with shore-based ASW helicopters and aircraft (and other small ASW surface units) for coastal defence. For these operations they carry a dipping sonar (of the type seen on the Kamov Ka-25

'Hormone-A' ASW helicopter) fitted to their transom. The sonar is particularly useful in the Baltic and Pacific areas for searching below thermal layers. Production for the Soviet navy stopped in 1979 after some 30 units had been produced, although a further six have subsequently been built for Cuba without the sonar and fitted with 533-mm (21-in) anti-ship torpedoes.

Specification
'P4' class
Operators: Albania (12), Benin (2), Bulgaria (4), China (60), Cuba (12), Egypt (4), North Korea (12), North Yemen (4), Syria (8), Tanzania (4), Vietnam (3) and Zaire (3).
Displacement: 25 tons full load
Dimensions: length 22.0 m (72.2 ft); beam 4.7 m (15.4 ft); draught 1.5 m (4.9 ft)
Propulsion: two diesels delivering 2,400 hp (1790 kW) to two shafts
Maximum speed: 42 kts

Complement: 12
Armament: two 457-mm (18-in) anti-ship torpedo tubes, one twin 12.7- or 14.5-mm (0.5- or 0.57-in) heavy machine-gun and between four and eight depth charges
Electronics: one 'Skin Head' search radar, one 'High Pole-A' IFF and one 'Dead Duck' IFF

Specification
'P6' class
Operators: Algeria (4), China (65), Cuba (6), Egypt (20), Equatorial Guinea (1), Guinea (4), Guinea-Bissau (1), Iraq (12), North Korea (64 plus 8 of a locally-built variant), Somalia (4), South Yemen (2), Tanzania (3) and Vietnam (3)
Displacement: 73 tons full load
Dimensions: length 26.0 m (85.3 ft); beam 6.0 m (19.7 ft); draught 1.5 m (4.9 ft)
Propulsion: four diesels delivering 5,800 hp (4325 kW) to four shafts
Maximum speed: 43 kts
Complement: 12
Armament: two 533-mm (21-in) anti-ship torpedo tubes, two twin 25 mm AA guns and eight depth charges

A 'Shershen' class torpedo attack craft. The Shershen class had become obsolete by the mid-1980s and were replaced by missile craft and hydrofoils.

Electronics: one 'Pot Head' search radar, one 'High Pole-A' IFF and one 'Dead Duck' IFF

Specification
'Shershen' class
Operators: Angola (4), Bulgaria (6), Cape Verde (2 without torpedo tubes), Congo (3 without torpedo tubes), East Germany (18), Egypt (6), Guinea (1), Guinea-Bissau (2 without torpedo tubes), North Korea (4), USSR (17), Vietnam (12) and Yugoslavia (4 plus 10 locally built)
Displacement: 180 tons full load
Dimensions: length 34.0 m (111.5 ft); beam 7.2 m (23.6 ft); draught 1.5 m (4.9 ft)
Propulsion: three diesels delivering 12,000 hp (8950 kW) to three shafts
Maximum speed: 47 kts
Complement: 23
Armament: four 533-mm (21-in) anti-ship torpedo tubes, two twin 30 mm AA guns and 12 depth charges
Electronics: one 'Pot Drum' search radar, one 'Drum Tilt' fire-control radar, one 'High Pole-A' IFF and two

'Square Head' IFF interrogators

Specification
'Mol' class
Operators: Ethiopia (2), Somalia (4 without torpedo tubes) and Sri Lanka (1 without torpedo tubes)
Displacement: 220 tons full load
Dimensions: length 39.0 m (128 ft); beam 7.7 m (25.3 ft); draught 1.7 m (5.6 ft)
Propulsion: three diesels delivering 15,000 hp (11190 kW) to three shafts
Maximum speed: 36 kts
Complement: 25
Armament: four 533-mm (21-in) anti-ship torpedo tubes and two twin 30-mm AA guns
Electronics: one 'Pot Head' search radar, one 'Drum Tilt' fire-control radar, one 'High Pole-B' IFF and one 'Square Head' IFF interrogator

Specification
'Turya' class
Operators: Cuba (8) and USSR (30)
Displacement: 240 tons full load
Dimensions: length 39.0 m (128 ft);

beam 7.2 m (23.6 ft) over the hull and 12.0 m (39.4 ft) over the foil; draught 1.8 m (5.9 ft) without the foil
Propulsion: three diesels delivering 15,000 hp (11190 kW) to three shafts
Maximum speed: 42 kts
Complement: 30
Armament: four 533-mm (21-in) anti-submarine torpedo tubes, one twin 57-mm AA gun and one twin 25-mm AA gun

The 'Turya' class hydrofoil, of which Cuba received eight by mid-1983. The 30 vessels in Soviet service have been given the designation torpedny kater (torpedo cutter).

Electronics: one 'Pot Head' search radar, one 'Muff Cob' fire-control radar, one 'High Pole-A' IFF, one 'Square Head' IFF interrogator and one helicopter-type dipping sonar

---

Former USSR

'Stenka', 'Zhuk' and 'Shmel' class patrol craft

Designated as a border patrol ship (PSKR, or *pogranichnyy storozhevoy korabl'*) by the Soviets, the **'Stenka' class** currently comprises the second largest coastal-force class in service, with some 90 vessels. These are primarily operated by the Maritime Border Guard Directorate of the KGB and were built from 1967 to 1977. The design utilizes the 'Osa' hull with the same machinery outfit as the 'Osa I' but a modified superstructure and bridge that reflect the operational role. Although used for maritime patrol, the craft have a useful ASW outfit with four single torpedo tubes for the 400-mm (15.75-in) electric-powered acoustic-homing ASW torpedo and two depth-charge racks for a total of 12 charges. A dipping sonar of the type carried on the 'Turya' class of hydrofoil is also carried. Several of the boats have had the torpedo tubes removed to make space for a motor launch, presumably for close inshore patrol where the mother ship cannot go.

To support the 'Stenkas' in their KGB role the Soviets began to build a small coastal patrol boat from 1970 onwards. Known as the **'Zhuk' class** the design is still in production primarily for export. Some 30 or more are in service with the KGB and Soviet navy, whilst over 65 have been built for transfer to 15 other countries.

The Soviets also have a great tradition in riverine and inland waterway warfare. During World War II they developed a series of improvised armoured craft for use on the Danube, Volga, Amur and Ussuri river complexes and the many large lakes found in the Soviet Union. They continued this practice with post-war designs, of which the most recent, built between 1967 and 1974, is the **'Shmel' class**. The most distinctive feature of the 85-vessel class is the forward 76-mm (3-in) gun turret, which is similar to that of the PT-76 light amphibious tank with its co-axial 7.62-mm (0.3-in) machine-gun. Behind the turret is an armoured bridge and enclosed space fitted with bulkheads, a heavy machine-gun position and several firing slits for small arms and LMGs. A twin 25-mm AA mounting with light protection is on the after deck. On a number of boats between this and the battle position are mounted one or two 17-tube BM-14 140-mm (5.5-in) multiple rocket-launcher systems for shore bombardment. It is estimated that for short-distance raiding missions, a platoon of

Naval Infantry or army special forces could be carried on three 'Shmels'.

Specification
'Stenka' class
Operators: USSR (90)
Displacement: 210 tons full load
Dimensions: length 39.5 m (129.6 ft); beam 7.7 m (25.3 ft); draught 1.8 m (5.9 ft)
Propulsion: three diesels delivering 12,000 hp (8950 kW) to three shafts
Maximum speed: 36 kts
Complement: 22
Armament: four 400-mm (15.75-in) anti-submarine torpedo tubes, two twin 30-mm AA guns and 12 depth charges on two racks
Electronics: one 'Pot Drum' search radar, one 'Drum Tilt' fire-control radar, one 'High Pole-B' IFF, two 'Square Head' IFF interrogators and one helicopter-type dipping sonar

Specification
'Zhuk' class
Operators: Algeria (1), Angola (1), Benin (4), Bulgaria (5), Cape Verde (1), Cuba (22), Ethiopia (2), Equatorial

Guinea (3), Iraq (5), Mozambique (5), North Yemen (4), Seychelles (2), Somalia (3), South Yemen (2), North Yemen (4), Syria (3), USSR (30+) and Vietnam (6)
Displacement: 50 tons full load
Dimensions: length 22.9m (75.1 ft); beam 4.9 m (16.1 ft); draught 1.5 m (4.9 ft)
Propulsion: two diesels delivering 2,400 hp (1790 kW) to two shafts
Maximum speed: 30 kts
Complement: 17
Armament: one or two twin 14.5-mm (0.57-in) heavy machine-guns
Electronics: one 'Spin Trough' search radar

Specification
'Shmel' class
Operator: USSR (85)
Displacement: 60 tons full load
Dimensions: length 28.3m (92.8 ft); beam 4.6 m (15.1 ft); draught 1.0 m (3.3 ft)
Propulsion: two diesels delivering 2,400 hp (1790 kW) to two shafts
Maximum speed: 22 kts
Armament: one 76-mm (3-in) gun in light tank turret, one twin 25-mm AA gun, one or two 17-tube 140-mm (5.5-in) rocket-launchers, plus provision for heavy and medium machine-guns, and for mines
Electronics: none

A 'Stenka' class patrol craft at speed. Some 35 Stenkas were still in Russian service in 1998

The Russian Navy still uses about 50 of these craft to patrol the nation's inland waterways

Spyships

Ranging in size from a few hundred tons to tens of thousands, spyships, or intelligence-gathering auxiliaries, were at the cutting edge of signals intelligence in the Cold War. No longer as essential as they were to the gathering of information in the modern era, spyships are being reassigned to other duties.

Throughout the long years of the Cold War, the gathering of naval intelligence remained a vital activity of both East and West, and although monitoring by surface vessels has largely given way to space-based systems, intelligence-gathering vessels still ply their trade on the world's oceans.

Dedicated 'spyships' are properly known as intelligence-gathering auxiliaries (AGIs), their principal task being to gather signals and electronic intelligence data; some are specially configured to monitor ballistic missile tests. The former Soviet Union made widespread use of AGIs, some of the craft operating in different guises, but the Americans lost interest in employing intelligence vessels following an attack on the USS *Liberty* during the Arab-Israeli war of 1967 and the capture of the *Pueblo* by North Korea some years later, switching to specialized aircraft and submarines for the task.

Russian AGI activity reached a peak in the 1960s, when the Soviet Navy adopted an increasingly bold fleet policy. In July 1961 the Soviet Navy

A former Soviet Navy 'Okean' class intelligence-gathering auxiliary, festooned with the aerials and antennae that characterized its role. These 650-ton vessels were converted trawlers.

held its first significant out-of-area exercise, when eight surface combatant units, associated support vessels, AGIs and submarines exercised in the north Norwegian Sea. A pattern of bi-annual exercises was established in 1963, by which time it had become clear that the Soviet Union intended to establish a

powerful 'blue water' navy – something they had lacked at the time of the Cuban missile crisis a year earlier. NATO's response was to step up the scope of its own maritime activity, which from then on was shadowed by Soviet AGIs as a matter of course.

With the signals intelligence (SIGINT) task now assumed by

satellites, many AGIs that functioned purely in the intelligence-gathering role during the Cold War are now used as research vessels, carrying out hydrographic and other survey work on behalf of various government departments. Such research work is likely to be their principal task in the future.

'Henri Poincaré' class

The **Henri Poincaré** is the sole ship of her type and the flagship of Force M, the French naval test and measurement group, which takes measurements and conducts experiments as requested by the navy or any other organization, civil or military. The Hen-

The Henri Poincaré is the flagship of Group M, the French navy's test and measurement unit, and is responsible for monitoring the French SSBS and MSBS strategic missile tests. She was due to be replaced by the research ship Monge in the late 1990s.

ri Poincaré's chief mission is to monitor and measure the trajectory of the SSBS (IRBMs) and MSBS (SLBMs) fired from the experimental station at Landes (or from missile-carrying submarines) in order to compute their flight characteristics, especially in the re-entry and impact stages. During such tests the Henri Poincaré also acts as the range safety and command ship by assisting

the flag officer-in-charge in controlling the naval and air elements in the test zone, particularly in the final descent and recovery phases.

Built originally as an Italian tanker, the Henri Poincaré was reconstructed at Brest between 1964 and 1967, a second major refit following between 1979 and 1980 to update her electronic systems. These include one Savoie and two Gascogne tracking radars, a fully automatic tracking station, celestial position-fixing equipment, a cine-camera-equipped theodolite, infrared tracking systems, Transit navigational and Syracuse satellite communications systems, meteorological and oceanographic equipment, a data collection and collation system, and hull-mounted sonar. For the vertical replenishment and communications

tasks she has a hangar and flightdeck aft for either two Aérospatiale SA321 Super Frelon heavy-lift or up to five Aérospatiale Alouette III light communications/transport helicopters.

Specification
'Henri Poincaré' class
Displacement: 19,500 tons standard and 24,000 tons full load
Dimensions: length 180.0 m (590.6 ft); beam 22.2 m (72.8 ft); draught 9.4 m (30.8 ft)
Propulsion: one geared steam turbine delivering 7457 kW (10,000 hp) to one shaft
Speed: 15 kts
Aircraft: two Aérospatiale SA321 Super Frelon or up to five Aérospatiale Alouette III helicopters
Armament: none
Electronics: navigation radars plus items mentioned in the text
Complement: 223

'Yuan Wang' class

First seen during the May 1980 ICBM test series in the central Pacific, the **'Yuan Wang' class** of satellite- and missile-tracking ships is an important part of China's space technology and missile-testing programme. The two vessels, the **Yuan Wang 1** and **Yuan Wang 2**, were built by the Jiangnan Shipyard at Shanghai and commissioned in 1979. For their tracking and monitoring duties they carry a large parabolic tracking antenna amidships, two log-

The Yuan Wang class was first observed during the 1980 Chinese ICBM tests in the central Pacific. They have a large helicopter landing platform aft, but no hangar for the French-built Aérospatiale SA321 Super Frelon heavylift helicopters normally embarked.

periodic HF antennae (fore and aft) shaped like 'fish-spines', two small missile-tracking radars and several precision theodolite optical tracking director stations. There are also several additional positions available for the later installation of equipment. For vertical replenishment and personnel transfer there is a large helicopter deck located aft, but this lacks hangar facilities. A helicopter type known to use the deck is the heavy-lift Aérospatiale SA321 Super Frelon. A bow thruster and retractable fin stabilizers are fitted for station-keeping and stability in rough seas.

To support these vessels the

Chinese Academy of Sciences also has a fleet of research ships sailing under the name **'Xiang Yang Hong'** (East is Red) and individual numbers. These vessels are capable of a wide variety of duties including general oceanographic, upper atmosphere, missile and satellite research, and also hydrometeorology. The gathering momentum of the Chinese space programme gave rise to a requirement for two improved vessels of this class; one was commissioned in April 1995 and the other in 1996. These ships have communications relay facilities between an orbiting manned space craft and ground stations.

Specification
'Yuan Wang' class
Displacement: 17,100 tons standard and 21,000 tons full load
Dimensions: length 190.0 m (623.4 ft); beam 22.6 m (74.1 ft); draught 7.5 m (24.6 ft)
Propulsion: one diesel powering one shaft
Speed: 20 kts
Aircraft: helicopter landing deck only
Armament: none
Electronics: navigation radars plus items mentioned in the text
Complement: 300-400

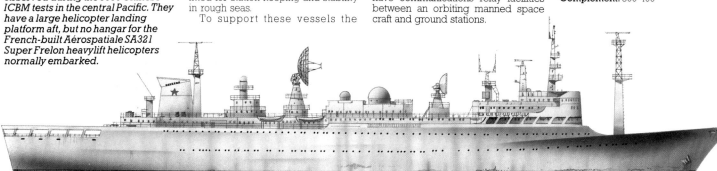

'Mod Kondor I' class

Two of a number of 'Kondor I' inshore minesweeper class conversions, the pair of **'Mod Kondor I' class** vessels produced between 1968 and 1970 are the **Komet** (D42) and **Meteor** (D43). These had their armament and minesweeping gear removed and various signal intelligence (Sigint) and electronic intelligence (Elint) antenna added, together with a deckhouse aft to accommodate the associated recording equipment. The vessels are used with a trawler-type unit, the Hydrograph (D41) of the Soviet 'Okean' design, to monitor NATO naval exercises in the Baltic, and regularly patrol

offshore near highly sensitive West German and Danish military installations to gather classified signal data and electronic order-of-battle information. They have also been known on a number of occasions to appear near neutral Swedish installations and warships on similar missions. Very often the trips near NATO bases are co-ordinated with East German air force intelligence-gathering missions by Mikoyan-Gurevich MiG-21 'Fishbed-H' visual and electronic reconnaissance fighters and Ilyushin Il-14 'Crate' Elint platforms; these simulate penetration flight profiles into NATO

airspace in order to trigger air-defence systems into revealing operating frequencies and procedures. The ships waiting offshore can thus record all the communications and signal traffic generated by the defending systems. Following the unification of Germany both vessels were taken over by the Bundesamt fur Seeschiffahrt und Hydrographie and are now used for oceanographic research.

Specification
'Mod Kondor I' class
Displacement: 245 tons standard and

320 tons full load
Dimensions: length 52.0 m (170.6 ft); beam 7.0 m (23.0 ft); draught 2.0 m (6.6 ft)
Propulsion: two diesels delivering 3729 kW (5,000 hp) to two shafts
Speed: 17 kts
Aircraft: none
Armament: SA-7 'Grail' SAMs, machine-guns and small arms
Electronics: one TSR333 navigation radar plus various unidentified Elint and Sigint systems
Complement: 40

The East Germans converted two of their 'Kondor I' coastal minesweepers (shown here) into intelligence-gathering units by removing all the sweeping gear and armament, fitting various antennaè and making several small changes to the superstructure. The 'Kondor I' Elint ships work in conjunction with East German air force aircraft as required.

POLAND

'Nawigator', 'Baltyk' and 'Piast' classes

The Polish navy uses two modified 'Moma' class survey ships, the Hydrograf and Nawigator, in the intelligence role in the Baltic to monitor West German, Danish and Norwegian naval exercises and shore installations for the Warsaw Pact.

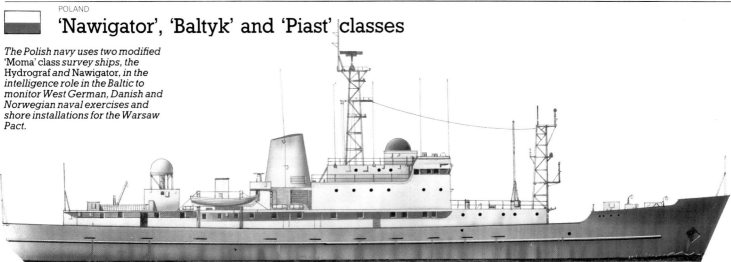

The two vessels that comprise the 'Nawigator' class, namely the **Nawigator** (262) and **Hydrograf** (263), and the 'Piast' class salvage vessels are all based on the Soviet-designed 'Moma' class survey ships. 'Nawigator' and 'Piast' class vessels mount a conspicuous lattice mainmast, the 'Nawigators' being distinguished by the addition of two large radomes, one immediately aft of the bridge atop the main superstructure and the other atop the aft superstructure. The Hydrograf differs slightly from her sister in having a much longer forecastle that is one deck higher. Although no armament is openly carried at present, there are

positions for four twin 25-mm AA guns, two forward and two aft. Both the masts are fitted with a variety of DF and signal-intercept antennae, but it is believed that no real-time analysis capability is carried. Thus all the data obtained have to be recorded for eventual analysis at a shore station fitted with the necessary equipment and computer systems. All the information received after processing is then fed into the Soviet intelligence network for future use.

There is a third vessel, the 1,200-ton 'B10' class Baltyk (264), a converted trawler which also serves in the AGI role with the Polish navy. Both the

'Nawigator' class units are quoted as navigational training ships, but like others are betrayed as to their real role by the enormous amount of electronic gear fitted.

Specification
'Nawigator' class
Displacement: 1,260 tons standard and 1,540 tons full load
Dimensions: length 67.0 m (219.8 ft); beam 10.5 m (34.4 ft); draught 4.0 m (13.1 ft)
Propulsion: two diesels delivering 2685 kW (3,600 hp) to two shafts
Speed: 17 kts
Aircraft: none

Armament: fitted for four twin 25-mm AA (not shipped), otherwise SA-7 'Grail' SAMs, machine-guns and small arms
Electronics: two RN231 navigation radars plus various unidentified Elint and Sigint systems
Complement: 60

Like the 'Nawigator' class of AGI, the 'Piast' class salvage vessel is based on the Soviet 'Moma' class survey ship. Note, however, the absence of radomes, the one lattice mast and the conspicuous diving bell together with its launching apparatus on the port side.

'Bal'zam' class

Designated by the Soviets as sudno svyazyy (SSV or communications vessels) the 'Bal'zam' class vessels were the first military ships purpose built for intelligence gathering and processing. Four vessels were in service by 1986, all having been completed at the Kalingrad Shipyard. The ships carry an array of intercept and direction-finding antennae that feed raw intelligence information into the onboard data analysis and processing equipment located within the extensive superstructure. The product can then be sent via the two satellite transmitting and receiving antennae located beneath the spherical radomes, either to shore stations or to the flagships of surface action battle groups for immediate action. For the extended sea periods which they serve, the ships are equipped to refuel underway and to transfer solid cargo and personnel via constant-tension transfer rigs on each side of the aft mast. The class was also the first Soviet AGI type to be defensively armed, the lead ship appearing in service during 1980 with two quadruple SA-N-5 'Grail' SAM launchers and a 30-mm six-barrel ADG6-30 CIWS. However, no radar fire-control systems are fitted (presumably to prevent interference with the electronic equipment already carried) so the weapons instead use a re-

mote 'Kolonka' pedestal director. The 'Bal'zams' were commonly seen at sea monitoring major NATO naval exercises in the North Atlantic and also American carrier battle groups. All vessels of the Bal'zam class were in active in 1999.

SSV 516 is the lead ship of a new class of very large AGIs given the NATO codename 'Bal'zam'. Armed with two quadruple SA-N-5 'Grail' SAM launchers and a 30-mm CIWS, the class also has elaborate at-sea underway replenishment facilities and real-time satellite transmitter and receiver installations beneath the two dome installations.

Specification
'Bal'zam' class
Displacement: 4,000 tons standard and 5,000 tons full load
Dimensions: length 105.0 m (344.5 ft); beam 15.5 m (50.9 ft); draught 5.0 m (16.4 ft)
Propulsion: two diesels delivering 6711 kW (9,000 hp) to two shafts
Speed: 22 kts
Aircraft: none
Armament: two quadruple SA-N-5 'Grail' SAM launchers with 16 missiles, and one ADG6-30 30-mm CIWS
Electronics: two 'Don Kay' navigation radars, various Elint and Sigint systems, two satellite transmitter/receiver systems, and one real-time intelligence-analysis centre
Complement: 200

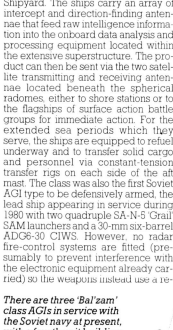

There are three 'Bal'zam' class AGIs in service with the Soviet navy at present, with a fourth unit building. Designated a Sudno Svyazyy (SSV or communications vessel) they are the world's best equipped intelligence-gathering ships.

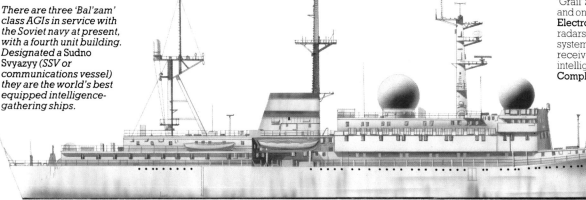

'Primor'ye' class

Although its units resemble small passenger liners in appearance, the 'Primor'ye' class of AGI was the first commercially-based intelligence-gathering design to have an onboard analysis capability. Based on the hull of the highly successful 'Mayakovskyy' series of stern trawler-factory ships, the six vessels are the *Kavkaz* (SSV591), *Krym* (SSV590), *Primor'ye* (SSV465), *Zabaykalye* (SSV464), *Zakarpatye* and *Zaporozhye* (SSV501). They have a distinctive superstructure with box-like structures fore and aft (to house electronic processing equipment) and three main masts (for the associated aerials and antennae). Two of the units, the *Krym* and *Kavkaz*, retain the trawler kingpost aft, while all six vessels differ among themselves in minor details of superstructure and antennae outfits. Most have now been refitted with platforms to carry one or two quadruple SA-N-5 'Grail' SAM launchers for local air defence, while as an interim measure they previously carried the Soviet army's shoulder-launched SAM-7 'Grail' SAM that had been issued to

Soviet naval infantry
The 'Primor'ye' class ships were often to be seen off both coasts of the USA, especially during missiles tests held off Florida by British and American SSBNs. Three of the 'Primor'ye' units were scrapped in 1995 followed by an other in 1997. The two remaining vessels were still active in the Black Sea in 1999.

Specification
'Primor'ye' class
Displacement: 2,600 tons standard and 3,700 tons full load
Dimensions: length 83.6 m (274.3 ft); beam 13.7 m (44.9 ft); draught 7.0 m (23.0 ft)
Propulsion: one diesel delivering 1491 kW (2,000 hp) to one shaft
Speed: 13 kts
Aircraft: none
Armament: one (SSV 590) or two (SSVs 464, 501 and 591) quadruple SA-N-5 'Grail' SAM launchers with eight or 16 missiles respectively (other ships to be fitted with launchers), machine-guns

The Zakarpatye of the 'Primor'ye' class shows the multitude of arrays and antenna that are required by an intelligence-gathering ship. Those

on the foremast are primarily of the direction-finding type so as to pinpoint the origin of an electronic transmission.

and small arms
Electronics: two 'Don Kay' or 'Don 2' navigation radars, various Elint and

Sigint systems, and one real-time intelligence-analysis centre
Complement: 160

The 'Primor'ye' class of AGI comprises six units, and is regularly seen attending NATO naval exercises and American space events and missile tests to gather electronic and photographic intelligence for use by Soviet designers on their own systems.

Former USSR

'India' class

Although said to be designed for the underwater-rescue role, with two small deep submergence recovery vessels (DSRVs) semi-recessed in wells on the deck abaft the sail structure, the two units of the **'India' class** diesel-electric submarine would in wartime or for certain clandestine intelligence-gathering operations probably operated with the Soviet navy's Spetsnaz special forces brigades to carry combat mini-subs and frogman units. The DSRVs normally carried were about 11 m (36.1 ft) long and were fitted out to lock onto the rescue hatches of submarines lying disabled on the seabed. For under ice covert operations direct access to and exit from the DRSVs in their wells was possible while the submarine was submerged. Although no torpedo armament is believed to have been carried, the hull of the submarine was designed for high surface speed operation in order to cut down on transit times to possible rescue areas. For operations in the extreme north where ices-floes are likely to be encountered, the bow was specially strengthened by the fitting of an ice guard. For convenience and better underwater manoeuvring in certain circumstances) the hydroplanes were fitted on the sides of the sail.

Only two 'India' class boats were in service, one in the Northern Fleet and the other with the Pacific Fleet. The former may have been detached to the baltic fleet on occasions for use in the various intrusions that were made into Swedish territorial waters in the late 1980s. It is believed that on this type of operation the 'India' class submarine carried two modified versions

of the Soviet Army's IPR tracked amphibious armoured engineer vehicle with diver lock-out facilities; this vehicle is capable of travelling along the seabed on tracks as well as using the more conventional swimming mode. The two India class vessels were withdrawn from use at the end of the Cold War and laid up. They were awaiting the breaker's yard in 1999.

Specification
'India' class
Displacement: 3,900 tons surfaced and 4,800 tons dived
Dimensions: length 106.0 m (347.8 ft); beam 10.0 m (32.8 ft); draught not known
Propulsion: three diesels delivering 8948 kW (12,000 hp) to two electric motors powering two shafts
Speed: 15 kts surfaced and 12.5 kts dived
Diving depth: mother craft 300 m (984 ft) operational and 500 m (1,640 ft) maximum; DSRVs 1000 m (3,281 ft) operational
Armament: demolition charges, small arms etc

Photographed in transit from the Pacific to the Northern Fleet, this 'India' class boat has landed both DSRVs and has been fitted with a built-up bow to cope with the rough conditions of the northern coast.

Electronics: one 'Snoop Plate' surface-search radar, one ESM system, one medium-frequency bow sonar, several types of underwater telephone and homing systems
Complement: 70 crew plus 120 passengers/divers

The 'India' class rescue submarines were equipped to carry and operate deep submergence rescue vessels and were believed to operate in support of the naval Spetsnaz special operations brigades when not being used in their primary role.

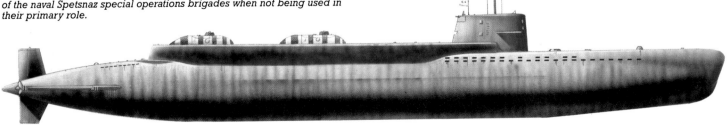

'Gagarin' class

The *Kosmonavt Yuriy Gagarin*, sole unit of the '**Gagarin' class**, is a space control monitoring ship based at the Black Sea port of Odessa. She is the world's largest vessel fitted for scientific studies and is also the largest ship with turbo-electric propulsion. Originally a 'Sofiya' class steam tanker, she was adapted before final completion to fulfil the research role. Built at Leningrad by the Baltic Shipbuilding and Engineering Works, she was completed in 1971 and is engaged in research into the conditions in the upper atmosphere and the problems associated with long-range communication, as well as undertaking space control and spacecraft communications activities. For this work the ship is fitted with two 27-m (88.6-ft) diameter 'Ship Shell' and two 12.5-m (41-ft) diameter 'Ship Bowl' stabilized communications and tracking dish antennae, two 'Vee Tube' HF communications systems and four 'Quad Ring' yagi arrays. With all the antennae deployed forward, the vessel suffers a loss in speed of 2 kts. To maintain the ship on station during a particular task, bow and stern thrusters are fitted. The ship is capable of staying at sea for 120 consecutive days without resupply, and for her crew's comfort she has three swimming pools, a theatre and a sports hall. The ship is named after the first man to travel in Earth orbit, and who was subsequently killed in an air crash in the Soviet Union during 1968.

Specification
'Gagarin' class
Displacement: 37,500 tons standard and 45,000 tons full load
Dimensions: length 235.9 m (774.0 ft); beam 31.0 m (101.7 ft); draught 9.2 m (30.2 ft)
Propulsion: one geared steam turbine delivering 14168 kW (19,000 hp) to an electric drive turning one shaft
Speed: 17.5 kts
Aircraft: none
Armament: none
Electronics: two 'Don Kay' navigation radars plus items mentioned in the text
Complement: 320

The 45,000-ton Kosmonavt Yuriy Gagarin is the largest Former Soviet research vessel, adapted from the unfinished hull of a tanker. Her powerful communication and detection equipment enable Former Soviet space missions to be controlled far from convenient ground stations.

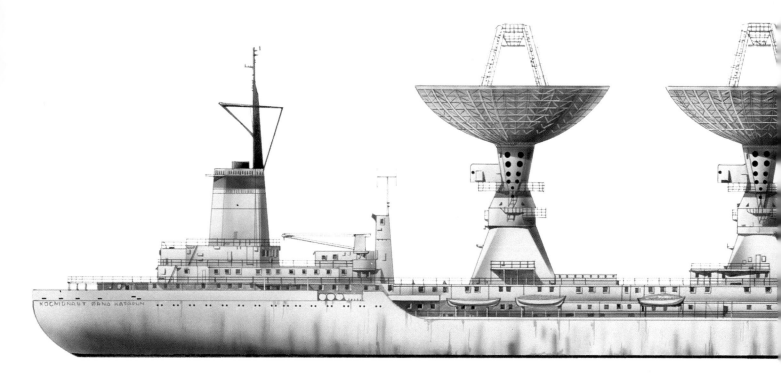

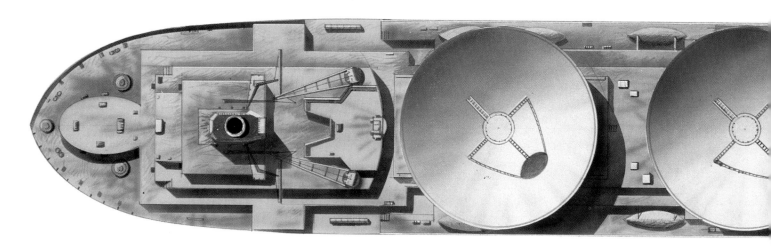

Kosmonavt Yuriy Gagarin

The Kosmonavt Yuriy Gagarin is the largest of the Former Soviet space event ships and is subordinated to the Academy of Science for assignments. Adapted from a tanker hull whilst still on the stocks, she is homeported at Odessa in the Black Sea but operates in many parts of the world. The four huge dish antennae can act as brakes, and when in the correct orientation actually reduce the speed of the ship by up to two knots. For the crew's comfort on long voyages she has three swimming pools, a gymnasium and a 300 seat theatre aboard.

'Okean' class

Built in East Germany from 1959 to the mid-1960s, the **'Okean' class** of 15 converted side trawlers is the largest and hence the most observed class of Soviet AGI. They are designated *gigrograficheskoye sudno* (GS, or survey ship) in the Soviet navy, and retain their trawler tripod mast forward and a pole mast well aft. These are festooned with the various aerials and antennae that characterize their role. It is vessels of this class (together with the eight larger trawler units of the 'Mayak' class and the four ex-whalers of the 'Mirnyy' class) that are regularly seen off the

Western nuclear submarine bases monitoring the coming and going of SSBNs in transit. There are many variations within the class. One modified subgroup of four (the **Linza, Lotlin, Reduktor** and **Zond**) has the port side superstructure enclosed and the starboard side open; these ships also have additional accommodation on the welldeck. The *Reduktor, **Alidada, Barometr, Ampermetr*** and **Gidrofon** have no installation for shoulder-launched SA-7 SAMs, while such has been added to the **Barograf, Deflektor, Ekholot, Krenometr,** *Linza, Lotlin,*

Repiter, Teodolit, Traverz and *Zond.* The *Barograf* also has two twin 14.5-mm (0.57-in) heavy machine-gun mountings to supplement the small arms carried by the crew. It is likely that the 'Okean' class will eventually be replaced by conversions of the **'Al'pinist' class** stern trawlers which are currently being built at the Leninskaya Kuznitsa Shipyard at Kiev and at the Volgograd Shipyard. At present there are five such units in service, with the former fish hold converted to allow extensive space for electronics and/or additional accommodation for specialist personnel.

Specification
'Okean' class
Displacement: 650 tons standard and 760 tons full load
Dimensions: length 51.0 m (167.3 ft); beam 8.8 m (28.9 ft); draught 3.7 m (12.1 ft)
Propulsion: one diesel delivering 403 kW (540 hp) to one shaft
Speed: 13 kts
Aircraft: none
Armament: see text
Electronics: one or two 'Don Kay' navigation radars, and various Elint and Sigint systems
Complement: 70

The Linza *of the 'Okean' class shadows the amphibious warfare ship HMS* Fearless. *The 'Okeans' are the most numerous of the Soviet*

AGIs, with the antenna outfits varying considerably between the units of the class so that they can perform different roles.

The 'Okean' class AGI Gidrofon. *Most of the class have now been fitted with two positions for quadruple SA-N-5 'Grail' SAM launchers. The* Barograf

has also been fitted with two twin 14.5-mm heavy machine-guns for use off such unfriendly areas such as the African coast and China.

'Okean' class intelligence collection ships cutaway drawing key

1 Aft wheel
2 Searchlight
3 Derrick
4 Steering compartment
5 Rudder post
6 Rudder
7 Single screw
8 Bulkhead/framing
9 Single shaft
10 Auxiliary engine
11 Dynamo
12 Engine room
13 540-bhp diesel engine
14 Exhaust uptake
15 Double bottom
16 Fuel
17 Officers'/crew quarters
18 Funnel
19 Mainmast
20 Disc cone omnidirectional receiver antenna
21 Radar receiver
22 Direction-finding loop
23 Air search
24 Folded dipole for HF reception
25 Coaxial feeder to wire dipole antenna
26 Vertical rod antenna
27 Don 2 navigation radar
28 Radar receiver
29 Ventilator
30 Bridge
31 Deck light
32 Chart room
33 Navigation light
34 Radar room
35 Extended space for information processing
36 Waterline
37 Forward hold
38 Tripod foremast
39 Bow light
40 Direction-finding loop with earthplane
41 Raised foredeck
42 Hull guard
43 Anchor
44 Winch
45 Lifeboat

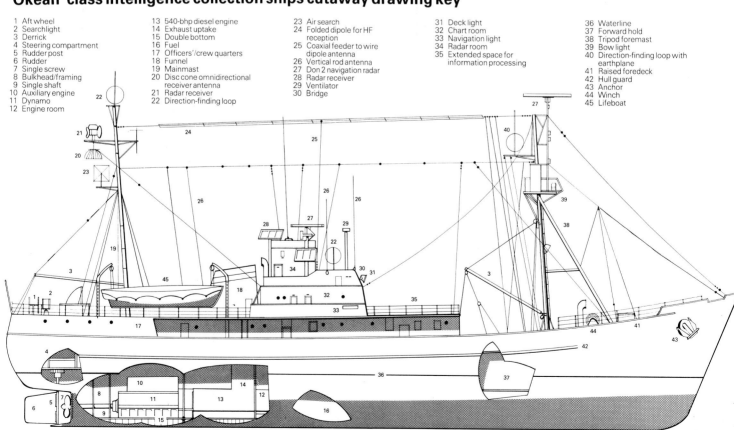

'Converted Compass Island' class

The USNS *Observation Island* (T-AGM23) is a former ballistic missile trials ship that was modified as a **'Converted Compass Island' class** range instrumentation ship during 1979-81. This was specifically for the purpose of carrying SPQ-11 'Cobra Judy' phased-array missile-tracking radar aft to collect data on Soviet and Chinese ballistic missile tests. Operated for the USAF Eastern Space Missile Center in the Pacific area by the Military Sealift Command, she is painted white. Two large parabolic signal-collection antennae are fitted beneath the pair of geodesic radomes atop the bridge. An extensive communications fit, which includes satellite receivers and transmitters, allows for the real-time transmission of raw and analysed data to distant shore stations if required. During her original career as a missile trials ship she fired the first ship-launched Polaris missile at sea on 27 August 1959 and then, following a refit in 1969, the first Poseidon missile on 16 December 1969. The massive 'Cobra Judy' radar carried is very similar in operational aspects to the even larger land-based 'Cobra Dane' radar, the phased transmissions allowing the system to detect and track objects at a very fast rate. The installation aboard the *Observation Island* weighs about 250 tons, and the radar itself is located in a mechanically-rotated pyramid-like steel structure, with the data analysis and storage computers (plus the display consoles) in compartments on the decks beneath it.

USNS Observation Island *is operated by MSC with a civilian crew and watches Soviet space and missile launches with her 'Cobra Judy' phased-array radar.*

Specification
'Converted Compass Island' class
Displacement: 13,060 tons light and 17,015 tons full load
Dimensions: length 171.9 m (564.0 ft); beam 23.2 m (76.0 ft); draught 7.6 m (25 ft)

Propulsion: geared steam turbines delivering 14355 kW (19,250 hp) to one shaft
Speed: 20 kts
Aircraft: none
Armament: none
Electronics: one Raytheon TM1650/9X navigation radar and one Raytheon TM1660/12S navigation radar, plus items mentioned in the text
Complement: 153

The large phased-array radar turret mounted on USNS Observation Island *when working in concert with the similar system based on land in Alaska is capable of simultaneously tracking up to 200 missile targets.*

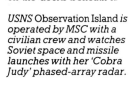

'Stalwart' class

The 18 vessels of the **'Stalwart' class** are to provide the gap-filling role for the American Sound Surveillance Under Sea (SOSUS) system in areas where there is no or only poor coverage. The sonar used by the 'Stalwarts' is the Surveillance Towed Array Sensor (SURTASS): this is a 1829-m (6,000-ft) long linear passive hydrophone array which is deployed over the ship's stern in a flexible, neutrally buoyant cable housing. The data picked up by the array is then instantaneously relayed to a shore monitoring station for processing and evaluation via a WSC-6 satellite communications link. The first seven ships are the USNS *Stalwart* (T-AGOS1), *Contender* (T-AGOS2), *Vindicator* (T-AGOS3), *Triumph* (T-AGOS4), *Assur-*

Unlike many ASW surveillance vessels, the 'Stalwart' class has no capacity for analysing data on board. Information picked up by the 1.8-km (1.2-mile) towed sonar array is transmitted via satellite to a ground station for further processing and action.

ance (T-AGOS5), *Persistent* (T-AGOS6) and *Indomitable* (T-AGOS7), and all have been completed; the USNS *Prevail* (T-AGOS8), *Assertive* (T-AGOS9), *Invincible* (T-AGOS10), *Dauntless* (T-AGOS11) and *Vigorous* (T-AGOS12) are building, and the remaining six are projected in batches of three under the Fiscal Years 1985 and 1986 naval building programmes. The ships are manned by Military Sealift Command civilian personnel, but carry a small six-man naval detachment to maintain the SURTASS and satellite communications link equipment. The class members are expected to conduct 90-day patrols at a time, with a total of 300 days per year at sea on such patrols or on trials.

Specification
'Stalwart' class
Displacement: 1,650 tons light and 2,285 tons full load
Dimensions: length 68.3 m (224.0 ft); beam 13.1 m (43.0 ft); draught 4.6 m (15.1 ft)
Propulsion: four diesels delivering 2386 kW (3,200 hp) to electric drives turning two shafts
Speed: 11 kts
Aircraft: none
Armament: none
Electronics: two navigation radars plus items mentioned in the text
Complement: 30

The 'Stalwart' class is being used by the US Navy to carry and tow a long-range passive sonar system that is designed to help fill the gaps in the SOSUS underwater monitoring network around the coasts of the USA and fellow NATO nations.

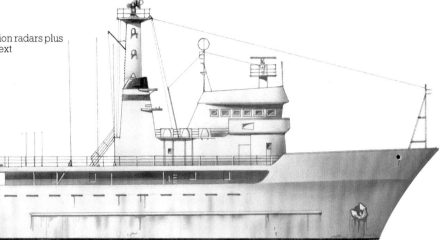

'Converted Haskell' class

The USNS *Range Sentinel* (T-AGM22) is a **'Converted Haskell' class** attack transport developed for specific use as a range instrumentation ship, to monitor first the Poseidon and then the Trident I/II SLBM development programmes. Converted from October 1969 to October 1971, the *Range Sentinel* operates as a unit of the US Navy's Military Sealift Command (MSC) fleet. She is fitted with an SPQ-7 and three other radar tracking systems on a single-deck superstructure laid over the forward cargo hold area. Since commissioning for this role the *Range Sentinel* has had several electronic equipment updates, and these have resulted in changes of appearance over the years.

There was also a second vessel of similar design converted from a **'Victory' class** merchant ship, the USNS *Wheeling*, which has now been struck off the naval register. The reason for the similarity is that the *Range Sentinel* has the VC2-S-AP5 'Victory' type hull design and propulsion plant. Under current planning, the US Navy intends in the Fiscal Year 1987 budget allocation to convert another large vessel to the range instrumentation role to replace one or more of the older vessels now used.

Specification
'Converted Haskell' class
Displacement: 8,853 tons light and 12,170 tons full load
Dimensions: length 138.7 m (455.0 ft); beam 18.9 m (62.0 ft); draught 7.9 m (26.0 ft)
Propulsion: geared steam turbines delivering 6338 kW (8,500 hp) to one shaft
Speed: 15.5 kts
Aircraft: none
Armament: none
Electronics: one Raytheon TM1650/9X navigation radar and one Raytheon TM1660/12S navigation radar, plus items mentioned in the text
Complement: 124

Originally commissioned in 1944, the converted attack transport Range Sentinel is based upon a 'Victory' ship hull, and is used in the SLBM test programmes. The forward radome has recently been lost following transfer from the Poseidon to the latest Trident range instrumentation ship.

Converted from a former US Navy amphibious transport, the Range Sentinel *(T-AGM 22) now operates in support of SSBN missile firing in the Atlantic as a missile range instrumentation vessel.*

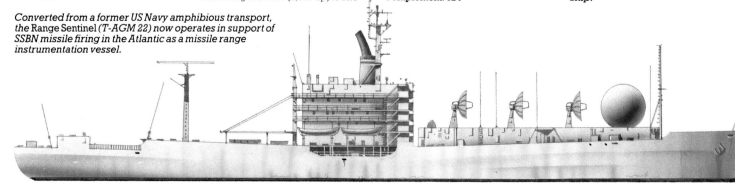

'Vanguard' class

The USNS *Redstone* (T-AGM20) is the surviving range instrumentation member of the three-ship **'Vanguard' class** following the striking of the *Mercury* from the navy list and the conversion of the *Vanguard* into the US Navy's test ship for fleet ballistic missile guidance and ship navigation systems. Converted between 1964 and 1966 from a Type T2-SE-A2 tanker (by inserting a 22-m/72.2-ft extension amidships) to serve as the tracking and communications ship for the NASA Apollo lunar manned spaceflight programme, she now operates in support of the US Air Force's Eastern Space Missile Center at Patrick Air Force Base, Florida. To fulfil her current missions she is fitted with two large communications dish antennae and two tracking radars, plus a number of HF communications systems. To monitor upper-atmosphere conditions which might affect her work she has a high-altitude meteorological balloon hangar and launch platform located aft. Approximately 450 tons of electronic equipment are installed to support the radars and communications antennae; most of this is below decks converted in hold areas. Vanguard has recently been reactivated and modified to replace Compass Island as the test ship for Fleet Ballistic Missile Guidance under a new classification.

Specification
'Vanguard' class
Displacement: 16,882 tons light and 24,710 tons full load
Dimensions: length 180.7 m (593.0 ft); beam 22.9 m (75.0 ft); draught 7.6 m (25.0 ft)
Propulsion: geared steam turbines delivering 6488 kW (8,700 hp) to an electric drive turning one shaft
Speed: 16 kts
Aircraft: none
Armament: none
Electronics: one Raytheon TM1650/9X navigation radar and one Raytheon TM1660/12S navigation radar, plus items mentioned in the text
Complement: 198

Above: USNS Mercury *is the only one of the three converted 'Mission' class tankers to have been struck from the navy list. The vessels were named after early US missile programmes, and were used during the manned space programme for tracking and communications relay tasks.*

Above: USNS Redstone *operates in support of the Trident fleet ballistic missile programme, serving as a tracking and communication ship.*

She also has some upper atmosphere meteorology capability, essential for the analysis of missile performance.

Above: The Vanguard *(T-AG 194) has taken part in a number of international upper atmosphere research exercises, including the GATE programme. Her sister ship* Redstone *(T-AGM20) now serves as the US Navy's navigation research ship, testing new systems.*

Below: Vanguard *(T-AG 194, formerly T-AGM19) supported the USAF missile-testing range in the Atlantic for a number of years, and is now temporarily laid up after conversion to ballistic missile guidance and ship navigation test ship in 1980.*

Naval Anti-Aircraft Weapons

Naval anti-aircraft weapons must be able to stop not only aerial but also surface targets at close range. Sophisticated technology and ammunition has ensured that this is possible, and warships now rely on a range of guns and missiles to protect them against anti-ship missiles and attack from the air.

Phalanx is a total weapon system which automatically, searches, detects, evaluates, tracks and fires at target threats. The six-barrelled 'Gatling' gun can fire 3,000 rounds per minute.

The introduction of the surface-to-air missile in the 1950s did not, as many believed, lead to the demise of conventional anti-aircraft artillery. 'Triple A' (AAA) played a massive role in defending the UK task force in the 1982 Falklands War, and proved the ongoing value of the gun as a close-range weapon.

As used in the Falklands, AA guns of all calibres were able to put up a heavy barrage over the ships of the task force, and even if it was not particularly accurate it discouraged a fair number of Argentine pilots from making precise bombing and rocket attacks. Anti-aircraft fire accounted for two confirmed kills, whilst an

unknown number of aircraft returned to their bases with flak damage.

There was a grim lesson to be learned from the Falklands War, too. It was that in order to survive in an environment dominated by anti-ship missiles, ships need a combination of quick-firing fully automatic guns and short-range point-

defence missiles, effectively creating a lethal zone through which missiles are unable to penetrate. Gun calibres in this field vary between 20-mm (0.8-in) and 30-mm (1.2-in) because of the rapid rate of fire demanded (up to 6,000 rounds per minute); but larger calibres, governed by sophisticated electronics and armed with proximity-fuzed fragmentation ammunition can also be used against missiles. A good example of this is the Emerlec 30-mm cannon system designed to stop both air and surface targets at close range. The cannon has 1970 rounds of ammunition stored below deck immediately beneath the operator's cabin, which is environmentally controlled. The system can fire a range of ammunition including armour-piercing incendiary shells, and the gun mount can swing through a complete circle.

It is an interesting fact that such close-in weapons systems (CIWS) were first developed by the Soviet Navy, which became aware of the potential of the sea-skimming missile before the Americans did. CIWS are now deemed indispensable by all the major navies.

Breda Twin 30-mm Naval Mount

Designed for the export market, the **Breda Twin 30-mm Naval Mount** uses two Mauser MK cannon set in a twin cradle within a turret. Some of the advanced features of the twin 40-mm L/70 mount described separately have been incorporated into the design to reduce reaction time to a minimum. The mount is completely automated, with sufficient ammunition reserves (2,000 belted ready-use rounds per mount) to meet both saturation and successive wave attacks without the need for human intervention to replenish stocks. Four versions are available to meet siting arrangements in various classes of warships. In each case the dimensions and weights have been reduced to the minimum to save topweight. The ammunition is the same as that developed for the American GAU-8 tank-buster cannon, and comprises two basic types: an HE-incendiary round with an impact fuse and an AP-incendiary round with the penetrator made out of depleted uranium. A production line was set up in anticipation of orders.

Specification
Breda 30-mm
Calibre: 30 mm
Number of barrels: two
Elevation: −13° to +85°
Muzzle velocity: 1040 m (3,412 ft) per second
Effective range: 3000 m (3,280 yards)
Rate of fire: 1,600 rounds per minute
Weight: varies according to the ship type fitted
Number of rounds carried on mount: 2,000

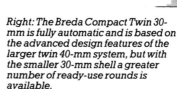

The Breda Compact Twin 30-mm Naval Mount is still in production and remains a very effective weapon. In the Background is a 'Lupo' class frigate with twin 40-mm turret visible.

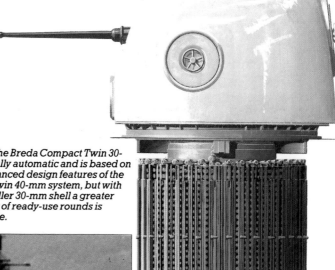

Right: The Breda Compact Twin 30-mm is fully automatic and is based on the advanced design features of the larger twin 40-mm system, but with the smaller 30-mm shell a greater number of ready-use rounds is available.

The general layout of the gunhouse and below-decks magazine for 2,000 ready-use rounds is seen in the cutaway drawings below. Already the Breda company has designed a single 30-mm naval mount along the same lines and firing the same GAU-8/A ammunition types.

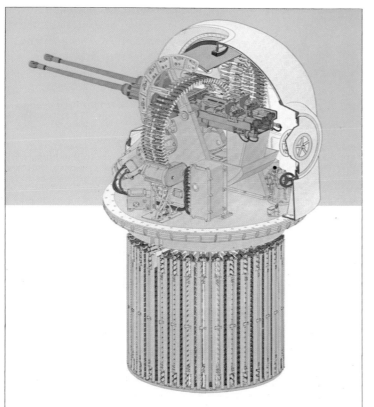

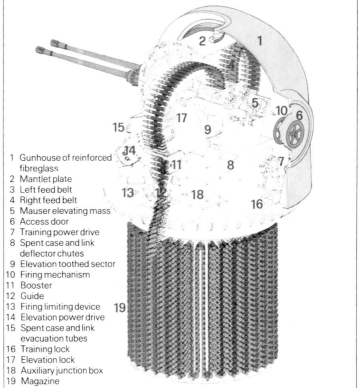

1 Gunhouse of reinforced fibreglass
2 Mantlet plate
3 Left feed belt
4 Right feed belt
5 Mauser elevating mass
6 Access door
7 Training power drive
8 Spent case and link deflector chutes
9 Elevation toothed sector
10 Firing mechanism
11 Booster
12 Guide
13 Firing limiting device
14 Elevation power drive
15 Spent case and link evacuation tubes
16 Training lock
17 Elevation lock
18 Auxiliary junction box
19 Magazine

40-mm L/70 Breda Compact Twin Naval Mount Type 70

The **40-mm L/70 Breda Compact Twin Naval Mount Type 70** is a joint venture by Breda Meccanica Bresciana and Bofors to produce a system intended for point-defence use against aircraft and anti-ship missiles. The mount is fully automatic in operation, and features a high rate of fire with a considerable ready-use ammunition supply to the two guns, which are laid by remote-control high-performance servo-units. The mount is available in two versions, the **Type A** and **Type B**, which differ only in weights and the amount of ammunition carried in the turret's magazine (736 rounds in the Type A and 444 in the Type B). In each variant the magazine itself is divided into two halves, each with hoist serving one barrel. Three types of ammunition are fired: 40-mm AP tracer, 40-mm HE direct action (with impact fuse) and 40-mm HE proximity-fused. Both turrets are in production and service with a number of navies worldwide, especially as secondary armament on missile craft. When the mount is coupled to a Selenia RTN-20X I/J-band fire-control radar with a direct electronic link to the ship's main surveillance radar and fire-control system, the weapon then forms part of the **Dardo** close-in weapon system designed specifically to counter high-speed late-detection attacks by anti-ship missiles. It does this by utilizing the turret's rapid-response characteristics and high rate of fire (together with proximity-fused ammunition) in order to ensure a kill. The Dardo CIWS is widely fitted in frigate-sized and larger vessels of the Italian navy, and has also been exported to several countries who have bought Italian frigates and missile corvettes.

Specification
L/70 Breda Compact
Calibre: 40 mm
Number of barrels: two
Elevation: −13° to +85°
Muzzle velocity: 1000 m (3,281 ft) per second
Effective range: 3500-4000 m (3,830-4,375 yards) depending upon target type
Rate of fire: 600 rounds per minute
Weight: (with ammunition) Type A 7300 kg (16,093 lb), and Type B 6300 kg (13,889 lb)
Number of rounds carried on mount: see main text

The Omani navy missile boat Al Mansur mounts a 40-mm L/70 Breda Compact Twin Naval Mount Type 70 'B' forward, carrying a total of 444 rounds in its magazine below decks. The weapon can be used in both the air defence and surface attack roles, a flexibility important in smaller navies.

Left: The heavier twin 40-mm Breda Type A variant of the L/70 Type 70 mounting is used on larger warships, as it has a more capacious magazine with 736 ready-use rounds below decks and is some 1000 kg (2,200 lb) heavier. More than 20 navies have adopted the Type 70.

Above: The Ecuadorean corvette Esmeralda is typical of the general-purpose vessels in service with many navies. It is armed with Exocet SSMs and an OTO-Melara 76-mm dual-purpose gun in addition to the AA armament of Albatros missiles and the 40-mm L/70 Type 70 twin gun.

20-mm Meroka Close-In Weapon System

Developed by CETME, the **20-mm Meroka CIWS** consists of a turret with two rows each of six 20-mm automatic Oerlikon cannon, a PDS-10 control console which incorporates a digital fire-control computer, a RAN-12/L search and target-designation radar, and an on-mount PVS-2 monopulse Doppler I/J-band tracking radar with low-light thermal-imaging TV camera. The combined rate of fire of the barrels is some 9,000 rounds per minute, although only 720 rounds are actually carried on the mount itself. An additional 240 rounds apiece are carried in each of three externally fitted boxes. The normal mode of action is by radar control, but the camera can be used for manual standby operations via a monitor unit and controls on the below-decks console. Twenty systems have been ordered by the Spanish navy in place of more expensive foreign CIWS such as the Phalanx. The allocation is four on the carrier Principe de Austurias, one for each of the six 'Descubierta' class frigates and one each of the five 'FFG-7' class missiles frigates. The remaining five were introduced on the five 'Baleares' class ASW frigates from 1985 onwards as they underwent their mid-life refits. The Meroka will be fitted on the stern. No export sales are expected.

Specification
Meroka
Calibre: 20 mm
Number of barrels: 12
Elevation: not known
Muzzle velocity: 1200 m (3,937 ft) per second
Effective range: 2000 m (2,185 yards)
Rate of fire: 9,000 rounds per minute
Weight: 4500 kg (9,921 lb)
Number of rounds carried on mount: 1,440

30-mm anti-aircraft guns

The first Soviet 30-mm mount was the **AK-230** 60-calibre system which entered service in 1960 to replace the elderly 25-mm 60-calibre twin anti-aircraft gun on new-build major and minor warship classes. The small enclosed turret is usually known by the nickname Dalek because of its physical appearance. The two 30-mm cannon fitted are fully automatic in operation, and the barrels are water-cooled. The theoretical maximum rate of fire for the guns is 1,050 rounds per minute, but the maximum realistic rate to prevent damage is actually in the region of 200-240 rounds per minute. The guns are usually used in conjunction with a 'Drum Tilt' fire-control radar or a remote optical director. On the smaller ships fitted with the AK-230 an anti-surface role is also assigned to the type, the maximum effective range being 2500 m (2,735 yards). A shell weighing 0.54 kg (1.2 lb) is used. The system has been widely exported to Soviet-supplied states as the gun forms the main armament of the 'Osa' class missile craft.

To counter the threat of missile attack the Soviets developed the 30-mm weapon further to produce a 'Gatling' gun version with six 30-mm barrels inside a larger barrel-like cylinder in a similar shaped mount known by the designation **AK-630**. This is designed to fire at a fast rate as large a number of the 0.54-kg (1.2-lb) shells as possible, with high-density metal penetrators to destroy cruise missile sized targets at relatively close range. Usually

mounted in pairs with a 'Bass Tilt' fire-control radar, the mount is in service on the 'Kiev', 'Kara', 'Udaloy', 'Sovremenny', 'Slava' and 'Kresta II' classes, and has been retrofitted to several older ships. On smaller warships it is usually found as a single mount together with a larger-calibre gun and a fire-control radar. Each mount also has a remote fire-control optical director.

Specification
AK-230
Calibre: 30 mm
Number of barrels: two
Elevation: 0° to +85°
Muzzle velocity: 1000 m (3,281 ft) per second
Effective range: 2500 m (2,735 yards)
Rate of fire: 1,050 rounds per minute

Specification
AK-630
Calibre: 30 mm
Number of barrels: six
Elevation: 0° to +85°
Muzzle velocity: 1000 m (3,281 ft) per second
Effective range: 3000 m (3,280 yards)
Rate of fire: 3,000 rounds per minute

Right: Soviet distribution of CIWS was liberal, with vessels such as the nuclear-powered 'Kirov' class being equipped with up to eight 30-mm Gatling types, the four-stern turrets being shown here. The Soviets also developed a high density penetrator round for the system.

Below: The 30-mm turret for twin automatic cannon is standard fit aboard Soviet light force units and is shown on the bow of a Soviet navy 'Osa I' class missile boat. The turret has also been exported widely to Soviet client states.

57-mm anti-aircraft guns

The oldest of the Soviet navy's **57-mm anti-aircraft guns** is a single-barrel 70-calibre mounting which can still be found on some 'Skory (Mod)' destroyers. This version was followed in the late 1950s by a twin-barrel version which is found on a number of the smaller warship classes such as the 'T-58' class patrol vessels and radar pickets. The final version of the weapon to appear was a quadruple mount with the barrels arranged in two superimposed pairs. All three systems can be controlled locally, the twin and quad guns using either 'Hawk Screech' or 'Muff Cob' fire-control radars to obtain target data for below-decks electronics. The guns fire a 2.8-kg (6.2-lb) shell which has in recent years

been fitted with a proximity fuse to increase its lethality against missile-type targets. The weapons can also be fired in the anti-surface target role, in which the maximum effective range is 8 km (5 miles).

In the early 1960s a new twin 57-mm 80-calibre water-cooled dual-purpose mount was introduced into service. This is fully automatic in operation from the below-decks ammunition handling room to the gun mount itself. Classes fitted with the gun include the 'Moskva', 'Kresta I', 'Kresta II', 'Poti', 'Grisha I/II/III', 'Nanuchka', 'Turya', 'Ropucha', 'Ugra' and 'Berezina'. The fire-control radars used are the 'Muff Cob' or 'Bass Tilt' systems, while the ammunition fired is of the same type as used by the

70-calibre gun.

Specification
57-mm L/70
Calibre: 57 mm
Number of barrels: one, two or four
Elevation: 0° to +90°
Muzzle velocity: 1000 m (3,281 ft) per second
Effective range: 4500 m (4,920 yards)
Rate of fire: 120, 240 or 480 rounds per minute

'Kanin' class units of the Soviet navy had two 57-mm quadruple mountings located forward and were supplied with proximity-fused ammunition.

Specification
57-mm L/80
Calibre: 57 mm
Number of barrels: two
Elevation: 0° to +85°
Muzzle velocity: 1000 m (3,281 ft) per second
Effective range: 6000 m (6,560 yards)
Rate of fire: 240 rounds per minute

The twin 57-mm turret mounted aft on the Soviet 'Grisha III' class corvette was first introduced in the 1960s. Water-cooled, it is a fully automatic weapon with increased maximum range from that of its predecessor.

40-mm L/60 and L/70 Bofors automatic guns

The original **40-mm L/60 Bofors** automatic anti-aircraft gun was introduced into use during the period of World War II, and today is still in service with a number of navies. It may also be fitted to some new-build warships in a reconditioned form as it is no longer in production. Present-day construction is now devoted to the higher performance **40-mm L/70 Bofors gun** variant, which is operational worldwide with more than 30 navies. Three basic types of single barrel mountings for the L/70 are offered, these differing in the amount of automation provided. Gun control can be either local or remote, the latter using either a below-decks fire-control system or an above-decks optical director.

To increase the lethality of the older L/60, two new types of ammunition have been developed by the Swedes, a prefragmented HE (PFHE) round with a proximity fuse and an armour-piercing high-capacity tracer (APHC-T) round. The L/70 has its own family of ammunition which includes PFHE, HCHE, HE-tracer (HE-T) and practice types. The pulse-Doppler radar proximity fuses fitted to the two PFHE round types allows missile targets to be engaged, the L/60 version having an effective detonation distance of between 4.5 and 6.5 m (14.76 and 21.33 ft) and the L/70 round of between 1 and 7 m (3.28 and 22.97 ft) depending upon target size and type. The L/70 addi-

tionally forms part of the Italian Breda 40-mm single- and twin-barrel gun mounts, which are currently used by more than 20 navies.

Specification
L/60 Bofors
Calibre: 40 mm
Number of barrels: one
Elevation: −10° to +80°
Muzzle velocity: 830 m (2,723 ft) per second
Effective range: 3000 m (3,280 yards)
Rate of fire: 120 rounds per minute
Weight: varies, but typically between

1200 and 2500 kg (2,646 and 5,511 lb)
Number of rounds carried on mount: varies according to mount type

Specification
L/70 Bofors
Number of barrels: one
Elevation: −10° to +90°
Muzzle velocity: 1005-1030 m (3,297-3,379 ft) per second according to round type
Effective range: 4000 m (4,375 yards)
Rate of fire: 300 rounds per minute
Weight: (without ammunition) SAK 40L/70-350 2890 kg (6,371 lb), SAK 40L/

The original 40-mm L/60 Bofors was one of the principal air defence weapons of the US Fleet in the Pacific war. It served well into the 1970s and was last mounted on such vessels as the attack transport USS Sandoval, which is seen shadowed by a 'T-143' class minesweeper of the Soviet navy.

70-315 1700 kg (3,748 lb) and SAK 40L/70-520 3790 kg (8,355 lb)
Number of rounds carried on mount: SAK 40L/70-350 96, SAK 40L/70-315 96 and SAK 40L/70-520 144

The Breda/Bofors 40-mm L/70 naval mount with a Breda 144 round automatic feed device allows the number of men required on-mount to be reduced to two, with a third on standby to reload the feed mechanism during lulls in firing.

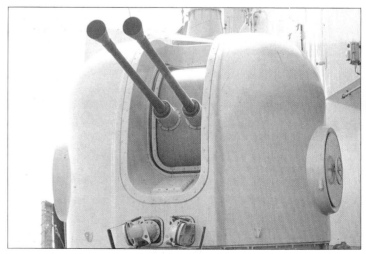

Among the most popular of Bofors mounts are those provided by Breda, the L/70 being used in both single and twin forms. The compact twin turret is currently in service or on order for more than 20 navies worldwide.

30-mm Goalkeeper Close-In Weapon System

The **30-mm Goalkeeper CIWS** naval air-defence system is an autonomous radar-directed short-range weapon designed for fully automatic defence against high-speed missile and aircraft. Built as a joint venture by the American company General Electric and the Dutch company Hollandse Signaalapparaten BV, the Goalkeeper has all its elements integrated on a single mount like the Phalanx system. The Goalkeeper consists of an I-band track-while-scan search-and-acquisition surveillance radar, a dual-frequency I/K-band tracking radar, fire-control electronics and a cannon with high rate of fire, namely the 30-mm seven-barrel GAU-8/A Sea Vulcan version of the aircraft Gatling gun. System operation is completely automatic from target detection, through target destruction and termination of the engagment, to detection of the next target. Missiles flying as low as 5 m (16.4 ft) have been successfully destroyed, and the tracking radar can also be used against high-elevation diving targets. For multiple attacks there is an automatic kill-assessment subsystem to assign target priorities. The AP discarding-sabot round has, instead of the original depleted-uranium penetrator, one made of a high-density tungsten alloy. For softer targets an HE-incendiary round is employed. A total of 1,190 rounds is carried in a linkless-feed/drum-storage system. To replenish this storage/feed arrangement a bulk loading system is used, but in an emergency manual reloading can be performed. The Goalkeeper system has been chosen by the Royal Netherlands navy for its 'Kortenaer', 'Jacob van Heemskerck' and future 'M' class frigates. The Royal Navy has also installed the weapon in its Broadsword class frigates and Type 42 destroyers.

Specification
Goalkeeper
Calibre: 30 mm

Left: Goalkeeper is able to engage multiple targets, the system having demonstrated kills of simulated supersonic anti-ship cruise missiles at ranges of 500 m and 400 m respectively within about one second of switching target.

Number of barrels: seven
Elevation: −25° to +85°
Muzzle velocity: 1021 m (3,350 ft) per second
Effective range: 3000 m (3,280 yards)
Rate of fire: 4,200 rounds per minute
Weight: (with ammunition) 6730 kg (14,837 lb)
Number of rounds carried on mount: 1,190

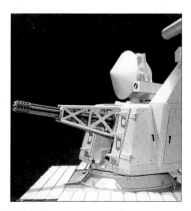

Left: A Goalkeeper CIWS is seen on a test rig during the trials stage. The system is now widely used in the warships of European NATO navies, and has proved its capability against sea-skimming missiles in numerous trials.

Right: The 30-mm Goalkeeper CIWS uses a modified version of the seven-barrel GAU-8/A aircraft Gatling gun, with integrated fire control and search radars on the same mount.

30-mm TCM-30 Twin Naval Gun

Built by a subsidiary of Israel Aircraft Industries, the **30-mm TCM-30 Twin Naval Gun** consists of a pair of 30-mm automatic cannon and their feed systems mounted in a stabilized electrically-actuated turret capable of high angular accelerations. The cannon are 30-mm Oerlikon models, and are carried on a barrel-support system which reduces longer-range shot dispersion to a minimum. The turret's positioning and traverse velocity can be controlled from the ship's fire-control system. Five different types of ammunition can be used in the two 125-round linked-ammunition boxes that are located on the gun cradle. Two reserve magazines provide a further 40 rounds for the system. The TCM-30 is gradually replacing the older single-barrel Bofors 40-mm mounts fitted to the Israeli navy's missile craft after the prototype was tested aboard the 'Aliyah' class *Geoula*. The same gun has also been adapted for land use on a towed carriage and armoured fighting vehicles, as well as being employed in the **Spider II** air-defence artillery system. Under Israeli government regulations it is also being offered for export.

The TCM-30 twin 30-mm naval air defence weapon is now in service with the Israeli navy aboard several of the missile boats of the SAAR 4.5 design. The gun acts as a CIWS and shares this duty with 14 20-mm Phalanx systems bought from the US Navy.

Specification
TCM-30
Calibre: 30 mm
Number of barrels: two
Elevation: −20° to +85°
Muzzle velocity: 1080 m (3,543 ft) per second
Effective range: 3000 m (3,280 yards)
Rate of fire: 1,300 rounds per minute
Weight: (with ammunition) not known
Number of rounds carried on mount: 290

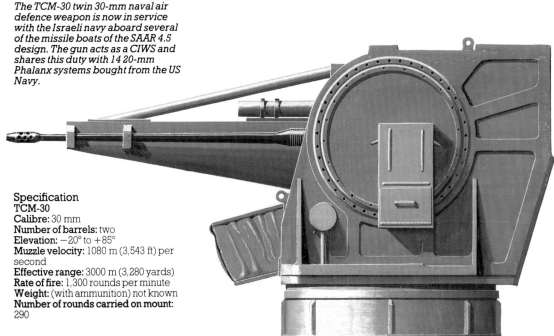

20-mm Naval Gun Type GAM-BO1 and 25-mm Naval Gun Type GBM-AO1

The single-barrel 20-mm GAM-BO1 is a simple unpowered locally-operated mount that uses the Oerlikon-Bührle KAA automatic cannon. It is capable of engaging surface targets out to 2000 m (2,185 yards) and aircraft-sized targets out to 1500 m (1,640 yards). A night sight can be fitted if required. Several navies use this weapon, including the Spanish navy's 'Lazarga' and 'Barcelo' class fast attack missile craft. The

Although a relatively simple weapon, the 20-mm Oerlikon Type GAM-BO1 has been chosen by a number of navies for its light weight and robustness. The Royal Navy uses it in conjunction with twin 30-mm mounts to boost close-range AA defences.

Below: Similar to the 20-mm weapon, the 25-mm GBM-AO1 fires a heavier shell. Its low weight makes it simple to instal aboard vessels down to the smallest of fast patrol craft, and no electrical power is required for operation.

Bottom: The widely-used 20-mm Oerlikon mounting of the World War II manual type is still in production and service worldwide. A more modern cannon and ring sighting system has been fitted, as on this gun in service with the Angolan navy aboard an ex-Portuguese 'Bellatrix' class patrol vessel.

Royal Navy's 'Invincible' class carriers; 'County', 'Type 42' and 'Type 82' destroyers; and 'Type 22 Batch 1/2' frigates each have two; and non-converted 'Leander Batch 3' class frigates (one apiece). The adoption of the gun by the Royal Navy was as a result of its experiences during the Falklands war.

For increased firepower there is the larger-calibre 25-mm GBM-AO1, which is similar in characteristics to the GAM-BO1 system but mounts the 25-mm KBA-C02 cannon with a double belt feed. The engagement ranges are the same as those of the 20-mm cannon but the shell is heavier. Several unidentified navies have adopted this weapon.

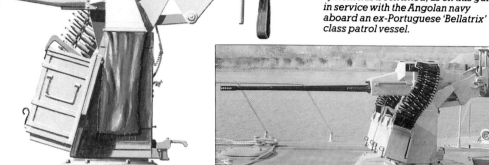

Specification
GAM-BO1
Calibre: 20 mm
Number of barrels: one
Elevation: −15° to +60°
Muzzle velocity: 1050 m (3,444 ft) per second
Effective range: see text
Rate of fire: 600 rounds per minute
Weight: (with ammunition) 500 kg (1,102 lb)
Number of rounds on mount: 200

Specification
GBM-AO1
Calibre: 25-mm
Number of barrels: one
Elevation: −15° to +50°
Muzzle velocity: 1100 m (3,609 ft) per second
Effective range: see text
Rate of fire: 570 rounds per minute
Weight: (with ammunition) 600 kg (1,323 lb)
Number of rounds on mount: 200

30-mm Twin Anti-Aircraft Gun Type GCM-A

The Oerlikon-Bührle 30-mm Type GCM-A is produced in three different versions: the GCM-AO3-1 with an enclosed gunner's position, stabilized control and optional remote control from a fire-control system; the GCM-AO3-2 which is essentially the same as the GCM-AO3-1 but with an open gunner's position; and the GCM-AO3-3 without a gunner's position and thus fitted only for remote control. The 30-mm KCB cannon used in the GCM-AO3 is also used in the American twin 30-mm EMERLEC-30 and the British Laurence Scott (Defence Systems)

As is increasingly common, the GCM-A has been designed for fitment to small surface vessels. The model AO3-2, with an open gunner's station, weighs only 2560 kg (5,644 lb) complete, and can be operated both locally and with remote control.

single-barrel LS30B systems. As a direct result of the lack of close-range air-defence guns during the Falklands war, to augment secondary armament the Royal Navy purchased a number of licence-built GCM-AO3-2 mounts from the British company BMARC for fitting to its sole 'Type 82' destroyer and the 12 'Type 42' destroyers remaining after HMS *Sheffield* and *Coventry* had been sunk. Unfortunately in the case of the 'Type 42s' the ships' boats have had to be removed in order to incorporate the two mountings required and prevent top-heaviness. A number of other navies are in the process of evaluating the mounts and are expected to place orders.

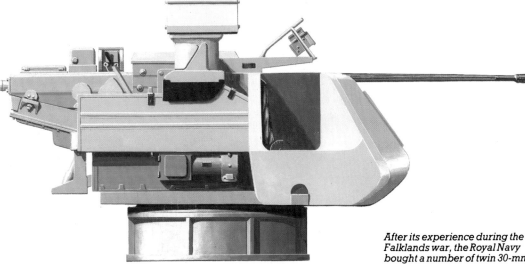

Specification
Type GCM-A
Calibre: 30 mm
Number of barrels: two
Elevation: −10° to +75°
Muzzle velocity: 1080 m (3,543 ft) per second
Effective range: 3000 m (3,280 yards)
Rate of fire: 1,300 rounds per minute

Weight: (with ammunition) GCM-AO3-1 2910 kg (6,415 lb), GCM-AO3-2 2515 kg (5,545 lb) and GCM-AO3-3 2560 kg (5,644 lb)

Number of rounds carried on mount: GCM-AO3-1/2 500, and GCM-AO3-3 640

After its experience during the Falklands war, the Royal Navy bought a number of twin 30-mm GCM-A mounts fitted with Ferranti gyroscopic lead angle computing sights from BMARC Ltd to supplement its close-range anti-aircraft armament.

SWITZERLAND
35-mm Twin Anti-Aircraft Gun Type GDM-A

Similar in concept and design to the highly successful Oerlikon twin 35-mm Type GDF land-based anti-aircraft guns, the naval **35-mm Type GDM-A** is intended primarily for use against air attacks, but if required can also be used to engage surface targets at sea and on land. The stabilized mount is an all-weather system with its electronic control units located below decks. The cannon fitted are of the KDC model, which are fully automatic in operation. The turret has three possible modes of use: fully automatic with control exercised from either a below-decks fire-control system or an upper-deck optical aiming unit fitted with an auxiliary computer; local operator control with the gunner using a joystick and gyro-stabilized gunsight; and emergency manual control using two hand wheels and the gunsight when power to the mount is cut. Each of the cannon has 56 ready-use rounds, with another 224 rounds in total reserve. At least five countries use this turret on their

warships, namely Ecuador, Greece, Iran, Libya and Turkey.

Specification
Type GDM-A
Calibre: 35 mm
Number of barrels: two
Elevation: −15° to +85°
Muzzle velocity: 1175 m (3,855 ft) per second
Effective range: 3500 m (3,830 yards)
Rate of fire: 1,100 rounds per minute
Weight: (with ammunition) 6520 kg (14,374 lb)
Number of rounds on mount: 336

Below: Produced as a private venture by OTO-Melara, the twin 35-mm OE/OTO mount uses the Oerlikon KDA 35-mm gun, which is similar to the KDC gun employed in the Swiss company's Type GDM-A system. At present only the Libyan navy has bought the mount for its 'Assad' class missile corvettes.

Above: The original Oerlikons were largely used as naval weapons, but the 35-mm KDC cannon used in the GDM-A is derived from a towed weapon developed in the late 1950s. The Italian model, known to Oerlikon as the GDM-C, uses a slightly heavier variant.

25-mm Seaguard Close-in Weapon System

The **25-mm Seaguard CIWS** naval air-defence system is an international project between countries from Italy, Switzerland and the United Kingdom. It consists of an above-decks tracker module, an independent search radar, a GMB-B1Z Sea Zenith mount with four KBB-R04/404 cannon, and a below-decks ammunition feed and operator's console with associated electronics. The sensor unit is fitted with a K-band radar, a forward-looking infra-red (FLIR) system and a laser sensor for the acquisition of missile-sized targets. Each of the cannon is independently fed from the below-decks ready-use supply, where sufficient rounds are available to engage 18-20 different targets without reloading. Typical engagement ranges are from 1500 m

(1,640 yards) down to 100 m (109 yards) against missiles and out to a maximum of 3500 m (3,830 yards) against aircraft. Ammunition types fired include an HE-incendiary round and a new Anti-Missile Discarding-Sabot (AMDS) round. If required the mount can be elevated to +127° to cover steep-diving targets. Three Seaguard CIWS systems were fitted to each of the four 'MEKO 200' frigates built for the Turkish navy.

Below: The first navy to adopt the 25-mm Seaguard CIWS was that of Turkey, which ordered the system for installation in four new frigates. Enough ammunition is provided on mount to engage 14 targets without reloading.

Specification
Seaguard
Calibre: 25 mm
Number of barrels: four
Elevation: −20° to +127°
Muzzle velocity: 1355 m (4,446 ft) per second
Effective range: 100-3500 m (109-3,830 yards)

Rate of fire: 3,400 rounds per minute
Weight: (with ammunition) 5700 kg (12,566 lb)
Number of rounds carried on mount: 1,660

The obvious difference between Seaguard and most other close-in weapon systems is the provision of four barrels independently fed with ammunition, instead of a single rotary cannon. This allows for redundancy in the feed system.

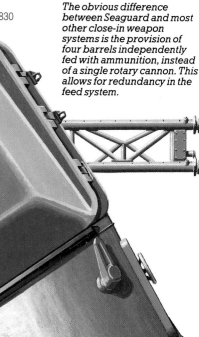

20-mm Mk 15/16 Phalanx Close-In Weapon System

The General Dynamics Corporation **20-mm Phalanx Mk 15/16 CIWS** is a total weapons system which automatically carries out search and detection, target threat evaluation, tracking and firing against high-performance anti-ship missiles and aircraft as a 'last-ditch' defence. The Phalanx is built around the General Electric 20-mm M61A1 six-barrel 'Gatling' gun, and is hydraulically powered. Production started in late 1977, the first operational units being installed aboard the aircraft-carriers USS *Enterprise* and *America* during 1980. The US Navy subsequently installed the system in more than 250 ships, with frigates having only a single system and the 'Iowa' class battleships four. In order to enhance the Phalanx's capabilities a product-improvement programme is under way to increase the search-area and target-detection performance, and to provide for greater flexibility. By the end of 1984 220 Phalanxes had been installed aboard 125 US Navy ships, while a further 52 had been supplied to foreign buyers. Amongst the navies known to have Phalanx either in service or on order are those of Australia, Canada, Israel, Japan, Saudi Arabia and the UK. In the case of the last the systems were apparently ordered before the Falklands war for the 'Invincible' class carriers, with the first delivery being

accelerated to equip HMS *Illustrious*. At present the *Invincible* and *Illustrious* carry two, while the newly completed *Ark Royal* has three. In live firing trials undertaken by the US Navy and the Royal Navy the Phalanx has proved capable of detecting and destroying MM.38 Exocet anti-ship missiles that may threaten Royal Navy ships in any future conflict in the South Atlantic.

Specification
Phalanx Mk 15/16
Calibre: 20 mm
Number of barrels: six
Elevation: −25° to +80°
Muzzle velocity: 1097 m (3,600 ft) per second
Effective range: 500-1500 m (545-1,640 yards)
Rate of fire: 3,000 rounds per minute
Weight: (with ammunition) 6092 kg (13,430 lb)
Number of rounds on mount: 1,000 (latest Block 1 version is believed to have 1,400-1,600)

The General Dynamics Phalanx uses a 20-mm six-barrel Gatling gun with magazine and integrated fire control radars on the same mount to produce a single modular weapon system package. It is fully automatic in operation, but manual override is possible.

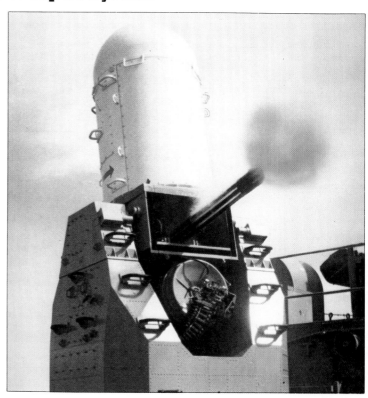

EMERLEC-30 Twin 30-mm Mounting

The operator's cabin of the EMERLEC is environmentally controlled, with windscreen demisting and the option of local or remote control. The sighting station visible within the cabin is fitted with a reflex optical lens and a gyro-stabilizer together with the usual gun controls, and can be fitted with night sights and variable fire rate selection.

Access to the operator's cabin is between the cannon cradle assembly.

The 30-mm Oerlikon automatic cannon fitted to the EMERLEC are of the KCB type, and are similar to those fitted to Oerlikon's own systems.

The KCB cannon can fire a range of ammunition, including the usual HE, incendiary and tracer rounds. It is also capable of firing a shell rejoicing under the title of APICT – Armour Piercing Incendiary Shell – with hardcore and tracer.

The mount is capable of a complete 360° turn, clockwise or anti-clockwise, with elevation ranging between −18° and +84°. Traverse rate is 80° per second, as is elevation rate.

The weapon mount and training gear are all fitted into the mount above deck. Below deck the ammunition storage is arranged around a 2.75-mm wide work area which is fitted with most of the system's electronics.

The training drive is located in a sponson above deck level, with access through sponson hatches. Elevating drives are in the main structure of the mount, inboard of the cannon cradle assemblies.

Access to the ammunition store is through below-deck panels. Reloading can be carried out by a single man, although a two-man loading team is recommended for maximum efficiency.

The electronics below decks comprise batteries, de-icing relays, servo systems, gun control relays and fire rate selection systems, as well as connections to the outside for remote or director control.

The EMERLEC-30 has 1,970 rounds of ready ammunition in the below-decks magazine, with 985 rounds per gun. All rounds of ready ammo can be fired even if ship's power is lost, and if the batteries are damaged there are hand crank mechanisms for fully-manual operation.

Designed and built by the Emerson Electric Company, the **EMERLEC-30 Twin 30-mm Mounting** was originally developed as the **EX-74 Mod O** for the US Navy to use aboard coastal patrol and interdiction craft. Based on two Oerlikon KCB cannon it has an environmentally controlled cabin for the gunner, day and/or night sights, and an integral below-decks magazine. The mount can also be operated by remote control using a standard shipboard fire-control system. In emergency an on-mount battery can provide all the power required to operate the guns and fire the full complement of ready-use ammunition carried. Manual gun controls are also fitted to provide further back-up if the battery fails. The mount has been in series production since 1976 and is known to be in service with the navies of Colombia, Ecuador, Ethiopia, Greece, Malaysia, Nigeria, the Philippines, South Korea and Taiwan. In most cases the fit has

been to missile attack craft or large patrol boats. The mounting is also capable of being used in the surface-to-surface role.

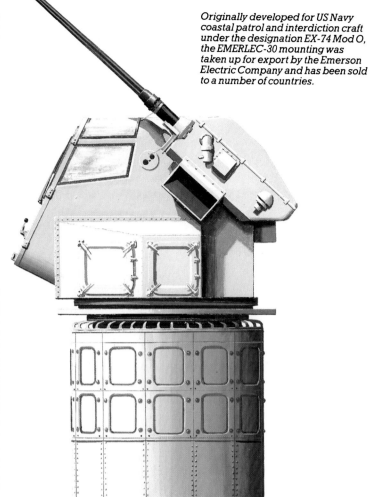

Originally developed for US Navy coastal patrol and interdiction craft under the designation EX-74 Mod O, the EMERLEC-30 mounting was taken up for export by the Emerson Electric Company and has been sold to a number of countries.

Specification
EMERLEC-30
Calibre: 30 m
Number of barrels: two
Elevation: −15° to +80°
Muzzle velocity: 1080 m (3,543 ft) per second
Effective range: 3000 m (3,280 yards)
Rate of fire: 1,200 rounds per minute
Weight: (without ammunition) 1905 kg (4,200 lb)
Number of rounds on mount: 1,970

Below: Designed for anti-missile, anti-aircraft and surface fire, the EMERLEC-30 comprises two Oerlikon 30-mm cannon with associated sights, below-decks ready-use magazine and an enclosed operator's cabin.

 UK
30-mm LS30R (Rarden) Naval Gun Mounting

The British firm Laurence Scott (Defence Systems) has developed a lightweight naval mounting for the RARDE-designed 30-mm Rarden automatic cannon. The gun is both power-driven and line-of-sight stabilized for use on small naval vessels as well as on large frigate or destroyer designs. An extensive series of tests were carried out by the Royal Navy both at sea (aboard the converted trials frigate HMS *Londonderry*) and on land (at the Fraser Gunnery Range at Portsmouth) to confirm the high accuracy of the weapon, which hit a 2-m² (21.5-sq ft) target some 80 per cent of the firing time at ranges between 1000 and 1300 m (1,095 and 1,420 yards) in good to poor visibility. If required the mount can be fitted with a predictor, image intensifier, IR camera and/or low-light TV camera for remote firing. The ammunition types used include HE, APSE and APDS rounds. The **LS30R** has been adopted for use by the Royal Navy, and will be used to replace the older 20-mm Oerlikons and 40-mm Bofors from 1986 onwards. The first fit will be to the Offshore Patrol Vessels. The basic mounting can also be used with other types of 30-mm cannon such as the Oerlikon KCB and the Mauser Model F, in which case the designations become respectively **LS30B** and **LS30F**.

Specification
LS30R
Calibre: 30 mm
Number of barrels: one
Elevation: −20° to +70°
Muzzle velocity: 1080-1200 m (3,543-3,937 ft) per second depending upon round type
Effective range: 4000 m (4,375 yards)
Rate of fire: 90 rounds per minute
Weight: (with ammunition) 800 kg (1,764 lb)
Number of rounds on mount: 6-22

The LS30R 30-mm (Rarden) naval gun mount has been chosen by the Royal Navy to replace all its 20-mm and 40-mm gun mounts, which have their origins in World War II. Its accuracy is sufficient to allow single shots at a target.

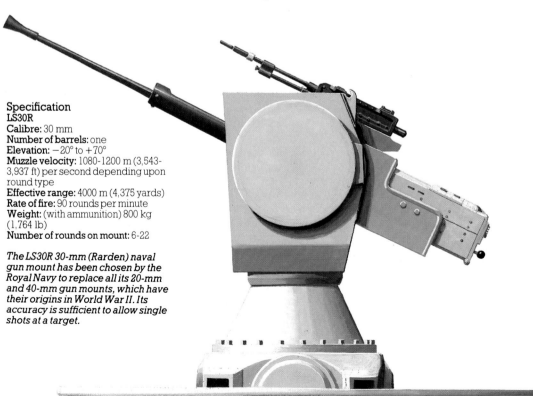

Naval Artillery

Despite the advent of long-range missiles and the eclipse of the big-gun battleship by the aircraft carrier, naval artillery still has a role to play, especially in providing fire-support for ground troops ashore. Indeed, the US Navy's 'Iowa' class World War II-vintage battlewagons were still in commission until the 1990s.

During World War II, although naval gunnery still played a major part in battles at sea, it was the carrierborne aircraft that became the major offensive weapon – particularly in the Pacific, where aircraft carriers dominated the action from first to last. Even then, naval gunfire support proved indispensable to the success of amphibious landing operations, from Sicily and Normandy to Okinawa.

Conflicts such as the 1982 Falklands War underlined the ongoing importance of the naval gun, and persuaded the British Ministry of Defence – which had planned to eliminate such weapons from future generations of warships in favour of missiles – that its retention was essential. The Americans and Russians, by way of contrast, not only retained their naval guns, but continued to update them. This lead was followed by the navies of both NATO and the Warsaw Pact, and some nations, notably France and Italy, found a lucrative market in manufacturing naval guns for export. The Italian 76-mm (3-in) OTO-Melara Compact, for example, was adopted by some 40 navies worldwide, and has proved its worth in action.

At the other end of the scale

The impressive 406-mm (16-in) main guns of a US Navy 'Iowa' class battleship in action. Big guns like these were used as recently as the 1980s to support US Marine Corps forces in Beirut.

are the 406-mm (16-in) guns of the 'Iowa' class battleships, which were reactivated for duty in the Korean and Vietnam wars. In the former conflict, the four battleships of this class proved invaluable for shore bombardment; again and again they were able to give rapid and precise fire support to ground troops, their biggest advantage

being their ability to loiter and resume bombardment if the enemy showed signs of further activity. This still holds good today; no matter what weight of ordnance can be delivered by aircraft they always have to return to base after a short interval, whereas a warship can remain in the area and available to provide more gunfire.

One of the American battleships, the USS *Missouri,* was also operational in the Gulf War, although her main function was as a cruise missile launcher. While the cruise missile is a long-range extension of the naval gun, it is not a replacement for it: naval artillery will still have a part to play in future conflicts.

100-mm Model 68-II gun

The 100-mm (3.9-in) **Model 1968-II** 55-calibre weapon is the latest version of a series of French 100-mm (3.94-in) guns which have the designations **Models 1953, 1964** and **1968-I**. Compared with these the Model 68-II is lighter and fully automatic, with the option of autonomous operation with a turret crew of only two. The barrel has a longer life than those of the previous guns because it is air-purged and water-cooled after each round has been fired. The gun can engage both air and surface targets, the former including sea-skimming anti-ship missiles. The round types fired include both a multi-purpose shell with either a time or proximity fuse, and a prefragmented shell with a proximity fuse. Apart from the

French navy, the Model 1968-II or its earlier variants serve with the navies of Belgium, Portugal, Argentina and Greece.

A 100-mm **Creusot-Loire Compact** variant (entirely automatic and possessing the same performance characteristics) has also been developed and sold to Saudi Arabia, Malaysia and the People's Republic of China.

Specification
Model 1968-II
Calibre: 100 mm (3.94 in)
Weight: 22 tons
No. of barrels: one
Elevation: −15° to +80°
Muzzle velocity: 870 m (2,854 ft) per second

Projectile weight: 13.5 kg (29.8 lb)
Total round weight: 23.6 kg (52 lb)
Maximum rate of fire: 60 rpm
Maximum effective ranges: surface fire 15 km (9.3 miles), and anti-aircraft fire 8 km (5 miles)

Above: Admiral Charner, *a frigate of the 'Commandant Rivière' class, is fitted with the standard 100-mm gun turret fore and aft, although one of the aft turrets has been replaced by Exocet launchers.*

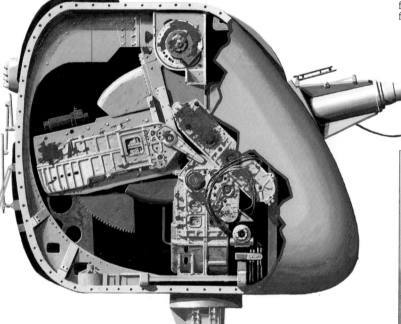

Derived from the standard 100-mm weapon used by the French navy, the 100-mm Compact has been developed by Creusot-Loire and offered to several countries. Entirely automatic, it has a similar performance to the Model 1968-II, but an all-up weight of some 17 tons allows for installation on relatively small vessels. A feature of all the French turrets is the ability to replenish the magazine while firing is in progress.

Above: The Mediterranean-based aviso (frigate) Quartier Maitre Anquetil *of the 'A69' class is equipped with a single 100-mm dual-purpose gun in the Model 1968-II mounting. This version of the turret is a lightened and completely automatic derivation of the Models 1953, 1964 and 1968-I.*

Below: Second Maitre Le Bihan, based in the Channel, displays her bow-mounted 100-mm main armament. The gun has a rate of fire of 60 rounds per minute (which can be sustained) and is designed to engage both surface and aerial targets. Sea-skimming missiles can also be engaged.

5-in Gun Mounting Mk 42

The dual-purpose radar-controlled single **5-in Gun Mounting Mk 42** was adopted in the late 1950s and early 1960s as the successor to the semi-automatic twin 127-mm (5-in) 38-calibre Mk 32 and single 127-mm 54-calibre Mk 39 mountings of World War II and the immediate post-war years respectively. The Mk 42 is capable of a much higher rate of fire and is fitted with an automatic ammunition feed system with two 20-round ready-use drums. Driven by electro-hydraulic power units, the Mk 42 can be operated in local or automatic control. Crew for the **Mk 42 Mod 7/8** is 14, of whom four are actually on the mount. Over 150 guns of this type are at sea with the US Navy and the navies of Australia, Japan, Spain and West Germany. All bar a few of the US guns have been upgraded to the **Mk 42 Mod 10** standard by kit additions, this bringing the mount up to the same equipment fit as the lighter **Mk 42 Mod 9** variant which was constructed for the 'Knox' class frigates. This has solid-state electronics, a 10 per cent reduction in power requirements and a crew of only two on the mount, reducing the overall total to 12. The 127-mm gun barrel fitted to the Mk 42 mounts is designated the Mk 18. A semi-active laser-guided projectile is in the procurement stage for these and the later Mk 45 mountings. The round is 1.548 m (5.08 ft) long, weighs 47.4 kg (104.5 lb), and is similar in concept to the US Army's Copper-

Above: The radar guided 5-in Gun Mounting Mk 42 is in widespread use, over 150 units of various models being at sea with the US Navy and the navies of four Allied countries. The gun crew required to operate the system (14, with four in the turret itself) is almost half that of preceding twin-gun turrets.

Right: The single 5-in (127-mm) Mk 42 gun aboard a 'Forrest Sherman' class guided missile destroyer is engulfed by heavy seas. It should be remembered that naval guns have to function in all conditions.

head projectile for its 155-mm (6.1-in) howitzers.

Specification
Mounting Mk 42
Calibre: 127 mm (5 in)
No. of barrels: one
Weights: Mod 7/8 65.8 tons, Mod 9 57.65 tons and Mod 10 63.9 tons
Elevation: −5° to +80°
Muzzle velocity: 810 m (2,657 ft) per second
Projectile weight: 31.8 kg (70 lb)
Maximum rate of fire: 20 rpm
Maximum effective ranges: surface fire 23.8 km (14.8 miles), and anti-aircraft fire 14.8 km (9.2 miles)

The helicopter-carrying destroyer Shirane is armed with two single 5-in (127-mm) Mk 42 guns mountings. Altogether 13 vessels of the Japanese Maritime Self-Defence Force carry the Mk 42.

5-in Gun Mounting Mk 45

The lightweight radar-controlled single **5-in Gun Mounting Mk 45** utilizes a Mk 19 gun barrel and represents what is essentially a quantum leap for US naval medium gun technology. It was designed for fitting to new-build warships and is fully automatic in operation, with only six men required in the fixed-ammunition handling room to reload the single 20-round ready-use drum. The mount embodies all the improvements to 127-mm (5-in) gun mounts that have been developed over the last 50 years or so since the 127-mm 38 calibre gun was first introduced. In the Mk 45 Md 1 version, produced in the 1980s the below decks reloading arrangements have been modified to allow remote and rapid round selection between several

types of ammunition carried on the drum. The gun has already seen extensive combat use in the shore bombardment role during the US Navy's involvement in Lebanon, and has proved to be exceptionally reliable and easily maintained. To date no other country has bought the weapon for its ships, although it is still in mass production for the US Navy as the main gun armament for the AEGIS-equipped 'Ticonderoga' class missile cruisers and the 'Arleigh Burke' class missile destroyers amongst others.

Specification
Mounting Mk 45
Calibre: 127 mm (5 in)
No. of barrels: one
Weight: 21.34 tons
Elevation: −5° to +65°
Projectile weight: 31.8 kg (70 lb)
Maximum rate of fire: 20 rpm
Maximum effective ranges: surface fire 23.8 km (14.8 miles), and anti-aircraft fire 14.8 km (9.2 miles)

Right: Built by the Northern Ordnance division of the FMC corporation, the single 5-in/54-calibre Gun Mounting Mk 45 is the most advanced of the turrets currently in service with the US Navy.

Below: One of the most important vessels to be commissioned in the last decade, USS Ticonderoga is equipped to command and control the air defences of a fleet. She is also equipped for surface action, with two Mk 45 mounts.

Above: The lean form of the 'California' class cruiser USS South Carolina cuts through the water. In common with all of the larger fighting ships of the US Navy built in the last 10 years, the 'Californias' are armed with Mk 45s, which may soon be capable of firing laser guided projectiles.

Above: USS Texas of the 'Virginia' class is amongst the most potent cruisers afloat. With weaponry that includes Tomahawk, Harpoon, ASROC and Standard missiles, together with gun systems including Phalanx CIWS and two Mk 45 5-in (127-mm), the class has anti-air, anti-surface, and anti-submarine capability in no small measure.

16-in Gun Turret Mk 7

Following the reactivation of the 'Iowa' class battleships the US Navy reintroduced to active service the largest-calibre naval guns in the world today. With nine radar directed **16-in Mk 7 Mod 0** guns in three 1,708-ton triple turrets, the 'Iowas' require a crew of 77 per mount alone plus an additional 30-36 men in the magazines. The ammunition fired is either High-Capacity High Explosive (HCHE) or Armour-Piercing (AP), the latter being capable of penetrating up to 9 m (29.5 ft) of reinforced concrete or 559 mm (22 in) of armour plate. Each battleship has a magazine load of 1,220 projectiles with a larger number of 49.9-kg (110-lb) full-

charge and 24-kg (52.8-lb) reduced-charge propellant bags. The length of each gun is 50 calibres, and the weight 108479 kg (239,156 lb) without its breech block. The guns can also be loaded, elevated and fired individually.

Since reactivation the USS *New Jersey* has used her guns in support of the Lebanese army and US Marines in and around Beirut, Lebanon, whilst during her previous Vietnam War activation the 406-mm gun proved one of the most accurate and deadly bombardment weapons of the whole war, hitting targets in direct support of ground troops and others which were

inland and heavily defended with respect to air attack. During the late 1950s a tactical nuclear round, the 15-kiloton yield Mk 23 'Katie', was developed for service and, although a number entered the active nuclear stockpile, it is thought that none were taken to sea. The 'Iowa's were equipped to carry 10 of these rounds in their magazines.

Specification
Turret Mk 7
Calibre: 406 mm (16 in)
No. of barrels: three
Weight: 1,708 tons
Elevation: −5° to +45°

Muzzle velocity: HCHE 762 m (2,500 ft) per second, and AP 579 m (1,900 ft) per second
Projectile weights: HCHE 862 kg (1,900 lb), and AP 1225 kg (2,700 lb)
Maximum rate of fire: 6 rpm
Maximum effective ranges: HCHE 38 km (23.6 miles), and AP 36.7 km (22.8 miles)

The need for powerful shore bombardment saw the re-activation of the class in both the Korean and Vietnam wars. New Jersey in 1968 was seen primarily as a gun platform, her 16-in (406-mm) guns being the only weapons manned.

Above: The most heavily-armoured US warships ever built, the 'Iowa' class was designed to withstand combat with the Japanese superbattleships Yamato *and* Musashi. *The main armament was also the most powerful available, in triple Mk 7 turrets.*

Below: The most recent activation has seen the 'Iowas' comprehensively refitted, and serving at the centre of surface action groups. The enormous main turrets are without parallel in today's navies, each barrel alone weighing over 100 tons.

Soviet naval rocket-launcher systems

For shore bombardment and defence suppression missions the Soviet navy has fitted some of its amphibious warfare vessels with modified versions of standard Soviet army multiple rocket-launcher systems. The oldest type used is an 18-tube 140-mm (5.51-in) launcher which is fitted amidships with blast shields in pairs on the 'Polnochny A/B/C' LSM classes. The rocket used is the spin-stabilized MF-14-0F, which weighs 39.6 kg (87.3 lb) and has an 18.8-kg (41.4-lb) HE-fragmentation warhead. The maximum range of the weapon is around 10 km (6.2 miles). It is believed that a smoke round can also be fired to screen an assault landing. The weapon has been exported aboard 'Polnochnys' to the navies of Algeria, Angola, Cuba, Egypt, Ethiopia, India, Iraq, Libya, Poland, Somalia, South Yemen, Syria and Vietnam.

In the late 1970s the Soviets introduced a new rocket-launcher aboard the 'Ivan Rogov' class LPD and the 'Alligator IV' class LST. Based on the 122-mm (4.8-in) BM-21, the naval system comprises a pedestal mount with two clusters of 20 loaded rocket tubes. Once fired, the empty tubes are discarded and the mount is automatically reloaded with two new pods from a below-deck magazine. Several of the East German's 'Frosch' class LSTs are also configured for this system. The standard rocket weighs some 77 kg (169.75 lb) and has a 19.4-kg (42.8-lb) HE-fragmentation warhead. Smoke and chemical rounds are available as options. The maximum range of the system is in the region of 20 km (12.4 miles), which allows the vessel to stand-off a fair distance to avoid return fire. In both cases the systems used can be fired individually, in multiples or complete salvoes.

Specification
122-mm launcher
Calibre: 122 mm (4.8 in)
No. of launcher tubes: 40 (two 20-round pods)
Weight of rocket: 77 kg (169.8 lb)
Types of rockets: HE, smoke, chemical
Reload time: 2-3 minutes
Maximum range: 20 km (12.4 miles)

Specification
140-mm launcher
Calibre: 140 mm (5.51 in)
No. of launcher tubes: 18
Weight of rocket: 39.6 kg (87.3 lb)
Types of rockets: HE, smoke
Reload time: 10 minutes
Maximum range: 10 km (6.2 miles)

Given previous Soviet practice in adapting naval systems for land use or vice versa, it should not be surprising to learn that the famous 'Katyusha' multiple rocket-launcher should appear on Soviet assault ships. On the Ivan Rogov, the rockets are pedestal-mounted high in front of the bridge.

76-mm guns

In the early 1960s the Soviet navy introduced into service on the 'Kynda' class missile cruisers a twin 76-mm 60-calibre rapid-firing dual-purpose gun mount which rapidly became the standard fit for a number of warship and auxiliary vessel classes. Now found on the 'Kiev' class aircraft-carriers, the 'Kara' and 'Kyunda' class missile cruisers, the 'Kashin' and 'Kildin' class destroyers, the 'Krivak I', 'Mirka' and 'Petya' class frigates and the 'Ivan Rogov' class amphibious warfare ships, the mount is usually associated with either an 'Owl Screech' or 'Hawk Screech' I-band fire-control radar. The system has also been exported to a number of Soviet client states on export version 'Kashin' class destroyers and 'Petya' and 'Koni' class frigates.

For smaller surface combatants such as the 'Matka' class missile craft and the 'Tarantul', 'Nanuchka III' and 'Pauk' class corvettes, the Soviets introduced in the 1970s a fully automatic single 76-mm 60-calibre dual-purpose gun which also had the option of local

The 76-mm Dual Purpose gun fitted to the rear of the superstructure of the Soviet carrier 'Kiev' is seen in the anti-aircraft position in this picture taken in the Mediterranean by a Royal Air Force Nimrod maritime patrol aircraft.

on-mount control by a gun crew if required. Fire-control for aerial targets is by a 'Bass Tilt' H-band radar, whilst surface targets need the use of a local sighting system in conjunction with the ship's search radar.

Specification
76-mm L/60
Calibre: 76 mm (3 in)
No. of barrels: two
Elevation: 0° to +80°
Muzzle velocity: 900 m (2,953 ft) per second
Projectile weight: 16 kg (35.3 lb)
Maximum rate of fire: 90 rpm
Maximum effective ranges: surface fire 8 km (5 miles), and anti-aircraft fire 6 km (3.7 miles)

Specification
76-mm L/60
Calibre: 76 mm (3 in)
No. of barrels: one
Elevation: −5° to +85°
Muzzle velocity: 900 m (2,953 ft) per second
Projectile weight: 16 kg (35.3 lb)
Maximum rate of fire: 120 rpm
Maximum effective ranges: surface fire 10 km (6.2 miles), and anti-aircraft fire 7 km (4.3 miles)

First appearing on 'Kynda' class cruisers in the early 1960s, the twin 76-mm DP gun also appeared on the contemporary 'Kashin' class destroyers. Classes since carrying it include 'Kiev', 'Kara' and 'Krivak'.

100-mm and 130-mm guns

In the early 1970s the 'Krivak II' class missile frigates were seen to be armed with two new-pattern single 70-calibre 100-mm dual-purpose gun mounts aft. The barrel is water-cooled and the mounting is assessed by NATO as being fully automatic in operation, with fire-control by either a 'Kite Screech' radar or an off-mount optronic sighting system. The new gun was subsequently seen to be adopted for the 'Udaloy' class ASW destroyers, the 'Krivak III' class missile frigates and the lead ship of the nuclear-powered battle-cruisers, the *Kirov* herself.

The 100-mm (3.9-in) gun was followed in the mid-1970s by a brand new gun design mounted initially on the 'Sovremenny' destroyer class, and found to be a 70-calibre twin 130-mm dual-purpose gun mount. The barrels are also water-cooled to prolong life. The fitting of the barrels close together would seem to indicate that they share a common cradle system. The guns have a greater maximum range than the older 152-mm (6-in) Soviet guns (28 km/17.4 miles, in comparison with 27 km/16.8 miles), and were fitted as the main armament for the larger

Soviet surface combatants such as the 'Slava' class missile cruisers and the second nuclear-powered battle-cruiser, the *Frunze*. Fire-control is similar to that of the smaller 100-mm gun.

Specification
100-mm L/70
Calibre: 100 mm (3.94 in)
No. of barrels: one
Elevation: −5° to +80°
Muzzle velocity: 900 m (2,953 ft) per second
Maximum rate of fire: 80 rpm
Maximum effective ranges: surface fire 15 km (9.3 miles), and anti-aircraft fire 8 km (5 miles)

Specification
130-mm L/70
Calibre: 130 mm (5.12 in)
No. of barrels: two
Elevation: −5° to +80°
Muzzle velocity: 950 m (3,117 ft) per second
Maximum rate of fire: 130 rpm
Maximum effective ranges: surface fire 18 km (11.2 miles), and anti-aircraft fire 10 km (6.2 miles)

Above: Unlike earlier Soviet 100-mm guns the weapon that appeared on later versions of the 'Krivak' class frigate was fully automatic. The only other vessel to be thus equipped were the battle cruiser Kirov and the large ASW destroyer Udaloy.

Below: The powerful surface warfare armament of the 'Sovremenny' class destroyers is enhanced by the fitting of two twin 130-mm (5.12-in) automatic gun turrets. Also fitted to 'Slava' class cruisers, the weapon outranges the old 152-mm (6-in) gun aboard the 'Sverdlovs'.

152-mm triple gun mounting

The Soviet Navy's 50-calibre 152-mm **triple mounting** featured the largest naval guns in service save that of the USA in the Cold War. The guns are of a 1938 design, and are fitted on the unmodified 'Sverdlov' class cruisers in a conventional two forward and two aft turret arrangement. The barrels can be individually elevated, loaded and fired if required. The loading phase is believed to be semi-automatic in nature, each barrel having a maximum rate of fire of 10 rounds per minute, though a more practical rate is thought to be 4-5 rounds per minute. The guns also have a limited anti-aircraft capability using barrage fire. At the rear of each turret top is installed an 8-m (26.25-ft) long optical rangefinder, whilst for radar fire-control purposes the turrets usually mount an 'Egg Cup' E-band ranging only radar. An additional two 'Top Bow' fire-control radars for the guns are included as part of the ship's main electronic fit. Recently a tactical nuclear capability has been associated with these guns, possibly as a direct result of its naval gunfire support role in Warsaw Pact amphibious assault operations.

The only other country to use this gun was Indonesia, which had the weapon aboard a 'Sverdlov' class cruiser which has now been scrapped.

Specification
152-mm triple gun mounting
Calibre: 152 mm (5.98 in)
No. of barrels: three
Weight: not known
Elevation: −5° to +50°
Muzzle velocity: 915 m (3,002 ft) per second
Projectile weight: 50 kg (110.2 lb)
Maximum rate of fire: 30 rpm
Effective ranges: surface fire 18 km (11.2 miles), and anti-aircraft fire 12 km (7.5 miles)

Right: The triple 152-mm gun mounting in service with the remaining 'Sverdlov' class cruisers of the Soviet Fleet are of the 1938 pattern, originally designed for the 'Chapayev' class. The 50-calibre guns are reported to have a maximum range of 27 km (16.8 miles), firing a projectile of some 50 kg (110 lb).

Right: This photograph dating from the 1970s contrasts the 'Sverdlov' class with the last British 6-in gun cruiser. The Soviet ship remains to all intents and purposes an unmodified World War II type, while HMS Blake bears little resemblance to any wartime forebears.

Below: Dzerzhinsky was altered in the early 1960s, being fitted with an SA-N-2 launcher in place of its X-turret. Presumably the conversion was not a great success, as no other 'Sverdlov' was so converted. Although an important part of the Soviet Navy's inventory for much of the Cold War period, the Sverdlovs became increasingly vulnerable to modern weaponry and were relegated to a second-line training role, no attempt having been made to update their missile defences by the addition of close-in weapon systems.

76-mm OTO Melara Compact gun

The 62-calibre **76-mm OTO Melara Compact** gun is now the most famous lightweight dual-purpose naval gun in the world. Developed from the 76-mm (3-in) **OTO Melara MMI** mount in the mid-1960s the gun first entered service in 1969 as a system intended for installation in ships of any size and class down to motor gunboats and hydrofoils. The fully automatic mounting consists of two parts, the shank and the turret assembly. The former is installed below deck and contains the 80-round rotating platform and hoist ammunition feed system to the gun in the turret above. This is covered by a watertight and NBC proof fibreglass shield. The only manpower required is in the main magazine, where ammunition handlers are needed to feed the drum in order to keep it loaded. The rate of fire is adjustable from a minimum of 10 to a maximum of 85 rounds per minute, although a new **Super Rapid** variant increases the latter to 100+ rounds per minute. The rate is adjusted on the operations room control console. Another option available is the ability to fit a stabilized line of sight local fire-control system if required.

The gun barrel is fitted with a muzzle brake and a fume extractor. Currently the gun is in service or on order with some 37 navies, and is being licence-built in the USA, Japan and Spain. The Israeli navy has used the weapon extensively in combat in the anti-ship and shore bombardment roles. It is believed that the Israelis have modified the gun for use in the latter role, possibly with locally produced ammunition.

A more modern variant with an autonomous turret-mounted Lince gun director and new prefragmented ammunition, for use against sea-skimming missiles, was developed by the Italians as a follow-on weapon.

Specification
76-mm OTO Melara Compact
Calibre: 76 mm (3 in)
No. of barrels: one
Weight: 7.35 tons
Elevation: −15° to +85°
Muzzle velocity: 925 m (3,035 ft) per second
Projectile weight: 6.3 kg (13.9 lb)
Maximum rate of fire: 85-100 rpm (according to variant)
Maximum effective ranges: surface fire 8 km (5 miles), and anti-aircraft fire 5 km (3.1 miles)

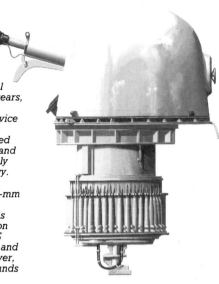

Right: One of the most successful naval weapons in the post-war years, the 76-mm (3-in) OTO-Melara Compact gun mounting is in service with, or is being delivered to, 35 navies or more. It is manufactured under licence in the USA, Japan and Spain, and it has been extensively combat-tested by the Israeli navy.

Below: The light weight of the 76-mm Compact has enabled it to be installed on vessels displacing as little as 60 tons. It was mounted on the 'Pegasus' class hydrofoil USS Aquila, and the gun gives Aquila and her sisters considerable firepower, being able to fire at up to 100 rounds per minute.

Below: With more than 60 built or projected, the US 'FFG-7' class is one of the most numerous frigate designs since the war. Unusually, the design placed the sole gun, a licence-built OTO-Melara Compact 76-mm, high up amidships. This is less than effective against sea-skimming missiles.

127-mm OTO Melara Compact gun

Design work for the **127-mm OTO Melara Compact** 54-calibre gun started in 1965 as a joint venture by OTO Melara with the Italian government. The first prototype was completed in May 1969 and the gun was adopted as the main armament for new-build Italian navy frigates and destroyers. The loading, ammunition, feeding and firing sequences are controlled by one man in the ship's opera-

tions room using a console. Ready-use ammunition is held in three 22-round loading drums below deck under the mount. This allows a choice between three different ammunition types, the gun's operator choosing the round appropriate to the action. The three drums are automatically reloaded via two hoists that are manually replenished in the main magazine. A drum can be reloaded even whilst the gun is

firing. The barrel itself is fitted with a muzzle brake. Apart from Italy the navies of Argentina, Canada, Iraq, Nigeria, Peru and Venezuela have guns of this type in service aboard frigates and destroyers.

Specification
127-mm OTO Melara Compact
Calibre: 127 mm (5 in)

No. of barrels: one
Weight: 34 tons
Elevation: −15° to +85°
Muzzle velocity: 807 m (2,648 ft) per second
Projectile weight: unknown
Total round weight: 32 kg (70.5 lb)
Maximum rate of fire: 45 rpm
Maximum effective ranges: surface fire 15 km (9.3 miles), and anti-aircraft fire 7 km (4.3 miles)

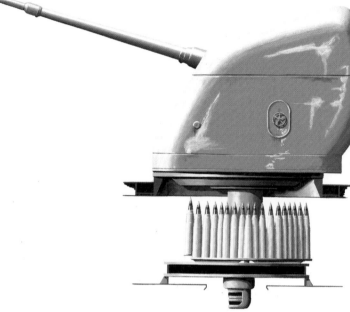

Left: OTO-Melara developed a compact, lightweight 127-mm (5-in) gun and turret for use as the main armament for frigates and destroyers. Blohm und Voss have adopted the gun for their 'Meko 360' class of destroyer, as seen here on Argentina's Almirante Brown.

Above: The major technical features of modern compact systems are the major use of light alloy structures, lightweight control mechanisms, and a higher rate of fire. This last feature requires an automatic loading sequence, with ready-use rounds close to hand and easily refillable.

105-mm Breda SCLAR rocket-launcher

The **105-mm Breda SCLAR** naval rocket-launcher system normally consists of two 20-tube launchers for 105-mm (4.13-in) countermeasures or assault rockets, an Elsag fire-control unit and a magazine filled with SNIA rockets. The two launchers are mounted one on each side of the ship so that they provide as wide a coverage as possible. A remote-control facility on the fire-control unit allows them to be automatically trained and elevated to respond to any incoming threats detected by the ship's own ESM sensors. To meet any threat, mixed rocket type salvoes can be loaded into the launcher tubes, automatic selection of the type, fuse setting and launch sequence being undertaken by the operator on the remote fire-control console. If necessary the countermeasures rockets can be offloaded and replaced by a variant fitted with HE warheads for shore bombardment and defence suppression purposes.

About 1,000 SCLAR mountings have been built to date for the navies of Argentina, Ecuador, Iraq, Italy, Nigeria, Peru, Venezuela and West Germany. The other rocket types used include the 105LR-C long-range (up to 12 km/7.5 miles) chaff distraction, the 105MR-C medium-range (up to 5 km/

Above: The Breda 105-mm rocket-launcher is usually fitted to a ship as one of a pair, primarily for use as a launch system for countermeasures; high explosive warheads can be fitted for assault purposes.

Right: Developed from the 105-mm launcher, the multi-calibre assault launcher fires both 105-mm and 51-mm rockets. The servos of the training mechanisms are more carefully protected against adverse weather conditions than in the original system.

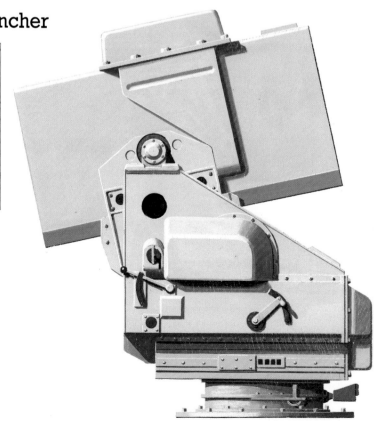

3.1 miles) chaff seduction and the 105LR-I illuminating with a maximum range of 4 km (2.5 miles).

Specification
SCLAR
Calibre: 105 mm (4.13 in)
No. of tubes per launcher: 20
Weight: 1.72 tons
Elevation: −5° to +60°
Rate of fire: 1 rocket per second
Rocket types: HE, chaff, illumination
Maximum range: 4-12 km (2.5-7.5 miles)

Seen aboard a 'Lupo' class frigate of the Italian navy, the Breda multi-calibre assault launcher retains the capacity to fire deception and countermeasure rockets from the 105-mm tubes. The 51-mm rockets are strictly for close range assault, however.

Vickers 4.5-in Mk 8 gun

The Royal Navy has been using the 114-mm (4.5-in) weapon as its standard medium calibre gun since World War II. In the mid-1960s RARDE began design development of a fully automatic version to replace the semi-automatic Mk 6 twin turret. Based on the British army's Abbot gun, the radar-controlled **4.5-in Mk 8** gun, as it became known, is a 55-calibre weapon fitted with a muzzle brake and fume extractor. The gun mounting itself is designed by Vickers and features a reinforced GRP gun shield with a simple ammunition feed system and remote power controls. A stockpile of ready-use rounds can be accommodated at the mounting and fired remotely from the operations room with no crew closed up on the reloading system below decks. Five types of

Below: The Vickers 4.5-in Mk 8 mounting is currently in service with the Royal Navy aboard Type 42 and Type 82 destroyers as well as Type 21 and Batch 3 Type 22 frigates, and will be fitted to the new Type 23 'Duke' class of frigate.

fixed ammunition can be fired: chaff, surface practice, anti-aircraft practice HE (with impact, close proximity, distant proximity or delay-action fuses) and illuminating. Apart from the Royal Navy the Mk 8 is in service with the Argentine, Brazilian, Iranian, Libyan and Thai navies. The Mk 8 saw extensive combat service in the 1982 Falklands war, mainly in the shore bombardment and close-support roles for troops in contact with the enemy, but it is also credited with destruction of an Argentine supply ship when HMS *Alacrity* sank the *Isla de los Estados*.

Specification
Mk 8 gun
Calibre: 114.3 mm (4.5 in)

With a maximum range of 23 km (14.3 miles) and a sustained rate of fire of 25 rounds per minute, the Mk 8 can fire a variety of differing rounds, including high explosive with four different types of fuse (impact, close proximity, distant proximity and delayed action).

No. of barrels: one
Weight: not known
Elevation: −10° to +55°
Muzzle velocity: 870 m (2,854 ft) per second
Projectile weight: 21 kg (46.3 lb)
Maximum rate of fire: 25 rpm
Maximum effective ranges: surface fire 23 km (14.3 miles), and anti-aircraft fire 6 km (3.7 miles)

SWEDEN
57-mm Bofors SAK gun

The 70-calibre **57-mm Bofors SAK Mk 1** dual-purpose gun can be used either in fully automatic remote-controlled or gyro-stabilized one-man local-control modes. The gun is housed in a plastic cupola and is designed for both surface and anti-aircraft fire. The barrel is liquid-cooled, whilst the feed system contains 40 ready-use rounds with another 128 rounds stowed in racks within the turret. The ammunition is of two types, a prefragmented round for use against aerial targets and a semi-armour-piercing round with a delay action fuse for use against surface targets. The turret can also be fitted with launching rails for 57-mm (2.24-in) illuminating rockets if required. The Mk 1 gun is in service with the navies of Sweden, Malaysia, Norway, Indonesia, Singapore, Thailand and Yugoslavia.

In the early 1980s a low-radar-signature variant, the all-purpose **57-mm Bofors SAK Mk 2**, was built. Using the same ammunition types it has a completely new automatic reloading system with 120 ready-use rounds in the cupola, and an improved electro-hydraulic remote-control system that greatly enhances the weapons accuracy against all types of targets, including sea-skimming anti-ship missiles. The Mk 2 is already in mass production for the navies of Sweden, Canada, Mexico and several unidentified countries.

Right: Designed for combating both surface and aerial targets, the all-purpose Bofors 57-mm SAK Mk 2 is fitted to a completely automatic fire control system and is enclosed in a compact plastic turret to provide as low a radar signature as possible.

Below: The single 57 mm L/70 automatic gun mounting fitted to the 'Spica' class fast patrol boat is equipped with rocket-launching rails for 57-mm (2-in) rockets. The elevation arc of the gun is −10° to +75°, rate of fire being as much as 200 rounds per minute.

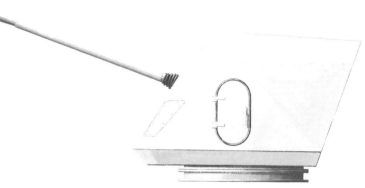

Specification
SAK Mk 1
Calibre: 57 mm (2.24 in)
No. of barrels: one
Weight: 6 tons
Elevation: −10° to +75°
Muzzle velocity: 1025 m (3,363 ft) per second
Projectile weight: 2.4 kg (5.3 lb)
Total weight of rounds: surface 6.8 kg (15 lb), and anti-aircraft 5.8 kg (12.8 lb)
Maximum rate of fire: 200 rpm
Maximum effective ranges: surface fire 13 km (8.1 miles), and anti-aircraft fire 5 km (3.1 miles)

Specification
SAK Mk 2
Calibre: 57 mm (2.24 in)
No. of barrels: one
Weight: 6 tons

Elevation: −10° to +75°
Muzzle velocity: 1025 m (3,363 ft) per second
Projectile weight: 2.8 kg (6.2 lb)
Total weight of round: 6.5 kg (14.3 lb)

Maximum rate of fire: 220 rpm
Maximum effective ranges: surface fire 17 km (10.6 miles), and anti-aircraft fire 6 km (3.7 miles)

SWEDEN
120-mm Bofors gun

The **120-mm Bofors** 46-calibre automatic gun was designed for use against surface and airborne targets. Housed in a 4-mm (0.16-in) thick steel turret, the gun has two ready-use magazines mounted on the elevating cradle, and these are manually filled from a hoist system from the main magazine. The alternative to the automatic control is a gyro-stabilized one-man local control console. For this telescopic sights are fitted, whilst the hoist, elevation and traverse mechanisms can be operated by hand. The gun barrel itself has an exchangeable liner, and is water-cooled to help prolong barrel life. At present only the Finnish and Indonesian navies have the gun in service on corvette- and frigate-sized vessels respectively. The Swedish navy instead uses an older radar-controlled twin 120-mm (4.7-in) mount on its sole sur-

The first post-war destroyer design for the Swedish navy was armed with twin turrets for its 50-calibre 120-mm (4.7-in) guns. HMS Halland is now in reserve, but the gun type is still active with the Dutch, Peruvian and Colombian navies.

viving destroyer. The same 67-ton 50-calibre mounts are used by the Dutch, Peruvian and Colombian navies on their destroyers.

Specification
120-mm Bofors
Calibre: 120 mm (4.72 in)
No. of barrels: two
Weight: 28.5 tons
Elevation: −10° to +80°
Muzzle velocity: 800 m (2,625 ft) per second
Projectile weight: 21 kg (46.3 lb)
Total round weight: 35 kg (77.2 lb)
Maximum rate of fire: 80 rpm
Maximum effective ranges: surface fire 12 km (7.5 miles), and anti-aircraft fire 7 km (4.3 miles)

Finland's very capable 'Turunmaa' class corvettes are equipped with the Bofors single L/46 120-mm (4.7-in) gun. Fully automatic, the weapon is capable of firing some 80 21-kg (46.3-lb) shells per minute, an extremely high rate for a gun of this size.

100-mm and 130-mm guns

In the late 1950s the People's Republic of China received the blueprints for the Soviet twin 130-mm (5.12-in) 58-calibre dual-purpose gun mounting. However, it was not until some 10 years later that the first units were produced to arm the 'Luda' class missile destroyers. The guns were built to a slightly modified design with rounded turret edges and an indigenous on-mount ranging radar. To date only the 'Luda' class have been so armed although an older Soviet single 130-mm **B-13-2C** 50-calibre weapon is used on the 'Anshan' class missile destroyers and the single refurbished ex-World War II Japanese 'Haishidate' class escort.

During the mid-1950s the Chinese also introduced into service the Soviet single **100-mm Bu-34** 56-calibre mount on its locally assembled 'Chengdu' (Soviet 'Riga' class) frigates. The design was subsequently manufactured in a modified form by the Chinese and used to arm the 'Jiangnan' and 'Jianghu I/II' series frigates and many of the refurbished ex-World War II escorts still in service. A twin-barrel variant has also been produced, and this has been fitted to the 'Jianghu III' and 'Jiandong' frigate classes. For the future the Chinese navy is known to be acquiring modern Western naval guns, and is thought to have ordered the French 100-mm (3.9-in) Compact gun for a new frigate class under construction.

Specification
100-mm Bu-34
Calibre: 100 mm (3.94 in)
No. of barrels: one
Elevation: −5° to +40°
Muzzle velocity: 875 m (2,871 ft) per second
Projectile weight: 13.5 kg (29.8 lb)
Maximum rate of fire: 15 rpm
Maximum effective ranges: surface fire 10 km (6.2 miles), and anti-aircraft fire 8 km (5 miles)

Specification
130-mm twin gun
Calibre: 130 mm (5.12 in)
No. of barrels: two
Elevation: −5° to +80°
Muzzle velocity: 945 m (3,100 ft) per second
Projectile weight: 33.4 kg (73.6 lb)
Maximum rate of fire: 20 rpm
Maximum effective ranges: surface fire 18 km (11.2 miles), and anti-aircraft fire 8 km (5 miles)

Specification
B-13-2C
Calibre: 130 mm (5.12 in)
No. of barrels: one
Elevation: −5° to +45°
Muzzle velocity: 875 m (2,871 ft) per second
Projectile weight: 27 kg (59.5 lb)
Maximum rate of fire: 12 rpm
Maximum effective range: surface fire 15 km (9.3 miles)

As with so much of their military equipment, current Chinese naval guns are modifications of Soviet designs of the 1950s, and as such are out of date.

Underwater Weapons

Advanced underwater weapons technology has seen the development of sophisticated anti-submarine hardware These weapons include long-range torpedoes delivered by guided missile and armed with either nuclear or conventional warheads and nuclear depth bombs that can be dropped from the air.

The Marconi Spearfish is an advanced wire-guided torpedo with a top speed of 60 knots. It carries a 249-kg (550-lb) HE warhead and has a range at full speed of 28.6 km (17.75 miles).

By the end of World War II enormous advances had been made in underwater weapons systems and their associated sensors. Since then, both submarines and surface vessels dedicated to the anti-submarine warfare role have acquired increasingly complex rocket and missile systems with substantially longer ranges.

There are two main types of anti-submarine projectile: the proximity and the contact weapon. The former, typified by the depth charge, which was first used in action by the Royal Navy in 1916, must carry an explosive charge large enough to damage a submerged target even at a considerable miss distance. The greatest lethal radius of weapons of this type is achieved by the nuclear depth charge, which can destroy or damage targets which are several thousand metres away from the point of detonation.

The second type of projectile, can be precisely guided to the target – as in the case of the homing torpedo – or delivered in such numbers that a hit is virtually guaranteed, so it does not need as large a warhead. The range and speed of torpedoes has steadily increased and the main development has seen the use of a guided missile to carry a torpedo or depth bomb to within striking distance of a target. Such systems can use either conventional or nuclear warheads; a good example is the American SUBROC. Launched from the torpedo tubes of attack submarines, it carried a one-kiloton nuclear warhead which had a lethal radius of 5–8 km (3–5 miles).

The Soviet Navy deployed three types of nuclear-armed missile and rocket for anti-submarine missions: the FRAS-1 (Free Rocket Anti-Submarine-1), the SS-N-15 Starfish nuclear depth bomb, and the SS-N-16 Stallion ASW missile. Twin-rail SUW-N-1 launchers with FRAS-1 are deployed in 'Kiev' class vessels, among others. The missile is a nuclear-only variant of the Soviet Army's FROG-7 short-range rocket.

The Soviet Navy also deployed at least two types of ASW nuclear depth bombs, which were deliverable by three types of land-based fixed-wing aircraft and two ship-based helicopters. According to estimates, the former Soviet Union had a stockpile of about 400 nuclear depth bombs.

AEG-Telefunken Seal, Seeschlange, SST4 and SUT torpedoes

These AEG-Telefunken weapons constitute a complete family of heavyweight torpedoes. The basic electric-powered dual-speed **Seal** and **Seeschlange** (sea snake) were developed specifically for use by the West German navy, and are currently in use aboard its 'Type 205/206' submarines, whilst the Seal is also employed on some light forces' missile craft. There is a high degree of equipment commonality between the two weapons, the major difference being that the smaller ASW Seeschlange has only half the propulsive battery capacity of the anti-ship Seal. An active/passive homing head is fitted with a dual-core wire-guidance system that allows rapid changing between speeds, attack patterns and guidance modes in order to meet the needs of developing tactical situations.

The Seal was then taken as the model for the **Special Surface Target (SST) 4** torpedo, which except for certain features unique to West German operational requirements is comparable in dimensions, construction and capabilities to its predecessors. Used as the standard anti-ship weapon sold with export 'Type 209' submarines and West German missile craft, the SST4 is found in various NATO and South American navies, and was used operationally by the Argentine submarine *San Luis* during the 1982 Falklands war in several abortive torpedo attacks against Royal Navy task force ships.

The Seal was then further developed to produce the export **Surface and Underwater Target (SUT)** torpedo. As a dual-purpose ASW/anti-ship weapon capable of being launched from surface ships, submarines or shore positions, the SUT has the same shallow-water and deep-diving engagement capabilities of the other members of the family plus the same contact and magnetic proximity fusing systems. Like the SST4 it is in production for export with the 'Type 209' submarines.

Specification
Seal
Dimensions: diameter 533 mm (21 in); length 6.08 m (19.95 ft), or 6.55 m (21.49 ft) with wire guidance casket
Weight: 1370 kg (3,020 ft)
Warhead: 260-kg (573-lb) HE
Performance: speed 23 or 35 kts; range 28 or 12 km (17.40 or 7.46 miles)

A missile-armed Type 143 fast attack craft of the West German navy makes a test launch of an AEG/Telefunken Seal torpedo. One of a family of weapons, it is designed for the engagement of surface targets, and is fitted to Type 142 and 143 boats as well as aboard Type 206 submarines.

Specification
Seeschlange
Dimensions: diameter 533 mm (21 in); length 4.15 m (13.62 ft), or 4.62 m (15.16 ft) with wire guidance casket
Weight: 800 to 900 kg (1,764 to 1,984 lb)
Warhead: 100-kg (220-lb) HE
Performance: speed 23 or 35 kts; range 14 or 6 km (8.70 or 3.73 miles)

Specification
SST4
Dimensions: diameter 533 mm (21 in);

Right: The Surface and Underwater Target (SUT) torpedo, seen being loaded aboard one of the widely exported 'Type 209' submarines, is the most versatile of the AEG-Telefunken heavyweight torpedo range. It is a dual-purpose weapon, wire guided for greater accuracy.

length 6.04 m (19.82 ft), or 6.50 m (21.33 ft) with wire guidance casket
Weight: 1414 kg (3,117 lb)
Warhead: 260-kg (573-lb) HE
Performance: speed 23 or 35 kts; range 28 or 12 km (17.40 or 7.46 miles)

Specification
SUT
Dimensions: diameter 533 mm (21 in); length 6.15 m (20.18 ft), or 6.62 m (21.72 ft) with wire guidance casket
Weight: 1414 kg (3,117 lb)

Warhead: 260-kg (573-lb) HE
Performance: speed 23 or 35 kts; range 28 or 12 km (17.40 or 7.46 miles)

Soviet sea mines

The USSR is the world's leading exponent of sea mine warfare, with over 400,000 of such weapons in its naval weapons inventory. The mine types used include small, medium and large defensive moored mines using contact, influence or antenna activating systems. Known types include the **YaRM** and **YaM** spherical contact mines for rivers and shallow waters, the **M08** and **KB** series contact mines for coastal waters, and the **KRAB** moored influence and **MAG** moored antenna mines for coastal and deeper continental shelf waters. All of these are likely to be in service with Soviet client states such as the other members of the Warsaw Pact, many nations in the Middle East, and also Vietnam and North Korea.

The offensive mines are mainly ground mines, of which the most important are the **AMD-500** and **AMD-1000** types (the number referring to the relevant mine's nominal weight in kilograms). The AMD-500 contains 300 kg (661 lb) and the AMD-1000 700 kg (1,543 lb) of HE. Using magnetic, acoustic, pressure or combination influence actuating systems, these weapons have also been widely exported, evidence being provided by recent wars in the Middle and Far East. The pressure types were almost certainly used only by the USSR and her most trusted Warsaw Pact partners, however because of the possibility of a technology compromise, and the fact that in other hands they may well have been used against their designers, eventually.

There were also substantial Soviet stocks of rising mines and underwater electrical potential mines for use in the offensive ASW roles against NATO targets. The two types of rising mine available could be used in a secondary anti-ship role. These two types are believed to be the '**Cluster Bay**' continental shelf and '**Cluster Gulf**' continental ledge types in NATO terminology. There is also a small stockpile of nuclear-armed mines with yields between 5 and 20 kilotons for use against very high-value surface ships or submarines such as nuclear-powered aircraft-carriers and 'Ohio' class SSBNs.

The primary offensive minelaying platforms available to the Soviet navy are its conventionally-powered submarines because of their covert laying capabilities. These would be backed by aircraft of the Soviet naval air force, whilst any defensive laying would be the responsibility of surface ship units.

Specification
M08
Dimensions: diameter 0.90 m (2.95 ft); maximum case length 6.096 m (20.00 ft)
Charge weight: 115 kg (253.5 lb)
Maximum laying depth: 130 m (427 ft)

Specification
KB1
Dimensions: diameter 0.9 m (2.95 ft); maximum case length 9.144 m (30.00 ft
Charge weight: 230 kg (507 lb)
Maximum laying depth: 275 m (902 ft)

Soviet torpedoes

Soviet torpedoes, like their Western counterparts, can be categorized into heavy and lightweight models for specific purposes. Of the former, two calibres are known: the standard 533 mm (21 in) and the relatively new 609.6 mm (24 in). The 533-mm (21-in) versions are thought to have been evolved from German World War II designs, and include straight- and pattern-running surface- and submarine-launched steam- or electric-powered models for anti-ship use, as well as acoustic/passive homing ASW/anti-ship versions. Surprisingly, most large modern surface combatants have multi-tube launchers for the ASW acoustic-homing versions. There is also a special 15-kiloton yield nuclear-armed non-terminal-homing 533-mm (21-in) torpedo in service on many of the submarines designed for use against high-value surface targets such as carriers or Very Large Crude Carriers. Similarly the huge 9.14-m (30-ft) long 609.6-mm (24-in) anti-ship **Type 65** torpedo has been introduced on board later-generation nuclear attack submarines for use against surface ship targets. It is believed to use wake-homing guidance methods and, with selectable 50- or 30-kt speeds, has ranges of 50 and 100 km (31 or 62 miles) respectively. With ranges like these, the Type 65 is being used to supplement the pop-up anti-ship cruise missile weapons of 'Charlie' class SSGNs, and the type's availability for the first time allows Soviet SSNs to fire torpedoes from outside the ASW screen of a convoy.

For air, shipboard and submarine ASW uses at close range a 400-mm (15.75-in) electric-powered lightweight torpedo has been in service for a number of years. This has now apparently been supplemented for use aboard ASW aircraft and helicopters by an even larger 450-mm (17.7-in) weapon which is believed to have a larger warhead and greater range to increase lethality. Both the air-launched weapons use parachutes to re-

Above: The Vitse-Admiral Kulakov *is the second of the large ASW destroyers of the 'Udaloy' class. In addition to her ASW missiles and helicopters, she is armed with two quadruple 533-mm (21-in) torpedo tubes, one of which is visible astern of the aft funnel structure.*

tard their entry into the water.

According to some reports there is also a short 400-mm (15.75-in) anti-ship torpedo which is found aboard the first-generation 'Hotel', 'Echo' and 'November' class nuclear submarines in their stern tubes. The later-generation nuclear submarine classes apparently have had several of their standard 533-mm (21-in) calibre torpedo tubes fitted with liners to fire the ASW version of the same weapon.

The standard fusing system fitted to Soviet torpedoes is an active magnetic proximity device (to ensure detonation under the target's hull so as to break its back) with a secondary contact unit for a direct hit.

Above: The 'Alfa' class submarine is considerably shorter than other Soviet SSN designs, so it is unlikely to have been fitted to fire the massive 610-mm (24-in) torpedo reportedly in service with the Soviet navy although it may be armed with the strategic SS-N-21 Cruise missile.

Below: Backbone of the Soviet anti-submarine force, the 'Krivak' class, like all major Soviet vessels, is fitted with torpedo tubes. The eight tubes abaft the bridge, in quadruple mounts port and starboard, probably fire acoustically-homing 533-mm (21-in) torpedoes.

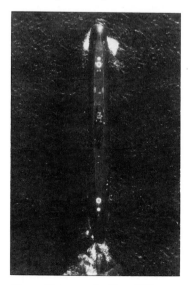

Above: Photographed by a US Navy F-14 fighter, this 'Victor III' SSN has fouled the towed array sonar of a 'Spruance' class destroyer off the coast of Georgia. These large boats may be fitted with the extremely long-ranged 610-mm (24-in) torpedo, which allows attacks from as far as 100 km (62 miles).

DTCN L3, L4 and L5 torpedoes

The electric-powered 550-mm (21.7-in) calibre L3 ship- or submarine-launched ASW homing heavyweight torpedo is currently in service with the French navy and was designed by the Direction Technique des Constructions Navales to attack submerged targets at depths up to 300 m (984 ft) and speeds from 0 to 20 kts. It is fitted with an AS-3T active acoustic guidance system that has a detection range of about 600 m (1,969 ft) in ideal conditions, and the warhead is detonated by an electro-magnetic proximity fusing system. A 533-mm (21-in) version with the same performance is available for export, length and weight being 4.318 m (14.17 ft) and 900 kg (1,984 lb). Apart from France, several of the countries (including Spain) which have bought 'Daphné' class submarines have also obtained the larger-calibre weapon.

Also in service with the French navy is the 533-mm (21-in) electric-powered L-4 air-launched torpedo for use with helicopters, aircraft and the Malafon ASW missile. Fitted with an active acoustic-homing system, it describes a circular search path upon entering the water until its seeker acquires the target. The warhead is detonated either by an impact fuse or a proximity acoustic influence fuse. French L4s have recently been modernized to improve shallow-water performance and its 0/20-kt target capability from periscope depth to around 300-m (984-ft) deep cruising. A version for surface ship launching has also been developed: this has a length of 3.30 m (10.83 ft) and a weight of 570 kg (1,257 lb).

The most recent of the L-series torpedoes is the electric-powered L5, which is available in four versions. The dual-purpose ASW/anti-ship L5 Mod 1 is carried by surface ships, whilst the similar-role but heavier L5 Mod 3 is used by submarines. A single-role variant, the ASW L5 Mod 4, has been derived from the Mod 1 and is used solely by surface ships. A further ver-

The Sintra-Alcatel-built L3 is a conventional ship- or submarine-launched active acoustic homing anti-submarine torpedo. Unusually, it has a diameter of 550 mm (21.65 in) but has been offered in the more standard 533 mm (21 in) for export. It is in widespread French naval service.

sion of this has been developed for the export market as the **L5 Mod 4P** multi-role torpedo. All versions are fitted with a Thomson CSF active/passive guidance system and are capable of various attack profiles including direct and programmed searches using either of the acoustic homing techniques available. Known operators of the L5 other than France include the Belgian navy (L5 Mod 3) and Spain (aboard submarines).

Specification
L3
Dimensions: diameter 550 mm (21.7 in); length 4.30 m (14.11 ft)
Weight: 910 kg (2,006 lb)
Warhead: 200-kg (441-lb) HE
Performance: speed 25 kts; range 7.5 km (4.66 miles)

Specification
L4
Dimensions: diameter 533 mm (21 in); length 3.033 m (9.95 ft), or 3.13 m (10.27 ft) with parachute pack
Weight: 540 kg (1,190 lb)
Warhead: 104-kg (229-lb) HE
Performance: speed 30 kts; range 5.5 km (3.4 miles)

Specification
L5
Dimensions: diameter 533 mm (21 in); length 4.40 m (14.44 ft)
Weight: (Mod 1) 1000 kg (2,205 lb), (Mod 3) 1300 kg (2,866 lb), (Mod 4) 920 kg (2,028 lb) and (Mod 4P) 930 kg (2,050 lb)
Warhead: 150-kg (331-lb) HE
Performance: speed 35 kts; range 9.25 km (5.75 miles)

Above: The L4 air-launched torpedo can function in shallow water against submarines manoeuvring at up to 20 kts. It also provides the warload for the Malafon ASW missile system, and a ship-launched version has been designed.

Below: The L5 series of multi-purpose torpedoes is fitted with Thomson-CSF active/passive homing heads, although the Mod 1 is intended for surface vessel use and the heavier Mod 3 version (shown here) equips submarines.

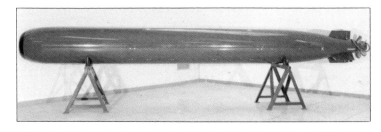

DTCN F17 torpedo

The **F17** is the first wire-guided heavyweight torpedo to be used by the French navy. Designed for use against surface ships from submarines, the weapon can be employed either in the wire-guided mode or in an autonomous passive homing mode, the capability for instant switching between the two modes being provided on a control panel aboard the launch platform. The terminal attack phase is normally of the passive acoustic type under the torpedo's own internal control. A dual-purpose surface- or submarine-launched variant, the **F17P**, has also been developed for the export market, and has been bought by Saudi Arabia for use aboard its 'Madina' ('Type F2000') class frigates, and by Spain for use aboard its 'Agosta' and modernized 'Daphné' class submarines. The F17P differs from the basic F17 in having an active/passive acoustic-homing seeker which allows completely autonomous operation if required.

Specification
F17
Dimensions: diameter 533 mm (21 in);

length 5.914 m (19.40 ft)
Weight: 1410 kg (3,108 lb)
Warhead: 250-kg (551-lb) HE
Performance: speed 35 kts; range 18 km (11.18 miles)

The wire-guided F17 heavyweight torpedo is an anti-shipping submarine-launched weapon, although an automatic homing head is standard. The F17P is a development capable of ship or submarine launch, and in addition to wire guidance is equipped for active or passive acoustic homing. In all the models, however, the terminal attack phase is usually autonomous.

FRANCE

Thomson-CSF sea mines

Thomson-CSF produces two types of operational sea mine. The **TSM3510** (or **MCC23**) is an offensive ground mine fitted with a multi-sensor fusing system based on two or all of the magnetic, acoustic and pressure actuating influences, and is shaped for launching from the standard torpedo tube of a submarine. The sensitivity of the fusing can be adjusted before laying to suit the depth of water and the type of target likely to be encountered. The mine is armed (by withdrawing two safety pins) before it is loaded into the tube and is activated by a preset timing delay to allow the submarine to clear the area. Two similarly shaped training mines, the **TSM3515** (**MCED23**) and the **TSM3517** (**MCEM23**), are also in service.

For defensive purposes there is the **TSM3530** (**MCT15**), which is a ground

As offensive mines have to be laid covertly, often in or near enemy waters, the most appropriate system for such work is the submarine. Hence the TSM 3510, in common with many other mines in production today, is designed to be ejected through standard torpedo tubes.

mine deployed from surface ships fitted with mine rails. It is checked in its descent to the sea bottom by a parachute-retarding device which ensures that correct orientation is achieved. It is armed by a preset timing delay which allows the laying platform to clear the area.

Both mines are in service with the French navy and have been sold abroad, especially the TSM3510 which is found in several of the countries that

have purchased 'Daphné' class submarines.

Specification
TSM3510
Dimensions: diameter 0.53 m (1.74 ft); length 2.368 m (7.77 ft)
Weight: 850 kg (1,874 lb)
Actuating sensors: combination magnetic acoustic, magnetic pressure, acoustic pressure, or magnetic acoustic pressure

Specification
TSM3530
Dimensions: diameter 1.20 m (3.94 ft); length 1.10 m (3.61 ft)
Weight: 1200 kg (2,646 lb)
Actuating sensors: combination magnetic acoustic, magnetic pressure, acoustic pressure, or magnetic acoustic pressure

---

UK

Marconi Stingray torpedo

Designed to supplement the American Mk 46 Mod 2 and to replace the Mk 44 torpedoes in British service, the **Marconi Stingray** lightweight torpedo was the sequel of the abortive MOD in-house lightweight Mk 30 and 31 programmes, which were cancelled in 1970. The Stingray is the first British torpedo to be developed entirely by private industry and incorporates a number of technical innovations. The weapon is capable of being launched from helicopters, aircraft and surface ships over a wide range of speeds and sea states and, as a result of its unique guidance system, can be used satisfactorily in both shallow and deep waters with an equally high single-shot kill probability, the former being demonstrated recently during a development trial shot when Stingray dropped from a BAe Nimrod of No. 42 Squadron hit and sank the decommissioned conventional submarine *Porpoise*, apparently whilst she was moored at periscope depth.

Although deployed operationally aboard several ships during the 1982 Falklands war, Stingray was not fired in anger and did not actually enter full-scale service with the Royal Navy and Royal Air Force until 1983. Since then the weapon has been sold to Thailand and Egypt. In terms of general performance it is similar to the Mk 46 though, it seems, the British torpedo has slightly deeper diving depth of 800 m (2,625 ft). The Stingray also possesses an onboard digital computer coupled to a multi-mode multi-beam active/passive sonar that effectively makes it a 'smart' weapon. Propulsion is by an electrically-driven pump-jet with a battery activated by sea water that ensures no speed loss as the depth increases. The warhead is of the directed-energy shaped-charge variety rather than blast type to ensure penetration of a Soviet submarine's double-hull construction.

In addition to its primary air launch mode. Stingray form as a part of the ASW armament of several classes of Royal Navy surface combatant, The torpedoes are launched from modified versions of the US Mk 32 triple tubes as shown here in a trial launch from the Type 21 frigate HMS Avenger.

Similar in size to the previous generation of lightweight torpedoes, the Marconi Stingray also has a similar performance. Where it differs is in the sophisticated guidance.

Specification (provisional)
Stingray
Dimensions: diameter 324 mm (12.75 in); length 2.6 m (8.52 ft)
Weight: 265.4 kg (585.2 lb)
Warhead: 40-kg (88-lb) shaped-charge HE
Performance: speed 45 kts; range 11.1 km (6.9 miles)

Right: The new generation of lightweight torpedo gives significant anti-submarine capability to relatively unsophisticated systems. The Britten-Norman Defender could carry Stingray and could use its sophisticated electronics to attack the most advanced of submarines.

Marconi Mk 24 Tigerfish torpedo

The origins of the **Mk 24 Tigerfish** heavyweight torpedo saga can be found as far back as 1959 in a British torpedo project codenamed 'Ongar'. By 1970 it was realized that the technology involved could not be handled solely by an in-house service approach, so the then Marconi Company was given the job of developing the weapon from 1972 onwards. This was five years after the originally envisaged in-service date. As a result of development and engineering problems the first version of the Tigerfish, the **Mk 24 Mod 0**, entered fleet service in 1974 with less operational capability than originally desired. It was only granted its full Fleet Weapon Acceptance certificate in 1979 after protracted evaluation.

To rectify the problems Marconi initiated development of a product-improved version, the **Mk 24 Mod 1**, during 1972 but this also encountered technical problems and finally entered limited service in mid-1978. By 1981 sufficient update kits were available to upgrade all the earlier Mod 0 weapons to this standard. Designed for submarine use against submerged (Mod 0 and 1) and surface (Mod 1) targets, the dual-speed electric-powered Tigerfish is guided in its initial stage by wire dispensed from both the submarine and the torpedo itself, using data derived from the launch platform's passive sonar sets. The roll-stabilized (by retractable mid-body stub wings) torpedo is guided in this fashion up to the point where its own three-dimensional active/passive sonar seeker head and computer can take over for the attack on the target. At present only the Royal and Brazilian navies use the Tigerfish. A further programme is under way to examine possible enhancements to the weapon's capabilities with a view to countering the new generation of Soviet nuclear submarines.

Specification
Mk 24 Tigerfish
Dimensions: diameter 533 mm (21 in); length 6.464 m (21.2 ft)
Weight: 1547 kg (3,410 lb)
Warhead: 134-kg (295-lb) HE
Performance: speed 24 or 35 kts; range 21 or 13 km (13.05 or 8.08 miles)

The Tigerfish is propelled by a two-speed electric motor driving a pair of contra-rotating propellers designed for high efficiency and low noise production. The 134-kg (295-lb) high-explosive warhead can be detonated by contact or by proximity fusing.

The end result of an unbelievably protracted development programme, the Tigerfish wire-guided heavyweight torpedo is a development of the Mk 24 torpedo, having a maximum speed variously estimated at 35 or 50 kts and a maximum range at low speed of some 21 km (13 miles).

Marconi Spearfish torpedo

Designed to meet Naval Staff Requirement 7525, the **Marconi Spearfish** is an advanced-capabilities wire-guided dual-role (ASW anti-ship) heavyweight torpedo. It was intended to engage the new generation of Soviet high-speed deep-submergence submarines using a new HAP-Otto fuel-powered Sundstrand 21TP01 gas turbine engine with a pump-jet outlet to achieve speeds in excess of 60 kts (up to 70 kts on trials). The warhead is of the directed-energy shaped-charge type and is capable of penetrating the latest Soviet developments in submarine double-hull construction which can be found aboard the 'Oscar' SSGN and 'Typhoon' SSBN classes. To ensure that the weapon actually contacts the target's hull the installed guidance system uses technology developed originally for the Stingray lightweight torpedo project. The computer will enable the torpedo to make its own tactical decisions during an engagement, optimizing the homing modes available to the underwater environment encountered and to the target's use of decoys and manoeuvring patterns.

Work on the development prototypes began in 1982, the first in water trials taking place in the following year. Production deliveries began in 1990, and Spearfish is now the primary torpedo armament of all British nuclear submarines.

Externally very similar to the Mk 24 Tigerfish wire-guided torpedo that it will eventually replace, the Marconi Spearfish is radically different internally and has a considerably enhanced performance.

Specification (provisional)
Spearfish
Dimensions: diameter 533 mm (21 in); length 8.5 m (27.9 ft)
Weight: 1996 kg (4,400 lb)
Warhead: 249-kg (550-lb) HE
Performance: speed 24 or 60 kts; range 46.25 or 28.6 km (28.75 or 17.75 miles)

Above: An early development model of the Spearfish is seen at the start of water trials. The torpedo guidance system is thought to make use of a digital computer (as in the Stingray), and the highly classified directed energy warhead is designed to cope with the latest Soviet submarines.

Left: Powered by an HAP-Otto fuelled gas turbine giving considerably more power density than electric motors, the Spearfish has achieved great speeds on trials, reaching more than 60 kts.

FFV Tp42 series torpedoes

Originally intended as the successor to the Royal Swedish navy's Tp41, the **Tp42** is the base model of a whole series of lightweight 400-mm (15.75-in) torpedoes built by FFV for the home market and for export. The basic model, the **Tp422**, entered service in mid-1983 and is intended primarily for ASW operations from the navy's small fleet of Boeing-Vertol 107 helicopters. It is unique amongst Western lightweight weapons in that it is capable of wire guidance after an air-launched delivery. The terminal attack phase is carried out by a passive sonar system. Propulsion is by an electric battery of the silver-zinc type, whilst the warhead is fitted with both proximity and contact fuses. The torpedo can be set to run at one of two speeds which are changeable after launch either via the guidance wire or as an instruction pre-programmed into the seeker unit. A similar model, the **Tp423**, is believed to be intended for launch from surface ships and submarines against submarine or ship targets. The export version of the Tp422/423 is known as the **Tp427**, and has internal/guidance changes which effectively introduce different sonar and proximity fuse frequencies in order not to compromise Swedish navy settings.

In 1984 the Swedish navy initiated a product improvement programme that has resulted in the **Tp432**, which is due to enter production in 1987. This is designed to use new digital microprocessor guidance units and is optimized to attack the new generation of Soviet conventional submarines oper-

ating in the quiet state in shallow waters. A new three-speed selectable propulsion system and increased guidance wire capacity have improved the maximum range of the weapon, at the slowest speed, by 33 per cent in comparison with the earlier Tp42 models. The equivalent export version is designated **Tp43XO** and will be able to use alternative propulsion systems if required. The lightest of the whole Tp43XO family will be the helicopter-launched variant which weighs 280 kg (617 lb), and because it has a smaller battery capacity this will have a maximum range in the order of 15-20 km (9.3-12.4 miles) at the slowest speed setting.

Specification
Tp422/427
Dimensions: diameter 400 mm (15.75 in); length 2.44 m (8.00 ft), or 2.60 m (8.53 ft) with wire guidance section
Weight: 298 kg (657 lb)
Warhead: 45-kg (99-lb) HE
Performance: speed 15 or 25 kts; range 20 or 10 km (12.43 or 6.21 miles)

Specification
Tp432/43XO
Dimensions: diameter 400 mm (15.75 in); length 2.60 m (8.53 ft), or 2.85 m (9.35 ft) with wire guidance section
Weight: 280 to 350 kg (617 to 772 lb)
Warhead: 45-kg (99-lb) HE
Performance: speed 15, 25 or 35 kts; range 30, 20 or 10 km (18.64, 12.43 or 6.21 miles)

Above: The Type 42 range of lightweight 400-mm (15.75-in) torpedoes is the only air-launched torpedo known to be wire-guided. It can be controlled by a hovering or cruising helicopter, although a variant has been designed for surface or submarine use. The Type 427 export version is illustrated.

Below: The advantage of lightweight torpedoes is that they can give a significant anti-submarine capability to the smallest of helicopters. The Type 422 has been launched from the Swedish navy's AB-406 helicopters, although the KV 107 (licence-built Boeing-Vertol CH-46) is the usual platform.

FFV Tp61 series torpedoes

Designed by FFV for use against surface ship targets, the **Tp61** entered service in 1967 as a non-terminal-homing wire-guided heavyweight torpedo for use by surface ships, submarines and coastal defence batteries. In 1984 the longer-range **Tp613** entered service as the Tp61's successor with essentially the same propulsion system and a terminal homing seeker that utilizes an onboard computer to oversee the attack and, if necessary, to initiate previously-programmed search patterns at the target's predicted location. The computer also guides the torpedo to the latter point and initiates a search even if the guidance wire is broken. The torpedo's thermal propulsion system combines hydrogen peroxide with ethanol to power a 12-cylinder steam motor which produces an almost invisible wake signature. Compared with modern electrically-powered weapons at similar speed, the maximum range attainable is between three and five times greater.

The earlier Tp61 is in service with Norway, whilst the Tp613 has recently been ordered by Denmark. Norway is also expected to purchase this variant in the near future. For other nations there is the **Tp617** export version which differs from the Tp613 only in

Unlike most modern heavyweight torpedoes, the FFV Tp61 is not powered electrically but by a hydrogen-peroxide/ethanol driven engine. Such systems are more unstable than battery power, but of much higher performance.

Norway is in the process of acquiring the improved Tp613 torpedo in place of the Tp61 already operated. The new weapon will probably equip the 'Type 207' submarines such as Uthaug, seen here, as well as the new 'Type 210' class which will enter service in the 1990s.

internal software changes to give sonar and proximity fuse settings different from Swedish ones. Each Tp61 series torpedo can be left in its tube for up to four months without requiring overhaul.

Specification
Tp61
Dimensions: diameter 533 mm (21 in); length 7.025 m (23.05 ft)
Weight: 1796 kg (3,959 lb) or (Tp613) 1850 kg (4,078 lb)
Warhead: 250-kg (551-lb) HE
Performance: speed 45 kts; range 20 km (1.43 miles) or (Tp613) 30 km (18.64 miles)

Snar, a 'Snogg' class fast attack craft, is fitted with four 533-mm (21-in) torpedo tubes in addition to Penguin anti-ship missiles. The torpedo and the missile have similar ranges and although the missile is much faster the torpedo does not appear on any radar screen.

 USA
Mk 37 torpedo

The original **Westinghouse Mk 37 Mod 0** heavyweight torpedo entered service in 1956 as a submarine- and surface ship-launched ASW acoustic-homing free-running torpedo. Fitted with studs along its sides, the 482.6-mm (19-in) calibre Mk 37 can be fired from standard 533-mm (21-in) torpedo tubes. As operational experience built up with the weapon, many Mod 0 torpedoes were refurbished and modified to bring them up to the **Mk 37 Mod 3** standard. Although useful in the ASW role these free-running weapons, which could dive to 300 m (985 ft), were not suited to really long sonar detection ranges as during the torpedo's run to a predicted target location it was possible that the target could perform evasive manoeuvres taking it out of the 640 m (2,100-ft) acquisition range of the weapon's seeker head. Thus wire guidance was fitted to the Mk 37 to produce the **Mk 37 Mod 1** version, which entered service in 1962 aboard American submarines. This was followed by the updated **Mk 37 Mod 2** conversion of Mod 1 weapons. Although the standard US Navy submarine-launched ASW torpedo for some 20 years, the Mk 37 is now found only aboard the diesel-electric boat USS *Darter*.

Many have been converted to Mk 67 submarine-launched mobile mine shells, whilst others have been put through major upgrading programmes before sale to other countries. The first such modification, in the mid-1970s, resulted in the **Northrop NT37C**, which incorporates a new thermo-chemical propulsion system based on that of the Mk 46 and has an anti-ship capability option. The NT37C is known to be in service with Canada and Israel aboard their submarine fleets. In 1979 Honeywell acquired the rights to the NT37C, and at the request of several NATO Mk 37 users further developed the weapon to the **Honeywell NT37E** standard which allows the fitting of several additional kits to produce **NT37E Mod 2** and **NT37E Mod 3** conversions of the basic Mk 37 variants. In general terms these new variants display a 40 per cent increase in speed, a 150 per cent increase in range, an 80 per cent increase in endurance and a 100 per cent increase in seeker detection range in comparison with the original Mk 37 models. At least 16 countries are known to use the various versions of the Mk 37 family including the above, plus West Germany, Spain, Argentina and the Netherlands.

Specification
Mk 37
Dimensions: diameter 484.6 mm (19 in); length (Mod 0 and 3) 3.52 m (11.55 ft) or (Mod 1 and 2) 4.09 m (13.42 ft)
Weight: (Mod 0 and 3) 649 kg (1,430 lb) or (Mod 1 and 2) 767 kg (1,690 lb)
Warhead: 150-kg (330-lb) HE
Performance: speed 16 or 24 kts; range (Mod 0 and 3) 16.5 or 7.3 km (10.25 or 4.5 miles), or (Mod 1 and 2) 8.7 km (5.4 miles)

Specification
NT37E
Dimensions: diameter 484.6 mm (19 in); length (Mod 2) 4.506 m (14.78 ft) or (Mod 3) 3,946 m (12.62 ft)
Weight: (Mod 2) 748 kg (1,650 lb) or (Mod 3) 640 kg (1,412 lb)
Warhead: 150-kg (330-lb) HE
Performance: speed 22.4 or 33.6 kts; range (Mod 2) 21.7 km (13.5 miles) or (Mod 3) 18.3 km (11.4 miles)

Above: Dutch seamen manoeuvre the long, heavy bulk of a NATO standard NT37 torpedo into one of the forward tubes of a 'Dolfijn' class submarine. The original Mk 37 entered service in the 1950s, but progressive modifications by Westinghouse and Northrop have upgraded the weapon's capability to an enormous extent.

Left: In its anti-ship version the NT37 can be programmed to explode on contact or be fitted with an acoustic proximity fuse. By adjusting the running depth this can ensure detonation immediately under the target, so breaking the ship's back. Had the trial torpedo seen here been armed, the explosion would have occurred immediately under the engines.

Mk 44, Mk 46 and Mk 50 torpedoes

The **Mk 44 Mod 0** lightweight torpedo was selected for production in 1956 and in the following year became the payload for the new ASROC ASW missile as well as the standard US Navy ship- and air-launched lightweight torpedo. The weapon is electrically powered, and utilizes a seawater-activated battery and an active-homing seeker with a detection range of 585 m (1,920 ft). A slightly modified version, the **Mk 44 Mod 1**, was produced at a latter date, and this model differed only in internal details. Several countries procured the weapon, but most have now replaced it with the Mk 46 although some like the UK have kept stocks because of the Mk 44's better shallow-water performance than its successor. The US Navy replaced it completely from 1967 onwards by the **Mk 46**.

The active/passive acoustic-homing Mk 46 programme began in 1960, the first production rounds of the air-launched **Mk 46 Mod 0** variant being delivered in 1963. The new torpedo achieved twice the range of the Mk 44, could dive deeper (460 m/1,500 ft versus 300 m/984 ft) and was 50 per cent faster (45 kts versus 30 kts) because of the use of a new type of propulsive system. In the Mod 0 this was a solid-fuel motor, but as a result of maintenance difficulties it had to be changed to the Otto-fuelled thermo-chemical cam engine in the follow-on **Mk 46 Mod 1** (which first entered service in 1967 for use in ASROC, surface ship and some airborne launching purposes) and the **Mk 46 Mod 2** that first appeared in 1972. There was no Mod 3, so the next variant to see service was the **Mk 46 Mod 4** intended specifically for use as the payload for Mk 60 CAP-TOR mines. However, because of Soviet submarine developments (primarily in the area of anechoic hull coatings to degrade active sonar acoustic transmissions) the US Navy had to develop a modification kit with new guidance and control units, engine improvements and an enhanced sonar transducer to restore the 33 per cent loss in the 550-m (1,800-ft) detection range suffered by Mk 46s when encountering such coatings. Known by the title **NEARTIP** (NEAR-Term Improvement Program), the **Mk 46 Mod 5** is being procured both as new-build weapons and as conversions of the earlier Mod 1 and Mod 2 weapons.

Apart from the US Navy, other users of the Mk 46 include Australia, Brazil, Canada, France, Greece, Indonesia, Iran, Israel, Italy, Morocco, the Netherlands, New Zealand, Pakistan, Saudi Arabia, Spain, Turkey, Taiwan, the UK and West Germany. The Mk 46 was used operationally by the Royal Navy on a number of occasions during the Falklands war with inconclusive results, although the threat of Mk 46s did help in the damaging and subsequent grounding of the Argentine submarine *Santa Fe* off South Georgia.

The replacement for the Mk 46 in US Navy service is the **Advanced Lightweight Torpedo (ALWT)**, which has now been given the designation **Mk 50 Barracuda** following a competitive evaluation. Fitted with a directed-energy shaped-charge warhead, the Mk 50 is roughly the same size and weight as the Mk 46 but will be faster at 55+ kts and be able to dive deeper (to 600 m/1,970 ft). It will also have a new stored chemical-energy propulsion system with a closed-cycle steam turbine in conjunction with a pump-jet arrangement. An onboard computer and advanced active/passive sonar will give the weapon 'smart' capabilities similar to those of the British Stingray. An in-service date of 1990 is anticipated.

Specification
Mk 44
Dimensions: diameter 324 mm (12.75 in); length (Mod 0) 2.54 m (8.33 ft) or (Mod 1) 2.57 m (8.44 ft)
Weight: (Mod 0) 192.8 kg (425 lb) or (Mod 1) 196.4 kg (433 lb)
Warhead: (Mod 0) 34-kg (75-lb) HE or (Mod 1) 33.1-kg (73-lb) HE
Performance: speed 30 kts; range 5.5 km (3.4 miles)

Specification
Mk 46
Dimensions: diameter 324 mm (12.75 in); length 2.6 m (8.5 ft)
Weight: (Mod 0) 257.6 kg (568 lb) or (Mod 1, 2, 4 and 5) 230.4 kg (508 lb)
Warhead: 43.1-kg (95-lb) HE
Performance: speed 40/45 kts; range 11 km (6.8 miles) at 15-m (50-ft) depth or 5.5 km (3.4 miles) at 457-m (1,500-ft) depth

Specification (provisional)
Mk 50 Barracuda
Dimensions: diameter 324 mm (12.75 in); length 2.9 m (9.5 ft)
Weight: 362.9 kg (800 lb)
Warhead: 45.4-kg (100-lb) shaped-charge HE
Performance: speed 55+ kts; range 13.7 km (8.5 miles)

More than 9,000 Mk 46 lightweight torpedoes have been produced by Honeywell for service with the US Navy and the naval forces of more than 20 other countries. It is launched from the air, the surface and by ASROC.

Above: The development of the dedicated anti-submarine helicopter, together with the lightweight acoustic homing torpedo, has immensely extended ASW radius. This Mk 46 torpedo, dropped by an SH-3A Sea King, is deploying a parachute to retard its speed.

Right: A Mk 46 torpedo is launched from one of the triple torpedo tubes fitted to all of the cruisers, destroyers and frigates of the US Navy.

The Israeli navy is one of several that have acquired Mk 46 torpedoes, and some of the 36 'Dabur' class coastal patrol craft operating in the Mediterranen and the Red Sea have been equipped with a pair of single tubes.

Mk 48 torpedo

The **Mk 48** heavyweight torpedo is the latest in a long line of US Navy 533-mm (21-in) calibre submarine-launched weapons. As a long-range selectable-speed wire-guided dual-role (ASW/anti-ship) weapon it replaced both the Mk 37 series wire-guided ASW torpedo and the US Navy's only nuclear-armed torpedo, the anti-ship Mk 45 ASTOR fitted with a 10-kiloton yield W34 warhead. Development of the Mk 48 began in 1957 when feasibility studies were initiated to meet an operational requirement eventually issued in late 1960. The weapon was intended as both a surface- and submarine-launched torpedo, but the former requirement was dropped when surface-launched weapons went out of favour. Two versions were produced to meet the range and speed performance figures needed to engage a 35-kt submerged target: the **Westinghouse Mk 48 Mod 0**, which used a gas turbine and was subsequently refined to the proposed production **Mk 48 Mod 2** variant, and the **Gould Mk 48 Mod 1** which used an Otto-fuelled piston (swashplate) engine and a redesigned acoustic-homing system. The latter was chosen for mass production, operational capability being achieved in 1972.

The next version to be built was the

The Mk 48 torpedo is carried by all US attack and ballistic missile submarines, a continual process of development having enhanced its performance in line with that of Soviet submarines in the past 15 years.

Mk 48 Mod 3, which had the same 762-m (2,500-ft) depth capability as the Mod 1 but introduced a new two-way TELECOM (rather than one-way) wire-guidance communication link that allowed the torpedo head to transmit its search data back to the launch platform for more accurate processing to produce what was in effect a track-via-torpedo guidance mode.

The latest production standard (to which most previous weapons are being upgraded) is the **Mk 48 Mod 4**. This has the same TELECOM facilities of the Mod 3, enhanced speed (to 55 kts) and depth (to 915 m/3,000 ft) capabilities, plus an additional fire-and-forget mode which can be initiated if the torpedo's own noise masks the launch submarine's passive sonar detection sets.

By 1978, because of an increasing awareness of the latest Soviet submarine capabilities in the area of speed and diving depth, an **ADvanced CAPability (ADCAP)** version of the Mk 48, the **Mk 48 Mod 5**, entered development. A new higher-powered sonar was fitted both to improve the target acquisition range from the current 3660 m (12,000 ft) and to reduce the effect of enemy decoys and anechoic coatings. The sonar is electrically steered to decrease the need for the torpedo to manoeuvre in the search phase. Together with a larger fuel load, this gives the new variant a longer range (using the same propulsion system) and a new under-ice capability. Further modifications are at present being researched to give an **Upgraded ADCAP** weapon for the next

decade: these developments include improved anti-ship homing features, an even greater maximum diving depth and a higher target speed engagement envelope. The operational date for the first ADCAP Mk 48 Mod 5 is expected to be 1986. Foreign users of the Mk 48 are limited to Australia and the Netherlands.

Specification
Mk 48
Dimensions: diameter 533 mm (21 in); length 5.8 m (19.17 ft)
Weight: 1579 kg (3,480 lb)
Warhead: 294.5-kg (650-lb) HE
Performance: speed (Mod 1 and 3) 48 kts, (Mod 4) 55 kts or (Mod 5) 60 kts; range (Mod 1 and 3) 32 km (20 miles), (Mod 4) 28 km (17.5 miles) or (Mod 5) 38 km (23.75 miles)

Above: Crewmen aboard the 'Sturgeon' class nuclear attack submarine USS Pargo carefully receive a Mk 48 Mod 1 torpedo into the torpedo room. Most current American SSNs have reduced torpedo armament to allow for missiles such as Subroc, Harpoon and Tomahawk, or tube-launched mines.

Above left: A Mk 48 torpedo is lowered into the torpedo room of the nuclear-powered ballistic missile submarine USS Stonewall Jackson at the Naval Submarine Support base at Kings Bay, Georgia. These submarines are armed with torpedoes for self-protection only.

Left: An artist's impression of the last stage in the life of a Mk 48, with the onboard sonar homing in on the hapless target at a maximum speed of close to 60 kts.

Whitehead Motofides A184 and A244 torpedoes

The **A184** is a dual-purpose ASW/anti-ship heavyweight wire-guided torpedo produced by Whitehead Motofides and carried by Italian navy submarines and surface ships. It has also been exported to Taiwan for use on its 'Guppy II' and 'Improved Zwaardvis' class submarines. The panoramic active/passive acoustic-homing head controls the torpedo's course and depth in the final attack phase whilst the initial wire guidance uses the launch platform's own sonar sensors to guide the weapon up to the point of acoustic acquisition. Like most modern electrically-powered torpedoes the A184 is fitted with a silver-zinc battery and has dual speed capabilities (low speed for the passive hunting phase and high speed for the terminal attack or active phase).

To complement the A184 and replace the American Mk 44 for operations in the notoriously difficult ASW environment of the Mediterranean the lightweight **A244** was developed. This is an electrically-driven weapon suitable for use by aircraft, helicopters or surface ships in normal or shallow waters. In its original form it was fitted with a Selenia AG70 homing head, but the latest variant, the **A244/S**, has a CIACIO-S advanced homing seeker. Using special signal-processing technique, this allows both active and passive operations which can discriminate between a real target and decoys. The A244 and A244/S have been sold to a number of countries including Argentina, Ecuador, India, Indonesia, Iraq, Libya, Nigeria, Peru and Venezuela. Whitehead is currently working on a replacement weapon for the A244 series, the 50-kt high-performance **A290**, which uses seeker technology derived from the A244/S weapon.

Capable of submarine or surface launch, the Whitehead A184 is capable of engaging both submarine and surface targets. Wire-guided, it is capable of operating at great depths and in a two-speed mode.

Specification
A184
Dimensions: diameter 533 mm (21 in); length 6.00 m (19.69 ft)
Weight: 1265 kg (2,789 ;b)
Warhead: 250-kg (551-lb) HE
Performance: 24 or 36 kts; range 25 or 10 km (15.53 or 6.21 miles)

Specification
A244/S
Dimensions: diameter 324 mm (12.75 in); length 2.70 m (8.86 ft)
Weight: 221 kg (487 lb)
Warhead: 34-kg (75-lb) HE
Performance: speed 30 kts; range 6.5 km (4.04 miles)

The Mediterranean is a very difficult environment for the effective use of torpedoes, and the A244 has been designed to replace the US-built Mk 44 in Italian service with that fact in mind.

Right: Designed for launch from surface ships, helicopters and aircraft, the A244 is capable of both active and passive operations, in a wide variety of attack patterns. The weapon has also been adapted as a potential warload for the Ikara anti-submarine missile system.

Below: The A184 is the latest heavyweight product of one of the world's oldest torpedo manufacturers. As with most modern torpedoes, it is electrically powered to a maximum speed of 36 kts, and has a maximum range of 10 km (6.21 miles) at that speed.

Modern Diesel Submarines

The development of the nuclear-powered submarine has not sounded the death-knell of the conventional diesel-powered boat, as some commentators predicted. Indeed, the diesel submarine has developed unique qualities of quietness and shallow-water performance to rival the nuclear-powered craft.

In some naval circles, it was thought that the advent of the nuclear submarine would mean the demise of the old-fashioned diesel-powered boats, craft which had carried the submarine through all the stages of its development since World War I. Such was not the case.

The Unites States Navy, for example, placed all its eggs in the nuclear submarine basket: its last three diesel-electric boats, known as SSKs, were built in the late 1950s. These were the 'Barbel' class, impressive boats of 2,140 tons surface displacement and capable of 21 knots for short periods. They were the first boats to have all their controls centralized in an 'attack centre'. An even larger diesel -electric boat, the 'Guppy III' was contemplated; this was a standard 'Guppy II', lengthened by 3.05 m (10 ft) to provide a larger control room. Nine boats were planned, all to be fitted with an updated fire-control system to enable them to fire the Mk 45 Astor nuclear anti-submarine torpedo. The only problem with this weapon was that its blast radius exceeded its range, so the attacker would probably have been destroyed along with the target.

The Russians on the other hand

HMS *Upholder* (S40) a 'Type 2400' submarine developed by Vickers shipbuilders. The first units were ordered by the Royal Navy in 1983 to replace the 'Oberon' class.

never lost faith in the SSK: they continued to develop it alongside their nuclear types. Most of their diesel-electric boats were held in reserve during the Cold War – something western analysts did not know at the time.

Today the diesel-electric submarine is still in active service. Only the richer nations can afford the costly nuclear powerplants that are necessary for long-endurance ocean patrol; for other countries, the diesel-electric boat provides a cost-effective solution to the problem of maintaining an undersea presence in territorial waters. Diesel-electric boats also have a considerable advantage in that they are very quiet when running on their electric motors underwater, which makes them very hard to detect.

Today, NATO navies, long dedicated to hunting Russian submarines in the ocean depths and now occupied with 'police actions' on behalf of the UN, often in restricted waters like the Adriatic, must face the threat of the small diesel submarine in potentially hostile hands.

'Agosta' class

Designed by the French Directorate of Naval Construction as very quiet but high performance ocean-going SSKs, the **'Agosta' class** boats are each armed with four bow torpedo tubes that are equipped with a rapid-reload pneumatic ramming system that can launch weapons with the minimum of noise signature. The tubes are of a completely new design which allows the submarine to fire its weapons at all speeds and at any depth down to its maximum operational limit.

The four boats in service with the French navy as its last conventionally powered submarines are the **Agosta** (S620), **Beveziers** (S621), **La Praya** (S622) and **Ouessant** (S623). All were authorized in the 1970-5 naval programme as the follow-on class to the 'Daphnés'. One, *La Praya*, has since been refitted with a removable swimmer delivery vehicle container aft of the sail to replace similar facilities that were available aboard the now-deleted submarine *Narval*. The Spanish navy built locally four 'Agostas' in the early 1980s, namely the **Galerna** (S71), **Sciroco** (S72), **Mistral** (S73) and **Tramontana** (S74) using French electronics and L5, F17 and E18 torpedoes. Pakistan purchased in mid-1978 two units (built originally for South Africa but embargoed) as the **Hashmat** (S135) and **Hurmat** (S136). Pakistan ordered three more boats of this class in September 1994. The French boats are armed with the Aerospatiale SM39 Exocet missile; 20 missiles and torpedoes can be carried in a mixed load. The Agostas were the first boats in the French Navy to be fitted with 533-mm (21-in) torpedo tubes. The two remaining French boats (**La Praya** and

Ouessant) have been based at Brest since June 1995 and assigned to the Atlantic Attack Submarine Group. La Praya was due to be paid off in 1999; Oussant was to remain in service until 2005 as a trials ship.

Specification
'Agosta' class
Displacement: 1,480 tons surfaced and 1,760 tons dived
Dimensions: length 67.6 m (221.8 ft); beam 6.8 m (22.3 ft); draught 5.4 m (17.7 ft)
Propulsion: two diesels delivering

3430 kW (4,600 hp) with one electric motor driving one shaft
Speed: 12.5 kts surfaced and 17.5 kts dived
Diving depth: 300 m (984 ft) operational and 500 m (1,640 ft) maximum
Torpedo tubes: four 550-mm (21.7-in) with 533-mm (21-in) liners
Basic load: 23 550-mm (21.7-in) or 533-mm (21-in) anti-submarine and anti-ship torpedoes, or 46 influence ground mines
Missiles: SM.39 Exocet underwater-to-surface anti-ship missiles

Agosta (S620) is lead ship of the last class of conventionally-powered submarines to be built for the French navy. All will be fitted to fire the SM-39 Exocet submerged launched anti-ship missile in the next few years.

Electronics: one DRUA 23 surface-search radar, one DUUA 2A sonar, or DUUA 1D sonar, one DUUX 2A sonar, one DSUV 2H sonar, one ARUR ESM system, one ARUD ESM system, and one torpedo fire-control/action information system
Complement: 54

'Daphné' class

In 1952 plans were requested from STCAN for a second-class ocean-going submarine to complement the larger 'Narval' class. Designated the **'Daphné' class**, the boats were purposely designed with reduced speed in order to achieve a greater diving depth and heavier armament than was possible with the contemporary 'Aréthuse' design of conventionally-powered hunter-killer submarines. To reduce the crew's workload the main armament was contained in 12 externally-mounted torpedo tubes (eight forward and four aft), which eliminated the need for a torpedo room and reloads. Further crew reductions were made possible by adopting a modular replacement system for onboard maintenance. The design uses the double-hull construction technique with the accommodation spaces split evenly fore and aft of the sail, below which is the operations and attack centre.

A total of 11 units was built for the French navy. The **Daphné** (S641), **Diane** (S642), **Doris** (S643), **Eurydicé** (S644), **Flore** (S645), **Galatée** (S646),

Minérve (S647), **Junon** (S648), **Vénus** (S649), **Psyché** (S650) and **Sirène** (S651) entered service between 1964 and 1970. Of these two were lost (the *Minérve* in 1968 and the *Eurydicé* in 1970) with all hands while operating in the western Mediterranean. The remaining boats all underwent an electronics and weapons modernization from 1970 onwards. Besides those for the French navy, a further 10 were built for export. Portugal received the **Albacore** (S163), **Barracuda** (S164), **Cachalote** (S165) and **Delfin** (S166), of which S165 was sold to Pakistan in 1975 as the **Ghazi** (S134). Pakistan also has the **Hangor** (S131), **Shushuk** (S132) and **Mangro** (S133). South Africa operates the **Maria Van Riebeeck** (S97), **Emily Hobhouse** (S98) and **Johanna**

Below: Once the 'Daphné' class units wear out they will not be replaced, as the French navy will concentrate on building only nuclear attack submarines for the future.

Above: Lead ship of the class, the Daphné (S641), runs on the surface with her diesels. Of the nine remaining units of the class, only the Daphné has not undergone a full mid-life modernization which changes the shape of the bow area by adding a larger sonar dome.

Van der Merwe (S99). A further four, the *Delfin* (S61), *Tonina* (S62), *Marsopa* (S63) and *Narval* (S64) were built under licence in Spain and are currently undergoing a modernization similar to that applied to the French boats. In 1971 the Pakistani submarine *Hangor* sank the Indian navy frigate *Khukri* during the Indo-Pakistan War; this was the first submarine attack since World War II.

Specification
'Daphné' class
Displacement: 869 tons surfaced and 1,043 tons dived
Dimensions: length 57.8 m (189.6 ft); beam 6.8 m (22.3 ft); draught 4.6 m (15.1 m)
Propulsion: two diesels delivering 1825 kW (2,448 hp) with two electric motors driving two shafts
Speed: 13.5 kts surfaced and 16 kts dived
Diving depth: 300 m (984 ft) operational and 575 m (1,886 ft) maximum
Torpedo tubes: 12 550-mm (21.7-in) located as eight in the bows and four in the stern
Basic load: 12 550-mm (21.7-in) anti-submarine and anti-ship torpedoes, or 24 ground influence mines
Electronics: one Calypso II surface-search radar, one DUUX 2 sonar, one DSUV 2 sonar, one DUUA 1 sonar, one DUUA 2 sonar, and one torpedo fire-control/action information system
Complement: 45

UK
'Oberon' class

Built in the late 1950s to the mid-1960s as the follow-on design to the 'Porpoise' class, the **'Oberon' class** was outwardly identical with its predecessor while internally there are a number of differences. These include the soundproofing of all the equipment for silent running and the use of a higher-grade steel for the hull to allow a greater maximum diving depth. A total of 13 units was commissioned into the Royal Navy between 1960 and 1967. They were HMS *Oberon* (S09), *Odin* (S10), *Orpheus* (S11), *Olympus* (S12), *Osiris* (S13), *Onslaught* (S14), *Otter* (S15), *Oracle* (S16), *Ocelot* (S17), *Otus* (S18), *Opossum* (S19), *Opportune* (S20) and *Onyx* (S21). The 'Oberon' has since been modified with a deeper casing to house equipment for the initial training of personnel for the nuclear submarine fleet. Several other units are also being modified for this role. The *Opossum* is now operating with a new GRP bow sonar dome and has been used recently as a trials vessel for an integrated combat operations centre that is under development for use in future submarine classes. The *Orpheus* has also been fitted with a special five-man lock-out diving chamber in its forecasing for covert operations, and for training by the Special Boat Squadron and Special Air Service. The *Onyx* served in the South Atlantic during the Falklands war on periscope beach reconnaissance operations and for landing special forces, and while performing these duties she rammed a rock, which caused a live torpedo to become stuck in one of her bow tubes. This weapon had to be removed in dry dock after she had returned to Portsmouth. The two shortened 533-mm (21-in) stern tubes that were used for Mk 20S anti-escort torpedoes have recently been converted to carry additional stores such as extra stocks of beer.

The 'Oberon' design has also been sold to several foreign navies. Chile bought the *O'Brien* (22) and *Hyatt* (23); Brazil the *Humaita* (S20), *Tonelero* (S21) and *Riachuelo* (S22); Canada the *Ojibwa* (72), *Onondaga* (73) and *Okanagan* (74); and Australia the *Oxley* (S57), *Otway* (S59), *Onslow* (S60), *Orion* (S61), *Otama* (S62) and *Ovens* (S70). The Canadian and Australian units have been modernized to a higher standard than that prevailing in the Royal Navy's units.

Specification
'Oberon' class
Displacement: 2,030 tons surfaced and 2,410 tons dived
Dimensions: length 90.0 m (295.25 ft); beam 8.1 m (26.5 ft); draught 5.5 m (18.0 ft)
Propulsion: two diesels delivering 5488 kW (7,360 hp) with two electric motors driving two shafts
Speed: 12 kts surfaced and 17.5 kts dived
Diving depth: 200 m (656 ft) operational and 340 m (1,115 ft) maximum
Torpedo tubes: eight 533-mm (21-in) located as six in the bows and two short in the stern
Basic load: 22 533-mm (21-in) anti-submarine and anti-ship torpedoes; British boats carry only 18 torpedoes
Electronics: one Type 1006 surface-search radar, one Type 187 sonar, one Type 2007 sonar, one Type 186 sonar, one torpedo fire-control/action information system, and one ESM system
Complement: 69

Although somewhat long in the tooth, the 'Oberon' class are still considered to be amongst the quietest conventional submarines ever built and will serve on into the 1990s as training boats.

UK
'Upholder' class

To meet a requirement for a new conventional submarine class for the Royal Navy, Vickers Shipbuilding and Engineering Ltd has developed the **'Type 2400'** or **'Upholder' class**. As with most new submarine classes, the emphasis has been placed on standardization and automation to reduce crew numbers. The first of the class was ordered in 1983 with an estimated completion date of 1988. A class total of 12 units was originally envisaged to replace most of the earlier 'Oberon' class vessels. Also included in the design are several advanced noise-reduction features that will reduce the radiated noise levels below those generated even by the very quiet 'Oberon' class. There will also be a reduction in the short time required to recharge the batteries to ensure the absolute minimum exposure time of any part of the masts above the water. The armament fit includes a new positive discharge and fully automated weapon-handling system which avoids the stability problems that arise at torpedo launch and the limitations that are sometimes made on the platform's speed and manoeuvrability. The weapons carried will include the heavyweight Tigerfish electric and the Spearfish thermal-powered dual-role wire-guided torpedoes, as well as the American Sub-Harpoon anti-ship missile. As part of the sensor fit a towed-array sonar will be carried, as will the Type 2040 active/passive bow sonar based on the French Thomson-CSF Argonaute set.

Specification
'Upholder' class
Displacement: 2,160 tons surfaced and 2,400 tons dived
Dimensions: length 70.3 m (230.6 ft); beam 7.6 m (25.0 ft); draught 5.4 m (17.7 ft)
Propulsion: two diesels with one electric motor driving one shaft
Speed: 12 kts surfaced and 20 kts dived
Diving depth: 300 m (984 ft) operational and 500 m (1,640 ft)

maximum
Torpedo tubes: six 533-mm (21-in) bow
Basic load: 18 533-mm (21-in) anti-submarine and anti-ship torpedoes, or 36 influence ground mines
Missiles: Sub-Harpoon underwater-to-surface anti-ship missiles
Electronics: one Type 1006 surface-search radar, one Type 2040 bow sonar, one Type 2024 towed-array sonar, one Type 2019 sonar, one DCC torpedo fire-control/action information system, and one ESM system
Complement: 44

Four units of the Upholder class were commissioned in the early 1990s: Upholder, Unsay, Ursula, and Unicorn. All are armed with Spearfish and Sub-Harpoon torpedoes.

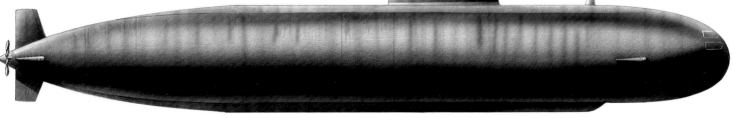

'Type 206' and 'Type 209' classes

Israel ordered three of the 'Type 640' variant from Vickers in Barrow, all being commissioned in 1977. They were originally to be fitted with the SLAM anti-aircraft missile system in the fin.

Studies began in 1962 by IKL for a follow-on development of the 'Type 205' design. The new **'Type 206' class**, built of high-tensile non-magnetic steel, was to be used for coastal operations and had to conform with treaty limitations on the maximum tonnage allowed to West Germany. New safety devices for the crew were fitted, and the armament fit allowed for the carriage of wire-guided torpedoes. After final design approval had been given, construction planning took place in 1966-8, and the first orders (for an eventual total of 18 units) were placed in the following year. By 1975 all the vessels, **U13** to **U30** (S192-199 and S170-179), were in service. Since then the class has been given extra armament in the form of two external GRP containers to carry a total of 24 ground mines in addition to their normal torpedo armament. From 1988 onwards 12 of the class are to be modernized with new electronics and torpedoes to form the **'Type 206A' class**.

In the mid-1960s IKL also designed a new class of submarine for the export market that became the **'Type 209' class** in 1967. Designed specifically for the ocean-going role, the 'Type 209' can, because of its relatively short length, operate successfully in coastal waters. The 'Type 209' and its variants have proved so popular that over 40 have been built or ordered to date by a number of foreign navies. Five variations have so far been constructed: the original **54.3-m 'Type 209'** 178.1-ft long version (960 tons surfaced and 1,105 tons dived), the **56-m 'Type 209'** 183.7-ft long version (980 tons surfaced and 1,185 tons dived), the **59.5-m 'Type 209'** 195.2-ft long version (1,000 tons surfaced and 1,285 tons dived), the **64.4-m** (211.3-ft) **'Type 1500'** variant (1,660 tons surfaced and 1,850 tons dived) and the smaller **'Type 640'** 45-m (147.6-ft) long coastal derivative (420 tons surfaced and 600 tons dived). The countries which have bought these vessels are Greece (four 54.3-m and four 56-m 'Type 209s'), Argentina (two 56-m 'Type 209s'), Peru (six 56-m 'Type 209s'), Colombia (two 56-m 'Type 209s'), Turkey (12 56-m 'Type 209s', most of which are being built locally with West German help), Venezuela (two 59.5-m 'Type 209s'), Chile (two 59.5-m 'Type 209s'), Ecuador (two 59.5-m 'Type 209s'), Indonesia (two 59.5-m 'Type 209s' plus a further four projected), Brazil (two 59.5-m 'Type 209s' plus a further one projected), India

(four 'Type 1500' plus two more projected) and Israel (three 'Type 640' plus three larger units projected). Each country can choose its own equipment fit and crew complement level according to the amount of money it is willing to spend.

During the 1982 Falklands war the Argentine Type 209 submarine *San Luis* made three unsuccessful torpedo attacks on vessels of the British task force, but because of her presence tied up considerable British ship and aircraft resources in trying to find her.

Specification
'Type 206' class
Displacement: 450 tons surfaced and 500 tons dived
Dimensions: length 48.6 m (159.4 ft); beam 4.6 m (15.1 ft); draught 4.5 m (14.8 ft)
Propulsion: two diesels delivering 895 kW (1,200 hp) with one electric motor driving one shaft
Speed: 10 kts surfaced and 17 kts dived
Diving depth: 150 m (492 ft)

operational and 250 m (820 ft) maximum
Torpedo tubes: eight 533-mm (21-in) bow
Basic load: eight 533-mm (21-in) anti-submarine or anti-ship wire-guided torpedoes, or 16 influence ground mines, plus another 24 mines in external containers
Electronics: one Calypso surface-search radar, one low-frequency bow sonar, one high-frequency attack sonar, one WM-8 torpedo fire-control/action information system, and one ESM system
Complement: 22

Specification
56-m 'Type 209' class
Displacement: 980 tons surfaced and 1,185 tons dived
Dimensions: length 56.0 m (183.7 ft); beam 6.2 m (20.3 ft); draught 5.5 m (18.0 ft)
Propulsion: four diesels delivering 1790 kW (2,400 hp) with one electric

The Greek navy 'Type 209' Amphitrite (S117) was part of the second batch of four procured. The first batch was the first export order placed for the design, and they were delivered in the period 1971-2, with the second group following in 1979-80 (built to the larger 56-m/183.7-ft length).

motor driving one shaft
Speed: 10 kts surfaced and 22 kts dived
Diving depth: 300 m (984 ft) operational and 500 m (1,640 ft) maximum
Torpedo tubes: eight 533-mm (21-in) bow
Basic load: 14 533-mm (21-in) anti-submarine and anti-ship wire-guided torpedoes, or 28 influence ground mines
Electronics: one surface-search radar, one low-frequency bow sonar, one passive intercept sonar, one torpedo fire-control/action information system, and one ESM system
Complement: 31-35

The Peruvian navy has taken delivery of a total of six 'Type 209' submarines in three batches between 1975 and 1983. The Casma (S31) carries a total of 14 American NT-37C dual anti-ship/ASW torpedoes as her main armament in preference to the normal West German weapons sold with the vessels.

'Romeo' class

Although it was the Soviets who built the first **'Romeo' class** submarines in 1958 at Gorky, as an improvement on their 'Whiskey' design, the construction coincided with the successful introduction of nuclear propulsion into Soviet submarines, so only 20 were actually completed out of the 560 boats originally planned.

However, the design was passed to the Chinese as part of the development of their weapons production industry, and the class has been built in China since 1964, the first boats being completed at the Wuzhang shipyard under the local designation **'Type 033'**. Three further shipyards, located at Guangzhou (Canton), Jiangnan (Shanghai) and Huludao, then joined the programme to give a maximum yearly production rate of nine units during the early 1970s. This rate has now been reduced to two vessels per year. A total of 98 'Romeos' has been constructed to date for the Chinese navy, while a further 10 have been exported to Egypt (six) and North Korea (four, with another 11 built locally with Chinese assistance).

Of the original Soviet boats only 10 remain operational with the Soviet navy. Six were transferred to the Egyptians in 1966-8, two to Bulgaria in the early 1970s and two were loaned to Algeria in 1982-3 for a five-year period as training boats, before Algeria's acquisition of more modern submarines. In physical appearance both the Chinese and Soviet 'Romeos' are essentially identical except that the Soviet boats tend to have extra sonar installations around the bow.

Specification
'Romeo' class
Displacement: 1,330 tons surfaced and 1,700 tons dived
Dimensions: length 77.0 m (252.6 ft); beam 6.7 m (22.0 ft); draught 4.9 m (16.1 ft)

Propulsion: two diesels delivering 2983 kW (4,000 hp) with two electric motors driving two shafts
Speed: 6 kts surfaced and 13 kts dived
Diving depth: 300 m (984 ft) operational and 500 m (1,640 ft) maximum
Torpedo tubes: eight 533-mm (21-in) located as six in the bows and two at the stern
Basic load: 18 533-mm (21-in) anti-ship

or anti-submarine torpedoes, or 36 AMD-1000 influence ground mines
Electronics: one 'Snoop Plate' surface-search radar, one medium-frequency Feniks bow sonar, one high-frequency Herkules bow sonar, and one 'Stop Light' ECM system
Complement: 60

With only a few 'Romeo' class units left in service, the Soviet navy has transferred six to Egypt, two to Bulgaria and two to Algeria. The latter are on loan and are being used to train Algerian naval personnel in submarine operations prior to transfer of more modern units such as the export 'Foxtrot'.

The Chinese have adopted the Soviet 'Romeo' class as their main submarine production type. China has managed to export the design to Egypt and North Korea.

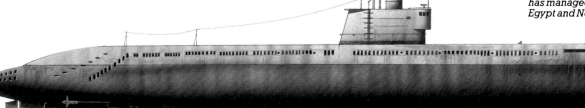

'Foxtrot' class

Built in the periods 1958-68 (45 units) and 1971-4 (17 units) at Sudomekh for the Soviet Union, the **'Foxtrot' class** is still in production at a slow rate for export. The class has proved to be the most successful of the post-war Soviet conventional submarine designs, a total of 62 entering service with the Soviet navy. Two were subsequently struck off as a result of damage sustained in accidents, one of them apparently caused by a collision with the Italian liner *Angelino Lauro* in the Bay of Naples on 10 January 1970, after which the unit was seen later at a Soviet naval anchorage off Morocco with 8 m (26.2 ft) of its bow missing. All four Soviet navy fleet areas operated 'Foxtrots' and the Mediterranean and Indian ocean squadrons regularly had

units attached to them as part of their subsurface forces.

The first foreign recipient of the type was India, which took eight brand new boats between 1968 and 1975. India was followed by Libya (with six units received between 1976 and 1983) and by Cuba (three boats handed over between 1979 and 1984). These differ from the standard Soviet units only in having export-grade electronic and weapon fits, although the Indian navy units are very close to the Soviet vessels.

Like all Soviet conventional and nuclear submarine classes, the 'Foxtrots' were fitted to carry the standard Soviet 15-kiloton yield anti-ship torpedo as part of its weapon load, but no liners for 400-mm (15.7-in) ASW torpedoes

have apparently not been fitted (contrary to several reports). The Soviet 'Foxtrots' were built in three distinct subclasses that differ only in the propulsion plant. The last group is thought to have served as prototypes for the follow-on 'Tango' 'design. All Russian Foxtrots were withdrawn from front-line service in the late 1980s.

Specification
'Foxtrot' class
Displacement: 1,950 tons surfaced and 2,500 tons dived
Dimensions: length 91.5 m (300.2 ft); beam 8.0 m (26.25 ft); draught 6.1 m (20.0 ft)
Propulsion: three diesels delivering 4474 kW (6,000 hp) with three electric

motors driving three shafts
Speed: 18 kts surfaced and 16 kts dived
Diving depth: 300 m (984 ft) operational and 500 m (1,640 ft) maximum
Torpedo tubes: 10 533-mm (21-in) located as six at the bows and four at the stern
Basic load: 22 533-mm (21-in) anti-ship and anti-submarine torpedoes, or 44 AMD-1000 influence ground mines
Electronics: one 'Snoop Tray' surface-search radar, one medium-frequency Feniks sonar, one high-frequency Herkules sonar, one torpedo fire-control/action information system, and one 'Stop Light' ECM system
Complement: 80

'Tango' class

Built as the Soviet navy's interim long-range successor to the 'Foxtrot' class in the Black Sea and Northern Fleet areas, the first unit of the **'Tango' class** was completed at Gorky in 1972. Since then a total of 18 have been constructed in two slightly different versions, the later type being several metres longer than the first in order to accommodate the fire-control systems necessary for launching the torpedo tube-launched SS-N-15, the Soviet equivalent of the American Subroc underwater-launched ASW missile with a nuclear warhead. The bow sonar installations appear to be the same as those fitted to the latter classes of contemporary Soviet nuclear attack submarines, while the propulsion plant is almost certainly the same as was tested on the last subgroup of the 'Foxtrot' design. The battery capacity is said to be much higher than in any preceding Soviet conventional submarine class as a result of the increased pressure hull volume, this allowing an underwater endurance in excess of a week before snorkelling is required. Coupled with the new armament and sensor fit, this made the 'Tangos' appear ideal for use in 'ambush' operations against Western nuclear submarines at natural 'choke points'.:Production of the 'Tango' class ceased in the early 1980s. Six remained in service in 1998, the rest having been paid off.

Specification
'Tango' class
Displacement: 3,000 tons surfaced and 3,700 tons dived
Dimensions: length 92.0 m (301.8 ft); beam 9.0 m (29.5 ft); draught 7.0 m (23.0 ft)
Propulsion: three diesels delivering 4474 kW (6,000 hp) with two electric motors driving two shafts
Speed: 16 kts surfaced and 15.5 kts dived
Diving depth: 300 m (984 ft) operational and 500 m (1,640 ft) maximum
Torpedo tubes: eight 533-mm (21-in) located as six in the bows and two at the stern
Basic load: 18 533-mm (21-in) anti-submarine and anti-ship torpedoes, or 36 AMD-1000 influence ground mines
Missiles: two SS-N-15 underwater-to-underwater anti-submarine missiles
Electronics: one 'Snoop Tray' surface-search radar, one low-frequency bow sonar, one medium-frequency torpedo and missile fire-control sonar, one torpedo fire-control/action information system, and one 'Brick Group' ESM system
Complement: 60

Evolved from the 'Foxtrot' class, the 'Tango' class long-range patrol submarine has been in service since the early 1970s. The example seen here was photographed off the US coast during the Soviet navy's 24th deployment to the Caribbean, in transit to Havana during late December 1984.

Production of the 'Tango ' class at the Gorky shipyard ended in the early 1980s. The design appears to be an improved 'Foxtrot' but with sensors and SS-N-15 ASW missiles of the third generation nuclear vessels.

The later 'Tango' class units were apparently built to a slightly longer length in order to accommodate all the systems associated with the ASW missile fire-control and targetting functions.

First seen at the July 1973 Sevastopol Naval Review in the Black Sea was the 'Tango' class prototype with the characteristic raised forecasing hump. The submarine to the front of the 'Tango' in the line is a 'Whiskey Twin Cylinder' cruise missile boat, which is used for training.

'Kilo' class

The **'Kilo' class** submarines were the replacements for the 'Whiskey' class which served in the Soviet Pacific Fleet, and as such are classed as medium-range vessels. Built at the river shipyard of Komsomolsk in the Soviet Far East, the first unit was launched in early 1980. At least a further five were in service by late 1984 with production believed to have been stepped up to two units per year. The shorter hull form, more advanced than the other contemporary Soviet conventional submarine designs, is more typical of Western teardrop-shaped designs, but is well suited to the enclosed waters off the Soviet Pacific coastlines and islands. In August 1983 the first operational 'Kilo' went to the vast Vietnamese naval base at Cam Ranh Bay for the testing of its weapons systems under tropical conditions, and in the following year the first sighting of a 'Kilo' in the Indian Ocean was disclosed by the Royal Australian Navy: the presence of the 'Kilo' class in that area is thought to be due to the replacement of the normal pair of 'Foxtrot' class submarines as an operational necessity, the new boats having far more sophisticated sonar systems. The armament is said to include some items of specialized minelaying equipment, possibly for the Soviet 'rising mine' weapons. The new low-frequency sonar is situated in the front of the bow above the six 533-mm (21-in) bow torpedo tubes. A probable class total of between 24 and 30 units is expected by the mid-1990s.

This 'Kilo' was seen in transit to the Indian Ocean from the Soviet naval base at Cam Ranh Bay in Vietnam. Fifteen 'Kilos' were still in Russian service in 1998. Kilo production continues at the rate of two a year for export.

Specification
'Kilo' class
Displacement: 2,500 tons surfaced and 3,200 tons dived
Dimensions: length 67.0 m (219.8 ft); beam 9.0 m (29.5 ft); draught 7.0 m (23.0 ft)
Propulsion: four diesels with two electric motors driving two shafts
Speed: 15 kts surfaced and 24 kts dived
Diving depth: 450 m (1,476 ft) and 650 m (2,133 ft) maximum
Torpedo tubes: six 533-mm (21-in) bow
Basic load: 18 533-mm (21-in) anti-submarine and anti-ship torpedoes, or 36 AMD-1000 influence ground mines, or a small number of 'rising mines'
Electronics: one 'Snoop Tray' surface-search radar, one low-frequency bow sonar, one medium-frequency torpedo fire-control sonar, one torpedo fire-control/action information system, and one 'Brick Group' ESM system
Complement: 60

Above: The 'Kilo' class is not precisely understood, although most reliable sources expect the class to be the successor to the elderly 'Whiskey/Foxtrot' units in, initially, the Pacific Fleet.

Below: Built at Komsomolsk at the rate of at least one a year, the 'Kilo' class is the first new operational diesel-electric powered design to be built for a number of years by the Soviets. It is believed that they have specialized mine-laying equipment as part of their armament.

'Enrico Toti' class

As the first indigenously-built Italian submarine design since World War II, the 'Enrico Toti' class had a chequered start as the actual plans had to be re-cast several times. With reasonable capabilities and performance, the four units are the *Attilio Bagnolini* (S505), *Enrico Toti* (S506), *Enrico Dandolo* (S513) and *Lazzaro Mocenigo* (S514), which entered service in 1968-9 for use in the notoriously difficult ASW conditions encountered in the central and eastern Mediterranean regions. For these operations the boats' relatively small size and minimum sonar cross-section stands them in good stead. The main armament carried is the White-head Motofides A184 533-mm (21-in) wire-guided torpedo. This is a dual ASW/anti-ship weapon with an active/passive acoustic-homing head that features enhanced ECCM to counter decoys launched or towed by a target. With a launch weight of 1300 kg (2,866 lb), a large HE warhead and a range in the order of 20 km (12.4 miles), the electrically-powered A184 can be used by the 'Enrico Totis' in 'ambush' situations at natural 'choke-points' to attack much larger opponents such as Soviet SSNs or SSGNs.

Specification
'Enrico Toti' class
Displacement: 524 tons surfaced and 591 tons dived
Dimensions: length 46.2 m (151.6 ft); beam 4.7 m (15.4 ft); draught 4.0 m (13.1 ft)
Propulsion: two diesels delivering 1641 kW (2,200 hp) with one electric motor driving one shaft
Speed: 14 kts surfaced and 15 kts dived
Diving depth: 180 m (591 ft) operational and 300 m (984 ft)

maximum
Torpedo tubes: four 533-mm (21-in) bow
Basic load: six A184 dual-role wire-guided torpedoes, or 12 ground influence mines
Electronics: one 3RM20/SMG surface-search radar, one IPD44 sonar, one MD64 sonar, one torpedo fire-control/action system, and one ESM system
Complement: 26

Third of the 'Enrico Toti' class was the Enrico Dandolo *(S513) which shows off the characteristic JP-64 active sonar system housing on the*

bow in this view. The crew for this relatively small class is four officers and 22 other ratings.

The 'Enrico Toti' class was designed specifically for the shallow water areas found around the Italian coastline. Armed with four bow torpedo tubes for the wire-guided A184 heavyweight torpedo, the four vessels have a top speed of 20 kts submerged for a short time, but can sustain 15 kts for one hour.

'Sauro' class

During the early 1970s it rapidly became apparent to the Italian navy that a new submarine design was required for defence against amphibious landings and for ASW and anti-shipping tasks in the local area. The result was the Italcantieri design for the 'Sauro' class, whose first two units were the *Nazio Sauro* (S518) and *Carlo Fecio di Cossato* (S519), which entered service in 1980 and 1979 respectively following major problems with their batteries. A further two units, the *Leonardo da Vinci* (S520) and the *Gugliermo Marconi* (S521) were then ordered, and these commissioned into service in 1981 and 1982. The class has a single pressure hull with external ballast tanks at the bow and stern and a buoyancy tank in the sail. The pressure hull is made from the US-developed HY80 high-tensile steel, which allows a deeper diving capability than on the previous 'Enrico Toti' design. The main armament is the Whitehead Motofides A184 dual-role

wire guided torpedo, but these can be replaced by Italian ground mines. Improved Sauros were commissioned in 1988-95: the *Salvatore Pelosi, Giuliano Prini, Primo Longobardo* and *Gianfrance Gazzana Priaroggia*. These have to have longer torpedo tubes to accommodate the US Sub-Harpoon anti-ship missile.

Specification
'Sauro' class
Displacement: 1,456 tons surfaced and 1,631 tons dived
Dimensions: length 63.9 m (209.6 ft); beam 6.8 m (22.3 ft); draught 5.7 m

The Leonardo da Vinci *(S520) is launched, in October 1979. The seven-bladed propeller used on the craft is noticeable, and is typical of the improvements made to submarines since the war in order to improve their speed and manoeuvrability.*

(18.7 ft)
Propulsion: three diesels delivering 2394 kW (3,210 hp) with one electric motor driving one shaft
Speed: 11 kts surfaced and 20 kts dived
Diving depth: 250 m (820 ft) operational and 410 m (1,345 ft) maximum
Torpedo tubes: six 533-mm (21-in) bow
Basic load: 12 A184 dual-role wire-guided torpedoes, or 24 ground influence mines
Electronics: one MM/BPS704 surface-

search radar, one IPD70 sonar, one Velox M5 sonar, one torpedo fire-control/action information system, and one ESM system
Complement: 45

The Nazario Sauro (S518). A third pair of this type was authorized in the 1983 budget, with longer torpedo tubes to accommodate the American Sub-Harpoon anti-ship missile. Future naval plans will include a fourth pair if funding permits.

JAPAN
'Yuushio' class

The 'Yuushio' class is the mainstay of a projected 14 boat submarine fleet that is armed with the American Sub-Harpoon anti-ship missile. All the classes incorporate Japanese built equipment, weapons and electronics into their designs.

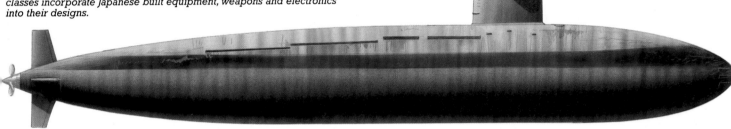

The latest in a long line of Japanese submarine designs, the **'Yuushio' class** is expected to total 14 units by the time construction is completed. It is essentially an enlarged version of the earlier tear-drop 'Uzushio' class with an increased diving-depth capability. Of double-hull construction, these Japanese boats follow the US Navy nuclear attack submarine practice of having a bow sonar array with the torpedo tubes moved to amidships and angled outwards. The first of the class, the *Yuushio* (SS573), entered service in 1980: *Mochishio* (SS574), *Setochio* (SS575), *Okishio* (SS576), *Nadashio* (SS577), *Hamashio* (SS578). These were followed by *Akishio, Takeshio, Yukishio* and *Sachishio*. From the *Nadashio* onwards the class is fitted to carry and fire the American Sub-Harpoon anti-ship missile, while to improve the torpedo armament indigenously-designed ASW and anti-ship

torpedoes are about to enter production for the submarine service. The electronics carried are of the latest designs, and are known to include several licence-built American systems. All the 'Yuushio' class were still in active service in international waters in 1998.

Specification
'Yuushio' class
Displacement: 2,200 tons surfaced and 2,730 tons dived
Dimensions: length 76.0 m (249.3 ft); beam 9.9 m (32.5 ft); draught 7.5 m (24.6 ft)
Propulsion: two diesels delivering 2535 kW (3,400 hp) with one electric motor driving one shaft
Speed: 12 kts surfaced and 20 kts dived
Diving depth: 300 m (984 ft) operational and 500 m (1,640 ft) maximum
Torpedo tubes: six 533-mm (21-in) amidships
Basic load: 18 anti-submarine and anti-ship torpedoes
Electronics: one ZPS-4 surface-search radar, one ZQQ-4 bow sonar, and one SQS-36(J) sonar
Complement: 75

The 'Yuushio' class was based on the earlier 'Uzushio' design, of which the Isoshio was the third unit. With a double-hull teardrop shape, the 'Uzushios' introduced the angled amidships torpedo tubes into service in the early 1970s.

The Yuushio (SS573) is equipped with automatic three-dimensional controls, remote engine control and a ZYQ-1 digital information processing system within its high-tensile steel teardrop hull structure. A new 2400-tonne type is projected to follow the 'Yuushio' class.

'Sjöormen' class

The first of the modern type of submarines for the Swedish navy was the **'Sjöormen' class** designed in the early 1960s by Kockums, Malmö and built by that company (three units) and Karlskrona Varvet (two units). The class comprises the *Sjöormen* (Sör), *Sjölejonet* (Sle), *Sjöhunden* (Shu), *Sjöbjörnen* (Sbj) and *Sjöhästen* (Shä). With an 'albacore' type hull for speed and a twin-deck arrangement the class is extensively used in the relatively shallow Baltic, where its excellent manoeuvrability and silent-running capabilities greatly aided the Swedish navy's ASW operations. The control surface and hydroplane arrangements were the same as those fitted to the latter Swedish submarine classes and it was these, together with the hull design that allowed the optimum manoeuvrability characteristics to be used throughout the speed range, though they were more noticeable at the lower end: for example 360° turn was achieved in five minutes within a 230 m (755 ft) diameter circle at a speed of 7 kts underwater; with increased speed to 15 kts the same turn took only two an a half minutes which mean the class could easily out-turn most of the Warsaw pact SASW escorts encountered in the Baltic as well as most of the NATO escorts.

Specification
'Sjöormen' class
Displacement: 1,125 tons surfaced and 1,400 tons dived
Dimensions: length 51.0 m (167.3 ft); beam 6.1 m (20.0 ft); draught 5.8 m (19.0 ft)
Propulsion: four diesels delivering 2,100 hp (1566 kW) with one electric motor driving one shaft
Speed: 15 kts surfaced and 20 kts dived
Diving depth: 150 m (492 ft) operational and 250 m (820 ft)

maximum
Torpedo tubes: four 533-mm (21-in) bow and two 400-mm (15.75-in) bow
Basic load: eight Type 61 533-mm (21-in) anti-ship wire-guided torpedoes or 16 influence ground mines, plus four Type 42 anti-submarine wire-guided torpedoes
Electronics: one Terma surface-search radar, one low-frequency sonar, one torpedo fire-control/action information system, and one ESM system
Complement: 18

The Sjölejonet *(Sle) of the 'Sjöormen' class runs on the surface in the submarine's major operating area of the Baltic. In such a region speed and manoeuvrability is of greater importance than diving depth, since much of the sea is relatively shallow.*

The Sjöbjörnen *(Sbj) shows the sail-mounted hydroplanes which increase the vessel's underwater manoeuvring capabilities. The class can, at medium speeds submerged, out-turn most of the West's and Warsaw Pact ASW vessels likely to be encountered in the Baltic.*

The five vessels of the 'Sjöormen' class were designated the Type-A11B by their builders. They were fitted with stern planes for increased manoeuvrability. In the mid-1990s they were replaced by three Gotland (A19) class boats.

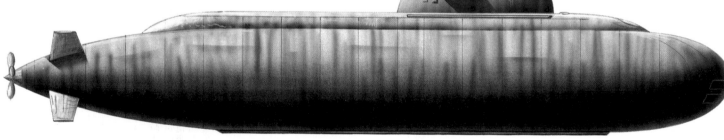

Sjöormen cutaway drawing key

1 Screw
2 Single shaft
3 X-configuration fin
4 Electric propulsion motor
5 Diesel generating set
6 Central monitoring station
7 Outer casing
8 Aft escape hatch with coupling for rescue craft
9 Crew quarters
10 Washroom
11 Battery room
12 Control room
13 Batteries
14 Torpedo loading hatch
15 Watertight communication hatch
16 Fuel tank
17 Keel
18 Ballast tank
19 Pump
20 Conning tower
21 Snorkel
22 Omnidirectional antenna
23 Directional antenna
24 Observation periscope
25 Attack periscope
26 Bridge fin with hoisting equipment
27 Access trunk
28 CIC
29 Radio room
30 Torpedo store
31 Periscope wells
32 Watertight bulkheads
33 Torpedo room
34 Torpedo tubes
35 Trim tank
36 Forward escape/access hatch
37 Compressed air store
38 Bow tube covers

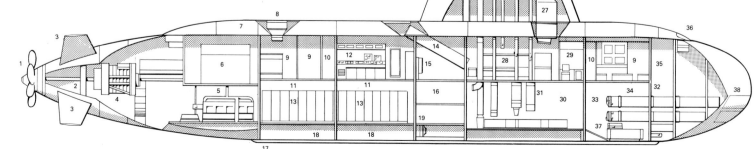

'Vastergötland' class

Designed by Kockums, Malmö under a 1978 contract, the four vessels of the '**A-17**' or '**Vastergötland**' class were ordered in 1981. The bows and sterns were built by the Karlskrona, Varvet shipyard and the mid-bodies and final assembly by Kockums. The ***Vastergötland*** (Vgd), ***Hälsingland*** (Hgd), ***Södermanland*** (Söd) and ***Östergotland*** (Ögd) all entered service in the period 1987-90. The internal arrangement of the two main watertight compartments allows sufficient space for six spare berths for trainee submariners. Each compartment is also provided with its own set of fittings for deep-diving rescue vessels such as the Swedish URF. The control surfaces

are arranged in an X-configuration that is connected in pairs to two separate hydraulic systems and, until fairly recently, was a purely Swedish submarine design feature. Only two of the control surfaces are used at any one time for manoeuvring, thus providing a high measure of redundancy except in the case of a direct hit right aft by a torpedo. Two hydroplanes are also fitted to the sail and are connected to a common control shaft. The torpedo tubes are arranged in the unique Swedish arrangment of the four long 533-mm (21-in) tubes over the two short 400-mm (15.75-in) tubes. Each tube set has its own reload compartment. The larger tubes can also be

used for influence ground mines in place of the torpedo load. The class may also be fitted in the sail with four vertical launch tubes for the RBS 17 anti-ship missile variant of the air-launched Bofors RBS 15 missile.

Specification
'Vastergötland' class
Displacement: 1,070 tons surfaced and 1,140 tons dived
Dimensions: length 48.5 m (159.1 ft); beam 6.1 m (20.0 ft); draught 6.1 m (20.0 ft)
Propulsion: two diesels delivering 1611 kW (2,160 hp) with one electric motor driving one shaft

Speed: 12 kts surfaced and 20 kts dived
Diving depth: 300 m (984 ft) operational and 500 m (1,640 ft) maximum
Torpedo tubes: four 533-mm (21-in) bow and two 400-mm (15.75-in) bow
Basic load: eight Type 61 533-mm (21-in) anti-ship wire-guided torpedoes or 16 influence ground mines, plus four Type 42 anti-submarine wire-guided torpedoes
Electronics: one Terma surface-search radar, one low-frequency sonar, one torpeo fire-control/action information system, and one ESM system
Complement: 21

'Zwaardvis' and 'Walrus' classes

Based on the US Navy's teardrop hulled conventional submarine 'Barbel' class, the ***Zwaardvis*** (S801) and ***Tijgerhaai*** (S807) of the '**Zwaardvis**' class were ordered in the mid-1960s. Because of the requirement to use indigenous Dutch equipment wherever possible, the design was modified. These modifications included the placement of all noise-producing machinery on a false deck with spring suspension for silent running. The two units entered service with the Dutch navy in 1972.

At the same time the need began to arise to start the design of a new class to replace the elderly 'Dolfijn' and 'Potvis' classes. The new design evolved as the '**Walrus**' class, and was based on the 'Zwaardvis' hull form with similar dimensions and silhouette but with more automation, a smaller crew, more modern electronics, X-configuration control surfaces and the French MAREI high-tensile steel hull material that allows a 50 per cent increase in maximum diving depth. The first unit, the ***Walrus*** (S802), was laid down in 1979 for commissioning in 1986 and the second, ***Zeeleeuw*** (S803), a year later for service entry in 1987. Two more units, the ***Delfin*** and ***Bruinvis***, were commissioned in 1993 and 1994 respectively. In 1981 Taiwan ordered a pair of '**Improved Zwaardvis**' class units for her navy and these were delivered in mid-1985 and mid-1986 respectively.

Specification
'Zwaardvis' class
Displacement: 2,350 tons surfaced and 2,640 tons dived
Dimensions: length 66.0 m (216.5 ft); beam 8.4 m (27.6 ft); draught 7.1 m (23.3 ft)
Propulsion: three diesels delivering 3132 kW (4,200 hp) with one electric motor driving one shaft
Speed: 13 kts surfaced and 20 kts dived
Diving depth: 300 m (984 ft) operational and 500 m (1,640 ft) maximum
Torpedo tubes: six 533-mm (21-in) bow

The Zwaardvis (S806) runs at speed on the surface. Based on the American 'Barbel' class with a teardrop hull, she uses a large proportion of Dutch-designed and -built equipment internally and has all noise-producing machinery mounted on a spring-suspended false deck.

Basic load: 20 Mk 37C anti-submarine and Mk 48 dual-role wire-guided torpedoes, or 40 influence ground mines
Electronics: one Type 1001 surface-search radar, one low-frequency sonar, one medium-frequency sonar, one WM-8 torpedo fire-control/action information system, and one ESM system
Complement: 67

Specification
'Walrus' class
Displacement: 2,390 tons surfaced and 2,740 tons dived
Dimensions: length 67.7 m (222.1 ft); beam 8.4 m (27.6 ft); draught 6.6 m (21.7 ft)

Propulsion: three diesels delivering 4101 kW (5,500 hp) with one electric motor driving one shaft
Speed: 13 kts surfaced and 20 kts dived
Diving depth: 450 m (1,476 ft) operational and 620 m (2,034 ft) maximum
Torpedo tubes: six 533-mm (21-in) bow

Basic load: 20 Mk 37C anti-submarine and Mk 48 dual-role wire-guided torpedoes, or 40 influence ground mines
Missiles: Sub-Harpoon underwater-to-surface anti-ship missiles can be carried in place of torpedoes
Electronics: one Type 1001 surface-search radar, one Octopus bow sonar, one Type 2024 towed-array sonar, one Gipsy III torpedo fire-control system, one SEWACO VIII action information system, and one ESM system
Complement: 50

Ordered in the late 1970s, the two 'Walrus' class submarines are much improved versions of the 'Zwaardvis' design, with more modern electronics, greater automation and a smaller crew.

Modern Missile Submarines

Lurking silent in the depths, awaiting the signal to strike, the nuclear-powered ballistic-missile submarine, or SSBN, is an awesome weapon of destruction: each of the missiles with multiple warheads carried today can destroy 60 per cent of a major city, and a US Navy 'Ohio' class boat can carry 16 missiles.

HMS *Vanguard,* constructed at Barrow-in-Furness by VSEL. It was the first in a new class of SSBNs developed for the Royal Navy and armed with the D5 Trident ballistic missile system.

The concept of the missile submarine is not new, dating as it does to German plans of World War II. But it was not until the 1950s that the Americans and Russians began to explore the concept of the nuclear-powered ballistic missile submarine, a vessel capable of remaining submerged for lengthy periods, making use of the polar ice-cap and various oceanic features to remain undetected. Armed with nuclear-tipped rockets, it would be the ultimate deterrent.

Although the Americans were the first nation to make the nuclear-powered submarine breakthrough, with an early class of boat based on the prototype *Nautilus*, what the US Navy really wanted was to merge the new technologies of ballistic missiles, smaller thermonuclear weapons, inertial guidance systems and nuclear power into a single weapon system. They succeeded with the deployment, in 1960, of the first Fleet Ballistic Missile (FBM) submarine, armed with the Polaris A1 missile.

The Russians were quick to respond, deploying the 'Hotel' class nuclear ballistic submarine. This was armed initially with three SSN-4 Sark missiles, with a range of only 650 km (350 miles), but after 1963 it converted to the SSN-5 Serb, with a range of 1200 km (650-miles).

The ballistic missile submarine race was on, and it would later be joined by Britain, France and China. In the late 1960s Britain deployed the 'Resolution' class SSBNs, built with British technology but carrying American Polaris A3 SLBMs; these were eventually replaced by the 'Vanguard' class armed with the Trident II. France, on the other hand, designed and built both the submarines and the missiles they carried. Her first SSBNs were the 'Le Redoubtable' class boats, five of which were built; they were replaced in the 1990s by four boats of the 'Le Triomphant' class. China initiated an SSBN programme in the late 1960s, and her first 'Xia' class boats were deployed in the mid-1980s.

By the 1980s, the nuclear-powered missile submarine had become an awesome weapon of destruction, capable of carrying up to 16 missiles, each with multiple warheads, that could rain nuclear destruction on targets 4,600km (2,500 miles) from their launch point.

'Yankee' class SSBN

The **'Yankee' class** was the first modern Soviet SSBN to be built. The design was apparently based on the plans of the US 'Benjamin Franklin' and 'Lafayette' classes that were covertly obtained by Soviet military intelligence (GRU) in the early 1960s. Thirty-four units were built between 1967 and 1974 at the shipyards in Severodvinsk and Komsomolsk, the peak year being 1970 when 10 vessels were completed. The 'Yankees' are distinguishable from the later 'Deltas' by having a smaller rise to the 'turtle-back' missile compartment abaft the sail. In 1976 one unit was converted to a **'Yankee II' class** configuration in which the original 16 missile tubes were replaced by 12 larger units for the experimental solid-propellant SS-NX-17 SLBM. The 'Yankee II' also differs from the similar 12-round 'Delta Is' by having a sloping forward edge to the 'turtle-back' casing of the missile tubes.

In order to comply with the SALT agreement a number of 'Yankee I' SSBNs have been deactivated as SLBM carriers. By mid-1984 10 had been so treated, a number being converted to SSNs by the complete removal of the missile section of the hull. Another has possibly become the trials platform for the highly accurate SS-N-21 533-mm (21-in) diameter 7-m (23-ft) long cruise missile with a single 200-kiloton yield warhead and a range of 3000 km (1,865 miles).

During the Cold War period three or four Yankee boats were on station at anyone time off the eastern seaboard of the USA, with at least one further unit either on transit to or back from a patrol area.

The forward deployed Yankees were assigned the wartime role of destroying time-sensitive area targets such as SAC bomber alert bases and carriers/SSBNs in port, and of disrupting the American higher command echelons as much as possible, to ease the task of follow up ICBM strikes. Despite the removal of the ballistic missile

section the overall length of the Yankee's hull has increased by 12 m (39.4 ft) with the insertion of a 'notch waisted' central section. This new section houses three tubes amidships on either side and the magazine holds up to 35 SS-N-21s or additional torpedoes and mines.

Specification
'Yankee' class
Displacement: 7,700 tons surfaced and 9,300 dived
Dimensions: length 130.0 m (426.5 ft); beam 11.6 m (38.1 ft); draught 8.0 m (26.3 ft)
Propulsion: two pressurized water-cooled reactors powering four steam turbines driving two shafts
Speed: 20 kts surfaced and 27 kts dived

Diving depth: 400 m (1,315 ft) operational and 600 m (1,970 ft) maximum
Armament: 16 ('Yankee I') or 12 ('Yankee II') launch tubes for 16 SS-N-6 ('Yankee I') or 12 SS-NX-17 ('Yankee II') submarine-launched ballistic missiles, and six 533-mm (21-in) bow tubes for a maximum of 12 533-mm (21-in) weapons, though the normal load is eight 533-mm (21-in) ASW/anti-ship torpedoes and six 406-mm (16-in) ASW torpedoes
Electronics: one 'Snoop Tray' surface-search radar, one low-frequency bow

sonar, one medium-frequency torpedo fire-control sonar, VHF/SHF/UHF communications systems, one VLF towed communications buoy, one ELF floating antenna, one 'Brick Group' ESM suite, and one 'Park Lamp' direction-finding antenna
Complement: 130

Apparently built with the aid of Polaris missile submarine plans stolen from the Americans, the 'Yankee I' class, with its SS-N-6 missiles, formed the major part of the Soviet SSBN fleet in the early 1970s.

A total of 34 'Yankee I' class submarines were constructed in a relatively short space of time at the Severodvinsk and Komsomolsk shipyards. Some 10 units of the class have now been converted to other duties.

SS-N-6 SLBM

The photographs that have been released of what NATO codenames **'Sawfly'** are in fact of a competitive prototype that was never taken into service. Such ruses are a common part of Soviet disinformation exercises. The actual **SS-N-6** was tested on a diesel-electric 'Golf' class submarine that was converted around 1970 to carry and fire six such weapons in a lengthened sail structure that was added to an 18-m (59-ft) extension to the hull. Being a third-generation weapon, the missile is actually something of a hybrid as it utilizes both components and technology derived from the land-based SS-11 ICBM. It is a single-stage SLBM with liquid-propellant propulsion. The original 2400-km (1,490-mile) range **SS-N-**

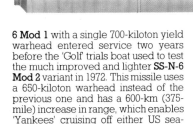

6 Mod 1 with a single 700-kiloton yield warhead entered service two years before the 'Golf' trials boat used to test the much improved and lighter **SS-N-6 Mod 2** variant in 1972. This missile uses a 650-kiloton warhead instead of the previous one and has a 600-km (375-mile) increase in range, which enables 'Yankees' cruising off either US seaboard to provide full target coverage from the 183-m (600-ft) contour. At the same time the **SS-N-6 Mod 3** began

development, initial deployment happening in 1974, one year after the SS-N-6 Mod 2. This third variant has the same range as its predecessor, but the single RV has been replaced by two 350-kiloton yield multiple re-entry vehicles (MRVs) for use against large area targets such as cities. By 1985 those 'Yankee Is' that were left in service had either SS-N-6 Mod 1 or SS-N-6 Mod 3 missiles in their tubes.

Now being used in its Mod 3 version with two Multiple Re-entry Vehicle warheads, the SS-N-6 arms the 'Yankee I' class of SSBN.

Specification
SS-N-6
Type: submarine-launched ballistic missile
Dimensions: length 10.0 m (32.8 ft); diameter 1.8 m (5 ft 10.9 in)

Launch weight: 18900 kg (41,667 lb)
Performance: range (Mod 1) 2400 km (1,490 miles) or (Mods 2 and 3) 3000 km (1,865 miles); CEP 1850 m (2,023 yards)
Warhead: one 700-kiloton yield re-entry vehicle in Mod 1, or one 650-kiloton yield re-entry vehicle in Mod 2, or two 350-kiloton yield MRVs in Mod 3
Propulsion: liquid-propellant rocket
Guidance: inertial

Predecessor to the SS-N-6 SLBM was the SS-N-5 'Serb'. This utilized a cold gas ejection system to fire the missile clear of the launch platform, where the main rocket motor was ignited. The 'Yankee' class SSBNs use a similar system to eject the SS-N-6 missiles from their launch tubes.

Former USSR

'Delta I', 'Delta II' and Delta III' class SSBNs

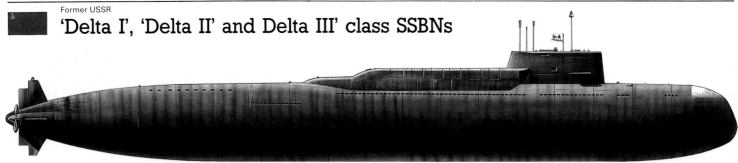

The **'Delta I' class** design was an enlargement of the previous 'Yankee' class design. Built initially at Severodvinsk and then at Komsomolsk in the Soviet Far East, the 'Delta I' was the world's largest undersea craft when the first unit was completed in 1972. The eighteenth and last of the class was completed at Komsomolsk in 1977. Designated a ballistic missile submarine (*podvodnaya lodka raketnaya krylataya* or PLRK) by the Soviets, the class carries two parallel rows of six missile tubes for the SS-N-8 missile aft of the sail, which is set forward with diving planes on each side.

In 1975 at Severodvinsk an interim batch of four **'Delta II' class** units was constructed. These were essentially the earlier design lengthened by 16.2 m (53.2 ft) to make possible the incorporation of a further four missile tubes to match contemporary Western SSBNs. These boats were followed in 1976 by the first units of the **'Delta III' class**. They are similar to the 'Delta II' boats but have the 'turtle-back' structure aft of the sail increased in height to accommodate the longer and more capable SS-N-18 in the missile tubes.

The last of the Delta class is the Delta IV, construction of which was first ordered in December 1975. The first of eight boats was launched and commissioned in 1984 at Severodvinsk and the programme was completed in late 1990. Names are being allocated to the Delta IVs; only two *Kareliya* and *Novo Moskovk* have been identified so far.

The submarines have a slim-fitting on the after fin which is a dispenser for as on a thin line towed array. The Delta IV has a diving depth of 300 m (1000 ft). Navigation systems include SAT-NAV, SINS, CodEye, and Pert Spring SATCOM. A modified and more accurate version of Delta IV's missile, SSN-23 (RSM54) was tested at sea in 1988; it has a range of 8300 km (4500 nm) and carries 4-10 MIRV each of 15 kT capacity. Delta IV also carries the Novator (SSN-15 Starfish) missile, with a 200 kT warhead and a range of 45 km (24 nm), or the Type 40 torpedo. Larger than the Delta III, the Delta IV is in reality new class of

submarine, which has been given the name Delfin (Dolfin). All units are based at Saida Guba with the Northern Fleet.

Specification
'Delta' class
Displacement: 8,750 tons surfaced and 10,000 tons dived for 'Delta I', and 9,750 tons surfaced and 11,000 tons dived for 'Delta II' and 'Delta III'
Dimensions: length 136.5 m (447.8 ft) for 'Delta I' and 152.7 m (501 ft) for 'Delta II' and 'Delta III'; beam 12.0 m (39.4 ft); draught 8.7 m (28.5 ft)
Propulsion: two pressurized water-cooled reactors powering four steam turbines driving two shafts
Speed: 20 kts surfaced and 26 kts ('Delta I'), 25 kts ('Delta II') or 24 kts ('Delta III') dived
Diving depth: 400 m (1,315 ft) operational and 600 m (1,970 ft) maximum
Armament: 12 ('Delta I') or 16 ('Delta II') launch tubes for 12 ('Delta I') or 16 ('Delta II') SS-N-8 submarine-launched ballistic missiles, or 16 launch tubes ('Delta III') for 16 SS-N-18 submarine-

launched ballistic missiles, and six 533-mm (21-in) bow tubes for a maximum of 12 533-mm (21-in) weapons, though the normal load is eight 533-mm (21-in) ASW/anti-ship torpedoes and six 406-mm (16-in) ASW torpedoes
Electronics: one 'Snoop Tray' surface-search radar, one low-frequency bow sonar, one medium-frequency torpedo fire-control sonar, VHF/SHF/UHF communications systems, one VLF towed communications buoy, one ELF floating antenna, one 'Brick Group' ESM suite, one 'Park Lamp' direction-finding antenna, and one 'Pert Spring' satellite navigation system
Complement: 130 ('Delta I') or 140 ('Delta II' and 'Delta III')

Only four 'Delta II' class submarines were built, as an interim design. The only difference between the vessels and the earlier 'Delta Is' is an increase in hull length.

Now in its fourth variant, the 'Delta' class ballistic missile submarine is essentially the 'Yankee' design lengthened to accommodate SLBMs.

'Typhoon' SSBN and 'SS-N-20' SLBM

A true monster of the deep, the Typhoon has been designed for operations under the polar ice. Its huge size enables it to be armed with missiles capable of hitting the continental USA without ever having to leave northern Soviet waters.

The **'Typhoon' class** boats are the largest undersea vessels yet built, and are believed to be based on a catamaran-type design that comprises two 'Delta III' hulls joined by a single outer covering to give increased protection against ASW weapons. In overall size a 'Typhoon' is almost half as long again as the US 'Ohio' class Trident missile-carrying submarines, and has a displacement some 9,500 tons greater when running on the surface. It is thought that the class has been built specifically for operations with the Soviet Northern Fleet in the Arctic ice-pack. The two parallel rows of missile tubes fitted forward of the stub-like sail aft of the craft's centre point, together with the high-rise hull and retractable bow hydroplanes, allows the submarine to break easily through the spots of thin ice (known as polnyas) within the Arctic ice shelf.

The first unit was laid down in 1975 at Severodvinsk and launched in 1980. It achieved operational status in 1983. In all six were commissioned 1980–1989; their designations: TK208, TK202, TK12, TK13, TK17 and TK20. Two were laid up in 1999 and two were awaiting refit. TK17 was damaged by fire during a missile loading accident in 1992 but was subsequently repaired.

To arm the 'Typhoon' the Soviets started to design a fifth-generation SLBM, the **SS-N-20**, from 1973. First-flight tested in 1980, the SS-N-20 is a three-stage solid-propellant MIRVed missile with a range of 8300 km (5,160 miles). This allows the submarine to fire the weapon from within the Arctic circle and still hit a target anywhere within the continental USA. Before the end of this decade the Soviets are due to test fly an improved version of the SS-N-20.

Specification
'Typhoon' class
Displacement: 26,000 tons surfaced and 30,000 tons dived
Dimensions: length 170.0 m (557.7 ft); beam 23.0 m (75.5 ft); draught not known
Propulsion: four pressurized water-cooled reactors powering four steam turbines driving four shafts
Speed: 20 kts surfaced and 30 kts dived
Diving depth: 400 m (1,315 ft) operational and 600 m (1,970 ft) maximum
Armament: 20 launch tubes for 20 SS-N-20 submarine-launched ballistic missiles, and six 533-mm (21-in) bow tubes for a maximum of 24 533-mm (21-in) weapons, though the normal load is 16 533-mm (21-in) ASW/anti-ship torpedoes and 14 407-mm (16-in) ASW torpedoes
Electronics: one surface-search radar,

The mammoth Typhoon SSBN is thought to be comprised of two 'Delta' class hulls in a side-by-side configuration with the missile tube compartment forward of the sail.

one ESM system, one low-frequency bow sonar, one medium-frequency torpedo fire-control sonar, VHF/SHF/UHF communications systems, one VLF towed communications buoy, and one ELF floating antenna
Complement: 150

Specification
SS-N-20
Type: submarine-launched ballistic

Such submarines are being built for operations beneath and within the polar ice regions of the northern hemisphere.

missile
Dimensions: length 15.0 m (49.2 ft); diameter 2.0 m (6 ft 6.7 in)
Launch weight: not known
Performance: range 8300 km (5,160 miles); CEP better than 1400 m (1,530 yards)
Warhead: between six and nine MIRVs of unknown yield
Propulsion: solid-propellant rocket
Guidance: stellar-inertial

SS-N-8, SS-N-18 and SS-NX-23 SLBMs

Introduced into operational service in 1972 aboard the 'Delta I' class SSBN, the **SS-N-8** is a fourth-generation SLBM that began flight trials back in 1969 aboard a lengthened 'Hotel' class nuclear-powered ballistic missile submarine (codenamed 'Hotel III') converted to carry and fire three of the missiles in an enlarged sail. A second trials vessel was converted in the early 1970s from a diesel-electric 'Golf' class ballistic missile submarine. Codenamed 'Golf III' and fitted to carry and fire six SS-N-8s, the vessel has now been dismantled under the SALT limitations. The SS-N-8 is a two-stage liquid-propellant missile that, in its **SS-N-8 Mod 1** form, has a range of 7800 km (4,845 miles). To ensure accuracy over that range, stellar-inertial guidance is used to update the navigation computer by utilizing two 'star fixes' for mid-course flight profile corrections. In 1977 an engineering improved variant, the **SS-N-8 Mod 2**, entered service with a range of 9100 km (5,655 miles) and the same warhead.

However, two years before this the Soviets had begun flight testing the fourth-generation 6500-km (4,040-mile) range storable liquid-propellant

SS-N-18 (Soviet designation **RSM-50**) which became operational on the 'Delta III' class in late 1976. The **SS-N-18 Mod 1** version was also the first Soviet SLBM to feature MIRV capability. This was followed in 1979 by the **SS-N-Mod 2** with a single warhead but much greater range. The SS-N-18 Mod 1 was then superseded in the same year by the **SS-N-18 Mod 3** which has a larger number of lower-yield MIRVs and the same range.

Another missile in this series, the liquid-fuelled **SSN-23 Skiff**, was developed as a back up to the SS-N20. It offers increased throw weight and greater degree of accuracy. It has a similar range and carries seven MIRV within the continental USA.

All the 'Typhoons' are in the Northern Fleet and based at Litsa Guba.

Specification
SS-N-8
Type: submarine-launched ballistic missile
Dimensions: length 12.9 m (42.3 ft); diameter 1.65 m (5 ft 5 in)
Launch weight: 20400 kg (44,974 lb)
Performance: range (Mod 1) 7800 km (4,845 miles) or (Mod 2) 9100 km (5,655 miles); CEP (Mod 1) 1410 m (1,540 yards) or (Mod 2) 1550 m (1,695 yards)
Warhead: one 800-kiloton re-entry vehicle
Propulsion: liquid-propellant rocket
Guidance: stellar-inertial

The SS-N-18 is now the mainstay of the Soviet SSBN force with the introduction into service of a version carrying Multiple Independent Re-entry Vehicle warheads.

Specification
SS-N-18
Type: submarine-launched ballistic missile
Dimensions: length 14.1 m (46.3 ft); diameter 1.8 m (5 ft 10.9 in)
Launch weight: 25000 kg (55,115 lb)
Performance: range (Mods 1 and 3) 6500 km (4,040 miles) or (Mod 2) 8000 km (4,970 miles); CEP (Mods 1 and 3) 1410 m (1,540 yards) or (Mod 2) 1550 m (1,695 yards)
Propulsion: liquid-propellant rocket
Guidance: stellar-inertial

'Le Redoutable' class SSBN

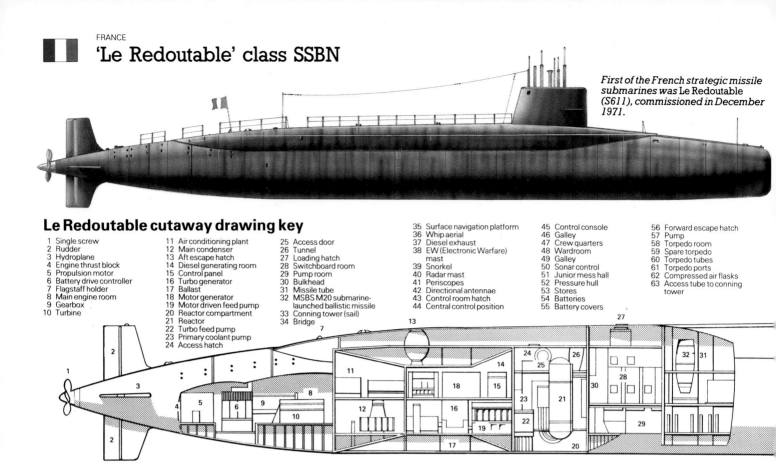

First of the French strategic missile submarines was Le Redoutable (S611), commissioned in December 1971.

Le Redoutable cutaway drawing key

1. Single screw
2. Rudder
3. Hydroplane
4. Engine thrust block
5. Propulsion motor
6. Battery drive controller
7. Flagstaff holder
8. Main engine room
9. Gearbox
10. Turbine
11. Air conditioning plant
12. Main condenser
13. Aft escape hatch
14. Diesel generating room
15. Control panel
16. Turbo generator
17. Ballast
18. Motor generator
19. Motor driven feed pump
20. Reactor compartment
21. Reactor
22. Turbo feed pump
23. Primary coolant pump
24. Access hatch
25. Access door
26. Tunnel
27. Loading hatch
28. Switchboard room
29. Pump room
30. Bulkhead
31. Missile tube
32. MSBS M20 submarine-launched ballistic missile
33. Conning tower (sail)
34. Bridge
35. Surface navigation platform
36. Whip aerial
37. Diesel exhaust
38. EW (Electronic Warfare) mast
39. Snorkel
40. Radar mast
41. Periscopes
42. Directional antennae
43. Control room hatch
44. Central control position
45. Control console
46. Galley
47. Crew quarters
48. Wardroom
49. Galley
50. Sonar control
51. Junior mess hall
52. Pressure hull
53. Stores
54. Batteries
55. Battery covers
56. Forward escape hatch
57. Pump
58. Torpedo room
59. Spare torpedo
60. Torpedo tubes
61. Torpedo ports
62. Compressed air flasks
63. Access tube to conning tower

The first French SSBN (or more correctly Sous-Marin Nucléare Lance-Engine or SNLE) *Le Redoutable* (S611) was authorized in March 1963, laid down in November 1964 and commissioned in 1971 after being employed for 2½ years on trials as the prototype for the French naval deterrent known as the Force de Dissuasion in official circles. She and her 'Le Redoutable' class sistership *Le Terrible* (S612) were initially equipped with the 2400-km (1,490-mile) range two-stage solid-propellant inertially-guided M1 SLBM that had a single 500-kiloton thermonuclear warhead and a CEP of 930 m (3,050 ft). In 1974 the third unit, *Le Foudroyant* (S610), was commissioned with the improved 3100-km (1,925-mile) range M2 missile with a more powerful second-stage motor but carrying the same warhead and having a similar CEP. The two previous vessels were then retrofitted with the M2 system during their normal

overhauls. The fourth boat, *L'Indomptable* (S613), was commissioned into service in 1977 with the vastly improved M20 missile that has the same range and accuracy as the M2 but carries a new 1.2-megaton yield specially hardened warhead with what is believed to be chaff dispensing penetration aids to confuse defending radar systems. The last vessel, *Le Tonnant* (S614) was completed with the M20 whilst the three units armed with the M2 were brought up to the same standard. Later, all units except *Le Redoutable* were armed with the Aérospatiale M4 three-stage solid fuel missile, which has a range of 5300 km (2860 nm) and carries six MIRV, each of 15 kT. The first operational launch of an M4 was made by *Le Tonnant* in 1987 in the Atlantic. The missiles can be discharged at twice the rate of the M20. *Le Redoutable* was withdrawn in 1991; two other boats, *L'Indomptable* and *Le Tonnant*, were upgraded and assigned to *L'Inflexible* class.

Le Foudroyant (S610) and her sisterships were designed and built in France without any help from the Americans, unlike the British Polaris boats, which required considerable design assistance.

'L'Inflexible' class SSBN

Ordered in September 1978, 'L'Inflexible' class was originally intended to be an intermediate design between 'Le Redoutable' and a new class of 14,000–15,000 tons SSBN, *Le Triomphant*. The 'Inflexible' retained most of the external characteristics of the earlier class, but with more advanced propulsion, better electronics and a more accurate weapon system. Laid down in March 1980, *L'Inflexible* (S616) achieved operational status in March 1985 and is set to serve until 2012. She was the sole true vessel of her class, the other two having been reassigned to teh 'Redoutable' class. In this way the

French navy not only saved costs, but fulfilled the requirement for three SSBNs to be continuously available of which two were on patrol.

The first boat of the new 'Le Triomphant' class was commissioned in 1997; three other boats are due to enter service, S617 *Le Temeraire* (1999), S618 *Le Vigilant* (2003) and S619 (unnamed) in 2007. French SSBNs normally undertake patrols of two months' duration, with three months as the absolute maximum. All the vessels are based at Ile Longue near Brest and have special protection when transiting to and from the port. This includes the French navy's sole Aérospatiale SA

321G Super Frelon ASW helicopter unit, Flottille 32F, which operates in groups of up to four helicopters to screen the boats, one helicopter dunking its sonar whilst the others stand back ready to attack if required.

Specification
'L'Inflexible' class
Displacement: 8,080 tons surfaced and 8,920 tons dived
Dimensions: length 128.7 m (422.2 ft); beam 10.6 m (34.8 ft); draught 10.0 m (32.8 ft)
Propulsion: one pressurized water-cooled reactor powering two steam turbines driving one shaft
Speed: 18 kts surfaced and 25 kts dived

Diving depth: 350 m (1,150 ft) operational and 465 m (1,525 ft) maximum
Armament: 16 launch tubes for 16 M4 submarine-launched ballistic missiles, and four 533-mm (21-in) bow tubes for 14 L5 ASW and F17 anti-ship torpedoes plus four SM.39 Exocet anti-ship missiles
Electronics: one surface-search radar, one passive ESM system, one DLT D3 torpedo and Exocet fire-control system, one DSUX 21 sonar, and one DUUX 5 underwater telephone
Complement: 135

Specification
'Le Redoutable' class
Displacement: 8,045 tons surfaced and 8,940 tons dived
Dimensions: length 128.7 m (422.2 ft); beam 10.6 m (34.8 ft); draught 10.0 m (32.8 ft)

Propulsion: one pressurized water-cooled reactor powering two steam turbines driving one shaft
Speed: 18 kts surfaced and 25 kts dived
Diving depth: 250 m (820 ft) operational and 330 m (1,085 ft) maximum
Armament: 16 launch tubes for 16 M20 submarine-launched ballistic missiles, and four 550-mm (21.7-in) bow tubes for 18 L5 ASW and F17 anti-ship torpedoes

Above: The French try to maintain a minimum of two SNLEs on patrol at any one time, with submarines such as Le Terrible (S612) being screened on departure and return by French navy surface units, submarines and ASW aircraft in order to maintain security.

Electronics: one Calypso surface-search radar, one DLT D3 torpedo fire-control system, one passive ESM system, one DSUV 23 sonar, and one DUUX 2 underwater telephone
Complement: 135

M20 SLBM

The **Mer-Sol Balistique Stratégique M20** is essentially a variant of the earlier two-stage M2 with the Rita 11/P6 second stage converted to carry a single re-entry vehicle (RV) with an MR60 1.2-megaton yield thermonuclear warhead and associated penetration aids. Since initial deployment in 1977 aboard *L'Indomptable*, the missile has been refitted to carry the lighter but similar-yield MR61 warhead. Both types were specially hardened to resist damage from the electromagnetic pulse (EMP) and fast radiation produced when nuclear-tipped anti-ballistic missiles (from systems such as the ABM-1 'Galosh' network around Moscow) explode in their vicinity. The M20 is ejected by compressed air, and is the culmination of a missile programme that started design development in 1959 and entered operational service as the MSBS M1 in 1971. The development progressed through the uprated M2 that entered service in 1974 to the present M20. The whole 16 M20 missile outfit of a French SSBN could be launched within 15 minutes. From 1985 the M20 was replaced aboard the last four boats of 'Le Redoutable' class by the M4, which carries a MIRV payload. The last M20s were phased out when *Le Redoutable* was decommissioned.

Eventually superseded by the M4, the M20 SLBM remained operational until Le Redoutable was decommissioned. It was armed with a 1.2 megaton yield thermonuclear warhead that was specially hardened against the effects of defensive ABM nuclear weapon systems.

Specification
M20
Type: submarine-launched ballistic missile
Dimensions: length 10.4 m (34.1 ft); diameter 1.5 m (4 ft 11 in)
Launch weight: 20054.6 kg (44,213 lb)
Performance: range 3100 km (1,926 miles); CEP 930 m (1,017 yards)

Warhead: one re-entry vehicle with an MR61 1.2-megaton weapon and penetration aids
Propulsion: solid-propellant rocket
Guidance: inertial

M4 SLBM

Twice the weight of the M20, the M4 can be fired more rapidly and from a greater operating depth than its predecessor. The missile entered service in 1985 aboard *L'Inflexible*, France's sixth ballistic missile submarine, allowing the French Navy to maintain three vessels on patrol at all times.

The design of the missile was started in 1976 and the missile was fired for the very first time from a landing pad in November 1980. The three stage solid propellant weapon had a payload of six 150-kiloton yield multiple independent re-entry vehicles (MIRVs) of greater circular error probability (CEP) accuracy than previous French single warhead SLBMs, with the added advantage of advance penetration aids to defeat enemy ballistic missile defences. In its original form the M4 had a range of 4,500 km (2425 nm), but an improved version with a range of 5000 km (2695 nm) entered service in 1987 on *Le Tonnant*, when that vessel completed its retrofit. The additional range was obtained by installing the lighter TN71 nuclear warhead. An advanced version of the M4, the Aérospatiale M45/TN75, arms the submarines of 'Le Triomphant' class. This in turn is to be replaced by the M51, with a range of 8000 km (4300 nm) in about 2001.

Specification
M4
Type: submarine-launched ballistic missile
Dimensions: length 11.05 m (36.25 ft); diameter 1.92 m (6 ft 3.6 in)
Launch weight: 35073.2 kg (77,323 lb)
Performance: range 4000 km (2,485 miles); CEP 460 m (503 yards)
Warhead: six 150-kiloton MIRVs

The M4 SLBM is due to enter service in early 1985 aboard the SNLE L'Inflexible (S615). The new missile has a longer range than previous French SLBMs.

Propulsion: solid-propellant rocket
Guidance: inertial

USA

'Benjamin Franklin' and 'Lafayette' class SSBNs

Although actually two classes, the 12 'Benjamin Franklin' class and 19 'Lafayette' class submarines are very similar in appearance. The main difference is that the former were built with quieter machinery outfits. All have diesel-electric stand-by propulsion, snort masts and an auxiliary propeller. As built, the first eight 'Lafayettes' carried 16 single 800-kiloton yield warhead 2775-km (1,725-mile) range Polaris A2 SLBMs, the rest receiving the Polaris A3 fitted with three 200-kiloton yield MRVs. Of the Polaris A2 boats four (SSBN620 and SSBN622-625) were rearmed with the Polaris A3 during refuelling overhauls in 1968-70. In August of the latter year SSBN627 became the first of the Poseidon C3 SLBM conversions, whilst between September 1978 and December 1982 12 units were further converted to carry and

fire the Trident I C4 SLBM. All 31 units serve with the Atlantic Fleet, several being forward-deployed to a submarine tender located at Holy Loch on the River Clyde in Scotland. Several units with Poseidon missiles have been reassigned to the theatre nuclear role in support of NATO. Each American SSBN is assigned two crews designated Blue and Gold, one manning the vessel during a 70-day patrol and helping during the following 32-day minor overhaul before the other crew takes the vessel out on patrol. Every six years each boat undergoes a complete overhaul and reactor refuelling that lasts about 22-23 months. The individual submarines that comprise the two classes are the USS *Lafayette* (SSBN616), USS *Alexander Hamilton* (SSBN617), USS *Andrew Jackson* (SSBN619), USS *John Adams*

(SSBN620), USS *James Monroe* (SSBN622), USS *Nathan Hale* (SSBN623), USS *Woodrow Wilson* (SSBN624), USS *Henry Clay* (SSBN625), USS *Daniel Webster* (SSBN626), USS *James Madison* (SSBN627), USS *Tecumseh* (SSBN628), USS *Daniel Boone* (SSBN629), USS *John C. Calhoun* (SSBN630), USS *Ulysses S. Grant* (SSBN631), USS *Von Steuben* (SSBN632), USS *Casimir Pulaski* (SSBN633), USS *Stonewall Jackson* (SSBN634), USS *Sam Rayburn* (SSBN635), USS *Nathaniel Greene* (SSBN636), USS *Benjamin Franklin* (SSBN640), USS *Simon Bolivar* (SSBN641), USS *Kamehameha* (SSBN642), USS *George Bancroft* (SSBN643), USS *Lewis and Clark* (SSBN644), USS *James K. Polk* (SSBN645), USS *George C. Marshall* (SSBN654), USS *Henry L. Stimson*

(SSBN655), USS *George Washington Carver* (SSBN656), USS *Francis Scott Key* (SSBN657), USS *Mariano G. Vallejo* (SSBN658) and USS *Will Rogers* (SSBN659). Those from SSBN640 onwards are of the 'Benjamin Franklin' subclass.

Specification
'Lafayette' and 'Benjamin Franklin' classes
Displacement: 7,250 tons surfaced and 8,250 tons dived
Dimensions: length 129.5 m (425.0 ft); beam 10.1 m (33.0 ft); draught 9.6 m (31.5 ft)
Propulsion: one S5W pressurized water-cooled reactor powering two steam turbines driving one shaft
Speed: 28 kts surfaced and 25 kts dived
Diving depth: 350 m (1,150 ft) operational and 465 m (1,525 ft) maximum
Armament: 16 launch tubes for 16 Trident I C4 (SSBNs 627, 629, 630, 632-634, 640, 641, 643, 655, 657 and 658) or for 16 Poseidon C3 (remainder) submarine-launched ballistic missiles, and four 533-mm (21-in) bow tubes for 12 Mk 48 ASW/anti-ship torpedoes
Electronics: one BPS-11A or BPS-15 surface-search radar, one ESM system, one BQR-7 sonar, one BQR-15 towed-array sonar, one BQR-19 sonar, one BQR-21 sonar, one BQS-4 sonar, and extensive communications and navigation systems
Complement: 140 ('Lafayette') or 168 ('Benjamin Franklin')

Left: The C4 Trident I-equipped 'Benjamin Franklin' class vessel USS Mariano G. Vallejo (SSBN658). Nowadays American SSBNs do not carry identifying pennant numbers for security reasons.

Below: Two operational boats of the 'Benjamin Franklin' class are in service. They are the Kamehameha *and* James K.Polk, *which are equipped for special operations in support of SEAL forces.*

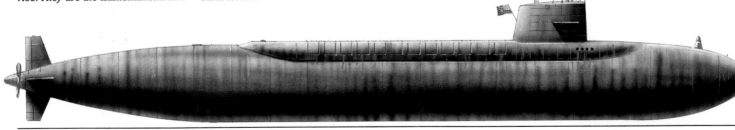

USA

Lockheed UGM-73A Poseidon C3 SLBM

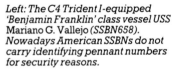

A C3 Poseidon SLBM just after launch. One problem for an SSBN commander is that he would prefer all his SLBMs to be launched in one go and not in several groups because each firing points to his location.

By 1964 two follow-on designs to the Polaris were under review. One subsequently evolved into the **Lockheed UGM-73A Poseidon C3** SLBM which could use the launch tubes of the existing fleet of SSBNs. Ultimately 31 out of the original 41 SSBNs built were refitted to carry the Poseidon, although some were later fitted to carry the Trident I. The Poseidon C3 entered operational service in 1970 after initial flight tests in 1968. The missile introduced the concept of MIRVing to American

SLBMs. Up to a maximum of 14 Mk 3 independently targeted RVs (each with a yield of 40 kilotons) can be carried over a range of 4000 km (2,485 miles), but with the normal loading of 10 MIRVs the range is increased to 5200 km (3,230 miles). Penetration aids to confuse defence systems are also carried. The two-stage solid-propellant missiles are targeted mainly against soft military and industrial targets such as airfields, storage depots, and above-ground command and

control facilities. A total of 619 operational missiles was bought, and 304 of these plus their 3,040 associated warheads are still afloat on the remaining 19 Poseidon-equipped SSBNs. Two or three Poseidon vessels are always assigned to the NATO high command for the theatre nuclear role in Europe and the Mediterranean. The Poseidon will eventually be replaced by the Trident II.

Specification
Poseidon C3
Type: submarine-launched ballistic missile
Dimensions: length 10.4 m (34.1 ft); diameter 1.9 m (6 ft 2 in)
Launch weight: 29030 kg (64,000 lb)
Performance: range 4000-5200 km (2,485-3,230 miles) depending on the number of MIRVs carried; CEP 553 m (605 yards)
Warhead: between 10 and 14 MIRVs each with a 40-kiloton weapon
Propulsion: solid-propellant rocket
Guidance: inertial

Still in service aboard 19 'Lafayette/ Benjamin Franklin' class SSBNs, the C3 Poseidon can carry up to 14 relatively low-yield warheads to attack independent targets.

 USA

'Ohio' class SSBN

Destined to become the mainstay of the American SSBN fleet in the next decade and after, the 'Ohio' class will eventually carry the D5 Trident II SLBM that will allow these submarines to operate in patrol zones close to the American coasts, where they can be protected more easily.

Designed in the early 1970s as the follow-on SSBN to the 'Benjamin Franklin' and 'Lafayette' classes, the lead ship of the **'Ohio' class**, the USS **Ohio** (SSBN726) was contracted to the Electric Boat Division of the General Dynamics Corporation in July 1974. As the result of an unfortunate series of problems both in Washington, DC, and at the shipyard, the lead vessel did not run her first sea trials until June 1981, and was not finally commissioned until November of that year, three years late. Since then further delays have occurred in the programme but the rate of production is now beginning to get back on schedule.

Each submarine is expected to have a 12-month reactor refuelling refit every nine years and will work a patrol period of 70 days with the next 25 days spent alongside a tender or jetty readying for the next patrol. Because of their longer-range Trident missiles, the 'Ohio' class boats have patrol areas in the remoter parts of the world's oceans, making effective Soviet ASW measures against them virtually impossible for the foreseeable future, especially as the boats are acoustically very quiet.

Eighteen Ohio class boats were in commission in the late1990s. These were the **Ohio** (SSBN726), **Michigan** (SSBN727), **Florida** (SSBN728), **Georgia** (SSBN729), **Henry M.Jackson** (SSBN730), **Alabama** (SSBN 731), **Alaska** (SSBN732), **Nevada** (SSBN733), **Tennessee** (SSBN734), **Pennsylvania** (SSBN735), **West Virginia** (SSBN736), **Kentucky** (SSBN737), **Maryland** (SSBN738), **Nebraska** (SSBN739), **Rhode Island** (SSBN740), **Maine** (SSBN741), **Wyoming** (SSBN742) and **Louisiana** (SSBN743). They are in both the Atlantic and Pacific Fleets. based at King's Bay Georgia and Bangor, Washington respectively.

Specification
'Ohio' class
Displacement: 16,764 tons surfaced and 18,750 tons dived
Dimensions: length 170.7 m (560.0 ft); beam 12.8 m (42.0 ft); draught 10.8 m (35.5 ft)
Propulsion: one S8G pressurized water-cooled natural-circulation reactor powering a turbo-reduction drive to one shaft
Speed: 20 kts surfaced and 24 kts dived
Diving depth: 300 m (985 ft) operational and 500 m (1,640 ft) maximum
Armament: 24 launch tubes for 24 Trident I C4 submarine-launched ballistic missiles, and four 533-mm (21-in) bow tubes for an unknown number of tube-launched weapons
Electronics: one BPS-15A surface-search radar, one WLR-8(V) ESM system, one BQQ-6 sonar, one BQS-13 sonar, one BQS-15 sonar, one BQR-19 sonar, one BQR-23 towed-array sonar, and extensive communications and navigation systems
Complement: 133

The USS Ohio (SSBN726) under way. This class represents the latest in American technology, and is designed to defeat all foreseeable ASW threats that the Soviets are known to possess or believed to be capable of developing.

Although constructed in the United Kingdom, the four 'Resolution' class SSBNs have a considerable amount of their internal systems based on American components that were used in the 'Lafayette' class.

Officially stated in February 1963 was the British government's intention to order four or five **'Resolution' class** Polaris missile-equipped 7,000-ton nuclear-powered submarines that would take over the nuclear deterrent role from the Royal Air Force's V-bomber force from 1968 onwards. The first two pairs of boats were ordered in May 1963 from Vickers Shipbuilding Ltd, Barrow-in-Furness, and Cammell Laird & Co. Ltd, Birkenhead; the option on a fifth unit was cancelled in February 1965. With characteristics very similar to the American 'Lafayettes' the lead ship HMS **Resolution** (S22) was launched in September 1966 and commissioned in October of the following year. The second vessel, HMS **Repulse** (S23), followed in September 1968, with the third, HMS **Renown** (S24), and fourth, HMS **Revenge** (S27), commissioning in November 1968 and December 1969 respectively. Early in 1968 the *Resolution* sailed to Florida in the United States for missile launch trials, making the UK's first successful Polaris launch on 15 February. Four months later she sailed on her first deterrent patrol. As in French and American SSBNs, two crews (Port and Starboard) are used to maximize the time spent at sea, each patrol lasting around three months. When not aboard the crews take leave and undergo refresher training at the 10th Submarine Squadron base at Faslane on the Clyde. In the1990s the 'Resolution' class boats were progressively replaced by the new 'Vanguard' class SSBNs, armed with the Trident II missile. The first of these was commissioned in August 1933. Their names are **Vanguard**, **Victorious**, **Vigilant** and **Vengeance**.

Specification
'Resolution' class
Displacement: 7,500 tons surfaced and 8,400 tons dived
Dimensions: length 129.5 m (425.0 ft); beam 10.1 m (33.0 ft); draught 9.1 m (30.0 ft)
Propulsion: one pressurized water-cooled reactor powering two steam turbines driving one shaft
Speed: 20 kts surfaced and 25 kts dived

Diving depth: 350 m (1,150 ft) operational and 465 m (1,525 ft) maximum
Armament: 16 launch tubes for 16 Polaris A3TK submarine-launched ballistic missiles, and six 533-mm (21-in) bow tubes for an unknown number of tube-launched weapons
Electronics: one Type 1003 surface-search radar, one type 2001 bow sonar, one Type 2007 sonar, one Type 2023 retractable towed-array sonar,

HMS Revenge (S27). In 1983 she became the second of Britain's Polaris submarines to operate with the upgraded Polaris A3TK Chevaline system designed to penetrate Soviet ABM defences around Moscow.

one ESM suite, and an extensive communications outfit
Complement: 135

USA/UK
Lockheed UGM-27C Polaris A3 SLBM

Now the sole user of the US-designed **Lockheed UGM-27C Polaris A3** SLBM, the Royal Navy has recently had its stockpile of Polaris missiles re-engined so that it can continue as the UK's nuclear deterrent force, with a range of 4748 km (2,950 miles). The British buy of the missile was, according to US Congressional records, 102 with another 30 purchased later to make up attrition. These were equipped with three British-designed and -built 200-kiloton yield MRVs for use against area targets such as cities and oilfields; the effect of a single high-yield warhead falls off rapidly with distance from the point of impact, where-

as several smaller-yield weapons around the target perimeter cause significantly more damage. However, as a result of Soviet developments in ABM defences it was decided in the early 1970s that countermeasures would have to be built into the Polaris system. The result was the **Polaris A3TK Chevaline** project, which had its roots in a cancelled US warhead programme called Antelope. Chevaline involves the replacement of the 200-kiloton MRVs with three 60-kiloton weapons hardened against EMP and fast radiation, as well as the modification of the carrier bus to present defending radar systems with a confusingly large number of credible threats at the same

Now used only by the United Kingdom, the Polaris A3 SLBM is undergoing a rocket-motor replacement programme.

ber of credible threats at the same time, with the result that the incoming warhead picture is swamped. Although not specified, these modifications are believed to include the fitting of chaff penetration aids and the possible carriage of decoys that on re-entry behave as real warheads do. The first submarine to be retrofitted with the new system was HMS *Renown*. As each boat comes in for refuelling she is converted to the new missile system.

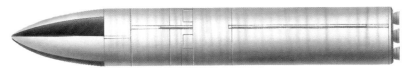

Specification
Polaris A3TK
Type: submarine-launched ballistic missile

Equipping the 'R' class submarines of the Royal Navy, the Polaris A3 is the last model of the pioneering SLBM to remain operational.

Dimensions: length 9.8 m (32.2 ft); diameter 1.4 m (4 ft 6 in)
Launch weight: 15876 kg (35,000 lb)
Performance: range 4748 km (2,950 miles); CEP 930 m (1,017 yards)
Warhead: three 60-kiloton yield MRVs plus an unknown number of decoys and chaff penetration aids
Propulsion: solid-propellant rocket
Guidance: inertial

USA

Lockheed UGM-96A Trident I C4 SLBM

The purpose of the **Lockheed UGM-96A Trident I C4** missile development programme was essentially to increase the range of American SLBMs to allow the use of larger and remoter patrol areas. A three-stage solid-propellant missile, the Trident I was flight tested in 1977, becoming operational two years later aboard the SSBN conversions of the 'Benjamin Franklin' and 'Lafayette' classes. The first two stages of the missile are essentially the same as those fitted to the earlier Poseidon C3 SLBM, but the third stage is fitted with stellar-inertial guidance to give the required accuracy over the longer range. The first eight 'Ohio class SSBNs were fitted to carry the Trident 1, but these were eventually retro fitted to carry the yet longer-ranged Trident II in the early 1990s. Rapid onboard targeting to another pre-planned target co-ordinates package is possible, but a far lengthier operation is required if the system has to be fed new target co-ordinates from an external source. As increased range was considered to be more important than accuracy improvement, a CEP comparable with that of the Poseidon was accepted. The use of higher-yield warheads, however, allows more hardened military and industrial targets to be engaged on a satisfactory basis than was possible with the earlier missile, and as such that one Trident-equipped submarine had its re-entry vehicles assigned to NATO for use in the theatre nuclear role. A total of 740 missiles were procured with eight MIRVs per missile. Eventually, in the next century, the American SSBN force will be a mix only of 'Ohio' class boats with Trident II missiles.

Specification
Trident I C4
Type: submarine-launched ballistic missile
Dimensions: length 10.4 m (34.1 ft); diameter 1.9 m (6 ft 2.8 in)

Launch weight: 31751 kg (70,000 lb)
Performance: range 6808 km (4,230 miles); CEP 549 m (600 yards)
Warhead: eight MIRVs each with a 100-kiloton weapon
Propulsion: solid-propellant rocket
Guidance: stellar-inertial

At enormous cost the Trident programme has provided the seaborne element of the US strategic deterrent for the foreseeable future. Trident 1 employs the 7400 km (4,600 mile) ranged C4 missile which has now been replaced by the D5.

Fitted to 12 of the 'Lafayette/ Benjamin Franklin' class SSBNs and the new 'Ohios', the C4 Trident 1 SLBM proves the nearest American equivalent to the long-range Soviet SLBMs but with more accurate payloads of MRV warheads.

USA

Lockheed Trident II D5 SLBM

The **Lockheed II D5** is the result of an improved accuracy programmes for American SLBMs begun in Fiscal Year 1975. The development go-ahead for Trident II was announced in 1982, and test flights started in early 1987. Trident II is the largest missile compatible with the launch tubes on Ohio-class SSBNs.

The Trident programme was aimed at increasing the number of warhead vehicles available to something like the total at the height of the Poseidon programme, but with greater megatonnage to match previous Soviet increases.

The missile was first deployed on schedule aboard the **Tennessee**, then in the 'Ohio' class submarine, in December 1989, and a total of 312 missiles had been deployed by 1989. The four British 'Vanguard' class Trident submarines incorporated a missile compartment based on that of the Ohio class boats, but with 16 rather than 24 launch tubes. Trident II D5 is able to carry up to 14 warheads per missile, each having sufficient accuracy to hit under-ground missile silos and command bunkers. Trident IIs maximum range

increases the area of ocean in which its carrier submarines can be deployed.

Specification
Trident II D5
Type: submarine-launched ballistic missile
Dimensions: length 13.96 m (45.8 ft); diameter 1.89 m (6 ft 2.4 in)
Launch weight: 57153 kg (126,000 lb)
Performance: range 7400-11100 km (4,600-6,900 miles) depending on number of MIRVs carried; CEP 92.5 m (101 yards)
Warhead: between eight and 14 MIRVs each with a 375-kiloton weapon
Propulsion: solid-propellant rocket
Guidance: stellar-inertial

Nuclear Attack Submarines

The nuclear attack submarine has high speed and phenomenal endurance: indeed, with virtually boundless range provided by its nuclear powerplant, the only limit on its operations is the need to feed its crew. A modern capital ship, a nuclear attack submarine now carries subsurface-to-surface and land attack cruise missiles.

USS *Buffalo* (SSN 715) is a 'Los Angeles' class nuclear attack submarine. Early Los Angeles class boats fire Tomahawk cruise missiles from their torpedo tubes; later boats have launchers.

For nearly three decades, NATO and Warsaw Pact submariners played a potentially deadly game of cat and mouse in the depths of the world's oceans. The tools of their trade were nuclear attack and hunter-killer submarines (SSNs), packed with advanced weaponry and sensors. Their targets were the nuclear-powered ballistic missile submarines (SSBNs) and naval task forces of the other side.

The development of nuclear-powered attack submarines began at about the same time in the United States and the Soviet Union, but the designs followed different paths. The Americans concentrated on anti-submarine warfare (ASW) and the Russians on a multi-mission role, which encompassed both ASW and surface attack using large anti-ship cruise missiles. Later on, the Americans also adopted a multi-mission capability with the deployment of submarine-launched weapons like Sub-Harpoon and the Tomahawk cruise missile, which were designed for anti-ship use and land attack.

In the 1960s a debate took place about the use of the SSN by the Soviets as escort for aircraft carriers. It was known they planned to use SSGNs (cruise missile submarines) and SSNs to counter a threat from US bombers. This prompted more design work in the US and ultimately resulted in the 'Los Angeles' class of submarine.

The main advantages of the nuclear attack submarine are its ability to remain submerged for virtually unlimited periods, its deep-diving capability, the sophisticated long-range sensor systems that it carries, and the high power output of its reactor that can be converted into very high underwater speeds. High speed was essential for the attacks on hostile submarines detected by sophisticated long-range acoustic detection systems. All of these advantages can be utilized to the full in modern submarine warfare.

The later generations of nuclear attack submarines are virtually underwater cruisers; the Russian 'Oscar' class, for example, was the underwater equivalent of the 'Kirov' class of battlecruiser. Their combat arena, in the main, lay under the Arctic ice cap, once considered to be a safe haven for SSBNs.

'Valiant' and 'Churchill' class SSNs

Essentially an enlarged 'Dreadnought' class design with all-British reactor plant and systems, HMS *Valiant* (S 102) was ordered in August 1960 as the lead boat of the **'Valiant' class** and completed in July 1966, a year later than planned because of the priority accorded to the British Polaris programme. Her sistership HMS *Warspite* (S 103) was followed by three others built to a modified design as **'Churchill' class** boats. These three are HMS *Churchill* (S 46), HMS *Conqueror* (S 48) and HMS *Courageous* (S 50), and are believed to be slightly quieter in service, having benefited from the experience gained in operating the earlier boats. All are fitted with the Type 2001 long-range active/passive LF sonar mounted in the 'chin' position, though the three boats will be retrofitted with the Type 2020 set as a replacement during future overhauls. It is also reported that the five boats can be fitted with a LF clip-on towed array since identified as the Type 2024 sonar system. Other sonars identified with the craft are the Type 2007 long-range passive set and the joint Anglo-Dutch-French Type 2019 Passive/Active Range and Intercept Sonar (PARIS). A Type 197 passive ranging sonar for detecting sonar transmissions is also carried. When the boats were built the main armament comprised the pre-World War II Mk 8 anti-ship torpedo, the 1950s technology wire-guided Mk 23 ASW torpedo and World War II Mk 5 ground and Mk 6 moored mines. Since then the armament has been modernized to include the Mk 8, the Mk 24 Tigerfish wire-guided dual-role torpedo, the Sub-Harpoon anti-ship missile and the new Stonefish and Sea Urchin ground mines. It was the *Chur-*

chill that tested the Sub-Harpoon for the Royal Navy. During the 1982 Falklands war the *Conqueror, Courageous* and *Valiant* were deployed to the Maritime Exclusion Zone, the first sinking the Argentinian cruiser *General Belgrano* on 2 May 1982. All five vessels were paid off in the late 1980s, following the full deployment of the 'Trafalgar' class SSNs.

Specification
'Valiant' and 'Churchill' classes
Displacement: 4,400 tons surfaced and 4,900 tons dived
Dimensions: length 86.9 m (285 ft 0 in); beam 10.1 m (33 ft 3 in); draught 8.2 m (27 ft 0 in)
Machinery: one pressurized-water reactor powering two steam turbines driving one shaft
Speed: 20 kts surfaced and 29 kts dived
Diving depth: 300 m (985 ft) operational and 500 m (1,640 ft) maximum
Torpedo tubes: six 533-mm (21-in) bow
Basic load: a mix of 32 Mk 8 and Mk 24 Tigerfish 533-mm (21-in) torpedoes or 64 Mk 5 Stonefish and Mk 6 Sea Urchin mines; this is being changed to 26 533-mm (21-in) torpedoes and six Sub-Harpoon anti-ship missiles
Missiles: none
Electronics: one Type 1006 surface-search radar, one Type 2001 sonar, one Type 2024 towed sonar, one Type 2007 sonar, one Type 2019 sonar, one Type 197 sonar, one direction-finding antenna, one ESM system, one DCB torpedo fire-control system, and one underwater telephone
Complement: 103

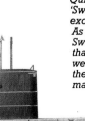

Essentially an enlarged version of the 'Dreadnought' design, HMS Valiant was built at the same time as the Polaris boats with an all-British PWR1 reactor plant and associated control systems.

Originally destined to remain in service until the early 1990s, the Valiant *and* Churchill *class of SSNs saw earlier retirement as more effective boats became operational.*

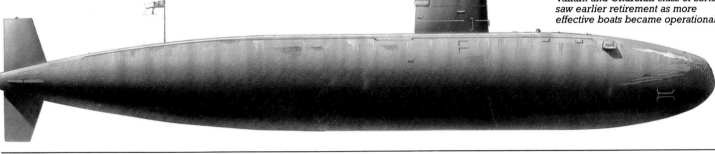

'Swiftsure' class SSN

In 1971 the first of the UK's **'Swiftsure' class** second-generation SSNs was launched at Vickers Shipyard at Barrow-in-Furness. Called HMS *Swiftsure* (S 126), the boat introduced a shorter and fuller hull-form than that of the 'Valiant' class in order to give a greater internal volume and a stronger pressure hull. Hence it can operate at greater depths and speeds than the previous class. The fin is smaller and the

retractable diving planes are located below the water line. The *Swiftsure* was followed by five sister ships, HMS *Sovereign* (S 108), HMS *Superb* (S 109), HMS *Sceptre* (S 104), HMS *Spartan* (S 105) and HMS *Splendid* (S 106); the class is currently used both in the ASW screening role for task forces, and in the independent anti-ship ASW roles because of the quieter machinery used. The sonar fit is the Type

Quieter than their predecessors, the 'Swiftsure' class have proved to be excellent ASW platforms in service. As a result of budget cuts the Swiftsure paid off in 1992 after less than 20 years' service, but the others were still operational in 1999. Two of the class are usually in refit or maintenance.

2074 (active/passive search and attack), Type 2007 (passive), Type 2046 (towed array), 2019 (intercept and ranging) and Type 2077 (short range) classification

The armament is reduced by one tube and seven torpedoes, but this reduction is balanced by the fact that it takes only 15 seconds to reload individual tubes. Emergency power is provided by the same 112-cell electric battery and associated diesel generator and electric motor as fitted in the 'Valiant' and 'Churchill' classes. In 1976 the *Sovereign* demonstrated the Royal Navy's ability to conduct ASW operations under the ice pack when she undertook a trip to the North Pole, the operational aspects being combined with a successful scientific voyage. The *Spartan* and *Splendid* were both involved in the Falklands war.

Specification
'Swiftsure' class
Displacement: 4,200 tons surfaced and 4,500 tons dived
Dimensions: length 82.9 m (272 ft 0 in); beam 9.8 m (32 ft 3 in); draught 8.2 m (27 ft 0 in)

Machinery: one pressurized-water reactor powering two steam turbines driving one shaft
Speed: 20 kts surfaced and 30 kts dived
Diving depth: 400 m (1,315 ft) operational and 600 m (1,970 ft) maximum
Torpedo tubes: five 533-mm (21-in) bow
Basic load: 20 Mk 8 or Mk 24 Tigerfish 533-mm (21-in) torpedoes plus five Sub-Harpoon anti-ship missiles, or 50 Mk 5 Stonefish and Mk 6 Sea Urchin mines
Missiles: SLCM Tomahawk Block III; SubHarpoon.
Electronics: Type 2074, Type 2007, Type 2046, Type 2019 and Type 2077 sonars (see main entry for details); Type 1006 H-band radar; DCB/DCG or SMCS tactical data handling system.
Complement: 97

To improve underwater performance, HMS Swiftsure *was introduced into service with a shorter and fuller hull form. This gives greater internal volume and a stronger pressure hull than earlier boats.*

UK
'Trafalgar' class SSN

Essentially an improved 'Swiftsure' design, the **'Trafalgar' class** constitutes the third generation of British SSNs to be built at Vickers Shipyard in Barrow-in-Furness. The lead boat, HMS *Trafalgar* (S 107), was launched in 1981 and commissioned into the Royal Navy in March 1983, serving with the 'Swiftsure' class boats at the Devonport naval base. The other vessels in the class are **Turbulent**, **Tireless**, **Torbay**, **Trenchant**, **Talent** and **Triumph**, all commissioned between 1984 and 1991. The major improvements over the 'Swiftsure' class include several features to reduce the underwater radiated noise. These comprise a new reactor system, a pump-jet propulsion system rather than a conventional propeller and the covering of the pressure hull and outer surfaces with anechoic tiles to give the same type of protection as afforded by the Soviet 'Clusterguard' coating in reducing noise. All the 'Trafalgar' class are being updated with the Type 2076 sonar systems, integrated with SMCS and countermeasures. This update also includes the Marconi 2077 short-range classification sonar. Tomahawk capability is being progressively fitted; the vessels will be armed with the Hughes Tomahawk Block III missile, which carries a 347 kg (765 lb)

shaped charge or submunitions and has a range of 1204 km (650 nm). Trafalgar was the trials boat for the Spearfish torpedo, which started production in 1992 and was first embarked operationally in *Trenchant* in early 1994. All of the class belong to the Second Submarine Squadron at Devonport. Two boats are usually in refit. The primary mission of the 'Trafalgar class boats is ASW, with a secondary anti-ship role.

Specification
'Trafalgar' class
Displacement: 4,700 tons surfaced and 5,200 tons dived
Dimensions: length 85.4 m (280 ft 3 in); beam 9.8 m (32 ft 3 in); draught 8.2 m (27 ft 0 in)

Right: Similar in many respects to the 'Swiftsure' class, HMS Trafalgar *is the first Royal Navy submarine to be covered with anechoic tiles that reduced underwater radiated noise.*

Below: With HMS Illustrious *in the background, HMS* Trafalgar *enters Devonport Naval Base to tie up at the 2nd Submarine Squadron berth.*

Machinery: one pressurized-water reactor powering two steam turbines driving one shaft with pump-jet propulsion
Speed: 20 kts surfaced and 29 kts dived
Diving depth: 400 m (1,315 ft) operational and 600 m (1,970 ft) maximum
Torpedo tubes: five 533-mm (21-in) bow
Basic load: 20 Mk 8 and Mk 24 Tigerfish

533-mm (21-in) torpedoes and five Sub-Harpoon anti-ship missiles, or 50 Mk 5 Stonefish and Mk 6 Sea Urchin mines
Missiles: Hughes Tomahawk Block III SLCM.
Electronics: Type 2020 or 2074 or 2076 hull-mounted active search and attack sonar; Type 2007 passive sonar; Type 2026 or 2046 towed array; Type 2019 or 2082 passive intercept and ranging sonar. Type 1007 I-band radar.

'Skipjack' class SSN

Although built in the late 1950s, the five 'Skipjack' class boats currently in service are still considered to be front-line operational boats and were, until the advent of the 'Los Angeles' class, the fastest submarines available to the US Navy. A sixth boat, the USS *Scorpion* (SSN 589, whose original hull was used in the construction of the first American SSBN, the USS *George Washington*), was lost in May 1968 south west of the Azores whilst en route from the Mediterranean to Norfolk, Virginia, with all 99 men aboard. The class is notable for being the first to use the S5W reactor design, which was subsequently used in all nuclear submarine classes built in the United States up to the 'Glenard P. Lipscomb' class. The 'Skipjack' class also introduced the classic teardrop hull shape, and as such acted as the model for the British 'Dreadnought' and 'Valiant/Churchill' classes, the long rearward taper of the hull forcing the designers to dispense with stern torpedo tubes and adopt a single-shaft propulsion arrangement. The diving planes were also relocated to the fin to increase underwater manoeuvrability, a feature which the British did not copy. All the engine room fittings except the reactor and steam turbines are duplicated to minimize breakdown possibilities. During their later years four boats (USS *Skipjack*, USS *Scamp*, USS *Sculpin* and USS *Shark*) served in the Atlantic Fleet and one (USS *Snook*) in the Pacific Fleet. The last boats were paid off in 1989.

USS Shark *at its maximum surface speed of 18 kts. With an underwater speed of 30 kts, the five remaining 'Skipjack' class vessels are still considered to be front-line submarines.*

Specification
'Skipjack' class
Displacement: 3,075 tons surfaced and 3,515 tons dived
Dimensions: length 76.7 m (251 ft 9 in); beam 9.6 m (31 ft 6 in); draught 8.5 m (27 ft 10 in)
Machinery: one Westinghouse S5W pressurized-water reactor powering two steam turbines driving one shaft
Speed: 18 kts surfaced and 30 kts dived
Diving depth: 300 m (985 ft) operational and 500 m (1,640 ft) maximum
Torpedo tubes: six 533-mm (21-in) bow
Basic load: 24 Mk 48 533-mm (21-in) dual-role torpedoes, or 48 Mk 57 moored mines
Missiles: none
Electronics: one surface-search radar, one modified BQS-4 sonar suite, one Mk 101 torpedo fire-control system, and one underwater telephone
Complement: 114

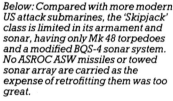

Below: Compared with more modern US attack submarines, the 'Skipjack' class is limited in its armament and sonar, having only Mk 48 torpedoes and a modified BQS-4 sonar system. No ASROC ASW missiles or towed sonar array are carried as the expense of retrofitting them was too great.

'Thresher' class (later 'Permit' class) SSN

The first of the SSNs in the US Navy with a deep-diving capability, advanced sonars mounted in the optimum bow position, amidships angled torpedo tubes with the SUBROC ASW missile, and a high degree of machinery-quieting, the 'Thresher' class was an important art of the US attack capability. The lead boat of this class, the USS *Thresher* (SSN 593), was lost with all 129 people on board during diving trials off the coast of New England on 10 April 1963, mid-way through the building period 1960-6. The class was then renamed the 'Permit' class after the second ship. As a result of the lessons learnt from the enquiry following the *Thresher*'s loss, the last three of the class were modified during construction with SUBSAFE features, heavier machinery and taller sail structures, essentially to act as the prototypes for the follow-on 'Sturgeon' class. In addition USS *Jack* (SSN 605) was built to a different design with two propellers on one shaft and a contra-rotating turbine without reduction gear to test a new method of reducing machinery-operating noises. This was unsuccessful, however, and the vessel was refitted with standard machinery. During

the normal refit programme the original Mk 113 torpedo fire-control system and the BQQ-2 sonar suite are to be replaced with the all digital Mk 117 FCS and the BQQ-5 sonar suite with clip-on towed sonar array facilities. All were intended to carry and fire the Sub-Harpoon and Tomahawk missiles. The SURBROC was to be replaced by a new stand-off ASW missile in the late 1980s, with the choice of either a nuclear depth bomb or an ASW torpedo as the payload. Eight 'Permit' class boats (USS *Permit*, USS *Plunger*, USS *Barb*, USS *Pollack*, USS *Haddo*, USS *Guardfish*, USS *Flasher* and USS *Haddock*) served in the Pacific with five (USS *Jack*, USS *Tinosa*, USS *Dace*, USS *Greenling* and USS *Gato*) in the Atlantic.

Specification
'Permit' class
Displacement: 3,750 tons surfaced and 4,311 tons dived, except *Jack* 3,800 tons surfaced and 4,470 tons dived, and *Flasher*, *Greenling* and *Gato* 3,800 tons surfaced and 4,642 tons dived
Dimensions: length 84.9 m (278 ft 6 in) except *Jack* 85.9 m (297 ft 5 in) and *Flasher*, *Greenling* and *Gato* 89.1 m

(292 ft 3 in); beam 9.6 m (31 ft 8 in); draught 8.8 m (28 ft 10 in)
Machinery: one Westinghouse S5W pressurized-water reactor powered two steam turbines driving one shaft
Speed: 18 kts surface and 27 kts dived, except *Jack*, *Flasher*, *Greenling* and *Gato* 18 kts surfaced and 26 kts dived

The first US Navy SSN class with a deep diving capability, advanced sonars, amidships torpedo tubes, and machinery quieting systems was the 'Permit' class. USS Plunger *is seen here off the coast of Hawaii during her first fleet deployment in 1963.*

USS Barb executes a high speed turn on the surface. Underwater, the submarine would be 'flown' using controls similar to those found aboard aircraft in order to exploit its maximum manoeuvrability and speed.

The 'Permit' class submarines are being upgraded with new sonars and weapon control systems in order that they might operate as first-line units into the 1990s to supplement the 'Los Angeles' class.

Diving depth: 400 m (1,315 ft) operational and 600 m (1,970 ft) maximum
Torpedo tubes: four 533-mm (21-in) amidships
Basic load: 17 Mk 48 533-mm (21-in) torpedoes and six SUBROC anti-submarine missiles (being modified to 15 Mk 48 torpedoes, four SUBROC missiles and four Sub-Harpoon anti-ship missiles), or 46 Mk 57, Mk 60 or Mk 67 mines: in the late 1980s the load will comprise 11 Mk 48 torpedoes, four

Sub-Harpoon missiles, four Tomahawk cruise missiles and four ASWSOW weapons.
Missiles: none, but see above
Electronics: one BPS-11 surface-search radar, one BQQ-2 or BQQ-5 sonar suite (the latter with towed array), one Mk 113 or Mk 117 torpedo fire-control system, one WSC-3 satellite communications system, one ESM system, and one underwater telephone
Complement: 122-134

'Sturgeon' class SSN

USA

Essentially an enlarged and improved 'Thresher/Permit' design with additional quieting features and electronic systems, the **'Sturgeon' class** SSNs built between 1965 and 1974 were the largest class of nuclear-powered warships built anywhere until the advent of the 'Los Angeles' class boats. Like the previous class they are intended primarily for ASW, and employ the standard American SSN amidships torpedo battery aft of the fin, with two tubes firing diagonally outwards from the hull on each side. This allows a larger torpedo handling room than in bow-battery boats, and facilitates fast access, weapon choice and reloading of the tubes. The last nine of the class were lengthened to accommodate more electronic equipment. What is not widely known, however, is that these are the boats used in one of the most closely guarded and classified naval intelligence programmes currently in operation. Codenamed 'Holy Stone', the programme was initiated in the late 1960s and involves the use of these submarines in highly specialized intelligence-gathering missions close to the coasts of nations unfriendly towards the United States. The addition-

al intelligence-gathering equipment is located in special compartments and is operated by National Security Agency personnel specifically carried for the task. During these operations several collisions with other underwater and surface craft have occurred, resulting sometimes in damage to the US boats involved; and on one occasion at least a 'Holy Stone' submarine was accidentally grounded for several hours during a mission within the territorial waters of the Soviet Far East. As in the case of the 'Thresher/Permit' class, the boast were retrofitted with MK 117FCS and BQQ-5 sonar suite. All 37 'Sturgeon' class boats were still in service in the late 1990s. In 1982 *Cavalla* was converted at Pearl Harbor to have a secondary amphibious assault role by carrying a swimmer deliver vehicle (SDV); *Archerfish, Silversides, Tunny* and *L. Mendel* are also similarly equipped. *William H. Bates, Hawkbill, Pintado, Richard B. Russell* and others have been modified in order to carry and support the Navy's Deep Submer-gence and Rescue vehicles. The 'Sturgeon' boats are named as follows:

USS *Sturgeon*, USS *Whale*, USS *Grayling*, USS *Sunfish*, USS *Pargo*, USS *Ray*, USS *Lapon*, USS *Hammerhead*, USS *Sea Devil*, USS *Bergall*, USS *Spadefish*, USS *Seahorse*, USS *Finback*, USS *Flying Fish*, USS *Trepang*, USS *Bluefish* and USS *Billfish*, while the 'Holy Stone' boats are probably the USS *Archerfish*, USS *Silversides*, USS *Batfish*, USS *L. Mendel Rivers* and USS *Richard B. Russell*. The Pacific Fleet's 15 'Sturgeon' class boats are the 'standard' USS *Tautog*, USS *Pogy*, USS *Aspro*, USS *Queenfish*, USS *Puffer*, USS *Sand Lance*, USS *Gurnard*, USS *Guitarro*, USS *Hawkbill*, USS *Pintado* and USS *Drum*, and the 'Holy Stone' USS *William H. Bates*, USS *Tunny*, USS *Parche* and USS *Cavalla*.

Specification
'Sturgeon' class
Displacement: 4,266 tons surfaced and 4,777 tons dived
Dimensions: length 89.0 m (292 ft 3 in) except *Archerfish, Silversides, William H. Bates, Batfish, Tunny, Parche, Cavalla, L. Mendel Rivers* and *Richard B. Russell* 92.1 m (302 ft 2 in); beam 9.65 m (31 ft 8 in); draught 8.9 m (29 ft 3 in)

Machinery: one Westinghouse S5W pressurized-water reactor powered two steam turbines driving one shaft
Speed: 18 kts surfaced and 26 kts dived
Diving depth: 400 m (1,315 ft) operation and 600 m (1,970 ft) maximum
Torpedo tubes: four 533-mm (21-in) amidships
Basic load: 17 Mk 48 533-mm (21-in) torpedoes and six SUBROC anti-submarine missiles (being modified to 15 Mk 48 torpedoes, four SUBROC missiles and four Sub-Harpoon anti-ship missiles), or 46 Mk 57, Mk 60 or Mk 67 mines; from the late 1980s the load comprised 11 Mk 48 torpedoes, four Sub-Harpoon missiles and four ASWSOW weapons.

Missiles: none, but see above
Electronics: one BPS-15 surface-search radar, one BQQ-2 or BQQ-5 sonar suite (the latter with towed array), one Mk 113 or Mk 117 torpedo fire-control system, one ESM suite, one WSC-3 satellite communication system, and one underwater telephone
Complement: 121-134

'Narwhal' and 'Glenard P. Lipscomb' class SSNs

These two single-ship classes are test-beds for major new submarine technology. The USS **Narwhal** (SSN 671) was constructed in 1966-7 to evaluate the natural-circulation S5G nuclear reactor plant. This uses natural convection rather than several circulator pumps, with their associated electrical and control equipment, for heat transfer operations via the reactor coolant to the steam generators, thus effectively reducing at slow speeds one of the major sources of self-generated radiated machinery noise within ordinary nuclear-powered submarines. In all other respects the boat is similar to a 'Sturgeon' and will be retrofitted with new equipment and missiles in the course of a regular refit.

In contrast the USS **Glenard P. Lipscomb** (SSN 685) was constructed in 1971-3 to a much larger design to evaluate a turbine-electric drive propulsion plant. This eliminates the noisy reduction gear of the standard steam turbine plant and introduces a number of new and quieter machinery systems into the boat. However, because the system is much larger and heavier than the normal plant, a penalty has had to be paid in terms of underwater speed in comparison with that of contemporary American SSN classes. The *Lipscomb* is being used in an ongoing project designed to allow an actual at-sea evaluation of noise reduction techniques as a counter to ASW measures. Several of the quieting techniques which do not result in an underwater speed loss have already been incorporated in the 'Los Angeles' class. The Narwhals operated until the late 1980s, when they were withdrawn.

Specification
USS *Narwhal*
Displacement: 4,450 tons surfaced and 5,350 tons dived
Dimensions: length 95.9 m (314 ft 8 in); beam 11.6 m (38 ft 0 in); draught 7.9 m (25 ft 11 in)
Machinery: one General Electric S5G pressurized-water reactor powering two steam turbines driving one shaft
Speed: 18 kts surfaced and 26 kts dived
Diving depth: 400 m (1,315 ft)

operational and 600 m (1,970 ft) maximum
Torpedo tubes: four 533-mm (21-in) amidships
Basic load: 17 Mk 48 533-mm (21-in) torpedoes and six SUBROC anti-submarine missiles (being modified to 15 Mk 48 torpedoes, four SUBROC missiles and four Sub-Harpoon anti-ship missiles), or 46 Mk 57, Mk 60 or Mk 67 mines; in the late 1980s the load will comprise 11 Mk 48 torpedoes, four Sub-Harpoon missiles, four Tomahawk cruise missiles and four ASWSOW weapons
Missiles: none, but see above
Electronics: one BPS-11 surface-search radar, one BQQ-2 or BQQ-5 sonar suite (the latter with towed

array), one Mk 113 or Mk 117 torpedo fire-control system, one WSC-3 satellite communications system, one ESM system, and one underwater telephone
Complement: 120

Specification
USS *Glenard P. Lipscomb*
Displacement: 5,800 tons surfaced and 6,840 tons dived
Dimensions: length 111.3 m (365 ft 0 in); beam 9.7 m (31 ft 9 in); draught 9.5 m (31 ft 0 in)
Machinery: one Westinghouse S5Wa pressurized-water reactor powering two steam turbines driving one shaft
Speed: 18 kts surfaced and 24 kts dived

USS Narwhal *(SSN671) is the testbed for the natural-circulation S5G nuclear reactor plant. The S5G uses natural convection rather than circulator pumps for heat transfer to the steam turbines in order to reduce the self-generated noise levels at low speeds.*

Diving depth: 400 m (1,315 ft) operational and 600 m (1,970 ft) maximum
Torpedo tubes: four 533-mm (21-in) amidships
Basic load: as for *Narwhal*
Missiles: none
Electronics: as for *Narwhal*
Complement: 120

'Los Angeles' class SSN

Destined to comprise the largest number of nuclear-powered warships built to one design, the **'Los Angeles' class** couples the speed advantage of the elderly 'Skipjack' class with the sonar and weapons capability of the 'Permit/Sturgeon' classes. The significant increase in size is mainly the result of doubling installed power available by the fitting of a new reactor design, the S6G, which is reportedly based on the D2G reactor fitted in the 'Bainbridge' and 'Truxtun' class nuclear-powered cruisers. Reactor refuelling will take place every 10-13 years. Few other improvements have been made apart

from a slight increase in the weapon stowage space and in the addition of various underwater quieting aspects. The boats, built on a continuing basis since 1974, are fitted with the BQQ-5 sonar suite with a spherical long-range active/passive bow array, three passive target-ranging hydrophone arrays on each side of the hull, a conformal long-range passive array and a clip-on (later to be a retractable system) towed long-range passive low-frequency array. Earlier submarines had weapons stowage problems. By 1991 75 per cent of the attack submarine force was equipped with the

Tomahawk SLCM as part of the normal weapons outfit; from SN719 (USS *Providence*) onwards all were equipped with the vertical launch system, which places 12 launch tubes external to the pressure hull behind the BQQ5 spherical array forward. While

in operational service, the class has proved to be an exceptionally good ASW platform, although on one occasion on the first out-of-area 'Alpha I' deployment the Soviet boat was easily able to outrun a trailing 'Los Angeles' class boat off Iceland just by using its superior underwater speed. Against

With a total of 62 boats built the 'Los Angeles' class design is the most numerous nuclear-powered warship class, as well as being the most expensive SSN type.

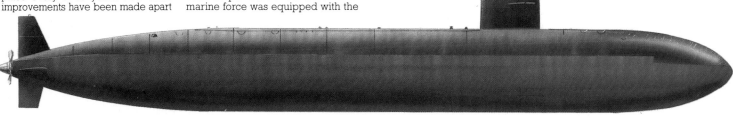

more conventional Soviet nuclear-powered boats the success rate of detection and tracking is quite high, the BQQ-5 system on one occasion acquiring and holding contact with two Soviet 'Victor' class SSNs for an extended time. The high underwater speed of the 'Los Angeles' class boats allows them to be the first American SSN units to be capable of providing an effective underwater escort capability for American carrier battle groups. Previous SSNs were too slow for most of the missions assigned to such escorts. The names are: USS *Los Angeles*, USS *Baton Rouge*, USS *Philadelphia*, USS *Memphis*, USS *Omaha*, USS *Cincinnati*, USS *Groton*, USS *Birmingham*, USS *New York City*, USS *Indianapolis*, USS *Bremerton*, USS *Jacksonville*, USS *Dallas*, USS *La Jolla*, USS *Phoenix*, USS *Boston*, USS *Baltimore*, USS *City of Corpus Christi*, USS *Alburquerque*, USS *Portsmouth*, USS *Minneapolis-St Paul*, USS *Hyman G. Rickover*, USS *San Francisco*, USS *Atlanta*, USS *Houston*, USS *Norfolk*, USS *Buffalo*, USS *Salt Lake City*, USS *Olympia*, USS *Honolulu*, USS *Providence*, USS *Pittsburgh*, USS *Chicago*, USS *Key West*, USS *Oklahoma City*, USS *Louisville*, USS *Helena*, USS *Newport News*, USS *San Juan*, USS *Pasadena*, USS *Albany*, USS *Topeka*, USS *Miami*, USS *Scranton*, USS *Alexandria*, USS *Asheville*, USS *Jefferson City*, USS *Annapolis*, USS *Springfield*, USS *Columbus*, USS *Santa Fe*, USS *Boise*, USS *Montpelier*, USS *Charlotte*, USS *Hampton*, USS *Hartford*, USS *Toledo*, USS *Tucson*, USS *Columbia*, USS *Greeneville* and one unnamed.

Specification
'Los Angeles' class
Displacement: 6,000 tons surfaced and 6,900 tons dived
Dimensions: length 109.7 m (360 ft 0 in); beam 10.1 m (33 ft 0 in); draught 9.85 m (32 ft 4 in)
Machinery: one General Electric S6G pressurized-water reactor powering two steam turbines driving one shaft
Speed: 18 kts surfaced and 31 kts dived
Diving depth: 450 m (1,475 ft) operational and 750 m (2,460 ft) maximum

Torpedo tubes: four 533-mm (21-in) amidships
Basic load: 26 533-mm (21-in) weapons (Mk 48 torpedoes, SUBROC anti-submarine missiles on the first six boats, Sub-Harpoon anti-ship missiles and Tomahawk cruise missiles) or 52 Mk 57, Mk 60 or Mk 67 mines
Missiles: (from 34th boat onwards) 15 Tomahawk cruise missiles
Electronics: one BPS-15 surface-search radar, one modified BQQ-5 sonar suite with towed array, one Mk 113 (first 13 units) or Mk 117 (later units, and to be retrofitted in first 13) torpedo

USS Birmingham (SSN695) shows off an emergency surfacing drill during her sea trials. Note the large volumes of water pouring from her sail and the sail-mounted diving planes. A normal surfacing is achieved gradually by selective blowing of ballast tanks.

fire-control system, one WSC-3 satellite communications system, one ESM suite, and one underwater telephone
Complement: 127

'Echo' class SSN and 'Echo II' class SSGN

The five **'Echo' class** SSNs were originally built at Komsomolsk in the Soviet Far East between 1960-2 as **'Echo I' class** SSGNs. Armed with six tubes for the SS-N-3C 'Shaddock' strategic cruise missile, they lacked the fire-control and guidance radars of the later **'Echo II' class**. As the Soviet SSBN force was built up so the need for these boats diminished, and they were converted to anti-ship attack SSNs between 1969 and 1974. The conversion involved the removal of the 'Shaddock' tubes, the plating over and streamlining of the hull to reduce the underwater noise caused by the tube system, and modification of the sonar systems to the standard carried by the 'November' class SSNs. All were then deployed with the Pacific Fleet, although one suffered some damage several years ago in an internal fire and had to be towed back to its base near Vladivostok for emergency drydocking.

The follow-on 'Echo II' class was built both at Severodvinsk (the lead yard, with 18 vessels built) and Komsomolsk (with 11 vessels built) between 1962 and 1967 as the Soviet Navy's primary anti-carrier missile submarines. They carry eight SS-N-3A 'Shaddock' anti-ship cruise missiles mounted in pairs above the pressure

hull, and for firing have to surface and elevate the pairs to about 25-30°. The forward section of the sail structure then rotates through 180° to expose the two 'Front' series missile-guidance radars. The firing in pairs of all eight missiles probably takes around 30 minutes, and the submarine then has to remain on the surface until the missile mid-course correction and final target-selection commands have been sent unless guidance can be passed over to a third party such as a naval air force Tupolev Tu-142 'Bear-D' fitted with the appropriate command guidance system. From the mid-1970s the 'Echo II' class boats have gradually been converted during routine overhauls to carry the longer-range and much faster SS-N-12 'Sandbox' anti-ship cruise missile in place of the 'Shaddocks'. The conversions can be distinguished by the fitting of bulges to each side of the sail and at the forward end of the mis-

Above: A Soviet 'Echo II' SSGN. A total of 29 of these vessels are in service, armed with SS-N-12 'Sandbox' or SS-N-3A 'Shaddock' anti-ship cruise missiles. Their major disadvantage is that they have to surface to fire and guide their missiles.

Below: The forward part of the 'Echo II' sail structure rotates through 180° to expose Front Piece and Front Door missile guidance radar antennae before firing. The many holes and hull protuberances makes for a very noisy boat under water.

sile tubes abreast the bridge. The 'Echo II' boats are split about evenly between the Pacific and Northern Fleets, with one unit of the latter normally to be found in the Mediterranean with a 'Juliett' class SSG.

Specification
'Echo' class
Displacement: 4,500 tons surfaced and 5,500 tons dived
Dimensions: length 110.0 m (360 ft 11 in); beam 9.0 m (29 ft 6 in); draught 7.5 m (24 ft 7 in)
Machinery: one pressurized-water reactor powering two steam turbines driving two four-blade propellers
Speed: 20 kts surfaced and 28 kts dived
Diving depth: 300 m (985 ft) operational and 500 m (1,640 ft) maximum
Torpedo tubes: six 533-mm (21-in) bow and two 406-mm (16-in) stern
Basic load: 20 533-mm (21-in) torpedoes (16 anti-ship or anti-

submarine HE and four anti-ship 15-kiloton nuclear) and two 406-mm (16-in) anti-ship torpedoes
Missiles: none
Electronics: one 'Snoop Tray' surface-search radar, one Hercules sonar, one Feniks sonar, one 'Stop Light' ESM system and one underwater telephone
Complement: 90

Specification
'Echo II' class
Displacement: 5,000 tons surfaced and 6,000 tons dived
Dimensions: length 115.0 m (377 ft 4 in); beam 9.0 m (29 ft 6 in); draught 7.5 m (24 ft 6 in)
Machinery: as for 'Echo' class
Speed: 20 kts surfaced and 25 kts dived
Diving depth: as for 'Echo' class
Torpedo tubes: as for 'Echo' class
Basic load: as for 'Echo' class
Missiles: eight SS-N-3A 'Shaddock' (four with 1000-kg/2,250-lb HE and four with 350-kiloton nuclear warheads) or

(in seven or eight converted boats) eight SS-N-12 'Sandbox' (four with 1000-kg/2,205-lb HE and four with 350-kiloton nuclear warheads)
Electronics: as for 'Echo' class, but with the addition of one 'Front Door' and one 'Front Piece' missile-guidance radar
Complement: 100

On 28 August 1976 an 'Echo II' class vessel collided with USS Voge, a 'Garcia' class frigate, in the Ionian sea. The 'Echo II' suffered severe hull lacerations and sail damage, and was patched up by a 'Prut' class submarine salvage vessel before sailing back to port for repairs.

Former USSR
'Charlie I', 'Charlie II' and 'Charlie III' class SSGNs

Designated PLARK by the Soviets, the first **'Charlie I' class** SSGN was launched at the inland shipyard at Gorki in 1967. Over the next five years a further 10 were completed there, with two banks of four missile tubes angled upwards on each side of the bow external to the pressure hull to give the class a distinctive blunt nose appearance. The tubes have large outer doors and are designed to carry the short range SS-N-7 submerged-launch anti-ship missile for the pop-up surprise attack on high-value surface targets such as a carrier. From 1972 to 1979 at Gorki an improved **'Charlie II' class** design was built with a 9-m (29.5-ft) hull insertion in the hull forward of the fin for the electronics and launch systems necessary for targeting and firing the SS-N-15 and SS-N-16 weapons. The four 'Charlie II' class boats also carry the longer-range SS-N-9 anti-ship missile in place of the SS-N-7. About 1980 the third and final variant of the design, the **'Charlie III' class**, appeared at Gorki, and this may be fitted to fire an underwater-launched variant of the SS-N-22 anti-ship missile, which is a longer-range and higher-speed development of the SS-N-9. In all three classes, once the missiles have been fired the boat has to be reloaded back at port, although the secondary torpedo armament and sonar systems allow each boat to be used as a useful anti-ship and ASW platform if required in the interim. The Charlie III production cycle, of five boats, is now ended. All Russian boats are now based in the Pacific Fleet. One is on lease to the Indian Navy.

Specification
'Charlie I' class
Displacement: 4,000 tons surfaced and 5,000 tons dived
Dimensions: length 93.9 m (308 ft 1 in); beam 10.0 m (32 ft 7 in); draught 7.8 m (25 ft 7 in)
Machinery: one pressurized-water reactor powering two steam turbines driving one five-blade main propeller and two two-blade quiet propellers
Speed: 20 kts surfaced and 27 kts dived
Diving depth: 400 m (1,315 ft) operational and 600 m (1,970 ft) maximum
Torpedo tubes: six 533-mm (21-in), two with 406-mm (16-in) liners, all bow
Basic load: maximum of 12 533-mm (21-in) torpedoes, but normally a mixture of four 533-mm (21-in) anti-ship or anti-submarine HE, six 406-mm (16-in) anti-submarine HE and two 533-mm (21-in) anti-ship 15-kiloton nuclear torpedoes plus two SS-N-15 15-kiloton anti-submarine missiles, or a total of 24 AMD-1000 ground mines
Missiles: eight SS-N-7 (four with 500-kg/1,102-lb HE and four with 200-kiloton nuclear warheads)
Electronics: one 'Snoop Tray' surface-search radar, one low-frequency bow sonar, one medium-frequency missile and torpedo fire-control sonar, one 'Brick Spit' and one 'Brick Pulp' passive intercept and threat-warning ESM system, one 'Park Lamp' direction-finding antenna, VHF and UHF communications, and one underwater telephone
Complement: 100

Specification
'Charlie II' class
Displacement: 4,500 tons surfaced and

5,500 tons dived
Dimensions: length 102.9 m (337 ft 7 in); beam 10.0 m (32 ft 10 in); draught 7.8 m (25 ft 7 in)
Machinery: as for 'Charlie I' class
Speed: 20 kts surfaced and 26 kts dived
Diving depth: as for 'Charlie I' class
Torpedo tubes: as for 'Charlie I' class but with the addition of two 618-mm (24.33-in) in the bows for SS-N-16
Basic load: as for 'Charlie I' class but with two SS-N-16 anti-submarine missiles
Missiles: eight SS-N-9 'Siren' (four with 500-kg/1,102-lb HE and four with 200-kiloton nuclear warheads)
Electronics: as for 'Charlie I' class but with the addition of one VLF towed communications buoy and one ELF floating communications antenna
Complement: 110

A 'Charlie I' class SSGN. This sub-class carries the SS-N-7 J-band active radar homing anti-ship missile in two banks of four missile tubes, angled upwards either side of the bow external to the pressure hull.

Specification
'Charlie III' class
Displacement: as for 'Charlie II' class
Dimensions: as for 'Charlie II' class
Machinery: as for 'Charlie II' class
Speed: as for 'Charlie II' class
Diving depth: as for 'Charlie II' class
Torpedo tubes: as for 'Charlie II' class
Basic load: as for 'Charlie II' class
Missiles: eight SS-N-22
Electronics: as for 'Charlie II' class
Complement: as for 'Charlie II' class

A total of 20 'Charlie' class SSGNs have been built in three sub-classes since 1967 at the Gorki shipyard. Primarily used for surprise pop-up missile attacks on high-value surface targets such as carriers, the 'Charlie' SSGNs also have a useful secondary ASW capability.

'Papa' and 'Oscar' class SSGNs

In 1970 the Soviet shipyard at Severodvinsk launched a single unit of what came to be known in NATO circles as the **'Papa' class**. The 'Papa' class boat was considerably larger and carried two more missile tubes (for an unidentified type of missile) than the contemporary 'Charlie' class SSGNs, and was for many years a puzzle to Western intelligence services. However, the answer appeared in 1980 at the same shipyard when the first of the even larger **'Oscar' class** of SSGN was launched; the 'Papa' class unit had been the prototype for advanced SSGN concepts with a considerably changed powerplant and revised screw arrangement. The missile system had been to test the underwater-launched version of the SS-N-9 'Siren' for the subsequent 'Charlie II' series of SSGN. The 'Oscar' design introduced yet further improvements, with two 12-round banks of submerged-launch long-range SS-N-19 anti-ship missile tubes set in elevation at an angle of 40° and external to the main pressure hull on each side of the fin. Assessed as the underwater equivalents to the battlecruiser 'Kirov' by several authoritative sources, the boats of the 'Oscar' class

are believed to be designed to operate in conjunction with surface battle groups built around those ships. Both types of SSGN are designated as PLARK (*podvonaya lodka atomnaya raketnaya krylataya*, or nuclear-powered cruise missile submarine) by the Soviets and operate with Northern Fleet from the Kola penninsula. Two Oscar 1s and four Oscar IIs units were still operational in the late 1990s.

Specification
'Papa' class
Displacement: 6,100 tons surfaced and 7,000 tons dived
Dimensions: length 109.0 m (357 ft 7 in); beam 11.5 m (37 ft 9 in); draught 7.6 m (24 ft 11 in)
Machinery: one pressurized-water reactor powering two steam turbines driving two shafts
Speed: 20 kts surfaced and 35-40 kts dived
Diving depth: 400 m (1,315 ft) operational and 600 m (1,970 ft) maximum
Torpedo tubes: six 533-mm (21-in), two with 406-mm (16-in) liners, all bow

Basic load: maximum of 12 533-mm (21-in) torpedoes, but normally a mixture comprising four 533-mm (21-in) anti-ship or anti-submarine HE, six 406-mm (16-in) anti-submarine HE and two 533-mm (21-in) anti-ship 15-kiloton nuclear torpedoes plus two SS-N-15 15-kiloton anti-submarine missiles, or a total of 24 AMD-1000 ground mines
Missiles: 10 SS-N-9 'Siren' (six with 500-kg/1,102-lb HE and four with 200-kiloton nuclear warheads)
Electronics: one 'Snoop Tray' surface-search radar, one low-frequency bow sonar, one medium-frequency torpedo and missile fire-control sonar, one 'Brick Spit' and one 'Brick Pulp' passive intercept and threat-warning ESM system, VHF/UHF communications, one 'Park Lamp' direction-finding antenna, and one underwater telephone
Complement: 110

Specification
'Oscar' class
Displacement: 10,000 tons surfaced and 14,000 tons dived
Dimensions: length 143.0 m (469 ft 2 in); beam 18.3 m (60 ft 0 in); draught

11.0 m (36 ft 1 in)
Machinery: two pressurized-water reactors powering two steam turbines driving two shafts
Speed: 20 kts surfaced and 30-35 kts dived
Diving depth: 500 m (1,640 ft) operational and 830 m (2,725 ft) maximum
Torpedo tubes: six 533-mm (21-in), two with 406-mm (16-in) liners, all bow
Basic load: maximum of 24 533-mm (21-in) torpedoes, but normally a mixture comprising 10 533-mm (21-in) anti-ship or anti-submarine HE, 14 406-mm (16-in) anti-submarine HE and four 533-mm (21-in) anti-ship 15-kiloton nuclear torpedoes plus two SS-N-15 15-kiloton anti-submarine missiles and two SS-N-16 anti-submarine missiles, or a total of 48 AMD-1000 ground mines and the two SS-N-16s
Missiles: 24 SS-N-19 (18 with 1000-kg/2,205-lb HE and six with 500-kiloton nuclear warheads)
Electronics: as for 'Papa' class except one new-type 'Snoop' series surface-search radar, one VLF towed communications buoy and one ELF floating communications antenna
Complement: 130

'November' class SSN

Built as the Soviets' first nuclear-powered submarine design from 1958 to 1963 at Severodvinsk, the 14-vessel **'November' class** was designed for the anti-ship rather than anti-submarine roles. Armed with nuclear torpedoes, the task of these boats was and still is to attack carrier battle groups in the hope of getting a clear shot at the carrier itself. The hull form, elderly reactor design and the many free flood holes in the casing make this type very noisy underwater. They are also considered to be, together with the 'Echo I' SSGN and 'Hotel' SSBN classes based on the 'November' design, something of a radiation hazard to their crews because of design defects and poor shielding. It is known that several specialist hospitals have been set up in the Soviet Union to treat the radiation casualties from these boats, and it is reported that they acquired the nickname 'widow-makers' amongst Soviet submarine crews. In April 1970 a 'November' class boat was lost south west of the United Kingdom after an internal fire, the crew being taken off before the boat sank, and there have also been numerous incidents of the three classes suffering machinery breakdowns whilst on operational patrol. At least one 'November' and two 'Hotel' class boats have been scrapped in recent years, while several other 'November' class units have been retired to reserve status. Retractable hydroplanes are carried just aft of the bow sonar systems, and two 406-mm (16-in) anti-escort torpedo tubes are fitted aft. The remaining 'November' class boats serve with the Pacific and Northern Fleets, and are expected to

pay off rapidly as new boats enter service over the next few years.

Specification
'November' class
Displacement: 4,200 tons surfaced and 5,000 tons dived
Dimensions: length 109.7 m (359 ft 11 in); beam 9.1 m (29 ft 10 in); draught 6.7 m (22 ft 0 in)
Machinery: one pressurized-water reactor powering two steam turbines driving two four- or six-bladed propellers
Speed: 20 kts surfaced and 30 kts dived
Diving depth: 300 m (985 ft) operational and 500 m (1,640 ft) maximum
Torpedo tubes: eight 533-mm (21-in) bow and two 406-mm (16-in) stern
Basic load: maximum of 24 533-mm (21-

in) torpedoes, normally a mixture of 18 533-mm (21-in) anti-ship or anti-submarine and six 533-mm (21-in) anti-ship 15-kiloton nuclear torpedoes, plus two 406-mm (16-in) anti-ship torpedoes
Missiles: none
Electronics: one 'Snoop Tray' surface-search radar, one 'Stop Light' ESM system, one medium-frequency Hercules bow sonar, one medium-frequency Feniks bow sonar, VHF/UHF communications and one underwater telephone
Complement: 86

The 'November' class SSN, the 'Echo' class SSN, 'Echo II' class SSGN and the 'Hotel II' class SSBN are characterized in Soviet navy service by the number of breakdowns they have suffered on operational patrol. The 'November' class boat seen here subsequently sank in April 1970.

Nicknamed 'widow-makers' in Soviet naval service because of poor reactor shielding, the 'November' class is expected to be retired rapidly over the next few years as more modern and much safer submarines enter service. Their primary armament is 15 kt yield 533-mm (21-in) anti-ship nuclear torpedoes.

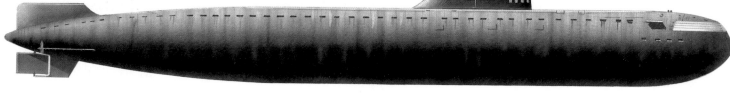

'Victor I', 'Victor II' and 'Victor III' class SSNs

The **'Victor I' class** is designated by the Soviets as a PLA (*podvodaya lodka atomnaya*, or nuclear-powered submarine), and together with the contemporary 'Charlie I' SSGN and 'Yankee' SSBN classes formed the second generation of Soviet nuclear submarines. The 'Victor' and 'Charlie' class boats were the first Soviet submarines built to the teardrop hull design for high underwater speeds. The first 'Victor' was completed in 1967 at the Admiralty Shipyard, Leningrad, where the last of 16 units was completed in 1974. The 'Victor I' boats are the fastest pressurized-water reactor-powered SSNs afloat, even with the advent of the American 'Los Angeles' class. The enriched uranium fuelled reactor is of the same type as installed in both the 'Charlie' and 'Yankee' class vessels. In 1972, the first of the improved **'Victor II' class** was built at the Gorki shipyard, being produced in alternate years to the 'Charlie II' design there. Four were built there, whilst another two were apparently constructed at the Admiralty Shipyard in 1975 as an interim measure whilst the first of the more complex **'Victor III' class** units were being laid down. Initially called the **'Uniform' class** by NATO, the 'Victor II' class is marked by a 6.1 m (20 ft) extension inserted into the hull forward of the sail for what is believed to be the original test fire-control and launch equipment for the SS-N-15/16 ASW missiles.

In 1976 the first of the 'Victor III' units was launched at the Admiralty Shipyard, and this class has subsequently been built there at the rate of one per year. In 1978 the Komsomolsk yard joined the production team, building two boats per year after the end of 'Delta I' class production. A total of 25 Victor III class boats was produced at the Admiralty shipyard, with all but one still operational in the 1990s. Its design successor was the **Akula** class (q.v.), the first of which was launched in 1984. The improvement over the 'Victor II' represented by the 'Victor III' class is a 3 m (9 ft 10 in) hull extension forward of the fin and a pod mounted atop the upper rudder for what is thought to be the first Soviet submarine-mounted towed sonar array. The extension probably provides the extra volume for the additional electronic equipment required to process the data from the array. All three classes are coated with the 'Clusterguard' anechoic coating developed to reduce the effectiveness of active sonar systems on NATO ships, submarines and ASW torpedoes. It is also known that there is a decrease in radiated noise levels as the design was improved, the 'Victor III' class being described officially in US Navy circles as the equivalent of the USS 'Sturgeon' class SSN in quietness. They also have bow hydroplanes that retract into the hull at high underwater speeds or when a boat is on the surface.

Like all boats after the 'Hotel' SSBN, 'Echo' SSGN and 'November' SSN classes, the 'Victor' class boats have had two of their 533-mm (21-in) tubes fitted with 406-mm (16-in) ASW torpedo liners for self-defence use. Two of these weapons are carried in the place of every 533-mm (21-in) reload offloaded. In recent months a 'Victor III' class boat was seen in difficulties on the surface near the USA's eastern coast before it was towed to Cuba for repairs. All three types serve in the Northern Fleet, whilst only the 'Victor I' and 'Victor III' classes serve in the Pacific Fleet.

A Soviet 'Victor I' class SSN in the Malacca Straits during 1974. The large number of personnel seen on the sail structure are sunbathing – a favourite pastime of Soviet sailors at sea or ashore in warm climate regions.

Specification
'Victor I' class
Displacement: 4,300 tons surfaced and 5,300 tons dived
Dimensions: length 93.9 m (308 ft 1 in); beam 10.0 m (32 ft 10 in); draught 7.3 m (23 ft 11 in)
Machinery: one pressurized-water reactor powering two steam turbines driving one five-blade propeller and two two-blade propellers
Speed: 20 kts surfaced and 32 kts dived
Diving depth: 400 m (1,315 ft) operational and 600 m (1,970 ft) maximum
Torpedo tubes: six 533-mm (21-in), two with 406-mm (16-in) liners, all bow
Basic load: maximum of 18 533-mm (21-in) torpedoes, but normally a mixture of eight 533-mm (21-in) anti-ship or anti-submarine, 10 406-mm (16-in) anti-submarine and two 533-mm (21-in) anti-ship 15-kiloton nuclear torpedoes plus two SS-N-15 anti-submarine 15-kiloton missiles, or a total of 36 AMD-1000 ground mines
Missiles: none
Electronics: one 'Snoop Tray' surface-search radar, one low-frequency bow sonar, one medium-frequency missile and torpedo fire-control sonar, one 'Brick Spit' and one 'Brick Pulp' passive intercept and threat-warning ESM system, VHF/UHF communications, one 'Park Lamp' direction-finding antenna and one underwater telephone
Complement: 100

Specification
'Victor II' class
Displacement: 4,700 tons surfaced and 5,700 tons dived
Dimensions: length 100.0 m (328 ft 10 in); beam 10.0 m (32 ft 10 in); draught 7.3 m (23 ft 11 in)
Machinery: as for 'Victor I' class
Speed: 20 kts surfaced and 31 kts dived
Diving depth: as for 'Victor I' class
Torpedo tubes: as for 'Victor I' class plus two 618-mm (24.33-in) bow
Basic load: as for 'Victor I' class but with two SS-N-16 anti-submarine
Missiles: none
Electronics: as for 'Victor I' class plus one towed VLF communications buoy and one floating ELF communications antenna

Complement: 110

Specification
'Victor III' class
Displacement: 5,000 tons surfaced and 6,000 tons dived
Dimensions: length 103.0 m (337 ft 11 in); beam 10.0 m (32 ft 10 in); draught 7.3 m (23 ft 11 in)
Machinery: as for 'Victor I' class
Speed: 20 kts surfaced and 30 kts dived
Diving depth: as for 'Victor I' class
Torpedo tubes: as for 'Victor II' class
Basic load: as for 'Victor II' class
Missiles: none
Electronics: as for 'Victor II' class but with one low-frequency retractable towed sonar
Complement: 115

Above: A windfall for Western naval intelligence, this Soviet 'Victor III' class SSN got into difficulties off the North Carolina coast in November 1983. The vessel had to be towed to Cuba for repairs after becoming the most photographed submarine in the Soviet navy.

Below: A Soviet 'Victor III' class vessel. The pod on the top of the upper rudder is for a towed sonar array, the first such installation on a Soviet submarine. To match the sonar's long range, the class carries both SS-N-15 and 16 ASW missiles.

'Alpha I' and 'Akula' class SSNs

The prototype of what is the world's fastest and deepest diving operational submarine, the **'Alpha I' class**, was launched at the Sudomekh shipyard, Leningrad in 1970-1 and underwent a series of trials with both the Baltic and Northern fleets. Major problems were encountered with both the powerplant and the hull, and the vessel was subsequently cut up for analysis in 1974, then scrapped. The reason for the problems were discovered by Western intelligence to be that the hull was suffering a severe cracking problem as it was constructed from a titanium alloy, a very difficult material to weld successfully, and that the reactor was of a very advanced type using a liquid-metal coolant as the heat exchange medium between the reactor and the secondary steam turbine systems, a type of reactor plant that the Americans had already tested and discarded as being too complex for submarine propulsion. However, by the mid-1970s solutions had been found to the problems, and the class entered slow series production at Sudomekh. A second production line may have started at Severodvinsk in the late 1970s to give a combined total of six or seven completed by mid-1983. The new propulsion plant endows the class with a confirmed underwater speed of 45 kts, which is sufficient to outrun most, if not all, of the current western ASW torpedoes and attack submarines. The Soviets have described the 'Alpha I' class as an underwater

'interceptor' type with a considerable amount of automation on the machinery side. The titanium alloy hull allows a very deep operational submergence whilst also considerably reducing the magnetic anomaly signature, as the only ferrous materials are in the fittings inside the hull itself. The underwater signature in terms of noise is said to be similar to other contemporary Soviet SSNs at low speeds. The boat is also coated with the 'Clusterguard' anechoic coating to reduce the efficiency of enemy active sonar transmissions. All the 'Alpha I' class boats serve with the Northern Fleet.

In late 1982 American spy satellites detected a new Soviet attack submarine under construction at Sudomekh. Designated **Akula** by NATO, this class eventually became operational at the end of 1985 and five boats were operational in the late 1990s, with four more laid up. The Akulas were built at the rate of one a year at Komsomolsk and Severodvinsk, but production ceased with the end of the Cold War. A multi-role SSN designed to follow the Victor III class, the Akulas are based in both the Northern and Pacific Fleets.

Specification
'Alpha I' class
Displacement: 2,800 tons surfaced and 3,680 tons dived

Dimensions: length 81.0 m (265 ft 9 in); beam 9.5 m (31 ft 2 in); draught 8.0 m (26 ft 3 in)
Machinery: one liquid-metal reactor powering two steam turbines driving one five-blade propeller
Speed: 20 kts surfaced and 45 kts dived
Diving depth: 600 m (1,970 ft) operational and 1000 m (3,280 ft) maximum
Torpedo tubes: six 533-mm (21-in), two with 406-mm (16-in) liners, all bow
Basic load: maximum of 18 533-mm (21-in) torpedoes, but normally a mixture of eight 533-mm (21-in) anti-ship or anti-submarine, 10 406-mm (16-in) anti-submarine and two 533-mm (21-in) anti-ship 15-kiloton nuclear torpedoes plus two SS-N-15 anti-submarine 15-

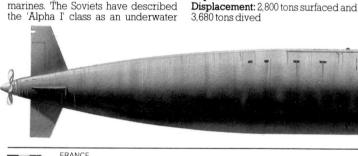

kiloton missiles, or a total of 36 AMD-1000 ground mines
Missiles: none
Electronics: one unidentified surface-search radar, one 'Park Lamp' direction-finding antenna, one unidentified third-generation ESM system, one low-frequency bow sonar, one missile and torpedo fire-control sonar (probably medium-frequency) and one underwater telephone
Complement: 45

An early shot of a Soviet 'Alpha I' class SSN, which has demonstrated underwater speed of 45 kts. The 'Alpha' class uses a highly automated liquid-metal-cooled reactor plant to achieve this speed.

The 'Alpha I' class introduced a titanium alloy hull into Soviet navy service. This is a notoriously difficult material to weld, and at least one 'Alpha' has been photographed by US reconnaissance satellites in dry dock with damage caused by hull cracking.

'Rubis' class SSN

In 1964 the French authorized the design of a 4,000-ton SSN. This was cancelled in 1968, however, just as construction was due to start. A new and smaller submarine design was then initiated, based on the hull form and overall layout of the conventional 'Agosta' class and with basically the same fire-control, torpedo-launching and sonar detection systems. The resulting **'SNA72' class** built at Cherbourg is the smallest SSN type in service with any navy, and was made possible by the French development of a small 48-megawatt integrated reactor-heat exchanger system driving two turbo-alternators and a main electric motor. The increased hull depth has allowed the typical three-deck layout of larger SSNs to be used for the areas forward and immediately aft of the fin. The forward diving planes

of the Agostas have been relocated to the fin to improve underwater manoeuvrability.

The French Navy operates two squadrons of Rubis boats, one based at Lorient to cover the SSBN base and the other at Toulon. Eight boats are in service; these are the **Rubis** (S601), **Saphir** (S602), **Casablanca** (S603), **Emeraude** (S604), **Amethyste** (S605), **Perle** (S606), **Turquoise** (S607) and **Diamant** (S608). The last five were built to a modified design, including a new bow form and a major silencing system, as well as new tactical and attack systems and improved electronics.

Specification
Rubis (S 601)
Displacement: 2,385 tons surfaced and

2,670 tons dived
Dimensions: length 72.1 m (236 ft 6.5 in); beam 7.6 m (24 ft 11 in); draught 6.4 m (21 ft 0 in)
Machinery: one 48-mW pressurized-water reactor (PWR) powering two turbo-alternators driving one shaft
Speed: 18 kts surfaced and 25 kts dived
Diving depth: 300 m (985 ft) operational and 500 m (1,640 ft) maximum
Torpedo tubes: four 550-mm (21.65-in),

all bow
Basic load: 14 F17 wire-guided anti-ship and L5 mod.3 active/passive ASW torpedoes, or 28 TSM3510 ground mines; from 1985 will be 10 F17/L5 mod.3 and four SM.39 or 28 mines
Electronics: one DRUA 23 surface-search radar, one DSUV 22 passive sonar, one DUUX 2 passive ranging sonar and one TUUM underwater telephone
Complement: 66

Currently the smallest of the world's front-line SSNs, the 'Rubis' class is powered by a French-developed and built 48 mW integrated reactor-heat exchanger system that fits well into what is essentially a heavily modified conventional 'Agosta' class submarine design.

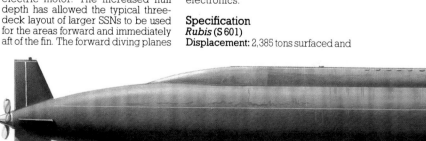

Military Hovercraft

Versatile, often capable of exceptional speeds, and even able to carry an impressive weapons fit, the Air Cushion Vehicle, otherwise known as the hovercraft, has been pressed into service as an assault vessel and logistic transport by several maritime forces worldwide.

Twenty years ago, experts believed that sea warfare was on the brink of a revolution as great as that sparked off by the introduction of the 'Dreadnought' battleship in 1906. It was thought that a British invention of the 1950s – the hovercraft – would give the surface combatant undreamed-of performance. Yet this has not happened.

The first country to really develop the hovercraft, or Air Cushion Vehicle (ACV), was the USSR. With an operational fleet of at least six different classes, the Soviet Navy quickly demonstrated the craft's versatility and viability as an assault vehicle and logistic transport. And the hovercraft was only the beginning, for the Russians soon began to explore the still more dramatic technology of the Surface-Effect Ship (SES) and the Wing in the ground effect (WIG) craft for military applications. The People's Republic of China also launched into an ACV construction programme, both for military purposes and research; its prototype craft the Type 722 'Jing-sah' class, was similar to a scaled-down version of the British SRN-4.

The US Navy also recognized the potential of the military hovercraft, but development was

The US Navy's Landing Craft Air Cushion (LCAC) is powered by four Textron Lycoming TF40 marine gas turbine engines.

slow, and it took the Vietnam War to speed it up. ACVs designed by Bell Aerospace Company (later Bell Textron) were used to patrol the Mekong Delta, and the river systems during that conflict. Today, Textron-built ACVs are in service with the US Army Troop Support Command and the United States Navy.

The sole British hovercraft

designed specifically for the navy and military is the BH7, which comes in the BH7 Mk 4 logistics version and the BH7 Mk 5A combat/logistics version. Designed for coastal defence operations, the latter carries medium-range surface-to-surface missiles, such as Exocet, and two roof-mounted 20-mm guns. It is fully amphibious, can operate

from relatively unprepared bases on beaches and can head directly toward its target on intercept missions regardless of the tidal state and marginal terrain. Also, since none of its solid structure is immersed, it is almost invulnerable to underwater defences such as acoustic, magnetic and pressure mines or to attack by torpedoes.

French air-cushion vehicles

The Dubigeon-Normandie **Naviplan N500** was a civilian passenger/car ferry ACV designed for use on cross-channel operations. Like the British SR.N4 hovercraft it could in wartime have been used safely as an emergency logistic transport on routes through suspected enemy minefields that would have stopped conventional ships. Although two craft were originally built, one (the **N500-1**) was written off after a severe fire that started

during minor repair work to its skirts. The second (**N500-02** *Ingenieur Jean Bertin*) was subsequently modified to incorporate a bi-conical skirt arrangement that increased the cushion area by some 10 per cent and enabled the bow/stern ramp-equipped craft to lift 418 passengers and 65 vehicles without any increase of installed power. Unfortunately the N500-2 was withdrawn from service in late 1983 because of continuous technical prob-

lems which caused high unserviceability. The N500 was characterized in appearance by an aft-mounted horizontal stabilizer that carried the three Avco Lycoming propulsion gas turbines in separate nacelles. Although no longer in use, the design was the largest ACV produced in France and provided much valuable data indirectly to the French navy for any future investment it may make in ACV technology.

Specification
Naviplan N500
Dimensions: length 50.0 m (164.1 ft); beam 23.0 m (75.1 ft)
Propulsion: five 3,200-shp (3877-kW) gas turbines driving two lift fans and three propellers
Weights: maximum 260 tons; payload see text
Speed: 75 kts
Electronics: one navigation radar

French SES types

As part of an overall plan to meet the needs of the French navy for the 1990s and beyond, the Direction Téchnique des Constructions Navales set up a special division to study surface-effect ships for use in the ocean-going ASW role. In 1981 a 5.4-ton 12.1-m (39.7-ft) long seagoing trial craft, called the MOLENES (Modèl Libre Expérimental de Navire à l'Effét de Surface) was launched to study all the systems required by an SES of a higher length-to-beam ratio, to confirm the data produced by water-tank model trials and to investigate the effect of acceleration and manoeuvrability on the structure, equipment and crew members. This is

to be followed into service by a 196.43-ton **NES-200** prototype which will confirm the feasibility of such craft in the ASW role and to investigate SES capabilities in other military and commercial roles. The design is being used to obviate the need for the development of any special components such as lift fans or propulsion plant as they can all be bought off-the-shelf for such craft. The information gained from both trials craft will, if satisfactory, be used in the construction of the projected 3,930-ton **NES-4000** SES warship for the next century. The vessel will be fitted with medium-calibre guns, CIWS, surface-to-surface missiles and

a large hangar and slight deck aft for a number of ASW helicopters. The latest French SES design is as 12,00-tonne craft intended for ASW.

Specification
NES-4000
Dimensions: length 111.2 m (364.8 ft); beam 30.9 m (101.4 ft); draught on cushion 2.7 m (8.8 ft)
Propulsion: two 40,000-shp (29824-kW) and one 16,750-shp (12489-kW) gas turbines driving two hydrojets and two lift fans respectively; hullborne propulsion uses two diesels delivering

4,800-hp (3579-kW) to two shafts
Weight: maximum displacement 3,930 tons
Speed: on cushion 65 kts, and hullborne 25 kts on gas turbines or 16 kts on diesels.
Armament: two single 76- or 100-mm (3- or 3.94-in) DP guns, one CIWS mounting, and ASW torpedo tubes
Aircraft: four to six ASW helicopters
Electronics: one air-search radar, one-surface-search radar, one navigation/helicopter-control radar, one action information system, one ESM suite and two sonar systems (including one towed-array type)
Complement: 130-150

SR.N4 'Mountbatten' class air-cushion vehicle

The **BHC SR.N4 Mk 2 'Mountbatten' class** ACV is a passenger/car ferry suitable for 185-km (115-mile) passages on coastal routes. Although civilian-owned, these craft could have an important wartime logistics role of ferrying reinforcement equipment and supplies across the English Channel without having to worry too much about damaged port facilities or enemy minefields. Only six 'Mountbatten' class craft have been built to date, of which four were converted from the original **SR.N4 Mk 1** to the Mk 2 standard whilst the remaining two went direct to the heavier **SR.N4 Mk 3 Super 4** configuration with a 16.76-m (55-ft) long insert amidships that also increased the beam slightly. The Mk 2s currently carry 282 passengers and 37 vehicles in a single lift, whilst the Mk 3s can carry 418 passengers and 60 vehicles. A military variant, the **Military 4**, was announced in 1980 and this can carry a payload of up to 165 tons of supplies and/or vehicles or a maximum of 1,000 fully-equipped troops at

speeds of around 65 kts. It is probable that if stripped of all interior furnishings a bow/stern ramp-equipped civilian SR.N4 could carry similar loads in the logistic transport role, which means for example that all the men of a Royal Marine Commando or an infantry battalion plus most of their equipment could be carried. The only limitation would be the sea state, which if too high would limit the craft's performance.

Specification
SR.N4
Dimensions: length (Mk 2) 39.68 m (130.17 ft) or (Mk 3) 56.38 m (185.0 ft); beam (Mk 2) 23.77 m (78.0 ft) or (Mk 3) 28.04 m (92.0 ft)
Propulsion: four 3,400-shp (2535-kW) gas turbines driving four lift fans and four propellers
Weights: maximum (Mk 2) 200 tons or (Mk 3) 300 tons; payload see text
Speed: (Mk 2) 70 kts (Mk 3) 65 kts
Electronics: two navigation radars

The British Hovercraft Corporation's SR.N4 is the largest hovercraft in regular service. In an amphibious assault role it can carry up to 1,000 fully-equipped troops, or light tanks. It is similar in size to the Soviet 'Aist' class, which is a purpose-designed amphibious assault craft.

SR.N4 'Mountbatten' class mine countermeasures hovercraft

The **BHC SR.N4 Mk 4 'Mountbatten' class** MCMH (mine countermeasures hovercraft) is identical in most respects to the British Hovercraft Corporation's SR.N4 Mk 2 civilian passenger/car ferry version but with a much larger fuel load. At its maximum weight it is capable of carrying up to 59875 kg (132,000 lb) of mission payload in addition to its fuel for a 10-hour sortie. As designed, it is able to perform all the tasks carried out by a conventional minesweeper with wire and/or influence sweeps, or a minehunter using towed sonar and either a Gemini dinghy with disposal divers or a remote-controlled PAP-104 submersible. The

operations room, crew quarters and workshops can be located in the twin side-cabin structures or on the central deck area forward of the main winch position. All the significant fittings in the cargo area are erected on palletized modules in order to facilitate role changes for MCM missions and conversion, if required, to the logistic transport role. A comprehensive communications and navigation fit is carried, as is an MCM-orientated action information system.

On an operation several MCMHs would normally be deployed to form a Forward Support Unit that would set up a Mobile Advanced Base for up to

three hovercraft within or very near to a suspected mined area. The craft would then sweep the region as conventional MCM forces would to clear a shipping lane.

If used in the logistic role a single MCMH can carry up to 90 tons of supplies, troops or vehicles in the form of seven loaded trucks and 250 troops, or one MBT, four light tanks and six 1-ton Land Rovers, or four light tanks, two laden and two unladen trucks, and two ambulances.

If the stern is rebuilt, an MCMH can be turned into a fast minelayer carrying some 110-120 ground mines and their trolleys for dropping in all depths

of water. To date no military version of the SR.N4 hovercraft has been purchased by any nation.

Specification
SR.N4 Mk 4
Dimensions: length 39.67 m (130.16 ft); beam 23.77 m (78.0 ft)
Propulsion: four 4,250-shp (3169-kW) gas turbines driving four lift fans and four propellers
Weights: maximum 223.4 tons; payload see text
Speed: 60/65 kts
Electronics: one navigation radar, one CAAIS action information system, and one Decca Hi-fix navigation system

SR.N6 'Winchester' class air-cushion vehicle

Designed originally as a fast ferry for operations in sheltered waters, the **BHC SR.N6 'Winchester' class** ACV has evolved into a number of variants over the years. Although extensively tested by the Royal Navy and British army all over the world, including the Falklands, the SR.N6 craft used were sold in 1982 following the demise of the Hovercraft Trials Unit. The basic **SR.N6 Mk 1** can accommodate either 38 passengers or 3 tons of supplies, and is in use with the Egyptian navy (one) and the Royal Saudi Arabian Frontier Force and Coast Guard (eight). This model was followed by the wholly military logistic support **SR.N6 Mk 2** and **SR.N6 Mk 3** variants, which feature a roof loading hatch and specially strengthened side decks for long loads weighing up to 0.5 ton; a roof-mounted armament of one 7.62- or 12.7-mm (0.3- or 0.5-in) machine-gun is carried for defensive purposes. The maximum payload is increased to 5 tons of supplies or between 20 and 30 fully armed troops. Only the Egyptian (two Mk 2s) and Iranian (two Mk 2s) navies have this type in service, though the former has had all three of its SR.N6s modified to carry six 500-kg (1,105-lb) ground mines if required. The Iranian navy also has six **SR.N6 Mk 4** variants in service. These are used for coastal defence duties and can carry either a 20-mm cannon or SS.12 wire-guided

missiles as alternatives to the more usual 7.62-mm medium machine-guns. The Iraqi customs service also uses the same hovercraft, but as the **SR.N6 Mk 6C** general-purpose model, with a larger cabin to accommodate up to 55 passengers or between 5 and 6 tons of supplies. Six are in use, and are known to have been used for combat duties in the Gulf War.

Saudi Arabia also has eight units of the **SR.N6 Mk 8** type in service. This is the latest of the military variants to be produced: it can carry up to 55 fully-equipped troops in the assault role, or have the same armament alternatives as the Mk 4 when used as a patrol craft. It differs from the earlier variants in having only a single propeller and the addition of two air conditioning units on the roof aft of the cockpit.

Specification
SR.N6 Mk 8
Dimensions: length 18.3 m (60.0 ft); beam 8.5 m (28.0 ft)
Propulsion: one 1,050-shp (785-kW) gas turbine driving one lift fan and one propeller
Weights: maximum 16.7 tons; payload see text
Speed: 50 kts
Electronics: one navigator radar

Above: SR.N6 'Winchester' is the military variant of the widely-used SR.N6 fast ferry. It can be used in the logistics role over swampy terrain or, as here, as a fast coastal patrol craft. It can be armed with 20-mm cannon or with short-range SSMs.

Left: The SR.N6 Mk 2/3 is a militarized version of the standard civil ferry, and unlike the later Mk 6 seen above is powered by a single propeller. This model was operated by the Royal Navy trials unit in locations as diverse as Hong Kong and the Falklands (ironically, practising amphibious landings!).

Variants of the SR.N6 are in service worldwide, involved in seismic survey, search and rescue, freight haulage, crash rescue and firefighting, amongst other tasks. The twin-propellered Mk 6 has a payload of between five and six tons of equipment or up to 55 passengers.

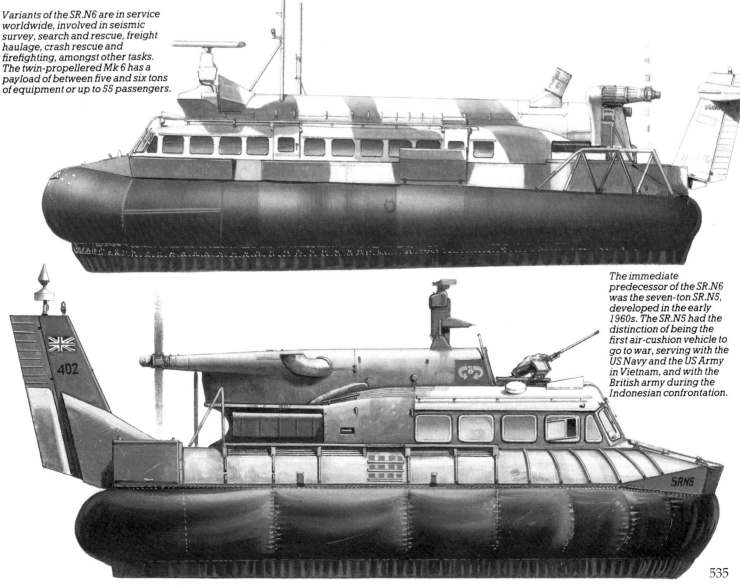

The immediate predecessor of the SR.N6 was the seven-ton SR.N5, developed in the early 1960s. The SR.N5 had the distinction of being the first air-cushion vehicle to go to war, serving with the US Navy and the US Army in Vietnam, and with the British army during the Indonesian confrontation.

BH7 'Wellington' class air-cushion vehicle

UK

The **BHC BH7 'Wellington' class** was designed specifically for navy and military use, the **BH7 Mk 2** prototype serving with the Royal Navy (from 1970 to late 1985, when funds ran out) as an advanced-technology trials craft to evaluate hovercraft in the logistic support, fishery protection, ASW and MCM roles. This machine was followed on the production line by two **BH7 Mk 4** logistic support and four **BH7 Mk 5** combat versions for the Iranian navy. The former, armed with medium machine-guns on each side of the cabin, can carry loads such as 170 fully-armed troops, or 60 troops with three Land Rovers and trailers, or two light armoured vehicles, or up to 14 tons of supplies. The Mk 5s were designed for coastal defence duties, and have recesses on their side decks for two medium-range anti-ship SSMs (such as the MM.38 Exocet) plus the ability to carry a radar-controlled twin 30-mm turret on the foredeck in front of the centre cabin, which is used as the operations centre. Although not armed as such in Iranian service, the Mk 5s and the logistic Mk 4s have seen considerable combat service during the Gulf War.

In 1982 the Saudi Arabian navy ordered eight **BH7 Mk 5A** combat/logistic hovercraft, which are essentially similar to the Mk 5 but retain the bow door of the logistic model in order to keep the load-carrying capability. However, instead of the 30-mm turret two single 20-mm cannon can be mounted on the roof positions previously used for machine-guns.

Major advances have enabled British Hovercraft Corporation to offer 10-tonne payload craft, the API-88, which could have a variety of military applications. It is in service with civilian operators.

Specification
BH7 Mk 5A
Dimensions: length 23.9 m (78.33 ft); beam 13.9 m (45.5 ft)
Propulsion: one 4,250-shp (3169-kW) gas turbine driving one lift fan and one propeller
Weights: maximum 55 tons; payload see text
Speed: 58 kts
Electronics: one navigation radar

Above: The latest variant of the BH7 'Wellington' is the Mk 20 Fast Attack Craft, which can carry an impressive weapon fit, in this case a pair of Rarden 30-mm cannon and four Sea Skua surface-to-surface missiles. Sea Cat SAMs or Exocet SSMs are alternative armaments.

Right: Seen here speeding past HMS Kent, the BH7 was evaluated by the Royal Navy from 1970 until 1985 in both combat and logistic support roles, but the funds for this important work ran out in 1985.

Below: The Mk 5 is capable of 58 kts and can carry four Exocet surface-to-surface missiles. The Iranians have made great use of their logistic support version, which can carry up to 170 fully-equipped troops.

VT2 air-cushion vehicle

The **Vosper Thornycroft VT2** hovercraft was extensively tested by the Royal Navy from the mid-1970s until 1982, when the Hovercraft Trials Unit (HTU) was disbanded as part of extensive defence cuts. Used originally in the logistic support role, the prototype **VT2-001 (P234)** was modified in 1978 to carry palletized cargo from ships lying offshore to a beach-head. The modifications included the fitting of a loading hatch in the main superstructure roof and the laying of roller tracking on the deck below the hatch for the movement of the cargo around the enclosed deck area. After several successful trials, the prototype was further rebuilt to investigate its operational capabilities in the MCM support role. This required the fitting of an electronic and communications outfit compatible in all respects to that of the contemporary 'Hunt' class MCM vessel, an Atlas 5002 hydraulic crane, a larger roof hatch and improved internal cargo-handling system and a 5.4-m (17.7-ft) long Sea Rider workboat. Again the craft proved highly successful, especially in the towing of various types of sweeping gear and in shock trials, in which it proved almost invulnerable to underwater explosions near or practically beneath the hull to simulate the detonation of various seamine types. Despite this and the success of the other hovercraft types used to test various roles the VT2 was sold to commercial concerns following the demise of the HTU, and the use of hovercraft within the Royal Navy and other armed services has been reduced to the barest minimum so that the forces can say that interest is still being shown.

Specification
VT2
Dimensions: length 30.18 m (99.0 ft); beam 13.3 m (43.6 ft)
Propulsion: two 4,250-shp (3169-kW) gas turbines driving four lift fans and two variable-pitch ducted drive fans
Weights: maximum 108 tons; payload 31.4 tons
Speed: 60/70 kts
Electronics: one navigation radar

The VT2 proved an enormous success in the MCM (Mine Countermeasures) role, but the Hovercraft Trials Unit was disbanded in the disastrous defence cuts made by the Government in 1982. The Royal Navy now shows only token interest in a minesweeper invulnerable to most mines.

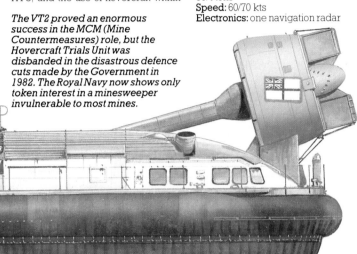

Skima series air-cushion vehicles

The Skima series of ACVs incorporates inflatable structures into its basic design, and this helps to reduce the overall weight and total cost. It also enhances the series' obstacle clearance, buoyancy and stability characteristics. The smallest of the craft offered for military use is the open-top **Skima 4**, which has been evaluated by the Royal Navy, US Navy and the US Coast Guard. Able to carry four persons, it can be transported on a light trailer or folded inside a pick-up truck and lifted off by the crew. Next in size is the **Skima 6** which has also been evaluated by the Royal Navy and bought by the Australian army and several police forces for patrol duties. It is car-sized in appearance and can be moved either on a large trailer or towed behind a light trailer as a single unit. An enclosed cabin is provided for the pilot and five passengers. The largest craft available is the **Skima 12**, which differs from the civilian version in having its controls moved amidships, in front of a mast arrangement carrying a small navigation/surface-search radar. With the controls aft the ACV can then carry a variety of weapons mounted in the space thus vacated. The Skima 12 can carry up to 12 people or around 998 kg (2,200 lb) of supplies. The Nigerian police are known to have bought several for river patrol work.

Specification
Skima 4
Dimensions: length 4.80 m (15.75 ft); beam 1.98 m (6.5 ft)
Propulsion: one 25-hp (18.6-kW) petrol or diesel engine driving a single lift and propulsion propeller

The Skima series of small air-cushion vehicles are based on the original Griffon designs now being manufactured by Vosper Hovermarine. The smallest of these craft can be transported on the back of a pick-up truck, and has been evaluated both in the UK and USA.

Weights: empty 225 kg (495 lb); payload see text
Speed: 30 kts

Specification
Skima 6
Dimensions: length 6.19 m (20.31 ft); beam 2.62 m (8.6 ft)
Propulsion: one 60-hp (44.7-kW) petrol or diesel engine driving a single lift and two propulsion propellers
Weights: empty 670 kg (1,474 lb); payload see text
Speed: 30 kts

Specification
Skima 12
Dimensions: length 7.77 m (25.5 ft); beam 3.5 m (11.5 ft)
Propulsion: one 250-hp (186-kW) petrol or diesel engine driving a single lift and propulsion propeller
Weights: empty 990 kg (2,178 lb); payload see text
Speed: 35 kts
Electronics: one navigation radar

The various Skima ACVs keep down their weight and reduce overall cost by incorporating inflatable structures into the basic design. This also gives improved buoyancy and stability, and endows them with impressive obstacle-crossing ability.

Ekranoplan wing-in-ground effect machines

Since 1965 the Soviets have been experimenting in the Caspian Sea area with what has become known as the **Ekranoplan** or 'Caspian Sea Monster'. This machine has a potential speed of 300 kts (556 km/h; 346 mph) or more, and operates at a height of between 3.5 to 14 m (11.5 to 46 ft) above water, marshland or other such terrain. With a main hull like that of a wide-body airliner, the Ekranoplan can carry a payload of over 90 tons, or some 900 fully-equipped troops or Naval Infantry. Its propulsion system comprises eight marinized gas turbines mounted above a forward stub wing and two propulsion turbines aft installed at the base of a dihedral tailplane. The mode of operation is that all the engines are used to start the Ekranoplan moving whilst the machine is in contact with the water; the forward engines are

then directed downwards so that their exhausts create an air-cushion effect under the vehicle's main wing. The growing lift then raises the vehicle clear of the water so that the forward engines can be reorientated to direct their blast back over the upper surface of the wing to establish additional lift and so rapidly increase the forward motion until the cruising speed at which flight can be sustained is established. By flying in and out of this ground-effect cushion the Ekranoplan can clear shipping, shorelines and other obstructions as required. Such a capability is particularly useful to the Soviet navy for amphibious assault and logistic support duties as this type of vehicle effectively overcomes the problems of sea conditions, tidal currents, underwater obstacles, and defensive sea and land minefields by

flying over them.

A smaller **Turboprop Ekranoplan** is also under test. Based on the 'sea monster' concept, this has improved aerodynamic shape and the rear-mounted gas turbines replaced by a single 15,000-shp (11184-kW) turbo-prop. The forward engines are also replaced by two internally-mounted gas turbines to provide the power augmentation for take-off and the initial lift. The new variant has also been used for amphibious assault trials with a swing-nose arrangement to allow for the carriage of vehicles and outsized loads. A missile attack variant (with two single underwing container-launchers for SS-N-22 anti-ship cruise missiles) has also been seen, although no production decision on any Ekranoplan version is believed yet to have been taken.

Specification (provisional)
Ekranoplan
Dimensions: span 40.0 m (131.23 ft); length 91.4 m (300.0 ft)
Propulsion: 10 gas turbines
Weights: maximum 307.4 tons; payload see text
Speed: 300 kts

Specification
Turboprop Ekranoplan
Dimensions: span 30.5 m (100.0 ft); length 60.9 m (200.0 ft)
Propulsion: one 15,000-shp (11184-kW) turboprop and two gas turbines
Weights: maximum 216 tons; payload 59 tons of cargo or 500 troops
Speed: 280 kts
Armament: see text

'Lebed' class air-cushion vehicle

The NATO reporting named **'Lebed' class** multi-duty surface-effect landing craft was first seen in prototype form in 1973 and entered series production in 1976-7. Used as amphibious initial assault landing and logistics-over-the-shore (LOTS), 'Lebeds' are normally carried in pairs by the 'Ivan Rogov' class LPDs in their stern well decks. For an assault the 'Lebeds' would be preloaded before embarking. The design is an original Soviet one, and is thought to have been undertaken by the Soviet navy's High-Speed Ship Design Bureau in Leningrad. Eighteen 'Lebeds' are in service, with some three or four more in varying states of completion. 'Lebeds' are now found with the Baltic, Black Sea and Pacific Fleets as well as aboard the LPDs. A bow ramp is provided for vehicle loading and unloading, whilst personnel can use doors located aft. Typical payloads include two PT-76 light amphibious tanks, two BTR-60/70/BMP-1/2 APCs, two loaded trucks up to a total weight of 34.38 tons, 120 Naval Infantry or some 40 tons of supplies.

In 1982 the prototype of what is expected to be the 'Lebed' successor, the 100-ton 'Tsaplya' class, was seen.

This is now believed to be entering series production on the construction line that was used for the 'Lebed' class.

Specification
'Lebed' class
Dimensions: length 24.8 m (81.4 ft); beam 10.8 m (35.4 ft)
Propulsion: three 3,600-shp (2684-kW) gas turbines driving four lift fans and two propellers
Weights: maximum 85 tons; payload see text
Speed: 70 kts (60/65 kts normal)

Armament: one ADMG6-30 six-barrel CIWS mounting on forward quarter of the starboard superstructure
Electronics: one navigation radar, and one 'High Pole-B' IFF system

The cockpit of the 'Lebed' is on the port side of the craft, balanced by a turret-mounted ADMG 30-mm remote-controlled Gatling-type cannon to the starboard. Typical payloads would include two PT-76 light tanks or two BMP infantry combat vehicles, or up to 35 tons of freight.

Mounted on the deck of a Soviet transport vessel, the 'Lebed' class of amphibious assault hovercraft is somewhat smaller than the American LCAC or the British Vosper VT2. The class has been designed to operate out of the docking wells of 'Ivan Rogov' class amphibious assault ships.

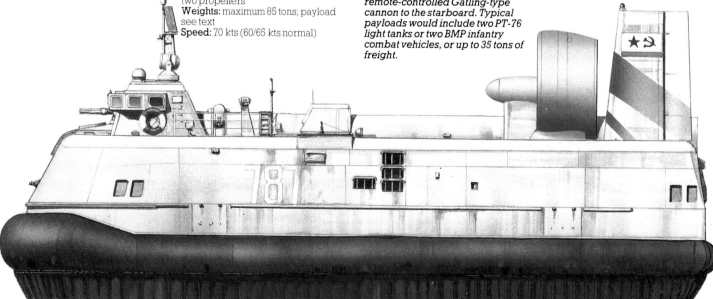

'Gus' class air-cushion vehicle

Former USSR

Developed from the 50-seater 'Skate' class amphibious passenger ferry ACV, the 'Gus' class logistic support ACV was tested in prototype form from 1969 onwards, series production of 36 craft taking place between 1970 and 1982 at a steady rate of two or three units per year. Deployed by all four Soviet fleets (the Northern, Baltic, Black Sea and Pacific), the 'Gus' can carry either a full Naval Infantry platoon of 25 men or several tons of supplies. It is used extensively for river patrol, special forces small-unit troop insertions, beach-head reconnaissance, and amphibious assault and logistic missions. For the last, the 'Ivan Rogov' class LPDs can each carry three 'Gus' class ACVs in place of the

two 'Lebed' class ACVs and one 'Ondatra' class LCM usually embarked. Some six or so of the 36 units were completed with two pilot positions and have been issued to the 'Gus' class ACV battalions of the fleets as operational conversion trainers. There has also been at least one further derivative of the design with twin ducted propellers, but this is believed not to have progressed beyond the prototype stage. It is likely that the long-term successor of the 'Gus' will be a WIG aircraft on the lines of the Ekranoplan.

Specification
'Gus' class
Dimensions: length 21.33 m (70.0 ft); beam 7.1 m (23.3 ft)
Propulsion: three 780-shp (582-kW) gas turbines driving one lift fan and two propellers
Weights: maximum 26.7 tons; payload see text
Speed: 60 kts (40 kts normal)
Armament: small arms and LMGs
Electronics: one navigation radar, and one 'High Pole-B' IFF system

The 'Gus' class logistic support ACV is roughly equivalent to the British SR.N6, although used by the Soviets in combat roles much more than those in the west. Used extensively by Soviet naval infantry on river patrol, small-unit insertions and assaults, the class serves with all Soviet fleets.

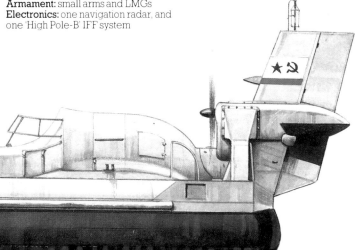

New Soviet air-cushion vehicles

Former USSR

In the early 1980s two new Soviet naval ACV prototypes were sighted by NATO reconnaissance units. The first, named the **'Tsaplya' class** by NATO, is thought to be the successor to the 'Lebed' class which is about to end its production run. It is similar in size, configuration and performance to the British BH7 Mk 4 and incorporates a bow door and central load well. Designed for use aboard the 'Ivan Rogov' class LPDs and their successors, the craft can carry one PT-76 light amphibious tank and 80 Naval Infantry, 160 Naval Infantry, or some 25 tons of cargo. The second design, named the **'Utenok'**

class, is slightly longer but smaller overall, and appears to be designed to carry one T-54/55/62/72/74 MBT as its primary payload. With two 'Utenoks' currently undergoing extensive testing along wiht the single 'Tsaplya', it is possible that both designs are actually complementary to one another with the aim that the 'Ivan Rogov' class LPDs will eventually have the ability to deliver MBTs beyond the water line of a beach-head rather than relying on the more conventional 'Ondatra' class LCM carried at present. This assumption has prooved correct: the LPDs carry mixed loads of 'Lebeds' and

'Utenoks' or 'Lebeds' or 'Tsaplya' and 'Utenoks', the precise load mix depending upon the operation to be mounted.

Specification (provisional)
'Tsaplya' class
Dimensions: length 24.0 m (78.75 ft; beam 14.0 m (45.9 ft)
Propulsion: not known
Weights: maximum 100 tons; payload see text
Speed: 65 kts
Armament: two 30-mm twin turrets
Electronics: one 'Spin Trough'

navigation radar, and one 'High Pole-B' IFF system

Specification (provisional)
'Utenok' class
Dimensions: length 26.3 m (86.3 ft); beam 13.0 m (42.7 ft)
Propulsion: not known
Weights: maximum 80 tons; payload see text
Speed: 65 kts
Armament: two 30-mm twin turrets
Electronics: one 'Spin Trough' navigation radar, and one 'High Pole-B' IFF system

'Aist' class air-cushion vehicle

Former USSR

Built at the Leningrad Shipyards, the air-cushion vehicle known to NATO as the **'Aist' class** is the Soviets' first large ACV design, and while similar in general appearance to the British SR.N4 Mk 2 'Mountbatten' class is much heavier. The prototype was launched in 1970 and following extensive testing the class entered series production in 1975. Since then several variants have been built, these differing in fin height, overall length, superstructure detail and armament configuration. Some 17 'Aists' are in service at present, and more are being built. Used as an amphibious assault and logistic supply ACV, the 'Aist' can deliver Naval Infantry, armoured vehicles and supplies to beach-heads which can be well inland. Only two of the Soviet fleets (the Baltic and Black Sea Fleets) deploy the 'Aists', the former having its units extensively photographed by NATO aircraft and ships during Warsaw Pact landing exercises. Large bow and stern loading ramps provide through-ship opera-

tions, and typical payloads for the craft are two MBTs of the T-54/T-55/T-62/T-72 or T-74 type, four PT-76 light amphibious tanks and 50 Naval Infantry, three BTR-60/70/BMP-1/2 APCs and 100 Naval Infantry, four trucks and 100 Naval Infantry, 220 Naval Infantry or up to 50 or 60 tons of supplies.

Specification
'Aist' class
Dimensions: length 47.8 m (156.8 ft); beam 17.5 m (57.4 ft)
Propulsion: two 24,000-shp (17894-kW) gas turbines driving four lift fans and four propellers
Weights: maximum 270 tons; payload see text
Speed: 80 kts (60/65 kts normal)
Armament: two twin 30-mm turrets over the bow
Electronics: one 'Spin Trough' navigation radar, one 'Drum Tilt' fire-control radar, one 'High Pole-B' IFF system, and one 'Square Head' IFF system

Seen operating with Mil Mi-8 'Hip' helicopters off the Baltic coast of the German Democratic Republic, the Leningrad-built 'Aist' class large amphibious ACV is about the same size as the 'Mountbatten' class used on the English Channel, although giving the impression of being more rugged.

Bell Model 7467 LACV-30

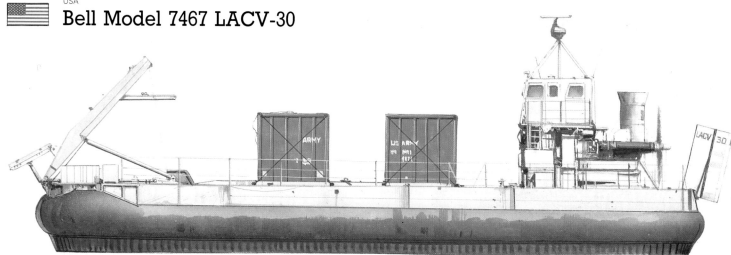

The **LACV-30** (Lighter Air-Cushion Vehicle 30-short ton payload) is a stretched version of Bell Aerospace Textron's Voyageur civilian model. A total of 24 of these vehicles (company designation **Bell Model 7476**) was delivered to replace the wheeled LARC-5 and the LARC-15 (Lighter Amphibious Resupply Cargo 5 and 15-ton) models then in service with the US Army's light and medium amphibian companies. The new craft was used as high-speed amphibious vehicles for LOTS (Lighter-Over-The-Shore) operations where no port facilities exist. The LACV-30 can travel over water, land, snow, ice, marshes, swamps, low brush and other small obstacles or through 2.44-m (8-ft) high surf carrying a variety of containerized cargo, wheeled or tracked vehicles, heavy engineering plant or other supplies such as fuel and water containers. It can be carried fully assembled on a ship, be launched by the crew and be fully operational within several hours or, alternatively, it can be broken down into 15 sections for carriage by truck, rail or aircraft and then reassembled at its destination. In the simple drive-on/drive-off role using its bow ramp the craft can carry the maximum load of 30 tons with an endurance of 2 hours. If, however, it is used as a self-unloading platform for supplies via its swing crane in the bows the load is reduced to 26.5 tons though endurance remains the same. Other roles (such as medical evacuation, troop transport and water or fuel resupply) give greater endurance, times of between 5 and 9 hours being possible depending upon the actual payload figure.

Specification
LACV 30
Dimensions: length 23.32 m (76.5 ft); beam 11.18 m (36.7 ft)
Propulsion: two 1,800-shp (1342-kW) gas turbines driving two lift fans and two propellers
Weights: maximum 51.34 tons; payload see text
Speed: 33.5 kts (normal)
Electronics: one navigation radar

The Bell Aerospace Canada Textron Voyageur heavy-haulage ACV was developed in 1971, and was used as the basis for development of the US Army's LACV-30.

Below: The LACV-30 is much more efficient than previous LOTS (Lighter Over The Shore) systems, and will eventually replace the LARC-5 and LARC-15 amphibious vehicles currently in service. Secondary roles could include coastal, harbour and riverine patrol, search and rescue and fire control.

Below: Operable over an enormous variety of terrains from the Arctic to the tropics, the LACV-30 can ensure dry landing of the wide range of cargoes carried. These can include ISO containers, tracked and wheeled vehicles, engineering equipment, pallets and barrels, water, fuel, firefighting equipment or troops.

Above: The first of 30 LACV-30s was delivered to MERADCOM (the US Army's Mobility Equipment Research and Development Command) in 1981. Unlike the same company's LCAC, the LACV is not an assault craft but is designed to be used solely for the transportation of goods from ship to shore.

Landing Craft Air Cushion (LCAC)

The **Bell Aerospace Textron LCAC** is the definitive production version of the **JEFF(B)** amphibious assault landing craft that was tested alongside the Aerojet-General JEFF(A) prototype for over five years by the US Navy. Incorporating the best attributes of both, 107 LCACs were to have been built, but this was cut to 87. Deliveries were made 1984–1996. Of the 17 LACs deployed to the Persian Gulf during the 1991, all were operational 100 percent of the time. LACs also provided relief to the outer islands of Bangladesh during the cyclone of 1991. The LCACs are being deployed in units of six to amphibious squadrons (PHIBRONS) and will be carried by the LHA, LPD, LHD and LSD classes (one, two, three and four craft respectively) to the disembarkation points. The open cargo deck area is 168.06 m² (1,809 sq ft) in area and capable of accommodating 60 tons of cargo under normal conditions or up to 75 tons in the maximum overload state with a consequent decrease in per-

formance. Typical loads include a 52-ton M60A1 MBT with five loaded jeeps, or a complete howitzer battery of six 105-mm/155-mm (4.13-in/6.1-in) guns and their loaded truck tractors and crews. The LCAC is fully skirted and can clear land obstacles up to 1.22 m (4 ft) high. Bow and stern ramps are fitted to allow ease of loading and unloading.

Specification
LCAC
Dimensions: length 26.82 m (88.0 ft); beam 14.33 m (47.0 ft)
Propulsion: four 3,070-shp (2289-kW) gas turbines driving four lift fans and two propellers
Weights: maximum 170 tons; payload see text
Speed: 50 kts, or 40 kts with maximum payload
Armament: small arms
Electronics: one surface-search/navigation radar

The first production LCAC enters the well deck of USS Pensacola (LSD 38) during the first underway mating of an LCAC and an LSD. The LCAC carries an M60 MBT, an M151 Jeep and an LAV-25 Light Armored Vehicle.

Below: With a range of 300 nautical miles (approximately 550 km) at a speed of 35 kts, the LCAC can ferry large loads fast from vessels standing well out to sea and can carry those loads (more than 60 tons, which could include an MBT and light vehicles, or a full artillery battery) safely inland.

Above: Operating off the coast of Florida, the Bell Aerospace Textron AALC (Amphibious Assault Landing Craft) JEFF(B) approaches the docking well of the Landing Ship Dock USS Spiegel Grove. The JEFF(B) formed the prototype for the US Navy's new LCAC.

Right: JEFF(B) underway off the coast of Florida early in 1984, with a cargo including an M60 MBT and two 155-mm howitzers. The LCAC programme will give the US Navy the capacity to land at high speed US Marine units with their heavy equipment, while standing some distance off the coast.

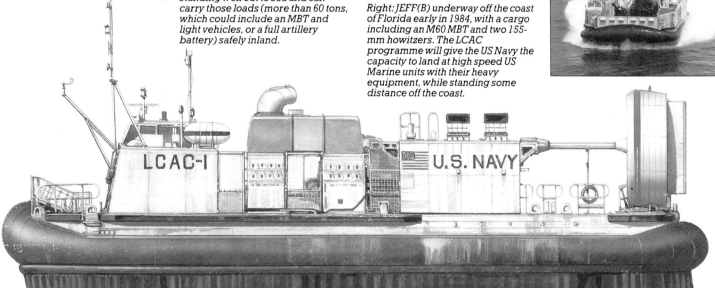

Glossary of Weapons

Tanks

American
M1 Abrams
M48A1 medium tank
M55s Sheridan
M60A1
M103 heavy
British
Alvis Scorpion
Centurion
Challenger 2
Chieftain
Conqueror
Vickers MBT
Vickers Mk 7 MBT
French
AMX-13 light tank
AMX-40
Leclerc MBT
German
Leopard I
Leopard II
Japan
Type 63
Type 74
Type 90
Russian
T-10
T-54
T-72
T-80
PT-76 amphib
Other
Argentine: TAM-1
Brazil: ENGESA Osorio MBT
China: Type 59
Italy: C-1 Ariete
Swiss: Pz68

Tank Destroyers

American
M50 Ontos
M56 Scorpion
Austrian
AK105 TD
British
Malkara Hornet

Reconnaissance Vehicles

American
Cadillac Gage Stingray
FMC CCV(L)
Lynx C&R vehicle
British
Alvis Saladin
Daimler Ferret
French
AMX-10RC Reconnaissance
vehicle
Panhard VB
Panhard AML-90
Panhard EBR
Panhard Sagaie
Panhard Sagaie 2
German
Spahpanzer 2 Luchs
Wiesel
Russian
ASU-57
BRDM-1
BRDM-2
Other
Engesa Cascavel
FIAT 6610

APCs, Tracked APCs & MICVs

American
FMC AIFV
M2 Bradley
British
FV-432
Warrior
French
AMX-10P
AMX-VC1
German
Marder
Russia
BMD
BMP-1
BMP-2
BTR-50PK
MT-LB
Other
Japan Type 73 APC
MOWAG Tornado
OTO-Melara VCC
Pvb-30
Steyr 4K7FA
Yugoslavia M980

Wheeled APCs

American
Cadillac Gage V-150 APC
Cadillac Gage V-300 APC
Cadillac Gage Commando
Ranger APC
Verne Dragoon APC
British
Alvis Saracen APC
BDX/Valkyr APC
Humber FV1600
Saxon APC
French
ACMAT APC
Berliet VXB-170
Panhard VCR
Panhard M3
Renault VAB
German
TM-170 APC
Transportpanzer 1
UR-416 APC
Russian
BTR-152
BTR-60P APC
Spanish
BLR-600 APC
BMR-600 IFV
Other
Condor APC
DAF YP408 AP
Egypt Fahd APC
Engesa EE-11 Urutu APC
FIAT-OTO Type 6614 APC
MOWAG Roland APC
MOWAG MR-8 series
MOWAG Piranha
OT-64 APC
PZH-4 APC
Ratel
SIBMAS APC

Amphibians and over-snow vehicles

American
LVTP7
LARC-5
LARC-15
Canadian
Bombardier over-snow

Russian
GAZ-46 MAV
PTS
Swedish
Bv202 over-snow
Bv 206 over-snow
Other
BAV-485
CAMAN-F Amphibian truck
EKW amphibian truck
FIAT Type 6640A
GT-2 tracked over-snow
K-61 amphib barrier
Type 60 over-snow

Light Vehicles

American
M37 truck
M38 truck
M151 Jeep
British
Land Rover cab-forward
French
Citroen Mehari
Hotchkiss M201 Jeep
Peugeot P4
German
Mercedes jeep
Volkswagen Iltis
Russian
GAZ-069
UAZ-469B
Other
DAF YA-126 weapons carrier
FIAT 1107 AD
Japanese light vehicles
Steyr 700 Haflinger

Multiple Rocket Launchers

American
MLRS
Brazilian
Various
Chinese
Types 63 and 81 107mm
Types 63 and 70 130mm
German
LARS
Russian
BM-21, BM-24, BM-22
Other
Czech RM-70
Egypt various
IMI (Israel)
Japan Type 67 M
South Africa Valkiri
Yugoslavia various

Self-Propelled Field Artillery

American
105-mm M61
105-mm M52
175-mm M107
203-mm M110
British
105-mm Abbot
Czech Republic
152-mm DANA wheeled
French
155-mm F3
155-mm GCT
Italian
155-mm Palmaria
Japanese
155-mm Type 75
Russian
155-mm M109
203-mm M1975 gun

Swedish
155-mm Bandkanon
Other
122-mm SP Howitzer
122-mm M1974
152-mm M1973
Israeli SP artillery

Self-Propelled Air Defence Artillery

American
M42 40-mm Twin
M163 20-mm Vulcan
M23740-mm Sgt York
British
Marconi Marksman
French
AMX-13 DCA
Panhard M3-VDA
German
Dragon twin 30-mm
Gepard twin 35-mm
Wildcat twin 35-mm
Russian
BTR-152A 14.5-mm
ZSU-23-4 23-mm
ZSU-57-2 57-mm
Other
Czech M53/59 30-mm
China 37-mm twin Type 63
Oerlikon GDF-CO3
OTOMATIC 76-mm

Towed Field Artillery

American
105-mm M102
155-mm M198
British
105-mm Light Gun
155-mm FH-70
French
155-mm TR-F1
Russian
122-mm D-30
130-mm M46
Other
105-mm M56 Yugoslavia
105-mm M56 OTO-Mel
155-mm Bofors FH-77A
155-mm CITEFA Model 77
  howitzer
155-mm G5 howitzer
155-mm GHN-45 gun-howitzer
155-mm Model 50 howitzer
155-mm Soltam M68 howitzer
180-mm S-23

Towed Air Defence Artillery

American
12.7-mm M55
20-mm Vulcan
French
20-mm Tarasque
German
20-mm Rh202
Russian
23-mm ZU-23
57-mm S-60
100-mm KS-19
Swedish
40-mm Bofors L/70
Swiss
20-mm GAI-BO1
20-mm GAI-DO1
Oerlikon 35-mm GDF
Other
FK-20 20-mm (Norway)
40-mm Breda 40L70

20-mm TCM-20 (Israel)
20-mm M55A2 (Yugo)
30-mm M53 (Czech)

Anti-Tank Weapons

American
Dragon
TOW
British
LAW-80
Swingfire
French
Aérospatiale SSII
HOT
MILAN
German
Cobra and Mamba
Russian
AT-2 Swatter
AT-3 Sagger
A-4 Spigot
AT-5 SPandrel
AT-6 Spiral
RPG-7
Swiss
ADATS
Other
Bofors Bantam
Carl Gustav
Folgore

Surface-to-Air Missiles

American
Chaparral M48
Improved HAWK MIM-23B
Patriot MIM-104
Stinger FIM-92A
British
Bloodhound
Blowpipe
Rapier
French
Crotale
Roland
Shahine
Japanese
TAN-SAM
Russian
Gainful SA-6
Ganef SA-4
Gaskin SA-9
Gecko SA-8
Grail SA-7
SA-11 SAM
SA-13 SAM
Swedish
RBS-70

Combat Pistols

American
Colt revolvers
Ruger revolvers
Smith & Wesson revolvers
Belgium
FN High Power
French
PA15
M1950
German
Heckler & Koch P7 series
Heckler & Koch P9, P7)
Heckler & Koch VP70M
Walther P1
Walther P5
Israeli
Desert Eagle
Italian
Beretta 951

Beretta 92 series
Beretta 93R
Russian
Makarovia
Swiss
SIG-Sauer P220

Sub-machine Guns

American
Ingram 10
British
Sterling L2A3
French
MAT49
German
MP5
Walther MPK/MPL
Italian
Beretta 12S
Swedish
Carl Gustav M45
Other
Argentine: PA3DM
Australia: F1
China Type 64 silent
Czech Republic: Skorpion
Israel: Uzi and Mini-Uzi
Poland: PM-63

Assault Rifles

American
Armalite AR-18
M16, M16A1, A2
Ruger Mini-14
British
SA-80
French
FA-MAS F-1
German
H&K G3
H&K G11
Italian
Beretta AR70/90
Russian
AK47, AKM
AK74
Other
Austria: Steyr AUG
Belgium: FN-FAL
Czechoslovakia: Vz-58
IsraeL: Galil/R4

Sniping Rifles

American
M21
M40A
Austrian
Steyr SSG69
British
L42A1
Parker-Hale 82
Belgium
FN 30-11
French
FR-1, FR-2
German
Mauser SP66
Mauser SP86
Walther WA2000
Israeli
Galil Sniper
Italian
Beretta Sniper
Russian
Dragunov
Yugoslavia
M76

Machine-Guns

American
M60
British
Bren
L86 LSW
Belgian
FN-MAG
FN Minimi

French
AA52
German
Heckler & Koch
MG3
Russian
PK
RPK
Other
SIG 710-3
Ultimax 100
Uru Mekanika
vz59

Modern Fighters

American
General Dynamics (now
  Lockheed Martin) F-16 Fighting
  Falcon
McDonnell Douglas (now
  Boeing) F-15 Eagle
McDonnell Douglas (now
  Boeing) F-4 Phantom II
Northrop F-E/F Tiger II
French
Dassault-Breguet Mirage 2000
Dassault-Breguet Mirage F.1
Dassault-Breguet Mirage
  III/5/50 series
International
Panavia Tornado ADV
Israeli
IAI Kfir
Russian
Mikoyan-Gurevich MiG-21
  'Fishbed'
Mikoyan-Gurevich MiG-23
  'Flogger'
Mikoyan-Gurevich MiG-25
  'Foxbat'
Sukhoi Su-15 'Flagon'
Tupolev Tu-128 'Fiddler'
Swedish
Saab JA37 Viggen

First Supersonic Fighters

American
Convair F-102 Delta Dagger
Convair F-106 Delta Dart
Lockheed F-104 Starfighter
McDonnell F-101 Voodoo
North American F-100 Super
  Sabre
Republic F-105 Thunderchief
British
BAC Lightning
French
Dassault Super Mystére
Dassault-Breguet Mirage III & 5
Russian
Mikoyan-Gurevich MiG-19
  'Farmer'
Shenyang J-6
Mikoyan-Gurevich MiG-21
Sukhoi Su-9 and Su-11 'Fishpot'
Yakovlev Yak-28 'Firebar'
Swedish
Saab J35 Draken

Modern Strike Aircraft

American
General Dynamics F-111
Rockwell B-1 Lancer
British
Hawker Siddeley (Blackburn/
  BAe) Buccaneer
British/West German/Italian
Panavia Tornado IDS
British/French
SEPECAT Jaguar
French
Dassault Mirage IV
Dassault-Breguet Mirage
  2000N
Israeli
IAI Lavi
Italian/Brazilian
Aeritalia/EMBRAER AMX

Russian
Sukhoi Su-24 'Fencer'
Tupolev Tu-22 'Blinder'
Tupolev Tu-22M/Tu-26 'Backfire'
Tupolev Tu-160 'Blackjack'
Swedish
Saab 37 Viggen

Modern Attack Aircraft

American
Fairchild Republic A-10
  Thunderbolt II
McDonnell Douglas F-4G
  'Wild Weasel'
McDonnell Douglas (now
  Boeing) F-15E Eagle
Vought A-7 Corsair II
British
British Aerospace Harrier
Chinese
Nanchang Q-5 and A-5 'Fantan'
Shenyang J-6
French
Dassault-Breguet Mirage 5 & 50
Dassault-Breguet Mirage F.1
Russian
Mikoyan-Gurevich MiG-23BN
MiG-27 'Flogger'
Sukhoi Su-7 'Fitter'
Sukhoi Su-17/20/22 'Fitter'
Sukhoi Su-25 'Frogfoot'
Swedish
Saab AJ37 Viggen
Yugosalvia/Romania
Soko/CNIAR Orao/IAR-93

Airborne Early Warning Aircraft

American
Boeing E-3 Sentry
Boeing EC-125
Lockheed EC-130 Hercules
British
British Aerospace (Avro)
  Shackleton AEW.Mk 2
British Aerospace Nimrod
  AEW.Mk 3
Westland Sea King AEW.Mk 2
Russian
Ilyushin A-50 'Mainstay'
Tupolev Tu-126 'Moss'

Strategic and Tactical Reconnaissance Aircraft

American
Grumman OV-1 Mohawk
Lockheed RF-104 Starfighter
Lockheed SR-71
Lockheed U-2/TR-1
Northrop RF-5 Tigereye
British
BAC Canberra
British/ French
SEPECAT Jaguar
French
Dassault-Breguet Mirage F.1CR
Dassault-Breguet Mirage IIIR
Italian
Aeritalia G91R
Russian
Mikoyan-Gurevich MiG-21R
  'Fishbed'
Mikoyan-Gurevich MiG-25R
  'Foxbat'
Swedish
Saab S35 Draken
Saab-Scania SF37 and SH37
  Viggen

Post-War Helicopters

American
Bell Model 47, H-13 Sioux and
  HTL
Piasecki H-21
Piasecki HUP Retriever
Hiller Model 360, UH-12 and
  H-23 Raven
Sikorsky S-55, H-19

Chickasaw, HO4S, HRS and
  Whirlwind
Sikorsky S-56, HR2S and H-37
  Mojave
Vought-Sikorsky R-4 and R-6
Vought-Sikorsky R-5
British
Bristol Type 171 Sycamore
Bristol Types 173 and 192
  Belvedere
French
Aérospatiale SE 313B Alouette II
Russian
Mil Mi-1 'Hare'
Mil Mi-2 'Hoplite'

Armed Combat Helicopters

American
Bell Model 209 Hueycobra,
  SeaCobra and SuperCobra
Hughes (now Boeing) AH-64
  Apache
Hughes Model 500 Defender
British
Westland Lynx (Army)
Westland Scout
French
Aérospatiale SA 316 and SA
  319 Alouette III
Aérospatiale SA 341 Gazelle
Italian
Agusta 109A
Agusta 129 Mangusta
West German
Messerschmitt-Balkow-Blohm
  BO 105
Russian
Mil Mi-24 'Hind'

Assault Helicopters

American
Bell OH-58 Kiowa
Bell UH-1 Iroquois
Boeing Vertol CH-47 Chinook
Sikorsky CH-3 and HH-3
Sikorsky CH-53 Sea Stallion
  and Super Stallion
Sikorsky CH-54 Tarhe
Sikorsky UH-60 Black Hawk
  and SH-60 Seahawk
British
Westland Commando
Westland Wessex
French
Aérospatiale SA 321 Super
  Frelon
Aérospatiale/Westland SA 330
  Puma
Russian
Mil Mi-6 'Hook' and Mi-10 'Harke'
Mil Mi-8 'Hip'

Post-War Carrier Aircraft

American
Douglas AD Skyraider
Douglas F3D Skyknight
Grumman AF Guardian
Grumman F7F Tigercat
Grumman F8F Bearcat
Grumman F9F Cougar
Grumman F9F Panther
McDonnell F2H Banshee
McDonnell FH Phantom
North American AJ Savage
North American FJ Fury
British
de Havilland Sea Hornet
de Havilland Sea Venom
Fairey Firefly
Hawker Sea Fury
Supermarine Attacker
Westland Wyvern

Carrierborne Aircraft

American
Grumman A-6 Intruder
Grumman C-2 Greyhound
Grumman E-2 Hawkeye

Grumman EA-6 Prowler
Grumman F-14 Tomcat
Lockheed S-3 Viking
McDonnell Douglas F/A-18
  Hornet
Vought A-7 Corsair II
American/British
McDonnell Douglas/British
  Aerospace AV-8B Harrier II
British
British Aerospace AV-8A/C
British Aerospace Sea Harrier
French
Breguet Alizé
Dassault-Breguet Super
  Etendard
Russian
Yakovlev Yak-38 'Forger'

Carrier Aircraft of the 1960s

American
Douglas (McDonnell Douglas)
  A-4 (A4D) Skyhawk
Douglas A-3 (A3D) Skywarrior
Douglas F-6 (F4D) Skyray
Grumman E-1 (WF) Tracer
Grumman S-2 (S2F) Tracker
McDonnell F-3 (F3H) Demon
McDonnell F-4 Phantom II
North American (Rockwell)
  A-5 (A3J) Vigilante
Vought F-8 (F8U) Crusader
British
Fairey (Westland) Gannet
Hawker (DH/BAe) Sea Vixen
Hawker Siddeley (de
  Havilland/BAe) Buccaneer
Supermarine Scimitar
French
Dassault Etendard

Maritime Aircraft

American
Grumman HU-16 Albatross
Grumman S-2 Tracker
Lockheed C-130 Hercules
Lockheed P-2 Neptune
Lockheed P-3 Orion
British
British Aerospace Nimrod
Pilatus Britten-Norman
  Maritime Defender
Brazilian
EMBRAER EMB-110 & EMB-111
Dutch
Fokker F.27 Maritime
French
Dassault-Breguet Atlantic
Japanese
Shin Meiwa PS-1 and US-1
Russian
Beriev Be-12 Tchaika 'Mail'
Ilyushin Il-38 'May'
Tupolev Tu-16 'Badger'
Tupolev Tu-95 and Tu-142 'Bear'
Myasischev M-4 'Bison'

Naval Helicopters

American
Kaman SH-2 Seasprite
Sikorsky S-61/H-3 Sea King
Sikorksy S-70/SH-60B
  Seahawk
Sikorsky S-65/H-53
British
Westland Wasp
Westland Wessex
Westland Sea King
Westland Lynx
French
Aérospatiale Dauphin
Aérospatiale Super Frelon
Italian
August-Bell AB.204, AB205,
  and AB.212
British/Italian
EH Industries EH101

American/Japanese
Boeing Vertiol 107
Russian
Mil Mi-14 'Haze'
Kamovc Ka-25 Hormone
Kamove Ka-32 'Helix'

Aircraft carriers

American
'America' class
'Forrestral' class
'Hancock' class
'Intrepid' class
'John F. Kennedy'class
'Kitty Hawk' class
'Midway' class
'Nimitz' Class
SS *Enterprise*
Argentinian
Veintincio de Mayo
Brazilian
Minas Gerais
British
HMS *Hermes*
'Invincible' class
French
'Clemenceau' class
Indian
Vikrant
Italian
Guiseppe Garibaldi
Russian
'Kiev' Class
Spanish
Dedalo
Principe de Asutrias

Modern Cruisers

American
'Bainbridge' Class
'Belknap' class
'California' class
'Iowa' class
'Leahy' class
'Long Beach' class
'Ticonderoga' class
'Truxtan' class
'Virginia' class
French
'Colbert' class
Italian
'Vittorio Veneto' class
Russian
'Kara' class
'Kirov' class
'Krasina' class
'Kresta I' c;ass
'Kresta II' class
'Kynda' class
'Moskva' class
'Sverdlov' class

Destroyers

American
'Arleigh Burke' class
'Charles F. Adams' class
'Kidd' class
'Spruance' class
Argentinian
'Meko 360H2' class
British
'County' class
Type 82 class
Types 42 class
Canadian
'Iroquois' class
French
'Suffren' class
Type C70 class
Italian
'Audace' class
Japanese
'Haruna' class
'Hatsuy Britishi' class
'Shirane' class
'Tachikaze' class
'Tatats Britishi' class

Russian
'Kashin (Mod)' class
'Kashin' class
'Sovremenny' class
'Udaloy' class

Modern Western Frigates

American
'Brooke' class
'Garcia' class
'Knox' class
'Oliver Hazard Perry' class
Belgian
'Weilingen' class
British
Type 22' Broadsword' class
Types 12 'Modified Leander' class
Types 21 'Amazon' class
British/Brazilian
'Niteroi' class
Chinese
'Jianghu' class
'Jiangnan' class
Dutch
'Jacob van Heemskerck' class
'Kortenaer' class
'Tromp' class
French
'Destienne d'Orves' (A69) class
French/Saudi Arabian
Type F2000 class
Dutch/Indonesian
'Fatahillah' class
Italian
'Esmeraldas' class
'Lupo' class
'Mastreale' class
Japanese
Chikugo class
'Yubai' class
Norwegian
'Oslo' class
Russian
'Graisha' class
'Koni' c;ass
'Krivak' class
'Mirka' class
'Nanuchka' classes
'Petya' classes
'Riga' Class
'Tarantul' class
West German
'Bremen' (Types 122) class
'Parchim' class
West German/Argentinian
'Meko140A16' class

Modern patrol craft

American
'Asheville' class patrol
  combatant
PB series patrol craft
PBR series patrol craft
PCF series patrol craft
'Pegasus' class patrol
  combatant hydrofoil
'Riverine' warfare class
British
British class patrol craft
'Ramadan' class fast attack
  craft
Shmel class patrol craft
Chinese
'Huchan' class fast attack craft
'Shanghai' class fast attack
  craft
French
Combattante II class fast
  attack craft
Combattante III class fast
  attack craft
Israeli
Alia fast attack craft
Reshef fast attack craft
Saar class fast attack craft
Italian
'Sparverio' class fast attack
  hydrofoil

South America
South American Riverine
  warfare craft
Swedish
'Spic' class fast attack craft

Russian
'Komar' class fast attack craft
'Matkas' fast attack craft
'Mol 'class fast attack craft
  (torpedoes)
'Osa 'fast attack craft
P4 class fast attack craft
  (torpedoes)
P5 class fast attack craft
  (torpedo)
'Shershen' class fast attack
  craft (torpedoed)
'Stenka' class patrol craft
'Turya' class fast attack craft
  (torpedoes)

Spyships

American
Corvette 'Compass Island'
  class
Corvette 'Haskell' class
'Stalwart' class
'Vanguard' class
Chinese
'Yaun Wang' Class
East German
'Mod Kondor I' class
French
'Henri Poincare' class
Polish
'Baltyk' class
'Nawigator' class
'Piast' class
Russian
'Bal'zam' class
'Gagarin' class
'India' class
'Okean' class

Naval Anti-aircraft weapons

American
EMERLEC-30 Twin 30-mm
  Mounting
20-mm Mk 15/16 Phalanx
Close-In Weapon system
British
30-mm LS30R (Rarden) Naval
  Gun Mounting
Dutch/American
30-mm Goalkeeper Close-in
  Weapon System
Italian
Breda Twin 30-mm Naval
  mount
40-mm L/70 Breda Compact
  twin naval Mount Type 70
Italian/Dutch/British
25-mm Close-In Weapon
  System
Israeli
30-mm TCM-30 Twin naval Gun
Swedish
40-mm L/60 abdl L/70 Bofors
  automatic guns
Swiss
20-mm naval Gun Type
  GAM-BOI
25-mm naval Gun Type
  GBM-Aoi
30-mm Twin Anti-Aircraft gun
  Type GCM-A
35-mm Twin Anti-aircraft Gun
  Type GDM-A
Russian
30-mm anti-aircraft guns
57-mm anti-aircraft gun

Naval Artillery

American
5-in Gun Mounting Mk42
5-in Gun Mounting Mk45

16-in Gun Turret Mk7
British
Vickers 4,5-in Mk8 gun
Chinese
100-mm gun
130-mm gun
French
100-mm Model 68-II gun
Italian
105-mm Breda SCLAR rocket
  launcher
76-mm OTO Melara Compact
  gun
127-mm OTO Melara
  Compact gun
Swedish
57-mm Bofors Sak gun
120-mm Bofors gun
Russian
Soviet Naval rocket launcher
  systems
76-mm guns
100-mm guns
130mm -guns
152-mm triple guns mounting

Underwater weapons

American
Mk 37 torpedo
Mk 44 torpedo
Mk 45 torpedo
Mk 48 torpedo
Mk50 torpedo
British
Marconi Mk24 Tigerfish
  torpedo
Marconi Spearfish torpedo
Marconi Stingray torpedo
French
DTCN F17 torpedo
DTCN L3 torpedo
DTCN L3 torpedo
DTCN L4 torpedo
DTCN L5 torpedo
Thomson-CSF sea mine
Italian
Whitehead Motofides A184
  torpedo
Whitehead Motofides A244
  torpedo
Swedish
FFV Tp42 series torpedo
FFV Tp61 torpedo
West German
AEG-Telefunken Seal torpedo
Seeschlange torpedo
SST4 torpedo
SUT torpedo
Russian
Soviet sea mines: YARM
Soviet torpedoes

Modern diesel submarines

British
'Oberon' class
'Upholder' class
Chinese
'Romeo' class
Dutch
'Swaardvis' class
'Walrus' class
French
'Agosta' class
'Daphne' class
Italian
'Enrico Toti' class
'Suaro' class
Japanese
'Yuushio' class
West German
Type 206 class
Type 208 class
Swedish
'Sjöormen' class
'Vastergotland' class
Russian
'Foxtrot' class

'Kilo' Class
'Tango' Class

Modern missile submarines

American
'Benjamin Franklin' class SSBN
'La Fayette' class SSBN
Lockheed trident II D5 SLBM
Lockheed UGM-73A Poseidon
  C3 SSBN
Lockheed UGM-96A Trident
  C4 SLBM
'Ohio' class SSBN
American/British
Lockheed UGM-27c Polaris
  A3 SLBM
British
'Resolution' class SSBN
French
'L'Inflexible' class SSBN
'Le Redoubtable' class SSBN
M20 SLBM
M4 SSLBM
Russian
'Delta I, II, III' class SSBN
SS-N-18
SS-N-20 SLBN
SS-N-6 SLBM
SS-N-8
SS-NX-23 SLBN
'Typhoon' class SSBN
'Yankee' class SSBN

Nuclear attack submarines

American
'Glenhard P. Liscomb' class SSN
'Los Angeles' class SSN
'Narwhal' class SSN
'Skipjack' class SSN
'Sturgeon' class SSN
'Thresher' class (later Permit
  class) SSN
British
'Churchill' class SSNS
'Swiftsure' class SSNS
'Trafalgar' class SSNS
'Valiant' class SSNS
French
'Rubis' class SSN
Russian
'Akula' class SSN
'Alpha' class SSN
'Charlie I' class SSGN
'Charlie II" class SSGN
'Charlie III class SSGN
'Echo' class SSN
'Echo II' class SSGN
'November' class SSN
'Oscar 'class SSGN
'Papas' class SSGN
'Victor I' class SSN
'Victor II' class SSN
'Victor III 'class SSN

Hovercraft

American
Bell model 7467 LACV-30
Landing Craft Air Cushion
British
BH7 Wellington class ACV
Skima series ACV
SR.N4 'Mountbatten' class
  mine countermeasure
  hovercraft
SR.N4 'Mountbatten' class air
  cushion vehicle
SR.N6 'Winchester' class ACV
VT2 ACV
French
French Air Cushion Vehicles
French SES types
Russian
Aist class ACV
Ekranoplan wing-in-ground
  effect machines
Lebed class ACV Gus class ACV
New Soviet ACV